Argentina

D1042922

Danny
Sandra Bao, Gregor Clark, Sarah Gilbert,
Carolyn McCarthy, Andy Symington, Lucas Vidgen

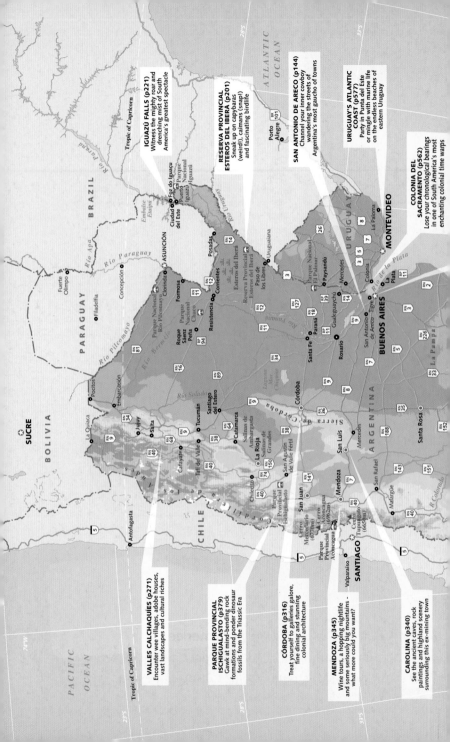

IGUAZÚ FALLS (p221)
Witness the mighty roar and drenching mist of South America's greatest spectacle

RESERVA PROVINCIAL ESTEROS DEL IBERÁ (p201)
Sneak up on capybaras (weird!), caimans (snap!) and fascinating birdlife

SAN ANTONIO DE ARECO (p144)
Channel your inner cowboy wandering the streets of Argentina's most gaucho of towns

URUGUAY'S ATLANTIC COAST (p577)
Party in Punta del Este or mingle with marine life on the endless beaches of eastern Uruguay

COLONIA DEL SACRAMENTO (p562)
Lose your chronological bearings in one of South America's most enchanting colonial time warps

VALLES CALCHAQUÍES (p271)
Encounter wee villages, adobe houses, vast landscapes and cultural riches

PARQUE PROVINCIAL ISCHIGUALASTO (p379)
Gawk at mind-bending rock formations and ponder dinosaur fossils from the Triassic Era

CÓRDOBA (p316)
Treat yourself to galleries galore, fine dining and stunning colonial architecture

MENDOZA (p345)
Wine tours, a hopping nightlife and some seriously big mountains - what more could you want?

CAROLINA (p340)
See the ancient caves, rock paintings and highland scenery surrounding this ex-mining town

CHOS MALAL (p387)
Explore volcanoes and hot spring geysers before heading up Ruta 40 to Mendoza

THE LAKE DISTRICT (p380)
Enjoy gorgeous scenery, skiing and more hiking than you could poke a trekking pole at

EL CHALTÉN (p483)
Hunker down in Argentina's coolest mountain town before tackling the Fitz Roy Range

GLACIER PERITO MORENO (p495)
See (and hear!) this mighty river of ice calving into icy Lago Argentino

BUENOS AIRES (p81)
Experience porteño passions: tango, soccer, food, fashion and fantastically frenzied nightlife

BEAGLE CHANNEL (p528)
Sail among the mystical islands of Tierra del Fuego aboard a chartered boat

PACIFIC OCEAN

ATLANTIC OCEAN

FALKLAND ISLANDS
(Islas Malvinas)

○ Stanley

ELEVATION
5000m
4000m
3000m
2000m
1000m
600m
200m
0

LEGEND
Tollway
Freeway
Primary Road
Secondary Road
Tertiary Road
Unsealed Road

0 — 400 km
0 — 250 miles

On the Road

DANNY PALMERLEE Coordinating author
Yep, traveling solo for extended periods makes you take droll self portraits, like this one in front of Mount Fitz Roy in Patagonia's Parque Nacional Los Glaciares (p483). Down here, when the rain finally stops, you should drop everything you're doing, take a picture of yourself and then hike like crazy.

GREGOR CLARK This was probably the peak moment of my whole Uruguay trip, saddling up a horse at Estancia La Sirena (p570) near Mercedes, and riding through wheat fields down to the Río Negro at sunset. We returned to a roaring fire, a huge barbeque and a brilliant sky full of stars.

SARAH GILBERT One of my last trips researching the Pampas & Atlantic Coast chapter – here I am atop Cerro de la Ventana (p154). Only a handful of other hikers were on the mountain on this warm December day, and I had the peak to myself, watching the blue dragonflies dart among the wildflowers.

CAROLYN McCARTHY The day was socked in but we hiked anyway, destination Hito XXIV in Parque Nacional Tierra del Fuego (p535). Southern forests have magic – crisp air and twisted lengas. We saw only two hikers on the whole trail, plus a handful of rabbits that scattered at the sound of our boots.

SANDRA BAO We were at a *parrilla* (steak restaurant) and I ordered my favorite – a *bife de chorizo* (sirloin), grilled *jugoso* (rare). My friend Jorge pretended to steal it from me. Like his own *tira de asado* (short ribs) wasn't huge enough – one serving was bigger than his whole plate!

LUCAS VIDGEN Transport on a Lonely Planet gig can take many forms, but there's always plenty of walking. So imagine my delight getting offered an electric scooter to check out Mendoza's wineries (p357). It's hard to look like a badass when your ride tops out at 25km/h, but I think I pulled it off.

ANDY SYMINGTON Heading off in a small boat to explore the fabulous wetlands of the Reserva Provincial Esteros del Iberá (p201), soon to be stunned by the rich birdlife, unsettled by the sinister toothy grins of numerous caimans, and highly amused at the cute, comical roly-poly capybaras.

For full author biographies see p648-9.

BEST OF ARGENTINA

Round up the best of Argentina – the wine, the fishing, the art, the mountaineering, the skiing, the literature, the beef, the architecture, the clubbing – and you have the building blocks for one of the most exciting journeys you'll ever take. No joke. While *so many* things in Argentina are exciting, some things are better defined as 'mind blowing.' We've cobbled together a collection of the latter. Put as many on your Go list as possible.

City Life

Buenos Aires might reign supreme in this category, but Argentina's other cities offer urban fun on an altogether different level. Despite being the country's next biggest cities, they exude a small-town feel, and friendliness seems to permeate most facets of life, from the nightclub floor to the local *parrilla*.

❶ Buenos Aires

The Argentine capital (p81) is one of the world's most exhilarating cities, with astounding art, fascinating neighborhoods, fabulous food and a passionate population blazingly devoted to having fun *all…night… long.*

❷ Córdoba

Argentina's second city (p316) boasts the country's finest colonial center, with a gorgeous central plaza and exquisite Jesuit architecture. And the people? They're some of the friendliest you'll find anywhere.

❸ Mendoza

Grab your corkscrew and venture to the heart of wine country. Basking in the sun beneath the Andes' highest peaks, Mendoza (p345) is a stunning city of shade trees and *vino* (wine).

❹ Salta

Only one thing beats an evening stroll around Salta's historic central plaza: drinking an ice cold beer at one of its outdoor cafés. On a hot summer's evening, beneath the old buildings, it's pretty close to perfect (p261).

Natural Wonders

With its head in the tropics and its toes in Antarctica, it's hardly surprising Argentina kicks out such a barrage of natural wonders. Few places in the world offer so many opportunities for jaw-dropping, speech-stopping encounters with planet earth. Although the journeys are long, access is usually easy. The rewards? Unforgettable.

① Iguazú Falls

There are waterfalls and there are waterfalls. And then there's Iguazú. Nothing can prepare you for the sight and sound of so much water falling so hard from so many jungle-clad cliffs (p221).

② Tierra del Fuego

Maybe it's the austral light, or just knowing that the next step south is Antarctica. Whatever it is, this trove of mystical islands (p518), cut off from the northern world by the Strait of Magellan, is indescribably magical.

③ Reserva Faunística Península Valdés

Never mind the Galápagos, this coastal Patagonian reserve (p436) is a wildlife lover's dream, with sea lions, elephant seals, guanacos, rheas, Magellanic penguins, seabirds and – most famously – endangered southern right whales.

④ Quebrada de Humahuaca

Etched into the Andes near the Bolivian border, this spectacular valley (p253) is home to traditional villages, epic views, unique food, and plenty of proof that erosion can be nature's greatest artist. No wonder it made Unesco's World Heritage list!

⑤ Valles Calchaquíes

From Parque Nacional Los Cardones, where fawn-colored guanacos dart among giant cacti, to the traditional adobe villages of Cachi and Molinos, this vast network of valleys (p271) cradles some of Argentina's most scenic treasures.

⑥ Glaciar Perito Moreno

What Iguazú Falls is to water, the Perito Moreno Glacier (p495) is to ice. This advancing Patagonian glacier calves with such force into the steel-blue waters of Lago Argentino you'll forever remember the sounds with glazed-over eyes.

⑦ Valle de Calingasta

You might look a little funny pulling off the road, getting out of your rental car, throwing your arms into the sky and spinning around in deranged, oblivious bliss – but you probably wouldn't be the first. This stretch of the Andes (p373) is *that* beautiful.

⑧ Reserva Provincial Esteros del Iberá

Vast wetlands, shimmering lagoons, fiery red sunsets, gauchos, capybaras, caimans, birds – this enormous provincial reserve (p201) is the stuff of dreams, where you can experience traditional Argentine life and some of the continent's most visible wildlife all in one go.

Classic Argentina

Whether it's as simple as *dulce de leche* (that delicious milk caramel Argentines spread on just about everything) or as complex as the tango, some things are quintessentially Argentine. These are the experiences that will plunge you deeper into life in Argentina and burn an eternal fondness for the place into your soul.

Author Tip

First-class overnight buses often provide wine with dinner. It's a welcome perk, but it's usually cheap swill. Bring your own bottle (and a corkscrew). Not only will it make dinner that much tastier, it'll make the ride that much more relaxing. Sleep well!

① Tango

Go on, give it a try. So what if it's one of the world's most sophisticated dances (p50). It's so sexy, you'll be fired up enough to make it through that long Buenos Aires night.

② Soccer

Take a deep breath and get ready for the most concentrated 90 minutes of emotional rollercoastering you've ever experienced. And pray for goals (p128)!

③ Estancias

There's something definitively Argentine about *estancias* – those don't-fence-me-in ranches with endless views, peace and quiet and plenty of home-cooked food. Opportunities for livin' the county life are ample, too (p603).

④ Gauchos

The gaucho is as much a state of mind as a cultural icon. You can experience both by heading into the pampas, to towns like San Antonio de Areco (p144) where tradition trumps all.

⑤ Bus Rides

Argentines are avid travelers, and they've mastered the art of bus travel (p625): imagine two stories of big, plush, fully reclining seats, complimentary meals, cheap wine and even aperitifs! Overnight rides have never been such fun.

⑥ Bariloche

Alpine aesthetics meet Latin American urban planning at Argentina's classic vacation town (p406). Set on the scenic shores of Lago Nahuel Huapi, in the Patagonian Lake District, it's home to snow sports, hiking and nature aplenty.

⑦ The Jesuit Missions

Journey to northeast Argentina – and even into Paraguay for the day – to wander among the astonishing ruins of the Jesuit missions (p214), which were built by indigenous laborers in the 17th century.

⑧ Argentines

Ultra friendly, fun-loving, engaging and warm, Argentines are, without a doubt, one of the highlights of any trip to Argentina. Just asking someone for directions can lead to loads of fun...

The Taste of Argentina

Argentines take barbequing and beef to heights you cannot imagine. They make fabulous red, white and sparkling wines. Their pizzas vie with those of New York, Naples and Chicago. The pasta? Superb. The coffee? Excellent. Best of all, you can eat big while spending surprisingly little.

❶ Beef

Whether you're dining on prime cuts in a swanky Buenos Aires *parrilla* (grill) or digging into a sizzling tabletop grill of chewy, flavorful, close-to-the-bone cuts in a family-style eatery, you're bound to get your fill of Argentina's most famous food (p55).

❷ Ice Cream

Argentine ice cream, from Buenos Aires to Patagonia, gives the French and Italian versions a run for their money. The capital's *heladerías* (ice cream parlors; p118) are a great place to start lickin'.

❸ Wine

Exploring Argentina by the glass will take you – and your palate – from the malbecs and cabernets of Mendoza (p357) to the crisp torrontés of Cafayate (p276) to the succulent syrahs of San Juan (p369). A bottle a day – make that your motto.

❹ Mate

Although most first-time *mate* drinkers can barely choke the stuff down, this strong green tea, sipped communally from a gourd with a filtering metal straw, is a cultural delight (p57).

Contents

Regional Map Contents

THE ANDEAN NORTHWEST p244

NORTHEAST ARGENTINA p178

MENDOZA & THE CENTRAL ANDES p346

CÓRDOBA & THE CENTRAL SIERRAS p315

URUGUAY p541

BUENOS AIRES pp82-3

THE PAMPAS & THE ATLANTIC COAST p139

THE LAKE DISTRICT p381

PATAGONIA p425

TIERRA DEL FUEGO p520

Destination Argentina

Get a few people free-associating on the word 'Argentina,' and it's quickly apparent why the country has long held travelers in awe: tango, Patagonia, beef, soccer, Tierra del Fuego, passion, the Andes. The classics alone make a formidable wanderlust cocktail.

Just wait till you get here. Arriving in Buenos Aires is like jumping aboard a moving train. Outside the taxi window, a blurred mosaic of drab apartment blocks and haphazard architecture whizzes by as you shoot along the freeway toward the center of the city. The driver – probably driving *way* too fast while chain-smoking and talking incessantly about government corruption – finally merges off the freeway. Then the people appear, the cafés, the purple jacaranda flowers draped over the sidewalks, *porteños* (residents of Buenos Aires) in stylish clothing walking purposefully past the newspaper stands and candy kiosks and handsome early-20th-century stone facades.

Despite the enormity of the capital city – which is home to a whopping 30% of the country's population – visitors seem to find its groove with surprising ease. The real shocker, after experiencing the art, music, cafés, shopping and all-night revelry of Buenos Aires, comes when you leave it. Aside from a handful of cities such as Rosario, Córdoba, Mendoza and La Plata, Argentina is pretty darn empty. Population centers are small, and even provincial capitals can have the feel of a friendly town. While these places can be worthy destinations in themselves, their real purpose is usually to springboard people into Argentina's greatest attraction: the natural world.

From the mighty Iguazú Falls in the subtropical north, to the thunderous, crackling advance of the Perito Moreno Glacier in the south, Argentina is a vast natural wonderland. The country beholds some of the Andes' highest peaks, several of which top 6000m near Mendoza and San Juan. It's home to wetlands that rival Brazil's famous Pantanal, massive ice fields in Patagonia, a vast, sweltering, thorn-riddled wilderness known as the Impenetrable, cool lichen-clad Valdivian forests, glacial lakes, deserts, Andean salt flats, a spectacular Lake District, penguins, flamingos, caimans, capybaras and more.

But Argentina's cosmopolitan and natural marvels are only part of the equation. Visitors will also experience a country at a crossroads – an Argentina emerging from its worst economic crisis ever with a renewed, forward-looking sense of self. Cristina Kirchner, the country's first elected female president, took office in 2007, following in the footsteps of her husband, Nestor Kirchner, who enjoyed higher approval ratings than any other president in recent years. There's a palpable optimism in the air. Yet there's also a real sense of urgency, one that's fueled by skepticism, by daily reminders of government corruption and by signs that economic recovery has been far from universal.

No one wants to make a wrong turn.

Travelers who dig beneath the tourist-office version of Argentina will find a cultural climate electrified by discussion, argument and creative fervor. Argentina is in the throes of reinvention, and many people have a lot at stake. More than ever, Argentines have a lot to argue about. Spend any amount of time here, and you'll find yourself wrapped up in the discussion too, hopefully with a couple of locals. Argentines are, after all, some of the most amicable, seductive, engaging folks on the planet.

FAST FACTS

Area: 2.8 million sq km

Population: 40,301,927

Capital: Buenos Aires

Primary language: Spanish

Secondary languages: Quechua, Aymara, Toba (Qom) & others

Time: GMT minus 3hr

GDP per capita (2007 est): US$15,795

Inflation: 10.9%, highly variable

Unemployment rate: 8.7%

Beef consumption per capita: 70kg per year

Getting Started

Forget everything you've heard about the challenges of travel in South America. Argentina is different. It's easy. Comfortable buses run on set schedules, petty theft is relatively rare, overnight buses are luxurious and streets are safe. But the country does have its quirks, and knowing a few particulars before you go will make your journey all the more enjoyable.

This section will help you know when to visit (wait, August is ski season?), how much you might spend (prices have skyrocketed) and where to go for more information (we'd like to help you surf the internet on the boss's time). Argentina is still a remarkable deal, and you can do it on a budget or live it luxuriously. It all depends on what you want out of your trip.

WHEN TO GO

See Climate Charts (p606) for more information.

Argentina's seasons are reversed from the northern hemisphere's. The best time to visit Buenos Aires is in spring (September through November), when the jacarandas are in bloom and temperatures are blissfully cool, and in fall (March through May). Summer (December through February) in the capital is hot and humid. Mendoza, Córdoba and the Lake District are all spectacular in fall: the leaves put on an epic display, temperatures are comfortable and the crowds are thin.

Summer is the best time to hit Patagonia, when the weather's milder and more services are available. In other seasons, public transport becomes trickier as services thin out. Northern Argentina can be brutally hot in summer and is best visited in spring. Winter (June through August) and fall in this region are also pleasant.

Ski season runs mid-June through mid-October, and the resorts are most expensive and most crowded in July and August when every *porteño* (person from Buenos Aires) seems to be on the slopes.

The most expensive times to travel are the Argentine vacation months of January, February and July.

COSTS & MONEY

After the economic collapse of 2001/02 Argentina devalued the peso and the country became instantly affordable. Travel was cheap. In the following years the economy stabilized, inflation reared its head and the world became hip to the Argentine bargain. Prices rose. Although Argentina has become pricier, it's still a great value, especially if you're traveling on the euro or the pound.

DON'T LEAVE HOME WITHOUT...

- Your passport (see p619)
- Checking the visa situation (see p616)
- Tampons – tough to find in smaller towns
- Ziplock bags – to waterproof your gizmos
- Duct tape – make a mini-roll around a pencil stub or lighter
- Handy wipes – great for overnight bus rides
- Swiss Army knife – must contain a corkscrew!
- Ear plugs
- Universal sink plug – a must for hand-washing clothes

RATES ON THE RISE

Lonely Planet aims to give its readers a precise idea of what things cost. Rather than slapping hotels or restaurants into vague budget categories (which can still leave you guessing), we publish the actual rates and prices that businesses quote to us during research. The problem is that prices change, especially somewhere like Argentina, where inflation runs rampant. But we've found that readers prefer to have real numbers in their hands so they can make the calculations once they're on the road and then apply them across the board. It's still more precise than price ranges.

Argentina is no longer the rock-bottom bargain it was before 2005, but it remains great value. Where else can you enjoy a steak dinner with a good bottle of wine for under US$10? Or an amazing scoop of ice cream for under US$2? Certainly not in Europe or the United States. Although we anticipate prices will continue to rise, we've still opted to provide the prices given us at the time of research. Our advice: call or check a few hotel or tour operator websites before budgeting your trip, just to make sure you're savvy about going rates.

If you're on a budget you can get by on AR$60 to AR$75 per day (outside Patagonia) by sleeping in hostels or cheap hotels and eating at the cheapest nontouristy restaurants. Things get pricier when you add tours and entertainment. Outside the capital and Patagonia, midrange travelers can get by comfortably on AR$160 to AR$200 per person per day, staying in a comfy hotel and eating at decent restaurants.

Buenos Aires and especially Patagonia are more expensive than the rest of Argentina. In the capital, good hotel rooms *start* at around AR$180 per double. In the provinces you can land a good hotel for AR$90 per double, while an extra AR$20 to AR$50 will get you something very comfortable.

Except in Patagonia, a pasta dinner can be as cheap as AR$8 per person at a no-frills family joint, while a full gourmet meal at a top-end restaurant can cost around AR$90 per person. In Patagonia a cheap restaurant meal starts at around AR$18.

HOW MUCH?

Midrange hotel
AR$60-180

Five-hour bus ride AR$45

Slice of pizza AR$3.50

Sirloin steak AR$15

Average in-city cab ride AR$6

TRAVELING RESPONSIBLY

Since our inception in 1973, Lonely Planet has encouraged our readers to tread lightly, travel responsibly and enjoy the magic that independent travel affords. International travel is growing at a jaw-dropping rate, and we still firmly believe in the benefits it can bring – but, as always, we encourage you to consider the impact your visit will have on both the global environment and the local economies, cultures and ecosystems.

Whenever you can, patronize the businesses listed in the Lonely Planet GreenDex (p672), which have proven they're dedicated to sustainable travel. In all situations, try to support local businesses rather than large and international chains – it keeps profits local. Whenever hiking, trekking, climbing, flying or otherwise enjoying the great outdoors, do your best to adhere as strictly as possible to the ethics of Leave No Trace (www.lnt.org), principles created by outdoor enthusiasts to minimize impact on the environments in which we play.

Although Argentina lacks a large indigenous population (unlike the Andean nations to the north), it does have its share of indigenous communities, primarily in the Chaco (p232). Whenever visiting or traveling through these communities, be sensitive to local beliefs and customs and avoid playing the gawker.

And don't forget the obvious: learn the language! Even if you blow it, you're attempt will be appreciated.

For more on sustainable travel, see p78.

TOP PICKS

LITERATURE

Be they works by Argentine authors or by foreigners writing about Argentina, the following works of fiction are perfect for those long bus rides across the Argentine pampas.

- *The Story of the Night* (1996), by Colm Tóibín
- *Hopscotch* (1963), by Julio Cortázar
- *Labyrinths: Selected Stories & Other Writings* (1962), by Jorge Luis Borges
- *The Tunnel* (1948), by Ernesto Sábato
- *Santa Evita* (1995), by Tomás Eloy Martínez
- *The Honorary Consul* (1973), by Graham Greene

MOVIES

Argentina has both inspired and produced countless outstanding movies. Here's our noninclusive, totally biased choice of six.

- *El Bonaerense* (2002), directed by Pablo Trapero
- *The Motorcycle Diaries* (2004), directed by Walter Salles
- *Intimate Stories (Histórias mínimas;* 2002), directed by Carlos Sorin
- *La ciénaga* (2001), directed by Lucrecia Martel
- *Nine Queens (Nueve reinas;* 2000), directed by Fabián Bielinsky
- *Blessed by Fire (Iluminados por el fuego;* 2005), directed by Tristán Bauer
- *Pizza, Beer & Smokes (Pizza, birra, faso;* 1998), directed by Adrián Caetano & Bruno Stagnaro

WEIRD & WACKY PLACES

After all, everywhere has its oddities. The following offbeat places will get you thinking just how *interesting* Argentina can be. *¡Que raro!*

- Museo Rocsen (p336)
- Difunta Correa Shrine (p373)
- Interpretation Center at San Ignacio Miní (p219)
- Gaucho Antonio Gil shrines (p201)
- Parque El Desafío, Gaiman (p447)

PARKS

Argentina is a nature-lover's dream, and its parks are truly one of the best reasons to be here. For a complete list see p66, but don't miss the following:

- Parque Nacional Los Glaciares (p483)
- Parque Nacional Iguazú (p223)
- Parque Nacional Tierra del Fuego (p535)
- Reserva Faunística Península Valdés (p436)
- Parque Provincial Ischigualasto (p379)

TRAVEL LITERATURE

After years out of print, Lucas Bridges' classic, *Uttermost Part of the Earth* (1947), was republished in 2008. Bridges brilliantly describes his life among the indigenous peoples of Tierra del Fuego – a must-read for anyone heading south.

Another newly released account of an old journey is Ernesto 'Che' Guevara's offbeat *The Motorcycle Diaries* (2003), in which the young medical student recounts his eye-opening journey by motorcycle in 1951–2 through Argentina, Chile, Brazil, Venezuela, Peru and Colombia.

In *Bad Times in Buenos Aires* (1999), Miranda France covers everything from Argentine condoms to psychoanalysis in a wry (and sometimes overbearingly negative) account of her stay in the capital while working as a journalist in the 1990s.

If you're going to be wandering down to Patagonia (and even if you're not), pick up Bruce Chatwin's *In Patagonia* (1977), one of the most informed syntheses of life and landscape for any part of South America. For a glimpse into some gripping Patagonian mountaineering, read Gregory Crouch's *Enduring Patagonia* (2001), in which the author details his ascents of Cerro Torre's brutal west face and several other wild climbs.

Nick Reding's *The Last Cowboys at the End of the World: The Story of the Gauchos of Patagonia* (2001) takes place mostly in Chile, but is equally pertinent to the conditions and changes in neighboring Argentine Patagonia.

Frequently reprinted, William Henry Hudson's *Idle Days in Patagonia* (1893) is a romantic account of the 19th-century naturalist's adventures in search of migratory birds. Also check out his *The Purple Land* (1885) and *Far Away and Long Ago* (1918).

'Ernesto 'Che' Guevara's offbeat *The Motorcycle Diaries* recounts his eye-opening journey by motorcycle in 1951–2'

INTERNET RESOURCES

The web is a great place to plan your trip. For websites about specific topics (such as hostels, relocating to Argentina or gay and lesbian resources), see the appropriate section in the Directory (p602). The following should get you started:

Argentina Turística (www.argentinaturistica.com) Packed with information in English and Spanish, this is one of the best general information sites on the web.

Buenos Aires Herald (www.buenosairesherald.com) An international view of the country and world can be found at the website of Buenos Aires' excellent English-language newspaper. Membership required.

Latin American Network Information Center (www.lanic.utexas.edu/la/argentina/) This site has a massive list of Argentine websites. If you can't find it here…well, never mind, 'cause you'll find it here.

Lonely Planet (www.lonelyplanet.com) Succinct summaries on traveling to most places on earth; postcards from other travelers; and the Thorn Tree bulletin board, where you can ask questions before you go or dispense advice when you get back.

Sectur (www.turismo.gov.ar) The official Argentine state tourist board's website offers a decent dose of information in English and Spanish.

Events Calendar

Although Argentina is less prone to wild festivals than other South American countries, there are several fiestas which – depending on your interests – might be worth planning your trip around. Aside from the festivals listed here, nearly every town in Argentina has its own fiesta, most of which are covered in each destination's Festivals & Events section throughout this book. For a list of national public holidays, see p610.

JANUARY

FESTIVAL NACIONAL DEL FOLKLORE late Jan
Near the city of Córdoba, in the Central Sierras, the town of Cosquín hosts the National Festival of Folk Music (p327; www.aquicosquin.org, in Spanish) during the last week of January. It's the country's largest and best known *folklórico* (folk music) festival.

FEBRUARY–MARCH

BUENOS AIRES TANGO late Feb–early Mar
During the last week of February and first week of March, Buenos Aires celebrates its native dance with masterful performances shown at different venues all over the city. For details, see www .festivaldetango.com.ar.

CARNAVAL late Feb–early Mar
Though the pre-Lenten festival is not as rockin' in Argentina as it is in Brazil, the celebration is rowdy in the northeast, especially in the cities of Gualeguaychú (p205) and Corrientes (p196). In the northwest (particularly the Quebrada de Humahuaca), there's more emphasis on traditional music and dancing, making it a particularly good place to be. Dates vary around the end of February and beginning of March.

FIESTA NACIONAL DE LA VENDIMIA late Feb–early Mar
Mendoza's National Wine Harvest Festival (p351) kicks off with parades, folkloric events and a royal coronation – all in honor of Mendoza's intoxicating beverage. The festival takes place in Mendoza city, the de facto capital of Argentina's wine country. For more information, see www .vendimia.mendoza.gov.ar in Spanish.

MAY

DÍA DE VIRGEN DE LUJÁN May 8
Thousands of devout believers make a 65km pilgrimage to the pampas town of Luján (p142) in honor of the Virgin Mary; other large pilgrimages to Luján take place in early October and on December 8, but May's is the largest.

AUGUST

FESTIVAL & MUNDIAL DE TANGO mid–late Aug
Buenos Aires' best tango dancers perform at venues throughout the city during the Tango Festival (p108). It's a much more local event than the internationally attended Mundial de Tango (World Tango Festival) the following week.

OCTOBER

FIESTA NACIONAL DE LA CERVEZA/OKTOBERFEST early Oct
Join the swillers and oompah bands at the National Beer Festival, Villa General Belgrano's Oktoberfest (p333) in the Central Sierras. For details, see http:// elsitiodelavilla.com/oktoberfest in Spanish.

EISTEDDFOD late Oct
This lively Welsh festival, featuring plentiful grub and choral singing, takes place in the wee Patagonian towns of Trelew (p444) and Trevelin (p473). It's a great one for inducing those wait-am-I-really-in-South-America? moments.

NOVEMBER

DÍA DE LA TRADICIÓN Nov 10
The Day of Traditional Culture festival kicks off with a salute to the gaucho and is especially significant in San Antonio de Areco (p146), the most classically gaucho of towns. It's also important – and decidedly less touristy – in the mountain town of San José de Jáchal (p377), in San Juan.

MARCHA DEL ORGULLO GAY mid Nov
Buenos Aires' Gay Pride Parade (www.marcha delorgullo.org.ar; p108) draws thousands of gay, lesbian, and transgendered citizens, as well as their supporters, who march (with the music up loud!) from Plaza de Mayo to the Congreso.

Itineraries
CLASSIC ROUTES

NORTHERN LOOP

Two to Four Weeks/Mendoza, the Andean Northwest & Iguazú Falls

From **Buenos Aires** (p81), head to **Mendoza** (p345), smack in the heart of wine country. Take a one-day side trip up RN 7 to **Puente del Inca** (p361) and the **Cristo Redentor** (p363) monument. Then, take an overnight bus to **Córdoba** (p316) to explore Argentina's finest colonial center.

Journey to **Tucumán** (p286) for some eclectic architecture and one of Argentina's liveliest street scenes. Head northwest to mellow lakeside **Tafí del Valle** (p293) for a day, then onto beautiful **Cafayate** (p275) to knock back some local torrontés wine. Sober up and drive the epic **Quebrada de Cafayate** (p286) to **Salta** (p261), whose central plaza is one of Argentina's finest. From there, journey into the otherworldly Valles Calchaquíes to the adobe villages of **Cachi** (p272) and **Molinos** (p273). Next up, the magnificently eroded Andean valley, **Quebrada de Humahuaca** (p253), where you can overnight in lively little **Tilcara** (p254).

Return to Salta. From there, bus across the Chaco or fly via Buenos Aires for the grand finale: two days at **Parque Nacional Iguazú** (p223).

Covering over 4000km, the Northern Loop takes you to four of Argentina's finest cities, through the forgotten Valles Calchaquíes to villages plucked from centuries past, and to one of South America's greatest natural spectacles, Iguazú Falls.

GRAND LOOP

The Grand Loop traverses over 8800km, from Tierra del Fuego and Los Glaciares in the south, through the beautiful Lake District, to the traditional villages and Andean scenery of northwest Argentina. From wine country to wildlife, you'll have seen the best of Argentina. Throwing a couple of flights into this itinerary makes it manageable in less time.

Six to 12 Weeks/Humahuaca to Tierra del Fuego

From **Buenos Aires** (p81), head south for whale watching at **Reserva Faunística Península Valdés** (p436). Take the long bus ride south to **Ushuaia** (p525) in Tierra del Fuego and on the way, stop for penguin watching at **Reserva Provincial Punta Tombo** (p448), dolphin spotting at **Reserva Natural Ría Deseado** (p457) and coastal bird watching at **Parque Nacional Monte León** (p460).

After finally reaching Ushuaia allow for several days of exploration. Then, follow the two-week Patagonian Passage itinerary (p27) before winding your way up to the **Lake District** (p380), with a chocolate stop in **Bariloche** (p406). Bump down the lake-studded **Ruta de los Siete Lagos** (Seven Lakes Route; p397) to the leafy resort of **San Martín de los Andes** (p395) before exploring the Valdivian forests of **Parque Nacional Lanín** (p400).

From San Martín, head to **Aluminé** (p388) for rafting or fly-fishing and then on to gorgeous little **Villa Pehuenia** (p389) for a day or two of hiking and relaxation. Next, explore the breathtaking volcanic landscapes around **Malargüe** (p366) and continue north to **Mendoza** (p345) for wine tasting and more mind-blowing Andean scenery. From Mendoza, journey via **San Juan** (p369) to **Parque Provincial Ischigualasto** (p379), and then head east to explore the colonial center of **Córdoba** (p316).

From Córdoba, cut north to **Tucumán** (p286), then through the wildly eroded canyon of **Quebrada de Cafayate** (p286) to **Salta** (p261). From there head into **Quebrada de Humahuaca** (p253) for a few days. Travel across the rugged Chaco, to visit **Reserva Provincial Esteros del Iberá** (p201). Continue northeast to the **Jesuit missions** (p217) near Posadas and finish beneath the massive falls of **Parque Nacional Iguazú** (p223). Fly back to Buenos Aires and party till your plane leaves.

ROADS LESS TRAVELED

RUTA NACIONAL 40 (RN 40) Four to Eight Weeks/The Argentine Andes

Argentina's quintessential road trip, RN 40 travels the length of the Argentine Andes through some of the country's remotest regions. Much of it remains un-paved, and requires perseverance, time and self reliance. As you travel it, you'll see an Argentina that most people – even most Argentines – never do. Much of the route is doable by bus, but some stretches require your own vehicle.

RN 40 starts immediately south of **Abra Pampa** (p259) in the Andean northwest, but the steep stretches before **Cachi** (p272), in the wildly scenic **Valles Calchaquíes** (p271), are impossible without a 4WD. Instead, start at Cachi. Further south, you'll hit lovely **Cafayate** (p275) before passing tiny **Huaco** (p377) and traditional **San José de Jáchal** (p377). Take a breather in **Mendoza** (p345) – you've been going *at least* a week now – and then explore the volcanic landscapes around **Malargüe** (p366). To avoid road closures from snow and rain, plan your trip so that you're traveling south of Malargüe in summer (December to March).

Continue south to tranquil **Buta Ranquil** (p388) and then explore the lagoons and hot springs around **Chos Malal** (p387). Detour to **Parque Nacional Nahuel Huapi** (p415) and **Parque Nacional Lanín** (p400) for epic hiking before stocking up on chocolate in **Bariloche** (p406). By car or travelers shuttle (p470), make the two- to four-day journey south to **El Calafate** (p490), where you can see the mind-altering Perito Moreno Glacier. Detour to **El Chaltén** (p483) for superb hiking in the Fitz Roy Range before continuing down RN 40 for a detour to **Puerto Natales** (p508), Chile. From there, explore **Parque Nacional Torres del Paine** (p512) before doglegging west to Río Gallegos to fly back to Buenos Aires.

RN 40 travels nearly the entire length of Argentina, over 5000km, from just south of the Bolivian border in the north, nearly to Tierra del Fuego in the south. Some stretches require a private vehicle, others a 4WD (or, sans the 4WD, good walking shoes, plenty of food and water and a need for adventure).

FORGOTTEN ANDES & PARKS   Two to Three weeks/San Luis to Corrientes

This journey off the beaten track will turn up tiny villages, empty roads and rarely visited provincial parks. Begin in the tiny provincial capital of **San Luis** (p337), from where you can visit **Parque Nacional Sierra de las Quijadas** (p339), whose wildly eroded lunar landscape is similar to San Juan's Parque Provincial Ischigualasto – sans the people. Bus over to **San Juan** (p369), rent a car and head for the hills: drive up to **Barreal** (p374) in the breathtaking Valle de Calingasta for hiking, rafting, climbing and land sailing beneath the country's highest peaks. Head up RP 412 to the traditional towns of **Rodeo** (p377), **San José de Jáchal** (p377) and **Huaco** (p377), and stop en route for a dip in the thermal baths of **Pismanta** (p378). Take RN 40 back to San Juan and bus out to the fascinating **Difunta Correa Shrine** (p373) – and don't forget to leave a bottle of water as an offering to this patron saint of truck drivers (especially if you hitchhike!).

> Just because the crowds head elsewhere doesn't mean this 2850km trip lacks sights. In fact, the forgotten back roads and little-visited villages and parks make this a very special trip through an Argentina that most foreigners never see.

From San Juan, take an overnight bus to **Córdoba** (p316), a colonial city that foreigners often skip. After a day or two exploring the city and the Jesuit *estancias* (ranches) of the **Central Sierras** (p325), grab an overnighter to **Resistencia** (p233), an odd city of sculptures and the nearest hub to **Parque Nacional Chaco** (p237). From **Corrientes** (p194), catch some live *chamamé* (folk music of northeast Argentina), and head to **Reserva Provincial Esteros del Iberá** (p201), a wetlands preserve and wildlife sanctuary comparable to Brazil's Pantanal.

By now you'll be aching for human contact: either join the crowds at **Iguazú Falls** (p223), a full day's travel away, or head back to Buenos Aires, flying from Corrientes or journeying overland.

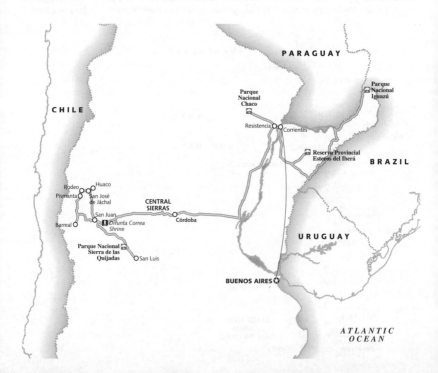

TAILORED TRIPS

PATAGONIAN PASSAGE   Patagonia, Tierra del Fuego & the Lake District

Though the sadistic manage this national parks circuit in 10 days, two weeks is really the minimum. It's the end of the world, after all, so don't sell yourself short. From Buenos Aires fly to **Ushuaia** (p525), in Tierra del Fuego, and visit nearby **Parque Nacional Tierra del Fuego** (p535). Take a hopper flight to **El Calafate** (p490) and visit spectacular Perito Moreno Glacier in **Parque Nacional Los Glaciares** (p483). Bus down to **Puerto Natales** (p508) and trek the famous **Parque Nacional Torres del Paine** (p512). Head north again to **El Chaltén** (p483) for mind-altering hikes in the **Fitz Roy area** (p483). Then back to El Calafate for your return flight to Buenos Aires. *Chau!*

With an extra two weeks, begin the trip by heading south by bus (rather than plane) and stop in **Puerto Madryn** (p431) on your way down for whale watching at **Reserva Faunística Península Valdés** (p436). After exploring the national parks mentioned above, fly from El Calafate up to **Bariloche** (p406). From here, hike yourself silly in the Lake District national parks of **Nahuel Huapi** (p415) and **Lanín** (p400). Before your flight back to Buenos Aires, you may even be able to squeeze in trips to nearby **Parque Nacional Lago Puelo** (p422) and **Parque Nacional Los Alerces** (p473).

ADVENTURES IN WINE   Mendoza, San Juan & the Andean Northwest

Prime your palate for this trip through Argentina's world-class wine countries. Following the oenologist's trail will not only give you a serious sampling of the country's finest libation, you'll be introduced to many of its most interesting regions. Uncork your trip in beautiful **Mendoza** (p345), Argentina's Andes-flanked wine capital. Be certain to stop at **Bodega La Rural** (p358), home of South America's largest (and best) wine museum. Squeeze in a day trip up RN 7 to **Puente del Inca** (p361) thermal baths and the lung-busting heights of the **Cristo Redentor** (p363), on the Chilean border.

Take a crack-of-dawn bus to **San Rafael** (p364), rent a bike and ride out to the city's wineries, making **Bianchi Champañera** (p364) your last stop for a bit of bubbly. The next day, head to **San Juan** (p369) to try the excellent syrah and regional whites produced near this leafy provincial capital. Squeeze in a day trip to **Parque Provincial Ischigualasto** (p379) or up RN 40 to **San José de Jáchal** (p377) if you have the time. From San Juan take an overnight bus to **Tucumán** (p286), and head the next day to lovely little **Cafayate** (p275) to hit a few wineries and dazzle your taste buds with the regional torrontés white wine. Return to Tucumán for your flight back to Buenos Aires.

History

Like all Latin American countries, Argentina has a tumultuous history, one tainted by periods of despotic rule, corruption and hard times. But it's also an illustrious history, a story of a country that was once one of the world's economic powerhouses, a country that gave birth to the tango, to international icons like Evita Perón and Che Guevara, and to some of the world's most important inventions (the public bus, the coronary bypass and the ballpoint pen all come to mind). Understanding Argentina's past is paramount to understanding its present and, most importantly, to understanding Argentines themselves.

NATIVE PEOPLES

Human migration to the Americas began nearly 30,000 years ago, when the ancestors of Amerindians, taking advantage of lowered sea levels during the Pleistocene epoch, walked from Siberia to Alaska via a land bridge across the Bering Strait. Not exactly speedy about moving south, they reached what's now Argentina around 10,000 BC. One of Argentina's oldest and impressive archaeological sites is Cueva de las Manos (Cave of the Hands; p480) in Patagonia, where mysterious cave paintings, mostly of left hands, date from 7370 BC.

By the time the Spanish arrived, much of present-day Argentina was inhabited by highly mobile peoples who hunted the guanaco (a wild relative of the llama) and the rhea (a large bird resembling an emu) with bow and arrow or *boleadoras* – heavily weighted thongs that could be thrown up to 90m to ensnare the hunted animal. (Today, replica *boleadoras* are sold at artisan shops throughout the country – pick up a set and give them a hurl at a stationary object for an idea of the skill required to take down a guanaco!)

The Argentine pampas was inhabited by the Querandí, hunters and gatherers who are legendary for their spirited resistance to the Spanish. The Guaraní, indigenous to the area from northern Entre Ríos through Corrientes and into Paraguay and Brazil, were semisedentary agriculturalists, raising sweet potatoes, maize, manioc and beans, and fishing the Río Paraná.

Of all of Argentina, the northwest was the most developed. Several indigenous groups, most notably the Diaguita, practiced irrigated agriculture in the valleys of the eastern Andean foothills. The region's inhabitants were influenced heavily by the Tiahanaco empire of Bolivia and by the great Inca empire, which expanded south from Peru into Argentina from the early 1480s. In Salta province the ruined stone city of Quilmes (p295) is one of the best-preserved pre-Incan indigenous sites, where some 5000 Quilmes, part of the Diaguita civilization, lived and withstood the Inca invasion. Further north in Tilcara (p254) you can see a completely restored *pucará* (walled city), about which little is known.

Journey back in time to the epoch of Patagonia's first human inhabitants, and see how their world changed in the centuries that followed, in *Patagonia: Natural History, Prehistory and Ethnography at the Uttermost End of the Earth* (1997), by Colin McEwen et al.

TIMELINE

10,000 BC	7370 BC	4000 BC
The estimated time when humans, having crossed the Bering Strait approximately 20,000 years earlier, finally reach the area of modern-day Argentina. The close of one of the world's greatest human migrations nears.	Estimated date when Toldense culture makes its first paintings of hands inside Patagonia's famous Cueva de las Manos. The paintings prove humans inhabited the region this far back – and had a preference for painting the left appendage.	Around this time, the indigenous Yaghan, later referred to as Fuegians by the English-speaking world, begin populating the southernmost islands of Tierra del Fuego. Humans could migrate no further south.

In the Lake District and Patagonia, the Pehuenches and Puelches were hunter-gatherers, and the pine nuts of the araucaria, or pehuén tree, formed a staple of their diet. The names Pehuenches and Puelches were given to them by the Mapuche, who entered the region from the west as the Spanish pushed south. Today there are many Mapuche reservations, especially in the area around Junín de los Andes (p393), where you can still sample foods made from pine nuts.

Argentina's national beer, Quilmes, is named after an indigenous group of northwest Argentina.

Until they were wiped out by Europeans, there were indigenous inhabitants as far south as Tierra del Fuego, where the Selk'nam, Haush, Yaghan and Alacaluf peoples lived as mobile hunters and gatherers. Despite frequently inclement weather they wore little or no clothing, but constant fires (even in their bark canoes) kept them warm and gave the region its Spanish name, Tierra del Fuego (Land of Fire).

ENTER THE SPANISH

Just over a decade after Christopher Columbus (Cristóbal Colón in Spanish) accidentally encountered the Americas, other Spanish explorers began probing the Río de la Plata estuary. (Columbus was actually Italian, but he was sailing under the Spanish flag). Most early explorations of the area were motivated by rumors of vast quantities of silver. Spaniard Sebastian Cabot optimistically named the river the Río de la Plata (River of Silver), and to drive the rumors home, part of the new territory was even given the Latin name for silver *(argentum)*. But the mineral riches that the Spanish found in the Inca empire of Peru never panned out in this misnamed land.

The first real attempt at establishing a permanent settlement on the estuary was made by Spanish aristocrat Pedro de Mendoza in 1536. He landed at present-day Buenos Aires and, not one to mince words, named the outpost Puerto Nuestra Señora Santa María del Buen Aire (Port Our Lady St Mary of the Good Wind). After the colonists tried pilfering food from the indigenous Querandí, the natives turned on them violently. Within four years Mendoza fled back to Spain without a lick of silver, and the detachment of troops he left behind beat it up river to the gentler environs of Asunción, present-day capital of Paraguay.

The most comprehensive, though not necessarily most readable, book on Argentine history is David Rock's *Argentina 1516–1987: From Spanish Colonization to Alfonsín* (1987). It's worth the grunt.

NORTHWEST SUPREMACY

Although Spanish forces reestablished Buenos Aires by 1580, it remained a backwater in comparison to Andean settlements founded by a separate and more successful Spanish contingency moving south from Alto Perú (now Bolivia). With ties to the colonial stronghold of Lima, capital of the viceroyalty of Peru, and financed by the bonanza silver mine at Potosí, the Spanish founded some two dozen cities as far south as Mendoza (1561), all during the latter half of the 16th century. Santiago del Estero, founded in 1553, is the country's oldest permanent settlement. The main force in this northward orientation was the

AD 1480s	1536	1553
Under the rule of Huayna Cápac, the Inca empire expands into present-day Argentina's Andean northwest. At the time, the region was inhabited by Argentina's most advanced indigenous cultures, including the Diaguita and Tafí.	Pedro de Mendoza establishes Puerto Nuestra Señora Santa María del Buen Aire on the Río de la Plata. But the Spaniards anger the indigenous Querandí, who soon drive the settlers out.	Francisco de Aguirre establishes Santiago del Estero, furthering Spain's expansion into present-day Argentina from Alto Perú. Today, the city is the country's oldest permanent settlement.

AN ABBREVIATED HISTORICAL WHO'S WHO

▪ **José de San Martín** (1778–1850) Argentina's great national hero, who lead the country and southern South America to independence from Spain. Best quote: 'I only want lions in my regiment.'

▪ **Domingo Faustino Sarmiento** (1811–88) Argentine author, educator and president of Argentina (1868–74). Famous words: 'It would be fun to make an offer to England, just to see how much muslin and cotton it would give to own these plains of Buenos Aires.'

▪ **General Julio Argentino Roca** (1843–1914) Minister of War (1877–79); President of Argentina (1843–1914). Famous for: wiping out much of Patagonia's indigenous population in the 1879 Conquest of the Desert.

▪ **Raúl Alfonsín** (1927–) First democratically elected president (1983–89) following the Dirty War. Famous quote: 'The house is in order.'

▪ **Ernesto Guevara de la Serna** (1928–67) Born in Rosario, Argentina, and known as Che Guevara, the most legendary of revolutionaries. Famous quote: 'I don't care if I fall as long as someone else picks up my gun and keeps on shooting.'

▪ **Juan Domingo Perón** (1895–1974) President of Argentina (1946–55); husband of Evita. Famous quote: 'The people are my only descendants.'

▪ **María Eva Duarte de Perón** (1919–52) Known to the world as 'Evita'; championed social rights as First Lady to President Perón. Famous quote: 'If I fall, look out for the crash. There won't be anyone left standing.'

▪ **Jorge Rafael Videla** (1925–) Former military general and leader of military coup that unseated Isabel Perón in 1976; de facto president until 1981.

protectionist King of Spain, whose mercantile policy decreed that commerce between Spain and the colonies had to be routed through Lima.

The two most important population centers at the time were Tucumán (founded in 1565) and Córdoba (1573). Tucumán lay in the heart of a rich agricultural region and supplied Alto Perú with grains, cotton and livestock. Córdoba became an important educational center, and Jesuit missionaries established *estancias* (ranches) in the surrounding sierras to supply Alto Perú with mules, foodstuffs and wine. Córdoba's Manzana Jesuítica (Jesuit Block; p317) is now the finest preserved group of colonial buildings in the country, and several Jesuit *estancias* in the Central Sierras (p325) are also exquisitely preserved. These sites, along with the central plazas of Salta (founded in 1582) and Tucumán, boast the country's finest colonial architecture.

South America's oldest university is Córdoba's Universidad Nacional de Córdoba, founded in 1613 and elevated to university status in 1622.

THE JESUITS

Northeast Argentina, along the upper regions of the Río Uruguay and Río Paraná, was colonized later with the help of Jesuit missionaries, who

1561	1565	1573
The city of Mendoza is founded by Spaniards traveling east from Santiago, Chile, during their push to establish access to the Río de la Plata, where Spanish ships could deliver more troops and supplies.	Diego de Villarroel founds the city of San Miguel de Tucumán (referred to today simply as Tucumán), Argentina's third-oldest. The city was relocated further east 120 years later.	The city of Córdoba is founded by Tucumán Governor Jerónimo Luis de Cabrera, establishing an important link on the trade routes between Chile and Alto Perú.

- **Carlos Menem** (1930–) President of Argentina (1989–99). Famous for: curbing inflation after the Dirty War, selling off state enterprises, corruption.
- **Domingo Cavallo** (1946–) Argentine Minister of Economy under Carlos Menem. Famous for: pegging the peso to the dollar in 1991 and instituting *el corralito* (a freeze on withdrawals) in 2001.
- **Alfredo Yabrán** (1944–1998) Powerful Argentine businessman with links to the Menem government. Found dead in his home amid investigation for the murder of photojournalist José Luis Cabezas. Catch: the gunshot to his face left him suspiciously unrecognizable.
- **José Luis Cabezas** (1962–97) Photojournalist who was murdered following his photographing of secretive businessman Alfredo Yabrán.
- **Fernando de la Rúa** (1937–) President of Argentina (1999–2001); resigned amid economic crisis that rocked Argentina. Best campaign ad: 'They say that I'm boring.'
- **Eduardo Duhalde** (1941–) Interim president (2002–03) following resignation of Fernando de la Rúa. Famous for: devaluing the peso in 2002.
- **Roberto Lavagna** (1942–) Minister of Economy (2002–05) under interim President Eduardo Duhalde. Credited with: handling the economic crisis and arranging Argentina's debt swap with the IMF.
- **Nestor Kirchner** (1950–) President of Argentina (2003–07). Nicknames: 'K' and 'El Pingüino' ('the penguin;' he hails from Patagonia).
- **Cristina Fernández de Kirchner** (1953–) Current president of Argentina; former First Lady to Nestor Kirchner.

concentrated the indigenous Guaraní in settlements. Starting around 1607, the Jesuits established 30 missions, including the marvelously preserved San Ignacio Miní (p219), which should be on every architecture-lover's hit list.

Perhaps as many as 100,000 indigenous people lived in the Jesuit settlements, which resembled other Spanish municipalities but operated with a political and economic autonomy that did not apply to other Iberian settlers. Wary of the Jesuits' accumulating wealth and power, the Spanish crown expelled them in 1767, and the mission communities disintegrated rapidly, almost fading into the wilderness.

The Mission (1986), starring Robert De Niro and Jeremy Irons, is an epic film about the Jesuit missions and missionaries in 18th-century South America. It's the perfect kickoff for a trip to northern Argentina's missions.

BUENOS AIRES: BOOTLEGGER TO BOOMTOWN

As the northwest prospered, Buenos Aires suffered the Crown's harsh restrictions on trade for nearly two centuries. But because the port was ideal for trade, frustrated merchants turned to smuggling, and contraband trade with Portuguese Brazil and nonpeninsular European powers flourished.

1580	1607	1767
Buenos Aires is reestablished by Spanish forces, but the city remains a backwater for years, in comparison with the growing strongholds of Mendoza, Tucumán and Santiago del Estero in central and northwestern Argentina.	Jesuits begin building missions in northeast Argentina, concentrating the indigenous Guaraní into settlements known as *reducciones*. The missions of San Ignacio Miní (1610), Loreto (1632) and Santa Ana (1633) date from this period.	The Spanish crown expels the Jesuits from all of New Spain, and the mission communities decline rapidly.

The increasing amount of wealth passing through the city fueled much of its initial growth.

For an interpretation of the gaucho's role in Argentine history, check out Richard W Slatta's book *Gauchos and the Vanishing Frontier* (1983).

With the decline of silver mining at Potosí in the late 18th century, the Spanish crown was forced to recognize Buenos Aires' importance for direct transatlantic trade. Relaxing its restrictions, Spain made Buenos Aires the capital of the new viceroyalty of the Río de la Plata – which included Paraguay, Uruguay and the mines at Potosí – in 1776.

Although the new viceroyalty had internal squabbles over trade and control issues, when the British raided the city in 1806 and again in 1807, the response was unified. Locals rallied against the invaders without Spanish help and chased them out of town.

The late 18th century also saw the emergence of the legendary gauchos of the pampas (see the boxed text, p147). The South American counterpart to North America's cowboys, they hunted wild cattle and broke in wild horses that had multiplied after being left behind by previous expeditions on the Río de la Plata.

INDEPENDENCE & INFIGHTING

Gargantuan in size and vast in scope, *The Argentina Reader* (2002), edited by Gabriella Nouzeilles and Graciela Mondaldo, is a thorough compilation of some of the most important essays, excerpts and stories from Argentine history and culture.

Toward the end of the 18th century, *criollos* (Argentine-born colonists) became increasingly dissatisfied and impatient with Spanish authority. The expulsion of British troops from Buenos Aires gave the people of the Río de la Plata new confidence in their ability to stand alone. After Napoleon invaded Spain in 1808, Buenos Aires finally declared its independence on May 25, 1810. To commemorate the occasion, the city's main square was renamed Plaza de Mayo.

Independence movements throughout South America soon united to expel Spain from the continent by the 1820s. Under the leadership of General José de San Martín and others, the United Provinces of the Río de la Plata (the direct forerunner of the Argentine Republic) declared formal independence at Tucumán on July 9, 1816.

Take a more personalized look into Argentina's past with Monica Szurmuk's *Women in Argentina* (2001), a collection of travel narratives by women – both Argentine and foreign – who traveled here between 1850 and 1930.

Despite achieving independence, the provinces were united in name only. With a lack of any effective central authority, regional disparities within Argentina – formerly obscured by Spanish rule – became more obvious. This resulted in the rise of the caudillos (local strongmen), who resisted Buenos Aires as strongly as Buenos Aires had resisted Spain.

Argentine politics was thus divided between the Federalists of the interior, who advocated provincial autonomy, and the Unitarists of Buenos Aires, who upheld the city's central authority. For nearly two decades bloody and vindictive conflicts between the two factions left the country nearly exhausted.

THE REIGN OF ROSAS

In the first half of the 19th century Juan Manuel de Rosas came to prominence as a caudillo in Buenos Aires province, representing the interests of

1776	1806–07	1810
Spain names Buenos Aires the capital of the new viceroyalty of the Río de la Plata. The territory includes the areas of present-day Paraguay, Uruguay and the mines at Potosí (Bolivia).	Attempting to seize control of Spanish colonies during the Napoleonic Wars, British forces raid Buenos Aires in 1806 and again in 1807. Buenos Aires militias defeat British troops without Spain's help, which kindles ideas of independence.	Buenos Aires declares its independence from Spain on May 25, although actual independence is still several years off. The city names the Plaza de Mayo in honor of the event.

rural elites and landowners. He became governor of the province in 1829 and, while he championed the Federalist cause, he also helped centralize political power in Buenos Aires and required that all international trade be funneled through the capital. His reign lasted more than 20 years (from 1829 to 1852), and he set ominous precedents in Argentine political life, creating the infamous *mazorca* (his ruthless political police force) and institutionalizing torture.

Under Rosas, Buenos Aires continued to dominate the new country, but his extremism turned many against him, including some of his strongest allies. Finally, in 1852, a rival caudillo named Justo José de Urquiza (once a staunch supporter of Rosas) organized a powerful army and forced Rosas from power. Urquiza's first task was to draw up a constitution, which was formalized by a convention in Santa Fe on May 1, 1853. Urquiza became the country's first president. The Constitution (still in force today despite its frequent suspension) pointed to the triumph of Unitarism, and subsequent economic developments confirmed Buenos Aires' power in the coming decades. In 1862 Buenos Aires was declared the capital of the Argentine Republic.

One of the best-known contemporary accounts of postindependence Argentina is Domingo Faustino Sarmiento's *Life in the Argentine Republic in the Days of the Tyrants* (1868). Also superb is his seminal classic, *Facundo, Or Civilization & Barbarism* (1845).

THE FLEETING GOLDEN AGE

Argentina's second president, Bartolomé Mitre, was concerned with building the nation and establishing infrastructure, but his goals were subsumed by the War of the Triple Alliance (or Paraguayan War), which lasted from 1865 to 1870. Not until Domingo Faustino Sarmiento, an educator and journalist from San Juan, became president did progress in Argentina really kick in (see the boxed text, p155). Sarmiento is still revered for his promotion of education, and his childhood home in San Juan is now a lovely museum (p371), honoring the man and displaying his colonial-style home.

Buenos Aires' economy boomed and immigrants poured in from Spain, Italy, Germany and Eastern Europe. The city's population grew more than sevenfold from 1869 to 1895. The new residents worked in the port, lived tightly in the tenement buildings and developed Buenos Aires' famous dance – the tango – in the brothels and smoky nightclubs of the port (see the boxed text, p50). Basque and Irish refugees became the first shepherds, as both sheep numbers and wool exports increased nearly tenfold between 1850 and 1880.

In 1901, tired of robbing trains and running from the US law, Butch Cassidy and the Sundance Kid packed it up and moved to Cholila, Argentina. They gave ranching a shot before abandoning it again for the gun.

Still, much of the southern pampas and Patagonia were inaccessible for settlers because of fierce resistance from indigenous Mapuche and Tehuelche. Argentina's next president, Nicolás Avellaneda, took care of that. In 1879 Avellaneda's Minister of War, General Julio Argentino Roca, carried out a ruthless campaign of extermination against the indigenous people in what is known as the Conquista del Desierto (Conquest of the Desert). The campaign doubled the area under state control and opened up Patagonia to settlement and sheep. Junín de los Andes' Vía Cristi memorial (p394) is

1816	**1829**	**1852**
After successful independence movements throughout South America, the United Provinces of the Río de la Plata (Argentina's forerunner) declares formal independence from Spain at Tucumán on July 9.	Federalist caudillo Juan Manuel de Rosas becomes governor of Buenos Aires province and de facto ruler of the Argentine Confederation. He rules the confederation with an iron fist for more than 20 years.	Federalist and former Rosas ally Justo José de Urquiza defeats Rosas at the Battle of Caseros and, in 1853, draws up Argentina's first constitution, making him president of a divided Argentine republic.

Built around a lesbian love story wracked with struggle, Judith Katz' interesting novel *The Escape Artist* (1997) transports the reader into the seamy underbelly of Jewish Buenos Aires at the start of the 20th century.

likely the region's most impressive and moving tribute to the Mapuche lives lost in this 'war.'

By the turn of the 20th century Argentina had a highly developed rail network (financed largely by British capital), fanning out from Buenos Aires in all directions. Still, the dark cloud of a vulnerable economy loomed. Because of inequities in land distribution, the prosperity of the late 19th century was far from broad. Industry could not absorb all the immigration. Labor unrest grew. As imports surpassed exports, the economy showed signs of stress. Finally, with the onset of the Great Depression (Great Slump), the military took power under conditions of considerable social unrest. An obscure but oddly visionary colonel, Juan Domingo Perón, was the first leader to try to come to grips with the country's economic crisis.

THE PERÓN DECADE

Juan Perón emerged in the 1940s to become Argentina's most revered, as well as most despised, political figure. He first came to national prominence as head of the National Department of Labor, after a 1943 military coup toppled civilian rule. In this post he organized relief efforts after a major earthquake in San Juan, which earned praise throughout the country. In the process he also met Eva (Evita) Duarte, the radio actor who would become his second wife and make her own major contribution to Argentine history (see the boxed text, opposite). With the help of Evita, Perón ran for and won the presidency in 1946.

Argentine writer Uki Goñi's *The Real Odessa* (2003) is the best and probably most meticulously researched book about Argentina's harboring of Nazi war criminals during the Perón administration.

During previous sojourns in fascist Italy and Nazi Germany, Perón had grasped the importance of spectacle in public life and also developed his own brand of watered-down Mussolini-style fascism. He held massive rallies from the balcony of the Casa Rosada, with the equally charismatic Evita at his side. Although they ruled by decree rather than consent, the Peróns legitimized the trade-union movement, extended political rights to working-class people, secured voting rights for women and made university education available to any capable individual.

Economic difficulties and rising inflation undermined Juan Perón's second presidency in 1952, and Evita's death the same year dealt a blow to both the country and the president's popularity. In late 1955 a military coup sent him into exile in Spain and initiated nearly three decades of catastrophic military rule.

For a glimpse into the life of Argentina's beloved Eva Perón, check out Julie M Taylor's *Eva Perón: The Myths of a Woman* (1981).

PERÓN'S EXILE & RETURN

During their exile, Perón and his associates constantly plotted their return to Argentina. In the late 1960s increasing economic problems, strikes, political kidnappings and guerrilla warfare marked Argentine political life. In the midst of these events, Perón's opportunity to return

1862	1865	1865–70
Bartolomé Mitre is elected president of the newly titled Argentine Republic and strives to modernize the country by expanding the railway network, creating a national army and postal system, and more.	Over 150 Welsh immigrants, traveling aboard the clipper *Mimosa,* land in Patagonia and establish Argentina's first Welsh colony in the province of Chubut.	The War of the Triple Alliance is fought between Paraguay and the allied countries of Argentina, Brazil and Uruguay. Paraguay loses the war, and Argentina gains control of territory along the Río de la Plata and upper Río Paraná.

EVITA, LADY OF HOPE

'I will come again, and I will be millions.'

Eva Perón, 1952

From her humble origins in the pampas, to her rise to power beside President Juan Perón, María Eva Duarte de Perón is one of the most revered political figures on the planet. Known affectionately to all as Evita, she is Argentina's beloved First Lady, in some ways even eclipsing the legacy of her husband, who governed Argentina from 1946 to 1955.

At age 15 Eva Duarte left her hometown of Junín for Buenos Aires, looking for work as an actor. After stints in theater and film she landed a job in radio. In 1944 Duarte attended a benefit at Buenos Aires' Luna Park for victims of an earthquake in San Juan. Here she met Colonel Juan Perón, head of the National Department of Labor, who was entranced by her intensity and vision. They were married by 1945.

Shortly after Perón won the presidency in 1946, Evita went to work in the office of the Department of Labor and Welfare. During Perón's two terms, Evita empowered her husband both through her charisma and by reaching out to the nation's poor, who came to love her dearly. She created the Fundación Eva Perón, through which she built housing for the poor, created programs for children, and extended subsidies and distributed clothing and food items directly to needy families. She fervently campaigned for the aged, urging her husband to add elderly rights to the constitution and successfully pushing through a law granting pensions to elderly people in need. The foundation created medical trains and buses that traveled the country, offering health services directly to the poor. Evita created the Partido Peronista Femenino (Peronista Feminist Party), and in 1947 successfully advocated for a law extending suffrage to women.

When Perón ran for his second term in 1952, thousands gathered in the streets of Buenos Aires demanding Evita be his running mate. She accepted publicly, but declined in a radio announcement the following day, due to opposition within the military government. The same year, at age 33, Evita died of cancer on July 26.

Although Evita is remembered for extending social justice to those she called the country's *descamisados* (shirtless ones), her rule with Perón was hardly free from controversy. Together they ruled the country with an iron fist, jailing opposition leaders and closing opposition newspapers. When *Time* magazine referred to her as an 'illegitimate child' she banned the publication, and when she traveled to Europe in 1947 she was refused entrance to Buckingham Palace. However, there is no denying the extent to which she empowered women at all levels of Argentine society and helped the country's poor.

When Evita said she'd return to 'be millions' in a speech shortly before her death, she probably had no idea of her words' prophetic truth. Today she enjoys near-saint status (many have petitioned the Vatican unsuccessfully) and has practically become a pop icon after the release of the Hollywood musical *Evita,* starring Madonna (a serious bone of contention in Argentina). She is loved throughout the world. In Argentina she was, for many, 'our Lady of Hope.'

To get a little closer to Evita, stop by the Museo Evita (p103) or visit her tomb in the Recoleta cemetery (p101).

1868	**1869–95**	**1872–79**
Domingo Faustino Sarmiento, an educator and journalist from the city of San Juan, is elected president. He encourages immigration to Argentina, ramps up public education and pushes to Europeanize the country.	The Argentine economy booms, immigration skyrockets and Buenos Aires' population grows from 90,000 to 670,000. The tango emerges in Buenos Aires and Italian and Spanish immigrants flood in.	Writer José Hernández publishes his epic poem, 'El Gaucho Martín Fierro,' in two parts: 'El Gaucho Martín Fierro' (1872) and 'La Vuelta de Martín Fierro' (1879). General Julio Roca slaughters thousands during his Conquest of the Desert.

finally arrived in 1973, when the beleaguered military relaxed their objections to Perón's Justicialist party (popularly known as the Peronistas) and loyal Peronista Hector Cámpora was elected president. Cámpora resigned upon Perón's return, paving the way for new elections easily won by Perón.

After an 18-year exile, Perón once again symbolized Argentine unity, but there was no substance to his rule. Chronically ill, Perón died in mid-1974, leaving a fragmented country to his ill-qualified third wife – and vice president – Isabel.

Eva Perón speaks for herself, to some degree, in her ghostwritten autobiography La Razón de Mi Vida *(My Mission in Life; 1951), well worth a read for Evitaphiles.*

THE DIRTY WAR & THE DISAPPEARED
In the late 1960s and early '70s, antigovernment feeling was rife, and street protests often exploded into all-out riots. Armed guerrilla organizations like the Ejército Revolucionario del Pueblo (ERP; People's Revolutionary Army) and the Montoneros emerged as radical opponents of the military, the oligarchies and US influence in Latin America. Perón's bumbling widow, Isabel, along with her adviser, José López Rega, created the Triple A (Alianza Argentina Anticomunista), a death squad to take on the revolutionary groups. With increasing official corruption exacerbating Isabel's incompetence, Argentina found itself plunged into chaos.

On March 24, 1976, a bloodless military coup led by army general Jorge Rafael Videla took control of the Argentine state apparatus and ushered in a period of terror and brutality. Videla's sworn aim was to crush the guerrilla movements and restore social order, and much of the Argentine press and public gave their support. During what the regime euphemistically labeled the Process of National Reorganization (known as El Proceso), security forces went about the country arresting, torturing, raping and killing anyone on their hit list of suspected leftists.

A fascinating, fictionalized version of the life of ex-president Juan Perón, culminating in his return to Buenos Aires in 1973, is Tomás Eloy Martínez' The Peron Novel *(1998).*

During the period between 1976 and 1983, often referred to as the Guerra Sucia or Dirty War, human-rights groups estimate that some 30,000 people 'disappeared.' To disappear meant to be abducted, detained, tortured and probably killed, with no hope of legal process. Ironically, the Dirty War ended only when the Argentine military attempted a real military operation: liberating the Falkland Islands (Islas Malvinas) from British rule.

THE FALKLANDS/MALVINAS WAR
Under military rule, Argentina's economy continued to decline and eventually collapsed in chaos. El Proceso was coming undone.

Hectór Olivera's 1983 film Funny Dirty Little War, *available on DVD, is an unsettling but excellent black comedy set in a fictitious town just before the 1976 military coup.*

In late 1981 General Leopoldo Galtieri assumed the role of president. To stay in power amid a faltering economy and mass social unrest, Galtieri played the nationalist card and launched an invasion in April 1982 to dislodge the British from the Falkland Islands, which had been claimed by Argentina as the Islas Malvinas for nearly a century and a half.

1926	1946	1952
Novelist and poet Ricardo Güiraldes publishes *Don Segundo Sombra*, a classic work of gaucho literature evoking the spirit of the gaucho and its impact on Argentine society.	With Eva Perón at his side, Juan Perón is elected president and makes sweeping changes to the Argentine political structure. Evita would soon embark on her social-assistance programs to help lower-class women and children.	Eva Perón dies of cancer on July 26 at age 33, one year into her husband's second term as president. Her death would severely weaken the political might of her husband.

LAS MADRES DE LA PLAZA DE MAYO

In 1977, after a year of brutal human-rights violations under the leadership of General Jorge Rafael Videla, 14 mothers marched into the Plaza de Mayo in Buenos Aires. They did this despite the military government's ban on public gatherings and despite its reputation for torturing and killing anyone it considered dissident. The mothers, wearing their now-iconic white head scarves, demanded information about their missing children, who had 'disappeared' as part of the government's efforts to quash political opposition.

The group, which took on the name Las Madres de la Plaza de Mayo (The Mothers of Plaza de Mayo), developed into a powerful social movement and was the only political organization that overtly challenged the military government. Las Madres were particularly effective as they carried out their struggle under the banner of motherhood, which made them relatively unassailable in Argentine culture. Their movement showed the power of women – at least in a traditional role – in Argentine culture, and they are generally credited with helping to kick start the reestablishment of the country's civil society.

After Argentina's return to civilian rule in 1983, thousands of Argentines were still unaccounted for, and Las Madres continued their marches and their demands for information and retribution. In 1986 Las Madres split into two factions. One group, known as the Founding Line, dedicated itself to recovering the remains of the disappeared and to bringing military perpetrators to justice. The other, known as the Asociación de Las Madres de la Plaza de Mayo (www.madres.org in Spanish), continued to march every Thursday afternoon on the Plaza in protest of continued government unaccountability. The association held its last protest march in January 2006, saying it no longer had an enemy in the presidential seat, but continues to hold silent vigils every Thursday afternoon in remembrance of the disappeared.

Overnight, the move unleashed a wave of nationalist euphoria that then subsided almost as fast. Galtieri underestimated the determined response of British Prime Minister Margaret Thatcher, and after only 74 days Argentina's ill-trained, poorly motivated and mostly teenaged forces surrendered ignominiously. In 1983 Argentines elected civilian Raúl Alfonsín to the presidency.

AFTERMATH OF THE DIRTY WAR

In his successful 1983 presidential campaign, Alfonsín pledged to prosecute military officers responsible for human-rights violations during the Dirty War. He convicted high-ranking junta officials for kidnapping, torture and homicide, but when the government attempted to also try junior officers, these officers responded with uprisings in several different parts of the country. The timid administration succumbed to military demands and produced a Ley de la Obediencia Debida (Law of Due Obedience), allowing lower-ranking officers to use the defense that they were following orders, as well as a Punto Final (Stopping Point), beyond which no criminal or civil

Nunca Más (Never Again; 1984), the official report of the National Commission on the Disappeared, systematically details military abuses from 1976 to 1983, during Argentina's so-called Dirty War.

1955	1976–83	1982
After the economy slides into recession President Perón loses further political clout and is finally thrown from the presidency and exiled to Spain after another military coup.	Under the leadership of General Jorge Videla, a military junta takes control of Argentina, launching the country into the Dirty War. In eight years an estimated 30,000 people were 'disappeared.'	With the economy on the brink of collapse once again, General Leopoldo Galtieri, now in control, invades the Falkland Islands, successfully unleashing a wave of nationalism and distracting the country from its current state.

Jacobo Timerman, an Argentine publisher and journalist who was outwardly critical of the 1976–83 military regime, was arrested and tortured by the military. He details the experience in his esteemed memoir *Prisoner Without a Name, Cell Without a Number* (1981).

prosecutions could take place. These measures eliminated prosecutions of notorious individuals such as Navy Captain Alfredo Astiz (the Angel of Death), who was implicated in the disappearance of a Swedish-Argentine teenager and the highly publicized deaths of two French nuns.

In December 1990 president Carlos Menem pardoned Videla and his cohorts even though the Argentine public overwhelmingly opposed it. During the 1995 presidential campaign, Dirty War issues resurfaced spectacularly when journalist Horacio Verbitsky wrote *The Flight: Confessions of an Argentine Dirty Warrior* (1996), a book based on interviews with former Navy Captain Adolfo Scilingo, in which Scilingo acknowledges throwing political prisoners, alive but drugged, into the Atlantic. In January 2005 Scilingo went to trial in Spain, facing numerous counts of human-rights abuses and becoming the first official associated with El Proceso to be tried abroad. He was convicted of crimes against humanity by the Spanish Supreme Court and is currently serving 30 years in prison (although he was sentenced to 640 years, 30 is the legally applied limit in Spain). In 2007 the Spanish upped his sentence to 1084 years.

Other than Scilingo, few have been convicted for crimes perpetrated during the Dirty War. One exception was the conviction of Héctor Febres, who worked at Buenos Aires' Naval Mechanics School, the country's most notorious detention center. In December 2007, days before he was to be sentenced in Argentina for human-rights violations, Febres was found dead from cyanide poisoning in his prison cell. Most of the criminals of El Proceso, however, still walk the streets, either in Argentina or abroad.

Set in the 1970s during Argentina's Dirty War, *Imagining Argentina* (1991) is an enthralling novel about a Buenos Aires playwright who acquires the ability to see *desaparecidos*, people who 'disappeared' at the hands of the military.

As frightening and as recent as this chapter in Argentine history is, most Argentines feel an atrocity such as the Dirty War could never happen again. Today, after more than 20 years of civilian rule, many visitors to the country find themselves amazed that it did happen.

THE MENEM YEARS

Carlos Menem, whose Syrian ethnicity earned him the nickname 'El Turco' (The Turk), was elected president in 1989. Menem quickly embarked on a period of radical free-market reform. In pegging the peso to the US dollar, he effectively created a period of false economic stability, one that would create a great deal of upward mobility among Argentina's middle class. Despite the sense of stability, his policies are widely blamed for Argentina's economic collapse in 2002.

Patricia Sagastizabal's award-winning *A Secret for Julia* (2001) is a gripping novel about a Dirty War survivor living in London years later when one of her former torturers tracks her down.

Menem's presidency was characterized by rampant government corruption and the privatization of state-owned companies. He sold off YPF (the national oil company), the national telephone company, the postal service and Aerolíneas Argentinas, all to foreign companies, and much of the profit was never accounted for.

Menem changed the constitution to allow himself to run for a second term (which he won), and unsuccessfully tried again so he could run for

1983	**1989–1999**	**1999–2000**
After the failure of the Falklands War and with an economy on the skids, Raúl Alfonsín is elected the first civilian leader of the country since 1976.	Carlos Menem serves as president of Argentina. During his presidency, he pegs the Argentine peso to the US dollar, sells off state-owned companies and paves the way for the economic crisis.	Fernando de la Rua succeeds Menem as president of Argentina, inheriting a failing economy. Agricultural exports slump and strikes begin occurring throughout the country. The IMF grants Argentina US$40 million in aid.

a third term in 1999. Amid accusations of corruption, Menem finally stepped down.

Adding to his scandals, Menem married Chilean Cecilia Bolocco, a former Miss Universe and 35 years his junior. In 2001 he was charged with illegally dealing arms to Croatia and Ecuador and placed under house arrest. After five months of judicial investigation, the charges were dropped and Menem was released from house arrest; the following day he announced he would run again for president. In 2003 he did, only to withdraw after the first round.

'LA CRISIS'

At the end of Menem's second term in 1999, the country faced economic crisis. Fernando de la Rua succeeded Menem in the 1999 elections, inheriting an unstable economy and US$114 billion in foreign debt. With the peso pegged to the US dollar, Argentina was unable to compete on the international market and exports slumped. A further decline in international prices of agricultural products pummeled the Argentine economy, which depended heavily on farm-product exports.

By 2001 the Argentine economy teetered on the brink of collapse, and the administration, with Minister of Economy Domingo Cavallo at the wheel, took measures to end deficit spending and slash state spending, including employee salaries and pensions. After attempted debt swaps and talk of devaluing the peso, middle-class Argentines began emptying their bank accounts. Cavallo responded to the bank run by placing a cap of US$250 per week on withdrawals, a measure that would become known as 'el corralito' (meaning small enclosure or playpen). It was the beginning of the end.

By mid-December unemployment hit 18.3% and unions began a nationwide strike. Things came to a head on December 20 when middle-class Argentines took to the streets banging pots and pans, in what became known as the *cacerolazo* (from the word *cacerola*, meaning pan), in protest of De la Rua's handling of the economic situation. Rioting spread throughout the country, leaving more than 25 dead, and President de la Rua finally resigned. Three interim presidents had resigned by the time Eduardo Duhalde took office in January 2002, becoming the fifth president in two weeks. Duhalde devalued the peso in January 2002 and announced that Argentina would default on US$140 billion in foreign debt, the biggest default in world history. For Argentina it was 'la crisis,' an economic collapse that sent poverty skyrocketing and foreign investors running.

Placing the blame squarely on neoliberalism and the IMF, Marcel López Levy's *We are Millions* is one of the only books published that tackles Argentina's economic crisis of 2000-2002.

ARGENTINA TODAY

After a low of AR$4 to the US dollar, Duhalde's Minister of Economy, Roberto Lavagna, stabilized the peso at about AR$3 to the dollar and negotiated a take-it-or-leave-it deal with the IMF in which Argentina would pay only the interest on its debts. Simultaneously, devaluation of the peso meant that

2001	2002	2003
The Argentine economy goes into tailspin; President de la Rua places caps on bank withdrawals – known as 'el corralito' – and later resigns amid violent protests throughout the country.	Interim president Eduardo Duhalde devalues the peso, and Argentina defaults on its US$140 billion international debt (including US$800 million owed to the World Bank), the largest default in world history.	Nestor Kirchner is elected president of Argentina after Carlos Menem bows out of the presidential race, despite winning more votes in the first round of elections.

Argentina's products were suddenly affordable on the world market, and by 2003 exports were booming. The surge was great for the country's GNP (its growth rate of nearly 9% was Latin America's largest), but prices at home skyrocketed, plunging more of Argentina's already shaken middle class into poverty – and those already in poverty into dire economic straits.

A presidential election was finally held in April 2003, and Santa Cruz Governor Nestor Kirchner emerged victoriously (and by default) after his opponent, former president Carlos Menem, bowed out of the election. Although Menem emerged from the first round of voting with more percentage points than Kirchner, it quickly became clear that Menem would lose horrendously.

By the end of his term in 2007, Kirchner – known affectionately as 'K' – had become one of Argentina's most popular presidents ever. Risking backlash from the military, Kirchner immediately reversed amnesty laws that protected members of the 1976–83 junta against being charged for atrocities committed during the Dirty War, and by 2008 several higher-ups had been arrested, tried and charged in both Argentina and Spain. He took a heavy stance against government corruption, impeaching two supreme-court justices and forcing the resignation of another. He steered the economy away from strict alignment with the US and realigned it with that of Argentina's South American neighbors. And in 2005 he paid off Argentina's entire debt to the IMF in a single payment. By the end of Kirchner's presidency in 2007, unemployment had fallen to just under 9% – from a high of nearly 25% in 2002.

Nestor Kirchner, president of Argentina from 2003 to 2007, was known as El Pingüino (the penguin), partially because he was from the Patagonia province of Santa Cruz, but also because of his – how would you say it? – beaklike nose.

Despite Kirchner's successes and the recovery of the Argentine economy – not to mention the great rise in optimism nationwide – poverty and inflation remain serious issues. Many from Argentina's middle classes have regained their footholds, but many others, particularly those who were already living at or below the poverty line, have found their economic shackles impossible to break.

When the presidential seat went up for grabs in 2007, Argentines expressed their satisfaction with Kirchner's policies by electing his wife, well-known Senator Cristina Fernández de Kirchner, as president. Cristina won the presidency with a whopping 22% lead over her nearest challenger and became Argentina's first elected female president. She and her husband were deemed 'the Clintons of the South.' At the time of research, Cristina faced two major challenges: tackling poverty (over 25% of the population still lived in poverty) and curbing inflation, which, officially estimated at 9%, hit levels closer to 15%. Nestor Kirchner will likely be his wife's chief advisor (just as she was his during his presidency), and it's expected the 'K' approach – both domestically and internationally – will continue.

2004	2005	2007
Argentina wins two Olympic gold medals, beating the US in basketball and Paraguay in soccer. Two international arrest warrants for Carlos Menem are issued by Argentina.	The Argentine Supreme Court overturns an amnesty law which, until now, protected former military officers suspected and accused of human rights abuses during the 1973–86 military dictatorship.	Former First Lady Cristina Fernández de Kirchner is elected president. Isabel Perón, former president and wife of Juan Perón, is arrested in Spain in connection with military crimes committed during the Dirty War.

The Culture

Whether it's for the country's world-famous tango or its renowned rock and roll, the paintings of Antonio Berni, or the prose of Jorge Luis Borges, Argentina is no less than a cultural goldmine.

THE NATIONAL PSYCHE

Throughout Latin America, Argentines endure a reputation for being a bit cocky. 'How does an Argentine commit suicide?' goes the old joke. 'By jumping off his ego.'

Traveling to Argentina, you'll find that the Argentine stereotype has a nugget of truth to it. But anyone who spends some time here finds the stereotype immediately challenged by warmth, friendliness and the gregarious social nature that more accurately defines the Argentine psyche. There's simply no denying the fact that Argentines are some of the most welcoming, sociable, endearing folks on the planet.

Opinionated, brash and passionate, Argentines are quick to engage in conversation and will talk after dinner or over coffee until the wee hours of the morning. Argentina's most visible customs are entirely social in nature. Look no further than the ritual of drinking *mate* (p57) and the famous *asado* (barbecue; p55).

While Argentines are friendly and passionate they also have a subtle broodiness to their nature, especially *porteños* (residents of Buenos Aires). This stems from a pessimism Argentines have acquired watching their country, one of the world's economic powerhouses during the late 19th and early 20th centuries, descend into a morass of immense international debt. They've endured military coups, severe government repression, and year after year they've seen their beloved Argentina, rich in resources, people and beauty, plundered by corrupt politicians.

But the broodiness is just a part of the picture. Add everything together and you get a people who are fun, fiery, opinionated and proud. And you'll come to love them for it.

LIFESTYLE

Although Buenos Aires holds more than one-third of the country's population, it's surprisingly unlike the rest of Argentina or, for that matter, much of Latin America. The city's core neighborhoods, especially the Microcentro, are more akin to Paris or New York than Caracas or Lima. As throughout the country, one's lifestyle in the capital depends mostly on money. A modern flat rented by a young advertising creative in Buenos Aires' Las Cañitas neighborhood differs greatly from a family home in one of the city's impoverished *villas* (poor neighborhoods), where electricity and clean water are luxuries and street crime comes in daily doses.

Geography and ethnicity also play an important role. Both of these Buenos Aires homes have little in common with that of an indigenous family living in an adobe house in a desolate valley of the Andean northwest, where life is eked out through subsistence agriculture and earth goddess Pachamama outshines Evita as a cultural icon. In regions such as the pampas, Mendoza province and Patagonia, a provincial friendliness surrounds a robust, outdoor lifestyle.

By Latin American standards, Argentina has a large middle class, though it shrank significantly after the economic crisis that began in 1999. Middle-class neighborhoods, quiet and tree-lined, are still common throughout the country, but large sectors of the population have yet to experience the

'Yo, Argentino' is a classic Argentinism, which literally means 'I'm Argentine' but is usually accompanied by a shrug of the shoulders and means 'Don't ask me. I've got nothing to do with it.'

Argentines almost always exchange a kiss on the cheek in greeting – even among men. In formal and business situations, though, it is better to go with a handshake.

Argentines tend not to shy away from stereotypes. Fair-complexioned people are called *Rusos* (Russians), Asians are called *Chinos* (Chinese) and if anyone is overweight, they may get a *gordo* (fatty).

economy's revival. On the other side of the spectrum, wealthy city dwellers are moving into *'countries,'* (gated communities that are found in a city's outlying countryside) in surprising numbers. In Buenos Aires alone, over 400 gated communities have been built since the crash. The question that remains is how this shift away from the city – from its cafés and other pillars of Argentine social life – will affect the cultural landscape.

One thing that all Argentines have in common is the devotion to family. The Buenos Aires ad exec joins her family for weekend dinners, and the café owner in San Juan meets cousins and friends out at the family *estancia* (ranch) for a Sunday among the álamos (poplars) and grapevines. Especially within the country's poorer households, children commonly live with their parents until they're married.

Argentine culture has long been known for its machismo and the accompanying dose of misogyny and homophobia. But things are changing. Women occupy 33% of Argentina's congressional seats (compared with about 15.5% in the US and 18.5% in France), while the workforce is over 40% female. In 2007 Argentina elected its first female president, Cristina Fernández de Kirchner (Isabel Perón was president from 1973–74 by succession, not election). Especially among the country's youth, women are breaking out of their traditional roles and men are becoming more accepting of that fact.

In 2002 Buenos Aires passed Latin America's first ordinance allowing gay civil unions, and in 2007 the capital hosted South America's first Gay World Cup. Outside the capital and the Atlantic's beach resorts, however, tolerance is less apparent (see p609).

ECONOMY

Since colonial times, the Argentine economy has relied on agricultural exports (hides, wool, beef and grains) gleaned from the fertile pampas. Until the late 19th century, the economy resembled that of most Latin American countries – with most of the land and profits in the hands of a few. After Argentina began reaping the benefits of exportation in the 1870s, the economy boomed. With the onset of WW I, foreign investment in Argentina ceased and exports plummeted and, after the Great Depression of 1929 delivered the final punch, Argentina's economy crumbled.

Juan Perón (p34) helped revive the Argentine economy by encouraging the development of a state-supported industrial base. Before long, however, many state enterprises became havens for corruption, including the proliferation of *'ñoquis,'* or ghost employees (see the boxed text, p45), which contributed to inflation rates often exceeding 50% per month.

Inflationary chaos was finally broken by Carlos Menem (1989–99; see p38), who reduced public sector employment, sold off state enterprises, restricted labor-union activities and, most importantly, pegged the peso to the US dollar. His approach eliminated short-term budget deficits, but finally collapsed by the end of his second term. After the peso was devalued in 2002, Argentina was once again able to compete on the world market. Today Argentina's economy is growing faster than any in Latin America. Its primary industries are food processing, motor vehicles and consumer durables, and agricultural products are largely dominated by sunflower seeds, lemons, soybeans, grapes, corn, tobacco, peanuts and livestock.

POPULATION

The great majority of Argentines live in cities. Of the country's population of over 40 million people, 12.4 million live in greater Buenos Aires alone. The country's second-biggest city is Córdoba (1,450,000), followed by Rosario (1,161,000), Mendoza (848,000, with the inclusion of greater Mendoza),

Argentina's fertility rate is 2.13 children per woman, which is higher than in Brazil, Chile and Uruguay but lower than in the rest of South American countries.

Argentina's 97.1% literacy rate is approximately the same as in the United States.

Three Argentines have won the Nobel Prize for Science, while two have won the Nobel Prize for Peace: Carlos Saavedra Lamas (1936) and Adolfo Perez Esquivel (1980).

SOCIAL DOS & DON'TS

When it comes to social etiquette in Argentina, there aren't many wildly obscure dos or don'ts (you won't be stoned for hiccupping in public or leaving a bite of steak on your plate). But knowing a few social intricacies will keep you doing the right thing.

Dos

- Greet people you encounter with *buenos días* (good morning), *buenas tardes* (good afternoon) or *buenas noches* (good evening).
- Use *usted* (the formal term for 'you') when addressing elders and in formal situations.
- Dress for the occasion.
- Accept and give *besos* (kisses) on the cheek.
- Tip the luggage handlers at bus stations, airports and taxi stands.
- Tip bathroom caretakers.
- In small villages, greet people on the street and when walking into a shop.
- Be seen eating ice cream at all times, especially in northern Argentina.

Don'ts

- Don't go clubbing in shorts or tennis shoes.
- Don't refer to the Islas Malvinas as the Falkland Islands (if you're British, don't refer to them at all).
- Don't cheer for the wrong team in the wrong place.
- Don't hand someone the salt when they ask you to pass it to them at the table; place the shaker on the table in front of them. (It's a superstition.)
- If you buy Argentines a round in a bar, don't expect it to come back – unlike in Britain or Australia, it's no faux pas if you don't reciprocate.
- Don't suggest Italian or US pizza might taste better than Argentine pizza.

Tucumán and La Plata. What's left is a country with *lots* of open space (which you'll have to cross any time you want to go somewhere).

Compared to countries like Bolivia, Peru and Ecuador, Argentina has a small indigenous population. Historically, native populations were relatively thin along the coast and in the pampas, and those who did not die from hard labor and disease were eradicated during the Conquista del Desierto (Conquest of the Desert; see p33). Unlike other Latin American countries, Argentina was built more on the backs of imported European labor – primarily Italian and Spanish – than indigenous or African slavery. The most visible indigenous cultures in Argentina today are found in the Lake District, the Andean northwest and in and around the Chaco.

SPORTS

Fútbol (soccer) is Argentina's passion and is far and away the most popular sport in the country. The national team has been to the World Cup final four times and has triumphed twice, in 1978 and 1986. Argentines (and the media) devote a great deal of time following the Boca Juniors, River Plate and other club teams, and the fanatical behavior of the country's *hinchas* or *barra brava* (hooligans) rival that of their European counterparts.

Rugby's popularity has exploded in Argentina ever since Los Pumas, Argentina's national team, beat France in the first game of the 2007 Rugby World Cup and *again* in the semifinals. As an indicator of just how popular

Keep up on Argentine soccer from home by logging on to www .argentinesoccer.com, which posts scores, standings, lineups, schedules and more.

Jimmy Burns' *The Hand of God* is the definitive English-language book about soccer legend Diego Maradona and makes for a great read even if you're not a soccer fanatic.

FÚTBOL & DIEGO MARADONA *Andy Symington*

You don't have to travel long in Argentina to realize that football (soccer) is the number one thing here; there are impromptu games everywhere, and paraphernalia of Boca Juniors, River Plate, or one of the other big sides (mostly based in Buenos Aires) is ubiquitous. The country is an assembly line of thoroughbred talent, the best of which quickly moves to Europe, where the salaries are many times higher; this weakens the local leagues but doesn't dim the passion of the supporters.

Argentine football traditionally combines a South American flair in attack with a rugged Italianate defense, a very effective synthesis that has won the national team two World Cups. Defensive rocks like Daniel Passarella, Oscar Ruggeri, and Roberto Ayala have been complemented by midfielders and attackers like twinkletoed Osvaldo Ardiles, lethal Gabriel Batistuta, or, more recently, unpredictable genius Juan Román Riquelme, muscular Carlos Tévez, and, perhaps destined to be the best of all, mercurial Lionel Messi.

Best of all bar one, that is. Debate rages over who is the sport's greatest-ever player. Many say Brazil's Pelé takes the garland, but just as many would award it to Diego Armando Maradona, whose life has been equal parts controversy and brilliance. Born in 1960 in abject poverty in a Buenos Aires shantytown, he played his first professional game for Argentinos Juniors before his 16th birthday. Transferring to his beloved Boca Juniors, he continued to prosper, and, after a good showing at the 1982 World Cup, moved to Barcelona in Spain, then Naples in Italy. This was the start of a phenomenal few years. His genius inspired unfashionable Napoli to two league titles, and in 1986 he single-handedly won a very average Argentina side the World Cup. In the quarter-final against England, he scored the first with his hand – later saying the goal was scored partly by the hand of God – and the second with his feet, after a mesmerizing run through the flummoxed English defense that led to it being named goal of the century by FIFA.

But the big-time also ruined Diego. Earning huge sums of money, Maradona became addicted to cocaine and the high life and, as his body began to feel the strain over the years, a succession of drug bans, lawsuits, and weight issues meant that by his eventual retirement in 1997 he had been a shadow of his former self for some years.

Since retiring, he has rarely been out of the news. Overdoses, heart attacks, detox, his own TV program, offbeat friendships and enmities: all par for the course in the Maradona circus these days. But it's all substantially outweighed by those numerous moments of magic in the number 10 shirt that have sealed his immortality.

Although Gabriel Batistuta will forever live in Diego Maradona's shadow, he scored a record 56 goals for the Argentine national soccer team, while Maradona scored 34.

Due to political conditions in Africa, the 2009 Dakar Rally will be held not in Africa, but in Argentina and Chile. The 15-day off-road race starts in Buenos Aires on January 3, 2009.

the sport has become, the Superclásico (the famed soccer match between Boca and River Plate) was rescheduled so it wouldn't conflict with Los Pumas quarterfinal match.

Horse racing, polo and boxing are also popular, followed by tennis, golf, cricket, basketball and auto racing. Among the best-known national sports figures are soccer legends Diego Maradona and Gabriel Batistuta (and soon-to-be legend Lionel Messi), tennis stars Guillermo Vilas and Gabriela Sabatini, the late boxers Oscar Bonavena and Carlos Monzón, ex-Formula One racers Juan Manuel Fangio (see p172) and Carlos Reutemann and basketball phenomenon Emanuel Ginobili, who holds a championship ring with the NBA's San Antonio Spurs. In 2007 Argentine golfer Ángel Cabrera won the US Open, the United States' most important golf tournament.

Argentina also has some of the best polo horses and players in the world. (The players, incidentally, are also known as relentless playboys who make cameo appearances at parties in New York City and nightclubs in Monaco.) For well over a century the Campeonato Argentino Abierto de Polo (Argentine Open Polo Championship) has been held in the Buenos Aires neighborhood of Palermo. Most polo events are open to the public and are often free of charge.

MULTICULTURALISM

According to the most recent census (2001), 97% of the Argentine population claims European descent (mainly Spanish and Italian). If this statistic is in fact true, Argentina is the least racially diverse country in the Americas. However, on a closer look, Argentina is a country that has been influenced by numerous cultures – cultures whose distinctive traits, although Argentinized, are still apparent today.

In the mid-19th century, Italians, Basques, English, Ukrainians and other European immigrants began flooding into Argentina. As a result, you'll still find Welsh-Argentines in Chubut province, German surnames and physical traits in Misiones province, Bulgarians and Yugoslavs in Roque Sáenz Peña, and Ukrainians in La Pampa province. Argentina also has a substantial Jewish population of about 300,000 (see p191). Middle Eastern immigrants, though fewer in number, have attained great political influence – the most obvious case being former president Carlos Menem, who was of Syrian ancestry.

Immigrants from Asia are a visible presence in Buenos Aires and increasingly in the interior. The first Japanese Argentines arrived during the late-19th-century immigration boom. Today they are a well-established community and there are even Japanese-Argentine sumo wrestlers. Koreans, who number in the tens of thousands, are a more recent immigrant group. The Chinese-Argentine population is not particularly well integrated into Argentine society, but there is a miniature Chinatown around Calle Arribeños beside the Belgrano train station in Buenos Aires.

According to Indec (Argentina's national census bureau), Argentina is home to over 600,000 self-recognized indigenous people. Some organizations estimate over a million indigenous people live in Argentina. Of the more than 30 recognized *pueblos indígenas* (indigenous groups), the largest is the northern Patagonia's Mapuche, with some 113,000 members. In northwest Argentina, mostly in and around the Quebrada de Humahuaca, there are over 70,000 Kolla (formerly Quechua and Aymara) and, in northern Argentina's Chaco province, nearly as many Toba. The country's other largest groups include the Wichí (over 40,000), the Diaguita (over 31,000) and the Mocoví (nearly 16,000) in Chaco province; the Guaraní (over 22,000), Ava Guaraní (over 21,000) and Tupí Guaraní (over 16,000) in northeastern Argentina; the Huarpe (14,633), Ranculche (10,149) and Comechingón (10,863) of central Argentina; and the Tehuelche (10,500) of northern Patagonia.

For more on the indigenous cultures of the Gran Chaco, see p233. For more on the Mapuche of northern Patagonia, see p402.

MEDIA

Since the end of the military dictatorship in 1983, Argentina has enjoyed a free press. Argentina today boasts over 150 daily newspapers, hundreds of radio stations and more than 40 TV stations. Nearly all are privately owned,

The first usable ballpoint pens were designed and created in Argentina by two Hungarian brothers, Lazro and George Biro. Hence the name biro (in Britain) and *birome* (in Argentina) for ballpoint pen.

Buenos Aires' Jewish community of a third of a million people is the largest of its kind in Latin America.

THE GNOCCHI BUREAUCRACY

Gnocchi is big in Argentina, and it gets its day in the spotlight on the 29th of each month, when it's traditionally served in Argentine households. In Argentina, the word *ñoquis* (gnocchi) has another meaning: it refers to government employees. The nickname arose during the Perón years, when many industries were state-operated and government employment was a source of government gratuity. The implication is that government employees appeared on the job just before monthly paychecks were due – once a month, gnocchi style. The term – and the tradition – persist today.

and many engage in a fair amount of political analysis and criticism. A few large conglomerates dominate print and TV, but smaller print publications bring a variety of opinions to the table. That said, there's a fair amount of self censorship among the largest TV stations and newspapers, which is where most folks get their news.

RELIGION

Roman Catholicism is the official state religion, though only a relatively small percentage of Argentines attend mass regularly. Even so, the church still holds much sway over the culture; up until recently, the president of Argentina had to be Catholic. As in the rest of Latin America, the religion sometimes morphs into fascinating blends of indigenous tradition or local belief and official church doctrine. Shrines adorned with water bottles and car parts and devoted to the female saint Difunta Correa (see p373) add color to roads throughout the country. You are also likely to see shrines decorated with red flags honoring the saintlike Gaucho Antonio Gil (p201), a sort of gaucho Robin Hood worshipped by many.

Argentina has one of the world's largest Jewish populations, and Buenos Aires has a large and active Jewish community. Other religions include Evangelical Protestantism, Jehovah's Witnesses, Hare Krishnas and Mormons.

Visitors to Recoleta and Chacarita cemeteries in Buenos Aires will see pilgrims going to the resting places of Juan and Eva Perón, psychic Madre María and tango singer Carlos Gardel. Followers come to communicate and to ask for favors by praying at the tombs and to leave offerings.

> Under the old Argentine constitution, Carlos Menem had to convert from Islam to Catholicism to become president.

WOMEN IN ARGENTINA

As throughout Latin America, Catholicism has, until recently, played a major role in defining women's place in society. Over the past few decades, Argentine women have made huge strides in their struggle for social and economic independence and equality. Although Argentina's famous machismo is still alive and well, men have been forced to take women seriously in the work place, and women are increasingly excelling in jobs across the entire economic spectrum. That said, glass ceilings still exist in some professions, and the core of many businesses remains a boys' club.

In the political realm, women have made huge impacts. One only need consider Eva Perón (Evita), the country's most enduring political icon. Women such as those involved with Las Madres de la Plaza de Mayo (p37) exerted a unique power through their roles as mothers. In 2007 Cristina Fernández de Kirchner became the country's first elected president.

For information on what to expect as a woman traveling to Argentina, see p617.

> Evita and Che – the world knows them both. But what about Mafalda, Argentina's politically astute, delightfully inquisitive comic-strip character, created by famed cartoonist Quino? She relentlessly challenges the adult world with her vision of a more humanitarian planet. Touché, Che!

ARTS

Artistically, Argentina is one of Latin America's most compelling countries, with a rich literary heritage and vibrant, evolving scenes in cinema, theater and music. And, of course, few places in the world attract so many people who simply want to learn to dance like the locals.

> For a brief survey of modern Argentine art in English, comb the internet for a copy of Jorge Glusberg's now out of print Art in Argentina (Milan, Giancarlo Politi Editore, 1986).

Literature

Despite its rich history, Argentine writing only reached an international audience during the Latin American literary explosion of the 1960s and 1970s, when the stories of Jorge Luis Borges, Luisa Valenzuela, Julio Cortázar, Adolfo Bioy Casares and Silvina Ocampo, among many others, were widely translated for the first time.

The two writers most responsible for creating international interest in Argentine literature are Jorge Luis Borges (1899–1986) and Julio Cortázar (1914–84). The pair's recognition as great Argentine writers is somewhat ironic, as neither considered themselves to be part of an Argentine national literary tradition.

As a half-Jewish, half-English Argentine who was educated in Europe, Borges was influenced by everything from Jewish cabalists to HG Wells, Cervantes and Kafka. His tight, precise, paradoxical *ficciones* are part essay and part story, blurring the line between myth and truth, underscoring the idea that reality is a matter of perception and that an infinite number of realities can exist simultaneously. His early stories like 'Death and the Compass' and 'Streetcorner Man' offer a metaphysical twist on Argentine themes, and his later works, such as 'The Lottery in Babylon,' 'The Circular Ruins' and 'Garden of the Forking Paths,' are works of fantasy.

Despite being discovered and influenced by Borges in the 1940s, Julio Cortázar's writing was considerably different. His short stories and novels are more anthropological and concern people living seemingly normal lives in a world where the surreal becomes commonplace. Cortázar's most famous book is *Hopscotch,* which requires the reader to first read the book straight through, then read it a second time, 'hopscotching' through the chapters in a prescribed but nonlinear pattern.

The contemporary, postboom generation of Argentine writers is more reality-based, often reflecting the influence of popular culture and directly confronting the political realities of the authoritarian Argentina of the 1970s. One of the most famous postboom Argentine writers is Manuel Puig (author of *Kiss of the Spider Woman).* In the Argentine tradition, Puig did much of his writing in exile, fleeing Argentina during the Perón years and ultimately settling in Mexico.

The late Osvaldo Soriano (1943–97), perhaps Argentina's most popular contemporary novelist, wrote *A Funny Dirty Little War* (1978), later adapted into a film, and *Winter Quarters* (1989). In Soriano's *Shadows* (1993), the protagonist is lost in an Argentina where the names are the same, but all the familiar landmarks and points of reference have lost their meaning. The youngster of the postboom generation is Rodrigo Fresán (1963–), whose novel *The History of Argentina* was an international bestseller.

Cinema

Since the end of the military dictatorship, film has emerged as one of Argentina's most vibrant and creative art forms. Argentine cinema has achieved international stature, and many Argentine films are available abroad.

One of the best places to start is Luis Puenzo's *The Official Story* (1985), which deals with the controversial theme of the Dirty War and won an Oscar for best foreign-language film. Perhaps the best internationally known film to deal with Argentina is Héctor Babenco's English-language, Oscar-winning *Kiss of the Spider Woman* (1985), based on Manuel Puig's novel.

Today's cutting-edge Argentine cinema includes director Lucrecia Martel, whose 2001 *La Ciénaga* (The Swamp) tells the story of the crises of two families in Salta, with almost a documentary-style realism. In 2004 she released the acclaimed *La Niña Santa* (The Holy Girl). Pablo Trapero's gritty and widely applauded *El Bonaerense* (2002) is the story of a young rural locksmith who is forced to leave his family to join the notoriously corrupt Buenos Aires provincial police force.

Mariano Llinás is another popular director, whose 2002 film *Balnearios* shows how the influx of outsiders shapes and changes people's existence

---

Doris Meyer's biography Victoria Ocampo: Against the Wind and the Tide *(1990) is one of the few opportunities that English readers will have to read Victoria Ocampo's essays.*

Jorge Luis Borges' short-story collections in English include Labyrinths, The Aleph, A Universal History of Iniquity *and – if you want it all in one big, not-so-backpackable tome –* Collected Fictions.

Federico Andahazi's sexually explicit but unquestionably literary The Anatomist *(1998) caused an uproar when the wealthy sponsor of a national literary prize tried to overturn the award her committee had given the author.*

Want to learn more about the history and beginnings of Argentine cinema? Check out www.surdelsur.com/cine/cinein/indexingles.html.

in little tourist towns. Two films by director Carlos Sorin – both released internationally – capture the quiet spirit and vast emptiness of Patagonia: *Historias mínimas* (Minimal Stories; 2002) and *El Perro* (Bonbón El Perro; 2004). Although little happens in either, both are outstanding. Tristán Bauer's powerful, award-winning *Illuminados por el fuego* (Blessed by Fire; 2005) tells the story of the 1982 Falklands War through the eyes of a young soldier both in the midst of and after the war.

Other recent Argentine films include Daniel Burman's *Derecho de familia* (Lost Embrace; 2006) and Damián Szifron's hilarious *Tiempo de valientes* (2005). For more films, see p20.

Music & Dance

Music and dance are unavoidable in Argentina, and none is more famous than the tango. But tango is a Buenos Aires thing. The rest of the country (and much of Buenos Aires, for that matter) grooves to different sounds, be it *chamamé* in Corrientes, *cuarteto* in Córdoba or *cumbia villera* in the poor neighborhoods of Buenos Aires.

Argentina's biggest film event is the Buenos Aires International Festival of Independent Film (Bafici), held in April. Check out www.bafici.gov.ar for more information.

TANGO

There's no better place to dive into tango than through the music of the genre's most legendary performer, singer Carlos Gardel (1887–1935). After gobbling up his CDs, check out violinist Juan D'Arienzo, whose *orquesta* (orchestra) reigned over tango throughout the 1930s and into the 1940s. Osvaldo Pugliese and Hector Varela are important bandleaders from the 1940s, but the real giant of the era was *bandoneón* (an accordion-like instrument) player Aníbal Troilo. Modern tango is largely dominated by the work of *bandoneón* maestro Astor Piazzolla who moved the genre from the dancehalls into the concert halls – *tango nuevo,* as it was called, was now for the ear. Piazzolla paved the way for the tango fusion which emerged in the 1970s and continues to this day with tango electrónica groups such as Bajofondo Tango Club. Tango has enjoyed a real resurgence among Buenos Aires' youth, and you'll hear plenty when you're there.

FOLK MUSIC

Traditional music is generally known as *folklore* or *folklórico.* It's sort of an umbrella genre that captures numerous styles and there are many contemporary branches *(chamamé, chacarera, carnavalito* and *copla)* that are popular throughout the countryside, claiming fans of all ages. Los Chalchaleros are a northern *folklórico* institution who have turned out more than 40 albums over a 50-plus year career. One of Argentina's greatest contemporary *folklórico* musicians is accordionist Chango Spasiuk, a virtuoso of Corrientes' *chamamé* music. Peteco Carabajal (master of the *chacarera*) and *charango* player Jaime Torres are both big names in *folklórico.* Atahualpa Yupanqui (1908–92) eclipses all of them and is by far Argentina's most important *folklórico* musician of the 20th century. Yupanqui's music emerged alongside the *nueva canción* (literally 'new song') movement that swept Latin America during the 1960s. *Nueva canción* was deeply rooted in folk music and its lyrics often dealt with social and political themes of the era. The genre's grande dame is Argentina's Mercedes Sosa.

Charly García's version of the Argentine national anthem does what Jimi Hendrix did for 'The Star-Spangled Banner,' but it earned García a court appearance for 'lacking respect for national symbols.'

ROCK & POP

Argentina is famous throughout the Spanish speaking world for its *rock en español* (Spanish-language rock). Musicians such as Charly García (formerly a member of the pioneering groups Sui Generis and Serú Giran), Fito Páez and Luis Alberto Spinetta are national icons. Soda Estereo, Sumo, Los Fabulosos

---

HOT HYBRID TUNES

These days it can be hard to categorize some musicians – for example, where do you put a tango-influenced band that plays Talking Heads covers? The easy answer: in our favorites list. Here's an abbreviated version:

- Juana Molina – Cocteau Twins meets Julieta Venegas
- Axel Krygier – grooves meet gauchos
- Arbolito – *folklórico* meets rock 'n' roll
- Pequeña Orquesta Reincidentes – Piazzolla meets The Pixies
- Kevin Johansen – Argentina meets Alaska
- Daniel Melingo – Tom Waits meets tango
- Miníno Garay y los tambores del sur – *murga* meets MC Solaar
- Lisandro Aristimuño – Radiohead meets an Argentine Dogo puppy

---

Cadillacs and Los Pericos rocked Argentina throughout the 1980s and maintain wild popularity. Bersuit Vergarabat, who put out its first album in 1992, endures as one of Argentina's best rock bands with a musical complexity that is arguably without peer. Other popular national groups include the off-beat Babasónicos; punk rockers Ataque 77; rockers Los Piojos, Los Redonditos, Divididos and Catupecu Machu; and metal-meets-hip-hop Illya Kuryaki and the Valderramas (cofounded by Dante Spinetta, son of Luis Alberto).

Born in Córdoba in the early 1940s, *cuarteto* is Argentina's original pop music: despised by the middle and upper classes for its arresting rhythm and off-beat musical pattern (called the '*tunga-tunga*'), as well as its working-class lyrics, it is definitely music from the margins. Although definitively *cordobés* (from Córdoba), it's played in working-class bars, dance halls and stadiums throughout the country.

Cumbia villera is a relatively recent musical phenomenon: a fusion of *cumbia* (originally a Colombian dance music) and gangsta posturing with a punk edge and reggae overtones. This spawn of Buenos Aires shantytowns has aggressive lyrics that deal with marginalization, poverty, drugs, sex and the Argentine economic crisis. Gauchin, Los Pibes Chorros, Yerba Brava and Damas Gratis are Argentina's best known *cumbia villera* groups.

If you really want to get an idea of just what makes Argentines tick – from what riles 'em up to what inspires them the most – have a local translate the lyrics of the rock anthem *Argentinidad al palo,* by Bersuit Vergarabat.

ELECTRÓNICA

Electrónica, or dance music, exploded in Argentina in the 1990s and has taken on various forms in popular music. Hybrid *bandas electrónicas* (electronic bands) are led by the likes of Intima, Mujik and Adicta. DJ-based club and dance music is increasingly popular. Argentina's heavyweights include Hernan Cattaneo, Ricky Ryan, Bad Boy Orange (the reigning king of Argentine drum 'n' bass), DiegoRo-K (who has been around since the mid-1980s, and is known as the Maradona of Argentine DJs), Fabian Dellamonica and Zucker.

CLASSICAL & BALLET

Buenos Aires' Teatro Colón is one of the world's premier opera houses and hosts top world talent. Tickets are unfortunately hard to come by, as many of the theater's 3500 seats are held by season ticketholders. However, it is sometimes possible to watch touring ensembles rehearse (see p98). One person who never has problems getting into Teatro Colón is Argentine Julio Bocca, one of the most important ballet dancers of the 20th century. Bocca danced a farewell performance in 2006 and planned to retire in 2007.

THE TANGO Sandra Bao

The air hangs heavy, smoky and dark. Streams of diffused light illuminate a large, open space. A lone woman, dressed in slit skirt and high heels, sits with legs crossed at one of the small tables surrounding a wooden dance floor. Her eyes dart at the figures all around her, casually looking here and there, in search of the subtle signal. Her gaze sweeps over several tables and suddenly locks onto a stranger's eyes, and there it is: the *cabezazo*, the signal, a quick tilt of his head. She briefly considers the offer, then nods with a slight smile. His smile is broader, and he gets up to approach her table. As he nears she rises to meet him, and the new pair head out toward the dance floor, reaching it just as the sultry music begins to play.

The tango hasn't always been quite so mysterious, but it does have a long and somewhat complex history. Though the exact origins can't be pinpointed, the dance is thought to have started in Buenos Aires in the 1880s. Legions of European immigrants, mostly lower-class men, arrived in the great village of Buenos Aires to seek their fortunes in the new country. They settled on the capital's *arrabales* (fringes), but missing their motherlands and the women they left behind, they sought out cafés and bordellos to ease the loneliness. Here the men mingled and danced with waitresses and prostitutes. It was a strong blend of machismo, passion and longing, with an almost fighting edge to it.

Small musical ensembles were soon brought in to accompany early tangos, playing tunes influenced by pampas *milonga* verse, Spanish and Italian melodies and African *candombe* drums. (The *bandoneón*, a type of small accordion, was brought into these sessions and has since become an inextricable part of the tango orchestra.) Here the tango song was also born. It summarized the new urban experience for the immigrants and was permeated with nostalgia for a disappearing way of life. Themes ranged from profound feelings about changing neighborhoods to the figure of the mother, male friendship and betrayal by women. Sometimes, raunchy lyrics were added.

The perceived vulgarity of the dance was deeply frowned upon by the reigning elites, but it did manage to influence some brash young members of the upper classes, who took the novelty to Paris and created a craze – a dance that became an acceptable outlet for human desires, expressed on the dance floors of elegant cabarets. The trend spread around Europe and even to the USA, and 1913 was considered by some 'the year of the tango.' When the evolved dance returned to Buenos Aires, now refined and famous, the tango finally earned the respectability it deserved. The golden years of tango were just beginning.

Gardel & the Tango

In June 1935 a Cuban woman committed suicide in Havana; meanwhile, in New York and in Puerto Rico two other women tried to poison themselves. And it was all over the same man – a man none of them had ever met. The man was tango singer Carlos Gardel, El Zorzal Criollo, the songbird of Buenos Aires, and he had just died in a plane crash in Colombia.

Though born in France, Gardel was the epitome of the immigrant *porteño*. When he was three his destitute single mother brought him to Buenos Aires. In his youth he worked at a variety of menial jobs, but he also managed to entertain his neighbors with his rapturous singing. A performing career began after he befriended Uruguayan-born José Razzano, and the two of them sang together in a popular duo until Razzano lost his voice. From 1917 onward, Gardel performed solo.

Carlos Gardel played an enormous role in creating the tango *canción* (song). Almost single-handedly, he took the style out of Buenos Aires' tenements and brought it to Paris and New York. His crooning voice, suaveness and overall charisma made him an immediate success in Latin American countries, and for a while his timing was perfect. His star rose in tango's golden

Architecture

Argentina lacks the great pre-Columbian architecture of Andean South America, though a few significant archaeological sites exist in the Andean northwest. This region has notable, if not abundant, Spanish colonial architecture in cities such as Salta and Tucumán, and in villages in isolated areas like the Quebrada de Humahuaca. Some of the country's most splendid colonial architecture is in Córdoba (p316), whose historic center is arguably years of the 1920s and 1930s and Gardel became a recording star. Unfortunately, his later film career was tragically cut short by that fatal plane crash.

Every day a steady procession of pilgrims visits Carlos Gardel's sarcophagus in the Cementerio de la Chacarita in Buenos Aires, where a lit cigarette often smolders between the metal fingers of his life-size statue. The large, devoted community of his followers, known as *gardelianos,* cannot pass a day without listening to his songs or watching his films. Another measure of his ongoing influence is the common saying that 'Gardel sings better every day.' Elvis should be so lucky.

Tango at a Milonga Today

Tango is not an easy dance to describe; it needs to be seen and experienced. Despite a long evolution from its origins, it's still sensual and erotic. The upper bodies are held upright and close, with faces almost touching. The man's hand is pressed against the woman's back, guiding her, with their other hands held together and out. The lower body does most of the work. The woman's hips swivel, her legs alternating in short or wide sweeps and quick kicks, sometimes between the man's legs. The man guides, a complicated job since he must flow with the music, direct the woman, meld with her steps and avoid other dancers. He'll add his own fancy pivoting moves, and together the couple flows in a communion with the music. Pauses and abrupt directional changes punctuate the dance. It's a serious business, which takes a good amount of concentration, and while dancing the pair wear hard expressions. Smiling and chatting are reserved for between songs.

At an established *milonga* (tango dance hall), choosing an adequate partner involves many levels of hidden codes, rules and signals that dancers must follow. After all, no serious *milonguera* (female regular at a *milonga;* the male equivalent is *milonguero*) wants to be caught dancing with someone stepping on her toes (and expensive tango heels). In fact, some men will only ask an unknown woman to dance after the second song, so as not to be stuck for the four tango songs that make a session. It's also considered polite to dance at least two songs with any partner; if you are given a curt *'gracias'* after just one, consider that partner unavailable to you for the rest of the night.

Your position in the area surrounding the dance floor can be critical. At some of the older *milongas,* the more-established dancers have reserved tables. Ideally, you should sit where you have easy access to the floor and to other dancers' line of sight. You may notice couples sitting further back (they often dance just with each other), while singles sit right at the front. And if a man comes into the room with a woman at his side, she is considered 'his' for the night. For couples to dance with others, they either enter the room separately, or the man may signal his intent by asking another woman to the floor. Then 'his' woman becomes open for asking.

The *cabezazo* – the quick tilt of the head, eye contact and uplifted eyebrows – can happen from way across the room. The woman to whom the *cabezazo* is directed either nods yes and smiles, or pretends not to have noticed. If she says yes, the man gets up and escorts her to the floor. If you're at a *milonga* and don't want to dance with anyone, don't look around too much – you could be breaking some hearts.

So what is the appeal of the tango? Experienced *milongueros* will tell you that the adrenaline rush you get from an excellent performance is like a successful conquest: it can lift you up to exhilarating heights. But watch out – the dance can become as addictive as an insidious drug. Once you have fallen for the passion and beauty of the tango's movements you may spend your life trying to attain a physical perfection that can never be fully realized. The true *milonguero* attempts to make the journey as graceful and passionate as possible.

Argentina's finest. Carmen de Patagones is also home to some outstanding colonial architecture. Buenos Aires itself has scattered colonial examples, but is essentially a turn-of-the-20th-century city, with architectural influences that are predominantly French.

Catholicism has provided Argentina with some of its finest monuments, from the lonely, picturesque churches of the Andean northwest to the colonial cathedral in Córdoba and the neo-Gothic basilicas of Luján and

La Plata, to the Jesuit ruins of Misiones province. Recent architecture tends to the large and impersonal, with modernistic glassy buildings dominating downtown areas, most notably the new high-rise developments of Buenos Aires' Puerto Madero.

Painting & Sculpture

Although the visual arts have waxed and waned over the years, they've always been a fundamental part of Argentine expression, and its painters and sculptors are on par with the world's best. Artists such as Lino Spilimbergo (1896–1964) and Antonio Berni (1905–81) are two of Argentina's greatest painters. Benito Quinquela Martín (1890–1977) put the working-class *barrio* of La Boca on the artistic map, by painting brightly colored oils of life on Buenos Aires' waterfront. Beyond classification, Xul Solar (see p102) was a multitalented phenomenon who (along with color-coded piano and a chess-inspired astrological board game) painted colorful Kandinsky- and Klee-inspired dreamscapes. Other Argentine masters include Tucumán-born Víctor Hugo Quiroga, *porteño* painter Guillermo Kuitca and multimedia artist Graciela Sacco.

Buenos Aires has a multitude of museums and galleries, but its streets, where graffiti and stencil art adorn buildings in many neighborhoods, can be just as inspirational as anything found indoors. A more traditional form of popular painting in Buenos Aires' is *filete*, the ornamental line painting that once graced the capital's horse carts, trucks and buses. It's enjoying a comeback today.

Given its French origins, official public sculpture tends toward hero worship and the pompously monumental, expressed through prominent equestrian statues of military figures. A welcome exception is the work of the late Rogelio Yrurtia, some of whose works deal sympathetically with the struggles and achievements of working people (such as his *Canto al Trabajo* in Plaza Eva Perón in San Telmo). Argentina's most influential sculptors include Alberto Heredia, Juan Carlos Distéfano and Yoël Novoa. The city of Resistencia (p233) is famous for its outdoor sculptures.

Theater

Theater is important in Argentina, not only in cosmopolitan Buenos Aires (whose historic Av Corrientes is the country's version of Broadway), but even in the most remote provinces. The country's legendary performers include Luis Sandrini and Lola Membrives, while its most famous contemporary playwrights and directors include Juan Carlos Gené, Ciro Zorzoli, Lorena Vega, José Muscari and Daniel Veronese. Buenos Aires has a vibrant off-Corrientes, independent theater scene that's well worth tapping (see p127). The official theater season is June to August, but there are always performances on Buenos Aires' Av Corrientes, and at smaller theater companies in the city. In summer, some of the best shows are seen in the provincial beach resort of Mar del Plata (see p170).

Whether you read Spanish or not, Rafael Squirru's beautifully illustrated *Arte Argentino Hoy* (Buenos Aires, Ediciones de Arte Gaglianone, 1983) is well worth owning for its profile of 48 contemporary painters and sculptors.

To appreciate one of Buenos Aires' most prolific forms of contemporary painting, you never have to step inside – just watch for the ubiquitous street stencils that adorn buildings throughout the capital, but especially in the neighborhoods of Palermo and San Telmo.

The palatial Teatro Colón opera house was built in France and then shipped part and parcel to Buenos Aires, where it was reassembled in 1908.

Food & Drink

Argentines love eating. A great deal of their social and political life involves a table, be it for a leisurely coffee, an informal meal or an elegant banquet. The food must meet two criteria: abundance and a good price-to-quality relationship. Sophistication is not a national feature, and beef and pasta are the two pillars upon which the national menu is based. That's not to say sophistication doesn't exit. On the contrary. In Buenos Aires and other Argentine cities, you'll find plenty of slick international restaurants – Japanese, Middle Eastern, Mexican, Southeast Asian, Brazilian, you name it – that serve intricately prepared dishes. But traditional Argentine food, which is rooted in Italian and Spanish cooking, is generally more modest.

As for libations, Argentina is fast becoming synonymous with wine – *good* wine. The number of wineries and vineyards, not just in Mendoza province (the heart of Argentine wine country) but in northwest Argentina and even northern Patagonia is skyrocketing. And with the current exchange rate, sampling fine wine has never been more affordable.

> Argentines eat a lot of beef. Per capita, they eat nearly 70kg of the stuff per year. Compare that to 43kg in the US and 31kg in Canada.

STAPLES & SPECIALTIES

Most visitors (unless they're vegetarian, heaven forbid) follow the same splurge-and-purge pattern when they get to Argentina: they arrive, gorge themselves on the country's famous beef, and then, by day four, start moaning for something different – *anything* but more beef! Rest assured, beef is only part of the story.

Beef

But first things first. When it comes to national cuisine, beef is the operative word. Argentina produces what is arguably the world's best, and it certainly consumes more per capita than most other countries. The most important thing to keep in mind when partaking in the experience is the difference between prime cuts (such as sirloin, tenderloin, ribeye and others) versus the cuts that Argentines favor for the grill. The former are usually tender and juicy and offer foreigners that uniquely orgasmic grilled-beef experience they expect. The latter include everything from short ribs and T-bone to small intestines, all of it with plenty of fat and grilled to a state of well-doneness far beyond anything most foreigners care to ingest. The result: lots of flavor and *lots* of chewing. It may not be your idea of tastiness. If not, stick with the prime cuts. For the complete lowdown in beef, read the boxed text, p55.

> *Mollejas* (the thymus glands of cows) are so popular in Argentine *asado* (barbecue) that they are imported from places like the USA, where they are less of a delicacy.

Italian

Thanks to Argentina's Italian heritage, the national cuisine oozes with influences carried across the Atlantic by the wave of Italian immigrants who entered the country during the late 19th century. Along with an animated set of speaking gestures, they brought their love of (and recipes for) pastas, pizzas, gelato, olive oil, and more.

Many restaurants make their own pasta – look for *pasta casera* (handmade pasta) – and those that don't almost invariably buy it fresh. *Ravioles* (ravioli), *sorrentinos* (large, round filled pastas), *ñoquis* (gnocchi), *fideos* (spaghetti) and *tallerines* (fettuccine) are just a few of the pastas you'll encounter. Standard sauces include *tuco* (tomato sauce), *estofado* (beef stew, popular on raviolis) and *salsa blanca* (béchamel). Perhaps as an Argentine touch (and to the

> Italian food is everywhere in Argentina, thanks to its rich Italian heritage, and the strongest influence is Genoese, since so many hail from Genoa.

chagrin of budget travelers), sauce is often *not* included in the price of the pasta – you pay for it separately.

Then, of course, there's the pizza. Big, piping-hot extra-cheesy *porciones* (slices) or whole pies are sold at *pizzerías* throughout the country. But pizza is especially popular (and arguably at its artery-clogging best) in Buenos Aires. The traditional way to polish off a couple of slices is by topping each with a slice of *fainá* (a sort of chickpea patty sliced to match) and washed down with a glass of *moscato* (muscatel). Most *pizzerías* also sell empanadas.

Spanish

Shirley Lomax Brooks' *Argentina Cooks! Treasured Recipes from the Nine Regions of Argentina* does a great job remaining true to its title.

Spanish cooking is the other bedrock of Argentine food. Most of the country's *guisos* and *pucheros* (types of stews) are almost all descendants of Spain. Paella is commonly found on menus, as are other typically Spanish preparations of seafood. (Beware that Argentine seafood is usually mediocre, at best). Although Italians might argue that empanadas – ubiquitous throughout Argentina – are the country's take on calzone, the empanada is actually Spanish in origin (though the Spanish originally got them from the Moors). Empanadas are prepared differently throughout Argentina (for example, you'll find spicy ground beef empanadas in the Andean northwest and ham-and-cheese empanadas in Buenos Aires) and make for a tasty quick meal.

Regional Dishes

Although it's the national food, beef is really a regional dish. It's a pampas thing. Cows don't stay tender roaming the barren Andean northwest, or the scrub forests of the Chaco, or the steppes of windswept Patagonia. When you're outside the provinces of Buenos Aires, Santa Fe, Córdoba and La Pampa – Argentina's cattle-producing region – it's best to try something different.

Smack in the middle of cow country, the pampas town of Tandil (p148) is famous for its cheeses and cured meats – two great reasons to go!

Although the term *comida típica* can refer to any of Argentina's regional dishes, it often refers to food from the Andean northwest. Food from this region, which has roots in pre-Columbian times, has more in common with the cuisines of Bolivia and Peru than with the Europeanized food of the rest of Argentina. It's frequently spicy (thanks to the liberal use of chilies) and is hard to find elsewhere (most Argentines are suspicious of anything spicier than a pinch of black pepper). Typical dishes from the northwest can include everything from *locro* (a hearty and often outstanding corn or mixed-grain stew with sausage or other meat), to tamales, *humitas* (sweet tamales) and fried empanadas.

In Patagonia, lamb and seafood (including delicious king crab and oysters) almost wipe beef off the map. In the west, the provinces of Mendoza, San Juan and La Rioja pride themselves on *chivito* (goat). The northeast also offers food dating far back, but it is milder and more bland. River fish, such as the dorado, pacú (a relative of the piranha) and surubí (a type of catfish), are staples in the northeast.

El Gaucho Gourmet (2001), by Dereck Foster, offers a brief, bilingual history of eating in Argentina.

Meals

Argentines are not great breakfast eaters, and bacon-and-eggs people may find themselves fighting hunger pangs by midmorning. A typical breakfast consists of *café con leche y medialunas* (coffee with milk and croissants), although hotels catering to tourists offer American-style breakfasts. The croissants come *dulce* (sweet) or *salada* (plain). *Tostadas* (toast), with *manteca* (butter) and/or *mermelada* (jam) is an alternative. *Facturas* (sweet pastries), which can be seen and bought at any *confitería* (café serving light meals) and most bars, are a common snack.

HERE'S THE BEEF *Sandra Bao*

You walk into a traditional *parrilla* (steak house), breezing past the stuffed bull and sizzling *asado* (barbecue grill) at the entrance, and sit down hungry, knife and fork in hand. You don't know a word of Spanish, you've never had to choose between more than two or three cuts of steak in your life and the menu has at least 10 different choices. What do you do? Don't fret. We'll give you a better idea of what will show up on your plate.

But first, you should have an idea of where Argentina's famous beef comes from. When the first Spaniards came over to Argentina from Europe, with the intention of colonizing the area, they brought some cows. Because stubborn locals were unwilling to let themselves be dominated, the Spaniards' first efforts at a colony proved unfruitful. They ended up abandoning their herds in the pampas and moving away. The cattle, on the other hand, found the bovine equivalent of heaven: plenty of lush, fertile grasses on which to feed, with few natural predators to limit their numbers. Things were great until the Europeans decided to start recolonizing the pampas and capturing the cattle for their own use. (The gauchos, however, had been taking advantage of these free-roaming meals-on-the-hoof all along.)

Today, intermixing with other European bovine breeds has produced a pretty tasty beef. Why is it so good? Any Argentine will say it's because free-range Argentine cows eat nutritious pampas grass, lacking in the massive quantities of corn, antibiotics and growth hormones that American or European stocks are given in feedlots. This makes for a leaner, more natural-tasting meat. (Though these days it's not entirely organic: efforts to reduce *aftosa*, or foot-and-mouth disease, have resulted in Argentina's need to inoculate its herds.)

The average intake of beef is around 70kg per person per year, though in the past Argentines ate even more. Most of this consuming takes place at the family *asado*, often held on Sunday in the backyards of houses all over the country. (If you are lucky enough to be invited to one, make sure you attend.) Here the art of grilling beef has been perfected. This usually involves cooking with coals and using only salt to prepare the meat. On the grill itself, which is often waist-high and made of bricks, slanted runners funnel the excess fat to the sides to avoid flare-ups, and an adjustable height system directs the perfect amount of heat to the meat.

Emerging from this family tradition, the commercial steak house offers a little bit of everything. The *parrillada* (mixed grill) might have an assortment of *chorizo* (beef of pork sausage), *pollo* (chicken), *costillas* (ribs) and *carne* (beef). It can also come with more exotic items such as *chinchulines* (small intestines), *tripa gorda* (large intestine), *molleja* (thymus gland or sweetbreads), *ubre* (udder), *riñones* (kidneys) and *morcilla* (blood sausage). You can order a *parrillada* for as many people as you want; the steakhouse adjusts its servings according to the party's size.

You could skip the mixed grill and dive right into the beef cuts. Here's a guide:

bife de chorizo	sirloin; a thick, juicy and popular cut
bife de costilla	T-bone; a cut close to the bone; also called *chuleta*
bife de lomo	tenderloin; a thinly cut, more tender piece
cuadril	rump steak; often a thin cut
ojo de bife	eye of round steak; a choice smaller morsel
tira de asado	a narrow strip of rib roast
vacío	flank steak; textured and chewy, but tasty

If you don't specify, your steak will be overcooked. Ask for it *a punto* (medium). To get it pink on the inside ask for *jugoso* (rare), and if you want it well done, say *bien hecho*. Be sure not to miss *chimichurri*, a tasty sauce often made of olive oil, garlic and parsley. Also try the *salsa criolla*, a condiment made of diced tomato, onion and parsley – it's harder to find.

Argentines make up for breakfast at lunch and dinner, although the three-course lunch is now far less common. While most places begin service around noon, the popular time to lunch is between 1pm and 1:30pm. Dinners can begin at 8pm, but an Argentine will seldom eat before 9pm (10pm is far more common), and meals can draw out long after midnight on weekends.

Sandwiches & Snacks

In big cities, it's easy to snack at any time on almost anything you desire. *Kioscos* (kiosks) are all over town and provide sweets, cookies, ice cream and well-packaged sandwiches. On many streets, *pancho* (hot dog) and *garapiñadas* (sugar-roasted peanuts) sellers prepare and sell their treats from carts. A more substantial snack is the aforementioned empanada, which is cheap and filling, and comes either *al horno* (baked) or *frito* (fried).

Sandwiches de miga (white-bread sandwiches, usually with cheese and ham) are practically a national obsession and are sold at kiosks and service stations throughout the country. At cafés, *migas* are often sold as *tostados*, which basically just means toasted *migas*. *Tostados* are a favorite for *la leche*, which literally means milk, but in Argentina also refers to the 5pm or 6pm snack that's necessary for making it to dinnertime without having a blood-sugar crash.

Pebetes (or PBTs) are heartier sandwiches made on oblong bread rolls. *Lomitos* (steak sandwiches) are by far the pinnacle of Argentine sandwiches, and few things can beat a really good, cholesterol-packed *super lomito* (a *lomito* served with a slice of ham and fried egg on top of the meat). The one thing that can: the *choripán*, a classic sandwich made with two ingredients: *chorizo* (pork or beef sausage) and *pan* (bread). Top it with *chimichurri* sauce, and you're set!

> *Chimichurri* is the classic steak and sausage condiment invented in Argentina. An old joke attributes the name to a Spanish-language corruption of 'Che, mi curry!' – what the British soldiers couldn't stop yelling in the 19th century.

Desserts & Sweets

Argentina consumes more sweets per capita than any nation in the world. From the multitude of candy bars that pour from streetside kiosks to the national addiction to *dulce de leche* (milk caramel), there's no shortage of sweetness in Argentina.

Two of Argentina's most definitive treats are *dulce de leche* and *alfajores* (round, cookie-type sandwiches stuffed with anything from apple preserves to *dulce de leche*). Each region of Argentina has its own version of the *alfajor*, and many argue that those from Santa Fe are the best.

Helado (ice cream) is outstanding in Argentina, especially in Buenos Aires. Based on the Italian tradition, there are three basic types: the large-scale, such as Frigor (Nestlé); the semi-artisanal, produced by chains like Freddo; and the artisanal, made by small *heladerías* (ice-creameries). *Helados* are eaten all year long and flavors are extremely varied. Heladería Jauja in Bariloche (p412) is often credited with making the country's best ice cream, but parlors such as Una Altra Volta and Persicco in Buenos Aires (p118) are arguably on par.

In restaurants, fruit salad and ice cream are almost always on the menu. *Flan* is a baked custard that comes with a choice of either cream or *dulce de leche* topping. *Queso y dulce* consists of slices of fresh cheese with candied *membrillo* (quince) or *batata* (sweet potato). The former is typical of northern Argentina and can be outstanding.

> Ice cream is one of Argentina's greatest treats, more akin to Italian gelato than its creamy counterparts in France and the US.

DRINKS
Alcoholic Drinks

Over the last decade Argentina has exploded onto the international wine map, and its reputation for producing fine wines continues to grow. Argentine wines scale the entire price range from very cheap (less than a soft drink) to very expensive. Mendoza is Argentina's premier wine region, but the provinces of San Juan, La Rioja and Salta (primarily around Cafayate) also produce excellent wines. Mendoza is known for its malbec, while San Juan is famous for its syrah and Cafayate for its torrontés, a crisp, dry white wine.

> With all the boutique wineries and newly planted varietals in Argentina, it's important to remember the past: Toro Viejo is the country's classic table wine. At about AR$3 per bottle, it's rough but cheap!

MATE & ITS RITUAL   *Sandra Bao & Danny Palmerlee*

Nothing captures the essence of *argentinidad* (Argentinity) as well as the preparation and con-sumption of *mate* (pronounced *mah*-tay), perhaps the only cultural practice that truly transcends the barriers of ethnicity, class and occupation in Argentina. More than a simple drink, *mate* is an elaborate ritual, shared among family, friends and coworkers. In many ways, sharing is the whole point.

Yerba mate is the dried, chopped leaf of *Ilex paraguayensis,* a relative of the common holly. Also known as Paraguayan tea, it became commercially important during the colonial era on the Jesuit missions' plantations in the upper Río Paraná. Europeans quickly took to the beverage, crediting it with many admirable qualities. The Austrian Jesuit Martin Dobrizhoffer wrote that *mate* 'provokes a gentle perspiration, improves the appetite, speedily counteracts the languor arising from the burning climate and assuages both hunger and thirst.' After the Jesuits' expul-sion in 1767, production declined, but since the early 20th century, production has increased dramatically.

Argentina is the world's largest producer and consumer of *yerba mate*. Argentines consume an average of 5kg per person per year, more than four times their average intake of coffee. It's also popular in parts of Chile, southern Brazil, Paraguay and, in particular, Uruguay, which consumes twice as much per capita as Argentina.

Preparing *mate* is a ritual in itself. In the past, upper-class families even maintained a slave or servant whose sole responsibility was preparing and serving it. Nowadays, one person, the *cebador* (server) fills the *mate* gourd almost to the top with *yerba*, heating but not boiling the water in a *pava* (kettle) and pouring it into the vessel. Drinkers then sip the liquid through a *bombilla*, a silver straw with a bulbous filter at its lower end that prevents the *yerba* leaves from entering the tube.

Gourds can range from simple calabashes to carved wooden vessels to the ornate silver museum pieces of the 19th century. *Bombillas* also differ considerably, ranging in materials from inexpensive aluminum to silver and gold with intricate markings, and in design from long straight tubes to short, curved models.

There is an informal etiquette for drinking *mate*. The *cebador* pours water slowly as he or she fills the gourd. The gourd then passes clockwise, and this order, once established, continues. A good *cebador* will keep the *mate* going without changing the *yerba* for some time. Each participant drinks the gourd dry each time. A simple *'gracias'* will tell the server to pass you by. Don't hold the *mate* too long before passing it on.

There are marked regional differences in drinking *mate*. From the pampas southwards, Argentines take it *amargo* (without sugar), while to the north they drink it *dulce* (sweet) with sugar and yuyos (aromatic herbs). Purists, who argue that sugar ruins the gourd, will keep separate gourds rather than alternate the two usages.

An invitation to *mate* is a cultural treat and not to be missed, although the drink is an ac-quired taste and novices may find it bitter and very hot at first. (On the second or third round, both the heat and bitterness will diminish.) Because drinking *mate* is a fairly complex process, it is rarely served in restaurants or cafés, except in teabag form. For a foreigner, it is therefore easy to spend an entire holiday in Argentina without ever experiencing it. The simple solution is to do what traveling Argentines do: buy a thermos (stores rarely lack a thermos shelf), a *mate* gourd, a *bombilla* and a bag of herb. The entire set-up will cost you AR$$20 to AR$$50, depending on the thermos you choose.

Before drinking from your gourd, you must first cure it by filling it with hot water and *yerba* and letting it soak for 24 hours. When it's ready, you have to fill your thermos; nearly all res-taurants, cafés and hotels are used to filling thermoses, sometimes charging a small amount. Simply whip out your thermos and ask: *'¿Podía calentar agua para mate?'* ('Would you mind heating water for *mate*?'). Even gas stations are equipped with giant tanks of precisely heated water for drinkers on the road. Once you have your water, you're off to the park to join the rest of the locals drinking *mate* in the shade.

The wine list is called *la carta de vinos* and most restaurants have one. Sommeliers are scarce. For more on Argentine wine, see p357.

If Argentina has a national beer, it's Quilmes. Following close behind are Isenbeck, Warsteiner, Andes and the Brazilian Brahma. Order a *porrón* and you'll get a half-liter bottle or a *chopp* and you'll get a frosty mug of draft. Unless you order it with a meal, beer is usually served with a free snack, such as peanuts or potato chips.

At the harder end of the spectrum, it's all about Fernet Branca, a bitter, herbed Italian digestif (45% alcohol), originally intended as medicine, but now gulped down as a Coca Cola cocktail by Argentines everywhere. *Fernet con Coke* is by far Argentina's favorite cocktail, and despite many claims that it won't give you hangover, it will (trust us).

Another popular beverage (and one that won't knock you on your ass) is Gancia, a locally produced aperitif of Italian origin. It hurts by itself, but when whipped up with soda and lemon, it makes a delicious summertime drink called *Gancia batido*. Unusual beverages, more popular in the country than in cities, are *caña*, distilled from sugar cane, and a local gin made by Bols and Llave.

Nonalcoholic Drinks

Argentines are great coffee drinkers, and they like it strong. They drink coffee and milk in the morning and innumerable cups of *café solo* (basically espresso, but weaker) during the day. An espresso with a drop of milk is *café cortado*, while a *lágrima* is mostly milk with a drop or two of coffee. *Cafe de filtro* is regular, nonespresso coffee, but it's rarely served in cafés.

Black and herbal teas are also available, such as *manzanilla* (chamomile) and *peperina* (an Argentine mint). In the cooler seasons, try a *submarino:* a bar of chocolate placed in a glass of very hot milk and allowed to melt slowly.

Although fresh fruit is plentiful in the markets, fruit juices in bars and *confiterías* are usually limited to *exprimido de naranja* (fresh-squeezed orange juice) and *pomelo* (grapefruit). A *licuado* is fruit liquefied in a blender with milk or water.

Gaseosas (soft drinks) are big business in Argentina, from Coke to *amargos Serrano* (a herbal infusion) and flavored mineral waters. Mineral waters come *con gas* (carbonated) and *sin gas* (plain). Tap water in the cities is drinkable, but if you have doubts, ask for *agua mineral* (mineral water) or *un sifón de soda* (carbonated water in a spritzer bottle), often used for mixing with cheap wine.

CELEBRATIONS

Food during the holidays in Argentina is similar to that in Europe and the US. At Christmas, stores begin to fill up with many of the items typical in the northern hemisphere, although here in the south it's hot, hot, hot this time of year. During *Semana Santa* (Holy Week), fish and seafood hold sway, but whatever the occasion, the *asado* almost always reigns supreme. You may need to make restaurant reservations during holiday periods.

WHERE TO EAT & DRINK

Argentines love to eat out, and there is no lack of places, from simple pubs to elegant restaurants. The simplest places and usually the most economical are cafés and bars, where simple snacks are available all day. Pubs, which are cafés with a pseudo-British touch, offer a few more choices. Café life is typical of Buenos Aires, and much financial, romantic, social and political business is conducted there.

Remember the handy mnemonic: San Juan with an 's' means syrah. Mendoza with an 'm' means malbec. That way you'll get the good stuff even when you're too looped to know where you are.

To learn more about *mate,* check out www .soygaucho.com/english/mate/index.html; for supplies, try www .gauchogourmet.com.

Various scientific studies have attributed numerous possible health benefits to *yerba mate,* including the ability to inhibit oral cancer, lower cholesterol, decrease heart disease and increase brain functions. Other studies suggest it may cause bladder or esophageal cancer. Either way, it's fun to drink!

Confiterías, open all day, offer a restricted menu, while restaurants, open only at meal times, have a more complete menu. When you tire of beef and *parrillas,* you can try one of Argentina's Chinese or Japanese restaurants (sushi has exploded in popularity). Or dine at a Middle Eastern restaurant (widespread in Buenos Aires and usually excellent); many are *tenedor libre* (all you can eat for a set price).

With few exceptions, Argentine restaurants are less formal than in the US or Europe. Reservations are taken but are necessary only on weekends at better restaurants, especially during peak times in hotspots like Mar del Plata or Bariloche. If in doubt, call ahead. Expect to linger over your meal and chat over coffee or drinks afterward. Your bill will rarely be presented until you ask for it, by saying, *'la cuenta, por favor'* ('The bill, please.'). A waiter is a *mozo* and a waitress *señorita* (or *moza*). Standard opening hours are 1pm to 3:30pm or 4pm, and 9pm to 1am or 2am, but many places are open earlier.

Menus come in two types: a regular menu and *menú fijo* or *menú del día,* which refer to fixed-price meals, sometimes including a drink. Many menus are 'translated' into English (and occasionally French) with results ranging from useful to hilarious to incomprehensible.

When your bill arrives you may note an item called *cubierto* (cover charge). This is not a tip, which is up to you to pay, usually around 10%. Free drinks such as a glass of sparkling wine or sherry are frequently offered at the start of a meal. In 2007 smoking was banned from restaurants throughout Argentina, and most establishments enforce the ban.

VEGETARIANS & VEGANS

Recently, health foods and organic products have become accessible in Argentine cities, but vegetarian restaurants are scarce. Most menus do include a few vegetarian choices, and pastas are a nearly ubiquitous (and usually excellent) option, provided you don't order a meat sauce, of course. At *parrillas,* salads, baked potatoes, *provoleta* (a thick slice of grilled provolone cheese) and, occasionally, roasted vegetables, all make good alternatives to meat. Outside the *parrilla,* you'll find plenty of vegetarian options, including *pizzerías* and *empanaderías* (empanada shops). At the latter, look for empanadas made with *acelga* (Swiss chard) and *choclo* (corn), both generally free of meat.

Sin carne means 'without meat,' and the words *soy vegetariano/a* ('I'm a vegetarian') will come in handy when explaining to an Argentine why you don't eat their delicious steaks.

For tips on where to eat *sin carne* in Buenos Aires, see p115.

EATING WITH KIDS

Argentines adore children, and eating out with the kids is common. A number of restaurants incorporate special menus for the junior brigade, but all (save perhaps the five-star outfits) will cater to your reasonable demands – from serving half portions to preparing something special in the kitchen.

EAT YOUR WORDS

Want to make sure you don't order cow brains or testicles? Get behind the cuisine scene by getting to know the language. For pronunciation guidelines, see p638.

Useful Phrases

I'd like to make a reservation.
Quisiera hacer una reserve.   kee·see·*air*·a a·*ser* oo·na re·*ser*·va
Do you accept credit cards?
¿Aceptan tarjetas de crédito?   a·*sep*·tan tar·*khe*·tas de *kre*·dee·to

Torta galesa (Welsh cake) is a delicious fruitcake unknown in Wales. Welsh settlers in Argentina created it to tide them over during the harsh Patagonian winters, when food was scarce.

Especially in Buenos Aires, look out for *panettone* (a sweet egg bread originally from Italy) around Christmas time – some of the loaves are as beautiful as they are delicious.

With its Central European heritage, Bariloche (p406) is Argentina's reigning capital of chocolate. Can't make it? Try a bar of Águila from any supermarket.

When do you serve (meals/breakfast/lunch/dinner)?
¿A qué hora sirven (comidas/desayuno/   a ke *o·*ra *seer·*ven (ko·*mee·*das/de·sa·*shu·*no/
almuerzo/cena)?   al·*mwair·*zo/*se·*na)

Table for ..., please.
Una mesa para ..., por favor.   *oo·*na *me·*sa *pa·*ra ... por fa·*vor*

Can I see the menu please?
¿Puedo ver el menú, por favor?   *pwe·*do ver el me·*noo,* por fa·*vor*

What do you recommend?
¿Qué me aconseja?   ke me a·con·*se·*kha

What's today's special?
¿Cuál es el plato del día?   kwal es el *pla·*to del *dee·*a

What's the soup of the day?
¿Cuál es la sopa del día?   kwal es la *so·*pa del *dee·*a

I'll try what she/he's having.
Probaré lo que ella/él está comiendo.   pro·ba·*ray* lo ke *e·*sha/el es·*ta* ko·*myen·*do

We'd like to share the salad.
Quisiéramos compartir la ensalada.   kee·*syair·*a·mos kom·par·*teer* la en·sa·*la·*da

What's in this dish?
¿Qué ingredientes tiene este plato?   ke een·gre·*dyen·*tes *tye·*ne *es·*te *pla·*to

Can I have a (beer) please?
¿Una (cerveza) por favor?   *oo·*na (ser·*ve·*sa) por fa·*vor*

Is service/cover charge included in the bill?
¿El precio en el menú incluye el servicio el *pre·*syo en el me·*noo* in·*cloo·*she el
de cubierto?   sair·*vee·*syo de coo·*byair·*to

Thank you, that was delicious.
Muchas gracias, estaba buenísimo.   *moo·*chas *gra·*syas es·*ta·*ba bwe·*nee·*see·mo

The bill, please.
La cuenta, por favor.   la *kwen·*ta por fa·*vor*

I'm a vegetarian.
Soy vegetariana/o.   soy ve·khe·tair·*ya·*na/o

I'd like ...
Quiero ...   *kyair·*o ...
  a knife
  un cuchillo   oon koo·*chee·*sho
  a fork
  un tenedor   oon te·ne·*dor*
  a spoon
  una cuchara   *oo·*na koo·*cha·*ra

Food Glossary

achuras	a·*choo·*ras	organ meats
alfajor	al·fa·*khor*	a sandwich biscuit (cookie) usually filled with *dulce de leche*
anchi	*an·*chee	a popular sweet dessert with cornflour and citrus fruit
arroz	a·*ros*	rice
bife	*bee·*fe	general name for steak (*bife de chorizo* is thick and boneless, similar to New York strip)
bifes a la criolla	*bee·*fes a la kree·*o·*sha	steaks slowly cooked in a casserole
boga	*bo·*ga	delicious freshwater fish
budin de choclo	boo·*deen* de *chok·*lo	a corn souffle
buseca	boo·*se·*ka	a tripe and vegetable soup
cabrito	ka·*bree·*to	goat (kid)
carbonada	kar·bo·*na·*da	typical beef, corn, pumpkin and vegetable stew, with peaches in season

When you order a beer at many restaurants, you often have to settle for a huge bottle, what's known as a *tres-quartos* (three-fourths), which is 0.75L. Smaller bottles are often unavailable. Ah shucks!

carre ahumado	*ka*·re a·oo·*ma*·do	smoked pork loin
cayote	ka·*sho*·te	fig-leaf gourd, eaten usually as jam or in syrup
centolla	sen·*to*·sha	southern king crab
cerdo	*sair*·do	pork
chanfaina	chan·*fai*·na	a stew with tomatoes, onions, peppers and (usually) lamb and liver; a Patagonian version is made with fish
charqui	*char*·kee	air-dried beef, similar to South African biltong
chimichurri	chee·mee·*choo*·ri	an Argentine herb marinade, also used as a dressing
chinchulines	cheen·choo·*lee*·nes	small intestine
chirimoya	chee·ree·*mo*·sha	apple custard
chivito	chee·*vee*·to	young goat (kid)
choripán	cho·ree·*pan*	Argentina's answer to the hot dog, made with spicy chorizo
chorizo	cho·*ree*·zo	sausage (also *salchicha* and *morcilla*)
churrasco	choo·*ras*·ko	grilled beef
ciervo	*syair*·vo	venison
cochinillo	ko·chee·*nee*·sho	suckling pig, younger than a *lechón*
cordero patagónico	kor·*dair*·o pa·ta·*go*·nee·ko	Patagonian lamb, celebrated for its lean, herb-flavored meat
corvina	kor·*vee*·na	sea fish, similar to a perch
criadillas	kree·a·*dee*·shas	testicles
dorado	do·*ra*·do	celebrated river fish, dear to anglers and gourmets alike
dulce de batata	*dool*·se de ba·*ta*·ta	sweet potato (yam) preserve, frequently eaten with cheese
dulce de leche	*dool*·se de *le*·che	caramelized milk, Argentina's most popular sweet
dulce de membrillo	*dool*·se de mem·*bree*·sho	quince preserve, frequently eaten with cheese
empanada	em·pa·*na*·da	pastry similar to a turnover, usually filled with beef and fried or baked
escabeche	as·ka·*be*·che	an oil, vinegar and herb marinade
garrapiñada	ga·ra·pee·*nya*·da	caramelized peanuts or almonds
gaznate	gaz·*na*·te	brandy-flavored pastry cone usually filled with *dulce de leche*
helado	el·*a*·do	ice cream
hígado	*ee*·ga·do	liver
jamón	kha·*mon*	ham
langostino	lan·gos·*tee*·no	prawn
lechón	le·*chon*	suckling pig
lengua	*len*·gwa	tongue
mantecol	man·te·*kol*	sweet made with ground peanuts and sugar
martineta	mar·tee·*ne*·ta	type of quail, found on the pampas and in Patagonia
matambre	ma·*tam*·bre	flank or skirt steak, usually stuffed, rolled up and eaten cold
medialuna	me·dya·*loo*·na	croissant
mollejas	mo·*she*·khas	either the thymus or pancreas, a popular part of an *asado*
morcilla	mor·*see*·sha	black pudding (blood sausage)

Make the wine snobs wince — order the house wine with a *sifón de soda* (bottle of soda water) and mix them over ice in the good ol' Argentine tradition.

A great reason to learn Spanish: recipes for over 2000 Argentine dishes are housed at www2 .informatik.uni -muenchen.de/recetas/, likely the web's longest list of Argentine culinary concoctions.

morron	mo·*ron*	red pepper
palta	*pal*·ta	avocado
pan dulce	pan *dool*·se	a sweet bread containing dried fruit, nuts and some brandy, similar to *panettone*
pavo	*pa*·vo	turkey
pejerrey	pe·khe·*ray*	a very fine river fish
pionono	pyo·*no*·no	a version of a Swiss roll with a savory filling
pollo	*po*·sho	chicken
puchero	poo·*chair*·o	local version of a French *pot au feu* or the Spanish *cocido*
salpicón	sal·pi·*kon*	a vegetable and meat (usually chicken, tuna or beef) salad eaten cold
sesos	*se*·sos	brains
surubí	soo·*roo*·bi	large, delicate river fish
ternera	tair·*nair*·a	veal
tocino del cielo	to·*see*·no de *sye*·lo	a rich, creamy egg and sugar dessert (also *yemas quemadas*)
torta galesa	*tor*·ta ga·*le*·sa	a rich fruit cake, created by the Welsh colony in Patagonia
ubre	*oo*·bre	udder
vizcacha	veez·*ka*·cha	a member of the chinchilla family, almost always eaten in a pickled form

Environment

Argentina. For anyone raised on *National Geographic* and adventure stories, the name is loaded with images: the Magellanic penguins of the Patagonian coast, the windswept mysteries of Tierra del Fuego, the vast emptiness of the pampas, the towering Andes, and the raging Iguazú Falls. Spanning from the subtropics to the edge of Antarctica, the country is simply unmatched in natural wonders.

THE LAND

Argentina is big – *really* big. With a total land area of about 2.8 million sq km, excluding the South Atlantic islands and the Antarctic quadrant claimed as national territory, Argentina is the world's eighth-largest country, only slightly smaller than India. It stretches from La Quiaca on the Bolivian border, where summers can be brutally hot, to Ushuaia in Tierra del Fuego, where winters are experienced only by seasoned locals and the nuttiest of travelers. It's a distance of nearly 3500km, an expanse that encompasses a vast array of environments and terrain. The Andean chain runs the length of Argentina, from the Bolivian border in the north to the South Atlantic, where it disappears into the islands of Tierra del Fuego.

The Central & Northern Andes

In the extreme north, the Andes are basically the southern extension of the Bolivian *altiplano*, a thinly populated high plain between 3000m and 4000m in altitude, punctuated by even higher volcanic peaks. Although days can be surprisingly hot (sunburn is a serious hazard at high altitude), frosts occur almost nightly. The Andean northwest (p243) is also known as the *puna*.

Further south, in the arid provinces of San Juan and Mendoza (p344), the Andes climb to their highest altitudes, with 6962m Cerro Aconcagua (p362) topping out as the highest point in the western hemisphere. Here, their highest peaks lie covered in snow through the winter. Although rainfall on the eastern slopes is inadequate for crops, perennial streams descend from the Andes and provide irrigation water, which has brought prosperity to the wine-producing Cuyo region (the provinces of Mendoza, San Juan and San Luis). Winter in San Juan province is the season of the *zonda*, a hot, dry wind descending from the Andes that causes dramatic temperature increases (see p376).

The Chaco

East of the Andes and the Andean foothills, much of northern Argentina consists of subtropical lowlands. This arid area, known as the Argentine Chaco, is part of the much larger Gran Chaco (p232), an extremely rugged, largely uninhabited region that extends into Bolivia, Paraguay and Brazil. The Argentine Chaco encompasses the provinces of Chaco, Formosa and Santiago del Estero, the western reaches of Jujuy, Catamarca and Salta provinces, and the northernmost parts of Santa Fe and Córdoba.

The Chaco has a well-defined winter dry season, and summer everywhere in the Chaco is brutally hot. Rainfall decreases as you move east to west. The wet Chaco, which encompasses the eastern parts of Chaco and Formosa provinces and northeast Santa Fe, receives more rain than the dry Chaco, which covers central and western Chaco and Formosa provinces, most of Santiago del Estero and parts of Salta.

At its mouth, the Río de la Plata is an amazing 190km wide, making it the widest river in the world.

In 2007 Greenpeace Argentina helped pass Argentina's first federal forest protection law, the Ley de Bosques, which will hopefully curb rampant deforestation in northeast Argentina.

Mesopotamia

Also referred to as the Litoral (as in littoral), Mesopotamia is the name for the region of northeast Argentina (p177) between the Río Paraná and Río Uruguay. It's a region defined, as its names suggest, by its rivers, both a dominant part of the landscape. Here, the climate is mild, and rainfall is heavy in the provinces of Entre Ríos and Corrientes, which make up most of Mesopotamia. Hot and humid Misiones province, a politically important province surrounded on three sides by Brazil and Paraguay, contains part of Iguazú Falls, which descend from southern Brazil's Paraná Plateau. Shallow summer flooding is common throughout Mesopotamia and into the eastern Chaco, but only the immediate river floodplains become inundated in the west. Mesopotamia's rainfall is evenly distributed throughout the year.

Iguazú Falls consists of more than 275 individual falls that tumble from heights as much as 82m.

The Pampas & Atlantic Coast

Bordered by the Atlantic Ocean and Patagonia and stretching nearly to Córdoba and the Central Sierras, the pampas (p138) are Argentina's agricultural heartland. Geographically, this region covers the provinces of Buenos Aires and La Pampa, as well as southern chunks of Santa Fe and Córdoba.

This area can be subdivided into the humid pampas, along the Litoral, and the arid pampas of the western interior and the south. More than a third of the country's population lives in and around Buenos Aires, where the humid climate resembles New York City's in the spring, summer and autumn. Annual rainfall exceeds 900mm, but several hundred kilometers westward it's less than half that. Buenos Aires' winters are relatively mild.

The pampas are an almost completely level plain of wind-borne loess (a fine-grained silt or clay) and river-deposited sediments. The absence of nearly any rises in the land to speak of makes the area vulnerable to flooding from the relatively few, small rivers that cross it. Only the granitic Sierra de Tandil (484m; p148) and the Sierra de la Ventana (1273m; p152), in southwestern Buenos Aires province, and the Sierra de Lihué Calel (p157) disrupt the otherwise monotonous terrain.

The largest dinosaur ever discovered was the *Argentinosaurus huinculensis,* uncovered in Neuquén province; the herbivore measured a massive 40m long and 18m high.

Moving south along the Atlantic coast from the Argentine capital, the province of Buenos Aires features the sandy, often dune-backed beaches that attracted the development of seaside resorts like Mar del Plata and Necochea. Inland it's mostly the grasslands of the pampas. South of Viedma, cliffs begin to appear but the landscape remains otherwise desolate for its entire stretch south through Patagonia.

Patagonia & the Lake District

Ever-alluring Patagonia is the region of Argentina south of the Río Colorado, which flows southeast from the Andes and passes just north of the city of Neuquén. The Lake District is a subregion of Patagonia. Province-wise, Patagonia consists of Neuquén, Río Negro, Chubut and Santa Cruz. It's separated from Chilean Patagonia by the Andes.

Join *National Geographic* photographer David McLain behind the shutter as he shoots Patagonia with writer Tim Cahill and shares his photo secrets with you. It's tucked away online at www.nationalgeographic.com/adventure/0305/photo_index.html.

The Andean cordillera is high enough that Pacific storms drop most of their rain and snow on the Chilean side. In the extreme southern reaches of Patagonia, however, enough snow and ice still accumulate to form the largest southern hemisphere glaciers outside of Antarctica.

East of the Andean foothills, the cool, arid Patagonian steppes support huge flocks of sheep, whose wool is almost all exported to Europe. For such a southerly location, temperatures are relatively mild, even in winter, when more uniform atmospheric pressure moderates the strong gales that blow most of the year.

Except for urban centers like Comodoro Rivadavia (the center of coastal Patagonia's petroleum industry) and Río Gallegos (the hub for wool and meatpacking), Patagonia is thinly populated. Tidal ranges along the Atlantic coast are too great for major port facilities. In the valley of the Río Negro and at the outlet of the Río Chubut (near the town of Trelew), people farm and cultivate fruit orchards.

Tierra del Fuego

The world's southernmost permanently inhabited territory, Tierra del Fuego (aka Land of Fire) consists of one large island (Isla Grande), unequally divided between Chile and Argentina, and many smaller ones, some of which have been the source of longtime contention between the two countries. When Europeans first passed through the Strait of Magellan (which separates Isla Grande from the Patagonian mainland), the fires stemmed from the activities of the now endangered Yaghan people; nowadays, the fires result from the flaring of natural gas in the region's oil fields.

The northern half of Isla Grande, resembling the Patagonian steppes, is devoted to sheep grazing, while its southern half is mountainous and partly covered by forests and glaciers. As in Patagonia, winter conditions are rarely extreme, although trekking and outdoor camping are not advisable except for experienced mountaineers. For most visitors, though, the brief daylight hours during this season may be a greater deterrent than the weather.

WILDLIFE

With such variances in terrain and such great distances, it's no wonder Argentina supports a wide range of flora and fauna. Subtropical rainforests, palm savannas, high-altitude deserts and steppes, humid-temperate grasslands, alpine and sub-Antarctic forests and rich coastal areas all support their own special life forms. The most exciting part is that visitors – especially those from the northern hemisphere – will find many of Argentina's plants and animals unfamiliar. Take the capybara, for instance, the world's largest rodent, or the araucaria (pehuén), a conifer appropriately deemed the monkey puzzle tree in English. To protect these environments, Argentina has created an extensive system of national and provincial parks (p68), which are often the best places to experience the country's unique wildlife.

> The spotted suede sold throughout Argentina is *carpincho*, made from capybara, the largest rodent in the world. Females weigh up to 66kg and reach 130cm in length.

Animals

Northeast Argentina boasts the country's most diverse animal life. One of the best areas on the entire continent to enjoy wildlife is the swampy Esteros del Iberá (p201), in Corrientes province, where animals such as swamp deer, capybara and caiman, along with many large migratory birds, are commonly seen. It's comparable – arguably even better – than Brazil's more famous Pantanal.

In the drier northwest the most conspicuous animal is the domestic llama, but its wild cousins, the guanaco and vicuña, can also be seen. Your odds of seeing them are excellent if you travel by road through Parque Nacional Los Cardones (p271) to Salta. Their yellow fur is often an extraordinary puff of color against the cactus-studded backdrop. Many migratory birds, including flamingos, inhabit the high saline lakes of the Andean northwest.

In less densely settled areas, including the arid pampas of La Pampa province, guanacos, foxes and even pumas are not unusual sights. Many bodies of water, both permanent and seasonal, provide migratory bird habitats.

Most notable in Patagonia and Tierra del Fuego is the wealth of coastal wildlife, ranging from Magellanic penguins, cormorants and gulls to sea lions, fur seals, elephant seals and whales. Several coastal reserves, from Río Negro province south to Tierra del Fuego, are home to enormous concentrations of wildlife that are one of the region's greatest visitor attractions. Inland on the

> Magellanic penguins, native to Patagonia and Tierra del Fuego, have approximately 27 feathers per sq cm – now that's a down jacket!

NATIONAL PARKS & PROTECTED AREAS

Park	Features	Activities	Best Time to Visit
Monumento Natural Laguna de los Pozuelos (p260)	High-altitude lake; abundant bird life including three species of flamingos	bird watching, walking, wildlife watching	Nov-Mar
Parque Nacional Baritú (p252)	Nearly virgin subtropical montane forest	walking, wildlife watching, visiting traditional communities	Jun-Sep
Parque Nacional Calilegua (p250)	Transitional lowland forest, subtropical montane forest and subalpine grassland	walking, wildlife watching, bird watching	May-Nov
Parque Nacional Los Cardones (p271)	Montane desert park with striking cardón cacti and wandering guanacos	walking, photography, geology	Sep-May
Parque Nacional El Rey (p252)	Lush subtropical forest and coniferous Andean forest	walking, wildlife watching, bird watching	May-Nov
Parque Nacional Río Pilcomayo (p241)	Subtropical marshlands and palm savannas; colorful birds, caimans and nocturnal mammals	swimming with piranhas, boat trips, bird watching	Jun-Sep
Parque Nacional Chaco (p237)	Dense, subtropical thorn forests, marshes, palm savannas and colorful birds; very accessible but rarely visited	walking, 4WD trips, tree admiration	Apr-Oct
Parque Nacional Iguazú (p223)	Home of the awesome Iguazú Falls; also subtropical rainforest and abundant birds, mammals and reptiles	walking, boat trips, gawking	Oct-Mar
Parque Nacional Mburucuyá (p199)	Quebracho and palm forests, estuaries and islands; capybaras, foxes, gazunchos, river wolves and swamp deer (swamp deer?!)	walking, wildlife watching, bird watching	year-round
Reserva Provincial Esteros del Iberá (p201)	Tranquil wetland reserve; arguably a better wildlife site than Brazil's famous Pantanal	boat trips, wildlife and bird watching, horseback riding	Mar-Dec
Parque Nacional El Palmar (p209)	On the Río Uruguay; home to the last extensive stands of yatay-palm savanna	walking, horseback riding, cycling, tree admiration	year-round
Parque Nacional Talampaya (p313)	Rich desert scenery and extraordinary geological, paleontological and archaeological resources	geology, cycling, 4WD trips, walking	Sep-Nov & Mar-May
Parque Nacional Copo (p300)	Dense dry Chaco forest, mostly flat, home to the last of the region's threatened wildlife	walking, wildlife and bird watching	Apr-Oct
Parque Provincial Ischigualasto (p379)	Known as Valley of the Moon; surreally scenic paleontological preserve with wild rock formations	trekking, bike tours, full moon tours	Apr-Sep
Parque Nacional El Leoncito (p376)	760 sq km of barren Andean precordillera; home to guanacos, foxes and peregrine falcons	hiking, landsailing, astronomy	year-round
Parque Nacional Quebrada del Condorito (p335)	Stunning rocky grasslands across the Pampa de Achala in the Sierras Grande; condors, condors, condors	trekking, hiking, condor watching	Apr-Sep
Parque Nacional Sierra de las Quijadas (p339)	Polychrome desert canyons and the site of major dinosaur discoveries; hiking, wonderfully quiet	photography, paleontology	Apr-Sep
Parque Provincial Aconcagua (p362)	Home of the western hemisphere's highest peak, 6960m Aconcagua	trekking, hiking, mountain climbing	Dec-Mar
Parque Provincial Volcán Tupungato (p364)	Centerpiece: 6650m summit of Tupungato, a more challenging climb than nearby Aconcagua	trekking, hiking, mountain climbing	Dec-Mar

Park	Features	Activities	Best Time to Visit
Parque Nacional Lihué Calel (p157)	Pinkish peaks, isolated valleys, petroglyphs and a surprising range of fauna and flora	hiking, archeological interest, wildlife-spotting	Sept-Oct, Mar-Apr
Parque Provincial Payunia (p368)	Boasts a higher concentration of volcanic cones (over 800 of them) than anywhere else in the world	hiking, photography, bird watching	year-round
Parque Nacional Laguna Blanca (p386)	Desolate lake, lots of nothingness; ancient volcanoes and lava flows, bird watching nesting colonies of black-necked swans, Andean flamingos	hiking, photography,	Sep-Dec
Parque Nacional Lanín (p400)	Extensive forests of monkey puzzle trees (araucaria) and southern beech capped by the perfect cone of Volcán Lanín	hiking, photography, visiting Mapuche communities	Dec-Mar
Parque Nacional Nahuel Huapi (p415)	An area of 7580 sq km around the exquisite Lago Nahuel Huapi; lakes, views, trees, fun – and lots of people	hiking, snow sports, fishing	Dec-Mar
Parque Nacional Los Arrayanes (p405)	Tiny park inside Parque Nacional Nahuel Huapi; protects stands of the unique arrayán tree	hiking, photography, boat cruises	Dec-Mar
Parque Nacional Lago Puelo (p422)	Lago Puelo, an aquamarine, low-altitude lake set among high Andean peaks	fishing, boating, hiking	Dec-Mar
Parque Nacional Los Alerces (p473)	Unique Valdivian forest, which includes impressive specimens of the redwood-like alerce tree	hiking, boating, fishing	Nov-Apr
Reserva Faunística Península Valdés (p436)	Wildlife enthusiast's dream; whales, sea lions, Magellanic penguins	wildlife watching, diving, boat tours	Jun-Dec
Reserva Provincial Punta Tombo (p448)	Known for its enormous nesting colony of burrowing Magellanic penguins	wildlife watching, walking	Sep-Mar
Parque Nacional Perito Moreno (p481)	Awesome glacial lakes, alpine peaks, Andean-Patagonian forest and hiking, guanaco; way off the beaten track	wildlife watching, horse-back riding	Nov-Mar
Monumento Natural Bosques Petrificados (p458)	Isolated park featuring immense specimens of petrified *Proaraucaria* trees	hiking, fossils	year-round
Parque Nacional Monte León (p460)	Argentina's first coastal national park outside Tierra del Fuego,	hiking, wildlife watching, bird watching	year-round
Parque Nacional Los Glaciares (p483 & p495)	Home to Argentina's must-sees: the famous Glaciar Perito Merino and the awesome pinnacles of the Fitz Roy Range	hiking, glaciers, backpacking, climbing	Nov-Mar
Parque Nacional Tierra del Fuego (p535)	Argentina's first shoreline national park: alpine glaciers and peaks, marine mammals, seabirds, shorebirds and extensive southern beech forests	hiking, kayaking	Nov-Mar

* Parks are listed generally north to south, west to east.

Patagonian steppe, as in the northwest, the guanaco is the most conspicuous mammal, but the flightless rhea, resembling the Old World ostrich, runs in flocks across the plains.

For more on Patagonia's wildlife, see the boxed text, p440.

Plants

When it comes to plant life, the country's most diverse regions are in northeast Argentina, the Lake District, the Patagonian Andes and the subtropical forests of northwest Argentina. The high northern Andes are dry and often barren, and vegetation is limited to ichu (sparse bunch grasses) and low, widely spaced shrubs, known collectively as tola. In Jujuy and La Rioja provinces, however, huge, vertically branched cardón cacti add a rugged beauty to an otherwise empty landscape. In the Andean precordillera, between the Chaco and the Andes proper, lies a strip of dense, subtropical montane cloud forest known as the Yungas. Spanning parts of Salta, Jujuy and Tucumán provinces, the Yungas are kept lush by heavy summertime rains, and are one of the most biologically diverse regions in the country. The Yungas are home to three national parks: Parque Nacional Calilegua (p250), Parque Nacional Baritú (p252) and Parque Nacional El Rey (p252).

The wet Chaco is home to grasslands and gallery forests with numerous tree species, including the quebracho colorado and caranday palm. The dry Chaco, although extremely parched, is still thick with vegetation. Its taller trees include the quebracho colorado, quebracho blanco, algarrobo, palo santo, and a dense understory of low-growing spiny trees and shrubs. Both quebracho and algarrobo trees produce highly valued hard woods that have lead to widespread deforestation throughout both regions of the Chaco.

In Mesopotamia rainfall is sufficient to support swampy lowland forests as well as upland savanna. Misiones' native vegetation is mostly dense subtropical forest, though its upper elevations are studded with araucaria pines.

The once lush native grasses of the Argentine pampas have suffered under grazing pressure and the proliferation of grain farms that produce cash crops such as soy beans. Today very little native vegetation remains, except along watercourses like the Río Paraná.

Most of Patagonia lies in the rain shadow of the Chilean Andes, so the vast steppes of southeastern Argentina resemble the sparse grasslands of the arid Andean highlands. Closer to the border there are pockets of dense *Nothofagus* (southern beech) and coniferous woodlands that owe their existence to the winter storms that sneak over the cordillera. Northern Tierra del Fuego is a grassy extension of the Patagonian steppe, but the heavy rainfall of the mountainous southern half supports verdant southern beech forests.

NATIONAL & PROVINCIAL PARKS

Argentina's national parks lure visitors from around the world. One of Latin America's first national-park systems, Argentina's dates from the turn of the 20th century, when explorer and surveyor Francisco P Moreno donated 75 sq km near Bariloche to the state in return for guarantees that the parcel would be preserved for the enjoyment of all Argentines. This area is now part of Parque Nacional Nahuel Huapi (p415) in the Andean Lake District.

Since then the country has established many other parks and reserves, mostly but not exclusively in the Andean region. There are also important provincial parks and reserves, such as Reserva Faunística Península Valdés (p436), which do not fall within the national-park system but deserve attention. In general, the national parks are more visitor-oriented than the

An estimated 3000 sq km of native Argentine forest is cleared every year in order to plant soy, Argentina's latest big-prize crop.

Founded by the former CEO of Patagonia clothing company, Conservación Patagónica (www .patagonialandtrust .org) has controversially purchased thousands of acres in Patagonia and Esteros del Iberá in order to preserve them. The website is excellent.

(Continued on page 77)

Argentina
Outdoors

A hiker's reward: the astounding beauty of Parque Nacional Los Glaciares (p483), Patagonia

GARETH MCCORMACK

Whether to the rugged wilderness of Patagonia or the massive peaks of the Andes, Argentina has long allured the world's most adventurous souls. For anyone with a little grit and a love of the great outdoors, it's more than just a magnet. It's a mecca. Mountaineering, hiking and fishing have long been Argentina's classic outdoor pursuits, but these days people – both from Argentina and abroad – are doing much more. They're kite surfing in the Andes, snowboarding in August near Bariloche, paragliding in the Central Sierras and sneaking up on caimans in Esteros del Iberá. And they're always, *always* having fun.

HIKING & TREKKING

Argentina is home to some seriously superb stomping. The Argentine Lake District is probably the country's most popular hiking destination, with outstanding day and multi-day hikes in several national parks, including Nahuel Huapi (p415) and Lanín (p400). Bariloche is the best base for exploring the former, San Martín de los Andes the latter.

Patagonia, needless to say, has out-of-this-world hiking. South of Bariloche, El Bolsón (p417) is an excellent base for hiking both in the forests outside of town and in nearby Parque Nacional Lago Puelo (p422). Parque Nacional Los Glaciares offers wonderful hiking in and around the Fitz Roy Range; base yourself in the town of El Chaltén (p483) and wait out the storms (drinking beer in the local brewery, of course).

If you've come this far south, you might as well head over to Parque Nacional Torres del Paine (p512), in Chile, for some of the continent's most epic hiking of all. Tierra del Fuego also has great hiking, primarily in and around Parque Nacional Tierra del Fuego (p535).

Then there are the high Andean peaks west of Mendoza (p345). Although these areas are more popular for mountaineering, there's some great trekking in the area as well. The northern Andes around the Quebrada de Humahuaca (p253) are also good.

The peaceful, mossy delights of trekking through lenga forest

GARETH McCORMACK

Most sizable towns in the Lake District and Patagonia have a hiking and mountaineering club, called a Club Andino. These can be outstanding places to get information, maps and current conditions. We've listed the clubs in Information sections throughout this book (Bariloche, Junín de los Andes, El Bolsón and Ushuaia all have one).

Lonely Planet's *Trekking in the Patagonian Andes* is a great resource to have along if you're planning some serious trekking.

MOUNTAINEERING

The Andes are a mountaineer's dream, especially in San Juan and Mendoza provinces, where some of the highest peaks in

The humbling peaks of Cerro Torre, Parque Nacional Los Glaciares (p483)

GARETH MCCORMACK

the western hemisphere are found. While the most famous climb is Aconcagua (p362), the highest peak in the Americas, there are plenty of others in the Andes – many of them more interesting and far more technical. Near Barreal in San Juan province (p374), the Cordón de la Rameda boasts five peaks over 6000m high, including the mammoth Cerro Mercedario which tops out at 6770m. The region is less congested than Aconcagua, offers more technical climbs and is preferred by many climbers. Also near here is the majestic Cordillera de Ansilta (p374), with seven peaks scraping the sky at altitudes between 5130m and 5885m.

The magnificent and challenging Fitz Roy Range (p483), in southern Patagonia, is one of the world's top mountaineering destinations, while the mountains of Parque Nacional Nahuel Huapi (p415), around Bariloche, offer fun for all levels.

ROCK CLIMBING

Patagonia's Parque Nacional Los Glaciares (p483), home to Cerro Torre and Mount Fitz Roy, is one of the most important rock-climbing destinations in the world. Cerro Torre, in fact, is considered one of the five toughest climbs on the planet. The nearby town of El Chaltén is a climbers haven, and several shops offer lessons and rent equipment. If you don't have the time or talent for climbs of the Cerro Torre magnitude, there are plenty of other options throughout the country. Los Gigantes (p327), in the Central Sierras, is fast becoming the country's de facto sport climbing capital, with lots of high-quality granite. Operators in Córdoba (p320) offer lessons and transportation. In Mendoza province, Los Molles (p368) is a small, friendly hub for rock climbing. In the pampas, there's a friendly rock-climbing scene in the town of Tandil (p148), although there's not a climb in the area over 600m.

FISHING
Where to Fish
Patagonia and the Lake District together constitute one of the world's premier fly-fishing destinations, where introduced trout species (brown, brook, lake and

Angling for a bite in Tierra del Fuego (p518)
MICHAEL T

rainbow) and landlocked Atlantic salmon reach massive sizes in cold rivers surrounded by spectacular scenery. Without a doubt, it's an angler's paradise.

In the Lake District, Junín de los Andes (p393) is the self-proclaimed trout capital of Argentina, and lining up a guide there to take you out to fish Parque Nacional Lanín's superb trout streams is easy. Nearby Aluminé (p388) sits on the banks of the Río Aluminé, one of the country's most highly regarded trout streams. Bariloche (p409) is another excellent base.

Further south, Parque Nacional Los Alerces (p473) has outstanding lakes and rivers. The Río Grande, on Tierra del Fuego's Isla Grande (p521), is famous for holding some of the largest sea-running brown trout in the world. Other important mainland Patagonian rivers include Río Negro, Río Gallegos and Río Santa Cruz.

In subtropical northeast Argentina (p177), the wide Río Paraná attracts fly-fishers, spin fishers and trollers (heaven forbid) from around the world, who pull in massive river species such as sábalo (a sort of umbrella name for several species of river fish native to northeast Argentina), surubí (a massive catfish) and dorado (a trout-like freshwater game fish). The dorado, not to be confused with the salt-water mahi mahi, is an extremely powerful swimmer and is said to be one of the most exciting fish to catch on a fly. Accordingly, it has earned the nickname 'fighting tiger of the Paraná.'

Guides & Services
A fly rod makes a great addition to any backpack. If you're traveling around Patagonia, especially the Lake District, you can easily throw a pack-rod into your bag and fish wherever you feel like (provided you're licensed, of course). But if you really want to fish, nothing can take the place of having a good guide. In smaller towns such as Junín de los Andes, you can usually go to the local tourist office and request a list of local fishing guides to contact yourself. Better yet, most tourist offices can set you up with a list of established fishing operators, or you can simply contact one that's listed in an Activities section of this book. Another good option for independent anglers heading to the Lake District is the **Asociación de Guías Profesionales de Pesca del Parque Nacional Nahuel Huapi y Patagonia Norte** (www.guiaspatagonicos .com.ar in Spanish), which maintains a list of licensed guides for northern Patagonia and the Lake District. It includes telephone numbers and links to the guides' websites.

In northern Argentina, which doesn't have a tourist infrastructure as accommodating as the Lake District's, it's virtually impossible to fish without a guide – and usually a boat.

For general information about fly-fishing in Argentina, contact **Asociación Argentina de Pesca con Mosca** (Argentine Fly Fishing Association; ☎ in Buenos Aires 011-4773-0821; www.aapm.org.ar in Spanish). For more about fishing in Tierra del Fuego, see p523.

Rules & Regulations

In the Lake District and Patagonia, the season runs November 1 to sometime between mid- and late-April. In the northeast the season runs February to October. Certain lakes and streams on private land may stay open longer.

Trout fishing is almost always mandatory catch and release. Throughout Patagonia (including the Lake District), native species should *always* be thrown back. These are usually smaller than trout and include perca (perch), puyen (common galaxias, a narrow fish native to the southern hemisphere), Patagonian pejerrey, and the rare peladilla.

Fishing licenses are required everywhere and are available at tackle shops, the local *club de caza y pesca* (hunting and fishing club) and sometimes at tourist offices and YPF (gas) stations. For most of the country, prices are AR$50 per day, AR$200 per week and AR$300 for the season. Trolling fees cost extra. In Tierra del Fuego, prices are higher. You must pay the regular fees mentioned here, plus an additional fee for preferential zones.

SKIING & SNOWBOARDING

Although still not as internationally known as the slopes in neighboring Chile, Argentina's mountains can be outstanding. Most locations offer superb powder, good cover and plenty of sunny days. Many resorts have large ski schools with instructors from all over the world, so even language is not a problem. At some of the older resorts equipment can be a little antiquated, but in general the quality of skiing more than compensates.

There are three main snow-sport areas: Mendoza, the Lake District and Ushuaia. Mendoza is home to Argentina's premier resort, Las Leñas (p369), which has the best snow, the

Shooting the dry-powder slopes of Las Leñas (p369)

CHRISTIAN ASLUND

driest snow and the longest runs. The Lake District is home to several low-key resorts, including Cerro Catedral (p416) near Bariloche and Cerro Chapelco (p399), near San Martín de los Andes. Although the snow doesn't get as powdery here, the resorts are more low-key and the views are far superior to Las Leñas. They're also much closer to their nearest towns, meaning food and lodging is cheaper, and you'll find more to do at night. The world's most southerly commercial skiing is near Ushuaia in Tierra del Fuego (see p529). The ski season everywhere generally runs mid-June to mid-October.

CYCLING

Cycling (road biking) is a popular activity among Argentines, and spandex-clad cyclists are a common site along the road, despite the fact that you'll never see a bicycle lane. There are some outstanding paved routes for cyclists, especially in the

Earn your tipple cycling between the vineyards of Mendoza (p357)
ANDREW PE

Lake District and, to a lesser extent, in the Andean northwest.

In the Lake District's Parque Nacional Nahuel Huapi (p415), near Bariloche, there are several excellent loops (including the Circuito Chico) that skirt gorgeous lakes and take in some of Patagonia's most epic scenery. Cyclists often take their bikes on the Cruce de Lagos (p414), a famous two-day boat/bus journey across the Andes to Chile. Instead of bussing the road stretches, they ride.

In the northwest, there are several excellent road routes, including the highway from Tucumán to Tafí del Valle; the direct road from Salta to Jujuy; and – arguably most spectacular of all – the Quebrada de Cafayate (p286). The Central Sierras (p325) are also great candidates for cycling, and the mostly paved network of roads roll past a countryside which is, at times, reminiscent of Scotland. Mendoza boasts some epic routes through the Andes, but most are doable only for the seasoned cyclist – those lacking thighs of glory can entertain themselves pedaling between wineries in Maipú (p358).

For more information on bike rentals and logistics on getting around Argentina on two wheels, see p623.

SLOPE OF THE WIND

From around the world, windsurfing and kite-surfing fanatics drag an insane amount of gear to an isolated spot in the central Andes: Dique Cuesta del Viento, literally 'slope of the wind reservoir' (p377). The reservoir, near the wee village of Rodeo, in San Juan province, is one of the best windsurfing and kite-surfing destinations on the planet. Its consistent and extremely powerful wind blows every afternoon – without fail – from October to early May. We checked it out, and it blew us away!

MOUNTAIN BIKING

The opportunities for mountain biking are endless. However, the sport is fairly undeveloped here, and you'll find few places that have true single tracks for mountain bikers. Most foreigners on mountain bikes are touring with them rather than bombing down hills. Even if you're leaving your bike at home, you'll find ample opportunity to ride. At most outdoor hubs (such as Bariloche) you can rent a mountain bike for a day of independent pedaling or for guided mountain bike rides, a fantastic way to see parts of an area you otherwise wouldn't. Places with mountain bike rentals and guides include La Cumbrecita (p334), La Cumbre (p328) and Villa General Belgrano (p332) in Córdoba; Villa la Angostura (p404), Bariloche (p406), El Bolsón (p417) and Junín de los Andes (p393) in the Lake District; Mendoza (p345), Cacheuta (p359) and Uspallata (p360) in Mendoza; Barreal (p374) in San Juan; and Tilcara (p254) in the Andean northwest.

For more on the logistics of pedaling around Argentina, see p623.

> ### SAILING: NO WATER NECESSARY
>
> In San Juan province's Parque Nacional El Leoncito (p376), the Pampa El Leoncito has become the epicenter of *carrovelismo* (land sailing). Here, people zip across the dry lake bed beneath Andean peaks in so-called sail cars. If you're interested, head straight to Barreal (p374).

WHITE-WATER RAFTING & KAYAKING

Although its rivers can't compare to neighboring Chile's when it comes to white-water action, Argentina does have some excellent river running. Currently, the Río Mendoza and Río Diamante, in Mendoza province (see p351), are the reigning white-water destinations, but for scenery, it's all about Patagonia. The Río Hua Hum and Río Meliquina near San Martín de los Andes (see p397), and the Río Limay and Río Manso near Bariloche (see p410) are both spectacular. So is the Río Aluminé, near the wee town of Aluminé (p388). From the Patagonian town of Esquel (p465) you can join a rafting trip on the incredibly scenic, glacial-fed Río Corcovado. A relatively unknown rafting destination is Barreal (p374), in the Andes, but it's more about the epic Andean scenery than the rapids. Scenic class II-III floats are possible on most of these rivers, while class IV runs are possible on the Ríos Mendoza, Diamante, Meliquina, Hua Hum and Corcovado. Experience is generally unnecessary for guided runs.

PARAGLIDING & SKYDIVING

Paragliding is popular in Argentina and it's a great place to take tandem flights or classes. Why? Firstly because it's so affordable here and secondly because there are some outstanding places to do it. Many agencies in Bariloche (p410) offer paragliding, and views are superb. Perhaps the best place of all, however, is La Cumbre (p329), in Córdoba's Central Sierras. Both La Cumbre and Córdoba (p320) are the places to go for the absurd rush of skydiving.

Soar sky-high over the mountains around Bariloche (p410)   © AARON BECK / ALAMY

Experience the thunderous power of Iguazú Falls (p224)

(Continued from page 68)

provincial parks, but there are exceptions: Parque Nacional Perito Moreno has few visitor services, for example, while Península Valdés has many.

Before seeing the parks, visitors to Buenos Aires should stop at the **national parks administration** (Administración de Parques Nacionales; www.parquesnacionales.gov.ar; Santa Fe 690) for maps and brochures, which are often in short supply in the parks; there may be a charge for some. Admission to most national parks is AR$12 for adults. It's less for Argentines and free for children under 12. Some are pricier: Parque Nacional Tierra del Fuego, for example, costs AR$20, and Parque Nacional Los Glaciares costs AR$30.

Admission to provincial parks varies between AR$9 and AR$35, but official fees can be deceiving. At some parks you'd have to set off flares just to find someone to pay; at others (such as Parque Provincial Ischigualasto in San Juan), you may be required to hire a guide, which can increase the price by anywhere from AR$15 to AR$175 per person. At Parque Provincial Aconcagua, trekking permits cost AR$90 to AR$150 and climbing permits AR$300 to AR$900.

With a special focus on Latin America, Ron Mader's Planeta (www.planeta.com) is the most comprehensible online resource for exploring ecotourism and environmental reporting; check out the Argentina pages.

ENVIRONMENTAL ISSUES

Although Argentina boasts one of South America's largest systems of parks and reserves, much of those areas – not to mention the extremely sensitive regions around and between them – face serious threats. Deforestation is a major issue in the Chaco, where genetically modified soy, sunflower crops and lumber outweigh the health of the forests. It's equally bad in the Yungas and the subtropical rainforests of Misiones, where tea plantations and timber companies continue to destroy some of Argentina's most biologically diverse regions. The result is that many of the country's protected areas, especially those in the Gran Chaco and the Mesopotamia, are virtual islands in a sea of environmental destruction.

For a close and outstanding look at Argentina's environmental problems, and to learn how to help, check out Fundación Vida Silvestre Argentina (www.vidasilvestre.org.ar), in Spanish and English.

The good news is that 2007 saw the passing of the Ley de Bosques (National Forest Law), which levied a one-year nationwide moratorium on clearing native forests. The law, largely a project of Greenpeace Argentina, was a major victory for environmentalists and, at least on paper, forced

---

UNESCO WORLD HERITAGE SITES

The UN Educational, Scientific and Cultural Organization (Unesco) has designated the following sites in Argentina World Heritage sites. The first was Parque Nacional Los Glaciares (1981), and the most recent was the magnificent Quebrada de Humahuaca (2003).

- Cueva de las Manos (p480)
- *Estancias* of Córdoba province: (p331, p331 and p331)
- Jesuit Missions of the Guaraní: San Ignacio Miní (p219), Santa Ana (p217), Loreto (p217)
- Manzana Jesuítica (Jesuit Block), Córdoba (p317)
- Parque Nacional Iguazú (p223)
- Parque Nacional Los Glaciares (p483 and p495)
- Parque Nacional Talampaya (p313)
- Parque Provincial Ischigualasto (p379)
- Quebrada de Humahuaca (p253)
- Reserva Faunística Península Valdés (p436)

GREEN ARGENTINA *Sarah Gilbert*

If you're in Argentina long enough, you're sure to hear a local say, in tones of either exasperation or resignation, that the root of the country's troubles is this: *'No hay control de nada!'* In other words, nothing is organized, and nothing is under control. One look at the filth floating in Buenos Aires' Río Riachuelo or the rampant urban development gobbling up the country's coastline confirms this theory.

The sad irony is that while Argentina has one of the best environmental protection regimes in South America, the rules are very poorly enforced. Conservationists say this is the single biggest problem facing Argentina's natural environment.

Argentina is a developing country with huge natural resources, large tracts of wilderness and around 10 million people in poverty. One third of those live in extreme poverty. Argentina needs to rapidly develop to lift its citizens' standard of living, but this often comes at the expense of the environment. After all, as long as huge revenues from soy crops are helping to offload Argentina's massive debt, who wants to worry about a bit of soil degradation? At the same time, cleaning up the rivers or protecting the forests can all too often seem less urgent than the many critical problems that take up the lion's share of government and social-sector resources. And as with most countries, the costs of failing to properly protect its natural resources is not effectively factored into Argentina's economic formulas.

Of course, it's not just domestic policy and development that are having an impact. Global climate change is affecting the weather in Argentina, too, with Patagonia's melting glaciers grabbing frequent headlines here. Argentina is already South America's second-highest carbon emitter, and increased development is creating ever more energy consumption. At the same time, according to Greenpeace, a football field's worth of the country's native forest is cut down each hour.

Conservation in Argentina

Super-rich in biodiversity, Argentina boasts 18 distinct ecological regions with 20,000 plants, 700 fish, 150 amphibian, 250 reptile, 360 mammal and 1000 bird species. Argentines are justifiably proud of this immense natural wealth and of the network of national parks and reserves that help protect it.

On the whole, though, Argentina's resources have been overexploited and imperiled over the 300-odd years since Europeans arrived. At the beginning of the 20th century there were 1.05 million sq km of native forest and jungle. There are now 320 000 sq km left, and what is left has been compromised. Forests, fish stocks, water and soil have all been overexploited and continue to be so, and environmental awareness remains fairly low.

On the bright side, however, Argentina has lost very few of its native species since colonization, and compared to most countries, it is still full of wild, untouched places. Meanwhile, important and creative conservation work is being done. Argentina's foremost environmental organization, Fundación Vida Silvestre (www.vidasilvestre.org.ar), has its own network of reserves, occasionally passing areas on to National Parks for protection. Vida Silvestre works closely with private landowners to create *refugios* (protected areas managed by joint agreement) that help preserve wildlife and indigenous plant species throughout the country.

Sustainable Travel

Tourism has grown exponentially since the 2001 currency crisis made Argentina affordable to a greater number of travelers. This is a plus for the economy, of course, but in many ways it's a plus for the environment, too. Argentina's extraordinary natural beauty is its main attraction, and the increase in tourism revenues proves that the country's wild places are worth preserving for economic as well as environmental reasons. Nonetheless, with the increase in visits to all national parks, it's important to note that the tourism boom places a strain on Argentina's fragile ecosystems.

Sustainable travel and ecotourism are still fairly novel concepts in Argentina, and are often misunderstood. If you see the *eco* tag attached to a tour group or lodge, it's as likely as not that it simply means 'something to do with nature.' As yet, there's no official certification program for the travel industry, and anyone can hang a tour-guide sign on their door. Until a proper scheme is in place, it's up to travelers to support those businesses that are helping develop a sustainable tourism industry.

While solar-powered eco-lodges may be thin on the ground, there are plenty of travel options in Argentina that contribute to the wealth and wellbeing of Argentina's people, cultural heritage and natural environment, whether it's a stay at a historic *estancia* (ranch) or buying organic wine from an Argentine-owned winery.

Sustainable travel also involves the kind of energy-saving and carbon-reducing practices you can adopt any time. Where possible, rent a bike or a horse rather than a car. While popular, activities like quad biking and jet-skiing can have a negative impact on wildlife and create unnecessary noise pollution. Even if locals don't always seem to get it, respectful travelers can easily take care with their garbage. In hotel rooms, try using the fan instead of the air conditioner.

The harsh truth for travelers who want to reduce their carbon footprint is that flying is the single worst thing you can do. Unfortunately, in a country as large as Argentina, it's hard for most of us to avoid planes, and the absence of a fast and reliable railway system doesn't help. Carbon offsetting schemes are one way to mitigate the negative effects of your flights (see p621).

Sustainable Gems

The popularity of rural tourism, resilience of indigenous communities and the creativity and enterprising spirit of Argentina's people all mean that you can find plenty of ways to contribute to the country's sustainable development while you're traveling here. For starters, see this book's GreenDex (p672).

Argentina has a rich agricultural history, and throughout the country you'll find historic *estancias*, or ranches, which often conserve large green spaces and forested areas, while helping to preserve part of the country's rural and architectural heritage. A few use alternative energy and nearly all of them are Argentine-owned, employing locals and buying produce from local farmers.

You'll find *estancias* listed throughout this guide, including standouts like **Estancia y Bodega Colomé** (www.estanciacolome.com; see the boxed text, p274), where alternative energy and Argentina's oldest grapevines help produce excellent organic wine; and the Unesco World Heritage–listed **Estancia Santa Catalina** (p331), whose owners blend tourism with heritage preservation and happily inform guests of the area's rich history.

Argentina's indigenous tribes may be less visible than their counterparts in neighboring countries like Peru and Bolivia, but they have held on to their traditions in many regions, particularly in the north. You can help support economic development in communities by buying handicrafts directly from indigenous artisans, some of whom run their own cooperatives, or by visiting enterprises like the Mapuche-operated **Batea Mahuida ski park** (p389).

Argentina's national parks (www.parquesnacionales.gov.ar in Spanish) offer an impressive array of spectacular landscapes to explore, while provincial and municipal parks protect green spaces and unique ecosystems. According to the Fundación Vida Silvestre, tourism is a threat to nearly all of Argentina's parks. Too often success is measured in terms of the volume of visitors, without considering the effect these volumes have on the wildlife and fauna of the parks. The worst example of this is Iguazú national park, which welcomes over a million visitors per year without measuring their impact. One park that's doing better at managing human intervention is the **Reserva Provincial Esteros del Iberá** (p201), where boat trips through the marshes are strictly controlled.

Frustratingly, interpretive material can be scant in many parks. Eco-conscious private tour companies offer an opportunity to learn more about the environment you're in. Worth recommending is **Seriema Nature Tours** (p158), which works closely with the Ornithological Association of Argentina and runs tours throughout the country for birdwatchers, botanists and nature photographers.

Environmental & Social Organizations

The two main environmental organizations operating nationally in Argentina are **Greenpeace** (www.greenpeace.org.ar in Spanish) and the **Fundación Vida Silvestre** (www.vidasilvestre.org.ar in Spanish), an Argentine NGO. Greenpeace does its usual crucial mix of public awareness and lobbying, while Vida Silvestre is on the ground, working with landowners and nature lovers to preserve important ecosystems throughout the country.

NGOs in the social sector are also participating. **Responde** (www.responde.org.ar) helps small villages to build healthy local economies, often in the form of sustainable tourism, thus preserving regional culture and stemming uncontrolled urban sprawl in the big cities, while the many NGOs in Buenos Aires' slums are campaigning to improve the quality of the urban environment.

For information on volunteering opportunities with NGOs for travelers, see p617.

the government to carry out environmental impact reports and the creation of forest management policies. Corruption, however, is as deadly for trees as chainsaws are, and it remains to be seen whether a true halt to deforestation will actually occur.

Another high-profile issue is global warming, which, according to scientists, is taking a major toll on the Southern Patagonian Ice Field, which is melting far faster today than it was before the 1990s. Ironically, global warming and glacial retreat have become such big news these days that more people than ever are booking tours to see Argentina's glaciers and Antarctica before they're…gone forever?

US environmentalist Doug Tompkins, founder of The North Face and Esprit clothing companies, owns 630 sq km of the Argentine Patagonian coast and over 2000 sq km of Esteros del Iberá.

As international headlines point south, national headlines point north – to the Botnia paper mill that opened in 2007 across the Río Uruguay from the Argentine town of Gualeguaychú (p204). Owned by Finnish company Botnia, the Uruguayan mill has sparked widespread protest from Argentina, which views it as an environmental catastrophe. For more, see p543.

The Canadian company Barrick Gold currently operates a massive goldmine in San Juan province that has taken a dramatic toll on both the landscape and the people. Locals and environmentalists in and around the town of San José de Jáchal (p377), as well as winemakers and other groups from the province, have fervently protested Barrick's use of highly toxic cyanide, which is contaminating both soil and groundwater. In 2008 the company was set to begin construction of its highly controversial Pascua Lama gold and silver mining project on the Argentine/Chilean border, though tax and permit issues were delaying the start of construction. The project received intense criticism after reports surfaced that Barrick planned to 'relocate' three Andean glaciers (by some estimates, that meant removal of 20 hectares of ice) in order to mine. Chile approved the mine but forbade the transfer of glaciers, and Barrick has stated no ice will be moved.

According to Greenpeace, Patagonian glaciers are shrinking, as a whole, at a rate of 42 cubic km annually – faster than anywhere else on the planet.

With Argentina's economic collapse and the country's subsequent ability to compete on the international market, production of soy has skyrocketed and become Argentina's single most important cash crop. Farmers throughout the pampas now plant monocrops of genetically modified, herbicide-resistant soy, which is rapidly depleting the ground of its minerals, and contributing to high levels of herbicide in soils throughout the region.

On a positive note, Argentines are becoming more environmentally aware, and protected areas are still increasing. The 2007 Ley de Bosques is just one example of how locals are demonstrating their frustration with the status quo.

Buenos Aires

Mix together a beautiful European-like city with attractive residents (call them *porteños*), gourmet cuisine, awesome shopping, a frenzied nightlife and top-drawer activities, and you get Buenos Aires, a cosmopolitan metropolis with both slick neighborhoods and equally downtrodden areas – but that's part of the appeal. It's an elegant, seductive place with a ragged edge, laced with old-world languor and yet full of contemporary attitude. BA is somehow strangely familiar, but unlike any other city in the world.

In between cutting-edge designer boutiques, ritzy neighborhoods and grand parks are unkempt streets full of spewing buses and bustling fervor. Seek out classic BA: the old-world cafés, colonial architecture, fun outdoor markets and diverse communities. Rub shoulders with the formerly rich and famous in Recoleta's cemetery, making sure to sidestep the ubiquitous dog piles on the sidewalks. Fill your belly at a *parrilla* (steak restaurant), then spend the night partying away in Palermo Viejo's trendiest dance club. Hunt for that antique gem in a dusty San Telmo shop, or visit on Sunday for the *barrio's* spectacularly popular fair. Learn to sweep your leg dancing the sultry tango, and then attend a super-passionate *fútbol* match between River and Boca. These unforgettable adventures (and many more) are just waiting for you to go out and experience them.

Everyone knows someone who has been here and raved about it. You've put it off long enough. Come to Buenos Aires and you'll understand why so many people have fallen in love with this amazing city, and even decided to stay. There's a good chance you'll be one of them.

HIGHLIGHTS

- Commune with BA's rich and famous dead at the **Recoleta cemetery** (p101)
- Marvel at those amazingly high leg kicks at a **tango show** (p123)
- Shop the fun and stylish designer boutiques in **Palermo Viejo** (p128)
- Feast on tasty steaks or more exotic cuisine in **Las Cañitas** (p118)
- Party all night long in BA's chic and super-happening **nightclubs** (p124)

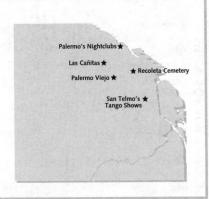

Palermo's Nightclubs ★

Las Cañitas ★

Palermo Viejo ★

★ Recoleta Cemetery

San Telmo's ★
Tango Shows

■ TELEPHONE CODE: 011　　■ POPULATION: THREE MILLION　　■ AREA: 200 SQ KM

REGIONAL BUENOS AIRES

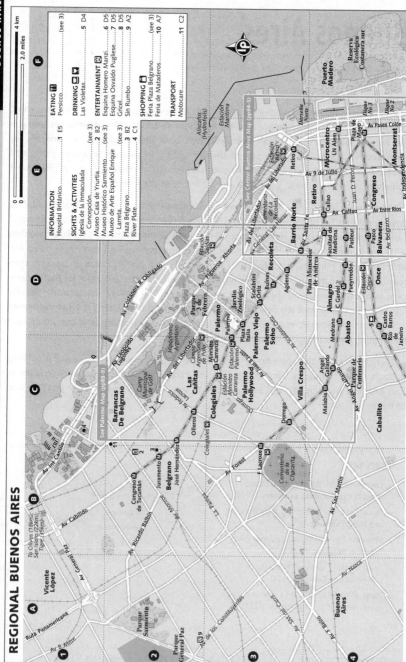

0   2.0 miles
0   4 km

INFORMATION
Hospital Británico......................1 E5

SIGHTS & ACTIVITIES
Iglesia de la Inmaculada
Concepción........................(see 3)
Museo Casa de Yrurtia............2 B2
Museo Histórico Sarmiento....(see 3)
Museo de Arte Español Enrique
Larreta...............................(see 3)
Plaza Belgrano.........................3 B2
River Plate...............................4 C1

EATING
Persicco..................................(see 3)

DRINKING
Las Violetas.............................5 D4

ENTERTAINMENT
Esquina Homero Manzi............6 D5
Esquina Osvaldo Pugliese........7 D5
Gricel.......................................8 D5
Sin Rumbo...............................9 A2

SHOPPING
Feria Plaza Belgrano...............(see 3)
Feria de Mataderos...............10 A7

TRANSPORT
Motocare...............................11 C2

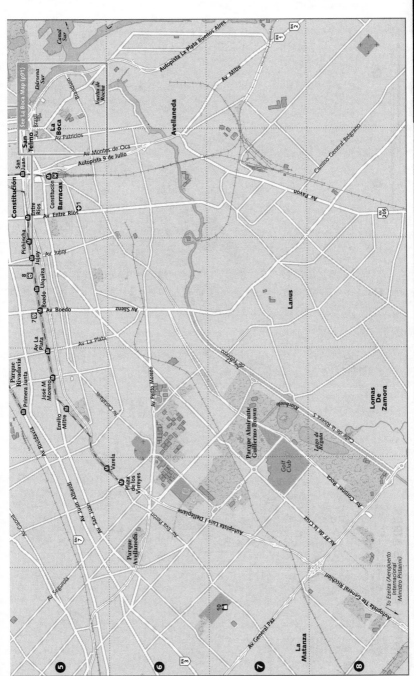

BUENOS AIRES

CENTRAL BUENOS AIRES

See Palermo Map (pp88-9)

CENTRAL BUENOS AIRES (pp84-5)

CENTRAL BUENOS AIRES (pp84-5)

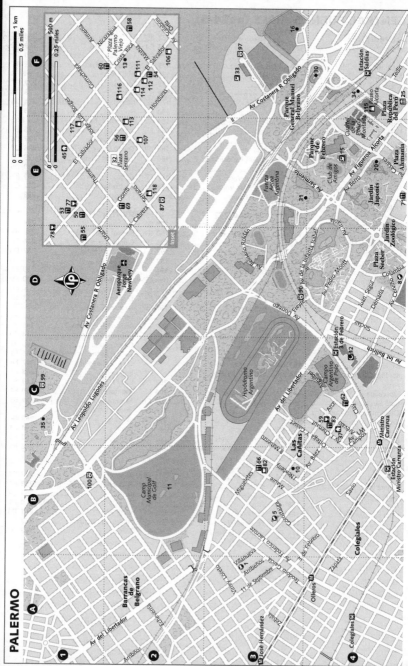

PALERMO

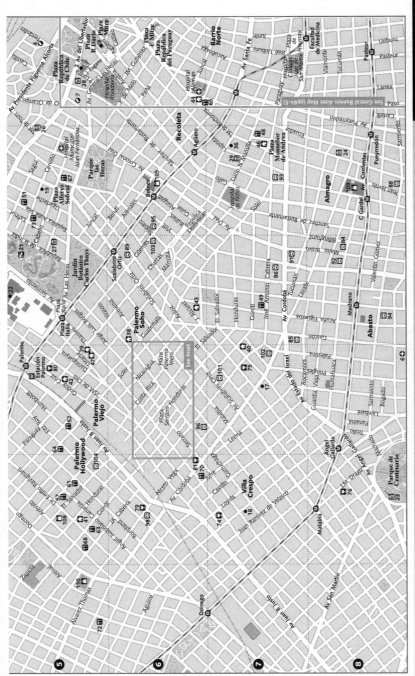

PALERMO (pp88-9)

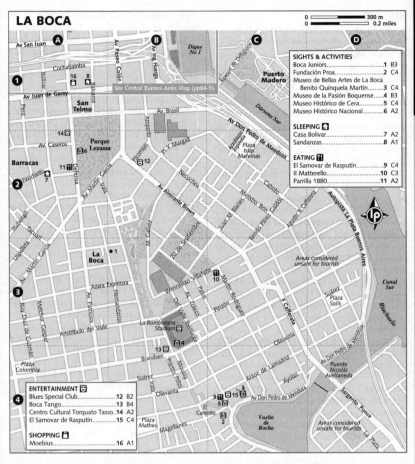

LA BOCA

0 ——— 300 m
0 ——— 0.2 miles

SIGHTS & ACTIVITIES
Boca Juniors...................................1 B3
Fundación Proa..............................2 C4
Museo de Bellas Artes de La Boca
  Benito Quinquela Martín.........3 C4
Museo de la Pasión Boquense......4 B3
Museo Histórico de Cera.............5 C4
Museo Histórico Nacional...........6 A2

SLEEPING 🏠
Casa Bolivar..................................7 A2
Sandanzas.....................................8 A1

EATING 🍴
El Samovar de Rasputín...............9 C4
Il Matterello.................................10 C3
Parrilla 1880................................11 A2

ENTERTAINMENT 📺
Blues Special Club......................12 B2
Boca Tango................................13 B4
Centro Cultural Torquato Tasso..14 A2
El Samovar de Rasputín.............15 C4

SHOPPING 🛍
Moebius......................................16 A1

HISTORY

Buenos Aires was settled in 1536 by Pedro de Mendoza, an adventurous and aristocratic Spaniard who financed his own expedition to South America. Food shortages and attacks by indigenous groups prompted Mendoza's hasty departure in 1537; to add insult to injury, he died at sea on the way home. Meanwhile, other expedition members left the settlement, sailed 1600km upriver and founded Asunción (now capital of Paraguay).

By 1541 the original settlement was completely abandoned. In 1580 a new group of settlers moved downriver from Asunción under Juan de Garay's command and repopulated Mendoza's abandoned outpost.

For the next 196 years Buenos Aires was a backwater and a smuggler's paradise, due to trade restrictions imposed by mother Spain. All the same, its population had grown to around 20,000 by 1776, the year Spain decreed the city capital of the enormous new viceroyalty of the Río de la Plata. Suddenly Buenos Aires was a very important place, and many *porteños* have had a notoriously high opinion of themselves and their city ever since.

After repelling British invasions in 1806 and 1807, *porteños* reckoned they could handle themselves without Spain's help (or interference). Napoleon's 1808 conquest of Spain led to BA's *cabildo* (town council) cutting ties with the mother country in May 1810. Decades of power struggles between BA and the other former viceregal provinces ensued, escalating more than once into civil war.

Finally in 1880 the city was declared the federal territory of Buenos Aires, a separate entity from the surrounding province of the same name, and the nation's capital forevermore.

Buenos Aires' population by then was nearly half a million, and waves of immigrants (chiefly Spanish and Italian) continued to roll in. Many of them settled on the southern edge of town, to work in the booming port and the meat-processing industry. The 1871 yellow-fever epidemic had already driven the wealthy northward, and now the middle class abandoned La Boca and San Telmo to the throngs of newcomers.

The nation's agricultural exports soared from 1880 to 1914, which resulted in great wealth accumulating in BA. Well-heeled *porteños* flaunted it by building opulent French-style mansions, and the government spent lavishly on public works, including parks, ornate offices and a subway line. Much of the unique look BA sports today dates from this period, although Av 9 de Julio's transformation into a block-wide megaboulevard didn't occur until the late 1930s.

But the boom times didn't last forever. Immigration burgeoned, export prices began to drop and workers became frustrated and militant. The Wall Street crash of 1929 dealt the final blow to the country's markets, and soon the first of many military coups took over. It was the end of Argentina's Golden Age.

Immigration to Buenos Aires kept climbing, but now it was mostly mestizos (people of mixed Indian and Spanish descent) from the rest of Argentina. Shanty towns popped up and social problems grew as the city failed to absorb its increasing population. The capital was the center of the country's economy, but as its prosperity waned there were no other centers of commercialism to help.

Pollution, poverty, unemployment and decaying infrastructure have been constant problems in the 19th century, and even today greater Buenos Aires holds an astounding third of Argentina's population. Extreme governments and a roller-coaster economy have been constant plagues, but at least the 20th century has seen a turn-around in the country's direction. For more on Argentina's roller-coaster history, see p28.

ORIENTATION

Buenos Aires is a huge city, but most places of interest to travelers are concentrated in just a few easily accessible neighborhoods.

At the heart of the city is the Microcentro, the downtown business center; it's small enough that you can walk around it fairly easily. Just south is San Telmo, known for its tango and its Sunday antiques market. Further south is La Boca, famous for its colorful houses clad in corrugated metal.

West of the Microcentro is Congreso, BA's seat of politics. To the north is Retiro and northwest, Recoleta, upscale areas of museums and fancy stores. Further north are Palermo and Belgrano, upper-middle-class suburbs with spacious parks and plenty of shopping.

For details on what to do after arriving at Ezeiza airport, see the boxed text, p133.

INFORMATION
Bookstores
El Ateneo (Map pp84-5; ☎ 4325-6801; Florida 340; ☺ 9am-10pm Mon-Fri, to 5pm Sat) Modern bookstore with several branches; see p131.
Walrus Books (Map pp84-5; ☎ 4300-7135; Estados Unidos 617; ☺ 10am-8pm Tue-Sun) The best English-language bookstore for quality new and used literature and nonfiction books.

Cultural Centers
Centro Cultural Borges (Map pp84-5; ☎ 5555-5359; www.ccborges.org.ar; cnr Viamonte & San Martín) One of BA's best, offering cheap art exhibits, music, classes and workshops.
Cuidad Cultural Konex (Map pp88-9; ☎ 4864-3200; www.ciudadculturalkonex.org; Sarmiento 3131) Stages theatrical performances and percussion shows; see p127.
Centro Cultural Recoleta (Map pp84-5; ☎ 4803-1041; www.centroculturalrecoleta.org; Junín 1930) Features art exhibits, a cinema, a kids' science museum and outdoor films in summer.
Centro Cultural Ricardo Rojas (Map pp84-5; ☎ 4954-5523; www.rojas.uba.ar; Corrientes 2038) Exceptionally good, offering a very wide range of quality, inexpensive classes.
Centro Cultural San Martín (Map pp84-5; ☎ 4374-1251; www.ccgsm.gov.ar; Sarmiento 1551) An excellent cultural resource, with many free or inexpensive offerings.

There are also several foreign cultural centers, all offering cultural events and classes:

Alianza Francesa (Map pp84-5; ☎ 4322-0068; www.alianzafrancesa.org.ar; Av Córdoba 946)
British Arts Centre (Map pp84-5; ☎ 4393-2004; www.britishartscentre.org.ar; Suipacha 1333)
Instituto Goethe (Map pp84-5; ☎ 4311-8964; www.goethe.de/hs/bue; Av Corrientes 319)

Emergency
Ambulance (☎ 107)
Police (☎ 101)
Tourist police (Comisaría del Turista; Map pp84-5; ☎ 4346-5748, 0800-999-5000; Av Corrientes 436; ☺ 24hr) Provides interpreters and helps victims of robberies and rip-offs.

Internet Access
Internet cafés and *locutorios* (private telephone offices) with internet access are very common everywhere in the center; you can often find one by just walking a couple of blocks in any direction. Rates are cheap and connections are quick. Many cafés (such as Havanna) and even restaurants have free wi-fi.

Internet Resources
The following websites are devoted to Buenos Aires; all are in English or have an English link:
Bue (www.bue.gov.ar) The city's official website.
What's up Buenos Aires (www.whatsupbuenosaires.com) Great for current happenings in the city; especially good hip music section.

BUENOS AIRES IN...

Two Days
Start with a stroll in **San Telmo** (p99) and duck into some antiques stores. Walk to **Plaza de Mayo** (p96) for a historical perspective, then wander the **Microcentro** (p95), perhaps veering east to **Puerto Madero** (p97) – a great spot for a break.
   Keep heading northward into **Retiro** (p100) and **Recoleta** (p101), stopping off at the **Museo Nacional de Bellas Artes** (p101) to admire some impressionism. Be sure to visit the **Cementerio de la Recoleta** (p101) to commune with BA's bygone elite. For dinner and nightlife, **Palermo Viejo** (p118) is hard to beat.
   On day two take a quick side trip to **La Boca** (p100) and watch a soccer game if your timing is right. Shop on **Av Santa Fe** (p129) or **Palermo Viejo** (p129), and at night catch a **tango show** (p123) or a performance at the **Teatro Colón** (p98).

Four Days
Follow the two-day itinerary, then on your third day add a trip to **Tigre** (p136). On the fourth day think about taking a **tango lesson** (see boxed text, p123), going to the **Mataderos fair** (see boxed text, p130) if it's a weekend, seeing more museums, walking around the **Congreso area** (p98) or checking out **Palermo's parks** (p102). Be sure to find yourself a good steak restaurant for your last meal.

Buenos Aires Expatriates Group (www.baexpats .com) Popular expat website.

Buenos Aires International Newcomers (BAIN; www.bainnewcomers.org) Popular expat website.

craigslist (www.buenosaires.en.craigslist.org) Find everything from an apartment to a job to a lover.

Salt Shaker (www.saltshaker.net) Best for its detailed restaurant reviews.

Libraries

Biblioteca Lincoln (Map pp84-5; ☎ 5382-1536; www .bcl.edu.ar; Maipú 672) Located inside the Instituto Cultural Argentino-Norteamericano; good for English newspapers, magazines and books.

Biblioteca Nacional (Map pp88-9; ☎ 4806-9764; Agüero 2502) BA's main library and downright ugly; occasionally hosts author talks.

The Alianza Francesa and Instituto Goethe also have foreign libraries (see p93 and p93).

Media

BA's most popular newspapers are the entertaining *Clarín* and the more moderate *La Nación*. The English-language daily *Buenos Aires Herald* covers Argentina and the world from an international perspective, and German speakers have *Argentinisches Tageblatt*. International newspapers like the *New York Times*, the *Guardian* and *Le Monde* are available at many newspaper kiosks, as are magazines like *Time*, *Newsweek* and the *Economist*.

English-language booklets and newspapers, aimed at tourists and expats, have been popping up lately. Good ones include the *Argentimes*, *BA Insider* and the *Traveller's Guru*; these can be found in hostels, some businesses and at the South American Explorers (see Tourist Information, opposite).

Cable TV lives a healthy life in Buenos Aires; international channels include CNN, BBC and ESPN. There are also plenty of reality shows, bimbo-led dance parties and *telenovelas* (soap operas). There are five regular channels:

Canal 2 (América TV) Heavy on the sports, news and entertainment.

Canal 7 State-run channel; known for its general-interest and cultural programming.

Canal 9 Smut at its best and expresses no shame in using sex to sell.

Canal 11 (Telefé) Popular for video queen Susana Giménez and USA imports.

Canal 13 Grupo Clarín's mainstream channel; hosts Marcelo Tinelli's *Videomatch*.

Dozens of FM stations serve BA: FM 92.7 has tango, 95.1 has entertainment news and dance, 98.3 has Argentine rock and 97.1 has the BBC in English.

Medical Services

Hospital Italiano (Map pp88-9; ☎ 4959-0200; www .hospitalitaliano.org.ar; Gascón 450) Highly regarded hospital.

Hospital Británico (Map pp82-3; ☎ 4304-1081; www .hospitalbritanico.org.ar; Perdriel 74) Also has a clinic at MT de Alvear 1573.

Blue Care (☎ 4822-7244, 011-15-4165-0024; www .bluecare.com.ar) On-call 24-hour service with English-speaking doctors and dentists; also has clinic services.

Dental Argentina (☎ 4828-0821; Av Santa Fe 2227, 12th fl Suite G) Dental services with English-speaking professionals.

Money

Banks and *cambios* (money-exchange offices) are common in the city center; banks have longer lines and more-limited opening hours but may offer better rates. ATMs are the way to go – they're everywhere and dispense pesos only. There may be limits per withdrawal (in 2008 it was AR$310), but you can withdraw several times per day (beware per-transaction fees!).

Even in Buenos Aires it's hard to change traveler's checks. Only a few fancy hotels and banks will take them, and you won't get a favorable rate. One exception is American Express (see following), but you'll have to line up.

The following local representatives can help you replace lost or stolen cards:

American Express (Map pp84-5; ☎ 4312-3000; Arenales 707) Also changes traveler's checks 10am to 3pm Monday to Friday.

MasterCard (Map pp84-5; ☎ 4348-7070; Perú 151)

Visa (Map pp84-5; ☎ 4379-3400; Corrientes 1437, basement fl)

Post

Correo Central (Map pp84-5; ☎ 4316-3000; www .correoargentino.com.ar; Sarmiento 151; ☒ 8am-8pm Mon-Fri, 9am-1pm Sat)

Correo Internacional (Map pp84-5; ☎ 4316-1777; Av Antártida Argentina; ☒ 10am-5pm Mon-Fri) For international parcels over 2kg.

DHL Internacional (Map pp84-5; ☎ 4314-2996; www .dhl.com.ar; Av Córdoba 783)

Federal Express (Map pp84-5; ☎ 0810-333-3339; www.fedex.com; Maipú 753)

OCA (Map pp84-5; ☎ 4311-5305; www.oca.com.ar; Viamonte 526) For domestic packages.

Telephone

The easiest way to make a phone call in BA is at a *locutorio* (small telephone office). Street phones require coins or *tarjetas telefónicas* (magnetic phone cards available at many kiosks). Faxes are cheap and widely available at most *locutorios* and internet cafés. For more information on telephone services, including cell phones, see p614.

Tourist Information

There are several small government tourist offices or kiosks in BA; hours vary throughout the year. The official tourism site of Buenos Aires is www.bue.gov.ar and the government site is www.buenosaires.gov.ar.

Florida tourist kiosk (Map pp84-5; Diagonal Norte & Perú)
Obelisco tourist office (Map pp84-5; Carlos Pellegrini & Juan D Perón)
Puerto Madero tourist kiosk (Map pp84-5; ☎ 4313-0187; Dique 4)
Recoleta tourist kiosk (Map pp84-5; Quintana 596)
San Telmo tourist office (Map pp84-5; Defensa 1250)
Secretaría de Turismo de la Nación (Map pp84-5; ☎ 4312-2232; www.turismo.gov.ar; Av Santa Fe 883; ☒ 9am-5pm Mon-Fri) Dispenses information on Buenos Aires, but focuses on Argentina as a whole.
South American Explorers (Map pp84-5; ☎ 4307-9625; www.saexplorers.org; Estados Unidos 577; ☒ 1-7pm Mon-Fri, to 6pm Sat & Sun) A plethora of information and services for the independent traveler, but requires annual membership.

Travel Agencies

The following agencies all arrange tours in BA and Argentina, and staff speak English. For tours, see p107.

Pride Travel (Map pp84-5; ☎ 5218-6556; www.pride-travel.com; Paraguay 523, Room 2E) Gay-oriented; also helps arrange short- or long-term stays in BA.
Say Hueque (Map pp84-5; ☎ 5199-2517; www.sayhueque.com; Viamonte 749, 6th fl) Friendly company that offers 'independent' packages around Buenos Aires and Argentina.
Tangol (Map pp84-5; ☎ 4312-7276; www.tangol.com; Florida 971, Suite 31) Do-all agency that offers city tours, tango shows, guides to *fútbol* games, hotel reservations, Spanish classes, air tickets and country-wide packages.
Wow Argentina (Map pp84-5; ☎ 5239-3019; www.wowargentina.com.ar; Av Santa Fe 882, 12th fl) Small agency catering to an upper-class clientele.

DANGERS & ANNOYANCES

Buenos Aires has been getting a bad rap these past few years. Crime does exist (as it does in any big city) and you'll notice that *porteños* are very security conscious, but in general BA is fairly safe. In many places you can comfortably walk around at all hours of the night, even as a lone woman. People stay out very late, and there's almost always somebody else walking down any street at any time. However, you should be careful at night in some neighborhoods, including Constitución (around the train station), the eastern border of San Telmo, and La Boca (where, outside tourist streets, you should be careful even during the day).

Crime against tourists is almost always of the petty sort, such as pickpocketing in crowded markets or buses, or bag snatches when you're not looking – things smart travelers can certainly guard themselves against. Minor nuisances include the lack of respect shown by cars toward pedestrians, lax pollution controls and high noise levels. For dealing with taxis, see p134. There is also a tourist police service that can help (see p93).

Remember that it's good advice to use your head wherever you are: don't flash any wealth, don't stagger around drunk, always be aware of your surroundings and look like you know exactly where you're going (even if you don't). And realize that if you're reasonably careful, the closest thing to annoyance you'll experience is being shortchanged, tripping on loose sidewalk tiles, stepping on the ubiquitous dog pile or getting flattened by a crazy bus driver. Watch your step.

SIGHTS
Microcentro

BA's Microcentro is where the big city hustles: here you'll see endless crowds of business suits and power skirts yelling into cell phones as they hasten about the narrow streets in the shadows of skyscrapers and old European buildings.

Florida, a long pedestrian street, is in some ways the main artery of this neighborhood. It's always jammed during the day with businesspeople, shoppers and tourists seeking vehicle-free access from north to south without the ubiquitous bus fumes and honking taxis. Buskers, beggars and street vendors thrive here as well, adding color and noise. Renovated old buildings, such as beautiful Galerías Pacífico (near Florida and Av Córdoba) add elegance to the area.

Further south is BA's busy financial district, where there are several museums to investigate. After that comes Plaza de Mayo, often filled with people resting on benches or taking photos of the surrounding historic sites.

GALERÍAS PACÍFICO

Covering an entire city block, this beautiful French-style **shopping center** (☎ 5555-5110; 10am-9pm Mon-Sat, noon-9pm Sun) dates from 1889 and boasts vaulted ceilings with paintings done in 1954 by muralists Antonio Berni, Juan Carlos Castagnino, Manuel Colmeiro, Lino Spilimbergo and Demetrio Urruchúa. All were adherents of the *nuevo realismo* (new realism) school of Argentine art. For many years the building was semiabandoned, but a joint Argentine-Mexican team repaired and restored the murals in 1992.

The beautiful structure, which is dotted with fairy lights at night, is now a central meeting place sporting upscale stores and a large food court. Tourist-oriented tango shows take place in front on pedestrian Florida, and the excellent Centro Cultural Borges takes up the top floor. Tours in English and Spanish take place every day at 11:30am and 4:30pm.

MUSEO MITRE

Bartolomé Mitre, who became Argentina's president in 1862, resided at this colonial house, now a **museum** (☎ 4394-8240; San Martín 336; admission free; 8am-7pm Mon-Fri). After leaving office, he founded the influential daily *La Nación*, still a *porteño* institution. The museum provides a good reflection of 19th-century upper-class life. It's full of Mitre's personal effects, such as home decorations and furniture.

MUSEO DE LA POLICÍA FEDERAL

In the heart of the financial district, this **museum** (☎ 4394-6857; San Martín 353, 7th fl; admission free; 2-6pm Tue-Fri) proudly displays a whole slew of uniforms, medals, guns, drug paraphernalia and gambling exhibits. Avoid taking your kids into the room way in back – grisly forensic photos, along with dummies of murder victims, are barf-bag specials.

MUSEO HISTÓRICO DR ARTURO JÁURETCHE

This **museum** (☎ 4331-1775; Sarmiento 364; admission free; 10am-6pm Mon-Fri) makes some sense of Argentina's chaotic economic history. Well-lit displays about paper money and counterfeiting are no doubt scrutinized by BA's current money forgers. The million-peso bill from 1981 gives an idea of the hyperinflation *porteños* had to deal with.

CORREO CENTRAL

The massive **main post office** (☎ 4316-3000; Sarmiento 151; 8am-8pm Mon-Fri, 9am-1pm Sat) fills an entire city block. It took 20 years to complete the impressive beaux arts structure, originally modeled on New York City's main post office. Architecture buffs should take a peek inside.

PLAZA DE MAYO

Planted between the Casa Rosada, the Cabildo and the city's main cathedral is grassy Plaza de Mayo, BA's ground zero for the city's most vehement protests. In the plaza's center is the **Pirámide de Mayo**, a small obelisk built to mark the first anniversary of BA's independence from Spain. Looming on the plaza's north side is the impressive **Banco de la Nación** (1939), the work of famed architect Alejandro Bustillo.

Today the plaza attracts camera-toting tourists, the occasional camera thief, and activists. And, on Thursdays at 3:30pm, the Madres de la Plaza de Mayo still march around the square in their unrelenting campaign for the government's accountability for Dirty War atrocities during the military dictatorship of 1976–83 (see p36).

CABILDO

The mid-18th-century town council, now a **museum** (Map pp84-5; ☎ 4342-6729; Bolívar 65; admission AR$1, Fri free; 10:30am-5pm Tue-Fri, 11:30am-6pm Sun & holidays) is not the size it once was, due to the building of surrounding avenues, but still has a section of the *recova* (colonnade) that once spanned Plaza de Mayo. The museum inside offers scanty exhibits, but a lively crafts market sets up in the patio on Thursday and Friday – and the café is a great place to relax. Call for tours.

CASA ROSADA

Taking up the whole east side of the Plaza de Mayo is the unmistakable pink facade of the Casa Rosada (Pink House). Though the offices of 'La Presidenta' Cristina Kirchner are here, the presidential residence is in the calm suburb of Olivos, north of the center.

The side of the palace facing Plaza de Mayo is actually the back of the building. It's from these balconies, however, that Juan and Eva Perón, General Leopoldo Galtieri, Raúl Alfonsín and other politicians have preached to throngs of impassioned Argentines. Pop celebrity Madonna also crooned from here for her movie *Evita*.

The salmon-pink color of the Casa Rosada, which positively glows at sunset, could have come from President Sarmiento's attempt to make peace during his 1868–74 term (blending the red of the Federalists with the white of the Unitarists). Another theory is that the color comes from painting the palace with bovine blood, which was a common practice in the late 19th century.

The Casa Rosada, like so many other government sites in Buenos Aires, was being renovated during research time for the city's bicentennial in 2010. Call (use the museum telephone number below) to see if tours are being offered, and in what language; advance reservations may be required.

Off to the side is the **Museo de la Casa Rosada** (☎ 4344-3802; Hipólito Yrigoyen 219; admission free; ☺ 10am-6pm Mon-Fri, 2-6pm Sun, tours 3pm & 4:30pm Sun), which provides displays of Perón memorabilia and a truncated chronology of Argentine presidents. You'll need your passport for both the tour and the museum.

CATEDRAL METROPOLITANA

BA's baroque **cathedral** (☎ 4331-2845; cnr Av Rivadavia & San Martín; ☺ 8am-7pm Mon-Fri, 9am-7:30pm Sat & Sun) is a significant religious and architectural landmark, but more importantly it contains the tomb of General José de San Martín – Argentina's most revered hero. Outside the cathedral you'll see a flame keeping his spirit alive.

Tours of the church and crypt are given at 3:30pm Monday to Saturday; tours of the just the crypt are at 11:30am Monday to Friday. All tours are in Spanish. Occasional free choir concerts are also on offer.

MANZANA DE LAS LUCES

The Manzana de las Luces (Block of Enlightenment) includes the city's oldest colonial church, the Jesuit Iglesia San Ignacio. During colonial times this was BA's center of learning, and it still symbolizes high culture in the capital. The first to occupy this block were the Jesuits, and two of the five original buildings of the Jesuit Procuraduría still remain. Dating from 1730, these build-ings include defensive tunnels discovered in 1912. The Universidad de Buenos Aires has occupied the site since independence in 1810. **Tours** (☎ 4331-9534; Perú 272; AR$5; ☺ 3pm Mon-Fri, 3pm, 4:30pm & 6pm Sat & Sun) in Spanish are available, but don't expect too much.

MUSEO DE LA CIUDAD

Wander among the permanent and temporary exhibitions on *porteño* life and history, including historical photographs and old furniture, in this **city museum** (☎ 4343-2123; Defensa 219; local/foreigner AR$1/3, Wed free; ☺ 11am-7pm Mon-Fri, 3-7pm Sat & Sun). Salvaged doors and ancient hardware found a home next-door at the museum's annex. Nearby, at the corner of Defensa, is the **Farmacia de la Estrella**, a functioning homeopathic pharmacy with gorgeous woodwork and elaborate late-19th-century ceiling murals.

MUSEO ETNOGRÁFICO JUAN B AMBROSETTI

This small but attractive **anthropological museum** (☎ 4331-7788; Moreno 350; admission AR$2; ☺ 1-7pm Tue-Fri, 3-7pm Sat & Sun) displays collections from the Andean northwest, Patagonia and elsewhere in South America. Beautiful indigenous artifacts, including intricate jewelry and Mapuche ponchos, are presented, while an African and Asian room showcases priceless items. Tours available in English and Spanish (call for hours).

BASÍLICA DE SANTO DOMINGO

Further south, at Defensa and Av Belgrano, the 18th-century Dominican Basílica de Santo Domingo has a colorful history. On its left tower are the replicated scars of shrapnel from fire against British troops who holed up here during the 1806 invasion. The **museum** (☎ 4331-1668; admission by donation; ☺ by appointment only) displays the flags that were captured from the British.

Puerto Madero

The newest and least conventional of the capital's 48 official barrios is Puerto Madero, located east of the Microcentro. Once an old waterfront, it's now a wonderful place to stroll, boasting cobbled paths and a long line of attractive brick warehouses that have been converted into ritzy new lofts, business offices and upscale restaurants. It carries a bumpy history, however.

In the mid-19th century competing commercial interests began to fight over the location of a modernized port for Argentina's burgeoning international commerce. Puerto Madero was finally chosen, and the city's mudflats were transformed into a series of modern basins and harbors consistent with the aspirations and ambitions of a cosmopolitan elite. It was completed in 1898, but Puerto Madero had exceeded its budget and was tarnished by scandal – suspicions arose from the sale of surrounding lands likely to increase in value. The practical side of the scheme didn't go so well either: by 1910 the amount of cargo was already too great for the new port, and poor access to the rail terminus at Plaza Once made things even worse. Only the 1926 completion of Retiro's Puerto Nuevo solved these problems.

Today you'll find BA's most expensive real estate in Puerto Madero, and tall buildings are popping up so quickly the skyline here seems to change by the month. Check with the artsy **Museo Fortabat** (Olga Cossettini 50) to see if it's finally open during your stay.

FRAGATA SARMIENTO

Over 23,000 Argentine naval cadets and officers have trained aboard this 85m **ship** (Map pp84-5; ☎ 4334-9386; Dique No 3; admission AR$2; ☽ 10am-8pm), which sailed around the world 40 times between 1899 and 1938 but never participated in combat. On board are records of its voyages, nautical items and even the stuffed remains of Lampazo (the ship's pet dog).

MUSEO DE LA INMIGRACIÓN

Located behind the immigration office in an industrial area, this rather bleak **museum** (Map pp84-5; ☎ 4317-0285; Av Antártida Argentina 1355; admission free; ☽ 10am-5pm Mon-Fri, 11am-6pm Sat & Sun) tells the story of the thousands of European immigrants who landed in BA beginning in the late 1880s. A smattering of old photos and memorabilia are on display.

RESERVA ECOLÓGICA COSTANERA SUR

The beautifully marshy land of this **nature preserve** (Map pp82-3; ☎ 4315-1320; Av Tristán Achával Rodríguez 1550; ☽ 8am-7pm Nov-Mar, to 6pm Apr-Oct) makes it a popular site for weekend outings, when hundreds of picnickers, cyclists and families come for fresh air and natural views. Bird watchers will adore the 200-plus bird species that pause to rest here, and a few lucky folks might spot a river turtle or a coypu. You

can rent bikes just outside the park entrance on the weekends (daily in summer).

Congreso

Congreso is an interesting mix of old-time cinemas and theaters, bustling commerce and hard-core politics. The buildings still hold that European aura, but there's more grittiness here than in the Microcentro: it has more local city feel, with an atmosphere of faded elegance and fewer fancy crowds.

Separating Congreso from the Microcentro is Av 9 de Julio, 'the widest street in the world!', as proud *porteños* love to boast. While this may be true – it's 16 lanes at its widest – the nearby side streets Cerrito and Carlos Pellegrini make it look even broader. At Avs 9 de Julio and Corrientes lies the city's famous **Obelisco**, 67m high and built in 1936 in only a month; it's the destination of *porteños* sports fans when they have a big win to celebrate.

Plaza Lavalle is surrounded by the austere neoclassical **Escuela Presidente Roca** (1902), the French-style **Palacio de Justicia** (1904) and the landmark **Teatro Colón.** Nearby is the **Templo de la Congregación Israelita**, Argentina's largest synagogue.

Finally, head around 10 blocks south of Plaza Lavalle to the **Palacio del Congreso**, together with its plaza and obligatory monument.

TEATRO COLÓN

Started in 1880 and finished in 1908, the **Teatro Colón** (Map pp84-5; ☎ 4378-7344; www.teatrocolon.org.ar; Libertad 621) is a major landmark and gorgeous world-class facility for opera, ballet and classical music. It was the southern hemisphere's largest theater until the Sydney Opera House was built in 1973. Opening night featured Verdi's *Aïda*, and visitors have been wowed ever since. Even through times of economic hardship, the elaborate Colón remains a high national priority – essentially, this place rocks.

Renovations halted the excellent tours (offered in several languages), but work should be finished in May 2008 for the Colón's 100th anniversary. Call ☎ 4378-7132 for an update.

PALACIO DEL CONGRESO

Colossal and topped with a green dome, the **Palacio del Congreso** (Map pp84-5; ☎ 4010-3000; Senado ext 3885; Hipólito Yrigoyen 1849) cost more than twice its projected budget and set a precedent for contemporary Argentine public-works projects. It was modeled on the Capitol

Building in Washington, DC, and was completed in 1906. Across the way, the **Monumento a los Dos Congresos** honors the congresses of 1810 in BA and 1816 in Tucumán, both of which led to Argentine independence.

Inside the Congreso, free guided tours are given of the **Senado** every day except Wednesday (call for hours and languages); go to the entrance on Hipólito Yrigoyen.

PALACIO DE LAS AGUAS CORRIENTES
About six blocks west of Plaza Lavalle, this gorgeous and eclectic Swedish-designed waterworks building (1894) is topped by French-style mansard roofs and covered in 170,000 glazed tiles and 130,000 enameled bricks. If you like quirky museums, check out the small **Museo del Patrimonio** (Map pp84-5; ☎ 6319-1104; cnr Córdoba & Riobamba; admission free; �ّ 9am-1pm Mon-Fri) on the 2nd floor; it's full of pipe fittings, tiles and odd toilets. Guided visits offer a backstage glimpse of the building's inner workings (Monday, Wednesday and Friday at 11am). Bring photo ID and enter via Riobamba.

San Telmo
Full of charm and personality, San Telmo is one of BA's most attractive and historically rich barrios. Narrow cobbled streets and low-story colonial housing retain an old-time feel, though the tourist dollar continues to bring about changes.

Historically, San Telmo is famous for the violent street fighting that took place when British troops, at war with Spain, invaded the city in 1806. British forces advanced up narrow Defensa, but an impromptu militia drove the British back to their ships. The victory gave *porteños* confidence in their ability to stand apart from Spain, even though the city's independence had to wait another three years.

After this San Telmo became a fashionable, classy neighborhood, but in the late 19th century a yellow-fever epidemic hit, driving the rich north into present-day Recoleta. Many older mansions were subdivided and became *conventillos* (tenements) to house poor families. A few years ago these *conventillos* attracted artists and bohemians looking for cheap rent, but these days they're likelier to be filled with fancy shops, new hostels, gay couples or rich expatriates.

The heart of San Telmo is **Plaza Dorrego**, which hosts its famous Sunday antiques market (see the boxed text, p130). Nearby, the baroque, neo-colonial **Iglesia Nuestra Señora de Belén** (Map pp84-5; Humberto Primo 340) was a Jesuit school until 1767, when the Bethlemite order took it over.

EL ZANJÓN DE GRANADOS
One of the more unique places in Buenos Aires is this amazing **architectural site** (Map p84-5; ☎ 4361-3002; Defensa 755; ½hr/1hr tour AR$12/30; ☑ tours 11am, noon, 1pm & 2pm Mon-Fri, every half hr 2-6pm Sun). Below the remains of a mansion, a series of old tunnels, sewers and water wells going back to 1730 were discovered. Meticulously reconstructed brick by brick, and very attractively lit, this 'museum' offers a fascinating glimpse into the city's architectural past. Choose between hour-long tours during the week or half-hour tours on Sundays. It's best to call and reserve ahead of time, especially if you need English-speaking guides.

MUSEO HISTÓRICO NACIONAL
This **national historical museum** (Map p91; ☎ 4307-1182; Defensa 1600; admission AR$2; ☑ 11am-6pm Tue-Sun) is located at the supposed site of Pedro de Mendoza's original founding of the city in 1536. Inside, you'll relive the Argentine experience, from its shaky beginnings and independence to the present, through a panorama of artifacts, paintings, weapons and period furniture. Major figures of Argentine historical periods, such as San Martín, Rosas and Sarmiento, are represented. There are also portrayals of the British invasions of 1806 and 1807, along with period knickknacks from late-19th-century *porteño* life. The museum was closed in 2008 for security upgrades; call to confirm hours.

MUSEO PENITENCIARIO
Just off the plaza, this **prison museum** (Map pp84-5; ☎ 4361-0917; Humberto Primo 378; admission AR$1; ☑ 2:30-5:30pm Wed-Fri, 1-7pm Sun) occupies a building that was first a convent, then a women's prison. Don't miss the tear-gas canisters used for riot control, the tennis balls used to hide drugs and the effeminate mannequins sporting past prison fashions. Cool old jail cells too.

MUSEO DE ARTE MODERNO
Housed in a former tobacco warehouse, this roomy **museum** (Map pp84-5; Av San Juan 350) exhibits the works of contemporary Argentine artists, as well as temporary exhibitions. In 2008 it was undergoing a major remodeling, with plans to integrate the old cinema museum next door. Contact the tourist office in San Telmo (Defensa 1250) for current information.

MUSEO DEL TRAJE

This small **clothing museum** (Map pp84-5; ☎ 4343-8427; Chile 832; admission free; ⏰ 3-7pm Tue-Fri & Sun) is always changing its wardrobe. You can hit upon civilian and military clothing from colonial times to the present, or '60s vintage hippie wear. Come by and see what hot fashions the dummies are wearing when you're in town.

La Boca

Blue collar and raffish to the core, La Boca is very much a locals' neighborhood. In the mid-19th century, La Boca became home to Spanish and Italian immigrants who settled along the Riachuelo, the sinuous river that divides the city from the surrounding province of Buenos Aires. Many came during the booming 1880s and ended up working in the many meat-packing plants and warehouses here, processing and shipping out much of Argentina's vital beef. After sprucing up the shipping barges, the port dwellers splashed leftover paint on the corrugated-metal siding of their own houses – unwittingly giving La Boca what would become one of its claims to fame. Unfortunately, some of the neighborhood's color also comes from the rainbow slick of industrial wastes on the river.

Caminito is the barrio's most famous street, and on weekends busloads of camera-laden tourists come here for photographs and to browse the small crafts fair while watching tango dancers perform for spare change. A riverside pedestrian walkway offers a close-up sniff of the Riachuelo, while a few museums provide mental stimulation. Four blocks inland is **La Bombonera** stadium, home of the Boca Juniors soccer team – the former club of disgraced superstar Diego Maradona.

FUNDACIÓN PROA

This elegant **art foundation** (Map p91; ☎ 4104-1000; www.proa.org; Av Don Pedro de Mendoza 1929; admission AR$1; ⏰ 11am-7pm Tue-Sun) exhibits works by only the most cutting-edge national and international artists in both traditional and more unusual mediums. Visit the rooftop terrace – views are excellent and you can grab a drink, too. It was remodeled in 2007; call to confirm hours.

MUSEO DE BELLAS ARTES DE LA BOCA BENITO QUINQUELA MARTÍN

On display at this modern **museum** (Map p91; ☎ 4301-1080; Av Don Pedro de Mendoza 1835; suggested donation AR$5; ⏰ 10am-6pm Tue-Fri, 11am-7pm Sat & Sun) are the works of Benito Quinquela Martín, which center on La Boca's port history. There are also paintings by more contemporary Argentine artists, along with a small but excellent collection of painted wood bowsprits (carved statues decorating the front of ships).

MUSEO DE LA PASIÓN BOQUENSE

High-tech and spiffy, this **fútbol museum** (Map p91; ☎ 4362-1100; www.museoboquense.com; Brandsen 805; admission AR$14; ⏰ 10am-7pm) chronicles La Bombonera stadium, some soccer idols' histories, past highlights (on many videos), the championships, the trophies and, of course, the goooooals. It's located right under the stadium; peek at the pitch for a few extra pesos.

MUSEO HISTÓRICO DE CERA

Reconstructions of historical figureheads (literally just their heads!) and dioramas of scenes in Argentine history are the specialty of this small and very tacky **wax museum** (Map p91; ☎ 4301-1497; www.museodecera.com.ar; Del Valle Iberlucea 1261; admission AR$10; ⏰ 10am-6pm Mon-Fri, 11am-8pm Sat & Sun). There are also stuffed snakes and creepy wax limbs depicting bite wounds – all barely worth the price of admission.

Retiro

Well-located Retiro is one of the ritziest neighborhoods in BA – but it hasn't always been this way. The area was the site of a monastery during the 17th century, and later became the *retiro* (country retreat) of Agustín de Robles, a Spanish governor. Since then, Retiro's current **Plaza Libertador General San Martín** – which sits on a bluff – has played host to a slave market, a military fort and even a bullring. Things are more quiet and exclusive these days.

French landscape architect Charles Thays designed the leafy Plaza San Martín, whose prominent monument is the obligatory equestrian statue of José de San Martín.

BOCA WARNING

La Boca is not the kind of neighborhood for casual strolls – it can be downright rough in spots. Don't stray far from the riverside walk, El Caminito or the Bombonera stadium, especially while toting expensive cameras. And certainly don't cross the bridge over the Riachuelo. There's nothing you'd really want to see outside the touristy areas anyway.

Surrounding the plaza are several landmark public buildings, such as the **Palacio San Martín**, an art nouveau mansion originally built for the elite Anchorena family and sometimes open to the public; the huge and beautiful **Palacio Paz** (also called the Círculo Militar; see below) and the 120m-high **Edificio Kavanagh** (1935), once South America's tallest building.

The 76m **Torre de los Ingleses**, across Av del Libertador from Plaza San Martín, was a donation by the city's British community in 1916. Opposite the plaza is the impressive and busy **Retiro train station** (Estación Retiro), built in 1915 when the British controlled the country's railroads. Don't wander behind the station – it's a shantytown.

PALACIO PAZ

This gorgeous **palace** (Map pp84–5; ☎ 4311-1071 ext 147; Santa Fe 750; tours in Spanish AR$10; ⏰ tours 11am & 3pm Tue-Fri, 4pm Wed & Thu, 11am Sat) was once the private residence of José C Paz, founder of the still-running newspaper *La Prensa*. Inside are ornate rooms, salons and halls with wood-tiled floors, marble walls and gilded details. Nearly everything was ordered from Europe and assembled here. Tours in English (AR$20) are Tuesday at 4pm and Thursday at 4.15pm.

MUSEO DE ARMAS

If you're big on weaponry, don't miss this extravagant **museum** (Map pp84–5; ☎ 4311-1071; Santa Fe 702; admission AR$5; ⏰ 1-7pm Mon-Fri) showcasing over 2000 bazookas, grenade launchers, machine guns, muskets, pistols, lances and swords – even the gas mask for a combat horse is on display. Don't miss the Japanese suits of armor.

MUSEO DE ARTE HISPANOAMERICANO ISAAC FERNÁNDEZ BLANCO

This neocolonial-era mansion turned **museum** (Map pp84–5; ☎ 4327-0228; Suipacha 1422; local/foreigner AR$1/3; ⏰ 2-7pm Tue-Sun) holds some gorgeous pieces of silverwork, religious paintings, Jesuit statuary and antiques. There's been no effort to place items in any historical context, but everything is in great condition, and an attractive garden provides a peaceful sanctuary.

TEATRO NACIONAL CERVANTES

Six blocks west of Plaza San Martín, you can't help but notice the lavishly ornamented **Teatro Cervantes** (Map pp84–5; ☎ 4816-8883; www.teatrocervantes.gov.ar; Av Córdoba 1155). The landmark building dates from 1921 and holds a historical theater

with a grand tiled lobby and plush red-velvet chairs. Enjoy the elegance – however faded – with a tour (call for current schedule).

MUSEO NACIONAL DEL TEATRO

Exhibits at this tiny, low-key **museum** (Map pp84–5; ☎ 4815-8883, ext 156; cnr Córdoba & Libertad; admission free; ⏰ 10am-6pm Mon-Fri) trace the history of Argentine theater from its colonial beginnings. Check out the gaucho suit worn by Gardel and the *bandoneón* that once belonged to Paquita Bernardo, Argentina's first musician to play this accordion-like instrument.

Recoleta & Barrio Norte

BA's wealthiest citizens live and breathe in Recoleta, the city's most exclusive and fashionable neighborhood. In the 1870s many upper-class *porteños* originally lived in southerly San Telmo, but during the yellow-fever epidemic they relocated north to here. Today you can best see the wealth of this sumptuous quarter on **Av Alvear**, where many of the old mansions (and newer international boutiques) are located.

Full of lush parks, classy museums and French architecture, Recoleta is best known for its **Cementerio de la Recoleta**. Next door to the cemetery, the 1732 **Iglesia Nuestra Señora del Pilar** (Map pp84–5) is a baroque colonial church with a small **museum** (☎ 4806-2209; ⏰ 10:30am-6:15pm Mon-Sat, 2:30-6:15pm Sun) upstairs, while just in front the **Plaza Intendente Alvear** hosts the city's most popular *feria artesanal* (crafts fair; see the boxed text, p130). A little further north is the sinuous sculptural flower **Floralis Genérica**, whose giant metal petals close up at night – if all the gears are working, that is.

CEMENTERIO DE LA RECOLETA

Wander for hours in this amazing **cemetery** (Map pp84–5; ☎ 4803-1594; cnr Junín & Guido; admission free; ⏰ 7am-6pm) where 'streets' are lined with impressive statues and marble sarcophagi. Crypts hold the remains of the city's elite: past presidents, military heroes, influential politicians and the rich and famous. Hunt down Evita's grave, and bring your camera – there are some great photo ops here. Tours are available (call for current schedule) or buy a copy of Robert Wright's excellent map (see www.recoletacemetery.com and click on 'walking tour map').

MUSEO NACIONAL DE BELLAS ARTES

Argentina's top **fine-arts museum** (Map pp84–5; ☎ 4803-8814; www.mnba.com.ar; Av del Libertador 1473;

admission free; 12:30-7:30pm Tue-Fri, 9:30am-7:30pm Sat, Sun & holidays) is a must-see for art lovers. It showcases works by Renoir, Monet, Gauguin, Cézanne and Picasso, along with many classic Argentine artists like Xul Solar and Edwardo Sívori. There are also temporary exhibits, a small gift shop and a cinema.

MUSEO XUL SOLAR

Xul Solar was a painter, inventor and poet, and this **museum** (Map pp88-9; 4824-3302; www .xulsolar.org.ar; Laprida 1212; admission AR$6; noon-8pm Tue-Fri, to 6:30pm Sat, closed Jan) highlights over 80 of his bizarre, surreal and even cartoonish paintings; the guy was in a class by himself.

Palermo

Palermo is heaven on earth for BA's middle class. Its large, grassy parks – regally punctuated with grand monuments – are popular destinations on weekends, when families fill the shady lanes, cycle the bike paths and paddle on the peaceful lakes. Many important museums and elegant embassies are also located here, and certain subneighborhoods of Palermo have become some of the city's hottest destinations for shopping and nightlife.

Palermo's green spaces haven't always been for the masses. The area around **Parque 3 de Febrero** was originally the 19th-century dictator Juan Manuel de Rosas' private retreat and became public parkland after his fall from power. Within these green spaces you'll find the **Jardín Japonés** (Map pp88-9; 4804-4922; www.jardinjapones .ar; cnr Avs Casares & Berro; admission AR$5; 10am-6pm), a peaceful paradise with koi ponds, teahouse, and cultural offerings; the surprisingly decent **Jardín Zoológico** (see opposite), BA's main zoo; and the nearby **Jardín Botánico Carlos Thays**, which will appeal to both botanists and cat-lovers (it's full of feral felines). There's also the **Planetario Galileo Galilei** (Map pp88-9; 4771-9393; www.planetario .gov.ar; cnr Avs Sarmiento & Belisario Roldán), a planetarium with shows throughout the week and summertime telescope viewings. Just south of the zoo and a major landmark is **Plaza Italia**, Palermo's main transport hub.

Roughly bounded by Av Santa Fe, Scalabrini Ortiz, Av Córdoba and Dorrego, **Palermo Viejo** is one of the capital's most trendsetting areas. It's further divided into Palermo Hollywood (north of the train tracks) and Palermo Soho (south of the tracks), both full of beautiful old buildings, leafy sidewalks and cobbled streets. Dozens of ethnic, ultramodern restaurants cater to anyone

yearning for Japanese, Vietnamese, Greek or even Norwegian food, though modern international cuisine tops the list (see p118). There are also great guesthouses, bars and clubs; hanging out in **Plaza Serrano** on any weekend night is a blast. And the shopping! Buenos Aires' most cutting-edge designers have opened up dozens of boutiques here, and there are also many fancy housewares stores and other fun themed shops. You can wander around for hours and even days in this exciting area.

Another popular but much smaller Palermo neighborhood, **Las Cañitas**, is further north. Many restaurants and other nightspots attract hordes of hip folk at night, when Av Baéz clogs with traffic. Southeast of Las Cañitas is the landmark **Centro Islámico Rey Fahd** (4899-0201; www.ccislamicoreyfahd.org.ar; Av Int Bullrich 55), built by Saudis on land donated by former president Carlos Menem. Tours in Spanish are offered on Tuesday and Thursday at noon (call to confirm, and dress conservatively).

MUSEO DE ARTE LATINOAMERICANO DE BUENOS AIRES (MALBA)

Sparkling inside its glass-and-cement walls, this airy **modern-arts museum** (Map pp88-9; 4808-6541; www.malba.org.ar; Av Figueroa Alcorta 3415; admission AR$12, free Wed; noon-8pm Thu-Mon, to 9pm Wed) is BA's fanciest. Art patron Eduardo Costantini displays his limited but fine collection, which includes work by Argentines Xul Solar and Antonio Berni, plus some pieces by Mexicans Diego Rivera and Frida Kahlo. A cinema screens art-house films, and there's an excellent café for watching the beautiful people.

JARDÍN ZOOLÓGICO

Artificial lakes, pleasant walking paths and over 350 species of animals entertain the crowds at this relatively good **zoo** (Map pp88-9; 4011-9900; www.zoobuenosaires.com.ar; cnr Avs Las Heras & Sarmiento; admission from AR$7, under 12 free; 10am-6pm Tue-Sun). Most of the enclosures offer decent spaces, and some buildings are impressive in themselves – check out the elephant house. An aquarium, a monkey island, a petting zoo and a large aviary are other highlights. Closes an hour earlier from April to September.

MUSEO NACIONAL DE ARTE DECORATIVO

Located in the stunning beaux arts mansion called Palacio Errázuriz (1911), this **museum** (Map pp88-9; 4802-6606; www.mnad.org; Av del Libertador 1902; admission from AR$2; 2-7pm Tue-Sun, closed Jan &

PRAYING FOR KITSCH

Lovers of the quirky and tacky will find heaven at **Tierra Santa** (Map pp88-9; ☎ 4784-9551; www .tierrasanta-bsas.com.ar; Av Costanera R Obligado 5790; ☺ 9am-9pm Fri, noon-11pm Sat, Sun & holidays Apr-Nov, 4pm-midnight Fri-Sun & holidays Dec-Mar; adult/3-11 yr AR$15/5), which boasts being 'the world's first religious theme park.' Roughly based on Jerusalem, this unique destination offers moving dioramas detailing the creation of the world, the manger scene at Bethlehem, the Last Supper and the Resurrection (every half hour!). *Porteños* are visibly moved by the spectacle, and when emotions overwhelm are happy to sit drinking coffee at the Baghdad Café served by employees dolled up in Middle Eastern garb. You won't find a place like this anywhere else on earth – and especially not in Jerusalem. To get to Tierra Santa, flag a taxi (AR$15 to AR$20 from downtown) or take buses 28, 33, 37, 42, 45, 107 or 160.

Feb) displays the posh belongings of Chilean aristocrat Matías Errázuriz. Everything from Renaissance religious paintings and porcelain dishes to Italian sculptures and artwork by El Greco and Rodin can be admired. The outside café in front is a fine place to refresh yourself on a sunny day. Admission prices vary according to the exhibition showing.

MUSEO EVITA
Everybody who is anybody in Argentina has their own museum, and Eva Perón is no exception. See her immortalized in **Museo Evita** (Map pp88-9; ☎ 4807-9433; Lafinur 2988; local/foreigner AR$3/10; ☺ 11am-7pm Tue-Sun Nov-Apr, 1-7pm May-Oct) through videos, historical photos, books, old posters and newspaper headlines – even her fingerprints are recorded. The prize memorabilia, however, would have to be her wardrobe: dresses, shoes, handbags, hats and blouses stand proudly behind shining glass, forever pressed and pristine.

MUSEO DE JOSÉ HERNÁNDEZ
This modest-sized **museum** (Map pp88-9; ☎ 4803-2384; www.museohernandez.org.ar; Av del Libertador 2373; admission AR$3, Sun free; ☺ 1-7pm Wed-Fri, 10am-8pm Sat & Sun) has permanent exhibitions on Mapuche crafts, such as exquisite ponchos and (at the opposite end of the spectrum) gaudy Carnaval costumes. Diverse changing exhibitions range from folk crafts to modern toys.

Belgrano
Bustling Av Cabildo, the racing heartbeat of Belgrano, is an overwhelming jumble of noise and neon; it's a two-way street of clothing, shoe and housewares shops that does its part to support the mass consumerism of *porteños*. For a bit more peace and quiet step away from the avenue, where Belgrano becomes a leafy barrio of museums, parks and good eateries.

Only a block east of Av Cabildo, **Plaza Belgrano** is the site of a modest but fun weekend market (see boxed text, p130). Near the plaza stands the Italianate **Iglesia de la Inmaculada Concepción**, a church popularly known as 'La Redonda' because of its impressive dome.

Just across the plaza is the **Museo de Arte Español Enrique Larreta** (Map pp82-3; ☎ 4784-4040; Juramento 2291; local/foreigner AR$1/3, Thu free; ☺ 3-8pm Mon & Wed-Fri, 10am-1pm & 3-8pm Sat & Sun), which displays the well-known novelist's gorgeous art collection. Also close by is the **Museo Histórico Sarmiento** (Map pp82-3; ☎ 4782-2354; www .museosarmiento.gov.ar; Juramento 2180; admission AR$2, Thu free; ☺ 2-6:30pm Mon-Fri, 3-6:30pm Sun), which displays the memorabilia of Domingo F Sarmiento, one of Argentina's most famous, forward-thinking presidents.

About five blocks north, the **Museo Casa de Yrurtia** (Map pp82-3; ☎ 4781-0385; O'Higgins 2390; admission AR$1, Tue free; ☺ 1-7pm Tue-Fri, 3-7pm Sun) honors the well-known Argentine sculptor Rogelio Yrurtia. His old house and garden is full of his large sculptures and other artists' works; look for Picasso's *Rue Cortot, Paris*.

Four blocks northeast of Plaza Belgrano, French landscape architect Charles Thays took advantage of the contours of **Barrancas de Belgrano** (Map pp88–9) to create an attractive, wooded public space on one of the few natural hillocks in the city. On Sunday evenings the bandstand is host to a *milonga* (dance school; see boxed text, p123).

Across Juramento (and the railroad tracks) from the Barrancas, Belgrano's tiny **Chinatown** takes up two to three blocks, offering decent Chinese restaurants and cheap goods.

Once & Caballito
BA's most ethnically colorful neighborhood is Once, with sizable groups of Jews, Peruvians

and Koreans. The cheap market around Once train station always bustles, with vendors selling their goods on sidewalks and crowds everywhere, and is a fun spot to wander around. The nearby **Museo Casa Carlos Gardel** (Map pp88–9; ☎ 4964-2071; Jean Jaurés 735; local/foreigner AR$1/3, Wed free; ☷ 11am-6pm Mon & Wed-Fri, 10am-7pm Sat & Sun) offers tango fans some insight into the dance's most famous singer.

For high-class shopping, wander through the **Mercado de Abasto** shopping mall (see p132); it has especially good kids' entertainment. West of Once is Caballito, a calm residential neighborhood. Here you'll find the **Museo Argentino de Ciencias Naturales** (Map pp82–3; ☎ 4982-6595; Ángel Gallardo 470; admission AR$1; ☷ 2-7pm), a good natural-science museum that's definitely worth a peek for its musty taxidermy and cool skeleton room.

ACTIVITIES

Extensive greenery in Palermo provides good areas for recreation, especially on weekends when the ring road around the rose garden is closed to motor vehicles. Recoleta has grassy parks also, if you can avoid the dog piles. Best of all is the Reserva Ecológica Costanera Sur (p98), an ecological paradise just east of Puerto Madero; it's excellent for walks, runs, bike rides and even a bit of wildlife viewing.

Cycling

Bike paths interlace Parque 3 de Febrero, where rental bikes are available in good weather; look for them on Av de la Infanta Isabel (Map pp88–9) on weekends in winter and daily in summer. The Reserva Ecológica Costanera Sur (p98) also has bike rentals with a similar schedule.

For safe family cycling, head to Nuevo Circuito KDT in Palermo's **Parque General Belgrano** (Map pp88–9; ☎ 4807-7700; Salguero 3450; admission AR$2). Here, **Sprint Haupt** (☎ 4807-6141; Salguero 3450; per hour AR$8; ☷ Tue-Sun) rents bicycles for use around a plain 1200m concrete bike path (bring your passport). Nearby there's a rather run-down, banked velodrome, but you'll have to bring your own specialized bicycle. They're both under the overpass and over the pedestrian bridge.

For information on bike tours, see p107.

Swimming

Some upscale hotels have decent-sized pools, but they charge hefty prices for non-

---

THE SPA LIFE

Scrub that dead skin off – you've earned it. Other than the places listed below, several hotels also have spa services, including the **Four Seasons** (p112), the **Park Hyatt** (p113) and **Home Hotel** (p114).

Aqua Vita Spa (Map pp84–5; ☎ 4812-5989; www.aquavitamedicalspa.com; Arenales 1965)

Espacio Oxivital (Map pp88–9; ☎ 4775-0010; www.oxivital.com.ar; Aguirre 864)

Evian Spa (Map pp84–5; ☎ 4807-4688; www.aguaclubspa.com; Cerviño 3626)

Spa de Piel (Map pp84–5; ☎ 4821-0230; www.spadepiel.com.ar; Ayacucho 1250)

---

guests to use their facilities – if they even allow them. It's better to find a health club with an indoor pool (see Health Clubs, opposite). Otherwise there's Palermo's **Club de Amigos** (Map pp88–9; ☎ 4801-1213; www.clubdeamigos.org.ar; Figueroa Alcorta 3885; admission AR$10-15, pool extra AR$19), which has a pool open December to February; **Punta Carrasco** (Map pp88–9; ☎ 4807-1010; cnr Costanera R Obligado & Sarmiento) has three outdoor pools, but they may or may not be open during your stay. For all these pools, call for public swimming times.

Golf & Tennis

BA's most convenient golf course is the 18-hole **Campo Municipal de Golf** (Map pp88–9; ☎ 4772-7261; Av Tornquist 1426; ☷ Tue-Sun). Practice your long shots at the **Costa Salguero Driving Range** (Map pp88–9; ☎ 4805-4732; cnr Avs Costanera & Salguero), which also has a golf store, a café and a 9-hole, family-friendly course.

There are both cement and clay tennis courts at **Punta Carrasco** (Map pp88–9; ☎ 4807-1010; www.puntacarrasco.com.ar; cnr Av Costanera Norte & Sarmiento). Rates are AR$15 to AR$35 per hour, depending on the day. You can buy balls here, and rental racquets are occasionally available. Nearby is **Parque General Belgrano** (Map pp88–9; ☎ 4807-7879; Salguero 3450; admission AR$2), with eight clay courts; rates are AR$12 to AR$14 per hour. Reserve 48 hours in advance; you'll need to bring your own equipment.

Another good option is **Salguero Tenis** (Map pp88–9; ☎ 4805-5144; Salguero 3350), near Paseo Alcorta shopping mall. **Club de Amigos** (Map pp88–9; ☎ 4801-1213; www.clubdeamigos.org.ar; Figueroa Alcorta 3885; admission AR$10-15, court hire AR$35-42) also has tennis courts.

Health Clubs & Climbing Walls

The king of BA's gyms is **Megatlon** (Map pp84-5; ☎ 4322-7884; www.megatlon.com; Reconquista 335; day/week/month AR$50/100/200), with about 15 branches throughout the city. Expect decent gym services, including many classes; some have an indoor pool. Hours vary depending on the branch. Other gyms include **Le Parc** (Map pp84-5; ☎ 4311-9191; www.leparc.com; San Martín 645; day-use fee AR$30), **Sport Club Cecchina** (Map pp84-5; ☎ 5199-1212; www.sportclub.com.ar; Bartolomé Mitre 1625; day-use fee AR$25) and **YMCA** (Map pp84-5; ☎ 4311-4785; www.ymca.org.ar; Reconquista 439; day-use fee AR$20).

Boulder (Map pp88-9; ☎ 4779-2825; www.elboulder.com.ar; Arce 730; ☼ 3-11pm Tue-Fri, to 9pm Sat & Sun; day-use fee AR$15) is a decent indoor climbing wall with a tiny bouldering cave. It rents harnesses; shoe use is free (it doesn't stock all sizes).

Yoga & Pilates

Most gyms and some cultural centers schedule yoga and Pilates classes. Even some health-oriented restaurants, like Arte Sano (see p117) offer yoga, tai chi and meditation.

Centro Valletierra (Map pp88-9; ☎ 4833-6724; www.valletierra.com; Costa Rica 4562) This slick Palermo Viejo studio has Hatha, Kri and Ashtanga yoga classes, meditation, tai chi, kung fu and qi gong.

Tamara Di Tella Pilates (Map pp88-9; ☎ 4813-1216; www.tamaraditella.com; cnr Juncal & R Peña; 4 sessions AR$117) The 'Pilates Queen' has over a dozen branches with modern facilities.

Vida Natural (Map pp88-9; ☎ 4826-1695; www.yogacentro.com.ar; Charcas 2852; 4 classes AR$95) This natural-therapy center in Palermo offers Ashtanga, Hatha and Iyengar yoga. Therapeutic massage, tai chi and harmonizing Tibetan bowls are also available.

WALKING TOUR

Start at leafy **Plaza San Martín** (**1**; p100), designed by French landscape architect Carlos Thays. If you like guns, swords and cannons, stop in at the **Museo de Armas** (**2**; p101). Otherwise, head

---

WALK FACTS

Start: Plaza San Martín
End: Heladería Cadore
Distance: 5km
Duration: about four hours, depending on breaks

CENTRAL BUENOS AIRES WALKING TOUR

down pedestrian Florida to the elegant **Galerías Pacífico** (**3**; p96), one of the capital's most beautiful malls. Take a peek inside at the ceiling murals, or watch one of the pass-the-hat tango shows that are often just outside.

From here you'll head west on Córdoba, crossing the impressive **Av 9 de Julio** (**4**). Soon you'll come to the lovely **Teatro Cervantes** (**5**; p101) and the notable **Templo de la Congregación Israelita** (**6**; p98). Walk south along Libertad to the **Teatro Colón** (**7**; p98), one of BA's most impressive buildings; take a tour if you've got time. Then keep going south and turn left at Av Corrientes. You'll soon bisect Av 9 de Julio again, but under the shadow of BA's famous **Obelisco** (**8**; p98). Just after you cross, turn left at Carlos Pellegrini and then right at pedestrian Lavalle; keep going until the junction at Florida.

If you need a break, stop at the classic café **Richmond** (**9**; p120) – the old atmosphere can't be beat. After your *café con leche* (coffee with milk), keep buzzing south on Florida and then down Diagonal Roque Sáenz Peña to **Plaza de Mayo** (**10**; p96). Tour the **Casa Rosada** (**11**; p96), then head west on Av de Mayo past **Café Tortoni** (**12**; p124), the city's most famous and touristy café, to the **Palacio del Congreso** (**13**; p98). Note the rococo **Confitería del Molino** (**14**), a now-defunct café that presently molders in BA's air. For a special treat, walk north four blocks and one block west to **Heladería Cadore** (**15**; p118) for a delicious ice-cream cone.

COURSES

Visitors have many opportunities to study almost anything in BA, from Spanish to cooking to tango (see the boxed text, p123). Most cultural centers (p93) offer classes at affordable rates, and South American Explorers (p616) has a wide variety of fun options also.

Those proficient in Spanish and seeking cooking classes can try the highly regarded **Instituto Argentino de Gastronomía** (Map pp84-5; IAG; ☎ 4816-1414; www.iag.com.ar; Montevideo 968) or **Mausi Sebess** (☎ 4791-4355; www.mausisebess.com; Av Maipú 594), located in BA's suburb of Vicente López.

Language

BA has become a major destination for students of Spanish, and good institutes are opening up all the time. Nearly all organize social activities and home-stay programs,

and all have private classes. Below are just a few institutes; it's always best to ask for current recommendations.

For something different, contact **Español Andando** (☎ 5278-9886; www.espanol-andando.com.ar). You'll walk around town with a guide, learning Spanish by interacting with *porteños* on the street.

CEDIC (Centro Estudio del Español; Map pp84-5; ☎ 4312-1016; www.cedic.com.ar; Reconquista 715, 11th fl, Suite E) Long-running school in the center.

DWS (Map pp88-9; ☎ 4773-1379; www.danielawasser.com.ar; Av Córdoba 4382) Friendly and has free internet computers.

Expanish (Map pp84-5; ☎ 4322-0011; www.expanish.com; Viamonte 927, 1st fl, suites A & B) Housed in a lovely building; offers good services.

IBL (Map pp84-5; ☎ 4331-4250; www.ibl.com.ar; Florida 165, 3rd fl) Very central and offers eight levels of Spanish instruction.

ILEE (Map pp84-5; ☎ 4372-0223; www.argentinailee.com; Callao 339, 3rd fl) Well-regarded school that rotates teachers to expose students to different learning methods.

One on One (Map pp84-5; ☎ 4815-4452; www.oneononeargentina.com.ar; Rodrígues Peña 736, 7th fl, Suite A) Tiny school with tailor-made courses.

University de Buenos Aires (UBA; Map pp84-5; ☎ 4343-5981; www.idiomas.filo.uba.ar; 25 de Mayo 221) Regular and intensive, long-term classes (one to four months). Italian, German, French, Portuguese and Japanese also taught. Cheap, but classrooms are run-down.

BUENOS AIRES FOR CHILDREN

Those with kids have it good in BA. On weekends Palermo's parks bustle with families taking walks or picnicking. Shopping malls fill with strollers, while zoos, museums and theme parks also make good child-friendly destinations.

Good green spots in the city include Palermo's **3 de Febrero park**, where on weekends traffic isn't allowed on the ring road around the rose garden (and you can rent bikes, boats and in-line skates nearby). Other good stops here include a planetarium (p102), a zoo (p102) and a Japanese garden (p102). If you're downtown and need a nature break, think about the Reserva Ecológica Costanera Sur (p98), a large nature preserve with good bird watching, pleasant gravel paths and no vehicular traffic.

Shopping malls make safe destinations for families (especially if it's raining), and most come with a playground, a video arcade, a multiplex and toy shops. **Paseo Alcorta** (Map pp88-9; ☎ 5777-6500; Salguero 3172; ⏰ 10am-10pm) is particularly good, while the Abasto (p132) boasts a full-blown children's museum (actually a fancy playground) and a mini-amusement park.

In San Telmo, check out the puppet museum, **Museo Argentino del Títere** (Map pp84-5; ☎ 4304-4376; Piedras 905; admission free; ⏰ 3-6pm Tue-Sun), which has inexpensive weekend shows (call for schedule) that will amuse the little urchins.

In Recoleta visit the **Museo Participativo de Ciencias** (Map pp84-5; ☎ 4806-3456; www.mpc.org.ar; Junín 1930; admission AR$10; ⏰ 3:30-7:30pm Tue-Sun), in the Centro Cultural Recoleta (p93). This hands-on science museum has interactive displays that focus on fun learning. Hours vary depending on the season. A bit outside the center, in Caballito, is the good Museo Argentino de Ciencias Naturales (natural science museum; p104).

Heading to Tigre (p136), just north of center, makes a great day excursion. Get there via the Tren de la Costa; it ends right at Parque de la Costa (p136), a typical amusement park with fun rides and activities. Take a boat trip on the Delta or wander the market (p136) for fruit and housewares.

Outside the city is the exceptional zoo, **Parque Temaikén** (☎ 03488-436-900; www.temaiken.com.ar; RP 25, Km 1, Escobar; adult/child 3-12 AR$25/15; ⏰ 10am-7pm Tue-Sun Dec–mid-Mar, to 6pm mid-Mar–Dec). Only the most charming animal species are on display (think meerkats, pygmy hippos and white tigers), roaming freely around natural enclosures. An excellent aquarium comes with touch pools, and plenty of interactive areas provide mental stimulation. Taxis from the center cost around AR$80 and take 40 minutes, or grab bus 60 marked 'Escobar' from Plaza Italia.

To help calm down temper tantrums, visit one of BA's dozens of ice-cream shops; see the boxed text, p118 for suggestions.

For more particulars on traveling with children in Argentina, see p605.

TOURS

There are plenty of organized tours, from the large tourist-bus variety to more intimate car trips to guided bike rides to straight-up walks. Other than the following listings, there are also travel agencies (p95), most of which broker tours or offer their own.

The city of Buenos Aires organizes **free monthly tours** (☎ 4114-5791) from August to December, with themes ranging from art to historic bars to particular neighborhoods. Stop by any government tourist office (p95) for a schedule.

If you have an MP3 player (such as an ipod) and are self-sufficient, check out www.mp tours.com. You can download unique self-guided tours and maps of BA neighborhoods for US$14.99 each, walking, stopping and listening at your leisure. The city also has good downloads (www.bue.gov.ar/audioguia; both in English and Spanish) and they're free, but not quite as offbeat or 'local' feeling.

All companies listed below offer tours in English and possibly other languages.

La Bicicleta Naranja (Map pp84-5; ☎ 4362-1104; www.bicicletanaranja.com.ar; Pasaje Giuffra 308; tours AR$70, bike rental per hr AR$7) Offers various bike tours around the city; tour price includes helmet, lock and guide.

BA Local (☎ 4361-8101, 011-15-4870-5506; www.balocal.com) Itinerary planning and custom tours (AR$310 for five hours) are available from superorganized Christina Wiseman, an ex–New Yorker.

Bob Frassinetti (☎ 011-15-6965-1955; bob@artdealer.com.ar; per person AR$125) Bohemian Bob speaks excellent English and offers tours to art galleries, artists' studios, second-hand shops, antique markets and private collectors.

Bitch Tours (☎ 011-15-6157-3248; www.bitchtours.blogspot.com) Agustina Menendey is actually not a bitch, and she will give off-beat custom tours at sliding fees for the right (cool) people.

Cultur (☎ 011-15-6575-4593; www.cultour.com.ar; per person from AR$55) Good tours run by teachers and students from UBA (University of Buenos Aires). Prepare to learn the historical and cultural facets of Buenos Aires.

Eternautas (☎ 5031-9916; www.eternautas.com) Three-hour city tours, including transport, cost AR$78 per person. Weekend walking tours (only in Spanish) are from AR$7 per person. Other tours (with historical, economic or cultural themes) also available.

Urban Biking (☎ 4568-4321; www.urbanbiking.com) Offers similar services to Bicicleta Naranja.

FESTIVALS & EVENTS

There are festivals happening in BA all the time, and they celebrate nearly everything – tango, horses, gauchos, cinema, art, wine, fashion and books. Spring is when the lion's share of these events occur. Check with tourist offices for exact dates as they vary from year to year. Palermo's La Rural (aka Predio Ferial;

Map pp88–9) is the venue for many of the city's bigger events.

January & February

Carnaval (late February) Get sprayed with foam while enjoying Afro-Latin *murga* (musical theater) rhythms on Av de Mayo. BA's Carnaval is relatively tame, but there's still a chance for water-balloon fights.

Chinese New Year (date depends on the lunar calendar) Head to Belgrano's tiny Chinatown for food, firecrackers and festivities.

April

Feria del Libro (www.el-libro.org.ar; La Rural) The largest book festival in Latin America, attracting over a million book-lovers for three weeks (April-May).

Festival International de Cine Independiente (www.bafici.gov.ar) Highlights national and international independent films at venues all around town.

May

arteBA (www.arteba.com; La Rural) Popular event that exposes general public to contemporary art, introduces exciting new young artists and shows off top gallery works.

July

La Rural (www.ruralarg.org.ar; La Rural) The mother of all livestock fairs, with lots of bull(s). Gaucho shows and agricultural machinery make this a quirky event. Late July-early August.

August

Fashion BA Four days spotlight the city's latest designer threads and hottest models. A fall collection shows in March; both events are at Palermo's La Rural.

Festival de Tango (www.festivaldetango.com.ar) Masterful performances shown at different venues all over the city; the Mundial de Tango follows the week after.

Mundial de Tango (www.mundialdetango.gov.ar; various venues) International couples compete fiercely for this most prestigious trophy – to be the world's best tango dancers.

September

Feria de Anticuarios (www.feriadeanticuarios.org) BA's ritziest (and priciest) antiques are exhibited and sold at this event, held in Recoleta's Palais de Glace.

Vinos y Bodegas (www.expovinosybodegas.com.ar; La Rural) A can't-miss event for wine aficionados, offering vintages from over 100 Argentine bodegas (wineries).

Casa Foa (www.casafoa.com) The city's top-notch architecture, design and decoration fair, located at a different renovated (and usually historical) building each year. Runs from September to November.

October

South American Music Conference (www.samc.net) BA's biggest electronic music party, featuring networking conferences during the day and 50,000 party-goers at night.

November

Maratón de Buenos Aires (www.maratondebuenos aires.com) A whole lot of running through BA's best sights and neighborhoods.

Marcha del Orgullo Gay (www.marchadelorgullo.org.ar) Thousands of BA's gay, lesbian and transgender citizens proudly march from Plaza de Mayo to the Congreso.

Gran Premio Nacional The country's biggest horse race and a fine family event, held in Palermo's opulent and French-styled *hipódromo*.

Día de la Tradición Located in San Antonio de Areco (see p144), but a worthwhile day-trip if you like gauchos.

Creamfields (www.creamfieldsba.com.ar) BA's answer to the UK's outdoor, all-night, cutting-edge electronic-music and dance party, with over 100 international DJs and bands.

December

Campeonato Abierto de Pato (www.fedpato.com.ar) Showcases Argentina's quirky traditional sport involving horseback riders wrestling over a handeled ball.

Campeonato Abierto de Polo (☎ 4343-0972; www.aapolo.com) Watch the world's best polo players thunder up and down Palermo's polo fields.

Festival Buenos Aires Danza Contemporánea (www.buenosairesdanza.com.ar) A major contemporary dance party that occurs every two years. Performances, seminars and workshops in various cultural centers and theaters.

SLEEPING

Buenos Aires' huge tourist boom, which began in 2002 after the peso plummeted, has seen the city's accommodation options increase exponentially. Boutique hotels and guesthouses, especially, have mushroomed in neighborhoods like San Telmo and Palermo, and hostels are a dime a dozen. You shouldn't have trouble finding the type of place you're looking for, but it's a good idea to make a reservation beforehand – especially during any holidays or the busy summer months of November through January.

Many places will help you with transportation to and from the airport if you reserve ahead of time. The most expensive hotels will take credit cards, but cheaper places might not (or may include a surcharge). Some kind of breakfast, whether it be continental or buffet, is included nearly everywhere; the same goes for internet access, wi-fi and air-con.

We've listed high-season prices (roughly November to February). Rates can skyrocket during peak seasons (Christmas and Easter) or drop during slow seasons.

Microcentro

As well as being very central, the Microcentro area has the best range and the largest number of accommodations in the city. Toward the north you'll be close to the popular pedestrian streets of Florida and Lavalle, as well as the neighborhoods of Retiro and Recoleta (and their upscale boutiques). The Plaza de Mayo area, however, contains the bustling banking district and many historical buildings, and is within walking distance of San Telmo. During the day the whole area is very busy, but nights are much calmer as businesspeople flee the center after work. Don't expect creative cuisine in this area – for that you'll have to head to Palermo.

BUDGET

HI Obelisco Suites (Map pp84-5; ☎ 4328-4040; www.hihos tels.com; Av Corrientes 830; dm AR$33, r AR$70-95; ✕ 🖳) This large hostel features large dorms (six to eight beds) and pleasant private rooms; every three rooms share a bathroom and a kitchenette. Common areas include a trendy bar-lounge with a pool table, and separate small rooms for Spanish classes and watching TV. Lots of activities are on offer; buy an HI card (AR$43) for a 10% discount.

Milhouse Youth Hostel (Map pp84-5; ☎ 4345-9604; www.milhousehostel.com; Hipólito Yrigoyen 959; dm/d AR$33/130; ✕ 🖳) Best known as a party hostel, this popular spot offers a plethora of activities and services. Dorms and private rooms are tiny but fairly well kept, and most surround a pleasant open patio. Common spaces are large and boisterous, and include a bar in the basement, a TV lounge on the mezzanine and a rooftop terrace above. A nearby annex is opening in 2008. Buy an HI card (AR$43) for a 10% discount.

Portal del Sur (Map pp84-5; ☎ 4342-8788; www.portal delsurba.com.ar; Hipólito Yrigoyen 855; dm AR$35-40, s/d AR$120/150; ✕ 🖳) Located in a charming old building, this is one of the city's best hostels. Beautiful dorms and sumptuous, hotel-quality private rooms surround a central well area, which features a kitchen and dining area. The highlight is the lovely rooftop deck with views

and attached airy common lounge. Free tango lessons, Spanish lessons and walking tour.

MIDRANGE

Hotel Alcázar (Map pp84-5; ☎ 4345-0926; Av de Mayo 935; s/d AR$90/110) One of BA's best budget deals, the old Alcazar now has awesome remodelled rooms (get one with an outside window) that are clean, good-sized and great value. It's centrally located on Av de Mayo and just steps away from the famous Tortoni Cafe, which is handy since breakfast isn't included. There are also some nice interior tiled patios. Reserve ahead.

Suipacha Inn (Map pp84-5; ☎ 4322-0099; www.hotel suipacha.com.ar; Suipacha 515; s/d AR$140/160; ✕) This well-located hotel is a good deal in the Microcentro – it's only a couple blocks from the Obelisco. It could use a facelift (ignore that hole in the comforter), but you do get small, basic and tidy rooms, most with a fridge, a microwave, a sink and a safe box. Treat yourself and upgrade to a more spacious 'special' room, as they don't cost too much more.

Hotel Frossard (Map pp84-5; ☎ 4322-1811; www.hotel frossard.com.ar; Tucumán 686; s/d AR$140/170; ✕ 🖳) If you don't mind iffy service and faded glory, this intimate hotel is a little gem, boasting 25 small but high-ceilinged rooms in a charming older building. Singles are tiny and doubles are small, but triples have more breathing room. The location is excellent; the pedestrian streets of Florida and Lavalle are just a block away.

TOP END

Reino del Plata (Map pp84-5; ☎ 5272-4000; www.hotel reinodelplata.com.ar; Hipólito Yrigoyen 647; d AR$450-489; ✕ 🖳) Just a skip away from Plaza de Mayo is this large, modern hotel with a shiny lobby and good services. The elegant rooms all have flat-panel TVs and safe boxes big enough for laptops. Get a 'superior' room for more light, more space and a small balcony – it's only AR$30 more. Best of all is the wonderful rooftop terrace with a Jacuzzi.

NH City & Tower (Map pp84-5; ☎ 4121-6464; www.nh -hotels.com; Bolívar 160; d AR$525; ✕ 🖳 ⛱) The NH chain's signature style is hip minimalism, with muted earth tones and natural design accents. Expect classy, tasteful rooms and excellent services – this particular hotel has a small but beautiful rooftop swimming pool with city views. Prices can vary at the several other NH branches in town.

Tryp Hotel (Melia; Map pp84-5; ☎ 4891-3808; www .solmelia.com; San Martín 474; d from AR$560; ✷ ▯) A good modern and upscale choice in the center, the Tryp (aka Melia) is a large hotel on the cutting edge of hip. On offer are large, contemporary rooms in cool earthy colors, featuring flat-panel TVs, glass desks and large elegant headboards framing comfortable beds. Business travelers should note the meeting room with attached rooftop deck. Book online for best rates.

Congreso

Congreso and Tribunales contain many of the city's older theaters, cinemas and cultural centers. Lively Av Corrientes has many modest shops, services and bookstores, and was BA's original theater district. The Plaza de Congreso area is always moving, sometimes with mostly peaceful public demonstrations. Generally, this area is not quite as packed as the Microcentro and has a less business and touristy flavor, but still bustles day and night.

BUDGET

Kilca Hostel (Map pp84-5; ☎ 4381-1966; www.kilcaback packer.com; Mexico 1545; dm/d AR$31/93; ▯) The casual and slightly artsy Kilca is in the upcoming Montserrat neighborhood, which is cool – fewer tourists and more local activity. It also has awesome vibes; it's a casual spot in an early 1900s house, and rooms feature exposed brick and high ceilings with beams. There's a funky kitchen, and small leafy courtyards that are good for relaxing.

Hotel Reina (Map pp84-5; ☎ 4381-2496; www.reinahotel .com; Av de Mayo 1120; s AR$90, d AR$100-120; ✷) This charming old building still has a subdued elegance that's apparent in the grand halls, the classic elevator and the original light fixtures. Some rooms are simple, while others are lovely – with high ceilings, wood floors and balconies (try for room 210). Tango classes are given in the airy salon.

Hotel Sportsman (Map pp84-5; ☎ 4381-8021; www .hotelsportsman.com.ar; Av Rivadavia 1425; s AR$105-186, d AR$186-280) For a taste of how backpacker lodgings in BA used to be, check into this oldie but still goodie. It's a classic, ancient hotel with a creaky wood staircase, an old iron elevator and mazelike hallways leading to basic but perfectly fine rooms with either shared or private bathrooms. Character abounds, and there's even a kitchen – but only for

heating up that *mate* (tea-like beverage). An awesome deal.

Hotel Turiluz (Map pp84-5; ☎ 4374-9112; molinohotel@ hotmail.com; Av Callao 164; s/d AR$110/150; ✷) Formerly known as Molino, Hotel Turiluz is excellent value and a popular choice in Congreso. The singles here are small and have open showers that get everything wet, but rooms in general are basic, neat and come with tasteful decor. The security is good and the lobby sparkles. Book ahead.

Fiamingo Apart Hotel (Map pp84-5; ☎ 4374-4400; www.fiamingoapart.com.ar; Talcahuano 120; s/d AR$170/200; ✷ ▯) Great for families, the Fiamingo features huge suites that lean more toward comfortable and convenient than fancy. All come with attached kitchenettes for heating up drinks or takeout foods (there are no stoves – just microwaves and sinks). Staff are friendly, and windows are double-paned for peace and quiet. It's a great deal for the price; reserve ahead of time.

TOP END

Crystal Suites (Map pp84-5; ☎ 5811-4169; www.crystalsuites .com.ar; Uruguay 820; r AR$220; ✷) If you need lots of room – and who doesn't? – there's this slightly odd-looking hotel, at least from the outside. Inside, huge suites come with limited-use kitchenettes and dining areas, and most have rounded balconies. It's not a really modern place, but for casual comfort and plenty of breathing room this is a good deal.

Design Suites (Map pp84-5; ☎ 4814-8700; www.design suites.com; MT de Alvear 1683; r AR$488-560; ✷ ▯) Futuristically elegant, with that minimalist style so popular in trendy BA hotels these days, Design Suites offers a great location and exclusive atmosphere. All suites have flat-panel TVs, gorgeous decor and small kitchenettes (no stoves, just microwaves). There's a roof atrium, and the downstairs lounge is elegant; too bad you can't dip into the pool.

San Telmo

South of the Microcentro, San Telmo has some of the most traditional atmosphere in Buenos Aires. Buildings are more charming, historical, and less modernized than those in the center, and tend to be only a few stories high. Many restaurants and fancy boutique stores have opened here in recent years, and there are some good bars, tango venues and other nightspots for entertainment. Most accommodation options here are hostels, humble hotels or upscale guesthouses rather than five-star hotels.

BUDGET

Garden House (Map pp84-5; ☎ 4305-0517; www.garden houseba.com.ar; San Juan 1271; dm AR$27-30, s/d AR$60/80; 🖳) A bit off the beaten tourist path is this friendly hostel with two dorms and six doubles (a couple with pretty patios) and some casual but cozy common spaces. Most rooms share bathrooms. It's a bit far from the center, but the good vibes are worth the trek. Cheap but excellent weekly *asados* (barbecues) take place on the terrace.

Art Factory (Map pp84-5; ☎ 4343-1463; www.artfactoryba .com.ar; Piedras 545; dm AR$27-30, s AR$60-80, d AR$80-100; 🗙 🖳) Friendly and uniquely art-themed, this fine hostel offers more private rooms than most – and all feature huge murals, painted and decorated by different artists from around the world. Even the hallways and water tanks have colorful cartoonish themes, and the 1850s mansion adds an elegant old touch to the atmosphere. Activities organized; great beds.

Che Lagarto Hostel (Map pp84-5; ☎ 4343-4845; www .chelagarto.com; Venezuela 857; dm AR$29-34, s AR$55, d AR$86-130; 🗙 🖳) Most rooms are nothing special at this large hostel, except for one 12-bed dorm in a huge and beautiful space. Plain doubles have either a shared or private bathroom. The best feature here is likely the downstairs party-bar-restaurant with backyard rock garden, though a future roof terrace might steal some thunder.

Sandanzas Hostel (Map p91; ☎ 4300-7375; www .sandanzas.com.ar; Balcarce 1351; dm AR$30-33, d AR$100-130; 🖳) This friendly hostel has just 28 beds and is enthusiastically run by its five young owners, all artists or social workers. It's a colorful place with good-sized dorms, six doubles (three with private bathroom) and occasional cultural events. The location is in a gritty blue-collar neighborhood near Plaza Lezama. Coffee and tea are served all day, and there are free bike rentals.

MIDRANGE

Lugar Gay (Map pp84-5; ☎ 4300-4747; www.lugargay.com .ar; Defensa 1120; s AR$125-170, d AR$155-235; 🖳) This intimate guesthouse is for gay men only, offering eight small but elegant rooms – half with shared bathrooms and most featuring stunning views of the pretty church in back. It's a maze of catwalks, spiral staircases and

sunny terraces (nude sunbathing welcome), plus a tango salon, a tiny café and a closet kitchenette. Two Jacuzzis—one indoor, one out—translate into fun nights.

TOP END

Casa Bolivar (Map p91; ☎ 4300-3619; www.casabolivar .com; Finochietto 524; d AR$220-375; 🖳 🗙) Fourteen spacious studios and loft apartments have been lovingly renovated into attractive and modern spaces at this amazing mansion, some with incredible original details like carved doorways or painted ceilings. Separate entrances join with common hallways connecting through the complex, and there are lovely garden patios in which to relax. Run by a gay French couple.

Mansion Dandi Royal (Map pp84-5; ☎ 4307-7623; www .hotelmansiondandiroyal.com; Piedras 922; d AR$330-695; 🖳 🗙 🌊) Catering to tango fanatics, this 1903 family mansion has been renovated into a luxurious themed hotel complete with murals, glass chandeliers and a curved wooden staircase. The 30 rooms are gorgeous; most come with antique furniture, claw-foot tubs and high ceilings. There's a small but lovely rooftop pool and a sunny patio, while tango classes, *milongas* and shows take place in the wonderful wood-floored basement studios or next-door salon.

Axel Hotel (Map pp84-5; ☎ 4136-9393; www.axelhotels .com; Venezuela 649; s/d from AR$775/860; 🖳 🗙 🌊) BA's first five-star gay hotel is certainly a showpiece – the lobby boasts a multistory wall fountain and a peek at the top-floor swimming pool – from the bottom up. Stairways are also glassy (watch that vertigo), and rooms are fabulously contemporary, with acid-concrete floors and glass-wall bathrooms. There's a large, decked-out back garden with another (outdoor) pool, two bar-lounges, a restaurant, saunas, Jacuzzis and a gym. Hetero-friendly to boot.

Retiro

Retiro is a great, central place to be, *if* you can afford it – many of BA's most expensive hotels, along with some of its richest inhabitants, are settled in here. Close by are leafy Plaza San Martín, the Retiro bus station and many upscale stores and business services. Recoleta and the Microcentro are just a short stroll away.

MIDRANGE

Hotel Central Córdoba (Map pp84-5; ☎ 4311-1175; www .hotelcentralcordoba.com.ar; San Martín 1021; s/d AR$110/130; 🅿 🗙) Possibly Retiro's most affordable hotel is the Central Córdoba. Rooms are neat and feature desk areas and tiled floors, but don't leave much space to move around. Ask for an inside room if you want quiet. The location is spot on – some key bars are within easy staggering distance – and it's very popular, so book well ahead.

TOP END

Aspen Suites (Map pp84-5; ☎ 4313-9011; www.aspen suites.com.ar; Esmeralda 933; d AR$450-600; ⊠ ▯) It's hardly luxurious – the halls could use a lick of paint and views out the window vary – but the modern, spacious suites all have fully equipped kitchenettes and are very comfortable. Bigger 'deluxe' suites and one-bedroom apartments are available; for best rates book online.

Hotel Bel Air (Map pp84-5; ☎ 4816-0016; www.hotel belair.com.ar; Arenales 1462; s/d AR$465/480; ⊠ ▯) The lobby bar here is downright sensuous, and the nearby lounge has upscale travelers and business folks sitting pretty. Upstairs, rooms are beautifully designed in warm colors and have modern furnishings. Robes in the bathrooms are a nice touch, but best of all is this hotel's location between the upscale neighborhoods of Retiro and Recoleta.

Dazzler Suites Arroyo (Map pp84-5; ☎ 4325-8200; www.dazzlersuites.com; Suipacha 1359; d from AR$490; ⊠ ▯ ▯) They're remodeling, so try to snag one of the newer suites – which more closely match the snazzy lobby area. New or old, all come with a kitchenette, and some have two bedrooms. Perks include an open-air swimming pool, a sauna, a modern gym and an international restaurant.

Four Seasons (Map pp84-5; ☎ 4321-1200; www.four seasons.com/buenosaires; Posadas 1086; d from AR$1480; ⊠ ▯ ▯) No surprise here – the Four Seasons offers all the perks that define a five-star hotel, such as great service and white terry-cloth robes. Rooms are large and beautiful, with contemporary furnishings and decorations, and the finest suites are located in an old luxurious mansion next door. There's also a gorgeous spa and an outdoor heated swimming pool.

Recoleta & Barrio Norte

Most of the accommodations in Recoleta (Barrio Norte is more of a subneighborhood) are expensive, and what cheap hotels there are tend to be full much of the time. Buildings here are grand and beautiful, befitting the city's richest barrio, and you'll be close to Recoleta's famous cemetery, along with its lovely parks, museums and boutiques.

BUDGET

Southernhouse Hostel (Map pp84-5; ☎ 4961-6933; www .southernhouseba.com; TM de Anchorena 1117; dm AR$31, s AR$84, d AR$93-140; ▯) This newer hostel attempts to be slick with a hip bar-lounge area, and it succeeds – kind of. Rooms are on the tiny side, but each has its own private bathroom. There's also a tiled outside patio, but the best thing here is likely the location, on the edge of upscale Recoleta.

MIDRANGE

Hotel Lion D'or (Map pp84-5; ☎ 4803-8992; www.hotel -liondor.com.ar; Pacheco de Melo 2019; s AR$115-140, d AR$145-175; ⊠) These digs have their charm, but what you get can be a crap shoot – some rooms are small, basic and dark, while others are absolutely grand and may include a modest (nonworking) fireplace. All are clean and good value, and while a few are a bit rough around the edges, most have been modernized for comfort. There's a great old marble staircase, and the elevator is just fabulous. Breakfast is not included; air-con extra.

Juncal Palace Hotel (Map pp84-5; ☎ 4821-2770; www .juncalpalacehotel.com.ar; Juncal 2282; s/d AR$120/150; ⊠) Reserve way ahead for this baby, 'cause it's a great deal and nearly always full. Small but pleasant and comfortable rooms come with homey flowery bedspreads, and some feature small balconies. The best part is the location – within walking distance of Recoleta cemetery and the busy shopping street Av Santa Fe.

TOP END

Art Hotel (Map pp84-5; ☎ 4821-4744; www.arthotel.com .ar; Azcuénaga 1268; d AR$202-530; ⊠ ▯) Stunningly beautiful, this boutique hotel features an art gallery near the lobby, a small outdoor patio with an interesting wall of mirrors, and a wonderful rooftop terrace with a Jacuzzi and a wood deck. Rooms are small but boast a contemporary mix of decor – think concrete floors, plasma TVs and ironwork details – along with romantic canopied beds and original high doors.

Onze Trendy Hotel (Map pp88-9; ☎ 4821-2873; www .onzehotelboutique.com; Ecuador 1644; d AR$375-530; ⊠ ▯) With a name like this, how can you resist?

Gorgeous from the get-go, this boutique hotel offers 11 rooms with unique touches like dressing rooms and traditional *mantas* (hand-woven blankets) for decoration. Floors are wood and some rooms have balconies. It's a lovely place with great service and an exclusive feel.

Palacio Duhau – Park Hyatt (Map pp84-5; ☎ 5171-1234; www.buenosaires.park.hyatt.com; Av Alvear 1661; d from AR$1500; ❄ 🖳 ⚓) One of the loveliest new hotels in Buenos Aires, the Park Hyatt consists of two wings – a newer building on Av Posadas and the renovated Palacio Duhau. In between is a gorgeously terraced grassy garden with fountains and patios, overlooked by the palace's large restaurant balcony. Rooms are luxuriously wonderful, and swanky amenities include a fine spa, an indoor pool, a wine and cheese bar, an art gallery and even a teahouse.

Alvear Palace Hotel (Map pp84-5; ☎ 4808-2100; www.alvearpalace.com; Av Alvear 1891; d from AR$2060; ❄ 🖳 ⚓) Ask any local to name the classiest, most traditional hotel in Buenos Aires, and they'll name this jewel. Treat yourself to old-world sophistication and superior service, while the bathtub Jacuzzi, Hermès toiletries and Egyptian cotton bedsheets aid your trip into dreamland. There are also three fine restaurants, an elegant tea room and an indoor swimming pool to luxuriate in, along with butler service.

Palermo

Despite being a short trek (about a 10-minute taxi ride) from the center, Palermo is the top choice for many travelers. Not only is it full of extensive parklands – which are great for weekend jaunts and sporting activities – but you'll have heaps of cutting-edge restaurants, designer boutiques and hip dance clubs at your fingertips. Many of these places are located in the extensive subneighborhood of Palermo Viejo, which is further subdivided into Palermo Soho and Palermo Hollywood. All are connected to the center by bus or Subte.

BUDGET
Palermo House Hostel (Map pp88-9; ☎ 4832-1815; www.palermohouse.com.ar; Thames 1754; dm AR$25-31, d AR$93-109; ❄ 🖳) It's a bit of an odd layout, with reception on the 3rd floor – but this is where everyone hangs out anyway. It's one big room, with a whole bank of windows making it bright and welcoming – and a deck is in the

plans, which will make a nice addition. Good dorms and private rooms with high ceilings are down one floor.

Casa Jardín (Map pp88-9; ☎ 4774-8783; www.casajardinba.com.ar; Charcas 4422; dm/s/d AR$35/50/90; 🖳) Despite its name there's no real garden at this small hostel, but the pleasant rooftop terrace is a great substitute. Common living areas are comfortable, and there are only 15 beds – which means you'll get to know everyone pretty well. It's basic but peaceful and well-located near transport options.

Hostel Suites Palermo (Map pp88-9; ☎ 4773-0806; www.hostel-inn.com; Charcas 4752; dm/d AR$36/130; ❄ 🖳) One of the more pleasant large cheapies in town is this HI hostel in a fine old mansion and former geriatric home. Maybe this explains why it's not a party place, but a rather peaceful spot with good, large dorms and 10 small, private rooms. There's a rooftop terrace for hanging out, and lots of events on offer. Buy an HI card (AR$43) for a 10% discount.

MIDRANGE
Gorriti 4290 (Map pp88-9; ☎ 4862-8300; www.gorriti4290.com.ar; Gorriti 4290; d AR$140-220; ❄ 🖳) For an intimate stay, seek out this small, friendly spot. There are only four rooms (three with shared bathrooms) and all are simple yet comfortable, with quality beds and linens. Common areas are spacious and even a touch industrial – there's an interesting catwalk above the dining room. The owners live on site and can help with area information.

Hotel Costa Rica (Map pp88-9; ☎ 4864-7390; www.hotelcostarica.com.ar; Costa Rica 4137; d AR$155-295; ❄ 🖳) One of few larger hotels in Palermo, this place manages to retain a sense of intimacy – the small bar in the lobby helps. It's run by a Frenchman, who has added contemporary details like slick raised sinks and modern decor while keeping some of the building's original details. Tiled hallways are narrow and plain, but there's a spacious rooftop patio. Cheaper rooms share bathrooms; breakfast costs extra.

Casa Alfaro B&B (Map pp88-9; ☎ 4831-0517; www.bandb.com.ar; Gurruchaga 2155; s/d AR$150-340; ❄ 🖳) Restful and very homey, this mazelike guesthouse offers a dozen simple, colorful rooms (including one large suite). The ones that look over the interior patios and garden are nicest and, consequently, much more expensive. It's a safe and friendly choice, and well-located in Palermo.

TOP END

ourpick **Home Hotel** (Map pp88-9; ☎ 4778-1008; www .homebuenosaires.com; Honduras 5860; s/d from AR$432; ✖ ▭ ☎) Sleek with Scandinavian designs, Home is a friendly, intimate little paradise of a hotel. Rooms come beautifully decorated with simple, modern lines and vintage wallpaper accents. The highlight is in the back, however; here you'll find an excellent bar and a grassy garden with a glorious pool. The basement spa is icing on the cake.

Vain Boutique Hotel (Map pp88-9; ☎ 4774-4215; www .vainuniverse.com; Thames 2260; d from AR$469; ✖ ▭) Located in a lovely renovated building, the Vain typifies the new Palermo Viejo style of boutique minimalism. The 15 rooms here have been tastefully done up along contemporary lines – black headboards, white bedspreads and simple furnishings. All have high ceilings and wood floors, and you get a welcome drink on arrival. They'll even shine your shoes.

248 Finisterra (Map pp88-9; ☎ 4773-0901; www .248finisterra.com; Av Báez 248; s/d from AR$520/565; ✖ ▭) Smack in the middle of Las Cañitas' nightlife lies this elegant, Zenlike boutique hotel. There are four classes of minimalist rooms, with most being good sized and all beautifully contemporary. Best of all is the rooftop terrace, with wood lounges and a Jacuzzi. Service is attentive, and security good.

Long-Term Rentals

Any hotel, hostel or guesthouse should significantly discount a long-term stay, so negotiate a deal in advance. There are also many guesthouses that specialize in weekly or monthly stays, and these offer a more intimate experience. If you're interested in spending time with a host family, check out www.coret.com .ar, where private rooms go for around AR$800 to AR$1200 per month (shared rooms are cheaper, and meals cost extra).

Traditionally you need a local's lien to help you cover rent for an apartment, but so many long-term foreigners are pouring into BA that a plethora of rental agencies and websites have popped up to help them find housing without this requirement. Expect to pay a much higher monthly rate for this service, however; locals usually commit to at least one or two years when obtaining a lease for unfurnished

apartments, and consequently pay less. Sites to check:

www.adelsur.com
www.alojargentina.com.ar
www.apartmentsba.com
www.buenosaireshabitat.com
www.bytargentina.com
www.friendlyapartments.com (gay oriented)
www.roomargentina.com
www.stayinbuenosaires.com
www.yourhomeinargentina.com.ar

EATING

Eating out in BA is a gastronomical highlight, and remains a great deal for those earning hard currency. Not only are the typical *parrillas* (steak houses) a dime a dozen, but the city's Palermo Viejo neighborhood boasts the most varied ethnic cuisine in the country. You can find Armenian, Brazilian, Mexican, Indian, Japanese, Southeast Asian and Middle-Eastern cuisines – and even fusions of several. Most are acceptable and some are exceptional, so be sure to try a few.

Microcentro eateries tend to cater to the business crowd, while nearby Puerto Madero is full of elegant and pricey restaurants. Congreso is pretty traditional, cuisine-wise, except for its 'little Spain' neighborhood. Recoleta is another expensive neighborhood with touristy dining options on RM Ortiz (near the cemetery). San Telmo keeps attracting more and more worthwhile restaurants.

Reservations are usually unnecessary except at the most popular restaurants – or if it's the weekend. The most thorough online guide to BA restaurants is www.guiaoleo.com, in Spanish; for English there's www.saltshaker.net.

Microcentro

Parrilla al Carbón (Map pp84-5; ☎ 4328-0824; Lavalle 663; mains AR$10-26; ☻ lunch & dinner) Cheap *parrilla* doesn't come easier than this. Go for a quick *choripan* (sausage sandwich, AR$3) at the counter in front of the grill. For more comfort and a better view of the TV, snag one of the few crowded tables and order a half-portion of the *vacío* (a chewy but tasty flank cut).

California Burrito Company (CBC; Map pp84-5; ☎ 4328-3057; Lavalle 441; mains AR$12-15; ☻ 8am-11pm Mon-Fri) At this modern Mexican joint, flour tortillas are loaded up with your choice of meat, rice, beans and salsa, and rolled into large San Francisco–style burritos the likes

---

MEATLESS IN BUENOS AIRES

Argentine cuisine is internationally famous for its succulent grilled meats, but this doesn't mean vegetarians – or even vegans – are completely out of luck.

Most restaurants, including *parrillas*, serve a few items acceptable to most vegetarians, such as green salads, omelettes, pizza and pasta. Key words to beware of include *carne* (beef), *pollo* (chicken), *cerdo* (pork) and *cordero* (lamb). *Sin carne* means 'without meat,' and the phrase *soy vegetariano/a* (I'm a vegetarian) will come in handy when explaining to an Argentine why in the world you don't want to tuck into a prime *bife de chorizo* (sirloin).

Luckily for nonmeat-eaters, vegetarian restaurants have become somewhat trendy in Buenos Aires recently. For cafeteria-style places close to the Microcentro there's **Granix** (below), **La Esquina de las Flores** (p117), **Lotos** (☎ 4814-4552; Córdoba 1577; mains AR$5-10; ☽ 11:30am-6pm Mon-Fri, 11:30am-4pm Sat) and **Arte Sano** (p117). The Palermo Viejo area has more upscale options, including **Bio** (p119) and **Artemesia** (p119). Finally, raw-food fans shouldn't miss **Verdellama** (p118).

---

of which BA has never before seen (go for the *fuego* salsa – it isn't that spicy). Tacos and salads are lighter options, and the house margaritas are a nice touch.

Broccolino (Map pp84-5; ☎ 4322-7754; Esmeralda 776; mains AR$20-35; ☽ lunch & dinner) Pick from over 25 sauces (including squid ink!) for your pasta, with a choice of rigatoni, fusilli, pappardelle and all sorts of stuffed varieties. If you can't decide your topper, try the delicious Sicilian sauce (spicy red peppers, tomato and garlic) or the pesto with mushrooms and garlic. Portions are large and the bread homemade.

La Estancia (Map pp84-5; ☎ 4326-0330; Lavalle 941; mains AR$20-50; ☽ lunch & dinner) Stop by the picture window and snap a photo of yourself in front of the huge roasting meat spits, then step into the large dining room and have a seat. This steak house has been serving up grilled goods for decades, and despite the tourist-trap feel serves pretty tasty *parrilla*.

Granix (Map pp84-5; ☎ 4343-4020; Florida 165, 1st fl; all-you-can-eat AR$25; ☽ lunch Mon-Fri) Stepping into this large, modern lacto-ovo-vegetarian eatery will make you wonder if *porteños* have had enough steak already. Pick from the many hot appetizers and entreés; there's also a great salad bar and plenty of desserts. It's only open for weekday lunches, and located in a shopping mall. Takeout available.

Sabot (Map pp84-5; ☎ 4313-6587; 25 de Mayo 756; mains AR$25-36; ☽ lunch Mon-Fri) Big mostly with businessmen power-lunching their way through the afternoon, this exceptional restaurant features well-prepared traditional food and the capital's best pepper steak and roasted goat. Service is professional and customers are like members of an old boys' club; reservations are a must after 1:30pm.

Puerto Madero

Estilo Campo (Map pp84-5; ☎ 4312-4546; Av Alicia Moreau de Justo 1840; mains AR$17-46; ☽ lunch & dinner) One of many elegant *parrillas* in Puerto Madero, Estilo Campo is as good as any. But the waiters here are dressed up like gauchos – making it easier to visualize yourself on the pampas. The *bandiola grillé* (grilled pork loin) is especially luscious and tender, while the *brochettes* (shish kebabs) aren't too shabby either. Serves pasta and seafood also.

Bice (Map pp84-5; ☎ 4315-6216; Av Alicia Moreau de Justo 192; mains AR$32-75; ☽ lunch & dinner) Homemade pastas are exceptional at this Italian restaurant – try the black fettuccini with shrimp and the risotto with artichokes and asparagus. End it all with a gelato, a crepe, mousse with pears or white chocolate semifreddo. Service is good; test it by asking for a table out back near the water.

Siga la Vaca (Map pp84-5; ☎ 4315-6801; Av Alicia Moreau de Justo 1714; lunch AR$38-52, dinner AR$46-52; ☽ lunch & dinner) Only the truly hungry should set foot in this excellent all-you-can-stuff *parrilla*. Work your way from the appetizer salad bar to the grill, where the meat hangs out. Eat slowly and pace yourself, and you'll only need to eat once that day. One drink and a dessert are included in the price, which varies depending on the meal and day.

Congreso

Pizzería Güerrín (Map pp84-5; ☎ 4371-8141; Av Corrientes 1368; slices AR$3.50; ☽ 11am-2am) Just point at a prebaked slice behind the glass counter and eat standing up with the rest of the guys. To be more civilized, sit down and order freshly baked – this way you'll also get to choose from a greater variety of toppings. Empanadas and plenty of desserts are also available.

Rocket Bar & Bistro (Map pp84-5; ☎ 4383-3833; Av Rivadavia 1285; mains AR$10-16; ☺ lunch & dinner) Countering the general stodgy restaurant scene in Congreso is Rocket, started by a British expat. Tandoori chicken, Thai green curry, seafood pie and creative salads are all available. However, it's the large range of deli-style sandwiches – roast beef, BLT and shrimp with avocado – that do a better job attracting homesick palates.

Cervantes II (Map pp84-5; ☎ 4372-5227; Juan D Perón 1883; mains AR$10-17; ☺ lunch & dinner) A modern and unpretentious spot with a touch of old-world atmosphere. Locals order an *agua de sifón* (soda water) to go along with their *bife de chorizo* (sirloin) or *ravioles con tuco* (ravioli with sauce). Short orders like *milanesas* (breaded steaks) and omelettes are also available. Portions are large and the service is efficient.

Chiquilín (Map pp84-5; ☎ 4373-5163; Sarmiento 1599; mains AR$17-35; ☺ lunch & dinner) Going strong for 80 years, Chiquilín is a large and comfortable restaurant with a classic atmosphere that adds a bit of personality. The best food here is the *parrilla* and the pasta, though specials like paella on Monday and *puchero* (a meat-and-vegetable stew) on Wednesday add welcome detours from the regular menu.

El Hispano (Map pp84-5; ☎ 4382-7534; Salta 20; mains AR$18-45; ☺ lunch & dinner) Tired of the same old steak? Then head to BA's Spanish neighborhood, where this classy restaurant offers choices from frogs Provençal to snails à la Andaluza…or just paella. Seafood is big; there's grilled trout, mussels and fried calamari. Traditional desserts include *natilla* (custard) and *arroz con leche* (rice pudding).

San Telmo & Constitución

Pride Café (Map pp84-5; ☎ 4300-6435; Balcarce 869; mains AR$8-12; ☺ 10am-10pm Sun-Fri) This small contemporary café is especially swamped with cute gay men on Sundays during San Telmo's antiques fair, attracting them with homemade pastries, healthy snacks and 'queer coffee.' Sushi nights add interest, though you might also tuck yourself away, martini in hand, to peruse the foreign magazines.

Parrilla 1880 (Map p91 ☎ 4307-2746; Defensa 1665; mains AR$10-22; ☺ lunch & dinner Tue-Sun) A good, solid *parrilla* away from the more touristy sections of San Telmo. The atmosphere is thick with history and locals come here to enjoy juicy cuts of meat from the open grill in front. The half portion of *bife de chorizo*

is plenty big for one person. Lots of other dishes, like pastas, omelettes and salads, are also available.

Bar El Federal (Map pp84-5; ☎ 4300-4313; Av Perú & Carlos Calvo; snacks AR$10-27; ☺ 8am-2am) This historic bar with classic atmosphere dates from 1864; check out the amazing counter area. The specialties here are sandwiches (especially turkey breast) and *picadas* (shared appetizer plates), but there are also pastas, salads and desserts. Sidewalk tables are the perfect perch for you to watch San Telmo go by.

Origen (Map pp84-5; ☎ 4362-7979; Humberto Primo 599; mains AR$14-28; ☺ 8:30am-8pm Mon-Tue, to 1am Wed-Sun) Modern but not pretentious, this stylish corner café features a wide range of offerings, from green-curry stir-frys and chicken satay to whole-wheat pizza, homemade soups and vegetarian options. There's also afternoon tea. Service is friendly and the sidewalk tables are especially welcoming on a warm day.

Bar Plaza Dorrego (Map pp84-5; ☎ 4361-0141; Defensa 1098; mains AR$15-30; ☺ 8am-2am Sun-Thu, to 3am Fri & Sat) You can't beat the atmosphere at this traditional joint; sip your *cortado* (coffee with milk) by a picture window and watch the world pass by. Meanwhile, traditionally suited waiters, tango music and scribbled graffiti on the counters take you back in time – at least until your hamburger lands on the table. Sitting at a sidewalk table is another experience in itself.

Casal de Catalunya (Map pp84-5; ☎ 4361-0191; Chacabuco 863; mains AR$24-55; ☺ lunch & dinner Mon-Fri, dinner Sat) Unsurprisingly big on seafood, this excellent Catalan restaurant offers garlic shrimp, mussels and clams in tomato sauce and fish of the day with *aioli* (garlic mayonnaise). Other typical Spanish dishes include *jamón serrano* (*prosciutto*-like ham), seafood paella and suckling pig. Don't miss the luscious *crema Catalana* for dessert.

Café San Juan (Map pp84-5; ☎ 4300-1112; Av San Juan 450; mains AR$28-40; ☺ lunch & dinner Tue-Sun) Some of San Telmo's best international cuisine can be found at this family-run restaurant. The pork *bandiola* is deliciously tender, and the crushed-almond shrimp is a real treat – but everything is good. This is a great spot to try seafood; it's brought in daily from Patagonia. Generous portions and great service; reserve for dinner.

La Boca

El Samovar de Rasputin (Map p91 ☎ 4302-3190; De Valle Iberlucea 1232; mains AR$10-18; ☺ 10am-8pm Tue-Fri & Sun, dinner Sat) On warm summer days choose the street seating at this atmospheric old joint, with great tourist-watching opportunities. The food is nothing new – basic pasta, sandwiches, *milanesas* (breaded cutlets) and *parrilla* – but there's good live rock and blues after midnight (see p127).

Il Matterello (Map p91; ☎ 4307-0529; Martín Rodríguez 517; mains AR$18-32; ☽ lunch Tue-Sun, dinner Tue-Sat) The food is exceptional at this Genovese trattoria. Try the *lasagne bolognese* or the *tagliatelle alla rucola* (tagliatelle with arugula). For a special treat, the house *tortelli verde* (small pasta pillows stuffed with cheese and garlic) is hard to beat.

Retiro

La Esquina de las Flores (Map pp84-5; ☎ 4811-4729; Av Córdoba 1587; mains AR$8-12; ☽ 8:30am-8:30pm Mon-Fri, to 3pm Sat) This modern restaurant also has a small health-food store that sells soy flour, whole-wheat breads and organic *mate*, among other things. There's a fast-food section, but to sit down, go upstairs and choose from the tasty and nutritious menu. Also at Gurruchaga 1630 in Palermo (Map p88-9).

Ligure (Map pp84-5; ☎ 4394-8226; Juncal 855; mains AR$15-40; ☽ lunch & dinner) Come to this old-school restaurant to savor traditional Spanish delicacies like the seafood paella, *ranas a la provencal* (frogs' legs in garlic) and *pulpo a la gallega* (Galician octopus). Steak lovers can select their *lomo* (tenderloins) in six kinds of sauce, while vegetarians should stick to the homemade pasta.

Filo (Map pp84-5; ☎ 4311-0312; San Martín 975; mains AR$22-40; ☽ noon-2am) Your choice is likely to be excellent at this artsy restaurant, as it does a great job cooking up the 20 varieties of pizza and 15 kinds of salads (try the smoked salmon). Other tasty choices include *panini*, pasta and meats, along with a whirlwind of desserts.

Empire Bar (Map pp84-5; ☎ 4312-5706; Tres Sargentos 427; mains AR$21-45; ☽ lunch & dinner) This trendy place is good for its tasty Thai cuisine, though the spice factor is toned down for Argentine taste buds. The kitchen puts out crispy wrapped prawns, *paneng* pork in red curry and *tom ka gai* (chicken-and-coconut-milk soup). Choose from nearly 100 vodkas, the largest selection in BA.

Gran Bar Danzón (Map pp84-5; ☎ 4811-1108; Libertad 1161; mains AR$25-60; ☽ dinner) It's hard to be hipper than this popular lounge-bar-restaurant. A cool-looking conservation system makes

it possible for many wines to be offered by the glass. The menu presents dishes like duck *confit* with *taleggio* cheese, rabbit ravioli and risotto with king crab. Trendy sushi is a bit sweet for true authenticity.

Recoleta & Barrio Norte

Pura Vida (Map pp88-9; ☎ 4806-0017; Uriburu 1489; juices AR$6-12, snacks AR$8-14; ☽ 11:30am-9pm Mon-Thu, till 8pm Fri, noon-9pm Sat) Step into this healthy juice bar for fruit blends and smoothies. The Green Monster (celery, cucumber, and apple) is especially refreshing, and you can add wheatgrass, yogurt, spirulina or bee pollen to your selection. Sandwiches, wraps and salads available. A second branch (Map pp84–5) has also just opened up in central BA at Reconquista 516.

Arte Sano (Map pp88-9; ☎ 4963-1513; Mansilla 2740; mains AR$8-15; ☽ 8am-10pm Mon-Sat) Vegetarian heaven, this small eatery cooks up excellent dishes, such as a zucchini, eggplant and tomato tart or veggie stir-frys. The tiny attached bakery sells brown rice, powdered ginger and whole-wheat breads. Also on offer are yoga, tai chi, dance classes and natural-food workshops.

Cumaná (Map pp84-5; ☎ 4813-9507; Rodriguez Peña 1149; mains AR$9-15; ☽ lunch & dinner) Cumaná specializes in these deliciously homey, stick-to-your-ribs pot stews, which are filled and baked with squash, corn, potatoes and/or meats, among other tidbits. Also popular are the pizzas, empanadas, pastas and calzones. Come early if you want a table.

El Sanjuanino (Map pp84-5; ☎ 4805-2683; Posadas 1515; mains AR$10-12; ☽ lunch & dinner) The cheapest food in Recoleta, attracting both penny-pinching locals and thrifty tourists. Sit at one of the 10 tables and order spicy empanadas (each AR$2), tamales or *locro*, or take your food to go – Recoleta's lovely parks are just a couple of blocks away.

Grant's (Map pp84-5; ☎ 4801-9099; Las Heras 1925; lunch AR$17-26, dinner AR$23-26; ☽ lunch & dinner) This *tenedor libre* (all-you-can-eat) offers a fantastic assortment of foods too numerous to mention. There are also plenty of *parrilla* and dessert selections. The price depends on the meal and on the day of the week; drinks are mandatory and cost extra. There's another branch at Riobamba 1068.

Munich Recoleta (Map pp84-5; ☎ 4804-3981; RM Ortiz 1871; mains AR$18-27; ☽ lunch & dinner Wed-Mon) This traditional old place hasn't changed much since Borges was a regular and enjoying its

LICKING YOUR WAY THROUGH BA

Because of Argentina's Italian heritage, Argentine *helado* is comparable to the best ice cream in the world. Amble into an *heladería* (ice-cream shop), order up a cone (pay first) and the creamy concoction will be artistically swept up into a mountainous peak. Important: *granizado* means with chocolate flakes.

Here are some of the tastiest *heladerías* in town:

■ **Dylan** (Map pp84–5; ☎ 0810-3333-9526; Perú 1086, San Telmo)

■ **Freddo** (Map pp84–5 ☎ 0810-33-Freddo; cnr Santa Fe 1600, Retiro) Many branches; check www .freddo.com.ar.

■ **Heladería Cadore** (Map pp84–5; ☎ 4374-3688, Av Corrientes 1695, Congreso)

■ **Persicco** (Map pp88–9; ☎ 0810-333-7377) Belgrano (**Vuelta de Obligado 2092**); Las Cañitas (**Migueletes 886**); Palermo (**Salguero 2591**)

■ **Una Altra Volta** (Map pp88–9; ☎ 4805-1818, Av del Libertador 3060, Palermo) Also at the corner of Quintana and Ayacucho (Recoleta) and Santa Fe 1826 (Barrio Norte).

■ **Vía Flaminia** (Map pp84–5 ☎ 4342-7737, Av Florida 121, Microcentro)

great food; try the *brochettes* (shishkebabs), grilled salmon or nine kinds of ravioli. Just make sure you can stomach the trophy animal heads looking down at you from the wall.

Oviedo (Map pp88–9; ☎ 4821-3741; Beruti 2602; mains AR$40-65; ☺ lunch & dinner) Chef Martin Rabaudino oversees one of the best kitchens in the city. This is a truly elegant place, with professional service and classy atmosphere. Fish and meat dishes are the specialty; choose from tempting and nonpretentious dishes like quail with mushrooms, shrimp risotto and seafood paella. The wine list is excellent.

Palermo
BUDGET
Providencia (Map pp88–9; ☎ 4772-8507; JA Cabrera 5995, Palermo Hollywood; mains AR$10-17; ☺ lunch Mon-Sat, dinner Mon-Fri) Casually funky, Providencia is also refreshingly grungy in that hippie-cool way. What's even better is the food – fresh, healthy, tasty and affordable. Try the huge veggie tortilla covered in rice, beets, potatoes and a goat-cheese salad. The homemade bread is awesome, as is the pitcher of (not too) sweet lemonade.

Las Cholas (Map pp88–9; ☎ 4899-0094; Arce 306, Las Cañitas; mains AR$10-20; ☺ lunch & dinner) Las Cholas found the golden rule of many successful restaurants: quality food, trendy design and bargain prices. Traditional Argentine foods like *locro* and *cazuelas* (meat and veggie stews) are worth a shot, but the *parrilla* is also excellent. Expect a wait and so-so service.

El 22 Parrilla (Map pp88–9; ☎ 4833-7876; Gorriti 5299, Palermo Soho; mains AR$10-23; ☺ lunch & dinner) Cheap

unpretentious *parrilla* isn't that easy to find in upscale Palermo Viejo. This casual family-style joint is an exception, serving up huge portions for great prices. The lunch menu is an even better deal, especially if you score a sidewalk table.

Sarkis (Map pp88–9; ☎ 4772-4911; Thames 1101, Villa Crespo; mains AR$10-24; ☺ lunch & dinner) There's a reason this long-standing, Middle Eastern restaurant is still around – the food is awesome. For appetizers, don't miss the *baquerones* (marinated sardines) or *parras rellenas* (stuffed grape leaves). Follow up with lamb in yogurt sauce. At night a fortune teller reads diners' coffee grounds.

MIDRANGE
Krishna (Map pp88–9; ☎ 4833-4618; Malabia 1833, Palermo Soho; mains AR$14-17; ☺ lunch Tue-Sun, dinner Wed-Sun) With colorful decor and low tables, Krishna offers a vegetarian Indian food experience with a multireligious theme – look for Ganesh mixing it up with Jesus, the star of David and even Jimi Hendrix. Order the *thali*, *koftas* (balls of ground vegetables) or stuffed soya *milanesa*, and there's chai, lassis and alcohol-free beer to help wash it all down.

Verdellama (Map pp88–9; ☎ 4554-7467; J Newberry 3623, Palermo Hollywood; mains AR$19-28; ☺ 10am-7pm Mon-Wed, to midnight Thu & Fri, to 5:30pm Sat) BA's first raw-food restaurant serves tasty 'spaghetti' (shredded zucchini), vegetable salads and a beet soup with almond milk. The excellent *licuados* can be supplemented with spirulina or a wheatgrass shot. Except for *chapati* bread, nothing here has been cooked over 40° centigrade.

Bio (Map pp88-9; ☎ 4774-3880; Humboldt 2199, Palermo Hollywood; mains AR$20-26; ☺ lunch & dinner Tue-Sun) The health-conscious should make a beeline to this casual corner joint, which specializes in healthy, organic and vegetarian fare. Feed your body and soul quinoa risotto, seitan curry, mushroom stir-fries and Mediterranean couscous with dried tomatoes.

Artemesia (Map pp88-9; ☎ 4863-4242; José Antonio Cabrera 3877, Palermo Soho; mains AR$20-32; ☺ dinner Tue-Sat) Serving mostly vegetarian fare, this restaurant in a less touristy part of Palermo is slightly fancy (but in an organic way). Tasty homemade bread with a squash spread is automatically brought to your table; follow it up with the grilled pear and goat cheese bruschetta. Main courses are flavorful and creative, and there are always a few selections for fish lovers.

Voulezbar (Map pp88-9; ☎ 4802-4817; Cerviño 3802; mains AR$27-32; ☺ breakfast, lunch & dinner Mon-Sat) It's worth the trek out to Palermo Chico to sit at this popular corner café. Fresh, creative cuisine includes salmon in mango salsa, and shrimp risotto. For lighter, less expensive fare, come for lunch – the baby calamari, grilled squash and lox salads are awe-inspiring, or try a burger or even the tasty *ceviche*.

Novecento (Map pp88-9; ☎ 4778-1900; Av Báez 199, Las Cañitas; mains AR$20-41; ☺ breakfast, lunch & dinner) Full breakfasts (a rarity in BA) are served at this elegant corner restaurant, but the selection is limited to eggs benedict, salmon bagels and – if you're lucky – waffles or chorizo-filled tortillas. Dinner means fancier options like fried calamari, penne with wild mushrooms or grilled trout over risotto. Fine romantic atmosphere.

TOP END

Miranda (Map pp88-9; ☎ 4771-4255; Costa Rica 5602, Palermo Hollywood; mains AR$25-35; ☺ lunch & dinner) Popular for its reasonably priced steaks, Miranda is a fashionable, modern *parrilla* with concrete walls, high ceilings and rustic wood furniture, but the food is the main attraction here. The meat is good quality and grilled to perfection, and if you score a sidewalk table on a warm day, life for a carnivore just doesn't get much better.

Bella Italia (Map pp88-9; ☎ 4802-4253; República Árabe Siria 3285; mains AR$27-42; ☺ dinner Mon-Sat) Start with a cheese plate or olive 'tasting,' then sink your teeth into the tagliolini with squid and scallops. Treats like braised rabbit and *grappa* also line the menu. Bella Italia also has a café just up the street on the next block, which serves similar fare at cheaper prices.

Olsen (Map pp88-9; ☎ 4776-7677; Gorriti 5870, Palermo Hollywood; mains AR$30-40; ☺ lunch & dinner Tue-Sat, 10:30am-8pm Sun) Olsen is famous for its Sunday brunch, but dinner isn't bad either; order venison ravioli with cherry compote or grilled tuna in yogurt dressing. Lunches are prix fixe and the best deal, plus you can see the peaceful garden better. The popular bar serves over 50 kinds of vodka, assiduously kept at 18° below zero.

Bar Uriarte (Map pp88-9; ☎ 4834-6004; Uriarte 1572, Palermo Soho; mains AR$30-40; ☺ lunch & dinner) One of Palermo's trendiest and best restaurants. Sample the rabbit risotto, *mojellas al grille* (grilled sweetbreads) or *noquis* de ricotta. There's also gourmet pizza baked in an adobe oven. And while the mains might not fill you to the brim, the luscious desserts certainly will – try the chocolate mousse with raspberries.

Green Bamboo (Map pp88-9; ☎ 4775-7050; Costa Rica 8502, Palermo Hollywood; mains AR$35-42; ☺ dinner) Just

---

THE SECRET'S OUT

A Buenos Aires culinary offshoot that has been getting a bit of press lately is the so-called 'closed-door restaurant' scene, or *puertas cerradas*. These restaurants are only open a few days per week, are pricey prix fixe and you have to ring a bell to enter. Most won't even tell you the address until you make reservations (mandatory, of course). But if you want that spine-tingling feeling brought on by discovering something off-the-beaten path – or just like being part of an exclusive group – these places are for you.

We'll let you in on the secret with a few starting points. At **Casa Saltshaker** (www.casasaltshaker .com) you'll be dining in the chef's actual apartment. Vegetarians shouldn't miss **Casa Felix** (www.diegofelix.com), which also serves fish. And for slick and glamorous, there's **647 Dinner Club** (www.club647.com) – more a private club than a closed-door restaurant, but hey, exclusivity is exclusivity.

a dozen or so mains grace the menu at this swank Vietnamese restaurant. Dishes are well-prepared and supremely tasty, and there are a few vegetarian options as well. Cocktails are especially good here, and the desserts luscious. Reserve, or you might sit at the bar.

Limbo (Map pp88-9; ☎ 4831-4040; Armenia 1820; mains AR$30-45, Palermo Soho; ☽ lunch & dinner) Sitting on the rooftop terrace on a hot day, looking over Plaza Palermo Viejo, you might just forgive Limbo for its average pasta and so-so service. Try the rack of lamb or one of the fancy salads instead, and hope for the best. A seat near the open front facade lets everyone see you're hanging with the hip crowd.

Cluny (Map pp88-9; ☎ 4831-7176; El Salvador 4618, Palermo Soho; mains AR$30-47; ☽ lunch & dinner) Cluny features a lovely front patio, comfortable white sofas and gorgeous contemporary atmosphere. Chef Lucas Dabrowski whips up delightful, top-notch cuisine – try the squash sorrentinos, Patagonian lamb or *magret de pato* (not for the queasy: it's the breast of *foie gras*–producing ducks).

our pick **Osaka** (Map pp88-9; ☎ 4775-6964; Soler 5608, Palermo Hollywood; mains AR$35-60; ☽ lunch & dinner Mon-Sat) Osaka slices up some of BA's most exquisite cold raw fish – and so much more. Catapulting Peruvian and Japanese cuisines into a whole new level of creative fusion, this amazing restaurant ponies up sublime dishes that look like works of art – and taste out of this world. Reserve a week in advance and load up the bank account.

DRINKING
Cafés

Cafés are an integral part of *porteño* life, and you shouldn't miss popping into one of these beloved hangouts to sip dainty cups of coffee and nibble biscuits with the locals. There are plenty of cafés in the city, and while you're walking around seeing the sights you're bound to run across one and find an excuse for a break. Some cafés are old classics and guaranteed to take you back in time.

Most cafés serve all meals and everything in between: breakfast, lunch, afternoon tea, dinner and late-night snack. For a background on these enduring legacies of the Argentine social history see the boxed text opposite.

La Puerto Rico (Map pp84-5; ☎ 4331-2215; Adolfo Alsina 416) One of the city's historic cafés, going strong since 1887. Located a block south of Plaza de Mayo, it serves great coffee and pas-

tries, the latter baked on the premises. Old photos on the walls hint at a rich past and the Spanish movies that have been filmed here. A good place to come that's not too touristy.

Richmond (Map pp84-5; ☎ 4322-1341; Florida 468) Feel like challenging the local male population to a billiards game or a chess match? Then head to the basement at this very traditional café. Better yet, go to the main room and sink into a leather chair to admire the Dutch chandeliers and English-style surroundings while sipping hot chocolate – just like Jorge Luis Borges did.

London City (Map pp84-5; ☎ 4343-0328; Av de Mayo 599) This swank and classy café has been serving java addicts for over 50 years, and claims to have been the spot where Julio Cortázar wrote his first novel. Your hardest work here, however, will most likely be choosing which luscious pastry to consume with your freshly brewed coffee.

El Gato Negro (Map pp84-5; ☎ 4374-1730; Av Corrientes 1669) Tea-lined wooden cabinets and a spicy aroma welcome you to this pleasant little sipping paradise. Enjoy cups of imported coffee or tea along with breakfast and dainty *sandwiches de miga* (thinly sliced white-bread sandwiches). Tea is sold by weight, and exotic herbs and spices are also on offer.

Café de los Angelitos (Map pp84-5; ☎ 4952-3078; Rivadavia 2100) Originally called Bar Rivadavia, this spot was once the haunt of poets, musicians…even criminals. Recently restored to its former glory, this historic café is now an elegant hangout, modernized by offering tango shows to tourists. Come during the day, order a cup of tea and enjoy a slice of the shady past.

La Biela (Map pp84-5; ☎ 4804-0449; Av Quintana 600) A Recoleta institution, this classic landmark has been serving the *porteño* elite since the 1950s – when race-car champions used to come here for their java jolts. The outdoor front terrace is unbeatable on a sunny afternoon, especially when the nearby weekend *feria* (street market) is in full swing – but it'll cost you 20% more.

Las Violetas (Map pp82-3; ☎ 4958-7387; Rivadavia 3899) Dating back to 1884, this historic coffeehouse was renovated in 2001. Lovely awnings and stained-glass windows, high ceilings, cream-colored ionic columns and gilded details make this café the most beautiful in BA. Breakfast, lunch and dinner service is available, along with a luxurious afternoon tea. Located in Almagro.

BUENOS AIRES' CAFÉS

Thanks to its European heritage, Buenos Aires has a serious café culture. *Porteños* will spend hours dawdling over a single *café cortado* (coffee with milk) and a couple of *medialunas* (croissants), discussing the economy, politics or that latest soccer play.

Some of the capital's cafés have been around for over a hundred years, and many still retain much of their original atmosphere. They've always been the haunts of Argentina's politicians, anarchists, intellectuals, artists and literary greats. **London City** (opposite) boasts that Julio Cortázar wrote his masterpiece *The Prizes* at one of its tables, while the **Richmond** (opposite) says Jorge Luis Borges drank hot chocolate there. The most famous is the **Café Tortoni** (p124), which is beautiful but way too touristy.

Most cafés offer a surprisingly wide range of food and drinks; you can order a steak as easily as a *cortado* (coffee with milk). Some double as bookstores or host live music, tango shows and other cultural events. Hanging out at one of these atmospheric cafés is part of the Buenos Aires experience – and also makes a welcome break from all that walking you'll be doing.

Clásica y Moderna (Map pp84–5; ☎ 4812-8707; Av Callao 892) Catering to the literary masses since 1938, this cozy and intimate bookstore-café continues to ooze history from its atmospheric brick walls. It's nicely lit, offers plenty of reading material and serves upscale meals. There are also regular live performances of folk music, jazz, bossa nova and tango.

Nucha (Map pp84–5; ☎ 4813-9507; Paraná 1343) There *must* be something in the tempting pastry counter – cheesecake, *medialunas* (croissants) or lightly layered afternoon cake – to go with your imported tea, iced coffee or *mate* at this cute café. Crowds flood in for afternoon tea, but breakfast is also served. Also at the corner of Maure and Migueletes in Las Cañitas.

Bars

In a city that never sleeps, finding a good drink (or cup of tea) is as easy as walking down the street. Whether you're into trendy lounges, Irish pubs, traditional cafés or sports bars, you'll find them all within the borders of Buenos Aires.

Argentines aren't huge drinkers and you'll be lucky to see one rip-roaring drunk. One thing they *do* do, however, is stay up late. Most bars and cafés are open until two or three in the morning, and often until 5am on weekends – or until the last customer stumbles out the door.

Many hotels and restaurants have great bars; try **Home Hotel** (p114) or **Casa Cruz** (☎ 4833-1112; Uriarte 1658). For the hippest scene in town, head to Plaza Serrano (in Palermo Viejo) and settle in at one of the many trendy bars surrounding the plaza.

Gibraltar (Map pp84–5; ☎ 4362-5310; Perú 895) One of BA's classic expat pubs, with cozy atmosphere and an excellent bar counter for those traveling alone. Great exotic food too – try the generous Thai, Indian or English dishes, or the sushi on Sunday. For a little friendly competition head to the pool table in back, grabbing a well-priced pint of beer along the way.

Mundo Bizarro (Map pp88–9; ☎ 4773-1967; Serrano 1222) This futuristically retro and stylishly slick lounge bar is open all night on weekends, when everything from old-time American music to hip DJs and jazz stir up the airwaves. Thursday night is ladies' night; if you feel lucky hop on the pole and grab some attention. For the hungry there are hamburgers, or sushi on Monday.

Milión (Map pp84–5; ☎ 4815-9925; Paraná 1048) This elegant and sexy bar is in a renovated mansion. The garden out back is a leafy paradise, overlooked by a solid balcony that holds the best seats in the house. There are elegant tapas to accompany the wide range of cocktails (pay first then catch the bartender's eye!), while downstairs a restaurant serves international dishes.

El Alamo (Map pp84–5; ☎ 4813-7060; Uruguay 1175) Open 24 hours a day all week long, El Alamo draws US expats with American football, baseball and basketball on TV. The music is good, there's pub food for the hungry and they've got a great way of attracting women – every day from noon to midnight, the ladies drink beer for free (really). Men have to pay – but only AR$5 per pint. Happy hour indeed.

Le Cigale (Map pp84–5; ☎ 4312-8275; 25 de Mayo 722) Sultry and moody downtown lounge very popular with both foreigners and *porteños*.

There's different music every night, with live bands on Thursdays and DJs on Saturday. But it's most popular on 'French Tuesday,' when electronica and French drinks draw the heavy crowds in.

Van Koning (Map pp88-9; ☎ 4772-9909; Av Báez 325) Great rustic spaces make this intimate Las Cañitas pub feel like the inside of a boat; after all, it's a 17th-century-style seafaring theme complete with dark-wood beams, flickering candles and blocky furniture. The bars on two floors serve 40 brews, with Heineken, Guinness and Quilmes on tap.

Rubia y Negra (Map pp84-5; ☎ 4313-1125; Libertad 1630) A true rarity in BA, this bar-restaurant also makes its own beer (eight kinds) – right on the premises. It's an upscale lounge sorta place however, so don't expect a homey pub-like atmosphere. Come on Monday, Tuesday or Saturday and see if the all-you-can-eat sushi (AR$55) goes with the suds.

El Carnal (Map pp88-9; ☎ 4772-7582; Niceto Vega 5511) The open-air roof patio, with its bamboo lounges and billowy curtains, can't be beat for a cool chill-out on a warm summer night. On Friday the reggae rocks, while Saturday means pop and '80s beats. Come earlier on for a meal down below.

Puerta Roja (Map pp84-5; ☎ 4362-5649; Chacabuco 733) There's no sign and you have to ring the bell, but once inside there's hot music and cool vibes, with low lounge furniture in the main room and a pool table tucked behind. Come early for a good seat and to munch on the excellent and cheap food options – there's little space to eat later, when the place starts to heave.

Debar (Map pp84-5; ☎ 4381-6876; Av Rivadavia 1132) A popular new bar in an area not known for its nightlife, Debar has some of BA's greatest rock and hip-hop beats. Businesspeople come for an after-work *trago* (drink), while travelers and expats hit it later in the evening. With a happy hour that runs until midnight every night, everyone is happy. Good DJs.

Congo (Map pp88-9; ☎ 4833-5857; Honduras 5329) The highlight at this beautiful and trendy bar is the back patio – *the* place to be seen on hot summer nights. The music is tops too, with DJs spinning from Wednesday to Saturday, and inside are elegant low lounges in creative spaces. Full food menu available, along with some tasty, stiff cocktails.

Kim y Novak (Map pp88-9; ☎ 4773-7521; Güemes 4900) Popular with the gay and expat crowds, this intimate corner bar has great *onda* (vibes). Come

before 2am if you want to chat, because it really gets packed in the early hours – especially later in the week when the basement dance floor opens. Strut your stuff any time on the stripper pole next to the counter for extra fun.

878 (Map pp88-9; ☎ 4773-1098; Thames 878) Enter into a wonderland of elegant, low lounge furniture and red-brick walls; if you're a whiskey lover, there are over 80 kinds to try. Tasty classic and original cocktails also lubricate the crowds, happy to revel in the jazz, bossa nova and good old rock music playing on the speakers.

ENTERTAINMENT

Nonstop Buenos Aires offers endless possibilities for entertainment. Dozens of venues offer first-rate theatrical productions, independent or contemporary movies, sultry tango shows, raging dance parties and exciting sports matches.

Most newspapers publish entertainment supplements on Friday; the *Buenos Aires Herald* does one in English called *Get Out*. Also check www.whatsupbuenosaires.com (in English) or www.adondevamos.com.

Major entertainment venues often require booking through Ticketek (☎ 5237-7200; www.ticketek.com.ar). The service charge is about 10% of the ticket price. At *carteleras* (discount ticket offices), you can buy tickets at 20% to 50% off for many entertainment events.

Cartelera Baires (Map pp84-5; ☎ 4372-5058; www.cartelera-net.com.ar; Av Corrientes 1382) In Cine Lorange.

LUNA PARK

If unique large-scale spectacles like the Beijing Circus, Tom Jones or the Pope come to town, Luna Park's dressing rooms are probably their destination. Originally a boxing stadium, **Luna Park** (Map pp84-5; ☎ 4324-1010; www.lunapark.com.ar; cnr Bouchard & Corrientes) has a capacity of 15,000 and hosted such historical moments as Carlos Gardel's wake (1935), Eva Duarte's meeting with Juan Perón (1944) and Diego Maradona's wedding (1989).

Other productions held here include fashion shows, ice-skating spectacles and mass religious baptisms, but Luna Park hasn't forgotten its roots; 25 boxing titles have been fought within the walls of this historic place, and even Ricky Martin can't match that record.

Cartelera Espectáculos (Map pp84-5; ☎ 4322-1559; www.123info.com.ar; Lavalle 742) Right on pedestrian Lavalle.
Cartelera Vea Más (Map pp84-5; ☎ 6320-5319; Paseo La Plaza, Local 2)

Tango

Tango is experiencing a renaissance, both at the amateur and professional levels and among all ages. Classes, *milongas* and shows are everywhere. For a wealth of information grab the free booklets *el tangauta* and *BA Tango*; they're often available from tango venues or tourist offices. Spanish-language website www.tango data.gov.ar also has lots of information, or try the bilingual www.letstango.com.ar.

Sensationalized tango shows aimed at tourists are common, and 'purists' don't consider them authentic – though this doesn't nec-

essarily make them bad. These shows cost around AR$175 (more with dinner included). Modest shows are more intimate and cost far less, but you won't get the theatrics, the costume changes or the overall visual punch.

For free (that is, donation) tango, head to Galerías Pacíficos, where there are daily performances in front on the pedestrian street. On Sunday in San Telmo, dancers do their thing in Plaza Dorrego (and it's *crowded* – watch your bag). Another good bet is weekends on Caminito in La Boca. All of these dancers are pretty good, so remember to toss some change into their hats.

For tango tours, check www.tangofocus .com or www.tangoafficionaldo.com. The following is a list of tango shows; for classes and *milongas*, see the boxed text, below.

MILONGAS & TANGO CLASSES

Tango classes are available just about everywhere, from youth hostels and cultural centers to all the *milongas* (dance halls or dance events). With so many foreigners flooding BA to learn the dance, many instructors now teach in English (group classes around AR$20).

Milongas start either in the afternoon or the evening. They're affordable, usually costing AR$12 to $20 entry. For a unique outdoor experience, head to the bandstand at the Barrancas de Belgrano, where the casual *milonga* 'La Glorieta' takes place on Sunday evenings at around 8pm (free tango lessons given earlier).

Confitería Ideal (Map pp84-5; ☎ 5265-8069; www.confiteriaideal.com; Suipacha 384) The mother of all historic tango halls, with many classes and *milongas* offered pretty much continuously. Live orchestras often accompany dancers; shows almost nightly (AR$40).

El Beso (Map pp84-5; ☎ 4953-2794; Riobamba 416) Another traditional and popular place that attracts some very good dancers. Located upstairs, with a good feel and a convenient bar as you enter.

Gricel (Map pp82-3; ☎ 4957-7157; www.clubgricel.com; La Rioja 1180) This old classic (far from the center, take a taxi) is open on weekends, attracting an older, well-dressed crowd. Wonderful dance floor and occasional live orchestras.

La Catedral (Map pp88-9; ☎ 15-5325-1630; Sarmiento 4006) If tango can be trendy and hip, this is where you'll find it. The grungy warehouse space is very casual, with funky art on the walls and jeans on the dancers. The best *milongas* are on Tuesdays and weekends.

La Marshall (Map pp84-5; ☎ 4912-9043; www.lamarshall.com.ar; Maipú 444) Everyone's welcome, but La Marshall is best known for its Tuesday night 'Tango Queer' – that's right, gay tango. Come at 10pm for a class, then at 11:30pm the *milonga* starts.

La Viruta (Map pp88-9; ☎ 4774-6357; www.lavirutatango.com; Armenia 1366) Located in the basement of the Asociación Cultural Armenia building. *Milongas* take place Wednesday through Sunday evenings. Good beginner tango classes are also available, as are tango shows.

Niño Bien (Map pp84-5; ☎ 4147-8687; Humberto Primo 1462) Takes place on Thursday and attracts a wide range of aficionados. It has beautiful atmosphere, a large ballroom and a good dance floor, but it still gets very crowded (come early and dress well). It's far from the center – take a taxi.

Salon Canning (Map pp88-9; ☎ 4832-6753; Av Scalabrini Ortiz 1331) Some of BA's finest dancers grace this traditional venue, with a great dance floor. Well-known tango company Parakultural (www.parakultural.com.ar) often stages good events here.

Sin Rumbo (Map pp82-3; ☎ 4571-9577; Tamborini 6157) One of the oldest tango joints in BA, Sin Rumbo has given rise to a few famous tango dancers. It's a local neighborhood place that attracts older professionals. Far from the center in Villa Urquiza; take a taxi.

Café Tortoni (Map pp84-5; ☎ 4342-4328; www.cafe tortoni.com.ar; Av de Mayo 829; show AR$40-50) Buenos Aires' landmark café has become overrun with tourists, but the tango shows are relatively good and still affordable. There are up to four shows nightly, but reserve ahead because they do fill up.

Café Homero (Map pp88-9; ☎ 4775-6763; www.cafe homero.cancionero.net; JA Cabrera 4946; shows AR$25-60) A cozy venue which features tango singers rather than dancers. It has great local flavor, and food is available; admission usually includes a drink. Tango sensation Adriana Varela has crooned here.

Centro Cultural Torquato Tasso (Map p91; ☎ 4307-6506; www.torquatotasso.com.ar; Defensa 1575; shows AR$10-20) One of BA's best live-music venues, with top-name tango *music* performances. Attracts bands that mix genres together, such as fusing tango or *folklore* with rock; keep an eye out for La Chicana, Sexteto Mayor or Fernández Fierro.

Piazzolla Tango (Map pp84-5; ☎ 4344-8201; www .piazzollatango.com; Florida 165; show & dinner AR$240, show only AR$180) This beautiful art nouveau theater used to be a red-light cabaret venue. Like at Ástor Piazzolla, the show here is a combination of old and new; it's based on tradition, but some moves are so athletic they seem more like circus acts.

El Balcón (Map pp84-5; ☎ 4362-2354; Humberto Primo 461, 1st fl) Located above Plaza Dorrego, this restaurant puts on free shows – but you have to order some food. Shows run Saturday at 10pm and on Sunday from 1pm to midnight.

Los 36 Billares (Map pp84-5; ☎ 4381-5696; www .los36billares.com.ar; Av de Mayo 1265; show AR$20) This traditional restaurant-bar is a good bet for cheap and atmospheric tango. A combination restaurant-café-bar-billiards-hall, it's been around for nearly 100 years, boasting pool tables in back and billiards tables in the basement. No shows Monday.

Boca Tango (Map p91; ☎ 4302-0808; www.boca tango.com.ar; Brandsen 923; show & dinner AR$240, show only AR$170) Pre-show theatrics include interacting with performers at a miniature representation of La Boca's colorful neighborhood, set up outside the main theater. Dinner is at a nearby casual dining room. Transport is included, fortunate since La Boca is an edgy barrio.

El Querandí (Map pp84-5; ☎ 5199-1770; www.querandi .com.ar; Perú 302; show & dinner AR$250, show only AR$175) This large corner tango venue is also an el-

egant restaurant with an upscale atmosphere. The excellent show is one of the better ones in town, taking you through the evolution of tango over the years. One plus is a high stage, which makes viewing easier.

Esquina Homero Manzi (Map pp82-3; ☎ 4957-8488; www.esquinahomeromanzi.com.ar; Av San Juan 3601; show & dinner AR$260, show only AR$145) An impressively refurbished old café, Homero Manzi was named after one of Argentina's most famous tango lyricists. Today you can take tango lessons here, then sit back and watch the show.

Esquina Osvaldo Pugliese (Map pp82-3; ☎ 4931-2142; Boedo 909; show AR$12-18) Also called Recuerdo Café, this casual venue has a small stage in more modest surroundings, with just a few performers doing the fancy footwork. It's at a fraction of the price of Homero Manzi's much fancier tango show, just a block away.

Nightclubs

BA's *boliches* (discos) are the throbbing heart of its world-famous nightlife. To be cool, don't arrive before 2am (or even 3am) and dress as stylishly as you can. Taking a nap before dinner helps keep you up all night. Admission sometimes includes a drink; women often pay less than men. Payment for admission and drinks is nearly always in cash only. Some clubs offer dinners and shows before the dancing starts.

Check out the website www.brandongay day.com.ar for current raves; there are many such last-minute parties happening in BA at any one time, so ask around. Massively popular annual event-parties include October's **South American Music Conference** (see p108) and November's **Creamfields** (see p108).

Asia de Cuba (Map pp84-5; ☎ 4894-1328; www.asia decuba.com.ar; Dealessi 750, Puerto Madero Este; ☾ nightly) An overpriced Puerto Madero restaurant by day, this beautiful spot turns into a flashy and snobby nightclub after midnight. Eclectic music, ranging from old hits and disco to Latin house, is a big draw for the dressy crowds, an even mix of tourists and Argentines. Breezy outside lounges offer romantic views of the dikes. Avoid the cover charge by grabbing dinner there beforehand.

Crobar (Map pp88-9; ☎ 4778-1500; Cnr Paseo de la Infanta Isabel & Freyre; ☾ Fri & Sat) The current darling of the Buenos Aires club world. Friday nights always feature international DJs mashing up the latest electronic selections, while Saturday has more commercial beats. There's also a back room for those who prefer classic rock, '80s remixes and occasional live bands, while the main levels are strewn with mezzanines and walkways for those perfect viewpoints.

Niceto Club (Map pp88-9; ☎ 4779-9396; www.nicetoclub .com; Niceto Vega 5510; 🕑 Thu-Sat) One of the city's biggest crowd-pullers, the can't-miss event at Niceto Club is Thursday night's Zizek. This cutting-edge DJ extravaganza features creative new sounds blending hip-hop, dancehall and electronic beats with cumbia, reggae, *folklore* and even Aboriginal chants. The artsy video installations are pretty cool too.

Club Aráoz (Map pp88-9; ☎ 4832-9751; www.araoz -club.com.ar; Aráoz 2424; 🕑 Thu-Sat) Also known as 'Lost,' this small club's finest hour is on Thursday, when hip-hop rules the roost and the regulars start break-dancing around 2am. It's popular with young Americans, and there's no dress code – a good thing, since it gets hot and sweaty. A great casual place to hang with friends, and drinks are well-priced as well.

Pachá (Map pp88-9; ☎ 4788-4280; www.pachabuenos aires.com; near cnr Av Costanera Norte & La Pampa; 🕑 Fri & Sat) Famous guest DJs from countries such as Israel and Germany spin tunes for the youthful, spruced-up and snobby crowds at this huge club. Laser lightshows and a great sound system keep the blissed-out masses entranced. Saturday nights are best, but don't come until after 4am – giving you time to party watching the sunrise on the terrace (bring your shades).

Museum (Map pp84-5; ☎ 4543-3894; Perú 535; 🕑 Wed, Fri & Sat) This cavernous disco is best known for its Wednesday night 'after-office' party, which starts at 8pm. It's a huge space with multiple balconies and a great sound system. Saturday nights feature incredible light shows and house music. Note the amazing building, an old factory designed by Eiffel (who also did that Parisian landmark).

Bahrein (Map pp84-5; ☎ 4314-8886; Lavalle 345; 🕑 Tue-Sat) Bahrein is hugely popular for its Tuesday night drum 'n' bass parties – highlighted with fast, aggressive electronic rhythms by resident DJ Bad Boy Orange. Trance, house and popular tunes round out the music menu, while an elegant upstairs restaurant provides much-needed energy. The club used to be a bank; check out the basement 'vault.'

Rumi (Map pp88-9; ☎ 4782-1307; Av Figuero Alcorta 6442; 🕑 Wed-Sat) If you're looking for glamour, fashion and possible celebrity sightings, then ultracool Rumi is your mecca. Dress well to satisfy the picky bouncers, then enter into a wonderland of electronica, hip-hop and house beats. Famous DJs spin on Wednesday night's Batonga party, but weekends are equally popular.

Maluco Beleza (Map pp84-5; ☎ 4372-1737; Sarmiento 1728; 🕑 Wed, Fri-Sun) Located in an old mansion is this popular Brazilian *boliche*. It gets really packed with crowds happily grinding to samba fusion music and watching lithe, half-naked dancers squirming on the stage. Upstairs it's darker and more laid-back. If you're craving Brazilian cuisine, get here at 8pm on Wednesday for the dinner.

Mint (Map pp88-9; ☎ 4771-5870; cnr Avs Costanera R Obligado & Sarmiento; 🕑 Fri & Sat) One of the older clubs in BA, Mint is still very fashionable with the beautiful people. Big-name DJs spin a good mix of hip-hop, electronica and trance to keep the young crowds riled, but beats can be loungey as well. The awesome riverside patio is best for kicking back. Friday nights are best, but don't get here earlier than 2am.

Classical Music

Teatro Colón (Map pp84-5; ☎ 4378-7344; www.teatrocolon .org.ar; Libertad 621) BA's premier venue for the arts, Teatro Colón has hosted prominent figures like Placido Domingo and Luciano Pavarotti. There's also ballet, opera and occasional free concerts. See also p98.

La Scala de San Telmo (Map pp84-5; ☎ 4362-1187; www.lascala.org.ar; Pasaje Giuffra 371) This small San Telmo venue puts on classical and contemporary concerts featuring piano, tango, musical comedy and musical-related workshops.

Teatro Avenida (Map pp84-5; ☎ 4384-0519; www.bali rica.org.ar; Av de Mayo 1222) This beautiful 1906 venue highlights mostly classical music, ballet and flamenco – but its biggest strength is opera.

Teatro San Martín (Map pp84-5; ☎ 0800-333-5254; www.teatrosanmartin.com.ar; Av Corrientes 1530) Along with art exhibitions, ballet, photography, cinema and theater, this large complex also hosts classical ensembles.

Teatro Coliseo (Map pp84-5; ☎ 4816-3789; www .fundacioncoliseo.com.ar; MT de Alvear 1125) Classical arts entertain here, with occasional surprises like Argentine-American rock star Kevin Johansen.

Live Music

ROCK & BLUES

The following are smaller venues that showcase mostly local groups; international stars tend to play at large venues like soccer stadiums or Luna Park (p122). Blues isn't as popular as rock, but still has its own loyal following.

La Trastienda (Map pp84-5; ☎ 5237-7200 for Ticketek; Balcarce 460; ☺ nightly) The large theater in the back of the restaurant here can entertain over 700 people, and showcases all sorts of live groups (mostly rock). Look for headers like Charlie Garcia, Los Divididos, Marilyn Manson and the Wailers.

Mitos Argentinos (Map pp84-5; ☎ 4362-7810; Humberto Primo 489; ☺ Wed-Sun) This cozy old brick house in San Telmo has lots of tables, a perfectly sized stage and a small balcony above. Known for its tributes to *rock nacional* (Argentine rock) bands. Limited dinner options can include all-you-can-drink.

Blues Special Club (Map p91; ☎ 4854-2338; Av Almirante Brown 102; ☺ Fri & Sat) Friday at this good-sized, semi-artsy venue is great for jam sessions; on Saturday at midnight the shows really start rockin'. Blues folk like Dave Meyers, Phil Guy, Eddie King and Aaron Burton have played here.

ND/Ateneo (Map pp84-5; ☎ 4328-2888; Paraguay 918; ☺ nightly) Theater with good acoustics and quality concerts, especially rock, jazz and folk. Also puts on films, theater and other artsy

GAY & LESBIAN BA

There is a live and kicking gay scene in BA, and it's become even livelier since December 2002, when Argentina became Latin America's first country to legalize same-sex unions. This is likely one reason Buenos Aires has outstripped Rio as South America's number one gay destination. And while BA's November Marcha del Orgullo Gay (gay pride parade; www.marchadelorgullo.org.ar) is pretty limited for now, other gay-oriented events – like an annual film festival (www.diversa.com.ar) and even a tango festival (www.festivaltangoqueer.com.ar) – have popped up. Let's not forget either that the 2007 gay World Cup took place here (www.iglfa2007.org).

For general information, there's **Lugar Gay** (p111) in San Telmo. It's a B&B but also acts as an information center and organizes activities for guests and nonguests alike. Other resources include **Grupo Nexo** (☎ 4374-4484; www.nexo.org) and **Comunidad Homosexual Argentina** (CHA; ☎ 4361-6382; www.cha.org.ar). The travel agency **Pride Travel** (Map pp84-5; ☎ 5218-6556; www.pride -travel.com; Paraguay 523, 2E) helps with travel plans. Gay websites in English include www.thegayguide .com.ar and www.buenosaires.queercity.info.

There are quite a few choices for gay-owned accommodations, such as **Casa Bolivar** (p111), the **Axel Hotel** (p111) and **Lugar Gay** (p111). For long-term apartments, check www.friendly apartments.com.ar.

There's lots of gay-oriented literature; keep an eye out for *Gay Maps*, *La Otra Guía* and *The Ronda*, available at many businesses. Heftier magazines such as *Guapo* and *Imperio* can be bought at newsstands.

There is plenty of nightlife to keep you out all night long. Gay-friendly restaurants include fancy **Chueca** (Map pp88-9; ☎ 4834-6373; Honduras 5255), **Empire Bar** (p117), **Rave** (Map pp88-9; ☎ 4833-7832; Gorriti 5092) and **La Farmacia** (Map pp84-5; ☎ 4300-6151; Bolívar 898).

Popular gay bars include the glitzy **Bulnes Class** (☎ 4861-7492; Bulnes 1250), loud **Sitges** (☎ 4861- 3763; Av Córdoba 4119) and casual **Flux** (☎ 5252-0258; MT de Alvear 980). **Pride Café** (p116) and **Kim y Novak** (p122) attract mixed crowds, while **Casa Brandon** (Map pp88-9; ☎ 4858-0610; LM Drago 236; ☺ Wed-Sun) is a restaurant-bar-art-gallery.

For clubbing, rough-and-tumble **Amerika** (Map pp88-9; ☎ 4865-4416; Gascón 1040; ☺ Thu-Sun), sexy **Glam** (Map pp88-9; ☎ 4963-2521; José Antonio Cabrera 3046; ☺ Thu-Sat) and fantasy-like **Alsina** (Map pp84-5; ☎ 4331-3231; Adolfo Alsina 940; ☺ Fri & Sat) are some of the best venues. Ask around for the most current hot gay cruising spots or parties, or check www.brandongayday.com.ar.

Lesbians don't have nearly as much choice as gay men. There's the long-running, intimate **Bach Bar** (Cabrera 4390) and, for dancing, trendy **Verona** (Map pp84-5; ☎ 15-5427-2962; Hipólito Yrigoyen 968; ☺ Fri & Sat) – best on Saturdays.

Finally, gay classes and *milongas* are given at **La Marshall** (see p123), **Tango Queer** (www .tangoqueer.com); Central Buenos Aires Perú 571; Palermo Luis María Drago 236) and Lugar Gay (p111).

shows, and in 2008 hosted the Buenos Aires International Jazz Festival.

El Samovar de Rasputín (Map p91; ☎ 4302-3190; Del Valle Iberlucea 1232; ⊗ Fri & Sat) Located across from its original location (where there are photos of Napo, the hippie-ish owner, with Keith Richards, Eric Clapton and Pavarotti). Argentine bands entertain with rock and blues most of the time. Bus 29 gets you here from the city center.

JAZZ

Clásica y Moderna (p121) occasionally hosts jazz groups.

Thelonious Bar (Map pp88-9; ☎ 4829-1562; Salguero 1884; ⊗ Fri & Sat) Cozily ensconced on the 2nd floor of an old mansion, this intimate, dimly lit and artsy jazz bar has high brick ceilings and a good sound system. Great jazz lineups, with DJs entertaining into the early morning hours. Come early for dinner and good seats.

Notorious (Map pp84-5; ☎ 4815-8473; Av Callao 966; ⊗ nightly) Slick and intimate, this is one of BA's premier jazz venues. Up front is a CD store; in back, the restaurant-café (overlooking a verdant garden) hosts live jazz shows every night.

FLAMENCO & FOLK

With so many *porteños* boasting Spanish ancestry, it's not surprising that there are a few flamenco venues in town. Most are located in Congreso's Spanish neighborhood, near the intersection of Salta and Av de Mayo.

Música folklórica also has its place in BA. There are several *peñas* (folk-music clubs) in the city, but other venues occasionally host folk music – keep your eyes peeled.

Cantares (Map pp84-5; ☎ 4381-6965; www.cantarestablao.com.ar; Av Rivadavia 1180; shows AR$35-65; ⊗ Wed-Sun) This intimate flamenco venue once hosted the Spanish poet Federico García Lorca. Dances are highly authentic. Either drinks or tapas are included; reserve ahead.

Ávila Bar (Map pp84-5; ☎ 4383-6974; Av de Mayo 1384; dinner-shows AR$70-90 ⊗ Wed-Sat) Long-running and cozy Spanish restaurant with pricey shows, but tasty meals are thrown in. Reserve on weekends.

Tiempo de Gitanos (Map pp88-9; ☎ 4776-6143; www.tiempodegitanos.com.ar; El Salvador 5575; dinner-shows AR$60-80 ⊗ Wed-Sun) This Palermo Hollywood venue offers excellent flamenco shows in an intimate restaurant setting, but – unlike the dancing – the tapas and seafood paella might be less than authentic. Reserve in advance.

Guayana (Map pp84-5; ☎ 4381-4350; Lima 27; min consumption AR$15; ⊗ daily, shows Fri & Sat) For great local working-class flavor, try this nondescript *confitería* with cheap food and surprisingly good music. Live tango and folk tunes play from 10pm on Friday and Saturday night. Reserve a table on Saturday night.

La Peña del Colorado (Map pp88-9; ☎ 4822-1038; Güemes 3657; ⊗ nightly) Nightly folkloric shows are awesome at this rustic, brick-and-stucco restaurant-bar, and afterwards audience members pick up nearby guitars to make their own entertainment. Try the tasty northern Argentine food, and wash it down with *mate*.

Theater

Av Corrientes, between Avs 9 de Julio and Callao, has traditionally been the capital's center for theater, but there are now dozens of venues throughout the city. The following venues include both the traditional and the alternative. See also Teatro Colón (p125) and Teatro San Martín (p125).

Abasto Social Club (Map pp88-9; ☎ 4862-7205; www.abastosocialclub.com; Humahuaca 3649) A small venue with weekend performances and concerts, along with a café-bar. Various classes and workshops.

Cuidad Cultural Konex (Map pp88-9; ☎ 4864-3200; www.ciudadculturalkonex.org; Sarmiento 3131) Has multidisciplinary performances that often fuse art, culture and technology. Amazing Monday-night percussion shows.

El Camarín de las Musas (Map pp88-9; ☎ 4862-0655; www.elcamarindelasmusas.com.ar; Mario Bravo 960) Trendy venue offering contemporary dance, plays and theatrical workshops. There's a good café in front.

Espacio Callejón (Map pp88-9; ☎ 4862-1167; www.callejonteatro.com.ar; Humahuaca 3759) A small independent venue showcasing new theater, music and dance, and offers a few classes.

Teatro Cervantes (Map pp84-5; ☎ 4816-4224; www.teatrocervantes.gov.ar; Libertad 815) Architecturally gorgeous theater featuring three halls, a grand lobby and red-velvet chairs – but could use a facelift. Has good productions at affordable prices. See also p101.

Teatro del Pueblo (Map pp84-5; ☎ 4326-3606; www.teatrodelpueblo.org.ar; Diagonal Roque Saénz Peña 943) Small independent theater with both classical and contemporary productions.

Teatro Gran Rex (Map pp84-5; ☎ 4322-8000; Av Corrientes 857) A huge theater seating 3,500, this place hosts a myriad of musical productions, from Cyndi Lauper to Kenny G.

Teatro Presidente Alvear (Map pp84-5; ☎ 4374-6076; www.teatrosanmartin.com.ar; Av Corrientes 1659)

GOING TO A FÚTBOL GAME   David Labi

In the land where Maradona is God, going to see a *futból* (soccer) match is a religious experience. The *superclásico* match between the two classic *porteño* teams, Boca Juniors and River Plate, has been called the number-one sporting event to do before you die; but even the less-celebrated games will give you an insight into a national passion.

Barring summer (January through February) and winter (July through August) breaks, two leagues and two international cup competitions provide plenty of opportunities every year for viewing silky ball-skills and learning some colorful vocabulary that you won't find in any phrasebook.

If you want to see a *clásico* – a match between two of the major teams – it is inadvisable to go to the stadium to buy tickets. People will have been waiting there all night, and the atmosphere is not exactly friendly. This goes triple for the *superclásico* itself. Instead, go with an agency (see Tangol, p95) or make (very good) friends with an Argentine who is a *socio* (member) of the club and therefore has priority in getting tickets.

But for smaller games, it's perfectly easy to get your own ticket. Keep an eye on the clubs' websites, which inform when and where tickets will be sold. This can be on match-day itself or up to a week in advance, and mostly at the stadium. Some clubs sell tickets for certain games online, at www.ticketek.com.ar.

Tickets for *populares* (terraces/bleachers) usually cost AR$14, and for *plateas* (seated stands) will range from AR$25 to AR$150. Agencies tend to charge more.

Try not to look too conspicuous when you go. Take just the money you need, don't bring anything of value, and don't flash your camera around. You probably won't get in with water bottles, and the food and drink sold in the stadium is meager, bad and expensive. You might be in the sun all day, so bring lotion and a hat. And most important – make sure you don't wear the opposing team's colors. Perhaps gray is the safest bet?

Bearing this in mind, you're ready to have some fun! The *superclásico* is justly the most famous game: get there hours before kick-off to witness the insane build-up. You can feel the Boca stadium, dubbed the *bombonera* (chocolate box) because of its shape, shake as the crowd jumps. And you might even glimpse God himself swinging his shirt above his head, in his special seat above an enormous hanging portrait. That's Maradona, just to make it clear.

David Labi is the editor of BA Insider magazine.

Inaugurated in 1942 and named after an Argentine president whose wife sang opera, this theater holds over 700 people and shows many musical productions, including tango.

Cinemas

BA is full of cinemas, both historical neon classics and slick modern multiplexes. The traditional cinema districts are along pedestrian Lavalle (west of Florida) and on Av Corrientes, but newer cineplexes are spread throughout the city; most large shopping malls have one. Tickets cost AR$12 to AR$17; matinees and midweek shows are cheapest.

Check out the *Buenos Aires Herald* for original titles of English-language films. Except for kids' films, most movies remain in their original language (with Spanish subtitles).

Sports

Fútbol is a national obsession, and witnessing a live game is part of the BA experience; see the boxed text, above, for pointers. For specifics on Argentine *fútbol*, check www.afa.org.ar and www.futbolargentino.com.ar (both in Spanish).

The most popular clubs are **Boca Juniors** (Map p91; ☎ 4362-2260; www.bocajuniors.com.ar; Brandsen 805) and **River Plate** (Map pp82-3; ☎ 4789-1200; www.cariverplate.com.ar; Presidente Figueroa Alcorta 7597), but Buenos Aires has two dozen professional football teams – the most of any city in the world.

Other popular spectator sports include rugby, basketball, polo and field hockey. *Pato* (like rugby on horseback) deserves an honorable mention for being the most 'traditional.'

SHOPPING

Despite a major drop in the purchasing power of the Argentine peso over the last few years, Buenos Aires' citizens continue to shop as if there's no tomorrow. Just a peek into the nearest mall on a weekend will make you wonder how people who seem to be making so little can spend so much. As the saying goes, 'An Argentine will make one peso and spend two.'

In the Microcentro, Florida is a multipurpose pedestrian strip that buzzes with shoppers, while Av Santa Fe is a bit less pedestrian-friendly but equally prominent as the city's main shopping artery. San Telmo is ground zero for antiques, and Av Pueyrredón near Once train station is *the* place for cheap (and low-quality) clothing. Jewelry shops are found on Libertad south of Corrientes. For the most unique and avant garde fashions, Palermo Viejo is the place to be. Here the city's youthful and up-and-coming designers have set up shop alongside trendy boutiques (not to mention dozens of fashionable restaurants). Not only are the fashions creative and beautiful, but compared with the US and Europe they're an absolute bargain.

As in other western countries, bargaining is not acceptable in most stores. High-price items like jewelry and leather jackets can be exceptions, especially if you buy several. At street markets you can try negotiating for better prices – just keep in mind you may be talking to the artists themselves, who generally don't make much money. San Telmo's antiques fair is an exception; prices here are often inflated for tourists.

One thing to be aware of is whether you're quoted in pesos or dollars. Most sellers quote in pesos, but a few unscrupulous ones switch to dollars after striking a deal. Make sure of your position if you have any doubts.

Antiques & Art

Gil Antiguedades (Map pp84-5; ☎ 4361-5019; Humberto Primo 412; ☻ 11am-1pm & 3-7pm Tue-Sun) Find antiques galore here, including baby dolls, china plates, old lamps, feather fans, Jesus figures and huge glass bottles. Best of all is the basement – it's stuffed with some amazing vintage clothing and accessories. Catherine Deneuve and Ferragamo have graced the aisles here.

Imhotep (Map pp84-5; ☎ 4862-9298; Defensa 916; ☻ 11am-6pm Sun-Fri) Come find the funkiest old knickknacks at this eccentric shop. Small oddities such as Indian statuettes, ceramic skulls, Chinese snuff boxes, precious stone figurines and gargoyles make up some of the bizarre trinkets here. Larger prize finds may include a boar's head and slot machine.

En Buen Orden (Map pp84-5; ☎ 011-15-5936-2820; Defensa 894; ☻ 11am-7pm) If you like sorting through endless shelves full of knickknacks such as old jewelry, little medals, old lace, musty shoes and antique figurines, then this place is for you.

Mercado de las Pulgas (Map pp88-9; cnr Álvarez Thomas & Dorrego; ☻ 10am-7pm Tue-Sun) This dusty and dim covered flea market sells antiques such as old furniture, glass soda bottles, ceramic vases, paintings, bird cages, elegant mirrors and metal garden furniture. Temporarily located just a block north of its permanent location, but in the future should return to its old premises at Álvarez Thomas and Dorrego.

Appetite (Map pp84-5; ☎ 4331-5405; Chacabuco 551; ☻ 2-7pm Mon-Sat) To see what's happening in the contemporary erotic art world, take a peek into this grungy space and expect fantasy, sexual and sometimes violent themes. For more of this, head around the corner to its sister gallery at Venezuela 638.

Galería Ruth Benzacar (Map pp84-5; ☎ 4313-8480; Florida 1000; ☻ 11:30am-8pm Mon-Fri, 10:30am-1:30pm Sat) The first contemporary art gallery in BA, this underground space shows off internationally known Argentine artists like Leandro Erlich, Jorge Macchi, Flavia Darin and Nicola Costantino. You're welcome to show up and have a look around.

Camping Equipment

Camping Center (Map pp84-5; ☎ 4314-0305; Esmeralda 945; ☻ 10am-8pm Mon-Fri, to 5pm Sat) This modern store carries new, high-quality camping and mountaineering equipment, rock-climbing gear and general backpacking products. There's also plenty of expensive, outdoor name-brand clothing from the USA.

BUENOS AIRES STREET MARKETS

Some of BA's best crafts and souvenirs are sold at its many street markets, often by the artists themselves. You may have to sort through some tacky kitsch, but you'll also find creative and original art. A plus is the 'free' (donation) entertainment from buskers and mimes.

Feria Artesanal (Map pp84–5; Plaza Intendente Alvear; 🕑 10am-7pm) Recoleta's hugely popular fair, with hundreds of booths and a range of creative goods. Hippies, mimes and tourists mingle; nearby restaurants provide refreshment. Biggest on weekends; located just outside the cemetery.

Feria de Mataderos (Map pp82–3; ☎ 4323-9532; www.feriademataderos.com.ar; cnr Avs Lisandro de la Torre & de los Corrales; 🕑 11am-9pm Sun & holidays Apr-Nov, 6pm-midnight Sat Dec-March) This unique market is far off in the barrio of Mataderos. There are shows of horsemanship, folk dancing and cheap authentic treats to be had. From downtown, take bus 155, 180 or 126 (one hour); taxis cost about AR$30.

Feria de San Telmo (Map pp84–5; Plaza Dorrego; 🕑 10am-5pm Sun) Locals and tourists alike come to this wonderful *feria*; you'll find antique seltzer bottles, jewelry, artwork, vintage clothing, collectibles and donation tango shows. Lots of fun, but keep an eye on your wallet.

Feria Plaza Belgrano (Map pp82–3; cnr Juramento & Cuba; 🕑 10am-8pm Sat, Sun & holidays) Belgrano's pleasant market is great on a sunny weekend. You'll find high-quality imaginative crafts, as well as some kitschy junk. Good for families as it's calmer and less touristy than more central *ferias*.

Feria Plaza Serrano (Map pp88–9; Plaza Serrano; 🕑 noon-7pm Sat-Sun) Costume jewelry, hand-knit tops, funky clothes, hippie bags and leather accessories fill the crafts booths at this small but lively fair on fashionable Plaza Serrano in Palermo Viejo.

Montagne (Map pp84–5; ☎ 4312-9041; Florida 719; 🕑 10am-8:30pm Mon-Sat, noon-8pm Sun) This shop sells outdoor clothing that is stylish, good quality and made in Argentina. Choose from a small selection of tents, backpacks and camping gear upstairs. There are several other Montagne branches.

Wildlife (Map pp84–5; ☎ 4381-1040; Hipólito Yrigoyen 1133; 🕑 10am-8pm Mon-Fri, 10am-1pm Sat) Crampons, knives, tents, backpacks, climbing ropes, foul-weather clothing and military gear can be found at this somewhat musty-smelling place. Sell your stuff here too.

Children

Recursos Infantiles (Map pp88–9; ☎ 4834-6177; Borges 1766; 🕑 3-8pm Mon, 8am-8pm Tue-Sun) Small but fun, this kids' store offers some pretty unique toys – and all are made in Argentina. Books in Spanish and a small rack of cute clothes keep mom busy, and a tiny café on the premises caters to hungry little bellies.

Owoko (Map pp88–9; ☎ 4502-9905; El Salvador 4694; 🕑 11am-8pm Mon-Sat, 3-7pm Sun) Every purchase at this small kids' clothes store comes with a free story booklet about Planet Owoko and its colorful characters, who are (conveniently) immortalized on cute T-shirts, pants and accessories.

Clothing & Accessories

Moebius (Map p91; ☎ 4361-2893; Defensa 1356; 🕑 10:30am-1:30pm & 3-8pm Tue-Sat, noon-8:30pm Sun)

Highly original bags, 'ugly' dolls, retro knick-knacks and ingeniously designed women's clothes are highlights here, but you'll never know exactly what you'll find. The recycled-material items are always the most fun.

Gabriella Capucci (Map pp84–5; ☎ 4815-3636; Av Alvear 1477; 🕑 10am-8pm Mon-Sat) All-original sequined T-shirts, wispy scarves, vintage tops, velvet pillows and eclectic accessories fill this girly boutique. Crocheted flowers decorate camouflage, satin and animal prints, and the costume jewelry is wild.

Hermanos Estebecorena (Map pp88–9; ☎ 4772-2145; El Salvador 5960; 🕑 11am-1pm & 1:30-9pm Mon-Fri, 11am-9pm Sat) The Estebecorena brothers apply their highly creative skills toward original, highly stylish, very functional men's clothing that makes the artsy types swoon. Selection is limited, but what's there really counts.

Bolivia (Map pp88–9; ☎ 4832-6284; Gurruchaga 1581; 🕑 11am-8pm Mon-Sat, 3-8pm Sun) There's almost nothing here that your young, hip and possibly gay brother wouldn't love, from the striped cut-off cowboy shirts to the floral Puma sneakers to the Mexican-bag-fabric plastic belts. Metrosexual to the hilt, and paradise for the man who isn't afraid of patterns, plaid or pastels.

Objeto (Map pp88–9; ☎ 4834-6866; Gurruchaga 1649; 🕑 11am-8pm Mon-Sat) The designers here display some of the wackiest, most outrageously fun clothes in town. Outfits are less frilly and more substantial than most of their *porteño* designer colleagues – think of dresses with multiple patterns accented with cartoons or silhouetted figures. Great gear for parties.

Rapsodia (Map pp88-9; ☎ 4832-5363; El Salvador 4757; ☯ 10am-8pm Mon-Sat, noon-9pm Sun) With fabrics from linen to leather, street casual to sequins, this larger boutique shop is a must for fashion mavens. There are cutting-edge jeans, wild bikinis and even a small kids' section, plus sofas for the guys.

Nadine Zlotogora (Map pp88-9; ☎ 4831-4203; El Salvador 4683; ☯ 11am-8pm Mon-Sat) Nadine Z's gorgeous dresses and tops combine feminine styles with nearly magical fabrics, creating fantastically romantic wearables. Thick and billowy base textiles are layered with lacy tulle and silky edging – a feast for the eyes as well as the skin.

Crafts & Souvenirs

Kelly's Regionales (Map pp84-5; ☎ 4311-5712; Paraguay 431; ☯ 10am-8pm Mon-Fri, to 3pm Sat) Cowhides, Mapuche ponchos, animal masks, alpaca knives and *mate* gourds are all good ethnic buys at this large souvenir shop, but plenty of cheap souvenir knickknacks also line the shelves.

Atípica (Map pp88-9; ☎ 4833-3344; El Salvador 4510; ☯ 2-8pm Mon-Fri, 11am-8pm Sat) This tiny shop stocks crafts from Argentine artists who use indigenous techniques for their works. All are handmade and unique, and include picture frames, wall hangings, mask replicas, gourd bowls, small boxes, textiles and jewelry. Quality is high and prices fair.

Housewares

Cualquier Verdura (Map pp84-5; ☎ 4300-2474; Humberto Primo 517; ☯ noon-8pm Thu-Sun) Located in a lovely, refurbished old house, this very fun store sells eclectic items from vintage clothing to entertaining soaps to recycled floppy-disc lamps to novelty toys. Note the *mate*-drinking Buddha above the fountain in the patio.

Calma Chicha (☎ 4831-1818; Honduras 4925; ☯ 10am-8pm Mon-Sat, noon-8pm Sun) Big on leather, this fun household spot has a variety of butterfly chair styles and brightly-colored cowhide rugs. Penguin pitchers, flowery plastic tablecloths and thick sheepskins are other must-haves. Also has a branch (Map pp84-5; Defensa 856) in San Telmo.

Music

El Ateneo (Map pp84-5; ☎ 4325-6801; Florida 340; ☯ 9am-10pm Mon-Fri, to 5pm Sat) Buenos Aires' landmark bookseller stocks a limited number of books in English (including Lonely Planet guidebooks) and also has a decent selection of music CDs. There are several branches within the city, including a gorgeous branch in the Gran Splendid, an old renovated cinema (Map pp84–5; Av Santa Fe 1860). Hours vary by store.

Musimundo (Map pp84-5; ☎ 4322-9298; Corrientes; ☯ 10am-9pm) With over 50 branches throughout the city, this is BA's largest music retailer; listening stations make selecting the hippest CDs a snap. There are many branches throughout the city; some sell event tickets as well.

Zival's (Map pp84-5; ☎ 5128-7500; www.tangostore.com; Av Callao 395; ☯ 9:30am-10pm Mon-Sat) One of the better music stores in town, especially when it comes to tango, jazz and classical music. Listening stations and a big sale rack are pluses, and it'll ship CDs, DVDs and sheet music abroad too (check the website). Also in Palermo Viejo at Serrano 1445 (see Map pp88–9).

Shoes & Leather Goods

Casa López (Map pp84-5; ☎ 4311-3044; MT de Alvear 640/658; ☯ 9am-8pm) Start up the limousine and make sure there's enough room for some of BA's finest selection of quality leather jackets, luggage, bags and accessories. A downside: service is almost too attentive. Another branch is at Galerías Pacífico (p132).

Mishka (Map pp84-5; ☎ 4833-6566; El Salvador 4673; ☯ 11am-8pm Mon-Sat) Well-regarded designer Chelo Cantón was an architect in a previous incarnation, but now creates glittery, low-heeled shoes with a retro-hip, feminine and slightly conservative vibe. Boots and booties are also on the plank but don't seem quite as cool.

Rossi y Carusso (Map pp84-5; ☎ 4814-4774; Av Santa Fe 1377; ☯ 9:30am-8pm Mon-Fri, 10am-7pm Sat) Fine leather goods line the shelves at this upscale shop. Choose from fancy boots, belts, bags, saddles, gaucho knives and the occasional silver *mate* vessel. All are made from Argentine materials, and most are exclusive designs.

Shopping Malls

Alto Palermo (Map pp88-9; ☎ 5777-8000; Av Coronel Díaz 2098; ☯ 10am-10pm) This popular, shiny mall offers dozens of clothing shops, bookstores, jewelry boutiques, and electronics and houseware stores. Look for Timberland, Lacoste, Hilfiger and Levis (plus many Argentine brands too).

Services include a food court, cinema complex and a good kids' area on the 3rd floor.

Mercado de Abasto (Map pp88-9; ☎ 4959-3400; cnr Corrientes & Anchorena; ☺ 10am-10pm) One of the most beautiful malls in BA, this remodeled old market holds more than 200 shops, a large cinema, a covered plaza, a kosher McDonald's, a good children's museum and even a small amusement park.

Buenos Aires Design (Map pp84-5; ☎ 5777-6000; Av Pueyrredón 2501; ☺ 10am-9pm Mon-Sat, noon-9pm Sun) The trendiest and finest home furnishings are all under one roof here. This is the ideal place to look for that snazzy light fixture, streamlined toilet or reproduction Asian chair. Also good for everyday appliances and housewares, along with cute décor and a few knickknacks.

Galerías Pacífico (Map pp84-5; ☎ 5555-5110; cnr Florida & Av Córdoba; ☺ 10am-9pm Mon-Sat, noon-9pm Sun) Centrally located right on pedestrian Florida, this gorgeous mall is always full of shoppers and tourists. Murals on the ceiling were painted by famous artists; for more information, see p96. Donation tango shows often play outside.

Galería Bond (Map pp84-5; Av Santa Fe 1670; ☺ 10am-9pm Mon-Sat) For the edgiest tattoos and piercings in town, you can't beat this grungy shopping center. Buenos Aires' skateboarder-wanna-bes and punk rockers come here to shop for the latest styles and sounds. Expect everything from Hello Kitty to heavy metal.

Wine

Winery (Map pp84-5; ☎ 4311-6607; Av Leandro N Alem 880; ☺ 9am-8:30pm Mon-Sat) One of several slick chain stores with a large selection of Argentine wines. Some branches have wine bars where you can taste certain selections; at this location sample up to 20 different wines by the glass (five for AR$30). There's another branch with just a café in the Microcentro (Map pp84-5; Av Corrientes 300).

GETTING THERE & AWAY
Air

Buenos Aires is Argentina's international gateway and easily accessible from North America, Europe and Australasia, as well as other capital cities in South America.

Almost all international flights arrive at BA's Ezeiza airport, about 35km south of the center. Ezeiza is a modern airport with decent services such as ATMs, restaurants and duty-free shops. There's also an overpriced internet café and iffy wi-fi. For more on arriving in Ezeiza see the boxed text, opposite.

Most domestic flights use Aeroparque Jorge Newbery airport, a short distance from downtown BA. Flight information for both airports, in English and Spanish, is available at ☎ 5480-6111 or www.aa2000.com.ar.

Boat

BA has a regular ferry service to and from Colonia (see p566) and Montevideo (see p560), both in Uruguay. Ferries leave from the **Buquebus terminal** (Map pp84-5; cnr Avs Antártida Argentina & Córdoba). There are many more launches in the busy summer season.

Bus

If you're heading out of town you'll probably have to visit BA's modern Retiro bus station (Map pp84–5). It's 400m long, three floors high and has slots for 75 buses. The bottom floor is for cargo shipments and luggage storage, the top for purchasing tickets and the middle for everything else. There's an **information booth** (☎ 4310-0700) that provides general bus information and schedules; it'll also help you with the local bus system. Other services include a **tourist office** (☺ 7:30am-1pm Mon-Sat), on the main floor under bus counter 105; telephone offices (some with internet access); restaurants; cafés; and dozens of small stores.

You can buy a ticket to practically anywhere in Argentina and departures are fairly frequent to the most popular destinations. Reservations are not necessary except during peak summer and winter holiday seasons (January, February and July). And remember to keep an eye on your bags at this station!

Here are some sample destinations; be aware that ticket prices vary widely according to bus company, class, season and inflation.

Destination	Cost (AR$)	Duration (hr)
Bariloche	180	22
Comodoro Rivadavia	189	27
Córdoba	85	10
Foz do Iguaçu (Brazil)	165	19
Mar del Plata	65	6
Mendoza	138	15
Montevideo (Uruguay)	90	8
Puerto Iguazú	175	17
Puerto Madryn	189	20
Punta del Este	120	9
Rosario	35	4
Santiago (Chile)	200	21

EZEIZA ARRIVAL & DEPARTURE TIPS

When you arrive at Ezeiza and want to change your money, don't go to the first *cambio* (exchange house) you see. Their rates are bad; for better rates, pass the rows of transport booths, go outside the doors into the reception hall and veer sharply to the right to find Banco de la Nación's small office; it's open 24 hours.

For shuttles and taxis from Ezieza to the center, see below. There's a **tourist information booth** (☎ 4480-0024; ☒ 8am-8pm) just beyond the city's taxi stand.

When you leave BA on an international flight you'll have to pay a departure tax of AR$56 (payable in Argentine pesos, US dollars and some credit cards). If you're heading to Montevideo or Punta del Este this tax will be AR$25. Most passengers pay this fee at the downstairs booth, but the upstairs booth (next to security) usually has shorter lines.

Train

Trains connect Buenos Aires' center to its suburbs and nearby provinces. They're best for commuters but not that useful for tourists, however. Several private companies run different train lines; here are the most central train stations (all served by Subte) and some destinations:

CONSTITUCIÓN TRAIN STATION
Ferrobaires (☎ 4306-7919; www.ferrobaires.gba.gov .ar) To Bahía Blanca and Atlantic beach towns.
Metropolitano (Roca line; ☎ 0800-1-2235-8736) To the southern suburbs and La Plata.

ONCE TRAIN STATION
Trenes de Buenos Aires (Sarmiento line; ☎ 0800-333-3822; www.tbanet.com.ar) To the southwestern suburbs and Luján.

RETIRO TRAIN STATION
Ferrovias (Belgrano line; ☎ 0800-777-3377; www .ferrovias.com.ar) To the northern suburbs.
Trenes de Buenos Aires (TBA, Mitre line; ☎ 0800-333-3822; www.tbanet.com.ar) To Belgrano, San Isidro, Tigre, Rosario and Córdoba.
Transportes Metropolitanos (San Martín line; ☎ 4011-5826; www.metropolitano.com.ar) To the northern suburbs.

The old *Gran Capitán* runs to Posadas' **train station** (☎ 436076) twice weekly; see p217 for more details.

GETTING AROUND
To/From the Airport
If you're alone, the best way to and from Ezeiza is to take a shuttle with transfer companies like **Manuel Tienda León** (MTL; Map pp84-5; ☎ 4315-5115; www.tiendaleon.com; cnr Av Eduardo Madero & San Martín). You'll see its stand immediately as you exit customs. Shuttles cost AR$32 to AR$35 one way, run every half hour from 6am to midnight and take about 40 minutes, depending on traffic. It'll deposit you either at its office (from where you can take a taxi) or at some central hotels. Avoid its taxi service, which is overpriced at AR$95; if you want to take a taxi just go past the transport 'lobby' area, through the doors to the reception area and – avoiding all touts – find the freestanding city taxi stand (blue sign), which charges AR$78 to the center. MTL also does shuttle transfers from Ezeiza to Aeroparque for AR$38.

Real shoestringers can take public bus 86, which costs AR$1.35 and can take up to two hours to reach the Plaza de Mayo area. Catch it outside the Aerolíneas Argentinas terminal, a short walk (200m) from the international terminal. You'll need change for the bus; there's a Banco de la Nación just outside customs.

To get from Aeroparque to the center, take public buses 33 or 45 (don't cross the street; take them going south). MTL has shuttles to the center for AR$12; taxis cost around AR$15.

Bicycle
BA is not a great city for cycling. Traffic is dangerous and hardly respectful toward bicycles; the biggest vehicle wins the right of way, and bikes are low on the totem pole. Still, some spots call out for two-wheeled exploration, such as Palermo's parks and the Reserva Ecológica Costanera Sur; on weekends and some weekdays you can rent bikes at these places. You can also join city bike tours (see p107).

Bus
BA has a huge and complex bus system. If you want to get to know it better, you'll have to buy a *Guia T* (bus guide); they're sold at any

newsstand, but try to find the handy pocket version (AR$2). Just look at the grids to find out where you are and where you're going, and find a matching bus number. Most routes (but not all) run 24 hours.

Save your change like it's gold; local buses do not take bills. Bus ticket machines on board will, however, give you small change from your coins. Most rides around town cost AR$0.80, so folks just say *ochenta* to the bus driver, who cues the ticket machine accordingly (short rides are AR$0.75). Offer your seat to the elderly, pregnant and women with young children.

Route	Bus no
Microcentro to Palermo Viejo	111
Microcentro to Plaza Italia (in Palermo)	29, 59, 64
Once to Plaza de Mayo to La Boca	64
Plaza de Mayo to Ezeiza airport	86 (placard says 'Ezeiza')
Plaza Italia to La Boca via Retiro & Plaza de Mayo	152, 29
Plaza Italia to Microcentro to San Telmo	29
Plaza Italia to Recoleta to Microcentro to Constitución	59
Plaza San Martín to Aeroparque airport	33, 45
Recoleta to Congreso to San Telmo to La Boca	39
Retiro to Plaza de Mayo to San Telmo	22

Car

Anyone considering driving in BA should know that most local drivers are reckless, aggressive and even willfully dangerous. They'll ignore speed limits, road signs, lines and traffic signals. They'll tailgate mercilessly and honk even before signals turn green. Buses are a nightmare to reckon with, potholes are everywhere, traffic is a pain and parking can be a bitch. Pedestrians seem to beg to be run over at times.

If, after all these warnings, you still insist on renting a car, expect to pay around AR$150 to AR$170 per day. You'll need to be at least 21 years of age and have a valid driver's license; having an international driver's license isn't crucial. You'll need to present a credit card and your passport, though.

Avis (Map pp84-5; ☎ 4326-5542; www.avis.com.ar; Cerrito 1527)

Hertz (Map pp84-5; ☎ 4816-8001; www.hertzargentina .com.ar; Paraguay 1138)

New Way (Map pp84-5; ☎ 4515-0331; www.new-way rentacar.com.ar; MT de Alvear 773)

Victory (Map pp84-5; ☎ 4381-4731; www.victoryrentacar .com.ar; Lima 509)

Motorcycle

For motorcycle rentals, head to **Motocare** (Map pp82-3; ☎ 4782-1500; www.motocare.com.ar; Av Libertador 6588). Honda Transalps 650 cost about AR$280 per day with a four-day minimum (it's cheaper by the month). Bring your own helmet and riding gear. Crossing into Chile, Uruguay, Paraguay and Brazil is allowed. If you buy a motorcycle here you can negotiate to sell it back, possibly saving money in the long term.

Subte (Underground)

BA's **Subte** (☎ 4555-1616; www.metrovias.com.ar) opened in 1913 and is the quickest way to get around the city, though it can get mighty hot and crowded during rush hour. It consists of Líneas (Lines) A, B, C, D and E; a new H line opened in 2007. Four parallel lines run from downtown to the capital's western and northern outskirts, while Línea C runs north–south and connects the two major train stations of Retiro and Constitución. Línea H runs from Once south to Av Caseros, with future plans to expand it from Retiro to Nuevo Pompeya.

One-ride magnetic cards for the Subte cost AR$0.70. To save time and hassle buy several rides, since queues can get backed up. If you're planning on staying in BA for awhile, the Subtecard (www.subte.com.ar) is a convenient, rechargeable card that you can use to enter the Subte, plus buy some products at the stations and get certain discounts. At some stations platforms are on opposite sides, so make sure of your direction *before* passing through the turnstiles.

Trains operate from 5am to (around) 11pm Monday to Saturday and 8am to (around) 10:30pm on Sundays and holidays. Service is frequent on weekdays; on weekends you'll wait longer.

Taxi & Remise

Buenos Aires' very numerous (about 40,000) and cheap taxis are conspicuous by their black-and-yellow paint jobs. In late 2007 meters started at AR$3.10 day or night. Drivers do not expect a big tip, but it's customary to let them keep small change. Taxis looking for passengers will have a red light lit on the upper right corner of their windshield.

Almost all cab drivers are honest workers making a living, but there are a few bad apples in the bunch. Try not to give them large bills; not only will they usually not have change, but

TRAM TRAVAILS

In July 2007 Buenos Aires inaugurated a new light rail system in Puerto Madero, called the Tranvía del Este. It's currently 2km long and has only four stops, with future plans extending the line from Retiro to Constitución. It only costs AR$1 to ride, but consider skipping it – and stroll down Puerto Madero's lovely cobbled lanes instead.

there have been cases where the driver quickly and deftly replaces a larger bill with a smaller one. One solution is to state how much you are giving them and ask if they have change for it (*'¿Tiene usted cambio de un veinte?'* – Do you have any change for a 20?). Be wary of receiving counterfeit bills; at night have the driver *prender la luz* (turn on the light) so you can carefully count and check your change (look for a watermark on bills).

Pretend to have an idea of where you're going; a few taxis offer the 'scenic' route (though also be aware there are many one-way streets in BA). A good way to do this is to give the taxi driver an intersection rather than a specific address. Also, if you are obviously a tourist going to or from a touristy spot, don't ask how much the fare is beforehand; this makes quoting an upped price, rather than using the meter, tempting.

Finally, make an attempt to snag an 'official' taxi. These are usually marked by a roof light and license number printed on the doors. Official drivers must display their license on the back of their seat or dashboard; you can write down the taxi's number and agency telephone in case of problems or forgotten items.

Most *porteños* recommend you call a *remise* instead of hailing street cabs. *Remises* look like regular cars and don't have meters. They cost a bit more than street taxis but are more secure, since an established company sends them out. Most hotels and restaurants will call a *remise* for you.

AROUND BUENOS AIRES

So you've spent days tramping on noisy and busy streets, visiting all the sights and smells of BA. You're ready to get away from the capital and experience something different and more peaceful. Where do you go?

Luckily for you, there are several trips that can be done in a day, but a few are better if you have more time to spare. Luján is a religious mecca, while San Antonio de Areco features peace and the occasional gaucho theme. For something different, head across the Rio de la Plata into neighboring Uruguay. Montevideo (p546) is a laid-back capital city with a much slower pace, while Colonia (p562) offers some cobbled streets and old-time atmosphere. The ritzy resort of Punta del Este (p582) provides sun, sand and stars – celebrities, that is.

SAN ISIDRO

About 22km north of Buenos Aires is peaceful and residential San Isidro, a charming suburb of cobblestone streets lined with graceful buildings. The historic center is at Plaza Mitre and its beautiful neo-Gothic cathedral; on weekends the area buzzes with a crafts fair. There's a **tourist office** (☎ 4512-3209; www .sanisidro.gov.ar; Ituzaingo 608) at the plaza near Av Libertador, next to the rugby museum.

A stroll through the rambling neighborhood streets behind the cathedral will turn up some luxurious mansions (as well as moremodest houses) and the occasional view over toward the coast. Close by is also the Tren de la Costa's San Isidro station, with a fashionable outdoor shopping mall to explore.

Once owned by Argentine icon, General Pueyrredón, the **Museo Histórico Municipal General Pueyrredón** (☎ 4512-3131; Rivera Indarte 48; admission free; ☾ 2-6pm Tue, Thu, Sat & Sun) is an old colonial villa set on spacious grounds with faraway views of the Río de la Plata. Don't miss the algarrobo tree under which Pueyrredón and San Martín strategized against the Spanish. To get here from the cathedral, follow Av Libertador five blocks, turn left on Peña and after two blocks turn right onto Rivera Indarte.

Even more glamorous is the Unesco site **Villa Ocampo** (☎ 4732-4988; www.villaocampo.org; Elortondo 1837; admission AR$10; ☾ 3-7pm Sat-Sun), a wonderfully restored mansion and reminder of a bygone era. Victoria Ocampo was a writer, publisher and intellectual who dallied with the literary likes of Borges, Cortázar, Sabato and Camus. The gardens are lovely here; tours and a café are also available.

Getting There & Away

The best way to reach San Isidro is via the **Tren de la Costa** (www.trendelacosta.com.ar), whose first station (called Maipú) is in the suburb of Olivos. Get to Maipú station on buses 59 or 152; some 60s also go (ask the bus driver). The Mitre train line from Retiro train station (downtown) also reaches Maipú station, but it's on a different line so you'll have to transfer in Olivos. You can also go directly to San Isidro with buses 60 and 168.

TIGRE & THE DELTA

The city of Tigre (35km north of BA) and her surrounding delta region is one of the most popular weekend getaways for weary *porteños*. The city itself has a few pleasant attractions, but it's really the delta just beyond Tigre that everyone's after. Latte-colored waters – rich with iron from the jungle streams flowing from inland South America – will hardly remind you of a blue paradise, but there are hidden gems in this marshy region. Boat rides into the delta offer peeks at local stilt houses and colonial mansions, and you can explore along some peaceful trails. Many lodgings are located throughout the region, making getaways complete. All along the shorelines are signs of water-related activity, from kayaking to wakeboarding, canoeing to sculling.

Information

Bonanza Deltaventura (☎ 4728-1674; www.delta ventura.com) Offers adventures that include walks, canoe trips, bike rides, horseback rides and *asados*.

Tourist Office (☎ 4512-4497; www.tigre.gov.ar; ☺ 9am-5pm) Located behind McDonald's; will help you sort out the complex delta region. There's a smaller booth (☎ 4512-4547; ☺ summer only) at the train station.

Sights & Activities

Tigre itself is very walkable and holds some attractions. Be sure to check out the **Puerto de Frutos** (Sarmiento 160; ☺ 10am-6:30pm), where vendors sell mostly housewares, wicker baskets and dried flowers, along with a modest selection of fruits. Weekends are best, when a large crafts fair sets up. Nearby is Tigre's amusement park, **Parque de la Costa** (☎ 4002-6000; www.parquedelacosta.com.ar; admission AR$28-36). Call for current hours.

The **Museo Naval de la Nación** (☎ 4749-0608; Paseo Victorica 602; admission AR$2; ☺ 8:30am-5:30pm Mon-Fri, 10:30am-6:30pm Sat-Sun) traces the history of the Argentine navy with an eclectic mix of historical photos, model boats and airplanes, artillery displays and pickled sea critters. Boat buffs can also visit the **Museo Histórico Prefectura Naval Argentina** (☎ 4749-6161; Liniers 1264; admission

free; ☺ 10am-noon & 2-6pm Wed-Sun), which has exhibits on the Argentine coast guard.

Tigre's fanciest museum, however, is the **Museo de Arte Tigre** (☎ 4512-4528; Paseo Victorica 972; admission AR$5; ☺ 9am-6pm Wed-Fri, noon-7pm Sat-Sun). Located in an old social club from 1912, this beautiful art museum showcases famous Argentine artists from the 19th and 20th centuries. The building itself is worth a visit.

The waterways of the delta offer a glimpse into how locals live along the peaceful canals, with boats as their only transportation. Frequent commuter launches depart from Estación Fluvial (located behind the tourist office) for various destinations in the delta (AR$11 to AR$19 round trip). A popular destination is the **Tres Bocas neighborhood**, a half-hour boat ride from Tigre, where you can take residential walks on thin paths connected by bridges over narrow channels. There are several restaurants and accommodations here. The **Rama Negra** area has a quieter and more natural setting with fewer services, but is an hour's boat ride away.

Several companies offer inexpensive boat tours (AR$14 to AR$30, 1½ hours), but commuter launches give you flexibility if you want to go for a stroll or stop for lunch at one of the delta's restaurants.

Sleeping & Eating

The huge delta region is dotted with dozens of accommodation possibilities, from camping to B&Bs to *cabañas* to beach resorts to activity-oriented places. The further out you are, the more peace and quiet you'll experience.

Since places are relatively hard to reach (you generally arrive by boat), the majority also provide meal services. The Tigre tourist office has photos of and information on all accommodation places, and many are listed on its website www.tigre.gov.ar (just click on 'turismo,' then on accommodation under 'Tigre delta').

The following places are in the city of Tigre itself. For all accommodations in the region, book ahead on weekends.

Tigre Hostel (☎ 4749-4034; www.tigrehostel.com.ar; dm AR$36, s AR$90, d 180-200; ☐) A great new addition to Tigre is this HI-affiliated hostel, located in an old mansion. It's a good place with large dorms and nice bunks, but the kitchen had iffy feng shui with its awkward access. Private rooms are either very spacious, with their own bathroom, or require you to walk through the dorms and share their bathrooms. A large garden and back deck are good hang-out areas. HI cards earn a 20% discount.

Casona La Ruchi (☎ 4749-2499; www.casonalaruchi .com.ar; Lavalle 557; s/d AR$110/160; 🖳 🖳) This family-run B&B is in a beautiful mansion that's show-ing its age (it was built in 1893). Most of the five romantic bedrooms have balconies; all have shared bathrooms with original tiled floors. There's a pool and large garden out back.

Villa Julia (☎ 4749-0642; www.villajulia.com.ar; Paseo Victorica 800; s/d AR$480/650; 🗙 🖳 🖳) Just five lux-urious rooms and suites are available at this classic 1913 mansion, where original tilework, large balconies and thick robes make for a very special stay. The atmosphere is lovely, and there's a swimming pool and restaurant.

As far as food goes, Tigre's cuisine is not cutting-edge, but it can be atmospheric. Stroll Paseo Victorica, the city's pleasant riverside avenue. For an upscale meal, try **Maria Luján** (☎ 4731-9613; mains AR$20-40; 🕑 lunch & dinner), which also has a great patio boasting river views.

Getting There & Away

There are three main ways to get to Tigre. From Retiro station (Map pp84–5) take a train straight to Tigre (one hour). You can also take No 60 (marked 'Panamericano') straight to Tigre (1½ hours).

The best way to reach Tigre, however, is via the **Tren de la Costa** (www.trendelacosta.com) – a pleasant electric train with attractive stations and some water views. This train line starts in the suburb of Olivos; to get here, take a train from Retiro station and get off at the Mitre station (then cross the bridge to the Tren de la Costa). Buses 59, 60 and 152 also go to the Tren de la Costa.

RESERVA NATURAL OTAMENDI
☎ 03489

Covering some 27 sq km on the banks of the Paraná de las Palmas river, the Reserva Natural Otamendi (Map p139) is just 70km from Buenos Aires along RN 9, just beyond the Tigre Delta.

The reserve takes in three habitats: the riverine forest with its native willows and brightly flowered coral trees; the floodplain with its variety of reeds and rushes where you'll find cabybaras and the rare marsh deer, as well as many bird species; and the tala woods with a small remnant of native pampas grassland beyond it.

The reserve also features remains of pre-Columbian settlements of fisherfolk and hunter-gatherers who left behind harpoon points and ceramics.

There are several marked trails throughout the reserve, and the **visitors' center** (☎ 447505; admission free, guided tours held weekends only AR$7) at its entrance offers written information in Spanish. The park is open from morning to late afternoon, but exact hours vary slightly depending on the season, as does the timing of weekend tours; contact the visitors center for details.

Getting There & Away

From Retiro, take the train along the Mitre line, changing at Villa Ballestar and getting off at Ing R Otamendi. Various bus companies run services from nearby Campana.

The Pampas & the Atlantic Coast

Evita's shirtless masses, the lawless and romantic gaucho, the wealthy landowner with his palatial country estate and the defiant Indian – all these classic Argentine characters have their origins in the pampas. In fact, in its early days, Argentina was the pampas – the fight for independence was born on the Río de la Plata, and Argentina's immigrant identity was forged by the Europeans who filled the pampean towns.

The seemingly endless fertile grasslands that make up this region financed Argentina's golden years, its natural grasses and easily cleared land yielding huge returns. The Buenos Aires province is still the nation's economic and political powerhouse – this is where all that juicy beef comes from, and it's also home to around 40% of Argentina's voters.

While the pampas is often overlooked by travelers, it does hold some hidden gems, many of which make worthwhile side trips from Buenos Aires. A visit to lovely San Antonio de Areco offers a taste of living gaucho culture, while the hills around Tandil and Sierra de la Ventana are a picturesque mix of the wild and the pastoral, with plenty of opportunities for hiking and climbing. And although the beaches can't compare with Brazil's, they make a good escape from the city's summer heat.

One of the best ways to get to know the pampas is to spend a day or so at one of the region's many historic *estancias*, where the huge sky and luscious green plains, the gauchos' horsemanship and the faded elegance of Argentina's belle epoque can all be experienced first hand.

HIGHLIGHTS

- Survey the endless plains from atop **Cerro de la Ventana** (p154)
- Soak up the sun in **Pinamar** (p159), where half of Buenos Aires' social scene sets up camp for the summer
- Sample some country life – and the cheese – in **Tandil** (p148)
- Go gaucho in **San Antonio de Areco** (p144), the prettiest town in the pampas
- Float on the lagoon, spot flamingos and hike the dunes at **Mar Chiquita** (p163)

- POPULATION: 15.4 MILLION
- AREA: 451,011 SQ KM

THE PAMPAS & THE ATLANTIC COAST

Climate

Temperatures on the pampas fluctuate wildly through the year, from lows of -6°C up to highs of 38°C, although such extremes are rare and the temperature is generally comfortable. The region is divided into two main climatic zones: the wet (or humid) pampas along the coast, where much of the rain falls, and the dry pampas to its west. There can be as much as 1000mm of rainfall per year (thanks to occasional heavy rainfalls rather than an extended rainy period), although drought is the largest single problem for farmers in the region.

National & Provincial Parks

The pampas and coast are home to a small but excellent selection of protected areas. The Parque Provincial Ernesto Tornquist (p154) is a hikers' paradise, where you can scale the peaks of Cerro de la Ventana (1186m) or check out the stunning Garganta del Diablo (Devil's Throat) gorge. Parque Nacional Lihué Calel (p157) is set in a near-desert landscape with surreal granite rock formations and is home to a wealth of animal species. More modest Parque Provincial Miguel Lillo (p172) is a leafy haven right by downtown Necochea.

Getting There & Away

There are flights from Buenos Aires to Bahía Blanca and Mar del Plata. Buses from nearly every town run to most destinations in the country although, of course, larger towns (such as Santa Rosa, La Plata and Mar del

Plata) will have better connections. Trains depart Buenos Aires' Constitución station for La Plata, Bahía Blanca, Villa Ventana and Mar del Plata, stopping at smaller towns along those routes.

NORTHERN PAMPAS

The pampas is both a general term for a large geographic region of fertile plains and the name of the province that lies to the west of Buenos Aires. The pampas grasslands roll southwards from the Río de la Plata to the banks of the Río Negro, stretching west towards the Andes and all the way up to the southern parts of Córdoba and Sante Fé provinces, taking in the entire Buenos Aires and La Pampa provinces.

The rich soil and lush natural grasses of the northern pampas make it Argentina's best cattle-raising country. The region yields plentiful hides, beef, wool and wheat for global markets, stamping Argentina on the world's economic map.

From the mid-19th century, the province of Buenos Aires was the undisputed political and economic center of the country. When the city of Buenos Aires became Argentina's capital, the province submitted to national authority but didn't lose its influence. By the 1880s, after a brief but contentious civil war, the province responded by creating its own provincial capital in the model city of La Plata.

Outside Buenos Aires, a dense network of railroads and highways connects the agricultural towns of the pampas, most of which resemble each other as much as any part of the endlessly flat pampas resembles another.

LA PLATA
☎ 0221 / pop 857,800

Barely an hour from Buenos Aires, this bustling university town has the same belle epoque architecture, gracious municipal buildings and leafy parks, all on a smaller scale. The big tourist draws are its natural-history museum, one of Argentina's best, and the imposing neo-Gothic cathedral.

When Buenos Aires became Argentina's new capital, Governor Dardo Rocha founded La Plata in 1882 to give the province of Buenos Aires its own top city. Rocha chose engineer Pedro Benoit's elaborate city plan, based upon balance and logic, with diagonal avenues crossing the regular 5km-square grid

pattern to connect the major plazas, creating a distinctive star design. Elegant on paper this blueprint creates confusion at many intersections, with up to eight streets going of in all directions. However, it probably made La Plata South America's first completely planned city.

Orientation

La Plata is 56km southeast of Buenos Aires via RP 14. Most of the public buildings are located on Plaza Moreno, which occupies four square blocks and sports the graffiti-covered Piedra Fundacional (Founding Stone), marking the city's precise geographical center. Most of the bustle occurs around Plaza San Martín. Navigation is confusing: some intersections have more than four corners and it's easy to become disoriented; keep checking street signs to make sure you haven't gone astray.

Address numbers run in sequences of 50 per block rather than the customary 100.

Information

ACA (Automóvil Club Argentina; cnr Av 51 & Calle 9; ☎ 482-9040) Argentina's auto club; good source for provincial road maps.

Alianza Francesa (☎ 483-1616; Calle 59, No 626; ⏱ 8:30am-1pm Wed, Thu & Sat, 2-8:30pm Mon-Fri) Cultural center.

Asatej (☎ 483-8673; cnr Calle 5 & Av 53) Argentina's student travel agency.

Instituto Cultural Británico-Argentino (☎ 489-9690; Calle 12, No 869) Located off the Plaza Moreno; hosts cultural events and Friday night films.

Locutorio Dardo Rocha (Calle 50, btwn Av 7 & Calle 8; per hr AR$1.50) Internet and telephones.

Municipal tourist office (Entidad Municipal de Turismo; ☎ 427-1535; www.laplata.gov.ar; ⏱ 10am-1pm & 2-5pm Mon-Fri, 10am-6pm Sat & Sun) Just off Plaza San Martín.

Post office (cnr Calle 4 & Av 51)

Sights

La Plata's main sights are all within walking distance. Near Plaza Moreno is the neo-Gothic **cathedral**, which was begun in 1885 but not inaugurated until 1932. The cathedral was inspired by medieval predecessors in Cologne and Amiens, and has fine stained glass and polished granite floors; tours are AR$5 and include an elevator ride to the top.

Opposite the cathedral is the **Palacio Municipal**, designed in German Renaissance style by Hanoverian architect Hubert Stiers.

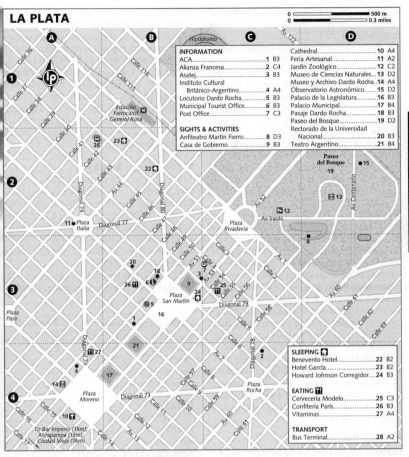

LA PLATA

0	500 m
0	0.3 miles

INFORMATION
ACA	1	B3
Alianza Francesa	2	C4
Asatej	3	B3
Instituto Cultural Británico-Argentino	4	A4
Locutorio Dardo Rocha	5	B3
Municipal Tourist Office	6	B3
Post Office	7	C3

SIGHTS & ACTIVITIES
Anfiteatro Martín Fierro	8	D3
Casa de Gobierno	9	B3
Cathedral	10	A4
Feria Artesanal	11	A2
Jardín Zoológico	12	C2
Museo de Ciencias Naturales	13	D2
Museo y Archivo Dardo Rocha	14	A4
Observatorio Astronómico	15	D2
Palacio de la Legislatura	16	B3
Palacio Municipal	17	B4
Pasaje Dardo Rocha	18	B3
Paseo del Bosque	19	D2
Rectorado de la Universidad Nacional	20	B3
Teatro Argentino	21	B4

SLEEPING
Benevento Hotel	22	B2
Hotel García	23	B2
Howard Johnson Corregidor	24	B3

EATING
Cervecería Modelo	25	C3
Confitería París	26	B3
Vitaminas	27	A4

TRANSPORT
Bus Terminal	28	A2

THE PAMPAS & THE ATLANTIC COAST

On the west side of the plaza, the **Museo y Archivo Dardo Rocha** (☎ 427-5591; Calle 50, No 933; admission free; ☼ 9am-5pm Mon-Fri) was the vacation house of the city's creator and contains period furniture and many of his personal knickknacks.

Two blocks northeast, the **Teatro Argentino** (☎ 0800-666-5151; www.teatroargentino.ic.gba.gov.ar; Av 51, btwn Calle 9 & Calle 10) is a somber concrete monolith, but boasts great acoustics and quality ballet, symphony and opera performances. Two blocks further northeast, in front of Plaza San Martín, is the ornate **Palacio de la Legislatura**, also in German Renaissance style. Nearby, catch the French Classic **Pasaje Dardo Rocha**, once La Plata's main railroad station and now the city's major cultural center, containing four museums. Also close by is the

Flemish Renaissance **Casa de Gobierno**, housing the provincial governor and his retinue. Over to the northwest a few blocks are the original buildings of the **Rectorado de la Universidad Nacional** (1905), which was once a bank but is now the university administrative offices. On Sundays, check out the crafts fair **Feria Artesanal** on Plaza Italia.

Plantations of eucalyptus, gingko, palm and subtropical hardwoods cover **Paseo del Bosque**, parkland expropriated from an *estancia* (ranch) at the time of the city's founding. It attracts a collection of strolling families, smooching lovers and sweaty joggers. Various interesting sights are strewn within, such as the open-air **Anfiteatro Martín Fierro** (marked Teatro de Aire Libre), that hosts music and drama performances; the **Observatorio Astronómico** (☎ 423-6593; 9am-4:30pm Mon-Fri); the modest **Jardín Zoológico** (☎ 427-3925; admission AR$4; 9am-6pm, closed Mon); and the **Museo de Ciencias Naturales** (☎ 425-7744; admission AR$12; 10am-6pm, closed Monday). Hugely popular with school groups, this notable museum has paleontological, zoological, archaeological and anthropological collections of famous Patagonian explorer Francisco P Moreno. Four floors and countless display rooms offer something for everyone: Egyptian tomb relics, Jesuit art, amusing taxidermy, amazing skeletons, mummies, ancient pottery, scary insects and reconstructed dinosaurs. There are daily tours in Spanish, but English tours must be arranged in advance.

Sleeping

Hotel García (Calle 2, No 525; s/d AR$48/60) Friendly and clean, this budget place near the bus station offers 15 small, basic rooms. Showers are open so everything in the bathroom gets wet – but the cable TV makes up for it.

Benevento Hotel (☎ 423-7721; www.hotelbenevento.com.ar in Spanish; Calle 2, No 645; s/d AR$115/178;) This renovated, old-style hotel offers high ceilings and wooden floors, and many rooms have balconies overlooking the busy street. Singles are tiny, but doubles are fairly comfortable.

Howard Johnson Corregidor (☎ 425-6800; www.hotelcorregidor.com.ar; Calle 6, No 1026; s/d AR$226/252;) No surprises here – modern rooms are pleasant and comfortable, and what you'd expect from a HoJos. Some have patios, and there's a small gym.

Eating & Drinking

Vitaminas (☎ 0211-15-555-9918; Diagonal 74, No 1640, btwn Calles 49 & 50; mains AR$9-15; lunch & dinner Mon-Sat) Well-priced fresh pastas, hearty salads, homemade burgers and meat dishes are served up at this cheerful, brightly decorated eatery.

Confitería París (☎ 482-8840; cnr Av 7 & Calle 49; mains AR$11-28; 7:30am-10pm) Delicious sweet treats abound at this classic café, where patrons sit in air-conditioned comfort observing the passing street life through huge windows. There's a larger-than-usual variety of lunch items like sandwiches and salads, with take-out service.

Cervecería Modelo (☎ 421-1321; cnr Calles 5 & 54; mains AR$15-32; breakfast, lunch & dinner) Dating from 1894, its walls adorned with retro beer ads and its ceiling hung with hams, this place serves ice-cold ales to a happy local crowd.

Modern touches include wi-fi and a big-screen TV for watching sports.

A little out of the center in a bohemian neighborhood popular with students you'll find **Bar Imperio** (☎ 453-3525; Calle 17 btwn 70 & 71), which along with its neighbors **Mirapampa** (cnr Calles 17 & 71) and **Ciudád Vieja** (☎ 452-1674; www.ciudadviejaweb.com.ar in Spanish; cnr Calles 17 & 71), offers live music from Thursday night through weekends, while on Sundays there are market stalls showcasing the creations of La Plata's young fashion designers.

Getting There & Away

Via Sur's bus 129 connects Buenos Aires with La Plata every 20 minutes. It leaves from Buenos Aires' Retiro train station, on Martín Zuvería, making stops along Ave 9 Julio and at Constitución train station. The 129 to Buenos Aires leaves frequently from La Plata's terminal, making several stops in the city before heading to the capital.

La Plata's bus terminal has plenty of connections to other parts of Argentina, including the following.

Destination	Cost (AR$)	Duration (hr)
Mar del Plata	50	5
Bahía Blanca	115	8
Córdoba	115	11
Mendoza	143	18
Bariloche	200	23

LUJÁN

☎ 02323 / pop 78,200

Luján is a sleepy riverside town that once a year overflows with pilgrims making their way to Argentina's most important shrine. It's worth visiting any time, though, with its gracious Spanish-style paved square and the imposing neo-Gothic cathedral, as well as a couple of interesting museums. The riverside area is lined with restaurants and barbecue stands selling *choripan* (a spicy pork sausage in a crunchy roll); you can rent boats for a paddle on the river (watch out for garbage and the odd dead rat) and on festive days there are games and rides. The chairlift carrying sightseers over the grubby river is an oddly charming touch.

On the first Saturday in October thousands of Catholics walk from the capital to honor Our Lady of Luján. Other large gatherings occur on April 21, May 8 (the Virgin's day), the third week of November and December 8 (Immaculate Conception Day).

OUR LADY OF LUJÁN

Argentina's patron saint is a ubiquitous presence – you can spot her poster on butcher shop walls, her statue in churches throughout the country and her image on the dashboards of many a Buenos Aires taxi, not to mention the countless shops and stands selling mini *virgincitas* in her hometown. She can be recognized by her stiff, triangular dress, the half-moon at her feet and the streams of glory radiating from her crowned head.

Her legend begins in 1630, when a Portuguese settler in Tucumán asked a friend in Brazil to send him an image of the Virgin for his new chapel. Unsure which kind of Virgin was required, the friend sent two – one of the mother and child, and one of the Immaculate Conception, her hands clasped before her in prayer. After setting out from the port of Buenos Aires, the cart bearing the statues got bogged near the river of Luján and only moved when the Immaculate Conception was taken off. Its owner took it as a sign, and left the statue in Luján so that a shrine could be built there. The statue of the mother and child continued its journey to the northwest.

Since then Our Lady and her humble terracotta statue have been credited with a number of miracles – from curing tumors to sending a fog to hide early settlers from warring Indians, to protecting the province from a cholera epidemic. She was rewarded for her trouble in 1886, when Pope Leo XIII crowned her with a golden coronet set with almost 500 pearls and gems.

The massive pilgrimage to her basilica, where the original statue is still venerated, happens on the first Sunday in October. Throngs of the faithful walk the 65km from the Buenos Aires neighborhood of Liniers to Luján – a journey of up to 18 hours. The cardinal says an early morning mass in Plaza Belgrano and from then on you can spot families of exhausted pilgrims snoozing in the square, enjoying barbecues by the river and filling plastic bottles with holy water from the fountain.

Orientation & Information

Luján is around 65km west of Buenos Aires on RN 7. Most places of interest are near the basilica, around Plaza Belgrano, though Plaza Colón, five blocks southeast via Calle San Martín, is another center of activity.

Post office (Mitre 575)

Tourist office (☎ 420453; ◷ 8am-6pm Mon-Fri, 10am-6pm Sat & Sun) Near the river at the west end of Lavalle, in the large domed building.

Sights
BASÍLICA NUESTRA SEÑORA DE LUJÁN

Every year five million pilgrims from throughout Argentina visit Luján to honor the Virgin for her intercession in affairs of peace, health, forgiveness and consolation. The terminus of their journey is this imposing **basilica** (☎ 420058; tours AR$1; ◷ tours hourly from noon-5pm Mon-Fri), built from 1887 to 1935. The neo-Gothic church is made from a lovely rose-colored stone that glows in the setting sun. The statue of the Virgin, which dates from 1630, sits in the high chamber behind the main altar. Devotees have lined the stairs with plaques acknowledging her favors. Under the basilica you can tour a **crypt** (AR$1; ◷ hourly 10am-5pm) inhabited by Virgin statues from all over the world. Masses take place in the basilica several times a day, mostly morning and evening.

Within the basilica, Irish visitors may be interested to find Gaelic inscriptions, Irish surnames and a side chapel dedicated to St Patrick.

COMPLEJO MUSEOGRÁFICO ENRIQUE UDAONDO

This gorgeous colonial-era **museum complex** (☎ 420245; admission AR$1; ◷ noon-6pm Wed-Fri, 10am-6pm Sat, Sun & holidays) rambles with display rooms, pretty patios, gardens and tiled outdoor walkways. The Sala General José de San Martín showcases Argentina's battles for independence with historic etchings, presidential bios and period items. The Sala de Gaucho contains some beautiful *mate* ware, ponchos, horse gear, guitars and other gaucho paraphernalia, as well as a reconstruction of Ricardo Güiraldes' (author of *Don Segundo Sombra*; 1886–1927) study. There's a Federal-era room, outlining Juan Manuel de Rosas' exploits and the 'conquest' of the desert (essentially the elimination of Patagonia's indigenous people). Near the entrance is a room portraying an old prison chamber, as the *cabildo* (town hall) used to be a lockup.

The nearby **Museo de Transporte** (☎ 420245; admission AR$1; ☯ noon-6pm Wed-Fri, 10am-6pm Sat, Sun & holidays) has a remarkable collection of horse-drawn carriages from the late 1800s, including some truly fit for Cinderella. Also on display are a 'popemobile,' the first steam locomotive to serve the city from Buenos Aires and a monster of a hydroplane that crossed the Atlantic in 1926. Some old wooden wagons and a brick windmill adorn the peaceful garden. The most offbeat exhibits, however, are the stuffed and scruffy remains of Gato and Mancha, the hardy Argentine criollo horses ridden by adventurer AF Tschiffely from Buenos Aires to Washington DC. This trip took 2½ years, from 1925 to 1928.

Note that these museums are closed on the Sunday of the pilgrimage.

Sleeping

Luján is probably best enjoyed as a daytrip out of the capital, as the town's hotels are unremarkable. Rates drop by around 30% during the week, and reservations are in order on weekends and holidays.

Hotel del Virrey (☎ 420797; San Martín 129; per room AR$120; ⊠ ⌨) Right near the basilica is this modern hotel offering 18 decent rooms and wi-fi in the dining area. There's pool access.

Hotel Hoxón (☎ 429970; www.hotelhoxon.com.ar in Spanish; 9 de Julio 760; s/d AR$78/128; ⊠ ⌨ ⌨) The best and biggest in town, with modern, clean and comfortable rooms and wi-fi throughout. The large swimming pool has a raised sun deck, and there's a gym as well.

Hotel de la Paz (☎ 424034; hoteldelapaz@hotmail .com; 9 de Julio 1054; r AR$130; ⊠) Well located and with friendly staff, Hotel de la Paz retains a faded sort of charm. The homey rooms are small and bathrooms have open showers.

Estancia San Ceferino (☎ 441500; www.estancia sanceferino.com.ar; RN 6, Lujan; día de campo AR$230, r per person AR$360; ⊠ ⌨ ⌨) About 20km out of town along RN 6, this modern *estancia* includes a spa and a museum with antique carriages and saddles. The large grounds feature playing fields and an ornamental pond, while the rooms are spacious and elegantly decorated.

Eating

Pilgrims won't go hungry in Luján – the central parts of San Martín, 9 de Julio and the riverfront are all lined with restaurants.

La Catedral (☎ 440668; 9 Julio 1074; mains AR$10-25; ☯ lunch & dinner Tue-Sun, lunch only Mon) Buzzing on weekends, this spot boasts a good AR$10 salad bar and delicious homemade pasta.

Café La Basilica (☎ 428376; San Martín 101; mains AR$15-30; ☯ 7am-7pm Sun-Thu, 7am-1am Fri & Sat) This classic old corner bar offers homemade breakfast pastries and a large selection of cocktails, as well as satisfying meals.

L'Eau Vive (☎ 421774; Constitución 2112; 3-course menu AR$25-28; ☯ lunch & dinner Tue-Sat, lunch only Sun) Just 2km from the center you'll find this friendly French restaurant run by Carmelite nuns from around the world. Taxis here cost around AR$5 or take bus 501 from the center.

Getting There & Away

Luján's **bus terminal** (☎ 420044; Av de Nuestra Señora de Luján & Almirante Brown) is just three blocks north of the basilica. From Buenos Aires, take Transportes Atlántida's bus 57 from outside the Plaza Italia or Once train stations, which leaves every half hour (AR$6.50, 1½ to two hours). There are also daily train departures from Estación Once in Buenos Aires, but you need to change trains in Moreno (AR$3).

SAN ANTONIO DE ARECO
☎ 02326 / pop 21,300

Nestled in lush farmlands, San Antonio de Areco is probably the prettiest town in the pampas. An easy drive from the capital, it welcomes many daytripping *porteños* (people from Buenos Aires), who come for the peaceful atmosphere and the picturesque colonial streets. The town dates from the early 18th century and to this day it preserves a great deal of the criollo and gaucho traditions, especially among its artisans, who produce very fine silverwork and saddlery. By day, men don the traditional *boina* (a kind of gaucho beret), while in the evenings locals head to the *peña*, a party with folk music and dancing. Gauchos from all over the pampas show up for November's Día de la Tradición where you can catch them and their horses strutting the cobbled streets in all their finery.

San Antonio de Areco's compact center and quiet streets are very walkable. Around the Plaza Ruiz de Arellano, named in honor of the town's founding *estanciero* (estancia owner), are several historic buildings, including the *iglesia parroquial* (parish church) and the Casa de los Martínez (site of the main house of the original Ruiz de Arellano *estancia*).

The *puente viejo* (old bridge; 1857), across the Río Areco, follows the original cart road

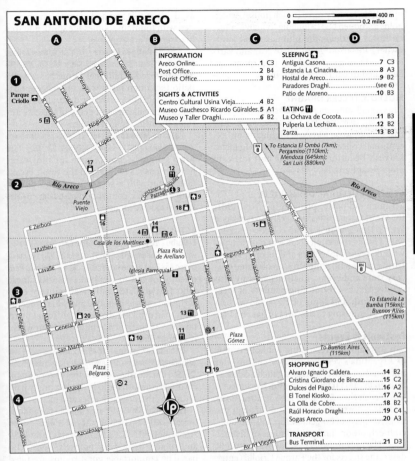

SAN ANTONIO DE ARECO

INFORMATION	
Areco Online..............................	**1** C3
Post Office.................................	**2** B4
Tourist Office............................	**3** B2

SIGHTS & ACTIVITIES	
Centro Cultural Usina Vieja............	**4** B2
Museo Gauchesco Ricardo Güiraldes.	**5** A1
Museo y Taller Draghi....................	**6** B2

SLEEPING	
Antigua Casona..........................	**7** C3
Estancia La Cinacina....................	**8** A3
Hostal de Areco..........................	**9** B2
Paradores Draghi........................	(see 6)
Patio de Moreno.........................	**10** B3

EATING	
La Ochava de Cocota..................	**11** B3
Pulpería La Lechuza...................	**12** B2
Zarza.......................................	**13** B3

SHOPPING	
Alvaro Ignacio Caldera................	**14** B2
Cristina Giordano de Bincaz..........	**15** C2
Dulces del Pago.........................	**16** A2
El Tonel Kiosko..........................	**17** A2
La Olla de Cobre.........................	**18** B2
Raúl Horacio Draghi....................	**19** C4
Sogas Areco..............................	**20** A3

TRANSPORT	
Bus Terminal.............................	**21** D3

THE PAMPAS & THE ATLANTIC COAST

---

to northern Argentina. Once a toll crossing, it's now a pedestrian bridge leading to San Antonio de Areco's main attraction, the Museo Gauchesco Ricardo Güiraldes.

Orientation

San Antonio de Areco is 113km west of Buenos Aires via RN 8. V Alsina is the main drag, though the town's numerous sites of interest and shops are scattered throughout the surrounding streets.

Information

There are a few banks with ATMs around the Plaza Ruiz de Arellano.

Areco Online (☎ 455698; Ruiz de Arellano 285; per hr AR$2) Internet access.

Post office (cnr Alvear & Av Del Valle)

Tourist office (☎ 453165; cnr E Zerboni & Ruiz de Arellano; ☺ 8:30am-10pm Mon-Fri, 8am-8pm Sat & Sun) In a white, stand-alone building in the park.

Sights

MUSEO GAUCHESCO RICARDO GÜIRALDES

Inaugurated by the provincial government in 1938, a decade after the death of Ricardo Güiraldes, author of the gaucho novel *Don Segundo Sombra* (see p147), this **museum** (☎ 455839; cnr R Güiraldes & Sosa; admission AR$3; ☺ 11am-5pm Wed-Mon) in Parque Criollo is a sort of gaucholand of restored or fabricated buildings, including an old flour mill, a re-created *pulpería* (tavern) and a colonial-style chapel. The main deal is a 20th-century reproduction of an 18th-century *casco* (ranch house), which holds a wooden bed belonging to Juan Manuel de Rosas (perhaps the ultimate rural landowner), lots of gorgeous horse gear and various works of gauchesco art. Two rooms are dedicated to Güiraldes himself.

MUSEO Y TALLER DRAGHI

This small **museum** and **workshop** (☎ 454219; Lavalle 387; admission AR$5; ⏰ 10:30am-1pm, 3:30-7:30pm, closed Sunday afternoons) highlights an exceptional collection of silver *facónes* (gaucho knives), beautiful horse gear and intricate *mate* paraphernalia.

CENTRO CULTURAL USINA VIEJA

Set in an old power plant dating from 1901, the **Centro Cultural Usina Vieja** (V Alsina 660; admission free; ⏰ 11am-5pm Tue-Sun) is an eclectic museum with a funky collection of ancient radios, typewriters, sewing machines and record players. Farm equipment, sculptures, an old-time grocery store and even a small airplane are also on display, as are rotating exhibits of local artists' work and some of Florencio Molina Campos' amusing caricatures of gaucho life.

Festivals & Events

San Antonio de Areco is the symbolic center of Argentina's vestigial cowboy culture, and puts on the country's biggest gaucho celebration on **Día de la Tradición** (in mid-November). If you're in the area, don't miss it; attractions include a horseback procession through the town, displays of horsemanship, folk dancing, craft exhibitions and guided tours of historic sites. The only drawback is that the townsfolk desert the streets for the Parque Criollo (entry AR$15) where the spectacles take place, and many of the stores and museums in town close for the day.

Sleeping

While San Antonio is a popular daytrip out of Buenos Aires, it's worth hanging around, as there are some lovely places to stay.

Hostal de Areco (☎ 456118; www.hostaldeareco.com.ar; Zapiola 25; d/tr AR$100/150) Clustered with two other hotels, which aren't as personable but do have pools, this hotel has a pleasant salon, complete with roaring fire in winter, which makes up for the smallish rooms.

Paradores Draghi (☎ 454219; reception at Lavalle 387; draghi@lq.com.ar; r AR$220; ✖ ✍ 🖳) Five large, gorgeous rooms (some with kitchenette) are

available at this tranquil place. A grassy garden with fountain soothes the spirit, and free bike rentals are available.

our pick **Antigua Casona** (☎ 456600; www.antiguacasona.com; Segundo Sombra 495; s/d/tr AR$120/250/360) This restored traditional home has a quiet patio that often hosts wine and cheese tastings, and just five rustically decorated rooms. Bikes are available, and many of the cute antique furnishings are for sale.

Patio de Moreno (☎ 445197; www.patiodemoreno.com; M Moreno 251; r AR$435-540; ✖ 🖳 ✍) The town's hippest hotel, once an old warehouse, boasts a fountain in the sunlit breakfast salon, with a serene patio and plunge pool, and slick contemporary design in the king-sized bedrooms.

ESTANCIAS

El Ombú (☎ 02326-92080, in Buenos Aires 011-4737-0436; www.estanciaelombu.com; RP 31, cuartel VI, Villa Lía; día de campo AR$150, r per person AR$270; ✍) This *estancia* once belonged to General Pablo Ricchieri, who first inflicted universal military conscription on the country. Stays here include unlimited drinks and bike rental. To get there, take RP 31 just outside of town, from where it's about 8km.

Estancia La Cinacina (☎ 452045; www.lacinacina.com.ar in Spanish; Mitre 9; día de campo AR$90, r per person AR$350; ✖ ✍) On the edge of town, this historic *estancia* offers comfortable lodgings in a pretty park setting, with horseback rides and bicycle use.

La Bamba (☎ 456293; www.la-bamba.com.ar; día de campo AR$200, d AR$1180; ✍) About 15km east of Areco along RN 8, La Bamba dates from 1830 and retains its original *pulpería*, or gaucho bar. The comfortable guest rooms are filled with antiques.

Eating

San Antonio de Areco has a considerable assortment of character-filled cafés and restaurants to choose from. Some host *peñas* on weekends – ask the locals or the people at the tourist office.

La Ochava de Cocota (☎ 452176; cnr V Alsina & LN Alem; mains AR$12-22; ⏰ breakfast, lunch & dinner Wed-Sat & Mon, dinner only Sun) Café serving homemade cakes and quiches by day, cocktail bar serving cheese plates and pizzas by night, this old corner bar has a welcoming, woody aroma and a laid-back feel.

Pulpería La Lechuza (☎ 454542; Costanera Aquiles Pazzaglia btwn Ruiz de Arellano & E Zerboni; mains AR$12-26;

THE GLORIOUS GAUCHO

If the melancholy *tanguero* (tango dancer) is the essence of the *porteño* (person from Buenos Aires), then the gaucho represents the pampa: a lone cowboy-like figure, pitted against the elements, with only his horse for a friend.

Perhaps the gaucho's chief claim to fame is as founder of Argentina's most beloved tradition. Gauchos enjoyed an all-beef diet, rigging the beast on the *asado a la cruz* (cross-shaped barbecue) and cooking it over hot embers. His only vegetable matter was *mate,* the caffeine-rich herbal tea that is sucked through a *bombilla* (metal straw) and shared among friends.

The word *gaucho* is thought to come from *huachu*, a Quechua term for vagabond. In the early years of the colony, the fringe-dwelling gauchos lived entirely beyond the laws and customs of Buenos Aires, eking out an independent and often violent existence in the countryside, slaughtering the cattle that roamed and bred unsupervised on the fertile pampas.

As the colony grew, cattle became too valuable to leave to the gauchos. Foreign demand for hides increased and investors moved into the pampas to take control of the market, establishing the *estancia* system where large landholdings were handed out to a privileged few. Many a free-wheeling gaucho became a *peón*, or exploited farmhand, while those who resisted domestication were dealt with by vagrancy laws threatening prison or the draft for gauchos without steady employment.

By the late 19th century, those in charge felt the gaucho had no place in modern Argentina. President Sarmiento (who governed from 1868–74; see p155) declared that 'fertilizing the soil with their blood is the only thing gauchos are good for' and already much gaucho blood had been spilled, their horsemanship making them excellent infantrymen for Argentina's civil war and the brutal campaigns against the Indians.

Like so many heroes, the gaucho only won love and admiration after his demise. The archetypal *macho,* his physical bravery, honor and lust for freedom are celebrated in José Hernández's 1872 epic poem *Martín Fierro* (now an animated film) and Ricardo Güiraldes' novel *Don Segundo Sombra.* His rustic traditions form part of Argentina's sophisticated folk art, with skilled craftspeople producing intricate silver gaucho knives and woven ponchos, while his image is endlessly reproduced – most amusingly in Florencio Molina Campos' caricatures that decorate many a bar and can be picked up in San Telmo's market. His sanitization reached its zenith when a cute soccer-playing *gauchito* became the mascot for the 1978 World Cup.

Alas, these days, the gaucho-for-export is much easier to spot than the real deal. But if the folkloric shows put on at many *estancias* (p150) are cheesily entertaining, the gaucho's true inheritors can be found among the men who work on cattle farms throughout the pampas – you can see them riding confidently over the plains in their dusty *boinas* (a kind of gaucho beret) and *bombachas* (caps and riding pants), while on special occasions like the Día de la Tradición (opposite) they sport their best horse gear and show off their extraordinary riding skills.

⊙ lunch & dinner) Enjoy a huge lunch of empanadas and barbecued beef under the trees or grab a *choripan* to go and enjoy it gaucho-style, by the riverbank. Located opposite the tourist office.

Zarza (☎ 453948; San Martín 361; mains AR$14-23; ⊙ dinner Wed-Mon, lunch & dinner Sat-Mon) Serving Argentine staples with a twist, this stylish restaurant offers plenty of inventive pasta options for vegetarians.

Shopping

San Antonio de Areco's artisans are known throughout the country, with many of their disciples practicing their trades in other cities and provinces. *Mate* paraphernalia, *rastras* (silver-studded belts) and *facónes*, produced by skilled silversmiths, are among the most typical. Wandering around the center you'll run into plenty of stores, but the following are must-sees.

Raúl Horacio Draghi (☎ 454207; Guido 391) Internationally known Raúl Horacio Draghi works in leather as well as silver.

Alvaro Ignacio Caldera (☎ 02325-15-654365; V Alsina, btwn Lavalle & Matheu) Alvaro is a top silversmith who claims to have made a belt buckle for ex-president and tabloid fodder Carlos Menem. Custom-made items here take weeks to make and can cost thousands of pesos.

THE PAMPAS & THE
ATLANTIC COAST

Sogas Areco (☎ 453797; General Paz near Italia) Check out this place for horse gear and gaucho clothing.

Cristina Giordano de Bincaz (☎ 452829; Sarmiento 112) There's a working loom here, plus some beautiful ponchos and *fajas* (intricate woven bands).

La Olla de Cobre (☎ 453105; Matheu near Zapiola) If you're looking for a gift of artisanal chocolates and tinned confections, come on over.

Dulces del Pago (☎ 454751; E Zerboni 280) This store offers a good variety of fruit preserves, as well as homemade *dulce de leche* (Argentina's national sweet).

El Tonel Kiosko (cnr R Güiraldes & Puente Viejo) For a funky good time, check out the second-largest wine barrel in Argentina; it's at the kiosk just across the Puente Viejo. Take a gander at the goods inside, or sit down for coffee or *mate*, but don't expect a traditional café or many tables; it's a very eclectic place run by an odd couple.

Getting There & Away

Buses run frequently from Buenos Aires to Areco (AR$21, two hours). General Belgrano, which leaves from the Don Seguno café, and Chevallier, which leaves from its small **bus terminal** (☎ 453904), are located almost next to each other on RN 8. Both serve as the town's bus terminal. A few long-distance services are available, including ones to Córdoba (AR$56, 10 hours) and Mendoza (AR$107, 12 hours).

SOUTHERN PAMPAS

Spreading out from the capital, the pampas region extends south beyond the borders of Buenos Aires province and west into the province of La Pampa.

In the southern part of Buenos Aires province, the endlessly flat plain is punctuated by sierras, or hills. The Sierras de Tandil are ancient mountain ranges, worn to soft, low summits whose heights barely reach 500m. A little to the west, Sierra de la Ventana's jagged peaks rise to 1300m, attracting hikers and climbers.

Further west again, in the province of La Pampa, are the modest granite boulders of Parque Nacional Lihué Calel.

The hillside towns of Tandil and Sierra de la Ventana offer lots of outdoor activities and a relaxing country atmosphere – both make good side trips from Buenos Aires. The provincial capital of Santa Rosa doesn't offer much in its own right, but is a decent resting point for overland travelers on their way west or south.

CHASCOMÚS
☎ 02241 / pop 30,800

This pretty town sits on the shores of Laguna Chascomús, a popular fishing spot. Its broad jacaranda-lined main street, Av Lastra, leads from RN 2, on the way to Mar del Plata, directly to the lagoon. Horses and bikes can be rented in town, and there's a paved trail all the way around the lagoon. The **tourist information office** (☎ 430405; 🕙 8:30am-8:30pm Dec-Feb, 9am-7:30pm Mar-Nov) provides maps and information on lodgings and activities.

Sights include the excellent **Museo Pampeano** (☎ 430982; Av Lastri & Muñiz; admission AR$1.50; 🕙 9am-3pm Tue-Fri, 10am-2pm & 5:30-7:30pm Sat & Sun Jan-Feb, 10am-4pm Sat & Sun Mar-Dec), filled with artifacts that represent the daily lives of the area's various former inhabitants – indigenous people, the gauchos and the wealthy landowners. Also worth a look is the **Capilla de los Negros** (Av Costanera & Presidente Perón). Here's a little-known fact: Buenos Aires province and the capital were once home to a significant African population that vanished in the 19th century – some say because they were conscripted into the war against Paraguay. In Chascomús, black people were refused entry to the main cathedral, so they built this chapel where you can still note their fusion of Catholicism with African beliefs.

There are several camping grounds near the lake, the pick of which is **Camping 6 de Septiembre** (☎ in Buenos Aires 011-15-5182-3836; www.seisdeseptiembre.com.ar in Spanish; per tent & per person AR$10; 🏊), which also offers *cabañas* (serviced cabins). There are several *parrillas* (grills) overlooking the lake on Av Costanera. **Estancia La Juanita** (☎ in Buenos Aires 011-15-5226-9158; www.estancialajuanita.com in Spanish; día de campo AR$120, r per person AR$215; 🏊) offers graciously simple accommodations, with a prime position right on the lake and the usual range of activities.

Daily trains to Chascomús leave from Constitución in Buenos Aires (AR$9, four hours), while Condor Estrella (☎ in Buenos Aires 011-4313-1700) runs several buses per day (AR$14, two hours).

TANDIL
☎ 02293 / pop 110,000

Tandil exudes a rare combination of laid-back country charm and the energy of a thriving regional city. The town sits at the northern edge of the Sierras de Tandil, a 2.5-million-year-old mountain range worn down to gentle, grassy peaks and rocky outcroppings, perfect for rock climbing and mountain biking.

The town arose from Fuerte Independencia, a military outpost established in 1823 by Martín Rodríguez. In the early 1870s, it was the scene of one of the province's most remarkable battles, when renegade gauchos, followers of the eccentric healer Gerónimo de Solané (popularly known as Tata Dios), gathered in the hills before going on a murderous rampage against landowners and recent immigrants.

The immigrants prevailed, and the culinary skills they brought from Europe have made the area an important producer of specialty foods. The hundreds of cheeses and cured meats made around Tandil can be sampled in eateries and stores throughout town.

The pretty town center is leafy and relaxed, with many places closing on Sundays and observing the afternoon siesta. Locals crowd the squares and streets of an evening, and there is plenty of cultural life, including a film festival each June (www.tandilcine.com.ar).

Orientation

Tandil is 384km south of Buenos Aires via RN 3 and RN 226, and 170km northwest of Mar del Plata via RN 226. The main commercial streets are Gral Rodríguez and 9 de Julio, while the center of social activity is Plaza

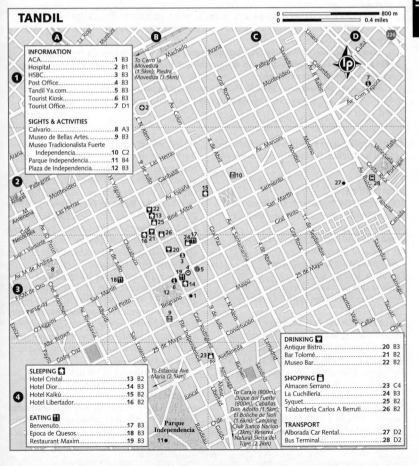

TANDIL

0 — 800 m
0 — 0.4 miles

INFORMATION
ACA...................................1 B3
Hospital............................2 B1
HSBC................................3 B3
Post Office.......................4 B3
Tandil Ya.com...................5 B3
Tourist Kiosk....................6 B3
Tourist Office...................7 D1

SIGHTS & ACTIVITIES
Calvario............................8 A3
Museo de Bellas Artes.......9 B3
Museo Tradicionalista Fuerte
   Independencia.............10 C2
Parque Independencia.....11 B4
Plaza de Independencia....12 B3

To Cerro la
Movediza
(1.5km); Piedra
Movediza (1.5km)

SLEEPING
Hotel Cristal......................13 B2
Hotel Dior.........................14 B3
Hotel Kaikú.......................15 B3
Hotel Libertador................16 B2

EATING
Benvenuto.........................17 B3
Epoca de Quesos...............18 B3
Restaurant Maxim..............19 B3

To Estancia Ave
Maria (2.5km)

To Carajo (800m);
Dique del Fuerte
(800m); Cabañas
Don Adolfo (1.5km);
El Boliche de Noli
(1.6km); Camping
Club Banco Nacion
(2km); Reserva
Natural Sierra del
Tigre (2.2km)

**Parque
Independencia**
11●

DRINKING
Antique Bistro...................20 B3
Bar Tolomé.......................21 B2
Museo Bar........................22 B2

SHOPPING
Almacen Serrano...............23 C4
La Cuchillería....................24 B3
Syquet..............................25 B2
Talabartería Carlos A Berruti....26 B2

TRANSPORT
Alborada Car Rental...........27 D2
Bus Terminal.....................28 D2

DÍA DE CAMPO

One of the best ways to enjoy the wide open spaces of the pampas is to visit an *estancia*, or cattle ranch. Argentina's late-19th-century belle epoque saw wealthy landowning families adorn their ranches with lavish, often fanciful homes and designer gardens, which they used as country retreats.

Those glorious days being long gone, a rich selection of these establishments is now open to tourists. The *día de campo* – or 'day in the country' – includes a huge *asado* (barbecue grill) lunch with drinks, a tour of the historic home and use of the property's horses, bicycles and swimming pool. Some places also offer a *show gauchesco*, featuring folk dances and traditional feats of horsemanship, while others host polo matches. *Estancias* are an excellent sustainable tourism option, helping to preserve part of the country's past while also providing an impressive guest-to-tree ratio. Overnight stays generally include all meals and activities. Here are some stand-out options in the pampas (rates include all meals and are per person):

La Candelaria (☎ 02227-424404; www.estanciacandelaria.com; RN 205, Lobos; día de campo AR$165, r AR$300; 🏊) The original family went bust building their French-style castle, whose grounds were designed by Charles Thays, responsible for many of Buenos Aires' public parks. Polo matches often held.

Santa Rita (☎ 02227-495026; www.santa-rita.com.ar; RN 205, Lobos; día de campo AR$150, r AR$400; 🏊) A somewhat eccentric restoration rescued this colonial-era home, whose chapel is one of the oldest in the province.

Juan Gerónimo (☎ 02221-481414; www.juangeronimo.com.ar; RP 36, Veronica; día de campo AR$200, r AR$400) Excellent horseback riding and bird watching at this working cattle farm, which includes a Unesco World Biosphere Reserve.

Bella Vista de Guerrero (☎ 02245-481234; www.bellavistadeguerrero.com; RN 2, Castelli; día de campo AR$272, r $544; 🏊) Boasts a magnificently restored mansion, gourmet cuisine, luxurious rooms and a day spa.

de Independencia, a two-block area bounded by Gral Rodríguez, Belgrano, Chacabuco and Gral Pinto.

Information

ACA (Automóvil Club Argentina; ☎ 425463; Gral Rodríguez 399) Argentina's auto club; good source for provincial road maps.

Hospital (Hospital Municipal Ramón Santamarina; ☎ 422210; Gral Paz 1406)

HSBC (cnr San Martín & 9 Julio) Has ATM.

Post office (Gral Pinto 621)

Tandil Ya.com (cnr 9 Julio & Gral Pinto; per hr $AR1; 🕐 9am-10pm Mon-Fri, 9am-1pm & 5-9pm Sat, closed Sun) Internet access.

Tourist kiosk (cnr Grals Pinto & Rodríguez, Plaza Independencia; 🕐 8am-6pm Mon-Sat, 9am-1pm Sun) Distributes a good city map and useful brochures.

Tourist office (Dirección de Turismo; ☎ 432073; www .tandil.gov.ar; Av Com Espora 1120; 🕐 8am-8pm Mon-Fri, 8am-8pm Sat, 9am-1pm Sun)

Sights

Tandil's museums include the historic **Museo Tradicionalista Fuerte Independencia** (☎ 435573; 4 de Abril 845; admission AR$5; 🕐 2-6pm Mar-Nov, 4-8pm Dec-Feb), which exhibits a large and varied collection on the town's history. Photographs (captioned in Spanish) commemorate major events, and the place is filled with relics – from carriages to ladies' gloves – donated by local families. The **Museo de Bellas Artes** (☎ 432067; Chacabuco 353; admission AR$1; 🕐 8:30am-12:30pm & 5-9pm Tue-Fri, 5-9pm Sat & Sun) holds a permanent collection of both European and Argentine art, including works by Antonio Berni and contemporary artist León Ferrari.

The walk to **Parque Independencia** from the southwestern edge of downtown offers good views of the city, particularly at night, while the central **Plaza de Independencia**, surrounded by the typical municipal buildings and church, is where the townspeople stroll in the evenings, often to the sounds of music from the bandstand.

At the north edge of town, where Tata Dios gathered his supporters over a century ago, the Piedra Movediza (a 300-ton 'rocking stone') once teetered precariously atop **Cerro La Movediza** for many years before falling in 1912. A 'replica,' non-moving stone was built in 2007, and a theme park is planned. Take bus 503 (blue).

Calvario, a hill ostensibly resembling the site of Christ's crucifixion, attracts masses of visitors at Easter, when a passion play is held.

The **Reserva Natural Sierra del Tigre** (☎ 1554-1803; at the end of Calle Suiza; ✷ closed Wed & rainy days) is just outside of town, off Av Don Bosco. The rocky hills are fun to climb, and in spring the reserve is filled with fragrant wild flowers. The peaks offer views of the town to one side and the patchwork pampean farms stretching out from the other. A somewhat incongruous collection of animals – llamas and donkeys among them – makes the park its home.

Activities

The **Dique del Fuerte**, only 12 blocks south of Plaza Independencia, is a huge reservoir where the Balneario Municipal runs three **swimming pools**. The Centro Nautico del Fuerte rents **canoes** and **kayaks** in summer.

To go horseback riding in the Reserva Natural Sierra del Tigre, call **Gabriel Barletta** (☎ 427725, 02293-15-584833; half-day tours per person AR$75).

Several tour agencies offer a range of activities around the town and the sierras. The highly trained guides at **Chao Tandil** (☎ 432542; www.chaotandil.com.ar in Spanish) offer trekking, canoeing, rappelling, mountain biking and rock climbing. **Kumbre** (☎ 434313; www.kumbre.com in Spanish) offers much the same, as well as walking tours taking in municipal and geographical history. Skydiving is offered by **Paracaidismo Tandil** (☎ 445005; www.paracaidismotandil.com.ar in Spanish).

Sleeping

Reservations are a must during summer, Easter week and holiday weekends. If you have your own transport, the many cabañas along Av Don Bosco are a good option – the tourist office provides lists of fully equipped cabins, many of which have pools.

Camping Club Banco Nacion (☎ 423125; Av Don Bosco & Yugoslavia; per person AR$10; ✷) Out of town, towards the *reserva*, this campground also offers dorm-style lodgings, as well as *parrillas* and outdoor activities.

Hotel Kaikú (☎ 423114; Bmé Mitre 902; per person AR$40) This modest and tidy hotel has been doing business here for 140 years and is in need of a facelift, but it's good value and by far the best budget bet in the center. Rates don't include breakfast.

Hotel Cristal (☎ 443970; hotelcristal_tandil@yahoo.com.ar; Gral Rodríguez 871; s/d/tr AR$82/112/132; ▣) A

basic but comfortable hotel, with a sunny garden where guests can enjoy breakfast.

Cabañas Don Adolfo (☎ 431030; www.cabaniasdonadolfo.com.ar; Don Bosco 800; 2-person cabin AR$120) A good-value option, offering cable TV, a wood-fired stove and outdoor *parrillas*.

Hotel Dior (☎ 431901; www.hoteldior.com; Gral Rodríguez 475; d/tr AR$205/259; ✷ ▣) This three-star's comfortable rooms feature bouncy beds, good-sized bathrooms and small balconies with lovely views of the square and the hills beyond town.

Hotel Libertador (☎ 422127; www.hotel-libertador.com.ar in Spanish; Bmé Mitre 545; s/d/tr AR$175/225/260; ✷) The smartest hotel in town is this modern four star, a couple of blocks from the plaza. Rooms are spacious and the restaurant isn't bad either.

Estancia Ave Maria (☎ 422843; www.avemariatandil.com.ar; d AR$590; ✷) This historic *estancia* offers home-cooked meals and elegant, comfortable rooms, some with views of the hills. Horseback rides and other outdoor activities included; *día de campo* is not offered. Take Juan B Justo just west of town; it's along Circuito Turistico, not far out of town.

Eating

Benvenuto (☎ 447001; cnr San Martín & L N Alem; pastas AR$9-14.50; ✷ lunch & dinner Tue-Sun) One of the few restaurants in the country doing only pasta, and they do it very well – it's all homemade and deliciously fresh. The *putanesca* sauce may have you hanging around town for a few unscheduled days.

Carajo (☎ 436669; Saavedra, at Club Nautico on the lake; mains $11-19; ✷ breakfast, lunch & dinner Wed-Mon) With a sunny outdoor terrace overlooking the lake, this place offers snacks like burgers and smoothies throughout the day and fires up the *parrilla* for lunch and dinner.

Restaurant Maxim (☎ 442444; cnr Grals Pinto & Rodríguez; mains AR$10-24; ✷ breakfast, lunch & dinner) Breakfast on the plaza? The Maxim is your spot: light and sunny, with heaps of sidewalk seating, but get there before the old guys grab all the tables.

our pick **Epoca de Quesos** (☎ 448750; cnr San Martín & 14 de Julio; mains AR$10-30; ✷ 9am-late) In one of Tandil's oldest buildings, Epoca de Quesos sells over 130 local cheeses and dozens of cured meats. You can taste and buy at the counter or dine in – in summer there's a sunny garden and on cold days customers huddle in the woodfire-warmed back rooms to enjoy the huge sampler plates and specialty beers.

El Boliche de Noli (cnr Don Bosco & Francia; 🕙 lunch & dinner Wed-Mon) Not far from the Reserva, this 100-year old former *pulpería* is another great place to taste the local cheeses, meats and beers, or to stock up on goods to take back to your *cabaña*.

Drinking

For a small town, Tandil has several good bars.

Bar Tolomé (☎ 422951; cnr Gral Rodríguez & Bmé Mitre; 🕙 7:30am-late) Dead midweek and lively on weekends, this relaxed bar serves pizzas and sandwiches when a beer's not enough.

Museo Bar (Gral Rodríguez 887; 🕙 7pm-late) There are pool tables and flat-screen TVs at this popular bar. Bands play most Friday nights and you can get two-for-one beers from 6pm to 11pm every evening.

Antique Bistro (☎ 449339; Gral Rodríguez 687; 🕙 7am-late, dinner show Wed) A sophisticated mood prevails at this tiny old-fashioned piano bar, where live folk and tango bands perform.

Shopping

Cold cuts and cheese are what Tandil is famous for, but there are also plenty of finely crafted gaucho knives that will come in handy when slicing the salami.

La Cuchillería (☎ 444937; San Martín 780) From 8cm whittlers to 36cm *facónes,* this high-end knife shop sells a wide array of quality handmade blades.

Talabartería Carlos A Berruti (☎ 425787; Gral Rodríguez 787) Especially good for leather, this store also stocks an assortment of *mates,* knives, silverwork and ponchos.

Almacen Serrano (☎ 448102; cnr Av Avellaneda & Gral Rodríguez) Sells cheese, salamis and hams from the region, as well as locally made beers and sweets.

Syquet (☎ 422122; cnr Bmé Mitre & Gral Rodríguez) More cheeses, meats and beers, plus a good selection of *dulce de leche,* jams and liqueurs made from chocolate and honey.

Getting There & Away

Several bus companies go to Buenos Aires daily from Tandil's **bus terminal** (☎ 432092; Av Buzón 650 at Portugal). There are buses every two hours to Mar del Plata and frequent services to other destinations along the coast. The following table shows approximate travel times and midseason fares for some popular destinations.

Destination	Cost (AR$)	Duration (hr)
Buenos Aires	53	5¼
Córdoba	124	14¾
Mar del Plata	24	3
Mendoza	178	14½
Necochea	24	2
Rosario	84	11
San Juan	186	18
San Luis	156	12
Santiago del Estero	186	18
Tucumán	207	20

Getting Around

Tandil's excellent public transportation system reaches every important sight. Bus 500 (yellow) goes to Dique del Fuerte, bus 501 (red) goes to the bus terminal, and bus 503 (blue) goes to Cerro La Movediza, the university and the bus terminal.

For car rental, try **Alborada** (☎ 441950; cnr Gral Pinto & Saavedra).

SIERRA DE LA VENTANA
☎ 0291 / pop 2000

The Río Sauce winding gently through it, this leafy town fills up on weekends, with families from around the province flocking to its pretty bathing spots and picturesque hills.

Sierra de la Ventana's main attraction is the wealth of outdoor activity it offers: hiking up the nearby peaks, trout fishing and bathing in the streams and pools, riding on horse or bicycle through the hills and climbing or rappelling among the rocks.

To reach the town from Bahía Blanca (125km to its south), take RN 33 to Tornquist, then RP 76. Sierra de la Ventana is divided into two sectors by Río Sauce Grande: Villa Tivoli has all of the businesses and services, while Villa Arcadia is a more residential area and also the locale for many hotels.

Information

Banco de la Provincia (San Martín 260) Has an ATM.

Cyber Intersierra (Av San Martín 403; per hr AR$2) Internet access.

Post office (cnr Av Roca & Alberdi)

Tourist office (☎ 491-5303; Av del Golf; 🕙 8:30am-1:30pm & 3:30-8:30pm) Across the tracks from the train station. Distributes a useful packet of maps and flyers and can help find accommodations.

Activities

Lots of outdoor pursuits are on offer in this region, and you can tackle some of them on your own. If you'd rather hire a guide, both **GeoTur** (☎ 491-5355; Av San Martín 193) and **Luan & Ventur** (☎ 491-5005; Av San Martín 140) offer tours to Garganta del Diablo (see p154), which is the only way to explore the gorge. They also offer hikes to Cerro Tres Picos (see p154), as well as activities like rappelling and horseback riding.

Eco Ventania (☎ 491-0245; 7 Colores btwn Pillahuinco & Cruz del Sur, Villa Ventana) offers similar activities as well as jeep tours and photographic safaris, while **Campo Equino** (☎ 0291-15-6431582; RP 76, Km 230) specializes in horseback riding.

Sleeping

Camping El Paraíso (☎ 0291-15-4074530; Los Paraísos & Diego Meyer; adult/child AR$10/5) This full-facility campground is opposite the river and the municipal swimming pool. It also offers dorms (double/triple AR$40/50).

Hospedaje La Perlita (☎ 491-5020; Calle E Morón; r AR$50) Basic, clean rooms cluster around an overgrown garden at this very friendly and secure hostel, but there's no breakfast or kitchen use.

Hostería AMOSBA (☎ 491-5071; cnr Punta Alta & Cnl Suarez; d/tr $70/120) This place in leafy Villa Arcadia offers simple, comfortable rooms as well as *cabañas* (AR$250) for up to five.

Hotel Provincial (☎ 491-5024; Drago 130; s/d AR$95/129; 🖳) Fans of crumbling grandeur won't want to miss this big old place. Dating from 1945, it's not in such a bad way, and the curving hallways and huge dining/ballroom add some real touches of class.

Hotel Atero (☎ 491-5002; fax 491-5344; cnr Av San Martín & Güemes; d/tr AR$120/180) Thoroughly remodeled rooms with balconies overlooking the street make this old hotel a favorite, so if you're coming in summer, book ahead.

Estancia El Retiro (☎ 491-5034; www.golfyestancias .com.ar/el_retiro.htm; s/d full board AR$180/270; 🖳) The *estancia* takes in a 70-hectare park and a golf course, while the Anglo-Norman castle built in 1904 is decorated with original antiques and enjoys sweeping views of the sierras. Activities include trout fishing, horseback riding, mountain biking, farm work and bird watching. Take RP 72, 3km south of town.

Eating

Parrilla Rali-Hué (☎ 491-5220; San Martín 307; mains AR$12-16; 🕒 lunch & dinner) Beef only at this plastic-tablecloth joint, where locals flock to dine on the *parrillada* (mixed grill) for two – great value at AR$28.

Hotel Provincial (☎ 491-5024; Drago 130; AR$12-28; 🕒 breakfast, lunch & dinner) Within this large hotel the attractive bar/restaurant is a worthwhile spot to enjoy a drink or snack while gazing over the rolling green hills.

Sher (☎ 491-5055; Güemes, near San Martín; mains AR$12-32; 🕒 lunch & dinner) Inventive dishes like *jabalí en escabeche* (a kind of wild boar stew) make this place a culinary adventure. Plenty of steak and pasta for the timid palate.

Sol y Luna (☎ 491-5316; Av San Martín 393; mains AR$13-29; 🕒 lunch & dinner) A huge menu offers everything from pastas and pizzas to *parrilla* and fresh trout. Vegetarians will welcome the soy burgers and other non-meat specials, all served in an attractive dining room.

Getting There & Away

Buses to Buenos Aires (AR$75, eight hours) and Bahía Blanca (AR$15, two hours) leave from Av San Martín, departing from the small kiosk near the gas station, which also sells tickets. **GeoTur** (☎ 491-5355) runs a door-to-door service between Sierra de la Ventana and Tornquist (AR$5, one hour), stopping at Saldungaray and Villa Ventana (AR$3), three times daily.

From the **train station** (☎ 491-5164; cnr Av San Martín & Roca), somewhat slow and unreliable trains leave three times a week for Buenos Aires (AR$20 to AR$35, 11 hours) and at 7am for Bahía Blanca (AR$7, two hours).

AROUND SIERRA DE LA VENTANA
☎ 0291

The hills around Sierra de la Ventana constitute Argentina's oldest mountain range, and are the site of much hiking, horseback riding, picnicking and general pleasure-seeking during the warmer months. Hiking trails can get very crowded during school holidays and weekends, and accommodations fill up fast in the high season.

Villa Ventana

Sierra de la Ventana's peaceful, woodsy neighbor offers a quieter base from which to explore the area's delights.

Just 17km southeast of Sierra de la Ventana, Villa Ventana's dirt roads are shaded by tall trees and curling ivy. The village is growing fast – while birdsong and the clip-clop of horses' hooves may be the only sounds during the week, long weekends and holidays see the serenity factor drop dramatically.

THE PAMPAS & THE
ATLANTIC COAST

SLEEPING

Hostería La Peninsula (☎ 491-0012; cnr Golondrina & Cruz del Sur; s/d AR$50/100; ☒) Right at the entrance to town, Villa Ventana's oldest hotel is pretty basic. The pool (when it's operating) is a welcome addition.

Posada Agua Pampas (☎ 491-0210; www.aguapampas.com.ar; cnr Calle Las Piedras & Canario; r AR$180-295; ☒) Definitely the town's best digs, this place is built from local stone and recycled wood, right down to the hollow-log bathtubs. It also boasts a chemical-free water recycling system that protects the nearby stream from pollution. Rooms are deliciously comfortable, each with its own deck looking towards the stream and the woods.

There are lots of cabins with kitchens to rent; ask the tourist office for a list and help with vacancies. Prices start around AR$120 for a double. Try the following for starters.

Del Molino (☎ 491-0090; www.del-molino.com.ar)
El Establo (☎ 491-0303)
Caramelo (☎ 491-0154)

There are grounds in town, but campers are better off heading to Cerro de la Ventana (right).

EATING

Rancho Villa (☎ 491-0052; cnr Cruz del Sur & Zorzal; mains AR$6-14; ☽ breakfast, lunch & dinner) This little teahouse has outdoor tables where you can snack on locally made *alfajores* (cookie-type sandwiches usually stuffed with *dulce de leche*) and quick meals like steak sandwiches.

Naposta (☎ 491-0178; cnr Cruz del Sur & Hornero; mains AR$12-36; ☽ lunch & dinner Tue-Sun) The small but varied menu includes delicious homemade pastas, along with meat, seafood and pizza. There are also *picadas* (appetizer plates) to share.

GETTING THERE & AWAY

Shuttles (AR$3, 20 minutes) connect Sierra de la Ventana (stops in front of the GeoTur office) with Villa Ventana (stops in front of Rancho Villa) three times a day – pick up a schedule at the tourist information office. A *remise* (telephone taxi) will cost around AR$50. From Bahía Blanca (AR$15, two hours), take the minivan that leaves for Sierra de la Ventana. Buses depart three times daily from the bus station – ask to be dropped off at Cerro de la Ventana, which is on the way.

Cerro Tres Picos

The 1239m Cerro Tres Picos, southwest of Villa Ventana but accessed from RP 76, is a worthwhile excursion. Since this is the private property of Estancia Funke, there is a charge – AR$8 to spend the day walking, cooking a barbecue lunch and enjoying the swimming spots, or AR$11 to make the 10-hour climb to the top of Cerro Tres Picos, where you can pitch your tent in a natural cave. Contact **Monica Silva** (☎ 494-0058) to arrange visits. Day hikers must begin by 9am; overnighters can start as late as 2pm. No food outlets here, so bring your own.

Parque Provincial Ernesto Tornquist

The 67-sq-km **Parque Provincial Ernesto Tornquist** (☎ 491-0039; admission AR$8; ☽ hikes 9am-5pm), 5km from Villa Ventana, draws visitors from throughout the province – on sunny weekends its hiking trails can be as busy as a Buenos Aires shopping strip. The **Centro de Visitantes** has a well-organized display on local ecology, enhanced by audiovisuals. The park's high point is the two-hour hike to 1186m **Cerro de la Ventana**, named for the window-shaped rock formation near its peak. The climb offers dramatic views of surrounding hills and the distant pampas, as well as glimpses of the wild guanacos that have been re-introduced to the park, along with the harder-to-spot puma. At the Cerro de la Ventana trailhead, rangers and volunteer guides collect the entry fee and register names. Those hiking to the top of Cerro de la Ventana must set out by 11am. Shorter, easier trails lead to small swimming holes. To visit the gorge at **Garganta del Diablo** (Devil's Throat), you must go with a private tour company (see p152). There's a kiosk near the base of the Cerro de la Ventana trail, but it's not always open – best to bring your own eats. Minibuses (AR$3) head from Sierra de la Ventana and Villa Ventana twice daily – pick up a schedule at the tourist office in either town.

SLEEPING & EATING

Campamento Base (☎ 491-0015; RP 76, Km 224; sites per person AR$10) This friendly campground at Cerro de la Ventana has shaded campsites and basic dorms with kitchens, clean bathrooms and excellent hot showers.

Hotel El Mirador (☎ 494-1338; RP 76, Km 226; s/d AR$160/205, 4-person cabin AR$350; ☒ ☒) A short distance from Cerro de la Ventana, pleasant

A-frame cabins and an ample hotel offer all the amenities, including an all-day restaurant. *Asado* is the house specialty, with meat dishes around $AR25 to AR$30, as well as local game meats. Pastas go for around AR$20.

SANTA ROSA

☎ 02954 / pop 82,000

About 600km from Buenos Aires – and a long way from pretty much anywhere else – Santa Rosa is unlikely to be of interest unless you find yourself traveling overland, in which case it's a convenient stopping point and transport hub. While Santa Rosa itself offers scant charms, it serves as a base for exploring Parque Nacional Lihué Calel, an isolated but pretty park that's home to a surprising assortment of vegetation and wildlife.

The area's native people were displaced, and many thousands killed, during General Roca's 'Conquest of the Desert' in 1879, but La Pampa is still home to the Ranquel people, who have regained some of their traditional lands and maintain their language and culture.

The city was founded in 1892 by French, Spanish and Italian immigrants who arrived with the expansion of the railroads at the turn of the 19th century. But one measure of Santa Rosa's continuing isolation and insignificance is that until 1951 the surrounding area remained a territory rather than a province.

Santa Rosa is also a university town, with the University of La Pampa attracting students from around the region.

Orientation

North of Av España, the city consists of a standard grid centered on the spotless but nearly shadeless Plaza San Martín. Most businesses are on the plaza and its surrounding streets, while the modern Centro Cívico, seven blocks east on Av Pedro Luro, is another center of activity.

CIVILIZATION OR BARBARISM?

In the early days of the Argentine Republic, one of its founding fathers, the journalist and statesman Domingo Faustino Sarmiento (1811–88), looked out onto the pampas and saw a problem. Mile upon countless mile of flat, fertile land, barely punctuated by any mark of civilization, filled instead with barbarians – from the illiterate gaucho to the remnants of Indian tribes clinging to their land, to the landowner who wielded feudal power, scorning the city-dweller and his enlightened plans for the nation. For Sarmiento, if Argentina were to become a modern democracy, the landscape itself would have to be overcome. 'Its own extent is the evil from which the Argentine republic suffers,' he wrote in *Civilizaton and Barbarism*, his 1845 treatise on the Argentine condition.

Throughout the pampa, each landowning family lived great distances from the next, without the civilizing influence of society or the benefits of education and religious ceremony. Their vast landholdings made them lazy: cattle simply ate the plentiful natural pasture, bred and were slaughtered. The people had no real occupation – young boys played at gaucho games and tormented the livestock, eschewing books and growing into savage men impervious to the rule of law.

Sarmiento was determined to stamp out feudal barbarism in Argentina and replace it with civilized village life. His answer was to populate the pampas, calling for the millions of immigrants who poured in from Europe to found the towns that now dot the plains. Meanwhile, President Sarmiento doubled student enrollment and built dozens of public libraries.

According to some, though, his project was in vain. Almost a century later Ezequiel Martínez Estrada answered Sarmiento with *X-Ray of the Pampa*, an essay condemning the rich 'lords of the nothingness' who continued to graze their cattle on the plains, never turning their energies to nation-building, and pitying the newly arrived immigrants who found an emptiness as wide and indifferent to their plight as the sea they had just crossed.

These days, while Sarmiento is credited with having founded modern Argentina, it's up for debate as to whether his vision of a civilized democracy ever really bore fruit. The country still struggles to industrialize and its democratic institutions remain fragile. Meanwhile, repeated financial crises have seen scores of villages disappear, their inhabitants leaving the interior to seek work in the capital, many building precarious homes in Buenos Aires' slums.

THE PAMPAS & THE ATLANTIC COAST

THE PAMPAS & THE ATLANTIC COAST

Information

You'll find several ATMs in the center.

ACA (☎ 422435; Av San Martín 102) Argentina's auto club; good source for provincial road maps. At the corner of Coronel Gil.

Alianza Francesa (☎ 423947; Lagos 67; ☽ 2-10pm Mon-Fri)

Post office (Hilario Lagos 258)

Tourist information center (☎ 436555; Luro 365; ☽ 24hr) In the bus terminal.

Tourist office (☎ 424404; www.turismolapampa .gov.ar; cnr Luro & San Martín; ☽ 7am-8:30pm Mon-Fri, 9:30am-1pm & 2-8:30pm Sat & Sun) Across the road from the bus terminal. Helpful staff speak some English.

Sights & Activities

The **Museo de Ciencias Naturales y Antropológicas** (☎ 422693; Pellegrini 180; admission free; ☽ 8am-5pm Mon-Fri, 5-9pm Sat & Sun) is heavy on the stuffed-animal collection, particularly featuring birds of the pampas. There's a good little live snake exhibit and a bit about local dinosaur fossil discoveries.

The **Museo de Bellas Artes** (☎ 427332; cnr 9 de Julio & Villegas; admission free; ☽ 7am-1:30pm & 2-8pm Tue-Fri, 6:30-9:30pm Sat & Sun) is an unexpectedly modern gallery featuring local and national artists, with five rooms of rotating exhibitions and a little sculpture garden out the back.

The **Teatro Español** (☎ 455325; Hilario Lagos 54; admission free; ☽ 10am-noon & 4-6:30pm Mon-Fri, hr vary Sat & Sun) is Santa Rosa's major performing-arts venue and dates from 1927.

Laguna Don Tomás, 1km west of the center, is the place for locals to boat, swim, play sports or just stroll.

Sleeping

Centro Recreativo Municipal Don Tomás (☎ 455358; Av Uruguay; sites free; 🖭) Camping facilities are excellent and include picnic tables, *parrillas*, a swimming pool, hot showers, a fitness course for joggers and shade trees. Bring repellent for the ferocious mosquitoes. From the bus terminal, take the local Transporte El Indio bus. It's at the west end of Av Uruguay.

Hotel San Martín (☎ 422549; www.hsanmartin .com.ar in Spanish; cnr Alsini & Pelligrini; s/d AR$80/120; 🖭) Opposite the sadly defunct train station, the San Martín offers clean and quiet rooms in a reasonably central location. Breakfast is a standard affair, but the coffee is excellent.

Hotel Calfucurá (☎ 433303; www.hotelcalfucura.com; San Martín 695; s/d AR$163/217; 🖭 🖭) The sedate atmosphere and handy location around the

corner from the bus terminal make this a winner. It's the best hotel in town by far, and the recently remodeled rooms are comfy.

Eating

La Recova (☎ 424444; cnr Hipólito Yrigoyen & Avellaneda; meals AR$14-25; ☽ breakfast, lunch & dinner) Good for breakfast, this sunny little place right on Plaza San Martín does the whole *confitería* (café) thing to perfection.

Club Español (☎ 439320; Hilario Lagos 237; all you can eat AR$28; ☽ lunch & dinner Tue-Sat) Don't let the name fool you – it's purely Argentine steaks, pastas and salads here, though the tiled courtyard with tinkling fountain is reminiscent of the old country.

Camelot (☎ 435566; Pueyrredón 25; meals AR$37-48; ☽ dinner Wed-Sat) Here's some geographical confusion for you – an Irish pub in the middle of Argentina named after an English castle. Still…the food's good and the Guinness is cold, so who cares?

Getting There & Away

It's AR$387 and it's actually an Aerolineas flight. Worth noting also that there's only one flight per week, on Wednesdays.

Aerolineas (☎ 433076; cnr Lagos & Moreno) flies to Buenos Aires (AR$387) once a week on Wednesdays. Taxis to the airport, which is 3km from town, cost about AR$7.

The **bus terminal** (☎ 422952, 422249; Luro 365) has departures for Bahía Blanca (AR$62, five hours), Buenos Aires (AR$96, eight hours), Puerto Madryn (AR$117, 10 hours), Mendoza (AR$127, 12 hours), Neuquén (AR$96, seven hours) and Bariloche (AR$140, 12 hours).

RESERVA PROVINCIAL PARQUE LURO
☎ 02954

Home to a mix of introduced and native species, as well as over 100 species of birds, the 75-sq-km **Reserva Provincial Parque Luro** (☎ 499000; www.parqueluro.gov.ar; admission AR$1; ☽ 9am-7:30pm, closed Mon) is a delightful spot to while away some easy hours.

The park's curious history explains its unusual assortment of beasts. At the turn of the 20th century, a wealthy local and keen hunter, Doctor Pedro Luro, created Argentina's first hunting preserve in these woods, importing exotic game species such as Carpathian deer and European boar. He also built an enormous French-style mansion (now a museum) to accommodate his European guests. As sport hunting fell out of vogue and the European aristocracy suffered the upheavals of WWI and the Great Depression, Luro went broke. The reserve was sold, then neglected, its animals escaping through the fence or falling victim to poachers (still a menace today). Later Luro's successor Antonio Maura exploited the forests for firewood and charcoal, grazing cattle and sheep, and breeding polo ponies.

Since its acquisition by the province in 1965, Parque Luro has served as a recreational and historical resource for the people of La Pampa, and a refuge for native species like puma and wild fox, along with exotic migratory birds, including flamingo. You reach the **Centro de Interpretación** by following the path from the entrance. There you'll find good material on local ecology and early forest exploitation, as well maps of the various hiking trails throughout the park.

Tours of the **Castillo Luro** (9am-7:30pm, closed Mon), as the museum is known, offer insight into the luxurious eccentricities that Argentine landowners could afford to indulge in the first half of the 20th century. Note, for instance, the walnut fireplace – an obsession that Luro was able to satisfy only by purchasing an entire Parisian restaurant.

Besides the museum, there are picnic areas, a small zoo, a restaurant and the **Sala de Caruajes**, a collection of turn-of-the-century carriages. Bikes can be rented near the restaurant on Sundays only.

Parque Luro is about 35km south of Santa Rosa, and is slightly tricky to get to without a car, except in January when a minibus heads out from the Santa Rosa bus terminal at around 8:30am and collects passengers at park closing time. Otherwise, ask at the terminal and catch a ride on a bus heading down RN 35 (AR$5) – they can drop you off near the park entrance.

PARQUE NACIONAL LIHUÉ CALEL
 02952
In the local indigenous language of Pehuenche, Lihué Calel means Sierra de la Vida or Range of Life, and describes the series of small, isolated mountain ranges and valleys that mark this nearly featureless pampean landscape.

While agriculture has driven native wildlife out of much of the pampas, this desert-like park is a haven for native cats like puma and yagouaroundi, which are still persecuted by local cattle farmers. You can easily spot armadillo, guanaco, mara (Patagonian hare) and vizcacha, while birdlife includes the rhea-like ñandú and many birds of prey such as the carancho (crested caracara). Though you're unlikely to encounter them unless you overturn rocks, be aware of the highly poisonous pit vipers commonly known as yarará.

Though Lihué Calel receives only about 400mm of rainfall per year, water is an important factor in the landscape. Sudden storms can bring flash floods and create brief but impressive waterfalls over granite boulders near the visitors center. Even when the sky is cloudless, the subterranean streams in the valleys nourish the *monte* (a scrub forest with a surprising variety of plant species). Within the park's 10 sq km exist 345 species of plants, nearly half the total found in the entire province.

Until General Roca's Conquest of the Desert, Araucanian Indians successfully defended the area against European invasion. Archaeological evidence, including petroglyphs, recalls their presence and that of their ancestors. Lihué Calel was the last refuge of the Araucanian leader Namuncurá, who eluded Argentine forces for several years before finally surrendering.

Located 226km southwest of Santa Rosa, the salmon-colored granite peaks do not exceed 600m, but still offer enjoyable hiking, and a variety of subtle environments that change with the seasons.

More information is available at the tiny **visitors center** (436595).

Sights & Activities
From the park campground, a signed nature trail follows an intermittent stream through a dense thorn forest of caldén and other typical trees. The trail leads to a petroglyph site, unfortunately vandalized. The friendly and knowledgeable rangers accompany visitors if their schedule permits.

A trail marks the gradual climb to the 589m peak, which bears the charming name **Cerro de la Sociedad Científica Argentina**. Watch for flowering cacti such as *Trichocereus candicans* between the boulders, but remember that the granite is very slippery when wet. From the summit, there are outstanding views of the entire sierra and its surrounding marshes and salt lakes, such as Laguna Urre Lauquen to the southwest.

If you have a vehicle, visit **Viejo Casco**, the big house of former Estancia Santa María, whose land the provincial government expropriated before transferring it to the national park system. It's possible to make a circuit via the **Valle de las Pinturas**, where there are some undamaged petroglyphs. Ask rangers for directions.

Sleeping

Near the visitors center is a comfortable and free campground with shade trees, firepits, picnic tables, clean toilets, cold showers (great in the baking-hot summer) and electricity until 11pm (bring a flashlight). Nearby you're likely to see foxes, vizcachas and many, many birds. Stock up on food before arriving; the nearest decent supplies are at the town of Puelches, 35km south.

ACA Hostería (☎ 436101; s/d AR$40/60) If you don't want to camp, you have one choice: this basic but functional place on the highway. There is a restaurant (which is nothing to get excited about) and the park entrance is a short walk away.

Getting There & Away

Buses head to the park from Santa Rosa's bus terminal (AR$27, 3¾ hours).

Driving is the best way to visit Parque Nacional Lihué Calel. Try **Rent Auto** (☎ 435770; cnr Luro & P Harris) in Santa Rosa.

ATLANTIC COAST

Argentines can justly claim Latin America's highest peak (Cerro Aconcagua), its widest street (9 Julio) and perhaps its prettiest capital, but its beaches are nothing to write home about. Nonetheless, while well-heeled *porteños* head to Uruguay and Brazil to while away the summer, most folks flock to the string of resort towns that dot the Atlantic Coast.

The coastal towns, for the most part, overflow in January and become very quiet – verging on depressing – in winter. As for the beaches, there's no white sand or turquoise waters here. The sand is darkish and the water cloudy but clean, while savage winds can turn sunbathers into *milanesas* in moments, sand sticking to their skins like crumbs on a schnitzel. Which explains the *balnearios* – beach clubs that offer a range of services from bathrooms to babysitters, but most importantly tents.

But while it's no paradise, the Atlantic coast does offer a quick escape from the steamy capital, and plenty of outdoor activities. Mar

del Plata is a bustling metropolis in its own right, with a rich cultural life and a great annual film festival. Pinamar attracts a hip summer crowd, while tiny Mar Chiquita boasts a worthwhile nature reserve.

Even by Argentine standards, prices are hard to pin down, rising sharply in December through February before declining until late March, when most lodgings close. Bargains can be found in the cooler months, though Easter marks an excuse to raise them briefly.

SAN CLEMENTE DEL TUYÚ
☎ 02252 / pop 11,050

With absolutely none of the glitz or glamour of the resorts down the coast, San Clemente is a favorite for low-key beachgoers. While eating and sleeping options are slim, they're good enough to keep you happy if you're on a short break from the big smoke.

The **tourist information office** (☎ 430718, 4212800; cnr San Martín & Calle 1) offers maps and useful brochures on local sights and activities, as well as full accommodations listings.

Sights & Activities

A few kilometers north of San Clemente del Tuyú are several protected areas, including **Reserva Natural Municipal Punta Rasa**, managed by the environmental NGO **Fundación Vida Silvestre** (☎ in Buenos Aires 4331-3631). At the tip of Cabo San Antonio, where the Río de la Plata meets the Atlantic, the park is essentially a beach with a wet pampas grassland beyond it. A path leads through the park, which is visited by more than 100,000 migratory birds each year – some from as far off as Alaska. This reserve and its neighboring parks area are some of the last protected areas of pampas grassland in the province. There's no public transport to the park, 10km from the center of town, and no visitors center. A *remise* will cost around AR$18. **Seriema Nature Tours** (☎ in Buenos Aires 011-4312-6345; www.seriemanaturetours.com) offers two-day bird-watching tours of the area.

Parque Nacional Campos del Tuyú was declared a national park in late 2007, and is the only national park in the Buenos Aires province. At the time of research, it was not yet open to visitors, though there are plans to make it accessible. Call **National Parks** (☎ in Buenos Aires 011-4311-0303; ☽ 9am-5pm Mon-Fri) to check.

Mundo Marino (☎ 430300; www.mundomarino.com.ar; admission AR$45; ☽ 10am-8pm daily in summer, rest of year Wed-Sun) is South America's largest marine park and home to a selection of marine and terrestrial mammals. It offers entertainment such as seal and dolphin shows.

The recreation center **Termas Marinas** (☎ 423000; www.termasmarinas.com.ar; admission AR$28; ☼ 10am-7pm summer, 10am-6pm winter), also referred to as Bahia Aventura, is just north of town and features mineral-rich thermal baths set in a leafy park. There's also a café and a beauty spa.

Sleeping & Eating

There are several **campgrounds** (per person AR$10) at the entrance to town.

Hotel 5 Avenue (☎ 421035; Calle 5, No 1561; s/d/tr AR$50/80/110) Just a block and a half from the beach, and a safe distance from the noise of downtown's bars and nightspots, this place offers sunny, cheerful rooms and tiny bathrooms. Rates don't include breakfast.

Gran Hotel Fontainebleau (☎ 421187; www.fontainebleau.com.ar; Calle 3, No 2290; s/d AR$255/285; ☒ ☒) The pick of the beachfront high-rises, the Fontainebleau has comfy if slightly dated rooms whose best features are undoubtedly the big balconies overlooking the sea.

Confiteria La Marca (☎ 521125; Calle 1, No 2385; meals AR$5-16; ☼ breakfast, lunch & dinner) The best cup of coffee in town, as well as tempting homemade cakes and pastries and the usual *confitería* meals.

Balneario Eden (☎ 430519; cnr Av 11 & the beach; mains AR$7-18; ☼ lunch & dinner, 24hr in Jan) With a wooden deck overlooking the sand and surf, this place offers burgers and snacks all day, with plenty of well-priced seafood and *parrilla* options.

La Querencia (☎ 423081; Calle 1, No 2453; meals AR$10-40; ☼ lunch & dinner Tue-Sun) In summer there are plenty of eating options, but this frequently recommended *parrilla* stays open year-round. It also does a great line in seafood and some excellent homemade pastas.

Getting There & Away

Frequent buses depart from the **bus terminal** (☎ 421340; cnr Calle 10 & Av San Martín) to Buenos Aires (AR$47, 4½ hrs). There are also buses down the coast toward Pinamar, Villa Gesell and Mar del Plata ($29.40, 3½ hrs).

PINAMAR

☎ 02254 / pop 25,000

Bathed by a tropical current from Brazil, Pinamar's waters are pleasantly warm, and its clean beaches slope gradually into a sea abundant with fish.

The town lacks the nightlife options of Villa Gesell and Mar del Plata, and its southern neighborhoods of Ostende and Valeria offer some semblance of tranquility along the teeming coast. Cariló's mansions, chic boutiques and fashionable restaurants make it the top end of town.

Pinamar was founded and designed in 1944 by architect Jorge Bunge, who figured out how to stabilize the shifting dunes by planting pines, acacias and pampas grass. It was the refuge for the country's upper echelons, but is now somewhat less exclusive, with the best-heeled beachgoers heading for Punta del Este (see p582), leaving Pinamar to a more laid-back crowd.

A new film festival, Pantalla Pinamar, takes place in December (www.pantallapinamar.com in Spanish) and there are concerts and parties on the beach around New Year.

Orientation

Pinamar sits 120km northeast of Mar del Plata via RP 11, and 320km southeast of Buenos Aires via RN 2. It was planned around an axis formed by Av Libertador, which runs parallel to the beach, and Av Bunge, which is perpendicular to the beach. On either side of Av Bunge, home to most of Pinamar's hotels and eateries, the streets form two large fans, making orientation tricky at first. The easiest way to keep track of your hotel is by picking and memorizing the nearest high-rise.

The Pinamar municipality takes in the towns – more like neighborhoods – that lie to Pinamar proper's south: **Ostende** and **Valeria**, and the woodsy **Cariló**, each with its own small commercial center.

Information

ACA (☎ 482744; Del Cazón 1365) Argentina's auto club; good source for provincial road maps.

Municipal Hospital (☎ 491770; Shaw 250)

Municipal tourist office (☎ 491680; Av Bunge 654 at Libertador; ☼ 8am-10pm summer, 8am-8pm rest of year) Has a good pocket-sized map with useful descriptions of Pinamar, Valeria, Ostende and Cariló.

Ojalá Café (☎ 480626; cnr Av Bunge & Marco Polo; per hr AR$3.50) Internet access and telephone.

Post office (Jasón 524)

Activities

The main activity in Pinamar is simply relaxing and socializing on the *balneario*-lined beach, which stretches all the way from north of the town down to Cariló. But the area also offers a wealth of outdoor activity, from windsurfing and waterskiing to horseback riding and biking. There are some wooded areas near the golf course, or you can ride through the leafy streets of nearby Cariló, but there is a distinct lack of nature reserves nearby to explore. Rental agencies and the tourist office both offer advice and maps.

Several shops in town offer rental for biking, including **Leo** (☎ 488855; Av Bunge 1111; per hr/day AR$7/20) and **Macca** (☎ 494183; Av Bunge 1075; per hr AR$7-10, per day $20-30).

The tourist office provides a list of folks who rent horses for riding in the summer. **Ismael** (☎ 497700; cnr Av Bunge & Av Intermedanos; per hr AR$40) is the only one open year-round, but call ahead if it's a winter weekday.

Boards for **surfing** can be rented during summer from the pier, a few blocks south of Av Bunge. If you want to learn how to **kite surf** (or just watch someone else) go to Sport Beach, the last *balneario* located about 5km north of Av Bunge.

Here's a good one: **sand boarding**. To give it a shot, follow jeep tours to nearby dunes or contact **Aventura Pinamar** (☎ 493531; www.aventura pinamar.com.ar; ☽ Sat & Sun).

Fishing, especially for shark and bass, is popular year-round, both from the pier and by boat. Cantina Tulumei (opposite) offers four-hour fishing excursions (AR$80 per person, 4 minimum).

Sleeping

Pinamar lacks real budget accommodations – it's worth heading to Ostende and Valeria where you'll find low-key lodgings close to the beach, but a little away from the action and bustle of Av Bunge. Reservations are a must in the high season. Prices below are for summer, but off-season rates are up to 40% lower.

BUDGET & MIDRANGE

Camping Saint Tropez (☎ 482498; cnr Quintana & Nuestras Malvinas, Ostende; 2 people in Jan/Feb AR$31) Due to its choice beachfront location, this small site fills up quickly in summer.

Albergue Bruno Valente (☎ 482908; cnr Mitre & Nuestras Malvinas, Ostende; members/nonmembers d AR$36/46) In Ostende, about eight blocks south of Pinamar's center, this large youth hostel gets packed in summer and cold and empty in winter. The kitchen is huge and the bathrooms

are institutional. The building itself is a decaying historic hotel built in 1926.

Hosteria Candela (☎ 486788; Coronel Nicolas Jorge 434, Valeria; d AR$$150; ☒) Just two blocks from the beach at Valeria, with good-sized rooms and private bathrooms, a lovely garden and delightful owners, this place is an excellent option.

If Hosteria Candela is full, get a similarly good deal next door at **Posada Amarela** (☎ 487428), or **Hosteria la Sirena** (☎ 486714), which has cable TV.

TOP END

Many of the hotels in Pinamar – and all of the hotels in Cariló – rent only by the week in high season, though you can sometimes negotiate.

Piedras Doradas (☎ 407708; www.hotelpiedras doradas.com.ar in Spanish; cnr Bathurst & Espora, Valeria; d AR$330; ☒ ☒) Four blocks from Valeria's beach, this place sports a quirky retro look and has a leafy, spacious pool deck.

Playas Hotel (☎ 482236; www.playashotel.com.ar; Av Bunge 250; d AR$420, 4-person apt AR$680; ☒ ☒ ☒) This old-school hotel just a block from the beach has a pleasant pool and sunbathing area, along with recently refurbished rooms.

Hotel Las Calas (☎ 405999; www.lascalashotel.com.ar; Av Bunge 560; d/tr AR$520/620; ☒ ☒) This boutique-style joint has clean, modern rooms with wooden floors, as well as a sundeck, games room and gym.

Terrazas al Mar (☎ 480900; www.terrazasalmar.com; cnr Av del Mar & Las Gaviotas; d with view AR$800; ☒ ☒ ☒) Boasting two pools, a gym, spa, restaurant and beachfront terrace, this huge modern tower books out months ahead of high season. It offers rooms as well as family-sized apartments, and wi-fi on the ground floor.

Eating

The beach is lined with *balnearios* serving fresh, inexpensive meals like fried calamari and burgers.

Viejo Lobo (☎ 483218; Av Bunge; mains AR$25-120; ☽ breakfast, lunch & dinner) With a beachside view, extensive wine list and menu complete with dishes including lightly crumbed calamari (AR$19), an excellent selection of fish and delicacies like Spanish-style octopus (AR$120), this is a great place for seafood. It's on the beach at the end of Av Bunge.

our pick **Acqua & Farina** (☎ 570278; cnr Cerezo & Boyero, Cariló; mains AR$12-21; ☽ dinner daily, lunch weekends

Dec-Feb, dinner Fri & Sat, lunch Fri-Sun Mar-Nov) Head to Cariló for the best thin-crust pizza around, as well as fresh salads and homemade pastas.

Cantina Tulumei (☎ 488696; Bunge 64; mains AR$22; ☯ lunch & dinner) This is the place for reasonably priced, quality seafood. In summer, get here early or make a reservation because it fills up fast and people tend to linger.

Tante (☎ 482735; De las Artes 35; mains AR$29-40, 3-course lunch AR$39; ☯ breakfast, lunch & dinner) This classy restaurant, bar and tea room was the home of a well-known soprano who wowed the crowds at Teatro Colón in the '50s.

Getting There & Away
Rapido del Sud runs up and down the coast several times a day, stopping at all coastal destinations between Mar del Plata (AR$15, 2½ hours) and San Clemente del Tuyú (AR$10, two hours). To reach Buenos Aires (AR$56, 4½ hours) take the bus from Pinamar's **bus terminal** (☎ 403500; cnr Jasón & Av Intermedanos).

Trains run to Pinamar's **Estación Divisadero** (☎ 497973) in January and February only. Get tickets to Constitución (Buenos Aires) at the bus terminal.

VILLA GESELL
☎ 02255 / pop 24,300
This beachside town is looking a little worn out alongside its newer, more upmarket neighbors, but it's still a hit with the younger crowd, and has a more bohemian feel than the flashier Pinamar.

In the 1930s, merchant, inventor and nature-lover Carlos Gesell designed this resort of zigzag streets, planting acacias, poplars, oaks and pines to stabilize the shifting dunes. Though he envisioned a town merging with the forest he had created, it wasn't long before high-rise vacation shares began their malignant growth and the trees started to disappear.

The town is known for its summer choral performances and rock and folk concerts, and there are plenty of outdoor activities to enjoy.

Orientation
Villa Gesell is 100km northeast of Mar del Plata via RP 11 and about 360km south of Buenos Aires via RP 11.

Av 3, Gesell's only paved road, parallels the beach and runs from Av Buenos Aires, north of town, south to the bus terminal and most of the campgrounds. Gesell's restaurant, shopping and entertainment center is along this thoroughfare between Paseos 102 and 110. Everything is within walking distance, including the beach, three blocks to the south.

With few exceptions, streets are numbered rather than named. Avenidas (all 11 of them) run east–west, parallel to the beach. Paseos, numbered 100 through 152, run north–south.

Information
There are many banks with ATMs on Av 3.

ACA (☎ 462273; Av 3 btwn Paseos 112 & 113) Argentina's auto club; good source for provincial road maps.

Gesell.net (Paseo 105, No 289; per hr AR$1.50) Internet access.

Hospital Municipal Arturo Illía (☎ 462618; cnr Calle 123 & Av 8)

Post office (Av 5 No 524)

Secretaría de Turismo (☎ 458596; www.gesell.com .ar in Spanish; Av Buenos Aires at Camino de los Pioneros, btwn RP 11 & Circunvalación; ☯ 8am-8pm Mon-Fri, 10am-6pm Sat & Sun) Friendly staff and reliable maps.

Tourist office (☎ 478042; Av 3, No 820; ☯ 8am-8pm summer only) The more conveniently located office.

Sights & Activities
The **Muelle de Pesca** (Playa & Paseo 129), Gesell's 15m fishing pier, offers year-round fishing for mackerel, rays, shark and other marine species.

Horseback riding is a popular activity, and you can rent horses at **La Peregrina** (☎ 457015; www.gesell.com.ar/laperegrina; cnr Calle 313 & Alameda 201). They also offer guided excursions to the dunes (AR$35 per hour) daily in summer and on weekends in winter.

For bicycle rentals, try **Casa Macca** (☎ 466030; cnr Av 3 & Paseo 126; per hr/day AR$8/25).

You can rent surf gear from **Windy** (Paseo 104) down on the beachfront.

The **beach** is very swimmable, with the usual string of *balnearios* renting tents.

Tours
El Ultimo Querandí (☎ 468989; cnr Av 3 & Paseo 110 bis; tours per person AR$37; ☯ tours 2pm Wed & Sat Mar-Dec, 3pm daily Jan-Feb) runs trips to **Faro Querandí**, the local lighthouse, carrying up to 10 passengers in 4WD jeeps on a four-hour, 30km trip over dunes, with stops along the way for photography, swimming and exploring. The lighthouse itself, one of the highest and most inaccessible in the country, soars impressively above the surrounding dense forest.

Sleeping

Villa Gesell has 200-plus hotels, *hosterías, hospedajes* (usually a large family home with a few extra bedrooms; the bathroom is shared), *aparthoteles* and the like. Many of these places close outside of summer; those listed here are open all year, but book ahead in January and February.

BUDGET

Los Medanos (☎ 463205; Av 5, No 549; r per person AR$45) One of the better budget options in town, with decent-sized rooms and modern, if minuscule, bathrooms. At AR$30, the *loft de señoritas* offers great value for single women.

Hospedaje Villa Gesell (☎ 466368; Av 3, No 812; r per person $65) The best part about this place is its centrality. The rooms are comfortable, though windowless, and the doors all open onto an interior patio. No breakfast, but all rooms come with private bathroom.

Villa Gesell's dozen campgrounds usually charge around AR$20 per person per night. Most close at the end of March, but three clustered at the southern end of town on Av 3 are open all year. They are **Camping Casablanca** (☎ 470771), **Camping Mar Dorado** (☎ 470963) and **Camping Monte Bubi** (☎ 470732).

MIDRANGE & TOP END

Residencial Viya (☎ 462757; residencialviya@gesell.com.ar; Av 5, No 582, btwn Paseos 105 & 106; s/d AR$65/130) Rooms are smallish, but pleasant, and open onto a small patio at this friendly, owner-operated *residencial* (cheap hotel) on a quiet street.

Hotel Tamanacos (☎ 468753; tamanacos@gesell.com .ar; cnr Paseo 103 & Av 1; r $195; ☒ ☒) A mere 100m away from the beach, this cute little hotel has some great common sitting areas, particularly the front balcony, and a good breakfast buffet. Rooms are on the small side, but good value for the price.

Achimalen (☎ 462380; Av 4 & Paseo 106; d/tr AR$210/250; ☒) Upstairs rooms have high ceilings and large bathrooms. Breakfast can be taken on the terrace and there's a bring-your-own-beef *parrilla* for guests' use.

Apart Hotel La Plaza (☎ 468793; Av 2 No 375, btwn Paseos 103 & 104; s/d/tr AR$110/220/310; ☒) Just a couple of blocks from both the beach and the bustle of Av 3, this place has clean, comfortable bedrooms, a sunny breakfast salon and friendly staff. Also on offer are family-sized apartments.

Hotel Merimar (☎ 462243; www.gesell.com.ar /hotelmerimar; cnr Paseo 107 & Playa; r AR$220; ☒) The Merimar's small but comfortable rooms are in an excellent location – rooms at the front have good balconies overlooking the whole beach scene.

Hotel ACA Spa (☎ 462960; www.gesell.com.ar/hotelaca in Spanish; Av 1 btwn Paseos 112 & 113; r AR$390; ☒ ☒) One of the more stylish of the ACA hotels, this one has good-sized rooms with ample balconies, a lovely breakfast area and, inexplicably, Indian decorations adorning the walls.

Hotel Bahia (☎ 462838; www.hotelbahia-gesell.com .ar in Spanish; Av 1, No 855 btwn Paseos 108 & 109; r AR$462; ☒ ☒) One of the better four-star high-rises down on the beachfront, the Bahia has spacious rooms with little sitting areas and good views. Plenty of extras, like the gym, sauna, breakfast buffet and heated pool.

Eating

Villa Gesell has a wide variety of restaurants, mostly along Av 3, catering to all tastes and budgets.

La Pachamama (☎ 468727; Av 2, No 411, at Paseo 104; mains AR$9-12; ☽ lunch & dinner) This hole-in-the-wall joint makes delicious Salta-style empanadas and fresh pizzas – perfect for a quick budget meal.

Sutton (☎ 460674; cnr Paseo 105 & Ave 2; mains AR$12-28; ☽ 9:30am-late) This lively café has wi-fi access and serves well-made classics like burgers and wok-fried noodles. There's live bossa nova and jazz at dinner, then a DJ in the later evening, when the place becomes a happening bar.

our pick Las Margaritas (☎ 456377; Av 2, No 484 btwn Paseos 104 & 105; mains AR$12-28; ☽ dinner) Charmingly cozy and quiet, this place serves excellent homemade pasta, including a shellfish and squid ink ravioli. The tiramisú is to die for. Reservations essential.

Sancho (☎ 462320; Av 3, No 349 btwn Paseos 104 & 105; mains AR$14-36; ☽ lunch & dinner) Locals recommend this place, which has an extensive menu filled with Argentine favorites as well as plenty of local seafood.

Entertainment

Villa Gesell comes alive with music in the summer months, when venues book everything from rock to choral music.

Cine Teatro Atlas (☎ 462969; Paseo 108, btwn Avs 3 & 4) Such rock-and-roll greats as Charly García and Los Pericos have played this small theater, which doubles as a cinema (www.cinesdela costa.com) during off-season months.

Anfiteatro del Pinar (☎ 467123; cnr Av 10 & Paseo 102) There are musical performances in January, February and Semana Santa. Gesell's Encuentros Corales, an annual gathering of the country's best choirs, takes place annually in this lovely amphitheater.

Pueblo Límite (☎ 452845; www.pueblolimite.com; Av Buenos Aires 2600; admission AR$12-30) A sort of small town megadisco, this complex has two dance clubs (one for Latino music, one for electronica), four restaurants, a bar and cheap food booths in the front.

Shopping

Feria Artesanal, Regional y Artística (Av 3, btwn Paseos 112 & 113; nightly mid-Dec–mid-Mar, Sat & Sun mid-Mar–mid-Dec) This is an excellent arts and crafts fair, with lots of handmade jewelry and decorative objects in carved wood and glass, as well as paintings and the usual range of souvenirs.

Getting There & Away

The **main bus terminal** (☎ 477253; cnr Av 3 & Paseo 140) is on the south side of town. Most buses stop here first and then at the **Parada Los Pinos Mini Terminal** (☎ 458059; cnr Blvd Silvio Gesell & Av Buenos Aires), closer to the center of town.

In summer there are several direct buses daily to Buenos Aires (AR$50, six hours), and Mar del Plata (AR$15, 1½ hours). Rápido del Sud has frequent buses to other coastal towns.

MAR CHIQUITA
☎ 0223 / pop 400

Despite being so very *chiquita*, this spot merits special mention as one of the best destinations for nature-lovers within an easy distance of Buenos Aires. It's a humble little gem of a place, with no high-rises, no *balnearios* and no stress. What makes it special is its lagoon, a unique ecosystem that's home to a wealth of bird and fish species.

Orientation

Along RP 11, 34km north of Mar del Plata, the town is a wedge-shaped set of streets arranged on a grid, bordered by the lagoon to the north and the beach to the east. You enter via the main street, Av San Martín. The visitors center overlooks the lake, on the corner of Belgrano and Rivera del Sol.

Information

There are no ATMs in Mar Chiquita, and it's difficult to get online. For more tourist information (in Spanish), see www.marchiquita.com.ar.

Tourist information & visitors center (☎ 469-1158; Rivera del Sol 1424, cnr Belgrano) Maps of the town, information on the reserve and accommodation listings available.

Sights & Activities

Most visitors come here to explore the **Reserva Mar Chiquita**, a Unesco World Biosphere Reserve. It takes in several types of landscapes and ecosystems, including the lagoon, pampean grasslands and the coastal dunes to the north (**Reserva Provincial Dunas del Atlantica Sur**). Tours of the area depart from the visitors center at 9am every day except Monday. The tour lasts around four hours and costs AR$25 per person.

Fed by creeks from the Sierras de Tandil and sheltered by a chain of sand dunes, the lagoon, **Albúfera Mar Chiquita**, alternately drains into the ocean or absorbs seawater, depending on the tides. This creates a unique ecosystem boasting huge biodiversity, and is the only lagoon of its kind in Argentina. The spot is a paradise for birdwatchers, with over 220 species, 86 of which are migratory, including flamingos. There are also over 55 fish species in the lagoon, making it a popular fishing spot.

While the lagoon is a great spot for canoeing, windsurfing and kite surfing, there are no rental agencies in the town. However, if you show up for a kite-surfing lesson, the teacher may lend you his gear. Classes take place weekends right in front of the visitors center.

Call **Charly** (☎ 156-801718) to explore the area on horseback.

The **beach** itself is unspectacular – narrow and windy, it doesn't offer as much as some of its neighbors.

Just 6km south of Mar Chiquita, **Mar de Cobo** offers another tranquil beach experience. Set in a pleasant wood, with its beach backed by dunes and featuring smooth rocks that make excellent beach furniture, the place has yet to be invaded by summer crowds. There are a couple of comfortable *hosterias*; the pick of them is **Posada del Solar** (☎ 469-1252; www.posadadelsolar.com.ar; d AR$200; 🐾), with simple rooms, a huge garden and a pool.

Sleeping & Eating

There are several campgrounds and hotels in town.

Hostería Bariloche (☎ 469-1254; Beltran 1190 & Echeverría; s/d AR$65/100; 🖳) Across the road from Hotel Mar Chiquita, this better-value, friendly establishment offers apartments, rooms and dorms, along with a library, sea-view lounge and spacious *parrilla* area for guests.

Hotel Mar Chiquita (☎ 469-1046; www.hotel -marchiquita.com.ar; Echeverria & the beach; s/d AR$130/260; 🖳 🖳) The rooms here are pretty basic, but the hotel's set right on the beach next to the lagoon and offers guests all the services of a *balneario*. Excellent games room with old-school arcade games.

Campgrounds include **Club de Regata y Pesca** (☎ 469-1409; River del Sol 1622; campsite per person AR$15). To rent a *cabaña* for up to five people, try **Palumbo Propiedades** (☎ 469-1237; San Martín 1907, cnr of Rojas; AR$150-200).

Of the three restaurants facing the lagoon along Rivera del Sol, **Parador Mor** (☎ 469-1167; Rivera del Sol & Belgrano; mains AR$12-24; 🕒 breakfast, lunch & dinner daily in Jan, Sat & Sun rest of the year) is the best value, with excellent homemade pastas and seafood dishes, and tasty cakes and pastries.

Getting There & Away

Rápido del Sud departs frequently to and from Mar Chiquita, connecting it with Mar del Plata and towns to the north. The cheaper local bus 221 (AR$3.60) leaves hourly from stops along Blvd Marítimo. Ask the driver; some 221 buses stop short.

MAR DEL PLATA

☎ 0223 / pop 700,000

It's worth going to Mar del Plata on a summer weekend if only so you'll never again be tempted to say 'gee this beach is crowded.' There's a couple of places where you could get a few strokes in without taking somebody's eye out, but mostly it's shoulder-to-shoulder sun-frazzled *porteños*. During the week, and especially in the nonsummer months, the crowds disperse, hotel prices drop and the place takes on a much more relaxed feel.

First impressions of the extremes to which this resort town has taken itself can be abhorrent. But, after spending a few days on its comically packed beaches, watching street performers on the beachside Plaza Colón or exploring the wonders of the port, it's hard not to give in to the adoration the country

feels for the place. If summer crowds aren't your bottle of lotion, visit in spring or autumn, when prices are lower and the area's natural attractions are easier to enjoy.

History

Europeans were slow to occupy this stretch of the coast, so Mar del Plata was a late bloomer. Not until 1747 did Jesuit missionaries try to evangelize the southern pampas Indians; the only reminder of their efforts is the body of water known as Laguna de los Padres.

More than a century later, Portuguese investors established El Puerto de Laguna de los Padres, with a pier and a *saladero* (slaughterhouse). Beset by economic problems in the 1860s, they sold out to Patricio Peralta Ramos, who founded Mar del Plata proper in 1874. Peralta Ramos helped develop the area as a commercial and industrial center, and later as a beach resort. By the turn of the century, many upper-class *porteño* families owned summerhouses, some of which still grace Barrio Los Troncos.

Since the 1960s, the skyscraper-building craze has nearly gotten out of control, leaving many beaches in the shade much of the day. As the 'Pearl of the Atlantic' has lost exclusivity, its architectural character and its calm, the Argentine elite have sought refuge in resorts such as nearby Pinamar or Punta del Este (Uruguay). Still, Mar del Plata remains the most thriving Argentine beach town.

Orientation

Mar del Plata, 400km south of Buenos Aires via RN 2, sprawls along 8km of beaches, though most points of interest are in the downtown area, bounded by Av JB Justo (running roughly west from the port), Av Independencia (runs roughly northeast–southwest) and the ocean. On street signs, the coastal road is called Av Peralta Ramos, but most people refer to it as Blvd Marítimo. *Peatonal* San Martín is the downtown pedestrian mall, and Rivadavia is pedestrianized through the summer. To the center's south lies the leafy neighborhood of Los Troncos, where along Av LN Alem you'll find another small commercial center.

Information
CULTURAL CENTERS

Alianza Francesa (☎ 494-0120; La Rioja 2065; 🕒 8:30am-1:30pm & 2:30-8pm Mon-Fri)

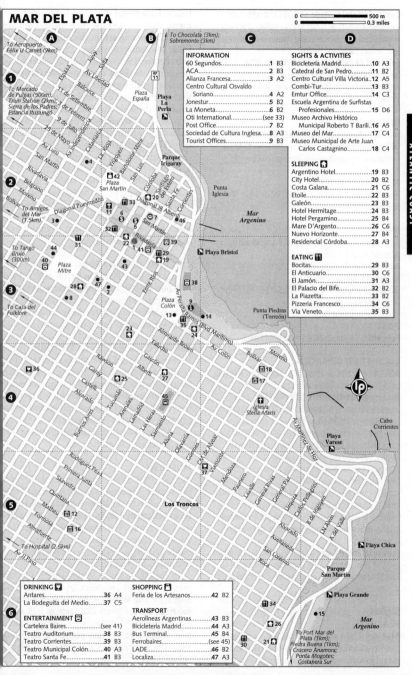

MAR DEL PLATA

| 0 | 500 m |
| 0 | 0.3 miles |

INFORMATION
60 Segundos......................................1 B3
ACA..2 B3
Alianza Francesa................................3 A2
Centro Cultural Osvaldo
  Soriano...4 A2
Jonestur..5 B2
La Moneta...6 B2
Oti International..........................(see 33)
Post Office...7 B2
Sociedad de Cultura Inglesa............8 A3
Tourist Offices...................................9 B3

SIGHTS & ACTIVITIES
Bicicletería Madrid..........................10 A3
Catedral de San Pedro.....................11 B2
Centro Cultural Villa Victoria...........12 A5
Combi-Tur..13 B3
Emtur Office.....................................14 C3
Escuela Argentina de Surfistas
  Profesionales.................................15 D6
Museo Archivo Histórico
  Municipal Roberto T Barili...........16 A5
Museo del Mar................................17 C4
Museo Municipal de Arte Juan
  Carlos Castagnino.........................18 C4

SLEEPING
Argentino Hotel...............................19 B3
City Hotel..20 B2
Costa Galana...................................21 C6
Etoile...22 B3
Galeón...23 B3
Hotel Hermitage..............................24 B3
Hotel Pergamino.............................25 B4
Mare D'Argento...............................26 C6
Nuevo Horizonte.............................27 B4
Residencial Córdoba........................28 A3

EATING
Bocitas...29 B3
El Anticuario....................................30 C6
El Jamón..31 A3
El Palacio del Bife............................32 B2
La Piazetta.......................................33 B2
Pizzeria Francesco............................34 C6
Via Veneto.......................................35 B3

DRINKING
Antares..36 A4
La Bodeguita del Medio...................37 C5

ENTERTAINMENT
Cartelera Baires........................(see 41)
Teatro Auditorium...........................38 B3
Teatro Corrientes.............................39 B3
Teatro Municipal Colón....................40 A3
Teatro Santa Fe...............................41 B3

SHOPPING
Feria de los Artesanos.....................42 B2

TRANSPORT
Aerolíneas Argentinas......................43 B3
Bicicletería Madrid..........................44 A3
Bus Terminal....................................45 B4
Ferrobaires................................(see 45)
LADE...46 B2
Localiza...47 A3

THE PAMPAS & THE
ATLANTIC COAST

Centro Cultural Osvaldo Soriano (☎ 499-7878; cnr Catamarca & 25 de Mayo) Offers a variety of activities ranging from film screenings and theater to popular music, jazz, *folklore*, tango and the like.

Sociedad de Cultura Inglesa (☎ 495-6513; San Luis 2498) Has a library with newspapers, magazines and books in English, as well as occasional films and lectures.

INTERNET ACCESS

You'll find plenty of *locutorios* in the downtown area.

60 Segundos (Santiago del Estero 1884; per hr AR$1) Twelve machines with reliable internet service.

MEDICAL SERVICES

Hospital (☎ 477-0262; JB Justo 6700, between Tres Arroyos & Calle 164)

MONEY

There are several money exchanges along San Martín and Rivadavia.

Jonestur (San Martín 2574)

La Moneta (Rivadavia 2623)

Oti International (☎ 494-5414; San Luis 1632) The Amex representative.

POST

Post office (Av Luro 2460 & Santiago del Estero)

TOURIST INFORMATION

ACA (☎ 491-2096; Av Colón 2450) Argentina's auto club; good source for provincial road maps.

Municipal tourist office (☎ 495-1777; www.mardelplata.gov.ar in Spanish; Blvd Marítimo 2400, Local 60; 🕑 8am-10pm mid-Dec–Semana Santa, 8am-8pm Semana Santa–mid-Dec) In the old Rambla Hotel Provincial, opposite Plaza Colón. Exceptionally helpful. Since the city gets so crowded in summer, staff cope with tourists in assembly-line fashion, but they have maps, informative brochures and a nifty monthly activities magazine. There is usually an English-speaker on duty. In summer, Emtur opens a branch at the bus terminal. If you read Spanish, the website is extremely helpful, listing most lodgings, activities and events around town.

Provincial tourist office (☎ 495-5340; Blvd Marítimo 2400; 🕑 9am-8pm Mon-Fri, 9am-1pm & 4-8pm Sat & Sun) Basic information on other coastal resorts and the rest of Buenos Aires province.

Sights

BEACHES

Mar del Plata's beaches are safe and swimmable, if impossibly crowded in the summer. Downtown fronts onto the most central beach, **Playa Bristol**, with its wharf and fishermen's club bearing the huge neon Quilmes sign. The next beach to the north is **Playa La Perla**, favored by a younger crowd and filled with *balnearios*. To the south of Playa de los Pescadores are **Playa Varese** and **Cabo Corrientes**, a pair of small waveless beaches, also public, that are protected by small rocky headlands. South of these, at the more fashionable end of town, lies **Playa Grande**, also crowded with *balnearios*. Just past the port you'll find the huge **Punta Mogotes** complex – slightly more chilled and favored by families, who fill the *balnearios* to overflowing in January.

Beyond the lighthouse and the limits of Mar del Plata proper is the **Costanera Sur**. This area is less urbanized, and though the beaches are filled with yet more *balnearios* in the summer, they're a quieter option if you're here outside of the peak season.

CATEDRAL DE SAN PEDRO

Facing the leafy **Plaza San Martín** at San Luis, this neo-Gothic building features gorgeous stained glass, an impressive central chandelier from France, English-tile floors and a ceiling of tiles from other European countries.

CENTRO CULTURAL VILLA VICTORIA

Victoria Ocampo (see the boxed text, opposite), founder of the literary journal *Sur*, hosted literary salons with prominent intellectuals from around the world at her summer chalet, now a **museum** and **cultural center** (☎ 492-0569; Matheu 1851; admission AR$3; 🕑 6-9pm Dec-Feb, 1-7pm Mon-Fri, 1-8pm Sat & Sun other times) that features changing exhibitions.

MUSEUMS

Built in 1909 as the summer residence of a prominent Argentine family, the Villa Ortiz Basualdo is now the **Museo Municipal de Arte Juan Carlos Castagnino** (☎ 486-1636; Av Colón 1189; admission AR$3, Tue free; 🕑 5-10pm Fri-Wed). Resembling a Loire Valley castle, its Belgian interior exhibits paintings, drawings, photographs and sculptures by Argentine artists.

In the Villa Emilio Mitre (1930), another former summer residence of the Argentine oligarchy, the **Museo Archivo Histórico Municipal Roberto T Barili** (☎ 495-1200; Lamadrid 3870; admission AR$3; 🕑 noon-5pm) houses a superb collection of late-19th-century photographs, along with other exhibits recalling Mar del Plata's colorful past.

LITERARY LADY OF LA PLATA

She was 'the most beautiful cow in the pampas' according to French novelist Pierre Drieu, and Jorge Luis Borges called her 'the most Argentine of women.' In the 1920s and 1930s, Victoria Ocampo gathered writers and intellectuals from around the globe to her home in Mar del Plata each summer, creating a formidable literary and artistic salon.

Victoria (1890–1979) was born to one of those upper-class Argentine families whose habit it was to escape the oppressive heat of Buenos Aires during summer and head for the coast. In keeping with the Europhilia of the time, the Ocampos' *veraneo*, or summer home, Villa Victoria (see opposite), was imported piece by piece from Scandinavia. Over the years, the house hosted such luminaries as Borges, Gabriela Mistral, Igor Stravinsky, Le Corbusier and Rabindranath Tagore.

She never went to university (her parents' social class regarded women's education as superfluous), but Victoria's voracious appetite for knowledge and love of literature led her to become Argentina's leading lady of letters. She founded the literary magazine *Sur*, which introduced writers like Virginia Woolf and TS Eliot to Argentine readers. She also helped introduce Latin American writers to Europe. She was an inexhaustible traveler and a pioneering feminist among incurable *machistas*.

Having no regard for convention, Ocampo was loathed as much as she was loved, scandalizing society by driving her own automobile when such a thing was unheard of among society women. A ferocious opponent of Peronism, chiefly because of Perón's interference with intellectual freedom, Victoria was arrested at Villa Victoria, and at the age of 63 locked up in a jailhouse in San Telmo, where she entertained herself and her fellow inmates by reading aloud and acting out scenes from novels and cinema.

If Victoria is remembered as a lively essayist and great patroness of writers, her younger sister, Silvina, was the literary talent, writing both short stories and poetry. As an aside, Mar del Plata was the scene of a separate key event in Argentina's literary life when poet Alfonsina Storni (1892–1938), suffering from cancer, threw herself off the rocks. You can see her monument at the southern tip of Playa La Perla.

As for the tradition of the *veraneo*, it's still going strong. Many wealthy families still have mansions in leafy Los Troncos, where Villa Victoria stands, but Argentines of all social classes save vacation time and cash to squeeze themselves onto a patch of sand, whether in humble San Clemente del Tuyú or upper-crust Cariló, and spend the summer running into everyone they know.

Housing the most extensive seashell collection you're ever likely to see, the **Museo del Mar** (☎ 451-3553; Av Colón 1114; admission AR$3; ⏰ 9am-2pm Dec-Mar, 8am-9pm Mon-Thu, 8am-midnight Fri & Sat, 9am-9pm Sun Apr-Nov) exhibits more than 30,000 shells, representing 6000 species from around the world. In a sleek new building, the museum also contains a small tide pool, an aquarium and a delightful café, complete with internet service.

PORT MAR DEL PLATA

Mar del Plata is one of the country's most important fishing ports and seafood-processing centers. At **Baquina de Pescadores** – the picturesque wharf hidden behind the ugly YPF fuel tanks – fisherfolk and stevedores follow their routine on and around kaleidoscopically colored wooden boats, monitored by sea lions who have established a large colony – mostly male – along one side of the pier.

In the early morning, unfazed by the chilly sea breeze, the fishermen load their nets and crates before spending the day at sea, escorted by the sea lions. At about 5pm, the pier gets noisy and hectic as the returning fishermen sort and box the fish, bargain for the best price and tidy up their boats and tools. The sea lions return to seek or fight over a resting spot. Braving their horrendous stench affords excellent opportunities for photography: separated by a fence, you can approach within a meter of the sea lions.

Just past the colony is the port's fantastic graveyard of **ruined ships**, half-sunken and rusting in the sun. Here the **Escollera Sur** (southern jetty) begins its long stretch some 2km out to sea, with panoramic views of the city from its tip. Climb the yellow ladders and walk on top of the sea wall for the best views. You can walk back to the **Centro Comercial Puerto** (the port's commercial center) and close the day in one of its great restaurants.

Local buses 221, 511, 522, 551, 561, 562 and 593 go to the wharf from downtown. A taxi costs AR$15.

SIERRA & LAGUNA DE LOS PADRES

A popular weekend destination for *marplatenses*, the lake and soft hills to its west offer a bucolic setting and a range of outdoor activities, including horseback riding, biking, trekking and rock climbing (see below). The spot was first settled in 1746 as a Jesuit Mission aimed at rounding up the nomadic tribes of the area – you can see a replica of the original chapel by the lake's shore. There are plenty of places to eat, and campgrounds as well. The lake is about 10km out of town along RN 226 (take bus 717 from Av Luro).

Activities

Mar del Plata and its surrounds offer plenty of opportunity to enjoy outdoor activities and adventure sports.

Biking is a good, green way to get around town. The streets of Los Troncos are relatively calm and pleasant for cycling. Bicycles can be rented from **Bicicletería Madrid** (☎ 494-1932; Yrigoyen 2249, Plaza Mitre; per hr/day AR$10/30; ☒ 10am-6:30pm).

The **Escuela Argentina de Surfistas Profesionales** (☎ 154-002072) offers **surfing** classes and rents boards at Playa Grande during the summer. Find them at the beach, near the Yacht Club.

The nearby Sierra de los Padres (see above) is a good spot for **horseback riding**, which can be arranged through **El Cobijo Cabalgatas** (☎ 463-0309), which leads rides of 1½ hours through the hills and around the lake.

As the sea lions attest, Mar del Plata is one of the best spots for **fishing** in Argentina. The rocky outcrop at **Cabo Corrientes**, just north of Playa Grande, is a good spot to try, as are the two breakwaters – **Escollera Norte** and **Escollera Sur** – at the port. Freshwater fishing is popular at Laguna de los Padres (see above), while **Mako Team** (☎ 493-5338; www.makoteam.com.ar) offers daily eight-hour ocean fishing ex-

cursions (US$150, including all meals, drinks and fishing gear). You can rent gear from **Complejo Recreativo Islas Malvinas** (☎ 0223-15-562 5430), right near the lake.

The rocky cliffs by the sea and the hills of Sierra de los Padres make for excellent **climbing** and **rappelling**. **Acción Directa** (☎ 474-4520) runs a school – they also offer **mountain biking**, **canoeing** and overnight active camping trips.

For those really looking to get the heart racing, there's a **skydiving** outfit just outside of town that offers daily jumps, weather permitting. Contact **Aeroclub Mar del Plata** (☎ 464-2151; RP 88, Km 96). Catch bus 715 or 720 there from the Mar del Plata neighborhood of Batán.

Tours

Combi-Tur (☎ 493-0732) Offers two-hour city tours (AR$15) daily at 10:30am, 3:30 & 5:30pm and excursions to nearby Sierra and Laguna del los Padres (AR$30; see left), leaving at noon and 3:30pm. Tours depart from Plaza Colón, at Colón and Arenales.

Crucero Anamora (☎ 489-0310; www.anamoracrucero.com.ar) The 30m boat offers one-hour harbor tours (AR$29) several times daily in summer and twice daily on weekends in winter from Dársena B at the port.

Emtur office (Blvd Marítimo) Emtur conducts free organized tours of various city sights; register one day in advance at the office.

Festivals & Events

Mar del Plata's elaborate tourist infrastructure guarantees a wide variety of special events throughout the year. It's worth being in town for the city's **International Film Festival** (www.mardelplatafilmfest.com), which used to take place each March but has now shifted to October. Launched in 1950, though interrupted for decades by Argentina's political and economic woes, it is South America's most important film festival, attracting participants from all over the world.

In January Mar del Plata also celebrates **Fiesta Nacional del Pescador** (Fisherman's Festival), which sees locals cooking up seafood feasts and a traditional procession where a statue of Our Lady, Star of the Sea – patron saint of fishermen – is carried through the streets.

Sleeping

It's worth reiterating that prices climb considerably from month to month during summer and drop in the off-season, when many of Mar del Plata's 700 hotels and *residenciales* close their doors. The cheapest accommodations are near the bus terminal.

BUDGET

Hotel Pergamino (☎ 495-7927; hotelpergamino@ciudad.com.ar; Tucumán 2728; dm/s/d AR$27/40/60) Secure, clean and comfortable budget rooms. If you've got a few spare pesos, it's definitely worth getting a room, although the dorms will do in a pinch. Wi-fi access.

Residencial Córdoba (☎ 495-7927; Córdoba 2337; dm/d AR$35/80) Rooms are basic but spotless in this rambling family-owned place, where oversized photos of beaming grandkids decorate the breakfast room.

Rates at Mar del Plata's crowded campgrounds, mostly south of town, are around AR$10 per person; the tourist office prints out information about their facilities.

MIDRANGE

Many of the larger hotels have their own parking lots and all include breakfast.

Nuevo Horizonte (☎ 494-2345; www.nuevohorizonte.com.ar; Lamadrid 2506; per person AR$70) Free parking and helpful staff at this nondescript hotel, which offers excellent half-price deals in the off-season.

Mare D'Argento (☎ 451-1223; LM Alem 3528; s/d AR$90/160) Close to Playa Grande at the smart end of town, the freshly updated rooms are smallish but comfortable. An easy walk to both the beach and the bars on LM Alem and Bernardo de Irigoyen.

Galeón (☎ 495-9200; www.hoteles-mardelplata.ar/galeon in Spanish; Buenos Aires 2431; d/tr AR$160/195) Positioned just south of Plaza Colón, this place has comfortable beds and simply decorated rooms.

Etoile (☎ 493-4968; Santiago del Estero 1869; d/tr AR$180/210) Its central location, plus the superspacious rooms and large bathrooms, make this place good value. Wi-fi's available in the lounge.

ourpick **City Hotel** (☎ 495-3018; www.cityhotelmardelplata.com; Diagonal JB Alberdi 2561; d AR$175-220) This worker-owned cooperative has an old-school feel and a delightful back garden. Keep in mind that it is worth paying a bit extra for the 'superior' rooms – they come with better beds and sunny balconies overlooking the street.

TOP END

Argentino Hotel (☎ 493-0091; www.argentinohotel-mdp.com.ar; Belgrano 2225; d AR$270; 🛱) This four-star property offers spacious, good-value rooms right in the center of the action.

Estancia Ituzaingó (☎ 460-0797; www.estanciaituzaingo.com.ar; día de campo AR$80; r AR$330; 🖭) This working farm is just 20 minutes drive from downtown. The Creole-style manor dates from 1862 and the six rooms are all decorated with original furnishings. Activities include horse and bike rides around the Laguna de los Padres, which once belonged to the *estancia*.

Hotel Hermitage (☎ 451-9081; www.hermitagehotel.com.ar; r with city/sea views AR$504/598; 🛱 🖳 🖭) Built in 1942, this is the grand old dame of Mar del Plata, with a majestic lobby that has sweeping ocean views, a casino, Turkish bath and slightly worn but comfortably refined rooms.

Costa Galana (☎ 410-5000; www.hotelcostagalana.com; Blvd Marítimo 5725; d AR$545-820; 🛱 🖳 🖭) At the Paris end of town overlooking Playa Grande, this European-style five-star fills up with *farándula* – Argentine models, celebrities and showbiz folk – in high summer, hosting fashion parades and the like. The spa boasts Jacuzzis with unbeatable beach views. Rooms are spacious and impeccably decorated.

Eating

Although Mar del Plata's numerous restaurants, pizzerias and snack bars usually hire extra help between December and March, they often struggle to keep up with impatient crowds, and there are always long lines. Around the bus terminal you can find very cheap *minutas* (snacks), while there's a bunch of restaurants at the port serving freshly cooked catch of the day.

BUDGET & MIDRANGE

Bocitas (Rivadavia 2262; mains AR$12-17; 🕑 24hr) This place can't be topped when it comes to cheap pizza; it's low on atmosphere, but you can't beat the opening hours, and the sidewalk tables are perfect for people-watching.

El Jamón (☎ 493-7447; cnr Bolívar & Bartolomé Mitre; mains AR$11-28; 🕑 lunch & dinner Mon-Sat) Cured hams and plastic plants swing from the beams at this neighborhood favorite, full every evening with locals enjoying the delicious lamb roast.

Via Veneto (☎ 494-8105; Blvd Maritimo 2451; AR$12-20; ☯ breakfast, lunch & dinner) Good coffee and *medialunas* (croissants; AR$6) can be found at this café, with well-priced daily specials posted on its windows.

Pizzeria Francesco (☎ 486-3137; cnr Bernardo de Irigoyen & Primera Junta; AR$12-22; ☯ dinner) This family-style place in Los Troncos is perfect for a quick bite before bar-hopping.

La Piazzetta (☎ 494-5113; San Luis 1652; mains AR$14-29; ☯ lunch & dinner) This Italian restaurant, a member of the International Slow Food Association, offers fine homemade pastas and a range of other dishes. A cheesy keyboard soloist is on hand to accompany your lunch.

El Palacio del Bife (☎ 494-7727; Córdoba 1857; mains AR$15-30; ☯ lunch & dinner) A highly recommended *parrilla* with a massive menu (that's also available in English). Come hungry and come wanting meat, although the homemade pastas are also worth a try.

Piedra Buena (☎ 480-1632; Centro Comercial Puerto, Port; mains AR$18-32; ☯ dinner daily Jan, lunch & dinner Wed-Sun Feb-Dec) Of the bunch of seafood restaurants down at the port, this is reputedly the best, and is certainly the most atmospheric. There's a huge range of seafood on offer, a good atmosphere and a seafood bisque (AR$26) that comes highly recommended.

TOP END

Amigos del Mar (☎ 491-6054; Guido 2056; sushi AR$40-50; ☯ lunch & dinner, closed Mon Easter-Nov) Apart from the hearty *'buenas noches'* greeting you on arrival, this Japanese restaurant is the real deal. Bamboo screens, jangly background music and a sushi sashimi platter that's worth the trek 1.5km west (or AR$15 taxi ride) on its own.

El Anticuario (☎ 451-6309; Bernardo de Irigoyen 3819; AR$25-98; ☯ dinner) A fancy restaurant at the fancy end of town, Anticuario has a private room perfect for special occasions and serves very good Mediterranean and local dishes, with excellent seafood platters to share.

Drinking

The area southwest of Plaza Mitre is particularly conducive to barhopping, as are Bernardo de Yrigoyen and LN Alem, between Almafuerte and Rodríguez Peña at the Playa Grande end of town.

Antares (☎ 492-4455; Córdoba 3025; ☯ 8pm-late) The six homebrews on tap at Mar del Plata's only microbrewery include imperial stout, pale ale and barley wine – excellent cures for

the Quilmes blues. Food is available and there is live music most weekends. Come early if you want a table out the front.

La Bodeguita del Medio (☎ 486-3096; Castelli 1252; AR$15-28; ☯ 6pm-late) Named after one of Hemingway's favorite haunts, the mojitos here do him proud and can be had two-for-one between 7pm and 9pm. The Cuban dishes, tapas and bar snacks all go down well.

Entertainment

NIGHTCLUBS

After tanning on the beach all day, Argentines take their hot, bronzed bodies to the nightclubs and dance until the morning hours. The most popular clubs are along Av Constitución, about 3km from downtown, and don't really get started until after 1am. Bus 551 from downtown runs along the entire avenue. Keep your eyes peeled during the day for discount flyers handed out along San Martín and Rivadavia.

Sobremonte (☎ 479-2600; Constitución 6690; admission AR$10-20; ☯ midnight-dawn Dec-Mar, midnight-dawn Thu-Sat off-season) Ground zero for the city's most fashionable summertime clubbers, Sobremonte is three throbbing discos, a Mexican restaurant and a lounge all under one roof.

Chocolate (☎ 479-4848; Constitución 4451; admission AR$10-20; ☯ midnight-dawn Dec-Mar, midnight-dawn Thu-Sat off-season) This is another long-time favorite, with two floors, a patio and a standard soundtrack covering everything from techno to *rock nacional* (Argentine rock).

For *tangueros*, there are occasional **milongas** (dance events) in the city, including the Sunday night's **Tango Brujo** (☎ 495-2196; Gascón 3540; AR$7). Check the notice board at the tourist information office for *milongas* and classes going on around town.

LIVE MUSIC

The tourist information office has information on current performances.

Casa del Folklore (☎ 472-3955; San Juan 2543; ☯ from 9pm summer, from 9pm Fri & Sat winter) Music usually gets underway after 11pm at this lively *peña* (folk music club) northwest of downtown, where there's plenty of food, drink and dancing.

THEATER

When Buenos Aires shuts down in January, many shows come from the capital to Mar del Plata. Theaters mostly cater to vacationers by showing comedies that range from café concert (stand-up comedy) to vulgar but popular burlesque. As in Buenos Aires, there are *carteleras* that offer half-price tickets to movies and theater presentations. The local branch of Cartelera Baires is at Santa Fe 1844, Local 33.

Teatro Auditorium (☎ 493-6001; Blvd Marítimo 2280) Part of the casino complex, this place offers quality musical theater.

Other venues include **Teatro Municipal Colón** (☎ 499-6210; Yrigoyen 1665), **Teatro Corrientes** (☎ 493-7918; Corrientes 1766) and **Teatro Santa Fe** (☎ 491-9728; Santa Fe 1854).

Shopping

Mar del Plata is famous for sweaters and jackets. Shops along Av JB Justo, nicknamed 'Avenida del Pullover,' have competitive, near-wholesale prices.

Feria de los Artesanos (Plaza San Martín) Vendors set up their stalls every afternoon on Plaza San Martín to sell everything from *mate* gourds and knives to sweaters and silverwork.

Mercado de Pulgas (Plaza Rocha; ☻ 11am-6pm Fri-Sun) This relaxed flea market, selling everything including the kitchen sink, is at 20 de Septiembre between San Martín and Av Luro, seven blocks northwest of Plaza San Martín.

Getting There & Away

AIR

Aerolíneas Argentinas (☎ 496-0101; Moreno 2442) has several daily flights to Buenos Aires (from AR$300).

LADE (☎ 470-3571; Corrientes 1537) has flights to various parts of the country.

Following are sample fares:

Destination	Cost (AR$)
Bahía Blanca	153
Bariloche	209
Buenos Aires	176
Calafate	451
Trelew	219
Ushuaia	451
Viedma	175

BUS

Mar del Plata's busy **bus terminal** (☎ 451-5406; Alberti 1602) is very central. Dozens of companies serve most major destinations throughout the country. There are generally two departures per week to Patagonian destinations south of

Bariloche. Rapido del Sud departs hourly for nearby coastal resorts.

Following are sample fares:

Destination	Cost (AR$)	Duration (hr)
Bahía Blanca	64	7
Bariloche	182	19
Buenos Aires	56	5½
Comodoro Rivadavia	230	24
Córdoba	145	18
Jujuy	240	27
La Plata	50	5
Mendoza	132	18
Miramar	5	1¼
Necochea	18	2
Neuquén	96	12
Paraná	102	12½
Pinamar	17	2½
Posadas	146	19
Puerto Madryn	127	16½
Rosario	72	7½
Salta	252	26
San Juan	215	20
Santa Fe	96	12
Santiago del Estero	205	20
Tandil	22	3
Trelew	182	18
Tucumán	230	24
Villa Gesell	13	2

TRAIN

The **train station** (☎ 475-6076; Av Luro 4700 at Italia; ☻ 6am-midnight) is about 2km from the beach. Tickets can also be purchased at the **Ferrobaires office** (☎ 451-2501; Alberti 1602; ☻ 8am-9pm) which is located at the bus terminal.

During summer, the tourist train *El Marplatense* travels seven times daily (eight on Sunday) to Buenos Aires. Reservations should be made far in advance, since it's usually booked solid through the season. One-way *turista* (2nd-class) fares cost AR$28; Super Pullman (1st-class) costs AR$55. There are daily departures through the slower seasons as well.

Getting Around

Despite Mar del Plata's sprawl, frequent buses reach just about every place in town. For information on local destinations, the tourist office can help.

Aeropuerto Félix U Camet (☎ 479-0194, 479-2787; RN 2 Km 396) is 10km north of the city. To get there by bus, take bus 542 from the corner of Blvd Marítimo and Belgrano. A taxi or *remise* costs about AR$30.

Car rentals are available at **Localiza** (☎ 493-3461; www.localizarentacar.com.ar in Spanish; Córdoba 2270), while bicycles can be rented from **Bicicletería Madrid** (☎ 494-1932; Yrigoyen 2249, Plaza Mitre; per hr/day AR$10/30; ☺ 10am-6:30pm).

AROUND MAR DEL PLATA
Museo del Automovilismo Juan Manuel Fangio
Named for Argentina's most famous race car driver, this **museum** (☎ 02266-425540; www.museo fangio.com; cnr Dardo Rocha & Mitre, Balcarce; adult/child AR$15/8; ☺ 10am-5pm Mon-Fri, 10am-6pm Sat & Sun), one of the country's finest, preserves a multimillion-dollar collection of classic and racing cars in Fangio's birthplace of Balcarce, 60km northwest of Mar del Plata via RN 226. Occupying an early-20th-century building, the museum stresses the worldwide exploits of Fangio and his contemporaries, but also makes an effort to put automotive history into a global context.

Fangio, who died in 1995 at the age of 84, is the subject of Stirling Moss and Doug Nye's biographical tribute *Fangio: a Pirelli Album*.

El Rápido runs frequent buses from Mar del Plata (AR$9, 1½ hours).

NECOCHEA
☎ 02262 / pop 88,200
Totally pumping in summer and near dead in winter, Necochea's beach-town feel is undisturbed by the high-rises that keep springing up. With 74km of beachfront, it's fairly certain that you'll be able to find a spot to lay your towel, and the place has the best waves on the coast, attracting surfers throughout the year. The foresty Parque Provincial Miguel Lillo is a great bonus here, as are the walking and horseriding opportunities out to the west of town.

Necochea lacks the woodsy allure of the smaller resorts of Pinamar and Villa Gesell, but it has some of the best-value lodging on the coast.

Orientation
Necochea is 128km southwest of Mar del Plata via RP 88, the direct inland route. Car-clogged RN 11 is the coastal route from Cabo Corrientes in Mar del Plata. It takes you past dramatic headlands as far south as the family resort of **Miramar** and then heads inland to RP 88.

The south-flowing Río Quequén Grande separates Neuquén, on its western bank, from the village of Quequén on the eastern side.

Though streets have both names and numbers, everyone just uses the numbers. Even-numbered streets run parallel to the sea; odd numbers run perpendicular.

The focus of tourist activity is in 'La Villa,' the newer part of town between Av 10 and the beach. Calle 83 (Alfredo Butti) is its main commercial street. The area is dead in winter. Banks and other year-round businesses are near Plaza Dardo Rocha in the old town (Centro); most of the shops and restaurants line the streets just northwest of the plaza.

Information
ACA (☎ 422106; Av 59, No 2073) Argentina's auto club; good source for provincial road maps.
Banco de la Nación (cnr Av 6 & Calle 83) Has ATM.
Municipal hospital (☎ 422405; Av 59, btwn Calles 100 & 104)
Municipal tourist office (☎ 430158; www.necochea net.com.ar; Av 2 & Calle 79; ☺ 9am-10pm, to 5pm winter) On the beach.
Nevada (Calle 4, No 4063; per hr AR$1) Internet access.
Post office (Av 6, No 4065)

Sights & Activities
The dense pine woods of **Parque Provincial Miguel Lillo**, a large greenbelt along the beach, are widely used for bicycling, horseback riding, hiking and picnicking. Horses and bikes can both be rented inside the park.

The Río Quequén Grande, rich in rainbow trout and mackerel, also allows for adventurous **canoeing**, particularly around the falls at **Saltos del Quequén**. At the village of **Quequén** at the river's mouth, several stranded shipwrecks offer good opportunities for exploration and photography below sculpted cliffs. The **faro** (lighthouse) is another local attraction.

The **beach** is, just for a change, overrun with *balnearios* in January, but relatively quiet at other times of year.

With the best waves on the Atlantic coast, Necochea is a hit with surfers. There's a surf school at the **Monte Pasuvio camping ground** (☎ 451482; Calle 502 No 1160), across the river in Quequén, where you can arrange classes and rent boards year-round.

Sleeping
Prices given here are for the January peak period; they can almost halve during the rest of the year.

Hospedaje La Casona (☎ 423345; Calle 6, No 4356; per person AR$45) This welcoming place offers

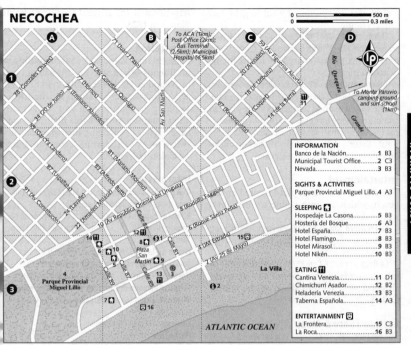

guests simple rooms, a spacious garden with a *parrilla*, as well as a games room and small library. There are also apartments for four with kitchenette (AR$160). The *hospedaje* is open only from 15 December to Easter.

Hotel Flamingo (☎ 420049; hotflamingo@mixmail .com; Calle 83, No 333; r AR$130) The Flamingo's rooms are surprisingly well decked out for a budget joint, with minibars and (relatively) large bathrooms.

Hotel Mirasol (☎ 4525158; Calle 4 bis, No 4133; d/tr AR$150/195) With an excellent location right on the square, this place has comfortable rooms, some with refrigerator and TV.

ourpick Hostería del Bosque (☎ 420002; Calle 89, No 350; r AR$230) Once home to a Russian princess, this *hostería* is by far the most atmospheric place to stay in town. Rooms are quaint and comfortable, bathrooms modern and Parque Lillo is right outside the front door.

Hotel España (☎ 422896; www.hotel-espana.com.ar; Calle 89, No 215; r AR$240) A small hotel with wonderfully comfortable rooms; some at the front have balconies overlooking the street, but all have good natural light.

Hotel Nikén (☎ 432323; www.hotelniken.com.ar in Spanish; Calle 87, No 335; s/d AR$186/240; ❄ ▯ ❷) The town's only four-star, the Nikén is outstandingly ugly from the outside, but interior charms like modern, spacious rooms and a ripping breakfast buffet make it excellent value.

Eating

There are plenty of dining options around Plaza San Martín, and while most are open seven days during the summer, their hours vary during the quieter months. Many of the *balnearios* have *confiterias* (cafés) where you can grab a bite beachside.

Heladeria Venezia (☎ 430300; Av 2, No 4190; ❧ daily) Pull up a swinging chair at this beach-front icecreamery and suck on one of 40 delicious homemade flavors.

Cantina Venezia (☎ 424014; Av 59, No 259; mains AR$14-28; ❧ dinner daily Jan & Feb, dinner Wed-Sun Mar-Dec) Still going strong after 40 years, this Italian/seafood restaurant is the pick of the seafood joints near the port. Prices are a little higher than the rest, but more than justified by the quality and size of the meals. It's not a great area, so you might want to get a taxi (AR$7) home.

Chimichurri Asador (☎ 420642; Calle 83, No 345; asado per person AR$20; ☑ lunch & dinner Sun) Carnivores only at this place, favored by locals for its delicious meats.

Taberna Española (☎ 525126; Calle 89, No 366; mains AR$22-40; ☑ lunch & dinner) For the Spanish take on the whole seafood thing, this is the place to come, and come hungry. The *picada de mariscos* (series of small seafood dishes; AR$39) is a gut buster – delicious fishy dishes just keep on coming. Reservations essential.

Entertainment

There are several dance clubs located on the beach, which are impossible to miss on a weekend night.

La Frontera (cnr Av 2 & Calle 75, Playa; ☑ Fri & Sat) Live bands play here during summer, from midnight onwards.

La Roca (cnr Av 2 & Calle 87, Playa; ☑ Fri & Sat) For salsa, cumbia, *rock nacional* and an overall good vibe, try this disco at the end of Calle 87.

Getting There & Away

The **bus terminal** (☎ 422470; Av 58, btwn Calle 47 & Av 45) is near the river. Several companies run daily buses to Buenos Aires (AR$76, seven hours). Empresa Córdoba Mar del Plata serves the interior, and there are often special services by other carriers in summer. El Rápido connects Necochea with Mar del Plata (AR$18, two hours), Bariloche (AR$180, 18 hours) and Tandil (AR$20, 2¾ hours). Rapido del Sud connects Necochea with other coastal destinations.

BAHÍA BLANCA

☎ 0291 / pop 314,500

Grandiose buildings, an attractive plaza and boulevards lined with shade trees and palms lend oft-overlooked Bahía Blanca the feel of a cosmopolitan city in miniature. While its chief advantage is as a resting point during overland trips from Buenos Aires to Patagonia, there are a few things to see in town, and plenty of good eating and entertainment options.

The hoards of sailors who dock here at what is now South America's largest naval base attest to Bahía Blanca's militaristic beginnings. In an early effort to establish military control on the periphery of the pampas, Colonel Ramón Estomba situated the pompously named Fortaleza Protectora

Argentina at the natural harbor of Bahía Blanca in 1828.

Orientation

Bahía Blanca is located 654km southwest of Buenos Aires via RN 3, 530km east of Neuquén via RN 22, and 278km north of Viedma via RN 3. Don't let the town's soothing grid layout fool you – like many other pampean towns, Bahia Blanca's streets have a habit of changing their names. They switch at Av San Martín/Zelarrayán and at Av Colón/H Irigoyen.

Information

ACA (☎ 455-0076; Chiclana 305) Argentina's auto club; good source for provincial road maps.

Alianza Francesa (☎ 455-1986; afbahiab@bvconline .com.ar; Fitzroy 49; ☑ 9:30am-8:30pm Mon-Thu, 11am-7pm Fri)

Banco de la Nación (Estomba 52) Includes Western Union branch and may also change traveler's checks.

Hospital Municipal (☎ 456-8484; Estomba 968)

Hospital Privado del Sur (☎ 455-0270; Las Heras 164)

Internet access (Alsina 108; per hr AR$2.90) Also has telephones.

Laverap (Av Colón 197) Laundry.

Post office (Moreno 34)

Pullman Tour (☎ 455-3344; San Martín 171) Change money and traveler's checks here.

Tije Travel (☎ 456-0666; www.tije.com in Spanish; Zelerrayan 267, Local 7) Sells discount international flights, issues student ID cards.

Tourist office (☎ 459-4007; Alsina 65; ☑ 8am-7pm Mon-Sat) In the basement of the Municipalidad.

Sights & Activities

On the outskirts of town, in the former customs building hardly noticeable among the massive grain elevators and fortress-like power plant of Puerto Ingeniero White, the **Museo del Puerto** (☎ 457-3006; Guillermo Torres 4131; admission by donation; ☑ 8:30am-12:30pm Mon-Fri, 3-7pm Sat & Sun) is an iconoclastic tribute to immigrants and their heritage, and includes an archive with documents, photographs and recorded oral histories. The best time to visit is for a weekend afternoon tea, when local groups prepare regional delicacies, each week representing a different immigrant group. Live music often accompanies the refreshments. Bus 504 from the plaza goes to the museum.

The neoclassical **Teatro Municipal** (cnr Alsina & Zapiola Dorrego), is the main performing-arts center in the city. In the same building is

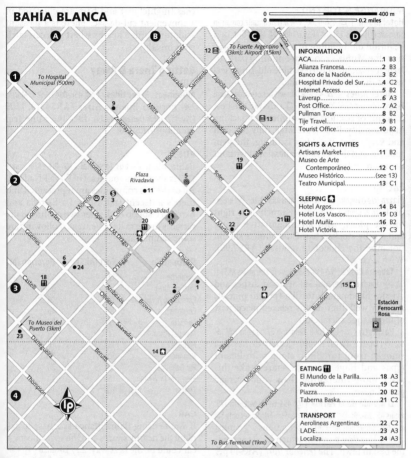

BAHÍA BLANCA

INFORMATION	
ACA	**1** B3
Alianza Francesa	**2** B3
Banco de la Nación	**3** B2
Hospital Privado del Sur	**4** C2
Internet Access	**5** B2
Laverap	**6** A3
Post Office	**7** A2
Pullman Tour	**8** B2
Tije Travel	**9** B1
Tourist Office	**10** B2

SIGHTS & ACTIVITIES	
Artisans Market	**11** B2
Museo de Arte Contemporáneo	**12** C1
Museo Histórico	(see **13**)
Teatro Municipal	**13** C1

SLEEPING	
Hotel Argos	**14** B4
Hotel Los Vascos	**15** D3
Hotel Muñiz	**16** B2
Hotel Victoria	**17** C3

EATING	
El Mundo de la Parilla	**18** A3
Pavarotti	**19** C2
Piazza	**20** B2
Taberna Baska	**21** C2

TRANSPORT	
Aerolineas Argentinas	**22** C2
LADE	**23** A3
Localiza	**24** A3

THE PAMPAS & THE ATLANTIC COAST

Museo Histórico (☎ 456-3117; Zapiola Dorrego 116; admission free; ⏲ 8am-noon & 4-8pm Tue-Fri, 4-8pm Sat & Sun). Displays include indigenous artifacts and collections that represent important episodes in the life of the town, such as its founding as a military base and the arrival of the railways. Also worth checking out is **Museo de Arte Contemporáneo** (☎ 459-4006; Sarmiento 454; admission free; ⏲ 2-8pm Tue-Fri, 4-8pm Sat & Sun), showcasing local and national artists.

On the weekends an **artisans market** takes over Plaza Rivadavia, situated opposite the Municipalidad.

Sleeping

Catering mainly to the business set, accommodations in Bahía Blanca are generally more expensive than in other Argentine towns its size; however, good deals can be found.

BUDGET

Hotel Los Vascos (☎ 452-0977; Cerri 747; s with/without bathroom AR$40/25, d AR$60/50) Across from the train station, Los Vascos is without doubt the best of the budget bunch in the area. Rooms are pleasant and basic, and the wooden floors and spotless shared bathrooms add to the appeal, as does the friendly family who run the place.

Hotel Victoria (☎ 452-0522; General Paz 84; s with/without bathroom AR$70/50, d AR$120/80) This well-kept old building has basic, comfortable rooms around a leafy central courtyard. Cable TV makes it a good deal.

MIDRANGE & TOP END

Hotel Muñiz (☎ 456-0060; www.hotelmuniz.com.ar in Spanish; O'Higgins 23; s/d AR$92/140; ✕ ▢) Set in a beautiful old building in a very central location, the Muñiz's rooms are nothing particularly special, but the irresistible old-timey feel makes the place worthwhile.

Hotel Argos (☎ 455-0404; www.hotelargos.com; España 149; s/d AR$170/200; ✕ ▢) By far the best in terms of comfort and shininess, if lacking in personality. Rooms are large, fully carpeted and very quiet. Breakfast is filling, the gym modern and the service professional without being pretentious.

Eating

Piazza (cnr O'Higgins & Chiclana; mains AR$12-26; ☾ breakfast, lunch & dinner) A popular lunch spot right on the plaza, with an imaginative menu and a fully stocked bar. Chocoholics should not miss the chocolate mousse (AR$7.90). Wi-fi access.

Taberna Baska (☎ 450-2500; Lavalle 284; mains AR$14-32; ☾ lunch & dinner Mon-Sat) Seafood dishes and classics like Spanish tortilla (potato omelet) are very well done at this relaxed place, part of the Basque social club.

Pavarotti (☎ 450-7000; Belgrano 272; mains AR$16-38; ☾ lunch & dinner) Sophisticated dishes like smoked-trout tortellini, along with lots of tapas and huge plates to share make this place more interesting than your average pasta house.

El Mundo de la Parilla (☎ 454-6446; Av Colón 379; mains AR$26-29; ☾ lunch & dinner Sun-Fri, dinner only Sat Mar-Dec, dinner only Jan-Feb) Reservations are a must at this buzzing *parrilla*, which locals agree is the best in town. The *tenedor libre* (AR$40 per person) sees an endless procession of succulent grilled meats brought to your table, along with salad and drinks.

Drinking

For a night out on the town in Bahía Blanca, head to **Fuerte Argentino**, about nine blocks northeast from Plaza Rivadavia, where *boliches* (nightclubs) and bars are clustered in a convenient cul-de-sac. There is a pleasant sculpture garden nearby where you can catch your breath.

Getting There & Away

AIR

Aerolineas Argentinas (☎ 456-0561; San Martín 298) hops to Buenos Aires (AR$437). **LADE** (☎ 452-1063; Darragueira 21) does the same trip for about AR$280.

BUS

Bahía Blanca's **bus terminal** (☎ 481-9615; Brown 1700) is about 2km southeast of Plaza Rivadavia. All of the bus companies are represented and there's a decent snack bar. La Estrella and Expreso Cabildo each offer two or three daily services to Sierra de la Ventana. Following are some sample fares:

Destination	Cost (AR$)	Duration (hr)
Bariloche	113	13
Buenos Aires	76	8-10
Comodoro Rivadavia	150	16
Córdoba	107	15
La Plata	93	9
Mar del Plata	74	7
Mendoza	153	16
Neuquén	50	7½
Río Gallegos	264	26
Sierra de la Ventana	15	2
Trelew	100	10

CAR

If you're using Bahia Blanca as a base to explore the nearby sierras and the coast, hiring a car could be the best way. Try **Localiza** (☎ 456-2526; Av Colón 194).

TRAIN

Trains leave from the **Estación Ferrocarril Roca** (☎ 452-9196; Av Cerri 750) for Buenos Aires daily at around 7pm (12 hours). Fares range from AR$23 *turista* (2nd class) to AR$40 for a Pullman (recliner) seat.

Northeast Argentina

Northeast Argentina is defined by its water. Muscular rivers roll southward through flat green pastureland that they flood at will, the crashing roar of spectacular waterfalls reverberates through the surrounding jungle, and fragile wetlands support myriad birdlife, snapping caimans and cuddly capybaras. The peaceful Iguazú river, meandering through the tropical forest between Brazil and Argentina, dissolves in fury and power in the world's most awe-inspiring cataracts – a sensual feast that cannot be missed. The river then merges gently into the Río Paraná, one of the world's mightiest watercourses which surges southward, eventually forming the Río de la Plata near Buenos Aires. Along its path are some of the country's most interesting cities: elegant Corrientes, colonial Santa Fe and booming Rosario, as well as Posadas, gateway to the ruined splendor of the Jesuit missions, whose humane dreams of social utopia in the jungle eventually foundered on the rocks of colonial realpolitik. The Paraná is joined by the Río Paraguay, west of which stretches the dry scrubland of the Chaco – whose more remote parts are tantalizingly named 'El Impenetrable' – and, eventually, the Río Uruguay, whose course down the Brazilian and Uruguayan border is interrupted by the unusual and spectacular Saltos del Moconá falls. Along its length are also several relaxed waterside towns: Colón, perhaps the region's most attractive settlement, and Gualeguaychú, whose exuberant Carnaval goes on for weeks.

Dotted throughout the region are excellent reserves and national parks, representative of the biological diversity of this sizable tract of country. The shallow freshwater lakes of the Esteros del Iberá harbor a stunning richness of wildlife, easily seen among the aquatic plants.

HIGHLIGHTS

- Drop your jaw in stunned amazement at the power of the **Iguazú Falls** (p221)

- Get personal with the mighty Paraná in livable, lovable **Rosario** (p179)

- Coo at the cute capybaras of the **Reserva Provincial Esteros del Iberá** (p201)

- Munch delicious freshwater fish by the Río Uruguay in pretty **Colón** (p208)

- Ponder a unique experiment in humanity at the ruined **Jesuit Missions** (p214)

Iguazú Falls

Jesuit Missions

Reserva Provincial
Esteros del Iberá

Colón

Rosario

■ POPULATION: 7,526,366 | ■ AREA: 501,487 SQ KM

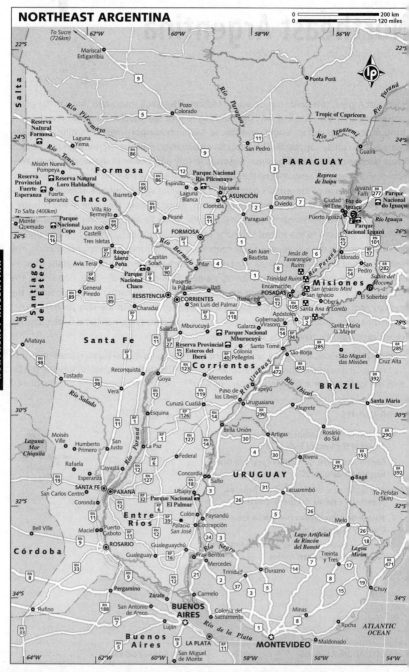

NORTHEAST ARGENTINA

Climate

Over such a large area, temperatures vary widely, getting more tropical as you head north. The riverside cities north of Rosario all tend to be humid, but the Chaco is particularly dry. Winter in the southern part of the region can be fairly cold, with occasional subzero temperatures.

National Parks & Reserves

There are some excellent national parks within the region, varying from the dry savannas of the Chaco to the rainforests of Misiones. In the far northeast, Parque Nacional do Iguaçu (p224) and Parque Nacional Iguazú (p223) are the access points for viewing the incredible Iguazú Falls, and also provide a habitat for orchids, big cats, birdlife and other flora and fauna.

Nowhere will you see as much wildlife as in the wetlands of Reserva Provincial Esteros del Iberá (p201) and its nearby counterpart Parque Nacional Mburucuyá (p199), while it's the haunting elegance of yatay palm trees that makes Parque Nacional El Palmar (p209) special.

Deforestation has denuded much of the Chaco area, so the scrub forests and marshes of Parque Nacional Chaco (p237) and Parque Nacional Río Pilcomayo (p241) are especially valuable, as are the natural reserves further west in the region (p239). Although Parque Nacional Copo (p300) is part of the dry Chaco ecoregion, the park is more easily reached from Santiago del Estero and is therefore covered in the Andean Northwest chapter.

Getting There & Away

There are flights from Buenos Aires to Rosario, Santa Fe, Posadas, Puerto Iguazú, Resistencia, Corrientes and Formosa. Bus connections are available from most towns to destinations all over the country.

ALONG THE RÍO PARANÁ

The mighty Río Paraná river, the continent's second longest at 4000km, dominates the geography of Northeast Argentina. Several of the nation's more interesting cities lie along it, and interact with it on a daily basis. All have their town centers a sensible distance above the shorelines of this flood-prone monster but have a *costanera* (riverbank) that's the focus of much social life. The river is still important for trade, and large oceangoing vessels ply it as far as Rosario, a city whose wonderfully friendly inhabitants and optimistic outlook make it a great destination.

Santa Fe and Paraná have a relaxingly sleepy feel – who can blame them with the humidity the Paraná generates? – and attractive traditional architecture, while beautiful Corrientes is the home of *chamamé* music (a local musical style derived from polka) and launchpad for the wonderful Esteros del Iberá wetlands.

The Paraná is the demesne of river fish – surubí, dorado and pacú among others – that grow enormous and attract sportfishers from around the world. Their distinctive flavor enlivens the menu of the region's restaurants; make sure you try them.

ROSARIO

☎ 0341 / pop 1,161,188

The boom times are back for Rosario, birthplace of both the Argentine flag and 'Che' Guevara, and an important riverport. The derelict buildings of the long *costanera* have been converted into galleries, restaurants and skate parks, and the river beaches and islands buzz with life in summer. The center – a curious mishmash of stunning early-20th-century buildings overshadowed by ugly apartments – has a comfortable, lived-in feel, and the down-to-earth *rosarinos* (people from Rosario) are a delight. All are very proud of the city's current claim to fame: Lionel Messi, a golden boy of world soccer, is Rosario born and bred.

History

Rosario's first European inhabitants settled here informally around 1720 without sanction from the Spanish crown. After independence Rosario quickly superseded Santa Fe as the province's economic powerhouse though, to the irritation of *rosarinos,* the provincial capital retained political primacy.

The Central Argentine Land Company, an adjunct of the railroad, was responsible for bringing in agricultural colonists from Europe, for whom Rosario was a port of entry. From 1869 to 1914 Rosario's population grew nearly tenfold to 223,000, easily overtaking the capital in numbers. The city's role in agricultural exports and its economic ties to the beef market of the Chicago Mercantile Exchange earned it the nickname 'Chicago Argentino.'

Though the decline of economic and shipping activity during the 1960s led to a drop

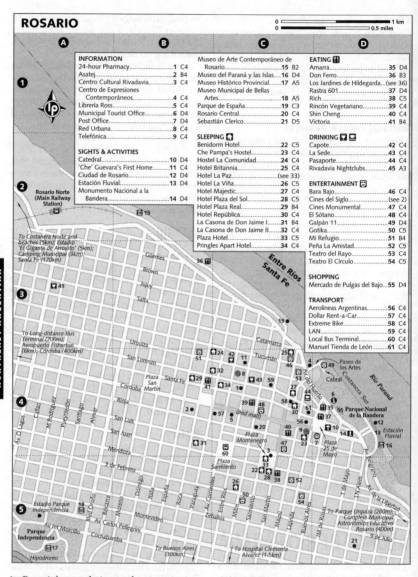

ROSARIO

0 _____ 1 km
0 _____ 0.5 miles

INFORMATION	
24-hour Pharmacy	1 C4
Asatej	2 B4
Centro Cultural Rivadavia	3 C4
Centro de Expresiones Contemporáneos	4 C4
Librería Ross	5 C4
Municipal Tourist Office	6 D4
Post Office	7 D4
Red Urbana	8 C4
Telefónica	9 C4

SIGHTS & ACTIVITIES	
Catedral	10 C4
'Che' Guevara's First Home	11 C4
Ciudad de Rosario	12 D4
Estación Fluvial	13 D4
Monumento Nacional a la Bandera	14 D4

Museo de Arte Contemporáneo de Rosario	15 B2
Museo del Paraná y las Islas	16 D4
Museo Histórico Provincial	17 A5
Museo Municipal de Bellas Artes	18 A5
Parque de España	19 C3
Rosario Central	20 C4
Sebastián Clerico	21 D5

SLEEPING 🏠	
Benidorm Hotel	22 C5
Che Pampa's Hostel	23 C4
Hostel La Comunidad	24 C4
Hotel Britannia	25 C4
Hotel La Paz	(see 33)
Hotel La Viña	26 C5
Hotel Majestic	27 C4
Hotel Plaza del Sol	28 C5
Hotel Plaza Real	29 B4
Hotel República	30 C4
La Casona de Don Jaime I	31 B4
La Casona de Don Jaime II	32 C4
Plaza Hotel	33 C5
Pringles Apart Hotel	34 C4

EATING 🍴	
Amarra	35 D4
Don Ferro	36 B3
Los Jardines de Hildegarda	(see 36)
Rastra 601	37 D4
Rich	38 C5
Rincón Vegetariano	39 C4
Shin Cheng	40 C4
Victoria	41 B4

DRINKING 🍷 🍺	
Capote	42 C4
La Sede	43 C4
Pasaporte	44 C4
Rivadavia Nightclubs	45 A3

ENTERTAINMENT 🎭	
Bara Bajo	46 C4
Cines del Siglo	(see 2)
Cines Monumental	47 C4
El Sótano	48 C4
Galpán 11	49 D4
Gotika	50 C5
Mi Refugio	51 B4
Peña La Amistad	52 C5
Teatro del Rayo	53 C4
Teatro El Círculo	54 C5

SHOPPING	
Mercado de Pulgas del Bajo	55 D4

TRANSPORT	
Aerolíneas Argentinas	56 C4
Dollar Rent-a-Car	57 C4
Extreme Bike	58 C4
LAN	59 C4
Local Bus Terminal	60 C4
Manuel Tienda de León	61 C4

in Rosario's population and power, its importance as a port was rivaled only by Buenos Aires. Its title as Argentina's second city, however, was later usurped by Córdoba – a status still hotly contested by *rosarinos*.

Nationalistic Argentines cherish Rosario, home of a monument to the nation's flag, as 'Cuna de la Bandera' (Cradle of the Flag).

Orientation

Rosario displays a very regular grid pattern, except where the curvature of the bluffs above the river channel dictates otherwise. Traditionally the focus of urban activities is Plaza 25 de Mayo, but the *peatonales* (pedestrian streets) of San Martín and Córdoba mark the commercial center. There are some

70 square blocks of open space in Parque Independencia, southwest of downtown.

Information

BOOKSTORES

Librería Ross (☎ 448-5378; Córdoba 1347) Has a small selection of classics in English.

CULTURAL CENTERS

Centro Cultural Rivadavia (☎ 480-2401; San Martín 1080) Situated on Plaza Montenegro, this is a good place to find out what's happening in town. It shows free or inexpensive films and hosts dance and theater events. Its galleries provide a showcase for the local arts community.
Centro de Expresiones Contemporáneas (☎ 480-2243; www.cecrosario.org.ar; cnr Av del Huerto & Paseo de los Artes) Consists of recycled historical buildings now providing space for special exhibitions.

INTERNET ACCESS

There are numerous places to get online, and plenty of spots offer wireless access, including the plane-shaded Plaza 25 de Mayo (password: mr_gratis).
Red Urbana (Av Corrientes 563; per hr AR$2; ☽ 24hr)
Telefónica (cnr Laprida & Córdoba; per hr AR$1.50; ☽ 7:30am-midnight)

MEDICAL SERVICES

There are several 24-hour pharmacies in the center of town, including one at the corner of San Lorenzo and Entre Ríos.
Hospital Clemente Alvarez (☎ 480-8111; Rueda 1110) Southwest of the city center.

MONEY

Banks and ATMs are all over, including a cluster along Santa Fe near Plaza 25 de Mayo. Exchanges along San Martín and Córdoba change cash and traveler's checks, the latter with commission. Street changers often pass false notes.

POST & TELEPHONE

Post office (Córdoba 721) There are many *locutorios* (private telephone offices) around the center, including the Telefónica office listed under Internet Access.

TOURIST INFORMATION

Municipal tourist office (☎ 480-2230; www.rosario turismo.com; Av del Huerto; ☽ 7am-7pm) Near the waterfront. Excellent bilingual brochures and a helpful attitude.

TRAVEL AGENCIES

Asatej (☎ 425-6002; Shopping del Siglo 2nd fl, Roca 848) Nonprofit student travel agency.

Sights & Activities

MUSEO DEL PARANÁ Y LAS ISLAS

Thanks to the romantic, engaging murals of local painter Raúl Domínguez, this **museum** (☎ 440-0751; Estación Fluvial; admission free; ☽ 3-7:30pm Wed-Sun), on the 1st floor of the waterfront Estación Fluvial, is worthwhile. Life on the islands of the Paraná so enchanted Domínguez that he created this small museum, filling it with photographs, artifacts, historical documents and his own paintings.

MONUMENTO NACIONAL A LA BANDERA

Manuel Belgrano, who designed the Argentine flag, rests in a crypt beneath this colossal 78m-high tower, a chillingly nationalistic construction in pitiless stone. The monument's redeeming attributes are its location near the Paraná waterfront and the dizzying views of the river and surrounds from its tower, accessed by elevator. Its **museum** (☎ 480-2238; Santa Fe 581; admission AR$1.50; ☽ 9am-6pm Tue-Sun, 2-6pm Mon) contains the original flag embroidered by Catalina de Vidal. For information about Rosario's yearly Flag Week celebrations see p183.

CATEDRAL

Near the flag monument, Rosario's **cathedral** (Plaza 25 de Mayo; ☽ 7:40am-12:30pm & 4:30-8:30pm Mon-Sat, 8am-1pm & 5-9:30pm Sun) is a slender construction with a high single nave and dome decorated with stained-glass panels depicting the life of the Virgin. It's one of several attractive buildings around this square, which is effectively the center of old Rosario.

MUSEO HISTÓRICO PROVINCIAL

The well-presented collection of this **museum** (☎ 472-1457; Parque Independencia; admission AR$2; ☽ 9am-5pm Tue-Fri, 3-7pm Sat & Sun) features plenty of postindependence exhibits plus excellent displays on indigenous cultures from all over Latin America. There are also colonial and religious artifacts and the most ornate collection of *mate* (a kind of tea-like beverage) paraphernalia you're ever likely to see.

MUSEO MUNICIPAL DE BELLAS ARTES

This **museum** (☎ 480-2542; cnr Av Carlos Pellegrini & Blvd Oroño; admission AR$2; ☽ 2-8pm Mon & Wed-Sat, 1-7pm Sun) is one of the better galleries in this part of Argentina. It houses a permanent collection of European and Argentine fine art, with occasional contemporary exhibitions.

MUSEO DE ARTE CONTEMPORÁNEO DE ROSARIO (MACRO)

Housed in a brightly painted grain silo on the waterfront, this **gallery** (☎ 480-4981; Av de la Costa at Blvd Oroño; donation AR$2; 2-8pm Tue-Sat) is the latest completed project of Rosario's impressive riverbank renewal. It features temporary exhibitions, mostly by young local artists, of varying quality, housed in small galleries spread over eight floors. There's a good view of the river islands from the *mirador* (viewpoint) at the top and an attractive café-bar, Davis, by the river.

LA COSTANERA

One of Rosario's most attractive features is its waterfront, where what was once home to derelict warehouses and train tracks is rapidly being reclaimed for the fun of the people. It stretches some 15km from its southern end at Parque Urquiza to the Embarcadero Costa Alta, near the city's northern edge, just short of the Rosario Victoria suspension bridge that crosses into Entre Ríos province. It's an appealing place to wander and watch what's going on, from the plentiful birdlife and impromptu football games to massive cargo ships surging past on the river.

The grassy **Costanera Sur**, just below downtown, includes plenty of space for jogging and courting, as well as La Fluvial (Estación Fluvial) building. This offers boats across to the islands as well as several upmarket eating and drinking options, and the Museo Del Paraná y las Islas.

Heading further north, you pass various cultural venues before reaching the **Parque de España** and its mausoleum-like edifice. Beyond here is a zone of bars and restaurants that gets lively at weekends, and then the Museo de Arte Contemporáneo de Rosario.

In summer, however, it's the **Costanera Norte** about 5km north of downtown that attracts the crowds, as this stretch, along with the islands, offers the best places to swim. The stretch along the busy Av Carrasco, north of Av Puccio, has the most to offer, including the **Rambla Cataluña**, a tree-lined riverfront with small sandy beaches, shoreline cafés, bars, volleyball nets and tanning sunbathers.

The widest beach is further north at **Balneario La Florida** (admission AR$2; Oct-Apr), with services including umbrellas, showers, clothing check and outdoor bars. The sidewalk stops at La Florida and picks up again at its northern edge at **Costa Alta**, where there

are more beaches and a pier with boats to the islands.

To get to Rambla Cataluña take bus 153 from the center of town 6km north to Av Puccio (here the bus turns inland).

RIVER ISLANDS

Rosario sits on the banks of the Río Paraná upper delta, an area characterized by largely uninhabited, subtropical islands and winding *riachos* (streams). **Isla Invernada** and **Isla del Espinillo**, the two main islands visible from Rosario's shore, are accessible by boat in summer. Out of season, you'll have to take a tour by kayak with a tour operator, such as Sebastián Clerico.

Boats from Costa Alta leave every 20 minutes (AR$3 roundtrip), from 9am to 8pm in summer, for the various *balnearios* (river beaches) along the western shore of Isla Invernada. They are all pretty similar, with sandy beaches, gregarious summer crowds, cafés, ice-cream stands, umbrella rentals, music, billboards and boats from the mainland. Bring plenty of sunblock.

From **Estación Fluvial** (Ferry Station; ☎ 447-3838; www.lafluvialrosario.com.ar) there are hourly boats (AR$11 roundtrip) to the southern *balnearios* (river beaches) of Costa Esperanza (which offers everything from quad bikes to boat trips), Vladimir and Oasis.

The **Ciudad de Rosario** (☎ 449-8688) offers two-hour cruises on the Paraná for AR$15; it leaves from Estación Fluvial on weekends and holidays at 2:30pm and 5pm, more often in summer.

COMPLEJO MUNICIPAL ASTRONÓMICO EDUCATIVO ROSARIO

Those interested in more distant environments can visit the planetarium at the **municipal observatory** (☎ 480-2554; Parque Urquiza; admission free), which has shows (AR$5) at 5pm and 6pm Saturday and Sunday from May to September. At 8:30pm Wednesday through to Sunday (clouds permitting), visitors can view the astral skies through its 2250mm refractor telescope and 4500mm reflecting telescope.

'CHE' GUEVARA'S FIRST HOME

This apartment building at Entre Ríos 480, designed by Alejandro Bustillo, was where Ernesto Guevara Lynch and Celia de la Serna lived in 1928 after the birth of their son, Ernesto Guevara de la Serna, popularly known as 'Che.' According to biographer Jon Anderson, young Ernesto's birth certificate was falsified (he was born more than a month before the official date of June 14), but this was certainly Che's first home, although briefly. It's now a private flat, so you can't go inside, but fans of this revolutionary figure will still enjoy such trivia, and may want to also check out the Guevara family home in Córdoba (see p332) which is now a museum.

Tours

Sebastián Clerico (☎ 0341-15-5713812; www.bikerosario .com.ar; Zeballos 327) offers recommended bike tours of the city and surrounds (AR$55, three hours) in several languages. Even better is the seven-hour trip (AR$105) which incorporates kayaking on the Río Paraná and around its islands.

Festivals & Events

Every June Rosario celebrates **Semana de la Bandera** (Flag Week), climaxing in ceremonies on June 20, the anniversary of the death of Manuel Belgrano, the flag's designer. In early October the **Semana del Arte** includes a poetry festival and theatre, comedy and dance performances. From mid-October to early November, the **Festival de Jazz** takes place in various venues around town. Pick up a copy of the *AC* (Agenda Cultural) magazine from the tourist office for event listings. Also in November, the national **Encuentro de las Colectividades**, a tribute to the country's immigrants, is celebrated with fancy dress, music and food stalls.

Sleeping

Booming Rosario has a huge number of places to stay. There are some 20 hostels (ask the tourist office for a list) and an ever-increasing herd of midrange hotels.

BUDGET

La Casona de Don Jaime (www.youthhostelrosario .ar; dm AR$25, d with/without bathroom AR$75/60; 🖳) | (☎ 527-9964; Roca 1051) & II (☎ 530-2020; San Lorenzo 1530) There's plenty of punch for your peso at this friendly pair of hostels. The original, on Roca, has darkish but comfortable dorms and rooms off a pretty central patio, as well as the offbeat Roots bar/restaurant out the front. The second, on San Lorenzo, is more modern and spacious and unlike the original, offers rooms with attached bathrooms. HI members get a 10% discount.

Hostel La Comunidad (☎ 424-5302; www.lacomunidad hostel.com; Roca 453; dm/s/d AR$27/60/70; 🖳) Occupying a gorgeous old Rosario building, this spot has lofty ceilings and a light, airy feel. The dorms have handsome wooden bunks and floorboards; a cute private room is also available. There's a bar, lounge area and peaceful vibe.

our pick **Che Pampa's Hostel** (☎ 424-5202; www .chepampas.com; Rioja 812; dm/d AR$30/90; 🕸 🖳) Designed with verve and panache, this is one of the best-looking hostels we've ever seen. Dark red is the color scheme of the comfortable dorms, which have a bit of road noise. There are also private rooms available, as well as almost any facility (DVDs, excellent kitchen, barbecue area, patio) you care to mention. The enthusiastic staff caps off an excellent place to stay.

Hotel Britannia (☎ 440-6036; San Martín 364; s/d AR$50/75) Handy for the river and tourist office, this likable old place features welcoming owners and a variety of rooms (some windowless) with TV and OK bathrooms. It's kept clean, but noise echoes, especially at weekends, when Bara Bajo next door goes until late.

Hotel La Viña (☎ 421-4549; 3 de Febrero 1244; s/d AR$60/90; 🕸) Sporting dark but spotless rooms with TV, and set around a patio that gives it a motel-like feel, this family-run joint is a likable place to crash. Rooms vary substantially in size, so check out a few.

The closest campsite to Rosario is at Granadero Baigorria, 9km north of the center. There the **Camping Municipal** (☎ 471-3705; sites per person AR$9) has a pleasant riverfront location and is popular with young Argentines. Take bus 35 from the center (Plaza Sarmiento is one option). In summer you can also camp at a couple of sites on the river islands, but don't rely on this, as members of the social clubs there get priority.

MIDRANGE & TOP END

Hotel La Paz (☎ 421-0905; Barón de Maua 36; s/d AR$75/90; 🕸 🖳) Well positioned on Plaza Montenegro, and still looking good after 60 years open, this welcoming hotel has resisted the price hikes in recent years and consequently offers excellent value. Family rooms at the front have balconies overlooking Plaza Montenegro.

Plaza Hotel (☎ 421-8300; www.hotelesplaza.com; Barón de Maua 26; s/d AR$149/179; 🕸 🖳) There's some serious '70s action going on in the lobby here, and

NORTHEAST ARGENTINA

if floral print means 'seethe' rather than 'soothe' for you, avoid the rooms, but otherwise it's a comfortable place with an excellent location on Plaza Montenegro. Service is helpful.

Pringles Apart Hotel (☎ 447-4050; www.pringles apart.com.ar; Santa Fe 1470; s/d $A165/185; 🕃 🔊) Put thoughts of potato snacks aside and book ahead for this top-value spot. The spacious apartments sleep up to three people and have a decent kitchen, comfy beds and a small balcony.

Hotel Plaza del Sol (☎ 421-3400; www.hotelesplaza .com; San Juan 1055; r AR$229; 🕃 🖥 🔊) The balconied rooms of this fine hotel are spacious, uninspired, but well equipped, and are shaded by the public areas, complete with strategically placed sculptures. There's a fabulous pool and sundeck area on the 11th floor. Service is good and the breakfast buffet is huge.

Hotel Plaza Real (☎ 440-8800; www.plazarealhotel .com; Santa Fe 1632; standard/superior/luxury r AR$240/288/ 500; 🕃 🖥 🔊) Perhaps Rosario's best hotel, this offers a range of luxurious rooms, apartments and suites in a modern building. It has fine facilities, a cracking breakfast and polite friendly service.

Also recommended:

Benidorm Hotel (☎ 421-9368; www.hotelbenidorm .com.ar; San Juan 1049; s/d AR$80/130) A decent no-frills option behind Plaza Montenegro.

Hotel Majestic (☎ 440-5872; www.hotelmajestic .ar; San Lorenzo 980; s/d/ste AR$145/175/220; 🕃 🖥) Stylish rooms in a stately old central building. The suites are much more spacious.

Hotel República (☎ 424-8580; www.solans.com; San Lorenzo 955; s/d AR$158/180; 🕃 🖥) Good-value rooms, some with city views, others that look out over the river.

Eating

Central Rosario seems empty come suppertime. That's because half the city is out on Av Carlos Pellegrini. Between Buenos Aires and Moreno there's a vast number of family-friendly eateries, including several barnlike *parrillas* (steak restaurants), dozens of pizza places, several all-you-can-eat buffets, and ice creameries. It's unsubtle but it's where everyone goes. Just stroll along and take your pick. Most have terraces on the street.

Rincón Vegetariano (☎ 411-0833; Mitre 720; all you can eat AR$11; 🕑 lunch & dinner Mon-Sat) With over 50 meat-free hot and cold dishes to eat-in or take-away, this is a real haven if barbecued meat ain't your thing. There are deals for two people.

Shin Cheng (☎ 411-0103; Rioja 954; 🕑 lunch & dinner Mon-Sat) Another good vegetarian option

where you pay by weight – there are many soya-based meat substitutes.

Rastra 601 (☎ 411-3303; Laprida 601, cnr San Lorenzo; lunch AR$13.90; 🕑 lunch & dinner) Get to this stylish but comfortable central spot early for lunch, as it tends to fill quickly. And deservedly so; the plates have a homecooked, cared-for feel that reminds the local businesspeople of their mum.

Los Jardines de Hildegarda (☎ 426-1168; riverbank near España; dishes AR$8-18; 🕑 noon-late Tue-Sun) Right by the river, this offbeat spot serves freshly caught fish as well as salads and the usual meats. The setting is delightful, some may say better than the food. Take the lift down from next to Don Ferro restaurant.

Victoria (☎ 425-7665; cnr San Lorenzo & Roca; mains AR$10-20; 🕑 7:30am-late Mon-Sat, 8pm-late Sun) This busy and atmospheric café-cum-bar in an old brick building offers a AR$15 lunch special and delicious salads. Also, it's a great place for a beer and has wi-fi.

Don Ferro (☎ 421-1927; riverbank near España; mains AR$10-28; 🕑 lunch & dinner) A very good-looking *parrilla* in what was once Rosario's train station, with a delightful terrace on the platform, excellent service and seriously delicious meat.

ourpick Amarra (☎ 447-7750; cnr Buenos Aires & Av Belgrano; mains AR$15-30; 🕑 lunch & dinner Mon-Sat) Smart but relaxed, this restaurant opposite the tourist office has a stylish split-level interior and serves up some very imaginative dishes, beautifully presented and prepared. Their specialty is fish, but the meat is also delicious. A huge paella for two people costs AR$36, there are tapas nights (AR$25) on Wednesday and Thursday, and the AR$9 weekday lunch is also great value.

Rich (☎ 440-8657; San Juan 1031; mains AR$20-35; 🕑 lunch & dinner Mon-Sat, lunch Sun) Specializing in exquisite Italian-influenced cuisine in a beautiful old building, Rich is one of the finest and most atmospheric restaurants in town. Budget-watchers shouldn't overlook the tasty *rotisería* (take-out shop) alongside.

Drinking

Rosario has a great number of *restobares*, which function as hybrid cafés and bars, and generally serve a fairly standard selection of snacks and plates. Many are good for either a morning coffee or an evening glass of wine – or anything in between.

Capote (☎ 448-5725; cnr Av Corrientes & Urquiza; snacks AR$6-10, pizza AR$6-15) Hard to miss with its pink neon sign, and decorated with tastefully framed posters, this is perhaps quieter than

Truman himself would have liked, but is a fine venue for wine and beer, and also offers salads, sandwiches and pizzas. One of four in town.

La Sede (☎ 425-4071; Entre Ríos 599) In a striking modernist building, this is a very Argentine café with a literary feel. Come here to read a book, enjoy the cakes and quiches or, at weekends, catch an offbeat live performance of something or other.

Pasaporte (☎ 448-4097; cnr Maipú & Urquiza; ☽ 8am-late Mon-Sat) A sublimely cozy spot with a pretty terrace and timeworn wooden furniture, including little window booths. It's a favorite for morning coffee with workers from the customs department opposite, but also has a great evening atmosphere, particularly when the rain's pouring down outside.

Entertainment

CINEMA

Cines del Siglo (☎ 425-0761; www.holidaycines.com.ar; Roca 848; AR$7-9) In the Shopping del Siglo center.

Cines Monumental (☎ 530-7070; San Martín 997, AR$9-11) Multiscreen complex in the *peatonal* in San Martín. You can smell the popcorn a block away.

LIVE MUSIC

El Sótano (Mitre 785) A moody downstairs venue with regular live acts, mostly hard rock and metal.

Galpán 11 (riverbank at Cabral) This is a big bare rock venue in an old riverside warehouse.

Mi Refugio (☎ 440-6186; España 445; ☽ 8pm-late Sat) The best place to go to listen (or dance) to tango music. There's often a live orchestra. Dinner is also available.

Peña la Amistad (Maipú 1111; ☽ 10pm-late Fri & Sat) For a different night out, head down to this folksy spot, where a harp and guitar duo bang out traditional music accompanied by the smell of roasting meat, stomping feet and corks being popped.

NIGHTCLUBS

Clubs open their doors shortly after midnight, but remain deserted until after 2am, when lines begin to form. There are several clubs northwest of downtown along Rivadavia. A cab from the center should cost around AR$15.

Bara Bajo (San Martín 370; admission AR$15; ☽ 2am-dawn Fri & Sat) This barlike dance club plays house, techno and Argentine rock and usually gets packed.

Gotika (Mitre 1539; admission AR$10-20; ☽ 24hr Thu-Sat) Set behind the imposing facade of a former church, this place kicks off at weekends with a variety of music from drum 'n' bass to house.

THEATER

Teatro El Círculo (☎ 448-3784; Laprida 1235) The city's main performing-arts venue located in a lovely building dating from 1904.

Teatro del Rayo (☎ 421-3980; San Martín 473; ☽ 8:30pm Wed, Thu, Sat & Sun, 5pm Fri) This cozy theater and bar with wooden tables shows art films and cult classics on a small screen. It also has occasional theater performances.

SPORTS

Rosario has two rival soccer teams with several league titles between them. **Newell's Old Boys** (☎ 421-1180; www.nob.com.ar) plays in red and black at **Estadio Parque Independencia**, where the club is based, and has a long, proud history of producing great Argentine footballers. **Rosario Central** (☎ 421-0000; www.rosariocentral.com; Mitre 857) plays in blue and yellow stripes at **Estadio 'El Gigante de Arroyito'** (☎ 438-9595; cnr Blvd Avellaneda & Génova). Buy tickets from the stadiums or Rosario Central's club office.

Shopping

Mercado de Pulgas del Bajo (Av Belgrano; ☽ from 3pm Sat & Sun) A picturesque flea market by the tourist office, where dealers sell everything from silverwork to leather goods.

Getting There & Away

AIR

Aerolíneas Argentinas (☎ 420-8138; Córdoba 852) flies four times weekly to Buenos Aires (AR$255). **Sol** (☎ 0810-444-4765; www.sol.com.ar) flies daily to Buenos Aires (AR$177) and Córdoba (AR$261). **LAN** (☎ 440-0060; San Lorenzo 1116) flies to Santiago (AR$1244) in Chile.

BUS

The long-distance **bus terminal** (☎ 437-3030; www.terminalrosario.com.ar, in Spanish; Cafferata & Santa Fe) is 25 blocks west of the center. From downtown, any bus along Santa Fe will do the trick.

Rosario is a major transport hub and there are direct daily services to nearly all major destinations, including international services to Paraguay, Brazil, Chile and Uruguay.

Manuel Tienda de León (☎ 0810-888-5366; www.tiendaleon.com.ar; Santa Fe 842) offers a direct service

NORTHEAST ARGENTINA

to and from Buenos Aires' international airport for AR$90. It does hotel pickups.

Some sample destinations:

Destination	Cost (AR$)	Duration (hr)
Buenos Aires	40	4
Córdoba	55	7
Corrientes	96	12
Mar del Plata	62	7½
Mendoza	115	11
Paraná	20	2
Posadas	103	16
Resistencia	93	10
Salta	144	16
Santa Fe	20	2
Santiago del Estero	89	10
Tucumán	110	12

TRAIN

From **Rosario Norte train station** (☎ 430-7272; Av del Valle 2700), unreliable services to Buenos Aires (AR$33, six hours) leave at 5:15am Monday to Friday, returning at 6:05pm. It's really for train buffs only. More interesting is the twice-weekly trip to Tucumán (see p292). Take bus 138 from San Juan and Mitre to the station.

Getting Around

To get to **Aeropuerto Fisherton** (Fisherton Airport; ☎ 451-1226), 8km west of town, take a *remise* (taxi), which costs AR$25 to AR$30. A reliable *remise* operator is **Primera Clase** (☎ 454-5454).

From the local bus terminal on Plaza Sarmiento, bus services run virtually everywhere. Buses (www.rosariobus.com.ar shows routes) accept the AR$1.25 fare in exact change; otherwise buy a *tarjeta magnética* (magnetic bus card) from any kiosk. To get to the city center from the long-distance terminal, take a bus marked 'Centro' or 'Plaza Sarmiento.'

To rent a car, try **Dollar Rent-a-Car** (☎ 011-4315-8800; www.dollar.com.ar; Paraguay 892) or one of the several at the airport.

To rent a bike, head to **Extreme Bike** (☎ 421-5952; www.extremebike.com.ar; San Lorenzo 981; ◴ 9am-1pm & 4-8pm Mon-Fri, 10am-1pm Sat, 4:30-8pm Sat Dec-Mar), where good-quality mountain bikes cost AR$25/35/45 for the day/24 hours/48 hours. You'll need to be 21, and bring a passport and either a credit card or AR$200 deposit.

SANTA FE

☎ 0242 / pop 454,238

There's quite a contrast between Santa Fe's relaxed center, where colonial buildings age gracefully in the humid heat and nobody seems to get beyond an amble, and a Friday night in the Recoleta district where university students in dozens of bars show the night no mercy. Capital of its province, but with a small-town feel, Santa Fe is an excellent place to visit for a day or two.

Santa Fe de la Veracruz, to give it its full title, was moved here in 1651 from its original location at Cayastá 75km to the north. The first Santa Fe was founded in 1573 by Juan de Garay but by the mid-17th century the location proved intolerable for the original Spanish settlers. Wearied by constant Indian raids, floods and isolation, they packed up the place and moved it to its current location on a tributary of the Río Paraná. Several picturesque colonial buildings remain.

In 1853 Argentina's first constitution was ratified by an assembly that met here, a source of great pride to the city. Santa Fe hit the headlines again in 2003, when a sudden flood caused havoc. About 100,000 people had to be evacuated, and 24 people perished.

Orientation

Santa Fe's remaining colonial buildings are within a short walk of Plaza 25 de Mayo, the town's functional center. Av San Martín, north of the plaza, is the major commercial street and part of it forms an attractive *peatonal* with palm trees and terraces.

To the east, a bridge across the river, then a tunnel beneath the Paraná connect Santa Fe with its twin city of Paraná in Entre Ríos province.

Information

Long-distance telephone services are in the bus terminal and at *locutorios* downtown. Several banks with ATMs can be found along the *peatonal*.

Hospital Provincial José María Cullen (☎ 457-3340; Av Freyre 2150)

Lavadero Junín (☎ 452-1096; Av Rivadavia 2834; ◴ Mon-Sat) Laundry.

Mr Jones (cnr Crespo & 25 de Mayo; per hr AR$1.50; ◴ 24hr) All night internet.

Municipal tourist office (☎ 457-4123; www.santafe-turistica.com.ar; Belgrano 2910; ◴ 7am-1pm & 3-9pm Mon-Fri, 7am-1pm & 2-8pm Sat & Sun) Located in the bus terminal.

Post office (La Rioja 2542) Near Av San Martín.

Provincial tourist office (☎ 457-4824; www.turismo-santafe.org.ar; cnr Amenábar & Av San Martín; ◴ 8am-

6pm Mon-Sat, 9am-6pm Sun) Fantastically helpful and enthusiastic. Deserves a gold star.

Tourfe (San Martín 2500; 8:15am-1:15pm & 4:30-7pm Mon-Fri, 9am-noon Sat) Collects 3% commission on traveler's checks.

Sights

CONVENTO Y MUSEO DE SAN FRANCISCO

The principal historical landmark is this Franciscan monastery and **museum** (459-3303; Amenábar 2257; admission by donation; 8am-noon & 4-7pm summer, 3:30-6:30pm winter), built in 1680. The walls, which are more than 1m thick, support a roof made from Paraguayan cedar and hardwood beams held together by fittings and wooden spikes, rather than by nails. While the museum section is mediocre, the church is beautiful, with an exquisite wooden ceiling and a fine polychrome Christ by the grumpy Spanish master Alonso Cano – it was sent as a sympathy gift to Santa Fe by the Queen of Spain when the town moved. Note also the tomb of Padre Magallanes, a priest who was killed by a jaguar that took refuge in the church when it was driven from the shores of the Paraná during the floods of 1825. The cloister has a carved wooden balustrade and is redolent with the perfume of flowers. The monastery is still home to one monk, who is helped out by a trio of priests.

MUSEO HISTÓRICO PROVINCIAL

In a lovable 17th-century building, this **museum** (457-3529; Av San Martín 1490; donation AR$1;

⊙ 8:30am-7pm Tue-Fri, 3-6pm Sat & Sun Apr-Sep, 8:30am-noon & 4-7pm Tue-Fri, 4:30-7:30pm Sat & Sun Oct-Mar) has a variety of possessions and mementos of various provincial governors and caudillos (provincial strongmen), as well as some religious art and fine period furnishings, including a sedan chair once used to carry around the Viceroy of Río de la Plata.

MUSEO ETNOGRÁFICO Y COLONIAL PROVINCIAL

Run with heartwarming enthusiasm, this **museum** (☎ 457-3550; 25 de Mayo 1470; donation AR$1; ⊙ 8:30am-7pm Tue-Fri, 3-6pm Sat & Sun Apr-Sep, 8:30am-noon & 4-7pm Tue-Fri, 4:30-7:30pm Sat & Sun Oct-Mar) has a chronological display of stone tools, Guaraní ceramics, jewelery, carved bricks and colonial objects. Highlights include a set of *tablas* – a colonial game similar to backgammon – and a scale model of the original Santa Fe.

PLAZA 25 DE MAYO

The center of colonial Santa Fe is a peaceful square framed by many fine buildings. The vast **Casa de Gobierno** (Government House) was built in 1909 and replaced the demolished colonial *cabildo* (town council), seat of the 1852 constitutional assembly. On the square's east side, the exterior simplicity of the Jesuit **Iglesia de la Compañia** masks an ornate interior. Dating from 1696, it's the province's best-preserved colonial church. On the square's north side the city's **cathedral** is a little underwhelming by comparison, and dates from the mid-18th century.

CERVECERÍA SANTA FE

The *santafesinos* are fond of a cold beer on one of their typical hot, humid days. Luckily, they have their own **brewery** (☎ 450-2237; Calchines 1401; tour free; ⊙ 8am-8pm) which produces the Santa Fe lager as well as brewing Budweiser and Heineken under license. If you call ahead, you can tour the plant for free and try the brew. Be sure to wear sturdy footwear and long pants.

GRANJA LA ESMERALDA

Nobody likes to see wild animals locked in confined spaces, but this **experimental zoo** (☎ 457-9202; Av Aristóbulo del Valle 8700; admission AR$2.50; ⊙ 9am-6pm Tue-Sun, to 7pm in summer) has a wild and woodsy feel to it that makes it stand apart from most other zoos in the country. Provincial native fauna is mainly represented, including toucans, pumas, jaguars and a giant anteater. Bus 10 bis, from Av Rivadavia, goes to the farm.

Sleeping

The vaguely seedy area around the bus terminal is the budget hotel zone. It's not dangerous – just the central location for various vice-fuelled transactions. Many hotels offer a discount for cash payment.

Hotel Constituyentes (☎ 452-1586; hotelconstituyentes@ciudad.com.ar; San Luis 2862; s/d with bath AR$60/80, without bath AR$40/60; ⊠ ▢) Plenty of value to be had at this relaxed place near the bus terminal. The rooms are spacious with cable TV and blasting hot showers. Rooms at the front suffer from street noise. Breakfast is a few pesos extra.

Gran Hotel España (☎ 455-2264; www.lineaverdedehoteles.com.ar; 25 de Mayo 2647; s/d AR$94/125; ⊠ ▢) There's nothing too fancy about the rooms here, but they're definitely good value, even more so when you consider that you can use the facilities at the Conquistador across the road.

Hotel Emperatriz (☎ 453-0061; emperatrizhotelsf@hotmail.com; Irigoyen Freyre 2440; r AR$129; ⊠) Sipping *mate* and chatting with the courteous old gentleman on the front desk, it's easy to fall in love with this curious other-era place. But it's competing with some of the better hotels in town at these prices, and you may feel it doesn't measure up. Solo travelers look elsewhere for better value.

Hostal Santa Fe de la Veracruz (☎ 455-1740; www.hostalsf.com; Av San Martín 2954; s/d AR$110/170, superior AR$160/190; ⊠ ▢) Decorated with indigenous motifs, this comfortable hotel offers spacious superior rooms and decent standards at a fair price. It'll soon be time for redecorating though; those dozen shades of beige are looking a little dated. Siesta fans will love the 6pm checkout.

our pick **Hotel Galeón** (☎ 454-1788; www.hotelgaleon.com.ar; Belgrano 2759; s/d AR$121/160; ⊠ ▢) Bright, unusual, and all curved surfaces and weird angles, this cheery place is a breath of fresh air. There's a variety of types of room, none of which is a conventional shape; the beds are seriously comfortable and the bathrooms pleasant. It's handy for the bus too.

Conquistador Hotel (☎ 400-1195; www.lineaverdedehoteles.com.ar; 25 de Mayo 2676; s/d AR$165/195; ⊠ ▢ ▢) The most modern hotel in town, the Conquistador lays on the charm, with sauna, hydromassage, fluffy bathrobes, gymnasium and a huge buffet breakfast. The beds in the twins and singles are happily queen-sized.

Also recommended:

Hotel Royal (☎ 452-7359; Irigoyen Freyre 2256; s/d with shared bathroom AR$40/60) Basic, with gloomy rooms, but it's cheap and near the bus terminal…it'll do for a night.

Hotel Zavaleta (☎ 455-1841; www.zavaletahotel .com.ar; Irigoyen Freyre 2349; s/d AR$100/125, superior AR$125/150; ☒) This welcoming hotel is right on a plaza, near the bus terminal.

Eating

On Belgrano, across from the bus terminal, several very good, inexpensive places serve Argentine staples, such as empanadas, pizza and *parrillada*.

Merengo (☎ 459-3458; Av General López 2634; alfajores from AR$1; ☹ 9am-6pm) Since 1851 little Merengo has been making some of the town's best *merengo alfajores* (Santa Fe's sugar-crusted version of the country's favorite snack). There's another branch on Av San Martín.

Las Delicias (☎ 453-2126; Av San Martín 2882; cakes & pastries from AR$1.50, mains AR$10-24; ☹ 8am-midnight) Delightfully old-fashioned and elegant, with a great shady terrace, this bakery offers some of the most sinful pastries and cakes imaginable, and it also does meals. Service is traditional and correct.

La Victoria (cnr 25 de Mayo & Santiago del Estero; pizza AR$6-10) Right in the middle of La Recoleta nightlife district and still pumping at 3am, the Victoria is the place to come before, after or in between bars to have a few drinks and load up on good pizza and snacks.

La Estaca (☎ 459-9361; Corrientes 2619; dishes AR$5-18; ☹ lunch & dinner) A cheap, traditional, hearty *parrilla*, with outdoor seating under a high awning. If you're not a vegetarian, it's mighty difficult to walk past when you can smell the grill going.

Club Social Sirio Libanés (25 de Mayo 2740; meals AR$10-22; ☹ lunch & dinner) In a rather aristocratic dining room, attentive waiters serve well-prepared Middle Eastern–style dishes; it's a pleasingly unusual place to eat. You enter down the end of a passageway.

Círculo Italiano (☎ 456-3555; Hipólito Yrigoyen 2457; meals AR$15-25; ☹ lunch & dinner) Part of the Italian social club, Círculo Italiano prepares good, moderately priced lunch specials (AR$18 to AR$20 Monday to Friday) and tasty pastas. Come for the ritzy atmosphere, the waiters in linen jackets, the complimentary pâté or the extensive wine list. Stay for the classic rock on the sound system.

Restaurante España (Av San Martín 2644; mains AR$10-30) This hotel restaurant has a huge menu that covers the range of fish (both locally caught and from the sea), steaks, pasta, chicken and crepes, with a few Spanish dishes thrown in to justify the name. The wine list is a winner, too.

El Quincho de Chiquito (☎ 460-2608; cnr Brown & Obispo Vieytes; set menu AR$30; ☹ lunch & dinner) This legendary place is a local institution, and *the* place to go to eat river fish. It's on the *costanera* some 6km north of downtown. There are few frills to the service, and no choice; four or five courses of delicious surubí, sábalo or pacú are brought out to you. You won't leave hungry. Drinks are extra but cheap. Think AR$10 each way in a cab (they'll call you one to take you back) or catch bus 16 from any point on the waterfront road.

Bodegas del Castelar (☎ 452-2229; Av San Martín 1601; mains AR$24-32; ☹ lunch & dinner) Run by the upmarket hotel of the same name, this spot appeals for its terrace on the stately Plaza 25 de Mayo – a fine spot for a sunset drink – as well as for its service and pricy but high-quality dishes, which include a couple of fondues (AR$40 to AR$55 for two people) and a copious platter of cheeses and meats (AR$42). Cheaper snacks are also available and there's plenty of wine to try.

Drinking & Entertainment

Santa Fe's nightlife centers around the intersection of 25 de Mayo and Santiago del Estero, the heart of the area known as La Recoleta, which goes wild on weekend nights, a crazy contrast to the sedate pace of life downtown. Places change name and popularity rapidly, so just head to the zone and take a look around the dozens of bars and clubs. Many have a cover charge redeemable for a drink. A few are listed to get you started.

Tarantino (25 de Mayo 3426) An attractive bar with a popular attached nightclub, Sivra. Dress smartish.

El Sheik (25 de Mayo 3452) Laid-back without being tranquil, this place attracts a young crowd with its cheap drinks and good music.

Passage (☎ 453-3435; Av San Martín 3243; admission AR$5) This venue has been dishing out rock, electronica and Latin grooves for years, and it is still a good place to cut loose.

EXPLORING SANTA FE PROVINCE

With perhaps a brief stop in Rosario or Santa Fe itself, most travelers bang straight on through this fascinating region, compass set for attractions further north. If you have more time, however, there are many things worth discovering, all within easy reach by bus or car from Santa Fe.

Some 43km south of the city, Coronda is famous for its strawberries *(frutillas)*. There are several places to try and buy and also a couple of fine river beaches. Further south, at Puerto Gaboto, you can see the reasonably conserved remains of the country's oldest Spanish fort, Sancti Spíritu, dating from 1527. It's a few kilometers east of the main road – turn or jump off the bus at Maciel.

Forty kilometers northwest of Santa Fe, the town of Esperanza has an interesting history. It was the first of the many planned agricultural colonies that were established in Argentina in the mid-19th century and peopled by immigrants from Central Europe. There's an interesting museum with the story of the settlement. Nearby, San Carlos Centro is worth a visit for its bell factory. The bells (mostly for churches) are carefully handcrafted in an intriguing process. Glassware and sweets are also produced in this hardworking community.

West of Esperanza, turn north at the booming town of Rafaela to explore the cheesemaking village of Humberto Primero, and the Jewish traditions of Moisés Ville. There are farmstay accommodations available in the area. For details, get in touch with the provincial tourist office in Santa Fe.

Suite (25 de Mayo 3249) Trendy lighting design and a roof terrace are the attractions at this handsome preclub venue.

THEATER

Teatro Municipal Primero de Mayo (☎ 459-7777; Av San Martín 2020) Designed in the French neo-renaissance style so common in Argentina at the turn of the 20th century, this theater presents both drama and dance performances.

SPORT

The city's football team, **Colón** (☎ 459-8025; www.clubcolon.com.ar), is in the top division. They play at the **Brigadier Estanislao López stadium** (cnr Dr Zavalla & Pietranera), where you can also pick up tickets.

Getting There & Away

AIR

Aerolíneas Argentinas (☎ 452-5959; 25 de Mayo 2287) has five weekly flights to Buenos Aires (AR$255). **Sol** (☎ 0810-444-4765; www.sol.com.ar) flies the same route Monday to Saturday (AR$200).

BUS

From the **bus terminal** (☎ 457-2490; www.terminalsantafe.com; Belgrano 2940) there are services throughout the country. The following are some sample fares.

Destination	Cost (AR$)	Duration (hr)
Buenos Aires	63	6
Córdoba	40	5
Corrientes	71	9
Mendoza	119	13
Paraná	3	40min
Paso de los Libres	41	9
Posadas	91	14
Resistencia	71	9
Rosario	20	2
Salta	133	16
Tucumán	97	11

Getting Around

For AR$1.50 city bus A goes to **Aeropuerto Sauce Viejo** (Sauce Viejo Airport; ☎ 457-0642), which is 7km south of town on RN 11. To rent a car, try **Hertz** (☎ 456-4480/1; www.hertz.com.ar; Lisandro de la Torre 2548).

AROUND SANTA FE
Cayastá

A fascinating daytrip from Santa Fe takes you to that city's original location, the **Cayastá ruins** (Santa Fe la Vieja; donation AR$1; ⊙ 9am-1pm & 3-7pm Tue-Fri, 10am-1pm & 4-7pm Sat & Sun), picturesquely set beside the Río San Javier, which has actually eroded away a good portion of them.

There's ongoing archaeological excavation and conservation here (and a campaign for Unesco status underway), but the most fascinating find by far has been the Iglesia de San Francisco. The Spanish and mestizo inhabitants of old Santa Fe were buried directly beneath the earth-floored church, and nearly 100 graves have been excavated, including those of Hernando Arias de Saavedra (known as 'Hernandarias'), the first locally born governor of Río de la Plata province, and his wife, Gerónima de Contrera, daughter of Juan de Garay, who founded Santa Fe and Buenos Aires.

You can also see the remains of two other churches and the *cabildo*, as well as a reconstructed period house. Near the entrance to the site is an attractive and excellent museum housing the finds from the site, including some fine indigenous pottery with parrot and human motifs.

Last entry is strictly one hour before closing.

Cayastá is 76km northeast of Santa Fe on RP 1. Paraná Medio bus company departs regularly from Santa Fe's bus terminal (AR$10; 1½ hrs). Ask the driver to drop you at 'las ruinas,' 1km short of Cayastá itself. There's a mediocre restaurant at the site and a couple of decent *parrillas* in town. If you want to stay, **Carlos Roberto** (☎ 493110; r per person AR$25) offers simple accommodations and boat trips on the river.

PARANÁ
☎ 0343 / pop 247,310
Comfortably down-at-heel and unpretentious, likable Paraná seems surprised at its own status as capital of Entre Ríos province. Perched on the hilly banks of its eponymous river, it's a sleepy, slow-paced city with little in the way of nightlife. The nicest part of town is the riverside where a pretty park slopes down to the *costanera*, where there are beaches, bars, boat trips, and hundreds of strollers and joggers. After the defeat of Rosas at the battle of Caseros, Paraná was the capital of the Argentine Confederation (which didn't include Buenos Aires) from 1853 to 1861.

Orientation
Paraná sits on a high bluff on the east bank of the Río Paraná, 500km north of Buenos Aires. A tunnel beneath the main channel of the Paraná connects the city to Santa Fe.

The city plan is more irregular than most Argentine cities, with diagonals and curving boulevards. Plaza 1 de Mayo is the town center and is crossed by the *peatonal* José de San Martín. Street names change on all sides of the plaza. At the northern end of San Martín, more than 1km of riverfront and the bluffs above it have been transformed into the lovely Parque Urquiza.

Information
There are several banks with ATMs within a couple of blocks of Plaza 1 de Mayo.
Hospital San Martín (☎ 423-4545; www.hospital sanmartin.org.ar; Presidente Perón 450)
Lavadero Belgrano (Av Belgrano 306) Laundry.

THE GAUCHO JUDÍO
The gaucho is one of Argentina's archetypal images, but it's a little-known fact that many a gaucho was of Jewish origin.

The first recorded instance of mass Jewish immigration to Argentina was in the late 19th century, when 800 Russian Jews arrived in Buenos Aires, fleeing persecution from Czar Alexander III.

The Jewish Colonization Association, funded by a wealthy German philanthropist, began to distribute 100-hectare parcels of land to immigrant families in the provinces of Entre Ríos, Santa Fe, Santiago del Estero, La Pampa and Buenos Aires.

The first major colony was in Moisés Ville in Santa Fe province, which became known at the time as Jerusalem Argentina. Today there are only about 300 Jewish residents left in town (15% of the population), but many Jewish traditions prevail: the tiny town boasts four synagogues, the bakery sells Sabbath bread and kids in the street use Yiddish slang like 'schlep' and 'schlock.'

These rural Jews readily assimilated into Argentine society, mixing their own traditions with those of their adopted country, so that it was not unusual to see a figure on horseback in baggy pants, canvas shoes and skullcap, on his way to throw a lump of cow on the *asado* (barbecue).

Many of their descendants have since left the land in search of education and opportunities in the cities. Argentina's Jews number about 300,000, making them Latin America's largest Jewish community.

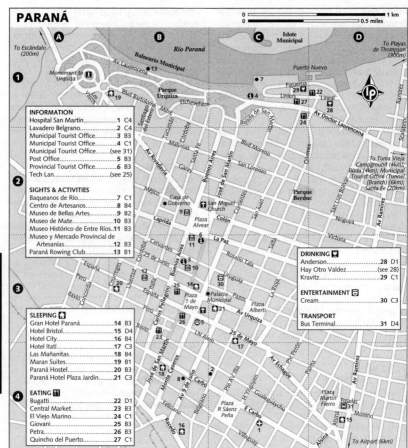

PARANÁ

Municipal tourist office (www.turismoenparana.com;
☎ 8am-8pm) Main office (☎ 423-0183; Buenos Aires
132); River branch (☎ 420-1837); Bus station branch
(☎ 420-1862; Av Ramírez 2300); Tunnel branch (Av
Uranga Acceso Túnel Subfluvial lado Paraná)
Post office (cnr 25 de Mayo & Monte Caseros)
Provincial tourist office (☎ 422-2100; www.turismo
.entrerios.gov.ar; Laprida 5; ☎ 8am-8pm) Don't rely on
it being open.
Tech Lan (Av Urquiza 1071; per hr AR$2) One of dozens
offering internet access and phone calls.

Sights & Activities
MUSEO HISTÓRICO DE ENTRE RÍOS
Flaunting local pride, this modern **museum** (☎ 420-7869; Buenos Aires 286; admission AR$2;
☎ 8am-12:30pm & 3-7pm Tue-Fri, 9.30am-noon & 5-7pm

Sat, 9.30am-noon Sun) on Plaza Alvear contains
well-arranged displays of artifacts of 19th-
century provincial life, including horse gear
and smoking paraphernalia, along with an
outstanding portrait collection.

MUSEO DE BELLAS ARTES
Oil paintings, illustrations and sculptures by
provincial artists are the focus of this subterranean **museum** (☎ 420-7868; Buenos Aires 355; admission
free; ☎ 9am-noon & 4-7:30pm Tue-Sat, 10am-noon Sun),
on Plaza Alvear.

MUSEO Y MERCADO PROVINCIAL DE ARTESANÍAS
Promoting handicrafts from throughout
the province, the **Museo y Mercado Provincial de**

Artesanías (☎ 422-4540; Av Urquiza 1239; admission free; ☾ 8am-1pm & 4-7pm Mon-Fri, 8am-1pm Sat, 9am-noon Sun) is a likable little place. Ask the curator to explain things to you; you'll be amazed at the intricacy of some of the work, like the hats made from tightly woven palm fibers. In December there are folk music performances in the garden.

Similar traditional *artesanía* (handicraft) is on display and sale at the **Centro de Artesanos** (☎ 422-4493; cnr Av 9 de Julio & Carbó; ☾ 9am-noon & 4-8pm daily, 5-9pm in summer).

MUSEO DE MATE

This cheeringly idiosyncratic **museum** (☎ 403-0244; 25 de Junio 72; admission AR$1; ☾ 8am-noon & 4-8pm Tue-Fri, 8am-noon Sat & Sun) is Paraná's most unusual. Thousands of pieces of *mate* paraphernalia fill the shelves, including the world's tallest and smallest *mate* gourds, and even some ornate pieces made in Germany, England and Austria.

RIVER ACTIVITIES

From the northern edge of downtown, Parque Urquiza slopes steeply downward to the banks of the Río Paraná. During the summer months the waterfront fills with people strolling, fishing, swimming and practicing other languorous methods of staying cool. Beware of *jejenes* (biting insects) along the river in summer.

There's a stretch of **beach** (some private, some public) west of the **Paraná Rowing Club** (☎ 431-2048), at which, for AR$15 per day, you can access facilities, including a private beach, swimming pool and showers. There's also a café-restaurant on the water.

A better beach, **Playas de Thompson**, is 1km further east, beyond the port.

Various operators offer boat trips, but the best is **Baqueanos del Río** (☎ 422-6042, 0343-15-611-2170; baqueanosdelrio@ecourbano.org.ar) which offers excursions in wooden boats and knows a hell of a lot about the river and its ecosystem. Ring or email to book a trip (A$15 per hour). Boats leave from the eastern end of the *costanera*, by the tourist office.

Festivals & Events

Every February Paraná hosts the **Fiesta Nacional de Música y Artesanía Entrerriana**, featuring regional folk music and crafts.

Sleeping

Paraná Hostel (☎ 422-1904; www.paranahostel .ar; Perú 342; dm/d AR$25/56; 🖳) Run smoothly by good-natured folk, this comfortable hostel has cozy male and female dorms, and a pretty double (shared bath) at the front. The rate includes breakfast, kitchen, internet and free *mate*; there's also a relaxing garden with a *parrilla* out the back.

Hotel City (☎ 431-0086; www.turismoentrerios .com/hotelcity; Racedo 231; s/d AR$35/60; 🖭) Spare a thought for this old hotel, which has suffered since the train station opposite went out of use. Clean and simple, it has a delightful patio garden and cool rooms with high ceilings and TV. A very good deal.

Hotel Itatí (☎ 423-1500; hoteles_itati@hotmail.com; Belgrano 135; s/d AR$40/65; 🖭) This curious hotel is an odd-looking design, but is nevertheless a reliable and pleasing budget choice. The dark rooms are fine for the price, have OK bathrooms and management is welcoming.

our pick **Las Mañanitas** (☎ 421-8324; www.lasmani anitas.com.ar; E Carbo 62; s/d AR$75/80; 🖭 🖳) There's a summer-house feel about this delightfully relaxed little place, which has nine rooms alongside a courtyard and garden with pool. The rooms are unremarkable but well priced, but it's the light style and grace of the whole ensemble that makes this a winner.

Paraná Hotel Plaza Jardín (☎ 423-1700; www.hoteles parana.com.ar; Av 9 de Julio 60; s/d AR$87/110, superior AR$132/154; 🖭 🖳) Set in a lovely old colonial building, this hotel has a peaceful patio that's great for a break from the midday heat. The superior rooms are much more spacious and stylish and worth the upgrade.

Gran Hotel Paraná (☎ 422-3900; www.hoteles parana.com.ar; Av Urquiza 976; s AR$106-198, d AR$145-250; 🖭 🖳) Fine service is a major plus at this large hotel on the main square. Bypass the unremarkable standards for a 'plus' room or the newly refurbished superior rooms, which are much bigger. If you don't mind a bit of traffic noise, try for a room with a balcony on the square. There's a health spa and a high-quality restaurant. The breakfast buffet is rocking.

Maran Suites (☎ 423-5444; www.maran.com.ar; cnr Av Rivadavia & Blvd Bartolomé Mitre; s AR$195-227, d AR$268-298; 🖭 🖳 🖭) Towering over the western end of Parque Urquiza, this sleek modern hotel has a rare combination of style and warm-hearted personal service. Try to get a room as high as possible for memorable city or river views. All the rooms are very spacious and decorated with flair; the 'presidential' suites (AR$685) are big enough to get lost in and boast a Jacuzzi with memorable vistas over the water.

Also recommended:

Toma Vieja Campground (☎ 424-7721; end of Av Blas Parera; sites AR$12) Scenic site of the old waterworks overlooking the river. Take bus 5 from the terminal.

Hotel Bristol (☎ 431-3961; bristolpna@yahoo.com.ar; Alsina 221; s/d with bathroom AR$45/85, without bathroom AR$25/45; ✖) Right by the bus station. Well kept and quiet.

Eating

Many restaurants in Paraná are closed on Mondays.

Petra (☎ 423-0608; 25 de Mayo 32; lunch/dinner AR$17/18; ☯ lunch & dinner) With a huge range of mostly Chinese food on offer, this redoubtable all-you-can-eat joint sits on the square. The standard is quite a lot better than you might expect – it's rather a bargain. Drinks not included.

Giovani (☎ 423-0527; Av Urquiza 1045; pasta AR$6-15, mains AR$17-30; ☯ lunch & dinner) With as-it-should-be service and thoughtful touches like free coffee, this stylish restaurant in the center of town serves excellent meats from the *parrilla* and delectable pastas. Fish isn't such a strong point.

El Viejo Marino (☎ 432-9767; Av Doctor Laurencena 341; most mains AR$10-20; ☯ lunch & dinner Wed-Mon) There's an uncomplicated, brightly lit and cheery atmosphere under the thatched roof at this restaurant near the river. It offers *milanesas* (breaded fish cutlets) and the like, river fish both filleted and whole, and a *parrillada* for AR$19 that'll feed two.

Quincho del Puerto (☎ 423-2045; Av Doctor Laurencena 350, fish AR$15-22; ☯ lunch & dinner Tue-Sun) This is a popular spot for river fish just back from the *costanera*. There are various options, including the tasty (but bony) pacú and surubí.

Bugatti (☎ 504-0770; cnr Güemes & Liniers; mains AR$18-33; ☯ lunch & dinner Tue-Sun) No surprises on the menu – meat, chicken, pasta and fish – but the elegance of the dining room in this renovated post office make it worth the trip. Even if you're not hungry, the veranda terrace is a great place to have a few drinks as the sun goes down.

The **central market** (cnr Carlos Pellegrini & Bavio) is good to buy food in the morning: there are a couple of cheap eateries around it as well.

Drinking & Entertainment

Paraná is very quiet midweek, but things get busier on Friday and Saturday nights. Most of the action is at the eastern end of the riverfront, by the port. Here, **Kravitz** (Figueroa s/n; ☯ 10pm-late Fri & Sat) plays the usual mix of mainstream *marcha*, house and salsa. **Anderson** (Lineal 334; ☯ Thu-Sat) is a spot for a drink or a dance, but only if you're 25 or over. Nearby **Hay Otro Valdez** (Lineal 376; ☯ Fri & Sat) has a bet each way, with a more mature crowd on Fridays and a student party on Saturdays. The real *discoteca* action can be found at **Cream** (Uruguay 190; ☯ Fri & Sat), where you'll feel ancient if you're over 30, **Escándalo** (Av Estrada s/n; ☯ Fri & Sat), on the river west of Parque Urquiza, and **Buda** (Av Blas Parera s/n at Toma Vieja s/n; ☯ Sat), by the campsite to the east of town.

Getting There & Around
AIR

The unreliable but cheap airforce airline **LADE** (☎ 0810-810-5233; www.lade.com.ar) flies once a week from Paraná's airport to Córdoba (AR$227), Buenos Aires (AR$144) and on southwards.

BUS

The **bus terminal** (☎ 422-1282; Av Ramírez) is opposite Plaza Martín Fierro. Buses 1, 4, 5 and 9 run between the terminal and the center for AR$1. Paraná is a hub for provincial bus services, but Santa Fe is more convenient for long-distance trips. Buses leave every 30 minutes for Santa Fe (AR$3, 40 minutes). Some other destinations:

Destination	Cost (AR$)	Duration (hr)
Buenos Aires	68	6½
Colón	26	4
Concordia	27	4½
Córdoba	55	6
Corrientes	76	10
Gualeguaychú	26	5
Paso de los Libres	40	6
Rosario	23	3

CORRIENTES
☎ 03783 / pop 316,782

Stately Corrientes sits below the confluence of the Paraná and Paraguay rivers just across the water from its twin city, Resistencia. One of the nation's most venerable cities,

Corrientes has dignity, with elegant balconied buildings dating from the turn of the 20th century lending a timeworn appeal to its colorful streets. Like many such cities, the *costanera* is everybody's destination of choice for strolling, licking ice creams or sipping *mate* with friends.

The city is famous for both its Carnaval, which attracts big crowds to its colorful parades, and for being the setting of Graham Greene's novel *The Honorary Consul*.

Corrientes is a magnet for regional indigenous crafts, which artisans sell in the evening on Plaza JB Cabral and in the Museo de Artesanías. Guaraní culture has a strong presence.

Corrientes was originally called Vera de los Siete Corrientes, after its founder Juan Torres de Vera y Aragón and the shifting *corrientes* (currents) of the Paraná. During colonial times Corrientes suffered repeated indigenous uprisings before establishing itself as the first Spanish settlement in the region.

Orientation

Corrientes has a regular grid, but the center is more spread out than in most Argentine cities. Plaza 25 de Mayo, near the river and its lively *costanera,* is one of the two main squares; the other is Plaza JB Cabral, from which the *peatonal* along Junín, the

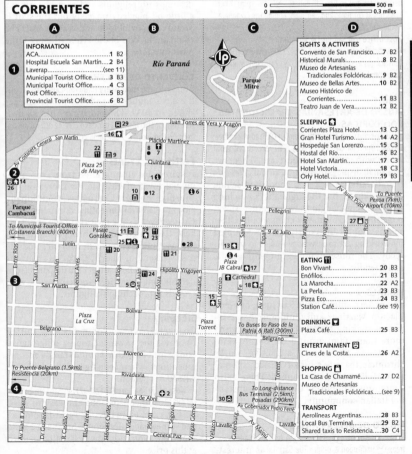

CORRIENTES

0 — 500 m
0 — 0.3 miles

INFORMATION
ACA..1 B2
Hospital Escuela San Martín....2 B4
Laverap..................................(see 11)
Municipal Tourist Office..........3 B3
Municipal Tourist Office..........4 C3
Post Office................................5 B3
Provincial Tourist Office..........6 B2

SIGHTS & ACTIVITIES
Convento de San Francisco......7 B2
Historical Murals.......................8 B2
Museo de Artesanías
   Tradicionales Folclóricas.......9 B2
Museo de Bellas Artes............10 B2
Museo Histórico de
   Corrientes...........................11 B3
Teatro Juan de Vera...............12 B2

SLEEPING
Corrientes Plaza Hotel............13 C3
Gran Hotel Turismo................14 A2
Hospedaje San Lorenzo..........15 C3
Hostal del Río.........................16 B2
Hotel San Martín....................17 C3
Hotel Victoria.........................18 C3
Orly Hotel..............................19 B3

EATING
Bon Vivant.............................20 B3
Enófilos..................................21 B3
La Marocha.............................22 A2
La Perla..................................23 B3
Pizza Eco................................24 B3
Station Café......................(see 19)

DRINKING
Plaza Café..............................25 B3

ENTERTAINMENT
Cines de la Costa....................26 A2

SHOPPING
La Casa de Chamamé..............27 D2
Museo de Artesanías
   Tradicionales Folclóricas...(see 9)

TRANSPORT
Aerolíneas Argentinas.............28 B3
Local Bus Terminal..................29 B2
Shared taxis to Resistencia.....30 C4

Río Paraná

Parque Mitre

Parque Cambacuá

Juan Torres de Vera y Aragón

Plácido Martínez

Plaza 25 de Mayo

Quintana

25 de Mayo

To Puente Pexoa (7km); Airport (10km)

Pellegrini

9 de Julio

To Municipal Tourist Office (Costanera Branch) (400m)

Pasaje González

Junín

Hipólito Yrigoyen

Plaza JB Cabral

Cathedral

Plaza La Cruz

Bolívar

Plaza Torrent

To Buses to Paso de la Patria & Itatí (300m)

Belgrano

Moreno

To Puente Belgrano (1.5km); Resistencia (20km)

Rivadavia

To Long-distance Bus Terminal (2.5km); Posadas (290m)

Av 3 de Abril

Av Gobernador Pedro Ferré

To Shared taxis to Resistencia

Av Costanera General San Martín

Entre Ríos
San Luis
Lucumán
Buenos Aires
Salta
La Rioja
San Juan
Mendoza
Córdoba
Catamarca
San Lorenzo
Santa Fe
Av España

Paraguay
Uruguay
Brasil
Roca
Perú

Av Juan Pujol

San Martín

Belgrano

Av Juan B Alberdi
Dr Gustavino
R Castillo
Blas Parera
Héroes Cívicos
JR Vidal
Pío XII
I Segovia
Vargas Gómez
Velazco
General Paz
Lavalle
Gutenberg
Av Maipú
Lavalle

main shopping street, heads westwards for six blocks.

On the west side of town, Puente Belgrano crosses the Río Paraná to Resistencia. To the east, RN 12 parallels the Paraná to Posadas, capital of Misiones province.

Information

Locutorios and internet places are easy to find. There are many banks with ATMs on 9 de Julio between La Rioja and Córdoba.

ACA (Automóvil Club Argentina; ☎ 422844; cnr 25 de Mayo & Mendoza) Maps and route information.

Hospital Escuela San Martín (☎ 420697; Av 3 de Abril 1251)

Laverap (Pasaje González 1071) Laundry.

Municipal tourist office (☎ 474733; www.ciudad decorrientes.gov.ar; Plaza JB Cabral; ☼ 7am-9pm) Other branches at cnr Junín and San Juan, and on the Costanera at the end of Junín.

Post office (cnr San Juan & San Martín)

Provincial tourist office (☎ 427200, www.corrientes turistica.gov.ar; 25 de Mayo 1330; ☼ 7am-9pm Mon-Fri, 8am-8pm Sat & Sun)

Sights

MUSEO DE ARTESANÍAS TRADICIONALES FOLCLÓRICAS

This intriguing **museum** (Quintana 905; admission free; ☼ 8am-9pm Mon-Sat) is set in a converted colonial house with an interior courtyard. There are two small displays of fine traditional *artesanía* (handicrafts) as well as a good shop selling craft products, but the highlight is watching students being taught to work leather, silver, bone and wood by master craftspeople. Other rooms around the courtyard are occupied by working artisans who will sell to you directly. The museum guides are enthusiastic and friendly.

MURALS

The eastern side of Calle San Juan, between Plácido Martínez and Quintana, has a series of striking **historical murals**, extending more than 100m around the corner onto Quintana. These very attractive works chronicle the city's history since colonial times; full marks to the council. There's also a monument honoring Corrientes' substantial Italian community.

MUSEO DE BELLAS ARTES

This **museum** (☎ 436722; San Juan 634; admission free; ☼ 9am-noon & 6-9pm Tue-Sat) is as interesting for the old house it occupies as for the artworks. The two front rooms have an eclectic permanent collection; the temporary exhibitions by young local artists tend to be avant-garde. Opposite, the **Teatro Juan de Vera** (☎ 427743; San Juan 637) is a striking belle epoque building; ask at the ticket office if you can have a peek inside to see the beautiful treble-galleried theater and its painted ceiling. The cupola retracts when they fancy a starlit performance.

MUSEO HISTÓRICO DE CORRIENTES

This **museum** (☎ 475916; 9 de Julio 1044; admission free; ☼ 8am-noon & 4-8pm Tue-Fri, 9am-noon & 4-7pm Sat) is set around an attractive patio and exhibits weapons, antique furniture, coins and items dealing with religious and civil history. It's a little bit higgledy-piggledy but the staff is proud of the exhibition and keen to chat. The room on the War of the Triple Alliance is the most interesting.

CONVENTO DE SAN FRANCISCO

This colonial **monastery** (Mendoza 450) dates from the city's founding, and was beautifully restored in 1939. The monastery has its own museum, the **Museo Francisco** (☎ 422936; admission free; ☼ 8am-noon & 5-9pm Mon-Fri).

Festivals & Events

Inspired by immigrants from the provincial town of Paso de los Libres on the Brazilian border, Corrientes' traditionally riotous **Carnaval Correntino** competes with Gualeguaychú's for the title of the country's best. Celebrated Friday through Sunday on the last three weekends in February and the first weekend of March, Carnaval's parades along the *costanera* attract participants from neighboring provinces and countries, with crowds approaching six figures.

Sleeping

Corrientes has few accommodations. During Carnaval, the provincial tourist office maintains a list of *casas de familia* (family accommodations) where lodging is about AR$20 to AR$30 per person.

Hospedaje San Lorenzo (☎ 421740; San Lorenzo 1136; s/d AR$40/50) Inconspicuous and easy to miss, the tiny entrance to this place guards compact and somewhat stuffy rooms, but it's in a good central location and is the best option in town at this price.

LA VIRGEN DE ITATÍ

One of Argentina's most revered figures, the Virgin of Itatí, resides 68km from Corrientes, beyond Paso de la Patria. Tradition has it that the figure was found by a group of Guaraní in 1615 atop a pillar of stone, accompanied by otherworldly light and music; a mission was built on the spot. Others say the wooden figure was sculpted by Guaraní at the mission. However she came to be, the Virgin of Itatí is now visited by up to two million people a year and has her home in a massive basilica, completed in 1950. It's quite a surreal sight in this remote riverside spot. There are numerous pilgrimages by different groups throughout the year. It's worth being here on July 9, when pilgrims arrive in horses and carts from San Luis del Palmar. Regular minibuses run to Itatí from the corner of Belgrano and Roca in Corrientes.

Gran Hotel Turismo (☎ 433174; Entre Ríos 650; s/d AR$90/120; ⊠ ⊠) Built in 1948, this stately old hotel is in low-slung Californian style and has an attractive restaurant, a large pool, a bar and an excellent riverside location. The rooms are slightly worn, but it's a charming old place, and a lot more atmospheric than other hotels in town.

Hotel San Martín (☎ 421061; hsanmartin@impsat1 .com.ar; Santa Fe 955; s/d AR$105/132; ⊠ ⊒) Right on Plaza JB Cabral, this place has reasonable rooms with excellent showers. Though none of the rooms face over the plaza, each floor has a shared balcony where you can sit and watch things going on down below. The hotel lets itself down with small meannesses; breakfast costs extra, and you virtually need a retina scan to get the remote for the TV from reception.

Orly Hotel (☎ 420280; hotelorly@gigared.com; San Juan 867; s/d AR$120/150; ⊠ ⊒) Spruce and spotless, this professional and attractive three-star job overlooks a small plaza, and has smallish but comfortable rooms with minibar and an appealing little café (Station Café) that does decent meals.

Corrientes Plaza Hotel (☎ 466500; www.hotel -corrientes.com.ar; Junín 1549; s/d AR$145/175; ⊠ ⊒ ⊠) The town center's second-swishest hotel (the Guaraní ranks higher), the Plaza has generous rooms that are a little heavy on the pastel paintwork, but otherwise very commodious. The staff is friendly, and this is a pretty good deal on the *peatonal*, particularly if you pay cash (10% discount). Excellent breakfast included.

Also recommended:

Hotel Victoria (☎ 435547; hotelvictoria1@hotmail .com; España 1050; s/d AR$70/80; ⊠ ⊒) One of two decent adjacent choices near Plaza JB Cabral.

Hostal del Río (☎ 436100; www.hotelhostaldelrio .ar; Plácido Martínez 1098; s/d AR$120/130; ⊠ ⊒ ⊠)

On the costanera near Plaza 25 de Mayo. All rooms have some river views.

Eating

La Perla (☎ 423008; cnr 9 de Julio & Mendoza; pastries from AR$2; ☉ 8am-1pm & 4-11pm Mon-Sat) An old-fashioned, Italian-style bakery and café, this serves mind-altering pastries and excellent coffee; each cup comes with *chipasitos* (small cheese pastries). All the yummy treats are warm when the doors open.

Station Cafe (☎ 420280; San Juan 867; meals AR$8-18; ☉ 7am-midnight) It looks huge, but it's all mirrors. Fine service, tasty *licuados* (fruit smoothies) and homemade pastas are on hand at this tastefully decorated café.

La Marocha (☎ 438699; cnr Salta & Quintana; meals AR$9-21; ☉ lunch & dinner) A cute little restaurant/bar right on Plaza 25 de Mayo with a wider-than-normal selection of salads, meat dishes and some excellent daily specials. Also a good range of wines and cocktails.

Pizza Eco (☎ 425900; Hipólito Yrigoyen 1108; pizzas AR$8-22; ☉ 7am-1pm & 5pm-3am) Both the atmosphere and the pizza rate well at this friendly spot, tucked in an attractive corner building. The tasy empanadas are also worthy of praise.

Bon Vivant (☎ 467902; Junín 918; mains AR$8-22; ☉ lunch & dinner) After the fierce heat of the *correntino* day, it's great to be able to eat outside once the sun goes down. With a terrace in the middle of the *peatonal*, good steaks, pizzas, warm service and more-than-fair prices, this place does the trick. It's also popular with young locals for a beer.

our pick Enófilos (☎ 439271; Junín 1260; dishes AR$18-44; ☉ lunch & dinner) An *enófilo* is an oenophile, or wine-lover, so the cellar gets plenty of attention at this attentive restaurant on the *peatonal*. Serving some of the most creative dishes available outside Buenos Aires, it's a

---

CHAMAMÉ

Tango? What's that? Up here they dance the *chamamé*, one of the country's most intoxicating musical forms. Rooted in the polka, which was introduced by European immigrants, it is also heavily influenced by the music and language of the indigenous Guaraní. Its definitive sound is the accordion, which is traditionally accompanied by the guitar, the *guitarrón* (an oversized guitar used for playing bass lines), the larger *bandoneón* (accordion) and the *contrabajo* (double bass). Of course, a *conjunto* (band) is hardly complete without a singer or two.

Chamamé is as much a dance as it is a musical genre, and it's a lively one. It is a dance for a couple, except when the man takes his solo *zapateo* (folkloric tap dance). Corrientes province is the heart of *chamamé* and is therefore the easiest place to find a live performance. Sitting in on an evening of music and dancing – or taking to the floor if you're brave – is one of the joys unique to the province.

Check out the Spanish-only website www.chamamecorrientes.com for details of performances, and online tunes to introduce you to the genre.

---

great place to get off the pizza, pasta, *parrilla* treadmill. There's a set menu available on weekdays for AR$40.

Drinking & Entertainment

The main nightlife area is around the intersection of Junín and Buenos Aires, where there are several bars and clubs pumping along at weekends. The *costanera* also sees some action.

Puente Pexoa (☎ 451687; RN 12 at Virgen de Itatí roundabout; ☽ from 8:30pm Fri & Sat) Corrientes is the heartland of the lively music and dance known as *chamamé* (see above), and seeing a live performance is memorable. This relaxed restaurant features dances every weekend and it can be outrageous fun when the dancing starts. Men and women show up in full gaucho regalia, and up to four *conjuntos* (bands) may play each night, usually starting around 11pm. A taxi costs around AR$20 or grab bus 102.

Cines de la Costa (☎ 460360; cnr 25 de Mayo & Av Costanera General San Martín) A cinema by the casino on the *costanera*. Shows both Hollywood hits and alternative choices.

Plaza Café (Junín 1070; ☽ 6pm-late) More bar than café, this is a lively bohemian spot with a terrace that's open quite late and sometimes has live music or shows.

Shopping

Museo de Artesanías Tradicionales Folclóricas (Quintana 905; ☽ 8am-noon & 4-9pm Mon-Sat) The shop attached to this museum sells a wide range of traditional handicrafts.

La Casa de Chamamé (Pellegrini 1790) This CD shop specializes in Corrientes' roots music, plus you can listen before you buy.

Getting There & Away

AIR

Aerolíneas Argentinas (☎ 428678; Junín 1301) flies to Buenos Aires daily (AR$504), and five times weekly to Asunción (AR$644), Paraguay. It also flies to Buenos Aires from nearby Resistencia. You can fly to Corrientes from Formosa (AR$ 123), but not the other way.

BUS

Nearby Resistencia has better long-distance bus connections, especially to the west and northwest (see p237). Buses to Resistencia (AR$2, 40 minutes) leave regularly throughout the day from the **local bus terminal** (cnr Av Costanera General San Martín & La Rioja). Faster are the shared taxis that zip you into Resistencia for AR$2.50. They leave from the same intersection, and also from the corner of Av 3 de Abril and Santa Fe. Buses to Paso de la Patria and Itatí leave from the corner of Belgrano and Roca.

Corrientes has a **long-distance bus terminal** (Av Maipú, btwn Manatiales & Nicaragua). Sample fares:

Destination	Cost (AR$)	Duration (hr)
Buenos Aires	118	12
Concordia	43	7
Córdoba	80	14
Mercedes	23	3½
Paraná	76	10
Paso de los Libres	41	6
Posadas	29	4
Puerto Iguazú	68	9
Rosario	96	12
Salta	117	14
Santa Fe	71	9

Getting Around

Local bus 105 (AR$1.25) goes to the **airport** (☎ 458684), about 10km east of town on RN 12. Bus 6 runs between the local bus terminal and the long-distance bus terminal on Av Maipú. Bus 103 connects the long-distance bus terminal with downtown.

PASO DE LA PATRIA

☎ 03783 / pop 3498

This humid but appealingly laid-back riverside town 38km northeast of Corrientes is a popular summer and weekend destination for *correntinos* (people from Corrientes) and *chaqueños* (people from Chaco). It's a sizable settlement stretching along the Río Paraná near its confluence with the Paraguay, but the population is small outside of high season.

The town's raison d'être is fishing, with some monster dorado, surubí, pacú and more being tempted by flies and lures. It makes a pleasant stop for a while, and has the added bonus of a large number of houses available for short-term rental.

The main street is Rioja, which runs from the entrance to town down to the river, where it meets 25 de Mayo (which runs along the riverfront).

The **tourist office** (☎ 494400; www.pasodelapatria turismoypesca.com; 25 de Mayo 425; ☒ 7am-9pm) is professional and helpful. Turn left from Rioja when you reach the riverfront, and it's five blocks down on the left.

Activities

Just about all the accommodations organize fishing trips on the Paraná. Various locals also run trips; try **Luis Macías** (☎ 494145; Córdoba 177). A whole day with everything included costs around AR$200 to AR$300 for two people; even novices regularly pull out some mighty impressive dorado. An hour's boat trip leaving the finned tribes unmolested costs about AR$20.

Festivals & Events

The annual **Fiesta Internacional del Dorado**, in mid-August, centers on a two-day competition for the largest specimens of the carnivorous dorado, known as the 'tiger of the Paraná' for its fighting nature. The dorado weighs up to 25kg, and the minimum allowable catch size is 75cm. Fish are thrown back after being weighed. Entry costs AR$300 for a three-person team; this includes tickets to a dinner

and show. You save AR$50 if you register by the end of July – contact the tourist office.

Sleeping & Eating

Several well-equipped campgrounds charge about AR$10 per tent. The best choice is one of the many houses available for rent, by the day or week. Prices start at AR$70 per day for a small house; the tourist office can arrange things. Other accommodations are regularly booked out by large fishing parties.

Hotel La Campana (☎ 03783-15-653019; lacampana hotel@hotmail.com; Rioja 261; s/d A25/50) Very central and near the river, this place has a river-fish restaurant, and small but rather sweet rooms. Prices go up significantly at the peak of the fishing season.

La Barra (La Rioja 262; meals AR$8-25; ☒ lunch & dinner) This place has a good airy dining area and shady sidewalk tables. While you're here, you have to try the local favorite: *surubí milanesa* (river fish covered in bread crumbs and fried).

Getting There & Away

There are buses every two hours to and from Corrientes (AR$3, one hour). Two operators, **Silvitur** (☎ 494260; Espana 926) and **Mir** (☎ 494654; Rioja & 12 Octubre) run hourly minibuses (AR$5, 40 minutes), which will pick you up and drop you off where you please. It's worth booking ahead. In Corrientes, these leave from the corner of Belgrano and Roca. A taxi from Corrientes to Paso is AR$45 fixed-fare.

PARQUE NACIONAL MBURUCUYÁ

☎ 03782

Well off the beaten track, this **national park** (☎ 498022; mburucuya@apn.gov.ar) lies about 180km southeast of Corrientes. It belongs to the same ecoregion as the Esteros del Iberá and although visitor services are nowhere near as advanced, it offers greater biodiversity.

The land was donated by Danish botanist Troels Pedersen, whose work in the area identified around 1300 species of plants, including some previously undiscovered. The park holds three natural regions: the Chaco, characterized by palm, carob and quebracho forests, pastures and riverine estuaries; the Paraná Forest, with magote islands, pindó palms and tacuarazú cane; and the Spinal Zone, with its xeróphilo forests, yatay palms and grasslands. There is an abundance of fauna: 150 species of birds have been spotted, as well as capybaras,

NORTHEAST ARGENTINA

caimans, foxes, swamp deer and the near-extinct maned wolf.

At present there are only two walking trails within the park. The Sendero Yatay passes through 2.5km of forests and grassland dotted with yatay palms to a lookout point on the Estero Santa Lucía. The Sendero Aguará Popé has explanatory signs along its 1.2km length as it winds through a variety of environments and crosses a small creek where caimans are often spotted.

The **visitor center** (9am-5pm) is 9km into the park. Both trails leave from near here.

Sleeping & Eating

Camping is the only option within the park itself. There's a small, rustic **campground** (free) with toilets and drinking water next to the visitor center.

The reasonable **Residencial Verón** (☎ 498006; Rivadavia 662; r per person AR$20) – in the small and friendly town of Mburucuyá, 12km west of the park – has basic rooms with shared bathroom and kitchen facilities for guests' use. There are simple eateries in town and a basic supermarket, as well as a small *chamamé* museum.

Getting There & Away

There are twice-daily buses from Corrientes to the town of Mburucuyá (AR$14, three hours). There, *remises* congregate on the plaza. The half-hour trip to the visitor center will cost around AR$50, a little more if you want the driver to wait while you walk the trails. Take note that the access road to the park is unpaved, sandy and often impassable after heavy rains, even in a four-wheel drive. Call the visitor center first to check on conditions.

MERCEDES

☎ 03773 / pop 30,961

The main access point for the spectacular Esteros del Iberá wetlands, Mercedes is a handsome gaucho town with a mighty easy pace to life. Its claim to fame is the nearby – and utterly surreal – roadside shrine to the gaucho Antonio Gil, an enormously popular religious phenomenon (see opposite), located 9km west of town.

The information office at the bus terminal is irregularly attended but has tourist information. The town's HI hostel also runs a helpful **information booth** (9-11am & 3:30-7pm) here. If they're not there, head to the hostel itself.

There are several telephone and internet places near the plaza, and various banks with ATMs.

Sleeping & Eating

Delicias del Iberá (☎ 423167; www.hostels.org.ar; Rivas 688; dm/s/d AR$30/70/90) Two blocks north of the plaza, this warmly welcoming hostel is a valuable fountain of information about the reserve, whether or not you are staying here. The comfortable and quiet dorms and rooms face a central patio, and there's a grassy garden out the back, past the kitchen. The hostel will pay your taxi from the bus station, where it also maintains an information office. There's 20% off for HI-members.

Hotel Itá Pucú (☎ 421015; Batalla de Salta 647; r per person AR$35;) Two blocks east of the plaza, this friendly low-roofed hotel has a sort of spaghetti-western feel, and OK rooms that open onto a grassy garden. Breakfast is extra.

Hotel Sol (☎ 420283; San Martín 519; s/d AR$70/90;) Around the corner from the Itá Pucú, this welcoming spot has good rooms for the price but the highlight is the stunning patio: a riot of plants, birdsong and gleaming chessboard tiles.

Mercedes Gran Hotel (☎ 421820; mercedesgranhotel@fibertel.com.ar; Guazú 750; s/d AR$70/120;) This once-appealing place on the north side of town has gone to the dogs recently. Nonetheless, it's still technically Mercedes' best. Smallish rooms are redeemed by big balconies and leafy, quiet grounds. The pool was too much trouble to maintain and is out of use.

El Quincho (☎ 420314; San Martín 1240; mains AR$8-18; lunch & dinner) This is the town's best eating option and is significantly cheaper than the decor (in the front room) and vaguely supercilious waiters would suggest. It wasn't doing fish at the time of research, but had a range of pasta, chicken, and steak with a variety of accompaniments.

Café de la Plaza (☎ 03773-15-627255; cnr Sarmiento & Pujol; light meals AR$6-10) This is a simple high-ceilinged place with a terrace; a reliable choice for burgers or beers.

Getting There & Away

The **bus terminal** (☎ 420165; cnr San Martín & Perreyra) is six blocks west of the plaza. Buses run regularly both ways. Destinations include: Buenos Aires (AR$96, nine hours), Paso de los Libres (AR$16, three hours), Resistencia

'GAUCHITO' GIL

Spend time on the road anywhere in Argentina and you're bound to see at least one roadside shrine surrounded by red flags and votive offerings. These shrines pay homage to Antonio Gil, a Robin Hood–like figure whose shrine and burial place just out of Mercedes attracts tens of thousands of pilgrims every year.

Little is known for sure about 'El Gauchito,' as he is affectionately known, but many romantic tales have sprung up to fill the gaps. What is known is that he was born in 1847 and joined the army – some versions say to escape the wrath of a local policeman whose fiancée had fallen in love with him – to fight in the War of the Triple Alliance.

Once the war ended, Gil was called up to join the Federalist Army but, unwilling to do so, he went on the run with a couple of other deserters. The trio roamed the countryside, stealing cattle from rich landowners and sharing it with poor villagers, who in turn gave them shelter and protection.

The law finally caught up with the gang, and Gil was hung by the feet from the espinillo tree that still stands near his grave, and beheaded.

So how did this freeloading, cattle-rustling deserter attain saintlike status? Moments before his death, Gil informed his executioner that the executioner's son was gravely ill. He told the soldier that if he were buried – not the custom with deserters – the man's son would recover.

After lopping off Gil's head, the executioner carried it back to the town of Goya where a judicial pardon awaited Gil. On finding that his son was indeed seriously ill, the soldier returned to the site and buried the body. His son recovered quickly, word spread and a legend was born.

'Gauchito' Gil's last resting place is now the site of numerous chapels and storehouses holding thousands of votive offerings – including T-shirts, bicycles, pistols, knives, license plates, photographs, cigarettes, hair clippings and entire racks of wedding gowns – brought by those who believe in the gaucho's miracles. January 8, the date of Gil's death, attracts the most pilgrims. If you are driving past, the story goes that you must sound your horn, or suffer long delays on the road or, more ominously, never arrive at all.

(AR$25, four hours) and Corrientes (AR$23, 3½ hours).

For information about transport to Colonia Pellegrini and the Esteros del Iberá, see p203

RESERVA PROVINCIAL ESTEROS DEL IBERÁ

This stunning wetland reserve is home to an abundance of bird and animal life, and is one of the finest places to see wildlife in South America. Although tourism has been increasing substantially in recent years, Esteros del Iberá remains comparatively unspoiled. The main base for visiting the park is the sleepy village of **Colonia Pellegrini**, 120km northeast of Mercedes; it offers a variety of excellent accommodations and trips to the reserve. Another, less-visited place to base yourself is Galarza, 80km further north.

The lakes and *esteros* are shallow, fed only by rainwater, and thick with vegetation. Water plants and other vegetation accumulate to form *embalsados* (dense floating islands), and this fertile habitat is home to a stunning array

of life. Sinister black caimans bask in the sun while busy capybaras (see p202) feed around them. Other mammals include the beautiful orange-colored marsh deer, howler monkeys (officially the world's noisiest animal), the rare maned wolf, coypu, otters and several species of bat.

There are some 350 species of bird present in the reserve, including colorful kingfishers, delicate hummingbirds, parrots, spoonbills, kites, vultures, several species of egret and heron (including the magnificent rufescent tiger-heron), cormorants, ducks, cardinals and the enormous southern screamer, which would really light up Big Uncle Bob's eyes at a Christmas roast. *Ibera: Vida y Color* (AR$18), on sale at La Cabaña, among other places, has beautiful photos of most of the birds, plants and animals you may see.

It's a delicate ecosystem, and environmentalists are understandably anxious that it not be harmed. To this end, US entrepreneur and environmentalist Doug Tompkins has been buying up large tracts of land around

---

CAPYBARAS

Treading, with its webbed feet, a very fine line between cute and ugly, the capybara is a sizable semiaquatic beast that you're bound to encounter in the Iberá area. Weighing in at up to 75kg, the *carpincho*, as it's known in Spanish, is the world's largest rodent.

Very much at home both on land and in the water, the gentle and vaguely comical creature eats aquatic plants and grasses in great quantity. They form small herds, with a dominant male living it up with four to six females. The male can be recognized by a protrusion on its forehead that emits a territory-marking scent. The lovably roly-poly babies are born in spring.

Though protected in the Iberá area, the capybara is farmed and hunted elsewhere for its skin, which makes a soft, flexible leather. The meat is also considered a delicacy in traditional communities.

---

the reserve and proposes to donate them to the Argentine government if it guarantees national park status for the area.

Information

The enthusiastic **municipal tourist office** (☣ 8am-1pm & 2-7pm) is at the entrance to the village, after crossing the causeway en route from Mercedes, and it's the best source of general information. The reserve's **visitor center** (☣ 7:30am-noon & 2-6pm), on the Mercedes side of the causeway, has an exhibition and an audiovisual presentation and a 400m monkey-spotting path opposite.

Note that as yet there is no bank or ATM in Colonia Pellegrini, so take plenty of cash. Internet access is currently limited to the more expensive posadas (inns).

Activities & Tours

The best way to appreciate the area is by boat. The classic trip is a two to 2½ hour excursion in a lancha, which takes you around the Laguna Iberá and its *embalsados*. You'll see myriad bird and animal life, elegant lilies, water hyacinths and other aquatic plants. There are abundant caimans and capybaras, and you also may see deer, otters, coypu and howler monkeys. Birdlife includes cormorants, grebes, several species of heron and egret, rails, kingfishers and ducks. The guide will punt you remarkably close to the creatures. You can also take a night trip; go prepared with plenty of insect repellent!

The short path opposite the visitor center gives you a sporting chance of seeing howler monkeys up close; longer, guided walks are also available, as are horseback rides, although these are more for the ride's sake than for wildlife spotting.

The Laguna Iberá is only a small part of the 13,000 sq km area of the Esteros. Some 80km north, at Galarza, is the Laguna Galarza and the larger Laguna de Luna, which can also be explored by boat.

Many of the lodges can organize these activities; if you are staying at one they are usually included in the price. If not, there are many other options. The standard boat trip costs AR$40 per person and can be arranged via the municipal tourist office or the campsite (from where most trips leave). There are several local, independent guides in town; the tourist office has a list. Note that few guides speak English; if you want an English-speaking guide, it's best to go through one of the lodges.

Sleeping

Colonia Pellegrini's accommodations are mushrooming, with more than 20 at last count. They are divided between *hospedajes*, usually simple rooms behind a family home, and posadas or *hosterías*, comfortable lodges that offer full-board rates, always including three meals a day plus afternoon tea. Most offer two free excursions daily, and provide bikes, canoes or kayaks for guests' use. All can book a transfer from Mercedes or Posadas for you.

Camping La Balsa (☎ 03773-15-628823) Right by the lake, and named for the raft-ferry that the causeway replaced, this campsite was closed for improvements at the time of research but will be up and running again by the time you read this.

Hospedaje Los Amigos (☎ 03773-15-493753; hospedaje losamigos@gmail.com; cnr Guasú Virá & Aguapé; s/d AR$25/50) The best of the budget choices, and with a kindly owner, this offers spotless rooms with big beds and decent bathrooms for a pittance. You can also eat simply but well here.

Hospedaje San Cayetano (☎ 03773-15-400929; cnr Yacaré & Aguapé; dm AR$25) This is a basic but friendly budget choice with comfortable-enough rooms; if there's space, you'll get your own room for the same price. The boss runs good boat trips. You can also camp in the grounds.

Posada Ypa Sapukai (☎ 03773-420155; www.ibera turismo.com.ar; Mburucuyá s/n; d with full board AR$500; ☀) Secluded and rustic, this has grounds (with hammocks and chairs for lounging) that stretch down to the lake and small rooms that are pretty good value. It wins points for the name, which means 'The Cry of the Lake.'

Hostería Ñandé Retá (☎ 03773-499411; www.nande reta.com; s/d with full board AR$390/660; ☐ ☀ ☀) This place has been around longer than any, and is still one of the most pleasing. Surrounded by pines and eucalypts, it's got a peaceful, hidden-away feel that is highly seductive. It's very family-friendly and the rooms are colorful.

Irupé Lodge (☎ 03752-438312; www.irupelodge.com .ar; Yacaré s/n; s/d with full board AR$465/725; ☀) On the lake near the causeway, this rustic lodge makes you feel very welcome straight away. While the rooms are satisfactory, artistic wooden furniture, a pool and views across the water are the highlights. The food cooked by the Swiss chef gets the thumbs-up too.

our pick **Posada de La Laguna** (☎ 03773-499413; www.posadadelalaguna.com; Guasú Virá s/n; s/d with full board AR$567/756; ☀) Highly elegant rooms in wide grounds by the lake at the end of town. The emphasis is on rural style and relaxation, and the staff pull it off, with warm and friendly service and great guided trips. The meals are excellent. The operators are proud of having no TV, and it's worth being proud of.

Posada Aguapé (☎ 03773-499412; www.iberaesteros .com.ar; Yacaré s/n; s in smaller/larger r AR$154/224, d AR$184/268, with full board AR$310/408 per person; ☀) This luxurious colonial-style posada is in a beautiful setting above the lake. It has more amenities than any other place in town, including a wide variety of excursions. Service is multilingual and excellent.

Estancia San Lorenzo (☎ 03756-481011; www.estancia sanlorenzo.com; d per person with full board & excursions AR$400; ☽ mid-Mar–Dec 20) In a remote area in the northeast sector of the park, this divine little eight-room *estancia* (ranch) in Galarza is run by its exceptionally friendly owners

who cook, talk, guide you on horseback and buzz you around the nearby lagoons to spy on caimans and capybaras. The food, all of it homemade, is superb (and seemingly endless). Considering what the price includes, it's great deal – and it just *feels* like the real thing. Visitors usually bus to the nearby town of Gobernador Virasoro (80km away), where the owners pick them up.

Eating

All of the midrange and top-end accommodations options put meals on for their guests. If you ask nicely in advance, and they have space, most of them will let nonguests eat. There are other simple options in town:

Yacarú Porá (☎ 03773-15-413750; cnr Caraguatá & Yaguareté; mains AR$10-15; ☽ 10am-midnight) Run with charm and enthusiasm, this attractive tin-roofed bungalow guarantees a warm welcome. The food is prepared to order and features generous portions of meat with tasty sauces, chicken dishes, empanadas, omelettes and *milanesas*. They should be offering rooms by the time you read this.

La Cabaña (cnr Yaguareté & Curupí; lomitos AR$4-6) Tiny *artesanía* shop that also does tasty *lomitos* (steak sandwiches) and coldish beer.

Getting There & Away

The road from Mercedes to Colonia Pellegrini (120km) is unsealed, and departures are limited. Bus services are unreliable and painfully slow, but theoretically leave Mercedes twice a day for Colonia Pellegrini (AR$20, four to five hours); check at the bus terminal information office.

A faster and more reliable way to get there is by combi or 4WD transport. At the time of research, these options were available departing Mercedes at 8am on Wednesday, Friday and Sunday (one-way/return AR$70/130) for the three-hour trip, returning from Colonia Pellegrini at 4:30pm on Tuesday, Thursday and Saturday. Check the schedule with the bus terminal or Delicias del Iberá hostel in Mercedes, or with **Cristian** (☎ 03773-15-730735), also contactable at Yacarú Porá restaurant in Colonia Pellegrini. At other times combis may leave according to demand. You can also charter your own transport; this costs AR$240 for as many people as you can fit in the vehicle. Arrange this through the hostel in Mercedes, or contact **Beto** (☎ 03773-15-515862), who lives opposite Hostería Ñandé Retá in Colonia Pellegrini. There may already be a trip arranged that you can join.

The road isn't as bad as everyone says it is, and is drivable in a normal car except after heavy rain. Plans are afoot to tarmac all but the last 40km on both the Mercedes and Posadas roads.

The road from Posadas is worse, but the same transport service leaves for Colonia Pellegrini at 8am on Wednesday, Friday, and Sunday (one-way/return AR$90/165; four to five hours), returning to Posadas at 4:30pm Tuesday, Thursday and Saturday. Drivers charge AR$480 for a charter to Posadas.

ALONG THE RÍO URUGUAY

The second of the two great rivers that converge above Buenos Aires to form the Río de la Plata, the Río Uruguay divides the country of the same name from Argentina, and also forms part of the border with Brazil. Bridges provide easy access to these neighbors, whose influences have blended with those of indigenous and immigrant groups in the area. The riverside towns on the Argentine side offer plenty and are very popular summertime destinations for *porteños* (people from Buenos Aires).

Gualeguaychú is famous for its Carnaval, while Colón is a fabulous little place within striking distance of the noble palms of Parque Nacional El Palmar. Peaceful little Yapeyú, meanwhile, has Jesuit ruins and is where José de San Martín, Argentina's great liberator, was born.

RN 14 runs north from Gualeguaychú roughly paralleling the Río Uruguay. It passes densely forested riverside areas and runs through grasslands where cattle graze alongside rheas.

GUALEGUAYCHÚ
☎ 03446 / pop 75,516

A mellow little riverside place, Gualeguaychú is very quiet out of season and you won't find much to do apart from stroll by the river or in the lush Parque Unzué – which makes it very appealing if you've just come from Buenos Aires, for example. Argentine holi-

daymakers begin to arrive in December, and in January and February the place really kicks off, with the country's longest and flashiest Carnaval celebrations.

Orientation

Some 220km north of Buenos Aires, Gualeguaychú sits on the east bank of its namesake river, a tributary of the Uruguay. Plaza San Martín, occupying four square blocks, is the center of its grid pattern; each block covers 50, rather than 100, street numbers. Nearby the General Libertador San Martín tollbridge leads to the Uruguayan city of Fray Bentos.

Information

There are several banks, most with ATMs, along Av 25 de Mayo.

ACA (☎ 426088; cnr Urquiza & Chacabuco) Argentina's auto club; good source for provincial road maps.

Hospital Centenario (☎ 427831; cnr 25 de Mayo & Pasteur)

Laverap (Bolívar 702) Laundry.

Post office (cnr Urquiza & Angel F Elías)

Telecentro (25 de Mayo 570; per hr AR$1.50; ⏰ 7:30am-11pm) Calls and internet

Tourist office (☎ 423668; www.gualeguaychuturismo .com; Plazoleta de los Artesanos s/n; ⏰ 8am-10pm summer, 8am-8pm winter) Thatched hut by the Av Costanera, south of Plaza Colón. A branch at the bus terminal keeps the same hours.

Sights & Activities

A handful of colonial buildings remain in Gualeguaychú, in addition to more recent ones important in Argentine political and literary history. The **Museo Aedo** (San José 105; admission free; ⏰ 9-11:45am Wed-Sat, Fri & Sat also 4-6:45pm Apr-Dec, 5-7:45pm from Jan-Mar), just off Plaza San Martín, is the municipal museum, occupying the oldest house in town (c. 1800). It features mostly antique furniture and weaponry. A free guided tour in rapid-fire Spanish is available.

In the mid-19th century, the colonial **Casa de Andrade** (cnr Andrade & Canonigo JJ Borques) belonged to *entrerriano* (from the province of Entre Ríos) poet, journalist, diplomat and politician Olegario Andrade. **Casa de Fray Mocho** (Fray Mocho 135) was the birthplace of José Álvarez, founder of the influential satirical magazine *Caras y Caretas* at the turn of the 20th century; Fray Mocho was his pen name. Dating from the early 20th century, the unusual **Casa de**

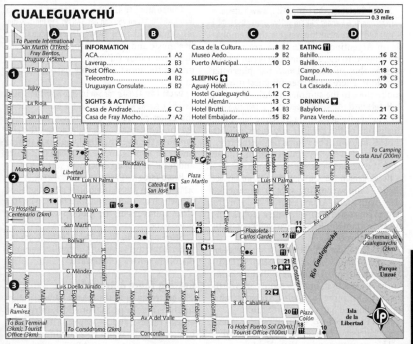

GUALEGUAYCHÚ

0 ━━━━━ 500 m
0 ━━━━━ 0.3 miles

INFORMATION			SLEEPING			EATING
ACA	1	A2	Aguaý Hotel	11	C2	Bahillo 16 B2
Laverap	2	B3	Hostel Gualeguaychú	12	C3	Bahillo 17 C3
Post Office	3	A2	Hotel Alemán	13	C3	Campo Alto 18 C3
Telecentro	4	B2	Hotel Brutti	14	B3	Dacal 19 C3
Uruguayan Consulate	5	B2	Hotel Embajador	15	B2	La Cascada 20 C3

Casa de la Cultura 8 B2
Museo Aedo 9 B2
Puerto Municipal 10 D3

SIGHTS & ACTIVITIES
Casa de Andrade 6 C3
Casa de Fray Mocho 7 A2

DRINKING
Babylon 21 C3
Panza Verde 22 C3

la Cultura (☎ 427989; 25 de Mayo) has occasional public exhibitions, and is the place to contact for entrance to the houses listed above.

Southwest of the center, the **Corsódromo** (Blvd Irazusta) is the main site for Gualeguaychú's lively Carnaval.

Gualeguaychú's highlight is **Parque Unzué**, a sizable and elegant riverside park across the bridge from the center. It's great for swimming, picnicking, camping, fishing and relaxing. Near the park are the **Termas de Gualeguaychú** (☎ 499167; www.gualeguaychutermal .com.ar; RP 42, km 2.5; admission AR$10; ☉ 8am-midnight), a popular complex of shallow thermal pools at various temperatures.

A stroll along Av Costanera yields views across the river to the park and various inlets and landscapes. Hour-long river cruises aboard the **Ciudad de Gualeguaychú** (☎ 423248; www.paseosnauticos.8m.com; AR$10) run in summer from the Puerto Municipal.

Festivals & Events

Gualeguaychú's summer **Carnaval** is big and brassy, so make a stop here any weekend from

mid-January to late February. Admission to the Corsódromo costs AR$20, plus another AR$7 to AR$15 to guarantee a seat.

Every October for more than 30 years, on the Día de la Raza weekend, high-school students have built and paraded floats through the city during the **Fiesta Provincial de Carrozas Estudiantiles**. Other local celebrations include numerous *jineteadas* (rodeos) throughout the year.

Sleeping

There's a string of decent budget hotels along Bolívar between Bartolomé Mitre and Monseñor Chalup. All prices are significantly lower out of season. On the eastern bank of the river in Parque Unzué are several clusters of cabins and bungalows. The simplest charge around AR$80 for up to four people. The tourist office will give you a list of them.

Camping Costa Azul (☎ 422672; Av Costanera s/n; 2-/4-person tent AR$25/35; ☉ Dec-Feb) This campground, 200m northeast of the bridge to Parque Unzué, has good facilities, but take plenty of mosquito repellent.

Hostel Gualeguaychú (☎ 424371; www.hostelguale guaychu.com.ar; G Méndez 290; dm incl breakfast AR$25; 🔧) A relaxed place near the water with an emphasis on Argentine *folklore*: there are musical instruments to use, and the owners run an impressive shop of artisanal *mate* paraphernalia next door. There's a kitchen for guest use and you're close to the summer nightlife.

Hotel Brutti (☎ 426048; Bolívar 571; s/d AR$40/65) A favorite of fifty-something traveling salesmen, this is one of the cheaper and more reliable choices in town. The rooms facing the front are lighter, but there's a bit of morning noise from the market opposite.

Hotel Alemán (☎ 426153; Bolívar 535; s/d AR$100/ 115; 🔧) This welcoming spot is a homelike place, with a faux-Alpine exterior and a bright central courtyard complete with a replica renaissance fountain. Rooms are well kept, with decent bathrooms.

Hotel Embajador (☎ 424414; www.hotel-embajador .com; cnr 3 de Febrero & San Martín; s/d AR$80/125; 🔧 💻) The central Embajador has a slightly careworn '70s feel to it, but the rooms are worth that little bit more for their extra space and marble-floored bathrooms with tub.

Hotel Puerto Sol (☎ 434017; www.hotelpuertosol .com.ar; San Lorenzo 477; d/tr AR$145/175; 🔧 💻) Cordial and bright, this spot near the water has an appealing summer-camp feel about it with its pastel paint job, outdoor sitting area, board games, solarium and dipping pool. Prices are a fair bit cheaper outside the height of summer, and single rates (AR$80) are available.

Aguaý Hotel (☎ 422099; www.hotelaguay.com.ar; Av Costanera 130; s/d AR$210/260; 🔧 💻 🔧) All rooms in this stylish modern hotel are spacious and have balconies (most with great views over the river) and excellent bathrooms. There's a small gym, a rooftop pool and spa. It's at least 60 pesos cheaper outside the summer months.

Eating & Drinking

Bahillo (ice-cream cones from AR$2.50-4.50; ⏰ 10am-9pm) Head to one of their two branches (corner of Av Costanera and San Lorenzo, and corner of Díaz and 25 de Mayo) for quality ice cream.

La Cascada (☎ 432451; Av Costanera near Av A del Valle; meat AR$6-16, fish AR$8-21; ⏰ lunch & dinner) Spacious, cheerful and simple, this place does the Entre Ríos basics well. Cheap *parrillada*, all the classic river fish (check out the photos of some of the monster surubí in the menu) and a range of salads – it's all here.

Campo Alto (☎ 429593; cnr San Lorenzo & Concordia; mains AR$10-18, all you can eat $AR19; ⏰ lunch & dinner) Thatched-roof bungalows, occasional live music and shady outdoor seating make this *asador libre* (all-you-can-eat barbecue) one of the most enjoyable eating options in town.

Dacal (☎ 427602; cnr San Lorenzo & Andrade; pasta AR$14-24, parrilla AR$15-30; ⏰ lunch & dinner) One of the better places to eat in town, but a little overpriced, Dacal looks right across the *costanera* to the river, has lively outdoor seating under an awning and serves good fish, pasta and meat. It fills up quickly in summer.

Panza Verde (cnr LN Alem & Luis Doello Jurado; ⏰ from 6pm Thu-Sun) A happening little neighborhood bar which also serves *picadas* (snacks). On a clear, balmy night, the rooftop terrace is the place to be.

Babylon (G Méndez 276; ⏰ nightly Dec-Feb) Near the waterfront, this is one of the livelier summer discobars, with a roof terrace.

Getting There & Around

The **bus terminal** (☎ 440688; Jurado & Artigas) is 3km southwest of the plaza. For AR$1, infrequent buses – routes 2 and 3 – stop on Artigas across from the terminal and take circuitous routes to the town center. For AR$7 a *remise* will drop you anywhere downtown.

The following table shows fares and schedules:

Destination	Cost (AR$)	Duration (hr)
Buenos Aires	32	3½
Colón	10	2
Concepción	7	1¼
Concordia	18	4
Fray Bentos (Uruguay)	9	1
Paraná	26	5
Paso de los Libres	34	7
Rosario	42	7½
Santa Fe	28	5½

CONCEPCIÓN

☎ 03442 / pop 65,954

Set around a stately plaza, Concepción del Uruguay (its full name) is a typical riverside town, wondering what to do with itself now that trade on the Río Uruguay has died off. It makes a decent stopover on the way north, has a couple of excellent places to stay, and boasts the sumptuous Palacio San José outside town. Unfortunately, its *costanera* is yet to be rejuvenated, but it's in the works.

Orientation

The parallel streets Rocamora, Galarza and 9 de Julio run east through the center of town to the river. On the way, Rocamora becomes pedestrianized and passes one block north of the central Plaza General Francisco Ramírez, Galarza runs along the northern edge of the plaza, and 9 de Julio hits the middle of the plaza, continuing on the other side.

Information

There is an ATM at the bus terminal and the Shell service station opposite has 24-hour internet access.

Municipal tourist office (☎ 425820; turismo@cdel uruguay.gov.ar; 9 de Julio 844; ☺ 7am-8pm Mon-Fri, 7am-10pm Sat & Sun) Well-prepared and helpful, but not clearly marked. Two blocks west of the plaza.

Sights

The principal sights are around the noble main plaza, where the earthy-pink colored **basilica** (☺ 8am-noon & 5-8pm) holds court. To the left of the altar, a sunken crypt (modeled on that of Napoleon in the Invalides in Paris) holds the remains of Justo José de Urquiza, first president of Argentina. Not far away, the **Museo Casa de Delio Panizza** (cnr Enterriano & Galarza; admission AR$2; ☺ 8am-noon & 4-8pm Mon-Fri, 9am-noon & 4-7pm Sat & Sun) dates from the late 18th century and holds a collection of 19th-century bric-a-brac.

Concepción has a long riverfront, but it doesn't offer much. The beaches are better to the northeast of town.

The region's primary attraction, however, is **Palácio San José**, 33km west of town.

Sleeping

Residencial Centro (☎ 427429; www.nuevorescentro .com.ar; Moreno 130; r AR$55; ⊠) The best budget deal in town has a variety of rooms around a courtyard. They vary slightly in price according to size and air-con; there's more light in the ones upstairs.

Apart Hotel Bonato (☎ 427621; www.turismo entrerios.com/aparthotelbonato; Rocamora 1266; r AR$75, apt AR$85-135; ⊠) If you don't feel like engaging with the whole Concepción scene (ie you're just here to see the palace), there's no shame in staying at this place across from the bus terminal. None at all. The apartments are a great deal with their fully equipped kitchens.

Grand Hotel (☎ 425586; www.grandpalaciotexier .com.ar; cnr Eva Perón & Rocamora; s/d AR$110/140; ⊠ 💻) This stately old place at the end of the pe-

CROSSING INTO URUGUAY

There are three main crossings linking Argentina with its eastern neighbor Uruguay (see p540). From south to north these are Gualeguaychú–Fray Bentos (opposite), Colón–Paysandú (p209), and Concordia–Salto (p212). All three are open 24 hours. Visitors from the USA, UK, Canada, Australia, New Zealand, Israel, and nearly all EU countries can enter Uruguay without a visa for an initial 90-day stay, which can be extended from within the country. An official list of countries that require no visa can be found in Spanish at: www.mrree.gub.uy/mrree /asuntos_consular/paisessinvisa.htm/.

destrian precinct has a charm from bygone years that plucks at the heartstrings. It's well priced, even though the rooms can be a little cramped. Try to picture the adjoining casino as it once would have been, without the ugly slot machines that disgrace it today.

our pick Antigua Posta del Torreón (☎ 432618; www.postadeltorreon.com.ar; Almafuerte 799; s/d AR$140/ 200; ⊠ 💷) This intimate and classy hotel a block west and four south of the plaza offers a real haven for a relaxing stay. It's an elegantly refurbished 19th-century mansion, with rooms surrounding a postcard-pretty courtyard replete with fountain and small swimming pool.

Eating & Drinking

El Remanso (☎ 428069; cnr Eva Perón & Rocamora; mains AR$10-22; ☺ lunch & dinner) Although it's showing its age a little, this is still one of the more traditional and atmospheric restaurants in town. Linen tablecloths and candlelight help make for a very agreeable mood.

Café de la Plaza (☎ 433292; www.cafedelaplazacdelu .com.ar; cnr Urquiza & Galarza; ☺ 8am-2pm & 4pm-late) On the northwest corner of the plaza, this offbeat place has a bit of everything, with a terrace, chessboard tiles, tasty coffee, wooden bench-booths, food and regular live music (AR$5 cover). The decor blends traditional and industrial, and pulls it off. Applause.

Frank Zappa (cnr Rocamora & Álvarez) This is a striking and massive bar-cum-nightclub near the river that sometimes has live music. With a beer garden, upstairs *boliche* (nightclub) and more intimate spaces, there's something for everyone.

NORTHEAST ARGENTINA

Getting There & Around

The **bus terminal** (☎ 422352; cnr Galarza & Chiloteguy) is 10 blocks west of the plaza. Bus 1 (AR$1) runs between them, a *remise* costs AR$2 to $AR3.

Regularly served destinations:

Destination	Cost (AR$)	Duration (hr)
Buenos Aires	43	4½
Gualeguaychú	7	1¼
Colón	4	¾
Concordia	14	3
Paraná	28.50	5
Paso de los Libres	25	6-7
Paysandú (Uruguay)	9	1½

PALACIO SAN JOSÉ
☎ 03442

Topped by twin towers and surrounded by elegant gardens, Justo José de Urquiza's ostentatious pink **palace** (☎ 432620; RP 39, Km 30; adult/child AR$3/1; ☻ 8am-7pm Mon-Fri, 9am-6pm Sat & Sun) is 33km west of Concepción via RP 39. Set around an elegant arched patio, with a walled garden out the back, it was built partly to show up Urquiza's arch rival in Buenos Aires, Juan Manuel de Rosas, and partly to show the power and wealth of Entre Ríos province. Local *caudillo* (provincial strongman) Urquiza, commanding an army of provincial loyalists, Unitarists, Brazilians and Uruguayans, was largely responsible for Rosas' downfall in 1852 and the eventual adoption of Argentina's modern constitution; he became effectively Argentina's first president.

Allies like Domingo Sarmiento and Bartolomé Mitre supped at Urquiza's 8.5m dining-room table and slept in the palatial bedrooms. Urquiza's wife turned the bedroom where López Jordán murdered her husband into a permanent shrine.

If you don't mind hitchhiking or walking the final 7km to the palace, you can get a Caseros-bound bus from Concepción and get the driver to drop you at the turnoff, but an easier option is to take a *remise* direct from Concepción. **Sarbimas** (☎ 427777) will take up to four people there and back, including a two-hour wait, for AR$48.

COLÓN
☎ 03447 / pop 19,288

The most appealing destination for riverside relaxation in Entre Ríos, Colón is a very popular summer getaway for Argentine holidaymakers. Its population almost doubles in January, but the pretty town takes it all in its stride. With numerous places to stay, a thriving handicrafts scene and worthwhile, out-of-the-ordinary restaurants, it's a great place to be. It's also the best base for visiting the Parque Nacional El Palmar.

One of three main Entre Ríos border crossings, Colón is connected to the Uruguayan city of Paysandú by the Puente Internacional General Artigas. The center of the action is Plaza San Martín, a block back from the river.

Information
Post office (cnr Artigas & 12 de Abril)
Tourist office (☎ 421996; www.colon.gov.ar; cnr Gouchón & Av Costanera; ☻ 6am-8pm Mon-Fri, 8am-8pm Sat & Sun) Occupies the former customs building, built by Urquiza. There is also an office open from 8am to 8pm in the bus terminal.

Sights & Activities
Strolling around the riverbank and quiet leafy streets is the highlight here. Check out beautiful Calle Alejo Peyret, a street back from the river; it's dotted with well-preserved 19th-century buildings, with their traditional green roofs and shutters. Old-style streetlamps give it a romantic cast at night. On the southern edge of town, **Parque Quirós** is handsome and tranquil.

There are numerous *artesanía* shops selling everything from *mate* gourds to pickled coypu. **La Casona** (☎ 425097; 12 de Abril 106; ☻ 9am-noon & 7-11pm Tue-Sun), on the corner of the plaza, is a cooperative selling a wide range of handmade goods. In February the city hosts the **Fiesta Nacional de la Artesanía**, a crafts fair held in Parque Quirós that features high-standard live folkloric entertainment.

The **Termas de Colón** (☎ 424717; www.termasdeentrerios.gov.ar; cnr Lavalle & Sabatier; admission AR$7; ☻ 8am-10pm), at the northern edge of town, is a thermal spa with 10 indoor and outdoor pools, ranging from 33°C to 40°C. The source is a 1500m-deep well drilled to tap the region's abundant geothermal aquifers.

There are various boat trips available to explore the river and the Islas Vírgenes. Expect to pay AR$15 to AR$20 for a one- to two-hour excursion.

It's also worth visiting the nearby village of **San José**, 8km west, where in 1857 European pioneers established the country's second agricultural colony. An interesting regional **museum** (☎ 470088; admission AR$2; ☻ 9:30am-

12:30pm & 3-5pm Tue-Sun) displays period tools and memorabilia.

Sleeping

Camping Municipal Norte (☎ 421917; cnr Alejo Peyret & Paysandú; 2-person site AR$20; ⏲ Oct-May) This campground is almost at the water's edge, and stretches north from the foot of Paysandú almost to the Termas de Colón complex. There is also more camping for the same price near the river on the south side of town.

our pick **Hostería 'Restaurant del Puerto'** (☎ 422698; www.hosteriadecolon.com.ar; Alejo Peyret 158; s/d AR$66/121;) In what has a strong claim to be Colón's loveliest house (on its prettiest street), this gorgeous spot has cracking characterful rooms decorated faithfully in keeping with the 1880 building, with enormous windows, plenty of wood and noble rustic furniture. The family duplexes (AR$170) are a great deal. All rooms surround a patio dominated by a fragrant Paraguay jasmine; there's also a heated pool and Jacuzzi. It's not a restaurant, despite the name.

Hotel Futuro (☎ 423712; Urquiza 168; s/d AR$50/90;) Despite the name, don't expect a glimpse forward in time, unless various shades of lime green come back into fashion in a big way. It's family run and comfortable enough, with a good location near the square. Some rooms are much better than others, with spacious bathrooms.

Hotel Palmar (☎ 421952; www.hotelpalmar.com.ar; Ferrari 295; r AR$120-170;) On the south side of town, the Palmar's rustic yet modern lobby leads on to some ordinary, but functional, motel-style rooms. Try to get one at the front for views of the lovely Parque Quirós.

Eating & Drinking

There are numerous places to eat. Hit Urquiza for traditional Argentine options, or Alejo Peyret for more unusual choices.

Verde Gourmet (☎ 424071; Alejo Peyret 168; mains AR$9-14; ⏲ lunch & dinner) Peaceful and welcoming, this fine little vegetarian spot has delicious crêpes and high-quality innovative mains, as well as duller soy-based 'meat' dishes. There are plenty of teas and great juices to drink, but nothing stronger.

El Sótano de los Quesos (cnr Chacabuco & Av Costanera; mixed plates AR$10-22; ⏲ 4-9pm Tue-Fri, 10:30am-9pm Sat & Sun) Near the tourist office, this intriguing spot serves a wide variety of artisanal cheeses and other delicacies at pretty thatched tables on a lawn looking over the port. There's also some tasty and unusual beers on hand.

our pick **La Cosquilla del Ángel** (☎ 423711; Alejo Peyret 180; pasta AR$18-26, mains AR$24-36; ⏲ lunch & dinner) Colón's best restaurant combines comfortably elegant decor, a big welcome and top service with a whimsical and unpretentious approach, particularly in the curiously named dishes, and the intriguing restaurant name, which translates to The Angel's Tickle. Many of the dishes combine sweet and savory flavors; try the *mollejitas* (sweetbreads) if you're a fan. The pastas are also highly recommended and the wine list is well above average.

Zalaka (☎ 424861; 12 de Abril 311; snacks AR$3-8; ⏲ 7pm-late Tue-Sun) Something of a Colón classic, this cozy pub on the main street would wear jeans and T-shirt if it were a person. It serves burgers and pizza, but it's better for drinks than food. There's a pool table upstairs.

Getting There & Around

Colón's **bus terminal** (☎ 421716; cnr Rocamora & 9 de Julio) is seven blocks inland (roughly west) of the river and eight blocks north of the main shopping and entertainment street, 12 de Abril. A *remise* into the center costs AR$3.

Destinations include Buenos Aires (AR$40, five hours), Gualeguaychú (AR$10, two hours) via Concepción (AR$3, 40 minutes), Concordia (AR$11, 2½ hours) via Ubajay (AR$6, 1½ hours), and Paysandú, Uruguay (AR$8, 45 minutes).

For details about visa requirements for crossing into Uruguay, see the boxed text, p207.

PARQUE NACIONAL EL PALMAR

☎ 03447

On the west bank of the Río Uruguay, midway between Colón and Concordia, 8500 sq km **Parque Nacional El Palmar** (☎ 493049; elpalmar@apn.gov.ar; RN 14, Km 199; admission Argentine/foreigner AR$7/20) preserves the last extensive stands of yatay palm on the Argentine littoral. In the 19th century the native yatay covered large parts of Entre Ríos, Uruguay and southern Brazil, but the intensification of agriculture, ranching and forestry throughout the region destroyed much of the palm savanna.

Most of the remaining palms in El Palmar are relics, some more than two centuries old, but under protection from grazing and fire they have once again begun to reproduce.

Reaching a maximum height of about 18m, with a trunk diameter of 40cm, the larger specimens clustered throughout the park accentuate a striking and soothing subtropical landscape that lends itself to photography. The grasslands and the gallery forests along the river and creeks shelter much wildlife, including birds, mammals and reptiles.

Park admission is collected at the entrance on RN 14 from 7am to 7pm, but the gate is open 24 hours.

Information

All the park's main facilities are 12km down the dirt road leading from the entrance. The **visitor center** (8am-7pm) has displays on natural history, including a small reptile house, and offers video screenings throughout the day. Guided bicycle tours (AR$10, one hour) of the park leave from a concession near the center.

Sights & Activities

To view the wildlife, your best bet is to go for walks along the watercourses or through the palm savannas, preferably in early morning or just before sunset. The most conspicuous bird is the rhea, but there are also numerous parakeets, cormorants, egrets, herons, storks, caracaras, woodpeckers and kingfishers. Among the mammals, the capybara and vizcacha are common sights, but there are also foxes, raccoons and wild boar.

Vizcachas inhabit the campground; their nocturnal squeaks and reflective eyes sometimes disturb campers, but they are harmless (as are the enormous toads that invade the showers and toilets at night). The same is not true of the yarará, a deadly pit viper that inhabits the savannas. Bites are rare, but watch your step and wear high boots and long trousers when hiking.

Arroyo Los Loros, a short distance north of the campground by gravel road, is a good place to observe wildlife. Five kilometers south of the visitor center is Arroyo El Palmar, a pleasant stream with a beautiful swimming hole, accessible by a good gravel road. It's a fine place to see birds and, crossing the ruined bridge, visitors can walk for several kilometers along a palm-lined road now being reclaimed by savanna grasses.

There is excellent access to the river for swimming and boating from the campground, as well as a series of short hiking trails.

Sleeping & Eating

Camping El Palmar (423378; per tent AR$6, plus per person AR$7) This campground across the parking lot from the visitor center is the only place to stay that's in the park. It has shady, level sites, hot showers, electricity and a small store. Rates vary with the season and numbers.

The nearest hotels are in Colón, some 58km south, and Concordia, 66km north.

There's a decent restaurant next to the visitor center, serving snacks and tasty full meals.

Getting There & Away

El Palmar is on RN 14, a major national highway, so there are frequent north–south bus services. Any bus running between Buenos Aires and Concordia, or between Concordia and Gualeguaychú, Concepción or Colón, will drop you at the park entrance, 12km from the visitor center. You could hitchhike from here or else stay on the bus a further 10km to Ubajay, from where a *remise* will cost you AR$20 to the visitor center.

Several agencies in Colón offer half-day trips to the park, which include a guided walk. **LHL** (422222; lhlColón@arnet.com.ar; 12 de Abril 119) near the plaza is one: the trip costs AR$45 plus the park entry fee. They can also arrange horseback riding in the park.

CONCORDIA

 0345 / pop 138,099

This pleasant agricultural service town on the Río Uruguay won't keep you spellbound for weeks at a time, but makes a convenient stop for a night. It's a working rather than a tourist town with a fine central plaza, interesting cathedral, and riverside beaches and fishing. It also offers a border crossing, via the Represa Salto Grande hydroelectric project, to the Uruguayan city of Salto.

The mainstay of the local economy is citrus fruit, and you can smell the tang in the air at times.

Information

There are several banks with ATMs in the vicinity of Plaza 25 de Mayo.

ACA (Pellegrini 801) Argentina's auto club; good source for provincial road maps.

Banco de la Nación (Pellegrini 651)

Cibercentro Colón (Pellegrini at Plaza 25 de Mayo; per hr AR$1.50) For phone calls and internet access.

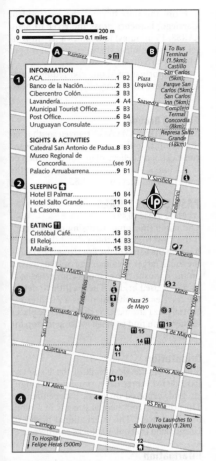

CONCORDIA

0 _____ 200 m
0 _____ 0.1 miles

INFORMATION
ACA..**1** B2
Banco de la Nación..................**2** B3
Cibercentro Colón...................**3** B3
Lavandería.............................**4** A4
Municipal Tourist Office.........**5** B3
Post Office.............................**6** B4
Uruguayan Consulate..............**7** B3

SIGHTS & ACTIVITIES
Catedral San Antonio de Padua.**8** B3
Museo Regional de
   Concordia.....................(see 9)
Palacio Arruabarrena..............**9** B1

SLEEPING
Hotel El Palmar.....................**10** B4
Hotel Salto Grande................**11** B4
La Casona.............................**12** B4

EATING
Cristóbal Café.......................**13** B3
El Reloj...............................**14** B3
Malaika...............................**15** B3

To Bus Terminal (1.5km); Castillo San Carlos (5km); Parque San Carlos (5km); San Carlos Inn (5km); Complejo Termal Concordia (8km); Represa Salto Grande (18km)

To Launches to Salto (Uruguay) (1.2km)

To Hospital Felipe Heras (500m)

(1919) is a fabulous building, blending French neo-renaissance architecture with art nouveau touches. It contains the **Museo Regional de Concordia** (☎ 421-1883; admission free; ☯ 8am-1pm & 2-8pm). The display is mostly about Italian immigration to the region, but there's also some fine furniture, including a mirror that belonged to Urquiza. The interior is badly in need of restoration but Concordia, hit hard by the economic crisis, has nowt in the bank. Readers?

In the riverside Parque San Carlos, at the northeastern edge of town, are the ruins of **Castillo San Carlos** (1888), built by a French industrialist who mysteriously abandoned the property years later. French writer Antoine de Saint-Exupéry briefly lived in the building; there's a monument to *The Little Prince* nearby. There's no charge for wandering around the ruins.

Concordia has a good thermal spa, the **Complejo Termal Concordia** (☎ 425-1963; www.termas concordia.com.ar; admission AR$18) to the north of town. Bus 7 runs there every half hour from San Lorenzo, near the bus terminal.

Festivals & Events

Fishing enthusiasts crowd Concordia during January's **Fiesta Nacional de la Boga**, in search of the region's tastiest river fish. The city holds its **Fiesta Nacional de Citricultura** (National Citrus Festival) the first week in December. Concordia's **Carnaval** celebrations (around February or March) are also lively. Carnaval Tuesday, the main day, is 47 days before Easter Sunday.

Sleeping

La Casona (☎ 400-1020; Pellegrini 443; s/d AR$40/60) By far the best budget choice, this friendly family-run spot offers spotless rooms with TV and bathroom three blocks south of the plaza. Book ahead, as it's popular. The family also runs a good cheap restaurant nearby.

Hotel El Palmar (☎ 421-6050; Urquiza 517; s/d AR$80/100, superior AR$110/144; ☒ ☐) A couple of blocks south of the plaza, the Palmer offers cramped rooms with balconies for reasonable prices. They're gradually being done up – the superior rooms offer plenty more space and modern convenience, but the standard rooms have that unmissable feel of gentle decline that characterizes so many Argentine hotels.

San Carlos Inn (☎ 431-0725; www.hotelsancarlosinn .com.ar; Parque San Carlos; s/d AR$147/170; ☒ ☐ ☒) Set

Lavandería (☎ 422-4375, cnr Urquiza & LM Alem) Laundry.
Municipal tourist office (☎ 421-2137; turismo@ concordia.gov.ar; Urquiza 636; ☯ 7am-midnight) Next to the cathedral. The information desk at the bus terminal also has tourist info.
Post office (Hipólito Yrigoyen)

Sights & Activities

On the west side of Plaza 25 de Mayo, the 19th-century **Catedral San Antonio de Padua** is the city's signature landmark. It's one of the region's more interesting cathedrals, with an ornate *retablo* (altarpiece) and stained-glass windows with scenes from the life of Christ.

Facing Plaza Urquiza, at the corner of Entre Ríos and Ramírez, the **Palacio Arruabarrena** in the lush grounds of the Parque Rivadavia, the resort-style San Carlos Inn's rooms are nothing special, but it's a quiet spot to rest up. Rooms have sweeping river views, as does the grassy sundeck.

Hotel Salto Grande (☎ 421-0034; www.hotel saltogrande.net; Urquiza 581; s/d AR$177/207, deluxe AR$209/244; 🍴 🖥 🖳) Concordia's fanciest hotel is just south of the main square and, although quite polished and modern, feels a little overpriced. The deluxe rooms have better views and minibar, but aren't a great deal better than the standards.

Eating

El Reloj (☎ 422-2822; Pellegrini 580; pizzas AR$11-19; 🕑 lunch & dinner) This spacious brick-walled pizzeria has good ambience and a staggering selection of options. A haven for the indecisive as they don't grumble about doing half and halves.

Malaika (☎ 422-4867; 1 de Mayo 59; dishes A$11-22; 🕑 lunch & dinner) Trendy eating has arrived in Concordia in the form of this relaxed and handsome café-bar on the square. It serves pizzas, but you should eschew them in favor of one of the daily specials, one of which is always vegetarian. Decent wines, caring service and a romantic mood seal the deal.

Cristóbal Café (☎ 421-5736; cnr Pellegrini & 1 de Mayo; mains AR$18-27; 🕑 breakfast, lunch & dinner) The terrace, complete with director's chairs and palm trees, is the best thing about this attractive, popular spot on the square. There's an interesting – if overpriced – menu, but the interior suffers from too much music and TV, and tables so closely packed you'll learn all about your neighbor's kidney complaints.

Getting There & Away

The **bus terminal** (☎ 421-7235; cnr Justo & Hipólito Yrigoyen) is 13 blocks north of Plaza 25 de Mayo. Four daily buses (none on Sunday) go to Salto, Uruguay (AR$8.50, 1¼ hours).

Other destinations:

Destination	Cost (AR$)	Duration (hr)
Buenos Aires	58	5½
Colón	11	2½
Concepción	14	3
Corrientes	43	7
Gualeguaychú	18	4
Paraná	27	4½
Paso de los Libres	24	4
Posadas	80	8

From the port beyond the east end of Carriego, launches cross the river to Salto (AR$8, 15 minutes) four times a day in winter, five in summer, between 9am and 6pm Monday to Saturday.

For information about visa requirements for crossing into Uruguay, see boxed text, p207.

Getting Around

Micro 2 (AR$1.25) takes Yrigoyen south from the terminal to the center. On its northward run catch it on Pellegrini in front of Banco de la Nación. A *remise* to the terminal from the center should cost about AR$5.

PASO DE LOS LIBRES
☎ 03772 / pop 40,494

The name (meaning 'Crossing of the Free') is the most romantic thing about this border town on the banks of the Río Uruguay. It faces the much larger Brazilian city of Uruguaiana on the opposite bank, and is connected to it by a well-used bridge. There's little to detain the traveler, but the town has a picturesque central plaza and a couple of reasonable places to stay if you find yourself looking to stop for the night.

Orientation

Situated on the west bank of the Uruguay, Paso de los Libres has a standard rectangular grid, centered on Plaza Independencia. The principal commercial street is Av Colón, one block west. The international bridge to Uruguaiana is about 10 blocks southwest.

Information

There's no tourist office, but try the ACA office near the border complex before the bridge or the Intendencia (town hall) on the plaza. There are maps of town all over the center. You'll find a bank with an ATM on the plaza.

Libres Cambio (Av Colón 901) Changes money.

Telecentro (Madariaga 660; per hr AR$1.50) Internet and phones half a block from the plaza.

Sleeping & Eating

Hotel Capri (☎ 421260; M Llanes s/n; s/d AR$35/60) Across the dirt lot from the bus terminal, the Capri is simple but OK if you need to sleep between buses.

Hotel Las Vegas (☎ 423490; Sarmiento 554; s/d AR$60/100; 🍴) Despite the burgundy carpets and '70s feel, this is a newish place in the center of town. The rooms are darkish but comfortable and have bathrooms with good showers. The rooms up the back have more light and space.

Hotel Alejandro Primero (☎ 424100; Coronel López 502; s/d AR$110/165; ✕ ▯ ☎) A surprisingly good hotel, this has a swish lobby and restaurant area and slightly less impressive but very spacious rooms. Ask for one with views over the river and Uruguaiana in Brazil on the other side.

La Farola (☎ 429945; Madariaga 802; mains AR$10-18; ✕ lunch & dinner) A cheerful blue-painted *parrilla* on the main plaza. It does a range of chicken, fish and meat dishes, and also tasty empanadas.

Getting There & Away

The **bus terminal** (☎ 425600) is at the corner of Av San Martín and Santiago del Estero. Several buses daily head to Buenos Aires (AR$86, 9½ hours) and Posadas (AR$45, six hours). Some go via Concordia, Colón, Concepción and Gualeguaychú. More buses bypass the town, but can drop you off at the Esso station on RN 14, where you can get a taxi to take you the last 16km to downtown.

Tata/El Rápido serves Corrientes (AR$41, six hours) via Mercedes (AR$16, three hours), from where you can visit the Esteros del Iberá.

Buses to Uruguaiana, Brazil (AR$1), leave frequently from 7am onwards, stopping on Av San Martín at Av Colón and across from the bus terminal (by the castlelike building).

Getting Around

The area between the bus terminal and downtown is a little dodgy at night. Minibuses (AR$1) run from the corner below the bus station into town. A taxi to the center is AR$6.

YAPEYÚ

☎ 03772 / pop 1650

It would be untruthful to call this delightfully peaceful place a one-horse-town; there are many horses, and the sound of their hooves thumping the reddish earth in the evening is one of the nicest things about it. Yapeyú was founded in 1626 as the southernmost of the Jesuit missions, and at its height had a population of more than 8000 Guaraní tending as many as 80,000 head of cattle. After the order was expelled in 1767, the mission started to decline, and was finally destroyed by Brazilian raiders in the early 19th century. Many houses

in the area are built of red sandstone blocks salvaged from mission buildings. Another historical note: José de San Martín, Argentina's greatest national hero and known as 'the Liberator,' was born here in 1778. Yapeyú is a great spot to relax; the sort of place where locals will greet you on the street.

Sights & Activities

Everything in town is within easy walking distance of the central Plaza San Martín. On its south side is the **Museo de la Cultura Jesuítica** (admission free; ✕ 8am-noon & 3-6pm Tue-Sun), set among the ruins of what was once the mission's church and cloister. If you read Spanish, it's an excellent museum, with a comprehensive overview of the missions in Argentina, Brazil and Paraguay and detailed information on all aspects of those fascinating communities. The photographic displays are also good, and the museum would make a useful first stop on a tour of the Jesuit zone.

It's a measure of the esteem that Argentines hold for the Liberator that they have built **Casa de San Martín** (admission free; ✕ 8am-noon & 2:30-6pm), an ornate building to protect the ruins of the house where he was born in 1778 and lived his first three years. The house actually dates from the early 17th century and was one of the Jesuit buildings. San Martín's parents' remains are here, and a campaign is underway to bring the man himself (he currently rests in the cathedral of Buenos Aires). No chance. Near the house, the incomplete arch is a Falklands War memorial and represents Argentina without the Malvinas.

On the southern edge of town, four blocks south of the plaza, the army barracks house another museum, the **Museo Sanmartiniano** (admission free; ✕ 8am-10pm). As well as various San Martín paraphernalia, it also has some objects from the Jesuit period, including a wooden Christ found in mud by the river. Charmingly, and typical of provincial museums in Argentina, there are also a couple of objects that aren't really on-message: an unusually twisted eucalyptus branch, for example.

On the west side of the plaza, the Gothic-spired parish **church** dates from 1899, but contains some important images from the Jesuit period.

Sleeping & Eating

Hotel San Martín (☎ 493120; Sargento Cabral 712; s/d AR$45/70; ☎) Handily located right on the plaza and next to the Jesuit ruins and San Martín's house, this is Yapeyú's only hotel. Rooms have TVs and face an echoey inner courtyard; there's not much natural light if you want privacy. The hotel also has a basic restaurant.

El Paraíso Yapeyú (☎ 493056; www.termasdeyapeyu .com.ar; cnr Paso de los Patos & San Martín; bungalow for 1/2/4 people AR$65/95/140; 🔀 🔊) This complex of comfortable modern bungalows (sleeping up to six) offers excellent value in a waterfront location – the Uruguay is mighty impressive right here. There's a pool and *parrilla* restaurant by the river.

Comedor del Paraíso (☎ 03772-15-433983; Gregoria Matorras s/n; mains AR$6-10; ⏰ 7am-midnight) This simple and friendly spot is just down from the Casa de San Martín on a street named after the Liberator's mum. There's no menu as such, just a limited choice from what's available. Portions are small but very cheap. If you ask a few hours beforehand, staff can organize other dishes for you. There are river views and out the front is a large, 300-year-old palo borracho tree, in which, they say, a young San Martín used to play. With a grand, bulbous and thorny trunk, this is a particularly fine example of this species, which is seen throughout Central and South America.

Getting There & Away

The small bus terminal is two blocks west of the plaza. There are four to five daily buses (AR$5 to AR$12; one hour) to Paso de los Libres, some continuing to Concordia (AR$29) and Buenos Aires (AR$92). In the other direction, there are daily services to Posadas (AR$38, five hours). More buses stop on the highway at the edge of the town.

For information about visa requirements for crossing into Uruguay, see boxed text, p207.

POSADAS & THE JESUIT MISSIONS

The narrow northeastern province of Misiones juts out like an Argentine finger between Brazilian and Paraguayan territory and is named for the Jesuit missions (p220) that were established in the region and whose ruins are a major attraction. Today San Ignacio Miní is the best restored; it and other ruins (including those across the border in Paraguay) are easily accessed from the provincial capital,

Posadas. Buses churn through Misiones en route to the Iguazú Falls in the north of the province, but a detour will take you to another stunning cascade – the Saltos del Moconá on the Río Uruguay.

The landscape here is an attraction. Approaching Misiones from the south you will see a change to gently rolling low hills, stands of bamboo, and papaya and manioc plantations. The highway passes tea and *mate* plantations growing from the region's trademark red soil – the province is the main producer of *mate*, Argentina's staple drink.

POSADAS

☎ 03752 / pop 279,961

Capital of Misiones, and a base for visiting the ruins of the Jesuit missions after which the province is named, Posadas is a modern city that gazes across the wide Río Paraná to Encarnación in Paraguay. Brightly colored street signs vie for attention on the bustling, humid streets, and shady trees stand guard in the several parks and plazas. Posadas is a stopover for travelers on their way north to Paraguay or Iguazú but has plenty of charm of its own, if little in the way of sights.

Posadas was the gateway to the pioneering agricultural communities of interior Misiones and in 1912 was linked with Buenos Aires by the Urquiza railway. The city lost some of its low-lying areas to flooding from the Yacyretá dam, a major hydroelectric project completed in 1997 that forced the relocation of 40,000 people.

Orientation

Posadas is on the south bank of the upper Río Paraná, 1310km north of Buenos Aires and 300km south of Puerto Iguazú. A handsome bridge links Posadas with the Paraguayan city of Encarnación.

Plaza 9 de Julio is the center of Posadas' standard grid; the impressive 19th-century facade of the Casa de Gobierno (Government House) stretches along almost its entire east side. Av Bartolomé Mitre is the southern boundary of the center and leads east to the international bridge.

Theoretically, all downtown street addresses have been renumbered, but new and old systems continue to exist side by side, creating great confusion for nonresidents, since many locals use the old system. The newer, four-digit street numbers are given here as

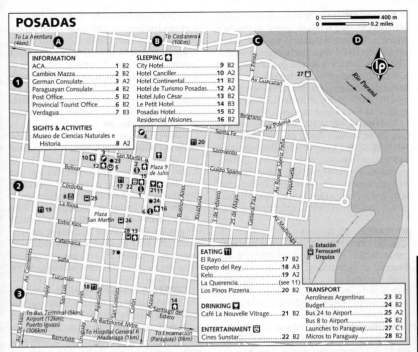

POSADAS

0 — 400 m
0 — 0.2 miles

INFORMATION
ACA..................................1 B2
Cambios Mazza...................2 B2
German Consulate................3 A2
Paraguayan Consulate...........4 B2
Post Office........................5 B2
Provincial Tourist Office.........6 B2
Verdagua...........................7 B3

SIGHTS & ACTIVITIES
Museo de Ciencias Naturales e
Historia..........................8 A2

SLEEPING
City Hotel..........................9 B2
Hotel Canciller...................10 A2
Hotel Continental................11 B2
Hotel de Turismo Posadas......12 A2
Hotel Julio César.................13 B2
Le Petit Hotel.....................14 B3
Posadas Hotel....................15 B2
Residencial Misiones.............16 B2

EATING
El Rayo.............................17 B2
Espeto del Rey...................18 A3
Kelo.................................19 A2
La Querencia..................(see 11)
Los Pinos Pizzeria................20 B2

DRINKING
Café La Nouvelle Vitrage.......21 B2

ENTERTAINMENT
Cines Sunstar.....................22 B2

TRANSPORT
Aerolíneas Argentinas..........23 B2
Budget.............................24 B2
Bus 24 to Airport................25 A2
Bus 8 to Airport.................26 B2
Launches to Paraguay...........27 C1
Micros to Paraguay..............28 B2

much as possible but some places still cling to their old three-digit addresses.

Information

There are several ATMs around the plaza, and call centers and internet places in the vicinity.

ACA (Automóvil Club Argentina; ☎ 436955; cnr Córdoba & Colón) Maps and route information

Cambios Mazza (Bolívar) Changes traveler's checks for a 1% commission plus AR$1 per check.

Hospital General R Madariaga (☎ 447775; Av López Torres 1177) About 1km south of downtown.

Post office (cnr Bolívar & Ayacucho)

Provincial tourist office (☎ 447539; www.turismo .misiones.gov.ar; Colón 1985; ☼ 8am-8pm Mon-Fri, 8am-noon & 4-8pm Sat & Sun) Well-informed staff.

Verdagua (☎ 433415; www.guayra.com.ar; San Lorenzo 2208) One of many operators (the tourist office will provide a list) offering half-day tours to the Jesuit missions (AR$120 to AR$160 for up to four), the Paraguayan missions, Saltos del Moconá and more.

Sights

The natural-history section of the **Museo de Ciencias Naturales e Historia** (☎ 423893; San Luis 384;

admission AR$1; ☼ 7am-noon & 2-8pm Mon-Fri, 9am-noon Sat & Sun) focuses on fauna and the geology and mineralogy of the province. The museum also has an excellent serpentarium (with demonstrations of venom extraction), an aviary and an aquarium. Its historical section stresses prehistory, the Jesuit missions and modern colonization.

Festivals & Events

Posadas celebrates **Carnaval** (in February or March, depending on the year) with great gusto, and seems to try to outdo other northern cities in the skimpiness of dancers' costumes.

Sleeping
BUDGET

Hotel de Turismo Posadas (☎ 437401; Bolívar 2176; s/d AR$25/38; ❀) This government-run place is scheduled for renovations but meanwhile it's the best bargain in the province. An aging but still comfortable hotel, it seems stuck in a time warp with its weird space-pod bathrooms and twilight-zone corridors. Luckily, the prices also come from another era.

Residencial Misiones (☎ 430133; Av Azara 1960; s/d AR$30/40) Offering seriously cheap rooms in a characterful central building, this is a budget option for those who aren't hygiene freaks. The mattresses are in reverse gear already, and neither the kitchen nor the bathrooms are up to much, but it gains points for the low prices and the staff's caring attitude. Rooms vary in quality, so have a look at a few.

La Aventura (☎ 465555; www.complejolaaventura .com; cnr Avs Urquiza & Zapiola; dm AR$25; cabins from AR$135; ✖ ▢ ▣) A sort of HI-affiliated holiday camp, 4km from the center (bus 3 or 13 from Ayacucho, or a AR$7 cab ride). Cabins sleep up to four; there are also dorm beds. In the large, leafy grounds are a river beach, a good restaurant, a pool, tennis court, minigolf and more.

MIDRANGE

ourpick Le Petit Hotel (☎ 436031; www.hotellepetit .com.ar; Santiago del Estero 1630; s/d AR$70/100; ✖) Peaceful and charming, this little place has clean, light and adequate rooms with big bathrooms and a leafy patio. The couple that run it are kind and helpful, and you'll feel right at home here. A great spot.

Hotel Continental (☎ 440990; www.hoteleramisiones .com.ar; Bolívar 1879; s/d AR$113/150, superior AR$149/ 193; ✖ ▢) A mite overpriced but bang on the plaza, this cavernous hotel has many rooms with superb views over the plaza to the river and Paraguay. Change the carpets please.

Posadas Hotel (☎ 440888; www.hotelposadas.com.ar; Bolívar 1949; s/d AR$125/160, deluxe AR$145/180; ✖ ▢) With by far the best-looking interior of any place in town, the Posadas has that gravitas missing from many modern hotels. Rooms are spacious, comfortable and well decorated.

Hotel Julio César (☎ 427930; www.juliocesarhotel.com .ar; Entre Ríos 1951; s/d AR$138/180; ✖ ▢ ▣) If you can rouse the staff from their torpor you'll find light, spacious, summery rooms with fridges and pleasing bathrooms. The slightly pricier superior rooms are identical but higher up.

Also recommended:

City Hotel (☎ 439401; www.misionescityhotel.com .ar; Colón 1754; s/d AR$60/98; ✖ ▢) Biggest sign in a big-sign town. Lino floors but on the plaza.

Hotel Canciller (☎ 440599; hotelcancillerposadas@ hotmail.com; Junín 1710; s/d AR$80/115; ✖) Low on character, OK on price, high on pastel colors.

Eating

El Rayo (☎ 439901; Bolívar 2089; medium pizzas AR$7-10; ✖ lunch & dinner) No-frills and effective, this joint is thronged at lunchtime for its delicious empanadas, lomitos and good-value pizzas. Service comes with a smile too. Thumbs up.

Los Pinos Pizzeria (☎ 423713; cnr Buenos Aires & Sarmiento; pizzas AR$9-18; ✖ 4pm-late) The place to go for pizza, draft beer or empanadas. There's a well-stocked bar and classical music on the sound system during the week; weekends things get a bit livelier. The lovely old building began as a pharmacy.

Espeto del Rey (☎ 436798; cnr Tucumán & Ayacucho; tenedor libre AR$20; ✖ lunch & dinner) It's somehow sad to see once-proud restaurants being forced to become *tenedor libre* (all you can eat). But there's no use crying over spilt milk; dry your eyes and tuck in. The salads are good, and there's an impressive wine list.

Kelo (☎ 429146; Av Corrientes 2051; tenedor libre AR$26; ✖ lunch & dinner) With its trademark *parrilla* smell, this isn't an easy place to walk past when you're hungry. It's even less easy to leave when you've eaten so much salad and meat for your 26 pesos you can hardly move.

ourpick La Querencia (☎ 437117; Bolívar 322; mains AR$12-29) On the plaza, this upmarket *parrilla* specializes in *galeto* (delicious chicken pieces with stuffing). Also memorable are the brochettes (giant spikes with various delicious meats impaled upon them). The salads are also unusually well prepared.

Drinking & Entertainment

Most of the weekend action is down at the new *costanera*, where a knot of eateries, bars and nightclubs go loud and late. Head north up Buenos Aires and its continuation for some nine blocks from the center. It's not particularly cheap, but it's where it's at.

Café La Nouvelle Vitrage (☎ 429619; Bolívar 1899) With a vaguely French feel, this amiable café on the plaza has a comfy interior and a terrace perfect for watching everyday life in Posadas go by.

Cines Sunstar (Bolívar 1981; admission AR$11) This cinema is a block west of the plaza.

Getting There & Away

AIR

Aerolíneas Argentinas (☎ 422036; Ayacucho 1728) flies five times weekly to the Aeroparque in Buenos Aires (AR$529).

BUS

Micros to Encarnación, Paraguay (AR$3), leave every 20 minutes from the corner of

San Lorenzo and Entre Ríos. With border formalities, the trip can take more than an hour, but is usually quicker.

Everyone gets out to clear Argentine emigration. The bus may leave without you; hang onto your ticket to catch the next one. The same happens on the Paraguayan side. There's a handy tourist office right by Paraguayan immigration, and official moneychangers hanging around. Make sure you get small denominations: a 100,000 guaraní note is hell to change. At time of research, the Paraguayan guaraní was running at 4525 to the US dollar and 1434 to the Argentine peso.

Launches (AR$3) cross Río Paraná to Encarnación from the dock at the east end of Av Guacurarí, but there is no immigration facility, so you're better off crossing the bridge.

For transport from Posadas to the Esteros del Iberá, see p203.

Posadas' **bus terminal** (☎ 425800; Quaranta, RN 12 & Av Santa Catalina) can be reached from downtown by buses 8, 15, 21 or 24 (AR$1).

All of the following destinations are served at least daily, most are served several times a day. Travel times are approximate.

Destination	Cost (AR$)	Duration (hr)
Asunción (Paraguay)	56	6
Buenos Aires	124	14
Corrientes	29	4
Paso de los Libres	45	6
Puerto Iguazú	30	5
Resistencia	31	5
Rosario	103	16
Santa Fe	91	14
Tucumán	107	18
Yapeyú	38	5

Bus services to San Ignacio (AR$5, one hour) begin at 5:15am and depart roughly half-hourly.

TRAIN

From Posadas' **Estación Ferrocarril Urquiza** (train station; ☎ 436076; General Madariaga s/n), the battered old Gran Capitán runs to Buenos Aires' Retiro train station on Sundays and Wednesdays at 7pm. It theoretically takes 26 hours, but usually takes many more. The cheapest class costs AR$39, while a sleeping berth costs AR$125.

Getting Around

Aerolíneas Argentinas runs its own minibus to the **airport**, 12km southwest of town. Bus 8

(AR$1.50) also goes there from San Lorenzo (between La Rioja and Entre Ríos), as does bus 24 from Junín, south of Córdoba. A *remise* costs about AR$17. **Budget** (☎ 432322; Colón 1909) is a central car-rental agency.

AROUND POSADAS
Santa Ana & Loreto

Atmospherically decaying in the humid forest, these two Jesuit missions are both off RN 12 between Posadas and San Ignacio, the site of another, better restored, mission.

At **Santa Ana** (☼ 7am-6pm), which was founded in 1633 but moved here in 1660, dense forest has been partially removed to reveal a settlement that had over 7000 Guaraní inhabitants at its peak. The enormous plaza, 140m square, attests to the importance of the settlement.

The muscular church's thick walls have been propped up with interior scaffolding and a few photogenic strangler figs grow atop them, lending a dramatic effect to what must have been a magnificent building, though none of its decorative embellishments remain. The church was designed by the Italian architect Brasanelli, who also worked on the San Ignacio church.

To the right side of the church is the cemetery, used by villagers into the latter half of the 20th century but now neglected. Crypts with doors agape reveal coffins fallen from their shelves and burst open; if this place doesn't give you the willies, you haven't watched enough horror movies.

Behind the church, a channel and reservoir remain from what was a sophisticated irrigation system.

Loreto (☼ 7am-6:30pm), founded in 1632, has even fewer visible remains than Santa Ana, and may not be worth the effort to visit via public transport. The old adobe latrine and a chapel are partially restored, but the jungle is king here again, and it's difficult to interpret the tumbled mossy stones among the trees. It's undeniably atmospheric though. It was one of the more important missions, and a printing press was built here – the first in the southern part of the continent.

Admission for both Loreto and Santa Ana is via a **joint ticket** (Argentines/other Latin Americans/others AR$7/9/12) that includes San Ignacio Miní and Santa María la Mayor. Both Santa Ana and Loreto are staffed by knowledgeable students, who give recommended tours, included in the admission price. The missions have small

NORTHEAST ARGENTINA

VISITING THE PARAGUAYAN MISSIONS

From Posadas there's a tempting and very rewarding day-trip to two of the Jesuit missions in Paraguay. The ruined but majestic churches at Trinidad and Jesús de Tavarangüe have been carefully restored and preserve some fabulous stonework.

From Posadas, cross to Encarnación (see p216) and get off the bus at the bus terminal (ask). From here, there are buses (most marked Ciudad del Este) every half-hour or so to Trinidad (G5000, 40 minutes). Get the driver to let you off at the turnoff to the ruins; it's then a 700m walk.

The **Trinidad ruins** (admission G5000; ⊗ 7am-7pm, to 5:30pm in winter) are spectacular, with the red-brown stone of the church contrasting strongly with the flower-studded green grass and surrounding hillscapes. Unlike at the Argentine missions, there is much decoration preserved here; the scalloped niches still hold timeworn sculptures, and the font and elaborate baroque pulpit are impressive. The doorways are capped with fine, carved decoration. You can climb to the top of one of the walls, but careful with the kids – there's no guardrail up there. An earlier church and belltower have also been restored here. There's a hotel and restaurant by the ruins.

For Jesús de Tavarangüe, walk back to the main road and turn right. At the petrol station 100m away is the turnoff to Jesús, 12km away. Shared taxis (G5000) wait here to fill, and buses (G4000) pass every two hours. You can get a taxi to take you to Jesús de Tavarangüe, wait for you, and bring you back to the turnoff for about G20,000.

The restored church at **Jesús de Tavarangüe** (admission G5000; ⊗ 7am-7pm, to 5:30pm in winter) was never finished. The spectacular trefoil arches (a nod to Spain's Moorish past) and carved motifs of crossed swords and keys make it perhaps the most picturesque of all the Jesuit ruins. The treble-naved church, with green grass underfoot, is on a similarly monumental scale as Trinidad. You can climb the tower for views of the surrounding countryside.

Head back to the main road by bus or taxi; buses back to Encarnación stop by the petrol station. Last stop is at or by the terminal; buses back to Posadas leave from the bus stop outside the terminal, opposite the school.

Note: you may need a visa to enter Paraguay. Currently, Americans, Canadians, Australians and New Zealanders do; Israelis, Brits and other EU citizens don't. A single-entry visa costs US$45 from the Paraguayan consulate in Posadas and can be ready in about an hour. You'll need passport photos, a copy of your passport and proof of an onward ticket. You can risk going through without getting your passport stamped, but the fine is US$75 if you get caught, which is possible on your way back through.

---

museums at their entrances and sell chips and drinks.

GETTING THERE & AWAY

Buses heading north from Posadas stop at the turnoffs on RN 12 for both sites. Santa Ana's is at Km 43, from where it's a 1km walk to the ruins. Loreto's is at Km 48, with a 3km walk. It can be intensely hot, so take plenty of water. You can get a *remise* from San Ignacio to take you to both, including waiting time, for about AR$60. If you can't see one around the center, call **Andi** (☎ 03752-15-273747), who knows plenty about the area.

Santa María la Mayor

Further afield, this is the fourth mission on the joint admission ticket for San Ignacio, Santa Ana and Loreto. Despite its smaller church and plaza, it was nevertheless a large

settlement and had a printing press as well as a prison, whose cells you can see next to the church.

The ruins are on the RP 2 road between Concepción de la Sierra and San Javier, 110km southeast of Posadas. To get there, take a bus from Posadas to Concepción de la Sierra. There, change to a San Javier–bound service and ask the driver to let you off at the ruins, which are some 25km down the road. You can get a San Javier–bound bus direct from Posadas but make sure it runs via the ruins – some go a different way.

SAN IGNACIO

☎ 03752 / pop 6312

The best preserved of the Argentine missions, San Ignacio Miní, is the central attraction of this small town north of Posadas. You could visit from Posadas or on your way to Iguazú, but a better idea is to stay the night; the hotels are comfortable, and you'll have a chance to check out the sound and light show at the ruins as well as Quiroga's house; both are worthwhile.

San Ignacio is 56km northeast of Posadas via RN 12. From the highway junction, the broad Av Sarmiento leads about 1km to the center, where Rivadavia leads six blocks north to the ruins. At the highway junction is a helpful **tourist office** (7am-9pm).

Sights

SAN IGNACIO MINÍ

These **mission ruins** (☎ 470186; www.misiones-jesuiticas .com.ar; entrance on Calle Alberdi s/n; admission Argentines/ Latin Americans/others AR$7/9/12; 7am-9:30pm) are the most complete of those in Argentina and impress for the quantity of carved ornamentation still visible and for the amount of restoration done. No roofs remain, but many of the living quarters and workshops have been reerected.

First founded in 1610 in Brazil, but abandoned after repeated attacks by slavers, San Ignacio was established at its present site in 1696 and functioned until the Jesuits finally gave in to the order of expulsion in 1768. The ruins, rediscovered in 1897 and restored between 1940 and 1948, are a great example of 'Guaraní baroque.' At its peak, the *reducción* had a Guaraní population of nearly 4000.

The entrance is on the north side on Calle Alberdi, where the first stop is the new **interpretation center**. It's an impressive display with plenty of unbiased information (in Spanish and English) about the missions from both the Jesuit and Guaraní perspectives. You can listen to Guaraní music, including some religious pieces composed at the missions, and inspect a virtual model of San Ignacio as it would have been.

Moving on to the ruins (via an informative free tour if you wish; guides speak English, some speak French and German), you pass between rows of Guaraní houses before arriving at the plaza, on one side of which is the enormous red sandstone church. Impressive in its dimensions, it is the focal point of the settlement. While the red-brown stone is very picturesque, the buildings were originally white. Before lime was widely available, it was obtained by burning snail shells.

By the church, the cloisters preserve some ornately carved balustrades, and the original flooring of some of the rooms off it. Just before the exit is another museum containing some excellent carved paving stones.

In summer it's worth trying to avoid visiting between 10am and 1pm, as the site gets particularly busy with tour groups at these times.

Every night there is a Luz y Sonido (sound and light show) at the ruins, included in the price of the ticket. The time varies slightly between 7pm and 8pm.

The admission ticket is valid for 15 days, and includes entry to the nearby ruins at Santa Ana and Loreto, and also to Santa María la Mayor, a little further afield.

CASA DE HORACIO QUIROGA

Horacio Quiroga was a poet and novelist who also dabbled in other activities, including snapping early photographs of the rediscovered ruins and farming cotton (unsuccessfully) in the Chaco. He lived in San Ignacio from 1910 to 1917, when his first wife committed suicide (as did Quiroga himself, terminally ill, 20 years later). Quiroga's regionally-based stories transcend time and place without abandoning their setting. Some of his short fiction is available in English translation in *The Exiles and Other Stories*.

Quiroga's house (☎ 470124; Av Quiroga s/n; admission AR$2.50; 8am-noon & 3-7pm) is at the southern end of town (a 20 to 30 minute walk), offering grand views of the Río Paraná. A small museum contains photos and some of the writer's possessions and first editions.

Quiroga's permanent **Casa de Piedra** is one of those simple but lovely houses that artists seem to inhabit, and holds various memorabilia, including butterfly specimens, an enormous snakeskin and the writer's rusted motorcycle. A replica of his initial wooden house, built for the 1996 biographical film *Historias de Amor, de Locura y de Muerte* (Stories of Love, Madness and Death), stands nearby.

Sleeping & Eating

Residencial Doka (☎ 470131; recidoka@yahoo.com.ar; Alberdi 518; s/d AR$30/50, 5-person cabin AR$100;) Located just a few steps from the ruins, the Doka has fairly nondescript rooms at a fair price. There are also a couple of cabins with kitchenette that are excellent value for groups or families. If there's nobody about, ask in the supermarket next door.

Hotel San Ignacio (☎ 470047; hotelsanignacio@arnet .com.ar; cnr Sarmiento & San Martín; s/d AR$40/60, 4-person cabana AR$80;) Located in the center near where the bus stops, this is an excellent choice

A TRIUMPH OF HUMANITY

For a century and a half from 1609, one of the world's great social experiments was carried out in the jungles of South America by the Society of Jesus (the Jesuits). Locating themselves in incredibly remote areas, priests set up *reducciones* (missions), where they established communities of Guaraní whom they evangelized and educated, while at the same time protecting them from slavery and the evil influences of colonial society. It was a utopian ideal that flourished and led Voltaire to describe it as 'a triumph of humanity which seems to expiate the cruelties of the first conquerors.'

For the Guaraní who were invited from the jungle to begin a new life in the missions, there were many tangible benefits, including security, nourishment and prosperity. Mortality declined immediately, and the mission populations grew rapidly. At their peak, the 30 Jesuit *reducciones* spread across what are now Argentina, Brazil, and Paraguay were populated by more than 100,000 Guaraní. Each mission had a minimum of Europeans: two priests was the norm, and the Guaraní governed themselves under the Jesuits' spiritual authority. The Jesuits made no attempt to force the Guaraní to speak Spanish and only sought to change those aspects of Guaraní culture – polygamy, and irregular cannibalism – which clashed with Catholic teaching. Each Guaraní family was given a house and children were schooled.

The typical *reducción* consisted of a large central plaza, dominated by the church and *colegio*, which housed the priests and also contained art workshops and storerooms. The houses of the Guaraní occupied the rest of the settlement in neat rows; other buildings might include a hospital, a *cotiguazú* (big house) which housed widows and abandoned wives, and a *cabildo*, where the Guaraní's chosen leader lived.

The settlements were self-sufficient; the Guaraní were taught agriculture, and food was distributed equally. As time went on and the missions grew, the original wooden buildings were replaced by stone ones, and the churches, designed by master architects with grandiose utopian dreams, were stunning edifices with intricate baroque stonework and sculpture comparable with the finest churches being built in Europe at the time.

Indeed, the missions' most enduring achievement was perhaps artistic. The Guaraní embraced the art and music they were introduced to and, interweaving European styles with their own, produced beautiful music, sculpture, dance and painting in the so-called 'Guaraní baroque' style. It was perhaps the Jesuits' religious music that most attracted the Guaraní to Catholicism.

However, mission life necessarily had a martial side. Raiding parties of *bandeirantes* from Brazil regularly sought slaves for sugarcane plantations, and the Jesuits were resented by both Spanish and Portuguese colonial authorities. There were regular skirmishes and battles until a notable victory over an army of 3000 slavers at Mbororó in 1641 ushered in a period of comparative security.

The mission period came to an abrupt end. Various factors, including envy from colonial authority and settlers and a feeling that the Jesuits were loyal to their own ideas rather than the crown's, prompted Carlos III of Spain to ban them from his dominions in 1767, following the lead of Portugal and France. With the priests gone, the communities were vulnerable, and the Guaraní gradually dispersed. The decaying missions were then ruined in the wars of the early 19th century.

The 1986 film *The Mission* is about the last days of the Jesuit missions. Most intriguing is the casting of a Colombian tribe, the Waunana, who had had almost no contact with white people, as the Guaraní.

Almost nothing remains of several of Argentina's 15 missions, but those well worth visiting include San Ignacio Miní (p219), Loreto & Santa Ana (p217), Yapeyú (p213) and Santa María la Mayor (p218). The fabulous Paraguayan missions at Jesús de Tavarangüe and Trinidad can be easily visited on a day-trip from Posadas (p218). There are others to visit not too far away in southern Brazil.

for its clean, quiet, comfortable rooms, great bathrooms, benevolent owners, and attached bar and internet café. The A-frame cabins out the back are great value for groups. The bar does simple tasty food; you'll never find it easier to be the best pool player in town, but the table football is a different story.

Hotel Portal del Sol (☎ 470005; www.portalsolhotel .com; Rivadavia 1115; dm/s/d AR$30/70/90; 🛱 🖳 🗐) Between the center and the ruins, this place is a fair bit better than it looks. The dorms are way overpriced, and the restaurant mediocre, but the rooms are rather attractive, with a contrast between the light linen and the dark wooden furniture. Guests can use the pool at the nearby Carpa Azul tent restaurant.

Don Valentín (☎ 03752-15-647961; Alberdi 444; mains AR$8-20; ⏱ 8am-5:30pm) Across from the entrance to the ruins, Don Valentín is a step up from the production-line operations serving tour groups along here. It has a shady terrace and cordial service, but doesn't stay open for dinner.

La Aldea (Los Jesuitas s/n; dishes AR$10-20; ⏱ 8am-midnight) Near the *artesanía* stalls at the ruins exit, this barn of a place has tables out the front, inside and on the rear deck. It serves excellent pizzas and *minutas* (snacks) and is one of the only eating options open late at night.

Getting There & Away

Fast buses on RN 12 stop at the arch on the main road, at the entrance to town, but plenty enter San Ignacio, stopping on Av Sarmiento in the center of town, by the church. Services between Posadas (AR$5, one hour) and Puerto Iguazú (AR$25, four to five hours) are frequent.

If you're not staying, the friendly kiosk next to the church, right where buses stop, will look after baggage for a couple of pesos.

IGUAZÚ FALLS

One of the planet's most awe-inspiring sights, the Iguazú Falls are simply astounding. A visit is a jaw-dropping, visceral experience, and the power and noise of the cascades live forever in the memory. An added benefit is the setting; the falls lie split between Brazil and Argentina in a large expanse of national park, much of it rainforest teeming with unique flora and fauna: there are thousands of species of insects, hundreds of species of birds and many mammals and reptiles.

The falls are easily reached from either side of the Argentine–Brazilian border, as well as from nearby Paraguay. Most visitors choose either to stay in Foz do Iguaçu, on the Brazilian side, or in Argentina's Puerto Iguazú. Both have a wide range of accommodation choices.

History & Environment

Álvar Núñez Cabeza de Vaca and his expedition were the first Europeans to view the

falls, in 1542. According to Guaraní tradition the falls originated when an Indian warrior named Caroba incurred the wrath of a forest god by escaping downriver in a canoe with a young girl, Naipur, with whom the god was infatuated. Enraged, the god caused the riverbed to collapse in front of the lovers, producing a line of precipitous falls over which Naipur fell and, at their base, turned into a rock. Caroba survived as a tree overlooking it.

Geologists have a more prosaic explanation. The Río Iguaçu's course takes it over a basaltic plateau that ends abruptly just short of the confluence with the Paraná. Where the lava flow stopped, thousands of cubic meters of water per second now plunge down as much as 80m into sedimentary terrain below. Before reaching the falls, the river divides into many channels with hidden reefs, rocks and islands separating the many visually distinctive cascades that together form the famous *cataratas* (waterfalls). In total, the falls stretch around for more than 2km.

Seeing the Falls

The Brazilian and Argentine sides offer different views and experiences of the falls. Go to both (perhaps to the Brazilian first) and hope for sun. The difference between a clear and an overcast day at the falls is vast, only in part because of the rainbows and butterflies that emerge when the sun is shining. Ideally you should allow for a multiple-day stay to have a better shot at optimal conditions.

THE OTHER FALLS

Iguazú's aren't the only spectacular falls in Misiones province; the remote and unusual **Saltos del Moconá** also live long in the memory. A geological fault in the bed of the Río Uruguay divides the river lengthwise, and water spills over the 10m shelf between the two sections, creating a waterfall some 2km long.

The falls are at the eastern edge of Misiones province roughly halfway between Posadas and Puerto Iguazú. From Posadas, several daily buses leave for El Soberbio (four hours); from here it's 73km to the falls, half paved.

There are several places to stay in El Soberbio for AR$20 to AR$30 per person, including **Hostal Del Centro** (☎ 03755-495133; cnr Rivadavia & San Martín) and **Hospedaje Messer** (☎ 03755-495191; Rivadavia 505).

More upmarket is the hilltop **Hostería Puesta del Sol** (☎ 03755-495161; www.hostpuestadelsol .com.ar; Suipacha s/n; s/d half-board AR$120/250; 🐷 🖵).

Several jungly lodges are closer to the falls. Accommodation in these places is in elegant rustic cabins; rates, except for Aldea Yaboty, include meals.

Aldea Yaboty (☎ 03755-15-553069; www.aldeayaboty.com; s/d AR$90/120, s/d in cabin AR$120/200)
Don Enrique Lodge (☎ 011-4790-7096; www.donenriquelodge.com.ar; s/d AR$300/460)
Posada la Bonita (☎ 03755-15-680380; www.posadalabonita.com.ar; s/d AR$270/420)
Posada La Misión (☎ 011-5199-0185; www.lodgelamision.com.ar; d AR$450)

The lodges organize trips to the falls and the various parks and reserves that protect the zone, as does friendly **Yaboti Jungle** (☎ 03755-495266; mocona4x4@yahoo.com.ar; Av Corrientes 481, El Soberbio), which charges AR$120 for a four-hour boat trip to the falls (AR$360 minimum). Operators in Posadas and Puerto Iguazú also arrange trips.

Most important: the falls aren't always visible; if the river is high then you're out of luck. Ring ahead to find out.

While the Argentine side – with its variety of trails and boat rides – offers many more opportunities to see individual falls close up, the Brazilian side yields the more panoramic views. You can easily make day trips to both sides of the falls whichever side of the border you choose to base yourself.

National Parks

The Brazilian and Argentine sides of the falls are both designated national parks; Parque Nacional do Iguaçu and Parque Nacional Iguazú respectively. High temperatures, humidity and rainfall encourage a diverse habitat, and the parks' rainforest contains more than 2000 identified plant species, countless insects, 400 species of birds and many mammals and reptiles.

Resembling the tropical Amazonian rainforest to the north, the forests of the falls region consist of multiple levels, the highest a closed canopy 30m high. Beneath the canopy are several additional levels of trees, plus a dense ground-level growth of shrubs and herbaceous plants. One of the most interesting is the guapoy (strangler fig), an epiphyte that uses a large tree for support until it finally asphyxiates its host.

Mammals and other wildlife are present but not easily seen in the parks, because many are either nocturnal or avoid humans – which is not difficult in the dense undergrowth. This is the case, for instance, with large cats such as the puma and jaguar. The largest mammal is the tapir, which is a distant relative of the horse, but most common is the coati, a relative of the raccoon. It is not unusual to see iguanas, and watch out for snakes.

Tropical bird species add a dash of color, with toucans and various species of parrot easily seen. The best time to see them is early morning along the forest trails.

Despite regular official denials, the heavy impact of so many visitors has clearly driven much of the wildlife further into the parks, so the more you explore, the more you'll see.

Dangers & Annoyances

The Río Iguaçu's currents are strong and swift; tourists have been swept downriver and drowned in the area of Isla San Martín. Of course, don't get too close to the falls proper.

The heat and humidity are often intense around the falls, and there's plenty of hungry insect life.

While you're very unlikely to see a jaguar, be aware that they are 'respect' beasts. Official jaguar tactics are: don't run, make yourself look big and speak loudly.

On both sides, you're almost certain to encounter coatis. Don't feed them; though these clownish omnivores seem tame, they become aggressive around food, and will bite and scratch. Both parks have a medical point in case of coati attack.

You are likely to get soaked, or at least very damp, from the spray at the falls, so keep your documents and camera protected in plastic bags.

PARQUE NACIONAL IGUAZÚ
☎ 03757

The **Argentine park** (☎ 491469; www.iguazuargentina .com; admission adult/child 6-12 yr AR$40/20, Mercosur AR$23, Argentines AR$14; ☼ 8am-6pm Apr-Sep, 7:30am-6:30pm Oct-Mar) has plenty to offer, and involves a fair amount of walking. The spread-out complex at the entrance has various amenities, including lockers, an ATM and a restaurant. There's also an **exhibition**, Ybyrá-retá, with a display on the park and Guaraní life essentially aimed at school groups. The complex ends at a station, where a train runs every half hour to the Cataratas station, where the waterfall walks begin, and to the Garganta del Diablo. You may prefer to walk: it's only 650m along the 'Sendero Verde' path to the Cataratas station, and a further 2.3km to the Garganta.

The train was a controversial project (despite announcements claiming that its construction caused minimal environmental impact) but, though birds and beasts flee from its noisy journey through the jungle, the vehicle traffic it has replaced was responsible for pollution and hundreds of road kill incidents every year. The decision to award the private company that built it rights to operate the visitor center and most of the amenities raised a few eyebrows.

There's more than enough here to detain you for a couple of days, and admission is reduced by 50% if you visit the park again the following day. You need to get your ticket stamped when leaving on the first day to get the discount.

Sights
Walking around is the best way to see the **falls**, with sets of paths offering different perspec-

tives over the cascades. While we normally wouldn't recommend such an early start, it really is worth getting here by 9am; the gangways are narrow and getting stuck in a conga line of tour groups in searing heat and humidity takes the edge off the experience.

Two circuits, the **Paseo Superior** (650m) and **Paseo Inferior** (1400m), provide most of the viewing opportunities via a series of trails, bridges and *pasarelas* (catwalks). The Paseo Superior is entirely level and gives good views of the tops of several cascades and across to more. The Paseo Inferior descends to the river (no wheelchair access), passing delightfully close to more falls on the way. At the bottom of the path a free launch makes the short crossing to **Isla Grande San Martín**, an island with a trail of its own that gives the closest look at several falls, including **Salto San Martín**, a huge, furious cauldron of water. It's possible to picnic and swim on the lee side of the island, but don't venture too far off the beach.

From Cataratas station, train it or walk the 2300m to the Garganta del Diablo stop, where an 1100m walkway across the placid Iguazú river leads to one of the planet's most spectacular sights, the **Garganta del Diablo** (Devil's Throat). The lookout platform is perched right over this amazingly powerful and concentrated torrent of water, a deafening cascade plunging to murky destination; the vapors soaking the viewer blur the base of the falls and rise in a smokelike plume that can often be seen several kilometers away. It's a place of majesty and awe, and should be left until the end of your visit.

Activities
Relatively few visitors venture beyond the immediate area of the falls to appreciate the park's forest scenery and wildlife, but it's well worth doing. On the falls trails you'll see large lizards, coatis and several species of birds, but you'll see much more on one of the few trails through the dense forest.

Along the road past the visitor center (you can also access it via a path from the Estación Central trailhead) is the entrance to the **Sendero Macuco** nature trail, which leads through dense forest to a nearly hidden waterfall, **Salto Arrechea**. The first 3km of the trail, to the top of the waterfall, is almost completely level, but a steep lateral drops to the base of the falls and beyond to the Río Iguaçu, about 650m in all. This part of the trail is muddy and slippery – watch your step and figure about 1½ hours each way from the trailhead. Early morning is best, with better opportunities to see wildlife, including toucans and bands of caí monkeys. Take insect repellent.

To get elsewhere in the park, hitch or hire a car to go out on RN 101 toward the village of **Bernardo de Irigoyen**. Few visitors explore this part of the park, and it is still nearly pristine forest.

Iguazú Jungle Explorer (☎ 421696; www.iguazujungle xplorer.com), with an office in the visitor center, is a well-run set-up which offers the following three excursions: a speedy inflatable boat ride to the bottom of several of the waterfalls, including a drenching under the San Martín torrent (AR$50, 15 minutes); a quiet dinghy ride down the upper Iguazú (AR$25, 30 minutes), and a one-hour trip combining a descent to the river in flatbed trucks along the Sendero Yacaratiá, and then a trip upriver through rapids to the falls (AR$100, one hour). Discounts are offered for combining any of these tours.

For five consecutive nights per month, **full moon walks** (☎ 491469; www.iguazuargentina.com; AR$80) visit the Garganta del Diablo. There are three departures nightly; the first one, at 8pm, offers the spectacle of the inflated rising moon; the last, at 9:30pm, sees the falls better illuminated. Don't expect to see wildlife. The price includes admission, and a cocktail and dinner afterwards. Extra bus departures from Puerto Iguazú cater for moonwalkers.

Sleeping & Eating

There's one hotel within the park. The numerous snack bars offer predictably overpriced snacks and drinks. The food is awful; bring a picnic or eat at one of the two restaurants, La Selva or El Fortín.

Sheraton International Iguazú (☎ 491800; www.sheraton.com/iguazu; r with forest/falls view AR$690/756; ✗ ☒ ☐ ☒) With a privileged position in the park itself and looking right up the river to the most spectacular section of the falls, the Sheraton backs it up with professional service and spacious rooms with balconies, though it looks a little tired in parts. You're paying for the view here, so you might as well upgrade to see the falls. Rooms are usually substantially cheaper booking online. Readers have been disappointed in the restaurant.

La Selva (☎ 491469; tenedor libre AR$45; ❥ 11am-5pm) During your visit, this restaurant will get talked-up so much you'll fear the worst, but

it's actually quite OK, with a decent buffet of hot and cold dishes, and all-you-can-eat *parrillada*. The information kiosks dotted around the complex sometimes give out vouchers offering a substantial discount.

El Fortín (☎ 491040; all-you-can-eat AR$30; ❥ 10am-5pm) Well located near the old hotel (now the park medical center), this offers a decent buffet spread with fairly mediocre *parrilla* choices. It's the closest acceptable lunch spot to the falls walkways. Doesn't appear on park maps.

Getting There & Away

The park is 20km southeast of Puerto Iguazú. From Puerto Iguazú's terminal, buses leave half-hourly for the park (AR$4, 40 minutes) between 6:40am and 7:40pm, with return trips between 7:20am and 8:20pm. The buses make flag stops at points along the highway. A cab from town to the park entrance is AR$40.

From Foz do Iguaçu tours to the Argentine park (US$50 to US$70) are overpriced but give you time to spend at the falls, without the hassle of waiting for bus connections (see p231).

PARQUE NACIONAL DO IGUAÇU (BRAZIL)

The **Brazilian park** (☎ 3521-4400; www.cataratas doiguacu.com.br; 7 years & older R$20.15, Brazilians R$12.65, ❥ 9am-7pm summer, 9am-5pm winter) is entered via an enormous visitor center, which has a snackbar, an ATM and big lockers, among other amenities. Parking here costs R$11.

Tickets can be purchased using Brazilian, Argentine and US currency and last admission is one hour before closing. Regional Mercosur-affiliated nationals (Argentines, Uruguayans, Paraguayans) can buy tickets for R$17.15. After buying tickets, you pass through to a new exhibition giving information (in Portuguese, English and Spanish) about the geology, history and biodiversity of the falls region. Behind the building, double-decker buses await to take you into the park proper. Keep your eyes peeled for animals.

The first stop is the **Trilha do Poço Preto** (☎ 3529-9626; www.macucoecoaventura.com.br; R$184), a 9km guided trek through the jungle on foot or by bike. The trail ends at Taquara Island, where you can kayak or take a boat cruise to Porto Canoas. You can also return via the Bananeiras Trail (below).

The second stop is for the two-hour **Macuco Safari** (☎ 3574-4244; www.macucosafari.com.br; R$156), which includes a 3km trailer ride through the jungle, a 600m walk to a small waterfall and then a boat ride up towards the falls. Don't confuse it with the Macuco trail on the Argentine side. Alight here too for the **Bananeiras Trail** (☎ 3529-9626; www.macucoecoaventura.com.br; R$86), a 2km walk passing lagoons and observing aquatic wildlife which ends at a jetty where you can take boat rides or silent 'floating' excursions in kayaks down to Porto Canoas. If you plan to do any of these, chat with one of the agents touting them around the park visitor center; they can get you a discount.

The third, and principal, stop is at the Hotel Tropical das Cataratas (see right). This is where the main waterfall observation trail starts. At the beginning of the trail is also **Cânion Iguaçu** (☎ 3529-6040; www.campodedesafios.com .br), an activity center offering rafting (R$80), abseiling (R$75), rock climbing (R$30) and a canopy tour (R$65).

From here you walk 1.5km down a paved **trail** with brilliant views of the falls on the Argentine side, the jungle and the river below. Every twist of the path reveals a more splendid view until the trail ends right under the majestic Salto Floriano, which will give you a healthy sprinkling of water via the wind it generates. A catwalk leads out to a platform with majestic vistas, with the Garganta del Diablo close at hand, and a perspective down the river in the other direction. If the water's high, it's unforgettable; a rainbow is visible in the spray on clear afternoons.

An elevator heads up to a viewing platform at the top of the falls at Porto Canoas, the last stop of the double-decker buses. Porto Canoas has a gift shop, a couple of snackbars (burgers R$4) and an excellent buffet restaurant (see right).

The local governor has been pushing to get a nightly sound-and-light show going at the falls, a move that has infuriated the Argentines and environmentalists. Hopefully it won't happen.

Activities

Just opposite the park entrance, **Helisul** (☎ 3529-7474; www.helisul.com) run 10-minute chopper jaunts at 450 meters over the Brazilian side of the falls. The environmental impact is debatable (the Argentines suspended their service for this reason), but it's undeniably exhilarating. There are open panels in the windows for photography. The ride costs US$70 per person; it's best done after you've visited the falls themselves. You can also charter the helicopter for a 35-minute trip that takes in the Itaipú dam and triple frontier. This costs US$700 for up to four.

Opposite Helisul, much-touted **Parque das Aves** (☎ 3529-8282; www.parquedasaves.com.br; admission R$18; 🕥 8:30am-6pm) is a large bosky bird park. While it's certainly overpriced, it does have a huge assortment of our feathered friends.

Sleeping & Eating

Hotel Tropical das Cataratas (☎ 3521-7000; www.hotel dascataratas.com.br; standard/superior/deluxe r US$235/260/295; 🕥 🖳 🖭) This elegant pinkish hotel, not as old as it looks, is right in the park and near the falls. It appeals enormously for its location, but the rooms are elegant and not much more; only a handful have views of the falls. The staff and facilities are, however, commendable. It's recently been bought up, so expect major improvements over the next few years. Don't miss climbing the belvedere for the view.

Porto Canoas (☎ 3521-4400; buffet R$30; 🕥 Tue-Sun 11:30am-4pm) After the falls, you (and your camera trigger finger) deserve a break. This spot is surprisingly good, with a long pleasant terrace overlooking the river just before it descends into maelstrom – a great spot for a beer – and a worthwhile buffet lunch with plenty of salads and tasty hot dishes.

Getting There & Around

'Parque Nacional' buses run from Foz do Iguaçu's urban bus terminal (you pay the fare entering the terminal) to the park entrance (R$2, 45 minutes) every 22 minutes between 6am and 7pm, and then every hour until midnight, making stops along Av Juscelino Kubitschek and Av das Cataratas.

A taxi from Foz to the park entrance costs around R$35.

To access the Brazilian park from Puerto Iguazú you can take a bus to Foz do Iguaçu's terminal and catch the Parque Nacional bus (also see p229) but, to save time, get off instead at Av das Cataratas, just beyond immigration on the Brazilian side of the bridge, and flag down the Parque Nacional bus there. If you're only planning to spend a day visiting the park, border formalities are minimal (see box p226).

PUERTO IGUAZÚ

☎ 03757 / pop 31,515

Little Puerto Iguazú sits at the confluence of the Ríos Paraná and Iguazú and looks across

ENTERING BRAZIL

If you're on a day trip, formalities are minimal. Argentine officials will stamp your passport as you leave the country, but Brazil usually unofficially tolerates day entry (even if you need a visa) without stamping you in.

If you are staying a while, or heading on into Brazil, you will need to get stamped in. Get off the bus at Brazilian immigration (then catch the next one on). Citizens of the USA, Australia, Canada and Japan, among others, will need a visa to officially enter Brazil. You can arrange one at the Brazilian consulate in Puerto Iguazú, or before you leave home.

to Brazil and Paraguay. It doesn't really feel like Argentina any more. There's no center and little feeling of community – everyone is here to see the falls or to make a buck out of them. Still, it's quiet, safe, has good transport connections, and has many excellent places to stay and eat.

Orientation

Some 300km northeast of Posadas via RN 12, Puerto Iguazú has an irregular city plan, but is small enough that you will find your way around easily. The main drag is the diagonal Av Victoria Aguirre, but most services are just north of this in a criss-cross of streets meeting at odd angles.

Information

Argecam (☎ 423085; Av Victoria Aguirre 1164) Changes money.
Banco de la Nación (Av Victoria Aguirre s/n) Has an ATM.
Hospital (☎ 420288; cnr Av Victoria Aguirre & Ushuaia)
Lavandería (P Moreno 211) Laundry.
Post office (San Martín 780)
Telecentro Internet (cnr Av Victoria Aguirre and Eppens; per hr AR$2) You guessed it: phone calls and internet.
Tourist office (☎ 420800; www.iguazuargentina.com; Av Victoria Aguirre 396; ⏰ 7am-9pm Mon-Fri, 8am-noon & 4-8pm Sat & Sun) Spare a thought for the staff here, who make do with hardly any brochures and no computer.

Sights

There's little to see in the town itself, but a kilometer west of the center along Av Tres

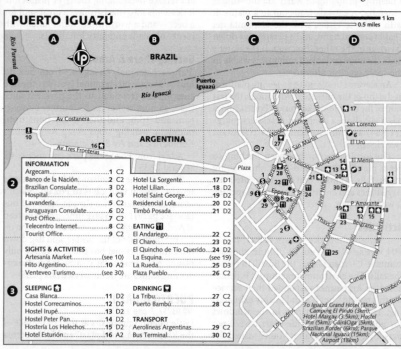

PUERTO IGUAZÚ

INFORMATION	
Argecam	1 C2
Banco de la Nación	2 C2
Brazilian Consulate	3 D2
Hospital	4 C3
Lavandería	5 D2
Paraguayan Consulate	6 D2
Post Office	7 C2
Telecentro Internet	8 C2
Tourist Office	9 C2

SIGHTS & ACTIVITIES	
Artesanía Market	(see 10)
Hito Argentino	10 A2
Venteveo Turismo	(see 30)

SLEEPING	
Casa Blanca	11 D2
Hostel Correcaminos	12 D2
Hostel Irupé	13 D2
Hostel Peter Pan	14 D2
Hostería Los Helechos	15 D2
Hotel Esturión	16 A2

Hotel La Sorgente	17 D1
Hotel Lilian	18 D2
Hotel Saint George	19 D2
Residencial Lola	20 D2
Timbó Posada	21 D2

EATING	
El Andariego	22 C2
El Charo	23 D2
El Quincho de Tío Querido	24 D2
La Esquina	(see 19)
La Rueda	25 D3
Plaza Pueblo	26 C2

DRINKING	
La Tribu	27 C2
Puerto Bambú	28 C2

TRANSPORT	
Aerolíneas Argentinas	29 C2
Bus Terminal	30 D2

To Iguazú Grand Hotel (3km);
Camping El Pindó (3km);
Hotel Margay (3.5km); Hostel
Inn (5km); CataraOpa (5km);
Brazilian Border (6km); Parque
Nacional Iguazú (15km);
Airport (18km)

THE RIDE OF A LIFETIME

If you think that the walkways give you a close-up view of Iguazú Falls, think again – you have actually missed out on a once-in-a-lifetime photo opportunity.

In the early days of Iguazú's popularity as a tourist attraction, you could hire a local with a rowboat who would take you right out to the edge of the falls and keep the boat there by rowing madly against the current while you and your friends took photos, spat and did all that other stuff you do at the edge of a waterfall.

But the inevitable has a way of happening, and so it was that one day in 1938 the rower found himself overpowered by the current, and the boat – with seven German tourists on board – went sliding over the edge. There were no survivors and these boat trips were immediately prohibited.

And so ends the history of a foolish but exhilarating sightseeing option.

Fronteras is the **Hito Argentino**, a small obelisk at the impressive confluence of the Ríos Paraná and Iguazú. From here you can see Brazil and Paraguay, with similar markers on their sides. A fairly desultory *artesanía* market is also here.

Five kilometers out of town on the way to the national park, **GüiráOga** (☎ 03757-15-465011; www.guiraoga.fundacionazara.org.ar; admission AR$30; ☼ 8:30am-6pm, last entry 4:30pm) is an animal hospital and center for rehabilitation of injured wildlife. They also carry out valuable research into the Iguazú forest environment, and have a breeding program for endangered species. You get driven around the park by one of the biologists and get to meet the creatures in a natural state. The visit takes about 80 minutes and is recommended.

Tours

Numerous local operators offer day tours to the Brazilian side of the falls (AR$50 to AR$110 depending on what's included), some taking in the Itaipú dam as well. **Venteveo Turismo** (☎ 424062; venteveoturismo@hotmail.com.ar) are one of many that have offices at the bus terminal, and have been recommended by readers.

Sleeping

There are many sleeping options for all budgets, including a string of resort-type hotels between town and the national park.

BUDGET

Hostel Correcaminos (☎ 420967; www.cchostel.com.ar; P Amarante 48; dm/d AR$20/60) You'll get an instant social life at this laid-back but upbeat hostel; there's a bar with drinks specials, regular *parrillas*, pool table and a boss who treats you like a friend rather than a client. The dorms

are fine and the private rooms (with bathroom) decent value; there's also a kitchen. 'Correcaminos' is the Road Runner.

Residencial Lola (☎ 423954; Av Córdoba 255, s/d AR$25/50) Plenty of price gouging goes on in Puerto Iguazú but it stops at Lola's front door. This cheap, cheerily run spot is very close to the bus station and features compact, clean rooms with bathroom for a pittance.

our pick **Hostel Peter Pan** (☎ 423616; www.peterpanhostel.com; Av Córdoba 267; dm/d AR$25/70; ⬛ 🖥 ⬛) In days past it may have seemed hostelling was about sleeping on beds of nails and scrubbing pots after a cold shower at six in the morning. Nothing like this, which has sparklingly clean and comfortable rooms and dorms surrounding a sizable swimming pool in a patio festooned with hammocks and swing seats. What is the world coming to? Happily, it's not even 'second star to the right and straight on till morning' but a block downhill from the bus station.

Hostel Inn (☎ 421823; www.hostel-inn.com; RN 12, Km 5; dm/r AR$33/130; ⬛ 🖥 ⬛) This is more resort than hostel, and you get a lot for 33 pesos (29 for HI-members), as the spotless place is set in expansive grounds, has a big pool, and all the backpacker-friendly facilities you can imagine. The dorms are commodious and air-conditioned. Most readers love it to bits; some complain about CHS (cool hostel syndrome); you'll know whether it's for you or not. It's 5km into town, but the falls buses (AR$1 to center) will stop right outside.

Also recommended:

Hostel Irupé (☎ 03757-15-535134; Misiones 80; dm/s/d AR$30/50/70) Good value for private rooms. Go for rooms at the back, which have more light.

Camping El Pindó (☎ 421795; elpindo@yahoo.com.ar; per tent AR$10 plus per person AR$8; ⬛) At Km 3.5 of RN 12 on the southern edge of town, easily reached on the bus.

MIDRANGE

Timbó Posada (☎ 422698; www.timboiguazu.com.ar; Av Misiones 147; s/d without bathroom AR$58/78, d with bathroom AR$140; ❄ 🖳) Cute and run with a warm smile, this place is tucked behind a shop of the same name in a central location. Rooms are on the dark side, but pretty cheery for all that. Breakfast is served outdoors. Dorm beds are also sometimes available (AR$31).

Hotel Lilian (☎ 420968; hotellilian@yahoo.com.ar; Fray Luis Beltrán 183; s/d AR$95/120; ❄ 🖳) Run by a hospitable family, this likable place offers plenty of value, with bright and cheerful rooms around a patio. The superior rooms only cost around AR$15 more, but have a balcony and heaps of natural light. All the bathrooms are spacious and spotless.

Hotel Margay (☎ 421340; www.hotelmargay.com.ar; RN 12, Km 3.5; s/d with half board AR$118/155; ❄ ❄) The Margay's low-slung hacienda vibe stops at the lobby, but the rooms are modern, spacious and comfortable. Big firm beds, mini-fridges, and a separate room for toilet and shower are added bonuses.

Hotel La Sorgente (☎ 424252; www.lasorgentehotel .com; Av Córdoba 454; s/d AR$140/165; ❄ 🖳 ❄) Book ahead for a real treat at this stylish but homey posada. Set around a verdant garden, life couldn't be easier here; if you can't face the long walk around the pool, take the bridge across it. The breakfast gets the seal of approval too.

Hotel Saint George (☎ 420633; www.hotelsaint george.com; Av Córdoba 148; s/d AR$239/298; ❄ 🖳 ❄) The Saint George has been around for years and is reliable for comfort, service and organization. It's right across from the bus terminal (some bus noise) and offers excellent facilities, including a garden and new spa complex. Superior rooms (s/d AR$315/350) are significantly larger, with two big double beds. Fifteen pesos more gets you a buffet dinner.

Also recommended:

Hostería Los Helechos (☎ 420338; www.hosteria loshelechos.com.ar; P Amarante 76; s/d AR$75/90; ❄ 🖳 ❄) Darkish rooms but good pool and garden. Air-con costs a little more. Dinner available.

Casa Blanca (☎ 421320; www.casablancaiguazu .com.ar; Av Guaraní 121; s/d AR$98/108; ❄ 🖳) A little somber but spotless and welcoming. Pool ready by the time you read this.

TOP END

For a luxury option inside the Parque Nacional Iguazú there's the Sheraton International Iguazú (p224).

Hotel Esturión (☎ 420100; www.hotelesturion.com; Av Tres Fronteras 650; r AR$315-385; ❄ 🖳 ❄) Set in spacious landscaped grounds near the triple frontier lookout, the Esturión has a great pool area, public areas, and tennis courts. The rooms feel tired, but some are better than others. Service is top class. They're building a cabaña annexe opposite.

Iguazú Grand Hotel (☎ 498050; www.casinoiguazu .com; RN 12, Km 1640; r from AR$1334; ❄ 🖳 ❄) Don't let the tacky ads for the attached casino put you off this classy place just short of the bridge across to Brazil. It's comfortably the most upmarket hotel on either side of the falls, with excellent service, pretty grounds and the town's best restaurant.

Eating

Plaza Pueblo (☎ 424000; Av Victoria Aguirre s/n; snacks AR$5-10; ⏱ 10am-10pm) This courtyard terrace is bang in the heart of town but, set back from the road, feels peaceful. They serve beer, pizza, and excellent burgers and lomitos, all with a smile.

El Andariego (☎ 03757-15-545963; Moreno 229; tenedor libre AR$27; ⏱ lunch & dinner) This impresses for the sheer quantity of food that is brought to your table. Some seven plates of empanada and salad are placed before you, and then a standard but decent *parrillada* is brought out. Outdoor tables but overpriced wine.

El Charo (☎ 421529; Av Córdoba 106; mains AR$8-22; ⏱ lunch & dinner) Another great place to sit and watch the world go by, El Charo has the usual range of *parrilla* offerings, with outdoor seating and some good-value set meals.

El Quincho de Tío Querido (☎ 420151; Bompland 110; mains AR$15-32; ⏱ dinner) Lively with the buzz of both tourists and locals, this popular *parrilla* has the usual grill favorites (*parrillada* for two: AR$43) as well as giant 'baby beef' steaks and a range of interesting specials with occasionally comic translations (we enjoyed 'loin with blow, camp bacon'). There's live music and limited outdoor seating. The wine list is pricy.

La Esquina (☎ 420633; cnr Av Córdoba & P Amarante; mains AR$17-38, buffet AR$35; ⏱ lunch & dinner) With a balmy, softly-lit terrace and solicitous service, La Esquina is a romantic dinner option that backs up the atmosphere with cracking food. There are some unusual combinations of flavors here with excellent results. Try the papaya, carrot, orange and palm-heart salad to kick things off.

our pick **La Rueda** (☎ 422531; Av Córdoba 28; mains AR$22-44; ⏲ lunch & dinner) A mainstay of upmarket eating in Puerto Iguazú, this culinary heavyweight still packs plenty of punch. The salads are imaginative and delicious, as are the river fish (dorado, pacú, and surubí) creations. The homemade pasta is cheaper but doesn't disappoint.

Drinking & Entertainment

Thanks to ever-increasing tourism, Puerto Iguazú's nightlife is livelier than it once was. The action centers around Avenida Brasil, where at **La Tribu** (Av Brasil 149) the drinks are expensive but the terrace appealing. **Puerto Bambú** (cnr P Moreno & Av Brasil) is a more down-to-earth place, with a great wooden bar to sit at outside and marvel at the traffic chaos on the six-way intersection.

Getting There & Away

Aerolíneas Argentinas (☎ 420168; Av Victoria Aguirre 295) flies from Iguazú six times daily to Buenos Aires (AR$627). **LAN** (☎ 424296) flies the route (AR$353) four times daily and five times more reliably.

The **bus terminal** (☎ 420854; cnr Avs Córdoba & Misiones) has departures for all over the country. The following are a sample of fares available; competition keeps them low on the popular routes.

Destination	Cost (AR$)	Duration (hr)
Buenos Aires	109	18
Córdoba	158	23
Corrientes	68	9
Paraná	116	15
Posadas	30	5
Resistencia	71	10
San Ignacio	25	4
Santa Fe	96	13

There are international services, as well as Brazilian domestic services, across the border in Foz do Iguaçu.

Getting Around

An Aerolíneas Argentinas bus leaves from the airline's office two hours before the plane's departure and does hotel pickups. A *remise* costs AR$30.

Frequent buses cross to Foz do Iguaçu, Brazil (AR$2 to AR$3/R$2 to R$3, 35 minutes), and to Ciudad del Este, Paraguay (AR$2/R$2/G5000, one hour), from the local side of the terminal. All will stop near the roundabout at the edge of town.

Groups of three or more wanting to see both sides of the falls (and the Itaipú dam) may find a taxi or *remise* a good idea; figure on it costing up to AR$250 for a full day of sightseeing. The tourist office may be able to arrange such trips for less. A taxi to Foz do Iguaçu costs around AR$50.

For information on entering Brazil see p226.

FOZ DO IGUAÇU (BRAZIL)

☎ 045 / pop 308,900

Hilly Foz is the main base for the Brazilian side of the falls, and also gives you a good chance to get a feel for a Brazilian town. It's much bigger and more cosmopolitan than Puerto Iguazú, and has a keep-it-real feel that its Argentine counterpart lacks. On the downside, it's noisier, more chaotic and has more crime. It's not a pretty place, but there's something appealing about it nonetheless.

In the '70s the Itaipú hydroelectric project led to the city's population exploding from 34,000, and commercial opportunities across the river in Ciudad del Este attracted many new ethnic communities. Today Foz is home to several thousand Lebanese, and smaller communities of Japanese and Koreans.

Orientation

Foz do Iguaçu is at the confluence of Río Iguaçu and Río Paraná; the Ponte Tancredo Neves links the city to Puerto Iguazú, Argentina, across the Río Iguaçu, while the Ponte da Amizade connects it to Ciudad del Este, Paraguay, across the Paraná. Fifteen kilometers upstream is Itaipú, the world's largest operating hydroelectric project.

Foz do Iguaçu's compact, hilly center has a fairly regular grid. Avenida/Rodovia das Cataratas leads 20km to the falls, passing the turnoff for the Argentine border on the way. BR 277 leads west to Ciudad del Este and northeast to Curitiba and beyond. The main downtown thoroughfare is Av Juscelino Kubitschek, often referred to simply as 'JK' (zho-ta-*ka*). Parallel to it is more pleasant Avenida Brasil, the main commercial street.

Information

Hotels and restaurants in town accept dollars, Paraguayan guaraníes and Argentine

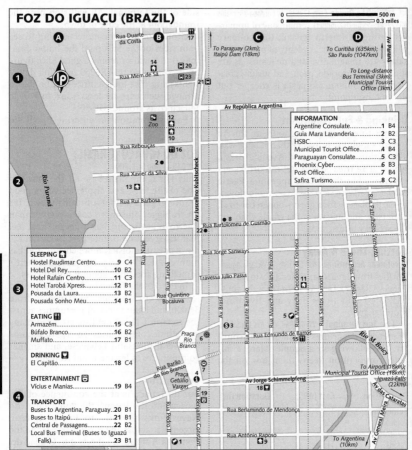

FOZ DO IGUAÇU (BRAZIL)

pesos, but it's always cheaper to pay in Brazilian reais.

Guia Mara Lavanderia (☎ 3523-9641; Rua Tarobá 834) Laundry.

HSBC (Av Brasil 1131) One of several banks with an ATM around this part.

Municipal tourist office (☎ 3521-1455; www .iguassu.tur.br; Praça Getúlio Vargas; ☼ 7am-10pm) Gives out a useful map and info sheet. Helpful. Also booths at the airport (☼ noon until the last plane) and long-distance bus terminal (☎ 3522-2590; ☼ 7am-6pm)

Phoenix Cyber (Rua Barão do Rio Branco 616; per hr R$2) One of many internet places.

Post office (cnr Juscelino Kubitschek & Rua Barão doRio Branco)

Safira Turismo (☎ 3523-9966; Av Brasil 567) Changes traveler's checks (6% commission) and cash.

Teletur (☎ 0800-451516; ☼ 7am-11pm) Maintains a tollfree information service with English-speaking operators.

Dangers & Annoyances

Don't make your way down to the Río Paraná; it's a sketchy neighborhood around the favela down there. Muggings of tourists are not unknown in Foz, so travel by taxi late at night.

Sights

With a capacity of 14 million kilowatts, the binational **Itaipú Dam** (Usina Hidrelétrica Itaipú) is still, for now, the largest hydroelectric project in the world. A controversial project, it plunged Brazil way into debt and necessitated large-scale destruction of rainforest and the displacement of 10,000 people. But it cleanly supplies nearly all of Paraguay's energy needs, and 25 percent of Brazil's.

The structure is highly impressive; at some 8km long and 200m high, it is a memorable sight. The **Centro de Recepção de Visitantes** (☎ 524-2533; www.itaipu.gov.br; Tancredo Neves 6702) is located 10km north of Foz. Regular tours (R$15) run daily at 8am, 9am, 10am, 2pm, 3pm and 3:30pm; more detailed ones (R$30) leave daily at 8am, 8:30am, 9:30am, 10am, 2pm, 2:30pm, 3:30pm and 4pm.

The bus stops 600m short of the visitor center, outside the **Ecomuseu** (☎ 520-5817; Tancredo Neves 600; ⏱ 8:30-11:30am & 2-5:30pm Tue-Sat, 2-5pm Sun), which is worth a look if you have time.

Across Av Juscelino Kubitschek from Foz's downtown local bus terminal, Conjunto C buses (R$2) run north every 10 minutes from 5:30am until 11pm. It's better to catch the bus on the street rather than from inside the terminal as the bus makes a long circuit of the city after leaving the terminal before passing by it again.

Tours

There are numerous travel agencies in Foz, and most hotels also have a tour desk. All can book you trips to either side of the falls, visits to Itaipú dam, walks and boat rides.

Sleeping

Hotels and pousadas in Foz will substantially lower their prices from those listed if they're not full. Ask!

Hostel Paudimar Centro (☎ 3028-5503; www .paudimarfalls.com.br; Rua Antônio Raposo 820; dm/r R$21/40; ❄ 🖳 🖭) This is an excellent HI hostel at the southern end of town. It's got bags of facilities, helpful staff and a lively atmosphere. You can also camp here. There's another branch in big grounds off the road to the falls, 13km from town.

Pousada da Laura (☎ 3572-3374; Rua Naipi 671; r per person R$25) This budget stalwart couldn't be more relaxed or welcoming. There's no luxury, but the clean, quiet, bright rooms with bathroom, tasty breakfast, and delightful people give it an appeal far beyond what you expect at first glance.

Pousada Sonho Meu (☎ 3573-5764; www.sonhomeu foz.com.br; Rua Mem de Sá 262; s/d R$80/120; ❄ 🖳 🖭) What from the outside looks like an administrative building becomes a delightful little oasis barely 50m from the local bus terminal. Guests have use of a kitchen and pool table, and are made to feel exceedingly welcome. Rooms are artistically decorated with bamboo. Rates almost halve out of season.

Hotel Del Rey (☎ 3523-2027; www.hoteldelreyfoz.com .br; Rua Tarobá 1020; s/d R$110/145; ❄ 🖳 🖭) A recent facelift has upgraded this friendly, spotless, and convenient hotel. The rooms are spacious and comfortable, facilities are excellent and the breakfast buffet is huge.

Hotel Tarobá Xpress (☎ 2102-7700; www.hoteltaroba .com.br; Rua Tarobá 1048; s/d R$110/145; ❄ 🖳 🖭) You'll likely need to book for this popular place handy for the bus terminal. Value is high here considering the facilities and professional staff; the tiled rooms are bright and spacious and all have mini-fridges and cable. There's also a sauna and small gym. Breakfast is excellent.

our pick Hotel Rafain Centro (☎ 3521-3500; www .rafaincentro.com.br; Rua Marechal Deodoro da Fonseca 984; s/d R$179/210; ❄ 🖳 🖭) Much more appealing than some of the hulking megahotels around town, the Rafain is a cracking four-star place with plenty of style, artistic detail and top-notch staff. Rooms have large balconies and fine facilities. Prices can come down substantially.

Eating

It's easy to eat cheap. Many places will do you a soft drink and *salgado* (baked or fried snack) for as little as R$2, and there are cheap local places where a buffet lunch costs around R$5 to R$8. Thanks to the Lebanese community, there are dozens of shwarma (kebab) places (R$4).

Muffato (☎ 2102-1800; Av Juscelino Kubitscheck 1565; per kg R$9; ⏱ 8:30am-10pm) Want to eat where the locals eat? Trust us on this one. Inside a hideous hypermarket near the bus station is a place with little atmosphere but one that serves a very typical, very tasty and cheap Brazilian pay-by-weight (the food, not you) buffet.

Armazém (☎ 3572-0007; www.armazemtrapiche.com .br; Rua Edmundo de Barros 446; mains R$15-30; ⏱ dinner) A block off Schimmelpfeng, this well-frequented restaurant serves top-shelf Brazilian food. As well as various chicken and beef dishes (all huge and just about enough for two) with a variety of tasty sauces, they offer more offbeat dishes such as wild boar, ostrich and caiman. There's a terrace outside and weekend live music.

Búfalo Branco (☎ 3523-9744; cnr Ruas Tarobá & Rebouças; tenedor libre R$42; ⏱ noon-11:30pm) This spacious Foz classic continues to draw locals and tourists alike for its classy *rodízio*, which features delicious roast meats, including excellent beef, as well as more unusual choices like chicken hearts and bull balls. The salad bar is truly excellent, and includes tasty Lebanese morsels and sushi rolls. There's a good choice of Brazilian wines.

Drinking & Entertainment

Make sure you have the classic Brazil experience: an ice-cold bottle of Skol in a plastic insulator served in a no-frills local bar with red plastic seats. Unbeatable. For a healthier tipple, the many juice bars give you the chance to try exotic fruits like acerola, açaí or cupuaçu. Nightlife centers around Av Jorge Schimmelpfeng a couple of blocks east of the tourist office. A buzzy and friendly staple around here is **El Capitão** (☎ 3572-1512; Av Jorge Schimmelpfeng s/n; pizzas R$20), which has a big terrace, well-poured *chopp*, and a menu of pizza and other food.

Vícius e Manias (☎ 523-9161; Rua Benjamin Constant 107; ⏰ 10pm–5am Thu–Sun) Popular central *discoteca* with reasonably priced drinks. There's no cover, but a R$5 minimum consumption, which is only one drink.

Getting There & Away

There are daily flights to Rio de Janeiro, Curitiba and São Paulo operated by **Gol** (www .voegol.com.br) and **TAM** (www.tam.com.br).

Long-distance bus destinations served daily from Foz include Curitiba (R$80, 10 hours), São Paulo (R$123, 17 hours) and Rio de Janeiro (R$185, 21 hours). You can buy tickets with a small surcharge at many central travel agencies, including **Central de Passagens** (☎ 3523-4700; www.centraldepassagens.com; Av Juscelino Kubitschek 526).

Getting Around

For the airport or falls, catch the 'Aeroporto/ Parque Nacional' bus from the local bus terminal or one of the stops along Av Juscelino Kubitschek; the trip takes 30 minutes and costs R$2, paid as you enter the terminal. A taxi costs about R$30.

Long-distance buses arrive and depart from the **bus terminal** (rodoviária; ☎ 3522-3336; Costa e Silva), 5km northeast of downtown. To get downtown, cab it for R$10 or walk downhill to the bus stop and catch any 'Centro' bus (R$2).

Buses to Puerto Iguazú (R$2 to R$3) run along Rua Mem de Sá alongside the local bus

terminal half-hourly from 8am until 8pm; they stop along Juscelino Kubitschek. Buses for Ciudad del Este, Paraguay (R$2), run every 15 minutes (half-hourly on Sundays); catch them on JK opposite the local bus terminal. The bridge can back up badly due to Paraguayan customs checks. Avoid sitting opposite the rear doors, as ne'er-do-wells on the bridge make a sport of tossing things through the doors at passengers.

THE GRAN CHACO

The Gran Chaco is a vast alluvial lowland, stretching north from the northern edges of Santa Fe and Córdoba provinces, across the entire provinces of Chaco and Formosa, and into western Paraguay, eastern Bolivia and along the southwestern edge of Brazil. It reaches west through most of Santiago del Estero province, drying up as it goes, and skirts the southeastern edge of Salta province. The western side, known as the Chaco Seco (Dry Chaco), has been deemed the Impenetrable, due to its severe lack of water across an endless plain of nearly impassable thorn scrub.

In the Chaco Húmedo (Wet Chaco), to the east, the gallery forests, marshes and palm savannas of Parque Nacional Chaco, as well as the subtropical marshlands of Parque Nacional Río Pilcomayo offer excellent birding opportunities. These areas are best visited in the cooler, drier months of April through November.

Resistencia, with a unique commitment to sculpture, is the most interesting city out here.

Crossing the Chaco from Formosa to Salta along the northern RN 81 is brutal and can take nearly two days; RN 16 from Resistencia is much faster.

History

In colonial times, Europeans avoided the hot, desolate Chaco, whose few hunter-gatherer peoples resisted colonization and were not numerous enough to justify their pacification for *encomiendas* (the colonial labor system). Today, about 85,000 Guaycurú (Toba, Mocoví) and Mataco peoples remain in the region.

Early Spanish settlements were soon abandoned after indigenous resistance. Later, Jesuit missionaries had some success, but the order's expulsion in 1767 again delayed European settlement.

INDIGENOUS GROUPS OF THE GRAN CHACO   Danny Palmerlee

One word inevitably arises alongside any discussion of the Toba: *olvidado* (forgotten). With nearly 70,000 members, the Toba of Argentina's Gran Chaco make up Argentina's second largest indigenous group. In 2008, amidst the country's applauded economic comeback, few Argentines had any idea some Toba were actually dying of starvation. They're not the only ones.

As a traveler, it's easy to zip through the sun-scorched Chaco without ever noticing the presence of *indígenas* (indigenous people), except, perhaps, for the crafts sold at government-sponsored stores or along the roadside. In Resistencia, the Toba live in *barrios* (neighborhoods) that are separated from the rest of the city. And those who don't live in the city either live in towns that travelers rarely visit (such as Juan José Castelli or Quitilipi) or deep within the Argentine Impenetrable, in settlements reached only by dirt roads that are impossible to navigate if you don't know the way. If you do know the way (or you go with someone who does), you'll find Toba *asentamientos* (settlements) that are unlike anything else in Argentina. People live in extreme poverty (although there's always a church) and, except for the occasional government-built health center, nearly all buildings are made of adobe, with dirt floors and thatched roofs.

The Toba refer to themselves as Komlek (or Qom-lik) and speak a dialect of the Guaycurú linguistic group, known locally as Qom. They are the most visible of the Chaco's indigenous groups and have a rich musical tradition (The Coro Toba Chelaalapi, a Toba choir founded in 1962, recently received Unesco World Heritage designation). Along with basket weaving and primitive ceramics, the Toba are known for their version of the fiddle, which they make out of a gas can.

The Gran Chaco's second most numerous indigenous group is the Wichí, with a population of over 40,000. Because the Wichí remain extremely isolated (they live nearly 700km from Resistencia, in the far northwest of Chaco province and in Formosa and Salta provinces) they are the most traditional of its groups. They still obtain much of their food through hunting, gathering and fishing. The Wichí are known for their wild honey and for their beautiful *yica* bags, which they weave with fibers from the chaguar plant, a bromeliad native to the arid regions of the Chaco. Like the Toba, most Wichí live in simple adobe huts. Due to the Wichí's isolation and self sufficiency, they were some of the only Argentines unaffected by the economic crash of 2001.

The Mocoví are the Gran Chaco's third largest indigenous group, with a population of nearly 16,000, concentrated primarily in southern Chaco province and Santa Fe province. Like the Toba, the Mocoví speak a dialect of the Guaycurú linguistic group. Until the arrival of Europeans, the Mocoví sustained themselves primarily through hunting and gathering, but today they rely mostly on farming and seasonal work. They are famous for their burnished pottery, which is the most developed of the Chaco's indigenous pottery.

For more information on the Toba, Wichí or Mocoví, stop by Resistencia's Centro Cultural Leopoldo Marechal (see p237), which has crafts exhibits sponsored by the Fundación Chaco Artesanal and helpful staff. The center is particularly worth a visit for the Toba fiddles and the Mocoví ceramics. To journey into the Argentine Impenetrable to visit the Toba or Wichí, contact Carlos Aníbal Schumann, an excellent guide based in Juan José Castelli, or Tantanacuy (see boxed text, p239, for details).

In the mid-19th century, woodcutters from Corrientes entered the region's forests to exploit the valuable hardwood quebracho, whose name literally means 'axe breaker.' This eventually opened the region to agricultural expansion, which has primarily taken the form of cotton and cattle production. Many new settlers came from Central Europe from the 1930s on.

Deforestation continues apace in the Chaco, with vast areas being cleared to plant soya, of which Argentina is now one of the world's major producers. This has impacted heavily on Toba tribes, whose traditional environment is being destroyed.

RESISTENCIA

☎ 03722 / pop 359,590

Poised on the edge of the barely populated wilderness of the Chaco (of which province it's the capital), baking-hot Resistencia isn't the most likely candidate for the garland of

NORTHEAST ARGENTINA

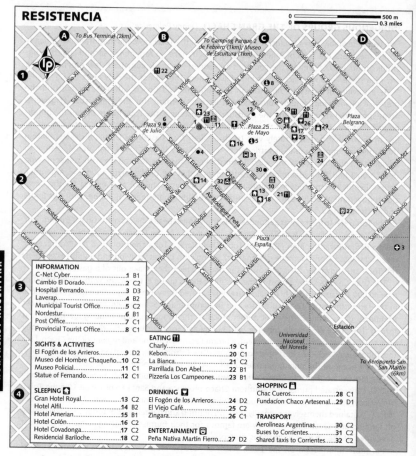

RESISTENCIA

INFORMATION
C-Net Cyber	1 B1
Cambio El Dorado	2 C2
Hospital Perrando	3 D3
Laverap	4 B2
Municipal Tourist Office	5 C2
Nordestur	6 B1
Post Office	7 C1
Provincial Tourist Office	8 C1

SIGHTS & ACTIVITIES
El Fogón de los Arrieros	9 D2
Museo del Hombre Chaqueño	10 C2
Museo Policial	11 C1
Statue of Fernando	12 C1

SLEEPING
Gran Hotel Royal	13 C2
Hotel Alfil	14 B2
Hotel Amerian	15 B1
Hotel Colón	16 C2
Hotel Covadonga	17 C2
Residencial Bariloche	18 C2

EATING
Charly	19 C1
Kebon	20 C1
La Bianca	21 C2
Parrillada Don Abel	22 B1
Pizzería Los Campeones	23 B1

DRINKING
El Fogón de los Arrieros	24 D2
El Viejo Café	25 C2
Zingara	26 C1

ENTERTAINMENT
Peña Nativa Martín Fierro	27 D2

SHOPPING
Chac Cueros	28 C1
Fundación Chaco Artesenal	29 D1

TRANSPORT
Aerolíneas Argentinas	30 C2
Buses to Corrientes	31 C2
Shared taxis to Corrientes	32 C2

artistic center of northern Argentina. Yet it has strong claims to that title; its streets are studded with sculpture – half a thousand by the time you read this – and there's a strong boho-cultural streak that represents a complete contrast to the tough cattle-and-dust solitudes that characterize the province.

First settled in 1750, Resistencia grew rapidly with the development of the tannin industry and subsequent agricultural progress. It acquired its name after successful resistance against numerous indigenous attacks throughout the 19th century.

Orientation
Enormous Plaza 25 de Mayo is the focus of the city center. It has fountains and numerous sculptures, and is planted with quebracho, ceibo, lapacho and other native trees.

Street names change at the plaza. Av Sarmiento is the main access route from RN 16, which leads east to Corrientes, and west to Roque Sáenz Peña and beyond. Av 25 de Mayo leads northwest from the plaza to RN 11, which goes north to Formosa and the Paraguayan border.

Information
There are several ATMs around Plaza 25 de Mayo.

C-Net Cyber (cnr Perón & Necochea; per hr AR$1.20) Fastish internet and phone calls.

Cambio El Dorado (Jose María Paz 36; ☼ Mon-Fri) Changes traveler's checks.

Hospital Perrando (☎ 452583; Av 9 de Julio 1099)
Laverap (☎ 424223; Vedia 23) Laundry.
Municipal tourist office (☎ 458289; www.resist encia.gov.ar; Plaza 25 de Mayo; ☺ 7am-1pm & 2-8pm Mon-Fri, 7am-1pm & 3:30-8pm Sat, 5-9pm Sun) In a kiosk on the southern side of the plaza. Helpful and knowledge-able staff, with good bilingual city information.
Nordestur (☎ 433429; Donovan 352) Helpful travel agent and tour operator.
Post office (Plaza 25 de Mayo at Av Sarmiento & Yrigoyen)
Provincial tourist office (☎ 423547; www.chaco.gov .ar/turismo; Santa Fe 178; ☺ 6.30am-8:30pm Mon-Fri, 8am-1pm & 2-7pm Sat & Sun) Good info about the Chaco.

Sights
SCULPTURES
At last count, there were 462 sculptures around the city, a number that is set to increase with every Bienal (see right). The streets are packed with them, especially around the plaza and north up Av Sarmiento. Calle Perón/Arturo Illia, a block south of the plaza, is also well endowed. Every Bienal, a brochure is printed with a sculpture walking tour around the city. The most likely place to get hold of the latest one is at the **Museo de Escultura** (☎ 436694; www .bienaldelchaco.com; admission free; ☺ 8am-noon & 3-8pm Mon-Sat) an open-air workshop on the north side of Parque 2 de Febrero. Several of the most impressive pieces are on display here, and this is where, during the Bienal, and quite frequently at other times, you can catch sculp-tors at work.

EL FOGÓN DE LOS ARRIEROS
Founded in 1942, this is a cultural center, art gallery and bar that for decades has been the driving force behind Resistencia's artis-tic commitment and progressive displays of public art. Still the keystone of the region's art community, it is now famous for its eclec-tic collection of art objects from around the Chaco and Argentina. The **museum** (☎ 426418; Brown 350; admission AR$5; ☺ 8am-noon Mon-Sat) also features the wood carvings of local artist and cultural activist Juan de Dios Mena.

OTHER MUSEUMS
The odd **Museo Policial** (☎ 421551; Roca 233; admission AR$3; ☺ 8am-noon & 5-9pm Mon-Fri summer, 8am-noon & 4-8pm Mon-Fri winter), the police museum, features grisly photos of auto accidents, tales of crimes of passion, and tedious drug-war rhetoric. It redeems itself with absorbing accounts of *cuatrerismo* (cattle rustling, still widespread

in the province) and banditry, including the tale of two 1960s' outlaws who, after killing a policeman, lived for five years on the run, helped by the Chaco's rural poor. Officers accompany visitors on guided tours.

The **Museo del Hombre Chaqueño** (Museum of Chaco Man; ☎ 426112; JB Justo 150; admission free; ☺ 9am-noon Mon-Sat) had just moved at the time of research and wasn't yet open, but focuses on the colonization of the Chaco and provides information and exhibits on the provincial indigenous cultures.

Festivals & Events
During the third week of July in even years, the **Bienal de Escultura** (www.bienaldelchaco.com) brings 10 renowned Argentine and inter-national sculptors to Resistencia. Arranging themselves around the fountain at the open-air museum in Parque 2 de Febrero, they have seven days to complete a sculpture under the public gaze. The medium changes every time, and there's a parallel competi-tion for students. The 2008 Bienal hoped to produce Resistencia's 500th sculpture.

Sleeping
Resistencia isn't over-endowed with ac-commodation choices, particularly in the budget sector.

Camping Parque 2 de Febrero (☎ 458276; Av Avalos 1100; sites AR$7) This well-staffed campground has good facilities, including shade, but can get crowded and noisy in high season – not least because of the dance clubs across the road. Bus 9 will get you there from the north side of the plaza.

Hotel Alfil (☎ 420882; Santa María de Oro 495; s/d AR$35/50; ☒) Situated a few blocks south of the plaza, the Alfil is a reasonable budget choice. The rooms are dark, and you have to pay AR$10 extra if you want air-con, but it's clean and quiet.

Residencial Bariloche (☎ 421412; Obligado 239; r AR$50; ☒) A good deal for two or more travel-ers, this simple but do-able place has quite reasonable rooms for a low price within easy striking distance of the plaza.

Hotel Colón (☎ 422861; hotelcolon@gigared.com; Santa María de Oro 143; s/d AR$71/93, apt AR$121; ☒ ▣) Art Deco fans mustn't miss this 1920s classic, a few steps south of the plaza. It's an amazingly large and characterful building with some en-ticingly curious period features. Rooms show

NORTHEAST ARGENTINA

A TOWN'S BEST FRIEND

Stray dogs wandering the streets of South American towns sometimes inspire fear, even outright panic. Not in Resistencia. In the late 1950s and early '60s, a stray dog inspired the love of the entire town, and Víctor Marchese's statue on Calle Mitre, in front of the Casa de Gobierno, immortalizes him.

His name was Fernando. As the story goes, he wandered the streets and slept in doorways and finally befriended a bank manager, who allowed Fernando to join him for breakfast every morning in his office. Before long, Fernando was the delight of downtown, inspiring people's daydreams with his daily, carefree adventures in the Plaza 25 de Mayo. In a town devoted to the arts, Fernando was bohemianism in fur, and was a welcome regular at El Fogón de los Arrieros. When Fernando died in 1963, the municipal band played a funeral march and people across town shut their shades in respect. He is buried at El Fogón de los Arrieros, where another sculpture by Marchese marks his grave.

---

their age, but the refurbished apartments are very spick and span. Rooms without TV are 10 pesos cheaper.

Hotel Covadonga (☎ 444444; www.hotelcovadonga .com.ar; Güemes 200; s/d AR$130/150; ✗ ☐ ☒) With an excellent location close to the square and restaurants, this upmarket hotel has fine facilities, including a pool, sauna, and jacuzzi, and personable staff. The public areas are slickly furnished, but the rooms – new wooden floors aside – are nothing to set the pulse racing.

Other recommendations include the following:

Gran Hotel Royal (☎ 439694; www.granhotelroyal .com.ar; Obligado 211; s/d AR$75/105; ✗) Spotless and comfortable rooms, if somewhat uninspired.

Hotel Amerian (☎ 452400; www.hotelcasinogala.com .ar; Perón 330; s/d AR$252/274; ✗ ✗ ☐ ☒) Casinohotel and the city's smartest choice, with various grades of room and slick service.

Eating

our pick **La Bianca** (☎ 443600; Colón 102; dishes AR$8-19; ✗ lunch & dinner) The exposed brick walls and cute wrought-iron mezzanine make this perhaps the town's most charming option. The menu is long, and features all the usual favorites, but the quality is very high – the *bife de lomo* (tenderloin) is exquisite – and the service very cordial. There's a terrace too.

Pizzería Los Campeones (☎ 443864; Perón 300; pizzas AR$12-20) This down-home pizzeria, with sidewalk seating on a very busy street, also serves unbeatable slices at AR$2 a pop.

Parrillada Don Abel (☎ 449252; Perón 698; meals AR$12-28; ✗ lunch & dinner, closed dinner Sun) This *parrilla* is inside a homey *quincho* (thatched-roof building) and serves substantial portions of pasta and grilled surubí (river fish), in addi-

tion to the usual grilled beef. It's got a convivial family buzz to it at the weekend.

Kebon (☎ 422385; cnr Güemes & Don Bosco; mains AR$16-32; ✗ lunch & dinner Mon-Sat) Popular and not lacking in quality, this corner restaurant has a wide choice of fish and meat dishes, with a series of elaborate sauces to choose from. Service is attentive and the portions generous, but the place somehow lacks a little bit of atmosphere. The take-out *rotisería* next door is a bargain.

Charly (☎ 434019; Güemes 213; mains AR$15-35; ✗ lunch & dinner Mon-Sat) Named after Chaplin, this is one of Resistencia's smarter restaurants with slightly lugubrious service but quality food. They take their river fish seriously here, and the carefully prepared dishes are praiseworthy. The restaurant has a cheap *rotisería* around the corner.

Drinking & Entertainment

El Fogón de los Arrieros (☎ 426418; Brown 350; ✗ 9.30pm-midnight) Stopping into El Fogón's friendly bar – a local institution for decades – is almost mandatory. The attached cultural center presents occasional live music and small-scale theatrical events (see p235).

El Viejo Café (☎ 459399; Pellegrini 109; ✗ 7am-late Sun-Thu, 1pm-late Fri & Sat) In an elegant old edifice, with an eclectically decorated interior, this is a fine choice at any time of day. Its terrace is a sweet spot for a sundowner, and it gets lively later on weekends. One request: it's one of the town's prettier buildings, so please lose the Quilmes sign...

Zingara (Güemes 279; ✗ 6pm-3am) Central and buzzy, this upbeat bar has a lively terrace, sound people running it, and a wide selection of music. They mix a decent drink too. A fine choice.

Peña Nativa Martín Fierro (☎ 423167; Av 9 de Julio 695) Try this traditional place on Friday or Saturday night after 10pm for live folk music and *parrillada*.

Shopping

There's a selection of *artesanía* stalls on the southern side of the plaza.

Chac Cueros (☎ 433604; Güemes 186) Chac Cueros specializes in high-quality goods made from the hide of capybaras, which is valued for the suede produced from their tan, naturally dimpled skin.

Fundación Chaco Artesanal (☎ 459372; Pellegrini 272; ☾ 9am-noon & 4-8pm Mon-Sat) This association, in the Centro Cultural Leopoldo Marechal, sells an outstanding selection of indigenous crafts.

Getting There & Away

AIR

Aerolíneas Argentinas (☎ 446802; JB Justo 184) flies to Buenos Aires' Aeroparque (AR$504, six times weekly). Three flights go to Asunción (AR$644, one hour), Paraguay.

BUS

Resistencia's **bus terminal** (☎ 461098; cnr MacLean & Islas Malvinas) serves destinations in all directions. Buses make the rounds between Corrientes and Resistencia (AR$2.50, 40 minutes) at frequent intervals throughout the day. You can also catch a bus to Corrientes from the center, on Av Alberdi just south of the plaza. Better are the shared taxis (AR$2.50, 20 minutes) that congregate at the corner of Frondizi and Obligado.

There are frequent daily services to the destinations listed below.

Destination	Cost (AR$)	Duration (hr)
Asunción (Paraguay)	28	5
Buenos Aires	118	13
Córdoba	113	12
Formosa	13	2
Mendoza	168	24
Mercedes	25	4
Posadas	38	5
Puerto Iguazú	71	10
Roque Sáenz Peña	14	2
Rosario	93	10
Salta	86	10
Santa Fe	71	9
Santiago del Estero	49	7½
Tucumán	74	12

Getting Around

The airport is 6km south of town on RN 11; take bus 2 from the northwest corner of the plaza. The bus terminal is a AR$6 taxi ride from the center, or you can take bus 3 or 10 from opposite the Hotel Colón. City buses cost AR$1.

PARQUE NACIONAL CHACO

Preserving several diverse ecosystems that reflect subtle differences in relief, soils and rainfall, this very accessible **park** (☎ 03725-499161; entrance free; ☾ visitor center 9am-7pm) protects 150 sq km of the humid eastern Chaco. It is 115km northwest of Resistencia via RN 16 and RP 9.

Ecologically, it falls within the 'estuarine and gallery forest' sub-region of the Gran Chaco, but the park encompasses marshes, grasslands, palm savannas, scrub forest and denser gallery forests. The most widespread ecosystem is the *monte fuerte*, where mature specimens of quebracho, algarrobo and lapacho reach above 20m, while lower strata of immature trees and shrubs provide a variety of habitats at distinct elevations. The hard-wooded quebracho colorado tree used to be widespread across northern Argentina, but overlogging almost led to its complete disappearance.

Scrub forests form a transitional environment to seasonally inundated grasslands, punctuated by caranday and pindó palms. Marshes and gallery forests cover the smallest areas, but they are biologically the most productive. The meandering Río Negro has left several shallow oxbow lakes where dense aquatic vegetation flourishes.

Mammals are few and rarely seen, but birds are abundant, including the rhea, jabirú, roseate spoonbill, cormorants, common caracaras and other less conspicuous species. The most abundant insect species is the mosquito, so visit during the cooler, drier winter and bring repellent.

Park service personnel are extremely hospitable and will accompany visitors if their duties permit.

Activities

Hiking and bird watching are the principal activities, best done in the early morning or around sunset. Some areas are accessible only while cycling or horseback riding; find out about the rental of cycles (AR$4 per hour) or horses and guides (AR$10 per hour) in Capitán Solari, 6km east of the park; ask at the *municipalidad* (town hall).

Sleeping & Eating

The *municipalidad* (city hall) in Capitán Solari provides information on locals who rent rooms to travelers at a fair price. One such is **Señora Nilda Ocampo** (☎ 03725-15-458977) who charges AR$20 per person. **Comedor El Quincho** (☎ 03725-421277; meals AR$7-10) is the town's principal place to eat.

Camping is the only option in the park. There are shaded sites with cold-water showers and toilets, and many ants and other harmless *bichos* (critters). There are fire pits with wood, and it's free.

Weekends can be crowded with visitors, but at other times you may have the park to yourself. On busy weekends a vendor from Resistencia sells meals, but it's better to bring everything you'll need.

Getting There & Away

Capitán Solari is 2½ hours from Resistencia by bus. La Estrella runs five buses daily each way (AR$7.50).

From Capitán Solari, you will have to walk/hitch the 5km to the park, or hire a horse or bike. A *remise* costs about AR$4. The road may be impassable for motor vehicles in wet weather.

ROQUE SÁENZ PEÑA

☎ 03732 / pop 76,794

Something of a frontier town, Presidencia Roque Sáenz Peña, its full cumbersome name, is well out in the Chaco, and is the gateway to the 'Impenetrable' beyond. It's known for its thermal baths, fortuitously discovered by drillers seeking potable water in 1937, and makes an appealing stop, with a rugged, friendly feel to the place.

Roque is primarily a service center for cotton and sunflower growers and, as the Chaco province grows nearly two-thirds of the country's total cotton crop, in May it hosts the **Fiesta Nacional del Algodón** (National Cotton Festival).

Orientation

The town straddles RN 16, which connects Resistencia with Salta. Its regular grid plan centers on willow-shaded Plaza San Martín; Av San Martín is the principal commercial street.

Information

Avenida San Martín has several banks with ATMs and numerous places to make phone calls or use the internet.

Post office (Belgrano 602, at Mitre)

Tourist office (Brown 541; ☉ 6am-noon & 2:30-8:30pm) In the thermal bath complex.

Sights

Roque's **Complejo Termal Municipal** (Thermal Baths Complex; ☎ 430030; www.elchacotermal.com.ar; Brown 545; ☉ 6:30-11:45am & 2:30-8:30pm) draws its saline water from 150m below ground. The center, around since the '30s, is now a top-class facility, offering thermal baths, saunas and Turkish baths (all AR$3 in the morning and AR$5 in the afternoon). Treatments on offer include kinesiology, massage and aromatherapy.

At the junction of RN 16 and RN 95, 3km east of downtown, the town's spacious and nationally renowned **Parque Zoológico** (☎ 424284; adult/child/vehicle AR$2/1/2; ☉ sunrise-sunset) and botanical garden emphasizes birds and mammals found in the Chaco region, rather than exotics. Featured species are tapir and jaguar, but there are also crocodiles, llamas, monkeys, a bafflingly large chicken pen, snakes, condors and vultures.

The zoo has two large artificial lakes frequented by migratory waterfowl. A small snack bar operates, but the aroma from nearby enclosures is a bit of an appetite killer. Bus 2 goes from Calle Moreno to the zoo (AR$1), a *remise* will cost AR$5; it's also within reasonable walking distance, if it's not too hot.

Sleeping

Orel Hotel (☎ 424139; ifmalina@yahoo.com.ar; cnr Saavedra & San Martín; s/d AR$40/60) The rooms are simple, clean and colorful, and have cable TV. Some have windows looking out on to the street (noisy), others face the hallway (and lack privacy). Still, it's not a bad deal.

Hotel Familiar (☎ 429906; Moreno 486; s/d AR$55/80; ☒) A welcoming little place a block from the main drag. The rooms are clean and quiet, if dark, and the people take an interest in their guests.

Hotel Gualok (☎ 420715; hotelgualok@hotmail.com; San Martín 1198; s/d AR$80/105; ☒ ☒) Right next to the spa complex, the fading elegance of the town's best hotel doesn't diminish the dignity and good-humored service to be found here. The spacious, light rooms still feel like a bargain at these prices.

PENETRATING THE IMPENETRABLE

If you've got a yen to get off the beaten track, the more remote areas of the Chaco are for you. Key access point for the Impenetrable is the town of Juan José Castelli, 115km north of Roque Sáenz Peña, and served by two daily buses from Resistencia (AR$20, five hours) via Roque. From Juan José Castelli, you can head west along *ripio* roads to remote Fuerte Esperanza (shared *remises* run this route), which has two nature reserves in its vicinity – Reserva Provincial Fuerte Esperanza, and Reserva Natural Loro Hablador. Both conserve typical dry Chaco environments, with algarrobo and quebracho trees, armadillos, peccaries, and many bird species. Loro Hablador, 40km from Fuerte Esperanza, has a good campsite and short walking trails with ranger guides. Fuerte Esperanza has two simple *hospedajes*. Further north, Misión Nueva Pompeya was founded in 1899 by Franciscans who established a mission station for Matacos in tough conditions. The main building, with its square-towered church, is a surprising sight in such a remote location.

Various operators offer excursions and packages, which include visits to the reserves, Misión Nueva Pompeya, and indigenous communities in the area. **Carlos Aníbal Schumann** (☎ 03732-15-440581; ecoturchaco@yahoo.com.ar; Av San Marín 500, Juan José Castelli) comes recommended and also runs a campsite and lodge in Villa Río Bermejito, a riverside settlement 67km northeast of Juan José Castelli. **Tantanacuy** (☎ 03722-15-640705; www.impenetrabletour.com.ar) is a *hostería* between Castelli and Fuerte Esperanza that offers packages including accommodation, transfers and excursions.

Heading west from Roque Sáenz Peña, RN 16 heads past the access to the Parque Nacional Copo (p300), which is part of the same ecoregion.

Hotel Presidente (☎ 424498; San Martín 771; s/d/tw AR$75/95/130; ❄ 🖳) With plush red carpet and mirrors everywhere, including on the doors of the rooms, this looks like a cross between a Colombian narcotrafficker's mansion and a top-of-the-market '70s brothel. It's a very pleasing place in the heart of town, with friendly staff and, for this price, excellent rooms with minibar and big comfortable beds.

Eating

Ama Nalec (☎ 420348; Moreno 601; ice creams from AR$2.50; ❄ 10am-3pm & 6pm-late) This busy corner place does tempting little pastries and very tasty ice cream, a godsend in Roque's paralyzing heat. They've got some unusual flavors – figs in cognac is worth a lick.

Bien, José! (25 de Mayo 531; mains AR$6-22; ❄ lunch & dinner) With an offbeat name, cheerily bright color scheme, and happy buzz of local families devouring low-priced meat, this is the town's best option for downmarket and tasty *parrilla*.

Giuseppe (☎ 425467; Moreno 680; small pizza AR$7-16, mains AR$8-18; ❄ lunch & dinner) This place has slightly staid décor but is very popular in the evening for its tasty pizzas and interesting pasta combinations. Try not to sit down the side – the kitchen belts out so much heat you expect brimstone and horned waiters.

Saravá (cnr San Martín & 25 de Mayo; dishes AR$8-16; ❄ 8am-midnight) A popular spot serving the regular range of steak, chicken, burgers and sandwiches, Saravá has a full bar and is located on a busy corner right in the heart of town, so the outdoor tables are the place to watch the Roque (horror?) show.

Getting There & Away

The **bus terminal** (☎ 420280; Petris, btwn Avellaneda & López) is seven blocks east of downtown; take bus 1 from Mitre. There are regular buses to Resistencia (AR$14, two hours), and services running west to Tucumán, Santiago del Estero, and Salta, also stop here.

FORMOSA
☎ 03717 / pop 198,074

Travelers heading to Formosa might get a mystified 'why?' from residents of other Argentine cities, but it's quite a sweet little city and provincial capital set on a horseshoe bend of the Río Paraguay. It makes a decent place to stop (far better than Clorinda) en route to Paraguay or Parque Nacional Río Pilcomayo. It's blazing hot in summer, with high humidity levels, but as the sun goes down, its riverside area makes a great place to stroll. You can even duck across the river for a taste of Paraguay if you wish.

Orientation

Formosa is 169km north of Resistencia and 113km south of Clorinda (on the border with Paraguay) via RN 11. It is also possible, though not easy, to cross the northern Chaco via RN 81.

Av Gutñiski, as RN 11 is called as it passes through town, heads eastward to Plaza San Martín, a four-block public park beyond which Av 25 de Mayo, the heart of the city, continues to the shores of the Río Paraguay.

Information

There are banks with ATMs along Av 25 de Mayo between the plaza and the river.

Post office (Plaza San Martín at 9 de Julio)

Provincial tourist office (☎ 425192; turismo@ formosa.gov.ar; Uruburu 820; ☺ 7am-8pm Mon-Fri) On the plaza. A foreign visitor makes their week.

Telecom (Av 25 de Mayo 242; per hr AR$1.50) Internet and phone calls.

Sights & Activities

In Casa Fotheringham, a pioneer residence that was the province's first government house, the **Museo Histórico** (cnr Belgrano & Av 25 de Mayo; admission free; ☺ 8am-noon Mon, 8am-noon & 3-7pm Tue-Sat, 9am-noon & 5-8pm Sat & Sun) focuses on the foundation and development of Formosa. It's small and well-organized. The province was part of the Paraguayan Chaco until the 19th-century War of the Triple Alliance, and the museum also houses uniforms, weapons and relics from the period. There are a few old indigenous weavings as well.

Six kilometers south of town, **Laguna Oca** is a wetland area that has a popular beach, with food kiosks and canoe hire; once you wander away from the weekend crowds, there's a great deal of birdlife to be spotted.

Festivals & Events

Formosa's annual **Fiesta del Río**, lasting a week in mid-November, features an impressive nocturnal religious procession in which 150 boats from Corrientes sail up the Río Paraguay.

In April, the **Encuentro de Pueblos Originarios de América** brings together delegations from various indigenous groups from Argentina, Paraguay, Bolivia, and further afield, with associated cultural spectacles.

Sleeping & Eating

Hotel San Martín (☎ 426769; Av 25 de Mayo 380; s/d AR$60/80; ✦) Good for the price, but otherwise

uninteresting, the San Martín is surprisingly quiet for its central location. Some rooms are definitely better than others, so have a look around if you can.

Hotel Plaza (☎ 426767; hotelplaza@elpajaritosa.com.ar; Uruburu 920; s/d AR$85/100; ✦ ☐ ✦) The name don't lie: it's right on the plaza, and has a welcoming feel to it. The rooms are nothing special, but there's a small swimming pool and good restaurant.

Hotel Interacional de Turismo (☎ 437333; www.hotelintdeturismo.com.ar; cnr 25 de Mayo & San Martín; s/d AR$135/160; ✦ ☐ ✦) Overlooking the river and the pretty, disused station, this large and somewhat impersonal hotel offers rooms with views across to Paraguay and decent facilities. Big balconies and an excellent swimming pool and sundeck are also on offer.

Yayita (☎ 431322; Av 25 de Mayo 787; dishes AR$8-15; ☺ lunch & dinner) Just off the square, this simple restaurant offers very acceptable and cheap meals and snacks. The menu changes slightly according to the day – the chicken and noodle stew is a banker.

Raíces (☎ 427058; Av 25 de Mayo 65; mains AR$11-32; ☺ lunch & dinner) Despite the garish sign, this is a refined and classy place, with a fine selection of surubí dishes, among many other well-prepared offerings, and a good wine list.

El Tano Marino (☎ 420628; Av 25 de Mayo 55; mains AR$12-30; ☺ lunch & dinner, closed dinner Sun) Nextdoor to Raíces, this similarly reliable restaurant has an Italian touch, but also features many of the usual Argentine favorites and correct service. It also has a decent wine list.

Shopping

Casa de las Artesanías (San Martín 82; ☺ 8am-1pm & 4-8pm Mon-Sat) In an historic building near the river, this artisans' cooperative sells wood carvings, weavings and other items that range from shoddy to beautiful. Proceeds go to the indigenous communities – the Mataco, Toba and Pilaga – who make the crafts.

Getting There & Away

AIR

Aerolíneas Argentinas (☎ 429314; Av 25 de Mayo 601) flies five times weekly to Buenos Aires (AR$564).

BOAT

Boats leave from the riverport for the rapid crossing to Alberdi, basically a typically sham-

bolic Paraguayan cheap-goods market. It costs
AR$4 to go and AR$3 to come back.

BUS
Formosa's modern **bus terminal** (☎ 451766; cnr
Gutñiski & Antártida Argentina) is 15 blocks west of the
plaza. Destinations include the following.

Destination	Cost (AR$)	Duration (hr)
Asunción (Paraguay)	11	2
Buenos Aires	122	16
Clorinda	8	1¾
Laguna Blanca	13	3
Resistencia	13	2

Getting Around
The airport is 4km south of town along RN
11, so cabs are inexpensive. The bus marked
Tejón passes by the bus terminal on its way to
the airport. A taxi between the terminal and
center costs AR$6.

CLORINDA
☎ 03718 / pop 47,004
Bustling Clorinda has a Paraguayan feel already with its street markets and intense heat,
and most visitors are indeed here to cross the
border to Asunción via the San Ignacio de
Loyola bridge. While the town's energy can
be briefly infectious, there's nothing much to
do or see. Two footbridges take you across to
the similar Paraguayan town of Nanawa on
the other side of the river.

There's inexpensive lodging at the **Hotel
San Martín** (☎ 421211; 12 de Octubre 1150; s/d AR$40/
60; 🔀), which, with its exposed brick walls
and understated décor, scrapes together a bit
of style. **La Pupuruchi** (☎ 425291; San Martín 548;
mains AR$6-12; 🕐 lunch & dinner) is a hugely popular
lunch spot on the main street with an excellent salad bar.

There are several bus terminals in Clorinda;
the most useful is the Godoy company's one at
San Martín and Paraguay. They have regular
cross-border departures to Asunción as well as
services south to Formosa (AR$8, 1¾ hours),
Resistencia (AR$20, 3¾ hours), and Buenos
Aires (AR$125, 18 hours).

LAGUNA BLANCA
☎ 03718 / pop 6508
The handiest base for visiting the Parque
Nacional Río Pilcomayo (see right), Laguna
Blanca is a spread-out settlement where people
move slowly, mostly on scooters and bicycles.

Cattle, horses, bananas, and citrus keep people
in business here, and the town is renowned for
its grapefruit, which are celebrated during the
Fiesta del Pomelo in mid-July. To the south of
town is a large reserve owned by the Toba.

Laguna Blanca is 55km west of Clorinda
and 126km northwest of Formosa. Most services are around the plaza. On its northeastern
side are a bank with ATM, and Maxi Compras
Plaza, a shop where *remises* congregate.

Sleeping & Eating
Residencial Guaraní (☎ 470024; cnr San Martín & Sargento
Cabral; s/d AR$35/45; 🔀) One of two places to stay,
this is a great little spot, with comfortable
rooms (AR$10 extra for air-con) with sizable
bathrooms set around a beautiful patio with
a well and shaded by mango trees. It also has
the best restaurant (dishes AR$8 to AR$18)
in town, which far exceeds expectations; it's
open for lunch and dinner.

El Monumental (25 de Mayo btwn RN 86 & San Martín;
meals AR$6-12; 🕐 lunch & dinner) A friendly local
with a simple dynamic: good cheap food, cold
beer, plastic tables outside, and the local radio
station belting out classic '80s rock.

Getting There & Away
Godoy and Tres Destinos run to Laguna
Blanca from Formosa five times daily
(AR$13); the trip takes three hours, a little less
via Riacho rather than Clorinda (AR$5, 1½
hours). Shared taxis (AR$9) shuttle between
Clorinda and Laguna Blanca, leaving from Av
San Martín in Clorinda, a block west of the
footbridge, and the plaza in Laguna Blanca.

PARQUE NACIONAL RÍO PILCOMAYO
East of Laguna Blanca are the wildlife-rich
marshlands of 600-sq-km Parque Nacional
Río Pilcomayo. Its outstanding feature is
shallow, shimmering **Laguna Blanca** (not to be
confused with the town) where, at sunset,
caimans lurk on the lake's surface. Other animals are likelier to be heard than seen; species
such as tapirs, anteaters, and the maned wolf
are present. Birds are abundant, with rheas,
parrots, cormorants, jabirú, and raptors easily spotted. The park has grasslands studded
with caranday palms, and thicker riverine
vegetation.

There are two distinct parts of the park
that you can access. The visitor center at
Estero Poí is 11km from the center of Laguna
Blanca, 3km east along the highway, and 8km

north along a dirt road. From the center, a roughish 14km vehicle track runs down to the Pilcomayo river; it's along here that you've got most chance of seeing wildlife.

The center at Laguna Blanca is 3km north of the main road from the turnoff 2km west of Laguna Naick-Neck, and 9km east of Laguna Blanca town. Here, there's a small nature display (from roadkills) and a boardwalk leading to the lake itself, where there's a rickety wooden observation tower, platforms out on the water, and boats that the rangers can take you out in. The water is shallow, and the caimans not a concern, but a sign advises swimming with footwear because of the piranhas… It's especially tranquil and appealing here late in the day, after picnickers and day-trippers have left, but take repellent.

Sleeping & Eating

Both the Estero Poí and Laguna Blanca centers have shady free campsites, with basic bathrooms, and barbecues with wood. The shower water is saline and most people prefer the lake. A shop sells basic food and cold drinks just outside the Laguna Blanca park entrance, but you're better off bringing supplies from Laguna Blanca town or Clorinda.

Getting There & Away

Buses between Clorinda and Laguna Blanca will drop you off at either of the national park turnoffs, but you'd have to walk or hitch from there. A *remise* from Laguna Blanca town to either park center will charge from AR$20, more if it waits for you. Ask at Maxi Compras Plaza in Laguna Blanca.

The Andean Northwest

Contrasting totally with the low, flat, humid northeast, Argentina's northwest sits lofty, dry and tough beneath the mighty Cordillera de los Andes. Nature works its magic here with stone: weird, wonderful and tortured rockscapes are visible throughout, from the imposing formations of the Parque Nacional Talampaya in the far south to the twisted strata of the Quebrada de Cafayate; from the jagged ruggedness of the Valles Calchaquíes to the palette of colors of the Quebrada de Humahuaca. And always to the west is the brooding presence of some of the Andes' most magnificent peaks.

The area has an Andean feel with its traditional handicrafts, Quechua-speaking pockets, coca leaves, llamas, the clear indigenous heritage of the inhabitants, Inca ruins and the high, arid puna (Andean highlands) stretching to Chile and north to Bolivia. The region's cities were Argentina's first colonial settlements and have a special appeal. The quiet gentility of Santiago del Estero recalls bygone centuries, Salta's beauty makes it a favorite stop for travelers, while resolutely urban Tucumán, a sugarcane capital, seems to look firmly to the future.

Several deservedly popular routes for visitors exist; from Salta you can march in time with the cactus sentinels of Parque Nacional Los Cardones on your way to gorgeous Cachi, and then head down through the traditional weaving communities of the Valles Calchaquíes to Cafayate, home of some of Argentina's best wines. Another route from Salta soars up into the mountains to the puna mining settlement of San Antonio de los Cobres, heads north to the spectacular salt plains of the Salinas Grandes, and then down to the visually wondrous and history-filled Quebrada de Humahuaca.

THE ANDEAN NORTHWEST

HIGHLIGHTS

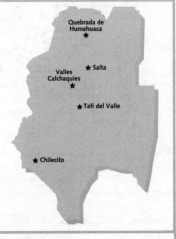

- Wonder at nature's palette in the **Quebrada de Humahuaca** (p253)
- Observe weavers working in the memorable **Valles Calchaquíes** (p271)
- Cleanse your lungs in the crisp mountain air of **Tafí del Valle** (p293)
- Discover the wonderful world of cactus in Wild West **Chilecito** (p310)
- Soak up the colonial ambience in sophisticated **Salta** (p261)

Quebrada de
Humahuaca
★

Valles
Calchaquíes
★

★ Salta

★ Tafí del Valle

★ Chilecito

■ POPULATION: 4.46 MILLION   ■ AREA: 559,864 SQ KM

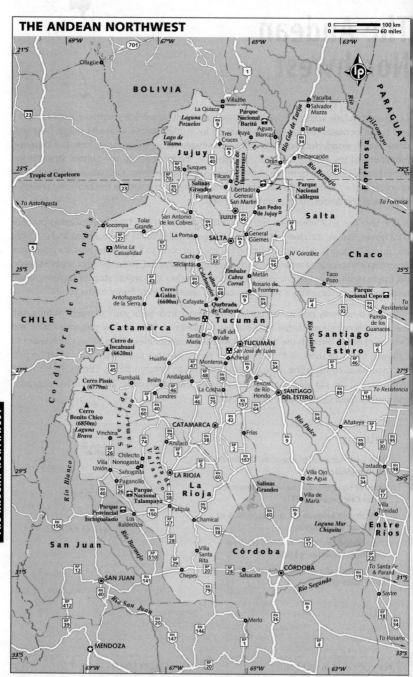

THE ANDEAN NORTHWEST

Climate

Dryness and the cold characterize the weather in the extreme northwest. Drought is often a problem here and many zones are virtual desert, receiving less than 250mm of rain per year. Although closest to the equator, the altitudes here keep things chilly. To the south and east of the region though, temperatures are much warmer, and you'll sweat it out in the steamy cloud forest of Parque Nacional Calilegua or the scorching summer of La Rioja.

National Parks

This region holds some important national parks, mostly in Jujuy and Salta provinces. Parque Nacional Calilegua (p250) preserves subtropical cloud forest and is home to an array of birdlife, as well as pumas and jaguars. The less accessible Parque Nacional El Rey (p252) is the most biologically diverse park in the country and teems with birdlife, including toucans. Far-flung Parque Nacional Baritú (p252) contains subtropical montane forest and is home to monkeys, big cats, otters and forest squirrels. Between Salta and Cachi, Parque Nacional Los Cardones (p271) is full of cactus-studded photo opportunities. Much further south, Parque Nacional Talampaya (p313) has aboriginal petroglyphs, photogenic rock formations and unique flora and fauna, while in the far east of the region, Parque Nacional Copo (p300) harbors anteaters, parrots and the fabulous quebracho colorado tree.

Getting There & Away

There are flights from Buenos Aires to Jujuy, Salta, Tucumán, Santiago del Estero, Catamarca and La Rioja. Salta has the most flights. Bus connections are generally available for destinations all over the country, particularly from the large cities of Tucumán and Salta.

JUJUY & SALTA PROVINCES

Intertwined like yin and yang, Argentina's two northwestern provinces harbor an inspiring wealth of natural beauty and traditional culture, of archaeological sites and appealing urban spaces, of national parks and wineries. Bounded by Bolivia to the north and Chile to the west, the zone climbs from the sweaty cloud forests of Las Yungas westward to the puna highlands and some of the most majestic peaks of the Cordillera de los Andes.

The two capitals, comfortable Jujuy and colonial, beloved-of-travelers Salta, are launchpads for exploration of the jagged chromatic ravines of the Quebrada de Cafayate and Quebrada de Humahuaca; for the villages of the Valles Calchaquíes, rich in artisanal handicrafts; for the stark puna scenery; for nosing of the aromatic Cafayate torrontés whites; or for rough exploration in the remote national parks of El Rey or Baritú.

JUJUY

☎ 0388 / pop 278,336 / elev 1201m

Of the trinity of northwestern cities, Jujuy lacks the colonial sophistication of Salta or urban vibe of Tucumán, but nevertheless shines for its livable feel, enticing restaurants and gregarious, good-looking locals. It's got the most indigenous feel of any of Argentina's cities. The climate is perpetually springlike; the city is the highest provincial capital in the country.

San Salvador de Jujuy (now commonly known simply as Jujuy) was founded in 1593 as the most northerly Spanish colonial city in present-day Argentina. It was the third attempt to found a city in this valley, after the previous two incarnations had been razed by miffed indigenous groups who hadn't given planning permission.

On August 23, 1812, during the wars of independence, General Belgrano ordered the evacuation of Jujuy. Its citizens complied in what is famously known as the *éxodo jujeño*. All possessions that could not be loaded on the mules were burned, along with the houses, in a scorched-earth retreat. Belgrano reported that most citizens were willing. They were able to return to what was left of their city in February 1813. The province of Jujuy bore the brunt of conflict during these wars, with Spain launching repeated invasions down the Quebrada de Humahuaca from Bolivia.

The city's name is roughly pronounced *hu-hui*; if it sounds like an arch exclamation of surprise, you're doing well.

Orientation

Jujuy sits above the Río Grande floodplain where the smaller Río Xibi Xibi meets it. It consists of two parts: the old city, with a fairly regular grid pattern between the Ríos Grande and Xibi Xibi, and a newer area south of the Xibi Xibi that sprawls up the nearby hills. All

THE ANDEAN NORTHWEST

JUJUY & SALTA PROVINCES

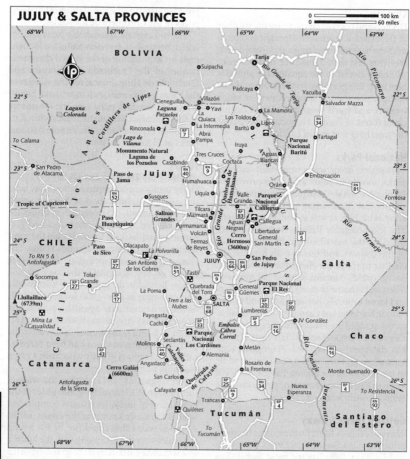

of interest is within walking distance of the main square, Plaza Belgrano.

Information

There are many central banks with ATMs. Call centers and internet places abound.

ACA (Automóvil Club Argentino; ☎ 422-2568; cnr Av Senador Pérez & Alvear) Maps and route information.

Hospital Pablo Soria (☎ 422-1228; cnr Patricias Argentinas & Av Córdoba)

La Zona (☎ 422-5233; Lavalle 340; per hr AR$1.25) Good cybercafé with extra facilities available.

Laverap (Belgrano 1214) Laundry.

Municipal tourist office (☎ 402-0254; Av Urquiza 354; ☒ 7am-10pm) Simple, friendly office in the old train station.

Post office (Belgrano 875)

Provincial tourist office (☎ 422-1343; www.turismo .jujuy.gov.ar; Gorriti 295; ☒ 7am-10pm Mon-Fri, 8am-10pm Sat & Sun) Excellent office with good brochures and staff.

Sights

CATEDRAL

Jujuy's 1763 **catedral** (cathedral; Plaza Belgrano; ☒ 8am-12:30pm & 5pm-8:30pm) replaced a 17th-century predecessor destroyed by the Diaguita. The outstanding feature, salvaged from the original church, is the gold-laminated baroque pulpit, probably built by local artisans trained by a European master.

MUSEO ARQUEOLÓGICO PROVINCIAL

The **Museo Arqueológico Provincial** (☎ 422-1315; Lavalle 434; admission AR$1; ☒ 8am-1pm & 4-8pm) is definitely worth a visit. The standout exhibit is a vivid 3000-year-old fertility goddess figure, depicted with snakes for hair and in the act of giving birth. She's a product of the advanced San Francisco culture, which existed in Las Yungas from about 1400 BC to 800 BC. There's also a selection of skulls with cranial deformities (practiced for cosmetic reasons) and mummified bodies displayed with what might have been their typical possessions. Staff hand out a booklet that has information in English.

CABILDO & MUSEO POLICIAL
On the north side of Plaza Belgrano is the **cabildo** (colonial town council) and **Museo Policial** (Police Museum; ☎ 423-7715; admission free; ☻ 8am-noon & 4-8pm Mon-Fri). The building and its colonnade deserve more attention than the museum housed within, which pays indiscriminate homage to authority, and glories in grisly photographs of crimes and accidents.

MUSEO HISTÓRICO PROVINCIAL
During Argentina's civil wars, a bullet pierced through the imposing wooden door of this colonial house, killing General Juan Lavalle, a hero of independence. The story of Lavalle unfolds in **Museo Histórico Provincial** (☎ 422-1355; Lavalle 256; admission AR$2; ☻ 8am-8pm). There is also religious and colonial art, as well as exhibits on the independence era, the evacuation of Jujuy and 19th-century fashion. There are some English labels, and guides on hand to answer questions.

IGLESIA Y CONVENTO SAN FRANCISCO
While the Franciscan order has been in Jujuy since 1599, **Iglesia y Convento San Francisco** (cnr Belgrano & Lavalle) dates only from 1912. Nevertheless, its **Museo Histórico Franciscano** (☎ 423-3434; admission AR$1; ☻ 8am-noon & 5-9pm), housed within, retains a strong selection of colonial art from the Cuzco school, which came about when monks taught indigenous Peruvians the style of the great Spanish and Flemish masters; this school gradually developed a high-quality style of its own that still exists today.

CULTURARTE
An attractive modern space, the **Culturarte** (☎ 424-9539; cnr San Martín & Sarmiento; admission free; ☻ 8:30am-1pm & 4.30pm-midnight) showcases exhibitions by well-established Argentine contemporary artists. There's also a café-bar with a great little balcony elevated over the street.

MERCADO DEL SUR
Jujuy's lively market, opposite the bus terminal, is a genuine trading post where indigenous Argentines swig *mazamorra* (a cold maize soup) and peddle coca leaves (see boxed text, p249). Upstairs eateries serve hearty regional specialties; try *chicharrón con mote* (stir-fried pork with boiled maize) or spicy *sopa de maní* (peanut soup).

Activities
Gimnasia y Esgrima de Jujuy (www.gyejujuy.com.ar; Lamadrid 451) better known as 'El Lobo' (the Wolf) is one of few provincial teams to regularly feature in the top division of Argentine football. Their **stadium** (General Savio s/n) is on the southern approaches to town.

Tours
Several Jujuy operators offer trips to the Quebrada de Humahuaca, Salinas Grandes and other provincial destinations.
Emilia Turismo (☎ 423-6742; www.emiliaturismo.com.ar; Independencia 859) Variety of tours, including treks in the Quebrada de Humahuaca area.
Noroeste (☎ 423-7565; www.noroestevirtual.com.ar; San Martín 155) Based at Club Hostel. Hits the Quebrada de Humahuaca area, Salinas Grandes and more.

Festivals & Events
In August, Jujuy's biggest event, the weeklong **Semana de Jujuy**, commemorates Belgrano's evacuation of the city during the wars of independence. The next largest gathering is the religious pilgrimage known as the **Peregrinaje a la Virgen del Río Blanco** on October 7. The March harvest festival is the **Festival de la Humita**, while May 25's **Fiesta de la Minería** honors the mining industry.

Sleeping
BUDGET
Club Hostel (☎ 423-7565; clubhostel@noroestevirtual.com.ar; San Martín 155; dm/d AR$23/65; ☐ ☑) There's a Caribbean feel to this upbeat Hostelling International (HI) hostel; it's probably the palm fronds and swimming pool. The friendly staff has laid on all backpacker-friendly facilities, and also operates a tour agency.
   Residencial Alvear (☎ 422-2982; csanchez@imagine.com.ar; Alvear 627; s/d with bathroom AR$45/75, without bathroom AR$25/50) A variety of rooms is tucked

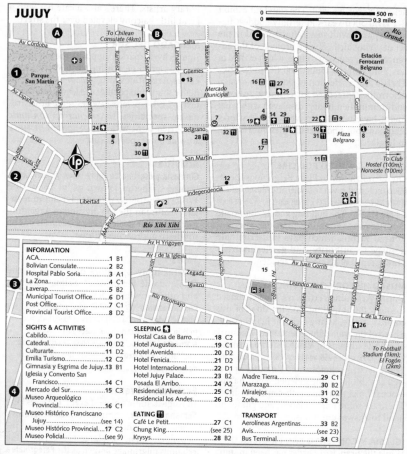

JUJUY

away behind the Chung King restaurant (the further back, the quieter it gets). They're OK for the price, but select carefully (upstairs) as some are a little poky.

Residencial los Andes (☎ 422-4315; República de Siria 456; s/d AR$35/50, d without bathroom AR$40) The best of the cluster of cheapies near the bus terminal, this has hardwood floors and spacious bathrooms. Rooms upstairs have much better light.

ourpick Hostal Casa de Barro (☎ 422-9578; www.casadebarro.com.ar; Otero 294; s/d without bathroom AR$40/60) Light-hearted and genuinely welcoming, this original and enjoyable place is a fine addition to Jujuy's accommodations spectrum. Rooms are bright and chirpy, and

shared bathrooms are very clean. The place is decorated throughout with rock-art motifs. There's a comfy lounge, a kitchen, and breakfast is included.

MIDRANGE

Hotel Avenida (☎ 423-6136; www.quintar.com.ar; Av 19 de Abril 469; s/d AR$70/100) There's a curious cast of characters at the aged Avenida, but they all mean well. Once quite upmarket, it's seen better days but is still a reasonable choice by the river. Rooms at the front have huge windows looking across to greenery, but suffer from street noise. Bag a discount.

Hotel Augustus (☎ 423-0203; www.hotelaugustus .com.ar; Belgrano 715; s/d AR$109/138; ❄ ▣) Smack on the pedestrian street (er, block), this offers personable service and value for money. The mattresses feel newish, and are draped with fleur-de-lis bedspreads. Half the rooms have pleasant balconies. You can use the pool at a hotel 15 minutes' cab-ride away.

Hotel Fenicia (☎ 423-1800; www.quintar.com.ar; Av 19 de Abril 427; s/d AR$110/180; ☒ ☐) This hotel overlooks the Xibi Xibi; its rooms are a bit rundown, but worth the price for the views from their great balconies. Modernized superior rooms are better value (singles/doubles AR$150/220), while the penthouse (AR$650) has the best views of all.

Hotel Internacional (☎ 423-1599; interjuy@imagine .com.ar; Belgrano 501; s/d AR$120/160; ☒) Perched on a corner of the plaza, this high-rise has smallish but bright cream-colored rooms with good-looking clean bathrooms. Some have spectacular views out over the plaza, and nice touches include a morning paper put under your door.

Posada El Arribo (☎ 422-2539; www.posadaelarribo .com.ar; Belgrano 1263; s/d AR$130/165; ☒ ☒) An oasis in the heart of Jujuy, this highly impressive family-run place is a real visual feast. The renovated 19th-century mansion is wonderful, with high ceilings and wooden floors; there's patio space galore and a huge garden. The modern annex behind doesn't lose much by comparison, but go for an older room if you can. A bargain.

Hotel Jujuy Palace (☎ 423-0433; jpalace@imagine .com.ar; Belgrano 1060; s/d AR$139/176; ☒ ☐) This well-appointed business hotel is attractively decorated and has a smart professional staff. The large rooms are spacious and modern, tastefully decorated with terrific views and the bathrooms feature good-sized tubs. There's a sauna and small gym.

Eating

Café Le Petit (Lavalle 415; cakes AR$4; ☻ 9am-8pm) A stately and well-loved salon with classic, refined decor, where you can take your well-deserved break for coffee and rather tasty cake.

Chung King (☎ 422-2982; Alvear 627; mains AR$11-26; ☻ lunch & dinner) This is a popular restaurant with an extensive Argentine menu and live *folklore* (folk music); it has an even more popular attached pizzeria. In fact, despite the name, about the only chow you can't get here is Chinese.

Miralejos (☎ 422-4911; Sarmiento 368; meals AR$11-29; ☻ 8am-midnight) This is plazaside dining at its finest. Miralejos offers the full gamut of steaks and pastas (with a wide choice of interesting sauces), with a few local trout dishes thrown in. The outside tables are a great place for breakfast and the eclectic music selection is interesting, to say the least.

Krysys (☎ 423-1126; Balcarce 272; mains AR$12-28; ☻ lunch & dinner Mon-Sat) The best *parrilla* (steak restaurant) option is this central, upscale place offering all your barbecued favorites in a relaxed atmosphere. The *bife de chorizo* (sirloin; AR$22) is particularly large, and you could get away with ordering a half, unless you're ravenous.

Marazaga (Av Senador Pérez 379; mains AR$13-29; ☻ lunch & dinner) Still teething when visited, this handsome place offers traditional Andean plates alongside trendy new creations. The vegetarian crepe starter is filling and tasty;

COCA CHEWING

Once you get seriously north, you see signs outside shops advertising coca and bica. The first refers to those leaves, mainly grown in Peru and Bolivia, which are used to produce cocaine. Bica refers to bicarbonate of soda, an alkaline that, when chewed along with the leaves (as is customary among Andean peoples) releases their mild stimulant effect and combats fatigue and hunger.

Though chewing coca is widespread and legal in Bolivia, its status in Argentina is confusing. Possession for personal use is legal, but the sale of it is not. Nor is its importation, so vast quantities are smuggled through from Bolivia to feed the *coqueo* (coca-chewing) custom of the indigenous population of Argentina's northwest. By all means chew some coca if invited by a local, but you'd be wise not to buy or carry any; those long bus searches by police are targeting coca leaves and their powdered derivative and you might find it tough to prove 'personal use' in an Argentine court. Taking the leaves into Chile is illegal, and the searches are dogged.

but the pork with honey-mustard sauce could do with a more dignified bed than crinkle-cut chips. But, as in Russian roulette, there are more positive than negative outcomes.

Zorba (☎ 424-3048; cnr Necochea & Belgrano; mains AR$15-22; ☒ 8am-1am) This is one of those hybrid places that always look good on paper but rarely work. Yet this one does. Big breakfasts (check out the Americano); an upmarket atmosphere for coffee or late drinks; and a hodge-podge of a menu featuring standard *minutas* (short orders or snacks), pastas and a few surprisingly tasty Greek dishes blend seamlessly into one.

ourpick Madre Tierra (☎ 422-9578; Belgrano 619; 4-course lunches AR$20; ☒ lunch Mon-Sat) This place is a standout. The vegetarian food – there's a daily set menu – is excellent and the salads, crepes and soups can be washed down with fresh juice. It's an earthy place where the simple, home-cooked food makes a welcome change. The bakery out the front does a range of wholesome breads.

Entertainment

Jujuy has several *peñas* (folk music clubs) to enjoy live *folklore* in a fairly traditional atmosphere. The best spots are located a little further away from the center; one of the better-known is **El Fogón** (☎ 425-2772; RN 9), on the southeastern edge of town, an AR$10 cab ride away. It is open for dinner from Thursday to Saturday.

Getting There & Away

AIR

Aerolíneas Argentinas (☎ 422-7198; Av Senador Pérez 355) flies from Jujuy (JUJ) to Buenos Aires' Aeroparque Jorge Newbery (AR$775) once daily. A shuttle service leaves from the Hotel Internacional two hours before flight departures (AR$9).

BUS

The **bus terminal** (☎ 422-1375; cnr Av Dorrego & Iguazú) has provincial and long-distance services, but Salta has more alternatives.

Chile-bound buses from Salta to San Pedro de Atacama (AR$124) and Calama pick up in Jujuy at 8:30am Tuesday, Thursday and Sunday; make reservations in advance at the Géminis or Pullman office at the terminal.

There are frequent services south to Salta and north to destinations in the Quebrada de Humahuaca as far as the Bolivian border at La Quiaca. Sample fares include the following:

Destination	Cost (AR$)	Duration (hr)
Buenos Aires	170	23
Catamarca	67	10
Córdoba	104	14
General Libertador San Martín	14	2
Humahuaca	13	3
La Quiaca	24	4-5
La Rioja	84	11
Mendoza	153	20
Purmamarca	7	1¼
Salta	13	2
Salvador Mazza	39	6-7
Santiago del Estero	59	7½
Susques	19	4-5
Tilcara	8	1¾
Tucumán	39	5

Getting Around

If you're after a rental car, **Avis** (☎ 423-0433; www.avis.com; Belgrano 1060) in Hotel Jujuy Palace, is one of a few choices.

AROUND JUJUY

Situated in a deep green valley above a mostly dry riverbed, the hot springs of **Termas de Reyes** are just 19km from Jujuy; the mineral-rich water emerges at a natural temperature of 50ºC. It is so named (Kings' Springs) because indigenous chiefs used to bathe in them for their magical properties.

There's a public pool (AR$3), and free campsite here, as well as the upmarket **Hotel Termas de Reyes** (☎ 0388-492-2522; www.termasdereyes .com; s/d AR$175/250; ☒ ☐ ☒), with a central-European feel, very comfortable rooms (views cost more) and spa treatments. They don't accept under-18s as guests.

Bus 1C runs hourly (AR$1.60, 45 minutes) from Calle Gorriti near the Jujuy tourist office.

PARQUE NACIONAL CALILEGUA

☎ 03886

Jujuy province's eastern portion is Las Yungas, a humid and fertile subtropical zone mostly devoted to the sugarcane industry. Here, arid, treeless altiplano gives way to the dense cloud forest of the Serranía de Calilegua, whose preservation is the goal of this accessible 760-sq-km park. At the park's highest elevations, about 3600m, verdant Cerro Hermoso reaches above the forest for boundless views of Chaco to the east. Birdlife is abundant and colorful, but the tracks of rare mammals, such as pumas, tapirs, and jaguars, are easier to see than the animals themselves.

INFORMATION

Park **headquarters** (☎ 422046; calilegua@apn.gov.ar; ☿ 7am-2pm Mon-Fri) is in Calilegua village, 5km north of the town of Libertador General San Martín. It has general park information and up-to-date road conditions. In the rainy season, you might as well just head straight to the park and talk to the ranger there.

The ranger at the **park entrance** (admission free; ☿ 9am-6pm) in Aguas Negras has information about trails and conditions. There's another ranger station at Mesada de las Colmenas, 13km past Aguas Negras and 600m higher. The trails are well marked.

Receiving 1000mm to 1800mm of precipitation a year, but with a defined winter dry season, Calilegua comprises a variety of ecosystems. The transitional *selva* (jungle), from 350m to 500m above sea level, consists of tree species common in the Gran Chaco, such as deciduous lapacho and palo amarillo. Between 550m and 1600m, the cloud forest forms a dense canopy of trees more than 30m tall, punctuated by ferns, epiphytes and lianas, often mist-covered. Above 1200m, the montane forest is composed of conifers, aliso and queñoa. Above 2600m this grades into moist grasslands, which become drier as one proceeds west toward the Quebrada de Humahuaca.

The 230 bird species at home in the park include condors, brown eagles, torrent ducks and colorful toucans. Important mammals include tapirs, pumas, jaguars, collared peccaries and otters. The presence of the road through the middle of the park, the nearby hydro-station and regular gravel-harvesting in the riverbed mean that, on the trails near Aguas Negras, there's little chance of spotting reclusive species.

ACTIVITIES

The best places for **bird and mammal watching** are near the stream courses in the early morning or late afternoon. From the ranger station at Mesada de las Colmenas, follow the steep, rugged trail down to a beautiful creek marked with numerous animal tracks, including those of large cats. The descent takes an hour, the ascent twice that.

There are seven marked trails in the park, from 20-minute strolls to tough four-hour hikes. From the campsite, a short Guaraní cultural trail, dotted with weird signboards, introduces you to the lower tropical forest. For waterbirds, head to La Lagunita, about 1½ hours' walk from Aguas Negras. The La Junta trail starts 3km up the road from Aguas Negras, and is a four-hour return walk with steepish climbs rewarded by great views over the park.

Vehicles with clearance can get right through the 23km of park, if there's been no rain. The road offers outstanding views of Cerro Hermoso and the nearly impenetrable forests of its steep ravines.

From Valle Grande, beyond the park boundaries to the west, it's possible to **hike** in a week to Humahuaca along the Sierra de Zenta, or to Tilcara.

SLEEPING & EATING

Nearby Libertador General San Martín is a sizable town devoted to processing sugarcane, whose sickly-sweet smell pervades all corners. The several places to stay include **Hotel Los Lapachos** (☎ 423790; Entre Ríos 400; s/d AR$80/100; 🅿), which tries hard with its scalloped hand-basins and wine-red carpets, and **Hotel Chosen** (☎ 425798; hotelchosen@cooperlib.com.ar; Ovejero 435; s/d AR$60/70; 🅿), offering decent rooms with fridge and bathroom. Both are a block from the plaza. Eating in town is dire. **Parador 34** (cnr Belgrano & RN 34; mains AR$7-15; ☿ 6am-midnight), on the highway in the center of town, is esteemed hereabouts, but offers little besides bright lights, internet, a huge TV and steak, chicken, and rabbit so overcooked it should be served in an urn.

Little Calilegua, 5km north, is a much more appealing place to stay, with a tumbledown tropical feel and a deafening chorus of cicadas. Near the park office, **Jardín Colonial** (☎ 430334; San Lorenzo s/n; s/d AR$20/40) is a lovely bungalow with rooms with shared bathroom, a shady porch and a verdant, sculpture-filled garden.

Camping is the only option in the park itself. The developed **campsite** (Aguas Negras) is some 300m from the ranger station at the entrance. It is free and has bathrooms and shower, but no shop. There are simple homestay accommodations at San Francisco, 39km from Aguas Negras, beyond the western end of the park.

GETTING THERE & AWAY

Numerous buses between Jujuy/Salta and the Bolivian border at Salvador Mazza stop at

BOLIVIA VIA SALVADOR MAZZA

RN 34 continues past Calilegua to Argentina's northernmost settlement, Salvador Mazza (also known as Pocitos, the name of the defunct station), one of the country's two major frontiers with Bolivia. Here you cross the **frontier** (⊙ 24hr), and take a shared cab 5km to the larger Bolivian settlement of Yacuiba, which has weekly flights to La Paz, and buses to Tarija (12 hours, US$12) and Santa Cruz (15 hours, US$9). There's no Bolivian consulate, so get your visa in Jujuy or Salta if you need one. At the time of research, US nationals needed a visa, but citizens of the EU, UK, Canada, Australia, New Zealand and South Africa did not. Salvador Mazza is served by numerous buses from Jujuy, Salta and other major northern cities. From October to April Bolivia is one hour behind Argentina.

Libertador General San Martín and Calilegua, and some will let you off on the highway at the junction for the park.

The access road heads west from the highway 3km north of Libertador, and 2km south of Calilegua. It's 8km to the ranger station at Aguas Negras; there's enough traffic to hitchhike.

A daily bus (at 8:30am) goes from Libertador General San Martín to Valle Grande (two hours) through the park. It passes the Aguas Negras ranger station at 9am. The return bus passes around 6pm; perfect for day trips to the park. It's also easy to get a taxi from either Libertador or Calilegua to Aguas Negras (AR$10 to AR$15).

PARQUE NACIONAL EL REY

Northeast of Salta, **Parque Nacional El Rey** (elrey@apn.gov.ar) is at the southern end of Las Yungas subtropical corridor and protects a habitat that is the most biologically diverse in the country. The park takes its name from the *estancia* (ranch) that formerly occupied the area and whose expropriation led to the park's creation.

The park's emblem is the giant toucan, appropriate because of the abundant birdlife, but the mosquito might be just as appropriate (check yourself for ticks, for that matter, although they don't carry disease). Most of the same mammals found in Calilegua and Baritú are also here.

There are various well-marked trails, some accessible by vehicle. **Laguna Los Patitos**, 2km from park headquarters, offers opportunities to observe waterbirds. Longer trails lead to moss-covered **Pozo Verde**, a three- to four-hour climb to an area teeming with birdlife. Two other trails are of similar day-trip length; rangers recommend a three-day stay to really get to know the park. Trails involve multiple

river crossings, so bring waterproof shoes or get your feet wet.

Entry is free and the best time to visit is between April and October.

There is free camping at the park's headquarters, with toilets, drinkable water, cold showers, and power from 7pm to 10pm. There is no shop. Contact the **National Parks Administration** (APN; ☎ 0387-431-2683; www.parquesnacionales.gov.ar; España 366; ⊙ 8am-3pm Mon-Fri) in Salta for up-to-date info.

It's tough to get here. Public transportation gets as far as Lumbreras, 91km short of the park. The last 46km are on rough *ripio* (gravel) road, almost impassable if it's been raining. Last fuel is at General Güemes, 160km from the park, so consider taking extra gas. If you aren't hiring a 4WD, the easiest way to get here is via guided tour from Salta (p265).

PARQUE NACIONAL BARITÚ

Hugging the Bolivian border, Baritú is the northernmost of the three Las Yungas parks conserving subtropical montane forest. Like Calilegua and El Rey, it harbors a large number of threatened mammals, including black howler and capuchin monkeys, southern river otters, Geoffroy's cats, jaguars and tapirs. The park's emblem is the forest squirrel, which inhabits the moist forest above 1300m. Admission is free and information can be obtained at Calilegua's **park headquarters** (☎ 03886-422046; calilegua@apn.gov.ar; ⊙ 7am-2pm Mon-Fri) or **National Parks Administration** (APN; ☎ 0387-431-2683; www.parquesnacionales.gov.ar; España 366; ⊙ 8am-3pm Mon-Fri) in Salta.

Here, Che Guevara's psychopathic disciple Masetti tried to start the Argentine revolution by infiltrating from Bolivia in 1963. The only road access is through Bolivia. From RN 34, 90km beyond Calilegua, head for Orán, through it, and on to Aguas Blancas. Crossing

THE ANDEAN NORTHWEST

into Bolivia, you hug the north bank of Río Bermejo, heading westward 113km, before crossing back into Argentina at La Mamora. A further 17km gets you to Los Toldos, and another 26km brings you to Lipeo, a hamlet at the northwest corner of the park. It has a ranger station but no other services. Los Toldos has accommodations, telephone and a supermarket. The drive to the park usually requires a 4WD.

From Lipeo, there are various trails, including to the **hot springs** of Cayotal, two hours away, and to the remote hamlet of **Baritú**, a four-hour walk each way through impressive cedar forest. You can rent horses in Lipeo for this ride. Locals in Lipeo and Baritú may offer you accommodations in their homes.

QUEBRADA DE HUMAHUACA

North of Jujuy, the memorable Quebrada de Humahuaca snakes its way upward toward Bolivia. It's a harsh but vivid landscape, a dry but river-scoured canyon overlooked by mountainsides whose sedimentary strata have been eroded into spectacular scalloped formations that reveal a spectrum colors in undulating waves. The palette of this Unesco World Heritage-listed valley changes constantly, from shades of creamy white to rich, deep reds; the rock formations in places recall a necklace of sharks' teeth, in others the knobbly backbone of some unspeakable beast. The canyon's southern stretches are overlooked by cardón cactus sentinels, but these peter out beyond Humahuaca as the road rises.

Dotting the valley are dusty, picturesque, indigenous towns that have a fine variety of places to stay; pretty, historic adobe churches; and homely restaurants serving warming *locro* (a spicy stew of maize, beans, beef, pork and sausage) and llama fillets. The region has experienced a tourism boom in recent years, and gets very full in summer.

There are many interesting stops along this colonial post route between Potosí (Bolivia) and Buenos Aires; buses along the road run every 40 minutes or so, so it's quite easy to jump off and on as required. The only spot to hire a car hereabouts is in Jujuy, or, further south, in Salta. The Quebrada de Humahuaca itself shows its best side early in the morning, when the colors are more vivid and the wind hasn't got up.

Look out for *Xuri*, a great little magazine published bimonthly with articles on regional culture and events.

Purmamarca

☎ 0388 / pop 510 / elev 2192m

Little Purmamarca, 3km west of the highway, sits under the celebrated Cerro de los Siete Colores (Hill of Seven Colors), a spectacular and jagged formation resembling the marzipan fantasy of a megalomaniac pastry chef. It and the surrounds offer a memorable range of hues.

The village is postcard-pretty, with ochre adobe houses and ancient algarrobo trees by the bijou 17th-century church. Its proximity to Jujuy makes it prime tour-bus territory; it's more enjoyable in the late afternoon, when you can stroll around in a more peaceful atmosphere.

There's a bank with ATM and, on the plaza is a little **information office** (🕙 8am-1pm & 2-7pm) with maps that include the easy but spectacular 3km walk around the *cerro* (hill), whose striking colors are best appreciated in the morning or evening sunlight.

SLEEPING & EATING

Hostería Bebo Vilte (☎ 490-8038; Salta s/n; s/d AR$50/80) Behind the church, this is a popular place offering basic rooms with bathroom, and a camping area with barbecues (AR$5 per person).

El Pequeño Inti (☎ 490-8089; elintidepurmamarca@hotmail.com; Florida s/n; s/d AR$60/70) Small and enticing, this is a fine little choice just off the plaza. Offering value (for two), it has unadorned rooms with comfortable beds and marine-schemed bathrooms.

Los Colorados (☎ 490-8182; www.loscoloradosjujuy.com.ar; Chapacal s/n; apt for 2/4 AR$240/300; 🖳) Looking straight out of a science-fiction movie, these strange but inviting apartments are tucked right into the *cerro,* and blend in with it. They are stylish and cozy; fine places to hole up for a while.

Behind the church, **Los Morteros** (☎ 490-8002; Salta s/n; mains AR$16-28; 🕙 lunch & dinner; 🖳), warmly lit and stylish, is considered the town's best restaurant and buzzes with chatter at weekends. If you fancy a bit of local music over your meal, **El Rincón de Claudia Vilte** (Libertad s/n; mains AR$10-24; 🕙 lunch & dinner) is the better of the two *folklore* choices.

GETTING THERE & AWAY

Buses to Jujuy (AR$7, 1¼ hours) run every one to two hours; others go to Tilcara (AR$3, 30 minutes) and Humahuaca (1¼ hours,

THE ANDEAN NORTHWEST

CHILE VIA SUSQUES

The paved road climbs doggedly from Purmamarca through spectacular bleak highland scenery to a 4150m pass, then crosses a plateau partly occupied by the Salinas Grandes. You hit civilization at **Susques**, 130km from Purmamarca, which has gas and an ATM.

Susques is well worth a stop for its terrific village **church** (admission by donation; ☼ 8am-6pm). Dating from 1598, it has a thatched roof, cactus-wood ceiling and beaten-earth floor, as well as charismatic, naïve paintings of saints on the whitewashed adobe walls. There's a tourist office on the main road, and basic places to stay and eat, including friendly **La Vicuñita** (☎ 03887-490207; lavicunita@arnet.com.ar; San Martín 121; d with bathroom AR$50, r per person without bathroom AR$20), opposite the bank, which serves up tasty meals too.

AndesBus and Empresa Purmamarca run Tuesday to Sunday from Jujuy to Susques (AR$19, four to five hours) via Purmamarca.

Beyond Susques, the road continues a further 154km (fuel up in Susques) to the Paso de Jama (4230m), a spectacular journey. This is the Chilean border, although Argentine **emigration** (☼ 8am-midnight) is some way before it. No fruit, vegetables or coca leaves are allowed into Chile – they check. The paved road continues toward San Pedro de Atacama, Calama and Antofagasta in Chile. Buses from Salta and Jujuy travel this route. Nationals of the USA, Canada, Australia, South Africa, New Zealand, and the EU do not need a visa to enter Chile. A fee is payable for US (US$131), Canadian (US$132), and Australian (US$56) citizens – that's what Chileans pay to apply for a visa for those nations.

AR$8). There's at least one bus every day (bar Monday) to Susques (AR$14, three to four hours) via Salinas Grandes.

Purmamarca has no gas station; the closest can be found 25km north, at Tilcara, or south, at Volcán. Westward, the next gas station is in Susques, 130km of steep climb away.

Tilcara

☎ 0388 / pop 4358 / elev 2461m

Picturesque Tilcara, 23km further up the valley from the Purmamarca turnoff, is many people's choice as their Quebrada de Humahuaca base and offers a wide accommodations choice from luxury boutique retreats to chilly hostels. The mixture of local farmers getting on with a centuries-old way of life and arty urban refugees looking for a quieter existence has created an interesting balance on the town's dusty streets.

Tilcara is connected by a bridge to RN 9. The main street, Belgrano, runs from the access road to the square, Plaza Prado, and on another block to the church.

INFORMATION

There are several central internet places and call centers as well as a bank with ATM just off the plaza on Lavalle.

Post office (Plaza Prado)

Tourist office (☎ 495-5135; mun_tilcara@cootepal .com.ar; Belgrano 366; ☼ 8am-1pm & 2-9pm Mon-Fri)

Good information on walks, and has a list of accommodation prices.

SIGHTS

Pucará

The reconstructed pre-Columbian fortification, the **pucará** (walled city; ☎ 495-5073; admission incl archaeological museum AR$5, Mon free; ☼ 9am-12:30pm, 2-6pm), is located 1km south of the center across an iron bridge. Its situation is undeniably strategic, commanding the river valley both ways and, though the site was undoubtedly used before, the ruins date from the 11th to 15th centuries. The 1950s reconstruction has taken liberties; worse yet is the earlier, ridiculous monument to pioneering archaeologists bang where the plaza would have been. Nevertheless, you can get a feel of what would have been a sizable fortified community. Most interesting is the 'church', a building with a short paved walkway to an altar; note the niche in the wall alongside. The site itself has great views and, seemingly, a cardón for every soul that lived and died here. For further succulent stimulation, there's a cactus garden by the entrance.

Museo Arqueológico

The Universidad de Buenos Aires runs the well-presented **Museo Arqueológico** (☎ 495-5006; Belgrano 445; admission incl pucará AR$5, Mon free; ☼ 9am-12:30pm & 2-6pm) of regional artifacts. There are some artifacts from the *pucará*, and exhibits give an insight into the life of people living around that time. The room dedicated to ceremonial masks is particularly impressive. The museum is in a striking colonial house on Plaza Prado.

Museo José Antonio Terry

Also located in a colonial building on Plaza Prado is **Museo José Antonio Terry** (☎ 495-5005; Rivadavia 459; admission AR$5, Thu free; ☼ 9am-7pm Tue-Sun), largely devoted to the work of a *porteño* (resident of Buenos Aires) painter whose themes were largely rural and indigenous; his oils depict weavers, market scenes and portraits.

ACTIVITIES

Of several interesting **walks** around Tilcara, the most popular is the two-hour hike to **Garganta del Diablo**, a pretty canyon and waterfall. Head toward the *pucará*, but turn left along the river before crossing the bridge. The path to the Garganta leaves this road to the left just after a sign that says '*Cuide la flora y fauna*'. **Swimming** is best in the morning, when the sun is on the pool.

Tilcara Mountain Bike (☎ 0388-15-5008570; tilcarabikes@hotmail.com; Belgrano s/n; ☼ 9am-7pm) is a friendly set-up that hires out well-maintained mountain bikes (AR$5/30 per hour/day) and provides a helpful map of trips in the area. If you fancy an early start it'll open for you.

There are several places for horseback riding with or without a guide. You'll see phone numbers for *cabalgatas* (horseback rides) everywhere, and most accommodations can arrange it.

TOURS

Based in the Posada de Luz, **Caravana de Llamas** (☎ 495-5326; www.caravanadellamas.com; cnr Alverro & Ambrosetti) is a recommended llama-trekking operator running half-day excursions (AR$120) around Tilcara, day trips in the Salinas Grandes (AR$180) and multiday excursions, including a five-day marathon from Las Yungas lowlands to Tilcara (US$500). The guide is personable and well-informed about the area. Llamas are pack animals: you walk, they carry the bags.

FESTIVALS & EVENTS

Tilcara celebrates several festivals during the year, the most notable of which is January's **Enero Tilcareño**, with sports, music and cultural activities. February's **Carnaval** is equally impor-

tant as in other Quebrada de Humahuaca villages, as is April's **Semana Santa** (Holy Week). August's indigenous **Pachamama** (Mother Earth) festival is worthwhile.

SLEEPING

Hostel Malka (☎ 495-5197; www.malkahostel.com.ar; San Martín s/n, Barrio Malka; dm AR$38, d AR$95) There's something very special about this rustic hostel 200m up a path, three blocks west of the church. The welcoming owners, secluded, shady situation and thoughtfully different dorms and cabins make it the sort of place you end up staying longer than you expected. There's a good breakfast included and you can take the bouncy dogs for walkies. There's a 15% discount for HI members.

Hotel de Turismo (☎ 495-5720; tilcahot@imagine.com.ar; Belgrano 590; s/d AR$80/120; ✖ 🖳 🖳) These government hotels always lack a little character, but the facilities are good for the price. The rooms aren't huge but some have little balconies. The central location, mountain views and good-sized pool (summer-only) make it a safe bet.

Posada de Luz (☎ 495-5017; www.posadadeluz.com.ar; cnr Ambrosetti & Alverro; r AR$175-190; 🖳) With a nouveau-rustic charm, this little place is a fantastic spot to unwind for a few days. More expensive rooms have sitting areas, but all feature pot-bellied stoves and individual terraces with deckchairs and views out over the valley. There are just six rooms, so book ahead.

ourpick Rincón de Fuego (☎ 495-5130; www.rincondefuego.com; Ambrosetti 445; s AR$170-250, d AR$250-312; ✖ 🖳) Romantic and welcoming, this posada is tucked away at the top of town; a fine spot to retreat to with someone you love. Effective, artistic use of bare stone and adobe lends much atmosphere; the rooms are darkish but seductive, with woodstoves. The common areas are exquisitely cozy, and breakfast features bread baked in the patio's clay oven.

The best budget accommodations in town are *casas de familia* (rooms in private homes with shared bathroom). They are invariably spotless, and you get a room to yourself for around AR$15 per person. The tourist office keeps a list; one is **Genara de Vargas** (☎ 495-5399; Lavalle 439), whose well-kept house is opposite the hospital.

EATING

El Patio (☎ 495-5044; Lavalle 352; mains AR$9-28, salads AR$7-15; ☼ lunch & dinner) Tucked away between the plaza and the church, this has a lovely shaded patio and garden seating. It offers a wide range of tasty salads, inventive llama dishes, and a far-from-the-madding-crowd atmosphere.

Música Esperanza (☎ 495-5318; Belgrano 547; dishes AR$8-19; ☺ lunch & dinner Tue-Sun) This outreach-via-music NGO puts on regular concerts and also runs a pretty little restaurant in this cultural center on the main street. Quinoa stew and local trout are among the dishes presented. Opening hours are somewhat irregular; call ahead or drop by.

Rincón del Colla (cnr Lavalle & Alverro; mains AR$10-27; ☺ lunch & dinner) Easily recognizable next to the church with its cheerful murals, this is a restaurant that has raucous live *folklorica* in the evenings. It's not to everyone's decibel comfort, but writers have highly praised the rabbit stew.

Los Puestos (☎ 495-5100; cnr Belgrano & Padilla; meals AR$12-26; ☺ lunch & dinner) Though a little touristy – we can't guarantee you won't be treated to a rendition of 'Sounds of Silence' on the pan-pipes – this makes up ground with its decor of local stone and chunky wood. Regional specialties feature heavily – barbecued llama (AR$16) is one – but it's small touches, such as tiny bread rolls straight from the clay oven, that win friends.

GETTING THERE & AWAY
The bus terminal is about 500m south of the town center. There are services roughly every 45 minutes to Jujuy (AR$8, 1¾ hours), and north to Humahuaca (AR$6, 45 minutes) and La Quiaca (AR$13, 3½ hours). There are several services daily to Purmamarca (AR$3, 30 minutes), and six to Salta (AR$19 four hours).

Around Tilcara
The town of **Maimará**, 8km south, is a typical adobe valley settlement set beneath the spectacular, and aptly-named Paleta del Pintor (Painter's Palette) hill. Just off the main road, its hillside cemetery is a surprising and different sight with a picturesque backdrop. Take photos respectfully; bear in mind that locals bury their loved ones here. The town also has a worthwhile anthropological and historical museum and places to stay if you fancy overnighting.

Part of a chain that ran from Lima to Buenos Aires during viceregal times, **La Posta de Hornillos** (admission AR$2; ☺ 8am-6pm Wed-Mon) is a beautifully restored staging post 11km

south of Tilcara. Founded in 1772, it was the scene of several important battles during the wars of independence, and remained an important stop on the road to Bolivia until 1908, when the La Quiaca railway opened. The interesting exhibits include leather suitcases, some impressively fierce swords and a fine 19th-century carriage. Someone should open a café here.

Some 15km north of Tilcara, the road crosses the **Tropic of Capricorn**, marked by a large sundial, *artesanía* (handcraft) offerings and a pair of photo-hungry alpacas.

Any of the frequent buses running north–south along the Quebrada will drop you off or pick you up at these spots.

Uquía
☎ 03887 / pop 525 / elev 2818m
It's not often that you imagine the heavenly hosts armed with muzzle-loading weapons, but in this roadside village's fabulous 17th-century **church** (admission by donation; ☺ 10am-noon, 2-4pm) that's just what you see. A restored collection of Cuzco school paintings – the *ángeles arcabuceros* (arquebus-wielding angels) – features Gabriel, Uriel et al putting their trust in God but keeping their powder dry. There's also a gilt *retablo* (retable) with fine painted panels. The village is perfect for arty 'exposed-adobe-wall-meets-late-afternoon-sun' photos. By the church, **Hostal de Uquía** (☎ 490508; hostaluquia@yahoo.com.ar; s/d AR$75/110; ☒) is a neat place with curious management but decent rooms and restaurant.

Humahuaca
☎ 03887 / pop 7985 / elev 2989m
The Quebrada's largest settlement is its most handsome, with atmospheric cobblestoned streets, adobe houses and quaint plaza. You can feel the nearby puna here, with chilly nights, sparse air and a quiet Quechua population. Humahuaca feels less affected by tourism than the towns further south, and is the better for it. There are good handicrafts shops around town, and folk musicians strum and sing in the more popular restaurants.

ORIENTATION
Straddling the Río Grande east of RN 9, Humahuaca is very compact. The town center is between the highway and the river. The disused railway runs through the middle of town. The main square, Plaza Gómez, has

---

TOREO DE LA VINCHA

You'll not see bullfighting in Argentina – it was banned in the 19th century – but the unusual fiestas of **Casabindo** feature a *toro* (bull) as the central participant. This tiny and remote adobe puna village celebrates the Assumption on August 15 in style, and thousands make the journey to see the main event – man against beast in a duel of agility and wits.

The bull's horns are garlanded with a red sweatband which contains three silver coins. *Promesantes* – young men from the village – armed with only a red cloth, then try to distract the animal's attention and rob it of its crown. The successful torero then offers the coins to the Virgin. The bull is unharmed. The festival has its origins in similar Spanish fiestas.

Casabindo is west of the Quebrada, accessible via a rough road beyond Purmamarca. Tour operators in Jujuy (p247) and Tilcara (p255) run trips to the festival.

---

the church and *cabildo*; another plaza, San Martín, is near the bus terminal.

INFORMATION

There are two places on Corrientes a block from the plaza that have internet access and open until midnight. There's an ATM on Plaza Gómez.

Locutorio (Jujuy 399) Behind the *municipalidad* (town hall). Make long-distance calls from here.

Post office (Buenos Aires) Across from the plaza.

Tourist office (Plaza Gómez s/n; 10am-9pm Mon-Fri) In the *cabildo*. The office on the highway is usually shut, but young rascals outside sell pamphlets that the other office gives out free.

SIGHTS

Built in 1641, Humahuaca's **Iglesia de la Candelaria** (Buenos Aires) faces Plaza Gómez. It contains an image of the town's patron saint, as well as 18th-century oils by Marcos Sapaca, of the Cuzco school.

The lovably knobbly **cabildo** is famous for its clocktower, where a life-size figure of San Francisco Solano emerges at noon to deliver a benediction. Be sure to arrive early; the clock is erratic.

From the plaza, a staircase climbs to the **Monumento a la Independencia**, a vulgarity produced by local sculptor Ernesto Soto Avendaño. The sculpture exemplifies *indigenismo*, a widespread tendency in Latin American art that romantically but patronizingly extols the virtues of native cultures overwhelmed by colonialism.

FESTIVALS & EVENTS

Besides **Carnaval**, which is celebrated throughout the Quebrada de Humahuaca in February, Humahuaca observes February 2 as the day of its patron, the **Virgen de Candelaria**.

SLEEPING

The boutique hotel boom hasn't yet hit Humahuaca, which keeps it real with cheap family-run accommodations and a couple of midrange hotels.

Posada La Churita (☎ 421055; balcazar@argentina.com; Buenos Aires 456; r per person AR$20, s/d AR$35/50) Run by warm-hearted, stout and motherly Olga, this is one of a few unheated cheapies on this street. In theory, the rooms are dorms, but you may well get one to yourself. The shared bathrooms are clean and hot water reliable. Guests have use of the kitchen and a common area with tables.

Posada El Sol (☎ 421466; elsolposada@imagine.com.ar; Barrio Milagrosa s/n; dm/d AR$25/70; 💻) In a peaceful location, signposted 800m across the river bridge, this curious, appealing adobe hostel has a variety of quirky dorm rooms, and pretty doubles under traditional cane ceilings. Some dorms are cramped, but this place is more than the sum of its parts. There's HI discount, and a kitchen.

Hotel de Turismo (☎ 421154; Buenos Aires 630; s/d AR$30/50; 🌊) With a 'Hotel California' vibe, this huge, echoing place is falling apart, and doesn't even appear open. It is, and the rooms are cheap for what they offer, as long as you don't get spooked by solitude in large buildings.

Residencial Colonial (☎ 421007; Entre Ríos 110; s/d AR$40/70) The price seems just for these compact, dark but clean rooms with TV, heating and bathroom around a reddish courtyard in the center of town. Bring something that makes a very loud noise if you arrive at siesta time.

Hostal La Soñada (☎ 421228; hostallasoniada@yahoo.com.ar; San Martín s/n; s/d AR$70/100) Just across the tracks from the center, this is run by a kindly local couple and features spotless rooms with colorful bedspreads and good bathrooms. Breakfast is served in the attractive common area, and guests feel very welcome.

EATING

Casa Vieja (cnr Buenos Aires & Salta; mains AR$10-20; ☼ lunch & dinner) This warm and attractive corner restaurant is hung with basketry and large dreamcatchers. It serves simple llama dishes, and also a tasty bean and quinoa stew. Portions are generous. There's live and decent music nightly from 9pm.

El Portillo (☎ 424-9000; cnr Tucumán & Corrientes; mains AR$12-25; ☼ 8am-midnight) Attractively decorated with cactus-wood furniture and booth tables, this popular restaurant has poor service and a simple menu, which mostly consists of llama in a variety of rather similar creamy sauces. Live music every night from 8pm.

SHOPPING

The handicrafts market, near the train station, has woolen goods, souvenirs and atmosphere. Near the plaza, **Manos Andinos** (cnr Buenos Aires 409), run by Cáritas, sells fair-trade artesanía.

GETTING THERE & AWAY

The **bus terminal** (cnr Belgrano & Entre Ríos) is three blocks south of the plaza. There are regular buses to Salta (AR$21, 4½ hours) and Jujuy (AR$11, 2¼ hours), and to La Quiaca (AR$12, three hours).

Transportes Mendoza (☎ 421442; cnr Belgrano & Salta) offers service to Iruya (AR$11, three hours). It leaves Humahuaca daily at 8:30am and 10:30am, and also 6pm Monday to Friday. Tickets are available from the bus terminal. The service is unreliable, especially in summer if rain has made the road impassable.

Around Humahuaca

Coctaca, 10km from Humahuaca, contains northwestern Argentina's most extensive pre-Columbian ruins. Although they have not yet been excavated, many of the ruins appear to have been broad agricultural terraces on an alluvial fan, though there are also obvious outlines of clusters of buildings.

The road may be impassable after rain; you can hike but take water, as tiny Coctaca has no shop. After crossing the bridge across the Río Grande in Humahuaca, follow the dirt road north and bear left until you see the village.

Iruya

☎ 03887 / pop 1070 / elev 2780m

There's something magical about Iruya, a remote village just 50km from the main road but a world away. It makes a great destination to relax for a few days, and also allows proper appreciation of the Quebrada de Humahuaca region away from the busy barreling highway.

The journey is worth the trip in itself. Turning off RN 9, 26km north of Humahuaca, the *ripio* road ascends to a spectacular 4000m pass that marks the Jujuy–Salta provincial boundary. Here, there's a massive *apacheta* (a cairn that accumulates stone by stone, left by travelers for luck). The plastic bottles are from liquid offerings to Pachamama.

The road then winds down into another valley, where smallholders farm potatoes, onions and beans, and reaches Iruya, with its pretty yellow-and-blue church, steep streets, adobe houses and spectacular mountainscapes (with soaring condors). It's an indigenous community with fairly traditional values, so respect is called for. Chatting with the friendly locals is the highlight of most travelers' experiences here. You can also trek in the surrounding hills – ask for a local guide – or visit other communities in the valley. In 2007, one of these, Colanzulí, was eagerly anticipating the arrival of electricity to the village. It was planning to build accommodations for travelers once the power was on – ask if there's any when you visit.

Iruya has a tourist office on Calle San Martín, but opening hours are irregular.

SLEEPING & EATING

There are many cheap places to stay in locals' homes. We won't recommend any –spreading the wealth is best here – but can confirm that they are spotless and value for money (AR$15 to AR$20 per person in a private room).

Federico III (☎ 1562-9152; www.complejofederico.com.ar; cnr San Martín & Salta; d AR$150) A more upmarket option, just above the plaza at the bottom of town; beds are much cheaper outside the January to February holidays.

Hostería Iruya (☎ 482002; www.hosteriadeiruya.com.ar; s/d AR$160/187, with view AR$190/220; ☒) At the top of the town, this place has light white rooms with wide beds, a spacious common area and a picturesque stone terrace with memorable views. There's a restaurant here.

BOLIVIA VIA VILLAZÓN

Crossing from La Quiaca to Villazón, Bolivia, walk, get a cab or local bus to the bridge, and then walk across, clearing **immigration** (7am-midnight). At time of research, US nationals needed a visa, but citizens of the EU, UK, Canada, Australia, New Zealand and South Africa did not. Bolivia is much nicer than Villazón promises, so head past the cut-price stalls and straight to the bus terminal or train station. A couple of cheap but reliable accommodation options are by the bus terminal and the plaza if you need them. Buses head to Tupiza (US$1.25, 2¼ hours), La Paz (US$20 to US$30, 20 hours) via Potosí (US$9, 10 hours), Oruro and Tarija (US$3.15, eight hours). The train station is 1.5km north of the border crossing – a taxi costs US$2. There are four weekly train services to Tupiza, Uyuni and Oruro. From October to April Bolivia is one hour behind Argentina. The rest of the year, Argentina operates on Bolivian time (only a bit more efficiently).

Pay cash. From the center of town, just head straight up the hill to the top of the village.

Several simple *comedores* (basic cafeterias) serve local cuisine. At **Comedor Iruya** (cnr Lavalle & San Martín; dishes AR$4-10; 10am-9pm), genial Juan and Tina serve delicious home-style meat and salad dishes in a cozy tin-roofed atmosphere.

GETTING THERE & AWAY

Buses from Humahuaca (AR$11, three hours) leave daily at 8:30am and 10:30am, and also 6pm Monday to Friday. The return service leaves Iruya at 1:30pm and 3:15pm daily, and 6am Monday to Saturday. Don't set your watch by it.

There is 50km of *ripio* road to negotiate off RN 9. In summer it often becomes impassable due to rain. You'll often see villagers hitchhiking – a good way to meet locals. A parking fee (AR$2) is charged entering Iruya.

LA QUIACA

03885 / pop 13,761 / elev 3442m

Truly the end of the line, La Quiaca is 5171km north of Ushuaia, and a major crossing point to Bolivia. It's a cold, windy place that has decent places to stay and eat but little to detain you. Once a bustling railroad terminus, La Quiaca's main sign of life these days is weary Bolivians trudging between the border and the bus terminal toting heavy bags. Nevertheless, it's not dangerous, and noble stone buildings recall more optimistic times.

The road to La Quiaca is intriguing. After leaving the Quebrada de Humahuaca, paved RN 9 passes through **Abra Pampa**, a forlornly windy town 90km north of Humahuaca, and climbs through picturesque and typi-cal altiplano landscapes. Nightly frosts make agriculture precarious, so people focus subsistence efforts on livestock (llamas, sheep, goats) that can survive on the sparse ichu grass. Look for the endangered vicuña off main routes.

La Quiaca is divided by its defunct train tracks; most services are west of them. North of town, a bridge across the river links La Quiaca with Villazón, Bolivia.

Information

Change money at the border and at the bus terminal. Call centers and internet places abound in town.

ACA (Automóvil Club Argentino; cnr Internacional & Bustamante) Maps and motorist services.

Banco Macro (Árabe Siria 445) Has an ATM.

Post office (cnr San Juan & Sarmiento)

Tourist office (422644; turismo@laquiaca.com.ar; cnr Pellegrini & Rivadavia; 7am-7pm) In the town hall on the other side of the railway. Also has branches at the border, and at the southern entrance to town.

Sleeping & Eating

Hospedaje Frontera (422269; cnr Belgrano & Árabe Siria; s/d without bathroom AR$20/30) Nights can get a little chilly here, but the darkish, motel-style rooms are clean and proper behind a popular local restaurant. Bathrooms (shared) have hot water, and management is welcoming.

Hotel de Turismo (422243; hotelmun@laquiaca .com.ar; cnr Árabe Siria & San Martín; s/d AR$50/90) A very good deal, the friendly government-run hotel offers handsome heated rooms with parquet floors and fine bathrooms. It's the best option in town.

Hostería Munay (423924; www.munayhotel.jujuy .com; Belgrano 51; s/d AR$70/85) Set back from the street in the heart of things, this is a reassuring option with cheery rooms decorated with *artesanía* and featuring small bathrooms, big beds and heating.

If coming from Bolivia: things get better eating-wise a few hours down the road. The Hotel de Turismo has a draughty *comedor* with fireplace; *bife de chorizo* with the works is AR$14, the set lunch AR$10. The **Frontera** (mains AR$8-14) has meat plates, Spanish omelet, decent *tallarines al pesto* (noodles with pesto), plus a four-course *menú económico* (cheap set meal) for AR$9. **Kasok** (Plaza Centenario s/n; mains AR$8-17; ⊙ lunch & dinner) is a handsome old building with an array of typical plates including *parrilla* options in the evening.

Getting There & Away
The chaotic La Quiaca **bus terminal** (cnr Belgrano & España) has frequent connections to Jujuy (AR$15, four to five hours) and Salta (AR$35, eight hours) and intermediate points. There is no transportation to Bolivia. Buy tickets directly from the bus company windows.

YAVI
☎ 03887 / pop 207 / elev 3440m
Picturesque, atmospheric, indigenous Yavi, 16km east of La Quiaca via paved RP 5, more than justifies a detour, and is a great little lazy hideaway. Apart from the tumbledown romanticism of its adobe streets, the village preserves two fascinating colonial-era buildings.

Yavi's is perhaps the most fascinating **church** (admission by donation; ⊙ 9am-noon & 3-6pm Tue-Fri, 9am-noon Sat, 3-6pm Mon) in northern Argentina. Built by the local marquis in the late 17th century, it preserves stunning altarpieces in sober baroque style, covered in gold leaf and adorned with excellent paintings and sculptures, mostly from the Cuzco school, but including one fine Flemish original. The translucent onyx windows also stand out.

Opposite, the **Casa del Marqués Campero** was the house of the marquis himself, a Spanish noble whose family dominated the regional economy in the 18th century. Now a **museum** (admission AR$2; ⊙ 9am-1pm & 2-6pm), it displays beautifully restored furniture, exhibits on more recent puna life and a lovable library. Restoration teams from Jujuy are working on further exhibits.

Near Yavi are several short walks in the Cerros Colorados, to rock paintings and petroglyphs at **Las Cuevas** or to springs at **Agua**

de Castilla. Ask for directions at the museum or the Hostal de Yavi.

There's a free campsite by the river. Locals offer basic accommodations in their homes; look for the signs along the apparently deserted main street. **Hostal de Yavi** (☎ 490523; hostaldeyavi@hotmail.com; Güemes 222; s/d AR$60/80; 💻) offers simple, comfortable rooms and an informal family atmosphere. Every need won't be anticipated before you voice it, but simple meals are available, and you can relax and chat to the personable kids.

Shared cabs and pickups (AR$3, 20 minutes) run to Yavi from La Quiaca's Mercado Municipal on Hipólito Yrigoyen; departures are frequent between 6am and 8am but slower after that. Otherwise, it's AR$20 to AR$25 in a taxi.

MONUMENTO NATURAL LAGUNA DE LOS POZUELOS
Three species of flamingos plus coots, geese, ducks and many other birds breed along the barren shores of this 160-sq-km lake, at an altitude of nearly 4000m. There's also a large vicuña population hereabouts. The lake has been declared a Ramsar site (an international conservation designation for wetland habitats and associated wildlife) because of its importance to waterbirds.

Because the park is so isolated, a car is the best transportation option, but carry extra fuel; there is no gasoline available beyond Abra Pampa, midway between Humahuaca and La Quiaca. Make sure you also take plenty of drinking water. Be aware that heavy summer rains can make the unpaved routes off the main highway impassable.

There are three main access routes to the lake: from just north of Abra Pampa; from La Quiaca west via Cieneguillas; and from La Intermedia, halfway between Abra Pampa and La Quiaca, where a road makes its way west over the hills to Pozuelos village.

There's a ranger station at Río Cincel, south of the lake. From near here, a 7km road heads north to a parking lot near the lakeshore. Or not; you may have to walk up to 3km depending on the water levels, which are highest in April and lowest in November. Take binoculars in any event, as you'll likely find yourself a long way from the flamingoes.

From Abra Pampa there are midmorning buses daily to Rinconada, west of the lake, where there are simple accommodations.

On request, the bus will drop you off at the ranger station, but you'll have to walk from there to the lake. Camping is possible on very exposed sites, with basic infrastructure, at the ranger station.

SALTA

☎ 0387 / pop 468,583 / elev 1187m

Sophisticated Salta is many travelers' favorite, smoothing ruffled psyches with its profusion of services, engaging active minds with its outstanding museums, and lighting romantic candles with its plaza-side cafés and the live *música folklórica* of its popular *peñas*. It offers the facilities of a large town, retains the comfortable vibe of a smaller place, and preserves more colonial architecture than most places in Argentina.

It's the most touristed spot in northwest Argentina, and has numerous accommodation options. The center bristles with travel and tour agents; this is the place to get things organized for onward travel. Nevertheless, there's a poorer Salta readily visible if you venture toward the city's outskirts, with a large population of indigenous farmfolk from the province and Bolivia searching, often in vain, for a better life in the big city.

History

Founded in 1582, Salta lies in a basin surrounded by verdant peaks. This valley's perpetual spring attracted the Spaniards, who could pasture their animals in the surrounding countryside and produce crops that it was not possible to grow in the frigid Bolivian highlands, where the mining industry created enormous demand for hides, mules and food. When the extension of the Belgrano railroad made it feasible to market sugar to the immigrant cities of the pampas, the city recovered slightly from its 19th-century decline. In recent years, growth has been rapid, as numerous families have settled here in search of work, fleeing the economic conditions in rural areas.

Orientation

Although Salta has sprawled considerably, most points of interest are within a few blocks of central Plaza 9 de Julio. North–south streets change their names on either side of the plaza, but the names of east–west streets are continuous. East of the center are the overlooks of Cerro 20 de Febrero and Cerro San Bernardo.

Information

BOOKSTORES

Feria del Libro (☎ 421-0359; Buenos Aires 83) Large selection.

Librería San Francisco (☎ 431-8456; Caseros 362) Decent selection of English books, mostly classics.

CULTURAL CENTERS

Alliance Française (☎ 431-2403; afsalta@sinectis.com .ar; Santa Fe 20; ⏰ 5-10pm Mon-Fri)

IMMIGRATION

Migraciones (☎ 422-0438; Maipú 35) Twelve blocks west of the plaza, near Caseros.

INTERNET ACCESS

There are hundreds of internet cafés. A central choice:

Cibercom (☎ 422-2514; Buenos Aires 97; per hr AR$1.50; ⏰ to 2am most days)

LAUNDRY

Laverap (☎ 432-0662; Pueyrredón 350, service wash AR$9) One of many. Most accommodations also have a (dearer) service.

MEDICAL SERVICES

Hospital San Bernardo (☎ 432-0445; Tobías 69)

MONEY

Banco de la Nación (cnr B Mitre & Av Belgrano) Cashes traveler's checks; it and several other banks around the plaza have ATMs.

Cambio Dinar (B Mitre 101) Changes traveler's checks (high commission) and cash.

POST

Post office (Deán Funes 140)

TELEPHONE

There are numerous call centers around town.

TOURIST INFORMATION

ACA (Automóvil Club Argentino; ☎ 431-0551; cnr Rivadavia & B Mitre) Road maps and route advice.

Municipal tourist office (☎ 437-3340; turismo@ municipalidad-salta.gov.ar; cnr Av San Martín & Buenos Aires; ⏰ 9am-9pm) Efficient multilingual staff. There's also a staff member at the information booth in the bus terminal.

National Parks Administration (APN; ☎ 431-2683; www.parquesnacionales.gov.ar; España 366; ⏰ 8am-3pm Mon-Fri) On the 3rd floor of the Aduana building, offers excellent information and advice on the region's national

THE ANDEAN NORTHWEST

SALTA

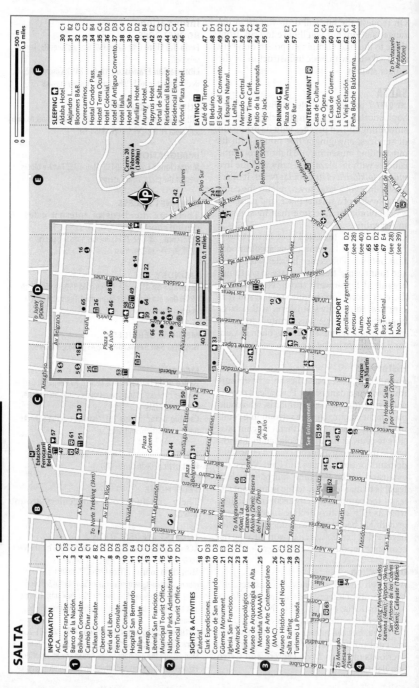

parks. Contact this place before going to the more remote parks such as El Rey or Baritú.

Provincial tourist office (☎ 431-0950; www.turismo salta.gov.ar; Buenos Aires 93; ☽ 8am-9pm Mon-Fri, 8am-8pm Sat & Sun) Friendly, efficient and multilingual. Top marks. Ask them about the condition of the roads if heading out in a rental car.

TRAVEL AGENCIES

There are numerous agencies along Buenos Aires, between Caseros and Alvarado, and all around the center, that can book airfares and bus tickets. See p265 for tour operators.

Sights
MUSEO DE ARQUEOLOGÍA DE ALTA MONTAÑA (MAAM)

Perhaps the premier museum in northern Argentina, **MAAM** (☎ 437-0499; www.maam.org.ar; Mitre 77; admission Argentines/foreigners AR$3/10, 9-10am Tue-Fri free; ☽ 9am-1pm & 4-9pm) has a serious and informative exhibition focusing on Inca culture and, in particular, the child sacrifices the Inca left on some of the Andes' most imposing peaks (see boxed text, p264).

The centerpiece of the display is the Doncella (Maiden), the mummified body of a 15-year-old girl, one of three children discovered at the peak of Llullaillaco during the 1999 expedition. It was a controversial decision to display the body (visitors may choose to view her or not) and it is a powerful experience to come face-to-face with her. Her intricately plaited hair and clothes are perfectly preserved, and her face reflects – who knows? – a distant past or a typical 21st-century Salta face; a peaceful passing or a tortured death. You decide.

The grave-goods that accompanied the children impress by their immediacy, with colors as fresh as the day they were produced. The *illas* (small votive figurines of animals and humans) are of silver, gold, shell and onyx, and many are clothed in textiles. It's difficult to imagine that a more privileged look at pre-Columbian South American culture will ever be offered us. Also exhibited is the 'Reina del Cerro', a mummy robbed from an Inca tomb in the 1920s that finally ended up here after a turbulent history. Some good videos give background information about the mummies and the expedition. Most of the museum's information panels are reproduced on laminated sheets in various languages. Take a jacket: comfortable mummy temperature

can be pretty chilly for the rest of us. There's a library as well as a café-bar with terrace and wi-fi.

MUSEO HISTÓRICO DEL NORTE

Set on the square in the *cabildo*, the **Museo Histórico del Norte** (☎ 421-5340; Caseros 549; admission AR$2; ☽ 9:30am-1:30pm & 3:30-8:30pm Tue-Fri, 9:30am-1:30pm & 4:30-8pm Sat, 9:30am-1pm Sun) has a collection that ranges from pre-Columbian ceramics through colonial-era religious painting and sculpture (admire the fine pulpit from Salta's Jesuit church), and displays on Salta in the 19th and 20th centuries. The endless series of portraits of Salta's governors wouldn't be out of place in a beard-and-moustache museum; the transportation collection includes a somber hearse used for children's funerals, and an enormous 1911 Renault that puts any Hummer to shame. The building itself, with cobbled patio and gallery overlooking the plaza, is lovely.

MUSEO DE ARTE CONTEMPORÁNEO (MAC)

The **MAC** (☎ 437-0498; Zuviría 90; admission AR$2; ☽ 9am-1pm & 5-9pm) has on display the work of contemporary artists from Salta, as well as other parts of Argentina and the wider world. The space itself is well lit and expertly curated. Exhibitions change regularly and are usually of high quality.

CATEDRAL

Salta's pink **catedral** (cnr España & B Mitre; ☽ 7am-noon & 4:30-8pm) was consecrated in 1878 and harbors the ashes of (among other notables) General Martín Miguel de Güemes, a *salteño* (resident of Salta) and independence hero; even today, the gauchos of Salta province proudly flaunt their red-striped *ponchos de güemes* (traditional Salta ponchos). The high baroque altarpiece is the other central feature.

IGLESIA SAN FRANCISCO

Two blocks east of the plaza, the magenta-and-yellow **Iglesia San Francisco** (cnr Caseros & Córdoba; ☽ 7:30am-noon & 5-9pm) is Salta's most striking landmark. The exuberant facade is topped by a slender tower; inside, the single nave is ornately painted to resemble stucco-work. There are several much-venerated images here, including the Niño Jesús de Aracoeli, a rather spooky crowned figure. There's a lovely garden cloister, accessed via guided tour (runs on demand in Spanish; donation appropriate)

THE CHILDREN GIVEN TO THE MOUNTAIN

The phrase 'human sacrifice' is sensationalist, but it is fact that the Inca culture from time to time offered the lives of high-born children to please or appease their gods. The Inca saw this as an offering to ensure the continued fertility of their people and the land. The high peaks of the Cordillera de los Andes were always considered sacred, and were chosen as sites for the sacrifices.

The children, carefully selected for the role, were taken to the ceremonial capital of Cuzco, where they were the centerpieces of a large celebration – the *capacocha*. Ceremonial marriages between them helped to cement diplomatic links between tribes across the Inca empire. At the end of the fiesta, they were paraded twice around the plaza, and then had to return home in a straight line – an arduous journey that could take months. Once home, they were feted and welcomed, and then taken into the mountains. They were fed, and given quantities of *chicha* (an alcoholic drink made from fermented maize) to drink. When they passed out, they were taken up to the peak of the mountain and left in their drunken sleep, presumably never to awaken.

Three such children were found in 1999 near the peak of Llullaillaco, a 6739m volcano some 480km west of Salta, on the Chilean border. It's the highest known archaeological site in the world. The cold, low pressure, and lack of oxygen and bacteria, helped preserve the bodies almost perfectly. The Doncella (Maiden) – displayed at Salta's Museo de Arqueología de Alta Montaña (MAAM) – was about 15 at the time of death, and was perhaps an *aclla* (a 'virgin of the sun'), a prestigious role in Inca society. The other two, a boy and girl both aged six to seven, had cranial deformations that indicated they came from high-ranking families. They were accompanied each by an *ajuar* (a selection of grave goods), which included textiles and small figurines of humanoids and camelids.

The mummies' transfer to Salta was controversial to say the least. Many felt they should have been left where they were discovered, but this, once the location was known, would have been impossible. Whatever your feelings on them, and the role of archaeology, they offer an undeniably fascinating glimpse of Inca religion and culture.

that takes in a mediocre museum of religious art and treasures.

CONVENTO DE SAN BERNARDO

Only Carmelite nuns may enter the 16th-century **Convento de San Bernardo** (cnr Caseros & Santa Fe), but visitors can approach the blindingly white-washed adobe building (consider sunglasses) to admire the carved, 18th-century algarrobo door. The nuns sell pastries (AR$3) through a traditional revolving cupboard that avoids their having direct contact with the outside world.

CERRO SAN BERNARDO

For outstanding views of Salta and its surroundings, take the **teleférico** (gondola cablecar; ☎ 431-0641; 1-way/roundtrip AR$6/12; ☺ 10am-7:45pm) from Parque San Martín to the top of Cerro San Bernardo. A trail that takes you up the hill begins at the Güemes monument at the top of Paseo Güemes. Atop this a *confitería* (café offering light meals), whose terrace has the best views, a watercourse and *artesanía* shops.

Just above the Güemes monument, on the lower slopes of Cerro San Bernardo, is the friendly **Museo Antropológico** (☎ 422-2960; cnr Ejército del Norte & Polo Sur; admission AR$2; ☺ 8am-7pm Mon-Fri, 8am-1pm & 3-7pm Sat). It has good representations of local ceramics, especially from the Tastil ruins (Argentina's largest pre-Inca town), and some well-designed displays in its attractive, purpose-built spaces.

RESERVA DEL HUAICO

This 60-hectare **cloud forest reserve** (☎ 497-1024; huaico1790@gmail.com; Mariano Moreno s/n, San Lorenzo; 4hr guided tour AR$30; ☺ 8am-6pm) is in San Lorenzo, 7km west of Salta, and run by a not-for-profit nature foundation. Entry is by prior appointment and includes a four-hour guided walk along the reserve's 15km of trails. Despite Salta's proximity, the bird watching is extraordinarily good; more than 205 species have been recorded, with 100 of those – including guans, tanagers, parrots, hummingbirds and woodpeckers – all common. A cab from Salta costs AR$15, or you can get any San Lorenzo-bound bus (AR$1). Get off at the *municipalidad* and it's a 1km walk along Mariano Moreno to the reserve.

Tours

Salta is the base for a range of innovative tours, offered by many companies. For city tours (AR$44) and excursions in the Salta area, try any of the travel agencies on Buenos Aires, between Caseros and Alvarado. Other popular trips head to Cafayate (AR$109), Cachi (AR$120), San Antonio de los Cobres (the Tren a las Nubes route; AR$151), Salinas Grandes (AR$252), and Humahuaca (AR$132). Several operators offer horseback riding, rafting and kayaking; paragliding, abseiling, climbing and hiking are also available. Full-day tours to Parque Nacional El Rey leave very early in the morning to give visitors the best possible opportunity to spot native birds and animals on guided walks in this remote forest.

Some operators:

Clark Expediciones (☎ 421-5390; www.clarkexpedi ciones.com; Caseros 121) Professional agency offering trips with highly competent English-speaking guides to the region's national parks and remote uplands. Bird watching is its specialty; trips include a day in Parque Nacional Caliegua (AR$120 to AR$160), a two-day excursion to Parque Nacional El Rey (AR$260 to AR$320), or multiday (or month-long) tailored itineraries. Book well ahead.

Movitrack (☎ 431-6749; www.movitrack.com.ar; Buenos Aires 28) Innovative and reliable operator, with a variety of daytrips and multiday excursions with fixed departure days. Some use a characterful open truck, while others go in a pressurized minibus that prevents altitude sickness.

Norte Trekking (☎ 436-1844; fedenorte@yahoo .com.ar; Libertador 1151, Barrio Grand Bourg) At time of research, one of only two agencies specifically approved for trips to Parque Nacional El Rey.

Salta Rafting (☎ 421-4114; www.saltarafting.com; Buenos Aires 88) Runs two-hour rafting trips on the Class III Río Juramento, 100km from Salta (AR$95 including a barbecue lunch, transportation to/from Salta AR$45 extra). At the same location are spectacular 400m ziplines across a canyon (four-line trip AR$50).

Turismo la Posada (☎ 421-6544; www.turismola posada.com.ar; Buenos Aires 94) This French- and English-speaking company has a good variety of trips, and offers horseback riding, trekking and rafting.

Sleeping

BUDGET

Camping Municipal Carlos Xamena (☎ 423-1341; Av Libano; sites per person/tent AR$2.50/3.75; 🖳) One of Argentina's best campgrounds, this has 500 tent sites and a huge pool (it takes a week to fill). It's typically loud in summer. From downtown, take southbound bus 13 (labeled 'Balneario'). There's a supermarket near the campsite.

Correcaminos (☎ 422-0731; www.cchostel.com .ar; Vicente López 353; dm AR$20, s/d AR$40/60; 🖳) 'Roadrunner' is a cheap-and-cheerful hostel which boasts a well-used bar and pool table out the back. Dorms are spacious if a little stuffy in summer; the location and laid-back vibe make this an appealing choice. Its card notes that it has been recommended by 'Looney Planet'.

Hostel Salta por Siempre (☎ 423-3230; www .saltaporsiempre.com.ar; Tucumán 464; dm/s/d AR$25/50/60; 🖳) A reader put us on to this place, a hostel-guesthouse run by a simpatico Argentine family. The quiet and handsome building has glisteningly clean colorful rooms, a proper kitchen and small garden. It's eight blocks south of the plaza, but it rents bikes. Breakfast included.

Hostel Terra Oculta (☎ 421-8769; www.terraoculta .com; Córdoba 361; dm/d AR$25/55; 🖳) Handily located between bus terminal and center, this laid-back, labyrinthine spot is an upbeat hostel that sensibly has its light, comfortable dorms well separated from the excellent rooftop bar, where the action can go loud and late.

Hostal Condor Pass (☎ 422-1050; condor_pass@hot mail.com; Urquiza 675; dm/d AR$25/70; 🖳) Two blocks from the plaza, this compact hostel has dorms with firm mattresses and rooms with bathroom around a narrow central patio. Kitchen use and breakfast is included, and it offers free transportation from the bus terminal.

MIDRANGE

Residencial Elena (☎ 421-1529; Buenos Aires 256; s/d AR$40/70) Set in a neocolonial building with a charming interior patio, this has a choice location not far south of the plaza. Though it's on a busy central street, it's very quiet, and the longtime Spanish owners keep it shipshape.

Residencial Balcarce (☎ 431-8135; www.residencial balcarce.com.ar; Balcarce 460; s/d AR$50/75) Just south of Plaza Güemes, a small entrance disguises a large interior at this value-packed place. In many ways, it's a standard *residencial*, with unadorned rooms with decent bathrooms, but the friendly service, grapevine-shaded patio and high hygiene levels make it a sound choice.

Munay Hotel (☎ 422-4936; www.munayhotel.jujuy .com; Av San Martín 656; s/d AR$70/85) With everything you could want in a budget hotel – a handy location; staff who are pleased to see you;

well-furnished, clean and modern bedrooms; shower curtains; and breakfast – this is one to book ahead.

Hotel Italia (☎ 421-4050; Alberdi 231; s/d AR$70/110) Right on a busy pedestrian street (but quiet), this hotel boasts darkish rooms with OK bathrooms. As usual, the shower seems designed to soak the toilet paper while keeping guests dry, but the location, staff and price here are fine; a fallback rather than a first choice. Try negotiating a discount.

Hotel Colonial (☎ 421-1740; www.saltahotelcolonial.com.ar; Zuviría 6; s/d AR$110/150; ✄ ☐) In a distant past – think BC – this might have been Salta's finest hotel, with fine public rooms and an ultracentral address. It's overpriced and needs a major refit now, but still has some character and a plazaside location. Make sure you pay the extra AR$20 (so-called 'superior' rooms) for street views; plaza views ('suites') cost more.

Victoria Plaza Hotel (☎ 431-8500; www.hotelvictoriaplaza.com.ar; Zuviría 16; s/d AR$115/160; ✄ ☐) The cheerful and bright rooms here have added touches of comfort, such as minibars, sofas and bathrooms with good-sized tubs. The rooms further up the building are more spacious and modern (singles AR$145 to AR$165; doubles AR$182 to AR$218) and have great city/mountain/plaza views.

Portal de Salta (☎ 431-7019; www.portaldesaltahotel.com.ar; Alvarado 341; s/d AR$122/158; ☐) A delightfully presented hotel done out in dark woods, gleaming brass and somber colors. Rooms are a bit cramped, but modern and comfortable nonetheless. Prices for foreigners are theoretically higher, but arguing the call usually works.

our pick **Bloomers B&B** (☎ 422-7449; www.bloomers-salta.com.ar; Vicente López 129; s AR$126, d AR$189-207; ✄ ☐) Break any or all of the Ten Commandments if needs be, but make sure you get one of the five rooms at this exquisitely stylish yet relaxed and comfortable guesthouse. The second B here stands for brunch, served until midday and replete with good things. The color-themed rooms are all different, and all delightful. The good company and laissez-faire environment makes you feel like a guest in a friend's home, but few of our friends have a place this pretty.

Marilian Hotel (☎ 421-6700; www.hotelmarilian.com.ar; Buenos Aires 176; s/d AR$129/159; ✄ ☐) Nestled among the tour agencies on this central street, this hotel offers bright and pretty white-tiled rooms with hanging headrests behind the beds. Bathrooms are small but new (a bathtub costs AR$10 extra) and the price (for Salta) feels fair.

Hotel del Antiguo Convento (☎ 422-7267; www.hoteldelconvento.com.ar; Caseros 113; r AR$135; ✄ ☐ ✄) There really is nothing *antiguo* (old) or conventlike about this place: rooms are modern and sunny and there's a great little pool area out the back. At these prices, it beats plenty of Salta's midrange options into a cocked hat.

Aldaba Hotel (☎ 421-9455; B Mitre 910; www.aldabahotel.com; r AR$170; ✄ ☐) A block away from the *peña* action of Calle Balcarce, this six-room place is nevertheless superbly quiet and tranquil. Run with a personal touch, it's decorated with restrained modern elegance, and boasts supercomfortable beds. Rooms vary widely in size (but not price).

TOP END

Hotel Salta (☎ 431-0740; www.hotelsalta.com; Buenos Aires 1; s/d AR$160/220; ✗ ✄ ☐ ✄) You pay extra for location here – but what a location – on a corner of the postcard-pretty central plaza, in a stately, traditional hotel. Facilities are good, but the rooms are a tad disappointing. Try to grab one with a view, although these are mostly suites (AR$395 to AR$570). Superior rooms are bigger than the compact standards, and have bathtubs.

Papyrus Hotel (☎ 422-7067; www.hotelpapyrus.com.ar; Linares 237; r AR$290-390; ✄ ☐ ✄) Discreetly tucked into a fold of the Cerro San Bernardo, this gorgeous boutique hotel offers both Salta at your feet (literally, the views are wonderful) and an ambience that feels withdrawn from the city, although it's only a few blocks to the center. The rooms higher up feel a little more vibrant, but all are excellent, and service is warm and faultless. Dinner – a AR$50 set menu – is also offered.

Alejandro I (☎ 400-0000; www.alejandro1hotel.com.ar; Balcarce 252; r standard/superior/executive AR$350/395/445; ✄ ☐ ✄) Astronauts, cosmonauts, or Google Earth aficionados might know whether Salta's most upmarket hotel is visible from orbit – it certainly is, for better or worse, from the whole city. The rooms are slick and modern, and get pricier and larger as you move higher up the building. The restaurant is reader-recommended, and service is swift and efficient.

Eating

Mercado Central (cnr Florida & Av San Martín) This large, lively market is very interesting as well as one of the cheapest places in town. You can supplement inexpensive pizza, empanadas and *humitas* (stuffed corn dough, resembling Mexican tamales) with fresh fruit and vegetables.

New Time Café (☎ 431-6461; Caseros 602; breakfast AR$3-6, snacks AR$3-9; ☺ 8am-late) In the race for the accolade of Salta's best plaza café, this two-level corner spot wins by several lengths. It offers shady (in the afternoon) tables, great views of the *cabildo*, Cerro San Bernardo and cathedral, and wi-fi…it also serves coffee and food, though it isn't the cheapest. Live music some nights.

El Beduino (☎ 421-2232; Deán Funes 61; dishes AR$3-9; ☺ lunch & dinner Tue-Sun) Authentic and delicious Lebanese food is here for the taking at bargain prices in this simple restaurant. Piquant tabouleh salad, exquisite *kebbe nayeh* (marinated raw mince), homemade pita, and creamy hummus – excellent. Dancers shake their bellies on weekend evenings.

La Esquina Natural (☎ 421-5771; Santiago del Estero 496; dishes AR$5-11; ☺ lunch & dinner Mon-Sat) This little vegetarian restaurant mostly functions as a take-out, but has a few simple wooden tables. Daily dishes are displayed at the glass counter.

ourpick La Leñita (☎ 421-4865; cnr Balcarce & A Alsina; mains AR$11-28; ☺ lunch & dinner) Tucumán's best *parrilla* has just reached Salta and hits the same heights on what is a hit-and-miss dining street. Fine meat, with a wide range of cuts, and solicitous service whether you're in a suit or singlet. The versatile staff serenade diners with Salta *folklore* halfway through dinner.

Portezuelo Restaurant (☎ 431-0104; Av de Turista 1; dishes AR$12-28; ☺ 7am-midnight) On a sunny day there's no better place to be than on the balcony of this restaurant in the Portezuelo Hotel, enjoying some of the best views in Salta. The food is well prepared, with welcome Mediterranean touches such as sun-dried tomatoes and calamari salad, and the service is excellent.

El Solar del Convento (☎ 421-5124; Caseros 444; most mains AR$16-28; ☺ lunch & dinner) Warmly decorated and popular, this reliable choice offers solicitous service – the free apéritif wins points – and a varied menu. It specializes in *lomo* (sirloin) with tasty sauces, and also has fish dishes and *parrillada* (mixed grill including steak) options. The wine list offers many excellent provincial choices. It wasn't quite up to its usual standards when last visited, but hopefully it was an aberration.

Viejo Jack (☎ 422-3911; Av Virrey Toledo 145; mains for 2 AR$18-32; ☺ lunch & dinner) Far enough out of the tourist zone to be authentic, but not so far it's a pain in the backside to get to, this is a down-to-earth spot very popular with locals for its *parrillada* and pasta. The serves are huge – designed for two – but they'll give you a single portion (still a big slab of meat) for 70% of the price.

Café del Tiempo (☎ 432-0771; Balcarce 901; dishes AR$22-35; ☺ 7pm-late) Decked out to resemble a Buenos Aires café, this has prices to match but offers a stylish terrace in the heart of the Balcarce zone; a top spot for a drink. There's some sort of performance or live music every night; most of the dishes – including international offerings such as chop suey, sushi and ceviche – are designed to share, and the *picadas* (shared appetizer plates) are great for a group.

It's a toss-up between Salta and Tucumán for Argentina's best empanadas, but they're wickedly toothsome in both places. Locals debate the merits of fried (in an iron skillet; juicier) or baked (in a clay oven; tastier). Numerous places specialize in them, including the *peñas*. Taxi-drivers' favorite is **Patio de la Empanada** (cnr San Martín & Islas Malvinas) where a dozen will set you back AR$7.50.

Drinking & Entertainment

See the boxed text (p268) for the classic Salta night-time experience. The two blocks of Balcarce north of Alsina, and the surrounding streets, are the main nightlife zone. Bars and clubs around here follow the typical boom-bust-reopen-with-new-name pattern, so just follow your nose.

Casa de Cultura (☎ 421-6042; Caseros 460) This cultural center near the plaza has regular live events. They run the whole gamut here: you're as likely to catch a Houdini-style magician as a classical ballet performance.

La Estación (Balcarce 872; ☺ Thu-Sat) Set right in the heart of the Balcarce nightlife strip, this one-time cinema is now one of several popular *discotecas* (nightclubs) in the zone.

Uno Bar (☎ 422-9120; Balcarce 926; ☺ 8pm-late) This intimate bar was popular at the time of research for its pricey but well-mixed drinks, terrace, cozy interior and trance/drum 'n' bass.

Plaza de Almas (☎ 422-8933; Pueyrredón 6; ☺ 9am-late Mon-Sat) Offering an eclectic mix of *artesanía*

THE ANDEAN NORTHWEST

PEÑAS OF SALTA

Salta is famous Argentina-wide for its *folklore* (folk music), which is far more national in scope than tango. A *peña* is a bar or social club where people eat, drink and gather to play and listen to *folklore*, which often traditionally took the form of an impromptu jam session.

These days, the Salta *peña* is quite a touristy experience, with scheduled performances, CD sales, tour groups and high prices, and it's difficult to find an authentic spot. There are a couple (ask around) where folk musicians hang out in their spare time, and you may catch a spontaneous performance.

Nevertheless, the standard Salta *peña* is a great deal of fun. Traditional fare is empanadas and red wine – delicious, but most of the places offer a wide menu including *parrillada* (mixed grill including steak) and 'Andean cuisine', with llama meat and quinoa featuring.

Peña heartland is Calle Balcarce, between A Alsina and the train station. There are several here, along with other restaurants, bars and *boliches* (nightclubs) – it's Salta's main nightlife zone. Things typically get moving at 9.30pm, but go on till late, especially at weekends.

Some *peñas* to get you started:

La Vieja Estación (☎ 421-7727; www.viejaestacion-salta.com.ar; Balcarce 885; mains AR$13-35; ☽ dinner) Best-established of the Balcarce *peñas*, with a stage, cozy wooden tables and three live shows per night. Tasty empanadas, and a wide range of other choices. There's a terrace to appreciate the show at a quieter volume.

La Casona del Molino (☎ 434-2835; Luis Burela 1; mains AR$18-35; ☽ 9pm-late) This former mansion, about 20 blocks west of Plaza 9 de Julio, is a Salta classic that goes sinfully late at weekends. It has several spacious rooms, each with different performers who work around the tables rather than on a stage.

Peña Boliche Balderrama (☎ 421-1542; www.boliche-balderrama.com.ar; Av San Martín 1126; mains AR$12-25; ☽ 8pm-late) With cheap but unremarkable food, this is Salta's most touristy *peña*. It can be a lot of fun, but feels contrived these days.

La Casa de Güemes (☎ 422-8978; España 730, mains AR$10-25; ☽ lunch & dinner) Central historic house once occupied by Güemes, a *salteño* independence hero who looms large in gaucho and *folklore* culture hereabouts. Decent, fairly-priced food, and good local music.

shops, a bar, lounge, café, and restaurant, this Tucumán classic has seamlessly moved into Salta. The most atmospheric place for a drink in town.

Cine Ópera (☎ 421-3520; Urquiza 560; movie ticket AR$6) This is the most central of Salta's several cinemas, showing Hollywood standards in original version.

Shopping

An artisan's market sets up every Sunday along Balcarce, stretching a couple of blocks south from the station.

Mercado Artesanal (☎ 439-2808; Av San Martín 2555; ☽ 8am-8:30pm) For souvenirs, this provincially-sponsored market is the most noteworthy place. Articles include native handicrafts such as hammocks, string bags, ceramics, basketry, leather work and the region's distinctive ponchos. To get here, take bus 2, 3 or 7 from downtown.

Getting There & Away

AIR

Salta's **airport** (SLA; ☎ 424-3115) is 9.5km southwest of town on RP 51. **Aerolíneas Argentinas** (☎ 431-1331; Caseros 475) flies four to five times daily to Buenos Aires' Aeroparque Jorge Newbery (AR$750). **LAN** (☎ 421-7330; www.lan.com; Buenos Aires 88) flies the same route once daily and much more reliably.

Andes (☎ 437-3514; www.andesonline.com; España 478) flies three times weekly to Buenos Aires, with onward connections to their other destination, Puerto Madryn. **Aerosur** (☎ 432-0149; www.aerosur.com; Buenos Aires 88) flies three times weekly to Santa Cruz, Bolivia (AR$670, one hour).

Flights are heavily oversubscribed, so try to book well ahead. As ever, don't rely on an Aerolíneas flight not being cancelled.

BUS

Salta's **bus terminal** (☎ 401-1248; Av Hipólito Yrigoyen), southeast of downtown, has frequent services to all parts of the country. The information desk is in the middle of the concourse.

Two companies, Géminis and Pullman, do the run to San Pedro de Atacama, Chile. Annoyingly, both leave at the same time: at 7am on Tuesday, Thursday, and Sunday. They go via Jujuy and the Paso de Jama, take 10 to

11 hours, and cost AR$136. It's worth reserving a few days before. The buses go on to service Calama, Antofagasta, Iquique and Arica.

El Quebradeño (☎ 427-1127) goes daily to San Antonio de los Cobres (AR$18, 5½ hours) and **Marcos Rueda** (☎ 421-4447) serves Cachi (AR$23.30, 4½ hours), departing daily at 7am, also at 1.30pm Tuesday to Saturday, at 3.30pm Thursday, and 5pm Sunday.

Sample fares to other destinations:

Destination	Cost (AR$)	Duration (hr)
Buenos Aires	150	20
Cafayate	23	3½
Catamarca	59	8
Córdoba	98	14
Jujuy	13	2
La Quiaca	35	8
La Rioja	76	10
Mendoza	142	18
Puerto Iguazú	226	21
Resistencia	86	10
Río Gallegos	405	48
Salvador Mazza	45	6
San Juan	127	16
Santiago (Chile)	198	25
Santiago del Estero	54	6
Tucumán	33	4½

CAR

Many travelers choose to rent a car for a few days in Salta in order to see the surrounding highlands and valleys. There are many agencies; it's worth getting a list from the tourist office of those that are officially registered. Cruise around getting quotes, as there are often special offers available. Typically, companies charge AR$120 to AR$200 per day for a week's hire, triple that for a 4WD. The stretches between San Antonio de los Cobres and La Poma (en route to Cachi), and north of Salinas Grandes toward Abra Pampa are basically 4WD only, but the *ripio* road between San Antonio and Salinas Grandes is normally passable in a standard car. Always check with the provincial tourist office for current conditions.

At the time of writing, only Argentine nationals could take rental cars into Bolivia. Companies required two to three days notice to process the paperwork required if you wanted to take the vehicle into Chile.

Some companies:

Alamo (☎ 422-8779; salta@alamoargentina.com.ar; Buenos Aires 176) Frequent weekly specials; attached to the Marilian Hotel.

Asís (☎ 431-1704; soruizar@yahoo.com.ar; Buenos Aires 68) Straight-talking and fairly priced.

Noa (☎ 431-7080; www.noarentacar.com; Buenos Aires 1) In the Hotel Salta.

TRAIN

Salta no longer has train services except the on-again, off-again Tren a las Nubes (below).

Getting Around

Buses running along RP 51 can leave you near the airport (AR$1), otherwise it's a AR$13 *remise* (taxi ride). There are also shuttle buses that leave from the Aerolíneas Argentinas office about one hour before flights (AR$8).

Local bus 5 connects the train station and downtown with the bus terminal.

TREN A LAS NUBES

Argentina's most famous train ride has been plagued with uncertainty in recent years, and service has been sporadic at best. At research time, latest word was that it was to recommence operation in mid 2008. The best place for up-to-date information is Salta's provincial tourist office (p263).

From Salta, the Tren a las Nubes (Train to the Clouds) leaves the Lerma Valley to ascend the multicolored Quebrada del Toro, continuing past the ruins of Tastil and stopping at San Antonio de los Cobres, before continuing a little further to the trip's highlight. A stunning viaduct 64m high and 224m long spans an enormous desert canyon at La Polvorilla; a magnificent engineering achievement unjustified on any reasonable economic grounds. The train stops here, but the track actually continues to the high Paso de Socompa on the Chilean border, 571km west of Salta.

When last in operation, the trip was a touristy one, with *folklore* performances and multilingual commentary. It ran once a week, less often in low season, and meals were available on board.

Many tour operators in Salta p265 run trips along the road that parallels the train's route, also a spectacular ascent; they include the viaduct.

SAN ANTONIO DE LOS COBRES

☎ 0387 / pop 4274 / elev 3775m

This dusty little mining town is on the puna 168km west of Salta, and over 2600m above it. It's suffered greatly since the deterioration of the region's mining and associated

THE ANDEAN NORTHWEST

railway, and relies heavily on tourism and the stop-start Tren a las Nubes for income. It's a very typical highland settlement, with adobe houses, almost deserted streets, and a serious drop in temperature as soon as the sun goes down. It's not the place for cutting-edge nightlife or street art, but is worth stopping in to get the feel of this facet of Argentine and South American life. You can head north from here to the Quebrada de Humahuaca via the Salinas Grandes and Purmamarca, but the road south to Cachi is very tough.

In colonial times, transportation from northwestern Argentina depended on pack trains; one route passed through here, crossing the rugged elevations of the Puna de Atacama to the Pacific and then on to Lima. It was a rugged journey, taking 20 days to cover the 800km.

There are two **tourist offices** (☉ 8am-8pm), one at the eastern and the other at the northern entrance to town; (the latter has a couple of simple rooms for AR$20 per person). They are not impartial recommending accommodations.

Sights

There's little to see in town – though the sunsets are spectacular – but 16km to the west is the viaduct at **La Polvorilla** (see p269), last stop of the Tren a las Nubes at 4200m above sea level. Though it seems underwhelming at first glimpse, it's very impressive once you get up close. From the parking lot, which has a couple of *artesanía* shops, you can climb up a zigzag path to the top of the viaduct and walk across it – watch the power lines! *Remises* in San Antonio charge about AR$30 for the return journey.

Sleeping & Eating

Choice of places to stay and eat is limited.

Hostal del Cielo (☎ 490-9912; www.vivirenloscobres .org.ar; Belgrano s/n; dm AR$20) This basic but very friendly hostel is on the edge of town, heading toward the viaduct. Buses from Salta will drop you here if you ask, otherwise it's about 1km from the center. There are two spotless, comfortable, gender-segregated dorms; HI members get breakfast included. There's a small anthropological museum next door.

El Palenque (☎ 490-9019; hostalelpalenque@hotmail .com; Belgrano s/n; r with bathroom AR$70, s/d without bathroom AR$30/50) Welcoming and tidy, this is a fine choice a few blocks from the center, past

the church. It looks closed from outside, but it's not. The rooms are insulated and (comparatively) warm, there's hot water and sound family ownership.

Hostería de las Nubes (☎ 490-9059; www.maresur .com; Caseros 441; s/d AR$120/150) The best place to stay and eat in town, this has attractively simple decoration in its comfortable rooms, which boast double-glazing and heating. Book ahead. The restaurant (mains AR$12 to AR$18; open noon to 2pm and 7pm to 10pm) serves a short menu of local dishes; all are well-prepared and nourishing.

El Águila (☎ 490-9108; Zavaleta s/n; dishes AR$6-12; ☉ lunch & dinner) This basic place near the central diagonal intersection serves simple local meals and doubles as a *locutorio* (private telephone office).

Getting There & Away

There are daily buses from Salta (AR$18, 5½ hours) with El Quebradeño. See also the Tren a las Nubes (p269). There's precious little transportation running over the Paso de Sico to Chile these days; if you are trying to hitchhike, ask around town for trucks due to leave.

SALINAS GRANDES

Bring sunglasses for this spectacular **salt plain** in a remote part of the puna, at some 3350m above sea level. What was once a lake dried up in the Holocene and is now a 525-sq-km crust of salt, which varies from 10cm to 50cm in thickness. On a clear day, the blinding contrast between the bright blue sky and the cracked and crusty expanse of white is spellbinding. Nearly all sense of distance and perspective is lost; you can take advantage and snap some creative photos if you have a couple of volunteers to stand at various distances.

The *salinas* (salt plains) are in Salta province but are most easily reached by heading west along the paved RP 52 from Purmamarca in Jujuy province. That road actually cuts across a narrow part of the salt flats, where there are a couple of places to buy drinks and food.

The good *ripio* road that runs north from San Antonio de Cobres to intersect with RP 52 (97km) passes very close to the southeastern edge of the *salinas* some 70km north of San Antonio, so you can easily walk across to them.

There's small-scale mining of the salt, but the inevitable 'salt hotel' hasn't appeared yet.

WESTERN SALTA PROVINCE

If you thought San Antonio de los Cobres was remote, think again. Hundreds of kilometers of Salta province stretch west of here, and include two passes to Chile, the barren **Paso de Sico**, and the remote rail crossing at **Socompa**. Sixty kilometers west of San Antonio, **Olacapato** is Argentina's highest village, at 4090m above sea level. All the area's settlements are mining camps or grew up around the railway that serviced the mines; many are abandoned now.

From Olacapato you can continue west to the Paso de Sico, or head southwest across salt flats to **Tolar Grande**, where there are accommodations in private homes. Beyond here it's 139km to the Paso de Socompa, or 131km southward to the abandoned mine of La Casualidad, the end of the road, and one of Argentina's most remote spots. Needless to say, it's a trip only possible in summer, and an arduous one. Take all your fuel needs from San Antonio, where you can buy 200L drums; and inform police of your plans. Don't wander off-road around Mina La Casualidad, as some landmines from a 1970s dispute with Chile are still around.

The closest places to stay are San Antonio and Susques. The only way of reaching the *salinas* by public transportation is to jump off a Susques-bound bus from Jujuy or Purmamarca. Check the timetables carefully before doing this; on some days it's possible to catch a bus back to Purmamarca a couple of hours later, but on other days it's not. This road has enough traffic to hitchhike.

Otherwise, hire a car, or take a tour from Jujuy or Salta. From the latter, it's a hellishly long day, unless you opt to overnight in Purmamarca.

The *salinas* are spectacular, but the otherworldly *salares* (salt flats) in southwestern Bolivia are even more so; if you're heading that way (or have already been) you might want to prioritize other attractions.

VALLES CALCHAQUÍES

The Valles Calchaquíes is one of Argentina's most seductive off-the-beaten-track zones, with a winning combination of rugged landscapes, traditional workshops, strikingly attractive adobe villages and some of Argentina's best wines. Small but sophisticated Cafayate, with its wineries and paved highway, presents quite a contrast to remoter settlements such as Angastaco or Molinos, while Cachi, accessible from Salta via a spectacular road that crosses the Parque Nacional Los Cardones, is another peaceful and popular base. The vernacular architecture in these valleys merits special attention – even modest adobe houses might have neoclassical columns or Moorish arches.

In these valleys, indigenous Diaguita (Calchaquí) put up some of the stiffest resistance to Spanish rule. In the 17th century, plagued with labor shortages, the Spaniards twice tried to impose forced labor obligations on the Diaguita, but found themselves having to maintain armed forces to prevent them from sowing their own crops and attacking pack trains.

Military domination did not solve Spanish labor problems, since their only solution was to relocate the Diaguita as far away as Buenos Aires, whose suburb of Quilmes bears the name of one group of these displaced people. The last descendants of the 270 families transported to the viceregal capital had died or had dispersed by the time of Argentine independence. The productive land that had sustained the Diaguita for centuries was formed by the Spaniards into large rural estates, the haciendas of the Andes.

Currently, you can't do the whole Calchaquí circuit by public transportation; the 37km stretch between Angastaco and Molinos isn't covered by a bus route. Short of doubling back through Salta – a lengthy detour – you might manage to hitchhike or find a ride on a pickup truck; it's much easier to ask around the towns rather than wait for hours on the road.

Parque Nacional Los Cardones

Occupying some 650 sq km on both sides of the winding RP 33 from Salta to Cachi across the Cuesta del Obispo, Parque Nacional Los Cardones takes its name from the candelabra cactus known as the cardón, the park's most striking plant species.

In the treeless Andean foothills and puna, the cardón has long been an important source of timber for rafters, doors, window frames and similar uses. You see it often in vernacular buildings and the region's colonial churches. According to Argentine writer Federico

Kirbus, clusters of cardónes can be indicators of archaeological sites; the indigenous people of the puna ate its sweet black seed, which, after passing through the intestinal tract, readily sprouted around their latrines. Certainly, many a *pucará* in the region bristles with these otherworldly sentinels.

Los Cardones is free to enter and still has no visitor services, but there is a **ranger office** (☎ 03868-496001; loscardones@apn.gov.ar; San Martín s/ n) in Payogasta, 11km north of Cachi. Take plenty of water and protection from the sun. Buses between Salta and Cachi will stop for you, but verify times. Most people disembark at Valle Encantada, which is the most accessible, picturesque part of the park.

Cachi
☎ 03868 / pop 2189 / elev 2280m
The biggest place by some distance hereabouts, enchanting Cachi is nevertheless little more than a village, albeit one surrounded by stunning scenery. Overlooked by noble mountains, it boasts fresh highland air, sunny days and crisp nights. The cobblestones, adobe houses, tranquil plaza and opportunities to explore the surrounds mean that it's the sort of place that eats extra days out of your carefully planned itinerary.

On the west side of the plaza, the **Mercado Artesanal** (☎ 491053; cachi@salnet.com.ar; Güemes s/n; ⏰ 8am-8pm) is both a handicraft shop and the tourist office.

Opposite, the simple but attractive **Iglesia San José** (1796) has graceful arches and a barrel-vaulted ceiling of cardón wood. The confessional and other features are also made of cardón, while the holy water lives in a large *tinaja* (a big clay vessel for storing oil).

Next door, Cachi's **Museo Arqueológico** (☎ 491080; admission by donation; ⏰ 8:30am-6:30pm Mon-Sat, 10am-1pm Sun) is a well-presented and professionally arranged account of the surrounding area's cultural evolution, with good background information on archaeological methods, all in Spanish. Don't miss the wall in the secondary patio, composed of stones with petroglyphs.

Two kilometers southwest of the center, on the edge of town, **Parque Temático Todo lo Nuestro** (☎ 03868-15-455711; www.parquetematicocachi.com.ar; admission AR$3; ⏰ 9am-6pm) is a labor of love that has constructed replica buildings from several phases of the valley's history. It's a fascinating project; in some of the buildings it really feels as if the occupants have just stepped out for a minute. There's a rustically styled restaurant here too, and possibly cabin accommodations by the time you read this.

ACTIVITIES
A short **walk** from Cachi's plaza brings you to its picturesque hilltop cemetery; nearby is a rather unlikely airstrip. A longer walk (one hour) takes you along the dirt road to Cachi Adentro, a tiny village where there's not a great deal to do save swing on the seats in the demi-plaza or sip a soda from the only store. It's a particularly lovely walk in summer, when the streams and cascades are alive with water. For more strenuous **hiking** and **mountaineering**, **Santiago Casimiro** (☎ 03868-15-638545; santiagocasimiro@hotmail.com; Barrio Cooperativa Casa 17) is a local guide. Many locals hire **horses**; look for signs or ask in the tourist office. After all that endeavor, you can always cool off in ACA Hostería Cachi's **pool** for AR$5.

SLEEPING & EATING
Albergue Municipal (dm with/without bathroom AR$12/8) On the same grounds as Camping Municipal, this place has very basic 10- to 15-bed dorms. Reservations must be made at the Mercado Artesanal tourist office.

Camping Municipal (☎ 491902; sites AR$15) On a hilltop about 1km southwest of the plaza, this

---

DON'T MISS: THE BUS TO CACHI

The bus ride from Salta to Cachi is one of the most spectacular you are ever likely to undertake. The bus grinds its way up narrow, winding roads that twist and curl around the imposing Cuesta del Obispo, giving passengers sweeping views of valley floors and peaks that seem to mirror endlessly into the distance. It's quite a sight, so try and make sure you get a window seat for the journey up and down the winding roads. Certainly locals know the real value of the scenery – they hold wailing kids up to the windows and the result is nearly always silence.

Before Cachi, you enter Parque Nacional Los Cardones, and the landscape levels out to plains of cardón cactus standing sentry in terrain reminiscent of a lunar landscape.

offers shaded sites surrounded by hedges; sites without hedges are AR$10.

Hotel Nevado de Cachi (☎ 491912; s/d with bathroom AR$50/60, without bathroom AR$20/40) Just off the plaza and right by the bus stop, this is a decent budget choice with rooms around a patio. Beds are comfortable, and bathrooms – both shared and private – work well enough. Prices are a bit negotiable and vary slightly by room.

ACA Hostería Cachi (☎ 491105; www.soldelvalle.com .ar; Av ACA s/n; s/d AR$130/206; ❄ ☐ ☎) With its hilltop position, this hotel has the best views in town (and a good restaurant), and there are worse ways to spend your day than relaxing poolside checking them out. Rooms are spacious and well-designed, with ultrahip bathrooms, and there's even a little zoo.

El Cortijo (☎ 491034; www.elcortijohotel.com; Av ACA s/n; s/d from AR$150/240; ❄) Opposite the ACA Hostería Cachi entrance, this stylish small hotel has gone up in the world in recent times. The rooms aren't large but are decorated with finesse, and some – particularly 'Los Padres', with its own private terrace with loungers (doubles AR$330) – have fabulous views of the sierra. There should be a pool by the time you read this.

El Molino de Cachi (☎ 491094; www.bodegaelmolino .com.ar; d AR$504; ☎) With just five rooms, this exquisite converted mill makes a highly relaxing rural base for exploring the area. Four kilometers from the center of Cachi, it's also a winery. The welcoming, cultured hosts make your stay very comfortable and personalized; they don't take walk-ups, so book ahead. No under-14s are admitted.

Luna Cautiva (☎ 491029; dishes AR$7-19; ☽ lunch & dinner) Run by a good-natured local couple, this offers interesting tapas options – sundried tomatoes with salami is one – and a short menu of local favorites. All dishes are a couple of pesos over the odds, but the *locro* gets an A+, and the ambience, in an historic house with cactus-wood ceiling, is intimate. Leave the plaza between the church and the archaeological museum, and it's on your left.

Oliver (☎ 491903; Ruíz de los Llanos 160; pizzas AR$8-18; ☽ 8am-midnight) On the square, this homey wooden-tabled restaurant offers very tasty pizzas, and a short list of creative meaty mains (AR$25 to AR$32). There's a small and cozy upstairs area, which doubles as a Colomé wine bar. Californians, South Africans and Australians longing for the taste of home can also indulge.

GETTING THERE & AWAY
Marcos Rueda (☎ 421-4447) buses run between Cachi and Salta. Buses to Salta (AR$23.30, 4½ hours) leave at 9.05am Monday to Saturday. There's a 3pm service on Monday, Wednesday and Friday, and a 3.30pm service on Sunday. There's a daily bus to Seclantás (AR$6.70, 1¼ hours) at 11.30am, and an extra Saturday service at 6pm. Molinos (AR$9.70, two hours) is served at 11.30am Monday, Wednesday, Friday and Sunday, and at 6pm on Saturday. Three buses a day run to Cachi Adentro (AR$2.20, 30 minutes). There are three weekly buses north to La Poma (AR$10, 1¼ hours), an old hacienda town that, for all practical purposes, is the end of the line. The road beyond, to San Antonio de los Cobres, is supersteep and impassable except for 4WD vehicles; it's much easier to approach San Antonio from Salta.

Seclantás
☎ 03868 / pop 306 / elev 2100m
Charming Seclantás is a quiet little place that's the spiritual home of the Salta poncho. There are many weavers' workshops in town, and north of here, along the road to Cachi, artisans' homes are marked with a sign indicating that you can drop in and peruse their wares; the stretch of road has been dubbed the **Route of the Artisans**. One of them, Señor Tero, is well-known hereabouts for having woven a poncho worn by Pope John Paul II.

Seclantás' church, pretty in yellow, dates from 1835; the evocative cemetery is at the top of town.

Places to stay in Seclantás are clustered around the plaza. Among them, **Hostería La Rueda** (☎ 498041, 0387-423-2587; cnr Cornejo & Ferreyra; s/d with bathroom AR$50/70, without bathroom AR$35/55) is hospitable and spotless, and features comfortable, pretty, common areas and decent rooms. The campsite is just behind the church, and has a pool that's open to the public for AR$1.

Buses leave Cachi for Seclantás daily, some continuing to Molinos. Return buses to Cachi leave at 7.30am Monday to Saturday, and 2.30pm Sunday.

Molinos
☎ 03868 / pop 927 / elev 2020m
If you thought Cachi was laid-back, wait until you see Molinos, a lovely little backwater with a collection of striking adobe buildings in

---

FINCA COLOMÉ

Some of Argentina's finest wines are produced at this ecological **bodega** (☎ 03868-494044; www .bodegacolome.com; tasting depending on quality AR$10-33; ◷ 10.30am-6pm), set, as they say hereabouts, 'where the devil lost his poncho' some 20km down a spectacular (and forgivingly smooth) *ripio* (gravel) road west from Molinos. Vineyards – including some ancient prephylloxera European vines – and hotel enjoy a stunning natural setting, surrounded by hills and mountains that seem to change color hourly. Forward thinking on environmental, social and cultural fronts is also in evidence; the complex is electrically self-sufficient, has funded substantial infrastructural improvements in the local community, and is due to inaugurate, in 2008, a museum designed by the avant-garde installation artist James Turrell, with a permanent exhibition of nine of his works drawn from the last 40 years.

The **hotel** (www.estanciacolome.com; d AR$812; ⌧ 🖳 🖳) features chic and relaxing rooms accompanied by excellent multilingual service and a raft of facilities, including a picturesque pool surrounded by the grapevines and beds of lavender. Apart from lolling about reading novels and enjoying the wine, you could also head off on some of the impressive criollo horses – really trained by whispering rather than the lash – to explore the surrounding hillscapes. The restaurant is open to visitors, and a meal (AR$17 to AR$35) includes a bodega tour.

---

gentle decline; a stroll through the streets will reveal some real gems. Its picturesque appeal is augmented by shady streets and a range of good accommodations.

Molinos takes its name from the still-operational flourmill on the Río Calchaquí. The town's restored 18th-century **Iglesia de San Pedro de Nolasco**, in the Cuzco style, features twin bell towers and traditional tiled roof. Like Angastaco, Molinos was a waystation on the trans-Andean route to Chile and Peru. Well into the 20th century, pack trains passed here with skins, wool and wood for sale in Salta and subsequent shipment to Buenos Aires.

About 1.5km west is the **Criadero Coquera** (☎ 0387-1540-71259) where the government's agricultural research arm raises vicuñas and manages to shear them without damaging their health; alongside is the **Casa de Entre Ríos**, part of the former Estancia Luracatao, where there's a fine artisans' market with spectacular *ponchos de güemes* for sale. There are two simple rooms (AR$15 per person) here.

Across from the church, the government-owned 18th-century **Hostal Provincial de Molinos** (☎ 494002) is under restoration, but due to reopen in 2008. It's also known as the Casa de Isasmendi, after Salta's last colonial governor, who was born, lived and died in this sprawling residence in a town that was a stronghold of royalist resistance. Expect prices of at least AR$200 for a double once the restoration is finished.

The *hospedajes* (family homes) scattered around town are more like homestays than anything. Right where the bus stops, **Los Cardones de Molinos** (☎ 494061; cardonesmolinos@ hotmail.com; r per person with/without bathroom AR$35/25) is an excellent choice, with comfortable rooms with cactus furniture. You're treated as one of the family and can use the kitchen; the exceptionally welcoming and accommodating owner can also prepare meals. Breakfast with homemade bread is included.

A bus runs from Salta to Molinos via Cachi and Seclantás on Monday, Wednesday and Friday at 7am, on Saturday at 1.30pm, and on Sunday at 7am (AR$29, six to seven hours). It returns from Molinos at 7am Tuesday, Thursday and Saturday, and 2pm on Sunday.

Angastaco

☎ 03868 / pop 881 / elev 1955m

Tiny Angastaco sits among some of the most dramatically tortuous rockscapes of the valley route. Forty kilometers south of Molinos, and 54km north of San Carlos, it resembles other oasis settlements placed at regular intervals in the Valles Calchaquíes, with vineyards, fields of anise and cumin, and the ruins of an ancient *pucará*.

Angastaco has gas but no bank. There is a tourist office located on the square, as well as an **archaeological museum** in the municipal building. Both are open irregular hours, but ask around in the *municipalidad* or police station and someone will help. **Horseback riding** (☎ 0387-1568-31322; per hr AR$15) is easily arranged by phone or via the Hostería Angastaco.

Angastaco's major fiesta is on December 8, the day of the Virgin of the Valley, the village's patron. On February 17 and 18, the **grape vintage** and making of foot-trodden *vino patero* is celebrated with a festival.

Hospedaje El Cardón (☎ 0387-1545-90021; per person with/without bathroom AR$15/12) is pretty basic, but you can't argue with the price. It's two houses to your right if you're standing facing the church. **Hostería Angastaco** (☎ 491123; s/d AR$65/95; ⚡), on the road into town, offers plenty more comfort, and has a restaurant.

At research time, the only public transportation was one daily bus that headed south to San Carlos and Cafayate. To reach Molinos, 37km north, you had to hitchhike or hike. Hitchhiking is slow hereabouts; take water.

San Carlos
☎ 03868 / pop 1887

A sizable traditional village, San Carlos, 22km north of Cafayate, is connected to it by paved road, a pleasant shock if you're arriving from the north. Most visitors push on through to Cafayate or Angastaco, but there's a special place to stay here in **La Casa de los**

Vientos (☎ 495073; Barrio Cemitigre; r AR$100), which is signposted off the main road at the Cachi end of town. Built in the traditional manner of adobe, with terracotta tiles and cane ceilings, it incorporates some ingenious environmental innovations. The owners are potters, and the rooms (all different) are decorated with rustic flair and beauty.

CAFAYATE
☎ 03868 / pop 10,714 / elev 1683m

Argentina's second center for quality wine production, Cafayate is a popular tourist destination but still has a tranquil small-town feel. It's easily reached from Salta via the spectacular Quebrada de Cafayate, and is also the southern terminus of the Valles Calchaquíes route. With a selection of excellent accommodations for every budget, and several wineries to visit in and around town, Cafayate invites laying up for a while to explore the surrounding area. It also has many young artists and craftspeople, so check out the *artesanía*.

Cafayate is famous for its torrontés, a grape producing aromatic but unexpectedly dry white wine, but the bodegas hereabouts

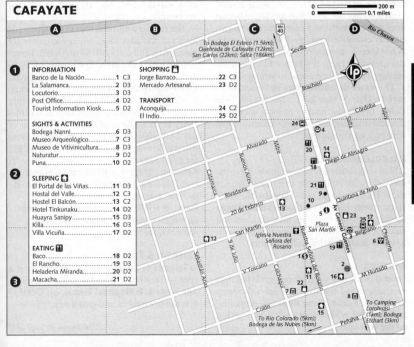

also produce some fine reds from cabernet sauvignon, malbec, and tannat.

Orientation

Cafayate sits at the foot of the Valles Calchaquí, near the junction between RN 40, which goes northwest to Molinos and Cachi, and RN 68, which goes to Salta through the Quebrada de Cafayate. Through town, RN 40 is Av General Güemes.

Information

Banco de la Nación (Plaza San Martín) ATM on the plaza, changes money.
La Salamanca (Av General Güemes; per hr AR$1.50) Internet access and horse rental. A fine combination.
Locutorio (Av General Güemes & Belgrano)
Post office (Av General Güemes & Córdoba)
Tourist information kiosk (Plaza San Martín; ☻ 8am-9pm) On the northeast corner of the plaza.

Sights & Activities
MUSEUMS

The late Rodolfo Bravo, an aficionado of the region, left an astounding personal collection of Diaguita ceramics to the **Museo Arqueológico** (☎ 421054; cnr Colón & Calchaquí; admission by donation; ☻ 11:30am-9pm Mon-Fri, 11:30am-3pm Sat). Also on display are colonial and more recent artifacts, such as elaborate horse gear and wine casks. While there's not much explanation, the material speaks for itself. If you're arriving outside opening times, phone ahead to arrange a visit.

The **Museo de Vitivinicultura** (Av General Güemes; admission AR$1; ☻ 10am-1pm & 5-8pm Mon-Fri), near Colón, details the history of local wine production and displays a range of antiquated winemaking equipment.

RÍO COLORADO

A 5km walk southwest of town leads you to the Río Colorado. Follow the river upstream for about 1½ hours to get to a 10m **waterfall**, where you can **swim**. Look out for hidden **rock paintings** on the way (for a small tip, local children will guide you). You could combine this walk with a visit to Bodega de las Nubes (right).

WINERIES

Several wineries offer tours and tastings in and around the town. Most only open Monday to Friday. Some are small, easygoing and friendly, while others are larger, with a cooler welcome.

The free tour and tastings are short and bright at **Bodega Nanni** (☎ 421527; www.bodega nanni.com; Chavarría 151; ☻ 9:30am-1pm & 2-6pm Mon-Sat, 11am-1pm & 2-4pm Sun), a small, central winery with a lovely grass patio. Its wines are organic, uncomplicated and drinkable.

Three kilometers south of town, 30-sq-km **Bodega Etchart** (☎ 421529; RN 40; ☻ 9am-noon & 1-5pm Mon-Fri) offers a free tour including tasting. Its 'Cafayate' midrange wines are a good deal.

Five kilometers west of town along the road to Río Colorado, small, organic and friendly **Bodega de las Nubes** (☎ 422129; ☻ 9:30am-5pm Mon-Sat) has a fabulous position at the foot of the jagged hills. The informative tour nominally costs AR$15, but if you buy wine it's not charged. There's also food here. Ring ahead to check it is open.

Michel Torino's **Bodega El Esteco** (☎ 421283; www.elesteco.com.ar; tours AR$15; ☻ tours 11am, noon, 2:30pm, 3:30pm & 4:30pm Mon-Fri), on the northern edge of town, is a smart and attractive winery producing some of the region's best wines and offering upmarket accommodations.

Tours

Some tour operators in town have a bit of a shonky feel, but those listed below are reliable.

The standard minibus tour of the Quebrada leaves in the afternoon, when the colors are more vivid, and costs AR$40 to AR$50. Three-to four-hour treks in the Quebrada (AR$100) and Río Colorado (AR$60) are also popular. Day-long trips to Cachi (AR$175) are tiring, while Quilmes (AR$60) can be visited cheaper in a cab if you're two or more. Horseback rides range from a couple of hours (AR$70) to all day (AR$200). Many places, including those listed following, hire bikes (AR$25 to AR$35 for a full day).
Naturatur (☎ 03868-15-452231; naturatur@gmail.com; Paseo Doña Ofelia, Av General Güemes) Organizes tours in the region, treks and bike excursions.
Puna (☎ 421808; www.punaturismo.com; San Martín 82) Runs the whole range of excursions and does so competently and honestly.

Festivals & Events

La Serenata de Cafayate, in late February, is a very worthwhile three-day *folklore* festival. The **Fiesta de la Virgen del Rosario**, on October 4, is the town fiesta and gets lively.

(Continued on page 285)

Mi Querida Argentina

My Beloved Argentina

The Gaucho

NAME	Don Manuel Pardo
OCCUPATION	Gaucho
RESIDENCE	*Estancia* near Bajo Caracoles
MUST SEE	Parque Nacional Perito Moreno

'The countryside is solitary... As soon as I'm outside, I am roaming – content.'

'In the north you can check on the cows by driving almost zero miles per hour in a truck – it's easy. Here, no. With 250 cows I need two hands to corral them because these animals roam 100 sq km without a fence.

'I learned in childhood [how to be a gaucho], well, by working. I went to work on an *estancia* and I ended up running it. Every day you are learning things until you come to your end. But the farm isn't a science – you try things. Then you teach: how to shoe a horse, how to shear a sheep…

'A gaucho? No-one wants to be a gaucho anymore. The countryside is solitary. I have no problem being here alone for three months. As soon as I'm outside, I am roaming – content. At 4pm I have to cook, feed the dogs and chickens, but that's it. All my days go by the same, but it makes me happy.

'Still, sometimes you want to take a truck and go...'

AS RELATED TO CAROLYN McCARTHY

In the saddle, beneath the mighty peaks of Cerro Mercedario (p375)

GRANT DIXON

FIVE WAYS TO TALK TO A GAUCHO

- Offer *mate amargo* (without sugar) or take some if offered

- Ask where he got his *facón* (the knife sticking out of the back of his pants)

- Don't ask about his family – they are probably far away

- Keep drinking *mate*…

- When all else fails (and it might, as a gaucho is a man of few words) ask how his livestock fared the winter

Roundin' up the sheep, on the banks of Lago Argentino (p495)

© DAVID R. FRAZIER PHOTOLIBRARY, INC. / ALAMY

How to catch the prime ingredient for the evening's *asado* (barbecue), gaucho style

MICHAEL COYNE

The Soul of Tango

NAME	Nora Schwartz
OCCUPATION	Tango teacher and dancer
RESIDENCE	Palermo, Buenos Aires
MUST SEE	Teatro Colón, a *fútbol* game, a tango cla...

'Everyone needs personal contact with others... Tango has *el abrazo* [the embrace] which mimics this; it's intimacy without compromise.'

'Tango has touched three centuries, the 19th to the 21st. It's lasted this long partly because each sex has a role to play, distinct and complementary – tango is against a unisex culture. It's not choreographed, but spontaneous and improvisational. It's playful, fun and sensual.

'Ultimately, we're all alone. But everyone needs personal contact with others; we like to be held and touched. This goes back to when we were babies, being rocked and comforted. Tango has *el abrazo* [the embrace] which mimics this; it's intimacy without compromise. Dances are only three minutes long, so there's little commitment.

'Tango banishes all age, social and cultural differences; there is no language, only *códigos* [dancing rules]. Youth and inquisitiveness keep you going. And it's very addictive: people have left their jobs, houses and families. I've been teaching tango for 20 years, and I teach with love. Take my work from me and I die.'

AS RELATED TO SANDRA BAO

The soulful steps of the tango (p50) reveal a seductive dance of passion and grace

MICHAEL TAYLOR

Vineland

NAME	Lucas Mendoza
OCCUPATION	Winemaker, Bodega Domaine St Diego
RESIDENCE	Maipú, Mendoza
MUST SEE	The wine country around Mendoza

'Winemaking is in my blood. My first memories are of harvesting grapes. My Father, Ángel Mendoza, is one of the famous winemakers. We've all followed him in some way. I make wines, my sister designs labels and my brother's a sommelier.

'We're not stuck in tradition, but we always take what's best from the old and the new. The foreigners who come with new methods have all my respect. That's the way our industry develops – with a dialogue between tradition and technology.

'We say that a great wine sells itself – it doesn't need explanation. We believe that wine is an expression of nature, a combination of all the elements. We're always looking to produce expressive grapes. They tell you when they need to be picked. Ninety percent of a good wine happens on the vine, and the other 10% happens in the bodega.'

AS RELATED TO LUCAS VIDGEN

'Wine is an expression of nature, a combination of all the elements.'

Behind the bottle: some of the fine vines around Cafayate (p275)

ANDY SYMINGTON

Traditional Life

NAME	Héctor 'Guiso' Morales
OCCUPATION	Weaver
RESIDENCE	Seclantás
MUST SEE	The Valles Calchaquíes and Salta province

'Many people think tango is typical of Argentina, but it barely exists up here. In Salta province, *folklórico* music is king.'

'I live in a traditional village, Seclantás (p273), in the northwest. We are Diaguita people, but have been Spanish-speaking for generations. They call me *'guiso'* (stew), because I can't eat enough of it! First mum's, now my wife's!

'Weaving's normally passed down through families, but my father was *muy gaucho* – he couldn't make anything! We were 10 children, so at 15 I had to work. I learned to weave. I use many traditional natural dyes. Willowroot gives blond; soot, surprisingly, gives warm yellow. Cholonga fruit gives beautiful gray.

'I'd recommend to anyone to visit Salta (p261) and the Calchaquí valleys (p271) to learn about this historic region. But it's also important we learn from them. In a small village, customs don't change, so it does us good to meet foreigners, who have a different mentality.

'Many people think tango is typical of Argentina, but it barely exists up here. In Salta province, *folklórico* music is king. You won't find a *salteño* who can't play the guitar!'

AS RELATED TO ANDY SYMINGTON

An indigenous Toba family's home in Argentina's Impenetrable region (p239)

DANNY PALMERLEE

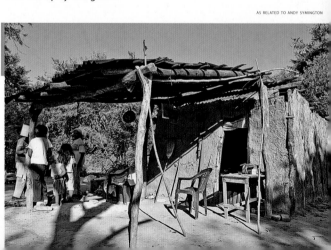

An indigenous Toba woman weaves wall hangings

DANNY PALMERLEE

Traditional adobe houses of Purmamarca (p253) beneath Cerro de los Siete Colores

MICHAEL TAYLOR

Musical Journeys

NAME	Agustín Ronconi
OCCUPATION	Musician; co-founder of group Arbolito
RESIDENCE	Buenos Aires
MUST SEE	Quebrada de Humahuaca

THE FESTIVAL BEAT

There are so many music festivals throughout Argentina, it's impossible to count them all. Three of the country's biggest music (and dance) festivals are the following.

Buenos Aires Tango (www.festivalde tango.gov.ar; p22) Buenos Aires' world-famous tango fest; held late February through early March.

Creamfields, Buenos Aires (p108) Dance music festival (of the electronica/house/techno sort) held in early November.

Festival Nacional de Folklore, Cosquín (www.aquicosquin .org; p327) National folk-music festival; held late January.

Sounds of the Gran Chaco (p233): Toba musicians in front of their adobe home

DANNY PALMERLEE

'Tango was born in Buenos Aires. Outside the capital, however, the music of Argentina is different. In the northwest there's *folklore norteño: zamba, chacarera, gato norteño, bailecito, cueca* and others, all of which are both rhythms and dances.

'In the Andean northwest, there's a real harmony between the music, the landscape and the people, and the Bolivian and Peruvian influences are strongly felt. In the northeast you'll find *chamamé* and polkas. Much less known is the indigenous music of Chaco and Formosa provinces, music of the indigenous Toba and Wichí. In Córdoba, *cuarteto* is supreme.

'There are numerous *folklore* festivals in Argentina, and they're well worth searching out. Cosquín (p327) is the best known, but it's not necessarily representative. There are many others. The Carnaval celebrations in the Quebrada de Humahuaca are celebrated with *bandas de sikuri* (a type of traditional Andean musical group). It's an experience entirely different from Brazilian Carnaval. And in Buenos Aires, there's everything: rock, *cumbia* and, of course, tango.'

AS RELATED TO DANNY PALMERLEE

(Continued from page 276)

Sleeping

Cafayate has excellent places to stay. Prices rise for the January–February high season but are much lower throughout the rest of the year. High-season prices are quoted here.

BUDGET

Camping Lorohuasi (☎ 421051; per person/tent AR$3/2; ☲) This municipal campground 10 minutes' walk from the center along Av General Guemes can get dusty when the wind blows. Facilities are OK, and there's a small grocery. Rough cabins sleeping up to four cost AR$20.

Huayra Sanipy (☎ 422311; hostelhuayra@hotmail.com; Nuestra Señora del Rosario 283; dm/d AR$25/50) Not too many of the stresses of life get past the front door of this cheery hostel, with clean, decent dorms and one private room. It's a very relaxed place; the back garden with mountain views is a spot that's hard to beat.

Hostel El Balcón (☎ 421739; 20 de Febrero 110; dm/d AR$30/90; ☲) Outside of summer, prices are much lower (dorm beds/doubles AR$20/60) at this well-equipped spot. There's a streetside balcony, and great roof terrace with views and a bar. It's kept very clean, including the kitchen, wood oven and *parrilla*, and it also hires bikes and runs tours.

El Portal de las Viñas (☎ 421098; www.portalvinias.com.ar; Nuestra Señora del Rosario 153; s/d AR$35/70; ☲) It's tough not to love this place, starting with the courteous and genuine welcome from the interesting owner, and continuing with the low prices, central location and general tranquility. The rooms are very good value, with terracotta tiled floors and spacious bathrooms; they're set around a vine-shaded courtyard.

MIDRANGE & TOP END

Hotel Tinkunaku (☎ 421148; Diego de Almagro 12; s/d AR$59/115; ☲ ☲) This well-priced if not rather stylish option has clean, modern rooms in a quiet, central location. The place has a relaxed family atmosphere and a huge pool out back.

our pick **Hostal del Valle** (☎ 421039; hostaldelvalle@nortevirtual.com; San Martín 243; s/d AR$65/100; ☲) A fabulous place, this offers myriad flowering pot plants, and pretty rooms with large, inviting beds and excellent bathrooms. There are a couple of smaller, darker rooms that are AR$20 cheaper but still worthwhile. Breakfast is served in a rooftop conservatory with privileged views.

Villa Vicuña (☎ 422145; www.villavicuna.com.ar; Belgrano 76; s/d AR$150/250; ☲) Peacefully set around twin patios, this offers an intimate retreat with beautiful, spotless rooms with big beds and reproduction antique furniture. Service and breakfast are good, and you can lose hours deciphering the offbeat mural sculpture in the courtyard.

Killa (☎ 422254; www.killacafayate.com.ar; Colón 47; s/d/ste AR$270/320/440; ☲ ☲ ☲) Classy, comfortable and well-run, this handsome and recommendable hotel has colonial style given warmth by creative use of natural wood, stone and local *artesanía*. The gorgeous rooms – not a TV in sight – have great bathrooms, and the upstairs suites have cracking views. The common areas are inviting and the hospitality impeccable.

Eating

Eating in Cafayate is somewhat limited.

Heladería Miranda (Av General Güeme; ice creams AR$3-5.50; ☼ 10am-10pm) A frequent dilemma in Argentina is whether to go for a rich red cabernet or a dry white torrontés, but it doesn't usually occur in ice-cream parlors. It does here: the Miranda's wine ice-creams are Cafayate's pride and joy.

Baco (☎ 0387-1540-28366; cnr Av General Güemes & Rivadavia; mains AR$8-23; ☼ lunch & dinner) Crammed full of rustic decorations, and with work by local artists on the walls, this is one of the most popular spots in town and certainly offers plenty of character. It serves up variations on Argentine standards, including tasty pasta, and has plenty of local wines to try at OK prices.

El Rancho (☎ 421256; www.elranchocafayate.com.ar; Toscano 4; mains AR$9-18; ☼ lunch & dinner) A cut above the string of hit-and-miss places around the plaza, this has a short, simple menu, including *locro* and some good chicken dishes. It's owned by a bodega, so competition wines are overpriced. It appeals on winter nights, with a crackling fire, and at weekends, when a blind guitarist plays unobtrusive *folklorica*.

Macacha (☎ 422319; Av General Güemes N28; mains AR$28-36; ☼ lunch & dinner) The jury's still out on this new 'gourmet' restaurant, so it's up to readers to decide. There are tables in a central courtyard and in intimate dining rooms off it. The menu is French-inspired, with some Andean dishes thrown in for the tourists. The starter assortment is generous and a good way to try a variety of dishes. Order wine by the bottle not the glass.

Shopping

There are numerous *artesanía* shops on and around the central plaza. The **Mercado Artesanal** (Av General Güemes; ⏰ 9am-10pm) cooperative features many locals' work. For fine silver, check out the workshop of **Jorge Barraco** (Colón s/n), next to the Museo Arqueológico.

Getting There & Away

El Indio (Belgrano s/n) has three to four buses daily to Salta (AR$17, 3½ hours). There are also three to four daily services to San Carlos (AR$3, 40 minutes), and one to Angastaco (AR$7, two hours), leaving at 11am Monday through Friday and 6.30pm on Saturday and Sunday. **Aconquija** (cnr General Güemes & Alvarado) leaves two to four times daily for Tucumán (AR$27.80, 6½ hours) via Tafí del Valle (AR$16.80, four hours); two buses go to Santa María (AR$16, two hours).

QUEBRADA DE CAFAYATE

North of Cafayate, the Salta road heads through the barren and spectacular Quebrada de Cafayate, a wild landscape of richly colored sandstone and unearthly rock formations. Carved out by the Río de las Conchas, the canyon's twisted sedimentary strata exhibit a stunning array of tones, from rich red ochre to ethereal green. While you get a visual feast from the road itself – it's one of the country's more memorable drives or rides – it's worth taking the time to explore parts of the canyon up close. The best time to appreciate the canyon is in the late afternoon, when the low sun brings out the most vivid colors.

A short way north of Cafayate, Los Médanos is an extensive dune field that gives way to the canyon proper, where a series of distinctive landforms are named and signposted from the road. Some, such as El Sapo (the Toad) are fairly underwhelming, but around the Km 49 mark, the adjacent Garganta del Diablo (Devil's Throat) and Anfiteatro (Amphitheatre) are much more impressive. Gashes in the rock wall let you enter and appreciate the tortured stone whose clearly visible layers have been twisted by tectonic upheavals into unimaginable configurations.

A few *artesanía* sellers hover around these landmarks, but there's no reliable place to buy food or water.

Getting There & Away

There are several ways to see and explore the canyon. The ideal option is renting a car (possible in Salta but not Cafayate) or a bicycle (Cafayate); you could also take the bus, hitchhike or walk. Tours from Salta are brief and regimented; it's much better to take a tour from closer Cafayate.

Here's the lowdown for those without a private vehicle: disembark from any El Indio bus (with your rental bike or by foot), tour around for awhile and then flag another bus later on. Be aware of the schedules between Salta and Cafayate and carry food and plenty of water in this hot, dry environment. A good place to start your exploration is the impressive box canyon of Garganta del Diablo; several other attractions are within easy walking distance of here.

TUCUMÁN & AROUND

Though it's the country's second-smallest province, Tucumán has played a significant role in Argentina's story. It was here that independence was first declared, and the massive sugar industry is of great economic importance. While this monoculture has enabled the province to develop secondary industry, it has also created tremendous inequities in wealth and land distribution, as well as ecological problems.

The city of Tucumán is full of heat and energy; a complete contrast to the lung-cleansing air of Tafí del Valle, up in the hills to the west. Beyond, Argentina's most important pre-Columbian site is Quilmes, on the Cafayate road. South of Tucumán, the Santiago del Estero province is a backwater with an enjoyably sleepy feel. The city itself merits a visit; you can also explore the far-flung Parque Nacional Copo.

TUCUMÁN

☎ 0381 / pop 738,479 / elev 420m

With nigh-on three-quarters of a million souls in its greater urban area, Tucumán, the cradle of Argentine independence, is the nation's fifth-largest city and feels like it, with a metropolitan bustle that can come as quite a shock after the more genteel provincial capitals elsewhere in the northwest. You may not like it at first, but don't be put off. This isn't the usual patter; Tucumán really rewards time

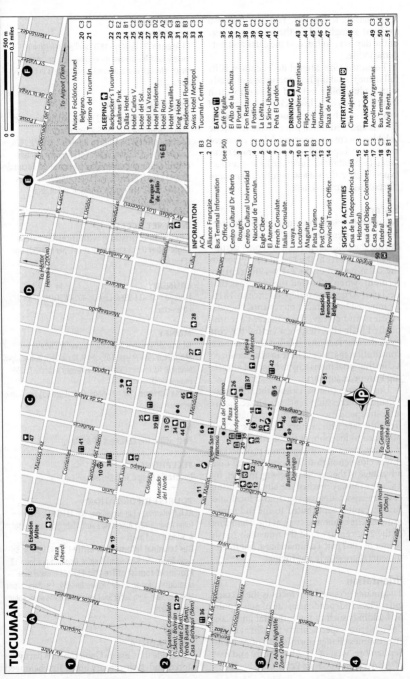

TUCUMÁN

INFORMATION

ACA....................................1	B3
Alliance Française...................2	D2
Bus Terminal Information	
Office...........................(see 50)	
Centro Cultural Dr Alberto	
Rougés.............................3	C3
Centro Cultural Universidad	
Nacional de Tucumán..........4	C2
Eagle Ciber.........................5	C2
El Ateneo...........................6	C2
French Consulate..................7	C3
Italian Consulate..................8	B2
Lavaya..............................9	B2
Locutorio...........................10	B1
Maguitur...........................11	B2
Patsa Turismo.....................12	B3
Post Office.........................13	C3
Provincial Tourist Office.........14	C3

SIGHTS & ACTIVITIES

Casa de la Independencia (Casa	
Historical)......................15	C3
Casa del Obispo Colombres.....16	E2
Casa Padilla.......................17	C3
Catedral............................18	C3
Montañas Tucumanas...........19	B1

SLEEPING

Museo Folclórico Manuel	
Belgrano.........................20	C3
Turismo del Tucumán............21	C3
Backpacker's Tucumán..........22	C2
Catalinas Park.....................23	E2
Dallas Hotel........................24	B1
Hotel Carlos V....................25	C2
Hotel del Sol......................26	C3
Hotel La Vasca....................27	C2
Hotel Presidente..................28	D2
Hotel Roni.........................29	A2
Hotel Versailles...................30	C3
King Hotel.........................31	B3
Residencial Florida................32	B3
Swiss Hotel Metropol............33	B3
Tucumán Center..................34	C2

EATING

Café Pigalle........................35	C3
El Alto de la Lechuza............36	A2
El Portal............................37	C3
Fon Restaurante..................38	B1
Il Postino...........................39	C2
La Leñita...........................40	C1
La Sirio-Libanesa..................41	C1
Peña El Cardón....................42	C3

DRINKING

Costumbres Argentinas..........43	B2
Filipo...............................44	C2
Harris..............................45	C2
Künstner...........................46	C3
Plaza de Almas....................47	C1

ENTERTAINMENT

Cine Majestic......................48	B3

TRANSPORT

Aerolíneas Argentinas............49	C3
Bus Terminal.......................50	D4
Móvil Renta........................51	C4

spent getting to know it. You may find you prefer it at night, when the fumes and heat of the day have lulled, and the cafés and bars come to life.

Tucumán (San Miguel de Tucumán is its full name) is baking hot, energetic and brash, with a blue-collar feel and a down-to-earth quality. It also has a lively cultural scene, and its stylish café-bars, great bookstores, art exhibitions and traditional *peñas* make its serene neighbors seem a bit provincial. Less advanced is the courtship behavior of the average *tucumano* (inhabitant of Tucumán) – women can expect higher-than-usual numbers of *piropos* (flirtatious remarks) here.

History

Founded in 1565, Tucumán and its hinterland were oriented toward Salta and Bolivia during the colonial period, and only distinguished itself from the rest of the region in the culmination of the early-19th-century ferment, when it hosted the congress that declared Argentine independence in 1816. Dominated by Unitarist merchants, lawyers, soldiers and clergy, the congress accomplished little else; despite a virtual boycott by Federalist factions, it failed to agree on a constitution that would have institutionalized a constitutional monarchy in hopes of attracting European support.

Unlike other colonial cities of the northwest, Tucumán successfully reoriented its economy after independence. Modern Tucumán dates from the late 19th century and owes its importance to location; at the southern end of the frost-free zone of sugarcane production, it was close enough to Buenos Aires to take advantage of the capital's growing market. By 1874 the railway reached the city, permitting easy transportation of sugar, and local and British capital contributed to the industry's growth. The economic crisis at the beginning of the 21st century (and the unusually harsh winter of 2007) hit Tucumán hard, but things in general are slowly improving.

Orientation

Tucumán's geographical focus is the rectangular Plaza Independencia, site of major public buildings such as the cathedral and Casa de Gobierno – spectacularly floodlit at night; street names change north/south of Av 24 de Septiembre, west of Av Alem/Mitre and east of Av Avellaneda/Sáenz Peña.

Information

BOOKSTORES

El Ateneo (25 de Mayo 182) Excellent selection of novels, local history and geography. Also has maps, a small selection of classics and airport novels in English, and a café.

CULTURAL CENTERS

Alliance Française (☎ 421-9651; aftucuman@arnet .com.ar; Mendoza 257; ☼ 5-9:30pm Mon-Fri)
Centro Cultural Dr Alberto Rougés (☎ 422-7976; Laprida 31) Has rotating exhibits of provincial painters.
Centro Cultural Universidad Nacional de Tucumán (☎ 421-6024; 25 de Mayo 265) Art exhibitions, crafts for sale, a café, and regular theatrical and musical performances.

INTERNET ACCESS

Tucumán is bristling with internet cafés.
Eagle Ciber (Crisóstomo Álvarez 381; per hr AR$2) One of the fastest.

LAUNDRY

Lavaya (☎ 431-2366; Laprida 460) Will deliver for a little extra.

MONEY

Many downtown banks have ATMs.
Maguitur (San Martín 765; ☼ 8:30am-2pm & 4-6:30pm Mon-Fri, 10am-noon Sat) Cashes traveler's checks (1.25% commission).
Patsa Turismo (☎ 421-6806; Chacabuco 38) The Amex representative.

POST

Post office (cnr Córdoba & 25 de Mayo)

TELEPHONE

Locutorio (Maipú 360; ☼ 24hr)

TOURIST INFORMATION

ACA (Automóvil Club Argentino; ☎ 431-1522; Crisóstomo Álvarez 901) Argentina's auto club; good source for provincial road maps.
Bus terminal information office (☎ 421-7634; Brígado Terán; ☼ 8am-9pm) Helpful. Opposite platform 12.
Provincial tourist office (☎ 430-3644; www.tucu manturismo.gov.ar; 24 de Septiembre 484; ☼ 8am-10pm Mon-Fri, 9am-9pm Sat & Sun) Helpful and knowledgeable. On the plaza.

Sights

CASA PADILLA

Alongside the Casa de Gobierno, this partly restored mid-19th-century house first belonged to provincial governor José Frías (1792–1874), then to his mayor son-in-law Ángel Padilla. A display of European art, Chinese porcelain and period furniture make up the collection housed by the **museum** (25 de Mayo 36; admission AR$3; 9:30am-12:30pm & 4:30-7:30pm Mon-Fri, 9am-noon Sat), closed for renovations at time of research.

CATEDRAL

Tucumán's neoclassical cathedral is a handsome presence on Plaza Independencia, and has a Doric facade with a pediment depicting the Exodus. Curiously, Moses is receiving bunches of grapes in the desert; a reference to the fertility of Tucumán's surrounding area. The interior has a petite wooden choir, cheerily alive ceiling paintings, and a canvas of the Annunciation behind the altar.

CASA DE LA INDEPENDENCIA (CASA HISTORICAL)

Unitarist lawyers and clerics (Federalists boycotted the meeting) declared Argentina's independence from Spain on July 9, 1816, in the dazzlingly whitewashed late-colonial **Casa de la Independencia** (431-0826; Congreso 151; admission AR$4; 10am-6pm). Portraits of the signatories line the walls of the room where the declaration was signed, the only actual original part of the structure – the rest has been rebuilt. There's plenty of information in Spanish on the lead-up to these seismic events, but you can also get a guided tour (free) in English.

There's a light-and-sound show nightly except Thursday at 8:30pm; entry is AR$5/3 per adult/child. The ticket office opens 15 minutes before the show.

MUSEO FOLCLÓRICO MANUEL BELGRANO

Occupying a colonial house, pleasant **Museo Folclórico Manuel Belgrano** (421-8250; Av 24 de Septiembre 565; admission AR$1; 9am-1pm & 3-7pm Mon-Fri, 4-10pm Sat & Sun) features a good collection of horse gear, indigenous musical instruments and weavings, Toba wood carvings, Quilmes pottery and samples of *randa* (an intricate lace resembling Paraguayan *ñandutí*) from Monteros, 53km south of Tucumán. Some items are for sale.

CASA DEL OBISPO COLOMBRES

In the center of Parque 9 de Julio (formerly Bishop Colombres' El Bajo plantation), 18th-century **Casa del Obispo Colombres** (452-2332; admission free; 8am-7pm Mon-Sat, 9am-7pm Sun) is a museum dedicated to the sugar industry, which the active cleric (an important figure in the independence movement whose promotion to Bishop of Salta arrived in the post a couple of hours after his death at 81) effectively set up. At the time of research a costly renovation was almost complete, so there'll likely be an admission charge levied on re-opening.

Tours

Tucumán province is hitching its horse firmly to the tourism wagon, and any number of tour operators offer excursions from sedate city strolls to canoeing, challenging treks and paragliding; the city hosted the 2007 Paragliding World Cup. The provincial tourist office will supply a fuller list or even offer themselves as guides.

Héctor Heredia (422-6205; Balcarce 1067) A reader-recommended mountain guide. Héctor (also known as 'El Oso' or 'the Bear') can arrange extended treks, including the beautiful, accessible four-day hike from Tucumán to Tafí del Valle.

Montañas Tucumanas (421-0660; www.montanas tucumanas.com; Catamarca 375) A cordial and professional set-up, this offers trekking, climbing, canyoning, rappelling, paragliding and more, both in locations near Tucumán and further afield.

Turismo del Tucumán (422-7636; tucumantur@ sinectis.com.ar; Crisóstomo Álvarez 435) This central agency offers guided trips to spots of interest around the province, including Tafí del Valle and Quilmes (AR$140) or a circuit in Las Yungas (AR$70).

Festivals & Events

Celebrations of **Día de la Independencia** (Argentina's Independence Day) on July 9 are vigorous in Tucumán, the cradle of the country's independence. *Tucumanos* also celebrate the **Batalla de Tucumán** (Battle of Tucumán) on September 24.

Sleeping

Most of Tucumán's hotels are overpriced, but you can negotiate substantial discounts in summer, particularly if paying cash. Half-a-dozen hostels in Tucumán offer dorm beds; the provincial tourist office can give a full list. Some cheap hotels around town are of the hourly variety.

BUDGET

Backpacker's Tucumán (430-2716; www.backpackers tucuman.com; Laprida 456; dm AR$24, s with/without bathroom AR$55/45; d with/without bathroom AR$75/65;) Formerly the Argentina Norte hostel, this is under new management and seems to be keeping the blend of airy charm and fine facilities alive. The dorms are spacious, the rooms tight but comfortable and the cool patio spaces make attractive common areas. HI members get 15% off.

Tucumán Hostel (☎ 420-1584; www.tucumanhostel .com.ar; Buenos Aires 669; dm AR$24, d with/without bathroom AR$70/60; 🖵 🏊) It's easy to like this breezy hostel seven blocks south of the plaza; with solid dorm beds and enthusiastic staff, it makes a fine base. The bathrooms are very clean, as is the kitchen; there's also a bar. If lounging around the pool at the back, be careful not to get brained by falling fruit from the avocado tree.

Casa Calchaquí (☎ 425-6974; www.casacalchaqui.com; Lola Mora 92, Yerba Buena; dm AR$25, d with/without bathroom AR$85/75; 🏊 🖵 🏊) Six kilometers west of the center in the upmarket barrio of Yerba Buena, this is a welcome retreat from the sweaty city. Hammocks, a wide green lawn, bar service and a minipool make it a top spot to relax. Add to that comfortable bunks and doubles, a kitchen and *parrilla*, and friendly multilingual hosts. Yerba Buena also has many good restaurants and nightlife choices. A cab costs AR$10 to AR$12, or grab bus 102 or 118 from opposite the terminal. Casa Calchaquí also hires bikes.

Residencial Florida (☎ 422-6674; Av 24 de Septiembre 610; s/d AR$30/50) On your honeymoon? Forget it. Love natural light? Shove off. Don't really mind where you sleep as long as it's cheap, central and has a private bathroom? This grungy, slightly weird place with dark fan-cooled rooms set around a courtyard might be for you.

Hotel Roni (☎ 421-1434; San Martín 1177; s/d AR$35/60) Cheap, clean, dark, friendly, with fans and manageable bathrooms; the rooms in this place tick all the usual budget boxes. But the lobby is way out there; you have to cross a small bridge over a pond to reach reception. Unbelievable.

Hotel La Vasca (☎ 421-1828; www.redcarlosv.com.ar; Mendoza 289; s with/without bathroom AR$55/45, d with/without bathroom AR$72/60) Everyone deserves to have 3m-high doors to their room, and you can in this central budget choice. Rooms are around two courtyards – go for an upstairs room at the back if you can – and decorated with original oils by the owner. The staff is welcoming.

MIDRANGE

King Hotel (☎ 431-0211; Chacabuco 18; s/d AR$58/78; 🏊) Traveling salespeople keep returning to this

hotel because it's comfortable, clean and in the heart of things. Prices are very fair by Tucumán standards. It often fills up by midafternoon, so you might want to book ahead.

Dallas Hotel (☎ 421-8500; www.dallashotel.com.ar; Corrientes 985; s/d AR$90/130; 🏊) Run with a smile, this likable place offers plenty of value. Padded doors give way softly to reveal sizable rooms with decent beds. There are plenty of popular bar-restaurants nearby; make sure you also check out the beautiful train station around the corner. It's 10% off if you pay cash.

Hotel Versailles (☎ 422-9760; www.hotelversaillestuc .com.ar; Crisóstomo Álvarez 481; s/d 114/142; 🏊) There is indeed a certain French elegance to this understated, old-fashioned hotel. The rooms are compact but have a stately quality, and the public areas are similarly appealing. It often will heavily discount prices if you ask.

Hotel Presidente (☎ 431-1414; www.hotelpresidente tuc.com.ar; Monteagudo 249; s/d AR$160/180; 🏊 🖵 🏊) A modern, comfortable hotel near the center, and set back slightly from the street, the Presidente is a solid choice. Some would say that two swimming pools are excessive, but that's just the way they do things in this town.

TOP END

Hotel Carlos V (☎ 431-1666; www.redcarlosv.com; 25 de Mayo 330; s/d AR$155/190; 🏊 🖵) There's something rather charming about the rooms here; it must be the parchment-colored walls and bright bedspreads, for they certainly aren't huge. Offering a fine central location and fairly classic ambience, as well as a busy café-restaurant, this is a decent Tucumán address.

Hotel del Sol (☎ 431-1755; www.hoteldelsol.com.ar; Laprida 35; s/d AR$160/200; 🏊 🖵 🏊) Tucumán's plaza, ringed by noisy three-lane roads, isn't the peaceful place it is in other cities, but there's still a certain cachet to staying on it. The bareish rooms are OK – weird color scheme aside – and the traffic noise is manageable, but only consider it if quoted substantially less than the rackrate listed here. Pool only in summer.

Swiss Hotel Metropol (☎ 431-1180; www.swisshotel metropol.com.ar; 24 de Septiembre 524; s/d AR$235/300; 🏊 🖵 🏊) The modern rooms and spacious bathrooms on offer here are perhaps slightly offset by the tiny balconies (standing room only). The fantastic rooftop pool makes up for a lot though, as does the very central location.

Catalinas Park (☎ 450-2250; www.catalinaspark .com; Av Soldati 380; s/d AR$250/280; 🏊 🖵 🏊) Several

Tucumán hotels charge this sort of price for what is barely three-star comfort. Not so at this spot by the large Parque 9 de Julio. Offering commodious (if not huge) rooms with great views, and a range of comforts that include a pleasant outdoor pool, babysitting service, sauna and anticipatory staff, this is as it should be. There's even a chopper should you fancy an aerial excursion.

Tucumán Center (☎ 452-5555; www.tucumancenter hotel.com.ar; 25 de Mayo 230; s/d AR$250/280, ste AR$448-499; ▣ ▣ ▣) It's hard to fault this upmarket, business-class hotel bang in the center of town. Service and facilities – including a small gym and outdoor pool – are first-rate, and the huge beds are mighty comfortable. Suites come with space to spare and a bathtub with bubbles. It offers big discounts in summer; check the website for specials.

Eating

Calle 25 de Mayo is eat-street, studded with modern café-bars sporting identical wooden pseudo-lyreback chairs and offering a variety of traditional and international cuisines.

El Portal (☎ 422-6024; Av 24 de Septiembre 351; dishes AR$2-19; ☻ 10am-11pm) Half a block east of Plaza Independencia, this rustic indoor/outdoor eatery has a tiny but perfectly formed menu, based around empanadas, *locro* and the like. Delicious!

Café Pigalle (25 de Mayo 24; ice creams AR$3-8; 9am-11pm) If you want to blend in in Tucumán, you'd better have an ice cream in your hand at all times. This place on the plaza does some of the best, and also offers a daily dessert special for AR$5 that is usually extremely sweet, sticky and good.

Peña El Cardón (☎ 430-8506; Las Heras 50; dishes AR$6-18; ☻ dinner) This historic and traditional *peña* gives a good idea of what these places were like before they started putting on touristy shows. There are regular cultural events, a pretty patio and delicious empanadas. It's authentic and not a tourist attraction; tread sensitively.

El Alto de la Lechuza (☎ 400-7171; Av 24 de Septiembre 1199; dishes AR$9-17; ☻ dinner Thu-Sun) Founded in 1939 and billing itself as Argentina's oldest *peña*, this place offers standard *parrilla* and pasta fare plus a few regional specialties. The real reason to come here, though, is the music; the venue has hosted many Argentine luminaries.

ourpick Il Postino (☎ 421-0440; cnr 25 de Mayo & Córdoba; pizzas AR$9-19, pastas AR$14-19; ☻ 11am-late) Pizza and pasta are served with panache in this atmospheric brick warehouse eatery. It's popular with all, and you often have to wait for a table. It's worth it; the standard (of the pizzas especially) is sky-high. It also serves various tapa-sized portions.

Fon Restaurante (☎ 421-8715; Maipú 435; all-you-can-eat AR$12; ☻ lunch Mon-Sat) The lunchtime buffet at this vegetarian restaurant has mostly Chinese dishes, with a few local favorites such as *ensalada rusa* (Russian salad) and empanadas thrown in. It's not gourmet, but it does the job.

La Leñita (☎ 422-9196; 25 de Mayo 377; mains AR$11-28; ☻ lunch & dinner) One of the best *parrilla* restaurants around in this part of the world, this wins few points for interior design but stands out for service and the sheer quality of the meat. Try *picanha* (rump steak) or the delicious *mollejitas* (sweetbreads). Sit strategically to avoid the air-con's arctic wind.

La Sirio-Libanesa (Maipú 575; set menus AR$14-26; ☻ lunch Mon-Sat, dinner Mon-Thu) The restaurant at the Syrian-Lebanese society offers tasty Levantine cuisine that makes a welcome change of scene. The set lunch is AR$14, and there are several other set menus, as well as à la carte.

Drinking & Entertainment

From Thursday to Saturday nights, most of the action is in the Abasto region, on Calle Lillo. Follow San Lorenzo west from the center, and you'll hit the middle of the zone three blocks west of our map. There are dozens of bars and nightclubs to choose from; take your pick. Other popular *boliches* (nightclubs) can be found in Yerba Buena, 6km west of the center (taxi AR$10 to AR$15). A controversial law means they shut at 4am.

Künstner (☎ 497-5597; Crisóstomo Álvarez 456) Blessed relief it is to step off this noisy, fume-filled street into the gentle aromas of malt and hops. Four tasty beers are brewed in this convivial spot, which also serves fine cheap food such as *milanesas* (breaded cutlets), pastas and pizzas, all very cheaply (AR$5 to AR$12). There's a AR$10 lunchtime set meal.

Harris (cnr Laprida & Mendoza; ☻ 8am-late) On a busy corner, this is a popular hangout for smartly-dressed *tucumanos*. The interior is padded seats and elegant dark wood; outside, the tables and chairs are at the very top of the Coca-Cola range. Excellent mixed drinks and good coffee; the food is also more than passable.

Filipo (Mendoza 501; espressos AR$3.50; ☻ 8am-midnight) Glasses gleaming on the gantry, outdoor tables and bow-tied waiters make this a great café. The espresso is superlative, and the apple-and-water *licuados* (fruit blended with milk or water) deserve a prize.

Plaza de Almas (Maipú 791; mains AR$9-15; ☺7pm-late) This intimate and engaging multilevel place is popular with bohemian young *tucumanos* and is one of the best of Tucumán's many combination café-bar-restaurant-cultural centers. The short but interesting menu offers a range of kebabs and salads among other choices.

Costumbres Argentinas (☎ 0381-15-6439576; San Juan 666; ☺9.30pm-4am Wed-Sun) Though the address seems like a contradiction in terms, this unusual, cozy and welcoming bar has an arty bohemian vibe and sometimes puts on live music.

Cine Majestic (☎ 421-7515; Av 24 de Septiembre) Close to the plaza, this is one of several central cinemas.

Getting There & Away

AIR
Aerolíneas Argentinas (☎ 431-1030; 9 de Julio 110) has three to five daily flights to Buenos Aires' Aeroparque Jorge Newbery (AR$687).

BUS
Tucumán's **bus terminal** (☎ 422-2221; Brígido Terán 350) is a major project with 60 platforms and plenty of shops and services. The bus **information booth** (☎ 430-6400) is outside, by the supermarket. The handy tourist office is opposite platform 12.

Sample destinations and fares:

Destination	Cost (AR$)	Duration (hr)
Buenos Aires	148	16
Cafayate	28	6½
Catamarca	27	4
Córdoba	69	7
Jujuy	39	5
La Quiaca	76	11
La Rioja	43	6
Mendoza	110	13
Posadas	107	18
Resistencia	74	12
Río Gallegos	342	40
Salta	33	4½
Salvador Mazza	75	10
San Juan	91	12
Santiago (Chile)	160	23
Santiago del Estero	15	2
Tafí del Valle	15	2½-3
Termas de Río Hondo	11	1

TRAIN
Argentina's trains aren't what they were, but Tucumán is still connected to Buenos Aires (via Santiago del Estero and Rosario) twice a week from the beautiful **Estación Mitre** (☎ 430-9220) in the northwest of town. Services frequently take several hours longer than advertised, but it's an experience a little like stepping back in time and might appeal to those in no hurry or on a strict budget.

At time of research, trains were leaving Buenos Aires' Retiro station at 10.40am on Monday and Friday, arriving in Tucumán at 11.40am the next day. From Tucumán, trains left at 5.40pm on Wednesday (arriving at 7.10pm Thursday), and 8.33pm (no joke) on Saturday, arriving at 10pm on Sunday.

The trip costs AR$35/45/66 in *turista* (2nd class)/1st class/Pullman (reclinable seats), or AR$200 in a sleeper.

Getting Around
Aeropuerto Benjamín Matienzo (TUC; ☎ 426-4906) is situated 8km east of downtown. Empresa 120 operates minibuses (AR$1.50) that leave from the bus terminal every 30 minutes during the day. A cab costs about AR$15 from the center.

For getting around the city, local buses (AR$1.50) clearly mark their major destinations on the front.

There are several car-rental places. A reliable choice is **Móvil Renta** (☎ 431-0550; www .movilrenta.com.ar; San Lorenzo 370).

AROUND TUCUMÁN
Until 1767 the ruins of **San José de Lules**, 20km south of Tucumán, was a Jesuit *reducción* (Indian settlement created by Spanish missionaries) among the region's Lule Indians. After the Jesuits' expulsion, the Dominicans assumed control of the complex, whose present ruins date from the 1880s and once served as a school. The small museum has replicas of colonial documents and a plethora of busts of various Argentine independence heroes. There are numerous ghost stories about the place, and legends of buried Jesuit treasure.

To get to Lules, a pleasant site for an outing, take the El Provincial bus from downtown Tucumán.

The fertile, hilly area northwest of Tucumán is known as **Las Yungas**, and offers plenty of appealing day trips that get you out of the hot, busy city. The tourist offices offer good information on destinations, which include the reservoir of **El Cadillal** (Dique Celestino Gelsi) offering swimming and windsurfing, or the **Parque Sierra de San Javier**, a university-operated reserve offering guided walks, including one to the small but pretty Río Noque waterfall. San Pedro (ticket office 69) runs regular buses from Tucumán's bus terminal to El Cadillal (one hour), while San Javier (no ticket booth, leaves from platforms 56 to 58) runs to San Javier (where there are a few places to stay) and the reserve. Tucumán tour operators also run trips out here.

TAFÍ DEL VALLE
☎ 03867 / pop 3300 / elev 2100m
The lovely hilltown of Tafí is where the folk of Tucumán traditionally head to take refuge from the summer heat. The journey from the city is a spectacular one; about 100km northwest of Tucumán the narrow gorge of the Río de los Sosas, with its dense, verdant subtropical forest on all sides, opens onto a misty valley beneath the snowy peaks of the Sierra del Aconquija. The precipitous mountain road is a spectacular trip – grab a window seat on the bus.

Tafí makes a fine spot to hang out for a few days, with crisp mountain air, many budget accommodations and a laid-back scene. There are also a couple of memorable historic ranches to stay at.

Orientation
Av Miguel Critto is the main street running east to west. If you turn left out of the bus terminal you soon join it. Off it, Av Perón is the center of activity, and Belgrano climbs from Perón past the church. A pedestrian street links Critto and Belgrano. Most public services are on or near the Centro Cívico, which features an unusual semicircular plaza.

Information
There's a *locutorio* at the bus terminal, one of several places offering phone calls and internet access.
Banco de la Provincia (Centro Cívico) Changes US dollars and has ATM.
Tourist office (Casa del Turista; Av Miguel Critto; ☉ 8am-9pm) Tourist information at the junction of the pedestrian street. Staff know exactly what you want, even if you try to convince them otherwise.

Sights & Activities
CAPILLA LA BANDA
This 18th-century **Jesuit chapel** (☎ 421685; Av José Frías Silva; admission AR$2; ☉ 8am-10pm summer, 8am-6pm winter), acquired by the Frías Silva family of Tucumán on the Jesuits' expulsion and then expanded in the 1830s, was restored to its original configuration in the 1970s. Note the escape tunnel in the chapel. A small archaeological collection consisting mostly of funerary urns, but also religious art of the Cuzco school, ecclesiastical vestments and period furniture that once belonged to the Frías Silvas is on display in the **museum** next door.

The chapel is a short distance south of downtown. Cross the bridge over the Río Tafí del Valle then follow the road around to the right onto José Frías Silva. Turn left onto the third dirt road along the left-hand side of José Frías Silva. The chapel is a little way along.

HIKING
Several nearby peaks and destinations make hiking in the mountains around Tafí del Valle an attractive prospect; try 3000m **Cerro El Matadero**, a four- to five-hour climb; 3800m **Cerro Pabellón** (six hours); and 4600m **Cerro El Negrito**, reached from the statue of Cristo Redentor on RN 307 to Acheral. The trails are badly marked, and no trail maps are available; you can hire a guide for about AR$10 an hour. Ask for more information at the tourist office. An easier hike climbs **Cerro Pelado** for views over the town. Cross the bridge toward the Capilla, and you'll see the path on your left immediately afterward. It takes about 1¼ hours to climb, and less to come down.

Several people around town hire out horses (look for *'alquilo caballos'*) for rides in the valley.

Tours
La Cumbre (☎ 421768; www.lacumbretafidelvalle.com; Perón 120) offers various two- to three-hour trips around the valley on 4WD tracks or taking in sights such as the menhir park near El Mollar and a traditional cheese factory (AR$50 to AR$70 per person). It also organizes more rigorous full-day trips and excursions to the Quilmes ruins.

Sleeping
There are many choices, including several budget places charging AR$20 to AR$25 per

person for dorm rooms without bathroom, and overpriced midrange options charging AR$150 to AR$180 a double. Prices drop out of season. Unheated rooms can get distinctly chilly.

Hospedaje Celia (☎ 421170; Belgrano 443; r per person AR$20) Set back from the road 100m uphill from the church, this place still seems to be being built but offers bright, white and comfortable-enough rooms with private bathroom. There are minor inconveniences – no sockets in the rooms and you have to tell staff when to turn the hot water on – but the price is right.

El Cardón Hostal (☎ 420129; hostalelcardon@hotmail.com; Los Faroles s/n; dm with/without bathroom AR$25/20, d AR$40-60) Named for the massive candelabra cactus opposite, and on the pedestrian street, this is fairly representative of budget choices in Tafí. Rooms are clean and decent, and breakfast is included except in high season.

Hostel la Cumbre (☎ 421768; www.lacumbretafidelvalle.com; Perón 120; dm/d without bathroom AR$25/50) The happy orange ochre color of the courtyard and views from the roof terrace make this a good choice. The rooms are cramped but clean, and there's a decent kitchen and welcoming staff.

Estancia Los Cuartos (☎ 0381-1558-74230; www.estancialoscuartos.com; Critto s/n; d AR$125) Oozing character from every pore, this lovely spot lies between the bus terminal and the center. Two centuries old, it feels like a museum, with venerable books lining antique shelves, and authentic rooms redolent with the smell of aged wood and woolen blankets. There are rooms in a new annex too, which offer more comfortable beds but less history, although they remain true to the feel of the place. Traditional cheeses are also made here.

Hotel Tafí (☎ 421007; www.hoteltafiweb.com.ar; Belgrano 177; s/d AR$125/170; ☒) Despair not when you see it from the street, for things improve once you get inside, with a ski-lodge feel and helpful staff. The medium-sized rooms have gleaming bathrooms, wood-tile floors, mountain views and tiny TVs. There's a pleasant rocky garden, and the huge fireplace makes the comfortable lounge area the place to be on a chilly night.

Hostería Lunahuana (☎ 421330; www.lunahuana.com.ar; Av Miguel Critto 540; s/d AR$140/180; ☒ ☐) This stylish and popular hotel has rooms decorated with flair – some have mezzanines accessed by spiral staircases. The whole place is decked out with interesting and tasteful decorations, and service is professional and friendly.

Las Tacanas (☎ 421821; www.estancialastacanas.com; Perón 372; s/d AR$230/280; ☐) Impeccably preserved and decorated, this fabulous historic complex was once a Jesuit *estancia* and is a most memorable place to stay. The adobe buildings, more than three centuries old, house a variety of tasteful, rustic rooms with noble furniture and beamed ceilings. Though it's in the center of town, it feels like you're in a country retreat, and there's a warm welcome from the family that has owned it for generations.

Eating & Drinking

Bar El Paraíso (☎ 0381-15-5875179; Perón 176; sandwiches AR$5-9, mains AR$8-19; ☒ lunch & dinner) This cozy bar is where locals congregate to dine cheaply and watch football or martial arts films. There is a pleasant terrace overlooking the street.

El Rancho de Félix (☎ 421022; cnr Belgrano & Juan de Perón; mains AR$10-22) A big warm barn of a place that's incredibly popular for lunch. Regional specialties such as *locro* and *humitas* feature heavily on the menu, but *parrilla* and pasta are also on offer.

Don Pepito (☎ 421764; Perón 193; mains AR$11-18; ☒ lunch & dinner) It looks touristy, the level of service varies here, and it charges too much for extras, but the meat is truly excellent. Bypass the set *parrillada* (for one/two AR$15/27) and order off the menu. Kidneys, *bife de chorizo* or *chivito* (goat) are all fine choices and are served in generous portions. There's often live entertainment (AR$2 extra).

The bar-restaurant at the bus terminal is an unexpectedly smart place, and locals head down there to socialize even if they've no intention to travel or spot buses.

Getting There & Away

Tafí's impressive **bus terminal** (☎ 421031; Miguel Critto), near the corner of Av Juan Calchaquí, is 400m east of the town center. Empresa Aconquija has eight buses a day to Tucumán (AR$15, three hours). Buses head the other way to Santa María (AR$14, 1½ hours, four to six daily) and Cafayate (AR$16.80, four hours, two daily) via Quilmes.

The road to Santa María, Quilmes and Cafayate is spectacular, crossing the 3050m pass known as Abra del Infiernillo (Little Hell Pass).

Getting Around

Hourly in summer (every three hours in winter), local Aconquija buses do most of the circuit around Cerro El Pelado, in the middle of the valley. One goes on the north side, another on the south side, so it's possible to make a circuit of the valley by walking the link between them.

AROUND TAFÍ DEL VALLE

In the valley around Tafí, there are several attractions, including **Parque de los Menhires** (AR$3; ☽ 8am-6pm), a collection of more than 100 carved standing stones found in the surrounding area. They were produced by the Tafí culture some 2000 years ago, but they have been somehow stripped of dignity by being removed from their original locations. The site lies 12km south of Tafí, near the village of El Mollar.

Santa María

☎ 03838 / pop 10,800 / elev 1900m

This seductive little town lies on the route between Tafí del Valle and Cafayate, and is the handiest base for exploring the ruins at Quilmes. It's actually the northernmost redoubt of Catamarca province (locals attribute their notable friendliness to this) and makes a fine stopover. You can also head south from here to Belén via Hualfin.

The plaza is the center of town, and lies nine blocks north of the bus terminal. A remarkably helpful **tourist office** (☎ 421083; ☽ 7am-11pm Mon-Fri, 8am-11pm Sat & Sun) with heroic opening hours, is located under the trees in the square itself. On one corner of the plaza, the recommended **Museo Arqueológico Eric Boman** (cnr Belgrano & Sarmiento; ☽ 9am-8pm Mon-Sat) has a worthwhile collection of ceramics from this important archaeological zone. Next door is an *artesanía* cooperative, selling woven goods and other handicrafts at more-than-fair prices. On the edge of town, **Cabra Marca** (☽ 8am-6pm Mon-Sat, 8am-2pm Sun) makes traditional goats' cheese, and is worth visiting for the free guided tour, which includes a chance to meet the horned beasts themselves. Nearby is a statue of Pachamama, the indigenous earth goddess whose **festival** on August 1 is celebrated in traditional manner with music, dancing, and a llama sacrifice to bless the next harvest.

There are many places to stay in town, including the welcoming **Residencial Pérez** (☎ 420257; San Martín 94; s/d AR$30/50) near the plaza (no sign), the basic but ultracheap **Albergue Municipal** (☎ 425064; dm AR$10), located at the campsite – bring your own bedding – and the somewhat surreal **Caasama** (☎ 421627; www.hotelcaasama.com.ar; cnr Marcial & 25 de Agosto; s/d AR$80/105; ☒ ☲) by the bus terminal, which offers comfortable and very unusual accommodations in a colorful provincial complex run by the Catamarca government that includes a big pool, floodlit tennis court and pumping *boliche*. You'll need to book ahead in summer months.

Eating options on the plaza include **El Colonial del Valle** (☎ 420897; cnr Esquiú & San Martín; meals AR$7-15; ☽ lunch & dinner), a traditional and attractive *confitería* which serves good coffee and tamales and fuller meals in the upstairs dining room.

There are several buses daily to Tucumán (AR$24, six hours) via Tafí del Valle (AR$14, 1½ hours) and two daily to Cafayate (AR$16, 2 hours) via Quilmes. Three buses a week go to Belén (AR$15, five hours) via Hualfin A *remise* from the terminal to the center is AR$2.

Quilmes

☎ 03892

Dating from about AD 1000, **Quilmes** (admission AR$5; ☽ 8am-6pm) was a complex indigenous urban settlement that occupied about 30 hectares and housed as many as 5000 people. The Quilmes locals survived contact with the Inca, which occurred from about AD 1480 onward, but could not outlast the siege of the Spaniards who, in 1667, deported the last 2000 inhabitants to Buenos Aires.

Quilmes' thick walls underscore its defensive purpose, but clearly this was more than just a *pucará*. Dense construction sprawls both north and south from the central nucleus, where the outlines of buildings, in a variety of shapes, are obvious even to the casual observer. For revealing views of the extent of the ruins, climb the trails up either flank of the nucleus, which offer vistas of the valley once only glimpsed by the city's defenders. Give yourself a few hours to explore the nucleus and the surrounding area.

There is a small **museum** at the entrance, which is well presented but poorly labeled. The admission charge entitles you to a free guided tour (English-speaking guides were available at time of research). The museum shop features a good selection of handicrafts.

SLEEPING & EATING

Parador de Quilmes (☎ 421075; s/d AR$93/126; ☲) This hotel blends so well into its surroundings that it's surprisingly inconspicuous from outside, but its high ceilings and skylights manage to convey the expansiveness of the

THE ANDEAN NORTHWEST

desert. It's beautifully decorated with Inca motifs and slate floors.

A large but stylish **bar-confitería** (mains AR$10-23; ☺ breakfast, lunch & dinner), just outside the ruins, offers *parrilla*, pasta and great views of the ruins.

GETTING THERE & AWAY

Buses from Cafayate to Santa María or Tafí del Valle will drop passengers at the junction, but from there you'll have to walk or hitch-hike (there is little traffic) 5km to the ruins. It will probably be easier to get a lift back to the highway, since you can approach any vehicle visiting the ruins.

Another option is to hire a taxi in Cafayate or Santa María. You should be able to bargain a driver down to about AR$100 for the roundtrip.

SANTIAGO DEL ESTERO

☎ 0385 / pop 327,974 / elev 200m

Placid Santiago del Estero enjoys the distinction of the title 'Madre de Ciudades' (Mother of Cities) for this, founded in 1553, was the first Spanish urban settlement in what is now Argentina. Sadly, it boasts no architectural heritage from that period but makes a pleasant stopover.

Santiagueños (residents of Santiago del Estero) enjoy a nationwide reputation for valuing rest and relaxation over work. A popular Argentine joke claims that they are world hammer-throwing champions, for they prefer to be as far away from anything work-related as possible. Nevertheless, there's plenty of bustle around the center, particularly in the evenings when life orbits around the pretty plaza and its adjoining pedestrian streets.

Orientation

Reflecting its early settlement, Santiago's urban plan is fairly irregular. The town center is Plaza Libertad, from which Av Libertad, trending southwest to northeast, bisects the city. South and north of the plaza, Av Independencia and the pedestrian malls Tucumán and Absalón Reyes are important commercial areas, but Av Belgrano is the main thoroughfare. Street names change either side of Avs Libertad and Belgrano. The Río Dulce runs to the northeast of the center. On the other side of the river, connected by bridges, is the twin town of La Banda.

Information

Several downtown banks have ATMs, and internet places are widespread.

ACA (Automóvil Club Argentino; ☎ 421-2270; cnr Avs Sáenz Peña & Belgrano) Argentina's auto club; good source for provincial road maps.

Banco Galicia (Avellaneda 159) Changes traveler's checks and cash. On Plaza Libertad.

Municipal tourist office (☎ 422-9800; www .santiagociudadmadre.com.ar; Plaza Libertad s/n; ☺ 8am-8pm) In a kiosk in the plaza itself. Helpful.

Post office (Buenos Aires s/n) Near the corner of Urquiza.

Provincial tourist office (☎ 421-3253; Av Libertad 417; ☺ 7am-10pm Mon-Fri, 8am-1pm & 4-9pm Sat & Sun) On the plaza. Displays work by local artists.

Sights

MUSEO DE CIENCIAS ANTROPOLÓGICAS Y NATURALES

An excellent collection founded by two French archaeologist brothers, the **Museo de Ciencias Antropológicas y Naturales** (☎ 421-1380; Avellaneda 355; admission free; ☺ 7:30am-8pm Mon-Fri, 10am-noon Sat) is by far the most interesting thing to see in town. There's a stunning array of indigenous ceramics – mostly sizable, noble funerary urns used for secondary burial (the remains were put in the pot after decomposition) – as well as jewelry, flutes and a large case filled with ornate loom weights. There are also some impressive fossils of glyptodonts, an extinct family of creatures that somewhat resembled large armadillos.

PARQUE AGUIRRE

Named for the city's founder and only 10 blocks from Plaza Libertad, this enormous park has a small **zoo**, camping areas, a swimming pool and, on the far side, a new *costanera* (riverside road) along the erratic Río Dulce. At time of research this was mostly recreational, but bars and restaurants tend to blossom in these places, so it might just be a happening place by the time you read this.

Tours

A competent and professional set-up, **Sumaq** (☎ 421-3055; www.sumaqturismo.com.ar; Tucumán 39) is currently the only operator offering tours to the remote Parque Nacional Copo; it also offers good trips to other parts of northwestern Argentina. The Copo tour costs AR$290 with a minimum of two people (give two to three days' notice). It includes an overnight stay in simple accommodations near the park. The office is in the same building as the Hotel

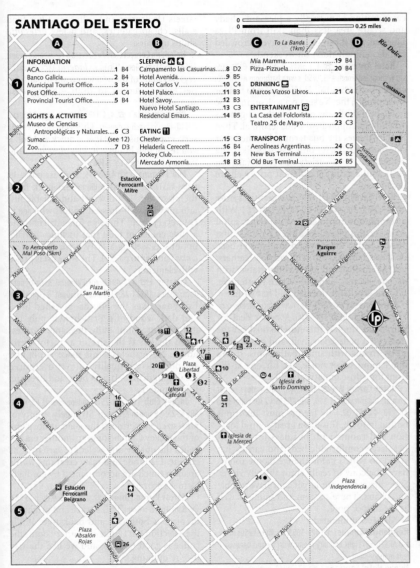

SANTIAGO DEL ESTERO

```
0                    400 m
0              0.25 miles
```

INFORMATION
ACA...1 B4
Banco Galicia..............................2 B4
Municipal Tourist Office............3 B4
Post Office...................................4 C4
Provincial Tourist Office.............5 B4

SIGHTS & ACTIVITIES
Museo de Ciencias
  Antropológicas y Naturales....6 C3
Sumac.....................................(see 12)
Zoo..7 D3

SLEEPING 🏕 🏠
Campamento las Casuarinas......8 D2
Hotel Avenida.............................9 B5
Hotel Carlos V............................10 C4
Hotel Palace...............................11 B3
Hotel Savoy.................................12 B3
Nuevo Hotel Santiago.................13 C3
Residencial Emaus......................14 B5

EATING 🍴
Chester...15 C3
Heladería Cerecett......................16 B4
Jockey Club..................................17 B4
Mercado Armonía........................18 B3

Mía Mamma..................................19 B4
Pizza-Pizzuela..............................20 B4

DRINKING 🍷
Marcos Vizoso Libros...................21 C4

ENTERTAINMENT 🎭
La Casa del Folclorista.................22 C2
Teatro 25 de Mayo.......................23 C3

TRANSPORT
Aerolíneas Argentinas..................24 C5
New Bus Terminal.........................25 B2
Old Bus Terminal..........................26 B5

THE ANDEAN NORTHWEST

Savoy – go through the restaurant and up a narrow spiral staircase.

Festivals & Events

Santiago's chaotic **Carnaval**, in February, resembles celebrations in the Quebrada de Humahuaca. During the entire last week of July, *santiagueños* celebrate the **founding of the city**. The centerpiece of this is the Marcha de los Bombos, a boisterous procession into the center of the city by some 2000 locals banging all manner of drums.

Sleeping

Campamento las Casuarinas (☎ 421-1390; Parque Aguirre; sites per person AR$5) This municipal campground is normally a pleasant, shady and secure area, less than 1km from Plaza Libertad, but it can be oppressively crowded and deafeningly noisy on weekends.

Hotel Avenida (☎ 421-5887; Pedro León Gallo 405; s/d without bathroom AR$30/50, s with bathroom AR$50-70, d with bathroom AR$60-100; ❄) You have to feel for these people; they've set up a welcoming little hotel, beautifully decorated with indigenous art and right opposite the bus terminal. Then the city moves the bus terminal to the other side of town. Still, it's only a short walk to the center. There's a variety of rooms (air-con costs a little extra) at different prices; all are decent value.

Hotel Savoy (☎ 421-1234; www.savoysantiago.com .ar, in Spanish; Tucumán 39; s/d AR$75/120; ❄) With a sumptuous entrance and gorgeous spiral staircase, this place looks like a palace at first glance. Sadly, there are no four-poster beds or slaves fanning you with ostrich feathers, but the smallish rooms are comfortable, with decent showers, and the service is attentive. It's also excellently located and has wi-fi.

Hotel Palace (☎ 421-2700; www.palacehotelsgo.com; Tucumán 19; s/d AR$80/118; ❄) A better deal for pairs than singles, this hotel is just off the plaza on a pedestrian mall, and has slightly stuffy rooms with small bathrooms. If you don't mind street noise, ask for one at the front for a dose of natural light.

Hotel Carlos V (☎ 424-0303; hotelcarlosv@arnet .com.ar; Independencia 110; s/d AR$150/230, superior d AR$290; ❄ ▢ ▣) By far the most luxurious option in town, this has a great central location and rooms with business-level facilities, large comfortable beds and carpet that could do with a color change. Some rooms have a balcony to really enjoy the city views. Superior rooms are larger and have a table and chairs. There's a gym and sauna as well as the indoor pool.

Also recommended:

Residencial Emaus (☎ 421-5893; Av Moreno Sur 675; s/d AR$30/55) Light and airy rooms with TV and benevolent management.

Nuevo Hotel Santiago (☎ 421-4949; nuevohotel santiago@arnet.com.ar; Buenos Aires 60; s/d AR$84/110; ❄ ▢) Smart impersonal place with good rooms a block from the plaza.

Eating & Drinking

Mercado Armonía (Tucumán) Santiago's art-deco market sits between the two pedestrian streets (Pellegrini and Salta), and has food stalls, cheap eateries, and a few *artesanía* shops upstairs.

Heladería Cerecett (cnr Av Libertad & Córdoba; ice creams AR$3; ❍ 11am-11pm) This *heladería* (ice creamery) has some of the best ice cream in Santiago del Estero, served in drab, no-nonsense surroundings.

Pizza-Pizzuela (☎ 424-1392; Absalón Rojas 78; pizzas AR$10-18; ❍ lunch & dinner) This central pizzeria serves up no-fuss food that is quick and hot. If you're not that hungry, it does *pizzetas* (minipizzas) for AR$5 to AR$7.

Mía Mamma (☎ 429-9715; 24 de Septiembre 15; mains AR$11-22; ❍ lunch & dinner) Set back from the plaza, this is a discreet and reliable restaurant with well-dressed waiters who see to your every need. There's a fine salad bar, and a wide choice of food that includes *parrilla* options as well as a tasty *arroz a la valenciana* (similar to paella). The wine list is priced with clemency.

Chester (☎ 422-4972; cnr Pelligrini & Av General Roca; mains AR$11-28; ❍ noon-3:30pm & 7pm-1am) Everyone likes the booths, polished brass and dark wood of a British-style pub, but it doesn't transmit quite the same coziness when the bar is the size of a tractor warehouse. Nevertheless, this place is popular and offers decent-quality but very overpriced meals and drinks. It gets busy and lively on Friday nights.

Jockey Club (☎ 421-7518; Independencia 68; mains AR$12-25; ❍ lunch & dinner) Strangely empty of pint-sized horseriders, the staid atmosphere of the Jockey Club belongs to another era but belies the quality and welcome variety of its cuisine. Elaborate and tasty creations with a Spanish touch are accompanied by cordially formal service.

Marcos Vizoso Libros (☎ 422-8166; 9 de Julio 181; ❍ 8am-1pm & 5-8pm) This spruce and bright little place is both café and bookstore. While the selection isn't huge on either count, the coffee is good (AR$3), and we like the way they're thinking.

Entertainment

La Casa del Folclorista (Pozo de Vargas, Parque Aguirre; admission AR$10) To the east of town, this is a big barn of a *peña* that has live folk bands some evenings, and a bargain *parrilla libre* for AR$10. The music tends to kick off around 11pm.

Teatro 25 de Mayo (☎ 421-4141; 25 de Mayo) In the same building as the Palacio Legislativo is Teatro 25 de Mayo, Santiago's prime theater venue.

Getting There & Away

AIR

Aerolíneas Argentinas (☎ 422-4335; 24 de Septiembre 547) flies four times weekly to Buenos Aires (AR$614).

BUS

Santiago's **old bus terminal** (☎ 421-3746; cnr Pedro León Gallo & Saavedra) is eight blocks southwest of Plaza Libertad. It's due to be replaced by a shiny new terminal in the north of town, at the corner of Av Rivadavia and Perú. They say early 2008, we say early 2009 at best. Sample destinations and fares:

Destination	Cost (AR$)	Duration (hr)
Buenos Aires	129	13
Catamarca	28	4½
Córdoba	54	6
Jujuy	63	7
La Rioja	47	7
Mendoza	125	17
Resistencia	49	7½
Rosario	89	10
Salta	54	6
Salvador Mazza	99	14
San Juan	107	14
Santa Fe	80	9½
Termas de Río Hondo	6	1
Tucumán	15	2

TRAIN

Santiago del Estero (actually, the adjacent twin town of La Banda) is on the Buenos Aires–Tucumán train line, which runs twice weekly. Trains run from La Banda **station** (☎ 427-3918) to Tucumán (4½ hours) twice weekly. They also leave twice weekly to Retiro (22 hours).

Getting Around

Bus 15 goes to **Aeropuerto Mal Paso** (SDE; ☎ 434-3651; Av Madre de Ciudades), situated 6km northwest of downtown. A taxi from the city center costs AR$7.

Central Santiago del Estero is compact and walking suffices for almost everything except connections to the airport. If you're weary, a taxi just about anywhere around town should cost AR$2 to AR$3.

AROUND SANTIAGO DEL ESTERO
Termas de Río Hondo
☎ 03858 / pop 27,838

Termas de Río Hondo, 70km northwest of its provincial capital Santiago del Estero, is famous for its thermal waters, and its nearly 200 hotels all have hot mineral baths. While it's very well known as a winter holiday destination for Argentines, it's an ugly, overdeveloped place of no interest unless you plan a spa treatment. The town has two unusual features: it has a triangular Plaza San Martín as well as one of the country's few public monuments to Juan and Evita Perón. There are numerous shops selling tasty chocolates and *alfajores* (filled sandwich cookies).

The town has many banks, internet places and other tourist facilities. There's a **tourist office** (☎ 421571; Caseros 132; ☼ 7am-9pm) just off the main Av Alberdi.

SLEEPING & EATING

Most of Río Hondo's hotels close in summer (ie from November to April), but a few remain open. Prices nearly halve in the low season. There are numerous restaurants.

Departamentos Ma & Cris (☎ 423495; departa mentos_macris@hotmail.com; Pasteur 180; d AR$80) With a quiet suburban feel, these apartments are very fairly priced and a good deal for couples or larger groups. There are two locations, basically identical, with a patio, grill, decent kitchen and comfortable beds. They're open all year.

Hotel Los Pinos (☎ 421043; www.lospinoshotel.com .ar, in Spanish; Maipú 201; r per person AR$264-334; ☼ Apr-Oct; ☒ ☐ ☒) This four-star property is in the most attractive building in town. The pool is huge, and you can also count on a sauna, gymnasium and tennis courts. There are two wings, styled slightly differently – the 'americano' is somewhat more expensive.

Express (☎ 423323; Rivadavia 170; mains AR$8-17; ☼ lunch & dinner) A pleasantly cool and dark place with an army of overhead fans working overtime to keep the air circulating. The menu runs the gamut of meats, pastas and excellent pizzas, and the place packs out later at night when it converts into a bar.

Giovanni Cremas Heladas has a couple of outlets around town, including one located on Rivadavia. Head here to sample Río Hondo's best ice cream. For those with an even sweeter tooth, head for La Bombonerie, a block north

THE ANDEAN NORTHWEST

of Av Alberdi, not far from the tourist office; if you get out of this place without a bag of chocolates, then you did better than most.

GETTING THERE & AWAY
The **bus terminal** (☎ 421513; Las Heras) is half-a-dozen blocks west of the plaza and two blocks north of Av Alberdi. Buses run regularly to Santiago del Estero (AR$5, one hour) and Tucumán (AR$4, one hour) as well as destinations further afield.

Parque Nacional Copo
Right in the northeast corner of Santiago del Estero province, on the edge of the Chaco, this 1150-sq-km national park was created in 2000. Like the Parque Nacional Chaco it is an important last redoubt of the quebracho colorado tree, of which there are some huge and noble examples in the park. Among the rich birdlife are several species of parrot, and unusual creatures include endangered tatú carretas (a large species of armadillo), ant-eaters and jaguars. When visiting the park, it's a sobering thought that this type of forest covered 80% of the province as recently as 1907. Less than a quarter remains.

You have to arrange a permit to visit beforehand. This is free and can be obtained from the **ranger office** (☎ 03841-491183; drnoa@apn.gov.ar; San Francisco Solano s/n) in Pampa de los Guanacos, where there are simple accommodations. Daily buses run through here from Santiago del Estero and Resistencia.

In the park itself, 24km west then north from Pampa, a short walking trail and an observation tower were being put in place at time of research. The rangers have cleared a camping area in the park, but there are no facilities. See p296 for tours to the park from Santiago del Estero.

CATAMARCA & LA RIOJA
Comparatively little visited by travelers, these provinces are great fun to explore, and are rich in scenery and tradition. Both were home to several important pre-Columbian cultures, mostly maize cultivators, who developed unique pottery techniques and styles, and the region has many important archaeological sites.

The town of Catamarca has an immediacy and lively feel that make it a definite on the 'to visit' list, while the remote poncho-making town of Belén, the mining heritage and fabulous surrounding scenery of Chilecito, and La Rioja's moving Tinkunaco celebration are other attractions well worth your while getting to know.

CATAMARCA
☎ 03833 / pop 171,923 / elev 530m
Vibrant Catamarca is booming at the moment, and has a very different feel to other towns of this size in the region. The local authorities have been energetically promoting the province's natural products, and trade fairs showcasing wines, walnuts, olive oils and jams mean the city's hotels are often full.

San Fernando del Valle de Catamarca, to give the city its full name, has a lovely central plaza, and noble buildings dot the streets. To the west of town, the huge eucalypts of Parque Navarro scent the air and are backed by the spectacular sierra beyond.

Orientation
Nearly everything is in walking distance in the city center, an area 12 blocks square circumscribed by four wide avenues: Belgrano to the north, Alem to the east, Güemes to the south and Virgen del Valle to the west. The focus of downtown is the beautiful Plaza 25 de Mayo. South of the plaza, Rivadavia is pedestrianized right down to Av Güemes.

Information
ACA (Automóvil Club Argentino; ☎ 424513; Av República 102) Argentina's auto club; good source for provincial road maps.
BBVA (Rivadavia 520) Cashes traveler's checks and has an ATM.
Cyber Web (San Martín 505; per hr AR$1.50; ☒ 10am-midnight) Internet and phone calls on the plaza.
Municipal tourist office (☎ 437413; turismocatamarca@cedeconet.com.ar; Av República 446; ☒ 8am-9pm) On the plaza; helpful. There's a desk in the bus terminal as well.
Post office (San Martín 753)
Provincial tourist office (☎ 455308; www.turismo catamarca.gov.ar; Av Virgen del Valle 901; ☒ 8am-8pm Mon-Sat) On the west side of town.

Sights
CATEDRAL BASÍLICA DE NUESTRA SEÑORA DEL VALLE
Overlooking Plaza 25 de Mayo, and dating from 1859, the cathedral shelters the Virgen

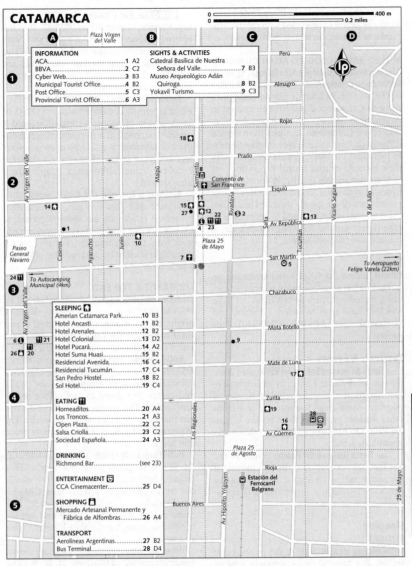

CATAMARCA

del Valle, who is the patron of Catamarca and one of northern Argentina's most venerated images since the 17th century. She sits atop a high altarpiece which is flanked by kitsch angels. Her diamond-studded crown can be seen in early April and on December 8, when multitudes of pilgrims converge on Catamarca to pay her homage. She is also, in a curious juxtaposition of the sacred and profane, the Patrona Nacional de Turismo.

The atmospheric cathedral also contains an elaborately carved altar to St Joseph, an ornate baroque pulpit and an exhibition of paintings of the Virgin.

THE ANDEAN NORTHWEST

The cathedral overlooks Plaza 25 de Mayo, a truly beautiful square filled with robust jacaranda, araucaria, citrus and palm trees.

MUSEO ARQUEOLÓGICO ADÁN QUIROGA

The fine **Museo Arqueológico Adán Quiroga** (☎ 437413; Sarmiento 450; admission AR$1; ✆ 7am-1pm & 2:30-8:30pm Mon-Fri, 10am-1pm Sat & Sun) is reason enough to come to Catamarca if you have an interest in Argentine indigenous culture. A superb collection of pre-Columbian ceramics from several different cultures and eras is on display. Some – in particular the black Aguada ceramics with their incised, stylized animal decoration – is of truly remarkable quality. A couple of dehydrated mummies found at 5000m are also present, as well as a spooky shrunken head from the Amazon, and trays used to snort lines of *rape* (finely-ground tobacco). There's also a colonial and religious section.

Tours

Yokavil Turismo (☎ 430066; www.yokavilturismo.com.ar; Rivadavia 916) arranges tours to area attractions, including Gruta de la Virgen del Valle (AR$60), and trips to Belén, Londres, and El Shincal ruins (AR$190 to AR$240). Kids go free.

Festivals & Events

The **Fiesta de Nuestra Señora del Valle** takes place for two weeks after Easter. In an impressive manifestation of popular religion, hordes of pilgrims come from the interior and from other Andean provinces to honor the Virgen del Valle. On her saint's day, December 8, she is similarly feted.

The **Fiesta Nacional del Poncho** is held in the last fortnight of July. A crafts and industrial fair accompanies this festival of *folklorica* and dance celebrating the importance of the poncho in the province.

Sleeping

BUDGET

Autocamping Municipal (RP 4; sites per tent/person AR$10/4; ✆) Around five kilometers west of town, in the Sierra de Ambato foothills, this is a pleasant spot by the Río El Tala. It's loud and crowded on weekends and holidays (forget about sleeping); and it has fierce mosquitoes. Bathrooms are clean and there is electricity. Take bus 101 (AR$1.10) from outside the Convento de San Francisco, or from by the bus terminal on Vicario Segura.

OUR PICK **San Pedro Hostel** (☎ 454708; www.hostelsanpedro.com.ar; Sarmiento 341; dm AR$25; ☐ ☎) One of two hostels in town, this is a great spot, with a big back garden that includes a *parrilla* and a tiny pool. Dorms are OK (mattresses are foam) but the overall package and cheery vibe make this a real winner.

Residencial Avenida (☎ 422139; Av Güemes 754; s without bathroom AR$25, d with/without bathroom AR$42/35) With plenty of rooms, arranged around a central courtyard, the Avenida, meters from the bus terminal, is a fine place to rest your legs and your pesos. Most of the rooms are excellent value, although a couple are a little rickety.

Residencial Tucumán (☎ 422209; Tucumán 1040; s/d AR$38/55; ✆) This well-run, immaculately presented *residencial* has spotless rooms, is excellent value and is about a one-minute walk from the bus terminal. For this reason you might want to book ahead. Air-con costs a little more.

MIDRANGE & TOP END

Sol Hotel (☎ 430803; solhotel@hotmail.com; Salta 1142; s/d AR$60/80; ✆) Clean and welcoming, the Sol's bright, cheery rooms are an OK deal if you want to be near the bus terminal. Some are much better than others; ask to see a few.

Hotel Colonial (☎ 423502; Av República 802; s/d AR$70/95; ✆) Cutely decorated in highland colonial style, with dimpled 'adobe' walls and cactus, this down-to-earth place represents value. The rooms are fairly ordinary, but there's space and everything works. Try to get one facing the rear for a bit more peace and quiet.

Hotel Pucará (☎ 431569; Caseros 501; s/d AR$85/120; ✆ ☐) Style gurus need not apply. This peaceful hotel on the west side of town stands out for its gloriously kitschy faux-Chinese knickknacks and ruffled bedspreads. The china dog on the stairs appeals and appalls in equal measure, but the place is comfortable and well-run.

Hotel Arenales (☎ 430307; www.hotel-arenales.com.ar; Sarmiento 542; s/d AR$112/138; ✆ ☐ ☎) The straight-down-the-line Arenales is reliable rather than spectacular. The rooms could do with more color, and some of the windows have irritating fixed louvres, but the facilities and treatment of guests are good.

Hotel Suma Huasi (☎ 435699; hotelescatamarca@hotmail.com; Sarmiento 541; s/d AR$119/130; ✆) Wise demonologists always keep their banishing skills one step ahead of their summoning skills. As should hotels with facilities and prices. While there's still something very appealing about this old-fashioned place, with its beige-colored rooms and dark wooden dignity, you're paying for character rather than mod-cons.

Hotel Ancasti (☎ 435951; hotelancasti@cedeconet.com.ar; Sarmiento 520; s/d AR$123/155; ✖ ▯) As ever, the handsome indigenous-art-inspired lobby of this upmarket central hotel is better than the rooms, which are comfortable but sparsely furnished, and showcase those toweling bedspreads normally seen in cheap *residenciales*. Cheerful service, mountain views, a gym and sauna, and excellent bathrooms go a long way to compensate.

Amerian Catamarca Park (☎ 425444; www.amerian.com; Av República 347; r AR$260; ✖ ▯ ▯) Catamarca's most upmarket hotel is well-appointed and coolly modern. Staff are overworked, but if you can grab a mountain-view room at the front of the building you'll be contented with your stay. Facilities include a gym and sauna. Single travelers once again fall victim of the cynical 'company pays so we'll charge them for a double' pricing policy.

Eating

There's a row of eateries along the north side of the plaza. Cheap burger and lomito joints are strung along Güemes west of the bus terminal.

Horneaditos (☎ 433586; Av Virgen del Valle 924; empanadas AR$1; ✖ 10am-10pm) The province's most legendary spot for empanadas – meat, cheese or chicken – this hole-in-the-wall cooks them on the street in two wood-fired clay ovens. A sight to see, and a Catamarca classic.

Los Troncos (☎ 434944; Mota Botello 37; dishes AR$6-26; ✖ lunch & dinner) Deservedly popular with locals, this typical restaurant and *parrillada* offers a great opportunity to try traditional Catamarcan cuisine. Tasty tamales and empanadas are on offer, and meaty options include *chivito* and *lechón* (suckling pig).

Open Plaza (☎ 404718; Av República 580; mains AR$7-22; ✖ 8am-late) This wins no marks for the name, but redeems itself with its classically restrained decor and no-nonsense filling food. Go for one of the daily specials (AR$12 to AR$18), available from noon till night.

Sociedad Española (☎ 431896; Av Virgen del Valle 725; meals AR$12-25; ✖ lunch & dinner Wed-Sat, lunch Sun)

The Spanish Society is always worth hunting down for traditional Spanish dishes, including seafood. It's a grand old place, worth the trek for some fine dining and formal service. It opens late for dinner, around 9.30pm.

Salsa Criolla (☎ 433583; Av República 546; all-you-can-eat AR$32; ✖ lunch & dinner) On the plaza, this bright and solicitous spot offers a high-class all-you-can-eat *parrillada*. They don't try to cynically stuff you with chorizo first like in some places – rather, they insist on tempting you with high-quality cuts long after you've insisted you don't want any more. The salad bar isn't so inspired though.

Drinking & Entertainment

Richmond Bar (☎ 423123; Av República 534; ✖ 9am-4pm & 8pm-1am) This mirrored-ceiling bar is a good place for a quiet drink; or if you like your entertainment livelier, things heat up on Saturday nights when there is tango from 11pm.

CCA Cinemacenter (☎ 423040; www.cinemacenter.com.ar) in the bus terminal shows the latest releases.

Shopping

Catamarca is enthusiastic in promoting its fine natural products; the region is well-known for wines, olive oil, walnuts, and various jams and conserves. There are several shops along Sarmiento and Rivadavia, in the first block north of the plaza, which stock these and other provincial products.

Mercado Artesanal Permanente y Fábrica de Alfombras (Av Virgen del Valle 945; ✖ 8am-noon) For Catamarca's characteristic hand-tied rugs, visit this morning market. Besides rugs, the market also sells a range of ponchos, blankets, jewelry, red onyx sculptures, musical instruments, hand-spun sheep and llama wool, and basketry.

Getting There & Away

AIR

Aerolíneas Argentinas (☎ 424460; Sarmiento 589) has three weekly flights to Buenos Aires (AR$589) and to La Rioja (AR$120). A minibus (AR$8) runs to **Aeropuerto Felipe Varela** (☎ 430080, 435582; RP 33), some 22km east of town, to coincide with flights.

BUS

Catamarca's spruce **bus terminal** (☎ 423415; Av Güemes 850) includes a shopping complex and cinema. Following are sample destinations and fares around the country.

Destination	Cost (AR$)	Duration (hr)
Belén	18	4
Buenos Aires	137	16
Córdoba	31	5
Jujuy	67	10
La Rioja	13	2
Mendoza	83	10
Rosario	103	11
Salta	59	8
Salvador Mazza	98	15
San Juan	65	8
Santiago del Estero	28	4½
Tucumán	27	4

AROUND CATAMARCA

According to local legend, in 1619 the image of the Virgen del Valle appeared in **Gruta de Choya**, 7km north of downtown Catamarca on RP 32. The present image is a replica of that in Catamarca's cathedral, and a protective structure shelters the grotto itself. Empresa Cotca's bus 104 goes to the Gruta de Choya every 40 minutes (AR$1.10).

Six kilometers out of town, not far from the campsite, **Pueblo Perdido de la Quebrada** is the ruins of a 9th-century-AD settlement built by an indigenous group who had moved south from the puna, perhaps driven by extreme climatic conditions. There's not a great deal to see, however; only low foundation walls remain. Take bus 101 (AR$1.10) from outside the San Francisco monastery.

The Sierra de Famatina, the province's highest mountain range, is visible from the road to picturesque **Villa Las Pirquitas**, near the dam of the same name, 29km north of Catamarca via RN 75. The foothills en route shelter small villages with hospitable people and interesting vernacular architecture.

Free camping is possible at the basic river beach, where the shallows are too muddy for swimming. The very attractive **Hostería Fray Mamerto Esquiú** (☎ 03833-492030; s/d AR$40/60) is government-run and hence great value, with clean and comfortable rooms.

From Catamarca's bus terminal, Empresa Cotca's bus 101 leaves hourly for the village.

BELÉN

☎ 03835 / pop 11,003 / elev 1250m

Slow-paced little Belén feels like, and is, a long way from anywhere, and will appeal to travelers who like things small-scale and friendly. It's got an excellent place to stay and is one of the best places to buy woven goods, particularly ponchos, in Argentina. There are many *teleras* (textile workshops) dotted around town, turning out their wares made from llama, sheep and alpaca wool. The nearby ruins of El Shincal are another reason to visit.

Before the arrival of the Spaniards in the mid-16th century, the area around Belén was Diaguita territory, on the periphery of the Inca empire. After the Inca fell, it became the *encomienda* of Juan Ramírez de Velasco, founder of La Rioja, but its history is intricately intertwined with nearby Londres, a Spanish settlement which shifted several times because of floods and Diaguita resistance. More than a century passed before, in 1681, the priest José Bartolomé Olmos de Aguilera divided a land grant among veterans of the Diaguita wars on the condition that they support evangelization in the area.

Orientation & Information

In the western highlands of Catamarca, Belén is 89km west of Andalgalá, 289km from the provincial capital and 180km southwest of Santa María. The **tourist office** (☎ 461304; turismobelencat@gmail.com; ☽ 8am-9pm Mon-Sat, 9am-10pm Sun) is by the bus terminal.

Sights

The neoclassical brick **Iglesia Nuestra Señora de Belén** dates from 1907 and faces Plaza Olmos y Aguilera, which is well shaded by pines and colossal pepper trees. Up some stairs at the end of a little shopping arcade, the **Museo Cóndor Huasi** (cnr Lavalle & Rivadavia; admission AR$1; ☽ 8:30am-12:30pm & 4:30-8:30pm Tue-Fri, 9am-noon & 5:30-8:30pm Sat, 8:30am-12:30pm Sun) has a well-presented archaeological collection, including some fine bronze axes, gold-leaf jewelry, and an illustrated information panel (in Spanish) on hallucinogen use among the Diaguita people.

Festivals & Events

On December 20, the town officially celebrates its founding, **Día de la Fundación**, but festivities begin at least a week earlier with a dance at the foot of the Cerro de la Virgen, three blocks west of the plaza. A steep 1900m trail leads to a 15m statue of the Virgin, side by side with a 4.5m image of the Christ child.

Sleeping & Eating

Hotel Gómez (☎ 461250; Calchaquí 213; s/d AR$35/50) One of a handful of cheap hotels around town, this spot on the main road has a plant-filled patio and basic rooms with bathroom and TV. The welcome isn't exactly effusive, but that's life.

Hotel Belén (☎ 461501; www.belencat.com.ar; cnr Belgrano & Cubas; s/d AR$75/105; ✹ 🖳) It's hard to believe that this superstylish hotel exists in Belén (thank the enlightened Catamarca government of a few years back), and with prices like this, you should try to take advantage, whatever your budget. The exposed rock bathrooms, with inlaid-tile mosaics on the floors and wall, and grottolike, extremely comfortable rooms are unusual and a delight. There are cheaper rooms (singles/doubles AR$40/60), but they're nothing special.

1900 (☎ 461100; Belgrano 391; mains AR$7-14; 🕑 breakfast, lunch & dinner) Beyond-the-call service is the key to this highly enjoyable restaurant a block down from the plaza. It's very popular, but they hate to turn people away, so a Tetrislike reshuffling of tables is a constant feature, bless 'em. Prices are more than fair, and there are a number of large platters designed to be shared.

El Único (cnr General Roca & Sarmiento; mains AR$8-19; 🕑 lunch & dinner) A block west of the plaza, this is the best *parrilla* in town. It features an attractive *quincho* (thatch-roof hut), and regional specialties such as *locro* are worth trying here.

On summer nights, restaurants near Plaza Olmos y Aguilera set up tables right on the plaza itself. There are several good ice creameries around the plaza.

Shopping

There's a marquee off the plaza with a number of friendly *artesanía* stalls selling ponchos, camelid-wool clothing and foot-trodden local wine. For more upmarket woven goods, **Cuna del Poncho** (☎ 461091; Roca 144) has reasonable prices, accepts major credit cards and arranges shipping.

Getting There & Away

Belén's **bus terminal** (cnr Sarmiento & Rivadavia) one block south and one block west of the plaza, is sadly underused, and Catamarca (AR$18, four hours) is the only long-distance destination served daily at a reasonable hour. There's a night service to La Rioja (AR$25, five hours) and Córdoba (AR$62, 14 hours), as well as three buses a week to Santa María (AR$15,

five hours) via Hualfin. Buses go Monday to Saturday to Andalgalá (AR$10, two hours). For Salta and Tucumán, you can change at Catamarca or Santa María.

Hotel Belén, among others, runs minibuses to Catamarca Monday to Friday.

AROUND BELÉN
Londres & El Shincal

Only 15km southwest of Belén, sleepy Londres (population 2134) is the province's oldest Spanish settlement, dating from 1558, though it moved several times before returning here in 1612; the inhabitants fled again during the Diaguita uprising of 1632. Its name (London) celebrated the marriage of the prince of Spain (and later King Philip II) to Mary Tudor, queen of England, in 1555. The **Festival Provincial de la Nuez** (Provincial Walnut Festival) takes place here the first fortnight of February.

Seven kilometers west of Londres, the Inca ruins of **El Shincal** (admission AR$2; 🕑 8am-sunset) are well worth visiting. Founded in 1470, the town occupied a commanding position in the foothills of the mountains and surveying the vast valley to the south. The setting is spectacular, with fantastic views and great atmosphere. The site was pretty thoroughly ruined when excavations began in 1991, but the *ushno* (ceremonial platform) and *kallanka* (possibly a barracks) have been restored, and you can climb two hillocks on either side of the central square. Aligned to the rising and setting sun, they probably served as both lookouts and altars. Entrance usually includes a tour by one of the welcoming family that lives here and looks after the site.

There are seven buses Monday to Saturday from Belén to Londres, that continue to a spot a short walk from the ruins. There's a campsite between Londres and the ruins, and some ugly-looking cabins that were soon to be opened at time of research. Londres also has a couple of basic *residenciales*.

Beyond Londres, you can head on south to Chilecito, 200km away in La Rioja province, if you have transportation. The drive is a spectacular one, with the imposing Sierra Famatina to the west, and the road is excellent.

Hualfin

About 60km north of Belén via spectacular RN 40, the grape-growing village of Hualfin – surprisingly green and fertile in the midst of a barren landscape – has an attractive pink chapel, dating from 1770, beneath a small promon-

THE ANDEAN NORTHWEST

tory whose 142-step staircase leads to a mirador with panoramic views of cultivated fields and the distant desert. Next to the chapel is a small archaeological museum. Two kilometers south, and a further 2km west, the Termas de la Quebrada is a small thermal bath complex; a little further south of the turnoff, amazing reddish rock formations stand proud above the usually dry river valley; the 'snowdrifts' on the mountains behind are actually cascades of fine white sand. Around town, look for locally grown paprika sprinkled on creamy slices of goats' cheese. **Hospedaje Alta Huasi** (☎ 03835-15-696275; r per person AR$20), 1km along the Santa María road from the church, offers simple accommodations. Minibuses run twice daily from Belén to Hualfín (AR$5, 1½ hours) from Monday to Friday; the thrice-weekly buses between Belén and Santa María also stop here.

LA RIOJA

☎ 03822 / pop 143,684 / elev 500m

Encircled by the graceful peaks of the Sierra de Velasco, La Rioja is quite a sight on a sunny day. And there are plenty of sunny days: summer temperatures rise sky-high in this quiet, out-of-the-way provincial capital.

Juan Ramírez de Velasco founded Todos los Santos de la Nueva Rioja in 1591. The Diaguita tribe who lived here were converted and made peace with the conquerors (see boxed text, p308), paving the way for Spanish colonization of what Vásquez de Espinosa called 'a bit of Paradise.'

The city's appearance reflects the conflict and accommodation between colonizer and colonized: the architecture combines European designs with native techniques and local materials. Many early buildings were destroyed in the 1894 earthquake, but the city has been entirely rebuilt.

Orientation

At the base of the picturesque Sierra de Velasco, La Rioja is relatively small, with all points of interest and most hotels within easy walking distance of each other.

North–south streets change their names at San Nicolás de Bari, but east–west streets are continuous.

Information

ACA (Automóvil Club Argentino; ☎ 425381; cnr Dalmacio Vélez Sársfield & Copiapó) Argentina's auto club; good source for provincial road maps.

Banco de Galicia (San Nicolás de Bari 604) One of many ATMs. Changes US dollars and does credit-card advances.

Lavadero Rocío (☎ 474706; Av JD Perón 954) Laundry.

Locutorio (529 Pelagio Luna; per hr AR$2; 7am-2am) On the plaza. Has internet facilities.

Post office (Av JD Perón 258)

Provincial tourist office (☎ 426345; www.larioja .gov.ar/turismo; Pelagio Luna 345; 8am-9pm) Will book accommodations for you.

Sights

LANDMARK BUILDINGS

La Rioja is a major devotional center, so most landmarks are ecclesiastical. Built in 1623 by the Diaguita under the direction of Dominican friars, the picturesque **Convento de Santo Domingo** (cnr Pelagio Luna & Lamadrid; 9:30am-12:30pm & 6-8pm Mon-Fri) is Argentina's oldest monastery. The date appears in the carved algarrobo doorframe, also the work of Diaguita artists.

The curious neo-Gothic **Convento de San Francisco** (cnr 25 de Mayo & Bazán y Bustos) houses the image of the Niño Alcalde, a Christ-child icon symbolically recognized as the city's mayor (see boxed text, p308).

The enormous and spectacular neo-Byzantine 1899 **catedral** (cnr Av San Nicolás de Bari & 25 de Mayo) contains the image of patron saint Nicolás de Bari, an object of devotion for both *riojanos* (people who live in La Rioja) and the inhabitants of neighboring provinces.

One of Argentina's greatest educators, and founder of the Universidad de La Plata, lived in the **Casa de Joaquín V González** (Rivadavia 952). The neoclassical **Escuela Normal de Maestros**, the teachers' school situated on Pelagio Luna between Catamarca and Belgrano, dates from 1884.

MUSEO FOLKLÓRICO

The hugely worthwhile **Museo Folklórico** (☎ 428500; Pelagio Luna 811; admission by donation; 9am-noon & 4-8pm Tue-Fri, 9am-noon Sat & Sun) is set in a wonderful early-17th-century adobe building, and has fine displays on various aspects of the region's culture. Themes include *chaya* (local La Rioja music) and the Tinkunaco festival, weaving – with bright traditional wall-hangings colored with plant extracts and winemaking. The *lagar* (stretched leather used for treading the grapes) is quite a sight, as is the room that deals with mythology, including a demanding series of rituals

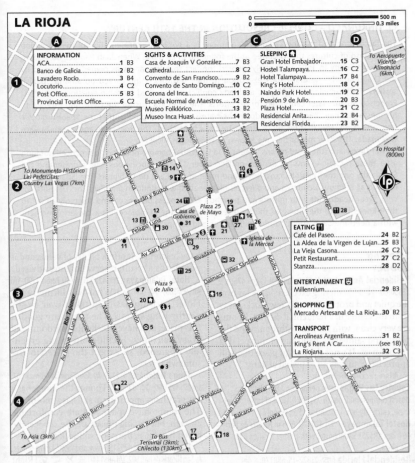

LA RIOJA

INFORMATION	
ACA	1 B3
Banco de Galicia	2 B2
Lavadero Rocío	3 B4
Locutorio	4 C2
Post Office	5 B3
Provincial Tourist Office	6 C2

SIGHTS & ACTIVITIES	
Casa de Joaquín V González	7 B3
Cathedral	8 C2
Convento de San Francisco	9 B2
Convento de Santo Domingo	10 C2
Corona del Inca	11 B3
Escuela Normal de Maestros	12 B2
Museo Folklórico	13 B2
Museo Inca Huasi	14 B2

SLEEPING	
Gran Hotel Embajador	15 C3
Hostel Talampaya	16 C2
Hotel Talampaya	17 B4
King's Hotel	18 C4
Naindo Park Hotel	19 C2
Pensión 9 de Julio	20 B3
Plaza Hotel	21 C2
Residencial Anita	22 B4
Residencial Florida	23 B2

EATING	
Café del Paseo	24 B2
La Aldea de la Virgen de Lujan	25 B3
La Vieja Casona	26 C2
Petit Restaurant	27 C2
Stanzza	28 D2

ENTERTAINMENT	
Millennium	29 B3

SHOPPING	
Mercado Artesanal de La Rioja	30 B2

TRANSPORT	
Aerolíneas Argentinas	31 B2
King's Rent A Car	(see 18)
La Riojana	32 C3

required to sell your soul to the Devil hereabouts. The informative guided tour is excellent if your Spanish is up to it.

MUSEO INCA HUASI

A couple of blocks from the plaza, this curious **museum** (Alberdi 650; admission AR$1; ☿ Tue-Sat 9amnoon), run by monks, has a notable collection of pre-Columbian ceramics from the region from a number of different cultures.

Tours

Several operators run excursions around the province, including visits to the Parque Nacional Talampaya, which invariably includes the nearby Parque Provincial Ischigualasto ('Valle de la Luna') in San Juan province. One such company is **Corona del Inca** (☎ 422142; www.coronadelinca.com.ar; Pelagio Luna 91), which also runs summer excursions up to high, remote parts of the Andes in the west of the province.

Festivals & Events

La Chaya, the local variant of Carnaval, attracts people from throughout the country. Its name, derived from a Quechua word meaning 'to get someone wet,' should give you an idea of what to expect. A particular style of local music, *chaya*, is associated with the festival.

Taking place at midday December 31, the religious ritual of **El Tinkunaco** is one of Argentina's most interesting ceremonies (see p308).

EL TINKUNACO – CONFLICT RESOLUTION IN THE 16TH CENTURY

The fascinating and moving Tinkunaco ceremony is a symbolic representation of the resolution of the clash of cultures that occurred at the founding of La Rioja. When Juan Ramírez de Velasco founded the city in 1591 he blithely ignored the fact that the land was owned and farmed by the Diaguita, who naturally took exception to their territory being carved up among Spanish settlers. They rebelled in 1593, and a bloody conflict was averted by the mediation of the friar Francisco Solano, later canonized for his efforts. The Diaguita trusted the cleric and listened to his message. They then agreed to down their arms on two conditions; that the Spanish *alcalde* (mayor) resign, and that his replacement be the Christ child. The Spaniards agreed, and peace was made. The new mayor became known as Niño Jesús Alcalde.

The Tinkunaco (the word means 'meeting' in Quechua) commemoration commenced not long after these historic events. At midday on December 31, two processions, one representing the Spaniards, one the Diaguita, cross town and meet at the Casa de Gobierno. The 'Spaniards' are dressed as religious penitents and *alféreces* (lieutenants) with uniform and flag. The 'Diaguita', or *aillis*, wear headbands with mirrors and ponchos. The processions meet, and solemnly all fall to their knees before the image of the Niño Jesús Alcalde, then embrace. It's a powerful moment with a deep message about cultural differences and compromises.

Sleeping

BUDGET

Residencial Anita (☎ 424836; Coronel Lagos 476; s/d AR$50/60; ❁ ⊠) Offering excellent value for two, the quiet and proper Anita is a few blocks away from the center in a residential district. Rooms are very clean, with spotless bathrooms, and the plant- and saint-filled patio and plump pet dog are bonuses. It's not the sort of place that will appreciate you rolling in pissed at 4am.

Also recommended:

Country Las Vegas (sites per person AR$7) Best and closest campground, on RN 75, Km 8, west of town; to get there, catch city bus 1 southbound on Perón.

Hostel Talampaya (☎ 420423; Av San Nicolás de Bari 464; dm AR$25) Small hostel with a great location near the plaza.

Residencial Florida (☎ 03822-15-688170; 8 de Diciembre 524; s/d AR$30/45, with bathroom AR$35/50) Dark but decent rooms with fan for a pittance.

MIDRANGE & TOP END

La Rioja's hotels often offer discounts if you pay cash and aren't afraid to bargain.

ᴏᴜʀ ᴘɪᴄᴋ Pensión 9 de Julio (☎ 426955; cnr Copiapó & Dalmacio Vélez Sársfield; s/d AR$60/90; ❁) Definitely a good deal, this place has clean and pleasant rooms in a central part of town. A shady, vine-covered patio overlooking the plaza of the same name is another bonus.

Gran Hotel Embajador (☎ 438580; www.granhotel embajador.com.ar; San Martín 250; s/d AR$65/85; ❁) This cheery place is very tidy; the rooms upstairs are larger and sunnier – a good thing if dark red color schemes oppress you – and some

have balconies. It offers plenty of value, and is popular as a result; reservations are advised.

Hotel Talampaya (☎ 422005; Av JD Perón 1290; s/d AR$95/160; ❁ ⊟ ▣) What was formerly the Hotel Turismo has been taken over by the nearby King's Hotel. The rooms are good at this price, and have excellent bathrooms and noisy balconies. Facilities are being gradually upgraded, so expect the prices to rise somewhat too.

King's Hotel (☎ 422122; Av Juan Facundo Quiroga 107; s/d AR$125/190; ❁ ⊟ ▣) Though the King's has a few gray hairs appearing, it still has atmosphere. The rooms have space and are comfortable enough, but the big pluses are the service, the buffet breakfast, the pool, sundeck and gym.

Plaza Hotel (☎ 425215; www.plazahotel-larioja.com.ar; Av San Nicolás de Bari 502; s/d AR$144/166; ❁ ⊟ ▣) Right on the plaza, this hotel looks a great deal better from inside than out. Rooms overlooking the plaza are much nicer than those looking onto internal lightwells. Superior rooms (singles/doubles AR$202/216) are also available; they've got a newer feel and king-sized beds.

Naindo Park Hotel (☎ 470700; www.naindoparkhotel .com; Av San Nicolás de Bari 475; s/d AR$305/339; ❁ ⊟ ▣) Just off the plaza, and dominating it assertively, La Rioja's finest hotel has an excellent level of service and comfort and prices to match. The rooms are particularly spacious, and many have good views.

Eating

Regional dishes to look for include *locro*, juicy empanadas, *chivito asado* (barbecued goat), *humitas, quesillo* (a cheese specialty) and olives. Don't miss the local bread, baked in *hornos de barro* (adobe ovens). There is also a good selection of dried fruits, preserves and jams from figs, apples, peaches and pears. Don't hesitate to order house wines, which are usually excellent.

Café del Paseo (☎ 422069; cnr Pelagio Luna & 25 de Mayo; sandwiches AR$5-9; ⏰ breakfast, lunch & dinner) This is your spot on the corner of the plaza to observe La Rioja life. The mobile-phone clique mingles with families and tables of older men chewing the fat over another slow-paced La Rioja day. It's a fine place to try Argentina's favorite aperitif – Fernet Branca with cola.

Petit Restaurant (Av San Nicolás de Bari 484; dishes AR$7-18; ⏰ 8am-midnight) No surprises are on the menu here at this simple but effective local eatery. Pasta, pizza, omelets and grilled meats are well-prepared and fairly priced. The fruit *licuados* are delicious.

La Aldea de la Virgen de Lujan (☎ 460305; Rivadavia 756, lunches AR$11-18; ⏰ breakfast, lunch & dinner) Serving good-value breakfasts and a fairly predictable range of dinner options, lunchtime is the place to be at this spot, when it offers a good range of regional specialties.

Stanzza (☎ 430809; Dorrego 1641; dishes AR$13-24; ⏰ lunch & dinner) One of the best places to eat in town, this friendly neighborhood restaurant serves up imaginative seafood and Italian dishes in an intimate environment.

La Vieja Casona (☎ 425996; Rivadavia 457; mains AR$14-29) Cheerfully lit and decorated, this is a cracking place with a great range of regional specialties, creative house choices, and a long menu of standard Argentine dishes – the *parrillada* here is of excellent standard. There's a fair selection of La Rioja wines too, and wonderful smells wafting from the busy kitchen.

Entertainment

If you're up for a late night, there are a number of discos where you can show the locals your latest moves. They all charge around AR$5/10 for girls/guys, although there are often promotions where women get in for free. All open about 1am or 2am on weekends and pound away until the early morning.

Two of the most popular options are **Millennium** (San Martín), opposite the Colegio Nacional, and packed and cheerful **Asia** (Av San Francisco).

Shopping

La Rioja has unique weavings that combine indigenous techniques and skill with Spanish designs and color combinations. The typical *mantas* (bedspreads) feature floral patterns over a solid background color. Spanish influence is also visible in silverwork, including tableware, ornaments, religious objects and horse gear. La Rioja's pottery is entirely indigenous; artists use local clay to make distinctive pots, plates and flowerpots. Fittingly for a place named after Spain's most famous wine region, La Rioja wine has a national reputation; Saúl Menem, father of the former president, founded one of the major bodegas.

La Rioja crafts are exhibited and sold at the excellent **Mercado Artesanal de La Rioja** (Pelagio Luna 792; ⏰ 8am-noon & 4-8pm Tue-Fri, 9am-noon Sat & Sun), as are other popular artworks at prices lower than most souvenir shops.

Getting There & Away

AIR

Aerolíneas Argentinas (☎ 426307; Belgrano 63) flies three times weekly to and from Buenos Aires (AR$589), stopping in Catamarca (AR$120 from Catamarca to La Rioja) on the way out.

BUS

La Rioja's brand new **bus terminal** (☎ 427911; Barrio Evita s/n) is an interesting building, picturesquely backed by the sierra. It's a long walk from the center of town.

Destination	Cost (AR$)	Duration (hr)
Belén	25	5
Buenos Aires	142	22
Catamarca	13	2
Chilecito	16	3
Córdoba	39	6
Jujuy	84	11
Mendoza	66	8
Salvador Mazza	115	18
Salta	76	10
San Juan	48	6
Santiago del Estero	47	7
Tucumán	43	6

For going to Chilecito, **La Riojana** (☎ 435279; Buenos Aires 154) minibuses run from its office in the center of town five times a day. The trip costs AR$20 and takes 2½ hours, a little quicker than the bus.

CAR
King's Rent A Car (☎ 422122; Av Juan Facundo Quiroga 107) is in the King's Hotel.

Getting Around
From Plaza 9 de Julio, bus 3 goes to **Aeropuerto Vicente Almonacid** (☎ 427239), 7km east of town on RP 5. An airport cab costs around AR$15. A taxi from the bus terminal to the city center costs about AR$6.

AROUND LA RIOJA
According to legend, San Francisco Solano converted many Diaguita at the site of **Monumento Histórico Las Padercitas**, a Franciscan-built colonial adobe chapel now sheltered by a stone temple, 7km west of town on RN 75. On the second Sunday of August, pilgrims convene to pay homage to the saint. Buses 1 and 3 go to the site.

Beyond Las Padercitas, RN 75 climbs and winds past attractive summer homes, bright red sandstone cliffs, lush vegetation and dark purple peaks whose cacti remind you that the area is semidesert.

CHILECITO
☎ 03825 / pop 29,453 / elev 1080m
With a gorgeous situation among low rocky hills and sizable snowcapped peaks, Chilecito is the province's second-largest settlement but nevertheless is just a small town. There are several interesting things to see, including the amazing cableway leading to a mine high in the sierra. It also makes a base for longer excursions to the Parque Nacional Talampaya or the remote hot springs at Fiambalá. With the intense heat, mining heritage and slopes around town dotted with cardón cactus, Chilecito can have a Wild West feel to it at times and is definitely the most appealing place to spend a few quiet days in this part of the country.

Founded as Villa Santa Rita in 1715 by Domingo de Castro y Bazán, who had been granted the land, it was little more than a hamlet until the mining took off in the late 19th century. It acquired the name Chilecito (Little Chile) because many from that country crossed the Andes to come and work the mines here.

Information
The plaza has three banks with ATMs.
Municipal tourist office (Pl Sarmiento s/n; ☒ 8am-9pm) In a kiosk on the plaza; helpful and friendly.
Post office (cnr Joaquín V González & Av Pelagio Luna)

Provincial tourist office (☎ 422688; D de Castro y Bazán 52; ☒ 8am-9pm) Has enthusiastic staff and good material. There is also a small kiosk on Plaza Sarmiento.
Telecentro (cnr Castro Barros & Plaza Sarmiento) Phone cabins and internet access.

Sights
MUSEO MOLINO DE SAN FRANCISCO
Chilecito founder Don Domingo de Castro y Bazán owned this colonial flour mill, whose **Museo Molino de San Francisco** (J Ocampo 63; admission AR$1; ☒ 8am-noon & 2-6pm Mon-Fri, to 7pm Sat & Sun) houses an eclectic assemblage of archaeological tools, antique arms, early colonial documents, minerals, traditional wood and leather crafts, plus weavings and paintings.

SAMAY HUASI
Joaquín V González, writer and founder of the prestigious La Plata university in Buenos Aires, used this *finca* (ranch), **Samay Huasi** (☎ 422629; samayhuasi@arnet.com.ar; admission AR$1; ☒ 8am-6:30pm Mon-Fri, 2-6:30pm Sat & Sun), 2km from Chilecito, as his country retreat. The verdant grounds counterpoint the rocky cactus hills around them. González' bedroom is preserved, as well as scrapbook material from his life. More interesting is a collection of paintings, mostly of the area; a canvas by González' friend Alberto Alice, *Claro de Luna,* stands out. Below is a somewhat depressing natural sciences, archaeology and mineralogy collection.

You can stay at the *finca,* which offers full-board accommodations for AR$60 per person. It needs to be booked in advance.

To get there, head out from town past the Chirau-Mita cactus garden and follow the main road as it bends around to the right. Keep going and you'll see the *finca* on your right.

LA RIOJANA WINERY
La Rioja is one of the best areas to taste the aromatic white torrontés, though it's far from the only wine the province has to offer. **La Riojana** (☎ 423150; www.lariojana.com.ar; La Plata 646; ☒ 8am-6pm Mon-Fri, 9am-1pm Sat) cooperative is the area's main wine producer, and a sizable concern. A good free tour (call or drop in to arrange a time; English spoken) shows you through the bodega – think large cement fermentation tanks rather than rows of musty barrels – and culminates in a generous tasting.

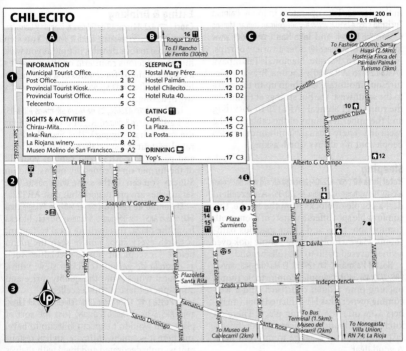

CHILECITO

INFORMATION
Municipal Tourist Office................1 C2
Post Office.......................................2 B2
Provincial Tourist Kiosk..................3 C2
Provincial Tourist Office................4 C2
Telecentro..5 C3

SIGHTS & ACTIVITIES
Chirau-Mita.....................................6 D1
Inka-Ñan..7 D2
La Riojana winery...........................8 A2
Museo Molino de San Francisco....9 A2

SLEEPING
Hostal Mary Pérez........................10 D1
Hostel Paimán................................11 D2
Hotel Chilecito...............................12 D2
Hotel Ruta 40................................13 D2

EATING
Capri...14 C2
La Plaza..15 C2
La Posta..16 B1

DRINKING
Yop's...17 C3

MUSEO DEL CABLECARRIL

The fascinating **Museo del Cablecarril** (admission by donation/tip; 8:30am-12:30pm & 2:30-6:30pm Mon-Fri, to 7:30pm Sat & Sun) and cable-car station documents an extraordinary engineering project that gave birth to the town of Chilecito at the beginning of the 20th century. To enable the mining of gold, silver and copper from the Sierra de Famatina, a German firm was contracted to construct a 35km cablecar running from here, at the end of the railway line, to La Mejicana, at an altitude of 4603m, more than 3.5km above Chilecito. With nine stations, a tunnel and 262 towers, the project was completed in 1904. Men and supplies were carried to the mine, operated by a British firm, in four hours. WWI put an end to this Anglo-German cooperation and the line started to decay, although local miners continued using it until the 1930s.

The picturesque museum preserves photos, tools and documents from the cablecar and mine, as well as communications equipment, including an early mobile phone. There's a detailed guided tour in Spanish, and you'll then be taken to the cablecar terminus itself – a rickety spiral staircase climbs to the platform, where ore carts now wait silently in line. It's worth going in the late afternoon, when the sun bathes the rusted metal and snowy sierras in rich hues.

The museum is on the main road at the southern entrance to town, a block south of the bus station.

CHIRAU-MITA

Even if you're not a fan of succulents, it's likely that you'll appreciate **Chirau-Mita** (424531; admission AR$10; 8am-noon & 4-7pm Tue-Fri, 8am-noon Sat), an impressive cactus garden a short stroll from town, where more than 1500 species have been grown from seeds and are elegantly showcased, divided by country of origin, in an attractive hillside setting. Entry is by informative guided tour (some English spoken), and the visit includes a handsomely presented museum, which has some stunning Patagonian fossils, prehistoric weapons and tools, and pre-Columbian ceramics.

Tours

The western portion of La Rioja province is fascinating, with plenty of intriguing destinations in the sierras. Two operators in town, **Paimán Turismo** (☎ 425102; www.fincadelpaiman.com.ar; Moreno 6, Barrio San Miguel) and **Inka Ñan** (☎ 423641; www .inkanan.com.ar; Martínez 49) offer a variety of trips, including to Parque Nacional Talampaya (AR$120 to AR$160); Laguna Brava, a picturesque mountain lake high up in the sierra to the southwest; the hot springs at Fiambalá; the ruins of El Shincal (AR$120 to AR$160); and the upper terminus of the cablecar at La Mejicana. There's usually a minimum of two people, but it's always worth asking.

Sleeping

Hotel Ruta 40 (☎ 422804; Libertad 68; s/d with bathroom AR$40/70, without bathroom AR$20/35) An excellent deal a couple of blocks from the square, this comfortable spot offers a variety of rooms with comfortable beds and clean spacious bathrooms. Have a look at a few – some look over a vine-covered patio to the hills beyond.

Hostel Paimán (☎ 429135; El Maestro 188; dm/s/d AR$22/30/45) With simple, comfortable rooms opening onto a quiet courtyard, and a welcoming owner, this HI-affiliated spot (members 10% off) is a relaxing place. There's a kitchen and laundry; prices include breakfast, and you can arrange tours from here. A good deal.

Hostal Mary Pérez (☎ 423156; hostal_mp@hotmail .com; Florencio Dávila 280; s/d AR$60/80) A neat little *residencial* in the northeast of town that is more like a family-run hotel. The place is spotless – you may get high on the smell of cleaning products – and rooms come with TV and telephone.

Hostería Finca del Paimán (☎ 425102; www .fincadelpaiman.com.ar; Moreno 6, Barrio San Miguel; s/d $60/95) Some 3.5km from the center in a fertile agricultural district, this peaceful *finca* is a place to relax with a decent novel for a couple of days. Breakfast is included, and there's a kitchen so you can prepare your own meals. You can also organize tours from here. Book ahead.

Hotel Chilecito (☎ 422201; hotel_acachilecito@hotmail .com; T Gordillo 101; s/d AR$71/94; ✷ ▢ ⊠) With a quiet location near where the town ends among rocky hills, this ACA establishment offers fine value for money. There's space to burn here, with a garden and cavernous recreation room (pool table). The rooms are light, bright and pleasant, with tiled floors and gleaming bathrooms. There's also a decent restaurant.

Eating & Drinking

Capri (☎ 422-441; cnr 19 de Febrero y Joaquín V González; lomitos AR$5-9; ✷ breakfast, lunch & dinner) You step back three to four decades in time as you walk into this spacious *confitería* on the plaza. It's a reliable standby for *lomitos* or a beer on the terrace. It often has specials of the day, so it's worth asking.

La Plaza (☎ 422696; 25 de Mayo 58; mains AR$8-15; ✷ breakfast, lunch & dinner) Right on the plaza (as the name may suggest), this warmly decorated restaurant specializes in tasty pizzas and pastas. For AR$9 you can eat your fill of the former on Wednesday nights, and on Sunday you can do the same with pasta. The set lunches are pretty good but cost AR$22.

El Rancho de Ferrito (☎ 422481; Av Pelagio Luna 647; mains AR$7-18; ✷ lunch & dinner) Seven blocks from the plaza, this inviting local restaurant is worth every step. You've seen the menu before – except for house specialties such as *cazuela de gallina* (chicken stew: yum), and local wines – but the quality, price and atmosphere make it truly excellent.

La Posta (☎ 425988; cnr 19 de Febrero & Roque Lanús; mains AR$15-30; ✷ lunch & dinner) Just the sort of place you wouldn't expect Chilecito to have, and here it is; a new, intimate, stylish restaurant warmly decorated and lined with shelves of deli products on sale. The dishes are innovative – stewed goat with torrontés for example – and attractively presented. The taste doesn't quite live up to the service or decor, but that will hopefully be corrected with experience.

Yop's (AE Dávila 70; ✷ 8am-2pm & 5pm-late Mon-Sat) Atmospheric and darkish, this bohemian spot is comfortably Chilecito's best café, serving fine coffee and decent mixed drinks. Watch the locals' epic chess battles.

Entertainment

If you're in Chilecito on a Saturday night, you'll want to check out castlelike **Fashion** (admission AR$10; ✷ 11pm-late Sat), the town's best *discoteca*. It's on the way to Samay Huasi about 1km out of town, and a lot of fun. Girls get in a little cheaper, and you may even win a motorbike or similar in the prize draw.

Getting There & Away

The new bus terminal is 1.5km south of the center, near the Museo del Cablecarril. There are regular services to La Rioja (AR$16, three hours), and beyond to Rosario, Buenos Aires and other cities. Various minibus services also do the La Rioja run for AR$4 more and half an hour less. There are no buses north to Belén.

PARQUE NACIONAL TALAMPAYA
☎ 03825 / elev 1300m

Though only a trickle of water winds through what, in the Quechua language, translates as the 'Dry River of the Tala', the spectacular rock formations and canyons of this national park are evidence of the erosive action of far greater quantities of water. It's a dusty desert of scorching days, chilly nights, infrequent but torrential summer rains and gusty spring winds.

Visitors may not use their own vehicles on park roads; only contracted guides with pickup trucks offer tours of sandy canyons where aboriginal petroglyphs and mortars adorn streambed sites. Nesting condors scatter from cliffside nests as vehicles invade their otherwise undisturbed habitat. On the usual two-hour tour from the park's headquarters, vehicles pass the dunes of **El Playón**, leading to the **Puerta de Talampaya** (Gate of Talampaya) entrance to the canyon.

Back on the road, the vehicles enter the red sandstone canyon, whose eastern wall reveals a conspicuous fault. The next major stops are the **Chimenea del Eco**, an extraordinary echo chamber where your voice seems to come back louder than your original call, and a nature trail to the **Bosquecillo** (Little Forest), a representative sample of native vegetation. On the return the major point is **El Cañón de los Farallones** (Canyon of Cliffs) where, besides condors and turkey vultures, you may see eagles and other birds of prey 150m above the canyon floor.

Longer four-hour excursions are possible to Los Pizarrones, as well as other sites such as Los Cajones, Ciudad Perdida and Los Chañares. These trips can be organized inside the park. If you can, sit in front with the guide one way, and in the back of the truck the other way.

Guided walks (two to three hours) and trips on bicycles are also available; these can be more appealing, particularly if you arrive here on a guided tour and have already spent hours in a car.

Orientation & Information

Talampaya is 141km southwest of Chilecito via a combination of RN 40's scenic Cuesta de Miranda route, RP 18 and RP 26. Via RP 26, it is 60km south of Villa Unión and 58km north of Los Baldecitos, the turnoff to San Juan's Parque Provincial Ischigualasto.

From the junction with RP 26, a paved eastbound lateral leads 14km to the Puerta de Talampaya entrance and the park's visitor center. Here you pay the AR$20 admission (AR$7 for Argentine citizens), and arrange vehicle tours of the park with guides. Two-hour excursions in the park cost AR$38.50 per person; proceeds go directly to guides. Four-hour trips cost AR$60 per person.

Villa Unión is the location of the park's **head office** (☎ 470356; www.talampaya.gov.ar; talampaya@apn.gov.ar; San Martín s/n).

Festivals & Events

In Villa Unión, a further 29km north of Pagancillo, **Festival del Viñador**, honoring local vintners, takes place at the beginning of the March grape harvest. During the festival there is music, dancing and tasting of regional wines, most notably the artisanal *vino patero*, made by traditional grape treading.

Sleeping & Eating

There are no accommodations in the park itself, but you can camp at the visitor center; there are toilets but no showers.

Pagancillo, just 29km north of the park, is the best place to stay. You should be able to get a lift to the park with one of the rangers, who live here. There are a few *casas de familia* as well as **Posada Talampaya** (☎ 431992; talampaya_olmo@hotmail.com; r per person AR$29), a very appealing place on the main road through town run by welcoming people. The price includes breakfast and other meals are available.

There's also a *confitería* serving meals and cold drinks in the park.

Getting There & Away

Travelers without their own cars can take the Transportes Rápido bus from La Rioja to Pagancillo, 29km from Talampaya, where most of the park personnel reside; from there the rangers will help you get to the park, where it is necessary to pay for the excursions. The bus goes on to Villa Unión, where the park headquarters is located.

THE ANDEAN NORTHWEST

Córdoba & the Central Sierras

Argentina's second city is bursting with life. Home to not one but seven major universities, Córdoba has a young population that ensures an excellent nightlife and a healthy cultural scene in general. Art is one of the city's strong points, and the four major galleries here are truly world-class. The business center of the country's most populous province, Córdoba also boasts a fascinating history, owing its architectural and cultural heritage to the Jesuits, who set up shop here when they first arrived in Argentina.

Outside of the city, the rolling hill country of the Central Sierras is dotted with towns that could grab your attention for a day or a month. The region boasts five Jesuit missions which have been declared Unesco World Heritage sites, each of them located in quaint little satellite towns that are an easy day trip from the capital.

Adventure buffs won't be left twiddling their thumbs, either – the paragliding is excellent at La Cumbre and Merlo and there's fantastic trekking to be done in two national parks – the fossil-strewn Sierra de las Quijadas and the condor haven of Quebrada del Condorito.

Further to the southwest, the Valle de Conlara and Sierras Puntanas offer a real chance to get away from the crowds and into the heart of the countryside. Highlights include the caves and rock art at Inti Huasi, the palm-filled valley of Papagayos and the picturesque ex-mining village of Carolina. Public transport in this part of the world is often rare and sometimes nonexistent, but the wealth of experiences that awaits far outweighs any inconvenience.

HIGHLIGHTS

- Soak in the culture and wander the gorgeous streets of the stately city of **Córdoba** (p316)

- Check out ancient caves, rock art and stunning highland scenery around **Carolina** (p340)

- Get high with the paragliding fanatics at **La Cumbre** (p329)

- Take a breather at the atmospheric 17th-century Jesuit *estancia* (ranch) of **Santa Catalina** (p331)

- Break in your hiking boots among the surreal rock formations of **Parque Nacional Sierra de las Quijadas** (p339)

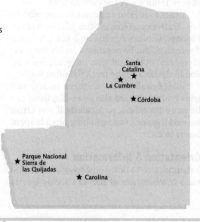

- POPULATION: 3,434,734
- AREA: 242,069 SQ KM

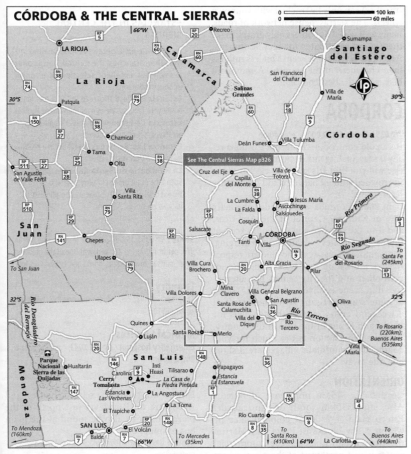

CÓRDOBA & THE CENTRAL SIERRAS

See The Central Sierras Map p326

Climate

Generally, November to February are the hottest months in the Central Sierras, when 29°C days are common, and nights are pleasantly warm. This is also the rainy season, but days are sunny enough for the hordes of sunbathers that descend on the sierras all summer. Winters are cool but get little precipitation and are often nice for outdoor pursuits. At higher altitudes (such as in La Cumbre), light snowfall is not uncommon. Fall and spring get more rain than winter, but temperatures are often ideal for hiking and biking.

National Parks

In San Luis province, the rarely visited Parque Nacional Sierra de las Quijadas (p339) is an excellent alternative to the better-known Parque Nacional Ischigualasto: getting there is far easier, and you'll often have the desert canyons and rock formations all to yourself. Parque Nacional Quebrada del Condorito (p335) is well worth a day trip from Córdoba to see the impressive Andean condors the park protects.

Getting There & Around

Córdoba makes an excellent stop if you're heading south or southwest toward Mendoza. The city has bus connections throughout the country.

The towns throughout the sierras are all easily accessible by public transport, but many tiny, remote towns and Jesuit *estancias* (ranches) can only be reached with your own wheels. The sierras' dense network of roads, many well paved but others only gravel, make them good candidates for bicycle touring; Argentine drivers here seem a bit less ruthless than elsewhere in the country. A mountain bike is still the best choice.

CÓRDOBA

☎ 0351 / pop 1,450,000 / elev 400m

It's an old guidebook cliché, but Córdoba really *is* a fascinating mix of old and new. Where else will you find DJs spinning electro-tango in crowded student bars next to 17th century Jesuit ruins?

In 2006, Córdoba was awarded the hefty title of Cultural Capital of the Americas, and it fit the city like a glove. Four excellent municipal galleries – dedicated to emerging, contemporary, classical and fine art respectively – are within easy walking distance of each other and the city center. The alternative film scene is alive and kicking. Young designers and artisans strut their stuff at a weekend crafts market that sprawls for blocks and is one of the best in the country. And if all this action is too much for you, quaint little mountain villages are a short bus ride away.

ORIENTATION

Córdoba is 715km northwest of Buenos Aires and 330km south of Santiago del Estero via RN 9. Most colonial sites lie within a few blocks of Plaza San Martín, the city's urban nucleus. The commercial center is just northwest of the plaza, where the main pedestrian malls – 25 de Mayo and Rivera Indarte – intersect each other. Obispo Trejo, just west of the plaza, has the finest concentration of colonial buildings. Just south of downtown, Parque Sarmiento offers relief from the bustling, densely built downtown.

East–west streets change names at San Martín/Independencia and north–south streets change at Deán Funes/Rosario de Santa Fe.

INFORMATION
Internet Access

Cyber cafés are tucked into *locutorios* (telephone kiosks) throughout the center, and they're everywhere in Nueva Córdoba.

ESTANCIAS IN THE CENTRAL SIERRAS

From rustic little getaways to sprawling, atmospheric ranches, the Central Sierras offer a small but excellent selection of *estancia* accommodations.

Estancia El Viejo Piquete (p329) A cozy ranch house with fabulous views over the Valle de Punilla.

Estancia La Estanzuela (p342) Wonderfully preserved, set on lush grounds.

Estancia Las Verbenas (p340) Set in a beautiful glade, a truly rustic experience.

La Ranchería de Santa Catalina (p331) Spend the night in the old slave quarters.

Puesto Viejo (p330) *Estancia* atmosphere at backpacker prices.

Stone (☎ 0351-15-547-6458; Av Marcelo T de Alvear 370; per hr AR$2; ☽ 10am-dawn) One of the grooviest cyber joints in town. Pizzas, drinks and empanadas too.

Laundry
Trapitos (☎ 422-5877; Independencia 898; full service about AR$10)

Medical Services
Emergency hospital (☎ 421-0243; cnr Catamarca & Blvd Guzmán)

Money
Downtown, *cambios* (exchange houses) and ATMs are on Rivadavia just north of the plaza; both can also be found at the main bus terminal and airport.

Cambio Barujel (cnr Rivadavia & 25 de Mayo) High commissions.

Maguitur (☎ 421-6200; 25 de Mayo 122) Charges 3% on traveler's checks.

Post
Main post office (Av General Paz 201)

Tourist Information
ACA (Automóvil Club Argentino; ☎ 421-4636; cnr Av General Paz & Humberto Primo) Argentina's auto club; good source for provincial road maps.

Casa Cabildo Tourist Information Office (☎ 428-5856; Independencia 30; ☽ 8am-8pm) Provincial and municipal tourist boards together maintain their main information office here in the historic Casa Cabildo.

Provincial tourist office airport (☎ 434-8390; Aeropuerto Pajas Blancas; ☽ 8am-8pm Mon-Fri); bus terminal (☎ 433-1980; ☽ 8am-9pm)

Travel Agencies

Asatej (☎ 422-9453; www.asatej.com in Spanish; Av Vélez Sársfield 361, Patio Olmos, Local 319) On the 3rd floor of Patio Olmos shopping center. Nonprofit student travel agency with a great staff. Open to all ages and nonstudents.

SIGHTS

There's plenty to see in Córdoba, so allow yourself at least a couple of days for wandering around. Most churches are open roughly from 9am to noon and from 5pm to 8pm. Museum opening hours change regularly depending on the season and the administration.

Centro

Downtown Córdoba is a treasure of colonial buildings and other historical monuments.

IGLESIA CATEDRAL

The construction of Córdoba's **cathedral** (guided visit AR$10; ◷ 9am-noon & 4-8pm) began in 1577 and dragged on for more than two centuries under several architects, including Jesuits and Franciscans, and though it lacks any sense of architectural unity, it's a beautiful structure. Crowned by a Romanesque dome, it overlooks Plaza San Martín, at Independencia and 27 de Abril. The lavish interior was painted by renowned *cordobés* (Córdoban) painter Emilio Caraffa. Guided visits leave hourly between 9am and 5pm from Psje Santa Catalina 61, the entry on the north side of the cathedral.

MUSEO DE LA MEMORIA

A chilling testament to the excesses of Argentina's military dictatorship, this **museum** (San Jerónimo s/n; admission free; ◷ 9am-noon & 2-8pm) occupies a space formerly used as a clandestine center for detention and torture. It was operated by the dreaded Department of Intelligence (D2), a special division created in Córdoba dedicated to the kidnap and torture of suspected political agitators and the 'reassignment' of their children to less politically suspect families.

The space itself is stark and unembellished, and the walls are covered with enlarged photographs of people who are still 'missing' after 30 years. There's not much joy here, but the museum stands as a vital reminder of an era that human rights groups hope will never be forgotten.

MANZANA JESUÍTICA

Córdoba's beautiful Manzana Jesuítica (Jesuit Block), like that of Buenos Aires, is also known as the Manzana de las Luces (Block of Enlightenment), and was initially associated with the influential Jesuit order.

Designed by the Flemish Padre Philippe Lemaire, the **Iglesia de la Compañía de Jesús** (cnr Obispo Trejo & Caseros; admission free) dates from 1645 but was not completed until 1671, with the successful execution of Lemaire's plan for a cedar roof in the form of an inverted ship's hull. Lemaire was once, unsurprisingly, a boat builder. Inside, the church's baroque altarpiece is made from carved Paraguayan cedar from Misiones province. The **Capilla Doméstica** (Domestic Chapel; guided visits per person AR$6; ◷ 10am, 11am, 5pm & 6pm), completed in 1644, sits directly behind the church on Caseros. Its ornate ceiling was made with cowhide stretched over a skeleton of thick taguaro cane and painted with pigments composed partially of boiled bones. Guided visits leave from inside the Universidad Nacional de Córdoba.

In 1613 Fray Fernando de Trejo y Sanabria founded the Seminario Convictorio de San Javier, which, after being elevated to university status in 1622, became the **Universidad Nacional de Córdoba** (☎ 433-2075; Obispo Trejo 242; ◷ 9am-1pm & 4-8pm). The university is the country's oldest and contains, among other national treasures, part of the Jesuits' Grand Library and the **Museo Histórico de la Universidad Nacional de Córdoba** (☎ 433-2075; guided visits per person AR$8; ◷ 10am, 11am, 5pm & 6pm Tue-Sun). Guided visits are the only way to see the inside and are well worth taking. They let you wander through the Colegio and peek into the classrooms while students run around.

Next door, the **Colegio Nacional de Monserrat** (Obispo Trejo 294) dates from 1782, though the college itself was founded in 1687 and transferred after the Jesuit expulsion. Though the interior cloisters are original, the exterior was considerably modified in 1927 by restoring architect Jaime Roca, who gave the building its present baroque flare.

In 2000, Unesco declared the Manzana Jesuítica a World Heritage site, along with five Jesuit *estancias* throughout the province.

MUSEO HISTÓRICO PROVINCIAL MARQUÉS DE SOBREMONTE

It's worth dropping into this **museum** (☎ 433-1661/71; Rosario de Santa Fe 218; admission AR$2; ◷ 10am-3pm Tue-Thu, 9am-2pm Sat), one of the most important historical museums in the country, if only to see the colonial house it occupies:

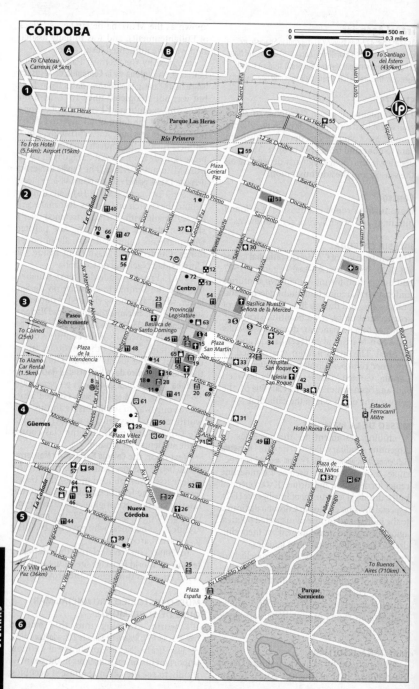

CÓRDOBA

an 18th-century home that once belonged to Rafael Núñez, the colonial governor of Córdoba and later Viceroyal of the Río de la Plata. It has 26 rooms, seven interior patios, meter-thick walls and an impressive wrought-iron balcony supported by carved wooden brackets.

CRIPTA JESUÍTICA

The Jesuits, at the beginning of the 18th century, built the **Cripta Jesuítica** (cnr Rivera Indarte & Av Colón; admission AR$1; 9am-7pm Mon-Fri). It was originally designed as a novitiate and later converted to a crypt and crematorium. Abandoned after the Jesuit expulsion, it was demolished and buried around 1829 when the city, while expanding Av Colón, knocked the roof into the subterranean naves and built over the entire structure. It remained all but forgotten until Telecom, while laying underground telephone cable in 1989, accidentally ran into it. The city, with a new outlook on such treasures, exquisitely restored the crypt and uses it regularly for musical and theatrical performances and art exhibits. Entrances lie

on either side of Av Colón in the middle of the Rivera Indarte pedestrian mall.

MUSEO MUNICIPAL DE BELLAS ARTES DR GENARO PÉREZ

This museum is prized for its collection of paintings from the 19th and 20th centuries. Works, including those by Emilio Caraffa, Lucio Fontana, Lino Spilimbergo, Antonio Berni and Antonio Seguí, chronologically display the history of the *cordobés* school of painting, at the front of which stands the museum's namesake, Genaro Pérez. The Palacio Garzón, an unusual late-19th-century building named for its original owner, houses the **museum** (433-1512; Av General Paz 33; admission free; 10am-8pm Tue-Sun), which also has outstanding changing contemporary art exhibits.

PLAZA SAN MARTÍN & AROUND

Córdoba's lovely and lively central plaza dates from 1577. Its western side is dominated by the white arcade of the restored **Cabildo** (colonial town-council building), completed in 1785 and containing three interior patios, as well

CÓRDOBA & THE CENTRAL SIERRAS

as basement cells. All are open to the public as part of the **Museo de la Ciudad** (☎ 433-1543; Independencia 30; admission free; ☼ 9am-9pm Tue-Sun).

Occupying nearly half a city block, the **Iglesia de Santa Teresa y Convento de Carmelitas Descalzas de San José** (cnr Caseros & Independencia; admission free; ☼ 6-8pm) was completed in 1628 and has functioned ever since as a closed-order convent for Carmelite nuns. Only the church itself is open to visitors. Once part of the convent, the **Museo de Arte Religioso Juan de Tejeda** (☎ 423-0175; Independencia 122; admission free; ☼ 9:30am-12:30pm Wed-Sat), next door, exhibits religious artifacts, as well as paintings by *cordobés* masters.

Nueva Córdoba

Before the northwestern neighborhoods of Chateau Carreras and Cerro de las Rosas lured the city's elite to their peaceful hillsides, Nueva Córdoba was the neighborhood of the *cordobés* aristocracy. It's now popular with students, which explains the proliferation of brick high-rise apartment buildings. Still, a stroll past the stately old residences that line the wide Av H Yrigoyen reveals the area's aristocratic past.

Paseo del Buen Pastor (Av H Yrigoyen 325; ☼ 10am-10pm) is a cultural center/performance space which was built in 1901 as a combined chapel/monastery/women's prison. In mid-2007 it was re-inaugurated to showcase work by Córdoba's young and emerging artists. There are a couple of hip café/bars in the central patio area where you can kick back with an Appletini or two. The attached chapel (which has been de-sanctified) hosts regular live music performances – stop by for a program, or check Thursday's edition of the local newspaper *La Voz del Interior* for details.

While you're in the neighborhood, pop across the road to see the marvelous neo-Gothic **Parroquia Sagrado Corazón de Jesús de los Capuchinos** (cnr Buenos Aires & Obispo Oro; admission free), built between 1928 and 1934, whose glaring oddity is its missing steeple (omitted on purpose to symbolize human imperfection). Among the numerous sculptures that cover the church's facade are those of Atlases symbolically struggling to bare the spiritual weight of the religious figures above them (and sins and guilt of the rest of us).

Nueva Córdoba's landmark building, the **Palacio Ferreyra** (Av H Yrigoyen 551; ☼ 8am-7pm, closed Mon) was built in 1914 and designed by Ernest Sanson in the Louis XVI style. The building itself is amazing, and has recently been converted into a fine-arts museum, featuring more than 400 works in 12 rooms spread over three floors. If you're into art or architecture, this place is a don't-miss.

One of the city's best contemporary art museums is the neoclassical **Museo Provincial de Bellas Artes Emilio Caraffa** (☎ 433-3414; Av H Yrigoyen 651; admission free; ☼ 11am-7pm Tue-Sun). It stands ostentatiously on the eastern side of Plaza España. Architect Juan Kronfuss designed the building as a museum and it was inaugurated in 1916. Exhibits change monthly. South of the museum the city unfolds into its largest open-space area, the **Parque Sarmiento**, designed by Charles Thays, the architect who designed Mendoza's Parque General San Martín.

Güemes

Once a strictly working-class neighborhood, Güemes is now known for the eclectic **antique stores** and **artisan shops** that line the main drag of Belgrano, between Rodríguez and Laprida. Its weekend *feria artisanal* (p324), one of the country's best, teems with antique vendors, arts and crafts and a healthy dose of Córdoba's hippies. It's within the same block as the **Museo Iberoamericano de Artesanías** (☎ 433-4368; cnr Belgrano & Av Rodríguez; admission free; ☼ 5-10pm Sat & Sun), which houses beautiful crafts from throughout South America. A good way back to the city center is along **La Cañada**, an acacia-lined stone canal with arched bridges.

COURSES

Córdoba is an excellent place to study Spanish; in many ways, being a student is what Córdoba is all about. Lessons cost about AR$40 per hour for one-on-one courses or AR$300 to AR$400 per week in small classes.

Coined (☎ 429-9402; www.coined.com.ar; Caseros 873)

Facultad de Lenguas (☎ 433-1073/5, ext 30; Av Vélez Sársfield 187) Part of the Universidad Nacional de Córdoba.

TOURS

City tours (in Spanish AR$10, in English AR$18) Absorb Córdoba's rich history by taking one of the guided city tours that depart daily at 9:30am and 4:30pm from the Casa Cabildo (p316). Reserve a day in advance if you want a tour in English.

Latitud Sur (☎ 425-6023; www.latitudsurtrek.com.ar; Fructuoso Rivera 70) Run by an enthusiastic young couple with boundless knowledge of both the sierras and the city,

Latitud Sur offers mountain-bike, trekking, rock-climbing and horseback-riding tours throughout the Sierras de Córdoba, including day trips to Los Gigantes and Parque Nacional Quebrada del Condorito (p335). Prices range from AR$90 to AR$120, including transport, guide and lunch. Paragliding costs AR$210 and skydiving AR$500 (including videotape of the big event). City tours are outstanding, fun and only cost AR$25 per person.

FESTIVALS & EVENTS

During the first three weeks of April, the city puts on a large **crafts market** (locally called 'FICO') at the city fairgrounds, on the town's north side near Chateau Carreras stadium. Bus 31 from Plaza San Martín goes there. Mid-September's **Feria del Libro** is a regional book fair.

SLEEPING

Hotels on and around Plaza San Martín (Centro) make exploring the center a cinch, but you'll have to walk several blocks for dinner and nightlife. Hotels along La Cañada and in Nueva Córdoba, on the other hand, mean going out to dinner and hitting the bars is a simple matter of walking down the street.

Centro

our pick Palenque Hostel (☎ 423-7588; www.palenque hostel.com.ar; Av General Paz 371; dm AR$22, d without bathroom AR$60; 🔌 🖳) By far the prettiest hostel in Córdoba, the Palenque occupies a classic old house and retains much of its original charm. Facilities are extensive, including laundry area, air-con and nightly cooking classes. Dorms are large, with plenty of room to move.

Baluch Backpackers (☎ 422-3977; www.baluch backpackers.com; San Martín 338; dm AR$22, d without bathroom AR$60; 🖳) Rightly boasting its status as the only hostel on a pedestrian street in Córdoba, the Baluch offers all the standard hostel amenities, plus an excellent rooftop bar/BBQ/chillout area.

Ritz Hotel (☎ 421-5031/2/3; www.ritzhotelcba.com.ar; San Jerónimo 495; s/d AR$100/120; 🔌) Step back into a dark and faded 1960s elegance at this 60-room hotel complete with dimly lit lounge, wood-paneled walls and big leather sofas. Suited bell-hops will lead you down wide, worn hallways to small but comfortable rooms whose main decoration is some wild floral wallpaper.

Hotel Victoria (☎ 421-0198; 25 de Mayo 240; www .granhotelvictoria.com.ar; s/d AR$100/130; 🔌) Grab a front room at this medium-sized hotel right

on the pedestrian strip and you'll have an awesome balcony without a sliver of street noise. Great views, terrible coffee.

Hotel Sussex (☎ 422-9070/5; www.hotelsussexcba .com.ar; San Jerónimo 125; s/d AR$130/160; 🖳) In a sophisticated building just off the main plaza, the Sussex is one of Córdoba's oldest hotels, though its remodeled rooms have a worn 1960s feel. The 11th-floor breakfast room has stunning views over the plaza, and the rooftop pool is open during summer.

Ducal Suites (☎ 570-8888; www.hotelducal.com.ar in Spanish; Corrientes 207; s/d AR$200/220; 🔌 🖳) This is another modern beauty, where guests have access to a fabulous rooftop pool with dozens of chaise longues around the deck. Spacious rooms have kitchenettes and ample bathrooms, but the TVs sure seem small.

Nueva Córdoba & La Cañada

Tango Hostel (☎ 425-6023; www.latitudsurtrek.com.ar in Spanish; Fructuoso Rivera 70; dm AR$25, d with/without bathroom AR$65/55) This immaculate and intimate hostel boasts a fabulous staff, clean dorm rooms with only four to five beds in each and spotless bathrooms. The well-equipped kitchen, comfy eating area and common room are all conducive to socializing, and the young owners know heaps about adventure tourism.

Hotel Viena (☎ 460-0909; www.hotelviena.com.ar; Laprida 235; s/d AR$130/150; 🔌 🖳) This modern hotel in the heart of Nueva Córdoba offers bright, clean rooms and an excellent breakfast buffet. Paying an extra AR$20 for a 'deluxe' gets you a big-screen TV, carpet and brand-new mattresses. There are lots of nooks for sitting in the lobby area, and there's a restaurant on the premises. Good choice.

Amerian (☎ 420-7000; www.amerian.com; Blvd San Juan 165; r from AR$320; 🔌 🖳 🖳) Straddling the border between the new town and the historic center, the Amerian is a big business hotel with an excellent location and all the comforts. Sunset drinks at the bar by the rooftop pool are near-obligatory.

Around the Bus Terminal

Hotel Viña de Italia (☎ 422-6589; www.hotelvinadeitalia .com.ar; San Jerónimo 611; s/d AR$90/120; 🔌) There's a bit of elegance left in this 150-room hotel, and the midsize rooms all include TV, telephone, air-con and heating. Light-blue satiny couches grace the lobby downstairs, and there's a decent restaurant attached.

LOVE BY THE HOUR

Every city in Argentina has *hoteles por hora* (hourly rate hotels), where people take their secret lovers for a romp in the good old proverbial hay. They vary from cheap, nondescript *residenciales* (cheap hotels) to deluxe love pads with black lights, wall-to-wall mirrors, nonstop sex-TV, Jacuzzis and room-service menus featuring every imaginable sex toy under the sun. These deluxe versions are a part of under-the-table Argentine culture that shouldn't be missed (provided you're traveling with a partner who's game, of course).

Córdoba boasts four deluxe *hoteles por hora* on the road to the airport, and if you haven't experienced one of these Argentine institutions, now's your chance. Although they're geared toward folks with cars, you can go in a taxi (trust us, we know). Here's a quick primer on how they work.

First, it's all about anonymity. As you drive into the hotel a big number flashes on a sign; that's your room number. Drive to the garage door with your number on it, pull in and close the garage door; if you're in a taxi, the driver will drop you in the garage and leave. Close the garage door and enter the room.

In five minutes the phone will ring, and the attendant will ask you if you'd like a complimentary beverage, which he or she then delivers through a tiny sliding door in the wall so no one sees anybody. When the attendant knocks on the door, you open it, take your drinks and pay for the room (AR$75 for two hours is the going rate). Ten minutes before your time is up, the attendant will courteously ring again to tell you it's time to get your gear back on.

Of the four hotels on the airport road, the best is **Eros Hotel** (Camino al aeropuerto, Km 5.5; 2hr AR$75). It has en-suite Jacuzzis, bedside control panels, all the right TV channels and *all* the fun stuff. And it's impeccably clean.

A taxi costs about AR$15 each way. If you take one, call a *remise* (telephone taxi) from your hotel and have the driver pick you up in two hours. They all know the drill – no pun intended.

Hotel Heydi (☎ 421-8906; www.hotelheydi.com.ar in Spanish; Blvd Illia 615; s/d AR$120/140; ☒) This is the best of the bunch near the bus terminal: a modern, immaculate place with a friendly, professional staff.

EATING

Mercado Norte (cnr Rivadavia & Oncativo; ☒ closed Sun) Córdoba's indoor market has delicious and inexpensive food, such as pizza, empanadas and seafood. Browsing the clean stalls selling every imaginable cut of meat, including whole *chivitos* (kid) and pigs, is a must.

La Vieja Esquina (☎ 424-7940; cnr Belgrano & Caseros; empanadas AR$1.50; ☒ closed Sun) Cozy little place serving excellent empanadas and other baked savories. The *locro* (spicy stew) is tempting but a little heavy on the oil. Great place.

Verde Siempre Verde (☎ 421-8820; 9 de Julio 36; lunch AR$9-15; ☒ lunch & dinner) Delicious vegetarian buffet that also serves set meals.

Bar San Carlos (Plazoleta San Roque, Salguero & San Jerónimo; mains AR$10-15; ☒ lunch & dinner) Neighborhood *parrillas* (steak restaurants) are fast disappearing in Córdoba, but the San Carlos is one of the best, and still hanging in there. Get there reasonably early and

beat the old guys out of a table on the small shady plaza.

El Ruedo (cnr Obispo Trejo & 27 de Abril; mains around AR$15; ☒ lunch & dinner) It doesn't stray too far from the steak, sandwich and pizza formula here, but the plaza-side spot under big shady trees is a winner, as are the *limonadas con soda* (lemon juice with soda water) on a hot day.

La Zete (cnr Corrientes & Salguero; mains AR$15; ☒ lunch & dinner) Adorned with posters from Syria and Lebanon, this Middle Eastern restaurant is the real deal, with delicious *kepe* (spiced minced meat), fried eggplant and a range of dips, among other temptations. The ample *picada* (sampler plate; AR$30) for two is a journey in deliciousness.

Mega Doner (Ituzaingó 528; doners AR$20; ☒ lunch & dinner) Conveniently located in Nueva Córdoba's bar district, this place specializes in real giro *doners*. Daily lunch specials are an excellent deal, starting at AR$8, and there's outdoor seating.

Las Tinajas (☎ 411-4150; Blvd San Juan 32; lunch AR$15 Mon-Fri, AR$18 Sat & Sun, dinner AR$23; ☒ lunch & dinner) The country's largest *tenedor libre* (all-you-can-eat restaurant) serves a mind-boggling array of international cuisine alongside a fake waterfall and indoor river.

our pick La Nieta 'e La Pancha (☎ 468-1920; Belgrano 783; mains AR$20-25; ❤ dinner) A wonderful staff prepares and serves a changing menu of delectable regional specialties, creative pastas and house recipes. Be sure to save room for dessert. Check out the lovely upstairs terrace, which catches breezes and gives ample people-watching ops on the street below.

Bursatil (San Jerónimo & Ituzaingó; mains AR$20-25; ❤ lunch & dinner) Stylish, modern cafés are starting to pop up in the old part of town, and Bursatil is one of the finest. There's a cool modern interior, good coffee and a small, Asian-inspired menu.

Alfonsina (☎ 427-2847; Duarte Quirós 66; pizzas AR$12-25; ❤ 8am-dawn, closed 4-8pm Sat) Slip into this laid-back bar-cum-pizzeria for great atmosphere and outstanding pizzas. Decorations are as eclectic as the crowd, and folks sit for hours smoking and talking. Great place to try *mate*.

La Parrilla de Raul (☎ 424-7865; Jujuy 278; mains AR$13-28 ❤ lunch & dinner) Of Córdoba's many *parrillas*, this is probably the most atmospheric: it's dimly lit, and the walls are stacked with Argentine wines. *Parrillada* (mixed grill) for two costs only AR$12 to AR$22, not including extras such as drinks or salad.

El Arrabal (☎ 460-2990; www.elarrabal.com.ar in Spanish; Belgrano 899; mains AR$18-30; ❤ lunch & dinner) One of the few old-style restaurants in Nueva Córdoba (ok, so it may be a reconstruction…), this place serves slightly pricey, imaginative regional and house specialties. It packs out for tango classes (AR$10) at 6pm nightly and the dinner tango show Thursdays to Saturdays at 11pm. Make a reservation.

Mandarina (☎ 426-4909; Obispo Trejo 171; mains AR$20-30; ❤ lunch & dinner) Decent Chinese dishes and tasty pizzas and pastas are all cooked with flare at this cozy hideaway with tables out on the pedestrian mall. Take a break from the meat and try one of the delicious salads.

Alcorta (☎ 424-7452; Av Alcorta 330; mains AR$30-55; ❤ lunch & dinner) This upmarket *parrilla*, esteemed for its grilled meats (many say they're the best in town), also serves delicious pasta and fish. Try the *mollejitas al sauvignan blanc* (sweetbreads in a white wine sauce).

DRINKING

Córdoba's drink of choice is Fernet (a strong, medicinal-tasting herbed liquor from Italy),

almost always mixed with Coke. If you don't mind a rough morning, start in on the stuff.

Nightlife in Córdoba basically divides itself into three areas – all the bright young things barhop in Nueva Córdoba – a walk down Rondeau between Avs H Yrigoyen and Chacabuco after midnight gives you a choice of dozens of bars, mostly playing laid-back electronic music.

North of the center, there's a string of live-music venues on Blvd Guzmán near the corner of Av General Paz.

Across the river on Av Las Heras between Roque Sáenz Peña and Juan B Justo (the area known locally as Abasto) are the discos and nightclubs. Go for a walk along here and you'll probably pick up free passes to some, if not all, of them.

Los Infernadas (Belgrano 631) A laid-back bar playing an eclectic range of music. Live music Thursday to Sundays and a big *patio cervecero* (beer garden) make this a standout.

But Mitre (www.butmitre.com; Av Marcelo T de Alvear 635) Extremely popular bar-cum–dance club on La Cañada. Check it out, especially on Thursday night.

Beep! (Sucre 171; entry incl drink AR$7; ❤ midnight-dawn Thu-Sat) The best gay club in the center is completely empty until 2am and completely slamming until sunup.

Ojo Bizarro (Igualdad 176; entry AR$8-13) In a semi-dodgy neighborhood, the Bizarro is one of the city's more bohemian hangouts. There's plenty of mood lighting, and a different DJ in each of the four rooms.

Barranga (Av Las Heras 58; entry AR$6-12) In the busy Albasto scene, this live music venue–cum-disco is a good place to start, if only for the fact that it gets a crowd before 1am. Fridays are Latin dance parties, Saturdays there are live bands.

ENTERTAINMENT

On Friday nights, the city hosts the **Patio del Tango** (admission AR$10, with dance lessons AR$20) on the outdoor Patio Mayor of the historic Cabildo (weather permitting), kicking off with two-hour tango lessons. Times vary, so it's best to stop by the Casa Cabildo Tourist Information Office (p316).

La Voz del Interior, Córdoba's main newspaper, has a reasonably comprehensive entertainment section every Thursday with show times and the like.

Teatro del Libertador General San Martín (☎ 433-2319; Av Vélez Sársfield 365; admission AR$20-150; ❤ box office 9am-9pm) It's well worth going to a performance here, if only to see the opulence of the country's most historic theater. The theater was completed in 1891, and the floor was designed to be mechanically raised and leveled to the stage, so seats could be removed, allowing for grand parties among the aristocracy of the early 1900s.

Cineclub Municipal Hugo del Carril (☎ 433-2463; www.ccmunicipal.org.ar in Spanish; Blvd San Juan 49; admission AR$6; ☻ box office 9am-late) For a great night (or day) at the movies, pop into this municipal film house which screens everything from art flicks to Latin American award winners and local films. Stop by for a program. There's also live music and theatrical performances.

SHOPPING

Antique stores line Calle Belgrano in barrio Güemes, where there is also a **feria artisanal** (artisans' market; cnr Rodriguez & Belgrano; ☻ 5-10pm Sat & Sun), one of the country's best. You'll find Argentine handicrafts at several stores downtown.

La Emilia (☎ 423-8402; Deán Funes 18) Though this shop has its share of shoddy souvenirs, there are still plenty of excellent regional crafts to choose from.

Pasaje Colonial (Belgrano 795; ☻ 10am-9pm Mon-Sat, 5-10pm Sun) To find out what the city's hip young designers have been working on, slip into this little arcade, featuring a variety of small shops selling clothes, homewares and jewelry.

Talabartería Crespo (☎ 421-5447; Obispo Trejo 141; ☻ closed Sun) Leather goods made from *carpincho* (a large rodent that makes a beautifully spotted leather) are the specialty here. Sweaters, knives and *mate* paraphernalia grace the shelves as well.

GETTING THERE & AWAY
Air

Córdoba's international airport, **Ingeniero Ambrosio Taravella** (☎ 434-8390), charges a AR$56 departure tax on all international departures from here.

Aerolíneas Argentinas/Austral (☎ /fax 482-1025; Av Colón 520) has offices located downtown and flies several times daily to Buenos Aires (from AR$285). **Lan Chile** (☎ 452-3030; Av Alcorta 206) flies daily to Santiago, Chile (one-way AR$930). **TAM** (☎ 424-4019; Av Colón 119, 3rd fl) flies daily to São Paulo, Brazil (AR$1050). **COPA** (☎ 0810-222-2672; www.copaair.com; Vélez Sársfield 478) plans to start flying out of Córdoba soon. Check the website for details.

Bus

Córdoba's **bus terminal** (NETOC; ☎ 423-4199, 423-0532; Blvd Perón 300) is about a 15-minute walk from downtown.

Sierras del Córdoba, Sierras de Calamuchita and Transportes La Cumbre all serve Córdoba's mountain hinterlands, including Villa General Belgrano (AR$12, two hours) and Mina Clavero (AR$17, three hours). Other nearby destinations in the Sierras are easier and more quickly reached from the Mercado Sud minibus terminal (below).

There are several daily departures to the destinations listed following. Check the **terminal tourist office** (☎ 433-1980) for the best deals, cheapest fares and highest services.

Destination	Cost (AR$)	Duration (hr)
Bahía Blanca	105	12
Bariloche	171	22
Buenos Aires	75	10
Catamarca	43	5-6
Comodoro Rivadavia	190	25
Corrientes	100	12
Esquel	220	25
Formosa	116	15
Jujuy	126	12
La Rioja	48	7
Mar del Plata	160	16
Mendoza	68	10
Merlo	45	5½
Montevideo (Uruguay)	160	15
Neuquén	141	15-16
Paraná	50	6
Puerto Iguazú	130	20
Puerto Madryn	152	18-20
Resistencia	100	11-12
Río Gallegos	290	36
Rosario	50	6
Salta	103	12
San Juan	52	8
San Luis	50	6
San Martín de los Andes	190	21
Santa Fe	47	5
Santiago del Estero	51	6
Tucumán	69	8

Several companies offer service to Chilean destinations including Santiago (AR$125, 16 hours) and Valparaiso (AR$125, 19 hours), though most involve changing buses in Mendoza.

Minibus

Frequent minibuses leave from **Mercado Sud minibus terminal** (Blvd Illia near Buenos Aires). Some of these go direct, while others stop at every little town along the way. It's worth asking, as this can shave an hour off your travel time. There are departures for Villa Carlos Paz (AR$5, one hour), Cosquín (AR$7, 1¼ hours), La Falda (AR$2, three hours), La Cumbre (AR$12, three hours), Capilla del Monte (AR$15, three hours), Jesús María (AR$5, one hour) and Alta Gracia (AR$4, one hour). There are a few direct buses to La Cumbrecita (AR$23, three hours), but it will probably be quicker going first to Villa General Belgrano (AR$12, two hours) and changing buses there. There are also buses to Mina Clavero (AR$17, three hours).

Train

Córdoba's **Estación Ferrocarril Mitre** (☎ 426-3565; Blvd Perón s/n) has reopened for business, much to the delight of train-lovers and bus-haters country-wide. Trains leave for Rosario (AR$18/24/36 in Turista/Primera/Pullman, eight hours) and Buenos Aires' Retiro station (AR$25/35/47/150 in Turista/Primera/Pullman/Camarote, 15 hours) on Wednesday and Sunday nights at 8pm. There is a dining car and bar on board. Tickets often sell out weeks in advance, especially in the *camarote* (two-person sleeping cabin), so book as soon as possible.

GETTING AROUND

The airport is 15km north of town via Av Monseñor Pablo Cabrera. From the main bus terminal, the Empresa Ciudad de Córdoba bus marked 'Salsipuedes' goes to the airport. A taxi into town shouldn't cost you more than AR$15.

Buses require *cospeles* (tokens), available for AR$1.10 from nearly every kiosk in town.

A car is very useful for visiting some of the nearby Jesuit *estancias* that cannot be reached by bus. Depending on seasonal demand, economy cars cost around AR$150 with 200km. Try the following:

Alamo (☎ 499-8436; Sheraton Hotel, Duarte Quirós 1300)

Europcar (☎ 422-4867, 481-7683; Entre Ríos 70) Inside Hotel Dora.

THE CENTRAL SIERRAS

Nowhere near as visually spectacular as the nearby Andes, the Central Sierras more than make up for it by being way more hospitable. The area is dotted with little towns that are worth a quick visit or a longer stay, and is connected by an excellent road network with frequent bus services.

From the hippy-chic of paragliding capital La Cumbre to the over-the-top kitsch of Villa Carlos Paz, you'd have to be one jaded traveler not to find something to your liking here. Kicking back is easily done – the riverside village of Mina Clavero is a favorite, as are the ex-Jesuit centers of Alta Gracia and Jesús María. Things get decidedly Germanic down south, and the pedestrian-only La Cumbrecita is not to be missed for *spaetzle* (German egg noodles), bush walks and swimming holes.

VILLA CARLOS PAZ
☎ 03541 / pop 74,200 / elev 600m

Not everybody gets a chance to go to Vegas, but you might be able to satiate a little of your thirst for kitsch in this summer resort town only 36km west of Córdoba. Villa Carlos Paz, set on the shores of so-called Lago San Roque (in reality a large reservoir), has architectural excesses including hotels shaped like pyramids and the Kremlin, and the town's pride and joy, a monstrous cuckoo clock (*reloj cu-cu* for the Spanish speakers out there). In summer, hordes of Argentines crowd Carlos Paz's lakeshores, pack its dance floors and whiz around in miniature trains on city tours. Foreigners generally find it less than appealing.

A **telesilla** (chairlift; ☎ 422254; Sanchez & San Antonio; return ticket AR$12; ☾ 9am-1pm & 3-5pm) takes you to the top of Cerro Carlos Paz for a bird's-eye view over town. There's a pricey café and a couple of short, well-signposted walking trails at the top.

The **tourist office** (☎ 436430; San Martín-Yrigoyen intersection; ☾ 7am-11pm summer, to 9pm rest of yr) distributes useful maps and guides to local services (which are plentiful).

Carlos Paz has some excellent hotels, but they're packed through the summer. **Carlos Paz Hostel** (☎ 436023; www.carlospazhostel.com.ar; Lugones 72; dm AR$30; ☐) is a modern house converted into a hostel, located up the hill from the bus terminal. The dorms are OK, the kitchen's well set up and there are awesome views from the rooftop terrace.

Nuevo Hotel Italiano (☎ 422202; www.nuevohotel italiano.com.ar; Uruguay 253; s/d AR$100/120; ☒ ☐) is a sweet little hotel oozing with character – a quantity in fairly short supply in this town. Rooms are cool and quiet, despite its central,

THE CENTRAL SIERRAS

main road location. The pool area (with bar service) is a definite bonus.

The *costanera* (waterfront) is lined with *parrillas, tenedor libres* and more upscale restaurants.

La Playa (Costanera s/n; mains AR$15-35; ☺ breakfast, lunch & dinner) This laid-back restaurant, with tables out on the waterfront shaded by palm thatch umbrellas, is one of the more atmospheric places to eat. Live bands play on weekend nights in summer.

Buses travel to Córdoba (AR$4.50, one hour, every 15 minutes) from the **bus terminal** (San Martín 400). There are also regular departures to Cosquín (AR$4, 40 minutes) and other towns throughout the Valle de Punilla, and to Buenos Aires (from AR$95, 11 hours).

LOS GIGANTES
☎ 03541 / elev 1800m

This spectacular group of rock formations 80km west of Córdoba is fast becoming Argentina's rock-climbing capital. The two highest peaks are the granite giants of Cerro de La Cruz (2185m) and El Mogote (2374m). There are numerous Andean condors – the park is only 30km from Parque Nacional Quebrada del Condorito, and the birds have slowly taken to this area as well. The area is home to the tabaquillo tree, with its papery peeling bark, which is endangered in Argentina and only found here and in Bolivia and Peru.

Getting to the area is complicated. **Sarmiento** (☎ 0351-433-2161) buses leave Córdoba's main bus terminal at 8am Wednesday to Monday and 6am on Tuesdays (AR$12, two hours). The bus pretty much turns around and comes back again, meaning you have to spend the night. Schedules change frequently, so be sure to check.

Get off at El Crucero (tell the driver you're going to Los Gigantes). From there it's a 3km walk to La Rotonda where there is a super-basic **hospedaje** (☎ 498370; ar.geocities.com/tanti aventura/rotonda.html; per person camping AR$3, per person kitchen use AR$3, dm AR$10) and a small store (beer, soft drinks and snacks only) which is open on weekends.

At La Rotonda you can hire guides (AR$25) to show you around the cave complexes and take you to the top of Cerro La Cruz. It's not a long hike, but there is some tricky rock scrambling involved. Guides are recommended because the maze of trails through the rocks can

be hard to follow and if the fog comes down, you can easily get lost.

Probably the best and easiest way to see the area is by taking a trip with Latitud Sur (p320) in Córdoba, whose excellent staff knows the area well. An overnight trip (AR$260) usually includes a big *asado* (barbecue grill) outside the *refugio* where you'll stay. Day trips cost around AR$140.

COSQUÍN
☎ 03541 / pop 19,000 / elev 720m

Cosquín is known countrywide for its **Festival Nacional del Folklore** (www.aquicosquin.org), a nine-day national folk-music festival which has been held in the last week of January since 1961. The town gets packed for the festival, stays busy all summer and goes pleasantly dead the rest of the year. The slightly more hard-core **Cosquín Rock Festival** used to be held here, until the neighbors decided that teenagers with wallet chains, studded wristbands and piercings weren't really the tourist trade they were looking for. The festival relocated a few years ago to the banks of the nearby (and aptly named) Lago San Roque.

East of town, 1260m **Cerro Pan de Azúcar** offers good views of the sierras and, on a clear day, the city of Córdoba. An **aerosilla** (chairlift; return ticket AR$20; ☺ 9am-1pm & 3-5pm) runs to the summit regularly in summer – check with the tourist office in the off season. A taxi to the base should cost about AR$20.

Across the river from the center of town (turn left after the bridge), Av Belgrano forms 4km of waterfront promenade – a great place for a stroll on a summer's day, dotted with swimming holes that pack out when the temperature rises.

The **municipal tourist office** (☎ 453701; San Martín 560; ☺ 8am-9pm Mon-Fri, 9am-6pm Sat & Sun) has a good map of the town.

Sleeping & Eating
Hostería La Tana (☎ 452239; Carranza 656; s/d with bathroom AR$30/60, without bathroom AR$25/50) Simple but clean rooms facing onto a narrow, sunny courtyard. Some of the rooms with private bathroom have a small kitchen.

Hospedaje Petit (☎ 451311; petithotel@infocosquin .com.ar; A Sabattini 739; s/d AR$80/100) Steepled roofs and lovely antique floor tiles in the lobby give way to some fairly ordinary, modern rooms on the interior. It's decent value, though – clean, spacious and central.

Hostería Siempreverde (☎ 450093; www.cosquin turismo.com.ar; Santa Fe 525; s/d AR$70/120) This lovely old house has good-sized, modern rooms out back. There's a big, shady garden and the breakfast/lounge area is comfortable and stylish.

Confitería Munich (cnr San Martín & Sarmiento; sandwiches from AR$10; ☺ lunch & dinner) An atmospheric plazaside café/bar, the Munich is a great place to grab a table in the late afternoon and watch the world go by.

Posta Maiten (Janer & Perón; mains AR$15-25; ☺ lunch & dinner) Cosquín's most frequently recommended *parrilla* looks like a barn from the outside, but the excellent service and warm atmosphere help lend it a touch of intimacy.

Getting There & Away

There are many daily departures north to La Falda (AR$4, 45 minutes) and La Cumbre (AR$4, 1¼ hours); and south every 20 minutes to Villa Carlos Paz (AR$4, 40 minutes) and Córdoba (AR$8, 1¼ hours). There are a few departures daily for Buenos Aires (AR$90, 11 hours).

LA FALDA

☎ 03548 / pop 15,100 / elev 934m

A woodsy resort town, La Falda is busier than its Central Sierra neighbors and not quite as interesting. It's worth a day or two, though, for walks in the hills and a wander around the grounds of the historic (and now defunct) Hotel Eden, built in 1897, where the guest list included Albert Einstein, the duke of Savoy and several Argentine presidents.

La Falda's main **plaza** (cnr Sarmiento & Rivadavia) is a charming, tranquil affair, all the more so for being removed from the main drag. Weekends and daily in summer, there's an **artisan market** (☺ daylight hr) here.

The **tourist office** (☎ 423007; Av España 50; ☺ 8am-8:30pm) is very helpful and has excellent maps of the area.

Sights & Activities

A favorite **hiking** trail takes about two hours to the nearby summit of 1350m Cerro La Banderita. And since you're here, take a guided tour of the once-extravagant, now-decaying **Hotel Eden** (admission by tour AR$8; ☺ 10am-noon & 2-4pm summer, 10am-noon & 2-4pm Fri-Sun winter).

A few blocks from Hotel Eden is a **Miniature Train Museum** (☺ 10am-6pm daily in summer, weekends only rest of yr), a strangely captivating museum

devoted to, you guessed it, very small trains. From the museum, follow signs to El Chorrito, a lookout with spectacular views out over the Sierras Chicas.

When the weather heats up, locals and tourists alike head for **7 Cascadas** (entry with transport from tourist office AR$5; ☺ daylight hr), which has three pools and a variety of swimming holes under waterfalls that were created when the local dam was built.

Sleeping & Eating

Hostería Marina (☎ 422640; Güemes 144; r per person AR$30; ☒) The rooms are on the small side, but this is an excellent budget deal – clean and quiet, with a decent sized swimming pool in the front yard.

Residencial Old Garden (☎ 422842; Capital Federal 28; s/d AR$80/120; ☒) Definitely one of the better accommodation deals in the country, this is a beautiful old house, lovingly maintained by the live-in owners. The whole place is charming, right down to the fuzzy dogs running around the large gardens.

La Bordolesa (cnr Sarmiento & Saavedra; mains AR$12-20) A laid-back, modern *parrilla* with two grills going – one inside and one out. If the weather's good, grab a table on the lawn and a platter of *picadas* (AR$25 for two) – it's a fine way to while away a few hours.

Getting There & Away

The bus terminal sits on RN 38, just north of Av Eden. There are regular buses and minibuses south to Cosquín (AR$4, 45 minutes), Villa Carlos Paz (AR$6, 1¼ hours), Córdoba (AR$9, two hours) and Mina Clavero (AR$15, 4½ hours); and north to La Cumbre (AR$2.50, 30 minutes) and Capilla del Monte (AR$4, one hour). There are regular long-distance runs to Buenos Aires (from AR$95, 12 hours) and other destinations.

LA CUMBRE

☎ 03548 / pop 7500 / elev 1141m

A favorite getaway for Córdoba dwellers and foreigners alike, La Cumbre packs a lot of character into a small space. It's an agreeable little town due to its wide streets and mild mountain climate, and there are plenty of adventures to be had in the surrounding hills. The town gained worldwide fame when it hosted the 1994 World Paragliding Cup, and enthusiasts of the sport have made La Cumbre their home, giving the town an international feel. The launch site,

380m above the Río Pinto, provides a spectacular introduction to the sport and there are plenty of experienced instructors around, offering both classes and tandem flights.

Information

Banco de la Provincia de Córdoba (cnr López y Planes & 25 de Mayo) Has an ATM.

Tourist office (☎ 452966; www.lacumbre.gov.ar in Spanish; Av Caraffa 300; ✆ 8am-9pm Apr-Jun & Aug-Nov, to midnight Dec-Mar & Jul) Across from the bus terminal in the old train station. Friendly staff will supply a handy map of the town and surroundings.

Sights & Activities

Head to the south side of town to the road known as **Camino de los Artesanos**, where more than two dozen homes sell homemade goodies, from jams and chutneys to wool, leather and silver crafts. Most homes open from 11am to sunset.

There are excellent views from the **Cristo Redentor**, a 7m statue of Christ on a 300m hilltop east of town; from the Plaza 25 de Mayo, cross the river and walk east on Córdoba toward the mountains – the trail begins after a quick jut to the left after crossing Cabrera.

PARAGLIDING & SKY DIVING

Flying from the launch at Cuchi Corral (and hanging out by the Río Pinto afterward) is truly a memorable experience. The launch site (La Rampa) is about 10km west of town via a signed dirt road off the highway. Pablo Jaraba (El Turco) at **Taller de las Nubes** (☎ 03548-15-570951; tallerdelasnubes@hotmail.com) and **Fechu** (☎ 03548-15-574568) both offer tandem flights and lessons. Everyone charges about the same. Tandem flights cost AR$180 for a half hour; full courses cost AR$2400.

At the **Aeroclub La Cumbre** (☎ 452544; Camino a los Troncos s/n), you can arrange everything from tandem flights to ultralights. Ask for Andy Hediger (former paragliding world champion) or Hernán Pitocco (number four in the world in paragliding acrobatics). You can also test your nerves parachuting with **Nicolás López** (☎ 452544; www.redbullaerobatix.com, in Spanish).

HORSEBACK RIDING, TREKKING & MOUNTAIN BIKING

La Chacra (☎ 451703; Pje Beiró s/n) and Estancia El Viejo Piquete (right) offer horseback excursions lasting from a few hours to multiple days. Prices run about AR$90 for a half-day

excursion and AR$450 for two days, including a full *asado* in the mountains.

Hacer Cumbre (☎ 452907; www.hacercumbrecom; Caraffa 270) rents quality mountain bikes (AR$30 per day) and offers guided rides in the breathtaking countryside around Cerro Ongamina, which you can combine with trekking, horseback riding and 4WD offroading. Day trips, including transfers and food, start at AR$300 for two people and become significantly cheaper if you get a group together.

Sleeping

The proprietors of all the following places can arrange any activities available in La Cumbre.

Camping El Cristo (☎ 451893; Monseñor P Cabrera s/n; sites AR$8) Below the Cristo Redentor east of town, La Cumbre's exceptional campgrounds are only a short tramp from the center.

El Condor (☎ 452870; el_condor_2001@yahoo.com .ar; Bartolomé Jaime 204; dm AR$25, d with/without bathroom AR$60/50) Thanks to its friendly owner and homey feel, this 1938 English-style home is easily the best deal in town. The house itself has a cozy living room and eight private rooms, some with private bathrooms and all with antique armoires and dressers. The small dorm area in back boasts a communal kitchen and an outdoor *parrilla*.

Hostería Plaza (☎ 451252; www.hosteriaplaza.com .ar; Cuesta 538; s/d AR$100/120; ☒) A friendly, family-run hotel on a quiet street overlooking the plaza. Rooms are spacious, if not quite palatial, and the whole place is decked out with homey decorations. The small pool in the front yard would serve for a quick dip.

Estancia El Viejo Piquete (☎ 03548-15-635948; elvie jopiquete@yahoo.com.ar; via Calle Mons Pablo Cabrera; d with full board AR$270) For a relaxing stay in a divine location about 2.5km north of town, treat yourself to a night or two at this remote three-room *estancia* with fabulous views over the Valle de Punilla. Horseback riding, hiking and other excursions are offered for guests and nonguests alike.

Eating & Drinking

Hacer Cumbre (Caraffa 270; sandwiches AR$9-13; ✆ breakfast & lunch) The café attached to this tour operator offers a small but enticing menu, featuring healthy sandwiches and yummy juices, smoothies and *lassis* (yogurt and iced-water drinks). Good breakfasts, too.

Kasbah (Alberdi & Sarmiento; mains AR$12-20; ✆ lunch & dinner) You may not be expecting a good Thai curry way out here, but this cute little triangular restaurant comes up with the goods. Also on offer are a range of Chinese and Indian dishes.

Casa Caraffa (cnr Caraffa & Rivadavia; mains AR$18-25) An excellent main-street restaurant serving up delicious homemade pastas and a divine *bife de chorizo* (sirloin steak) with Roquefort sauce (AR$22).

El Pungo (☎ 451378; www.elpungopub.com.ar in Spanish; Camino de los Artesanos s/n; cover AR$10-15; ✪ noon-late Sat & Sun) This somewhat legendary watering hole attracts musicians from all over the country (Argentine folk musicians Charly Garcia and Fito Paez have both played here).

Getting There & Away

Buses depart regularly from La Cumbre's convenient **bus terminal** (General Paz near Caraffa), heading northward to Capilla del Monte (AR$3, 30 minutes) or south to La Falda (AR$3, 30 minutes), Cosquín (AR$5, 1¼ hours), Villa Carlos Paz (AR$8, 1½ hours) and Córdoba (AR$11, 2½ hours). Minibuses (which take

about half an hour less) are the fastest way to Córdoba. There is also direct service to Buenos Aires (AR$85, 12½ hours).

AROUND LA CUMBRE

Capilla del Monte is an attractive town (elevation 979m) 18km north of La Cumbre on the RN 38. It not only attracts paragliders and outdoor enthusiasts to its surrounding countryside, but reputedly receives frequent visits from *Ovnis* (UFOs) as well, most frequently to the nearby 1950m-**Cerro Uritorco**, the highest peak in the Sierras Chicas. The 3km hike to the top affords spectacular views.

Capilla del Monte itself has plenty of restaurants and lodging, and there's a **tourist office** (☎ 03548-481903; Rivadavia 540). There is frequent bus service south to Córdoba (AR$15, three hours), stopping at all towns on the RN 38, and long-distance service to Buenos Aires.

Estancia Puesto Viejo

Billing itself as the only youth hostel set on an *estancia* in Argentina, this working ranch (☎ 05348-423809, 05348-15-566504; www

---

CLOSE ENCOUNTERS

It's not just the freaks and hippies. Even normal-looking people in Capilla del Monte have stories about strange lights appearing in formation in the night skies over nearby Cerro Uritorco. The stories go way back, too. In 1935 Manuel Reina reported seeing a strange being dressed in a tight-fitting suit while he was out walking on a country road. In 1986, Gabriel and Esperanza Gómez saw a spaceship so big that its lights illuminated the surrounding countryside. The next day a burn mark measuring 122m by 64m was found at the point where it reportedly landed.

A couple of years later, 300 people witnessed another ship, which left a burn mark 42m in diameter. And in 1991, another burn mark was found. This one measured 12m in diameter, with a temperature of 340°C. Geologists were called in and they claimed that nearby rocks had recently been heated to a temperature of 3000°C.

Why all this activity around Capilla del Monte? This is where it gets really weird. One theory is that *Ovnis* (UFOs) visit the area because Cerro Uritorco is where the knight Parsifal brought the Holy Grail and the Templar Cross at the end of the 12th century. He did this to lay them beside the Cane of Order, which had been made 8000 years before by Lord Voltán of the Comechingones, the indigenous tribe that inhabited this region.

Another theory offers that they are drawn here because underneath Uritorco lies Erks, a subterranean city which, according to 'hermetic scientists' is where the future regeneration of the human species will take place. Inside you'll find the Esfera Temple and the three mirrors used to exchange data with other galaxies, and where you can see the details of the life of every human being.

The official explanation? Good ol' meteorological phenomena, caused by supercharged ion particles in the atmosphere, mixed in with a healthy touch of mass hysteria.

Whatever you believe, one thing's for sure – all this hype isn't hurting little Capilla del Monte's tourist industry one bit. A few years ago, the only people climbing Uritorco were goatherds and a few interested townsfolk. These days, numbers can approach 1000 per day, all hoping to catch a glimpse of the mysterious lights.

.estanciapuestoviejo.com; dm/d AR$30/100) gives you the chance to live the gaucho dream without paying the deluxe prices that usually accompany it. All the farm-life activities are here – herding cattle, horseback riding etc or you can just kick back and enjoy the scenery. Also on offer are 4WD tours to the little-visited Jesuit mission at La Candelaria, gold mine tours and trekking on the Cerro Colorado. Simple, hearty meals (AR$55 per day) are available and you can use the kitchen. Access is a little tricky – from La Cumbre you have to take a taxi (one-way AR$40, 24km), but call first to see if the owners are in town and can give you a ride.

JESÚS MARÍA
☎ 03525 / pop 27,000

Sleepy little Jesús María earns its place on the map by being home to one of the most atmospheric Jesuit *estancias* in the region – the **Museo Jesuítico Nacional de Jesús María** (☎ 420126; admission AR$5; ⏰ 8am-7pm Tue-Fri, 10am-noon & 3-7pm Sat & Sun). The church and convent were built in 1618 and are set on superbly landscaped grounds. The Jesuits, after losing their operating capital to pirates off the Brazilian coast, sold wine they made here to support their university in colonial Córdoba. The museum has good archaeological pieces from indigenous groups throughout Argentina, informative maps of the missionary trajectory and well-restored (though dubiously authentic) rooms.

Jesús María is also home to the annual **Fiesta Nacional de Doma y Folklore** (www.festivaljesusmaria.com, in Spanish), a 10-day celebration of gaucho horsemanship and customs beginning the first weekend of January. The festival draws crowds from all over the country, and accusations of animal cruelty from animal rights groups, who argue that whipping horses and making them perform acrobatics in front of noisy crowds under bright lights is tantamount to torture. Or gaucho culture.

Most people do Jesús María as a day trip from Córdoba. Frequent buses (AR$5, one hour) leave Córdoba's Mercado Sud and main bus terminals (see p324) daily.

ESTANCIA SANTA CATALINA
☎ 03525

One of the most beautiful of the Sierra's Unesco World Heritage sites, the Jesuit *estancia* of **Santa Catalina** (☎ 421600; www.santacatalina.info; admission AR$3-9; ⏰ 10am-1pm & 2-6pm Tue-Fri, closed Jan, Feb, Jul & Semana Santa), some 20km northwest of Jesús María, is a quiet, tiny place, where the village store occupies part of the *estancia*, and old-timers sit on the benches outside and watch the occasional gaucho ride past on a horse. Much of the *estancia* is off-limits to visitors, but guided **tours** (each site AR$3) are available, taking in the chapel, cloisters and novitiate, where unmarried slave girls were housed.

The grounds themselves, while a fraction of their former selves, are lovely and well-maintained and you can easily while away an hour or two wandering around. Outside the *estancia*, around the back, is the original reservoir built by the Jesuits, now slowly being overtaken by tall-stemmed lilies.

Santa Catalina is the only Unesco World Heritage *estancia* still under private ownership. Part of the family owns and operates **La Ranchería de Santa Catalina** (☎ 424467, 03525-15-538957; r per person without bathroom AR$90), a lovely inn, restaurant (meals around AR$25) and crafts store in the *ranchería*. It has only two rooms, which occupy the former slave quarters and, while small, are carefully decorated and retain their original stone walls. Three more rooms with private bathrooms are being constructed, using traditional techniques (so don't expect them to be finished any time soon). The place is run by a friendly couple who are more than willing to fill you in on the illustrious story of the *estancia*, from Jesuit times to present.

A taxi out here from Jesús María costs about AR$60.

ALTA GRACIA
☎ 03547 / pop 41,000 / elev 550m

Set around a 17th-century Jesuit reservoir, Alta Gracia is a tranquil little mountain town of winding streets and shady parks. The star attraction here is the 17th-century Jesuit *estancia*, whose exquisite church, nighttime lighting, and lovely location between a tiny reservoir and the central plaza make it one of the most impressive of Córdoba's World Heritage sites. Revolutionary Che Guevara spent his adolescence in Alta Gracia and his former home is now a museum. Most visitors find a day enough and head back to Córdoba for the night.

The **tourist office** (☎ 428128; www.altagracia.gov.ar in Spanish; Reloj Público; cnr Av del Tajamar & Calle del Molino; ⏰ 7am-10:30pm summer, to 7pm winter) occupies an office in the clock tower.

Sights & Activities

THE JESUIT ESTANCIA

From 1643 to 1762, Jesuit fathers built the **Iglesia Parroquial Nuestra Señora de la Merced** (west side of Plaza Manuel Solares; admission free), the *estancia's* most impressive building. Directly south of the church, the colonial Jesuit workshops of **El Obraje** (1643) are now a public school. Beside the church is the **Museo Histórico Nacional del Virrey Liniers** (☎ 421303; www.museoliniers.org.ar; admission AR$3, Wed free; 9am-8pm Tue-Fri, 9:30am-12:30pm & 5-8pm Sat, Sun & holidays), named after former resident Virrey Liniers, one of the last officials to occupy the post of Viceroy of the River Plate. If you want to know every last historical detail, guided tours in English (AR$30 per person; 10am, 11:30am, 3:30pm and 5pm) are available and recommended – call to reserve one day in advance. If you just have a passing interest, each room has an information sheet in English, which gives you a fair idea of what's going on.

Directly north of the museum, across Av Belgrano, the **Tajamar** (1659) is one of the city's several 17th-century dams, which together made up the complex system of field irrigation created by the Jesuits.

MUSEO CASA DE ERNESTO CHE GUEVARA

In the 1930s, the family of youthful Ernesto Guevara moved here because a doctor recommended the dry climate for his asthma (see the boxed text, opposite). Though Che lived in several houses – including the house in Rosario (p182) where he was born – the family's primary residence was Villa Beatriz, which was recently purchased by the city and restored as the **museum** (☎ 428579; Avellaneda 501; admission AR$3, Wed free; 9am-7pm Tue-Sun). Its cozy interior is now adorned with a photographic display of Che's life, and a couple of huge photos commemorating a recent visit from Fidel Castro and Hugo Chávez. If you think you've been on the road for a while, check out the map detailing Che's travels through Latin America – whatever you think of the man's politics, you have to admit he was well-traveled. A small selection of Che paraphernalia (including cigars, of course) is on sale.

ADVENTURE ACTIVITIES

If all Alta Gracia's history makes you feel like throwing yourself out of a plane, contact recommended local outfit **Paracenter** (☎ 03525-15-5413816; www.paracenter.com.ar), which offers tandem skydives for AR$400.

Rent a Bike (☎ 494194; www.altagraciarentabike.com.ar) does pretty much what its name suggests, for AR$20 per day. Alta Gracia is a good place for bike riding – not much traffic and the two main sights are just far enough apart for it to be a pain to have to walk it.

Sleeping & Eating

A number of hip café/bar/restaurants with sidewalk seating are scattered along Av Belgrano in the three blocks downhill from the Jesuit museum.

Alta Gracia Hostel (☎ 428810; www.altagraciahostel.com.ar; Paraguay 218; dm AR$25) Five short blocks downhill from the Jesuit museum, Alta Gracia's hostel offers a fair deal. Dorms are roomy enough and the kitchen should meet your needs. One bizarre inconvenience: you can't check in until noon.

Hostal Hispania (☎ 426555; Av Vélez Sársfield 57; s/d AR$100/120;   ) Located in a handsome late-19th-century wooden building, this place boasts spacious rooms which open onto a covered porch (complete with chaise longues) overlooking the large garden. The attached Spanish restaurant is worth a look in, too.

Sol de Polen (☎ 427332; www.hectorcelano.com.ar; Avellaneda 529; mains AR$10-15) A few short steps from the Che museum, this Cuban-themed restaurant serves up a couple of Cuban dishes alongside all the Argentine standards. Friday nights there's live music and if you really like the place, it rents out basic double rooms at the back for AR$50.

Trattoria Oro (☎ 425619; España 18; mains AR$13-22) Varied menu and excellent service; opposite Plaza Manuel Solar.

Getting There & Away

Minibuses depart regularly for Córdoba (AR$4, one hour) from in front of the clock tower near the main plaza. The **bus terminal** (Tacuarí at Perón) near the river also has departures for Córdoba, as well as Villa Carlos Paz (AR$4, one hour) and Buenos Aires (AR$75, 13 hours). Buses to Villa General Belgrano stop every hour on RP 5, about 20 blocks along Av San Martín from the center.

VILLA GENERAL BELGRANO

☎ 03546 / pop 6000 / elev 820m

More a cultural oddity than a full-blown tourist attraction, Villa General Belgrano flaunts its origins as a settlement of unrepatriated sur-

---

THE LEGEND OF CHE GUEVARA

One of Cuba's greatest revolutionary heroes, in some ways even eclipsing Fidel Castro himself, was an Argentine. Ernesto Guevara, known by the common Argentine interjection 'che,' was born in the city of Rosario in 1928 and spent his first years in Buenos Aires. In 1932, after Guevara's doctor recommended a drier climate for his severe asthma, Guevara's parents moved to the mountain resort of Alta Gracia, where the young Guevara would spend his adolescence.

He later studied medicine in the capital and, in 1952, spent six months riding a motorcycle around South America, a journey that would steer Guevara's sights beyond middle-class Argentina to the plight of South America's poor. The journal he kept during his trip, now known as *The Motorcycle Diaries*, hit bookstore shelves around the world and inspired the movie of the same name, staring Mexico's Gael García Bernal.

After his journey, Guevara traveled to Central America and fatefully landed in Mexico, where he met Fidel Castro and other exiles. Together the small group would sail to Cuba on a rickety old yacht and begin the revolution that overthrew Cuban dictator Fulgencio Batista in 1959. Unable to resign himself to the bureaucratic task of building Cuban socialism, Guevara tried, unsuccessfully, to spread revolution in the Congo, Argentina and finally Bolivia, where he was killed in 1967.

Today Che is known less for his eloquent writings and speeches than for his striking black-and-white portrait as the beret-wearing rebel – an image gracing everything from T-shirts to CD covers – taken by photojournalist Alberto Korda in 1960. Although these commercialized versions of Che are hardly a poke at the belly of global capitalism, they have managed to irritate some: Korda sued Smirnoff in 2000 for using his famous photograph to sell vodka, and a 1998 Taco Bell ad, in which a talking, beret-wearing Chihuahua barks 'Viva Gorditas' to a cheering crowd, sparked furor in Miami's Cuban-American community.

In 1997, on the 30th anniversary of Che's death, the Argentine government issued a postage stamp honoring Che's Argentine roots. You can take a look as the stamps, as well as other government-sponsored tributes from around the world, by visiting Alta Gracia's modest but lovely Museo Casa de Ernesto Che Guevara (see opposite), inaugurated June 14, 2001, on what would have been Che's 73rd birthday.

---

vivors from the German battleship *Graf Spee*, which sank near Montevideo during WWII.

The annual **Oktoberfest** (elevated in 1972 to status of *Fiesta Nacional de la Cerveza*; National Beer Festival; see http://elsitiode-lavilla.com/oktoberfest in Spanish), held during the first two weeks of October, draws beer lovers from all over the world. In summertime, the village slowly fills with holidaymakers enjoying the tranquil streets and evergreen-dotted countryside. Unless you're really excited about microbrew beer, *torta selva negra* (black forest cake) and goulash, Villa General Belgrano makes a fine day trip from Córdoba or nearby La Cumbrecita. Despite its decidedly Germanic flavor, you'd be lucky to hear any of the modern-day inhabitants speaking the language of the old country.

For an overview of the town, make your way up the **tower** (admission AR$1; ☼ 9am-8pm) attached to the tourist office.

The **tourist office** (☎ 461215; www.vgb.gov.ar; Plaza José Hernández; ☼ 8am-8:30pm) is on the main strip.

Activities

To go horseback riding, look for Sr Martinez, who sets up behind the bus terminal in summer and charges around AR$20 an hour. Otherwise contact **Pituco Sanchez** (☎ 463142), who offers horseback riding year-round at similar prices. **Rapisenda** (☎ 463740; Ojo de Agua 90) rents mountain bikes for about AR$30 per day.

If you're up for a stroll, a lovely path runs between Corrientes and El Quebracho alongside the Arroyo La Toma, a creek one block downhill from the main street.

Sleeping & Eating

In the December-to-March high season, hotel prices rise and rooms book quickly. Unless you book weeks before Oktoberfest, plan on hitting the festival as a day trip from Córdoba.

CÓRDOBA & THE CENTRAL SIERRAS

There are numerous restaurants along the main strip of Julio A Roca and San Martín.

Albergue El Rincón (☎ 461323; rincon@calamu chitanet.com.ar; sites AR$10, dm AR$30, r per person with bathroom AR$36) This beautiful Dutch-owned hostel, surrounded by forest, has excellent, spacious dorm rooms, outdoor and indoor kitchens, a *parrilla* and its own biodynamic farm. Outstanding breakfasts cost AR$10, and lunch and dinner AR$20. It's a good 600m walk from behind the bus terminal to the entrance gate; follow the signs.

Posada Emanuel (☎ 463238; Koch 38; s/d AR$80/100; ✖ ▨) Bright, modern rooms in a new brick building on the edge of town. It's a few blocks from the action, but a lovely quiet location and rooms are much more spacious than those in the center.

Berna Hotel (☎ 461097; www.bernahotel.com.ar; Sarsfield 75; s/d from AR$190/220; ✖ ▯ ▨) Fairly ordinary rooms (it's worth paying an extra AR$40 for a suite) but excellent grounds, with an indoor and outdoor swimming pool, tennis court and manicured lawns. Sauna use is included in the price and spa treatments (extra) are available.

Arte Bar (☎ 463522; Julio A Roca 88; mains AR$15-25; ☽ lunch & dinner) Breaking the German mold that so defines General Belgrano, Arte Bar is a refreshing café serving tasty sandwiches for lunch and a changing menu for dinner. Live music starts at 10:30pm on Friday and Saturday.

Blumen (Julio A Roca 373; mains AR$20-30 ☽ lunch & dinner) With one of the widest menus in town, Blumen serves up good, tasty, if slightly expensive, dishes. It's a great spot for a few drinks – the huge shady beer garden is all wooden tables and pagodas, with plenty of space in between and the microbrew beer flowing readily.

Getting There & Away

The **bus terminal** (Av Vélez Sársfield) is uphill from San Martín, the main thoroughfare. Buses leave every hour for Córdoba (AR$12, two hours), and daily for Buenos Aires (AR$95, 11 hours). **Pajaro Blanco** (☎ 461709; cnr San Martín & Sarsfield), just down the hill from the bus terminal, has daily departures for La Cumbrecita (AR$12, two hours).

LA CUMBRECITA
☎ 03546 / pop 200

The pace of life slows waaaay down in this alpine-styled village, nestled in the forest in the Valle de Calamuchita. The tranquility is largely thanks to the town's pedestrian-only policy. It's a great place to kick back for a few days and wander the forest trails leading to swimming holes, waterfalls and scenic lookouts.

Visitors must park their cars in the dirt parking lot (AR$6) before crossing the bridge over Río del Medio by foot.

The helpful **tourist office** (☎ 481088; www.lacumbre cita.gov.ar in Spanish; ☽ 8:30am-9pm summer, 10am-6pm winter) is on the left, just before you cross the bridge into town.

Sights & Activities

The best reason to visit La Cumbrecita is to hike. Short trails are well marked and the tourist office offers a crude but useful map of the area. A 25-minute stroll will take you to **La Cascada**, a waterfall tucked into the mountainside. **La Olla** is the closest swimming hole, surrounded by granite rocks (people jump where it's deep enough). **Cerro La Cumbrecita** (1400m) is the highest point in town, about a 20-minute walk from the bridge. Outside town, the highest mountain is the poetically named **Cerro Wank** (1715m); a hike to the top takes about 40 minutes.

For guided hikes further into the mountains, as well as horseback riding (AR$50 for three hours), trout fishing and mountain biking, contact **Cumbrecita Viajes** (☎ 481087, 03546-15-475168; Las Truchas s/n), which has an office on the main road in town. The company can also take you trekking to the top of **Cerro Champaquí** (2790m), the highest peak in the sierras, for about AR$80 per person.

If the whole Disneyland feel of La Cumbrecita isn't enough for you, check out **Peñon del Aguila** (☎ 0351-15-552-5232; www.penonde laguila.com.ar; child/adult AR$10/20; ☽ 11am-7pm daily in summer, weekends only rest of yr), a theme park offering 'alpine adventures'. Rappelling, ziplining, a canopy boardwalk, nature trails and waterfalls are all in abundance, cheerfully guided by folks in Tirolese outfits. The whole show wraps up with a sunset song and dance spectacular paying homage to Gambrinus, the king of beer. We kid you not.

Sleeping & Eating

La Cumbrecita has more than 20 hotels and *cabañas* in the surrounding hills; the tourist office is a good resource. Make reservations in summer (January and February), during Easter and during Villa General Belgrano's

Oktoberfest (see p333). Hard-core budget travelers will find few options.

Hospedaje Casa Rosita (☎ 481003; Calle Pública s/n; s/d with/without bathroom AR$120/60) A humble little *hospedaje* (family home) set in a charming house by the river at the entrance to the village. If you can, go for room 1, which has a bay window overlooking the river.

La Campana (☎ 481062; lacampana@lacumbrecita.info; r AR$120) Tucked away in the center of town, this cozy place offers giant rooms with fully equipped kitchenettes.

Hotel La Cumbrecita (☎ 481052; www.hotelcumbre cita.com.ar; s/d AR$220/250; 🖭 🖭) Built on the site of the first house in La Cumbrecita, this rambling hotel has some excellent views out over the valley. Rooms aren't huge, but most have fantastic balconies. The extensive grounds include a gym and tennis courts. Half pensión (breakfast and dinner) is available for AR$25.

Confitería Tante Liesbeth (☎ 481079; 🕙 4-7:30pm Thu-Sun summer, 4-7:30pm Sat & Sun winter) On the north side of town, on the way to Cerro Wank, this is the village's most traditional teahouse, set creekside among the trees. It's about a 10-minute walk from the entrance to town.

El Paseo (☎ 03546-15-650395; mains AR$10-20) Marvelous outdoor deck right above La Olla swimming hole. Great for afternoon beer.

Restaurante Bar Suizo (Calle Pública s/n; mains AR$12-25; 🕙 breakfast, lunch & dinner) Pull up a wooden bench under the pine tree and try some of the excellent Swiss German options like *spaetzle* with wild mushroom sauce (AR$15).

Getting There & Away

From Villa General Belgrano, **Transportes Pajaro Blanco** (☎ 461709; cnr San Martín & Sarsfield), across and just downhill from the bus terminal, has departures to La Cumbrecita (AR$12, two hours, 7am, 10am, noon, 4pm and 6:50pm Monday through Friday, 8am, 10am, noon, 4pm and 6:50pm Saturday and Sunday). There are occasional minibuses (AR$23, three hours) from Córdoba's Mercado Sud terminal (see p324).

PARQUE NACIONAL QUEBRADA DEL CONDORITO

elev 1900-2300m

This national park protects 370 sq km of stunning rocky grasslands across the Pampa de Achala in the Sierras Grandes. The area, particularly the *quebrada* (gorge) itself, is an important condor nesting site and flight training ground for fledgling condors. A 9km, two-

to three-hour hike from the park entrance at **La Pampilla** leads to the Balcón Norte (North Balcony), a cliff top over the gorge where you can view the massive birds circling on the thermals rising up the gorge. You can visit easily as a day trip from Córdoba or on your way to Mina Clavero.

Any bus from Córdoba to Mina Clavero will drop you at La Pampilla (AR$15, about 1½ hours), where a trailhead leads to the gorge. To return to Córdoba (or on to Mina Clavero), flag a bus from the turnout. Latitud Sur (p320) offers recommended day tours to the park for AR$100 per person.

For more information contact **Intendencia del PN Quebrada del Condorito** (☎ 03541-433371, 03541-15-621727; www.quebradacondorito.com.ar; Sabattini 33) in Villa Carlos Paz.

MINA CLAVERO

☎ 03544 / pop 6850 / elev 915m

Really jumping in summertime, Mina Clavero pretty much empties out for the rest of the year, leaving visitors to explore the limpid streams, rocky waterfalls, numerous swimming holes and idyllic mountain landscapes at their own pace.

Mina Clavero is 170km southwest of Córdoba via RN 20, the splendid Nuevo Camino de las Altas Cumbres (Highway of the High Peaks). It sits at the confluence of Río de Los Sauces and Río Panaholma, in the Valle de Traslasierra.

The Río Mina Clavero splits the town in two – if you arrive at the bus terminal and are headed for Residencial El Parral or La Casa de Pipa, take the pedestrian bridge across the river – from there it's only a couple of blocks to the former and a short taxi ride to the latter. Otherwise you have to go the long way around.

The **tourist office** (☎ 470171; www.minaclavero.gov .ar in Spanish; Av San Martín 1464; 🕙 7am-midnight Dec-Mar, 9am-9pm Apr-Nov) has standard brochures and a useful map of town.

Sights & Activities

Mina Clavero's *balnearios* (swimming areas) get mobbed in the summer, but are often empty the rest of the year. The magnificent, boulder-strewn gorges of the Río Mina Clavero are easily explored. A lovely *costanera* has been constructed, running from the pedestrian bridge all the way to the **Nido de Aguila**, the best swimming hole around – this makes for a great afternoon stroll or bike ride. From there head west along the Río de Los Sauces and you'll hit **Los Elefantes**, a *balneario* named for its elephant-like rock formations. A 3km walk south along the river will take you to the village of **Villa Cura Brochero**, where you'll find black pottery characteristic of this region.

Bicicletas Racing (Intendente Vila & Uruguay) rents bikes for AR$15 per day. **Traslasierra Aventura** (☎ 471516; www.traslasierramix.com.ar; San Martín 1241) offers tours of the nearby Comechingones mountains, condor spotting and horse trekking.

Sleeping

Many accommodations close around the end of March, when the town almost rolls up the sidewalks.

Residencial El Parral (☎ 470005; Av Intendente Vila 1430; s/d AR$70/80; ☺ Oct-May) Run by a delightful older woman, this small *residencial* (cheap hotel) has plain rooms and a small backyard. It's no frills but it's comfortable, clean and the best price you'll find in town. It's one block uphill from San Martín.

Hotel Palace (☎ 470390; www.comprasvirtual.com /hotelpalace; Mitre 847; s/d AR$70/100) The highlight of this 40-room French-owned hotel is the huge backyard that slopes to the riverside. Shade trees and lounge chairs make it tough to leave the grounds. Rooms are slightly worn, but the garden makes up for it.

La Casa de Pipa (☎ 470480; www.lacasadepipa.com, in Spanish; Hernán Cortés at Colón; s/d AR$140/180; ☺ closed May & Jun; ☒ ☒) A beautiful *hostería* (lodging house) set on mildly sloping grounds. There's plenty of shady spots, a good pool, a couple of barbecues and a lovely sunny breakfast room with views out over the mountains. It's about five blocks uphill from San Martín.

Hotel Rossetti (☎ 470012; www.hotelrossettiyspa.com .ar; Mitre 1434; all-inclusive packages AR$360) A sparkling hotel/spa complex in a slightly unfortunate location on a busy thoroughfare. Summer prices include meals, drinks and spa treatments. Off-season, doubles go for AR$80 (room only) and individual spa treatments cost AR$25 each.

Eating

Most of Mina Clavero's restaurants are along San Martín.

Palenque (San Martín 1191; mains AR$15-23; ☺ lunch & dinner) Funky works of art on the walls and live music on the weekends make this a popular spot. It's a great place for drinks and the Tex Mex flavored snacks and meals are a good deal, too.

Cuba Bar (San Martín 1270; mains AR$15-20; ☺ breakfast, lunch & dinner) Out the back of the Galería Mina Clavero, the Cuba is noteworthy for three things – real breakfasts (including scrambled eggs – AR$10), a pool table and a great deck overlooking the river.

Don Alonso (cnr San Martín & Recalde; mains AR$18-25; ☺ lunch & dinner) The most frequently recommended *parrilla* in town, the Don serves up tasty empanadas and good-value set meals in front of the plaza.

Rincón Suizo (☎ 470447; Champaqui 1200; mains AR$20-30; ☺ lunch & dinner) This comfy teahouse on the river prides itself on its homemade ice creams, delicious Swiss food (including fondue, raclette and ratatouille) and *torta selva negra*.

Getting There & Away

The **bus terminal** (Mitre 1191) is across the Río Mina Clavero from the town center. There are several daily buses to Córdoba (AR$20, three hours), Villa Carlos Paz (AR$14, 2½ hours) and at least three a day to Merlo (AR$17, 2½ to three hours). Minibuses to Córdoba are faster (AR$20, 2½ hours). **TAC** (☎ 470420) has daily service to Buenos Aires (AR$90, 13 hours). For destinations in San Juan and Mendoza, go to nearby Villa Dolores (AR$6, one hour).

AROUND MINA CLAVERO
Museo Rocsen & Nono

Operated by Juan Santiago Bouchon, an anthropologist, curator and passionate collector who first came to Argentina in 1950 as cultural attaché to the French embassy, this eclectic **museum** (☎ 03544-498218; www.museorocsen .org; admission AR$5; ☺ 9am-sunset) reveals just how strange the world really is. It contains more than 11,000 pieces including antique motorcycles, mounted butterflies, Esso gas pumps, human skulls, Buddha statues, film projectors, Catholic altars, 19th-century instruments of torture, a shrunken head and a 1200-year-old Peruvian mummy. It's truly a one-of-a-kind museum, and requires plenty of time to explore.

The museum is 5km outside the pastoral village of **Nono**, a one-time indigenous settlement 8km south of Mina Clavero. There are regular minibuses from Mina Clavero to Nono's main plaza, from where you'll have to take a taxi (about AR$10 one way) or walk to the museum. If you do take a taxi, arrange for the driver to come back for you. A taxi from Mina Clavero to Nono costs AR$15.

SAN LUIS & AROUND

The little-visited province of San Luis holds a surprising number of attractions, made all the better by the fact that you'll probably have them all to yourself.

The province is popularly known as La Puerta de Cuyo (the door to Cuyo), referring to the combined provinces of Mendoza, San Luis and San Juan (see also the boxed text, p347).

The regional superstar is without doubt the Parque Nacional Sierra de las Quijadas, but the mountain towns along the Valle de Conlara and Sierras Puntanas are well worth a visit if you're looking to get off the tourist trail.

SAN LUIS

☎ 02652 / pop 153,350 / elev 700m

Even people from San Luis will tell you that the best of the province lies outside of the capital.

That said, it's not a bad little town – there are a few historic sights and the central Plaza Pringles is one of the prettiest in the country. The town's main nightlife strip, Av Illia, with its concentration of bars, cafés and restaurants, makes for a fun night out.

Orientation

On the north bank of the Río Chorrillos, San Luis is 260km from Mendoza via RN 7, 456km from Córdoba via RN 148 and 850km from Buenos Aires via either RN 7 or RN 8.

The commercial center is along the parallel streets of San Martín and Rivadavia between Plaza Pringles in the north and Plaza Independencia in the south.

Information

Several banks, mostly around Plaza Pringles, have ATMs.

ACA (Automóvil Club Argentino; ☎ 423188; Av Illia 401) Argentina's auto club; good source for provincial road maps.

Ciber Max (cnr Pedrera & Caseros; per hr AR$2; ⏰ 8am–5am) For that late-night email binge. There are countless other cybercafés downtown.

CÓRDOBA & THE CENTRAL SIERRAS

Las Quijadas Turismo (☎ 431683; San Martín 874) Tours to Parque Nacional Sierra de las Quijadas, La Angostura and Inti Huasi.

Post office (cnr Av Illia & San Martín)

Regional hospital (☎ 422627; Av República Oriental del Uruguay 150) On the eastward extension of Bolívar.

Tourist office (☎ 423957, 423479; www.turismoensanluis.gov.ar; intersection of Junín, San Martín & Av Illia; ☻ 8am-8pm) The helpful staff can supply a good map of the town and its attractions.

Sights & Activities

The center of town is the beautiful tree-filled Plaza Pringles, anchored on its eastern side by San Luis' handsome 19th-century **cathedral** (Rivadavia). Provincial hardwoods such as algarrobo were used for the cathedral's windows and frames, and local white marble for its steps and columns.

On the north side of nearby Plaza Independencia is the provincial **Casa de Gobierno** (government house). On the south side of the plaza, the **Iglesia de Santo Domingo** (cnr 25 de Mayo & San Martín) and its convent date from the 1930s, but reproduce the Moorish style of the 17th-century building they replaced. Take a peek at the striking algarrobo doors of the attached **Archivo Histórico Provincial** around the corner on San Martín.

Dominican friars at the **mercado artesanal** (cnr 25 de Mayo & Rivadavia; ☻ 8am-1pm Mon-Fri), next to Iglesia de Santo Domingo, sell gorgeous handmade wool rugs as well as ceramics, onyx crafts and weavings from elsewhere in the province.

Also stroll over to the handsome former **train station** (Avs Illia & Lafinur) for a look at its green corrugated-metal roofs and decorative ironwork dating from 1884. Rumors abound that the bus terminal may be moving here, but so far there's no sign of that happening.

Sleeping

San Luis' better hotels cater to a business crowd, filling up quickly on weekdays and offering discounts on weekends.

San Luis Hostel (☎ 424188; www.sanluishostel.com.ar; Falucho 646; dm AR$20) San Luis' best and most central hostel has it all, from pool table to DVD library, excellent kitchen and shady backyard with barbecue. The 16-person dorms (segregated for male and female) could be a bit more atmospheric, but apart from that it's pure gold.

Hotel Castelmonte (☎ 424963; Chacabuco 769; s/d AR$60/80; 🖳) An excellent-value midrange hotel.

Spacious rooms have wooden parquetry floors and firm new beds. It's central, but set back from the road, keeping things nice and quiet.

Hotel Aiello (☎ 425609; www.hotelaiello.com; Av Illia 431; s/d AR$130/170; 🖳 🖳) With its low-slung hacienda vibe the Aiello has what so many of San Luis' hotels are lacking – character. It's all very comfortable here, with patios spread around and an excellent pool area featuring a kids' pool, a good-sized main pool and a shady grassy corner with deck chairs.

Hotel Quintana (☎ 438400; Av Illia 546; s/d AR$160/230; 🖳 🖳 🖳) The best setup hotel in town, the Quintana lays it all out for the business set with a serene lobby area leading on to restaurants, bars and a small pool area out back. Rooms are comfortable but nothing special.

Eating & Drinking

Traditional San Luis dishes include *locro, empanadas de horno* (baked empanadas) and *cazuela de gallina* (chicken soup).

Bahia Café (cnr Pringles & Av San Martín; mains AR$10-20; ☻ breakfast, lunch & dinner) For plazaside café action and frenzied, middle-aged waiters, you can't go past the Bahia. At night they put tables out on the plaza in front, making it a great spot for drinks, snacks and people watching.

Las Pircas (Pringles 1417; mains AR$10-20; ☻ lunch & dinner) A friendly neighborhood *parrilla* with excellent prices (maybe thanks to an outrageous amount of advertising on the menu) – try the *bife de chorizo* (AR$15) or a whole grilled kid goat (AR$24).

La Plazoleta (cnr Av Illia & Lavalle; mains AR$20-35; ☻ lunch & dinner) San Luis' most frequently recommended restaurant is a definite step above the competition in terms of service and atmosphere. The menu is fairly standard, with the odd Mediterranean or Middle Eastern surprise thrown in.

There are numerous laid-back bars along Av Illia. As is the deal all over the country, they start late and end late. Go for a stroll and see which one you like.

Getting There & Around

AIR

The **San Luis airport** (☎ 422427/57) is only 3km northwest of the center; taxis cost around AR$15.

Aerolíneas Argentinas (☎ 425671, 437981; Av Illia 472) flies twice daily to Buenos Aires (AR$490) via San Rafael (AR$200) except weekends, when there's one flight daily.

BUS & CAR
Unless it's suddenly moved to the old train station (cnr Avs Illia & Lafinur), San Luis' **bus terminal** (☎ 424021; España, btwn San Martín & Rivadavia) is about six blocks north of the main plaza. Provincial destinations including Merlo (AR$15, four hours), El Volcán (AR$3, 30 minutes), Carolina (AR$8, two hours), Inti Huasi (AR$2, 30 minutes), La Toma (AR$6 1½ hours) and Balde (AR$3, 45 minutes) are served by local operators, whose ticket offices are in a separate building just in front of the main terminal complex.

There are long distance departures daily to the destinations in the following table. For destinations such as Neuquén and Bariloche, you must head to Mendoza or San Rafael.

Destination	Cost (AR$)	Duration (hr)
Buenos Aires	95	11
Córdoba	50	6
Mar del Plata	140	18
Mendoza	30	4
Paraná	90	11
Resistencia	88	12
Rosario	90	7
San Juan	30	4
San Rafael	28	4
Santa Fe	85	10

Hertz (☎ 02652-15-549002; Av Illia 305) is the local car rental agency.

AROUND SAN LUIS
Balde
☎ 02652
This small village, 35km west of San Luis, is remarkable only for its thermal baths. The municipal complex is a decidedly down-at-heel affair, while a new spa resort offers oodles of comfort in gorgeous surrounds.

Centro Termal Municipal (☎ 499319; Av Esteban Agüero s/n; 1hr baths per person AR$6, cabins for 2 people AR$50, camp sites AR$5; ⏰ baths 8am-6pm) is a budget-friendly alternative to Los Tamarindos up the road, offering small rooms with a bath and a bed to relax, rented by the hour. They're clean enough and decent value for a quick dip. Cabins (located across the road) are spacious for two, with kitchen facilities, but no thermal water piped in.

Los Tamarindos (☎ 499319; Av Esteban Agüero s/n; r AR$120, cabins s/d AR$120/160; ⏰ baths 8am-6pm) is a wonderful thermal baths complex featuring a couple of public pools for day use – an out-door one at 26°C (AR$15 per person) and a lovely, clean indoor one (AR$25 for both). The rooms here are standard, with small baths fed by hot spring water, but the cabins are a real treat – they're much more spacious and have a separate tub where you can get neck deep in the water. Hotel guests have access to the hot baths included in the price and there are a variety of spa treatments (mudpacks, massages etc) available. The whole complex is set on leafy grounds and is pure relaxation, especially midweek.

Regular buses run to and from San Luis' bus terminal to the bus terminal at Balde (AR$3, 45 minutes), which is a short walk to either of the complexes.

El Volcán
☎ 02652 / pop 1420
A small village nestled in the hills outside of San Luis, El Volcán (there is no volcano here, by the way) is a laid-back summer getaway spot. The star attraction is the river that runs through the middle of town, where Balneario La Hoya, a series of natural rock pools, offers shady swimming spots and picnic areas.

El Volcán is close enough to San Luis to make it an easy day trip, but there are plenty of cabins for rent, especially during summer.

Hotel El Volcán (☎ 494044; Banda Norte s/n; s/d AR$150/180; ✖ ⛄) is the only real hotel in the village. It's a sprawling complex set on shady grounds that run down to the river. The hotel closes off-season – call ahead to make sure it's open. **El Mantial** (Balneario La Hoya; mains AR$12-20; ⏰ breakfast, lunch & dinner) has decent food and great views out over the river. Portions are big and service is quick, if somewhat impersonal.

Regular buses run to and from San Luis' main bus terminal (AR$2.50, 30 minutes).

PARQUE NACIONAL SIERRA DE LAS QUIJADAS
Fans of the Road Runner cartoon will feel oddly at home among the red sandstone rock formations in this rarely visited **national park** (admission AR$20). The park comprises 1500 sq km of canyons and dry lake beds among the Sierra de las Quijadas, whose peaks reach 1200m at Cerro Portillo. Recent paleontological excavations by the Universidad Nacional de San Luis and New York's Museum of Natural History unearthed dinosaur tracks and fossils from the Lower Cretaceous, about 120 million years ago.

Despite the shortage of visitors here, access to the park is excellent: buses from San Luis to San Juan will drop visitors just beyond the village of Hualtarán, about 110km northwest of San Luis via RN 147 (which is the highway to San Juan, 210km to the northwest). At this point, a 6km dirt road leads west to a viewpoint overlooking the **Potrero de la Aguada**, a scenic depression beneath the peaks of the sierra that collects the runoff from much of the park and is a prime wildlife area. It's sometimes possible to catch a lift from the junction, where the park rangers have a house, to the overlook.

Hiking possibilities are excellent in the park, but the complex canyons require a tremendous sense of direction or, preferably, the assistance of a local guide. Even experienced hikers should beware of summer rains and flash floods, which make the canyons extremely dangerous. Guides can be hired at the park entrance.

There's a shady **campground** (sites free), near the overlook, and a small store with groceries and drinks, including very welcome ice-cold beer.

Buses traveling from San Luis to San Juan will drop you at the park entrance and ranger station (AR$10, 1½ hours), from where it's a 6km walk to Portrero de la Aguada, where you can hire guides. Two-hour, 3km treks to see the famous dinosaur footprints leave hourly between 9am and 4pm and cost AR$17 per person. Four-hour treks to a 150m-deep canyon in the park leave at 1:30pm and cost AR$25. A minimum group size of two people applies to both treks. Buses from San Juan to San Luis pass every hour or so, but they don't always stop.

VALLE DE LAS SIERRAS PUNTANAS

From San Luis the RP 9 snakes its way northwards, following the course of the Río Grande. Along the way, small villages are slowly developing themselves as tourist destinations while still retaining much of their original character. The picturesque mining town of Carolina and nearby Inti Huasi cave are highlights of the region, and the landscapes higher up in the valley, with their rolling meadows and stone fences, probably resemble the Scottish highlands more than anything you've seen in Argentina so far.

Estancia Las Verbenas

Set in a gorgeous glade in the Valle de Pancanta, this **estancia** (☎ 02652-430918; RP 9, Km 68; per person with full board AR$75) does rustic to the hilt, with

plenty of hearty food served up among animal-skin decoration and rough-hewn furniture. Rooms are basic but comfortable. Two-hour horseback-riding tours (AR$25 per person) to a nearby waterfall are bound to be a highlight of your stay here. The signposted entrance to the property is just after the bridge on the highway, from where it's another 4km to the farmhouse. If you're coming by bus, call and they'll pick you up from the highway.

Carolina
☎ 02651 / pop 200 / elev 1610m

Nestled between the banks of the Río Grande and the foothills of Cerro Tomalasta (2020m), Carolina is a photogenic little village of stone houses and dirt roads. Take away the power lines and you could be stepping back in time 100 years. The region boomed in 1785 when the Spanish moved in to exploit local gold mines that had first been used by the Inca. Nobody uses street addresses in Carolina – the town is small enough to navigate without them.

SIGHTS & ACTIVITIES

One of the quirkier museums in the country, **Museo de Poesia** (admission free; ⏰ 10am-6pm Tue-Sat) honors San Luis' favorite son, poet Juan Cristofer Lafinur. The museum has a few artifacts from the poet's life, plus handwritten homages to the man by some of Argentina's leading poets.

Across the creek and up the hill from the poetry museum is a small **stone labyrinth**, set on the hilltop. It should provide you with an hour or so of entertainment (or, if your sense of direction is really bad, days of frustration).

Huellas Turismo (☎ 02652-431683; www.huellas turismo.com.ar) is the local tour operator – it can set you up with tours of the local gold mine (AR$20, two hours), rock climbing and rappelling trips on Cerro Tomalasta, and tours of Inti Huasi, La Casa de la Piedra Pintada and La Angostura.

SLEEPING & EATING

Formal accommodations are light on the ground in Carolina. If the hotel isn't open (or too pricey), ask in the restaurants for a *casa de familia*; rooms with shared bathroom rent for around AR$20 per person.

La Posta del Caminante (☎ 490223; www.laposta delcaminante.com.ar; RP 9 s/n; s/d AR$120/150; ▣) Carolina's one true hotel is set in a gorgeous stone building on the edge of town. A lovely seminatural rock swimming pool out the back completes the picture. The hotel is open mainly in summer, so if you're set on staying here, call ahead.

La Tomalasta (mains AR$10-15; ☾ breakfast, lunch & dinner) Good-value home-cooked meals. If it looks like it's closed, go around the back to the general store and ask them to open up.

GETTING THERE & AWAY
Regular buses run from Carolina to San Luis (AR$8, two hours), passing through El Volcán. Some continue on to Inti Huasi (AR$2, 30 minutes).

Around Carolina
INTI HUASI
This wide, shallow **cave** (admission free; ☾ daylight hr), whose name means 'house of the sun' in Quechua, makes an interesting stop, as much for the gorgeous surrounding countryside as the cave itself. Radiocarbon dating suggests that the cave was first inhabited by the Ayampitín some 8000 years ago. There are regular buses here from San Luis (AR$9, 2½ hours), passing through Carolina (AR$2, 30 minutes).

LA CASA DE LA PIEDRA PINTADA
Coming from Carolina, 3km before the Inti Huasi cave, a dirt track turns off to Paso de los Reyes. From the turnoff, it's an easy 5km sign-posted walk to **La Casa de la Piedra Pintada** (admission free), where more than 50 rock carvings are easily visible in the rock face. Follow the signs until you reach an open meadow at the base of Cerro Sololasta and you see the new cable-and-wood walkway up the cliff face that gives you access to the site. Once you're finished with the rock art, continue up the hill for spectacular views out over the Sierras Puntanas.

If you're unsure about getting here on your own, there's usually someone around at Inti Huasi who will guide you for a nominal fee.

LA ANGOSTURA
This site, 22km north of El Trapiche, holds one of the most extensive collections of indigenous rock art in the region. There's somewhere around 1000 examples here, painted and carved onto a shallow concave cliff face. Some are wonderfully preserved, while others fade with exposure to the weather. Keep an eye out for three mortar holes carved into the rock floor; they were most likely used to grind grain.

The site is tricky to access, even with a private vehicle. On the El Trapiche–Paso de los Reyes road, a signpost leads off to the right, through a closed (but not locked) gate. From there, it's 2.5km along a very bad dirt road to an abandoned stone farmhouse where the road ends.

The trail to the site is unmarked, but if you head uphill, veering right, you'll reach a stone bluff on the hilltop, giving excellent views out over the valley. Descending on the right side of the bluff, you'll see the wire fence set up to protect the works of art.

Tour operators in Carolina (see opposite) and San Luis (see p337), including the San Luis Hostel (p338), come out here, but it's not a popular excursion – get a group together, or expect to pay top dollar.

VALLE DE CONLARA
Heading northeast to Merlo from San Luis, the landscape changes dramatically as the road climbs into the hills. Around La Toma the land is arid and desertlike, Papagayos has its own unique vistas, punctuated by palm trees, and Merlo is a lush mountain town, comprising (as you'll no doubt be told more than once), a microclimate.

La Toma
☎ 02655 / pop 6660
A dusty little town plonked down by the side of RP 20, La Toma owes its existence to the mineral riches in the surrounding hills. This is the only place in the world where green onyx is mined. The stone is soft and hard to work, so not much jewelry is made out of it, but several shops around town sell souvenirs made from green onyx and other local stones.

Tours of the local mines can be arranged at the **Cooperativa Telefónica office** (☎ 421400; Belgrano & Moreno; 2hr tours AR$20). Tours leave at 10am, Monday to Friday.

If you're interested in seeing the workshops (and the working conditions therein), drop in to **Onix Olimpia** (☎ 421732; H Yrigoyen & Av Centenario) and ask about a free tour. Workers will whip up a Holy Mary head right before your eyes, in about two minutes.

Hostería El Indio (☎ 421393; www.hosteriaelindio.com.ar; cnr Av San Martín & 7 de Mayo; s/d AR$35/65; ☑) is the best place to stay in town, featuring large, cool rooms with leopard-skin-print bedspreads.

Italia Hotel (Belgrano 644; mains AR$15-25) is the town's one true restaurant, serving up some reasonable set meals and tasty empanadas.

Estancia La Estanzuela

Set on a Jesuit mission dating from 1750, this gorgeous **estancia** (☎ 02656-420559; www.estanzuela .com.ar; per person with full board AR$180; 🔊) has been left in near-original condition from the days when it was a working farm. Floors are wood or stone, walls are meter-thick adobe and many ceilings are constructed in the traditional gaucho style. The house is decorated like a museum, with antique furniture, paintings and family heirlooms galore. A small pond that the Jesuits built for irrigation serves for romantic rowboating outings and there is plenty of horseback riding and nature walking to be done. This is a very special – near-magical – place and the minimum three-night stay would not be hard to adhere to. Prices include meals, drinks and activities. The property is located 2km off RP 1, between Villa del Carmen and Papagayos. The closest public transport is to Papagayos (see following). Reservations are essential and must be made at least two days in advance. If you don't have your own transport, ask about getting picked up in Papagayos or San Luis.

Papagayos

☎ 02656 / pop 275

Possibly the last thing you're expecting to see in this part of the world is a valley full of palm trees, but that's exactly where this small town is located. The town is located on the banks of the Arroyo Papagayos and has huge Caranday palms surrounding it, giving the area a certain notoriety for handicrafts made from their trunks and branches.

Small stores (mostly attached to workshops) selling these *artesanías en palma* are scattered around town. Rosa López (in front of plaza) has the best range. The tourist office can provide a map showing all the store locations, along with other local attractions.

The Arroyo (creek) is a good place to cool off – its length is dotted with swimming holes. For a more formal swimming environment, the Balneario Municipal offers swimming pools, picnic and BBQ areas.

For horseback riding and trekking to local waterfalls and swimming spots out of town, ask at the tourist office or Hostería Los Leños.

The **Oficina de Turismo** (☎ 480093; www.papagayos .gov.ar; RP 1 s/n; 🕐 8am-8pm) is useful for contacting guides and arranging tours, and has decent maps of the town.

Hostería Los Leños (☎ 478289; www.hosterialoslenios .com.ar; Av Comechingones 555; s/d AR$120/150; 🔊) is the best-looking hotel in town, featuring fresh new rooms with spacious bathrooms and a good sized swimming pool. Also on offer are excellent home-cooked meals (mains AR$15 to AR$30) and staff can set you up with a picnic lunch if you're off on a day trip.

From Papagayos' main plaza there are regular buses to Merlo (AR$3, one hour).

Merlo

☎ 02656 / pop 12,000 / elev 890m

Merlo is a growing resort known for its gentle microclimate (the local tourist industry buzzword) in a relatively dry area. The town is located 200km northeast of the city of San Luis, tucked into the northeast corner of San Luis province.

The **municipal tourist office** (☎ 476078; Coronel Mercau 605; 🕐 8am-8pm) has maps and information on hotels and campgrounds.

SIGHTS & ACTIVITIES

For a sweeping view of the town and valley, head up to the Mirador del Sol. Buses leave from the old bus terminal and cost AR$4 for the 40-minute ride. If you've got your walking shoes on (or better, have a private vehicle), you can continue on this road another 12km to the Mirador de los Condores, which is up on the mountain ridge, and gives views in both directions. There's a **confitería** (mains AR$10-20) up here and if the wind is right, you can watch the parasailing maniacs taking off from the nearby launchpad.

Two kilometers from the center, in Rincon del Este, on the road to the Miradors, the **Reserva Natural de Merlo** (admission free; 🕐 daylight hr) is a lovely spot for creekside walks up to a couple of swimming holes. The obligatory ziplines have been installed here and you can go whizzing through the canopy overhead for AR$30. **El Rincon del Paraiso** (set meals AR$12-30; 🕐 breakfast & lunch), about 400m from the park entrance, is a beautiful, shady restaurant in the middle of the park – a great place for lunch or a couple of drinks.

Volando Bajo (☎ 476248; Pringles 459) is the most established of the plethora of tour operators in town. It offers tours to the nearby archaeological/paleontological park at Bajo de Veliz (half-day AR$50) and a trip combining the Nature Reserve, and Miradors de Sol and de los Condores (half-day AR$40). Tandem parasailing flights cost around AR$180 and last 20 to 30 minutes, depending on wind conditions.

SLEEPING

Posada del Angel (☎ 479724; Av de los Incas 440; s/d AR$70/90; 🌐 🐾) In the leafy suburbs of Piedra Blanca just north of the center, this friendly little posada offers good-sized, modern rooms. Some have bunk beds and a mezzanine, meaning you could squeeze in four people.

Hostería Cerro Azul (☎ 478648; cerroazul2003@yahoo.com; cnr Saturno & Jupiter; s/d AR$120/150; 🐾) This bright new hotel just off the main drag offers big rooms with spacious bathrooms and tiny TVs. The lounge/dining area is gorgeous, with high cathedral ceilings.

Hotel Casa Blanca (☎ 475084; www.casablancamerlo.com.ar; Av del Sol 50; s/d from AR$180/210; 🌐 💻 🐾) A large business-style hotel right in the center. The slightly faded rooms are compensated for by two hectares of woodsy grounds and the covered swimming pool, which is open year-round.

EATING & DRINKING

Cirano (Av del Sol 280; mains AR$12-24; 🕐 lunch & dinner) Ignore the flashing fairy lights – there are some good-value eats on offer here, and an excellent set lunch or dinner for AR$16.

Giorgio (Av del Sol s/n; mains AR$18-35; 🕐 lunch & dinner) Some excellent, creative mixes here, along with hearty standards such as wild mushroom risotto (AR$24) and *bife de chorizo* (AR$19). Leave room for the tiramisu.

La Cerveceria (Av del Sol 515) If you're looking for a beer, this is your spot – there's eight different types of microbrew on offer, plus

the national and imported standbys, sidewalk seating and snacks.

GETTING THERE & AWAY

Long distance buses leave from the **new terminal** (RN 1 at Calle de las Ovejas), about eight blocks south of the center. Departures include the following.

Destination	Cost (AR$)	Duration (hr)
Buenos Aires	80	12
Córdoba	33	6
El Volcán	14	4
La Toma	10	3
Mendoza	70	7
Mina Clavero	20	3
Papagayos	3	1
San Luis	28	4
Villa Carlos Paz	30	5

GETTING AROUND

Local buses leave from the **old bus terminal** (☎ 492858; cnr Pringles & Los Almendres) in the center of town. There are departures for the Mirador del Sol (AR$4, 40 minutes), Piedra Blanca (AR$1.50, 20 minutes), Bajo de Veliz (AR$6, one hour), Papagayos (AR$3, one hour) and the nearby artisan village of Cerro de Oro (AR$1.50, 30 minutes).

Merlo Rent a Car (☎ 473949; www.merlorentacar.com.ar; cnr Av del Sol & Pelligrini) is the local car-rental operator.

Center Bikes (☎ 02656-15-641805; Pringles 586) rents bikes for AR$15 per day. Call to arrange drop off and pick up at your hotel.

Mendoza & the Central Andes

A long, narrow sliver of desert landscape jammed up against the eastern foothills of the Andes, this region gains its fame from all that is good about traveling in Argentina. To start with, this is where 70% of the country's wine is produced, and even if you have only a passing interest in the nectar of the gods, Mendoza is pretty much an obligatory stop on your itinerary. It's a lively, cosmopolitan city whose tasting rooms and wine stores are unrivaled in the country. In the surrounding area, hundreds of wineries offer tours – an educational (and occasionally intoxicating) way to spend an afternoon or a month.

If you can put your glass down for a minute, there's plenty more to keep you busy here. The nearby Andes are home to Aconcagua, the Americas' highest peak and a favorite for mountain climbers the world over. A couple of ski resorts give you the chance to drop into fresh powder with Argentina's jet set, or go off-piste on rugged Nordic or dogsledding expeditions. If none of that's ringing your bell, a slew of Mendoza-based operators offer rafting, mountain biking and paragliding, among other adventures.

To the north, San Juan province is often overlooked, but well worth a visit, as much for its small but important selection of wineries (producing some of the country's top syrah and whites) as for the Parque Provincial Ischigualasto, a near-surreal desert landscape whose cartoonlike eroded rock forms hold fossils dating from the first life forms to the Triassic era. Or make your way to Rodeo, one of the windiest places on earth, for some high-speed windsurfing action.

HIGHLIGHTS

- Carve tracks in fresh powder on the world-class slopes of **Las Leñas** (p369)
- Grab some wheels and treat yourself to a tour of the wineries in **Maipú** (p358)
- Get away from the crowds and into the stunning Valle de Calingasta in **Barreal** (p374)
- Discover dinosaur fossils embedded in bizarre rock formations in **Parque Provincial Ischigualasto** (p379)
- Make the scene in any number of hip bars on Av Arístides in **Mendoza** (p354)

★ Parque Provincial Ischigualasto

★ Barreal

MENDOZA
★ Maipú

★ Las Leñas

■ POPULATION: 2,199,674   ■ AREA: 238,478 SQ KM

Climate

Mendoza and the Central Andes is definitely a year-round destination. The region gets little rain through most of the year. Summer (December to March) in Mendoza is hot and dry. This is climbing season for the region's highest peaks. Fall is spectacular, thanks to the autumnal colors of Mendoza's introduced trees and grapevines. Winter (June through August) is ski season. Though the cities of Mendoza and San Juan never get snow, the highest passes to Chile close regularly during winter. Spring is lovely with warm days and cool nights.

National & Provincial Parks

The region's most famous park is Parque Provincial Aconcagua (p362), home of 6962m Cerro Aconcagua, the highest peak outside the Himalayas. Nearby Parque Provincial Volcán Tupungato (p364) is another favorite climbing destination. For mind-blowing volcanic landscapes, visit the little-known Parque Provincial Payunia (p368) near Malargüe. In neighboring San Juan province Parque Provincial Ischigualasto (p379) is world famous for its dinosaur remains as well as its spectacular desert rock formations. Also in San Juan, Parque Nacional El Leoncito (p376) occupies 76 sq km of dry Andean precordillera and is famous for its observatory and land sailing on the nearby flats of Pampa El Leoncito.

Getting There & Away

With flights to/from nearby Santiago (Chile), Mendoza has the region's only international airport. From Buenos Aires there are regular flights to Mendoza, San Juan and San Luis. During ski season there are usually flights to Malargüe, near Las Leñas ski resort. Bus transport is excellent throughout the province. If you're heading south to the Lake District, the fastest way is to head to Neuquén city, but if you don't mind taking it slow, a seldom-explored section of RN 40 between Mendoza and Neuquén provinces can be a worthwhile detour.

MENDOZA

☎ 0261 / pop 110,000 / elev 703m

A bustling city of wide, leafy avenues, atmospheric plazas and cosmopolitan cafés, Mendoza is a trap. Even if you've (foolishly) only given it a day or two on your itinerary, you're bound to end up hanging around, captivated by the laid-back pace while surrounded by every possible comfort.

Ostensibly it's a desert town, though you wouldn't know unless you were told – *acequias* (irrigation ditches) that run beside every main road and glorious fountains that adorn every main plaza mean you'll never be far from the burble of running water.

Lively during the day, the city really comes into its own at night, when the bars, restaurants and cafés along Av Arístides fill up and overflow onto the sidewalks with all the bright young things, out to see and be seen.

All over the country (and in much of the world), the name Mendoza is synonymous with wine, and this is the place to base yourself if you're up for touring the vineyards, taking a few dozen bottles home or just looking for a good bottle to accompany the evening's pizza.

The city's wide range of tour operators also makes it a great place to organize rafting, skiing and other adventures in the nearby Andes.

Orientation

Mendoza is 1050km west of Buenos Aires via RN 7 and 340km northwest of Santiago (Chile) via the Los Libertadores border complex.

Strictly speaking, the provincial capital proper is a relatively small area with a population of only about 110,000, but the inclusion of the departments of Las Heras, Guaymallén and Godoy Cruz, along with nearby Maipú and Luján de Cuyo, swells the population of Gran Mendoza (Greater Mendoza) to nearly one million.

The city's five central plazas are arranged like the five-roll on a die, with Plaza Independencia in the middle and four smaller plazas lying two blocks from each of its corners. Be sure to see the beautifully tiled Plaza España.

Av San Martín is the main thoroughfare, crossing the city from north to south, and Av Las Heras is the principal commercial street.

A good place to orient yourself is the **Terraza Mirador** (free; ☯ 9am-1pm), which is the rooftop terrace at **City Hall** (9 de Julio 500), offering panoramic views of the city and the surrounding area.

Information

BOOKSTORES

Centro Internacional del Libro (☎ 420-1266; Lavalle 14) Small selection of classics and best-sellers in English.

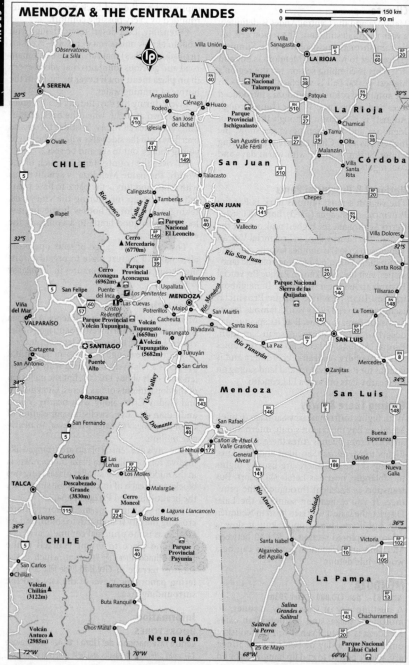

CUYO

The provinces of Mendoza, San Juan and, to some extent, neighboring San Luis (covered in the Córdoba & the Central Sierras chapter) are traditionally known as the Cuyo, a term which is derived from the indigenous Huarpe word *cuyum,* meaning 'sandy earth.' The Huarpes were the original practitioners of irrigated agriculture in the region, a legacy still highly visible throughout the region today. The term is one you'll encounter often, whether in the names of local bus companies, businesses and newspapers, or in everyday conversation.

Rubén Simoncini Libros (☎ 420-2988; San Juan 1108) One of many bookstores around the intersection of San Juan and Garibaldi; some English books in stock.
SBS (Gutiérrez 54) A large range of novels in English, Lonely Planet guidebooks, maps and wine-related literature. Also TOEFL resources and textbooks for Spanish students.

EMERGENCY
Servicio Coordinado de Emergencia (☎ 428-0000) Call for an ambulance.

IMMIGRATION
Immigration office (☎ 424-3512; Av San Martín 1859) In Godoy Cruz, south of the city center.

INTERNET ACCESS
Internet cafés are ubiquitous throughout the center, and all charge about AR$2 per hour. There are several large ones along the Av Sarmiento *peatonal* (pedestrian street).
Telefónica (cnr Avs Sarmiento & San Martín; per hr AR$2) Serves coffee and has telephones too.

LAUNDRY
La Lavandería (☎ 429-4782; San Lorenzo 352; full service about AR$12)
Laverap (☎ 423-9706; Av Colón 547; full service about AR$11)

MEDIA
La Guía This free monthly events magazine is a must-have if you plan on keeping up with Mendoza's hectic cultural scene. Pick up a copy at any tourist office.

MEDICAL SERVICES
Hospital (☎ 420-0600, 420-0063; cnr José F Moreno & Alem)

Wine Republic (www.wine-republic.com) An excellent English-language magazine focusing on wine but also featuring good reviews of up-and-coming restaurants, Mendoza gossip and a couple of entertaining articles. Pick up a copy at The Vines of Mendoza (p354) or Trout & Wine (p351).

MONEY
There are many ATMs downtown. The following two banks are architectural landmarks; Banco Mendoza is massive.
Banco de la Nación (cnr Necochea & 9 de Julio)
Banco Mendoza (cnr Gutiérrez & San Martín)
Cambio Santiago (Av San Martín 1199) Charges 2% commission on traveler's checks.

POST
Post office (Av San Martín at Colón)

TOURIST INFORMATION
ACA (Automóvil Club Argentina; ☎ 420-2900; cnr Av San Martín & Amigorena) Argentina's auto club; good source for provincial road maps.
Municipal tourist offices (www.turismo.mendoza .gov.ar in Spanish) bus terminal (☎ 431-5000, 431-3001; ☻ 7am-11pm); City Hall (☎ 449-5185; fax 449 5186; 9 de Julio 500; ☻ 8:30am-1:30pm Mon-Fri); Garibaldi ☎ 420-1333; Garibaldi sidewalk, near Av San Martín; ☻ 9am-9pm) The head office is at City Hall but the Garibaldi office is best for most questions.
Provincial tourist office (☎ 420-2800; www.turismo .mendoza.gov.ar in Spanish; Av San Martín 1143; ☻ 8am-10pm Mon-Fri) Good maps, plenty of brochures.

TRAVEL AGENCIES
Asatej (☎ /fax 429-0029/30; mendoza@asatej.com.ar; Av Sarmiento 223) Recommended student and discount travel agency. Also representative of Argentina Rafting Expediciones, which is based in Potrerillos (p359).
Isc Viajes (☎ 425-9259; www.iscviajes.com; Av España 1016) Travel agent and Amex representative.

Dangers & Annoyances
Mendoza has long been one of Argentina's safer destinations, but economic woes have caught up here, too, resulting in an increased number of street crimes. Tourists are rarely the target here and the city is still an incredibly safe place, but there are a few things to watch out for. Bag snatching and pickpocketing (particularly when the victim is wandering around with their hands full) is on the rise, as is the practice of snatching MP3 players from joggers in the park.

The areas around the bus terminal and on Cerro de la Gloria (in Parque General San

MENDOZA

INFORMATION

ACA	1 C5
Asatej	(see 24)
Banco de la Nación	2 C4
Banco Mendoza	3 C4
Cambio Santiago	4 C4
Centro Internacional del Libro	5 D4
German Consulate	6 C5
Hospital	7 E5
Isc Viajes	8 C5
Italian Consulate	9 A3
La Lavandería	10 B5
Laverap	11 A6
Municipal Tourist Office	12 C5
Municipal Tourist Office	13 B6
Municipal Tourist Office	(see 86)
Post Office	14 C6
Provincial Tourist Office	15 C5
Rubén Simoncini Libros	16 D5
SBS	17 C4
Telefónica	18 C5
Terraza Mirador (City Hall)	(see 13)

SIGHTS & ACTIVITIES

Acuario Municipal Mendoza	19 F4
Amparo Wine Tours	20 A4
Argentina Rafting Expediciones	21 C5
Aymará Turismo	22 C5
Betancourt Rafting	23 D4
Bus Turístico	(see 12)
Campo Base Travel & Adventure	24 C5
Centro Anaconda Serpentario	25 E4
Chamonix	26 C2
City Bike	27 C5
Esquí Mendoza Competición	28 B3
Extreme	29 A5
Huentata	30 B3
Iglesia, Convento y Basílica de San Francisco	31 C4
Museo Histórico General San Martín	32 D3
Museo Municipal de Arte Moderno	33 B4
Museo Popular Callejero	34 B3
Ríos Andinos	35 A4
Trout & Wine	36 C5

SLEEPING

Alcor Hotel	37 C3
B&B Plaza Italia	38 A5
Break Point Hostel	39 B6
Damajuana Hostel	40 B6
Hotel Aconcagua	41 B5
Hotel Argentino	42 B4
Hotel Casino	43 A4
Hotel City	44 D3
Hotel Crillón	45 A4
Hotel del Sol	46 C3
Hotel Horcones	47 C3
Hotel Laser	48 C3
Hotel San Martín	49 B4
Itaka Hostel	50 A6
Palace Hotel	51 C4
Park Hyatt Mendoza	52 B4
Punto Urbano Hostel	53 C3

Martín) now have an increased police presence, but are still considered dangerous at night. Increased caution is recommended during the early afternoon, too, as police tend to take the siesta along with everybody else. There have been several reports of people picking locks on hostel lockers – if you have something really valuable, leave it at your hostel's reception or, better yet, in its safe.

Sights

MUSEO FUNDACIONAL & AROUND

Mendoza's **Museo Fundacional** (☎ 425-6927; cnr Alberdi & Videla Castillo, Ciudad Vieja; admission AR$5; ☺ 8am-8pm Mon-Sat, 3-10pm Sun) protects excavations of the colonial *cabildo* (town council), destroyed by an earthquake in 1861. At that time, the city's geographical focus shifted west and south to its present location. A series of small dioramas depicts Mendoza's history, working through all of human evolution as if the city of Mendoza were the climax (maybe it was).

Walk to the museum from downtown and you'll pass some bizarre sights near **Parque Bernardo O'Higgins**. First check out the **Acuario Municipal Mendoza** (Municipal Aquarium; ☎ 425-3824; cnr Ituzaingó & Buenos Aires; admission AR$3; ☺ 9am-9pm, to 10pm in summer). Nothing at this small underwater freak show seems to have changed since its inauguration in 1945 (except the algae levels on the glass). But it's hard not to gaze in awe at the motionless, tongueless albino frogs or the 'armored pig,' a very ugly fish from the Río Paraná. Skip the crocodile exhibit. Across the street, the **Centro Anaconda Serpentario** (☎ 425-1393; Ituzaingó 1420; adult/child under 12 AR$5/3; ☺ 9:30am-1pm & 3:30-8pm) houses some 50 snakes (in equally small cages), including a giant yellow Burmese python.

OTHER MUSEUMS

Underground at the Plaza Independencia, the **Museo Municipal de Arte Moderno** (☎ 425-7279; Plaza Independencia; admission AR$4; ☺ 9am-8pm Tue-Sat, 4-8pm Sun & Mon) is a relatively small but well-organized facility with modern and contemporary art exhibits. Free concerts and theatrical performances are usually held here on Sunday night at 8pm – stop by for the weekly program.

Museo Popular Callejero (Av Las Heras, btwn 25 de Mayo & Perú; admission free; ☺ 24hr) is an innovative sidewalk museum. It consists of a series of encased streetside dioramas with odd clay sculptures depicting changes in one of Mendoza's major avenues since its 1830 creation in a dry watercourse.

Museo Histórico General San Martín (☎ 425-7947; Remedios Escalada de San Martín 1843; admission AR$5; ⊗ 9am-1pm & 4-8pm Mon-Fri) honors José de San Martín, the general who liberated Argentina from the Spanish and whose name graces parks, squares and streets everywhere in Argentina; the Libertador is especially dear to Mendoza, where he resided with his family and recruited and trained his army to cross into Chile. It's in a small arcade just off Av San Martín.

IGLESIA, CONVENTO Y BASÍLICA DE SAN FRANCISCO

Many *mendocinos* (people from Mendoza) consider the image at this **church** (Necochea 201; admission AR$2; ⊗ 9am-1pm Mon-Sat) of the Virgin of Cuyo, patron of San Martín's Ejército de los Andes (Army of the Andes), miraculous because it survived Mendoza's devastating 1968 earthquake. In the Virgin's semicircular chamber, visitors leave tributes to her and to San Martín. A mausoleum within the building holds the remains of San Martín's daughter, son-in-law and granddaughter, which were repatriated from France in 1951.

PARQUE GENERAL SAN MARTÍN

Walking along the lakeshore and snoozing in the shade of the rose garden in this beautiful 420-hectare park is a great way to enjoy one of the city's highlights. Walk along Mitre/Civit out to the park and admire some of Mendoza's finest houses on the way. Pick up a park map at the **Centro de Información** (☎ 420-5052, ext 22; cnr Avs Los Platanos & Libertador; ⊗ 9am-5pm), just inside the impressive entry gates, shipped over from England and originally forged for the Turkish Sultan Hamid II. The park was designed by Charles Thays, who designed Parque Sarmiento in Córdoba, in 1897. Its famous **Cerro de la Gloria** has a monument to San Martín's Ejército de los Andes for its liberation of Argentina, Chile and Perú from the Spaniards. On clear days, views of the valley make the climb especially rewarding.

Bus 110 ('Favorita') from around Plaza Independencia or Plaza España goes to the park. From the park entrance, open-air buses called *bateas* carry visitors to the summit of Cerro de la Gloria for AR$6 one way.

Activities

Once you've sucked down enough fine wine and tramped around the city a bit, get yourself into

the Andes, Mendoza's other claim to fame, for some of the most beautiful mountain scenery you'll ever lay your eyes upon. Numerous agencies organize climbing and trekking expeditions, rafting trips, mule trips and cycling trips. For Aconcagua guides, see p363.

Aymará Turismo (☎ 420-2064; 9 de Julio 1023) Mule trips, trekking, rafting.

Betancourt Rafting (☎ 429-9965; www.betancourt .com.ar; Lavalle 35, Local 8) Rafting, mountain biking, paragliding.

Campo Base Travel & Adventure (☎ 425-5511; www.campobase.com.ar; Av Sarmiento 231) Offers all adventures imaginable from trekking to paragliding (AR$210) to more conventional day trips.

Gabriel Cabrera Expediciones (☎ 452-0641; www .aconcagua2002.com.ar; Caseros 1053, Godoy Cruz) Climbing, skiing, expeditions, adventure courses.

Ríos Andinos (☎ 429-5030; www.riosandinos.com.ar; Sarmiento 721) Based in Potrerillos, it specializes in rafting on Río Mendoza. Rafting AR$60 (35 minutes, class I-II) to AR$190 (five hours, class III-IV). Combined rafting and trekking AR$160 per day.

CLIMBING & MOUNTAINEERING

Mendoza is famous for Cerro Aconcagua, the highest mountain in the Americas, but the majestic peak is only the tip of the iceberg when it comes to climbing and mountaineering here. The nearby Cordón del Plata boasts several peaks topping out between 5000m and 6000m, and there are three important rock-climbing areas in the province: Los Arenales (near Tunuyán), El Salto (near Mendoza) and Chigüido (near Malargüe).

Pick up a copy of Maricio Fernandez' full-color route guide (Spanish only), *Escaladas en Mendoza*, at **Inka Expediciones** (☎ 425-0871; www.inka.com.ar; Av Juan B Justo 345, Mendoza). For up-to-date information, contact the **Asociación Argentina de Guiás de Montaña** (☎ 445-3755; www .aagm.com.ar). See p363 for a list of the most experienced guides operating throughout the province.

For climbing and hiking equipment, both rental and purchase, visit **Chamonix** (☎ 425-7572; www.chamonix-outdoor.com.ar in Spanish; Barcala 267).

SKIING & SNOWBOARDING

Los Penitentes (p361) has the best skiing near Mendoza. To rent or buy ski and snowboard equipment, try **Esquí Mendoza Competición** (☎ 429-7944; Av Las Heras 583), **Extreme** (☎ 429-0733; Av Colón 733) or any of the shops along Las Heras.

All charge AR$30 to AR$40 per day for a skis-boots-poles package and about AR$60 per day for a snowboard with boots. Most rent gloves, jackets and tire chains, as well.

WHITE-WATER RAFTING

The major rivers are the Mendoza and the Diamante, near San Rafael. Most agencies mentioned earlier offer trips ranging from 35-minute runs (AR$60) or half-day descents (from AR$190) to overnight (from AR$320) and three-day expeditions (from AR$600). Well-regarded Argentina Rafting Expediciones is based in Potrerillos (p359) with a Mendoza **office** (☎ 429-6325; www.argentina rafting.com; Primitivo de la Reta 992, Local 4).

Courses

IAIM Instituto Intercultural (☎ 429-0269; www.intercul tural.com.ar in Spanish; www.spanishcourses.com.ar; República de Siria 241) offers 20 hours of private Spanish-language classes to foreigners for AR$860.

Tours

Huentata (☎ 425-7444; www.huentata.com.ar; Av Las Heras 699) is one of several conventional travel agencies that organize trips in and around town. Among the possibilities are half-day tours of the city (AR$35); tours of the wineries and Dique Cipoletti (AR$45); or full-day tours to Villavicencio (AR$55) or the high cordillera around Potrerillos, Vallecito and Uspallata (AR$130).

CITY TOURS

Bus Turístico (Tourist Bus; ☎ 420-1333) If you're here during the summer months, get a route map of the city's Bus Turístico (AR$10) from the Garibaldi municipal tourist office and take in Mendoza's sights from a red double-decker. Good for 24 hours, the ticket allows you to board and reboard at any of several fixed stops throughout the city. The circuit begins at the corner of Garibaldi and Av San Martín, near the municipal tourist office, and goes as far as the summit of Cerro de la Gloria.

City Bike (☎ 0261-15-469-2795; Av San Martín 1070, Local 3) rents bikes/mopeds for AR$35/45 for four hours, including a city map and MP3 player with audio bike tour of the city.

WINE TOURS

For the casual sipper, a self-guided tour of Maipú (see boxed text, p358) or any of the bo-dega tours offered by various travel agencies around town will likely satisfy. Moving several rungs up the ladder, there are a couple of companies operating out of Mendoza offering deluxe wine tours. They're not cheap, but the benefits are obvious – small group sizes (usually no more than six people), a knowledgeable English-speaking guide (as well as the winery guides, whose English is sometimes rough and occasionally nonexistent) and access to some of the more exclusive (ie better quality) vineyards. Winemakers are much more likely to be getting the good stuff down off the top shelf for you on these tours, too. The two listed below also offer tours of the Uco Valley, an important new winegrowing region 150km south of Mendoza that's near-impossible to explore by public transport and doesn't yet appear on any tour agency itinerary.

Trout & Wine (☎ 425-5613; www.troutandwine.com; Av Sarmiento 133, Local 12) organizes custom-designed full-day tours of Luján de Cuyo (AR$350), Maipú (AR$420) and the Uco Valley (AR$500). Maximum group size of six, also offering private tours across the border to Chilean wineries. From November to March it runs fly-fishing tours in the Uco Valley for AR$800, including all gear and a barbecue lunch out in the highlands accompanied by – you guessed it – some very fine wines.

Amparo Wine Tours (☎ 429-2931; www.winetours mendoza.com; Av Sarmiento 647) is a well-established operation that concentrates on midrange and top-end wines. It has tours leaving every day (sometimes two) to Luján de Cuyo and Maipú (AR$360) and the Uco Valley (AR$420). Tours focus more on tasting than winemaking techniques.

Festivals & Events

Mendoza's biggest annual event, the **Fiesta Nacional de la Vendimia** (National Wine Harvest Festival), lasts about a week, from late February to early March. It features a parade on Av San Martín with floats from each department of the province, numerous concerts and folkloric events, and it all culminates in the coronation of the festival's queen in the Parque General San Martín amphitheater.

Sleeping

Mendoza has abundant accommodations in all categories. For March's Fiesta Nacional de la Vendimia, reservations are highly advisable.

BUDGET

Hotel Laser (☎ 425-9285; hotellaser@hotmail.com; General Paz 360; s/d AR$40/60) A truly back-to-basics budget hotel. There's a formidable sag factor on the beds, but rooms are spacious, with cable TV and a few sticks of furniture.

Itaka Hostel (☎ 423-9793; www.itakahostel.com.ar; Av Arístides Villanueva 480; dm/d from AR$25/80; ⚒ ▭ ⚑) A gorgeous hostel in the busy bar district, this bright, modern building features spacious dorms and reasonable doubles. Call for free pick up from the bus terminal.

Punto Urbano Hostel (☎ 429-5281; www.puntourbano hostel.com; Godoy Cruz 332; dm/d AR$30/90; ▭) Just north of the city center, this newish hostel maintains an air of intimacy despite its grand proportions. The dorms are regular, but the doubles are extremely good value – spacious, with wide-screen TVs and tastefully decorated bathrooms. The large backyard – good for smoking, drinking, barbecuing and generally hanging out – is an added bonus.

Hotel City (☎ 425-1343; General Paz 95; s/d AR$60/90; ⚒) One of Mendoza's classic budget stand-bys, the Hotel City has hiked its prices without doing a whole lot to justify it. Still, if slightly crumbly doesn't bother you, the big, comfortable rooms here are a good deal.

Break Point Hostel (☎ 423-9514; www.breakpointhostel .com.ar; Av Arístides Villanueva 241; dm/d AR$33/100; ▭ ⚑) In the middle of Mendoza's bustling bar strip, this is one hostel with the lot – an excellent pool, comfy lounge/TV area, huge kitchen, balconies and a hip little streetside bar/café. Dorms have nine beds and private bathrooms.

Damajuana Hostel (☎ 425-5858; www.damajuana hostel.com.ar; Av Arístides Villanueva 282; dm/d from AR$35/100; ▭ ⚑) The best-looking of the Arístides hostels, this one doesn't miss a beat with great common areas, an excellent pool/garden area and functional dorms and doubles.

MIDRANGE

Hotel Casino (☎ 425-6666; Gutiérrez 668; s/d AR$100/120; ⚒) Facing on to Plaza Chile, the Hotel Casino offers some good, spacious rooms and some smallish, ordinary ones. They're all clean and comfortable, but have a look at a few before deciding.

Hotel Horcones (☎ 425-0045; www.hotelhorcones .com; Av Las Heras 145; s/d AR$110/140; ⚒) Set back off the busy avenue, the Horcones offers good value for this part of town. Rooms are unrenovated, but clean and quiet, with a few touches of charm and plenty of space.

Hotel del Sol (☎ 438-2032; hoteles@ciudad.com.ar; Av Las Heras 212; s/d AR$120/140) On busy Las Heras, this 28-room hotel, in a well-preserved old building, offers fair-sized rooms with ample bathrooms and small, stark lounge areas on each floor. Good deal.

Alcor Hotel (☎ 438-1000; www.alcorhotel.com.ar; General Paz 86; s/d AR$120/150; ⚒ ▭) One block from busy Av Las Heras, this is a recently renovated hotel that has maintained a few of its original charms. Rooms are big, light and well proportioned, with some comfy touches.

Hotel San Martín (☎ 438-0677; hotelsanmartin@hot mail.com; Espejo 435; s/d AR$130/160; ⚒ ▭) Fronting the plaza, this three-story brick hotel offers solid value. There's plenty of tasteful tile work and rooms are spacious and comfortable with modern bathrooms and big windows.

Palace Hotel (☎ 423-4200; Av Las Heras 70; s/d AR$120/160; ⚒) Another big ol' hotel on the main drag, the Palace brings some stately touches to the table. Rooms are generously sized with good, functional bathrooms. Those at the front boast views out over the busy avenue.

Hotel Argentino (☎ 405-6300; www.argentino-hotel .com in Spanish; Espejo 455; s/d AR$160/180; ⚒ ▭ ⚑) One of three hotels on the Plaza Independencia, the newly remodeled Argentino has small but immaculate rooms, decor that looks like it's straight out of an Ikea catalog and a back patio with a miniature pool.

Hotel Crillón (☎ 429-8494; www.hcrillon.com.ar; Perú 1065; s/d AR$170/190; ⚒ ⚑) This is a modern, unpretentious place with carpeted rooms, firm beds, good bathrooms (complete with towel-warmers) and a great swimming pool across the street.

ourpick B&B Plaza Italia (☎ 423-4219; www .plazaitalia.cjb.net; Montevideo 685; r AR$240; ⚒) This six-room B&B is hard to beat when it comes to friendliness and delicious breakfasts. The house is lovely, the owners (who speak English) are divine, and the living room is just right for reading. It's like being at home.

TOP END

Hotel Aconcagua (☎ 420-4455; www.hotelaconcagua .com; San Lorenzo 545; s/d AR$290/320; ⚒ ▭ ⚑) Four-star Hotel Aconcagua has it all, with manicurists and hairstylists on premises, a sauna and pool and some multilingual staff. It's the second biggest in town, built in 1978 for the soccer World Cup.

Park Hyatt Mendoza (☎ 441-1234; www.mendoza .park.hyatt.com; Chile 1124; r from AR$350, ste from AR$1050;

⊠ ⊠ ▣ ▨) Facing Plaza Independencia, Mendoza's only five-star hotel is a real beauty, and walk-in rates can be surprisingly affordable (from the splurge perspective) considering the quality and comfort of the ultrachic rooms.

Eating

Some of Mendoza's best restaurants, often with outdoor seating and lively young crowds, are along Av Arístides Villanueva, the western extension of Av Colón. West of Plaza Independencia, Av Sarmiento is lined with the city's most traditional, albeit touristy, *parrillas* (grills), while east of the plaza along the Sarmiento *peatonal*, you'll find numerous sidewalk cafés with outdoor seating. The Sarmiento cafés are required visiting for coffee.

Kato (Av E Civit 556; mains AR$10-15; ☽ lunch & dinner) Tired of the Arístides squeeze? This mellow neighborhood café/bar/restaurant is *way* hipper than all those places, and there's no fighting for a table. Empanadas, pizzas and sandwiches in a super-chic environment. Those in the know head straight for the lounging action on the sofas out the back.

Cocina Poblana (Av Arístides Villanueva 217; dishes AR$10-18; ☽ lunch & dinner Mon-Sat) The very tasty, inexpensive Middle Eastern food (hummus, felafel, dolmas) comes as a welcome break from all that steak. The shish kebab served with tabouleh salad is a definite winner.

Allure (Av Belgrano 1169; mains AR$20; ☽ lunch & dinner) Excellent, freshly prepared dishes in modern, tranquil surrounds. The ambience is hyper-zen and the food doesn't quite live up to that level of creativity, but the smoked meats platter (AR$15) and mixed kebabs (AR$20) are mouth-wateringly good.

de un Rincón de La Boca (Av Las Heras 485; mains AR$10-20; ☽ lunch & dinner) Many argue this is the best pizza in town (it's the crust). The wine list is very average, but there's no corkage charge, so grab a bottle before you come.

La Barca (Espejo 120; mains AR$12-20; ☽ lunch & dinner) There's nothing fancy going on here – just good honest food at reasonable prices. Excellent homemade pastas and a range of super-tempting daily specials.

our pick **Casa 3** (San Lorenzo 490; mains AR$15-20; ☽ lunch & dinner Mon-Sat) A hip little bar/restaurant that wouldn't look out of place in downtown Barcelona. There are sofas on the sidewalk, after-work happy hours and some good, inventive cooking.

Quinta Norte (Av Mitre & Espejo; mains AR$10-25; ☽ lunch & dinner) Sidewalk dining right across from the plaza. The menu's not huge, but there are some good dishes and the AR$10 set lunches are some of the best in town. A great place to grab a coffee and recharge the batteries.

La Mira (Av Belgrano 1191; mains AR$20-28; ☽ lunch & dinner) Delicious, innovative dishes in a relaxed and casual environment. Each dish comes as a full meal (some even with side orders of vegetables) and there's a small but respectable wine list.

El Palenque (Av Arístides Villanueva 287; mains AR$15-30; ☽ lunch & dinner Mon-Sat) Don't miss this superb, extremely popular restaurant styled after an old-time *pulpería* (tavern), where the house wine is served in traditional *pinguinos* (white ceramic penguin-shaped pitchers). The food and appetizers are outstanding, and the outside tables are always full and fun.

Decimo (Av San Martín & Garibaldi, 10th fl; mains AR$25-30; ☽ lunch & dinner) Up on the 10th floor in the middle of town, this modern restaurant/wine bar offers a good range of well-cooked dishes with distinctly un-Argentine ingredients like quinoa, alongside sushi and risotto. If the meals seem pricey, the coffee (AR$3) is a good enough excuse to soak up the views from the sunny terrace. Catch the elevator in the Gómez building on Garibaldi. Don't bother looking for the sign – there isn't one.

Tommaso Trattoria (Av Sarmiento 762; mains AR$18-30; ☽ lunch & dinner) An excellent, trilingual (Italian, Spanish and English) menu featuring a good range of creative regional Italian dishes. The wine list is impressive and the tables out front are the place to be on a balmy evening.

La Marchigiana (Patricias Mendocinas 1550; mains AR$20-30; ☽ lunch & dinner) Mendoza's most frequently recommended Italian restaurant. The decor may seem stark, but the service is warm and a few Argentine twists to the classic Italian menu keep things interesting.

Azafrán (☎ 429-4200; Av Sarmiento 765; mains AR$30-40; ☽ lunch & dinner Mon-Sat) It's hard to figure what's the bigger draw here – the rustic-chic decor, the small but creative menu or the extensive wine list. Who cares? Enjoy them all.

La Barra (☎ 0261-15-654-1950; Av Belgrano 1086; mains AR$35-50; ☽ lunch & dinner) Skip the slow service and mediocre food of the *parrillas* along Av Sarmiento and head straight for La Barra, where the owner personally tends the grill, cooking his meats with two types of wood (one for flavor, one for heat), while his partner tends to the blissed-out diners in front. The *matambre de cerdo* (pork) is truly sublime.

La Tasca de Plaza España (☎ 423-3466; Montevideo 117; mains AR$30-55; ⏲ lunch & dinner) With excellent Mediterranean and Spanish tapas (mostly seafood), great wines, intimate atmosphere, good art and friendly service, La Tasca is one of Mendoza's best.

Drinking

For a great night on the town, walk down Av Arístides Villanueva, where it's bar after bar; in summer, entire blocks fill with tables and people enjoying the night.

Por Acá (☎ 420-0346; Av Arístides Villanueva 557) Purple and yellow outside and polka-dotted upstairs, this bar-cum-lounge gets packed after 2am, and by the end of the night, dancing on the tables is not uncommon. Good retro dance music.

El Punto (Av Arístides Villanueva 305) A sea of white vinyl upholstery and laid-back electronica make this little bar a favorite for mixed drinks and cocktails.

Fin Sin (http://finsin.spaces.live.com; Primitivo de la Reta 1053; ⏲ Thu-Sat) For the nightowls, this is the best, most reliable live music venue in town. Things kick off around 11pm with happy hour, heat up around 1am when the first band hits the stage and keep going til sunup. Stop by for the weekly program.

WINE BARS

Wine is available pretty much everywhere in Mendoza (right down to gas stations), but there are a few places that specialize.

The Vines of Mendoza (☎ 438-1031; www.vinesof mendoza.com; Espejo 567; ⏲ 3-10pm) This friendly, central wine bar (where everybody, down to the security guards, seems to speak English) offers flights (tastings of five selected wines; AR$30) and Reserve Tastings (top shelf private tastings; AR$120). It also offers wine appreciation classes (AR$45, one hour) which give you an idea of how to taste wine – a great idea before hitting the bodegas. Every Wednesday there's a 'meet the winemaker' night (AR$15). Monday is wine and cheese night (AR$50 for five wines paired with five cheeses) and Friday is sparkling wine night – four sparkling wines for AR$35.

Juan Cedrón (Av Sarmiento 786) An intimate little combination wine bar/wine store. Occasional tastings and sidewalk tables.

Marcelino (Benegas & M Zapata; ⏲ 7pm Mon; AR$100 per person) The Wine Club Republic meets at this wine store every Monday to taste eight to 10 top-end wines. The atmosphere is very informal, with plenty of English spoken and winemakers from the region putting in regular appearances. Visitors welcome.

Entertainment

Check the tourist offices or museums for a copy of *La Guía,* a monthly publication with comprehensive entertainment listings. *Los Andes,* the daily rag, also has a good entertainment section.

DANCE CLUBS

Finding a dance floor generally means abandoning downtown for one of two areas: the northwest suburb of El Challao, or Chacras de Coria, along the RP 82 in the southern outskirts. The former is reached by bus 115 from Av Sarmiento. Chacras de Coria is reached from the stop on La Rioja between Catamarca and Garibaldi by taking bus 10, *interno* (internal route number) 19, or from the corner of 25 de Mayo and Rivadavia by taking bus 10, *interno* 15. In both cases simply asking the driver for *los boliches* (the nightclubs) is enough to find the right stop. The nightclubs in both El Challao and Chacras de Coria are all right next to each other, and you can walk along to take your pick from the ever-changing array. **Alquimia** (⏲ Wed-Sat; admission AR$10-40) was the hot club at the time of research – it may still be there by the time you arrive.

Something to watch for here: at the time of writing, the Mendoza government was trialing a law that prohibited dance clubs from allowing patrons to enter after 2:30am, making timing a tricky balancing act – get there after the place starts to fill up (1am at the earliest), but before they stop letting people in.

Many visitors to Mendoza (and *mendocinos* for that matter) find the effort involved getting to these places far outweighs the fun they have while there, often opting for the smaller bars along Av Arístides Villanueva. One club that has a regular buzz and is within a short cab ride from downtown is **Apeteco** (J Barraquero & San Juan; admission AR$8-15).

THEATER & LIVE MUSIC

Soul Café (☎ 425-7489; San Juan 456; admission AR$5-15) Grab a table and enjoy everything from live *ock en español* (Spanish-language rock) to azz and theater. Shows start after 10pm.

The main theaters in town are **Teatro Quintanilla** (☎ 423 2310; Plaza Independencia), alongside the Museo Municipal de Arte Moderno; the nearby **Teatro Independencia** (☎ 438-0644; cnr spejo & Chile); and **Teatro Mendoza** (☎ 429-7279; an Juan 1427).

Shopping

CRAFTS

Av Las Heras is lined with souvenir shops, leather shops, chocolate stores and all sorts of places to pick up cheap Argentine trinkets. Items made of *carpincho* (spotted tanned hide of the capybara, a large rodent) are uniquely Argentine and sold in many of the stores.

Plaza de las Artes (Plaza Independencia; 5-11pm Fri-Sun) Outdoor crafts market in the Plaza Independencia.

Feria Artesanal Plaza España (Plaza España; 5-10pm Fri-Sun) Crafts fair in Plaza España with mediocre-quality goods.

Raices (☎ 425-4118; España 1092) High-quality weavings, *mates* (tea-like beverages), jewelry and more. There is another location on Av Sarmiento 162.

Mercado Artesanal (☎ 420-4239; Av San Martín 1143; Mon-Sat) This cooperative offers provincial handicrafts, including vertical-loom weavings (Huarpe-style) from northwest Mendoza, horizontal looms (Araucanian-style) from the south, woven baskets from Lagunas del Rosario, and lots of braided, untanned leather horse gear. The Mercado Artesanal is located below the provincial tourist office.

WINE STORES

Unless you are looking for a very obscure top of the range bottle (or a sales assistant

---

GRABBING A BOTTLE: THE MENDOZA SHOPPING LIST

Time to put the beer down and see what all the fuss is about. That's right: wine. While nearly every restaurant in the country has some sort of wine list, choices quite often tend toward the lower end of the market and markups can be hefty. In all but the finest restaurants you can bring a bottle, pay a nominal corkage fee (between AR$5 and AR$10) and enjoy a sublime experience.

Something else worth considering is that while it's illegal to post wine from Argentina, countries like the US and Canada have no restriction on how much you can bring home in your luggage, provided you pay duty. And duty can be as low as US$5 for 40 bottles.

If you are planning on transporting wine, it's best to stop in at a specialty wine store (see above) where they can pack bottles to avoid breakage (remember that most airlines no longer allow bottles in hand luggage). If you're just looking for a bottle to have with dinner, supermarkets around town have an excellent selection in the under-AR$100 range. Listed below are some of our top picks. Don't worry about vintages – Mendoza's incredibly consistent weather means a good wine is a good wine, regardless of the year.

Reds

Callia Alta Syrah (AR$12) One of the bigger bargains on the market, this bold spicy wine could easily sell for double the price.

La Celia Malbec (AR$32) From one of the oldest vineyards in the Uco Valley, this is a classic malbec, with a deep palate and a soft finish.

Prodigo Malbec Reserva (AR$65) An intense floral nose leads to a long, long finish.

Cuvelier Los Andes Gran Vin (AR$95) Drink it now or cellar it for five years – this medium-bodied wine with a long, dry finish will get better and more complex with age.

Whites & Sparkling Wines

Huarpe Lancatay Chardonnay (AR$21) A delicate blend of oak and tropical fruit flavors, with a dry citric finish.

Navarras Coreas (AR$25) A fine sparkling wine with a spicy edge – could easily compete with its French counterparts.

Chandon (AR$28) From the makers of the famed Moët & Chandon, this local bubbly has all the character for a fraction of the price.

Domaine St Diego Brut Xero (AR$30) A fine, creamy sparkling wine built on a base of young malbec grapes. It's got a limited production, so if you see a bottle, grab it.

who knows what they're talking about), the best place to buy wine in town, in terms of price and variety, is the supermarket **Carrefour** (Avs Las Heras & Belgrano; ☼ 8am-10pm). The places listed below stock finer wines, speak at least a little English and can pack your bottles up for shipping.

Juan Cedrón (Av Sarmiento 786) A small but well-chosen selection lines the walls. Doubles as a wine bar. Occasional tastings and sidewalk tables.

Marcelino (Benegas & M Zapata) An almost staggering array of mostly reds. Tastings on Monday night.

Getting There & Away
AIR
Aerolíneas Argentinas/Austral (☎ 420-4185; Av Sarmiento 82) share offices; Aerolíneas flies several times daily to Buenos Aires (from AR$400).

Lan Chile (☎ 425-7900; Rivadavia 135) flies twice daily to Santiago, Chile, (from AR$960), the only international flights from Mendoza.

BUS
Mendoza is a major transport hub so you can travel to just about anywhere in the country. Mendoza's **bus terminal** (☎ 431-5000, 431-3001; cnr Avs R Videla & Acceso Este, Guaymallén) has domestic and international departures.

Domestic
Several companies send buses daily to Uspallata (AR$13, two hours) and Los Penitentes (AR$15, four hours), the latter for Aconcagua.

During the ski season several companies go directly to Las Leñas (about AR$30, 6½ hours); **Mendoza Viajes** (☎ 461-0210; Sarmiento 129) leaves from Av Sarmiento and 9 de Julio, rather than the terminal.

A number of companies offer a morning bus service to the Difunta Correa Shrine (p373; AR$13 roundtrip, departs 7:30am) in San Juan province; the journey's three hours each way and the bus waits three hours before returning. Buses to Maipú leave from the stop on La Rioja between Garibaldi and Catamarca.

There are daily departures from Mendoza's **bus terminal** (☎ 431-5000, 431 3001; cnr Avs R Videla & Acceso Este, Guaymallén) to the destinations in the following table, and sometimes upwards of 10 to 20 per day to major cities. Prices reflect midseason fares.

Destination	Cost (AR$)	Duration (hr)
Bahía Blanca	160	16
Bariloche	180	20
Buenos Aires	100	13-17
Catamarca	90	10
Comodoro Rivadavia	300	30
Córdoba	90	10
Jujuy	150	22
Maipu	1.10	45
Malargüe	35	6-7
Mar del Plata	170	19
Neuquén	110	10-12
Puerto Iguazú	290	36
Puerto Madryn	210	23-24
Resistencia	220	24
Río Gallegos	400	41
Rosario	80	12
Salta	190	18
San Agustín de Valle Fértil	36	6
San Juan	15	2½
San Luis	30	3½
San Martín de los Andes	180	19-20
San Rafael	17	3
Santa Fe	130	14
Tucumán	130	14
Zapala	165	9½

International
Numerous companies cross the Andes every day via RN 7 (Paso de Los Libertadores) to Santiago, Chile, (AR$45, seven hours), Viña del Mar (AR$45, seven hours) and Valparaíso (AR$50, eight hours). The pass sometimes closes due to bad winter weather; be prepared to wait (sometimes days) if weather gets extreme.

Several carriers have connections to Lima, Perú (AR$405, 60 to 70 hours), via Santiago, Chile, and there are at least two weekly departures to Montevideo, Uruguay (from AR$140, 22 hours), some with onward connections to Punta del Este and Brazil.

International buses depart from the main bus terminal. Companies are in the eastern end of the terminal.

Getting Around
TO/FROM THE AIRPORT
Plumerillo International Airport (☎ 448-2603) is 6km north of downtown on RN 40. Bus 68 ('Aeropuerto') from Calle Salta goes straight to the terminal.

BUS
Mendoza's **bus terminal** (☎ 431-5000, 431-3001; cnr Avs R Videla & Acceso Este, Guaymallén) is really just

cross the street from downtown. After arriving, walk under the Videla underpass (it's lined with merchandise stalls) and you'll be heading toward the center, about 15 minutes away. Otherwise, the 'Villa Nueva' trolley (actually a bus) connects the terminal with downtown.

Local buses cost AR$1.10 – more for longer distances such as the trip to the airport – and require a magnetic Mendobus card, which can be bought at most kiosks in denominations of AR$2 and AR$5. Most *lineas* (bus lines) also have *internos* (internal route numbers) posted in the window; for example, *linea* 200 might post *interno* 204 or 206; watch for both numbers. *Internos* indicate more precisely where the bus will take you.

CAR

Rental-car agencies are at the airport and along Primitivo de la Reta.

Avis (☎ 447-0150; Primitivo de la Reta 914)
Localiza (☎ 429-6800; Primitivo de la Reta 936, Local 4)
National/Alamo (☎ 429-3111; Primitivo de la Reta 928)

AROUND MENDOZA

Sites in this section are Mendoza's closest major attractions, but you could easily visit Puente del Inca and Las Cuevas (near the Chilean border; see p363) in a day.

Wineries

Thanks to a complex and very old system of river-fed aqueducts, land that was once a desert now supports 70% of the country's wine production. Mendoza province is wine country, and many wineries near the capital offer tours and tasting. Countless tourist agencies offer day tours, hitting two or more wineries in a precisely planned day, but it's also easy enough to visit on your own. Hiring a *remise*

GETTING THE JUICE ON MENDOZA WINE

If you've been paying any attention to the wine world in the last few years, you will have noticed that Argentine wines are hitting the global market with a vengeance.

There's a few reasons for their meteoric rise to fame: for one, the wine industry here is becoming more sophisticated. As domestic consumption drops (in favor of beer and, incredibly, soft drinks), more wineries are looking to export their product. At last count there were over 300 wineries in the region exporting, a dramatic increase from the '60s, when only a handful did so.

Quality is another factor. Argentine wines are good and they just keep getting better. One of the keys to successful winemaking is controlled irrigation. A big rain before a harvest can spoil an entire crop, but winemakers in the desertlike Mendoza region don't have to worry about that – nearly every drop of water is piped in, and comes as beautiful fresh snowmelt from the Andes.

Another advantage of the region is the variation in altitudes. Different grapes grow better at different heights, and the area around Mendoza has vineyards at altitudes between 900m and 1800m above sea level. Mendoza's flagship grape will probably always be malbec, but local winemakers are having good results with tempranilla, bonarda, syrah, chardonnay and sauvignon blanc.

Desert vineyards have another advantage – the huge difference between daytime and nighttime temperatures. Warm days encourage sugar production and help the grapes grow a nice thick skin. Cool nights ensure good acidity levels. Another bonus is low humidity levels, meaning bugs and fungus aren't a problem.

Overall quality is improving as techniques are refined. Back in the day, it was all about quantity, but now winemakers are looking to produce fewer grapes of higher quality. Better hygiene standards, the replacement of old 'criollo' vines with 'noble' varieties like malbec, cabernet sauvignon, merlot and syrah and the practice of aging wines in smaller oak barrels (with a lifespan of a few years) rather than large barrels (which would be used for up to 70 years) have all had their positive effects.

And you can't talk about Argentine wines without talking price to quality ratio. The country's economic crash in 2001 was a boon for exporters as prices plummeted and Argentine wine all of a sudden became a highly competitive product. Land here is (relatively) cheap and labor so inexpensive that nearly every grape in the country is hand picked, a claim that only the top-end wines in other countries can make.

For a list of recommended wines from the Mendoza region, see the boxed text, p355.

MAIPÚ: A GOURMET EXPERIENCE

The small town of Maipú, just out of Mendoza, is so packed with wineries, olive oil farms and other gourmet businesses that it's easy to hit five or six in a day. All offer tours and most finish proceedings with at least a small sampling of their produce.

Accordingly, a few companies in Maipú rent bikes and electric scooters, making a day tour of the area an excellent outing, and a lot more fun than the often rushed half-day wine tours on offer from Mendoza tour agencies.

To get to Maipú, catch the 173 bus from the bus stop on La Rioja in Mendoza and get off at the triangular roundabout. The best bike hire company is **Coco Bikes** (☎ 481-0862; Urquiza 1781; bikes/scooters per day AR$20/50). They'll supply you with a (basic) map of the area and take you in a van to your furthest point, meaning you only have to make your way back.

All of the following are open 10am to 5pm Monday to Friday and 10am to 1pm Saturdays. Reservations are not necessary at any.

Carinae (☎ 499-0470; www.carinaevinos.com; Aranda 2899; tours AR$10) is the furthest south you really want to go – it's a small, French-owned winery producing a lovely rosé and some good reds. Tour fees are deducted from any wine purchases you make.

Across the road is **LAUR** (☎ 499-0740; www.laursa.com.ar; Aranda 2850; tours AR$5), a 100-year-old olive farm. The 15-minute tour tells you everything you need to know about olive oil production and is followed by a yummy tasting session.

Heading back to Urquiza, go past the big roundabout and north. The first winery you come to is **Di Tomasso** (☎ 499-0673; Urquiza 8136; tours AR$10), a beautiful, historic vineyard dating back to the 1830s. The tour includes a quick pass through the original cellar section.

Heading north again, take a right on Moreno to get to **Viña del Cerno** (☎ 481-1567; www .elcerno.com.ar; Moreno 631; tours AR$15), a small, old-fashioned winery supervised by its two wine-maker owners. The underground cellar complex is atmospheric, but tastings can be a little rushed.

Back out on Urquiza, it's a little under 3km to Zanichelli, where you turn left and travel another 1km to get to **Almacen del Sur** (Zanichelli 709; set meals AR$35-120; ☺ lunch). This working farm produces and exports gourmet deli goods that are grown and packed on the premises. Free tours of the production process are available. There's also an excellent restaurant here, serving delicious set lunches (the more expensive ones come accompanied by local wines) in a leafy garden setting.

Head back to Urquiza and continue north until you get to the big roundabout. Turn right and follow the signs to **Historia y Sabores** (Carril Gómez 3064). Seven families run this little chocolate- and liqueur-making operation. Tours are brief, but the lovely rustic surrounds and comfy bar (where you're invited to a free shot of liqueur) make it a worthwhile stop.

Along Urquiza, keep heading north until you get to where you got off the bus, take a right on Montecaseros and continue for 500m to reach **Bodega La Rural** (☎ 497-2013; www.bodegalarural .com.ar; Montecaseros 2625; tours AR$10). Winery tours here are fairly standard (and you probably have the idea by now) but the museum (admission free) is fascinating – there's a huge range of winemaking equipment from over the years on display, including a grape press made from an entire cowskin. Tours in Spanish leave on the hour. If you want one in English, call ahead, or you can simply walk around on your own.

(telephone taxi) is also feasible. All winery tours and tastings are free, though some push hard for sales at the end, and you never taste the *good* stuff without paying. Malbec, of course, is the definitive Argentine wine.

With a full day it's easy to hop on buses and hit several of the area's most appealing wineries in the outskirts of neighboring Maipú, only 16km away. See the boxed text, above for a self-guided tour. Another option is the area of Luján de Cuyo, 19km south of Mendoza, which also has many important wineries. Buses to Maipú leave from La Rioja, between Garibaldi and Catamarca in downtown Mendoza; buses to wineries in Luján de Cuyo leave from Mendoza's bus terminal.

Mendoza's tourist office on Garibaldi near Av San Martín provides a basic but helpful map of the area and its wineries. Also look for the useful three-map set *Wine Map: Wine and Tasting Tours* (Wine Map, 2004–05).

Bodega Escorihuela (☎ 0261-424-2744; www.escoriuela.com; cnr Belgrano & Pte Alvear, Godoy Cruz; ☼ tours 9:30am, 10:30am, 11:30am, 12:30pm, 2:30pm, 3:30pm), founded in 1884, is one of the country's oldest wineries. It has an art gallery, a restaurant and a famous barrel from Nancy, France, with an impressive sculpture of Dionysus. Take bus 'T' from Mendoza's Av Sarmiento at Av San Martín.

Luigi Bosca (☎ 0261-498-0437; www.luigibosca.com ar; San Martín 2044, Luján de Cuyo; guided visits Mon-Sat with reservation only), which also produces Finca La Linda, is one of Mendoza's premier wineries. If you're into wine, don't miss it. Tours are available in Spanish and English. Take bus number 380 (AR$1, one hour) from platform 53 in Mendoza's bus terminal.

The modern **Bodegas Chandon** (☎ 0261-490-9900; www.bodegaschandon.com.ar; RN 40, Km 29, Agrelo, Luján de Cuyo; guided visits Mon-Sat with reservation only) is popular with tour groups and known for its sparkling wines (champagne). Tours are available in Spanish and English. Take bus 380 (AR$1, one hour) from platform 53 in Mendoza's bus terminal.

Catena Zapata (☎ 0261-490-0214; www.catenawines.com; Calle Cobos 5519, Agrelo, Luján de Cuyo; visits/tours by appointment 10am-6pm Mon-Sat) is one of Argentina's most esteemed wineries; its pioneering owner, Nicolás Catena, is often likened to California's Robert Mondavi. Tours are fairly mundane but can be conducted in English, German or Spanish. Tasting – if you put down the cash – can be educational indeed. Get there by taxi (cheaper if you bus to Luján and grab one from there).

Cacheuta
☎ 02624 / elev 1237m
About 40km southwest of Mendoza, in the department of Luján de Cuyo, Cacheuta is renowned for its medicinal thermal waters and agreeable microclimate.

Complejo Termal Cacheuta (☎ 429133; www.termascacheuta.com; RP 82, Km 41; admission Mon-Sat AR$15, Sun AR$20; ☼ 10am-6pm) This excellent, open-air thermal baths complex is one of the best in the country, due to its variety of pools and dramatic setting on the side of a valley. Midweek is the best time to come as

weekends get crowded with kids splashing around on the waterslide and in the wave pool and the air runs thick with the smoke from a thousand *parrillas*.

There is lodging at the lovely **Hotel & Spa Cacheuta** (☎ 490152/3; www.termascacheuta.com; RP 82, Km 38; s/d with full board Sun-Thu AR$360/600; 🏊), where prices include a swimming pool, hot tubs, massage and mountain bikes, in addition to optional recreation programs. Nonguests may use the baths for AR$120 per person.

Campers can pitch a tent at **Camping Termas de Cacheuta** (☎ 482082; RN 7, Km 39; per person AR$20).

Expreso Uspallata (in Mendoza ☎ 0261-438-1092) runs daily buses to Cacheuta (AR$4, 1½ hours).

Potrerillos
☎ 02624 / elev 1351m
Set above the newly built Potrerillos reservoir in beautiful Andean precordillera, Potrerillos is one of Mendoza's white-water meccas, usually visited during a day's rafting trip from the capital.

Located about 1km uphill from the ACA campground, **Argentina Rafting Expediciones** (☎ 482037; www.argentinarafting.com in Spanish; Ruta Perilago s/n; day trips with transfer from Mendoza AR$100) offers rafting and kayaking on the Río Mendoza. Trips range from a 5km one-hour Class II float to a 50km, five-hour Class III-IV descent over two days (AR$200). Set up trips at the Mendoza **office** (☎ 0261-429-6325; Primitivo de la Reta 992, Local 4) or at the base here in Potrerillos.

El Puesto Hostel (☎ 02624-15-655-9937; Av Los Condores s/n; dm AR$30) This newish hostel has 4- to 6-bed dorms in a tranquil setting. Table tennis and darts are on hand to keep you entertained and hearty traditional meals are available (AR$20 to AR$40).

Camping del ACA (☎ 482013; RN 7, Km 50; sites members/nonmembers AR$12/15, extra tent AR$4) offers shady sites near the reservoir just below the new town.

For delicious traditional cooking, don't miss friendly **El Futre** (☎ 482006; Ruta Perilago s/n; mains AR$15), at the same location as Argentina Rafting.

Villavicencio
☎ 0261 / elev 1800m
If you've ordered mineral water from any restaurant or café in Argentina, odds are you've ended up with a bottle of Villavicencio on

your table. These springs are the source, and their spectacular mountain setting once hosted the prestigious thermal baths resort of the **Gran Hotel de Villavicencio** (admission free; ☼ 8am-8pm). Popular with the Argentine elite during the middle of the 20th century, the resort has been closed for more than a decade; promises have floated around for years that it would 'soon' reopen.

Panoramic views from the hair-raising winding turns leading to Villavicencio make the journey an attraction in itself. There is free camping alongside the attractive **Hostería Villavicencio** (☎ 424-6482; meals AR$15-25), which has no accommodations but serves light meals, coffee and beer.

There is no public transport to the valley. Nearly every tour operator in Mendoza offers half-day tours (AR$35) that take in the hotel grounds, the bottling plant and short walks in the surrounding countryside.

USPALLATA

☎ 02624 / pop 3200 / elev 1751m

A humble little crossroads town on the way to the Chilean border, Uspallata is an oasis of poplar trees set in a desolate desert valley. The polychrome mountains surrounding the town so resemble highland Central Asia that director Jean-Jacques Annaud used it as the location for the epic film *Seven Years in Tibet*, starring Brad Pitt.

The town first gained fame as a low-budget base for the nearby ski fields at Los Penitentes, but has recently been coming into its own with a few companies offering treks, horseback riding and fishing expeditions in the surrounding countryside.

There's a post office and a Banco de la Nación, which has an ATM. The tiny **tourist office** (☎ 420009; RN 7 s/n; ☼ 9am-8pm) is across from the YPF station. It has good information on local sights and activities and some very basic (but still useful) area maps.

Sights & Activities

A kilometer north of the highway junction in Uspallata, a signed lateral leads to ruins and a museum at the **Museo Las Bóvedas** (admission AR$1.50; ☼ 10am-7pm Tue-Sun), a smelting site since pre-Columbian times. On view are unintentionally comical dioramas of battles that took place during General Gregorio de Las Heras' campaign across the Andes in support of San Martín.

An easy 8km walk north of town bring you to Cerro Tunduqueral, where you'll find sweeping views and Incan rock carvings.

Pizarro Expeditions (☎ 0261-15-594-8994; www .pizarroexpediciones.com.ar) offers a range of out door activities including horseback riding, mountain bike tours, rock climbing, trekking and 4WD off-roading. Prices generally run at AR$60/100 for half-/full-day trips, depending on group size. It also rents mountain bikes for AR$7 per hour.

Fototravesías 4x4 (☎ 420185; www.fototravesias4x4 .com in Spanish; day trips per person AR$50-100), near the main intersection, offers exciting 4WD tours in the surrounding mountains. The owner is a photographer and is especially sensitive to getting good shots.

Sleeping & Eating

In the summer high season (when climbers from around the world descend on the area), reservations are wise.

Hospedaje Mi Casa (☎ 420358; hospedajemicasa@ hotmail.com; RN 7 s/n; s/d AR$50/70) A cute little *hospedaje* (family home) with very homey-feeling rooms and super-friendly owners. It's a few hundred meters east of the junction, next to the post office.

Hostel Uspallata (in Mendoza ☎ 0261-15-466-7240; www.hosteluspallata.com.ar; RN 7 s/n; dm/d AR$30/100) Friendly hostel 5km east of town with plain but comfortable rooms, a Ping-Pong table and a café. There's good hiking from the hostel. Ask the bus driver to drop you at the front before you hit Uspallata.

Hotel Viena (☎ 420046; Av Las Heras 240; s/d AR$90/130) Making an extremely ordinary first impression, this little hotel actually has some of the cutest rooms in town. Lots of wooden furniture, big TVs and real floorboards await. Bathrooms are large and modern.

Hostería Los Cóndores (☎ 420002; www.loscon doreshotel.com.ar in Spanish; Las Heras s/n; s/d AR$150/180; ✗ ▨) Close to the junction, this is the finest hotel in the center of town. There's plenty of space, modern furnishings, and a gut-busting breakfast buffet is included in the price.

Gran Hotel Uspallata (☎ 420006; hoteluspallata@ atahoteleria.com.ar; RN 7, Km 1149; s/d from AR$160/230; ✗ ▨) Though it looks a bit shopworn since its Peronist glory days, this resort hotel, about 1km west of the junction, offers an interesting taste of old-school Argentine tourism and some serious attitude from the desk staff. The hallways are large, almost daunting, there's a bowling alley, and the rooms come complete with pink chenille bedspreads.

Café Tibet (cnr RN 7 & Las Heras; mains AR$10-20; ☺ breakfast, lunch & dinner) No visit to Uspallata would be complete without at least a coffee in this little oddity. The food is nothing spectacular, but the decor, comprising leftover props from the movie, is a must for fans of the surreal.

La Bodega del Gato (cnr RN 7 & Cerro Cahacay; mains AR$14-25; ☺ lunch & dinner) An intimate little *parrilla* restaurant serving up good pizzas and a delicious grilled trout (AR$22).

Getting There & Away

Expreso Uspallata (☎ 420045) runs several buses daily to and from Mendoza (AR$13, 2½ hours). Buses continue to Las Cuevas (from Uspallata AR$12, two hours), near the Chilean border, and stop en route at Los Penitentes, Puente del Inca and the turnoff to Laguna Los Horcones for Parque Provincial Aconcagua. They can be flagged from all of these locations on their return to Uspallata from Las Cuevas.

Andesmar has daily morning departures to Santiago (AR$40, six hours) and Valparaíso (AR$45, seven hours) in Chile.

All buses leave from the Expreso Uspallata office in the little strip mall near the junction.

LOS PENITENTES
☎ 02624

So named because the pinnacles resemble a line of monks, **Los Penitentes** (☎ 420229; www.lospenitentes.com in Spanish) has both excellent scenery and snowcover (in winter). It's 165km west of Mendoza via RN 7, and offers downhill and cross-country skiing at an altitude of 2580m. Lifts (AR$80 to AR$130 per day) and accommodations are modern, and the vertical drop on some of its 21 runs is more than 700m. Services include a ski school (lessons run around AR$100), equipment rentals (skis AR$50 per day, snowboards AR$60) and several restaurants and cafeterias. For transportation details, see above.

In high ski season (July and August) and during peak climbing season (December through March), make reservations up to a month in advance for all of the following options.

Hostel Los Penitentes (☎ 664-7097; www.penitentes .com.ar; dm AR$35) This cozy converted cabin,

owned by Mendoza's HI Campo Base, accommodates 20 people in extremely close quarters, and has a kitchen, wood-burning stove and three shared bathrooms. It's all good fun with the right crowd. Lunch and dinners are available for AR$20 to AR$30 each.

Hostería Los Penitentes (in Mendoza ☎ 0261-438-0222; d with half-board AR$150) This modest *hostería* (lodging house) with plain, comfortable rooms has a restaurant and bar and offers full board with ski passes (AR$1800 per week with full board and unlimited skiing).

Refugio Aconcagua (in Mendoza ☎ 0261-424-1565; www.refugioaconcagua.com.ar; r per person with half-board AR$100) There's nothing fancy about these rooms, but they're an OK size and considering you're in the middle of the resort, with a private bathroom and two meals a day, they're a good deal. The restaurant here serves up big, hearty set meals (AR$20 to AR$30) and is open year-round.

Hotel & Hostería Ayelén (in Mendoza ☎ 0261-427-1123; www.ayelen.net; s/d hostería AR$120/150, hotel AR$170/250) Four-star resort hotel with comfortable accommodations in the main hotel and cheaper rooms in the *hostería* alongside. The lobby and restaurant are great, but the wallpaper in the rooms could use a change.

PUENTE DEL INCA
☎ 0264

One of Argentina's most striking natural wonders, this stone bridge over the Río de las Cuevas glows a dazzling orange from the sediment deposited by the warm sulfuric waters. The brick ruins of an old spa, built as part of a resort and later destroyed by flood, sit beneath the bridge, slowly yielding their form to the sulfuric buildup from the thermal water that trickles over, around and through it. Due to the unstable nature of the structure, the area has been closed off and you can't cross the bridge or enter the hot baths any more, but you can still get some fairly wild photos.

Puente del Inca, 2720m above sea level and 177km from Mendoza, sits between Parque Provincial Aconcagua and Parque Provincial Volcán Tupungato. It enjoys a spectacular setting, and whether or not you climb, it's a good base for exploring the area. Trekkers and climbers can head north to the base of Aconcagua, south to the pinnacles of Los Penitentes, or even further south to 6650m Tupungato (p364).

About 1km before Puente del Inca (directly across from Los Puquios), the small **Cementerio Andinista** is a cemetery for climbers who died on Aconcagua.

In summer, free camping is possible at the nearby mini ski resort of **Los Puquios** (☎ 420190; www.lospuquios.com.ar). There are two accommodations options at Puente del Inca.

Refugio La Vieja Estación (☎ 0261-15-526-0392; dm AR$25; meals AR$30) is a rustic hostel in Puente del Inca's old wooden train station, built in the late 1800s. It's popular with climbers during peak season but can be wonderfully quiet other times of the year. If you're up for some outdoor action, these are the guys to ask – they'll take you trekking for one to three days (AR$60 per day) in summer or point you in the direction of the best backcountry skiing in winter – a six-hour walk uphill for two hours of downhill, track-carving bliss.

Hostería Puente del Inca (☎ 420266; RN 7, Km 175; s/d AR$120/140, with half-board AR$160/220) has comfortable rooms and a huge restaurant (with an overpowering smell of budget air-freshener) serving AR$25 set meals. It's the most comfortable in the area and fills up fast in climbing season.

For transportation details, see p361.

PARQUE PROVINCIAL ACONCAGUA

North of RN 7, nearly hugging the Chilean border, Parque Provincial Aconcagua protects 710 sq km of the wild high country surrounding the western hemisphere's highest summit, 6962m Cerro Aconcagua. Passing motorists (and those who can time their buses correctly) can stop to enjoy the view of the peak from **Laguna Los Horcones**, a 2km walk from the parking lot just north of the highway.

There's a ranger available at Laguna Los Horcones from 8am to 9pm weekdays, 8am to 8pm Saturday. There are also rangers at the junction to Plaza Francia, about 5km north of Los Horcones; at Plaza de Mulas on the main route to the peak; at Refugio Las Leñas, on the Polish Glacier Route up the Río de las Vacas to the east; and at Plaza Argentina, the last major camping area along the Polish Glacier Route.

Only highly experienced climbers should consider climbing Aconcagua without the relative safety of an organized tour.

Cerro Aconcagua

Often called the 'roof of the Americas,' the volcanic summit of Aconcagua covers a base of uplifted marine sediments. The origin of

the name is unclear; one possibility is the Quechua term Ackon-Cahuac, meaning 'stone sentinel,' while another is the Mapuche phrase Acon-Hue, signifying 'that which comes from the other side.'

Italian-Swiss climber Mathias Zurbriggen made the first recorded ascent in 1897. Since then, the peak has become a favorite destination for climbers from around the world, even though it is technically less challenging than other nearby peaks. In 1985 the Club Andinista Mendoza's discovery of an Incan mummy at 5300m on the mountain's southwest face proved that the high peaks were a pre-Columbian funerary site.

Reaching the summit requires a commitment of at least 13 to 15 days, including acclimatization time; some climbers prefer the longer but more scenic, less crowded and more technical Polish Glacier Route.

Potential climbers should acquire RJ Secor's climbing guide Aconcagua (Seattle, The Mountaineers, 1999). The web page www .aconcagua.com.ar is also helpful.

Nonclimbers can trek to **base camps** and **refugios** (rustic shelters) beneath the permanent snow line. On the Northwest Route there is also the rather luxurious **Hotel Refugio Plaza de Mulas** (☎ 02642-490442; www.refugioplaza demulas.com.ar; dm AR$70, r per person AR$100, with full board AR$250; ☉ Nov-Mar), the highest hotel in the world.

PERMITS

From December to March permits are obligatory for both trekking and climbing in Parque Provincial Aconcagua; park rangers at Laguna Horcones will not permit visitors to proceed up the Quebrada de los Horcones without one. Fees vary according to the complex park-use seasons. Permits cost AR$90/150 for trekkers (three/seven days), and AR$900 for climbers (20 days) during high season, from December 15 through January 31; AR$60/120 for trekkers and AR$600 for climbers during midseason, from December 1 to December 14 and February 1 through February 20; and AR$40/60 (trekking) and AR$300 (climbing) in low season, from November 15 through November 30 and February 21 through March 15. Argentine nationals pay half price at all times.

Organized tours rarely, if ever, include the park entrance fee. Fees must be paid in Argentine Pesos or US dollars only, and you must bring your original passport with you when you pay the fee. The permit start-date takes effect when you enter the park.

The three-day trekking permit can be purchased directly at Horcones ranger station, but hikers with the three-day permit are not allowed above 4200m. All other permits are available only in Mendoza at the Provincial Tourist Office (p347).

ROUTES
There are three main routes up Cerro Aconcagua. The most popular one, approached by a 40km trail from Los Horcones, is the **Ruta Noroeste** (Northwest Route) from Plaza de Mulas, 4230m above sea level. The **Pared Sur** (South Face), approached from the base camp at Plaza Francia via a 36km trail from Los Horcones, is a demanding technical climb.

From Punta de Vacas, 15km southeast of Puente del Inca, the longer but more scenic **Ruta Glaciar de los Polacos** (Polish Glacier Route) first ascends the Río de las Vacas to the base camp at Plaza Argentina, a distance of 76km. Climbers on this route must carry ropes, screws and ice axes, in addition to the usual tent, warm sleeping bag and clothing, and plastic boots. This route is more expensive because it requires the use of mules for a longer period.

MULES
The cost of renting cargo mules, which can carry about 60kg each, has gone through the roof: the standard fee among outfitters is AR$380 for the first mule from Puente del Inca to Plaza de Mulas, though two mules cost only AR$400. A party of three should pay about AR$700 to AR$1000 to get their gear to the Polish Glacier Route base camp and back.

For mules, contact Rudy Parra at Aconcagua Trek or Fernando Grajales, following. If you're going up on an organized tour, the mule situation is, of course, covered.

TOURS
Many of the adventure-travel agencies in and around Mendoza arrange excursions into the high mountains (see p350). It is also possible to arrange trips with overseas operators.

The following are the area's most established and experienced operators.

Daniel Alessio Expediciones (www.alessio.com.ar) Located in Mendoza, contact online.
Fernando Grajales (www.grajales.net) Contact online. Fernando operates from Hostería Puente del Inca (opposite) from December to March.

Inka Expediciones (☎ 0261-425-0871; www.inka .com.ar; Juan B Justo 345, Mendoza) Fixed and tailor-made expeditions. Airport to airport costs AR$7000 to AR$8000.
Rudy Parra's Aconcagua Trek (in Mendoza ☎ /fax 0261-429-5007; www.rudyparra.com) Contact Rudy by telephone. Rudy operates at nearby Los Puquios (opposite) from December to March.

Several guides from the **Asociación Argentina de Guías de Montaña** (www.aagm.com.ar in Spanish) lead two-week trips to Aconcagua, including **Pablo Reguera** (pabloreguera@hotmail.com) and **Mauricio Fernández** (info@summit-mza.com.ar).

All guides and organized trips are best set up online or by telephone *at least* a month in advance. Everything – guides, mules, hotels etc – must be booked far in advance during peak climbing months.

Getting There & Away
The two park entrances – Punta de Vacas and Laguna Los Horcones – are directly off RN 7 and are well signed. The Los Horcones turnoff is only 4km past Puente del Inca. If you're part of an organized tour, transport will be provided. To get here by bus, take an early morning Expreso Uspallata bus (see p361) from Mendoza. Buses bound for Chile will stop at Puente del Inca, but often fill up with passengers going all the way through.

From Los Horcones, you can walk back along the RN 7 to Puente del Inca or time your buses and catch a Mendoza-bound bus back down.

LAS CUEVAS & CRISTO REDENTOR
Pounded by chilly but exhilarating winds, situated nearly 4000m above sea level on the Argentine–Chilean border, the rugged high Andes make a fitting backdrop for Cristo Redentor, the famous monument erected after a territorial dispute between the two countries was settled in 1902. The view is a must-see either with a tour or by private car (a tunnel has replaced the hairpin road to the top as the border crossing into Chile), but the first autumn snowfall closes the route. You can hike the 8km up to El Cristo via trails if you don't have a car.

In the nearby settlement of Las Cuevas, 10km east of the Chilean border and 15km from Puente del Inca, **Arco de Las Cuevas** (☎ 0261-426-5273; www.arcodelascuevas.com.ar; mains AR$25; dm AR$30) has extremely basic bunks and only two bathrooms (which everyone in the restaurant uses as well). The restaurant, however, serves what one traveler called the 'best lentil soup ever' (hunger and cold make mighty good sauces).

PARQUE PROVINCIAL VOLCÁN TUPUNGATO

Tupungato (6650m) is an impressive volcano, partly covered by snowfields and glaciers, and serious climbers consider the mountain a far more challenging, interesting and technical climb than Aconcagua. The main approach is from the town of **Tunuyán**, 82km south of Mendoza via RN 40, where the **tourist office** (☎ 02622-488097, 02622-422193; República de Siria & Alem) can provide info. Many of the outfitters who arrange Aconcagua treks can also deal with Tupungato (see p363).

SAN RAFAEL

☎ 02627 / pop 112,000 / elev 690m

Arriving by bus at San Rafael's scruffy terminal, you're bound to be underwhelmed. Persevere, though – a few blocks away lies a busy, modern town whose streets are lined with majestic old sycamores and open irrigation channels. It's not exactly Mendoza, but it's getting there.

There is nothing to do in town (part of its allure) except wander its shady streets and plazas or while the day away in a café. There are, however, several esteemed wineries within biking distance that are well worth a visit. The city has also become a popular base for exploring (or driving through) the nearby Cañon de Atuel (p366) and for scenic rafting on the Río Atuel.

Orientation

San Rafael is located 230km southeast of the city of Mendoza via RN 40 and RN 143, and 189km northeast of Malargüe via RN 40. Most areas of interest in town are northwest of the Av H Yrigoyen and Av San Martín intersection.

Information

Banco de Galicia (Av H Yrigoyen 28) Several banks along Av H Yrigoyen have ATMs, including Banco de Galicia.
Cambio Santiago (Almafuerte 64) Charges 2.5% on traveler's checks.
Hospital Teodoro J Schestakow (☎ 424490; Emilio Civit 151)
Municipal tourist office (☎ 424217; www.sanrafael -tour.com; Av H Yrigoyen 745; ☼ 8am-8pm) Helpful staff and useful brochures and maps.
Post office (cnr San Lorenzo & Barcala)

Sights & Activities

San Rafael is flat (hence the proliferation of bike riders here), and when in Rome…get a bike. Try **Bicipartes** (☎ 430260; Chile 445; per half-day/day AR$20/30; ☼ 8am-1pm & 4-9pm Mon-Sat).

There are numerous tourist agencies offering standard local excursions to Valle Grande and nearby wineries. **Leufú** (☎ /fax 428164; Cabildo 1483) does rafting, mountain biking and other activities.

There are three wineries within walking or cycling distance of town offering free tours and tasting. Head west on RN 143, which has a welcome bike path (really!) along its side. The modern and highly regarded **Bianchi Champañera** (☎ 435600; www.vbianchi.com; cnr Ruta 143 & Calle Valentín Bianchi; ☼ 9am-12:30pm & 2-5pm) is the furthest west, but still only 6km away. Tours are friendly, offering visitors a glimpse into the making of sparkling wine (champagne), and English is spoken.

Only about 4km out, **Fincas Andinas** (Salafia; ☎ 430095; www.fincasandinas.com.ar; Av H Yrigoyen 5800; ☼ guided visits every half hr 9:30am-4pm Mon-Fri) makes excellent sparkling wine as well as malbec and cabernet.

Halfway between Fincas Andinas and San Rafael, **Suter** (☎ 421076; www.sutersa.com.ar in Spanish; Yrigoyen 2850; short tours free; ☼ 9:30am-12:30pm, 1:30-5pm Mon-Sat) is a rather unromantic, modern affair, but a worthwhile stop for some discounted wine. For AR$100 you can set up a half-day tour, visiting the vineyards with an agronomist, tasting specialty wines and eating a big lunch in the vineyard.

If wineries and bikes aren't your thing, the nearby Cañon de Atuel (p366) is an easy, scenic daytrip from San Rafael. The canyon also has plenty of accommodation options should you want to stay.

Sleeping

Trotamundos (☎ 432795; www.trotamundoshostel .com.ar; Barcala 300; dm AR$30) The best hostel in town is a few blocks from the bus terminal and features small dorms, a good common area and a well-stocked kitchen. The young staff has plenty of local info on things to do around town.

Hotel España (☎ 424055; hotelespanasrl@volsinectis.com .ar; Av San Martín 270; s/d AR$60/80) It may not scream 'Spain,' but the mod 1960s-ish interior is definitely unique. Rooms in the 'colonial' sector open onto a delightful patio area, making them

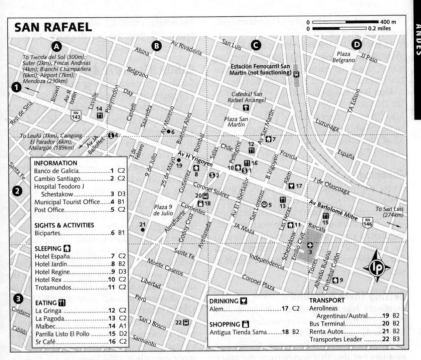

SAN RAFAEL

0 —————— 400 m
0 —————— 0.2 miles

INFORMATION
Banco de Galicia.................1 C2
Cambio Santiago.................2 C2
Hospital Teodoro J
Schestakow....................3 D3
Municipal Tourist Office.....4 B1
Post Office........................5 C2

SIGHTS & ACTIVITIES
Bicipartes...........................6 B1

SLEEPING
Hotel España......................7 C2
Hotel Jardín.......................8 B2
Hotel Regine.......................9 D3
Hotel Rex 10 C2
Trotamundos.....................11 C2

EATING
La Gringa..........................12 C2
La Pagoda.........................13 C2
Malbec..............................14 A1
Parrilla Listo El Pollo.........15 D2
Sr Café.............................16 C2

DRINKING
Alem................................17 C2

SHOPPING
Antigua Tienda Sama........18 B2

TRANSPORT
Aerolíneas
Argentinas/Austral........19 B2
Bus Terminal.....................20 B2
Renta Autos......................21 B2
Transportes Leader 22 B3

---

more attractive (and a better deal) than the spacious rooms in the pricier 'celeste' sector.

Hotel Rex (☎ 422177; www.rexhotel.com.ar; Av H Yrigoyen 56; s/d AR$60/90; ✿) The Rex has seen better days, but it has plenty of fading charm, including squeaky floorboards and huge bathrooms with tub.

Hotel Jardín (☎ /fax 434621; hoteljardin@speedy .com.ar; Av H Yrigoyen 283; s/d AR$140/170; ✿) There is indeed a garden here – or better said, a courtyard – filled with baroque touches like fountains and sculptures of nude Greek figures. Rooms face onto it and are big and comfortable, if slightly soulless.

Hotel Regine (☎ 421470; www.hotelregine.com.ar; Independencia 623; s/d AR$180/220; ☖) A bit of a walk from the center, but well worth it for the big stylish rooms. The palm-shaded pool/café/bar area is a real bonus.

Camping El Parador (☎ 427983; Isla Río Diamante; sites AR$18) Located 6km south of downtown.

Eating & Drinking

Parrilla Listo El Pollo (Av Bartolomé Mitre s/n; parrilla AR$20; ✹ lunch & dinner) The roadside *parrilla* is an Argentine classic and this one's a great example. Grab a sidewalk table (not that there's any choice) and knock elbows with taxi drivers while feasting on big cheap chunks of meat.

Tienda del Sol (☎ 425022; Av H Yrigoyen 1663; sandwiches AR$10-15; ✹ lunch) Stylish sandwich shop (try the Tienda del Sol with chicken and blue cheese) with outdoor tables and massive, creative hot sandwiches.

La Pagoda (Av Bartolomé Mitre 188; tenedor libre AR$15; ✹ lunch & dinner) Anybody familiar with the all-you-can-eat scene in Argentina won't find too many surprises here, but the food (Argentine and Chinese) is fresh enough – get there early – and there's plenty of it.

Sr Café (Av San Martín 49; sandwiches AR$12, mains AR$15-20; ✹ lunch & dinner) The most stylin' little café in the center, this is a good place for coffee and a sandwich anytime. Weekend nights, pull up an outside table and enjoy the live music.

Malbec (Av H Yrigoyen & Pueyrredón; mains AR$15-20; ✹ lunch & dinner) San Rafael's most frequently recommended *parrilla* holds no surprises, but has a good range of pastas and salads and, yes, some big juicy steaks.

La Gringa (Chile near Av San Martín; mains AR$18-25; ⏰ lunch & dinner) Despite its rather unappealing name, this is the go-to place in town for pastas, pizza and *parrilla*. Good salads, too.

Alem (Alem & Av Bartolomé Mitre; ⏰ 10pm-late Wed-Sat) Do your best to drop into this bar for the long list of cocktails and what's likely to be the most stylishly designed interior you'll find in all of Mendoza province. It's hard to believe it's San Rafael.

Shopping

There are numerous crafts stores around town, all of which stock the usual souvenirs. For something a bit more authentic, pick up a pair of *bombachas* (commonly worn gaucho-influenced pants with button-cuff bottoms) for about AR$60 at friendly **Antigua Tienda Sama** (Godoy Cruz 123); they're subtle enough to wear anywhere.

Getting There & Around

Aerolíneas Argentinas/Austral (☎ 438808; Av H Yrigoyen 395) flies daily except Sunday to/from Buenos Aires (from AR$600).

If you're headed to Patagonia, there's one minibus per day that leaves from the office of **Transportes Leader** (☎ 421851; Perú 65) for Buta Ranquil (AR$65, eight hours) in Neuquén province via Malargüe. It leaves at 6pm and spaces sell out quickly – it's recommended to book (and pay) a couple of days in advance. If you're in a hurry, it's actually quicker to go the long way around, via Neuquén.

San Rafael's **bus terminal** (Coronel Suárez) is conveniently located downtown. There are regular daily departures to the following destinations.

Destination	Cost (AR$)	Duration (hr)
Bariloche	150	14-15
Buenos Aires	130	13
Córdoba	65	12
El Nihuil	7	1½
Las Leñas	19	3
Malargüe	17	3
Mar del Plata	130	16
Mendoza	3.50	3
Neuquén	85	10
Rosario	80	13
San Juan	40	6
San Luis	30	4
Valle Grande/ Cañon del Atuel	6	1

Renta Autos (☎ 424623; rentaautos@infovia.com.ar; 25 de Mayo 380) offers the best deals on car rentals in town.

CAÑON DEL ATUEL & VALLE GRANDE

South of San Rafael along the Río Atuel, RP 173 passes through a multicolored ravine that locals compare to Arizona's Grand Canyon, though much of the 67km **Cañon del Atuel** (www .atuelcanon.com) has been submerged by four hydroelectric dams. Nevertheless, there is whitewater rafting on its lower reaches, and several operators at the tourist complex of **Valle Grande**, midway down the canyon, do short but scenic floats down the river, and other trips.

Sport Star (☎ 02627-15-581068; www.sportstar.com.ar; RP 173, Km 35) offers the widest range of activities, including trekking, horseback riding, kayaking, mountain bike tours, canoes and rappelling.

There are numerous places to stay in Valle Grande itself. Most of them cater to large groups and are rather unpleasant, but the small **Cabañas Balcón del Atuel** (☎ 02627-426265; www.elbaqueano.org/balcondelatuel in Spanish; RP 173, Km 24; d AR$120, cabaña for 6 AR$180) has three comfortable *cabañas* and one double (all with kitchens), with a lovely grassy area over the river – a great spot to while away a day or two in the sun, especially in off-season.

Camping Rio Azul (☎ 02627-423663; RP 173, Km 25; sites AR$15) offers the best facilities for campers and has a restaurant on the grounds.

RP 173 leads past the dam at Valle Grande, through the scenic Cañon del Atuel to the podunk village of **El Nihuil**, 79km from San Rafael.

Numerous San Rafael tour companies run day trips to Valle Grande, starting at AR$60. For bus service to Valle Grande, Transportes Iselín leaves from the bus terminal in San Rafael (see left; AR$6, one hour). Buses to El Nihuil take the alternative RP 144, which doesn't go through the canyon.

MALARGÜE

☎ 02627 / pop 23,000 / elev 1400m

Despite serving as a base for Las Leñas, one of Argentina's snazzier ski resorts, Malargüe is a mellow little town that even gets a little rough around the edges. For skiers it's a cheaper alternative to the luxury hotels on the mountain, and people staying here get a 50% discount on lift tickets (hotels provide vouchers). The dry precordillera that surrounds the town is geologically distinct from the Andes proper and two fauna reserves, Payén and Laguna Llancancelo, are close by. Caving is possible at Caverna de las Brujas and Pozo de las Animas. The nearby Parque Provincial Payunia is a 4500-sq-km reserve with the highest concentration of volcanic cones in the world.

Information

Banco de la Nación (cnr San Martín & Inalicán) One of several banks downtown with ATMs.

Post office (cnr Adolfo Puebla & Saturnino Torres)

Tourist office (☎ 471659; www.malargue.gov.ar; RN 40, Parque del Ayer; ☼ 8am-11pm) Helpful tourist office with facilities at the northern end of town, on the highway.

Sights

If the exterior of Malargüe's soon-to-be-opened **Planetarium** (Villegas & Aldeo) is anything to go by, we're in for a treat. The main building has been constructed to look as if it's sinking into the ground and the front yard features, among other things, a giant blue plastic pyramid. It should be open by the time you get there. Check it out.

Activities & Tours

Several companies offer excellent 4WD and horseback-riding excursions, and if you don't have a car, these are generally the best way to get into the surrounding mountains (see p368). Possible day trips include Caverna de las Brujas (AR$80 per person, which includes AR$20 park entrance fee and obligatory guide), Los Molles (AR$50), and the marvelous Laguna Llancancelo (AR$60). One of the most exciting drives you might ever undertake is the 12-hour 4WD tour through Parque Provincial Payunia (AR$190); be sure your tour stops at all the sites – those that combine the visit with Laguna Llancancelo only visit half the sites in Payunia.

Amulén (☎ 470019; www.amulenturismo.com.ar in Spanish; San Martín 540) offers half-day horseback or hiking trips to the spectacular **Volcán Malacara** (AR$80), which you should do your best to see. The company also offers a two-day trip through Parque Provincial Payunia complete with an *asado* (barbecue) under the stars.

Huarpes del Sol (☎ 02627 -15-557878; www.huarpes delsol.com.ar in Spanish; San Martín 85) and **Receptivo Malargüe** (☎ 471524; www.receptivomalargue.com.ar in Spanish; San Martín 328) have both received excellent reports for their trips; the latter offers a wide array of adventure trips. The owner of **Karen Travel** (☎ /fax 470342; www.karentravel.com.ar; San Martín

54) speaks English and the company trips have received rave reviews.

Sleeping

Malargüe has abundant, reasonably priced accommodations. Prices quoted here are for ski season (June 15 through to September 15) and drop by up to 40% the rest of the year. Get a discount voucher from your hotel if you plan to ski at Las Leñas. Singles are nonexistent during ski season, when you'll likely be charged for however many beds are in the room.

Hostel Nord Patagonia (☎ 472276; Fray Inalican 52 este; dm AR$40) Friendly hostel in a small converted house with fireplace and big wooden tables in a little common room.

Hotel Theis (☎ 470136; Av San Martín 938; s/d AR$100/120) Taking the opposite tack to the Pehuén, the Theis looks very ornery on the outside but features some of the sweetest rooms in town. They're spacious and well kept, with tiled floors, big TVs and modern bathrooms.

Hotel de Turismo (☎ 471042; Av San Martín 224; s/d AR$100/120) The Turismo's a good standby – there are plenty of rooms (which are nothing special) so it rarely fills up. The downstairs restaurant/café lifts the tone with a few charming touches.

Hotel Pehuén (☎ 02627-15-587-7024; Ruibal & A Puebla; s/d AR$110/140) Although the exterior is a lot better looking than the interior, the Pehuén still has some good-sized rooms (which vary – have a look at a few if you can) with fading carpet and floral bedspreads.

Hotel El Cisne (☎ 471350; Civit & Villegas; s/d AR$120/140) A new, ultramodern hotel with a good central location. Rooms are big, with plenty of furnishings and attractive pine-lined ceilings.

Hotel Bambi (☎ 471237; Av San Martín 410; s/d AR$150/180) Friendly hotel with clean but faded rooms with basic bathrooms. It's the most comfortable place downtown.

Camping Municipal Malargüe (☎ 470691; Alfonso Capdevila s/n; sites AR$10; ☼ year-round) At the north end of town, 300m west of Av San Martín, this is the closest place to camp.

Eating & Drinking

Don Gauderio (San Martín & Torres; mains AR$12-20; ☼ breakfast, lunch & dinner) A hip little nouveau-rustic bar on the plaza. Meal-sized sandwiches are the standouts here, but the pizzas and savory crepes deserve a mention too.

La Posta (☎ 471306; Av Roca 374; mains AR$15-20; ☺ lunch & dinner) A friendly neighborhood *parrilla*, La Posta comes up with the goods in the juicy steak, wine list and televised football department.

El Quincho de María (San Martín 440; mains AR$15-25; ☺ lunch & dinner) The finest dining in the center is at this cozy little *parrilla* where everything from the gnocchi to the empanadas is handmade. Don't miss the mouth-watering shish kebabs for AR$25.

Getting There & Around

There are charter flights to and from Buenos Aires in ski season only, leaving from the **Malargüe airport** (☎ 470098) at the south end of town. They're usually sold as part of an accommodation package for Las Leñas, but if there's space, they can squeeze you in. Contact the **Las Leñas office** (in Buenos Aires ☎ 011-4819-6000; www.laslenas.com; Cerrito 1186, 8th fl) for details.

There's a **bus terminal** (cnr Av General Roca & Aldao). There are several direct buses to Mendoza daily (AR$34, seven hours), plus others requiring a change in San Rafael (AR$17, three hours). In summertime, there's one departure daily for Los Molles (AR$6, one hour) and Las Leñas (AR$10, 1½ hours).

Transportes Leader (☎ 470519; San Martín & Roca) has one minibus leaving daily for Buta Ranquil (AR$55, five hours) in Neuquén at 9pm. Seats sell out fast – it's recommended that you book (and pay) at least two days in advance.

For winter transportation to Los Molles and Las Leñas ski resorts, contact any of the travel agencies listed on p367. They offer a roundtrip shuttle service, including ski rentals, from AR$30 to AR$50 per person.

AROUND MALARGÜE
☎ 02627

Geologically distinct from the Andean mountains to the west, the volcanically formed landscapes surrounding Malargüe are some of the most mind-altering in Argentina and have only recently begun to receive tourist attention. Visiting the following places is impossible without your own transportation, though Malargüe's excellent travel agencies arrange excursions to all of them.

Just over 200km south of Malargüe on the RN 40, the spectacular **Parque Provincial Payunia** is a 4500-sq-km reserve with a higher concentration of volcanic cones (over 800 of them) than anywhere else in the world. The scen-

ery is breathtaking and shouldn't be missed. The 12-hour 4WD tours or three-day horseback trips offered by most of the agencies in Malargüe (p367) are well worth taking.

Lying within its namesake fauna reserve about 60km southeast of Malargüe, **Laguna Llancancelo** is a high mountain lake visited by more than 100 species of birds, including flamingos.

Caverna de Las Brujas is a magical limestone cave on Cerro Moncol, 72km south of Malargüe and 8km north of Bardas Blancas along RN 40. Its name means 'Cave of the Witches.' The cave complex stretches for 5km. Guided tours (admission and flashlights included in the price) take two to three hours. Tours depart with a minimum group size of two, although getting more people together will bring down the per-person cost. Check with tour operators in Malargüe for details.

Los Molles

Before Las Leñas took over as the prime ski resort in the area, Los Molles was the only place around where you could grab a poma. These days it's a dusty windswept village that would be slowly sinking into obscurity if not for its reasonably priced accommodation alternatives for those wishing to be near, but not in, Las Leñas, and its favored status for rock climbers, hikers and other rugged outdoor types. The village straddles RP 222, 55km northwest of Malargüe. **Turismo Nuestra Tierra** (☎ in Buenos Aires 011-4831-8149; www.nuestratierraweb .com.ar) operates out of the Club Hualam Hotel in summer time, offering trekking, mountain biking, rock climbing and horseback riding trips in the dramatic countryside that surround the village.

Hostel Piriá (☎ 02627-15-516757; dm AR$30) Across the bridge and up the valley from the highway, this little *refugio* offers reasonable dorms, a big common area, cheap meals and kitchen access. Also on site, a 'mountain school' teaches rock climbing and ice climbing, depending on the season.

Hotel Los Molles (☎ 02627-499712; www.losmolleshotel .com.ar; RP 222, Km 30; r per person AR$120) The most modern and best equipped of the hotels here, this one features big rooms with balconies facing out over the valley. A decent restaurant serves good-value set meals (AR$30).

Buses heading between Malargüe (AR$6, one hour) and Las Leñas (AR$4, 30 minutes) pass through the village.

LAS LEÑAS

☎ 02627

Designed primarily to attract wealthy foreigners, **Las Leñas** (☎ 471100; www.laslenas.com; ⏱ mid-Jun–late-Sep) is Argentina's most self-consciously prestigious ski resort. Since its opening in 1983 it has attracted an international clientele who spend their days on the slopes and nights partying until the sun comes up. Because of the dry climate, Las Leñas has incredibly dry powder.

Las Leñas is 445km south of Mendoza, 200km southwest of San Rafael and only 70km from Malargüe, all via RN 40 and RP 222.

Its 33 runs cover 33 sq km; the area has a base altitude of 2200m, but slopes reach 3430m for a maximum drop of 1230m.

Outside the ski season Las Leñas is also attempting to attract summer visitors who enjoy week-long packages, offering activities such as mountain biking, horseback riding and hiking.

Lift Tickets & Rentals

Prices for lift tickets vary considerably throughout the ski season. Children's tickets are discounted about 30%. One-day tickets range from AR$100 in low season to AR$152 in high season (week passes AR$528 to AR$813). Also available are three-day, four-day, two-week and season passes. Anyone lodging in Malargüe receives 50% off lift tickets (make sure you get a voucher from your hotel).

Rental equipment is readily available and will set you back about AR$100 per day for skis and AR$60 per day for snowboards.

Sleeping & Eating

Las Leñas has a small village with four luxury hotels and a group of 'apart hotels,' all under the same management. They are generally booked as part of a week-long package, which includes lodging, unlimited skiing and two meals per day. Despite the country's economic troubles, rates for foreigners staying in Las Leñas have changed little. All booking is done online at www.laslenas.com or centrally through **Ski Leñas** (☎ in Buenos Aires 011-4819-6000/60; ventas@laslenas.com; Cerrito 1186, 8th fl).

Virgo Hotel & Spa (AR$4800-11,000) The newest hotel in the village, this one goes all out, with a heated outdoor swimming pool, sushi bar, whirlpool bath and cinema.

Hotel Escorpio (AR$4200-12,000) This 47-room hotel is nominally three stars, but still top-notch, with an excellent restaurant.

Hotel Aries (AR$4600-10,000) Aries is a four-star hotel with a sauna, gym facilities, a restaurant and luxuriously comfortable rooms.

Hotel Piscis (weekly adult package rates per person AR$5400-15,000; ☻) The most extravagant of Las Leña's lodging is the five-star, 99-room Hotel Piscis. This prestigious hotel has wood-burning stoves, a gymnasium, sauna, an indoor swimming pool, the elegant Las Cuatro Estaciones restaurant, a bar, a casino and shops. Rates depend on time of the season, and are based on double occupancy.

Apart Hotel Gemenis (weekly per person AR$3100-4200) and **Apart Hotel Delphos** (weekly per person AR$3100-4200) offer similar packages without meals but do have well-equipped kitchenettes.

There are also small apartments with two to six beds and shared bathrooms, equipped for travelers to cook for themselves. Budget travelers can stay more economically at Los Molles, 20km down the road, or at Malargüe, 70km away.

Restaurants in the village run the comestible gamut, from cafés, sandwich shops and pizzerias to upscale hotel dining rooms. The finest restaurant of all is Las Cuatro Estaciones, in the Hotel Piscis.

Getting There & Away

In season, there are charter flights from Buenos Aires to Malargüe, including transfers to and from Las Leñas. These are most commonly booked as part of an accommodation package with one of the Las Leñas hotels.

There is bus service operating in season from Mendoza (AR$30, 6½ hours), San Rafael (AR$19, three hours) and Malargüe (AR$10, 1½ hours).

SAN JUAN

☎ 0264 / pop 460,200 / elev 650m

Living in the shadow of a world-class destination like Mendoza can't be easy and, to its credit, San Juan doesn't even try to compete. Life in this provincial capital moves at its own pace, and the locals are both proud and humble about their little town.

No slouch on the wine production front, San Juan's wineries are refreshingly low-key after the Mendoza bustle, and the province's other attractions are all within easy reach of the capital. Most come here en route to Parque Provincial Ischigualasto (p379).

In 1944 a massive earthquake destroyed the city center, and Juan Perón's subsequent

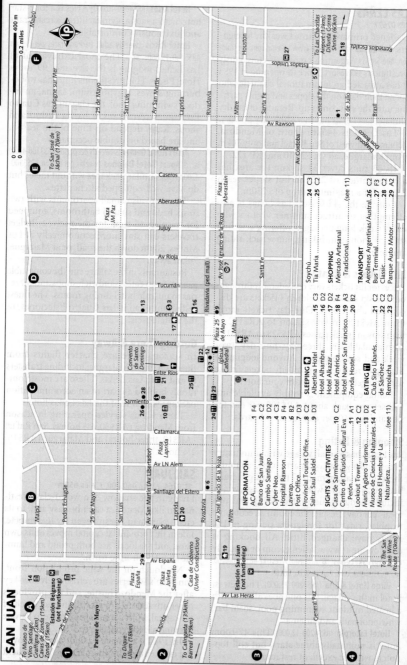

SAN JUAN

relief efforts are what first made him a national figure. The city goes dead in summer, especially on Sunday, when all of San Juan heads to the nearby shores of Dique Ullum for relief from the sun.

Orientation

San Juan is 170km north of Mendoza via RN 40 and 1140km from Buenos Aires. Like in most Argentine cities, San Juan's grid pattern makes orientation very easy; the addition of cardinal points – *norte* (north), *sur* (south), *este* (east) and *oeste* (west) – to street addresses helps even more. East–west Av San Martín and north–south Calle Mendoza divide the city into these quadrants. The functional center of town is south of Av San Martín, often referred to as Av Libertador.

Information

ACA (Automóvil Club Argentina; ☎ 422-3781; 9 de Julio 802) Argentina's auto club; good source for provincial road maps.

Banco de San Juan (cnr Rivadavia & Entre Ríos) Has ATM.

Cambio Santiago (General Acha 52 Sur) Money exchange.

Cyber Neo (cnr Mitre & Entre Ríos; per hr AR$2) One of countless internet cafés in San Juan.

Hospital Rawson (☎ 422-2272; cnr General Paz & Estados Unidos)

Laverap (Rivadavia 498 Oeste; full laundry service about AR$8)

Post office (Av José Ignacio de la Roza 259 Este)

Provincial tourist office (☎ 422-2431, 421-0004; www.turismo.sanjuan.gov.ar in Spanish; Sarmiento 24 Sur; 🕑 7am-8pm Mon-Fri, 9am-8pm Sat & Sun) Has a good map of the city and its surroundings plus useful information on the rest of the province, particularly Parque Provincial Ischigualasto.

Sights & Activities

If you need a little perspective on things, make your way up the **Lookout Tower** (Mendoza & Rivadavia; admission AR$2; 🕑 9am-1pm, 5-9pm) for a sweeping view out over the town and surrounding countryside.

Museum hours change often, so check with the tourist office for updated information.

The **Casa de Sarmiento** (☎ 422-4603; Sarmiento 21 Sur; admission AR$3; 🕑 9am-7pm Tue-Fri, 9am-2pm Sat, 9am-9pm Sun) is named for Domingo Faustino Sarmiento, whose prolific writing as a politician, diplomat, educator and journalist made him a public figure both within and beyond Argentina. Sarmiento's *Recuerdos de Provincia* recounted his childhood in this

house and his memories of his mother, Doña Paula Albarracín, who paid for part of the house's construction by weaving cloth in a loom under the fig tree that still stands in the front patio. The house is now a museum.

The most interesting specimen at the **Museo de Ciencias Naturales** (Museum of Natural Sciences; ☎ 421-6774; admission free; 🕑 9am-1pm) is the skeleton of the dinosaur Herrerasaurus from Ischigualasto, though there are plenty of provincial minerals, fossils and other exhibits to mull over. The museum is next to the old train station on Av España at Maipú.

Museo de Vino Santiago Graffigna (☎ 421-4227; museograffigna@adsw.com; Colón 1342 Norte; 🕑 9am-6pm Mon-Sat, 10am-4pm Sun; wine bar 9am-2am Fri & Sat) is a wine museum well worth a visit. It also has a wine bar where you can taste many of San Juan's best wines. Bus 12 'A' passes by the front door.

At Av España and 25 de Mayo, the now-defunct Estación Belgrano (train station) has been recycled into the **Centro de Difusión Cultural Eva Perón**, a cultural center that includes the anthropological museum, **Museo El Hombre y La Naturaleza** (admission AR$3; 🕑 9am-noon & 4-7pm), a combination museum/gift shop showcasing weavings and pottery finds from the region.

Tour operators in San Juan provide lots of options for taking in the sights in and around town.

Mario Agüero Turismo (☎ 422-3652; General Acha 17 Norte) Offers organized tours including Parque Provincial Ischigualasto.

Saitur Saul Saidel (☎ 422-2700; saitur@saulsaidel .com; Av José Ignacio de la Roza 112 Este) Offers city tours and day trips to Ischigualasto (AR$175) and elsewhere.

Sleeping

Zonda Hostel (☎ 420-1009; www.zondahostel.com.ar; Laprida 572 Oeste; dm AR$25) A well-set-up hostel, with good kitchen and common areas and a great backyard. Also organizes wine tours and activities like kite surfing, wind sailing and trekking. One room has a balcony over the street.

Hotel Nuevo San Francisco (☎ 422-3760; www .nuevo-sanfrancisco.com.ar in Spanish; Av España 284 Sur; r AR$90; 🖳) Excellent value for money, with big modern rooms set close to the park. Also offers 'apartments' with kitchenette for AR$170.

Hotel América (☎ 421-4514; www.hotel-america.com .ar; 9 de Julio 1052 Este; s/d AR$90/110; 🖳 🖳) This is excellent value in a drab location. It conveniently offers excursions through an on-site tour operator and is a popular place with a good restaurant.

Hotel Alhambra (☎ 421-4780; www.alhambrahotel .com.ar; General Acha 180 Sur; s/d AR$90/130; ☒) Cozy, carpeted rooms with splashes of dark wood paneling giving them a classy edge. Little touches like leather chairs and gold ashtray stands in the hallways give it a kitschy appeal and the central location seals the deal.

Albertina Hotel (☎ /fax 421-4222; www.hotel albertina.com; Mitre 31 Este; s/d AR$120/140; ☒ ☐) A slick, business-class hotel right on the plaza. Stay for more than two nights and you get free massages, gym access and yoga classes. The tiny rooms are a bit of a let down, but the bathrooms are big. Fair deal.

Hotel Alkazar (☎ 421-4965; www.alkazarhotel.com.ar in Spanish; Laprida 82 Este; s/d AR$220/260; ☒ ☐) San Juan's most upscale hotel teeters on corporate blandness, but pulls it off in the end, with big, stylishly decorated rooms. Services include a spa, sauna and on-site masseuse.

Eating

Most restaurants are right downtown, and many of the city's hippest eateries are around the corner of Rivadavia and Entre Ríos.

Soychú (☎ 422-1939; Av José Ignacio de la Roza 223 Oeste; tenedor libre AR$17; ☺ noon-4pm & 9pm-midnight Mon-Sat, lunch only Sun) Excellent vegetarian buffet attached to a health-food store selling all sorts of groceries and a range of teas. Arrive early for the best selection.

Remolacha (Av Ignacio de la Roza & Sarmiento; mains AR$10-20; ☺ lunch & dinner) One of the biggest *parrillas* in town, the dining room is extremely ordinary, but eating in the garden is a lush experience. Get a table by the picture windows looking into the kitchen and you'll be able to see your meal being hacked off the carcass before getting thrown on the flames. Excellent salads, too.

Tia Maria (Entre Ríos 175 Sur; mains AR$16-20; ☺ lunch & dinner) An indoor/outdoor restaurant on a relatively quiet street. There's a better-than-average range of pastas and some semi-gourmet mains like rabbit cannelloni in gruyère sauce, and seafood crepes.

Club Sirio Libanés (☎ 422-3841; Entre Ríos 33 Sur; mains AR$18-24; ☺ lunch & dinner) The Syrian-Lebanese club has by far the best-looking restaurant in town, with plenty of arched roofs and Moorish tile work. The menu's good, if a little light on Middle Eastern fare, but the tabouleh, hummus and kibbeh are all worth a try.

de Sánchez (Rivadavia 61; mains AR$30-40; ☺ lunch & dinner) San Juan's snootiest restaurant is actually pretty good. A creative menu with a smattering of seafood dishes, an adequate wine list (featuring all the San Juan heavy hitters) and a hushed, tranquil atmosphere.

Shopping

The **Mercado Artesanal Tradicional** (Traditional Artisans Market; Centro de Difusión Cultural Eva Perón) is an excellent local handicrafts market including ponchos and the brightly colored *mantas* (shawls) of Jáchal.

Getting There & Away

AIR

Aerolíneas Argentinas/Austral (☎ 421-4158; Av San Martín 215 Oeste) flies twice daily to Buenos Aires (AR$600) except Sunday (once only).

BUS

From San Juan's **bus terminal** (☎ 422-1604; Estados Unidos 492 Sur) there are international services to Santiago (AR$60, 10 hours), Viña del Mar and Valparaíso, Chile, but they require a change of bus in Mendoza.

Except in summer, when there may be direct buses, service to Patagonian destinations south of Neuquén requires a change of bus in Mendoza, though through-tickets can be purchased in San Juan.

Various companies serve the following destinations daily.

Destination	Cost (AR$)	Duration (hr)
Barreal	23	4
Buenos Aires	120	14
Calingasta	20	3½
Catamarca	75	8
Córdoba	52	9
Huaco	22	4
Jáchal	13	5
Jujuy	134	18
La Rioja	48	6
Mendoza	16	3
Neuquén	120	15½
Pismanta	20	4
Rodeo	20	6
Rosario	100	14
Salta	163	17
San Agustín de Valle Fértil	20	4½
San José de Jáchal	13	3
San Luis	25	4
San Rafael	40	6
Tucumán	110	13

Getting Around

Las Chacritas Airport (☎ 425-4133) is located 13km southeast of town on RN 20. A taxi or *remise* costs AR$25. For car rental, try **Classic** (☎ 422-4622; Av San Martín 163 Oeste) or **Parque Auto Motor** (☎ 422-6018; cnr Avs San Martín & España).

AROUND SAN JUAN
Dique Ullum

Only 18km west of San Juan, this 32 km sq reservoir is a center for nautical sports: swimming, fishing, kayaking, waterskiing and windsurfing (though no rental equipment is available). *Balnearios* (beach clubs) line its shores, and hanging out for a day in the sun is part of being in San Juan. At night, many of the *balnearios* function as dance clubs. Bus 23 from Av Salta or Bus 29 from the San Juan bus terminal via Av Córdoba both go hourly to the dam outlet.

Difunta Correa Shrine

At Vallecito, about 60km southeast of San Juan, the shrine of the Difunta Correa, a popular saint, is one of the most fascinating cultural phenomenons in all of Argentina, and visiting the shrine is a mandatory stop if you're in the area.

Empresa Vallecito goes daily from the bus terminal in San Juan to the shrine (AR$12 roundtrip, 1¼ hours each way) at 8:30am and 4pm Monday through Saturday, and waits about an hour and 15 minutes before returning. On Sunday there are roundtrip buses at 8am, 10:30am, 11:45am, 3:30pm, 4:15pm and 7pm. Any other eastbound bus heading toward La Rioja or Córdoba will drop passengers at the entrance. There are also departures from Mendoza (see p356).

VALLE DE CALINGASTA

The Calingasta Valley is a vast smear of scenic butter cradled between the Andes and the rumpled, multicolored precordillera, and is one of the most beautiful regions in both San Juan and Mendoza provinces.

With the completion of two new reservoirs, the spectacular cliffside RP 12 is now closed. Most maps will show the old road, but drivers have to take RP 5 north to Talacasto, then the RP 149, which snakes around west and then south to Calingasta.

Calingasta

☎ 02648 / pop 8100 / elev 1430m

Calingasta is a small agricultural town shaded by álamos (poplars) on the shores of Río de los Patos. There's little to do, though a visit to the 17th-century adobe chapel **Capilla de Nuestra Señora del Carmen** makes a nice stop on the way to Barreal. Looming on the horizon 7km out of

---

DIFUNTA CORREA

Legend has it that during the civil wars of the 1840s Deolinda Correa followed the movements of her sickly conscript husband's battalion on foot through the deserts of San Juan, carrying food, water and their baby son in her arms. When her meager supplies ran out, thirst, hunger and exhaustion killed her. But when passing muleteers found them, the infant was still nursing at the dead woman's breast. Commemorating this apparent miracle, her shrine at Vallecito is widely believed to be the site of her death.

Difunta literally means 'defunct,' and Correa is her surname. Technically she is not a saint but rather a 'soul,' a dead person who performs miracles and intercedes for people; the child's survival was the first of a series of miracles attributed to her. Since the 1940s her shrine, originally a simple hilltop cross, has grown into a small village with its own gas station, school, post office, police station and church. Devotees leave gifts at 17 chapels or exhibit rooms in exchange for supernatural favors. In addition, there are two hotels, several restaurants, a commercial gallery with souvenir shops, and offices for the nonprofit organization that administers the site.

Interestingly, truckers are especially devoted. From La Quiaca, on the Bolivian border, to Ushuaia in Tierra del Fuego, you will see roadside shrines with images of the Difunta Correa and the unmistakable bottles of water left to quench her thirst. At some sites there appear to be enough parts lying around to build a car from scratch!

Despite lack of government support and the Catholic Church's open antagonism, the shrine of Difunta Correa has grown as belief in her miraculous powers has become more widespread. People visit the shrine all year round, but at Easter, May 1 and Christmas, up to 200,000 pilgrims descend on Vallecito. Weekends are busier and more interesting than weekdays.

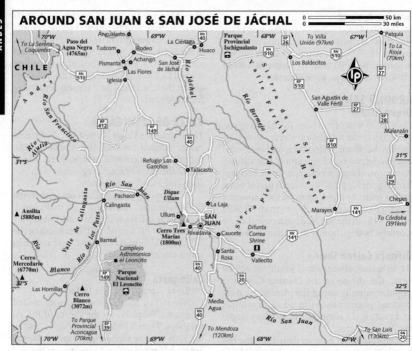

AROUND SAN JUAN & SAN JOSÉ DE JÁCHAL

town is **Cerro El Calvario**, the site of an indigenous cemetery where several mummies have been found. One example can be seen in Calingasta's small **Archaeological Museum** (admission AR$2; ⏰ Tue-Sat 10am-1pm & 4-8pm), just off the main plaza.

The folks at Calingasta's **tourist information office** (RP 12), at the entrance to town from San Juan, are helpful for sights and lodging in the area.

If you wish to spend the night, lay your head at the modest **Hospedaje Nora** (☎ 421027; on the main plaza; s/d AR$30/60), featuring simple but spacious rooms in a family house. Those in the building out the back are a better deal. There's a **Municipal Campground** (sites AR$8) down by the river. The meals at **Doña Gorda** (Calle Principal; mains AR$10-20) will keep you from starving – on offer are tasty empanadas and good-value set meals.

Two buses a day roll through town, heading for San Juan (AR$20, 3½ hours) and Barreal (AR$4, 30 minutes).

Barreal
☎ 02648 / pop 1900 / elev 1650m

Barreal's divine location makes it one of the most beautifully situated towns you'll likely ever come across. Sauces (weeping willows),

álamos and eucalyptus trees drape lazily over the dirt roads that meander through town, and views of the Cordillera de Ansilta – a stretch of the Andes with seven majestic peaks ranging from 5130m to 5885m – are simply astonishing. Wandering along Barreal's back roads is an exercise in dreamy laziness.

Presidente Roca is the main drag through town, a continuation of RP 149 that leads from Calingasta to Barreal and on to Parque Nacional El Leoncito. Only a few streets have names; businesses listed without them simply require asking directions.

INFORMATION
Banco de la Nación (Presidente Roca s/n) Has an ATM.
IWS Comunicaciones (San Martín s/n; per hr AR$2) Internet access. Slow.
Tourist office (☎ 441066; municipalidadecalingasta@ hotmail.com; Presidente Roca s/n; ⏰ 9am-1:30pm & 3-8pm) Located beside the main plaza; offers list of excursion operators and accommodations.

SIGHTS & ACTIVITIES
Wander down to the **Río de los Patos** and take in the sweeping views of the valley and the

Cordillera de Ansilta, whose highest peak, **Ansilta**, tops out at 5885m. To the south, **Aconcagua** and **Tupungato** are both visible, as is the peak of **Cerro Mercedario** (6770m).

At the south end of Presidente Roca is a sort of triangular roundabout. Follow the road east (away from the Andes) until it leads into the hills; you'll see a small shrine and you can **hike** into the foothills for more stunning views. Follow this road for 3km and you'll come to a mining site (the gate should be open). Enter and continue for 1km to reach a **petrified forest**.

Rafting is excellent – more for the scenery than for the rapids themselves – and most trips start 50km upriver at **Las Hornillas**. Contact **Condor Expediciones** (☎ 441144), the best-established rafting operator in town.

Las Hornillas (site of two *refugios* and a military outpost) also provides **climbing** access to the Cordón de la Rameda, which boasts five peaks over 6000m, including Cerro Mercedario. Climbing here is more technical than Aconcagua and many mountaineers prefer the area. Ramon Ossa, a Barreal

---

RUTA DEL VINO DE SAN JUAN

San Juan's winery tourism industry isn't quite as developed as that of Mendoza, but in a lot of ways that's a good thing. There are no crowds for one thing, and tours are occasionally conducted by the winemakers themselves. A few wineries have got together to promote the Ruta del Vino de San Juan (The San Juan Wine Route). The best way to do it, if you want to hit them all in one day, is by hire car. Starting from downtown San Juan, it's about a 40km round trip stopping at all the places listed below. It is feasible to do it by public transport and taxi, too. None of the wineries listed below require reservations.

The first stop on the route should be **Las Marianas** (☎ 423-1191; Calle Nuevo s/n; 9am-5pm Mon-Fri, 9am-1pm Sat). One of the prettiest wineries in the region, this one was built in 1922, abandoned in 1950 and reinstated in 1999. The main building is gorgeous, with thick adobe walls and a few examples of the original winemaking equipment lying around. The mountain views out over the vineyard are superb. If you're coming by bus, catch the 16 (AR$1.10, 40 minutes) near the corner of Santa Fe and Mendoza in San Juan. Get off at the corner of Calle Aberastain and Calle Nuevo, where you'll see a signpost to the winery (an 800m walk).

Making your way back to Calle Aberastain, turn right and follow the road south for 500m to **Viñas de Segisa** (☎ 492-2000; www.saxsegisa.com.ar; Aberastain & Calle 15; 9am-5pm Mon-Fri, 9am-1pm Sat). This stately old winery has more of a museum feel than others. The tour of the underground cellar complex is excellent and tastings are generous. This is one of the few wineries who actually admit to 'chipping' (adding oak chips to young wines to improve flavor).

If you're not up for a walk, now's the time to call a *remise*. If you are, make your way back north to Calle 14, turn right and continue for 5km until you hit RN 40. Turning left, after about 1km you'll come to **Fabril Alto Verde** (☎ 429-1905; RN 40 btwn Calle 13 & 14; 9am-5pm Mon-Fri, 9am-1pm Sat). A big, state-of-the-art winery that sells 90% of its wine for export; tours here are in English or Spanish and come accompanied by a very dreary promotional video. The award-winning organic brands of Buenas Hondas and Touchstone are produced here.

Next, catch a 24 bus heading north on RN 40 up to Calle 11. Turning right down Calle 11 for 300m brings you to **Miguel Mas** (☎ 422-5807; miguelmas@infovia.com.ar; Calle 11 s/n, 300m east of RN 40; 9am-5pm Mon-Fri, 9am-1pm Sat). This small winery makes some of the country's only organic champagne and other wine. The whole process – apart from inserting the cork in bottles – is done by hand. Tours (in Spanish only) take you through every step of the process.

Making your way back out to RN 40, flag down a 24 bus, which will take you back to the bus terminal in San Juan.

If you've still got a thirst up when you get back to the bus terminal, consider hopping on bus 23 to check out one of South America's most curious wineries, **Cavas de Zonda** (☎ 494-5144; Zonda; 9am-5pm Mon-Fri, 11am-5pm Sat & Sun), in a cave about 16km west of San Juan, via the RP 12, near the town of Zonda. This champagne-maker boasts having the only wine cellar in South America whose 'roof is a mountain' and, true or not, its temperatures are perfect for cellaring its excellent sparkling wines. And hey…it's a darn good marketing tool. Bus 23 leaves the San Juan bus terminal from platform 20 six times daily.

JUST A LOAD OF HOT AIR

While traveling through San Juan, especially in fall and winter, you may become acquainted – through hearsay if not through experience – with one of the region's meteorological marvels: el zonda. Much like the Chinook of the Rockies or the foehn of the European Alps, the zonda is a dry, warm wind that can raise a cold day's temperatures from freezing to nearly 20°C (68°F). The zonda originates with storms in the Pacific that blow eastward, hit the Andes, dump their moisture and come whipping down the eastern slopes, picking up heat as they go. The wind, which varies from mild to howling, can last several days; *sanjuaninos* (people from San Juan) can step outside and tell you when it will end – and that it will be cold when it does. It's a regular occurrence, giving the region – and the *sanjuaninos* – severe seasonal schizophrenia, especially in winter.

---

native, is a highly recommended mountain guide and excursion operator who knows the cordillera intimately; contact him at **Cabañas Doña Pipa** (☎ 441004; www.ossaexpedicion.com, www .fortunaviajes.com.ar in Spanish). He can arrange trips to Cerro Mercedario, including mules and equipment.

Fortuna Expediciones (☎ 0264-15-404-0913; www .fortunaviajes.com.ar) offers tours of the El Leoncito National Park, fishing trips and 4WD treks.

Barreal is best known for **carrovelismo** (land sailing), an exhilarating sport practiced on a small cart with a sail attached. Fanatics come from miles away to whizz around out on the gusty, cracked lake bed at Pampa El Leoncito, about 20km from town and adjacent to the national park. **Rogelio Toro** (☎ 0264-15-671-7196) hires the necessary equipment and also gives classes.

For access to the *refugio* at Las Hornillas, climbing information, guide services and **mountain bike** rental, visit Maxi at Cabañas Kummel (below).

SLEEPING & EATING

Posada Don Lisandro (Av San Martín s/n; s/d with shared bathroom AR$30/60) This new posada (inn) is actually a 100-year-old house. The original cane and mud ceilings are still there, as are a few sticks of room furniture. There's a kitchen for guest use and lovely, shady grounds to lounge around in.

Cabañas Kummel (☎ 441206, in San Juan 0264-15-670-8273; Presidente Roca s/n near Hipolito Yrigoyen; cabaña for up to 6 AR$150) Simple but delightful little *cabañas* with kitchens, grass outside and plenty of shade trees.

El Alemán (☎ 441193; d AR$150, cabaña for up to 4 AR$180; mains AR$30-50; ☽ breakfast, lunch & dinner) Down by the river, with sweeping views of the Andes, this German/Argentine–owned complex has some of the best-looking rooms in town. Cabins are more like small houses, spread out over the property and allowing for a sense of privacy. Rooms are cute and cozy. There's an excellent restaurant (mains AR$20 to AR$30) on the premises, serving hearty dishes and superb breakfasts made from the freshest ingredients. Jerome microbrew from Potrerillos is sold.

Posada San Eduardo (☎ 441046; cnr San Martín & Los Enamorados; s AR$130-150, d AR$150-180) This handsome adobe inn offers refreshing rooms with whitewashed walls set around a beautiful shady courtyard. Rooms have a quiet elegance, with natural poplar bed frames and chairs. Pay a little extra and you get your very own fireplace.

Restaurant Isidoro (Presidente Roca s/n; mains AR$15-20; ☽ lunch & dinner) Offers a fairly standard range of meats and pastas and some delicious meat empanadas. Also a good selection of wines from the San Juan region.

Pizzeria Alonso (Presidente Roca s/n; mains AR$10-18; ☽ dinner), next door to the Isidoro, cooks up some decent pies and turns into a bar later on.

GETTING THERE & AWAY

Barreal's right at the end of the line, but there are two departures per day for San Juan (AR$23, four hours), which pass through Calingasta (AR$4, 30 minutes).

Parque Nacional El Leoncito

The 76-sq-km Parque Nacional El Leoncito occupies a former *estancia* (ranch) 22km south of Barreal. The landscape is typical of the Andean precordillera, though it's drier than the valley north of Barreal. Lately, its primary attraction is the Pampa de Leoncito, where a dry lake bed makes for superb land sailing. The high, dry and wide-open valley rarely sees a cloud, also making for superb stargazing. Hence, the park is home to the Complejo Astronomico el Leoncito, which contains two important observatories: **Observatorio El Leoncito** (☎ 02648-441088; admission AR$5; ☻ guided visits 10am, 11am, 3pm, 4pm & 5pm) and **Observatorio Cesco** (☎ 02648-441087; admission AR$3; ☻ guided visits 10am, noon, 4pm & 6pm). Night visits must be scheduled ahead of time by contacting **Sra Marina Grosso** (☎ in San Juan 0264-421-3653 int 113; ☻ 8am-2pm).

Camping is not permitted here, but in the northwest corner of the park, **Cascada El Rincon** is a lovely, small waterfall set in a shallow canyon. If you're looking for somewhere to picnic and splash around on a hot day, this is your spot.

There is no public transport to the park, and with 17km of entrance road added to the 22km to get here from Barreal, it's certainly too far to walk and probably too far to ride. If you don't have your own transportation, contact Ramon Ossa in Barreal (p375), whose informative tours of the park have been heartily recommended.

SAN JOSÉ DE JÁCHAL
☎ 02647 / pop 21,000

Founded in 1751 and surrounded by vineyards and olive groves, Jáchal is a charming village with a mix of older adobes and contemporary brick houses. *Jachalleros* (the local residents) are renowned for their fidelity to indigenous and gaucho crafts traditions; in fact, Jáchal's reputation as the Cuna de la Tradición (Cradle of Tradition) is celebrated during November's **Fiesta de la Tradición**. Except during festival season, however, finding these crafts is easier in San Juan than it is here.

Across from the main plaza the **Iglesia San José**, a national monument, houses the **Cristo Negro** (Black Christ), or Señor de la Agonía (Lord of Agony), a grisly leather image with articulated head and limbs, brought from Potosí in colonial times.

Jáchal's accommodation scene isn't what you'd call thriving, but the **Hotel San Martín** (☎ 420413; hsanmartin_jsj@yahoo.com.ar; Echegaray 367; s/d AR$40/80, with shared bathroom AR$20/40), a few blocks from the plaza, does the job. It's not quite as contemporary as it looks from the outside, but rooms are big and comfortable and the bathrooms are modern.

La Taberna de Juan (San Martín s/n; mains AR$10-25; ☻ lunch & dinner) is a bright and cheery *parrilla* facing the plaza. Meat is the go here, but there's a range of pastas and salads, too.

There are several daily buses to San Juan (AR$12.50, three hours) and Mendoza (AR$16, four hours) from Jáchal's **bus terminal** (cnr San Juan & Obispo Zapata).

AROUND SAN JOSÉ DE JÁCHAL

Continuing north on RN 40, visitors pass through a beautiful landscape that is rich with folkloric traditions and rarely seen by foreigners. East of Jáchal RN 40 climbs the precipitous **Cuesta de Huaco**, with a view of Los Cauquenes dam, before arriving at **Huaco**, a sleepy village 36km from Jáchal whose 200-year-old Viejo Molino (Old Mill) justifies the trip. Some visitors get captivated by Huaco's eerie landscape and middle-of-nowhere atmosphere. If you're one of them, you can stay at **Eco Hostel** (☎ 0264-421-9528; www.ecohostel.com.ar; d/r AR$20/70; ☻)

One bus daily from Huaco heads to San Juan (AR$22, four hours), passing though Jáchal (AR$12, one hour) on the way.

Backtracking to RN 510 and heading westward, you pass through the town of Rodeo and into the department of Iglesia, home of the precordillera thermal baths of **Pismanta** (see p378). RN 510 continues west to Chile via the lung-busting 4765m **Paso del Agua Negra** (open summer only). South of Pismanta, RP 436 returns to RN 40 and San Juan.

Rodeo
☎ 02647 / elev 2010m

Rodeo is a small, ramshackle town with picturesque adobe houses typical of the region, 42km west of San José de Jáchal. There are several *cabañas* and *hosterías* in town, and Pismanta is only about 20km away.

Rodeo has recently become famous – world famous – for **windsurfing**. The town is only 3km away from one of the best windsurfing sites on the planet: **Dique Cuesta del Viento**, a reservoir where, between mid-October and early May, wind speeds reach 120km per hour nearly every afternoon, drawing surfers from around the globe. Even if you don't take to the wind, it's worth spending a day or two wandering around Rodeo and hanging out on the beach absorbing the spectacular views and watching the insanity of airborne windsurfers.

Inside the town hall, the **tourist office** (municipalidad_iglesia@yahoo.com.ar; ☻ 8am-8pm) provides a list of places to stay and information on local attractions.

On Playa Lamaral, on the shore of the reservoir, HI affiliate **Rancho Lamaral** (☎ in San Juan 422-5566, 15-671-8819; rancholamaral@arnet.com.ar; dm HI members/nonmembers AR$25/30; d with shared bathroom AR$60) offers simple rooms in a refurbished adobe house, and offers windsurfing classes (three/five days AR$230/260) and rents all equipment. Nearby, the bar and shop Puerto de Palos also rents equipment and offers classes.

El Viejo Carretón (☎ 493151; www.elviejocarreton.com; Enrique Paoli s/n; cabañas for 4-6 AR$130-180) is one of the many places in town offering cabins, but these are by far the sweetest deal. More like self-contained cottages, they're spacious and come with everything you could want, down to your own *parrilla* alongside and Direct TV.

Xipacote (mains AR$12-20; 🕐 lunch & dinner), on the main street in the center of town, is a laid-back pizzeria/café/bar that does reasonable steaks and a huge *milanesa à la suprema* (schnitzel with ham and melted cheese; AR$12).

From San Juan's bus terminal, there are several departures daily for Rodeo (AR$20, 5½ hours).

Pismanta
☎ 02647

Part of the **Hotel Termas de Pismanta** (☎ 497091/02; www.pismantahotel.com.ar in Spanish; s/d with full board AR$160/200; 🏊) and recently refurbished, this thermal baths complex offers stylish if slightly cramped rooms. The baths are all indoors, in small, clean tiled cubicles. Temperatures range from 38°C to 42°C. Access to the baths costs AR$6 for nonguests and there is a variety of spa treatments available.

If the complex is too pricey for a night, try **Hospedaje La Olla** (☎ 497003; r per person AR$20), a basic place with large rooms, low wooden ceilings and the odd animal skin thrown around for decoration. It's across the highway and up a side street from the thermal baths.

Iglesia SRL minibuses leave the San Juan bus terminal four times a week, and take RP 149 to Jáchal, stopping at Iglesia and Pismanta (AR$20, four hours).

SAN AGUSTÍN DE VALLE FÉRTIL
☎ 02646 / pop 6800

Reached by comically undulating highways that cut through the desert landscape, San Agustín de Valle Fértil makes an excellent base for trips to the nearby Parque Provincial Ischigualasto. It's a measure of just how dry the countryside is that this semiarid valley gets called 'fertile.'

Apart from visiting the park, there's not much to do around here, but the ponderous pace of life here, where people sit on the sidewalks on summer evenings greeting passersby, has mesmerized more than one visitor.

Orientation & Information

San Agustín lies among the Sierra Pampeanas, gentle sedimentary mountains cut by impressive canyons, 247km northeast of San Juan via RN 141 and RP 510, which continues to Ischigualasto and La Rioja. San Agustín is small enough that locals pay little attention to street names, so ask directions.

Cámara de Turismo (Mitre, btwn Entre Ríos & Mendoza) A private tourist office that maintains an office in the bus terminal.

Municipal tourist office (General Acha; 🕐 7am-1pm & 5-10pm Mon-Fri, 8am-1pm Sat) Directly across from the plaza. Can help arrange car or mule excursions into the mountain canyons and backcountry.

Post office (cnr Laprida & Mendoza)

Turismo Vesa (☎ 420143; turismo_vesa@yahoo.com.ar) For tours to Parque Provincial Ischigualasto, El Chiflón and horseback riding.

Sleeping & Eating

Campo Base (☎ 420063; www.hostelvalledelaluna.com.ar; Tucumán s/n; dm AR$20; 🏊) A cozy little hostel with four-bed dorms, kitchen access and good common areas. Can arrange good-value tours to local sights, including Parque Provincial Ischigualasto.

Hostería & Cabañas Valle Fértil (☎ 420015; www.alkazarhotel.com.ar in Spanish; Rivadavia s/n; s/d in hostería AR$140/160, 4-person cabañas AR$200) This place has the wraps on lodging in town, with a well-sited *hostería* above the reservoir and fully equipped *cabañas* nearby. The *hostería* also has a good restaurant (mains AR$15 to AR$25) serving food from 6am to 11pm. Both are reached from Rivadavia on the way to the river.

The *hostería* also owns the town's best campground, **Camping Valle Fértil** (Rivadavia s/n; sites AR$15). It's shaded by a monotone cover of eucalyptus trees, and gets very crowded during long weekends and holidays, but it's quiet enough off-season and midweek.

If the *hostería* is too much of a walk for you, there are good, simple restaurants along Rivadavia, leading west from the plaza. The plazaside **La Cocina de Zulma** (Rivadavia s/n; mains AR$10-25; ⓧ lunch & dinner) gets good reviews.

Getting There & Away
From San Agustín's **bus terminal** (Mitre, btwn Entre Ríos & Mendoza) daily buses head to San Juan (AR$20, 4½ hours). Monday and Friday buses to La Rioja (AR$17) can drop off passengers at the Ischigualasto turnoff.

PARQUE PROVINCIAL ISCHIGUALASTO
Also known fittingly as **Valle de la Luna** (Valley of the Moon; admission AR$35), this park takes its name from the Diaguita word for land without life. Visits here are a spectacular step – or drive, as the case may be – into a world of surreal rock formations, dinosaur remains and glowing red sunsets. The park is in some ways comparable to North American national parks like Bryce Canyon or Zion, except that here, time and water have exposed a wealth of fossils (some 180 million years old, from the Triassic period).

The park's **museum** displays a variety of fossils, including the carnivorous dinosaur Herrerasaurus (not unlike Tyrannosaurus rex), the Eoraptor lunensis (the oldest-known predatory dinosaur) and good dioramas of the park's paleoenvironments.

The 630-sq-km park is a desert valley between two sedimentary mountain ranges, the Cerros Colorados in the east and Cerro Los Rastros in the west. Over millennia, at every meander in the canyon, the waters of the nearly dry Río Ischigualasto have carved distinctive shapes in the malleable red sandstone, mono-chrome clay and volcanic ash. Predictably, some of these forms have acquired popular names, including **Cancha de Bochas** (The Ball Court), **El Submarino** (The Submarine) and **El Gusano** (The Worm) among others. The desert flora of algarrobo trees, shrubs and cacti complement the eerie landforms.

From the visitor center, isolated 1748m **Cerro Morado** is a three- to four-hour walk, gaining nearly 800m in elevation and yielding outstanding views of the surrounding area. Take plenty of drinking water and high-energy snacks.

Tours
All visitors to the park must go accompanied by a ranger. The most popular tours run for three hours and leave on the hour (more or less), with cars forming a convoy and stopping at noteworthy points along the way, where the ranger explains (Spanish only) exactly what it is you're looking at.

If you have no private vehicle, an organized tour is the only feasible way to visit the park. These are easily organized in San Agustín (opposite). Otherwise ask the tourist office there about hiring a car and driver. Tour rates (not including entry fees) are about AR$175 per person from San Juan (through any travel agency in town), or about AR$20 per person from San Agustín. Tours from San Juan generally depart at 5am and return well after dark.

A variety of other tours are available from the visitor center here. They cost AR$15 per person, and the group pays a one-off AR$30 fee for the guide. Options include spectacular full moon tours in the five days around the full moon (2½ hours), treks to the summit of Cerro Morado (three to four hours) and a 12km circuit of the park on mountain bikes.

Sleeping & Eating
There is camping at the **visitor center** (per person AR$3), which also has a *confitería* serving simple meals (breakfast and lunch) and cold drinks; dried fruits and bottled olives from the province are also available. There are toilets and showers, but because water must be trucked in, don't count on them. There is no shade.

Getting There & Away
Ischigualasto is about 80km north of San Agustín via RP 510 and a paved lateral to the northwest. Given its size and isolation, the only practical way to visit the park is by private vehicle or organized tour. Note that the park roads are unpaved and some can be impassable after a rain, necessitating an abbreviated trip.

The Lake District

Home to some of the country's most spectacular scenery, the Lake District hosts thousands of visitors each year. People come to ski, fish, climb, trek and generally bask in the cool, fresh landscapes created by the huge forests, glacier-fed lakes and cute little alpine-style villages. Don't get the idea that the region is overrun, though – spaces are so wide here you'll only end up bumping shoulders with other travelers in the main population centers.

The city of Neuquén – the largest in the region – provides transportation links to all over the country. What it lacks in beauty it makes up for in surrounding attractions. Just out of town are some world-renowned paleontological sites and outstanding wineries. Way, way south is the resort town of Bariloche, with its picture-postcard location on the banks of the Lago Nahuel Huapi. This is ground zero for the outdoor adventure crew, both in summer and wintertime. Bariloche is the chief transportation hub for southern Patagonia and Chile, and a short ride from the laid-back hippie haven of El Bolsón.

Those looking to get off the track and away from the crowds won't find it hard to do here. Villa Traful and San Martín de los Andes, both lakeside villages nestled among pehuén (araucaria) forests fill up for a short time in summer and are blissfully quiet the rest of the year. To the north, the little-visited ex-Provincial capital of Chos Malal makes an excellent base for exploring nearby volcanoes, lagoons and hot springs, as well as an important stopover for those traveling northwards on the RN 40 to Mendoza.

HIGHLIGHTS

- Drive the **Ruta de los Siete Lagos** (RN 234; p400), a breathtaking road winding between alpine lakes and pehuén forests
- Soak your worries away in a bubbling mudbath in the thermal resort town of **Copahue** (p391)
- Base yourself in **Bariloche** (p406) for some fun mountain adventures
- Get off the tourist trail in **Chos Malal** (p387) and out into its spectacular surrounds
- Follow in the footsteps of dinosaurs at **Lago Barreales** (p386)

- POPULATION: 1,026,977
- AREA: 297,091 SQ KM

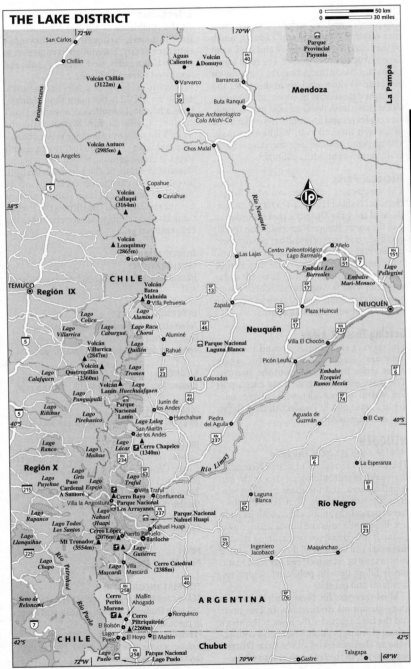

THE LAKE DISTRICT

Climate

Except for central and eastern Neuquén province (around Neuquén and Zapala), much of the Lake District is snowy and cold from June to August or September. The most scenic mountain roads (including the Ruta de los Siete Lagos) close regularly at this time, and the highest passes may not open until October. Fall sees warmish days and cold nights, while turning leaves and fewer tourists make it one of the best times to visit. Wildflowers make spring hiking beautiful. Summer days are generally quite warm, with cool nights.

National Parks

The spectacular but often crowded Parque Nacional Nahuel Huapi (p415) is the cornerstone of the Lake District's parks. Bordering it to the north, Parque Nacional Lanín (p400) gets fewer trail trampers and has equally spectacular sights, including Volcán Lanín and humbling pehuén forests. The tiny Parque Nacional Arrayanes (p405) is worth a day trip from Villa la Angostura to check out its beautiful cinnamon-colored arrayán trees. See p68 for more on Argentina's parks.

Getting There & Away

The region's two primary ground transport hubs are Neuquén and Bariloche, where buses arrive from throughout the country. The main airports are in these cities, plus San Martín de los Andes, while smaller ones are in Zapala and El Bolsón. All have flights to/from Buenos Aires.

NEUQUÉN

☎ 0299 / pop 251,000 / elev 265m

There's only two reasons to stop in Neuquén – the wealth of paleontological sites in the surrounding area, and the three excellent wineries just out of town. That said, the town has a strangely hypnotic effect, with its wide, tree-lined boulevards and liberal smattering of plazas. If you *do* find yourself hanging around, make sure you take a stroll through the central park, a strip of reclaimed railway land that is slowly filling up with public art, sculptures, fountains and galleries.

Most travelers hit Neuquén en route to more glamorous destinations in Patagonia and the Lake District – the town is the area's principal transport hub, with good connections to Bariloche and other Lake District destinations, to the far south and to Chile.

Orientation

At the confluence of the Río Neuquén and the Río Limay, Neuquén is the province's easternmost city. Paved highways go east to the Río Negro valley, west toward Zapala, and southwest toward Bariloche.

Known as Félix San Martín in town, east–west RN 22 is the main thoroughfare, lying a few blocks south of downtown. Don't confuse it with Av San Martín (sans the 'Félix'), the obligatory homage to Argentina's national icon. The principal north–south street is Av Argentina, which becomes Av Olascoaga south of the old train station. Street names change on each side of Av Argentina and the old train station; most of the old rail yard now constitutes the Parque Central. Several diagonal streets bisect the conventional grid.

Information

IMMIGRATION
Immigration office (☎ 442-2061; Santiago del Estero 466)

INTERNET ACCESS
Telecentro (Av Argentina at Ministro González; per hr ARS2; ☺ 24hr)
Telecentro del Comahue (Av Argentina 147; per hr ARS2)

LAUNDRY
Lavisec (Roca 137; wash & dry ARS10) Full service or DIY.

MEDICAL SERVICES
Regional hospital (☎ 443 1474; Buenos Aires 421)

MONEY
Several banks along Av Argentina, between Parque Central and Roca, have ATMs. Zanellato (opposite) is an Amex representative.
Banca Nazionale del Lavoro (Av Argentina & Rivadavia)
Cambio Olano (cnr Juan B Justo & H Yrigoyen) Money exchange.
Cambio Pullman (Ministro Alcorta 144) Money exchange.

POST
Post office (Rivadavia & Santa Fe)

TOURIST INFORMATION
ACA (Automóvil Club Argentino; ☎ 442-2325; diagonal 25 de Mayo at Rivadavia) Argentina's auto club; good source for provincial road maps.
Provincial tourist office (☎ 442-4089; www .neuquentur.gov.ar; Félix San Martín 182; ☺ 8am-10pm) Great maps and brochures.

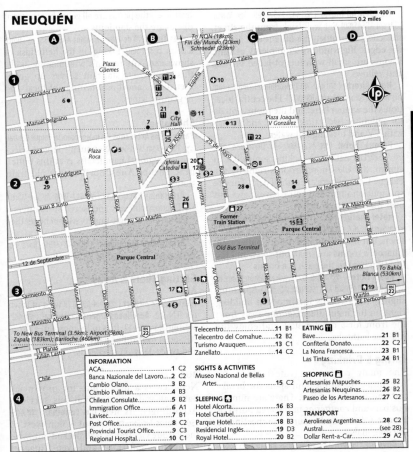

NEUQUÉN

TRAVEL AGENCIES

Neuquén's dozens of travel agencies are almost all near downtown.

Turismo Arauquen (☎ 442-6476; www.arauquen.com; Ministro González 165) Offers guided visits to paleontology sites of Lago Barreales, Plaza Huincul and Villa El Chocón. Prices are about AR$85 per person (minimum four), including the taxi fare; it's cheaper if you have your own vehicle.
Zanellato (☎ 443-0105; www.zanellatoviajes.com.ar; Av Independencia 366) Amex representative; reliable for airline tickets and the like.

Sights

Just outside of town are three of the most important Patagonian wineries – **NQN** (☎ 489-7500; www.bodeganqn.com.ar; RP 7, Picada 15), **Fin del Mundo** (☎ 485-5004; www.bodegadelfindelmundo.com;

RP 8, Km 9, San Patricio Del Chañar) and **Schroeder** (☎ 508-6767; www.familiaschroeder.com; Calle 7 Nte, San Patricio del Chañar). Access to the vineyards is almost impossible without your own vehicle, but Turismo Arauquen can get you out there, often in combination with paleontological tours.

Museo Nacional de Bellas Artes (☎ 443-6268; Bartolomé Mitre & Santa Cruz; admission free; ⏰ 10am-8pm Tue-Sat, 4-8pm Sun) showcases fine arts from the region and often features traveling exhibitions from Argentine and international artists.

Sleeping

Neuquén's hotels mainly cater to the business set, and are fairly unexciting in all ranges and less than great value for budget travelers.

THE LAKE DISTRICT

Residencial Inglés (☎ 442-2252; Félix San Martín 534; s/d AR$45/80) Set well back from the street, this cheapie is quiet, if a little rough around the edges. Big windows let in plenty of light. Rooms are small with lots of faded browns and yellows.

Hotel Alcorta (☎ 442-2652; alcortahotel@infovia.com.ar; Ministro Alcorta 82; s/d AR$60/80) The central location's the winner here, and the rooms will do for a night or two – they're clean and newish with TV and blasting hot water.

Parque Hotel (☎ 442-5806; Av Olascoaga 271; s/d AR$70/110) Although lacking somewhat in charm, the tile-floored rooms right by the Parque Central here are a good deal. They're spacious enough, and most have views out over the busy street below.

Hotel Charbel (☎ 442-4143; hotelcharbel@hotmail.com; San Luis 267; s/d AR$80/140) Not the best deal in town, but not a complete ripoff, either. The Charbel's rooms are small but clean and the location next to the park is a bonus.

Royal Hotel (☎ 448-8902; www.royalhotel.com.ar; Av Argentina 143; s/d AR$150/180; 🕸 🖳) Spacious, slightly stark rooms in a modern building right on the main drag. Get one away from the front for a quieter stay, and enjoy the full-size bathtubs.

Eating & Drinking

The many *confiterías* (cafés) along Av Argentina are all pleasant spots for breakfast and morning coffee. There are numerous bars and *confiterías* in the area north of Parque Central and around the meeting of the diagonals.

Bave (H Yrigoyen 375; schwarmas AR$10; 🕙 noon-late) For a quick schwarma/souvlaki/doner kebab/giro/whatever you want to call it, drop into this little take-out joint in the middle of Neuquén's *Zona Viva* (nightclub area).

Confitería Donato (☎ 442-6950; Juan B Alberdi & Santa Fe; snacks AR$8-12; 🕙 7am-3am Sun-Thu, 7am-5am Fri-Sat) Plenty of dark wood paneling and brass fittings give this place an old-timey feel and the wraparound seats may have you lounging around for hours on end. The menu runs the usual *confitería* gamut, with plenty of sandwiches, cakes and coffee on offer. There is live music Friday to Sunday nights and the occasional tango show – drop in for the schedule.

La Nona Francesa (☎ 430-0930; 9 de Julio 56; mains AR$20-30; 🕙 lunch & dinner) Some of Neuquén's finest dining can be found at this French/Italian trattoria – the pastas are all good, but the trout dishes are the standouts.

Las Tintas (9 de Julio 59; mains AR$25-35; 🕙 lunch & dinner, closed Sun) Taking on the hefty task of showcasing the region's winemaking skills, this wine-bar/restaurant serves up gourmet dishes and hosts tastings of local and Argentine wines.

Shopping

Paseo de los Artesanos (Av Independencia, Parque Central; 🕙 10am-9pm Wed-Sun) Neuquén's largest selection of regional handicrafts is at this outlet, near Buenos Aires, north of the old train station.

Artesanías Neuquinas (☎ 442-3806; Av San Martín 57) This provincially sponsored store offers a wide variety of high-quality Mapuche textiles and wood crafts.

Artesanías Mapuches (☎ 443-2155; Roca 76; 🕙 Mon-Sat) More quality local crafts.

Getting There & Away

AIR

Neuquén's **airport** (☎ 444-0525) is west of town on RN 22. **Aerolíneas Argentina/Austral** (☎ 442-2409/10/11; Santa Fe 52) flies to Buenos Aires (from AR$600) four times daily Monday to Friday and twice daily on weekends.

BUS

Neuquén is a major hub for provincial, national and international bus services. Accordingly, its new **bus terminal** (☎ 445-2300; Planas Teodoro s/n), about 3.5km west of the Parque Central, is well decked out, with restaurants, gift stores and even a luggage carousel!

Several carriers offer service to Chile: **Plaza** (☎ 446-5975) and Igi-Llaima go to Temuco (AR$70, 7 hours) via Zapala and Paso Pino Hachado; between them there are nightly departures except on Wednesday. Igi-Llaima and Nar Bus combine service to Temuco (AR$92, 14 hours) over Paso Tromen via Junín de los Andes nightly at 11pm. Andesmar goes three times a week to Osorno (AR$130, 12 hours) and Puerto Montt (AR$120, 13 hours) via Paso Cardenal A Samoré.

Neuquén is a jumping-off point for deep-south, Patagonian destinations. Northern destinations such as Catamarca, San Juan, Tucumán, Salta and Jujuy require a bus change in Mendoza, though the entire ticket can be purchased in Neuquén.

The following table lists daily departures to nearly all long-distance destinations; provincial destinations are served numerous times daily.

Destination	Cost (AR$)	Duration (hr)
Aluminé	36	6
Bahía Blanca	42	7½
Buenos Aires	110	17
Chos Malal	53	6
Comodoro Rivadavia	150	15-17
Córdoba	130	18
El Bolsón	76	9
Esquel	100	10
Junín de los Andes	53	6
Mar del Plata	90	14
Mendoza	100	10-12
Puerto Madryn	110	11
Río Gallegos	320	29
Rosario	160	21
San Martín de los Andes	57	6
San Rafael	85	10
Viedma	48	8
Villa la Angostura	66	8
Zapala	23	3

Getting Around

Neuquén is a good province to explore by automobile, but foreigners should be aware that RN 22, both east along the Río Negro valley and west toward Zapala, is a rough road with heavy truck traffic. On that note, try **Dollar Rent-a-Car** (☎ 442-0875; Carlos H Rodríguez 518), the only rental downtown.

ZAPALA

☎ 02942 / pop 31,800 / elev 1200m

Taking its name as an adaptation of the Mapuche word *Chapadla* (dead swamp), Zapala got off to a bad start, image-wise. Not much has changed. This is a humble little place where the locals amuse themselves with walks up and down the main street, punctuated by lengthy pauses on street corners.

The main excuse for rolling through town is to visit the nearby Parque Nacional Laguna Blanca (p386), with its awesome array of birdlife, or to take advantage of the town's bus connections for the rarely visited northern reaches of the Lake District.

Zapala's main drag is Av San Martín, which is an exit off the roundabout junction of RN 22 (which heads east to Neuquén and north to Las Lajas) and RN 40 (heading southwest to Junín de los Andes and north to Chos Malal).

Information

Banco de la Provincia del Neuquén (San Martín & Etcheluz) Bank and ATM.

Laguna Blanca national park office (☎ 431982; lagunablanca@zapala.com.ar; Av Ejercito Argentino 260; 8am-3pm Mon-Fri) For information on Parque Nacional Laguna Blanca.

Tourist office (☎ 424296; www.zapaladigital.com.ar in Spanish; RN 22, Km 1398; 7am-9pm) Located on the highway, 2km west of town center.

Sights

Zapala's **Centro Cultural** (San Martín & Chaneton; 5-10pm), in front of the plaza, shows work by local artists, recently released Hollywood blockbusters and hosts concerts.

Festivals

Zapala's **Feria de la Tradición**, held in the second week in November, showcases regional culture, with plenty of folk music, gaucho horse skill demonstrations, handicraft exhibits and regional food on sale.

Sleeping & Eating

Zapala has very limited accommodations.

Hotel Pehuén (☎ 423135; Etcheluz & Elena de la Vega; s/d AR$55/100) This is the best deal in town, conveniently near the bus terminal, with clean rooms, an attractive (classy, even) lobby and a good restaurant below.

Hotel Hue Melén (☎ 422344; hotelhuemelen@hotmail.com; Almirante Brown 929; s/d AR$100/150;) This three-star old-timer was undergoing renovations at the time of research (which included the addition of the near-obligatory casino). It should be open by the time you get there, offering the best lodgings in town.

El Chancho Rengo (☎ 422795; Av San Martín & Etcheluz; breakfast, lunch & dinner) It's likely half the town saunters in here for an espresso each day. Outdoor tables and good coffee and sandwiches make it great for a light bite.

Mayrouba (Monti & Etcheluz; mains AR$15-20; breakfast, lunch & dinner) The best-looking restaurant in town also serves up some of the tastiest fare. There's shades of Middle Eastern influence on the menu and Patagonian faves like smoked trout (AR$20). If you're up for a few drinks, it turns into a bar later on, with an impressive cocktail list.

Getting There & Away

Austral (☎ 430134; Uriburu 371) flies to Buenos Aires (from AR$590).

THE LAKE DISTRICT

BIG, BIG BONES

In 1989 a local Neuquenian named Guillermo Heredia discovered a dinosaur bone on his property 7km east of the town of Plaza Huincul. Paleontologists investigated the site and later unearthed a dozen bones belonging to what they named *Argentinosaurus huinculensis* – the largest known dinosaur in the world. The gargantuan herbivore, dating from the mid-Cretaceous period, measured an incredible 40m long and 18m high.

The sheer size of the *Argentinosaurus huinculensis* is difficult to fathom, which is why stopping to gawk at the replica skeleton at Plaza Huincul's **Museo Municipal Carmen Funes** (☎ 0299-496-5486; museocarmenfunes@copelnet.com.ar; Córdoba 55; admission AR$2; ⏰ 9am-7:30pm Mon-Fri, 9am-8pm Sat & Sun) is a humbling lesson in size.

Along with Parque Provincial Ischigualasto (p379) in San Juan province, Neuquén is one of the earth's dinosaur hot spots. Here, three important paleontology sites – Plaza Huincul, Villa El Chocón and Centro Paleontológico Lago Barreales – lie within a couple of hours' drive from Neuquén city and will delight anyone even slightly interested in dinosaurs.

About 80km southwest of Neuquén city, Villa El Chocón boasts the remains of the 100-million-year-old, 14m, eight-ton, meat-eating *Giganotosaurus Carolinii*, the world's largest known carnivore. Discovered in 1993 by fossil hunter Rubén Carolini, the dinosaur is even bigger than North America's better known *Tyrannosaurus rex*. El Chocón is also home to giant dinosaur footprints along the shore of Ezequiel Ramos Mexía reservoir. (One local confessed how families used to fire up *asados* – barbecues – in the footprints before they knew what they were!)

For true dino-freaks, the best place to satiate the hunger for bones is the **Centro Paleontológico Lago Barreales** (Costa Dinosaurio; ☎ 0299-15-404-8614; www.proyectodino.com.ar in Spanish; RP 51, Km 65; museum admission AR$20; ⏰ 9am-4pm), located 90km northwest of Neuquén. Here you can actually work – as in get your hands dirty digging – on-site with paleontologists in one of the world's only fully functioning dinosaur excavation sites *open to the public*. You can visit the museum and take a guided tour of the site in about 1½ hours, but the real pleasure comes from the unique opportunity offered by sticking around. Prices (which help fund research) are AR$120 for one day, AR$550 for two days/one night, or about AR$1200 for five days/four nights. Bear in mind that this is a working archaeological site, and visits (even day trips) should be organized well in advance. Under the supervision of renowned paleontologist and project director Jorge Calvo, you'll spend your days dusting off Cretaceous-period bones and picking at fossils, and your nights in the silence of the desert. As Calvo says, 'when you set to work picking at the soft rock, uncovering fossilized leaves and bones that are 90 million years old, you forget about the rest of the world – some people even forget to eat.'

Getting There & Away

From Neuquén, **Cooperativa El Petroleo** (☎ 0299-446-2572) runs regular buses to Plaza Huincul (AR$14, 1¾ hours), and all buses between Neuquén and Zapala stop there. There are also regular buses to Villa El Chocón from Neuquén (AR$12, 1¼ hours). Centro Paleontológico Lago Barreales is a bit more difficult to reach; contact the site for driving directions or possible transportation options (there are no buses to the site). If you drive, take RP 51, not RN 7.

The **bus terminal** (Etcheluz & Uriburu) is about four blocks from Av San Martín. Westbound buses from Neuquén en route to Junín de los Andes (AR$30, 3 hours), San Martín de los Andes (AR$34, 3½ hours) and Temuco, Chile (AR$60, 6 hours), pass through Zapala. Most services to Buenos Aires (AR$150, 18 hours) require changing buses in Neuquén (AR$23, three hours), the nearest major hub. There is daily service to Laguna Blanca (AR$10, ½ hour) and Aluminé (AR$18, three to 3½

hours). Depending on the season, there are at least two buses daily for Chos Malal (AR$30, three hours), Villa Pehuenia (AR$33, 4 hours) and Coviahue (AR$20, three hours). During summertime there are frequent departures for Copahue (AR$26, 4 hours).

AROUND ZAPALA
Parque Nacional Laguna Blanca

At 1275m above sea level and surrounded by striking volcanic deserts, Laguna Blanca is only 10m deep, an interior drainage lake that formed when lava flows dammed two small streams. Only 30km southwest of Zapala, the lake is too alkaline for fish but hosts many bird species, including coots, ducks, grebes, upland geese, gulls and even a few flamingos. The 112.5-sq-km park primarily protects the habitat of the black-necked swan, a permanent resident.

Starting 10km south of Zapala, paved and well-marked RP 46 leads through the park toward the Andean town of Aluminé. If you're catching a bus, ask the driver to drop you off at the information center. For more bus details, see p385. If you don't have your own transport, ask at the National Parks office in Zapala if you can get a ride out with the rangers in the morning. A taxi to the park should charge around AR$100, including two hours' waiting time.

There is a small improved campground with windbreaks, but bring all your own food. There's a visitor center (open in the morning) with information displays and maps of walking trails, but there's no place to eat.

CHOS MALAL
☎ 02948 / pop 11,700 / elev 862m

Cruising through the stark, desertlike landscape north of Zapala doesn't really prepare you for arrival at this pretty little oasis town. Set at the convergence of Río Neuquén and Río Curi Leuvú, Chos Malal's one claim to fame is that it was Neuquén province's capital until 1904. Perhaps this explains why the town has so many stately old buildings and the present-day capital has so few.

The two main plazas in town bear the names of the two superheroes of Argentine history – San Martín and Sarmiento. Around the former is the majority of the historic buildings, including the Fuerte IV Division fort (go around the back for sweeping views out over the river valley). Five blocks south is Plaza Sarmiento, where you'll find banks and businesses.

Information
Banco de la Nación (Sarmiento & Urquiza) Has an ATM.
Hospital Zonal Gregorio Avárez (☎ 421400; Entre Ríos & Flores) English-speaker usually onsite.
Laco (Sarmiento 280; ☑ 9am-8pm; per hr AR$3) Provides internet access.
Tourist Information (☎ 421425; turnorte@neuquen .gov.ar; 25 de Mayo 89; ☑ 8am-8pm) Has good maps of the town and surrounds.

Activities
The only tour operator in town, **Tunduca** (☎ 422829; www.tunduca.com.ar; Jujuy 60) offers everything from fly-fishing, horse-back riding and rafting to day trips to the geysers and hot springs (p388) north of town and the rock carvings at Colo Michi-Co archaeological park (p388). It can also arrange 5-day treks to the summit of Volcán Domuyo (4710m), the highest volcanic peak in Patagonia.

Sleeping & Eating
Most accommodations are located in between the two plazas.

Hospedaje Lemus (☎ 421133; Lavalle 17; s/d AR$50/70, with shared bathroom AR$30/40) A no-frills *hospedaje* with big, clean rooms and friendly owners. Shared bathrooms are OK, but there's only two, so get in quick.

Hostería Don Costa (☎ 421652; hostdoncosta@hot mail.com; s/d AR$90/120; ☒ ☐) Attractive, modern rooms set well back from the road in case Chos Malal ever has a noisy night. Rooms are on the small side (like, door-bumping-bed small), but excellent value for the price. Get one upstairs for a balcony, sunlight and ventilation.

People in Chos Malal eat a lot of goat, and you may find yourself doing the same while you're there.

Bahia Café (Urquiza 305; breakfast AR$5, snacks AR$7-15; ☑ breakfast, lunch & dinner) Just off the Plaza Sarmiento, this cozy little café serves up the best coffee in town, along with hamburgers, sandwiches, pastas and good-value set lunches.

El Viejo Caicallén (☎ 421373; General Paz 345; mains AR$15-30; ☑ lunch & dinner) The best *parrilla* in town is at this happy place, offering all sorts of meat dishes, pastas, salads and sandwiches, along with a couple of regional faves like black butter trout (AR$30) and grilled kid goat (AR$25).

Getting There & Around
Chos Malal is small enough to walk around, which is lucky – there's a serious taxi shortage. To get to the center of town from the bus terminal, walk two blocks down Neuquén and take a right on 25 de Mayo. Plaza Sarmiento is six blocks straight ahead.

Regular buses depart for Zapala (AR$30, three hours), Neuquén (AR$53, six hours) and Varvarco (AR$20, three hours). Three minibuses a day leave between 4:30pm and 5pm for Buta Ranquil (AR$12.50, two hours).

THE LAKE DISTRICT

AROUND CHOS MALAL
Parque Archaeologico Colo Michi-Co

This small, rarely visited archaeological site features one of the most important collections of Pehuenche rock art in Patagonia. There are over 600 examples here, carved with symbolic figures and abstract designs. Getting to the site without a private vehicle is tricky. Buses leave Chos Malal Fridays at 8am for the village of Varvarco (AR$18, two hours). From there, it's 9km south on the RP 39 to the Escuela Colo Michi-Co, where you'll see a signpost leading to the park. A moderate 8km walk over undulating countryside will bring you to the site. Bring everything – there's nothing out here.

If all that walking doesn't excite you, contact **Sra La Gallega** (☎ 02948-421329) in Varvarco – there aren't any *remises* (taxis) there, but the Señora should be able to hook you up with a car and driver, charging around AR$3 per kilometer, plus waiting time. Hitchhiking is also common practice in the area, but be prepared for long waits.

Aguas Calientes

These excellent, natural outdoor hot springs located at the foot of the Volcán Domuyo are spread over 20 sq km and feature three main sites. The main one at Villa Aguas Calientes is suitable for swimming; Las Olletas to the north is a collection of bubbling mud pits and Los Tachos are geysers, spurting up to heights of two meters. The site is 40km north of Varvarco, where the last public transport terminates. If you don't have your own wheels, your best way of getting here is with Tunduca (p387) in Chos Malal. If you can get to Varvarco on your own, you can ask about hiring a driver with **Sra La Gallega** (☎ 02948-421329) – the going rates are around AR$3 per kilometer, plus waiting time.

BUTA RANQUIL
☎ 02948 / pop 2200 / elev 850m

A small, dusty town on the border of Neuquén and Mendoza provinces, Buta Ranquil owes its existence to three oilfields operating just out of town. There's not a great deal (well, OK, nothing) to do here, but it's an important stopover on the little-traveled RN 40 between Chos Malal and San Rafael. Despite what everybody else in the country will tell you, the roads are in good shape – paved nearly all the way from Barrancas to Malargüe, with only a couple of smooth, unmade sections.

Hospedaje Bujos (☎ 493092; Carreño s/n; r per person AR$40) A very basic *hospedaje* with reasonable rooms and sagging beds. Best cheapie in town.

Residencial del Viento (☎ 493114; Moyano s/n; s/d AR$140/200) The fanciest place in town, set up for visiting oil company bigshots. If they're not in town, rates may halve, making it a good deal. The attached restaurant (mains AR$15 to AR$25) is about the only place you'd want to eat in town, with good pasta and *parrilla* and yummy homemade empanadas.

Transportes Leader (☎ 493268; Malvinas & Jadull) has one minibus daily going north on the RN 40. It leaves town at 11pm, passing Malargüe (AR$55, 4½ hours) and ending in San Rafael (AR$65, 7½ hours). Seats sell out quickly on this route – you should book (and may have to pay) at least one day in advance.

ALUMINÉ
☎ 02942 / pop 4000 / elev 400m

Time seems to have stopped for Aluminé, and although it's an important tourist destination, it is less visited than destinations to the south. The town itself has a very local flair, with the main plaza alive with families and children on weekends. Most of the buildings are whitewashed brick, faded with time, and the streets are nearly all dirt, all a relief from the chalet-lined streets of San Martín and Bariloche. Situated 103km north of Junín de los Andes via RP 23, it's a popular fly-fishing destination and offers access to the less-visited northern sector of Parque Nacional Lanín. The Río Aluminé also offers excellent white-water rafting and kayaking.

Information

Banco del Provincia del Neuquén (cnr Conrado Villegas & Torcuato Mordarelli) Bank and ATM.

Nex Sur (☎ 496027; Av RIM 26 848; per hr before 6pm AR$1.50, after 6pm AR$2) Internet access; uphill from plaza.

Tourist office (☎ 496001; intendencia@alumine.com.ar; Christian Joubert, Plaza San Martín; 🕐 8am-8pm mid-Mar–Nov, 9am-9pm Dec–mid-Mar)

Sights & Activities

The nearby Mapuche communities of **Aigo** and **Salazar**, on the 26km rolling dirt road to **Lago Ruca Choroi** (in Parque Nacional Lanín) sell traditional weavings, araucaria pine nuts, and, in summer time, *comidas tipicas* (traditional dishes). Salazar is an easy, signposted 12km walk or bike ride out of town – just follow the river. Aigo is another 14km along.

For rafting on the Río Aluminé (best in November), as well as kayaking, fly-fishing, trekking and rock climbing, contact **Aluminé Rafting** (☎ 496322; aluminerafting@yahoo.com.ar; Conrado Villegas 610).

Mali Viajes (☎ 496310), in front of the tourist office on the plaza, hires bikes for AR$10/40 per hour/day. During summer it offers scenic tours to Mapuche communities, circumnavigating Lago Ruca Choroi en route to Villa Pehuenia.

The tourist office keeps a list of available **fishing** guides and sells licenses (AR$40/180 per day/week).

Sleeping & Eating

If you're traveling in a group, the tourist office keeps a list of self-catering cabins – some just out of town – that offer good value for three or more people. High season coincides with the November-through-April fishing season.

Nid Car (☎ 496131; nidcaralumine@yahoo.com.ar; C Joubert & Benigar; s/d AR$40/75) Very standard and slightly spacious rooms just uphill from the plaza. Cheapest in town and not a bad deal.

Hostería Aluminé (☎ 496174; hosteriaalumine@hotmail.com; Christian Joubert 336; s/d AR$85/110, with shared bathroom AR$60/80) Probably a good-looking hotel once upon a time, the lobby and restaurant areas here are still impressive, but the rooms are functional and slightly drab. The attached restaurant (meals AR$15 to AR$22) serves good food, especially the mixed pasta dish with *salsa de piñon y hongos* (pine nut and mushroom sauce).

Hotel Pehuenia (☎ 496340; hotelpehuenia@uol.com.ar; RP 23 & Crouzielles; s/d from AR$150/190; 🖳) A sprawling brick wonderland out on the highway (a two-minute walk from the center of town), the Pehuenia is comfortable enough with modern, slightly cramped rooms. It's definitely worth paying the extra AR$30 for the river views.

Los Araucarias (Candelaria & C Joubert; mains AR$15-25; 🕑 lunch & dinner) This standard *parrilla* restaurant offers a down-home atmosphere and an impressive wine list.

Restaurante Sauco (☎ 496357; Av RIM 26 & Candelaria; mains AR$15-30; 🕑 lunch & dinner) A cozy little restaurant uphill from the plaza serving up a range of trout dishes (the owner is a fly-fishing enthusiast), regional specialties, Patagonian oddballs like pickled rabbit and your standard range of pasta, pizza, *parrilla* and sandwiches.

Getting There & Away

Aluminé's **bus terminal** (☎ 496048) is just downhill from the plaza, an easy walk to any of the hotels listed here. Aluminé Viajes and Albus go daily to/from Neuquén (AR$36, 7 hours), Zapala (AR$18, three to 3½ hours), Villa Pehuenia (AR$14, one hour) and San Martín de los Andes (AR$20, 4½ hours).

VILLA PEHUENIA
☎ 02942 / pop 500 / elev 1200m

Villa Pehuenia is an idyllic little lakeside village on the shores of Lago Aluminé. There are several Mapuche communities nearby, including the community of Puel, located between Lago Aluminé and Lago Moquehue. The *villa* lies at the heart of the Pehuen region, named of course after the pehuen (araucaria) trees that are so marvelously present. If you have a car, the Circuito Pehuenia is a great drive; it's a four- to six-hour loop from Villa Pehuenia past Lago Moquehue, Lago Ñorquinco, Lago Pulmarí and back around Lago Aluminé.

The drive from Zapala on RP 13 via Primeros Pinos is spectacular with sweeping vistas across the high Pampa de Lonco Luan, where the tip of Volcán Lanín is visible off to the left and the double peaks of Volcan Llaima (3125m) in Chile.

Orientation & Information

Villa Pehuenia is 102km north of Junín de los Andes (via RP 23 and Aluminé) and 120km west of Zapala, via RP 13. *Hosterías* and *cabañas* are spread around the Peninsula de los Coihues, which dangles nearly 2km into Lago Aluminé. Most services such as supermarkets and restaurants are in and around the *centro comercial*, which is just above the peninsula.

Banco de la Provincia del Neuquén (RP 13 s/n) Next to the police station; has an ATM.
Oficina de Turismo (☎ 498044; www.villapehuenia .org; RP 13) At the entrance to town, is extremely helpful and provides good maps of the region.

Sights & Activities

From the top of nearby **Volcán Batea Mahuida** (1960m) you can see eight volcanoes (from Lanín to the south to Copahue to the north) in both Argentina and Chile. Inside Batea Mahuida is a small crater lake. You drive nearly to the top (summer only) and then it's an easy two-hour walk to the summit. This is the location of the small Mapuche-operated **Batea Mahuida ski park**

(☎ 02942-15-664745), which is little more than a few snowy slopes with a T-bar and a poma. If you're a Nordic skier, you're in better luck – a circuit goes around the park, taking in awesome views of the volcano and lakes.

Brisas del Sur (☎ 02942-15-692737; www.brisasdelsur.8m .com) gives boat tours of Lago Aluminé (AR$35, 1½ hours), leaving from the small peninsula in front of the Laguna El Manzano.

Los Pehuenes (☎ 498029; Centro Comercial), the local adventure tourism operator, offers rafting, trekking, horse-back riding and 4WD off-roading trips.

In nearby Moquehue, **LM Aventura** (☎ 02942-15-664705; www.llienanmapu.com.ar, guillermoluna@yahoo .com.ar; Arroyo Las Animas, RP 11, Km 18) offers dog-sledding trips (40 minutes to three days) through the araucaria forests in wintertime.

LAGUNA TERMAL TREK

This day trip, which should be possible in around eight hours, is easy enough to do on your own, leaving from Copahue. Due to snow conditions, it's only possible from December to April unless you bring special equipment. If you'd like to take the side route to the peak of Volcán Copahue, it's recommended that you go with an experienced guide. Caviahue Tours (see p392) are among the many tour operators offering guides on this route.

From the Hotel Valle del Volcán at the upper (southwest) edge of the village, cross the little footbridge and climb briefly past a lifesize statue of the Virgin. The well-worn foot track leads across a sparsely vegetated plain towards the exploded cone of Volcán Copahue, dipping down to lush, green lawns by the northern shore of the Lagunas Las Mellizas' western 'twin.' Follow a path along the lake's north side past black-sand beachlets and gushing springs on its opposite shore to reach the start of a steam pipeline, one to 1¼ hours from the village. The roaring of steam from the subterranean Copahue Geothermal Field entering the vapoducto and irregular explosive blasts of discharging steam can be heard along much of the trek. Cross the lake outlet – further downstream is a wide, easy ford – then cut up southwest over snowdrifts past a tarn to meet a 4WD track at the edge of a small waterlogged meadow. Turn right and follow this rough road up around left (or take a vague trail marked with white paint splashes to its right until you come back to the road on a rocky ridge below a wooden cross). The 4WD track continues westward up through a barren volcanic moonscape to end under a tiny glacier on the east flank of Volcán Copahue, 1¼ to 1½ hours from the pipeline.

Ascend southwest over bouldery ridges, crossing several small mineral-and-meltwater streams. To the northwest, in Chile, the ice-smothered Sierra Velluda and the near-perfect snowy cone of Volcán Antuco rise up majestically. From the third streamlet (with yellowy, sulphur-encrusted sides), cut along the slope below a hot spring then climb to the top of a prominent gray-pumice spur that lies on the international border. Ascend the spur until it becomes impossibly steep, then traverse up rightward over loose slopes into a gap to reach Laguna Termal, 1¼ to 1½ hours from the end of the 4WD track (3½ to 4¼ hours from Copahue).

Filling Volcán Copahue's eastern crater, this steaming hot lake feeds itself by melting the snout of a glacier that forms a massive rim of ice above its back wall. Sulphurous fumes often force trekkers to retreat from the lake, but these high slopes also grant a wonderful vista across the vast basin (where both villages are visible) between the horseshoe-shaped Lago Caviahue (Lago Agrio) and the elongated Lago Trolope to the northeast. From here, more experienced trekkers can continue up to the summit of Volcán Copahue.

To get back to Copahue, retrace your ascent route. If you have a decent map of the area, you can follow the Arroyo Caviahue (Río Agrio) and RN 26 back to town.

Warning

Particularly on windy days, acrid fumes rising from Laguna Termal can be overpowering due to sulphur dioxide gas (which attacks your airways). Approach the lake cautiously – don't even consider swimming in it. Less-experienced trekkers are advised to go with an organized tour (see p392).

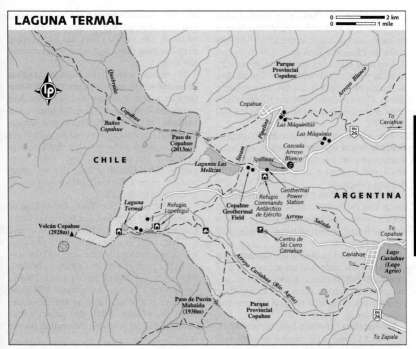

LAGUNA TERMAL

Sleeping & Eating

Many businesses in Villa Pehuenia close down off season. Those listed below are open year-round.

Hostería de las Cumbres (☎ 02942-498097; puerto delascumbres@yahpoo.com.ar; r AR$150) Right down by the waterfront in the main part of town, this cozy little *hostería* has smallish rooms coming off way-narrow corridors. Lake views from the front rooms, however, make this one a winner.

Hostería la Balconada (☎ 02942-15-473843; www .hosterialabalconada.com.ar; r AR$340-370) One of the finest, coziest accommodation options in town, this one sits out on a cliff on the peninsula. It's worth paying the extra AR$30 for the lake views.

Iñaki (☎ 498047; snacks from AR$8; ☺ lunch & dinner) A cool little restaurant/tapas bar near the lakefront in the main part of town. Vegetarian food and good-value set meals are available. On a sunny day, the deck out front is the place to be.

Parrilla Los Troncos (☎ 498006; Centro Comercial; mains AR$15-25; ☺ lunch & dinner) The most reliable *parrilla* in town cooks up some great burgers and excellent fries. Also *parrilla*, sandwiches

and more. They can set you up with a packed lunch if you're off on an outing.

Between the Centro Comercial and the tourist office, the **Fabrica de Alfajores** (☎ 498090; RP 13 s/n; ☺ 9am-6pm daily in summer, weekends only rest of year) makes and sells delicious *alfajores de piñon*, (*alfajores* made with pine nut flour) and serves up a mean cup of coffee or hot chocolate.

Getting There & Around

Exploring the area is tough without a car, though hitching is definitely feasible in summer. **Destinos Patagonicos** (☎ 498067; Centro Comercial) is the representative for Albus, the only bus company currently serving the village. There are daily buses to Zapala (AR$33, 4½ hours), Neuquén (AR$60, 7 hours) and Aluminé (AR$14, 1 hour).

COPAHUE

☎ 02948 / elev 2030m

Copahue is a small thermal springs resort, standing on the northeastern side of its namesake volcano among steaming, sulphurous pools including a bubbling hot mud pool, the popular **Laguna del Chancho** (⏰ 8am-6pm; AR$6). The setting, in a natural amphitheater formed by the mountain range, is spectacular, but the town isn't much to look at.

Copahue has been gaining in popularity over the years, mainly with Argentine tourists, as the rapid growth in tourist infrastructure shows. Due to snow cover, the village is only open from the start of December to the end of April.

The village centers on the large, modern **Complejo Termal Copahue** (☎ 495049; www.termas decopahue.com; Ortiz Velez; baths AR$8, spa treatments from AR$20), which offers a wide range of curative bathing programs.

Residencial Codihue (☎ 495151; codihue@futurtel .com.ar; Velez s/n; s/d AR$60/100) is the best budget option in town, with simple rooms just down the road from the thermal baths complex. Full board is available.

The best hotel in the village, **Copahue Hotel** (☎ 495117; www.copahuehotel.com.ar; Bercovich s/n; s/d from AR$200/250), features modern rooms, atmospheric common areas and an excellent restaurant serving traditional Argentine and regional foods.

Parrillada Nito (☎ 495040; Zambo Jara; mains AR$15-35; ⏰ lunch & dinner) is the most frequently recommended *parrilla* restaurant in town.

In summer, one bus daily runs to Neuquén (AR$48, seven hours) via Zapala (AR$25, four hours). There are no scheduled departures for the rest of the year.

CAVIAHUE
☎ 02948 / pop 500 / elev 1600m

On the western shore of Lago Caviahue, the ski village of Caviahue lies at the southeast foot of Volcán Copahue. A better-looking village than Copahue, this one is growing rapidly too – construction noise fills the air during summertime.

Information
Cyber Caviahue (Las Lengas s/n; per hr AR$3; ⏰ 8am-1pm & 4-9pm) Internet access.
Oficina de Turismo (☎ 495036; www.caviahue -copahue.com.ar; 8 de Abril s/n) In the municpalidad. Good maps and up-to-date info on local accommodations.

Activities
There are some good short walks from the village, including a popular day trek that goes up past the Cascada Escondida waterfall to Laguna Escondida. Another walk to

the four waterfalls known as Cascadas Agrio starts from across the bridge at the entrance to town. The tourist office has an excellent map showing these and other walks around the area.

If you have a taste for adventure, **Caviahue Tours** (☎ 495138; www.caviahuetours.com; Av Bialous Centro Comercial lcl 11) organizes treks, including to Laguna Termal and Volcán Copahue, while **La Huella** (☎ 495116; viatursur@yahoo.com.ar; Bungalow Alpino Sur 2) rents mountainbikes for AR$40 per day in summer and offers dog-sledding trips in winter. For those that fancy some pampering, Hotel Caviahue has a day spa where you can enjoy a thermal bath for AR$10 and treatments from AR$20.

A little under 2km from the village of Caviahue, the ski resort Centro de Ski Cerro Caviahue has four chairlifts, two pomas and a T-bar, with another three lifts planned, which will eventually take skiers all the way up to the peak of Volcán Copahue (2958m). At present, the highest lifted point is 2068m. Equipment hire (skis/snowboard AR$50/60 per day) is also available on the mountain or in the village. Adult day passes range from AR$70 to AR$130, depending on the season.

Sleeping & Eating
Hebe's House (☎ 495237; lacabanadehebe@ciudad.com .ar; Mapuche & Puesta del Sol; dm/d AR$35/100; ⏰ Dec-Sep) With the only hostel for miles around, Hebe crams them in to cozy but cramped dorms. It's set in a cute alpine building and offers kitchen access, laundry facilities and plenty of tourist information. If you're coming in winter, book well ahead.

Hotel Caviahue (☎ 495044; hotelcaviahue@issn.gov .ar; 8 de Abril s/n; s/d AR$130/200) A rambling, older-style hotel set up the hill, with views out over the village, lake and mountains. It's the only hotel open in the village year-round. Rates drop around 30% off-season. Also on the premises is the only restaurant (mains AR$15 to AR$20) in town to stay open year-round.

Getting There & Away
One bus daily runs to Neuquén (AR$40, 6½ hours) via Zapala (AR$20, 3½ hours). If you're headed for Chos Malal, you can shave a couple of hours off your travel time by getting off in Las Lajas (AR$15, 2½ hours) and waiting for a bus there. Check your connection times with the bus company **Cono Sur** (☎ 421800), though –

if you're going to get stranded, Zapala is the place to do it.

JUNÍN DE LOS ANDES
☎ 02972 / pop 11,000 / elev 800m

A much more humble affair than other Lake District towns, Junín's a favorite for fly fishers – the town deems itself the trout capital of Neuquén province and, to drive the point home, uses trout-shaped street signs. A couple of circuits leading out of town take in the scenic banks of the Lago Huechulafquen, where Mapuche settlements welcome visitors. Outside of peak season, these circuits are best done by private vehicle (or incredibly enthusiastic bike riders), but travel agents based here offer reasonably priced tours.

Orientation
Paved RN 234 (known as Blvd Juan Manuel de Rosas in town) is the main thoroughfare, leading south to San Martín de los Andes and 116km northeast to Zapala via RN 40. North of town, graveled RP 23 heads to the fishing resort of Aluminé, while several secondary roads branch westward to Parque Nacional Lanín.

The city center is between the highway and the river. Do not confuse Av San Martín, which runs on the west side of Plaza San Martín, with Félix San Martín, two blocks further west.

Information
Banco de la Provincia de Neuquén (Av San Martín, btwn Coronel Suárez & General Lamadrid) Opposite the plaza.

bits (Coronel Suárez 445 btwn Domingo Milanesio & Don Bosco; per hr AR$2) Internet access.

Club Andino Junín de los Andes (☎ 491207; hgonzalez@fronteradigital.net.ar) Provides information on the Volcán Tromen climb and other excursions within the national park.

Laverap Pehuén (Ginés Ponte 340) Laundry services.

Locutorio (Domingo Milanesio 540) Opposite the plaza. It's easiest to make local or long-distance calls from this office.

Park office (☎ 491160; Domingo Milanesio at Coronel Suárez; � 9am-8:30pm Mon-Fri, 2:30-8:30pm Sat & Sun) Next to the tourist office. Has information on Parque Nacional Lanín.

Post office (Coronel Suárez & Don Bosco)

Tourist office (☎ 491160, 492575; Domingo Milanesio 596 at Coronel Suárez, Plaza San Martín; � 8am-11pm Nov-Feb, 8am-9pm Mar-Oct) Enthusiastically helpful staff.

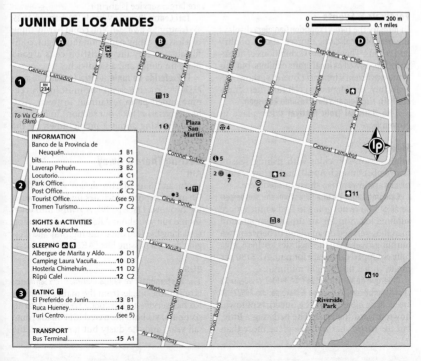

JUNIN DE LOS ANDES

0 — 200 m
0 — 0.1 miles

Fishing permits (AR$30/150 per day/week, AR$200 season pass) and list of licensed fishing guides available.

Tromen Turismo (☎ 491469; Coronel Suárez 445) Recommended tour operator for trips into Parque Nacional Lanín and tours of Mapuche communities. Also rents mountain bikes for AR$15/30 per half/full day and rock-climbing gear.

Sights & Activities

Junín's surroundings are more appealing than the town itself, but the **Museo Mapuche** (Ginés Ponte & Joaquín Nogueira; admission free; ☾ 10am-noon & 4-8pm Mon, Wed & Fri), which boasts Mapuche weavings and archaeological pieces, is well worth seeing.

West of town, near the end of Av Antártida Argentina, a wide dirt path called the **Vía Cristi** winds its way up the small Cerro de La Cruz (to get there, follow the cross) with impressive sculptures, bas-reliefs and mosaics vividly depicting the Conquest of the Desert, Mapuche legends, Christian themes and indigenous history.

The area around Junín is prime trout-fishing country, and the Río Aluminé, north of Junín, is an especially choice area. Catch-and-release is obligatory. Fishing permits are available through the tourist office.

Festivals & Events

In January the **Feria y Exposición Ganadera** displays the best of local cattle, horses, sheep, poultry and rabbits. There are also exhibitions of horsemanship, as well as local crafts exhibits, but this is the *estanciero's* (*estancia* owner's) show.

In July, the Mapuche celebrate their crafts skills in the **Semana de Artesanía Aborígen**.

The **National Trout Festival** takes place in November.

Sleeping

High season coincides with fishing season (November through April); during low season, prices are lower than those quoted here.

Camping Laura Vacuña (Ginés Ponte s/n; sites per person AR$5) You're not going to find a more sublime location for an urban campground than this, perched on an island in between two burbling creeks. All the facilities are here, plus fully equipped cabins are for rent, AR$180 per night, with a three-night minimum.

Albergue de Marita y Aldo (☎ 491042; casademarita yaldo@hotmail.com; 25 de Mayo & Olavorría; dm AR$22) A sweet little *albergue* on the outskirts of town, down toward the river. The beds sag a little, but the rustic charm of the place more than

makes up for that. Your hosts are fly fishers and meat smokers, which may give you something to talk about.

Rüpú Calel (☎ 491569; www.rupucalel.com.ar; Coronel Suárez 560; s/d AR$90/120) While they may look big and bare to some, the rooms here have a pleasing simplicity and are sparkling clean, as are the spacious bathrooms.

Hostería Chimehuín (☎ 491132; www.interpata gonia.com/hosteriachimehuin in Spanish; Coronel Suárez & 25 de Mayo; s/d AR$130/150) A beautiful spot a few minutes from the center of town. Book early and you'll have a good chance of snagging a room with a balcony overlooking the creek. Either way, rooms are big, warm and comfortable and the whole place has a tranquil air to it.

Eating

Junín has fairly mediocre restaurants, though local specialties like trout, wild boar or venison may be available.

Ruca Hueney (☎ 491113; Domingo Milanesio 641; mains AR$15-22; ☾ lunch & dinner) Ruca Hueney, Junín's oldest restaurant, is reliable and has the most extensive menu in town. Portions are large; service is abrupt.

Turi Centro (Domingo Milanesio 590; mains AR$15-25; ☾ breakfast, lunch & dinner) You could hardly think of a less appealing name, but this bright, comfortable café by the tourist office is a good place for coffee and a sandwich.

El Preferido de Junín (General Lamadrid 20; mains AR$20-30; ☾ lunch & dinner) The most highly recommended pasta restaurant in town. Also has a *rotisería* (take-out section) in case you were thinking about a picnic down by the creek.

Getting There & Away

AIR

Junín and San Martín de los Andes share Chapelco airport, which lies midway between the two towns (see p399). A *remise* into town should run you about AR$25. Another option is walking the 1km out to the highway and flagging down a passing bus (AR$6, 25 minutes).

BUS

The **bus terminal** (☎ 492038; Olavarría & Félix San Martín) is only three blocks from the main plaza. Ko-Ko has service to Bariloche (AR$30, four to six hours) via both the paved Rinconada route (all year) and the dusty but far more scenic

EXCURSIONS TO PARQUE NACIONAL LANÍN

In summer, buses leave the terminal several times a day for destinations within Parque Nacional Lanín (see p400), allowing you to hit the trails and camp in some beautiful areas. The buses run three 'circuits' and charge AR$12 for the return trip.

Lago Huechulafquen & Puerto Canoa (via RP 61)

From Puerto Canoa, on the north shore of the lake, there are three worthwhile hikes, including a 1½-hour roundtrip walk to the Cascada del Saltillo and a seven-hour roundtrip hike to **Cara Sur de Lanín** (south face of Volcán Lanín). For the latter, park rangers require you set out by 11am. Ranger stations are at both the entrance to Huechulafquen and at Puerto Canoa. From Puerto Canoa, the boat **Jose Julian** (☎ 421038, 429539) offers boat trips on the lake. Buses depart Junín's terminal twice in the morning (usually around 8am and 11am) and once in the afternoon (around 4pm). Be sure to catch the last bus back unless you plan to camp.

Circuito Tromen (via RN 23 & RP 60)

Buses depart twice daily to **Lago Tromen**, from where there is a 1½-hour roundtrip walk along the river, passing a fine araucaria forest and a lookout with fabulous views of the lake. Another 45-minute walk takes you to the base of **Volcán Lanín's Cara Norte** (north face). This is one departure point for the two- to three-day ascent of Lanín. Park rangers inspect equipment and test any climbers who plan to go without a guide. To hire a guide, contact the tourist office in Junín. This is the access point for the CAJA *refugio* (shelter) and two military-owned *refugios*. Lago Tromen can also be reached by taking any bus that goes to Chile and getting off at Tromen.

Circuito Curruhué (via RP 62)

Buses depart once or twice daily for **Lago Curruhué** and **Lago Epulafquen**; near the latter is a trailhead that leads to the **Termas de Lahuen-Có** (☎ 424709; www.lahuenco.com), about one hour's walking time from the head. Package tours out here, including transport, lunch and spa treatments cost around AR$450 and can be organized through the center or through tour operators in town. You can also hike to the crater of Volcán Achen Niyeu.

Siete Lagos alternative (summertime only). El Petróleo goes Tuesday to Aluminé (AR$24, three hours). To Mendoza you must change buses in Neuquén. Empresa San Martín crosses the Andes to Temuco, Chile (AR$46, six hours), via Paso Tromen (also known as Mamuil Malal). There are daily services to the following destinations:

Destination	Cost (AR$)	Duration (hr)
Bahía Blanca	85	13
Buenos Aires	150	22
Córdoba	176	22
Neuquén	53	6
San Martín de los Andes	5	1
Zapala	30	3

SAN MARTÍN DE LOS ANDES
☎ 02972 / pop 26,000 / elev 645m
Like a mellower version of Bariloche, San Martín has two peak periods – winter for

skiing at Cerro Chapelco and summer for trekking, climbing, etc in the nearby Parque Nacional Lanín. Brave souls also swim in the chilly waters of Lago Lácar on the western edge of town. Between these times, it's a quiet little town with a spectacular setting that retains much of the charm and architectural unity that once attracted people to Bariloche. A boat ride on the lake is pretty much a must if you're passing through, and if the snow's cleared (anytime from December onwards) and you're heading south, you should seriously think about leaving town via the scenically neck-straining Ruta de los Siete Lagos (RN 234), which runs south to Villa la Angostura and Bariloche.

Orientation
Nestled in striking mountain scenery, San Martín de los Andes straddles RN 234, which passes through town southbound to

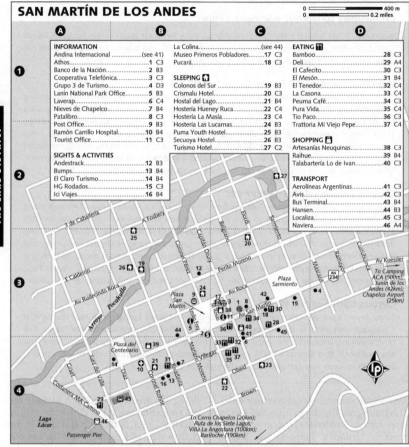

SAN MARTÍN DE LOS ANDES

0		400 m
0		0.2 miles

INFORMATION
Andina Internacional	(see 41)	
Athos	**1**	C3
Banco de la Nación	**2**	B3
Cooperativa Telefónica	**3**	C3
Grupo 3 de Turismo	**4**	D3
Lanín National Park Office	**5**	B3
Laverap	**6**	C4
Nieves de Chapelco	**7**	B4
Patalibro	**8**	C3
Post Office	**9**	B3
Ramón Carrillo Hospital	**10**	B4
Tourist Office	**11**	C3

SIGHTS & ACTIVITIES
Andestrack	**12**	B3
Bumps	**13**	B4
El Claro Turismo	**14**	B4
HG Rodados	**15**	C3
Ici Viajes	**16**	B4

La Colina	(see 44)	
Museo Primeros Pobladores	**17**	C3
Pucará	**18**	C3

SLEEPING
Colonos del Sur	**19**	B3
Crismalu Hotel	**20**	C3
Hostal del Lago	**21**	B4
Hostería Hueney Ruca	**22**	C4
Hostería La Masía	**23**	C4
Hostería Las Lucarnas	**24**	B3
Puma Youth Hostel	**25**	B3
Secuoya Hostel	**26**	B3
Turismo Hotel	**27**	C2

EATING
Bamboo	**28**	C3
Deli	**29**	A4
El Cafecito	**30**	C3
El Mesón	**31**	B4
El Tenedor	**32**	C4
La Casona	**33**	C4
Peuma Café	**34**	C4
Pura Vida	**35**	C4
Tío Paco	**36**	C3
Trattoria Mi Viejo Pepe	**37**	C4

SHOPPING
Artesanías Neuquinas	**38**	C3
Raihue	**39**	B4
Talabartería Lo de Ivan	**40**	C3

TRANSPORT
Aerolíneas Argentinas	**41**	C3
Avis	**42**	C3
Bus Terminal	**43**	B4
Hansen	**44**	B3
Localiza	**45**	C3
Naviera	**46**	A4

Villa la Angostura and Lago Nahuel Huapi. Northbound RN 234 heads to Zapala via Junín de los Andes. Almost everything in San Martín de los Andes is within walking distance of the *centro cívico* (civic center), and the shady lakefront park and pier are a delightful place to spend an afternoon. Av San Martín is the main commercial street, running north from the lakefront toward the highway to Junín.

Information

BOOKSTORES

Patalibro (☎ 421532; patalibro@yahoo.com.ar; Av San Martín 866) Good selection of books on Patagonia in Spanish; some Lonely Planet titles and novels in English. Carries the excellent *Sendas Y Bosques* park trail maps (AR$12).

INTERNET ACCESS

Athos (☎ 429855; Av San Martín 808; per hr AR$2) Internet access in kiosk, upstairs.

LAUNDRY

Laverap (☎ 428820; Capitán Drury 880; full service about AR$10)

MEDICAL SERVICES

Ramón Carrillo Hospital (☎ 427211; Coronel Rohde & Av San Martín)

MONEY

Andina Internacional (☎ 427871; Capitán Drury 876) Money exchange.
Banco de la Nación (Av San Martín 687) Has an ATM.

POST

Post office (Av Roca & Coronel Pérez)

TELEPHONE

Cooperativa Telefónica (Capitán Drury 761)

TOURIST INFORMATION

ACA (☎ 429430; Av Koessler 2175) Argentina's auto club; good source for provincial road maps.

Lanín national park office (Intendencia del Parque Nacional Lanín; ☎ 427233; www.parquenacionallanin.gov.ar in Spanish; Emilio Frey 749; 🕑 8am-2pm Mon-Fri) The office provides limited maps as well as brochures.

Nieves de Chapelco (☎ 427825; www.cerrochapelco.com; Rivadavia 880) Provides information and sells lift tickets for the Cerro Chapelco ski resort.

Tourist office (☎ 425500, 427347; www.smandes.gov.ar; cnr Av San Martín & Rosas; 🕑 8am-9pm, to 10pm Dec-Mar) Provides surprisingly candid information on hotels and restaurants, plus excellent brochures and maps.

TRAVEL AGENCIES

The agencies listed (right), as well as many others along Av San Martín, Belgrano and Elordi, offer standard services as well as excursions.

Grupo 3 de Turismo (☎ 428453; San Martín 1141, Local 1) The Amex representative.

Sights

MUSEO PRIMEROS POBLADORES

Regional archaeological and ethnographic items such as arrowheads, spear points, pottery and musical instruments are the focus of the **Museo Primeros Pobladores** (M Rosas; admission AR$1; 🕑 2-7pm Mon-Fri), located two doors north of the tourist office, on M Rosas near Av Roca.

RUTA DE LOS SIETE LAGOS

From San Martín, RN 234 follows an eminently scenic but rough, narrow and dusty route past numerous alpine lakes to Villa la Angostura. It's known as the Ruta de los Siete Lagos (Seven Lakes Route) and its spectacular scenery has made the drive famous. Sections of the 110km route close every year due to heavy snowfalls – December to May is the best time to schedule this trip, but ask around for current conditions. Full day tours from San Martín, Villa la Angostura and Bariloche regularly do this route, but there's also a scheduled bus service (p399) and, with a little forward planning, it's possible to drive/cycle it yourself (see p400).

Activities

Mountain biking is an excellent way to explore the surrounding area and a good way to travel the Ruta de los Siete Lagos. Rent bikes at **HG Rodados** (☎ 427345; Av San Martín 1061) or **Ici Viajes** (☎ 427800; Villegas 459). Both charge about AR$20 per day.

For rafting on the Río Meliquina, south of San Martín, or the Río Hua Hum to the west, contact Ici Viajes, **El Claro Turismo** (☎ 428876, 425876; www.elclaroturismo.com.ar; Diaz 751) or **Pucará** (☎ 427218; Av San Martín 941). They all charge about AR$90 for the all-day trip, including transfers. The river is spectacular and suitable for kids.

There are also excellent opportunities for trekking and climbing in Parque Nacional Lanín. **Andestrack** (☎ 420588; www.andestrack.com.ar; Perito Moreno 722) is a young, enthusiastic company that has been highly recommended for mountain biking, canoeing, snowshoeing and dogsledding in the park.

Skiing and snowboarding at nearby Cerro Chapelco attracts enthusiastic winter crowds (see p399). In San Martín, rental equipment is available at **Bumps** (☎ 428491; Villegas 459) and **La Colina** (☎ 427414; Av San Martín 532). Skis rent for AR$60 to AR$80 per day and snowboards for AR$80 to AR$100. You can also rent equipment on the mountain.

Festivals & Events

San Martín celebrates its founding on February 4 with speeches, parades and other festivities; the **parade** itself is an entertainingly incongruous mix of military folks, firefighters, gauchos, polo players and foxhunters.

Sleeping

As a tourist center, San Martín is loaded with accommodations, but they're relatively costly in all categories, especially in summer high season (January to March) and peak ski season (mid-July and August), when reservations are a must. Quality, however, is mostly high. In low season, prices can drop by 40%.

BUDGET

Secuoya Hostel (☎ 424485; Rivadavia 411; dm AR$33, d with shared bathroom AR$80) A beautiful new hostel with plenty of space, free internet and an abundantly fitted-out kitchen. It's located in front of a park in a residential neighborhood, so there's plenty of tranquility on offer.

Puma Youth Hostel (☎ 422443; www.pumahostel.com.ar; A Fosbery 535; dm AR$35, d AR$95) This pleasant, well-kept HI-affiliated hostel offers spacious dorms with private bathroom. There are a couple of good common areas and a well-stocked kitchen. Transfers to Cerro Chapelco are available.

Camping ACA (☎ 427332; Av Koessler 2640; sites per person with 2-person minimum fee AR$10) Spacious campground on the eastern outskirts of town. Avoid sites near the highway, however.

MIDRANGE

Hostería Las Lucarnas (☎ 427085; fax 427985; Coronel Pérez 632; s/d AR$110/150) A sedate little *hostería* in the center of town. Wood-beamed ceilings and big bathrooms are definite bonuses; try for a spot upstairs.

our pick **Hostal del Lago** (☎ 427598; hostallago@ hotmail.com; Coronel Rhode 854; s/d AR$120/150) This cute little alpine house has been converted into a cozy hostel. There are only six rooms, and all are upstairs with sloping ceilings. There's plenty of space, a charming sitting area downstairs and super-friendly management.

Crismalu Hotel (☎ 427283; Rudecino Roca 975; s/d AR$120/150) This huge hotel hasn't been renovated since the '70s (or if it has, it was a very retro fitout), so green carpet and chunky room phones are the go. Get a room out front with a balcony overlooking the huge araucaria tree and you'll be happy.

Turismo Hotel (☎ 427592; hotelturismo@smandes .com.ar; Mascardi 517; s/d AR$130/150) A classic '70s ski lodge, right down to the stuffed deer's head and old-school pool table in the lobby. Rooms are comfortable enough, but best avoided if you have problems with glaring yellow paintjobs.

Colonos del Sur (☎ 427106; www.colonosdelsur.com .ar; Rivadavia 686; r AR$160) A big, modern hotel pleasingly constructed in the alpine style. Rooms are spacious and bright, with large modern bathrooms, firm beds and faux wooden floorboards.

Hostería Hueney Ruca (☎ 421499; www.hueneyruca hosteria.com.ar; Obeid & Coronel Pérez; s/d AR$150/180) The big, terracotta-tiled rooms here look onto a cute, well-kept little backyard. Beds are big and firm and bathrooms spacious, with glass-walled showerstalls.

TOP END

Hostería La Masía (☎ 427688; www.hosterialamasia .com.ar in Spanish; Obeid 811; s/d AR$180/240) Taking the whole edelweiss thing to the next level, La Masía offers plenty of dark wood paneling, arched doorways and cast-iron light fittings.

Rooms are big and comfortable and most have mountain views. Fireplaces warm the lobby, and the owners are usually around to make sure everyone feels at home. Superb.

Eating & Drinking

BUDGET & MIDRANGE

Deli (☎ 428631; cnr Villegas & Costanera MA Camino; mains AR$8-12; ⊙ breakfast, lunch & dinner) Cheapest place on the lakeside with outdoor seating and reliable food. Good for afternoon beer and French fries. Very popular.

El Cafecito (San Martín 961; sandwiches AR$15; ⊙ breakfast & lunch) Cute, sunny little café on the main street. Good vegetarian options.

Pura Vida (☎ 429302; Villegas 745; mains AR$10-18; ⊙ lunch & dinner daily, closed lunch Sun) A small (mostly) vegetarian restaurant guaranteed to cure your *parrilla* blues. The menu is wide, featuring pizzas, savory pies, pastas, heaps of salads and a couple of meat dishes.

Tio Paco (☎ 427920; cnr Av San Martín & Capitán Drury; mains AR$10-20; ⊙ lunch & dinner) Great little bar-café with a full menu and a long list of mixed drinks, including coffee drinks (with booze), wine and cocktails. The menu's not all that exciting, but on a sunny day, the upstairs deck overlooking the main drag is the place to be.

Peuma Café (Av San Martín 853; mains AR$12-20; ⊙ lunch & dinner) If you're after that traditional ambience (and a televised soccer game), check out this local favorite – you can be sure that all the old guys in town will be there. The menu pushes all the right buttons, with steaks, pizzas and delicious raspberry waffles (AR$10).

our pick **Trattoria Mi Viejo Pepe** (Villegas 725; mains AR$15-25; ⊙ lunch & dinner) For homemade pastas, this is the place to come. The huge range of sauces and styles is matched by a near-encyclopedic wine list.

El Mesón (Rivadavia 888; mains AR$20-30; ⊙ lunch & dinner) This cute little place has one of the most creative menus in town, with plenty of trout dishes, paella and a couple of vegetarian options.

La Casona (Villegas 744; mains AR$16-40; ⊙ lunch & dinner) The cozy atmosphere belies the wide menu, with some good twists on regional favorites. Try the boar stew in black beer sauce (AR$32) or the lamb and wild mushroom risotto (AR$31).

TOP END

El Tenedor (Villegas 760; all you can eat AR$28; ⊙ lunch & dinner) San Martín's *tenedor libre* holds its own, and throws venison and trout into the mix, along with good-value set meals (AR$22).

Bamboo (Belgrano & Villegas; mains AR$28-40; ☽ lunch & dinner) One reader claims this up-market *parrilla* serves 'the best meat in all of Argentina.' We haven't tried all the meat in Argentina (yet), so you be the judge.

Shopping
Many local shops sell regional products and handicrafts.

Artesanías Neuquinas (☎ 428396; M Rosas 790) Mapuche cooperative with high-quality weavings and wood crafts on offer.

Talabartería Lo de Ivan (☎ 420737; Capitán Drury 814) Specializes in gaucho regalia.

Raihue (☎ 423160; Av San Martín 436) Artisan knives, sweaters, leather, purses and ponchos.

Getting There & Away
AIR
Flights from **Chapelco airport** (☎ 428388; RN 234) to Buenos Aires cost about AR$700 if booked well in advance. **Aerolíneas Argentinas** (☎ 427003/04; Capitán Drury 876) flies daily except Wednesday.

BOAT
Naviera (☎ 427380; naviera@smandes.com.ar) sails from the **passenger pier** (Muelle de Pasajeros; Costanera MA Camino) on Av Costanera as far as Paso Hua Hum on the Chilean border, daily at 10am. A dock is currently being constructed at Hua Hum – when it is completed, passengers will be able to disembark to cross the border there. For now, you have to get off at Chachin, about an hour's walk from Hua Hum. Departure times change annually; call the ferry company or check with the tourist office. The fare is AR$100 plus AR$15 national park fee.

BUS
The **bus terminal** (☎ 427044; Villegas & Juez del Valle) is a block south of the highway and 3½ blocks southwest of Plaza San Martín.

On Monday, Wednesday and Friday at 6am, Igi-Llaima takes RP 60 over Paso Tromen (also known as Mamuil Malal) to Temuco, Chile (AR$50, six hours), passing the majestic Volcán Lanín en route; sit on the left for views.

From San Martín there is direct service in summer via RN 231 over Paso Cardenal A Samoré (Puyehue) to Osorno and Puerto Montt.

If you're heading to Villa Traful or Bariloche in summertime, Transportes Ko-Ko regularly takes the scenic Ruta de los Siete Lagos (RN 234) instead of the longer but smoother Rinconada route. To get to Aluminé you must first change buses in Zapala.

There are frequent daily departures to the destinations listed in the following table.

Destination	Cost (AR$)	Duration (hr)
Bahía Blanca	90	15-16
Bariloche	37	4½
Buenos Aires	155	20-23
Córdoba	180	21
Junín de los Andes	5	1
Mendoza	100	17
Neuquén	50	6
San Rafael	73	14-15
Viedma	110	18
Villa la Angostura	45	4
Villa Traful	20	2½
Zapala	39	4

Getting Around
Chapelco airport (☎ 428388; RN 234) is midway between San Martín and Junín. **Al Sur** (☎ 422 903) runs shuttles between San Martín and the airport; call for hotel pickup.

Transport options slim down during low season. In summer Transportes Airen goes twice daily to Puerto Canoa on Lago Huechulafquen (AR$15) and will stop at campgrounds en route. Albus goes to the beach at Playa Catritre on Lago Lácar (AR$3) several times daily, while Transportes Ko-Ko runs four buses daily to Lago Lolog (AR$4) in summer only.

San Martín has no lack of car-rental agencies.

Avis (☎ 427704; Av San Martín 998)
Hansen (☎ 427997; Av San Martín 532)
Localiza (☎ 428876; Villegas 977)

AROUND SAN MARTÍN DE LOS ANDES
Cerro Chapelco
Located only 20km southeast of San Martín, **Cerro Chapelco** (☎ 02972-427845; www.cerrochapelco .com) is one of Argentina's principal wintersports centers, with a mix of runs for beginners and experts, and a maximum elevation of 1920m. The **Fiesta Nacional del Montañés**, the annual ski festival, is held the first half of August.

Lift-ticket prices vary, depending on when you go; full-day passes run from AR$73 to

RIDING THE ROAD THROUGH THE SEVEN LAKES

While there's no shortage of tour operators willing to take you on a quick day trip on the Ruta de los Siete Lagos from San Martín de los Andes to Villa la Angostura, the best way to do it is with your own wheels (see Map p416). It's a 110km trip, so it can be done in a day by car, but this isn't scenery to race through – there are a couple of lovely *hosterías*, some organized and 'bush' campsites along the way. If you've got the legs for it, a mountain-bike trip isn't out of the question. Depending on your pedal power, you could do the trip in three long days minimum, but factor in a lot more if you tend to get sidetracked by breathtaking scenery. If you're riding, take water and snacks, and if you're planning on camping, be aware that it can get very cold at night, even in summer. October and November are the best time to do the ride, for lack of traffic and dust. March and April are also good. If you're planning on staying at the *hosterías*, book well ahead.

Starting at San Martín de los Andes, head out of town on the RN 234, skirting the banks of Lago Lácar and passing the Mapuche town of **Curruhuinca**. After 20km you'll come to the lookout at **Arroyo Partido**. From here it's a 5km downhill coast to a bridge over the Río Hermoso. Two short climbs and 5km later, you'll reach the dark blue **Lago Machónico**.

A further 5km brings you to a turnoff to the right, where it's 2km of dirt road to **Lago Hermoso**, surrounded by mixed ñire and radale forests and the southernmost strand of pehuén trees in the Parque Nacional Lanín. Colored deer are common in this area, as are hunters, so be on the lookout (for both) when walking in the woods. The charming **Refugio Lago Hermoso** (☎ 02944-15-569176; www.refugiolagohermoso.com; dm/r AR$160/360; ☽ Nov-Apr) is here, offering every comfort imaginable, including some very welcome hot showers, a good restaurant, canoes and horseback-riding trips. There are also organized and free campsites.

Entering the Parque Nacional Nahuel Huapi, it's 15km to the **Cascada Vullignanco**, a 20m waterfall made by the Río Filuco. Two kilometers on, the road runs between **Lago Villarino** and **Lago Falkner**, which has a wide sandy beach and free campsites. **Hostería Lago Villarino** (☎ 02972-427483; www.hosteriavillarino.com.ar; r AR$250; ☽ Nov-Mar), on the banks of Lago Falkner is a gorgeous place, with cozy rooms and cabins with fireplaces. Two kilometers further on is **Lago Escondido**, from where it's 8km of downhill zigzag to a turnoff to the left. Follow this side (dirt) road for 2km to get to the north end of **Lago Traful**. This is a popular camping and fishing spot, but there are no services here.

Heading back to the turnoff, say goodbye asphalt, hello dirt road. After 30km of fairly constant uphill, you'll see a turnoff for **Villa Traful** (see p403). It's 27km down a good dirt road, passing scenic bush campgrounds on the lakeshore.

Sticking to the main road, though, after 20km you'll come to a bridge and a disused *hostería*. Just before that, turn right and take the uphill road that ends at **Lago Espejo Chico** after 2km. The grassy banks of this emerald green lake make it an excellent campsite, but there are no facilities.

Continuing south, you'll catch glimpses of **Lago Espejo Grande** on the right through the trees. There are several lookouts along the road.

Five kilometers on, you'll see **Lago Correntoso**. There are cabins and *hosterías* here, but if you feel like pushing on, it's another 15km to a crossroads where you turn left, and 10km on asphalt to **Villa la Angostura** (p404).

AR$133 for adults, AR$57 to AR$107 for children. The slopes are open from mid-June to early October. The low season is mid-June to early July and from August 28 to mid-October; high season is around the last two weeks of July.

The resort has a downtown information center (p397) that also sells lift tickets. Rental equipment is available on site as well as in town (p397).

Transportes Ko-Ko runs two buses each day (three in summer; AR$15 return) to the park from San Martín's bus terminal. Travel agencies in San Martín also offer packages with shuttle service, or shuttle service alone (AR$20 to AR$30); they pick you up at your hotel.

PARQUE NACIONAL LANÍN

Dominating the view in all directions along the Chilean border, the snowcapped cone of

3776m Volcán Lanín is the centerpiece of Parque Nacional Lanín, which extends 150km from Parque Nacional Nahuel Huapi in the south to Lago Ñorquinco in the north.

Protecting 3790 sq km of native Patagonian forest, the Lanín park is home to many of the same species that characterize more southerly Patagonian forests, such as the southern beeches – lenga, ñire and coihue. More botanically unique to the area, however, are the extensive stands of the broadleaf, deciduous southern beech, raulí, and the curious pehuén, or monkey puzzle tree *(Araucaria araucana)*, a pine-like conifer whose nuts have long been a dietary staple for the Pehuenches and Mapuches. Note that only indigenous people may gather *piñones* (pine nuts) from the pehuenes.

The towns of San Martín de los Andes, Junín de los Andes and Aluminé are the best starting points for exploring Lanín, its glacial lakes and the backcountry.

Information

The Lanín national park office (p397) in San Martín produces brochures on camping, hiking and climbing in various parts of the park. Scattered throughout the park proper are several ranger stations, but they usually lack printed materials. The national park's website (www.parquenacionallanin.gov.ar in Spanish) is full of useful information.

Lago Lácar & Lago Lolog

From San Martín, at the east end of Lago Lácar, there is bus service on RP 48, which runs along the lake to the Chilean border at Paso Hua Hum. You can get off the bus anywhere along the lake or get off at Hua Hum and hike to Cascada Chachín; bus drivers know the stop. From the highway, it's 3km down a dirt road and then another 20 minutes' walk along a trail to the waterfall. It's a great spot for a picnic.

Fifteen kilometers north of San Martín de los Andes, Lago Lolog offers good fishing in a largely undeveloped area. You'll find pleasant camping at **Camping Puerto Arturo** (free). Transportes Ko-Ko runs four buses daily, in summer only, to Lago Lolog from San Martín; the bus costs AR$4.

Lago Huechulafquen

The park's largest lake is also one of its most central and accessible areas. Despite limited public transport, it can be reached from San

PARQUE NACIONAL LANÍN

Martín and – more easily – Junín de los Andes. RP 61 climbs from a junction just north of Junín, west to Huechulafquen and the smaller Lago Paimún, offering outstanding views of Volcán Lanín and access to trailheads of several excellent hikes.

From the ranger station at **Puerto Canoa**, a good trail climbs to a viewpoint on Lanín's shoulder, where it's possible to hike across to Paso Tromen or continue climbing to either of two *refugios*: the **RIM refugio** belongs to the army's Regimiento de Infantería de Montaña, while the **CAJA refugio** belongs to the Club Andino Junín de los Andes (p393). Both are fairly rustic but well kept and can be bases for attempts on the summit (for more detail, including information about permits,

THE MAPUCHE

The Lake District's most prevalent indigenous group, the Mapuche, originally came from Chilean territory. They resisted several attempts at subjugation by the Inca and fought against Spanish domination for nearly 300 years. Their move into Argentina began slowly. Chilean Mapuche were making frequent voyages across the Andes in search of trade as far back as the 17th century. Some chose to stay. In the 1880s the exodus became more pronounced as the Chilean government moved into Mapuche land, forcing them out.

Another theory for the widespread move is that for the Mapuche, the *puelmapu* (eastern land) holds a special meaning, as it is believed that all good things (such as the sun) come from the east.

Apart from trade, the Mapuche (whose name means 'people of the land' in Mapudungun, their language) have traditionally survived as small-scale farmers and hunter/collectors. There is no central government – each extended family has a *lonko* (chief), and in times of war families would unite to elect a *toqui* (axe-bearer) to lead them.

The role of *Machi* (Shaman) was and still is an important one in Mapuche society. It was usually filled by a woman, whose responsibilities included performing ceremonies for curing diseases, warding off evil, influencing weather, harvests, social interactions and dreamwork. The *Machi* was also well-schooled in the use of medicinal herbs, but as Mapuche access to land and general biodiversity in the region has decreased, this knowledge is being lost.

Estimates of how many Mapuche live in Argentina vary according to the source. The official census puts the number at around 300,000, while the Mapuche claim that the real figure is closer to 500,000.

Both in Chile and Argentina, the Mapuche live in humble circumstances in rural settings, or leave the land to find work in big cities. It is estimated that there are still 200,000 fluent Mapudungun speakers in Chile, where nominal efforts are made to revive the language in the education system. No such official program has been instituted in Argentina, and while exact numbers are not known, it is feared that the language here may soon become extinct.

Apart from loss of language, the greatest threat to Mapuche culture is the loss of land, a process that has been underway ever since their lands were 'redistributed' after the Conquest of the Desert and many Mapuche relocated to reserves – often the lowest-quality land, without any spiritual significance to them. As with many indigenous peoples, the Mapuche have a special spiritual relationship with the land, believing that certain rocks, mountains, lakes and so on have a particular spiritual meaning.

Despite a relatively well-organized land rights campaign, the process continues today, as Mapuche lands are routinely re-assigned to large commercial interests in the oil, cattle and forestry industries. Defiant to the end, the Mapuche aren't looking like fading away any time soon. They see their cultural survival as intrinsically linked to economic independence, and Mapuche-owned and -operated businesses are scattered throughout the Lakes District.

equipment and the *refugios*, see opposite). The initial segment follows an abandoned road, but after about 40 minutes it becomes a pleasant woodsy trail along the **Arroyo Rucu Leufu**, an attractive mountain stream. Halfway to the *refugio* is an extensive **pehuén forest**, the southernmost in the park, which makes the walk worthwhile if you lack time for the entire route. The route to RIM's *refugio*, about 2450m above sea level, takes about seven hours one-way, while the trail to CAJA's *refugio* takes a bit longer.

Another good backcountry hike circles **Lago Paimún**. This requires about two days from Puerto Canoa; you return to the north side of the lake by crossing a cable platform strung across the narrows between Huechulafquen and Paimún. A shorter alternative hike goes from the very attractive campground at **Piedra Mala** to **Cascada El Saltillo**, a nearby forest waterfall. If your car lacks 4WD, leave it at the logjam 'bridge' that crosses the creek and walk to Piedra Mala – the road, passable by any ordinary vehicle to this point, quickly worsens after a harsh winter. Horses are available for rent at Piedra Mala. Transportes KoKo runs buses to Piedra Mala daily in summer from the San Martín bus terminal (p399).

Campsites are abundant along the highway; travelers camping in the free sites in the narrow area between the lakes and the highway must dig a latrine and remove their own trash. If you camp at the organized sites (which, though not luxurious, are maintained), you'll support Mapuche concessionaires who at least derive some income from lands that were theirs before the state usurped them a century ago. Good sites include **Camping Raquithue** (per person AR$12), **Camping Piedra Mala** (per person AR$9-15) and **Bahía Cañicul** (with/without electricity AR$15/12).

Noncampers should treat themselves to a stay at **Hostería Refugio Pescador** (Puerto Canoa ☎ 02972-490210, Junín de los Andes 02972-491132; r per person with full board AR$200) or the three-star **Hostería Paimún** (☎ 02972-491211; adelvalle@jandes .com.ar; r per person with full board AR$250); both cater to fishing parties.

Lago Tromen

This northern approach to **Volcán Lanín**, which straddles the Argentine–Chilean border, is also the shortest and usually the earliest in the season to open for hikers and climbers. Before climbing Lanín, ask permission at the Lanín national park office in San Martín (p397) or, if necessary, of the *gendarmería* (border guards) in Junín. It's obligatory to show equipment, including plastic tools, crampons, ice axe and clothing – including sunglasses, sunblock, gloves, hats and padded jackets.

From the trailhead at the Argentine border station, it's five to seven hours to the **CAJA refugio** (capacity 14 people), at 2600m on the Camino de Mulas route; above that point, snow equipment is necessary. There's a shorter but steeper route along the ridge known as the Espina del Pescado, where it's possible to stay at the **RIM refugio** (capacity 20 people), at 2450m. Trekkers can cross the Sierra Mamuil Malal to Lago Huechulafquen via Arroyo Rucu Leufu (see p401).

Contact Andestrack (p397) in San Martín to organize guides for climbing Lanín. The hike usually takes two days: you leave early the first and stay at the RIM *refugio*, rise before dawn the following day, hike to the summit and walk down. If you want to go up in winter, Andestrack can set you up with guides to hike up and board or ski down.

Lago Quillén

Situated in the park's densest pehuén forests, this isolated lake is accessible by dirt road from Rahué, 17km south of Aluminé, and has many good **campsites**. Other nearby lakes include **Lago Rucachoroi**, directly west of Aluminé, and **Lago Ñorquinco** on the park's northern border. There are Mapuche reservations at Rucachoroi and Quillén.

Getting There & Away

Although the park is close to San Martín and Junín, public transport is minimal; see p399 and p395 for details. With some patience, hitchhiking is feasible in high season. Buses over the Hua Hum and Tromen passes, from San Martín and Junín to Chile, will carry passengers to intermediate destinations but are often full.

VILLA TRAFUL

☎ 02944 / pop 500 / elev 720m

This little village enjoys an almost achingly beautiful location surrounded by mountains on the southern banks of Lago Traful. The place really packs out in January, February and Easter, when booking accommodation three months in advance is advised. The rest of the year, you may just have it to yourself. Depending on what you're into, November, December, March and April are great times to be here.

Getting here is half the fun – Villa Traful is 80km north of Bariloche via unpaved RP 65. Continuing east of Traful along the Río Traful to RN 237, you roll through spectacular countryside with wild, towering rock formations very distinct from the areas to the south.

The **tourist office** (☎ 479099; ☿ daily summer, Sat-Wed winter) is on the eastern side of the village.

Banco de la Provincia de Neuquén in the middle of the village has an ATM that accepts Visa and MasterCard.

Sights & Activities

Guides can easily be hired through the tourist office for horseback riding and hiking in the surrounding mountains. Everything books quickly during fishing season (November to April) and in January and February.

Eco Traful (☎ 479048; www.ecotraful.com.ar) is a recommended agency that leads trips to Lagunas Las Mellizas (AR$100/140 per person walking/horseback) and Cerro Negro (AR$40 per person), and organizes boat rides and fishing trips.

CASCADAS DE ARROYO BLANCO & COA CÓ

These two waterfalls are a moderately easy, two-hour round-trip walk from town that can be done without a guide. Walk uphill on the street running beside the *guardaparque* (park ranger) office and then follow the signs. From where the path forks at the open field it's 500m on the left to the 30m-high Coa Có. Return and take the other fork for 1km to the smaller Cascadas de los Arroyos Blancos. Far more spectacular than the actual waterfalls are the lookouts along the way, which give you a bird's-eye view of the forest, lake and mountains beyond.

LAGUNAS LAS MELLIZAS

Starting with a boat ride across the lake, this trek of moderate difficulty begins with a 2½-hour climb through cypress forests before reaching a lookout with views of the Lagunas Azul and Verde (Blue and Green Lagoons). If you've still got the legs for it, fording a stream gets you to an area with a variety of well-preserved Tehuelche rock paintings, dated at around 600 years old.

Eating & Sleeping

There are only a few places to stay unless you rent a *cabaña* (the tourist office has a complete listing).

Albergue & Camping Vulcanche (☎ 479028; www .vulcanche.com; camping per person AR$15, dm AR$30, d with shared bathroom AR$100, cabañas AR$120-140) In a beautiful wooded area on the eastern edge of the village, this grassy campground/hostel has decent dorms, a good kitchen and a huge living area overlooking the lake and mountains. The cabins, which come with kitchenette and private bathroom, are a particularly good deal.

Hostería Villa Traful (☎ 479005; s/d AR$100/160, 4-6 person cabañas AR$300-380) A pleasant little mom-and-pop-run operation on the western edge of town. Rooms are aging but comfortable, there's a good restaurant on the premises and the owners organize boating and fishing trips.

Walnor (breakfast AR$6, mains AR$18-25; ☼ breakfast, lunch & dinner) A cute little restaurant/café/bar overlooking the lake in the center of the village. It serves up tasty sandwiches, fresh trout and spicy empanadas, and an afternoon beer on the deck overlooking the lake is a fine way to end the day.

There are a couple of restaurants tucked into the trees and a general store to buy groceries.

Getting There & Away

Albus has daily services to Villa la Angostura (AR$18, 2 hours) and Bariloche (AR$18, 2 hours) and summertime services to San Martín de los Andes (AR$20, 2½ hours).

VILLA LA ANGOSTURA

☎ 02944 / pop 8,000 / elev 850m

An upmarket resort town on the northwestern shore of Lago Nahuel Huapi, Villa la Angostura provides accommodations and services for nearby Cerro Bayo, a small but popular winter-sports center.

It's worthwhile stopping by in summer, too, for lake cruises, walks in the small but incredibly diverse Parque Nacional Los Arrayanes – a small peninsula dangling some 12km into the lake, and because this is the southern starting point for the breathtaking trip along the Ruta de los Siete Lagos (Seven Lakes Route; see the boxed text, p400).

The village consists of two distinct areas: El Cruce, which is the commercial center along the highway, and La Villa, nestled against the lakeshore, 3km to the south. Though La Villa is more residential, it still has hotels, shops, services and, unlike El Cruce, lake access.

Orientation

Villa la Angostura is near the junction of RN 231 from Bariloche and RN 234 to San Martín de los Andes (100km). The junction gives the commercial strip of town the name of **El Cruce** (The Crossroads). Through town, RN 231 is known as Av Arrayanes and Av Siete Lagos. **La Villa** is a 3km walk toward the lake on Blvd Nahuel Huapi.

La Villa and its surrounds are easily seen on foot, but if you're venturing further out, taxis are the best means of getting to the trailheads, although some are served by local buses. Both leave from the local terminal on Av Siete Lagos, just north of Av Arrayanes.

Information

Banco de la Provincia (Calle Las Frambuesas btwn Cerro Belvedere & Nahuel Huapi, El Cruce) Has an ATM.

HoraCero (☎ 495055; Av Arrayanes 45, El Cruce; internet per hr AR$3) Pizzeria with internet in back.

Park administration office (☎ 494152; Nahuel Huapi, La Villa)

Post office (Las Fucsias 40, lvl 3, El Cruce)

Tourist office (☎ 494124; www.villalaangostura.gov.ar in Spanish; Av Siete Lagos 93, El Cruce; ☼ 8:30am-9pm)

Sights & Activities

Trekking, horseback riding and guided mountain-bike rides are all offered by several outfitters in town, and the tourist office provides information on all. Mountain biking is a great way to explore the surrounding area; for rentals, try **Free Bikes** (☎ 495047; per hr/day AR$7/30; La Villa Blvd Nahuel Huapi 2150; El Cruce Topa Topa 102). For horseback riding (half-day to multiday trips), contact Tero Bogani at **Cabalgatas Correntoso** (☎ 02944-15-510559; www.cabalgatacor rentoso.com.ar), who brings the gaucho side of things to his trips. Prices start at AR$40 for a one-hour outing. For sailboat rides around the lake (which can be rippin' on a windy day), contact Captain **Jorge Rovella** (☎ 02944-15-512460; velaaventura@yahoo.com.ar); a three-hour trip costs about AR$280 for up to four people.

La Angostura's **Museo Histórico Regional** (Nahuel Huapi & El Calafate; admission free; ☼ 9:30am-5pm Tue-Sat, guided visits at 11am, 1 & 3pm), on the road to La Villa, is worth popping into for a spot of Mapuche history, historical town photographs and old climbing relics.

PARQUE NACIONAL LOS ARRAYANES
This inconspicuous, often overlooked **park** (admission AR$20), encompassing the entire Quetrihué peninsula, protects remaining stands of the cinnamon-barked arrayán, a member of the myrtle family. In Mapudungun, language of the Mapuche, the peninsula's name means 'place of the arrayanes.'

The park headquarters is at the southern end of the peninsula, near the largest concentration of arrayanes, in an area known as **El Bosque**. It's a three-hour, 12km hike from La Villa to the tip of the peninsula, on an excellent **interpretive nature trail**; brochures are available in the tourist office at El Cruce. You can also hike out and get the ferry back from the point (p406), or vice versa. There are two small lakes along the trail. Regulations require hikers to enter the park before midday and leave it by 4pm in winter and around 6pm to 7pm in summer.

From the park's northern entrance at La Villa, a very steep 20-minute hike leads to two **panoramic overlooks** of Lago Nahuel Huapi.

CERRO BELVEDERE
A 4km **hiking trail** starts from Av Siete Lagos, northwest of the tourist office, and leads to an **overlook** with good views of Lago Correntoso, Nahuel Huapi and the surrounding mountains. It then continues another 3km to the 1992m summit. After visiting the overlook, retrace your steps to a nearby junction that leads to **Cascada Inayacal**, a 50m waterfall.

CENTRO DE SKI CERRO BAYO
From June to September, lifts carry skiers from the 1050m base up to 1700m at this relatively inexpensive **winter resort** (☎ 494189; www.cerrobayoweb.com in Spanish; full-day pass AR$72-140), 9km northeast of El Cruce via RP 66. All facilities, including rental equipment (AR$30 to AR$60), are available on site.

Sleeping
Except for camping and Angostura's growing hostel scene, accommodations tend to be pricey; in summer, single rooms are almost impossible to find – expect to pay for two people.

Camping Cullumche (☎ 494160; Blvd Quetrihué s/n; sites per person AR$10-15) Well signed from Blvd Nahuel Huapi, this secluded but large lakeside campground can get very busy in summer, but when it's quiet, it's lovely.

Italian Hostel (☎ 494376; www.italianhostel.com.ar; Los Marquis 215, El Cruce; dm AR$30) With plenty of space and all the comforts you'd expect, this is the town's standout hostel. The kitchen is well equipped, you can use the *parrilla* and the lounge is comfy in a rustic kinda way. The only drawback – the 18-bed dorm.

Hostel La Angostura (☎ 494834; www.hostella angostura.com.ar in Spanish; Barbagelata 157, El Cruce; dm AR$30, d AR$100) Forget the short uphill slog to get here – it's worth it. Staying in this place feels like being out in the woods and there are great views from the balconies, a bar, ping pong table, bike rental – the list goes on. Dorms are cramped but reasonable and have private bathrooms.

Residencial Río Bonito (☎ 494110; riobonito@ciudad .com.ar; Topa Topa 260, El Cruce; s/d AR$90/120) Bright and cheery rooms in a converted family home a few blocks from the bus terminal. The big, comfortable dining/lounge area is a bonus, as are the friendly hosts.

Verena's Haus (☎ 494467; verenashaus@infovia.com .ar; Los Taiques 268, El Cruce; s/d AR$140/180) With all the heart-shaped motifs and floral wallpaper, this one probably doesn't qualify as a hunting lodge, but it is a good deal for couples looking for a quiet, romantic spot. Rooms are big, spotless and packed with comfy features.

Hotel Angostura (☎ 494224; www.hotelangostura .com; Blvd Nahuel Huapi 1911, La Villa; s/d AR$190/220, bungalows AR$320-510) Ignore the squishy rooms and the deer antler light fittings – it's an awesome location. It's perched up on a clifftop overlooking the bay and the national park;

your biggest problem here is going to be neck crick from checking out the view – no matter which way you're walking.

Eating

There are several restaurants and *confiterías* in El Cruce along Los Arrayanes and its cross-streets.

Gran Nevada (Av Arrayanes 104, El Cruce; mains AR$12-24; ☺ lunch & dinner) With its big-screen TV (quite possibly showing a football game) and big, cheap set meals, this is a local favorite. Come hungry, leave happy.

La Oveja Negra (Av Arrayanes s/n, El Cruce; mains AR$15-25; ☺ lunch & dinner) This little place, tucked away in an arcade just near the main roundabout, offers good homestyle cooking with a couple of Middle Eastern inspired dishes thrown in. The set meals (AR$28) can be a good deal if you choose wisely.

Los Troncos (Av Arrayanes 67, El Cruce; mains AR$20-30; ☺ breakfast, lunch & dinner) Specializing in 'mountain food,' this lovely little place serves up a range of tempting dishes like deer stew, trout with almond sauce and wild mushroom stew.

La Encantada (☎ 495515; Cerro Belvedere 69, El Cruce; mains AR$20-30; ☺ lunch & dinner) A cute little cottage offering all the Patagonian and Argentine favorites. The food is carefully prepared and beautifully presented and the atmosphere is warm and inviting. The *ojo de bife* (eye fillet steak; AR$37) for two is a definite winner if you're a couple of carnivores.

Tinto Bistro (☎ 494924; Nahuel Huapi 34, El Cruce; mains AR$30-45; ☺ lunch & dinner) Besides the fact that the food (regional cuisine prepared with European flair) is excellent, the owner, Martín Zorreguieta, is the brother of Máxima, princess of the Netherlands. Feast on that.

Getting There & Away

Villa la Angostura's **bus terminal** (junction of Av Siete Lagos & Av Arrayanes, El Cruce) is across the street from the tourist office in El Cruce. Some buses stop in El Cruce on runs between Bariloche and San Martín de los Andes.

For Chile, **Andesmar** (☎ 495217) and Via Bariloche go over Paso Cardenal Samoré to Osorno (AR$55, four hours) and on to Puerto Montt (AR$55, five hours).

There are numerous daily departures to Bariloche (AR$14, two hours) and two daily departures to Neuquén (AR$76, seven to nine hours). Albus and Turismo Algorrobo go several times daily in summer to San Martín de los Andes (AR$45, 4½ hours) by the scenic Ruta de los Siete Lagos.

Getting Around

Transportes 15 de Mayo runs hourly buses from the terminal to La Villa (AR$1, 15 minutes), up Av Siete Lagos to Lago Correntoso (AR$1, 15 minutes), and south down Av Arrayanes to Puerto Manzano on Lago Nahuel Huapi (AR$1, 15 minutes). From July through September, and December through March, 15 de Mayo runs six or seven daily buses to the ski resort at Cerro Bayo (AR$8, one hour).

Two companies run daily ferries from the dock (next to Hotel Angostura in La Villa) to the tip of Quetrihué peninsula, Parque Nacional Los Arrayanes (AR$78 return, AR$43 one-way, plus AR$20 national park entrance), meaning you can hike the peninsula and take the boat back (or vice versa). Purchase tickets at the dock before hiking out, to secure a space on the return. Check with the tourist office for ever-changing ferry times. The ride takes 45 minutes.

BARILOCHE

☎ 02944 / pop 98,200 / elev 770m

Strung out along the shoreline of Lago Nahuel Huapi, in the middle of the national park of the same name, Bariloche (formally San Carlos de Bariloche) has one of the most gorgeous settings imaginable. This, combined with a wealth of summer and wintertime activities in the surrounding countryside, has helped it become, for better or worse, the Lake District's principal destination.

The soaring peaks of Cerros Catedral, López, Nireco and Shaihuenque (to name just a few) – all well over 2000m high – ring the town, giving picture-postcard views in nearly every direction.

These mountains aren't just for gazing, though – excellent snow coverage (sometimes exceeding 2m at the *end* of the season) makes this a winter wonderland, and a magnet for skiers and snowboarders from all over the world.

In summertime the nature buffs take over, hitting the hills to climb, hike trails, fish for trout and ride mountain bikes and horses.

There's so much fun to be had that this has become the destination for Argentine high school students' end of year celebrations.

THE LAKE DISTRICT

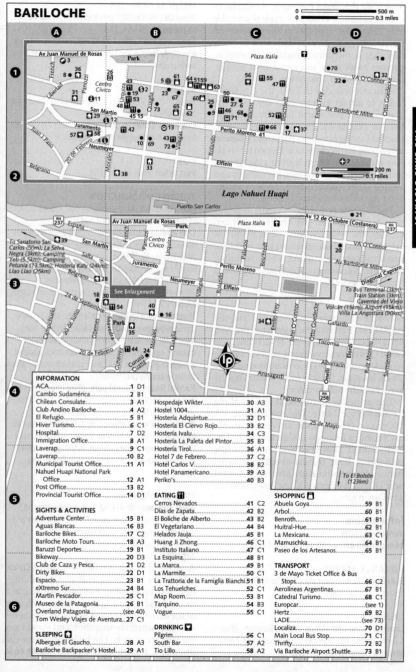

BARILOCHE

INFORMATION	
ACA	1 D1
Cambio Sudamérica	2 B1
Chilean Consulate	3 A1
Club Andino Bariloche	4 A2
El Refugio	5 B1
Hiver Turismo	6 C1
Hospital	7 D2
Immigration Office	8 A1
Laverap	9 C1
Laverap	10 B2
Municipal Tourist Office	11 A1
Nahuel Huapi National Park Office	12 A1
Post Office	13 B2
Provincial Tourist Office	14 D1

SIGHTS & ACTIVITIES	
Adventure Center	15 B1
Aguas Blancas	16 B3
Bariloche Bikes	17 C2
Bariloche Moto Tours	18 A3
Baruzzi Deportes	19 B1
Bikeway	20 D3
Club de Caza y Pesca	21 D2
Dirty Bikes	22 D1
Espacio	23 B1
eXtremo Sur	24 B4
Martín Pescador	25 C1
Museo de la Patagonia	26 B1
Overland Patagonia	(see 40)
Tom Wesley Viajes de Aventura	27 C1

SLEEPING	
Albergue El Gaucho	28 A3
Bariloche Backpacker's Hostel	29 A1
Hospedaje Wikter	30 A3
Hostel 1004	31 A1
Hostería Adquinte	32 D1
Hostería El Ciervo Rojo	33 B2
Hostería Ivalu	34 C3
Hostería La Paleta del Pintor	35 B3
Hostería Tirol	36 A1
Hotel 7 de Febrero	37 C2
Hotel Carlos V	38 B2
Hotel Panamericano	39 A3
Periko's	40 B3

EATING	
Cerros Nevados	41 C2
Días de Zapata	42 B2
El Boliche de Alberto	43 B2
El Vegetariano	44 B4
Helados Jauja	45 B1
Huang Ji Zhong	46 C1
Instituto Italiano	47 C1
La Esquina	48 B1
La Marca	49 B1
La Marmite	50 C1
La Trattoria de la Famiglia Bianchi	51 B1
Los Tehuelches	52 C1
Map Room	53 B1
Tarquino	54 B3
Vogue	55 C1

DRINKING	
Pilgrim	56 C1
South Bar	57 A2
Tío Lillo	58 A2

SHOPPING	
Abuela Goya	59 B1
Arbol	60 B1
Benroth	61 B1
Huitral-Hue	62 B1
La Mexicana	63 C1
Mamuschka	64 B1
Paseo de los Artesanos	65 B1

TRANSPORT	
3 de Mayo Ticket Office & Bus Stops	66 C2
Aerolíneas Argentinas	67 C1
Catedral Turismo	68 C1
Europcar	(see 1)
Hertz	69 B2
LADE	(see 73)
Localiza	70 D1
Main Local Bus Stop	71 C1
Thrifty	72 B2
Via Bariloche Airport Shuttle	73 B1

And if all this wasn't enough, Bariloche is also Argentina's chocolate capital and the only thing that approaches the amount of storefront window space dedicated to fresh chocolate is the infinite number of peculiar gnomes of all sizes and demeanors sold in nearly every shop downtown.

Officially founded in 1902, the city really began to attract visitors after the southern branch of the Ferrocarril Roca train line arrived in 1934 and architect Ezequiel Bustillo adapted Central European styles into a tasteful urban plan. Bariloche is now known for its alpine architecture, which is given a Patagonian twist through the use of local hardwoods and unique stone construction, as seen in the buildings of Bustillo's civic center.

The flip side of Bariloche's gain in popularity is uncontrolled growth: in the last two decades, the town has suffered as its quaint neighborhoods have given way to high-rise apartments and time-shares. The silver lining is that many accommodations have remained reasonably priced.

Orientation

Bariloche is 460km southwest of Neuquén via RN 237. Entering the town from the east, RN 237 becomes the Av 12 de Octubre (also called Costanera), continuing westward to the lakeside resort of Llao Llao. Southbound Calle Onelli becomes RN 258 to El Bolsón, on the border of Chubut province.

The principal commercial area is along Av Bartolomé Mitre. Do not confuse VA O'Connor (also known as Vicealmirante O'Connor or Eduardo O'Connor) with similarly named John O'Connor, which cross each other near the lakefront. Similarly, Perito Moreno and Ruiz Moreno intersect near Diagonal Capraro, at the east end of the downtown area.

Information

IMMIGRATION
Immigration office (☎ 423043; Libertad 191)

INTERNET ACCESS
El Refugio (Av Bartolomé Mitre 106, 1st fl; per hr AR$2) Upstairs; fast connection.

LAUNDRY
Laverap Rolando (☎ 432628; btwn Av Bartolomé Mitre & Perito Moreno; full service AR$10); Quaglia (btwn Perito Moreno & Elflein; full service AR$10-12)

MEDICAL SERVICES
Hospital (☎ 426100; Perito Moreno 601) *Long* waits, no charge.
Sanatorio San Carlos (☎ 429000/01/02, emergency 430000; Av Bustillo, Km 1; consultations AR$40) Excellent medical clinic.

MONEY
Banks with ATMs are ubiquitous in the downtown area.
Cambio Sudamérica (Av Bartolomé Mitre 63) Change foreign cash and traveler's checks here.

POST
Post office (Perito Moreno 175)

TOURIST INFORMATION
ACA (☎ 423001; Av 12 de Octubre 785) Argentina's auto club; good source for provincial road maps.
Club Andino Bariloche (☎ 527966; www.activepatagonia.com.ar, www.clubandino.com.ar in Spanish; 20 de Febrero 30; ⏰ 9am-1pm & 4-8:30pm Dec-Mar, Mon-Fri only Apr-Nov) Best source of hiking information on Nahuel Huapi. Takes reservations and gives information on hikers' refuges in the park. For park details, see p415.
Municipal tourist office (☎ 423022, 423122; www.barilochepatagonia.info; Centro Cívico; ⏰ 8am-9pm) It has many giveaways, including useful maps and the blatantly commercial but still useful *Guía Busch*, updated biannually and loaded with basic tourist information about Bariloche and the Lake District.
Nahuel Huapi national park office (Intendencia del Parque Nacional Nahuel Huapi; ☎ 423111; San Martín 24; ⏰ 8am-4pm Mon-Fri, 9am-3pm Sat & Sun)
Provincial tourist office (☎ 423188/89; secturrn@bariloche.com.ar; cnr Av 12 de Octubre & Emilio Frey) Has information on the province, including an excellent provincial map and useful brochures in English and Spanish.

TRAVEL AGENCIES
Hiver Turismo (☎ 423792; Av Bartolomé Mitre 387) One of numerous agencies along Av Bartolomé Mitre and immediate cross-streets. Amex representative.

Sights

A stroll through Bariloche's **Centro Cívico**, with its beautiful log-and-stone buildings designed by architect Ezequiel Bustillo, is a must. Besides, posing for a photo with one of the barrel-toting Saint Bernards makes for a classic Argentine snapshot, and views over the lake are superb. The buildings house the municipal tourist office and the **Museo de la**

Patagonia (☎ 422309; Centro Cívico; admission AR$3; ☉ 10am-12:30pm & 2-5pm Tue-Fri, 10am-6pm Sat). The last is filled with archaeological and ethnographic materials, lifelike stuffed animals and enlightening historical evaluations on such topics as Mapuche resistance to the Conquest of the Desert.

Cavernas del Viejo Volcán (☎ 529909; Villegas 246, 1st fl in Bariloche; with/without transport AR$46/35; ☉ tours 11:30am, 1:30 & 3pm) is a cave complex, 15km from Bariloche, which was inhabited for nearly 8000 years by the Mapuche and other tribes. Parts of the cave feature reasonably well-preserved rock art specimens. A guided tour is compulsory, and takes you 130m into Cerro Leones then out onto the summit where there is a lookout with majestic views of the surrounding countryside. It is possible (but not a whole lot cheaper) to make your own way there on public transport. Either way, reservations are essential – contact the Bariloche office for more information.

Activities

Bariloche and the Nahuel Huapi region are one of Argentina's major outdoor recreation areas, and numerous operators offer a variety of activities, particularly horseback riding, mountain biking and white-water rafting. The following have excellent reputations:

Overland Patagonia (☎ 461564; www.overland patagonia.com; Morales 555) Numerous trips throughout Patagonia. Also ski transfers for AR$16 from any hotel in town. Owner of Periko's (p411).

Tom Wesley Viajes de Aventura (☎ /fax 435040; Av Bartolomé Mitre 385) Riding, mountain biking; long in the business. Also at Av Bustillo, Km 15.5.

MOUNTAINEERING & TREKKING

The national park office distributes a brochure with a simple map, adequate for initial planning, that rates hikes as easy, medium or difficult and suggests possible loops. Many of these hikes are detailed in Lonely Planet's *Trekking in the Patagonian Andes*, by Clem Lindenmayer.

The Club Andino Bariloche (opposite) provides loads of information, and issues obligatory permits for trekking in Parque Nacional Nahuel Huapi. For AR$15, its *Mapa General de la Guía de Sendas y Picadas* is cartographically mediocre, but has good trail descriptions and is indispensable for planning. It sells three additional trekking maps, all of which include mountain-bike trails.

SKIING

Nahuel Huapi's ski resort, **Cerro Catedral** (☎ 409000; www.catedralaltapatagonia.com), was once South America's trendiest, and has been superseded only by Las Leñas (near Mendoza) and resorts in Chile. Las Leñas has far superior snow (dry powder), but it lacks Catedral's strong point: views. There's nothing like looking over the shimmering lakes of Nahuel Huapi from its snowy slopes.

If you need lessons, stop into the ski schools at Cerro Catedral or the Club Andino Bariloche (opposite). Three-hour classes run at about AR$240. For rental equipment, try Baruzzi Deportes or Martín Pescador (below). Equipment is also available on site. Standard skis, boots and poles sets rent for between AR$40 and AR$52, depending on the season.

MOUNTAIN BIKING

Bicycles are ideal for the Circuito Chico (though this 60km loop demands endurance; see p415) and other trips near Bariloche; most roads are paved and even the gravel roads are good. Mountain-bike rental, including gloves and helmet, costs AR$30 to AR$50 per day at a number of places. Try **Bariloche Bikes** (☎ 424657; Perito Moreno 520; ☉ Mon-Sat), **Bikeway** (☎ 424202; www.bikeway.com.ar; VA O'Connor 867) or **Dirty Bikes** (☎ 425616; www.dirtybikes.com .ar; VA O'Connor 681). Guided tours with bilingual guides run at about AR$150 per day.

FISHING

Fly-fishing draws visitors from around the world to Argentina's accessible Andean-Patagonian parks, from Lago Puelo and Los Alerces in the south to Lanín in the north.

On larger lakes, such as Nahuel Huapi, trolling is the preferred method, while fly-fishing is the rule on most rivers. The season runs mid-November to mid-April. For more information, contact the **Club de Caza y Pesca** (Hunting & Fishing Club; ☎ 422785; Costanera 12 de Octubre & Onelli). For rental equipment and guide hire, try **Baruzzi Deportes** (☎ 424922; Urquiza 250) or **Martín Pescador** (☎ 422275; martinpescador@ bariloche.com.ar; Rolando 257). Both offer guided fishing trips for about AR$1100 per day for one or two people (price is the same either way and includes all equipment, lunch, transport and guide). Fishing licenses (AR$35/160 per day/week) are required and available at these shops.

THE LAKE DISTRICT

HORSEBACK RIDING

Most travel agencies along Av Bartolomé Mitre offer horseback riding trips. For something special, contact the amiable Carol Jones at **Cabalgatas Carol Jones** (☎ 426508; www.caroljones.com.ar), who offers half-day horseback riding from her family *estancia* outside of town for AR$180 per person. The price includes transport to/from town and an excellent *asado* outside. She also offers multi-day pack trips by horse for AR$420 per person per day. Carol speaks English. All trips require a minimum of two people.

RAFTING & KAYAKING

Rafting and kayaking on the Río Limay and the Río Manso have become increasingly popular in recent years. The best time to be on the rivers is November through February, though you can raft October through Easter.

In business since 1991, **eXtremo Sur** (☎ 427301, 524365; www.extremosur.com in Spanish; Morales 765) offers several trips on the Río Manso: the Manso Inferior (class II to III, AR$165 per person) is suitable for all ages; the Manso a la Frontera (class III to IV, AR$230 per person, ages 14 and up) is a fun and beautiful stretch of the river before the Chilean border. There's also a three-day Expedición Río Manso (class III to IV, AR$1100 or AR$1300), where you camp riverside at excellent facilities. For the last, *asados* and all food and drink are included in the price.

Aguas Blancas (☎ 432799, 02944-15-601155; www .aguasblancas.com.ar; Morales 564) also has an excellent reputation and offers similar trips. Located inside Albergue Patagonia Andina.

Pura Vida Patagonia (☎ 400327; www.puravida patagonia.com) offers kayaking trips on the Lago Nahuel Huapi, ranging from half-day stints to overnight camp-n-kayak trips, custom designed to match your skill level.

PARAGLIDING

The mountains around Bariloche make for spectacular paragliding. If you wish to take to the sky, it will cost you around AR$200 for a 20-minute to half-hour tandem flight with, among others, **Luis Rosenkjer** (☎ 427588, 02944-15-568388) or **Parapente Bariloche** (☎ 02944-15-552403; Cerro Otto base).

Tours

Countless tourist agencies along and near Av Bartolomé Mitre, such as Catedral Turismo (see boxed text, p414), run minibus tours to the national park and as far south as El Bolsón. Prices range from AR$30 for a half-day trip along the Circuito Chico to AR$95 to San Martín de los Andes via the scenic Ruta de los Siete Lagos.

Overland Patagonia (p409) offers a series of well-received camping tours; they range from the four-day Safari Siete Lagos (AR$600 plus AR$140 for food kitty) to the 18-day Safari del Fin del Mundo (AR$4500 plus AR$520 for food), which goes all the way to Tierra del Fuego. Its local tours always offer a little more kick (like hikes) than those offered by most agencies.

Adventure Center (☎ 428368; www.adventurecenter .com.ar; Perito Moreno 30) offers four-day trips down the fabled Ruta Nacional 40 (RN 40) as far as El Calafate for AR$600 per person. Trips run from the end of September to April. Prices include accommodation and one meal per day, but national park entries are separate.

Bariloche Moto Tours (☎ 431324; www.barilochemoto tours.com; Güemes 643) organizes custom-tailored motorbike tours to everywhere between southern Patagonia and northern Chile.

Espacio (☎ 431372; www.islavictoriayarrayanes.com; Av Bartolomé Mitre 139) offers cruises on lake Nahuel Huapi in its 40ft catamaran Cau Cau during summer. Reserve your place two days in advance.

Tren a Vapor (☎ 423858; www.trenhistoricoavapor .com.ar; adult AR$50-100, child AR$35-75) runs full-day trips (a 40km circuit) in a five-wagon steam train built in 1912, stopping for photo ops at a bridge on the river Nirihau, Perito Moreno station, Laguna Los Juncos and Cerro Elefante. Buy tickets at the train station near the bus terminal.

Festivals & Events

For 10 days in August, Bariloche holds its **Fiesta Nacional de la Nieve** (National Snow Festival). In January and February the **Festival de Música de Verano** (Summer Music Festival) puts on several different events, including the **Festival de Música de Cámara** (Chamber Music Festival), the **Festival de Bronces** (Brass Festival) and the **Festival de Música Antigua** (Ancient Music Festival). May 3 is the **Fiesta Nacional de la Rosa Mosqueta**, celebrating the fruit of the wild shrub used in many regional delicacies.

Sleeping

From camping and private houses to five-star hotels, Bariloche's abundant accommodations make it possible to find good value even in high season, when reservations are a good idea. Prices peak during ski season (July and August), drop slightly during high season (January and February) and are lowest the rest of the year. The following are high season prices.

BUDGET
Bariloche has numerous excellent hostels; all of the hostels listed here arrange excursions in Nahuel Huapi and offer weekend *asados*.

La Selva Negra (☎ 441013; Av Bustillo, Km 2.9; sites AR$25) Located 3km west of town on the road to Llao Llao, this is the nearest organized camping area. It has good facilities, and you can step outside your tent to pick apples in the fall.

Periko's (☎ 522326; www.perikos.com; Morales 555; dm AR$26, d AR$100; 🖳) A good-time party hostel with spacious dorms, which have a maximum of six beds. The four doubles all have private bathrooms and the communal kitchen is huge. The owner rents bikes and operates tours throughout Patagonia (he owns Overland Patagonia, p409).

Hostel 1004 (☎ 432228; www.penthouse1004.com.ar; San Martín 127, 10th fl, Bariloche Center bldg; dm AR$30) Up on the 10th floor, this hostel has the most awesome views of any of the hotels in town. Dorms are spacious, with three or six beds and there's a giant living room, complete with sofas, fireplace and big wooden tables. There's no sign; enter the Bariloche Center, take the elevator to the 10th floor, and look for room 1004.

Albergue El Gaucho (☎ 522464; www.hostelelgaucho .com; Belgrano 209; dm AR$30; ✖ 🖳) Immaculate hostel with two kitchens and two common rooms and plenty of space. Most rooms have only four beds, and there are three double rooms. The interior is slightly plain, but the rooms are comfortable.

Bariloche Backpacker's Hostel (☎ 428683; San Martín 82; dm AR$30; ✖) The most central backpacker's hostel in town is also one of the best – a well-stocked kitchen, huge, comfortable lounge area and a mellow little patio outside for smoking purposes.

Other campgrounds between Bariloche and Llao Llao include **Camping Yeti** (☎ 442073; Av Bustillo, Km 5.6; sites AR$24) and **Camping Petunia** (☎ 461969; Av Bustillo, Km 13.5; sites AR$24).

MIDRANGE
Hospedaje Wikter (☎ 423248; Güemes 566; s/d AR$40/70) Up the hill away from the center, this friendly little *hospedaje* offers spacious rooms in a bright, modern building. Bathrooms are bigger than most in this price range and some rooms have good views.

Hostería Ivalu (☎ 423237; Emilio Frey 535; s/d AR$60/110) Up the hill overlooking town, this friendly little *hostería* offers spacious, slightly aging rooms, kept spotless by its friendly owner.

Hostería Adquintue (☎ 522229; VA O'Connor 766; s/d AR$70/120) Spacious, if slightly plain rooms on the edge of the busy downtown district. Good value for the location.

Hostería La Paleta del Pintor (☎ 422220; 20 de Febrero 630; s/d AR$70/120) Everything about this place screams 'cute,' but the rooms are big and airy, with small but spotless bathrooms and big-screen TVs.

Hotel 7 de Febrero (☎ 422244; www.hotel7defebrero .com.ar; Perito Moreno 534; s/d AR$130/140) Nothing too exciting going on decor-wise, but the rooms are big, the fittings new and overall it's a good deal for the price. Get a room out the back for stunning lake views.

ourpick Hostería El Ciervo Rojo (☎ 435241; www .elciervorojo.com in Spanish; Elflein 115; s/d AR$130/160) Book in advance if you'd like to shack up at this pleasant, attractively restored *hostería*. Slate-floored rooms with plenty of homey touches and spacious bathrooms make it a popular choice. Upstairs rooms are superior to those downstairs. The lobby is excellent.

Hostería Katy (☎ 448023; www.gringospatagonia.com; Av Bustillo Km 24.3; s/d AR$150/170) One of the closest *hosterías* to the national park, this one's set in a charming family home. It's a family-run operation – the rooms are warm and comfortable, with big bathrooms and firm beds.

TOP END
Hostería Tirol (☎ 426152; www.hosteriatirol.com.ar; Libertad 175; s/d AR$150/180) Right in the middle of town, this charming little lodge offers comfortable, spacious rooms. Those out the back have spectacular views out over the lake and to the mountain range beyond, as does the bright sitting/breakfast area.

Hotel Carlos V (☎ 425474; www.carlosvpatagonia.com .ar; Morales 420; s/d AR$180/220; 🖳) At first glance a fairly standard business hotel, the Carlos V has plenty of hidden charm. That, the central location and good-sized rooms make it hard to beat.

Hotel Panamericano (☎ /fax 425850; www.pan americanobariloche.com; San Martín 536; r from AR$370/460;

⊠ ⊠ ⊡ ⊒) Bariloche's biggest hotel (covering nearly three city blocks with over-street bridges connecting the different sectors) pulls out all the stops – a couple of restaurants, a casino, piano bar, etc. Rooms are all you'd expect for the price, with a couple of surprising flaws, like cracked tiles and fraying carpet.

Eating

Bariloche has some of Argentina's best food, and it would take several wallet-breaking, belt-bursting and intestinally challenging weeks to sample all of the worthwhile restaurants. Regional specialties, including *cordero* (lamb, cooked over an open flame), *jabalí* (wild boar), *ciervo* (venison) and *trucha* (trout), are especially worth trying.

BUDGET & MIDRANGE

Helados Jauja (Perito Moreno 14; ice cream AR$2-5) Ask anyone in town who serves the best ice cream in Bariloche and they'll reply with one word: 'Jauja.' Many say it's the best in the country.

Huang Ji Zhong (Rolando 268; mains AR$10-25; ☺ lunch & dinner) There's exactly one Chinese restaurant in town, and it's not bad – all the usual suspects at decent prices.

El Vegetariano (☎ 421820; 20 de Febrero 720; set meals AR$15-25; ☺ lunch & dinner) This cozy vegetarian restaurant serves sublime set lunches and dinners, including tea.

Los Tehuelches (Beschtedt 281; mains AR$18-25; ☺ lunch & dinner) The best-value *parrilla* in town, this no-frills place attracts a lot more locals than tourists. The range of set meals is impressive and a *bife de chorizo* (sirloin) with salad for AR$18 is nothing to be sneered at in this town. The house red is not recommended, except for fans of the very rough hangover.

Cerros Nevados (Perito Moreno 338; all you can eat AR$25; ☺ lunch & dinner) Every Argentine town has at least one gut-busting *tenedor libre*; Bariloche's lays it on thick, with plenty of *parrilla* items, pastas, salads and *fiambres* (cold meats).

Instituto Italiano (Beschdedt 141; mains AR$15-30; ☺ lunch & dinner) The local Italian Club serves up some *autentico* dishes, exquisite pastas, offers all you can eat pizza for AR$15 and has good-value set lunches.

La Esquina (Urquiza & Perito Moreno; mains AR$15-30; ☺ breakfast, lunch & dinner) The most atmospheric *confitería* in town has good coffee, reasonably priced sandwiches and burgers and some good regional specialties.

Map Room (Urquiza 248; mains AR$20-30; ☺ 11am-1am) A cozy little pub/restaurant with a good range of beers and some interesting menu items. The American breakfast is the real thing – a real belly-buster. Check out the 'after work' happy hours, when beers are half price.

our pick La Trattoria de la Famiglia Bianchi (Av Bartolomé Mitre 240; mains AR$20-35; ☺ lunch & dinner) Finally, an Italian restaurant that offers something a little different. Excellent, creative pastas, a good range of meat dishes and some wonderful risottos, with ingredients like seafood and wild mushrooms (AR$32).

Tarquino (☎ 421601; 24 de Septiembre & Saavedra; mains AR$20-35; ☺ lunch & dinner) Built entirely of Patagonian cypress, this esteemed restaurant resembles a hobbit house with its wood stairway, carved wooden doorway, fireplace and troll-like architecture. The small menu is almost entirely *parrillada* (including a delicious *cordero*, or grilled lamb), though a pasta and a trout dish grace the menu as well. One of Bariloche's best.

TOP END

El Boliche de Alberto (☎ 431433; Villegas 347; mains AR$25-30; ☺ lunch & dinner) It's worth dining at this esteemed *parrilla* simply to see the astonished look on tourists' faces when a slab of beef the size of a football lands on the table; it's the AR$30 *bife de chorizo* (the AR$20 portion is plenty).

Vogue (☎ 431343; Palacios 136; mains AR$25-30, ☺ lunch & dinner) One of the fullest menus in town, offering pizza, pasta, meats, calzones, *milanesas* (schnitzels) and an excellent smoked meat and cheese platter for two (AR$32), featuring regional goodies like venison and boar salami.

La Marca (Urquiza 240; mains AR$25-35; ☺ lunch & dinner) Upscale *parrilla* with reasonable (for Bariloche) prices. Choose from the impressive range of brochettes (shasliks) – beef, chicken, venison, lamb and salmon. On a sunny day grab a garden table at the side.

Días de Zapata (☎ 423128; Morales 362; mains AR$25-35; ☺ lunch & dinner) A warm and inviting little Mexican restaurant. Dishes tend more toward the Tex Mex than you would think (the owners hail from Mexico City) but the flavors are good and the servings generous.

La Marmite (☎ 423685; Av Bartolomé Mitre 329; mains AR$25-40; ☺ lunch & dinner) A trusty choice for Patagonian standards like trout and venison. Also the place to come for chocolate fondue (AR$52 for two), in case you haven't eaten enough of the stuff cold.

Drinking

For a rundown on cultural events, live music, etc, pick up a copy of *La Puerta*, a free weekly events magazine available in cafés and bars around town.

Tío Lillo (cnr Juramento & 20 de Febrero) A laid-back little corner bar serving a good range of local microbrewery beers at excellent prices. The music's cool, service, uh, laid-back, and the decor eclectic.

Pilgrim (Palacios 167) This pub is a good place to knock back a few beers in a friendly atmosphere. Try the Cervecería Blest brews on tap.

South Bar (Juramento s/n) Mellow local pub where you can actually have a conversation while you drink your beer. Darts too.

Shopping
CHOCOLATE

Bariloche is renowned for its chocolates, and dozens of stores downtown, from national chains to mom-and-pop shops, sell chocolates of every style imaginable. Quality of course varies, so don't get sick on the cheap stuff.

Mamuschka (☎ 423294; Av Bartolomé Mitre 216) Quite simply, the best chocolate in town. Don't skip it. Seriously.

Benroth (☎ 424491; Av Bartolomé Mitre 150) In our humble opinion, the best one after Mamuschka. Definitely try it.

La Mexicana (☎ 422505; Av Bartolomé Mitre 288) Bariloche's first chocolate store, started by the Ritter family in 1948, still produces delicious chocolates and fine *dulces* (jams). It's still owned by the same family, though the chocolate is no longer imported from Mexico, but from Ecuador and Brazil.

Abuela Goya (☎ 433861; Av Bartolomé Mitre 248) Another of Bariloche's longtime chocolate makers. Still small and still worth trying.

CLOTHING & CRAFTS

Arbol (☎ 423032; Av Bartolomé Mitre 263; ☺ Mon-Sat) For the latest in high Patagonian fashion, drop by this Bariloche original, which produces beautifully designed fleeces, woolens, hats and jackets, as well as ceramics and decorative pieces. It has some beautiful clothing, especially for women.

Huitral-Hue (☎ 426760; Villegas 250; ☺ Mon-Sat) Good selection of traditional ponchos, textiles and wool sweaters.

Paseo de los Artesanos (Villegas & Perito Moreno) Local craftspeople display wares of wool, wood, leather, silver and other media here.

Getting There & Away
AIR

Aerolíneas Argentinas (☎ 422425; Av Bartolomé Mitre 185) has flights to Buenos Aires (AR$500) twice daily Monday through Wednesday and three times daily the rest of the week. In high season there are direct weekly flights to Córdoba and El Calafate and possibly Ushuaia.

LADE (☎ 423562; Quaglia 238/242, Via Firenze center) flies at least once a week to Mar del Plata (from AR$310), El Bolsón (AR$70), Esquel (AR$110), Comodoro Rivadavia (AR$210), and Buenos Aires (AR$400).

BOAT

It's possible to travel by boat and bus to Chile aboard the Cruce de Lagos tour. See the boxed text, p414.

BUS

Bariloche's **bus terminal** (☎ 426999) and train station are located across the Río Ñireco on RN 237. Shop around for the best deals, since fares vary and there are frequent promotions. During high season, it's wise to buy tickets at least a day in advance. The bus terminal tourist office is helpful.

The principal route to Chile is over the Cardenal A Samoré (Puyehue) pass to Osorno (AR$60, 5 hours) and Puerto Montt (AR$60, 7 hours), which has onward connections to northern and southern Chilean destinations. Several companies make the run.

For northern destinations such as San Juan, La Rioja, Catamarca, Tucumán, Jujuy and Salta you must go to Mendoza. Buses to northeastern destinations usually connect through Buenos Aires, though you could also head to Rosario where there are frequent services northeast.

To San Martín de los Andes and Junín de los Andes, Albus, KoKo and **Turismo Algarrobal** (☎ 427698) take the scenic (though often chokingly dusty) Ruta de los Siete Lagos (RN 234; see p397) during summer, and the longer,

THE LAKE DISTRICT

THE LAKE DISTRICT

THE CRUCE DE LAGOS

One of Argentina's classic journeys is the Cruce de Lagos, a scenic 12-hour bus-and-boat trip over the Andes to Puerto Montt, Chile. Operated exclusively by **Catedral Turismo** (☎ 425444; www.crucedelagos.cl; Palacios 263; fee per person AR$500), the trip begins around around 8am in Bariloche (departure times vary) with a shuttle from Catedral's office to Puerto Pañuelo near Hotel Llao Llao. The passenger ferry from Puerto Pañuelo leaves immediately after the shuttle arrives, so if you want to have tea at Llao Llao, get there ahead of time on your own (but make sure you bought your ticket in advance). Service is daily in the summer and weekdays the rest of the year. In winter (mid-April to September), the trip takes two days, and passengers are required to stay the night in Peulla, Chile, where the only hotel will cost you an additional AR$480. You may be able to stay at **Hotel Puerto Blest** (☎ 425443; r AR$250), which is a fair bit cheaper. Ask about this option at Catedral Turismo. If you just visit Puerto Blest (boats leave from Puerto Pañuelo) and are not overnighting as part of the two-day lake crossing, the hotel charges AR$180; essentially the price is higher for those who are taking the full lake-crossing.

Bicycles are allowed on the boats, and sometimes on the buses (provided you dismantle them), so cyclists may end up having to ride the stretches between Bariloche and Pañuelo (25km), Puerto Blest and Puerto Alegre (15km), Puerto Frías and Peulla (27km), and Petrohué and Puerto Montt (76km); the tourist office may have info about alternative transport between Petrohué and Puerto Montt for cyclists hoping to avoid the ride.

In winter it's not possible to purchase segments of the trip (except that between Puerto Pañuelo and Puerto Blest; AR$70). During summertime (from December to April), it's possible to buy just the boat sections (AR$180). Either way, if you're cycling, Catedral Turismo will cut your rate slightly since you won't be riding the buses. Though the trip rarely sells out, it's best to book it at least a day or two in advance.

paved La Rinconada (RN 40) route during the rest of the year.

The following services have at least three departures per day.

Destination	Cost (AR$)	Duration (hr)
Bahía Blanca	97	12-14
Buenos Aires	180	20-23
Comodoro Rivadavia	110	14
Córdoba	180	22
El Bolsón	15	3
Esquel	32	4½
Junín de los Andes	30	4
Mar del Plata	160	18-20
Mendoza	180	19
Neuquén	70	6
Puerto Madryn	160	14-18
Río Gallegos	200	28
Rosario	200	23-24
San Martín de los Andes	37	4½
San Rafael	150	17
Trelew	150	13-19
Viedma	65	12
Villa la Angostura	14	2

TRAIN

The **Tren Patagonico** (☎ 422450; www.trenpatagonico.com.ar in Spanish) leaves the **train station** (RN 237), across the Río Ñireco next to the bus termi-

nal. Departures for Viedma (16 hours) are Thursday and Sunday at 5pm; fares are AR$30 *turista*, AR$70 Pullman (reclining chair) and AR$120 *camarote* (1st-class sleeper). Departure times change frequently so it's best to check with the tourist office beforehand.

Getting Around

TO/FROM THE AIRPORT

Bariloche's **airport** (☎ 422767) is 15km east of town via RN 237 and RP 80. **Via Bariloche** (☎ 429012; Quaglia 238/242, Via Firenze center) shuttles connect the airport with town (AR$10, 15 minutes); buses leave every hour, starting at 9:30am, from in front of the airline offices at Quaglia 242. A *remise* costs about AR$35.

BUS

At the main local bus stop, on Perito Moreno between Rolando and Palacios, Codao del Sur and Ómnibus 3 de Mayo run hourly buses to Cerro Catedral for AR$1.10 one-way. Codao uses Av de los Pioneros, while 3 de Mayo takes Av Bustillo. Some bus fares are cheaper when bought inside the **3 de Mayo ticket office** (☎ 425648; Perito Moreno 480), where you can also pick up handy *horarios* (schedules) for all destinations.

From 6am to midnight, municipal bus 20 leaves the main bus stop every 20 minutes for the attractive lakeside settlements of Llao Llao and Puerto Pañuelo (AR$2.60, 40 minutes). Bus 10 goes to Colonia Suiza (AR$2.60, 50 minutes) 14 times daily. During summer three of these, at 8:05am, noon and 5:40pm, continue to Puerto Pañuelo, allowing you to do most of the Circuito Chico (right) using public transport. Departure times from Puerto Pañuelo back to Bariloche via Colonia Suiza are 9:40am, 1:40pm and 6:40pm. You can also walk any section and flag down buses en route.

Ómnibus 3 de Mayo buses 50 and 51 go to Lago Gutiérrez (AR$5) every 30 minutes, while in summer the company's Línea Mascardi goes to Villa Mascardi/Los Rápidos (AR$2.60) three times daily. Ómnibus 3 de Mayo's Línea El Manso goes twice Friday to Río Villegas and El Manso (AR$10), on the southwestern border of Parque Nacional Nahuel Huapi.

Buses 70, 71 and 83 stop at the main bus stop, connecting downtown with the bus terminal (AR$1).

CAR

Bariloche is loaded with the standard car-rental agencies and is one of the cheapest places to rent in the country. Prices vary greatly depending on season and demand, but usually come in under AR$150 per day with 200km.

Catedral Rent-a-Car (☎ 441488, 02944-15-602999; www.autoscatedral.com.ar in Spanish; Pioneros 5645) Call for them to drop car off.

Europcar (☎ 456594, 02944-15-569518; aireservas@arnet.com.ar; Av 12 de Octubre 785)

Hertz (☎ 423457; bariloche@hertzargentina.com.ar; Quaglia 352)

Localiza (☎ 435374; cnr Emilio Frey & VA O'Connor)

Thrifty (☎ 427904; www.thrifty.com.ar; Villegas 355)

HITCHHIKING

It's easy to hitch along Av Bustillo as far as Km 8, after which traffic thins out and catching a lift means waiting longer. In summer it's usually not to difficult to get around the Circuito Chico by thumb.

TAXI

A taxi from the bus terminal to the center of town costs around AR$8. Taxis within town generally don't go over the AR$5 mark.

PARQUE NACIONAL NAHUEL HUAPI
☎ 02944

One of Argentina's most visited national parks, Nahuel Huapi occupies 7500 sq km in mountainous southwestern Neuquén and western Río Negro provinces. The park's centerpiece is Lago Nahuel Huapi, a glacial remnant over 100km long that covers more than 500 sq km. To the west, a ridge of high peaks separates Argentina from Chile; the tallest is 3554m Monte Tronador, an extinct volcano that still lives up to its name (meaning 'Thunderer') when blocks of ice tumble from its glaciers. During the summer months, wildflowers blanket the alpine meadows.

Nahuel Huapi was created to preserve local flora and fauna, including its Andean-Patagonian forests and rare animals. Tree species are much the same as those found in Parque Nacional Los Alerces (p473), while the important animal species include the huemul (Andean deer) and the miniature deer known as pudú. Most visitors are unlikely to see either of these, but several species of introduced deer are common, as are native birds.

A good source of information about the park is the national park office in Bariloche (see p408).

Books

For trekking maps and information about hiking in the region, see Lonely Planet's *Trekking in the Patagonian Andes*, by Clem Lindenmayer or, if you read Spanish, the locally published *Las Montañas de Bariloche*, by Toncek Arko and Raúl Izaguirre.

Circuito Chico

One of the area's most popular and scenic driving excursions, the Circuito Chico begins on Av Bustillo, on Bariloche's outskirts, and continues to the tranquil resort of **Llao Llao**, named for the 'Indian bread' fungus from the coihue tree. At **Cerro Campanario** (Av Bustillo, Km 18), the **Aerosilla Campanario** (☎ 427274) lifts passengers to a panoramic view of Lago Nahuel Huapi for AR$20.

Llao Llao's **Puerto Pañuelo** is the point of departure for the boat and bus excursion across the Andes to Chile, as well as to Parque Nacional Los Arrayanes on Península Quetrihué, though you can visit Los Arrayanes more easily and cheaply from Villa la Angostura (p404).

PARQUE NACIONAL NAHUEL HUAPI

Even if you don't plan to spend a night in the state-built **Hotel Llao Llao** (☎ 448530; www.llaollao .com.ar; d from AR$1100, studios AR$2300, cabañas AR$2600), Argentina's most famous hotel, take a stroll around the grounds. From Llao Llao you can head across to **Colonia Suiza**, named for its early Swiss colonists. A modest *confitería* has excellent pastries, and there are several campgrounds.

The road passes the trailhead to 2076m **Cerro López**, a three-hour climb, before returning to Bariloche. At the top of Cerro López it's possible to spend the night at Club Andino Bariloche's **Refugio López** (☎ in Bariloche for reservations 527966; info@ activepatagonia.com.ar; dm about AR$30; ☑ mid-Dec–mid-Apr), where meals are also available.

Although travel agencies offer the Circuito Chico as a half-day tour (AR$30 through most

agencies in Bariloche), it's easily done on public transportation or, if you're up for a 60km pedal, by bicycle (p409).

Cerro Otto

Cerro Otto (1405m) is an 8km hike on a gravel road west from Bariloche. There's enough traffic that hitchhiking is feasible, and it's also a steep and tiring but rewarding bicycle route. The **Teleférico Cerro Otto** (☎ 441035; Av de Los Pioneros, Km 5) carries adult passengers to the summit for AR$35, children for AR$20; a free bus leaves Bariloche from the corner of Av Bartolomé Mitre and Villegas or Perito Moreno and Independencia to the mountain base. Bring food and drink – prices at the summit *confitería* are nearly as painful as the walk up there.

Piedras Blancas (☎ 425720, ext 1708; Cerro Otto, Km 6) is the nearest ski area to Bariloche, and a popular area for summertime hiking.

There's a trail from Piedras Blancas to Club Andino's **Refugio Berghof** (☎ in Bariloche for reservations 527966; info@activepatagonia.com.ar; dm AR$30-40), at an elevation of 1240m; make reservations, since there are only 20 beds. Meals are available here. The *refugio* also contains the **Museo de Montaña Otto Meiling** (guided visit AR$8), named for a pioneering climber.

Cerro Catedral

This 2388m peak, 20km southwest of Bariloche, is the area's most important snow-sport center, open from mid-June to mid-October. Several chairlifts and the **Aerosilla Cerro Bellavista** (AR$40) carry passengers up to 2000m, where there's a restaurant/*confitería* offering excellent panoramas.

There is a good mix of easy, intermediate and advanced skiing runs, with steep advanced runs at the top and some tree runs near the base. Lift lines can develop at this very popular resort, but the capacity is substantial enough that waits are not excessive.

The rates for lift passes vary from low to mid to high season, starting at AR$75 and going up to AR$125 per day for adults, AR$60 to AR$105 for children. One-week passes cost AR$395 to AR$690 for adults, and AR$325 to AR$570 for children. Basic rental equipment is cheap, but quality gear is more expensive. There are several on-site ski schools.

The **Aerosilla Lynch** (adults AR$40, children AR$28) also takes passengers up the mountain during summer, from 10am to 5pm daily except Monday. Several trekking trails begin near the top of the lift: one relatively easy four-hour walk goes to Club Andino's **Refugio Emilio Frey** (☎ in Bariloche for reservations 527966; info@activepatagonia.com.ar; dm AR$30-40), where 40 beds and simple meals (AR$15 to AR$60) are available, as are kitchen facilities (AR$5). This *refugio* itself is exposed, but there are sheltered tent sites in what is also Argentina's prime **rock-climbing** area.

Hostería Knapp (☎ 460021; per person AR$100) is at the base of the lifts. Alternatively you can stay in Bariloche; public transport from there is excellent, consisting of hourly buses from downtown with Ómnibus 3 de Mayo (p414).

Monte Tronador & Pampa Linda

Traveling via Lago Mascardi, it's a full-day trip up a dusty, single-lane dirt road to Pampa Linda to visit the **Ventisquero Negro** (Black Glacier) and the base of Tronador (3554m).

The area around Tronador resembles, in some ways, California's Yosemite Valley – you have to set your sights above the hotels, *confiterías* and parking lots to focus on the dozens of waterfalls that plunge over the flanks of the extinct volcanoes.

From Pampa Linda – the starting point for several excellent hikes – hikers can approach the snow-line Club Andino **Refugio Otto Meiling** (☎ in Bariloche for reservations 527966; info@activepatagonia.com.ar; dm AR$30-40) on foot (about four to six hours' hiking time) and continue to Laguna Frías via the **Paso de las Nubes**; it's a five- to seven-hour walk to an elevation of 2000m. It's also possible to complete the trip in the opposite direction by taking Cerro Catedral's ferry from Puerto Pañuelo to Puerto Blest, and then hiking up the Río Frías to Paso de las Nubes before descending to Pampa Linda via the Río Alerce. The *refugio* itself prepares delicious meals (AR$15 to AR$60, kitchen use AR$10) and is well stocked with good wine and beer. You can hire a guide at the *refugio* to take you on a number of excursions, which range from a three-hour hike to a nearby glacier to the multiday ascent of Cumbre Argentina on Tronador.

Climbers intending to scale Tronador should anticipate a three- to four-day technical climb requiring experience on rock, snow and ice. Hostería Pampa Linda (right) arranges horseback riding in the area.

The road to Pampa Linda passes **Los Rápidos**, after which it becomes extremely narrow. Traffic is therefore allowed up to Pampa Linda until 2pm. At 4pm cars are allowed to leave Pampa Linda for the return. For AR$60 each

way, the Club Andino Bariloche (p408) has summer transport (end of November to April) to Pampa Linda daily at 8:30am and 10am, returning around 5pm, with **Expreso Meiling** (☎ 529875). Buses depart from in front of the Club Andino, and the 90km ride takes about 2½ hours. Park entry fees (AR$15) must be paid en route at the ranger station at Villa Mascardi (the bus stops so you can do this).

Sleeping

In addition to those campgrounds in the immediate Bariloche area, there are sites at Lago Gutiérrez, Lago Mascardi, Lago Guillelmo, Lago Los Moscos, Lago Roca and Pampa Linda. *Refugios* charge AR$25 to AR$40 per night, about AR$10 for day use, and sometimes about AR$5 extra for kitchen privileges. *Refugios* are open from December to the end of April.

Within the park are a number of hotels tending to the luxurious, though there is also the moderately priced **Hostería Pampa Linda** (☎ 490517; s/d AR$220/300, with half-pension AR$320/380). For a real treat, stay at the secluded **Hotel Tronador** (☎ 441062; www.hotel-tronador.com; s/d AR$490/550; ☼ Nov–mid-Apr), at the northwest end of Lago Mascardi on the Pampa Linda road.

Getting There & Around

For transport information from Bariloche, see p414. For road conditions in and around the national parks, call **Parque Nacional Estado de Rutas** (☎ 105) toll-free from any telephone.

EL BOLSÓN

☎ 02944 / pop 18,000 / elev 300m

It's not hard to see why the hippies started flocking to El Bolsón back in the '70s. It's a mellow little village for most of the year, nestled in between two mountain ranges. When summer comes, it packs out with Argentine tourists who drop big wads of cash and disappear quietly to whence they came.

In the last 30 years El Bolsón has been declared both a non-nuclear zone and an 'ecological municipality' (are you getting the picture yet?). What's indisputable is that just out of town are some excellent, easily accessible hikes that take in some of the country's (if not the world's) most gorgeous landscapes.

The town welcomes backpackers, who often find it a relief from Bariloche's commercialism and find themselves stuffing their bellies with natural and vegetarian foods and the excellent

THE LAKE DISTRICT

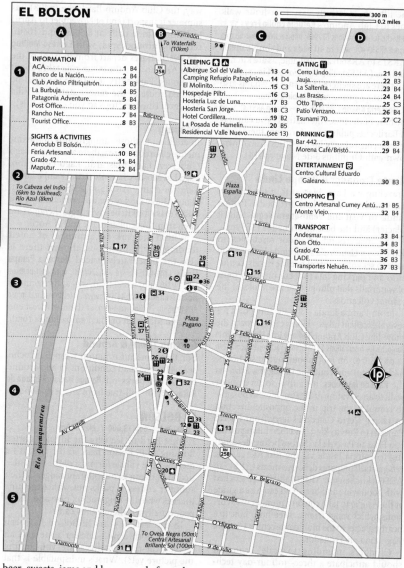

EL BOLSÓN

0 ———— 300 m
0 ———— 0.2 miles

INFORMATION
ACA...1 B4
Banco de la Nación..........................2 B4
Club Andino Piltriquitrón...............3 B3
La Burbuja...4 B5
Patagonia Adventure.......................5 B4
Post Office..6 B3
Rancho Net..7 B3
Tourist Office...................................8 B3

SIGHTS & ACTIVITIES
Aeroclub El Bolsón...........................9 C1
Feria Artesanal...............................10 B4
Grado 42..11 B4
Maputur...12 B4

SLEEPING
Albergue Sol del Valle....................13 C4
Camping Refugio Patagónico......14 D4
El Molinito......................................15 C3
Hospedaje Piltri..............................16 C3
Hostería Luz de Luna.....................17 B3
Hostería San Jorge........................18 C3
Hotel Cordillera.............................19 B2
La Posada de Hamelin...................20 B5
Residencial Valle Nuevo.........(see 13)

EATING
Cerro Lindo......................................21 B4
Jauja...22 B3
La Salteñita......................................23 B4
Las Brasas..24 B4
Otto Tipp...25 C3
Patio Venzano.................................26 B4
Tsunami 70......................................27 C2

DRINKING
Bar 442..28 B3
Morena Café/Bristó.......................29 B4

ENTERTAINMENT
Centro Cultural Eduardo
   Galeano.......................................30 B3

SHOPPING
Centro Artesanal Cumey Antú......31 B5
Monte Viejo.....................................32 B4

TRANSPORT
Andesmar..33 B4
Don Otto...34 B3
Grado 42..35 B4
LADE...36 B3
Transportes Nehuén.......................37 B3

beer, sweets, jams and honey made from the local harvest.

Rows of poplars lend a Mediterranean appearance to the local *chacras* (farms), most of which are devoted to hops (El Bolsón produces nearly three-quarters of the country's hops) and fruits.

Motorists should note that El Bolsón is the northernmost spot to purchase gasoline at Patagonian discount prices.

Orientation

Near the southwestern border of Río Negro province, El Bolsón lies in a basin surrounded by high mountains, dominated by the longitudinal ridges of Cerro Piltriquitrón to the east and the Cordón Nevado along the Chilean border to the west. On the east bank of the Río Quemquemtreu, it is roughly midway between Bariloche and Esquel, each about 130km via RN 258 from Bolsón.

From the south, RN 258 enters town as Av Belgrano and becomes north–south Av San Martín through town. The principal landmark is the ovoid Plaza Pagano. Most services are nearby.

Information

ACA (☎ 492260; cnr Avs Belgrano & San Martín) Argentina's auto club; good source for provincial road maps.
Banco de la Nación (Av San Martín & Pellegrini) Has an ATM.
Club Andino Piltriquitrón (☎ 492600; Sarmiento, btwn Roca & Feliciano; ☾ Dec-Mar) Visitors interested in exploring the surrounding mountains can contact this office. Occasionally open 6pm to 8pm off season.
La Burbuja (☎ 02944-15-639241; Paso 425; wash & dry AR$10; ☾ Mon-Sat) Laundry service.
Patagonia Adventure (☎ 492513; Pablo Hube 418) Travel agency.
Post office (Av San Martín 2806)
Rancho Net (Av San Martín at Av Belgrano; per hr AR$2) Internet access.
Tourist office (☎ 492604, 455336; www.bolson turistico.com.ar in Spanish; Av San Martín & Roca; ☾ 9am-9pm, in summer to 10pm) At the north end of Plaza Pagano. It has a good town map and brochures, plus thorough information on accommodations, food, tours and services. Maps of the surrounding area are crude but helpful. Superb staff.

Sights & Activities

Local craftspeople sell their wares at the **Feria Artesanal**, along the south end of Plaza Pagano from 10am to 4pm every Tuesday, Thursday and Saturday. The market boasts over 320 registered (and countless unregistered) artists, who make and sell everything from sculpted wooden cutting boards and handcrafted *mate* gourds to jewelry, flutes and marionettes. With numerous food vendors (all adhering to the regulation that everything sold in the market must be handmade), it's also an excellent opportunity to sample local delicacies. On sunny Sundays the *feria* operates about half-tilt.

For adventures in the surrounding countryside, **Grado 42** (☎ 493124; www.grado42.com in Spanish;

Av Belgrano 406) offers extensive trekking, mountain biking and other tours around El Bolsón, as does **Maputur** (☎ 491440; Perito Moreno 2331), which also rents mountain bikes for AR$5/25 per hour/day. Both also offer rafting on the Río Manso. Trips on the Manso Inferior (class II to III) cost AR$160 per person (including lunch); on the Manso a la Frontera (class II to IV) trips cost AR$220 (including lunch and dinner).

Aeroclub El Bolsón (☎ 491125; www.aeroclub elbolson.8k.com; San Martín & Puyrredon) offers aerial tours of the area for AR$54 to AR$360 per person on 10- to 110-minute scenic flights in a Cessna 182. Clouds tend to form in the afternoon, so it's best to go in the morning for stunning views of the national parks, lakes and unexplored (and therefore unnamed) glaciers of the region.

Festivals & Events

Local beer gets headlines during the **Festival Nacional del Lúpulo** (National Hops Festival), which takes place during four days in mid-February. El Bolsón also hosts a weekend **jazz festival** (www.elbolsonjazz.com.ar in Spanish) in December; dates vary.

Sleeping

BUDGET

Budget travelers are more than welcome in El Bolsón, where reasonable prices are the rule rather than the exception.

Camping Refugio Patagónico (☎ 02944-15-635463; Islas Malvinas s/n; sites per person AR$8) Not bad as far as campgrounds go – basically a bare field, but a pleasant stream burbles alongside it. Services are good, including *asados* and a clean, modern toilet block.

Albergue Sol del Valle (☎ 492087; 25 de Mayo 2485; dm AR$30) It's back to basics in El Bolsón's most central dorm rooms, but if you've got a sleeping bag and want to use a kitchen, it's good value for money.

Hospedaje Piltri (☎ 455305; Saavedra 2729; s/d with shared bathroom AR$50/60) Tucked away in a quiet little corner of town, the Piltri's definitely seen better days, but the friendly, enthusiastic owner makes up for whatever minor comforts may be lacking.

Hostería Luz de Luna (☎ 491908; www.luzdeluna elbolson.com.ar; Dorrego 150; s/d AR$60/70) Although spacious, the rooms here manage to retain a pleasant, homelike feel. Individual decoration and spotless bathrooms add to the appeal. Go for one upstairs for better light and views.

MIDRANGE & TOP END

our pick El Molinito (☎ 493164; 25 de Mayo & Dorrego; s/d AR$45/90) These newcomers offer quite possibly the sweetest deal in the entire Lake District – spacious rooms, firm beds, squeaky clean bathrooms *and* kitchen use. Check them out before they raise the prices.

Residencial Valle Nuevo (☎ 492087; 25 de Mayo 2345; s/d AR$50/100) With spotless bathrooms, big-screen TVs and rocking views out the back onto mountain peaks, these are some of the best budget rooms in town. If you're coming in summer, book well ahead.

La Posada de Hamelin (☎ 492030; posadadehamelin@elbolson.com; Granollers 2179; s/d AR$100/130) A beautiful little rustic getaway. There are only four rooms, but they're all gorgeous, with exposed beams and rough hewn walls. The sunny upstairs dining area is a great place to munch on an empanada.

Hostería San Jorge (☎ 491313; www.elbolson.com /sanjorge; Perito Moreno & Azcuénaga; s/d AR$130/160) Big, spotless rooms, filling breakfasts and comfy inside and outside sitting areas make this a winner in this price range. English spoken.

Hotel Cordillera (☎ /fax 492235; cordillerahotel@elbolson.com; Av San Martín 3210; s/d AR$170/200) The charm of the lobby/bar area is topped only by the mountain views from the 2nd floor – if you're booking ahead, make sure you tell them you want a room with a balcony. The rooms themselves are OK – spacious enough, but suffering slightly from Orange Carpet Syndrome.

Eating

El Bolsón's restaurants lack Bariloche's variety, but food is consistently good value and often outstanding, thanks to fresh, local ingredients and careful preparation. *Trucha arco iris* (rainbow trout) is the local specialty.

The Feria Artesanal (p419) is by far the best, most economical place to eat. Goodies here include fresh fruit, Belgian waffles with berries and cream, huge empanadas for AR$1.50, sandwiches, frittatas, *milanesa de soja* (soy patties), locally brewed beer and regional desserts.

La Salteñita (☎ 493749; Belgrano 515; empanadas AR$1.50-3; ☒ 10am-9pm) For spicy northern empanadas, try this cheap rotisserie.

Jauja (☎ Av San Martín 2867; mains AR$15-30; ☒ breakfast, lunch & dinner) The most dependable *confitería* in town serves up all your faves with some El Bolsón touches (like homemade bread and strawberry juice) thrown in. Daily specials are always worth checking out – the risotto with lamb and wild mushrooms is divine.

Las Brasas (☎ 492923; Av Sarmiento & Pablo Hube; mains AR$18-30; ☒ lunch & dinner) Probably the finest dining option in town. Las Brasas' signature dish is Patagonian lamb, but the place offers all your other *parrilla* favorites, plus a good variety of trout dishes.

Tsunami 70 (Av San Martín 3275; mains AR$20-30; ☒ lunch & dinner) Specializing in seafood, but offering an interesting range of meat dishes, this tiny, Spanish-influenced restaurant has a great atmosphere and serves up some of the best paella (AR$22) in town.

Cerro Lindo (☎ 492899; Av San Martín 2524; mains AR$20-30; ☒ lunch & dinner) Proving that you can stick a 'nouveau' in front of just about anything, this place offers 'Nouveau Patagonian' – plenty of lamb, beef, rabbit, venison and trout, accompanied by a jus, reduction, etc. Also features a good but pricey wine list.

Otto Tipp (☎ 493700; Roca & Islas Malvinas; mains AR$20-30; ☒ lunch & dinner in summer, dinner Wed-Sun rest of year) After a hard day of doing anything (or nothing for that matter) there are few better ways to unwind than by working your way through Mr Tipp's selection of microbrew beers. Guests are invited to a free sampling of the six varieties on arrival and there's a good selection of regional specialties on hand, such as smoked trout and Patagonian lamb cooked in black beer, should you happen to get peckish.

Patio Venzano (Av Sarmiento & Pablo Hube; mains AR$20-35; ☒ lunch & dinner) Sunny days in the high season, you'll want to arrive a little early to guarantee yourself an outside table. No surprises on the menu (pasta, *parrilla*), but the atmosphere's a winner.

Drinking & Entertainment

Morena Café/Bristó (☎ 455353; Av San Martín & Pablo Hube) Friendly café-cum-bar that sometimes has live music.

Bar 442 (☎ 492313; Perito Moreno & Dorrego) This venue doubles as a disco on Friday nights and often has live music on Saturday nights.

Oveja Negra (Av San Martín 1997) Laid-back pub with friendly atmosphere.

Centro Cultural Eduardo Galeano (☎ 491503; cnr Dorrego & Onelli; admission varies) Small performance space featuring local (and sometimes international) theater, music and dance. Stop by for a program or ask around town.

Shopping

El Bolsón is a craft hunter's paradise. Besides the regular Feria Artesanal (p419), there are several other outlets for local arts and crafts.

Centro Artesanal Cumey Antú (☎ 02944-15-412614; Av San Martín 2020) This outlet sells high-quality Mapuche clothing and weavings.

Central Artesanal Brillante Sol (☎ 02944-15-412614; San Martín 1920) Cooperative of 25 Mapuche women who spin and weave their woolen textiles on wooden looms in back and sell the products in front.

Monte Viejo (☎ 491735; Pablo Hube at Av San Martín) High-quality ceramics, wood crafts, silver, knives and Mapuche textiles.

Getting There & Away

AIR

LADE (☎ 492206; Perito Moreno at Plaza Pagano) flies Thursday to Bariloche (AR$68) and Tuesday to Comodoro Rivadavia (AR$206) and Esquel (AR$68). All flights leave from El Bolsón's small **airport** (☎ 492066) at the north end of Av San Martín.

BUS

El Bolsón has no central bus terminal, but most companies are on or near Av San Martín.

Andesmar (☎ 492178; Av Belgrano & Perito Moreno) goes to Bariloche (AR$15, two hours) and Esquel (AR$20, two to three hours), and to points north of there, usually with a change in Neuquén (AR$60, nine hours).

TAC, represented by **Grado 42** (☎ 493124; Av Belgrano 406), goes to Bariloche (AR$15, two hours) and Neuquén (AR$58, 9 hours); the company sells tickets to Mendoza, Córdoba and other northern destinations, though you'll have to change buses in Neuquén.

Don Otto (☎ 493910; cnr Av Sarmiento & Roca) goes to Bariloche and Comodoro Rivadavia, with connections in Esquel for Trelew and Puerto Madryn. **Transportes Nehuén** (☎ 491831; Sarmiento, near Roca) goes to El Maitén, Bariloche and Los Alerces.

Getting Around

BUS

Local bus service to nearby sights is extensive during the busy summer months, but sporadic in fall and winter, when you'll have to hire a taxi or take a tour. The tourist office

provides up-to-date information. Local buses cost AR$1.20.

Transportes Nehuén (☎ 491831; Sarmiento, near Roca) has summer bus services to many local destinations.

La Golondrina (☎ 492557) goes to Cascada Mallín Ahogado, leaving from the south end of Plaza Pagano; and to Lago Puelo, leaving from the corner of Av San Martín and Dorrego.

TAXI

Taxis (remises) are a reasonable mode of transport to nearby trailheads and campgrounds. Companies include **Radio Taxi Glaciar** (☎ 492892), **Patagonia** (☎ 493907) and **Suremiss** (☎ 492895); call for rides.

AROUND EL BOLSÓN

The outskirts of El Bolsón offer numerous ridges, waterfalls and forests for hikers to explore. If you give yourself plenty of time, and pack food and water, some of the following places can be reached by foot from town, though buses and remises to trailheads are reasonable. Mountain biking is an excellent way to get out on your own; for rentals try **Maputur** (☎ 491440; Perito Moreno 2331; per hr/day AR$5/25), in El Bolsón.

Cabeza del Indio

On a ridge-top 8km west of town, this metamorphic rock resembles a toothless hippie as much as it does a stereotypical profile of a 'noble savage,' from which the name 'Indian Head' was derived. The 7km trail up to the rock is reached by walking west on Azcuénaga from town. Part of it traverses a narrow ledge that offers the best views of the formation itself, but by climbing from an earlier junction you can obtain better views of the Río Azul and, in the distance to the south, Parque Nacional Lago Puelo.

Cascada Mallín Ahogado

This small waterfall, on the Arroyo del Medio, is 10km north of town, west of RN 258. Beyond the falls, a gravel road leads to Club Andino Piltriquitrón's **Refugio Perito Moreno** (☎ 493912; per night with/without bedclothes AR$40/25), a great base for several outstanding hikes. The refugio has capacity for 80 people; meals are an additional AR$15.

From the refugio, it's 2½ hours to the 2206m summit of **Cerro Perito Moreno** (☎ 493912; lift pass

AR$35, ski rental AR$25, snowboard rental AR$40). In winter there's skiing here at the Centro de Deportes Invernales Perito Moreno, where the base elevation is 1000m. The T-bar lifts reach 1450m.

Cascada Escondida

Downstream from the Cascada Mallín Ahogado, this waterfall is 8km from El Bolsón. There is a footpath beyond the bridge across the river at the west end of Av Pueyrredón.

Cerro Piltriquitrón

Dominating the landscape east of Bolsón, the 2260m summit of this granitic ridge yields panoramic views westward across the valley of the Río Azul to the Andean crest along the Chilean border. After driving or walking to the 1000m level (the 11km trip from El Bolsón costs about AR$30 by taxi), another hour's steep, dusty walk leads through the impressive **Bosque Tallado** (Sculpture Forest) to the Club Andino's **Refugio Piltriquitrón** (☎ 492024; dm AR$13). Beds here are outstanding value, but bring your own sleeping bag. Moderately priced meals are available.

From the *refugio*, a steep footpath climbs along the rusted tow bar, then levels off and circles east around the peak before climbing precipitously up loose scree to the summit, marked by a brightly painted cement block. On a clear day the tiring two-hour climb (conspicuously marked by paint blazes) rewards the hiker with views south beyond Lago Puelo, northwest to Monte Tronador and, beyond the border, the snow-topped cone of Volcán Osorno in Chile. Water is abundant along most of the summit route, but hikers should carry a canteen and bring lunch to enjoy at the top.

Cerro Lindo

Southwest of El Bolsón a trail from Camping Río Azul (a small campground reached by a secondary road from El Bolsón) goes to **Refugio Cerro Lindo** (☎ 492763; dm AR$20; closed in winter), where you can get a decent bed; meals are extra. It's about four hours to the *refugio*, from which the trail continues to the 2150m summit.

El Hoyo

Just across the provincial border in Chubut, this town's microclimate makes it the local 'fresh fruit capital.' Nearby Lago Epuyén has good camping and hiking. La Golondrina in El Bolsón (p421) has daily service to El Hoyo (AR$4, 1 hour).

Parque Nacional Lago Puelo

In Chubut province, only 15km south of El Bolsón, this windy, azure lake is suitable for swimming, fishing, boating, hiking and camping. There are regular buses from El Bolsón in summer, but there's reduced service on Sunday and off-season, when you may have to hitchhike.

Peuma Hue (☎ 499372; www.peuma-hue.com.ar; r AR$140) is a lakeside resort complex nestled between two rivers with great views of the mighty Piltriquitrón mountain range. Rooms are heavy on the wood theme, but comfortable and spacious. Delicious meals are prepared with local organic ingredients where possible and the grounds are notable for the many species of native plants that the owners are seeking to help save from extinction. Book well ahead if you're coming in summer.

There are both free and fee campsites at the park entrance, including **Camping Lago Puelo** (☎ 499186; per person AR$8).

The Argentine navy maintains a trailer close to the dock, where the launch **Juana de Arco** (☎ 493415) takes passengers across the lake to Argentina's Pacific Ocean outlet at the Chilean border (AR$60, three hours). For hardcore hikers heading to Chile, it's possible to continue by foot or horseback to the Chilean town of Puelo on the Seno de Reloncaví, with connections to Puerto Montt. This walk takes roughly three days. Contact the **Intendencia** (☎ 499432) in Lago Puelo for maps, trail conditions and recommended local guides.

For AR$40 the launches also take passengers to El Turbio, at the south end of the lake, where there's a campground.

EL MAITÉN

☎ 02945 / pop 3800

In open-range country on the upper reaches of the Río Chubut, about 70km southeast of El Bolsón, this small, dusty town is the end of the line for La Trochita, the old narrow-gauge steam train running between Esquel and El Maitén. It's also home to the workshops for La Trochita and a graveyard of antique steam locomotives and other railroad hardware – a train aficionado's dream.

Every February the **Fiesta Provincial del Trencito** commemorates the railroad that put El Maitén on the map and keeps it there; it now doubles as the **Fiesta Nacional del Tren a Vapor** (National Steam Train Festival). Drawing people from all over the province and the country, it features riding and horse-taming competitions, live music and superb produce and pastries, including homemade jams and jellies.

El Maitén has a helpful **tourist office** (☎ 495150; turismai@ar.inter.net).

Camping Municipal (per person AR$8), directly on the river, gets crowded and noisy during the festival. **Hostería Refugio Andino** (☎ 495007; San Martín 1317; per person AR$30; 🖳) is simple but clean and has an attached restaurant.

Getting There & Away

Transportes Jacobsen buses connect El Maitén with Esquel at 8am Monday, Tuesday, Friday and Saturday. There's also regular minibus service to and from El Bolsón with Transportes Nehuén.

Train schedules change regularly for **La Trochita** (☎ 495190; www.latrochita.org.ar), so contact El Bolsón's tourist office (p419), Grado 42 in El Bolsón (p419), the train offices in either El Maitén or Esquel, or the tourist office in Esquel. At time of writing, it went only once a month to/from Esquel. Rest assured, you can still ride the rails from Monday to Saturday at 10am when La Trochita spins its 2½-hour **Paseo Turístico** (AR$50), which departs and finishes in Esquel. In low season it runs only on Saturday at 2pm.

Patagonia

A star-riddled sky and snarled grasses dwarf the rider on the steppe as his horse closes the gap on the horizon. In South America's southern frontier, nature, long left to its own devices, grows wild, barren and beautiful. Spaces are large, as are the silences that fill them. For those who come here, an encounter with such emptiness can be as awesome as the sight of jagged peaks, pristine rivers and dusty backwater oases.

The paving of Ruta Nacional 40 (RN 40) is well under way, but it remains among the world's loneliest stretches, a spellbinding road to nowhere that has stirred affection in personalities as disparate as Butch Cassidy and Bruce Chatwin. On the eastern seaboard, RN 3 shoots south, connecting oil boomtowns with the remains of ancient petrified forests, Welsh settlements and the spectacular Península Valdés. The map will tell you that Patagonia is a very large place, but motoring its distant horizons offers a whole other level of insight.

Then there is the other, trendy Patagonia: the tourist hubs studded with Ray-Ban shops and reggae bars, where you will meet a dozen other travelers before one local. El Calafate and El Chaltén boast spectacular sights, but they remain a world apart from the mythical RN 40.

This chapter covers the region from its political start at the mouth of Río Negro, continuing through Chubut and Santa Cruz provinces south to the Strait of Magellan. Chile's Punta Arenas, Puerto Natales and Parque Nacional Torres del Paine are also included.

HIGHLIGHTS

- Gaze upon the blue-hued **Glaciar Perito Moreno** (p495) as icebergs crumble in thunderous booms
- Explore millennial forest in the eternal green of **Parque Nacional Los Alerces** (p473)
- Trek the toothy **Fitz Roy Range** (p483) near El Chaltén in the northern sector of Parque Nacional Los Glaciares
- See southern right whales up close in the waters of **Reserva Faunística Península Valdés** (p436)
- Ride the wide-open range and feast on fire-pit-roasted lamb at an **estancia** (p479)

Reserva Faunística Península Valdés

★ Parque Nacional Los Alerces

★ Estancias

★ Fitz Roy Range
★ Glaciar Perito Moreno

- POPULATION: 838,620
- AREA: 475,000 SQ KM

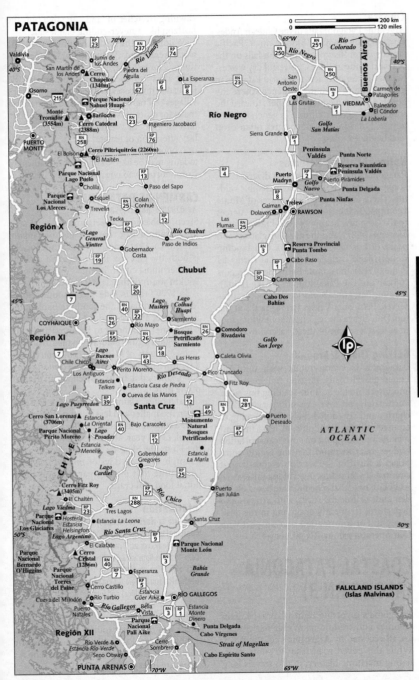

PATAGONIA

Climate

Argentine Patagonia sits in the Chilean Andes' rain shadow, which blocks most Pacific storms. After heavy precipitation falls on the seaward Andean slopes, powerful dry westerlies gust incessantly across the arid Patagonian plains. Due to oceanic influence where the South American continent tapers toward the south, the region's climate is generally temperate, but winter temperatures often drop well below freezing.

National Parks & Reserves

Patagonia's national parks boast diverse landscapes, immense solitude and incredible wildlife. There are the coastal treasures of Monte León (p460), the ancient forests of Los Alerces (p473), the raw beauty of little-known Perito Moreno (p481), and the dazzling glaciers and peaks of Los Glaciares (p483). Outstanding Chilean parks included here are the Torres del Paine (p512), the remote Bernardo O'Higgins (p512) and the Paleolithic Pali Aike (p507). Among Patagonia's world-class natural reserves, Península Valdés (p436) ranks at the top. Don't leave the region without setting foot in at least a couple of these natural wonders.

Getting There & Around

Patagonia is synonymous with unmaintained gravel roads, missing transport links and interminable bottom-scalding bus rides. Fortunately, an ever-expanding network of charter and scheduled flights is emerging to connect all the highlights, at least in summer. Before skimping on your transportation budget, bear in mind that the region comprises a third of the world's eighth-largest country. If you're bussing it along the eastern seaboard, note that schedules are based on the demands of Buenos Aires, with arrivals and departures frequently occurring in the dead of night. For information on transport with tour operators along RN 40, see p470.

COASTAL PATAGONIA (ALONG RN 3)

Patagonia's cavorting right whales, penguin colonies and traditional Welsh settlements are all accessed by Argentina's coastal RN 3. While this paved road takes in some fascinating maritime history, it also travels long yawning stretches of landscape that blur the horizon like a never-ending blank slate.

Wildlife enthusiasts shouldn't miss the world-renowned Península Valdés, the continent's largest Magellanic penguin colonies at Reserva Provincial Punta Tombo and Río Deseado's diverse seabird population. The quiet villages of Puerto San Julián and Camarones make for quiet seaside retreats, while Gaiman tells the story of Welsh settlement through a lazy afternoon of tea and cakes.

A booming petroleum industry means that lodging may be hard to find in the oil towns of Comodoro Rivadavia and Caleta Olivia.

CARMEN DE PATAGONES

☎ 02920 / pop 27,938

Steep cobblestone streets and colonial stylings breathe a little romance into this languid river town. Patagones, as it is known locally, is both the gateway into Patagonia and the southernmost city in Buenos Aires province, 950km south of the capital via RN 3.

In 1779 Francisco de Viedma founded the town of Viedma on the southern bank of the Río Negro, and a fort on the northern bank, which later expanded to became Patagones. The region's first colonists hailed from the Spanish county of Maragatería in León (to this day, townspeople are still called *maragatos*) and fashioned their first dwellings in the side of the hills.

Patagones' claim to fame came in 1827, when its smaller and less-equipped forces repelled superior invaders during the war with Brazil. Every year, at the beginning of March, the Fiesta del Siete de Marzo celebrates this triumph with ten days of *música folklórica* (Argentine folk music), parades and traditional food and crafts.

Information

Banco de la Nación (Paraguay 2) Has a 24-hour ATM.
Municipal tourist office (☎ 461777, ext 253; turismopatagones@speedy.com.ar; Bynon 186; ☻ 7am-7pm Mon-Fri, 10am-1pm & 6-9pm Sat & Sun Dec-Feb)
Post office (Paraguay 38)
Telefónica (cnr Olivera & Comodoro Rivadavia) *Locutorio* (private telephone office) and internet access.

Sights

Check out the eager tourist office for maps and brochures. Patagones has more historic buildings than most Patagonian towns and it's a pleasure to explore them on foot.

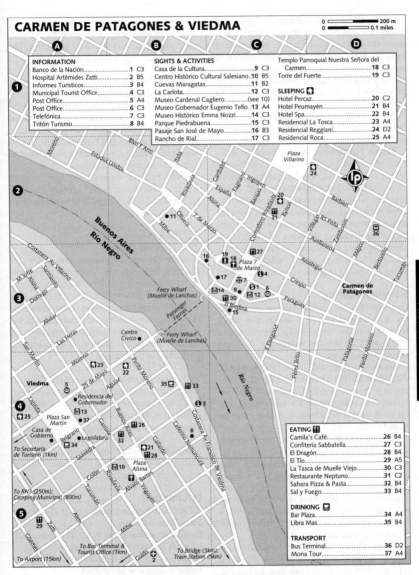

CARMEN DE PATAGONES & VIEDMA

| 0 | 200 m |
| 0 | 0.1 miles |

INFORMATION	
Banco de la Nación...................1 C3	
Hospital Artémides Zatti...............2 B5	
Informes Turisticos...................3 B4	
Municipal Tourist Office...............4 C3	
Post Office...........................5 A4	
Post Office...........................6 C3	
Telefónica...........................7 C3	
Tritón Turismo.......................8 B4	

SIGHTS & ACTIVITIES	
Casa de la Cultura...................9 C3	
Centro Histórico Cultural Salesiano..10 B5	
Cuevas Maragatas...................11 B2	
La Carlota..........................12 C3	
Museo Cardenal Cagliero..........(see 10)	
Museo Gobernador Eugenio Tello...13 A4	
Museo Histórico Emma Nozzi.......14 C3	
Parque Piedrabuena.................15 C3	
Pasaje San José de Mayo.............16 B3	
Rancho de Rial......................17 C3	

Templo Parroquial Nuestra Señora del Carmen.............................18 C3	
Torre del Fuerte....................19 C3	

SLEEPING	
Hotel Percaz........................20 C2	
Hotel Peumayén.....................21 B4	
Hotel Spa...........................22 B4	
Residencial La Tosca.................23 A4	
Residencial Reggiani.................24 D2	
Residencial Roca....................25 A4	

EATING	
Camila's Café.......................26 B4	
Confitería Sabbatella................27 C3	
El Dragón..........................28 B4	
El Tío..............................29 A5	
La Tasca de Muelle Viejo.............30 C3	
Restaurante Neptuno................31 C2	
Sahara Pizza & Pasta................32 B4	
Sal y Fuego........................33 B4	

DRINKING	
Bar Plaza..........................34 A4	
Libra Mas..........................35 B4	

TRANSPORT	
Bus Terminal.......................36 D2	
Mona Tour.........................37 A4	

Begin at **Plaza 7 de Marzo**; its original name, Plaza del Carmen, was changed after the 1827 victory over the Brazilians. Salesians built the **Templo Parroquial Nuestra Señora del Carmen** in 1883. Its image of the Virgin, dating from 1780, is southern Argentina's oldest, and two of the original seven Brazilian flags captured in 1827 are on the altar. Just west of the church,

Torre del Fuerte is the last vestige of the 1780 fort that once occupied the entire block.

Below the tower twin cannons, once used to guard the Patagonian frontier, flank the 1960s **Pasaje San José de Mayo** staircase leading to the riverside. At the base of the steps, the **Rancho de Rial** (Mitre 94) is an 1820 adobe that belonged to the town's first elected mayor. Three blocks west, the **Cuevas Maragatas** (Maragatas Caves; Rivadavia s/n), excavated in the riverbank, sheltered the first Spanish families who arrived in 1779. Return to the base of the stairs and walk two blocks east, where the early-19th-century **Casa de la Cultura** (Mitre 27) was the site of a *tahona* (flour mill). Across the street, **La Carlota** (cnr Bynon & Mitre) is a former private residence (c 1800) decorated with typical 19th-century furnishings; ask about guided tours at the museum.

Parque Piedrabuena has a bust of Luis Piedrabuena, the naval officer responsible for saving countless shipwrecked sailors. A block west, the **Museo Histórico Emma Nozzi** (☎ 462729; admission AR$1.50; ☺ 10am-noon & 2:30-4:30pm Mon-Fri, 5-7pm Sat) houses an impressive collection of artifacts from Argentina's southern frontier, including details on the town's former black slave population. Along the river are recreational *balnearios* (river beaches), popular spots for swimming and picnics in summer.

Sleeping & Eating

Options for accommodations are better in Viedma, but it is worth the short ferry ride across the river for a meal and a stroll on Carmen de Patagones' historic colonial waterfront.

Residencial Reggiani (☎ 461384; Bynon 422; s/d/tr AR$45/85/110) This rambling 20-room home is favored for its friendliness and location. The rooms with TV are warm but a bit dark and stale. There is also a recently added restaurant.

Hotel Percaz (☎ 464104; cnr Comodoro Rivadavia & Irigoyen; s/d/tr with breakfast AR$70/115/170) Kudos go to the staff at this old-fashioned hotel, who even help travelers find lodging when theirs is full. The clean, carpeted, no-frills rooms can be cramped, but there is central heating, twice-daily housekeeping service and wireless internet. Food at the 24-hour *confitería* (café offering light meals) is good.

Confitería Sabbatella (Comodoro Rivadavia 218; mains AR$15; ☺ to 2am) Locals linger at Sabbatella for a shot of coffee and simple café fare. Its billiard table is the best place to hustle pool sharks.

Restaurante Neptuno (Comodoro Rivadavia 310; mains AR$15-28; ☺ 7pm-late) When locals want options they head to this old-fashioned dining room, where the offerings range from tortillas and pizza to well-prepared meat dishes.

La Tasca de Muelle Viejo (JJ Biedma 30; mains AR$22; ☺ dinner only) Whipping up tasty empanadas

and traditional dishes like *puchero,* a hearty stew thick with veggies, this bohemian riverside café overflows with warm ambience. The owner's paintings adorn the walls.

Getting There & Around

Most travelers make bus, train and plane connections in Viedma. But most northbound buses also stop at Patagones' **bus terminal** (☎ 462666; cnr Barbieri & Méjico), with plenty of service to Bahía Blanca and Buenos Aires. Tickets for Tren Patagónico (Viedma to Bariloche) can be purchased at the bus terminal.

Two bridges connect Patagones with Viedma. The *balsa* (ferry) crosses the river to Viedma (AR$1) every few minutes, from 6:30am to 10pm.

VIEDMA
☎ 02920 / pop 80,000

Sharing the lush Río Negro with sister city Carmen de Patagones, Viedma, as the capital of Río Negro province, is comparatively bustling and prosperous. For travelers, it is a less-picturesque but more convenient base than next door, with a greater number of services and amenities. Social gatherings center on the riverfront, with upscale cafés and a jogging path close to downtown.

In 1779 Francisco de Viedma put ashore to found the city after his men started dying of fever and lack of water at Península Valdés. In 1879 it became the residence of the governor of Patagonia and the political locus of the country's enormous southern territory. A century later, the radical Alfonsín administration proposed moving the federal capital here from Buenos Aires but was crushingly defeated.

Information

ATMs and internet cafés are in the center along Buenos Aires.

Hospital Artémides Zatti (☎ 422333; Rivadavia 351)

Informes Turísticos (☎ 427171; www.viedma.gov.ar in Spanish; Av Francisco de Viedma 51) Offers local and regional information on the waterfront.

Post office (cnr 25 de Mayo & San Martín)

Secretaría de Turismo (☎ 422150; www.rionegrotur .com.ar; Caseros 1425) Located 15 blocks southwest of the plaza, with brochures for the entire province.

Tourist office (☎ 427171; bus terminal) Offers lodging and transportation details.

Tritón Turismo (☎ 431131; Ceferino Namuncurá 78) Changes traveler's checks, rents cars and runs tours.

Sights & Activities

Summer activities include **kayaking** on the Río Negro and weekend **catamaran rides** (AR$10). Ask individual launch operators at the pier about kayak rentals and river cruises.

The season for **sport fishing** on the Río Negro runs from November to early July, with rainbow trout (catch and release), silverside and carp. For information and licenses, consult Informes Turisticos, the Direccion de Pesca de Río Negro (☎ 420326) or fishing guides Eduardo Urriza (☎ 02920-15-626719) and Constantino Mikitiuk (☎ 426328).

In addition to exhibits on European settlement, the **Museo Gobernador Eugenio Tello** (☎ 425900; San Martín 263; admission free; ☼ 9am-1pm & 5:30-8pm Mon-Fri, 10am-12:30pm & 5-7pm Sat) displays Tehuelche tools, artifacts, deformed skulls and skeletons.

The Salesian **Museo Cardenal Cagliero** (☎ 424190; Rivadavia 34; admission free; ☼ 7am-1:30pm Mon-Fri) features incredible ceiling paintings and a neat fish-vertebrae cane (check out the cardinal's office). It is housed in the **Centro Histórico Cultural Salesiano**, the former Vicariato de la Patagonia, a massive 1890 brick structure on the corner of Colón.

The tourist offices and Tritón Turismo organize tours of nearby attractions, including fishing trips and visits to El Cóndor parrot colony.

Festivals & Events

In mid-January, the weeklong **Regata del Río Negro** (www.regatadelrionegro.com.ar) features the world's longest kayak race, a 500km paddle from Neuquén to Viedma.

Sleeping

Camping Municipal (☎ 421341; RN 3 riverside at Río Negro; per person AR$4; ☼ Nov-Mar) This shady riverside campground, 10 blocks west of RN 3, offers drab gravel sites and hot showers. Arrive via taxi (AR$5) or the Comarca bus from downtown.

Hotel Spa (☎ 430459; spaiturburu@rnonline.com.ar; 25 de Mayo 174; s/d/tr with breakfast AR$55/90/120; 🐾) Given the name, you might expect more glamour. Nonetheless, this hotel with small, average rooms and hardwood floors is popular. Ask about fees for hot and dry saunas, or sneak a spin on the treadmill in the hallway.

Residencial Roca (☎ 431241; residencialtosca@hotmail.com; Roca 347; s/d/tr AR$68/105/145; 🐾) The family-friendly Roca is a throwback to another time, but rooms are cavernous and desk attention is good. Rooms have delirious wallpaper designs and old TVs. Breakfast costs AR$7 extra.

Residencial La Tosca (☎ 428508; residencialtosca@hotmail.com; Alsina 349; s/d/tr AR$89/130/175) This elegant brick building with an old-fashioned lobby has an air of retirement home about it. Still, the rooms are large and snug, with carpeted walls and TVs. Basketball matches in the next-door gym mean some noisy evenings.

Hotel Peumayén (☎ 425222/234; Buenos Aires 334; s/d/tr AR$89/130/190; ⌨) This old business hotel is dated but well kept, with mint-green walls and carpeted rooms. Each floor has a small kitchen for *mate* (a tealike beverage) breaks. Your best bet is a 4th-floor room or those overlooking the plaza.

Eating & Drinking

Camila's Café (cnr Saavedra & Buenos Aires; snacks AR$8; ☼ breakfast, lunch & dinner; ⌨) A pleasant, homey atmosphere best for breakfast, which branches out from *medialunas* (croissants) with fruit and egg plates. Popular for coffee, sandwiches or drinks.

Bar Plaza (☎ 428842; cnr Belgrano & Tucumán; snacks AR$9; ☼ closed Sun) Probe Viedma's soul by eavesdropping on *ñoquis* (meaning literally gnocchis or government employees) quibbling about the economy over coffee and cigarettes. Look for live blues and tango on weekend evenings.

El Tío (cnr Zatti & Colón; mains AR$9-15; ☼ 8:30pm-midnight, closed Mon) Don't hit the Tío in a rush. This hole-in-the-wall hangout is the perfect place to split a big bottle of beer and indulge in slow-cooked *parrilla* (mixed grill) – steaks, sausages and innards – tended by the owner himself.

Libra Mas (☎ 427181; Costanero Av Villarino 110; sandwiches AR$10; ☼ 9am-3am) Settle into a sleek white leather armchair at this modern café-pub, perfect for sharing a *tabla* (cutting board with meat and cheeses) or fried calamari with drinks. It is the newest addition to the riverfront scene.

El Dragón (☎ 430691; Buenos Aires 366; buffet AR$14; ☼ noon-3pm & 8:30-11:30pm) This palatable all-you-can eat buffet is as authentic as Patagonian-Chinese gets, with staff playing mah-jongg at spare tables in their off-hours. Meals are a bargain but drinks can be spendy.

Sal y Fuego (☎ 431259; Costanero Av Villarino; mains AR$28) This hip riverfront hangout offers classic Argentine dishes with a few surprises (like chicken in sweet-and-sour plum sauce or fresh coleslaw). In good weather you can sit outside.

Sahara Pizza & Pasta (☎ 421530; Saavedra 336; pizzas AR$30) Pizzas go upscale at this white-linen pizzeria that also serves quality pastas. Try the pineapple and Serrano ham pizza.

Getting There & Around
AIR
Aeropuerto Gobernador Castello (VDM; ☎ 422001) is 15km southwest of town on RP 51; a taxi to the center costs AR$8. **Aerolíneas Argentinas** (☎ 423033) flies three times a week to Buenos Aires (AR$484). **LADE** (☎ 424420) lands here en route to Trelew (AR$158), Mar del Plata (AR$175), Comodoro Rivadavia (AR$192) and Buenos Aires (AR$243).

BOAT
From the pier at the foot of 25 de Mayo, a frequent ferry service (AR$1) connects Viedma and Carmen de Patagones from 6:30am until 10pm.

BUS
Viedma's **bus terminal** (☎ 426850) is 13 blocks southwest of the plaza, a 20-minute walk.

To Puerto Madryn, **Don Otto** (☎ 425952) and **El Cóndor** (☎ 423714) offer the best service. To Bariloche, **3 de Mayo** (☎ 425839) goes via RN 23, while **El Valle** (☎ 427501) takes longer via RN 22 and RP 6.

For Balneario El Cóndor (AR$3, half hour) and La Lobería (AR$5, one hour), **Ceferino** (☎ 426691) leaves from Plaza Alsina six times daily in summer.

Destination	Cost (AR$)	Duration (hr)
Bahía Blanca	25	3
Bariloche	110-150	14-15
Buenos Aires	80-150	13
Comodoro Rivadavia	121-144	10-13
Las Grutas	20	2½
Puerto Madryn	61-73	5-6
Trelew	69-81	8

TRAIN
Among the last of Argentina's great long-distance trains, **Tren Patagónico** (☎ 422130; www .trenpatagonico.com.ar in Spanish) offers service replete with dining and cinema cars. It crosses the plains to Bariloche (economy/1st class/Pullman/bed AR$40/53/93/160, 17 hours)

Mondays and Fridays at 6pm; children five to 12 pay half. Trains depart from the station on the southeast outskirts of town. Check the website for the current schedule, which changes often.

Tickets can also be purchased at **Mona Tour** (☎ 422933; info@monatur.com.ar; San Martin 225)

COASTAL RÍO NEGRO
La Ruta de los Acantilados occupies a beautiful stretch along Río Negro's 400km Atlantic coastline. Repeated wave action has worn the ancient cliff faces (three to 13 million years old) to reveal a wealth of fossils. While the area teems with activity in the summer, it shuts down off-season.

Balneario El Cóndor, a resort 31km southeast of Viedma at the mouth of the Río Negro, has what's considered the largest parrot colony in the world, with 35,000 nests of burrowing parrots in its cliff faces. Don't miss the century-old lighthouse, Patagonia's oldest. Lodging options include **Hospedaje Río de los Sauces** (☎ 02920-497193; Calle 20 bis; d with breakfast AR$100) and the RV-friendly **Camping Ina Lauquen** (☎ 02920-497218; cnr Calle 87 & Costanera; per person AR$7; 🖳), with grills, picnic tables, fast food and even internet.

There's a permanent southern sea lion colony at **La Lobería** (Reserva Faunística de Punta Bermeja), 60km from Viedma via RP 1, on the north coast of Golfo San Matías. The population peaks during the spring mating season, when males come ashore to fight other males and establish harems of up to 10 females. The females give birth from December onward. Visitors will find the observation balcony, directly above the mating beaches, safe and unobtrusive. Buses from Viedma pass within 3km of the colony.

At the northwest edge of Golfo San Matías, 179km west of Viedma along RN 3, the crowded resort of **Las Grutas** (The Grottos; www .balneariolasgrutas.com in Spanish) owes its name to its eroded sea caves. Thanks to an exceptional tidal range, the beaches can expand for hundreds of meters or shrink to just a few. The **tourist office** (☎ 02934-497470; Galería Antares, Primera Bajada) has tide schedules. Buses leave hourly to San Antonio Oeste, 16km northeast, with more lodging.

Besides free meals for bus drivers, **Sierra Grande**, 125km south of Las Grutas, only has one thing going for it: gasoline at subsidized *precios patagónicos* (Patagonian prices). Given that, most everyone fills up their tank, grabs an uninspired snack and carries on.

PUERTO MADRYN
☎ 02965 / pop 57,791

This sheltered port facing Golfo Nuevo is best known as the gateway to the wildlife sanctuary of Península Valdés. Fast-growing with tourism and industry, it does retain a few small-town touches: the radio announces lost dogs and locals are welcoming and unhurried. Madryn holds its own as a modest beach destination, but from June to mid-December visiting right whales take center stage. From July to September the whales are so close they can be viewed without even taking a tour, from the coast 20km north of town or the 500m pier in town.

Founded by Welsh settlers in 1886, the town takes its name from Love Parry, Baron of Madryn. Statues along the *costanera* (seaside road) pay tribute to the Welsh: one to the role women have played, and the other, at the south end of town, to the Tehuelche, who helped the Welsh immigrants survive. Madryn's campus of the Universidad de la Patagonia is known for its marine biology department, and ecological centers promote conservation and education. The city is the second-largest fishing port in the country and home to Aluar, Argentina's first aluminum plant, built in 1974.

Orientation

Puerto Madryn is just east of RN 3, 1371km south of Buenos Aires, 439km north of Comodoro Rivadavia and 65km north of Trelew. The action centers along the *costanera* and two main parallel avenues, Av Roca and 25 de Mayo. Bulevar Brown is the main drag alongside the beaches to the south.

Information

Call centers and internet cafés abound in the center. Some travel agencies accept traveler's checks as payment for tours.

Banco de la Nación (9 de Julio 117) Has ATM and changes traveler's checks.

Burbuja's (☎ 472217; Gobernador Maíz 440; ☽ closed Sun) Full- or self-service laundry.

Dirección de Cultura (Av Roca 444; showers AR$1.50) Showers available downstairs, beneath the Museo de Arte Moderno.

Hospital Subzonal (☎ 451999; R Gómez 383)

Post office (cnr Belgrano & Gobernador Maíz)

Presto-lav (☎ 451526; Blvd Brown 605) Laundry pickup and delivery available.

Recreo (cnr 28 de Julio & Av Roca) Stocks a good selection of regional books, maps and a few English-language novels and guidebooks. There is another branch on the corner of 25 de Mayo and Roque Sáenz Peña.

Telefónica (cnr Av Roca & 9 de Julio; ☽ 8am-midnight) Big call center with internet access.

Thaler Cambio (☎ 455858; Av Roca 493; ☽ 9:30am-1pm & 6-8pm Mon-Fri, 10am-1pm & 7-9pm Sat & Sun) Poorer rates for traveler's checks.

Tourist office (☎ 453504, 456067; www.madryn .gov.ar/turismo in Spanish; Av Roca 223; ☽ 7am-10pm Mon-Fri, 8am-11pm Sat & Sun Dec-Feb, reduced hours off-season) Helpful and efficient staff, and there's usually an English or French speaker on duty. Check the *libro de reclamos* (complaint book) for traveler tips. There's another helpful desk at the bus terminal.

Sights
ECOCENTRO

Celebrating the area's marine treasures, **Ecocentro** (☎ 457470; www.ecocentro.org.ar in Spanish; J Verne 3784; adult/concession AR$21/5; ☽ 10am-6pm Tue-Sun) is a masterpiece of interactive displays that combine artistic sensitivity with extensive scientific research. Exhibits explore the area's unique marine ecosystem, the breeding habits of right whales, dolphin sounds, stories of southern elephant-seal harems, a touch-friendly tide pool and more. Grab an English-language guide to the exhibits at the front desk. The building itself is equally impressive. The three-story tower acts as a library, with the top story, all glass and comfy couches, a great place to read, write or contemplate the fragile ocean community. Whales may be spotted from here.

It's an enjoyable 40-minute walk or 15-minute bike ride along the *costanera* to the Ecocentro. Shuttles run three times daily from the tourist office on Av Roca, or you can catch a Línea 2 bus to the last stop (La Universidad) and walk 1km.

MUSEO PROVINCIAL DE CIENCIAS NATURALES Y OCEANOGRÁFICO

Feeling up strands of seaweed and ogling preserved octopus are part of the hands-on approach of this **museum** (☎ 451139; cnr Domecq García & Menéndez; admission AR$6; ☽ 9am-1pm & 3-7pm Mon-Fri, 3-7pm Sat & Sun) in the 1917 Chalet Pujol. A winding staircase leads into nine small rooms of marine and land mammal exhibits and preserved specimens, plus collections of Welsh wares. The explanations are in Spanish and

PATAGONIA

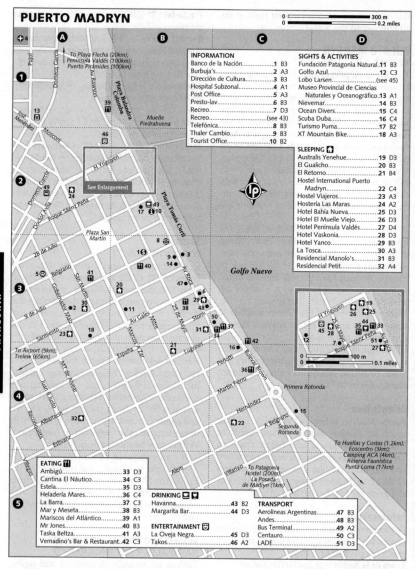

PUERTO MADRYN

0 — 300 m
0 — 0.2 miles

INFORMATION	
Banco de la Nación	1 B3
Burbuja's	2 A3
Dirección de Cultura	3 B3
Hospital Subzonal	4 A1
Post Office	5 A3
Presto-lav	6 B3
Recreo	7 D3
Recreo	(see 43)
Telefónica	8 B3
Thaler Cambio	9 B3
Tourist Office	10 B2

SIGHTS & ACTIVITIES	
Fundación Patagonia Natural	11 B3
Golfo Azul	12 C3
Lobo Larsen	(see 45)
Museo Provincial de Ciencias	
Naturales y Oceanográfico	13 A1
Nievemar	14 B3
Ocean Divers	15 C4
Scuba Duba	16 C4
Turismo Puma	17 B2
XT Mountain Bike	18 A3

SLEEPING	
Australis Yenehue	19 D3
El Gualicho	20 B3
El Retorno	21 B4
Hostel International Puerto	
Madryn	22 C4
Hostel Viajeros	23 A3
Hostería Las Maras	24 A2
Hotel Bahía Nueva	25 D3
Hotel El Muelle Viejo	26 D3
Hotel Península Valdés	27 D4
Hotel Vaskonia	28 D3
Hotel Yanco	29 B3
La Tosca	30 A3
Residencial Manolo's	31 B3
Residencial Petit	32 A4

EATING	
Ambigú	33 D3
Cantina El Náutico	34 C3
Estela	35 D3
Heladería Mares	36 C4
La Barra	37 C3
Mar y Meseta	38 B3
Mariscos del Atlántico	39 A1
Mr Jones	40 B3
Taska Beltza	41 A3
Vernadino's Bar & Restaurant	42 C3

DRINKING	
Havanna	43 B2
Margarita Bar	44 D3

ENTERTAINMENT	
La Oveja Negra	45 D3
Takos	46 A2

TRANSPORT	
Aerolíneas Argentinas	47 B3
Andes	48 B3
Bus Terminal	49 A2
Centauro	50 C3
LADE	51 D3

geared to youth science classes, but it's visually informative and creatively presented. Twist up to the cupola for views of the port.

FUNDACIÓN PATAGONIA NATURAL

This well-run nongovernmental **organization** (☎ 451920; www.patagonianatural.org in Spanish; Marcos A Zar 760; ⏱ 9am-4pm Mon-Fri) promotes conservation and monitors environmental issues in Patagonia. In a converted house, volunteers diligently nurse injured birds and marine mammals back to health. The friendly staff is happy to answer questions about coastal areas in the region.

Activities

DIVING

With interesting shipwrecks and sea life nearby, Madryn and the Península Valdés have become Argentina's diving capitals. **Lobo Larsen** (☎ 02965-15-516314, 15-681004; www.lobolarsen.com; H Yrigoyen 144) and **Scuba Duba** (☎ 452699; www.scubaduba.com.ar in Spanish; Blvd Brown 893) are both quality PADI-affiliated operators. **Golfo Azul** (☎ 471649; www.pinosub.com in Spanish; H Yrigoyen 200) sells equipment. Most of the *balnearios* also have operators offering diving, including **Ocean Divers** (☎ 472569, 02965-15-660865; www.oceandivers.com.ar in Spanish; Balneario Yoaquina). Dives start at around AR$120; some agencies also offer courses, night dives and multiday excursions.

WINDSURFING & KAYAKING

In high season, a hut next to **Vernadino's** (Blvd Brown 860) offers lessons and rents out regular and wide boards and kayaks by the hour. South of Muelle Piedrabuena, **Playa Tomás Curti** is a popular windsurfing spot.

BIKING & HIKING

XT Mountain Bike (☎ 472232; Av Gales btwn Gobernador Maiz & San Martín) rents beach cruisers and mountain bikes (AR$30 per day) in good shape. Several other outfits along Av Roca advertise rentals and guided tours; inspect the gears before heading out on a long ride. Guide service **Huellas y Costas** (☎ 02965-15-680515; www.huellasycostas.com; Blvd Brown 1900) offers coastal hiking, mountain biking, kayaking and camping adventures in small groups with bilingual guides.

Tours

Countless agencies sell tours to Península Valdés (p436), costing from AR$90 to AR$150 (not including the AR$40 park admission fee or whale watching, which ranges from AR$75 to AR$150). Most hotels and hostels also offer tours; it's always best to get recommendations from fellow travelers before choosing. Ask how large the bus was, if it came with an English-speaking guide, where they ate and what they saw where – different tour companies often visit different locations. Remember to take water, as it's a long drive to the reserve.

Those most interested in wildlife should bring binoculars and may find it more enjoyable to stay overnight in Puerto Pirámides (p437). Tours to Punta Tombo (p448) from Puerto Madryn cost about the same as those offered from Trelew (p444), but they require a couple of hours extra driving time and thus less time with the penguins.

Recommended tour companies:

Nievemar (☎ 455544; www.nievemartours.com.ar in Spanish; Av Roca 493) Amex representative. Excursions include whale watching and visits to sea lion colonies and the petrified forest.

Turismo Puma (☎ 471482; www.turismopuma.com in Spanish; 28 de Julio 46) Small groups, nature walks and excursions incorporating whale watching.

Sleeping

Reserve ahead, especially if you want a double room. If you are caught short, check with the tourist office, which posts a comprehensive lodging list with prices that include nearby *estancias* (ranches) and rental apartments (double occupancy from AR$100 per day). Budget rates don't generally include breakfast, and midrange accommodations charge solo travelers the double rate in high season. High-season rates (given here) apply from mid-October through March.

BUDGET

All hostels have kitchens and offer pickup from the bus terminal, but most are a short, flat walk away.

Camping ACA (☎ 452952; Camino al Indio; s/d occupancy AR$21/26; closed May-Aug) These 800 gravel sites are sheltered by trees to break the incessant wind. Although there are no cooking facilities, a limited selection of snacks (and sometimes prepared meals) is available. From downtown, city bus 2 goes within 500m of the campground; get off at the last stop, called 'La Universidad.'

our pick **La Tosca** (☎ 456133; www.latoscahostel.com; Sarmiento 437; dm AR$30, d AR$85-95) A cozy guesthouse where the owners greet you by name, La Tosca is the creation of a well-traveled couple. Although dorm beds are short, they sport good mattresses and convenient shelves. Perks include a grassy courtyard, bike rentals and the option of dinner (AR$25) featuring healthy mains, fresh veggies and dessert. It is now open year-round.

El Retorno (☎ 456044; www.elretornohostel.com.ar; Mitre 798; dm/d AR$32/120) This spotless refurbished home feels cozy and familiar – travelers will recognize Gladys, the host, as an eager den mother. Dorms have lockers and some have en suite bathrooms. Extras include an upstairs

PATAGONIA

solarium, barbecue area, laundry, bike rental and table tennis.

El Gualicho (☎ 454163; www.elgualicho.com.ar in Spanish; Marcos A Zar 480; dm/d AR$35/130; 💻) Boasting a hip and highly attentive staff, this hostel has nice dorms with wood-frame bunks. Ample shared spaces, including an interior patio and comfy living and dining areas, further the appeal. Some doubles share a bathroom.

Hostel Viajeros (☎ 456457; www.hostelviajeros.com; Gobernador Maíz 545; dm/d AR$35/120; 💻) Consider it a practical option: these plain, no-nonsense rooms have TVs and bathrooms, though doubles are scrunched in. Benefits include a large *quincha* (cabaña) with dining area and barbecue, plus free pickup from the bus terminal.

Patagonia Hostel (☎ 450155; www.hipatagonia.com in Spanish; Av Roca 1040; dm/d AR$40/130) Guests are easily at ease in this cool and cozy suburban-style home, the newest hostel in Madryn. It's a bit off the grid, but host Gaston goes the extra mile to help travelers, and the ambience of the grassy yard and well-cared-for shared spaces is inviting.

Residencial Manolo's (☎ 472390; manolos@speedy .com.ar; Av Roca 763; d/tr AR$45/60) The secret is out on this yellow house surrounded by high-rises; it's nearly always full. Inveterate bargain hunters should bring the phrasebook and try out their '*vos*' – English speakers are quoted higher rates.

MIDRANGE

Hotel Vaskonia (☎ 472581; buce23@infovia.com.ar; 25 de Mayo 43; s/d/tr AR$60/80/100) Style fatigue besets this longtime lodging with satin bedcovers and mismatched tiles. But it is super clean and central.

Hostería Las Maras (☎ 453215; www.hosterialas maras.com.ar; Marcos A Zar 64; s/d/tr standard with breakfast AR$63/74/88, superior AR$80/90/105; 💻) Brick walls, exposed beams and wicker furniture craft an intimate setting ideal for couples. Standards are bright and prim, but the space is tight. Superior rooms boast king-sized beds, flat-screen TVs and stylish design elements. All rooms have cable TV.

Residencial Petit (☎ 451460; hotelpetit@arnet.com .ar; MT de Alvear 845; d AR$110) These immaculate whitewashed motel rooms seem straight out of Florida. The management is attentive and rooms are furnished with desks and ceiling fans. Though it's more than a 10-minute walk to the *costanera*, drivers will appreciate the roomside parking.

Hotel El Muelle Viejo (☎ 471284; www.muelleviejo .com in Spanish; H Yrigoyen 38; s/d/tr AR$105/125/145) A pleasant couple have this older hotel ship-shape, with crisp linen curtains, plump beds and pale wood furniture. Rooms have bathtubs and cable TV. In high season they require a three-night stay for reservations and don't offer single rates. Superior rooms run AR$20 extra.

Hotel Yanco (☎ 471581; hotelyanco@hotmail.com; Av Roca 626; s/d/tr AR$110/130/168) This old-style charmer has an ancient switchboard and tidy rooms that don't look much newer. Showers have low separations so watch for overflow. Rooms facing the *avenida* are noisy, while whales have been spotted from those facing the ocean.

Hostel International Puerto Madryn (☎ 474426; http://usuarios.advance.com.ar/hi-pm; 25 de Mayo 1136; d/tr/apt AR$120/150/200; 🕙 closed May-Sep) While most lodging in town is bustling, this property remains quiet. On spacious grounds in a residential neighborhood, this former hostel has been converted to large private rooms with bathrooms. Guests get shared kitchen access and bus terminal pickups.

Hotel Península Valdés (☎ 471292; www.hotelpenin sula.com.ar; Av Roca 155; d with/without view AR$172/152; ❌ 💻) Ample rooms have comfy quilted bedding, temperature controls, piped-in music and cable TV. This high-rise caters to tour groups with a spa, massage and beauty parlor and ocean views – request a room above the tree line.

TOP END

La Posada de Madryn (☎ 474087; www.la-posada.com .ar; Mathews 2951; s/d AR$198/232; 💻) This modern inn amid rolling green lawns offers a quiet alternative to lodging in town. Its prim rooms with bright accents have heating controls and cable TV. It's in a residential neighborhood – catch a taxi from the center.

Hotel Bahía Nueva (☎ 450045/145; www.bahianueva .com.ar; Av Roca 67; s/d with breakfast AR$320/405; 💻) Stretching to resemble an English countryside retreat, Bahía Nueva distinguishes itself with a foyer library and flouncy touches. Its 40 rooms are well groomed, but only a few have ocean views. Highlights include a bar with billiards and a TV (mostly to view movies and documentaries), and tour information. The breakfast buffet offers fresh regional pastries. Non-Argentines booking ahead may be quoted higher rates.

Australis Yenehue (☎ 471496; Av Roca 33; www.austral iset.com.ar; s/d with view AR$678/754) A stylish new addition, this towering hotel-spa offers great sea views and a comfortable glassed-in 2nd-floor lounge. However, service can be sluggish and the pricing excessive for what's on offer.

Eating & Drinking

Havanna (☎ 473373; cnr Av Roca & 28 de Julio; snacks AR$6-12; 🖳) This smart, smoky café can cure your energy slump with sugar-bomb *alfajores* (cookie sandwiches) and specialty coffees.

Heladería Mares (☎ 470705; Martin Fierro 85; ice cream AR$9; 🕙 10am-midnight) Doing a brisk business in creamy *helados* (ice creams), this excellent beachfront parlor also offers delivery. Unless you're thirsty, avoid the beer flavor.

Margarita Bar (☎ 475871; www.margaritapub.com in Spanish; cnr Av Roca & Roque Sáenz Peña; set lunch AR$19; 🕙 11am-4am) With a trendy edge, this low-lit brick haunt has a laundry list of cocktails, a friendly bar staff and live music (such as jazz, bossa nova or drumming) on Wednesdays. The set lunches are healthy and good value.

Cantina El Náutico (☎ 471404; Av Roca 790; lunch special AR$25) This popular nook (see the photos of Argentine celebs) offers old-fashioned ambience, from the polished bar to the white linens. Lunch specials offer the best deals; drinks are expensive.

Estela (☎ 451573; Roque Sáenz Peña 27; mains AR$25-40; 🕙 noon-2:30pm & 8pm-midnight, closed Mon) The sweet smell of garlic sautéeing in the kitchen will stop you in your tracks if you're outside. Billed as the town's best *parrilla* (steak restaurant), Estela also does nice pastas in an intimate, unpretentious setting often packed with locals.

our pick **Mr Jones** (☎ 475368; 9 de Julio 116; mains AR$28; 🕙 dinner) With a wealth of yummy stouts and reds, homemade pot pie and sausages, Mr Jones will satiate your appetite for all things German. The food is good and reasonably authentic; the pub atmosphere of wooden booths and crowded passages proves fun.

Mariscos del Atlántico (☎ 02965-15-552500; Av Rawson 288; mains AR$28-40) You might expect a bit more from the only seafood restaurant in town stocked by artisan fisherman, but there is good local ambience. It is hidden behind Club Nautico, 20m past the arches and upstairs.

Vernadino's Bar & Restaurant (☎ 473715; Blvd Brown 860; set menu AR$35; 🕙 breakfast, lunch & dinner) With unbeatable beachfront atmosphere, Vernadino's white-linen tables are a hot spot for drinks and dinner. Tempura vegetables and wok dishes are some of the savory offerings. There's patio seating too.

Mar y Meseta (☎ 458740; Av Gales 32; mains AR$35) Colorful and cozy, this elegant seafood restaurant dishes up clever creations for a handful of tables. The service is good, although the food is not always spot-on. Reserve ahead to guarantee a table.

Ambigú (☎ 472451; cnr Av Roca & Roque Sáenz Peña; mains AR$40) With a focus on fresh ingredients and creative combinations, Ambigú masters a gamut of dishes, including seafood – try the *langostinos* (prawns) in sea salt – and pizza. The setting is an elegant renovation of a historic bank building, backlit by warm colors.

La Barra (☎ 454279; Blvd Brown 779; mains AR$40) Fashionable but somewhat overpriced, La Barra feels like a date destination offering fussy service and a wide selection, including *parrilla*, thin-crust pizzas and heaping salad bowls.

Taska Beltza (☎ 02965-15-668085; 9 de Julio 345; mains AR$50; 🕙 closed Mon, dinner only Tue) For a big night out, try the Basque cooking of Chef Negro, who expertly steams fish and crafts tasty pastas. Portions are small, leaving room for homemade banana ice cream drizzled with dark chocolate and *dulce de leche* (milk caramel). Reservations are advised.

Entertainment

Bars and dance clubs come and go, so ask locals what's *de moda* (in) for the moment.

Takos (☎ 02965-15-401665; P Escardo 171) With a hearty dose of *rock nacional* (Argentine rock) and pool tables, this hotspot offers a casual atmosphere for the twenty-something crowd.

La Oveja Negra (H Yrigoyen 144) This intimate bar is decked in burlap and revolutionary paraphernalia – long live rock and folk, which keep the crowds bubbling over at this fun bar. It also serves hearty pub grub.

Getting There & Away

Due to limited connections, it pays to book in advance, especially for travel to the Andes.

AIR

Though Puerto Madryn has its own modern airport, most commercial flights still arrive in Trelew (see p445), 65km south.

Aeropuerto El Tehuelche (PMY; ☎ 456774) is 5km west of town, at the junction with RN 3. From here, **LADE** (☎ 451256; Av Roca 119) puddle

PATAGONIA

jumps to Esquel (AR$181), El Calafate (AR$374), Río Gallegos (AR$371), Buenos Aires (AR$258), Río Grande (AR$400) and Ushuaia (AR$427).

Newcomer **Andes** (☎ 452355; www.andesonline .com; Av Roca 624) flies to Buenos Aires' Aeroparque (AR$665) three times a week. **Aerolíneas Argentinas** (☎ 451998; Av Roca 427) flies only to nearby Trelew – but it does have a ticketing representative here.

BUS
Puerto Madryn's full-service **bus terminal** (☎ 451789; Doctor Avila, btwn Independencia & Necochea), behind the historic 1889 Estación del Ferrocarril Patagónico, has an ATM and a helpful tourist information desk.

Bus companies include **Andesmar/Central Argentino** (☎ 473764), **Don Otto** (☎ 451675), **28 de Julio** (☎ 472056), **Mar y Valle** (☎ 472056), **Que Bus** (☎ 455805), **Ruta Patagonia** (☎ 454572), **TAC** (☎ 474938) and **TUS** (☎ 451962).

The bus to Puerto Pirámides leaves at 9:30am and returns to Madryn at 6:30pm.

Destination	Cost (AR$)	Duration (hr)
Bariloche	120-162	14-15
Buenos Aires	182-208	18-20
Comodoro Rivadavia	59-88	6-8
Córdoba	160	18
Esquel	88-118	7-9
Mendoza	163-224	23-24
Neuquén	110	12
Puerto Pirámides	11	1½
Río Gallegos	134-169	15-20
Trelew	7.50	1
Viedma	61-73	5-6

Getting Around
Renting a bicycle (see p433) is ideal for travel in and around town.

TO/FROM THE AIRPORT
Southbound 28 de Julio buses to Trelew, which run hourly Monday through Saturday between 6am and 10pm, will stop at Trelew's airport on request.

Flamenco Tour (☎ 455505) runs a door-to-door shuttle service (AR$10) to Madryn's airport, while **Eben-Ezer** (☎ 472474) runs a service (AR$20) to Trelew's airport.

CAR
Before renting a car to visit Península Valdés, consider that a roundtrip is a little over 300km.

A group sharing expenses can make a rental a relatively reasonable and more flexible alternative to bus tours – if you don't have to pay for extra kilometers.

Rental rates vary, depending on the mileage allowance and age and condition of the vehicle. The family-owned **Centauro** (☎ 02965-15-340400; www.centaurorentacar.com.ar; Av Roca 733) gets high marks as an attentive and competitively priced rental agency. Basic vehicles run AR$199 per day, with insurance and 400km included.

Northbound motorists should note that the last station with cheap gas is 139km north in Sierra Grande.

AROUND PUERTO MADRYN
Home to a permanent sea lion colony and cormorant rookery, the **Reserva Faunística Punta Loma** (admission AR$20) is 17km southwest of Puerto Madryn via a good but winding gravel road. The overlook is about 15m from the animals, best seen during low tides. Many travel agencies organize two-hour tours (AR$50) according to the tide schedules; otherwise, check tide tables and hire a car or taxi, or make the trek via bicycle.

Twenty kilometers north of Puerto Madryn via RP 1 is **Playa Flecha** observatory, a recommended whale-watching spot.

RESERVA FAUNÍSTICA PENÍNSULA VALDÉS
Unesco World Heritage site Península Valdés is one of South America's finest wildlife reserves. More than 80,000 visitors per year visit this sanctuary, which has a total area of 3600 sq km and more than 400km of coastline. The wildlife viewing is truly exceptional: the peninsula is home to sea lions, elephant seals, guanacos, rheas, Magellanic penguins and numerous seabirds. But the biggest attraction is the endangered ballena franca austral (southern right whale). The warmer, more enclosed waters along the Golfo Nuevo, Golfo San José and the coastline near Caleta Valdés from Punta Norte to Punta Hércules are prime breeding zones for right whales between June and mid-December. For details on the region's wildlife, see p440.

One doesn't expect lambs alongside penguins, but sheep *estancias* occupy most of the peninsula's interior, which includes one of the world's lowest continental depressions, the salt flats of Salina Grande and Salina Chica, 42m below sea level. At the turn of the 20th

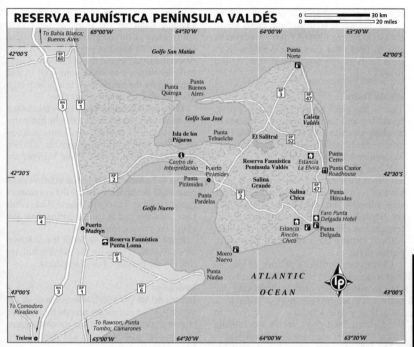

RESERVA FAUNÍSTICA PENÍNSULA VALDÉS

0 _____ 30 km
0 _____ 20 miles

To Bahía Blanca; Buenos Aires

Golfo San Matías

Punta Norte

Punta Quiroga

Punta Buenos Aires

Golfo San José

Isla de los Pájaros

Punta Tehuelche

El Salitral

Centro de Interpretación

Puerto Pirámides

Punta Pirámides

Reserva Faunística Península Valdés

Estancia La Elvira

Caleta Valdés

Punta Cerro

Punta Cantor Roadhouse

Salina Grande

Salina Chica

Punta Hércules

Punta Pardelas

Golfo Nuevo

Puerto Madryn

Reserva Faunística Punta Loma

Morro Nuevo

Estancia Rincón Chico

Faro Punta Delgada Hotel

Punta Delgada

Punta Ninfas

ATLANTIC OCEAN

To Comodoro Rivadavia

To Rawson; Punta Tombo; Camarones

Trelew

century, Puerto Pirámides, the peninsula's only village, was the shipping port for the salt extracted from Salina Grande.

About 17km north of Puerto Madryn, paved RP 2 branches off RN 3 across the Istmo Carlos Ameghino to the entrance of the **reserve** (admission AR$40; valid for 2 days). The **Centro de Interpretación** (8am-8pm), 22km beyond the entrance, focuses on natural history, displays a full right whale skeleton and has material on the peninsula's colonization, from the area's first Spanish settlement at Fuerte San José to later mineral exploration. Don't miss the stunning panoramic view from the observation tower.

If you are sleeping in Puerto Madryn but plan to visit the park on two consecutive days, ask a ranger to validate your pass before you exit the park so you can re-enter without charges.

Puerto Pirámides

 02965 / pop humans 250, whales 400-600

Set amid sandy cliffs on a bright blue sea, this sleepy old salt port now bustles with tour buses and visitors clad in orange life jackets.

Whales mean whopping and ever-growing tourism here, but at the end of the day the tour buses split and life in this two-street town regains its cherished slug's pace.

Av de las Ballenas is the main drag, which runs perpendicular to Primera (1era) Bajada, the first road to the beach, stuffed with tour outfitters. A small **tourist office** (495084; www.puertopiramides.gov.ar; 1era Bajada) helps with travelers' needs. New additions include internet at the **Telefónica** (Av de las Ballenas) and a cash machine at **Banco de Chubut** (Av de las Ballenas).

ACTIVITIES

While most visitors focus on whale watching, adventure options – including **diving**, **snorkeling** and **mountain biking** – are growing. Friendly **Patagonia Explorers** (02965-15-340619; www.patagonia explorers.com; 1era bajada) offers guided treks and sea-kayaking trips (AR$90, two hours). Area *estancias* offer **horseback riding**. But you don't have to stray far from town to find adventure: just join the local kids at the **sandboarding** hill at the end of the second road down to the beach.

Visitors can walk to the **sea lion colony** less than 5km from town (though mostly uphill).

It is a magnificent spot to catch the sunset, occasional whale sightings and views across the Golfo Nuevo toward Puerto Madryn. Be sure to time your visit with the tides (high tides finds all the sea lions swimming out to sea).

Whale Tours

This is the place to glimpse spy-hopping, breaching and tailing cetaceans on a **whale-watching excursion** (AR$75 to AR$150, children under 12 half-price), arranged in Puerto Madryn or Puerto Pirámides.

When choosing a tour, ask other travelers about their experiences and check what kind of boat will be used: smaller, Zodiac-style inflatable rafts offer more intimacy than the larger bulldozer variety. By law, outfitters are not allowed within 100m of whales without cutting the motor, nor allowed to pursue them.

Check your outfitter's policies. When the port is closed due to bad weather, tour bookings are usually honored the following day (although these days are more crowded too). Outside of whale-watching season (June to December), boat trips aren't worthwhile unless you adore sea lions and shorebirds.

The following is a partial list of reputable outfitters:

Bottazzi (☎ 474110; www.titobottazzi.com in Spanish; 1era Bajada; sunset cruise AR$150) Well worth the cost – especially if you can go out with Tito himself, an old sea dog with ample experience. Sunset cruises include a *picada* (shared appetizer plate) and glass of wine at Restingas afterwards.

Hydrosport (☎ 495065; www.hydrosport.com.ar; 1era Bajada) Runs sunset tours and has naturalists and submarine audio systems on board.

Whales Argentina (☎ 495015; www.whalesargentina .com.ar; 1era Bajada; catamaran/semi-rigid raft AR$75/150) Offers quality trips with a bilingual guide.

SLEEPING

If you're interested in watching wildlife, it's worth staying overnight, instead of trying to see everything in a daylong sprint from Puerto Madryn. Campers gloat about hearing whales' eerie cries and huffing blow holes in the night – it can be a truly extraordinary experience.

You will have to get a voucher from your hotel if you plan to exit and re-enter the park, so as to not pay the park entry fee twice. Watch for signs advertising rooms, cabins and apartments for rent along the main drag.

Budget

Camping Municipal (☎ 495084; per person AR$4) Convenient sheltered gravel sites with clean toilets, a store and hot pay showers (AR$2), down the road behind the gas station. Come early in summer to stake your spot. Avoid camping on the beach: high tide is very high and has washed sleeping logs away.

Hostel Bahía Ballenas (☎ 474110; Av de las Ballenas s/n; dm with breakfast AR$35; 🖳) Bright but barebones, this brick hostel is a welcome addition to a town with few budget services. Kitchen use, lockers with keys, TV and internet are included.

Casa de Tía Alicia (☎ 495046; Av de las Ballenas s/n; per person AR$60) Backpackers praise the *buena onda* (good vibes) at this old tin house. The rooms have windows and share two bathrooms. Ask about the private tours.

Hospedaje El Medano (☎ 495032; Av de las Ballenas s/n; s/d AR$35/50) If Casa de Tía Alicia is full, try this nearby option, of similar quality.

Midrange

Estancia del Sol (☎ 495007; Av de las Ballenas s/n; d/tr AR$120/145) The earnest owners do their best to ensure a pleasant stay in the modest rooms. It's popular with students and families and has a decent eatery.

Refugio de Luna (☎ 495083; Av de las Ballenas s/n; d/tr AR$150/250) Choose from spacious and inviting rooms in the main house, or a crunched but lovely guest cabin, perched above the house with excellent views. Breakfast, including homemade wholemeal bread, is extra and afternoon tea may be available to nonguests.

Motel ACA (☎ 495004; Av Roca s/n; s/d/tr AR$110/160/195) The 16 noisy beachfront motel rooms have heating and cable TV. The attached restaurant has good views and serves fresh seafood.

Top End

Restingas Hotel (☎ 495101; www.lasrestingas.com; 1era Bajada; d garden/oceanview AR$183/240; meals AR$50; 🖳) Mixed reviews beset this lavender luxury hotel with spa. While service appears lax and sanitation could bear improvement, watching whales from your bedroom is a big plus. Guests do praise the abundant buffet breakfast, and the oceanfront restaurant is open to nonguests.

Paradise (☎ 495030; www.hosteriaparadise.com.ar; 2da Bajada; s/d AR$314/377; 🖳) These 12 attractive, tiled, brick-walled rooms are expansive and cool. Some have views and Jacuzzi tubs. The more informal cabins are good options for groups and families. Outside of the whale-watching season, rates are 50% lower.

EATING & DRINKING

Restaurants flank the beachfront, down the first street to the right as you enter town. Note that water here is desalinated: sensitive stomachs should stick to the bottled stuff. If self-catering, it's best to haul your groceries from Puerto Madryn.

Towanda (1era Bajada; mains AR$15; ◷ 9am-6pm) This friendly café is ideal for an espresso and pressed sandwiches while waiting for your tour to depart.

Quimey Quipan (☎ 458609; 1era Bajada; mains AR$15-31; ◷ breakfast, lunch & dinner) Breakfast, towering sandwiches and no-frills set seafood menus are dished out from this average café to a steady stream of passersby.

La Estación (☎ 495047; Av de las Ballenas s/n; mains AR$17-28; ◷ breakfast-late) This happy house is the spot to knock back drinks; there are also good pasta dishes and breakfast service. It's opposite the YPF gas station, with a wooden deck for outdoor dining.

Pub Paradise (☎ 495030; Av de las Ballenas s/n; mains AR$21-40) This popular tour-group stop is also a hit with the locals. Few come for the food; instead, grab a cold one and enjoy the buzz of activity while sunset paints the bluffs.

Margarita Bar (Av de las Ballenas s/n; ◷ 8pm-late) This sleek bar specializes in cocktail o'clock, with a deep shelf of hard liquor and a long drinks list. There are also branches in Trelew and Puerto Madryn.

GETTING THERE & AROUND

During summer, the Mar y Valle bus service travels from Puerto Madryn to Puerto Pirámides (AR$11, 1½ hours) at 9.30am and returns to Madryn at 6.30pm, with more limited service in the off-season. Bus tours from Puerto Madryn may allow passengers to get off at Puerto Pirámides.

Around Puerto Pirámides

If you're driving around the peninsula, take it easy. Roads are *ripio* (gravel) and washboard, with sandy spots that grab the wheels. If you're in a rental car, make sure you get all the details on the insurance policy. Hitchhiking here is nearly impossible and bike travel is long and unnervingly windy.

ISLA DE LOS PÁJAROS

In Golfo San José, 800m north of the isthmus, this bird sanctuary is off-limits to humans, but visible through a powerful telescope. It contains a replica of a chapel built at Fuerte San José. See the boxed text, below, to find out how this small island figures into Antoine de St-Exupéry's *The Little Prince*.

THE LITTLE PRINCE

From an apartment in Manhattan in 1941, a French pilot and writer, in exile from the battlefields of Europe, scripted what would become one of the most-read children's fables, *The Little Prince*. Antoine St-Exupéry, then 40 years old, had spent the previous 20 years flying – in the Sahara, the Pyrenees, Egypt and Patagonia, where he was director of Aeropostal Argentina from 1929 to 1931. Intertwined in the lines of *The Little Prince* and Asteroid B612 are images of Patagonia that stayed with him while flying over the barren landscape and braving the incessant winds.

It has become popular legend that the shape of Isla de los Pájaros, off the coast of Península Valdés, inspired the elephant-eating boa constrictor (or hat, as you may see it), while the perfectly conical volcanoes on the asteroid owe their shape to the volcanoes St-Exupéry flew over en route to Punta Arenas, Chile. The author's illustrations show the little prince on the peaks of mountains, unquestionably those in the Fitz Roy Range (one such peak now bears his name). And, possibly, meeting two young daughters of a French immigrant after an emergency landing in Concordia, near Buenos Aires, helped mold the character of the prince.

St-Exupéry never witnessed the influence his mythical royal character would have. In 1944, just after the first publication of *The Little Prince,* he disappeared during a flight to join French forces-in-exile stationed in Algiers.

St-Exupéry's years in Patagonia also figure in two critically acclaimed novels, *Night Flight* and *Wind, Sand and Stars*, both worthwhile reads on long Patagonia trips. Or simply watch the miles go by and, every now and then, as the little prince requested, try to draw a sheep.

PATAGONIA WILDLIFE

You don't have to be a whale groupie to be awed by the animals along Southern Argentina's rugged coast. The chance to view a cast of wild characters – penguins, dolphins, killer whales, sea lions and elephant seals – up close makes these lonely Atlantic shores a must to visit.

Magellanic Penguin

What: *Sphenicus magellanicus;* in Spanish pingüino magellánico
When: August to April, peak season December through February
Where: Península Valdés, Punta Tombo, Cabo Dos Bahías, Seno Otway (Chile)

Referred to locally as the jackass penguin for its characteristic braying sound, the Magellanic penguin is black to brown in shading and has two black-and-white bars going across the upper chest. They average 45cm in height and weigh about 3.15kg. Winters are spent at sea, but males arrive on land in late August, followed by territorial fights in September as burrows and nests are prepared. In October females lay their eggs. Come mid-November, when eggs are hatched, males and females take turns caring for and feeding the chicks with regurgitated squid and small fish. In December it's a madhouse of hungry demanding chicks, adults coming in and out of the sea with food, and predatory birds trying to pick out the weaklings. In January chicks start to molt and take their first steps into the sea, and by February it's a traffic jam at the beach as chicks take to the water. By March juveniles start their migration north, followed in April by the adults.

Penguins are awkward on land, but in the water they are swift and graceful, reaching speeds of up to 8km/h. They are also naturally curious, though if approached too quickly they scamper into their burrows or toboggan back into the water. They will bite if you get too close. The least disruptive way to observe them is to sit near the burrows and wait for them to come to you.

Over a million pairs of these penguins exist, but their populations are threatened by human activity and oil spills.

Southern Right Whale

What: *Eubalaena australis;* in Spanish ballena franca austral
When: June to mid-December, peak season September and October
Where: Golfo Nuevo and Golfo San José, Península Valdés

Averaging nearly 12m in length and weighing more than 27 tonnes, southern right whales enter the shallow waters of Península Valdés in the spring to breed and bear young. Females, which are larger than males, will copulate a year after giving birth. A female may pick out the best partner by fending off the pack of males trailing her for hours to see which one endures. For the past three decades, researchers have been able to track individual whales by noting the pattern of callosities, made white against the black skin by clusters of parasites, found on the whale's body and head. Right whales don't have teeth, but trap krill and plankton with fringed plates (baleen) that hang from the upper jaw.

The slow-moving right whale was a favorite target of whalers because, unlike other species, it remained floating on the surface after being killed. After more than half a century of legal protection, South Atlantic right whale populations are now slowly recovering.

Killer Whale

What: *Ornicus orca;* in Spanish orca
When: June to mid-December, peak season September and October
Where: Península Valdés

These large dolphins, black with white underbellies, live in pods consisting of one male, a cluster of females and the young. Upon maturity, the males leave the pod to create their own. Males, which can reach more than 9m in length and weigh as much as 6000kg, live an average of 30 years, while females, substantially smaller at 7m and about 4000kg, live about 50 years, calving approximately every 10 years. The ominous dorsal fin can reach nearly 2m high.

Killer whales prey on fish, penguins, dolphins and seals, and will hunt in groups to prey upon larger whales. At Punta Norte on Península Valdés they hunt sea lions and elephant seals by almost beaching themselves and waiting for the waters to wash a few unfortunates their way. In the 1970s groups concerned with the livelihood of the sea lions requested the whales be shot, to either kill or scare them away, before they decimated the sea lion colonies. Fortunately, this reaction was short-lived and made clear the inevitability of the food chain.

Southern Sea Lion
What: *Otaria flavescens;* in Spanish lobo marino
When: year-round
Where: widely distributed along Patagonia coasts
Aggressive southern sea lions feed largely on squid and the occasional penguin. No matter how tempting, don't approach them too closely for photo ops. The bull (male) has a thick neck and large head with longer hair around the neck, creating the appearance of a lion's mane. An adult male can weigh 300kg and measure 2m, while females weigh around 200kg. Bulls fight to control their harems and breed with up to 10 females per season. Females give birth once each season and are ready for mating again in less than a week. Unlike the elephant seal, pups nurse only from their mothers.

Southern Elephant Seal
What: *Mirounga leonina;* in Spanish elefante marino
When: year-round; births and mating between September and November
Where: widely distributed along Patagonia coasts
Elephant seals take their common name from the male's enormous proboscis, which does indeed resemble an elephant's trunk. Bulls (males) reach nearly 7m in length and can weigh over 3500kg, but females are substantially smaller. They spend most of the year at sea, and have been observed diving to a depth of 1500m and staying submerged for over an hour in search of squid and other marine life. (The average dive depth and duration are 1000m and 23 minutes.)

Península Valdés has the only breeding colony of southern elephant seals on the South American continent. The bull comes ashore in late winter or early spring, breeding after the already pregnant females arrive and give birth. Dominant males known as 'beachmasters' control harems of up to 100 females but must constantly fight off challenges from bachelor males. Females give birth to a pup once a year, each pregnancy lasting 11 months. For 19 days after the birth the female nurses the pup, during which time she will lose close to 40% of her body weight, while the pup's increases by 300%. Pups will sometimes nurse from other females. After the 19 days, the mother may breed again.

Commerson's Dolphin
What: *Cephalorhynchus commersonii;* in Spanish tonina overa
When: year-round; breeding season November to February
Where: Puerto San Julián, Playa Unión, Puerto Deseado
Outgoing and acrobatic, the Commerson's dolphin is a favorite along shallow areas of coastal Patagonia. Adults are quite small, about 1.5m in length, and brilliantly patterned in black and white with a rounded dorsal fin. Young dolphins are gray, brown and black; the brown slowly disappears and the gray fades to striking white. In small groups, they play around the sides of boats, breaching frequently and sometimes riding the bow. Commerson's dolphins eat shrimp, squid and bottom-dwelling fish. In Argentina they are illegally captured to use as crab bait.

PUNTA DELGADA

In the peninsula's southeast corner, 76km southeast of Puerto Pirámides, sea lions and, in spring, a huge colony of elephant seals are visible from the cliffs. Enter the public dirt road right of the hotel for viewings.

The luxury **Faro Punta Delgada Hotel** (☎ 02965-406304, 02965-15-406304; www.puntadelgada.com; d half/full board AR$760/886) occupies a lighthouse complex that once belonged to the Argentine postal service. Horseback riding, 4WD tours and other activities are available. Nonguests can dine at the upscale restaurant serving *estancia* fare (mains AR$15 to AR$60). The quality is good, although it is often taken over by tour groups. Free guided naturalist walks down to the beach leave frequently in high season.

With a prime location for wildlife watching, **Estancia Rincón Chico** (☎ 02965-471733, 02965-15-688302; www.rinconchico.com.ar; d with half-pension AR$885; ☯ Aug-Mar) hosts university marine biologists, student researchers and tourists. Lodging is in a modern, corrugated-tin ranch house with eight well-appointed doubles and a *quincho* (thatched-roof building) for barbecues. In addition to guided excursions, there are paths for cycling and walking on your own.

PUNTA CANTOR & CALETA VALDÉS

In spring, elephant seals haul themselves onto the long gravel spit at this sheltered bay, 43km north of Punta Delgada. September has females giving birth to pups, while males fight it out defending their harem – making for dramatic sightings from the trails that wind down the hill. You may even see guanaco strolling along the beach.

Tour groups fill up the **Roadhouse** (☎ 02965-15-406183; www.laelvira.com.ar; meals AR$22), a decent self-service restaurant offering a salad bar, coffee, drinks and rest rooms. It is part of **Estancia La Elvira** (☎ 02965-474248; www.laelvira.com.ar; d with breakfast AR$330), a comfortable lodging whose modern construction lacks the romance of a seasoned guesthouse. Activities include horseback riding, agrotourism and nature strolls. A few kilometers north of the Roadhouse, there's a sizable colony of burrowing Magellanic penguins.

PUNTA NORTE

At the far end of the peninsula, Punta Norte boasts an enormous mixed colony of sea lions and elephant seals. Its distance means it is rarely visited by tour groups, and for that reason it offers visitors the treat of solitude.

But the real thrill here is the orcas: from mid-February through mid-April these 'killer whales' come to feast on the unsuspecting colonies of sea lions. Chances are you won't see a high-tide attack in all its gory glory, but watching their dorsal fins carving through the water is enough to raise some goosebumps.

There's a small but good museum focusing on marine mammals, with details on the Tehuelche and the area's sealing history.

TRELEW

☎ 02965 / pop 93,386

Though steeped in Welsh heritage, Trelew isn't a postcard city. In fact, this midsized hub, convenient to so many attractions, is poised to be touristy, but isn't. You might find that good or bad, but in its very uneventfulness Trelew does offer the traveler a welcome pause. After the obligatory visit to the city's top-notch dinosaur museum, you're free to frequent the ice-cream parlors, lounge on the verdant square and check out a few historic buildings. The region's commercial center, it is also a convenient base for visiting the Welsh villages of Gaiman and Dolavon. Founded in 1886 as a railway junction to unite the Río Chubut valley with the Golfo Nuevo, Trelew (tre-*ley*-ooh) owes its easily mispronounced name to the Welsh contraction of *tre* (town) and *lew* (after Lewis Jones, who promoted railway expansion). During the following 30 years, the railway reached Gaiman, the Welsh built their Salón San David (a replica of St David's Cathedral, Pembrokeshire), and Spanish and Italian immigrants settled in the area. In 1956 the federal government promoted Patagonian industrial development and Trelew's population skyrocketed.

Orientation

Trelew is 65km south of Puerto Madryn via RN 3. The center of town surrounds Plaza Independencia, with most services on Calles 25 de Mayo and San Martín, and along Av Fontana. East–west streets change names on either side of Av Fontana. Semipedestrian passageways go between the main north–south streets.

Information

ATMs and *locutorios* with internet are plentiful downtown and around the plaza.
ACA (Automóvil Club Argentino; ☎ 435197; cnr Av Fontana & San Martín) Argentina's auto club; good source for provincial road maps.

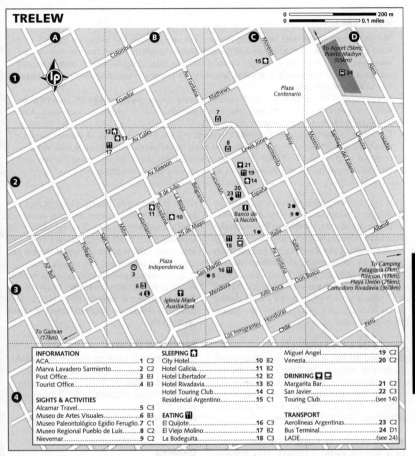

TRELEW

Marva Lavadero Sarmiento (Sarmiento 363) Self- and full-service laundry and dry cleaners.

Post office (cnr 25 de Mayo & Mitre)

Tourist office (☎ 426819; www.trelewpatagonia.gov .ar; Mitre 387; ☼ 8am-9pm) Helpful and well stocked, with some English-speaking staff, and brochures.

Sights

The tourist office sometimes has an informative walking-tour brochure, in Spanish and English, describing most of the city's historic buildings.

MUSEO PALEONTOLÓGICO EGIDIO FERUGLIO

Showcasing the most important fossil finds in Patagonia, this natural-history **museum**

(☎ 420012; www.mef.org.ar; Av Fontana 140; admission AR$16; ☼ 10am-8pm) offers outstanding life-sized dinosaur exhibits and more than 1700 fossil remains of plant and marine life. Nature sounds and a video accent the informative plaques, and tours are available in a number of languages. The collection includes local dinosaurs, such as the tehuelchesaurus, patagosaurus and titanosaurus. Museum researchers were part of an international team that recently discovered a new and unusual species called *brachytrachelopan mesai*, a short-necked sauropod. Feruglio was an Italian paleontologist who came to Argentina in 1925 as a petroleum geologist for YPF.

Kids aged eight to 12 can check out the 'Explorers in Pyjamas' program, which invites

PATAGONIA

WELSH LEGACY

The Welsh opened the door to settling Patagonia in 1865, though the newfound freedom cost them dearly. Few had farmed before and the arid steppe showed no resemblance to their verdant homeland. After nearly starving, they survived with the help of the Tehuelche, and eventually occupied the entire lower Chubut valley, founding the towns and teahouses of Rawson, Trelew, Puerto Madryn and Gaiman.

Today about 20% of Chubut's inhabitants have Welsh blood, though it logically grows thinner with each generation, 'or pretty soon you're marrying your cousin,' jokes one descendant. What you wouldn't expect is that a recent revival of Welsh culture is dragging it back from the grave. According to Welsh historian Fernando Coronato, 'For the old principality of Wales, Patagonia meant its most daring venture.' This renewed bond means yearly British Council appointments of Welsh teachers and exchanges for Patagonian students. Welsh tourists come curious, as if time-traveling in their own culture, thanks to Patagonia's longtime isolation.

---

kids to sleep over and explore the museum by flashlight. The museum also sponsors interesting group tours to **Geoparque Paleontológico Bryn Gwyn** (admission AR$8; ☺ daylight hours), in the badlands along the Río Chubut (25km from Trelew, or 8km south of Gaiman via RP 5). The three-hour guided visits are a walk through time, along a well-designed nature trail past a wealth of exposed fossils dating as far back as the Tertiary, some 40 million years ago.

MUSEO DE ARTES VISUALES
Adjoined to the tourist office, this small visual-arts **museum** (San Martín 351; admission free; ☺ 8am-8pm Mon-Fri, 2-8pm Sat & Sun) features works on loan from the Museo Nacional de Bellas Artes in Buenos Aires, as well as polished relics from Welsh colonization.

MUSEO REGIONAL PUEBLO DE LUIS
In a former railway station, this **museum** (☎ 424062; cnr Av Fontana & 9 de Julio; admission AR$2; ☺ 7am-1pm & 3-9pm Mon-Fri) displays historical photographs, clothing and period furnishings of Welsh settlers. More explanations would be welcome. The train stopped running in 1961, but the antique steam engine and other machinery outside are worth a stop.

Tours
Several travel agencies run excursions to Reserva Provincial Punta Tombo (around AR$125, plus AR$30 admission), some passing by Puerto Rawson on the way back to see toninas overas (Commerson's dolphins) when conditions are agreeable. The actual time at Punta Tombo is only about 1½ hours. Full-day trips to Península Valdés are also on

offer, but going to Puerto Madryn first is a better bet: there are more options, prices are similar and there's less driving time. Note that distances to all these sites are very long and more time is spent in transit than at the attractions; take water and snacks.

Local agencies worth checking out include Amex representative **Nievemar** (☎ 434114; www .nievemartours.com.ar in Spanish; Italia 20), which accepts traveler's checks, and **Alcamar Travel** (☎ 421448; San Martín 146).

Festivals & Events
Gwyl y Glaniad On July 28 the landing of the first Welsh is celebrated by taking tea in one of the many chapels.
Eisteddfod de Chubut (☎ 430156) A Welsh literary and musical festival, held in late October. The tradition started in 1875.
Aniversario de la Ciudad October 20; commemorates the city's founding in 1886.

Sleeping
Trelew's accommodations are largely dated and geared toward the business traveler; in addition, spots fill up fast. Travelers can find greater variety in nearby Puerto Madryn.

BUDGET
Camping Patagonia (☎ 02965-15-406907, 02965-15-350581; per person AR$7) Shady and spacious, this green campground has a small convenience store, electricity and hot showers, but limited public transport. It's 7km from town on RN 7, off the road to Rawson.

MIDRANGE
Hotel Rivadavia (☎ 434472; www.cpatagonia.com/riva davia in Spanish; Rivadavia 55; s/d/tr AR$60/80/90) Up on a hill, this small family-run hotel offers good

value, though the rooms with gauzy curtains are somewhat faded. Breakfast (AR$6) is served in the TV-oriented lobby.

Residencial Argentino (☎ 436134; Moreno 93; s/d/tr AR$60/90/110) This place has a kitsch throwback feel: rooms feature chrome chairs and fluorescent tube lamps. It is worn around the edges (particularly the bathrooms) but provides affordable value close to the bus terminal and fronts a pleasant park.

Hotel Touring Club (☎ 433997/98; htouring@ speedy.com.ar; Av Fontana 240; d with breakfast AR$140; 🖳) Expectations are high when you climb the curved marble staircase of this historic hotel, but most of the grandeur goes into the lobby. Touring Club feels retro but furnishings are probably original. Rooms are small but adequate, with the downside of lumpy mattresses.

City Hotel (☎ 433951; hotelcitytrelew@speedy.com .ar; Rivadavia 254; s/d/tr with breakfast AR$80/150/210; 🖳) There is not a speck of dust about this urban hotel, though it retains all the charm of a government institution. The shuttered rooms are plain but comfortable and include TV and wi-fi. Parking is free.

Hotel Galicia (☎ 433802; www.hotelgalicia.com.ar in Spanish; 9 de Julio 214; s/d/tr/q ARS$120/150/175/220) A marble staircase and gold trim bring a swanky touch to this popular hotel. The wood-paneled rooms have firm mattresses, carpet and cable TV. Staff are friendly and parking is AR$15 extra.

TOP END

Hotel Libertador (☎ 420220; www.hotellibertadortw.com; Rivadavia 31; s/d/ste AR$154/185/214; 🔀 🖳) Rooms in this business hotel are comfortable, with soft decor, firm beds and ample light, but no one ever updated the fire-engine red carpet! Tubs, phones and TVs come with all rooms, but VIP ones are more spacious. Breakfast in the restaurant is buffet-style and parking is free.

Eating

Venezia (25 de Mayo 21; snacks AR$6; 🕑 7:30am-10pm Mon-Sat, 9am-1pm & 4-8pm Sun) This bakery and ice-cream shop tempts passersby with a window view of mousses and chocolate creations to drool over. They also make fresh *facturas* (pastries).

El Quijote (Belgrano 361; mains AR$14-28) This traditional downtown *parrilla* is a bit frilly around the edges, but the meats are expertly handled and just right with a side of french fries.

La Bodeguita (☎ 436276; Belgrano 374; mains AR$15-30) A popular stop for meats, pasta and seafood, this restaurant boasts attentive service and a family atmosphere.

El Viejo Molino (☎ 428019; Av Gales 250; mains AR$21; 🕑 closed Mon) Iron lamps and brickwork restore the romance to this 1914 flour mill, a must if you're in town. On weekends it's packed, with the main attraction, the wood-fired *parrilla*, grilling steaks and even vegetables to perfection. There's an extensive wine list and salads too.

Miguel Angel (Av Fontana; mains AR$28; 🕑 closed Mon) This chic eatery departs from the everyday with yummy dishes like gnocchi with wild mushrooms, and popular sushi Wednesdays, but its staples are the homemade pastas and pizzas.

Drinking

Touring Club (☎ 433997/98; Av Fontana 240; snacks AR$12; 🕑 6:30am-2am; 🖳) Old lore exudes from the pores of this historic *confitería*, from the Butch Cassidy 'Wanted' poster to the embossed tile ceiling and antique barback. Even the tuxedoed waitstaff appear to be plucked from another era. It's too bad the sandwiches are only so-so, but it's worth stopping in for coffee or beers.

Margarita Bar (☎ 432126; Av Fontana 230; mains AR$28; 🕑 noon-3pm & 8pm-1am) A cool nightspot with brick walls and slick white-leather booths, Margarita also dishes up surprisingly tasty food in good portions. On weekends it can stay open until 6am. Occasional live acts include tango and *rock nacional*.

San Javier (☎ 423474; San Martín 57) The front part offers café fare and ice cream, but Guinness and Kilkenny are served in the dark-wood watering hole out back.

Getting There & Away

AIR

Trelew's **airport** (TRE; ☎ 428021) is 5km north of town off RN 3. Airport tax is ARS$6.

Aerolíneas Argentinas (☎ 420210; 25 de Mayo 33) flies direct daily to Buenos Aires (AR$537) and several times a week to Esquel (AR$425), Bariloche (AR$1334), Ushuaia (AR$1014) and El Calafate (AR$820).

LADE (☎ 435740), based at the bus terminal, flies to Comodoro Rivadavia (AR$170) on Wednesdays and Buenos Aires (AR$258) on Thursdays, in addition to other northern Patagonian destinations.

PATAGONIA

BUS

Trelew's full-service **bus terminal** (☎ 420121) is six blocks northeast of downtown.

For Gaiman (AR$3), **28 de Julio** (☎ 432429) has 18 services a day between 7am and 11pm (reduced weekend service), with most continuing to Dolavon (AR$5, half hour). Buses to Rawson (AR$2.20, 15 minutes) leave every 15 minutes.

Mar y Valle (☎ 432429) and 28 de Julio run hourly buses to Puerto Madryn (AR$7.50, one hour). Mar y Valle goes to Puerto Pirámides (AR$16.50, 2½ hours) daily at 8:15am, with additional service in summer. **El Ñandú** (☎ 427499) goes to Camarones (AR$20, three hours) at 8am Monday, Wednesday and Friday.

Long-distance bus companies include **El Cóndor** (☎ 431675), **Que Bus** (☎ 422760), **Andesmar** (☎ 433535), **TAC** (☎ 431452), **TUS** (☎ 421343) and **Don Otto** (☎ 429496).

Of several departures daily for Buenos Aires, Don Otto has the most comfortable and most direct service. Only Don Otto goes to Mar del Plata, while TAC goes to La Plata. TAC and Andesmar service the most towns. For Comodoro Rivadavia there are a few daily departures with TAC, Don Otto or Andesmar, all of which also continue on to San Julián and Río Gallegos.

Destination	Cost (AR$)	Duration (hr)
Bahía Blanca	97-116	12
Bariloche	116-150	13
Buenos Aires	188-214	18-21
Caleta Olivia	62-77	6
Comodoro Rivadavia	62-82	5-6
Córdoba	166-216	19
Esquel	80-105	8-9
La Plata	188-195	19
Mar del Plata	181-216	17-21
Mendoza	207-258	24
Neuquén	99-124	10
Puerto Madryn	7.50	1
Río Gallegos	155-186	14-17
Viedma	69-81	8

Getting Around

From the airport, taxis charge AR$15 to downtown, AR$40 to Gaiman and AR$110 to Puerto Madryn. Car-rental agencies at the airport include **Avis** (☎ 434634) and **Localiza** (☎ 430070).

AROUND TRELEW

Rawson, 17km east of Trelew, is Chubut's provincial capital, but nearby **Playa Unión**, the region's principal playground, has the capital attraction: toninas overas (Commerson's dolphins; see p441). Playa Unión is a long stretch of white-sand beach with blocks of summer homes. Dolphin tours (AR$70, 1½ hours) depart **Puerto Rawson** from April to December. For reservations, contact **Toninas Adventure** (☎ 02965-15-666542).

Empresas Rawson and 28 de Julio buses depart from Trelew for Rawson (AR$2.20) frequently from Monday to Friday and every 20 to 30 minutes on weekends. Get off at Rawson's plaza or bus terminal and hop on a green 'Bahía' bus, which heads to Puerto Rawson before turning around.

GAIMAN
☎ 02965 / pop 5753

Cream pie, dainty tea cakes, *torta negra* (a rich, dense fruit cake) and a hot pot of black tea – most visitors take an oral dose of culture when visiting this quintessential Welsh river-valley village. Today, about a third of the residents claim Welsh ancestry and teahouses persist in their afternoon tradition, even as their overselling sometimes rubs the charm thin. Gaiman's homey digs provide great value for lodgers, but the town offers little in the way of diversion beyond quiet strolls past stone houses with rose gardens after a filling teahouse visit.

The town's name, meaning Stony Point or Arrow Point, originated from the Tehuelche who once wintered in this valley. After the Welsh constructed their first house in 1874, the two groups peacefully coexisted for a time. Later immigrant groups of criollos, Germans and Anglos joined the Welsh and continued cultivation of fruit, vegetables and grains in the lower Río Chubut valley.

Orientation & Information

Gaiman is 17km west of Trelew via RN 25. The town's touristy center is little more than a crisscross of streets snuggled between the barren hills and Río Chubut. Av Eugenio Tello is the main road, connecting the main town entrance to leafy Plaza Roca. Most of the teahouses and historic sites are within four blocks of the plaza. Across the river are fast-growing residential and industrial areas.

There's one ATM on the plaza at Banco del Chubut but it does not always work, so bring cash. *Locutorios* and internet can be found along the main drag.

Post office (cnr Evans & Yrigoyen) Just north of the river bridge.

Tourist office (Casa de Informes; ☎ 491571; www .gaiman.gov.ar in Spanish; cnr Rivadavia & Belgrano; ☟ 9am-9pm Mon-Sat, 2-8pm Sun) Ask here for a map and guided tours of historic houses.

Sights

Gaiman is ideal for an informal walking tour, past homes with ivy trellises and drooping, oversized roses. Architecturally distinctive churches and chapels dot the town. **Primera Casa** (cnr Av Eugenio Tello & Evans; admission AR$2; ☟ by request at tourist office) is the first house, built in 1874 by David Roberts. Dating from 1906, the **Colegio Camwy** (cnr MD Jones & Rivadavia) is considered the first secondary school in Patagonia.

The old railway station houses the **Museo Histórico Regional Gales** (☎ 491007; cnr Sarmiento & 28 de Julio; admission AR$2; ☟ 3-7pm Tue-Sun), a fine small museum holding the belongings and photographs of town pioneers.

The **Museo Antropológico** (cnr Bouchard & Jones; admission free; ☟ by request at tourist office) offers humble homage to the indigenous cultures and history. Nearby is the 300m **Túnel del Ferrocarril**, a brick tunnel through which the first trains to Dolavon passed in 1914.

Don't miss **Parque El Desafío** (www.eldesafiogaiman .com.ar in Spanish; Av Brown 52; admission AR$10, children under 10 free; ☟ dawn-dusk), the perfect remedy to long-distance travel fatigue. Its octogenarian owner Joaquín Alonso, the 'Dali of Recycling,' fashioned some 80,000 bottles, cans and soda containers into whimsical folk art with some 30,000 hours of work. Though he created the park to entertain his grandchildren, adults can appreciate it just as well. Plaques (some translated into English) with folk sayings and quotes from Seneca and Plato offer wit and reflection for all amid this symphony of junk. As one proclaims, '*Si quieres vivir mejor, mezcla a tu sensatez unos gramos de locura*' ('If you want to live better, mix up your sensibility with a few grams of craziness'). The park gained Guinness World Record status in 1998 as Earth's largest 'recycled' park. Visitors can't help but leave El Desafío (translated as 'the achievement') without a smile, a whimsical notion or whiff of inspiration, which is its own testament. It is located at the western entrance to town.

Sleeping

Camping Bomberos Voluntarios (☎ 491117; cnr Av Yrigoyen & Moreno; per person AR$5, children under 12 free) The volunteer firefighters put together this agreeable campground with hot-water showers and fire pits.

Unelem (☎ 491663; www.unelem.com in Spanish; cnr Av Eugenio Tello & 9 de Julio; s/d AR$80/98) Downplaying its original elegance, this old building offers four patterned rooms that are enormous and airy, with room for a table and dresser. There is a cheap *comedor* (restaurant) inside. It sits in front of the YPF.

Dyffryn Gwyrdd (☎ 491777; www.dwhosteria.com .ar in Spanish; Av Eugenio Tello 103; s/d/tr AR$80/100/120) This canary-yellow home creates an inviting atmosphere of bright and simple rooms with carpet, fans and throw pillows. The bathrooms are dated but spotless and there's a quiet bar and TV area.

Hostería Gwesty Tywi (☎ 491292; www.advance .com.ar/usuarios/gwestywi; Chacra 202; s/d/tr/q with breakfast AR$90/110/130/150; ☐) Diego and Brenda run this wonderful Welsh B&B with large gardens and snug, frilly rooms. Breakfast includes a selection of jams, cold meats and bread. They are glad to help with travel planning and occasionally fire up the barbecue to the delight of guests.

El Cuenco (☎ 02965-15-505963; www.hostalelcuenco .com.ar in Spanish; Fontana 300; 4-person cabin AR$150) Previously inhabited by gnomes, this sprightly wooden A-frame cabin offers a welcome retreat in the middle of town. It's located across the bridge from the plaza on a quiet residential street.

Eating

Tarten afal, tarten gwstard, cacen ffrwythau, spwnj jam and *bara brith* and a bottomless pot of tea – hungry yet? Afternoon tea is taken as a sacrament in Gaiman – though busloads of tourists get dumptrucked in teahouses without warning. The best bet is to look for places without buses in front, or wait for their departure. Whatever you do, eat a light lunch, or simply skip it. Tea services usually run from 2pm to 7pm.

Breuddwyd (☎ 491133; Yrigoyen 320; snacks AR$8, tea AR$25) A modern café whose best feature is the flower garden out back, brimming with blooms and a fountain. Ask about rooms for rent upstairs.

Plas y Coed (☎ 02965-15-629343; www.plasycoed.com .ar; MD Jones 123; tea AR$25) Run by the original owner's great-granddaughter in a gorgeous brick mansion, Plas y Coed pleases the palette and senses, with friendly service, fresh cakes and serious crochet cozies for that steaming-hot pot.

PATAGONIA

La Vieja Cuadra (☎ 02965-15-682352; cnr Av Eugenio Tello & MD Jones; mains AR$20-30; ☼ 8:30pm-midnight Tue-Sat, 12:30-3pm Sun) Considered Gaiman's best restaurant, it serves homemade pastas and well-seasoned meat dishes that are consistently good. Service is attentive.

Ty Nain (☎ 491126; Yrigoyen 283; tea AR$30; ☼ closed May) With the endorsements of the *Washington Post* and *Los Angeles Times* plastered on the front lawn, who needs our two cents? Inside an ivy-clad 1890 home, Ty Nain persists as one of the country's most traditional teahouses. The adjoining museum has some interesting Welsh artifacts.

Ty Cymraeg (☎ 491010; Matthews 74; tea AR$30) Teatime in this riverside house includes sumptuous pies and jams. Breakfast is available with reservations.

El Ángel (☎ 491460; Rivadavia 241; mains AR$36) Combining sweet and savory in tasty concoctions, stylish Ángel is a favorite for romantic *tête-à-têtes*. Hours can be very sporadic so reserve ahead.

Getting There & Away

During the week, 28 de Julio buses depart for Trelew (AR$3) frequently from Plaza Roca, from 7am to 11pm; weekend services are fewer. Most buses to Dolavon (AR$3) use the highway, but some take the much longer gravel 'valley' route. *Remise* (taxi) service is cheaper in Gaiman than in Trelew; the trip to Trelew costs AR$75 for up to four passengers.

AROUND GAIMAN

To experience an authentic historic Welsh agricultural town, head to the distinctly nontouristy **Dolavon** (population 2500), 19km west of Gaiman via paved RN 25. Welsh for 'river meadow,' the town offers pastoral appeal, with wooden waterwheels lining the irrigation canal, framed by rows of swaying poplars. The historic center is full of brick buildings, including the 1880 **Molino Harinero** (☎ 02965-492290; romanogi@infovia.com.ar; Maipú 61; guided tour per person AR$10) with still-functioning flour mill machinery. It also has a café-restaurant (meals AR$30) serving handmade breads and pastas with local wines and cheeses. Call owner Romano Giallatini for opening hours.

RESERVA PROVINCIAL PUNTA TOMBO

Continental South America's largest penguin nesting ground, **Punta Tombo** (admission AR$30; ☼ dawn-dusk Aug-Apr) has a colony of more than half a million Magellanic penguins and attracts many other birds, most notably king and rock cormorants, giant petrels, kelp gulls, flightless steamer ducks and black oystercatchers.

Trelew-based agencies run daylong tours (around AR$125, not including entrance fee), but may cancel if bad weather makes the unpaved roads impassable. If possible, come in the early morning to beat the crowds. Most nesting areas in the 200-hectare reserve are fenced off: respect the limits and remember that penguins can inflict serious bites.

There's a bar and *confitería* on-site, but it's best to bring a picnic lunch.

Punta Tombo is 110km south of Trelew (180km south of Puerto Madryn) via well-maintained gravel RP 1 and a short southeast lateral. Motorists can proceed south to Camarones via scenic but desolate Cabo Raso.

CAMARONES

☎ 0297 / pop 1300

In the stiff competition for Patagonia's sleepiest coastal village, Camarones takes home gold. Don't diss its languorous state: if you've ever needed to run away, this is one good option. Its empty beaches are conducive to strolling and the sociable townsfolk are masters in the art of shooting the breeze. It is also the closest hub to the lesser-known Cabo Dos Bahías nature reserve, where you can visit 25,000 penguin couples and their fuzzy chicks.

Spanish explorer Don Simón de Alcazaba y Sotomayor anchored here in 1545, proclaiming it part of his attempted Provincia de Nueva León. When the wool industry took off, Camarones became the area's main port for wool and sheepskins. The high quality of local wool didn't go unnoticed by justice of the peace Don Mario Tomás Perón, who operated the area's largest *estancia*, Porvenir, on which his son (and future president) Juanito would romp about. The town flourished as a port, but after Comodoro Rivadavia finished its massive port, Camarones was all but deserted.

The very helpful oceanfront **tourist office** (☎ 496-3040; Tomas Espora s/n) offers maps, good tips on scenic outings and lodging information. Contact **Jorge Kriegel** (☎ 496-3056) at Camping Municipal for fishing excursions and outings to see dolphins and nearby islands. Every February, Camarones hits its stride with the **Fiesta Nacional del Salmón**, a weekend of deep-sea fishing competitions

---

DO IT YOURSELF: MI CAMARONES

- Look for the historic Perón family home (or enjoy chatting up locals while doing so)
- Explore the sandy beaches and rocky cliffs north of town
- Gaze out at the great view where Cabo Dos Bahías splits two bays

---

featuring a free Sunday seafood lunch for all and the crowning of Miss Salmoncito.

Locals anticipate the inauguration of RN 1 in 2009, which will mean direct buses from Comodoro Rivadavia, and probably a good deal more tourism. If you hurry, you can say you knew Camarones way back when.

Sleeping & Eating

Camping Camarones (San Martín; per person/vehicle AR$3/5) At the waterfront port, this peaceful campground offers shade to a few campers. Hot showers and electricity are other perks.

El Viejo Torino (☎ 496-3003; cnr Av Costanera & Brown; r per person AR$55) This attractive house down by the water is sometimes let out to long-term workers, but provides good-value rooms and meals on occasion.

Hotel Indalo Inn (☎ 496-3004; www.indaloinn.com.ar; cnr Sarmiento & Roca; s/d AR$100/130) Remodeled rooms are a bit of a squeeze but feature good bedding and snug comforts. The showers demonstrate gale force and breakfast includes *café con leche* (coffee with milk). Internet is AR$5 per hour for computer use or wi-fi. The attached restaurant (mains AR$30) is just OK for the price.

Pick up groceries at **Mercado Mica** (cnr Roca & Sarmiento).

Getting There & Away

At a gas-station junction 180km south of Trelew, RP 30 splits off from RN 3 and heads 72km east to Camarones. El Ñandú buses go to Trelew (AR$20, three hours) on Monday, Wednesday and Friday at 4pm. For transport to Cabo Dos Bahías, chat with Don Roberto at Hotel Indalo Inn.

CABO DOS BAHÍAS

Thirty rough kilometers southeast of Camarones, the isolated **Cabo Dos Bahías** (admission AR$20; ☺ year-round) rookery attracts far

fewer visitors than Punta Tombo, making it an excellent alternative. You'll be rewarded with orcas, a huge colony of nesting penguins in spring and summer, whales in winter and a large concentration of guanacos and rheas. Seabirds, sea lions, foxes and fur seals are year-round residents.

Inside the reserve, the friendly tourist complex **Caleta Sara** (☎ 0297-447-1118, 0297-15-422-2270; www.tramotours.com.ar in Spanish; camping per person AR$15, dm AR$35; ☺ Sep-Feb) offers dorm beds with sheets and blankets in trailers as well as camping. Cafeteria fare depends on the catch of the day. Car transfers can be arranged from the crossroads with RN 3 (AR$150) or Camarones (AR$80).

You can pitch a tent for free at Cabo Dos Bahías Club Naútico or on any of the beaches en route from Camarones.

COMODORO RIVADAVIA

☎ 0297 / pop 140,682

Surrounded by dry hills of drilling rigs, oil tanks and wind-energy farms, tourism in the dusty port of Comodoro (as it's commonly known) usually means little more than a bus transfer. What this modern, hardworking city does provide is a gateway to nearby destinations with decent services. It sits at the eastern end of the Corredor Bioceánico highway that leads to Coyhaique, Chile.

Founded in 1901, Comodoro was once a transport hub linking ranches in nearby Sarmiento. In 1907 the town struck it rich when workers drilling for water struck oil instead. With the country's first major gusher, Comodoro became a state pet, gaining a large port, airport and paved roads. Today it is a powerhouse in the now-privatized oil industry. Although the recession hit hard in 2001, this boomtown rebounded with a flashy casino, elegant shops and hot rods on the streets.

Commerce centers on the principal streets Av San Martín and Av Rivadavia. Av San Martín between Mitre and Belgrano has up-scale boutiques and shops unknown to most of Patagonia. A climb up 212m to the mirador atop Cerro Chenque, smack dab in the middle of the city, offers views to Golfo San Jorge.

Information

Locutorios abound around downtown.

ACA (Automóvil Club Argentino; ☎ 446-0876; cnr Dorrego & Alvear) Maps and road info.

PATAGONIA

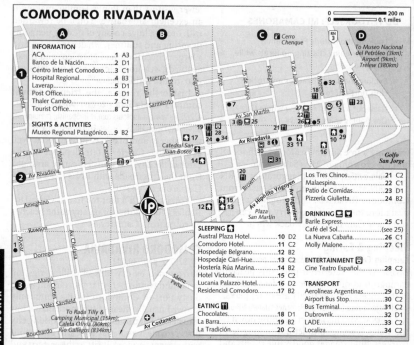

COMODORO RIVADAVIA

0 _____ 200 m
0 _____ 0.1 miles

INFORMATION
ACA...................................1 A3
Banco de la Nación................2 D1
Centro Internet Comodoro.......3 C1
Hospital Regional..................4 B3
Laverap.............................5 D1
Post Office.........................6 D1
Thaler Cambio.....................7 C1
Tourist Office......................8 C2

SIGHTS & ACTIVITIES
Museo Regional Patagónico.....9 B2

SLEEPING
Austral Plaza Hotel...............10 D2
Comodoro Hotel...................11 C2
Hospedaje Belgrano..............12 B2
Hospedaje Cari-Hue..............13 C2
Hostería Rúa Marina..............14 B2
Hotel Victoria.....................15 C2
Lucania Palazzo Hotel............16 D2
Residencial Comodoro............17 B2

EATING
Chocolates.........................18 D1
La Barra...........................19 B2
La Tradición.......................20 C2

Los Tres Chinos....................21 C2
Malaespina.........................22 C1
Patio de Comidas.................23 D1
Pizzería Giulietta..................24 B2

DRINKING
Barile Express......................25 C1
Café del Sol.......................(see 25)
La Nueva Cabaña..................26 C1
Molly Malone......................27 C1

ENTERTAINMENT
Cine Teatro Español...............28 C2

TRANSPORT
Aerolíneas Argentinas............29 D2
Airport Bus Stop...................30 C2
Bus Terminal......................31 C2
Dubrovnik.........................32 C1
LADE...............................33 C1
Localiza............................34 C2

Golfo San Jorge

To Museo Nacional
del Petróleo (3km);
Airport (9km);
Trelew (380km)

To Rada Tilly &
Camping Municipal (15km);
Caleta Olivia (80km);
Río Gallegos (834km)

PATAGONIA

Banco de la Nación (cnr Av San Martín & Güemes) Most of Comodoro's banks and ATMs, including this one, are along Av San Martín or Av Rivadavia.

Centro Internet Comodoro (Av San Martín 536) Stays open late.

Hospital Regional (☎ 444-2287; Av Hipólito Yrigoyen 950)

Laverap (Av Rivadavia 287) Centrally located laundry.

Post office (cnr Av San Martín & Moreno)

Thaler Cambio (Mitre 943) Changes traveler's checks.

Tourist office (☎ 446-2376; www.comodoro.gov .ar/turismo in Spanish; Av Rivadavia 430; ☼ 8am-3pm Mon-Fri) Friendly, well stocked and well organized. A desk at the bus terminal is open 8am to 9pm.

Sights

MUSEO NACIONAL DEL PETRÓLEO

Intransigent petroleum fans head to **Museo Nacional del Petróleo** (☎ 455-9558; admission AR$5; ☼ 9am-6pm Tue-Fri, 2-6pm Sat & Sun), for an insider look at the social and historical aspects of petroleum development. Don't expect balanced treatment of oil issues – the museum was built by the former state oil agency YPF (it is now managed by the Universidad Nacional de Patagonia). While its historical photos are

interesting, the detailed models of tankers, refineries and the entire zone of exploitation are best left to the die-hard. Guided tours are available.

The museum is in the suburb of General Mosconi, 3km north of downtown. Take a *remise* from downtown (AR$9), or bus 7 'Laprida' or 8 'Palazzo' (AR$1.50, 10 minutes); get off at La Anónima supermarket.

MUSEO REGIONAL PATAGÓNICO

Decaying natural-history specimens at this **museum** (☎ 477-7101; cnr Av Rivadavia & Chacabuco; admission free; ☼ 10am-6pm Mon-Fri, 3-7pm Sat & Sun) nearly overshadow the small yet entertaining archaeological and historical items, including well-crafted pottery, spear points and materials on early South African Boer immigrants.

Tours

Several agencies arrange trips to Bosque Petrificado Sarmiento (p453) and Cueva de las Manos (p480).

Ruta 40 (☎ 446-5337; www.ruta-40.com) organizes well-informed and personalized 4WD trips on RN 40 and in other parts of Patagonia. It's run by Mónica Jung and Pedro Mangini, a dynamic duo who speak English, German and Italian.

The urban train tour **Circuito Ferroportuario** (admission free) takes visitors on a circuit from the tourist office to visit containers, warehouses, historical installations and workshops on the port.

Sleeping

Catering mainly to business travelers and long-term laborers, lodging here fits two categories: the ritzy and the run-down (and often full). Try reserving your spot well in advance.

BUDGET

Camping Municipal (☎ 445-2918; Rada Tilly; www.rada tilly.com.ar/turismo-camping.html in Spanish; per person AR$5) At the windy beach resort of Rada Tilly, 15km south of Comodoro, this campground has sites with windbreaking shrubs. The wide beach is one of Patagonia's longest and there's a sea lion colony near the south end below Punta del Marqués. Frequent buses leave from Comodoro's bus terminal.

Hospedaje Belgrano (☎ 447-8439; Belgrano 546; s with/without bathroom AR$90/45) Run by a stern matron, this cavernous, high-ceiling classic offers basic, old-fashioned rooms, nice hallways and the tweeting of parakeets.

MIDRANGE

Hostería Rúa Marina (☎ 446-8777; Belgrano 738; s/d/tr/q with breakfast AR$60/126/154/180) Reminiscent of an old YMCA, Rúa Marina has small but OK rooms that are on the dark side. The best options are rooms 18, 19 and 20, with outside windows.

Hospedaje Cari-Hue (☎ 447-2946; Belgrano 563; s/d without bathroom AR$80/120, with bathroom AR$160/180) Tidy rooms flank an indoor patio that's strewn with plants and garden gnomes. It's central, albeit noisy.

Hotel Victoria (☎ 446-0725; Belgrano 585; s/d/tr AR$140/170/210) The friendliest hotel on the block. Soothing, good-sized rooms have firm twin beds, desks and cable TV.

Residencial Comodoro (☎ 446-2582; tilsamen dieta55@hotmail.com; España 919; s/d/tr/q with breakfast AR$130/180/195/240) A tidy and serviceable old hotel. Rooms have high ceilings and tile floors but clear tape mends the armchairs.

TOP END

Comodoro Hotel (☎ 447-2300; www.comodorohotel .ar in Spanish; 9 de Julio 770; s/d standard AR$191/218, superior

AR$231/270; ▣) Once the only game in town, this high-rise could use updating. Remodeled superior rooms offer larger bathrooms, while standard rooms remain a little drab for their price tag. Rates include a buffet breakfast and internet access.

Austral Plaza Hotel (☎ 447-2200; www.australhotel .com.ar in Spanish; Moreno 725; s/d standard AR$200/225, superior AR$410/435; ▣) Enter the labyrinth of this business hotel and convention center and you will find boxy standard rooms. Slicker suites await in the newer Plaza wing, with attentive staff and a big breakfast buffet adding to the sparkle. Its restaurant, Tunet, does gourmet seafood impeccably and the desserts are award-winning. Pack your polo shirt – guests also have access to a golf and tennis club.

Lucania Palazzo Hotel (☎ 449-9300; www.lucania -palazzo.com in Spanish; Moreno 676; s/d/ste AR$420/488/493; ▣) Comodoro's answer to the Trump Towers, the sparkling Palazzo offers ocean views from every room and tasteful modern decor, although ventilation could be better. There are six presidential suites (just in case OPEC comes to town), a business center and a haute Mediterranean seafood restaurant.

Eating

Travelers will find more in the way of restaurant selections than hotels – the oil boom has bankrolled a taste for fine dining. You can find the free *Sabores del Sur* restaurant directory in some hotels.

Chocolates (Av San Martín 231; cones AR$8) Ice-cream junkies can appreciate this parlor's selection of velvety chocolate and rich *dulce de leche* flavors.

Patio de Comidas (cnr Güemes & Av San Martín; meals AR$9) Meet some oil workers while you dine cheap and cafeteria-style, with burgers made to order. It's next to the grocery store.

Malaespina (☎ 446-0667; 9 de Julio 859; mains AR$15-25; ☯ 10am-late Mon-Sat, 7pm-late Sun; ▣) A chic restaurant-bar catering to playful palates, Malaespina is lustrous and low-lit with ample lounge space in the back. A wide selection of salads, pizza and gourmet sandwiches fills the menu. Try the Hendrix, with *jamon crudo* (cured ham), avocado and cheese on wheat bread.

La Barra (Av San Martín 686; mains AR$15-25) This modern café is a popular stop for an after-work *café con leche*. At mealtimes you'll find a good selection of salads, fancy burgers and meats, along with plenty of cocktails.

PATAGONIA

Los Tres Chinos (☎ 444-1168; Av Rivadavia 341; buffet AR$16) Hook up with this enormous *tenedor libre* (all-you-can-eat restaurant) for vegetarian fare as well as grilled meats. Drinks can be expensive.

Pizzería Giulietta (☎ 446-1201; Belgrano 851; mains AR$21) The place for pizzas, Giulietta also makes noteworthy spinach pasta and gnocchi, offered with your choice of several cream- or tomato-based sauces.

La Tradición (☎ 446-5800; Mitre 675; mains AR$28-45; ☎ closed Sun) This elegant *parrilla* grills excellent meats in a setting of white linens and oil paintings (literally, since their subjects are oil rigs!). The chicken in red-wine sauce has subtle, rich flavor. Save room for dessert.

Drinking & Entertainment

Barile Express (Av San Martín 514; snacks AR$8) Grab a newspaper and take your jolt of caffeine alongside the other patrons downing warm *medialunas*. The meringue pies look tempting.

Café del Sol (☎ 440-0034; Av San Martín 502; breakfast & snacks AR$6-15) This hip café offers mellow nightlife and also serves breakfast.

Molly Malone (☎ 447-8333; Av San Martín 292; mains AR$9-21) Run by the Golden Oldies rugby club, this funky little resto-pub is a pleasant stop for breakfast, set lunch or an evening Quilmes.

La Nueva Cabaña (9 de Julio 821; ☺ 8pm-6am Tue-Thu, 10pm-6am Fri & Sat) This rustic, bare-bones pub and dance spot attracts a young crowd for *música electrónica*, rock, folk and pop.

Cine Teatro Español (☎ 447-7700; www.cinecr.com.ar in Spanish; Av San Martín 668; admission AR$12) Offers a wide selection of Hollywood flicks.

Getting There & Away

The Corredor Bioceánico – RN 26, RP 20 and RP 55 – is a straight highway link to Coyhaique, Chile, and its Pacific port, Puerto Chacabuco. Developers are promoting this commercial transport route as an alternative to the Panama Canal, since the pass is open year-round and it is the continent's shortest distance between ports on both oceans. Paved RN 26, RP 20 and RN 40 lead to Esquel and Bariloche.

AIR

Aeropuerto General Mosconi (CRD; ☎ 454-8190) is 9km north of town. Airport tax is AR$6.

Aerolíneas Argentinas (☎ 444-0050; Av Rivadavia 156) flies a couple of times daily to Buenos Aires (AR$358) and a couple of times a week to Neuquén (AR$1209).

Comodoro is the hub for **LADE** (☎ 447-0585; Av Rivadavia 360), which wings it at least once a week to Bariloche (AR$209), El Calafate (AR$202), Esquel (AR$183), Río Gallegos (AR$210), Trelew (AR$179), Ushuaia (AR$286), Viedma (AR$192) and Buenos Aires (AR$296) and points in between. Schedules and routes change as often as the winds.

BUS

The chaotic **bus terminal** (☎ 446-7305; Pellegrini 730) receives all buses plying RN 3. Stop at the helpful tourist desk for maps and travel assistance.

Most bus schedules are divided into northbound and southbound departures. **Andesmar** (☎ 446-8894) departs five times daily (between 1:15am and 3pm) for points north including Trelew, Rawson, Puerto Madryn and San Antonio Oeste, then heads inland toward Córdoba. **TAC** (☎ 444-3376) follows the same route north through Patagonia, leaving at 6:20am, 7:20am and 2pm, but continues to Bahía Blanca, La Plata and Buenos Aires. For points south, TAC departs at 9:30pm for Caleta Olivia, Puerto San Julián and Río Gallegos.

Etap (☎ 447-4841) runs to Sarmiento four times daily (8:30am, 1pm, 6pm and 7pm), to Esquel at 9:30pm, to Río Mayo once daily, to Coyhaique on Wednesdays and Saturdays at 8am, and to Río Senguer four times weekly.

For Los Antiguos and connections to Chile Chico, via the town of Perito Moreno, **La Unión** (☎ 446-2822) has services at 5:30am and 4:45pm. **Marga** (☎ 447-0564) goes to Los Antiguos at 8pm. Marga also has a new service to El Calafate at 8pm daily. For other Chilean destinations, **Turíbus** (☎ 446-0058) goes to Coyhaique Wednesday and Saturday at 8am.

Destination	Cost (AR$)	Duration (hr)
Bahía Blanca	150-208	15
Bariloche	92-128	14
Buenos Aires	236-320	24
Caleta Olivia	14	1
Esquel	60-85	8
El Calafate	110	8
Los Antiguos	58	6
Puerto Deseado	44	4-5
Puerto Madryn	59-88	6-8
Río Gallegos	100-127	9-11
Trelew	49-75	5-6
Viedma	121-144	10-13

Getting Around

Bus 8 'Directo Palazzo' (AR$1.50) goes directly to the airport from outside the downtown bus terminal.

Expreso Rada Tilly links Comodoro's bus terminal to the nearby beach resort (AR$2) every 20 minutes on weekdays and every 30 minutes on weekends.

Rental cars are available from **Avis** (☎ 454-8483; at airport) and **Localiza** (☎ 446-3526; Av Rivadavia 535). **Dubrovnik** (☎ 444-1844; www.rentacardubrovnik .com; Moreno 941) rents 4WD vehicles.

SARMIENTO

☎ 0297 / pop 10,000

Sarmiento is a sleepy, picturesque outpost of berry and cherry plantations, where half the roads are gravel and cars dodge the dogs napping in the middle of them. Once Tehuelche territory, Argentina's southernmost irrigated town has been an agricultural center since its founding in 1897. These days it is also an oil hub surrounded by derricks, a reality most farmers prefer to ignore. For the visitor, it is the gateway to the petrified forests, 30km southeast, and a tranquil spot for the road-weary to rejuvenate. It sits between Lago Musters and Lago Colhué Huapi. As Comodoro's water source, Colhué Huapi has become a puddle of its former self and its compromised ecosystem is of serious concern to ecologists.

The eager **tourist office** (☎ 489-8220; turismo@ coopsar.com.ar; cnr Infanteria 25 & Pietrobelli; ⏲ 8am-7pm Mon-Fri, 11am-5pm Sat & Sun) is helpful and provides maps of the town and region. Tourist agency **Santa Teresita** (☎ 489-3238; cnr Roca & Uruguay) makes excursions (AR$70) to see rock art at Alero de los Manos, 55km from Sarmiento. **Cabaña del Futuro** (☎ 489-3336) raises quarter horses and runs horseback-riding trips (AR$15 per hour) in summer.

Facing the plaza, the **Museo Regional Desiderio Torres** (Coronel 355; admission free; ⏲ 10am-1pm & 5-8pm Mon-Sat, 10am-5pm Sun) offers interesting archaeological and paleontology displays, as well as indigenous artifacts with an emphasis on weaving. Just before the entrance to town on the way to the petrified forest, **Granja San José** (☎ 489-3733; tours AR$6) is a hydroponics farm selling exquisite jams.

Anglers can while away their time on **Lago Musters**, a 60m-deep, sandy-bottom lake with good year-round fishing for trout, perch and silverside. Licenses (AR$40) are available at the tourist office.

Comfortable campsites can be found at **Camping Río Senguer** (☎ 489-8482; per tent/car/ person AR$5/2/3), located 1km from the center on RP 24. In town, find the mint-green facade of the well-scrubbed **Hotel Ismar** (☎ 489-3293; Patagonia 248; s/d/t AR$60/90/110) for narrow motel rooms with linoleum floors.

Working cherry farm **Chacra Labrador** (☎ 489-3329, 0297-15-509-3537; www.hosterialabrador.com.ar; d AR$180) is a charming 1930s homestead offering bed and breakfast. Rooms are few but luxuriant, with big cozy beds, antique furniture, pots of tea and crackling fires. Attentive owners Annelies and Nicholás speak Dutch and English, provide meals on request and organize excursions to nearby attractions. Reserve in advance. If you're driving, it's 10km west of Sarmiento (past the turnoff for town if you're coming from Comodoro), 1km before the Río Senguer bridge. Otherwise call for pickup from town.

Sarmiento is 148km west of Comodoro along RN 26 and RP 20. Etap buses run daily to Comodoro Rivadavia (AR$15, two hours) at 8am, 1pm, 7pm and 10pm. Buses to Río Mayo (AR$26, 1½ hours) go at 9:30pm daily.

BOSQUE PETRIFICADO SARMIENTO

Fallen giants scattered in a pale sandstone landscape, this **petrified forest** (admission AR$20; ⏲ dawn-dusk), 30km southeast of Sarmiento, are a curious sight to explore. From the visitor center, a trail leads through ethereal grounds with the appearance of a lumberyard gone mad: 'wood' chips cover the ground and huge petrified logs, up to 100m in length and 1m wide, are scattered about. Unlike the petrified forest in Santa Cruz, these trunks were scattered here by strong river currents, which brought the trees from the mountainous regions about 65 million years ago. The most impressive area of the park has a handful of large trunks set against the red and orange striated bluffs. For travelers, this area is much more accessible than the Monumento Natural Bosques Petrificados further south.

Tour buses usually leave by 5pm. Try to stay through sunset, when the striped bluffs of Cerro Abigarrado and the multihued hills turn brilliantly vivid. Rangers guide tours and, if they are suspicious, will ask you to empty your pockets as you leave to expose any stolen pieces. A 'box of shame' shows what some have tried to sneak out. Ask at the tourist office in Sarmiento for *remise* rates for the 1½-hour roundtrip.

CALETA OLIVIA
☎ 0297 / pop 37,000

Slightly seedy but nevertheless authentic, Caleta Olivia earns its living refining oil and processing fish. High winds plague the port, but are preferable to its sporadic dust storms. Located south of Comodoro on costal RN 3, Caleta Olivia is, however, a convenient place to change buses to more inspiring locales, such as the petrified forests, Puerto Deseado or Los Antiguos.

The port was built in 1901 as part of a plan to run the telegraph along the coast, and was named after the only woman on board that first ship to land here. Discovery of oil in 1944 turned the face of industry from wool and sheep transport to petroleum, as evidenced by the eerie 10m-high Monumento al Obrero Petrolero that lords over the downtown traffic circle. Colloquially called 'El Gorosito,' the muscular oil worker looks north, symbolizing the link between this area's industry and Argentina's oil-poor northern reaches.

Orientation

Entering town from the north, RN 3 becomes Av Jorge Newbery, then Av San Martín (the main thoroughfare), continuing after the traffic circle along southeast diagonal Av Eva Perón. The southwest diagonal Av Independencia, the center of teenage cruising, becomes RP 12. Most streets run diagonal to San Martín, except in the northeast quadrant. The port and pebbly beach are four blocks east of the traffic circle.

Information

Banks along San Martín have ATMs but don't change traveler's checks. *Locutorios* and internet cafés also line San Martín.

Post office (cnr 25 de Mayo & Yrigoyen)

Tourist office (☎ 485-0988; caletaolivia@santacruz .gov.ar; cnr San Martín & Güemes; ☺ 7am-9pm) Enthusiastic office near the monument, with a map of the town.

SLEEP SPOT SHORTAGES

Travelers should carefully coordinate their overnight stops south on RN 3. Due to a petroleum industry boom, housing shortages in Caleta Olivia and Comodoro Rivadavia mean that many lodgings are booked out to seasonal workers. Make your reservations well in advance or coordinate your arrival with the departure of the next bus out.

Sleeping & Eating

A housing shortage means oil workers are filling up the budget hotels and travelers may have a tough time finding a space. Rates are steep for what's on offer, and breakfast is usually extra. Av Independencia has lots of bars, cafés and ice-cream shops.

Camping Municipal (☎ 485-0999, ext 476; cnr Brown & Guttero; per person/car AR$4/6) In an exposed gravel lot near the busy beach, the campground lacks privacy but has 24-hour security, hot showers and barbecue pits.

Posada Don David (☎ 857-7661; Yrigoyen 2385; d with/ without bathroom AR$100/90) Fronted by a lively café filled with male drinkers, these basic rooms line a tight corridor. While the bathrooms need work, this posada (inn) is at least clean. The casual eatery in front serves good grilled food and pastas (AR$15; closed Sunday).

Residencial Las Vegas (☎ 485-1177; Yrigoyen 2094; d/tr/q AR$120/150/200) This friendly basic lodging fills up with oil workers frequently. Ceilings are high and the back rooms quiet, but there's little ventilation.

Hotel Robert (☎ 485-1452; hrobert@mcolivia.com .ar; San Martín 2151; s/d/tr standard AR$137/157/167, superior AR$173/193/208) Considered the best lodging in town, the Robert put all its glitz into the mirrored marble lobby, leaving little cheer for the rooms. Standard rooms are cramped, with peeling wallpaper. The desk staff is gracious and there's a 10% cash discount.

Hotel Capri (☎ 485-1132; Hernández 1145; s/d AR$150/200) For the better half of a century, the fun-loving owners have offered basic rooms (upstairs are best) off a central hallway.

Buonna Pizza (☎ 485-5500; Independencia 52; pizzas AR$21) This family-friendly pizzeria provides an upbeat setting for pizza and empanadas, and it's less smoky than its nearby counterparts.

El Puerto (☎ 485-1313; Independencia 1060; mains AR$35) Crisp linens and elegant seafood platters are the order of the day. To get today's catch, ask waiters '¿Que es lo más fresco?' If you are up for a spendy power lunch, it's the best bet in town.

Getting There & Away

The **bus terminal** (cnr Bequin & Tierra del Fuego) is 3km northwest of downtown (AR$4 by remise). The main north–south carriers leave for Comodoro Rivadavia (AR$14, one hour) hourly from 7am to 11pm, with fewer services on Sunday, and for Río Gallegos (AR$90, seven to 10 hours) four times daily between

8:30pm and 2am, passing Puerto San Julián. **Sportsman** (☎ 485-1287) and **La Unión** (☎ 485-1134) serve Puerto Deseado (AR$36, 3½ hours), Perito Moreno (AR$48, four hours) and Los Antiguos (AR$59, five hours) in the early morning and late afternoon.

PUERTO DESEADO
☎ 0297 / pop 12,000

Some 125km southeast of the RN 3 junction, RN 281 weaves through valleys of rippling pink rock, past guanacos in tufted grassland, to end at the serene and attractive deep-sea fishing town of Puerto Deseado. While the town is ripe for revitalization it is also apparent that change takes a glacial pace here: witness the vintage trucks rusting on the streets like beached cetaceans. But the draw of the historic center plus the submerged estuary of Ría Deseado (p457), brimming with seabirds and marine wildlife, make Puerto Deseado a worthy detour.

In 1520 the estuary provided shelter to Hernando de Magallanes after a crippling storm waylaid his fleet; he dubbed the area 'Río de los Trabajos' (River of Labours). In

1586 English privateer Cavendish explored the estuary and named it after his ship *Desire,* and this time the name stuck. The port attracted fleets from around the world for whaling and seal hunting, compelling the Spanish crown to send a squadron of colonists, under the command of Antonio de Viedma. After a harsh winter, more than 30 of them died of scurvy. Those who survived moved inland to form the short-lived colony of Floridablanca. In 1834 Darwin surveyed the estuary, as did Perito Moreno in 1876.

Orientation

Puerto Deseado is two hours southeast of the RN 3 junction at Fitz Roy via dead-end RN 281. The center of activity is the axis formed by main streets San Martín and Almirante Brown.

Information

Banks, ATMs, *locutorios* and internet are all found along San Martín.

Banco de la Nación (San Martín)

CIS Tour (☎ 487-2864; San Martin 916) Handles local tours and flight reservations.

PATAGONIA

PUERTO DESEADO

0   500 m
0   0.3 miles

INFORMATION	
Banco de la Nación	1 C2
CIS Tour	2 C2
Ecowash	3 D2
Hospital Distrital	4 C3
Post Office	5 C2
Ría Deseada Tourist Office	6 B2
Vagón Histórico Tourist Office	7 C2

SIGHTS & ACTIVITIES	
Club Náutico	8 B3
Estación del Ferrocarril Patagónico	9 D2
Los Vikingos	10 B2
Museo Padre Beauvoir	11 C2
Museo Regional Mario Brozoski	12 C3
Sociedad Española	13 C2
Vagón Histórico	(see 7)

SLEEPING	
Cabañas Las Nubes	14 B2
Camping La Costanera	15 D3
Hotel Isla Chaffers	16 C2
Hotel Los Acantilados	17 A2
Residencial Las Bandurrias	18 B2
Residencial Los Olmos	19 D2

EATING	
El Pingüino	20 D2
El Refugio del Marino	21 B2
Juniors	22 D2
Maca	23 C2
Puerto Crystal	24 A2

DRINKING	
Quinto Elemento	25 D2

ENTERTAINMENT	
Jackaroe Boliche	26 C2

To Puerto Darwin (500m);
Darwin Expediciones (500m);
Camping Cañadón Giménez
(4km); RN 3 (127km);
Caleta Olivia (214km)

To Bus
Terminal
(150m)

Plaza
Centenario
9 de Julio

Ría Deseado

Punta
Cascajo

Muelle de
Ramón

Av Costanera

Ecowash (☎ 487-0490; Piedra Buena 859; ☒ closed Sun) Full-service laundry.

Hospital Distrital (☎ 487-0200; España 991)

Post office (San Martín 1075)

Ría Deseada Tourist Office (☎ 487-0220; www .puertodeseado.gov.ar in Spanish; San Martín 1525; ☒ 10am-1pm & 5-8pm Mon-Fri) There's another English-speaking desk at the bus terminal.

Vagón Histórico Tourist Office (cnr San Martín & Almirante Brown; ☒ 9am-9pm)

Sights & Activities

A self-guided **walking tour** is a good start to catching the vibes of Deseado. Pick up a *Guía Historica* map (in Spanish) from either tourist office.

Puerto Deseado was once the coastal terminus for a cargo and passenger route that hauled wool and lead from Chilean mines from Pico Truncado and Las Heras, 280km northwest. Choo-choo fans can check out the imposing English-designed **Estación del Ferrocarril Patagónico** (admission by donation; ☒ 4-7pm Mon-Sat), off Av Oneto, built by Yugoslav stonecutters in 1908.

In the center of town, the restored 1898 **Vagón Histórico** (cnr San Martín & Almirante Brown) is famous as the car from which rebel leader Facón Grande prepared the 'Patagonia Rebellion.' In 1979 the car was almost sold for scrap, but disgruntled townspeople blocked the roads to stop the sale. A few blocks west is the attractive **Sociedad Española** (San Martín 1176), c 1915.

The **Museo Regional Mario Brozoski** (☎ 487-0673; cnr Colón & Belgrano; admission free; ☒ 10am-5pm Mon-Fri, 3-7pm Sat) displays relics of the English corvette *Swift*, sunk off the coast of Deseado in 1776. Divers continue to recover artifacts from this wreck, located in 1982. Named for a Salesian priest, **Museo Padre Beauvoir** (☎ 487-0147; 12 de Octubre 577; admission free; ☒ 10am-5pm Mon-Fri) shows an eclectic combination of native relics, stuffed birds and objects donated by pioneer families.

Paddling and windsurfing can be enjoyed in summer. On the waterfront, **Club Naútico** (☎ 0297-15-419-0468) rents boards and kayaks (summer only). Depending on current conditions, sport fishing can be an option; inquire at the pier.

Tours

Darwin Expediciones (☎ 0297-15-624-7554; www .darwin-expeditions.com; Av España 2601) Offers sea-kayaking trips, wildlife observation and multiday nature and archaeology tours with knowledgeable guides. Their best seller is the tour of Reserva Natural Ría Deseado.

Los Vikingos (☎ 487-0020, 0297-15-624-5141/4283; www.losvikingos.com.ar; Estrada 1275) Offers excursions on land and sea. Tours, some led by marine biologists, include Reserva Natural Ría Deseado and Monumento Natural Bosques Petrificados.

Sleeping

Ask the tourist office about (relatively) nearby *estancias*.

Camping La Costanera (☎ 0297-15-625-2890; Av Costanera; per person AR$10, trailer bunks per person AR$30; ☒ year-round) Rates at this waterfront campground vary by site. It has good toilets and showers, but incessant winds can be a nuisance and some campsites are stony.

Camping Cañadón Giménez (☎ 0297-15-673-6051; RN 281; per person/tent AR$2/10, cabins AR$50-80; ☒ year-round) Four kilometers northwest of town, but only 50m from the Ría Deseado, this campground is sheltered by forest and high rocky walls. Bare-bones cabins sleep four; the upgrade gets you heating and kitchen basics. Showers, hot water and basic provisions are available.

Residencial Las Bandurrias (☎ 487-0745; acantour@ speedy.com.ar; Sarmiento 9050; s/d with breakfast AR$80/105) The cavernous dimensions give this tiled building a slightly institutional feel, but its plain rooms are kept impeccably clean and its hostess is divine. Matrimonial beds are few.

Residencial Los Olmos (☎ 487-0077; Gregores 849; s/d/tr/q AR$72/108/132/160) A solid budget option kept shipshape by a vigilant matron, this brick house has 17 small rooms with TV, heat and private bathrooms.

Hotel Isla Chaffers (☎ 487-2246; cnr San Martín y Mariano Moreno; s/d/tr AR$140/170/190) Just the setting of this dark downtown hotel inspires a yawn, with its soft light and flower patterns. If you don't make it to your room, there are huge purple chaises in the hallway that beckon for lounging.

Hotel Los Acantilados (☎ 487-2167; www.hotellos acantilados.com.ar in Spanish; cnr Pueyrredón & Av España; d AR$140-220, suite AR$400) More inspiring from outside than in, these clifftop digs do boast an extensive lounge with fireplace, the perfect spot to chill out. Superior rooms and the dining room look out on the waterfront, while standard rooms are plain with dated bathrooms. There's a good café and conscientious staff.

Cabañas Las Nubes (☎ 0297-15-403-2677; Ameghino 1351; d/q cabins AR$200/220) Currently the nicest lodging in town, these deluxe two- and three-story wooden cabins bring you in reach of cloud nine. They sit on a hilltop, and some have ocean views, fully equipped kitchens and ample living space – ideal for groups and families.

Eating

Maca (☎ 487-2134; San Martín 1263; sandwiches AR$15; ☿ 1-3pm & 7:30-10pm, closed Mon) This brick café serves cheesy pizzas and sandwiches to fans of all ages. The ice cream comes highly recommended.

El Refugio del Marino (☎ 0297-15-621-5290; Pueyrredón 224; tapas AR$15; ☿ to 2am) Cheap *vino tinto* (red wine) and tapas feed the tale-swapping of the sailors and fishermen who gather at this friendly bar.

Juniors (☎ 0297-15-419-1297; 12 de Octubre 859; mains AR$15-22; ☿ 9am-3am) *Milanesas* (breaded fish), empanadas and home-cooked meals are served in this casual trophy-packed social club. Kids play table tennis in the back while pops serves cold ones on a bar top painted with Curly, Larry and Mo.

El Pingüino (☎ 487-2105; Piedra Buena 958; mains AR$21; ☿ closed Sun) This local institution cooks up fresh fish and pasta in an animated setting kept in check by the gregarious owner. There's also a set menu and good wine list.

Puerto Crystal (☎ 487-0378; Av España 1698; mains AR$25-38; ☿ noon-3pm & 8pm-midnight, closed Wed lunch) Seafood looms large on the menu (fried calamari, paella and hearty soups), but steaks are also worth trying. The pink restaurant overlooks a small pond as you enter the center.

Puerto Darwin (☎ 247554; Av España 2581; menu del día AR$35; ☿ 9am-2am; 🖳) Featuring sandwiches, *picadas* and fish dishes, this café run by Darwin Expediciones has an easygoing atmosphere topped by unparalleled views of the port. At sunset it is a prime spot to crack open a beer.

Drinking & Entertainment

Late-night drinking and dancing spots include the pub **Quinto Elemento** (cnr Don Bosco & 12 de Octubre) and the swanky disco **Jackaroe Boliche** (Mariano Moreno 663), in an unfortunate building.

Getting There & Away

LADE (☎ 487-2674), at the bus terminal, can arrange flights leaving from Comodoro Rivadavia.

The **bus terminal** (Sargento Cabral 1302) is on the northeast side of town, nine long blocks

and slightly uphill from San Martín and Av Oneto. Taxis to/from the center should cost around AR$12.

There are five departures daily to Caleta Olivia (AR$31, three hours) at 4:15am, 6am, 1pm, 7pm and 7:30pm. All continue to Comodoro Rivadavia (AR$44, four hours). Sportman's 7:30pm bus to Comodoro Rivadavia is timed to link with Sportman connections to El Calafate. Leaving on the 1pm bus (which doesn't run Sunday) allows for the quickest connection to Perito Moreno and Los Antiguos. Travelers headed to San Julián must connect through Caleta Olivia.

If you're thinking of getting off at godforsaken Fitz Roy (where locals claim the only thing to see is the wind!) to make progress toward Comodoro or Río Gallegos, think again: buses arrive at a demonic hour and the only place to crash is the campground behind Multirubro La Illusion.

RESERVA NATURAL RÍA DESEADO

Flanked by sandy cliffs, these aquamarine waters create sculpted seascapes you won't forget. Moreover, it's considered one of South America's most important marine preserves. Ría Deseado is the unique result of a river abandoning its bed, allowing the Atlantic waters to invade 40km inland and create a perfect shelter for marine life.

The marine life is abundant. Several islands and other sites provide nesting habitats for seabirds, including Magellanic penguins, petrels, oystercatchers, herons, terns and five species of cormorants. Isla Chaffers is the main spot for the penguins, while Banco Cormorán offers protection to rock cormorants and the striking gray cormorant. Isla de los Pingüinos has nesting rockhoppers and breeding elephant seals. Commerson's dolphins, sea lions, guanacos and ñandús (ostrichlike rheas) can also be seen while touring the estuary.

The best time to visit the reserve is from December to April. Darwin Expediciones (opposite) runs circuits that take in viewing of Commerson's dolphins, Isla Chaffers, Banco Cormorán and a walk to a penguin colony (AR$90, 2½ hours). The main attraction of the all-day Isla de los Pinguinos excursion (AR$250) is the punked-out rockhopper penguins with spiky yellow and black head feathers, but the tour also includes wildlife watching, sailing and hiking. There's a four-to five-person minimum and tours leave

PATAGONIA

depending on tides, usually early morning or midafternoon. Los Vikingos (p456) makes similar excursions with bilingual guides and organizes overland trips.

MONUMENTO NATURAL BOSQUES PETRIFICADOS

During Jurassic times, 150 million years ago, this area enjoyed a humid, temperate climate with flourishing forests, but intense volcanic activity buried them in ash. Erosion later exposed the mineralized *Proaraucaria* trees (ancestors of the modern *Araucaria*, unique to the southern hemisphere), up to 3m in diameter and 35m in length. Today, the 150-sq-km **Monumento Natural Bosques Petrificados** (Petrified Forests Natural Monument; admission free; 9am-9pm year-round) has a small visitor center, English-language brochure and short interpretive trail, leading from park headquarters to the largest concentration of petrified trees. Until its legal protection in 1954, the area was plundered for some of its finest specimens; please don't perpetuate this unsavory tradition.

Other parts of the scenic desert park also merit exploration, but consult with park rangers before heading toward the peak of Madre e Hija. Bring water; there's none at the site.

The park is 157km southwest of Caleta Olivia, accessed from the good gravel RP 49, leading 50km west from a turnoff at Km 2074 on RN 3. There's no public transport directly to the park. Buses from Caleta Olivia will drop you at the junction, but you may wait several hours for a lift into the park. Los Vikingos (p456) runs tours from Puerto Deseado.

There's basic camping, as well as provisions, at **La Paloma**, 20km before the park headquarters. Camping in the park is strictly prohibited.

PUERTO SAN JULIÁN

☎ 02962 / pop 6143

The perfect desolate-yet-charismatic locale for an art film, this small town sits baking in bright light and dust, stark against Bahía San Julián's startling blue. Considered the cradle of Patagonian history, the port of San Julián was first landed in 1520 by Magellan. His encounter with local Tehuelches provided the region's mythical moniker (see the boxed text, opposite). But he was not the last to make his mark. Following him, Viedma, Drake and Darwin all ventured onto this sandy spit. While its human history is proudly put forth, the landscape speaks of geologic revolutions, with its exposed, striated layers, rolling hills and golden cliffs.

Puerto San Julián's first non-native settlers came from the Falkland Islands with the late-19th-century wool boom. Scots followed with the San Julián Sheep Farming Company, which became the region's primary economic force for nearly a century. Recent growth has the city, 350km south of Caleta Olivia, developing like never before, with mining and seafood-processing industries. For travelers, the port is a relaxed and welcoming stop, as well as the place to see Commerson's dolphins.

Information

Banco Santa Cruz (cnr San Martín & Moreno) Has Link ATM.

Dirección de Turismo (☎ 454396; www.sanjulian .gov.ar in Spanish; Magallanes s/n; 7am-9pm Mon-Fri, 5-9pm Sat & Sun) There's also a high-season kiosk at San Martín 500.

Post office (cnr San Martín & Belgrano)

Telefónica (cnr San Martín & Rivadavia) *Locutorio* with internet.

Sights & Activities

One small local adventure is to take a *remise* or your own poor abused rental car on the incredibly scenic 30km **Circuito Costero**, following Bahía San Julián on a dirt road. A series of golden bluffs divide beautiful beaches with drastic tides. The area includes a sea lion colony and the penitent attraction of Monte Cristo (with its stations of the cross). If you are in your own vehicle, make sure it is equipped with a spare tire.

Relive Magellan's landing at **Museo Nao Victoria** (admission AR$8), a museum-cum-theme-park with life-sized figures cloaked in armor and shown celebrating mass and battling mutiny. Reproductions of everyday items provide some interest. You can't miss it – it's at the port on a boat, a reproduction of the *Nao Victoria*.

The last census found 130,000 penguins inhabiting Banco Cormorán, which you can visit by boat. Two-hour excursions on Bahía San Julián (AR$80 per person) are run by **Expediciones Pinocho** (☎ 454600; cnr Mitre & 9 de Julio). The penguins stick around from September to April. The tour also stops at Banco Justicia, to see the cormorant rookeries and other seabirds. From December to March there's a good chance you'll see the Commerson's dolphin (p441), known as the world's smallest dolphin.

BIG FEET, TALL TALES

Say 'Patagonia' and most think of fuzzy outdoor clothes, but the name that has come to symbolize the world's end still invites hot debate as to its origin.

One theory links the term 'Patagón' to a fictional monster in a best-selling 16th-century Spanish romance of the period, co-opted by Magellan's crew to describe the Tehuelche as they wintered in 1520 at Puerto San Julián. The moniker is traced to Italian nobleman Antonio Pigafetta, a crew member who described one Tehuelche as 'so tall we reached only to his waist…He was dressed in the skins of animals skillfully sewn together…His feet were shod with the same kind of skins, which covered his feet in the manner of shoes…The captain-general [Magellan] called these people Patagoni.'

Another theory suggests that the name comes from the Spanish *pata*, meaning paw or foot. No evidence corroborates the claim that the Tehuelche boasted unusually big feet (it's possible that the skins they wore made their feet seem exceptionally large). But it's good fodder for the genre of travelers' tales, where first impressions loom larger than life.

Another option is **trekking** the coastline and checking out the abundant birdlife. If you have a friend (or make one), you can rent **tandem bicycles** (☎ 02962-15-532312; per hr AR$10) to explore the area. For more information on either activity, consult the tourist information kiosk.

Sleeping & Eating

Camping Municipal (☎ 452806; Magallanes 650; per person/car AR$3/5) On the waterfront at the north end of Vélez Sarsfield, this full-service campground has hot showers (AR$1.50), laundry and windbreaks.

Hostería Municipal (☎ 452300; 25 de Mayo 917) At the time of writing, this waterfront mainstay was closed for renovations. Call for rates.

Hotel Álamo (☎ 454092; RN 3; d AR$70) Next to the EG3 gas station (there's no sign; inquire inside) and the RN 3 junction, Álamo is a small, adequate place with dark shuttered rooms, a good restaurant and private bathrooms.

La Casona (☎ 452434; miramar@videodata.com.ar; Magallanes 650; s/t/q AR$60/95/110) You can't miss this red corrugated house by the point. What appears to be the perennial haunt of fishermen is now the lodging of students and backpackers. If no one answers the door, ring the bell at the house directly behind it.

Posada Kau Yenu (☎ 452431; cnr San Martín & Calafate; s/d AR70/100) Don Ernesto fills this cozy home with good spirits and homemade bread for breakfast. If you are coming unannounced, be aware that the door is only attended in the evening and early-morning hours.

Hotel Sada (☎ 452013; www.hotelsada.com.ar in Spanish; San Martín 1112; s/d/t AR$80/125/140) An abundant breakfast and friendly service add considerable cheer to this dated, boxy hotel with dreary hall paneling and baby-blue furniture. Carpeted rooms feature thick duvet covers, small TVs and phones.

Hotel Ocean (☎ 452350; San Martín 959; s/d/t AR$95/130/150) This bright, remodeled brick building has attractive rooms with firm beds and a backdrop of tropical tones. Service is so-so and some rooms lack windows, but triples are unusually spacious.

Hotel Bahía (☎ 454028; www.hotelbahiasanjulian.com.ar in Spanish; San Martín 1075; s/d/t/ste AR$130/165/190/290; 🖳) This lovely, glass-front hotel feels decadent in a place like San Julián. Rooms are modern and beds firm. TV and laundry service are perks. The café-bar is an appealing setting for breakfast or just coffee.

La Rural (☎ 454066; Ameghino 811; mains AR$16-25) Service is friendly but the hearty food mediocre; still, the whole town seems to congregate at this unpretentious spot. Fare ranges from meat and potatoes to grilled fish and pastas.

La Juliana (☎ 454149; Zeballos 1130; mains AR$40; 🕑 dinner Tue-Sun) This renovated old home offers well-prepared versions of popular meals, but guests are mostly paying for the cool ambience.

Getting There & Away

AIR

LADE (☎ 452137), located at the bus terminal, soars on Tuesdays for Puerto Deseado (AR$65), continuing to Comodoro Rivadavia (AR$138).

BUS

Most RN 3 buses visit San Julián's **bus terminal** (☎ 452082; San Martín 1552) at insane hours. **Via Tac** (☎ 454453) goes to Puerto Madryn (AR$110,

12 hours) at 12:20am via Trelew (AR$102). **Andesmar** (☎ 454403) goes to Comodoro Rivadavia (AR$50) at 11:25pm. **Taqsa** (☎ 454667) goes to Río Gallegos (AR$45) at 2am, where travelers can make connections south. It also has a 1:20am bus that travels to Caleta Olivia (AR$45), Perito Moreno (AR$85) and Los Antiguos (AR$95).

There are slightly more expensive door-to-door service options, all operating Monday to Saturday, for around AR$50. **Sur Servicio** (☎ 454044, in Comodoro Rivadavia 02962-454044; San Martín 1380) goes to Comodoro Rivadavia at 2:30am; **Gold Tour** (☎ 452265; San Martín 1075) goes to Río Gallegos at 4:30am; and **Cerro San Lorenzo** (☎ 452403; Berutti 970) serves Gobernador Gregores at 7:30am.

Bus schedules may change, so always confirm departures ahead of time.

ESTANCIA LA MARÍA

Some 150km northwest of Puerto San Julián on the Patagonia steppe, **Estancia La María** (www .arqueologialamaria.com.ar) is an important area of archaeological research, studied for clues of life in the Pleistocene epoch. It has 84 caves with excellently preserved rock paintings dating back 12,600 years. Three different cultures, predating the Tehuelche, created the *arte rupestre* (cave paintings), today seen as Patagonia's most important discovery of this kind. The only way to see these treasures is by guided tour (AR$110) with the *estancia* owners.

This is also a great opportunity for budget travelers to sample a night on an *estancia*. Contact the kind owners **Pepa and Fernando Behm** (☎ in San Julián 02962-452233, 15-449827; Saavedra 1168; d with/without bathroom AR$88/47, per tent incl hot shower AR$16; ☼ Oct-May) for reservations and transport options. The ranch house has 21 beds in six rooms, with breakfast available (AR$6). La María is accessed via RP 25 and RP 77.

PARQUE NACIONAL MONTE LEÓN

Inaugurated in 2004, this fine coastal national park protects over 600 sq km of striking headlands, archetypal Patagonian steppe, and 40km of dramatic coastline with bays, beaches and tidal flats. Once a hunting ground for nomads, and later frequented by the Tehuelche, this former *estancia* is home to abundant Magellanic penguins, sea lions, guanacos and pumas. Bring binoculars: the wildlife watching is prime.

Hiking along the coastline, with its unusual geographic features, is best when low tide exposes stretches of sandy and rocky beach. In October 2006 the park's signature landscape attraction, **La Olla** (a huge cavelike structure eroded by the ocean), collapsed from repeated tidal action. Accessible at low tide, **Isla Monte León** is a high offshore sea stack heavily mined for guano between 1933 and 1960. Now it has been recolonized by cormorants, Dominican gulls, skuas and other seabirds. Use caution and know the tide tables before setting out; the tidal range is great, exposed rocks are slippery and the water returns fast.

Nature trails split off from the main road, leading to the coast. The **penguin trail** crosses the steppe, leading to an overlook of the rookery. It's forbidden to go off-trail, but seeing these 75,000 couples shouldn't be difficult. The roundtrip takes 1½ hours. Cars can reach the prominent cliff **Cabeza de León** (Lion's Head), where a 20-minute trail leads to the sea lion colony.

There is free camping on the beach, with access to picnic tables, but visitors must bring their own water. The other option is the charming **Hostería Monte León** (☎ in Buenos Aires 011-4621-4784, in Ushuaia 02901-431851; www.monteleon -patagonia.com; full board s/d AR$670/1005; ☼ Nov-Apr), a refurbished century-old home that was the *casco* (ranch house) of an 1895 *estancia*, now run by the original owner's granddaughter. The four-bedroom house retains the spartan style of the Patagonian farmhouse, with rod iron beds, basic tasteful furnishings and an open kitchen with iron wood stove. The *hostería* also offers all-day boat excursions (AR$250 with lunch) and fly-fishing for steelhead.

The park entrance is 30km south of Comandante Luis Piedrabuena or 205km north of Río Gallegos, directly off RN 3. Watch for it carefully since signage is poor. A visitor center is in the works.

RÍO GALLEGOS
☎ 02966 / pop 79,114

Hardly a tourist destination, this coal-shipping, oil-refining and wool-raising hub is a busy port with a few merits worth mentioning. Since the reign of the Kirchners, the capital city of their home province has been spruced up and spit-polished – recent prosperity is palpable. Outside of town, visitors can find some of the continent's best fly-fishing, traditional *estancias* and amazingly low tides (retreating 14m). Traveler services are good here but most visitors quickly pass through en route to El Calafate, Puerto Natales or Ushuaia.

Río Gallegos has an opportunist past. As the wool industry boomed in the early 1900s, fortune-hungry Brits and Chileans came seeking land – foreigners totaled 80% of the original population. The port stayed active with the narrow-gauge railway when coal was discovered 230km away in Río Turbio. Gallegos' economy now revolves around nearby oilfields, with coal deposits shipped to ocean-going vessels at Punta Loyola. Home to a large military base, the city played an active role during the Falklands War.

Information

Banks on Av Roca have ATMs. Internet is widely available in cybercafés and restaurants.

ACA (Automóvil Club Argentino; ☎ 420477; Orkeke 10) Gas station, maps and traveler services.

Aike Lavar (☎ 420759; Corrientes 277) Serviced laundry.

Centro de Informes Turístico (☎ 422365; Av San Martín s/n; ☼ Oct-Apr) Useful info kiosk on median.

Hospital Regional (☎ 420025; José Ingenieros 98)

Immigration office (☎ 420205; Urquiza 144; ☼ 9am-3pm Mon-Fri)

Municipal tourist office (☎ 436917/20; www .riogallegos.gov.ar; cnr Av Roca & Córdoba; ☼ 9am-3pm Mon-Fri) A desk at the bus terminal keeps longer hours.

Post office (Av Roca 893)

Provincial tourist office (☎ 422702; www.santacruz .gov.ar in Spanish; Av Roca 863; ☼ 9am-7pm Mon-Fri,

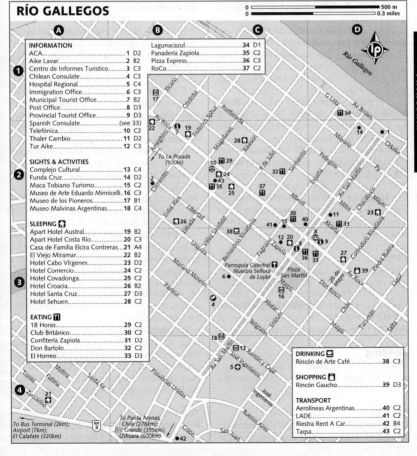

RÍO GALLEGOS

0 — 500 m
0 — 0.3 miles

10am-1pm & 5-8pm Sat & Sun) Most helpful, with maps, bilingual staff and detailed info.

Telefónica (Av Roca 1328) One of several late-night *locutorios* on Av Roca with internet access.

Thaler Cambio (Av San Martín 484; ⏱ 10am-3pm Mon-Fri, 10am-1pm Sat) Changes traveler's checks.

Tur Aike (☎ 422436; turaiketurismo@ciudad.com.ar; Zapiola 63) Helpful for airline bookings.

Sights

The pretty **Plaza San Martín** offers quiet benches in the shade of poplars and purple-blossom jacarandas.

Satiate your appetite for dinosaur dioramas and modern art at **Complejo Cultural** (☎ 423290; Ramón y Cajal 51; admission free; ⏱ 10am-7pm), offering exhibits on anthropology, paleontology, geology and fine arts. The Tehuelche ethnology exhibit includes fascinating photographs and local history.

With a mission to educate through art, **Museo de Arte Eduardo Minnicelli** (☎ 436323; Maipú 13; admission free; ⏱ 8am-7pm Tue-Fri, 3-7pm Sat & Sun) shows rotating exhibits from larger museums and paintings by Santa Cruz artists. It is also a good spot to get news on local cultural gatherings. Perhaps a must-see for Brits, the **Museo Malvinas Argentinas** (☎ 420128; Pasteur 74; admission free; ⏱ 1:30-7pm Mon-Fri) gets inside the Argentine claim to the Islas Malvinas.

In a prefabricated 1890s metal-clad house shipped from England, the **Museo de los Pioneros** (☎ 437763; cnr Elcano & Alberdi; admission free; ⏱ 10am-8pm) has good displays on early immigrant life. **Funda Cruz** (G Lista 60) is another attractive, imported, prefabricated wooden house. Once a customs office, it now hosts cultural activities as well as a *salón de té* (teahouse).

Tours

The large penguin rookery at Cabo Vírgenes, 140km southeast of Río Gallegos, can be visited from October to March. Excursions can be booked through **Maca Tobiano Turismo** (☎ 422466; Av Roca 998); an eight-hour trip costs AR$145 (plus AR$10 park admission).

Sleeping

Since hotels cater mainly to business travelers, good-value budget accommodations are scarce.

BUDGET

Casa de Familia Elcira Contreras (☎ 429856; Zuccarino 431; dm AR$30, d with bathroom AR$90) This friendly hostel offers clean, homey dorms with kitchen access, and one double room. It's far from the center but a 10-minute walk from the bus terminal.

MIDRANGE

Hotel Covadonga (☎ 420190; hotelcovadongargl@hotmail .com; Av Roca 1244; d/tr/q with bathroom AR$110/140/170, d/tr without bathroom AR$85/110) Good value and grandmotherly, the tidy Covadonga has appealing large rooms with creaky floors, and a sunny living room with worn leather sofas. Rooms with private bathrooms are worth the upgrade. Cash discounts are offered.

Hotel Cabo Vírgenes (☎ 422134/41; hotelcabo virgenes@speedy.com.ar; Comodoro Rivadavia 252; s/d/tr/q AR$85/115/170/190) A good-value option just a few blocks from the river, this yellow house features tiled rooms off narrow hallways. With the exception of family rooms, most can be cramped, but all are quiet.

La Posada (☎ 436445; hosterialaposada@infovia.com .ar; Ameghino 331; s/d AR$100/120) Cool, carpeted and clean rooms surround a well-cared-for internal garden at this attractive inn. Meals are served in the ranch-style dining area.

El Viejo Miramar (☎ 430401; Av Roca 1630; d AR$135) Snug carpeted rooms and spotless bathrooms make this affable choice a good one. Its personable owner makes guests at ease. Rates include breakfast (but not a second cup of coffee).

Hotel Sehuen (☎ 425683; www.hotelsehuen.com in Spanish; Rawson 160; s/d/tr/q AR$98/146/161/192) Boasting national-level service awards, modern Sehuen provides all-round good value. Bright and airy, the breakfast area has vaulted ceilings and the day's newspaper. Rooms are plain but well kept and have TVs.

Hotel Croacia (☎ 422997; hotelcroaciarg1@yahoo.com .ar; Urquiza 431; s/d/tr/apt AR$126/160/170/200; ▣) This former Yugoslav community center is now a popular family-oriented hotel. While its faux-wood walls and pleather armchairs are not for all, the carpeted rooms are pleasant and quiet time is respected. Breakfast is available in the 24-hour *confitería*.

Apart Hotel Austral (☎ 435588; www.apartaustral.com in Spanish; Av Roca 1505; d/apt AR$180/200; ⊠ ▣) Clean and modern, these pastel rooms boast good showers, stylish duvets and crisp linens. The hotel is nonsmoking and has wi-fi throughout. Mini-apartments have basic kitchens.

TOP END

Hotel Santa Cruz (☎ 420601/2; http://usuarios.advance .com.ar/htlscruz; cnr Av Roca & Comodoro Rivadavia; s/d/tr

AR$153/223/265; ⬚) Remodeling for a sleeker, suit-and-tie ambience, this downtown monolith is impeccably clean but currently a little short on charm (see the rubber shower curtains). Rooms have wi-fi and there's a busy café downstairs. Opt for the rooms along the internal patio. A small fee gets you time in the sauna.

Hotel Comercio (☎ 422458; hotelcomercio@infomacionrgl.com.ar; Av Roca 1302; s/d/tr AR$160/223/274; ⬚) Comercio caters to your inner businessperson with pleasant rooms with airtight shutters. The main drawback is the lingering smell of cigarettes. The brassy café-bar does brisk business. Cash payment earns a 10% discount.

Apart Hotel Costa Río (☎ 423027; Av San Martín 673; d/tr/q AR$310/412/484; ⬚) The '80s motif plays a big hand in this apartment hotel under siege by flower prints and heavy drapes. The apartments include kitchenettes, living rooms and separate bedrooms. Desk staff speak English and the hotel is family-friendly. Rates include breakfast and sauna, and cash payment nets a 15% discount.

Eating & Drinking

Panadería Zapiola (cnr Rawson & Zapiola; snacks AR$5; ☾ 24hr) Choose from dozens of sweet and savory confections at this bustling corner bakery. It's best to come early while the selections are still warm.

Rincón de Arte Café (Bernadino Rivadavia 131; snacks AR$9; ☾ 3-8pm Mon-Fri) Adjoined to an excellent gallery, this ambient coffee shop gets the creative juices flowing. It features regular art talks and courses, and sells beautiful blown glass and jewelry.

Pizza Express (☎ 434400; Av San Martín 650; mains AR$10) Cheap and casual, this is where students and families dine on burgers, gnocchi and salads. The signature pizzas can be oily.

Confitería Zapiola (☎ 420797; Chacabuco 104; sandwiches AR$17) Brick styling and alt rock bring freshness to this neighborhood snack spot, prized by local youth.

18 Horas (☎ 434541; Av Roca 1315; menu del día AR$20) A true neighborhood joint with cracked vinyl chairs and Boca football memorabilia. Half the fun is the seasoned waiter who addresses clients as 'captain' or 'old man.' There is a hearty daily special, but chicken Provencal with fries is also a good choice.

Don Bartolo (☎ 427297; Sarmiento 124; pizzas AR$21) Serious *parrilla* and stone-oven pizzas with fresh toppings are the highlights here. Create-your-own salads are good veggie options.

Lagunacazul (☎ 444114; cnr G Lista & Sarmiento; mains AR$16-32; ☾ closed Mon) Innovative and artsy, Lagunacazul dares to take Patagonian cuisine to new places, with stir-fried trout and pesto-encrusted lamb. Reservations are recommended.

RoCo (☎ 420203; Av Roca 1157; mains AR$30; ☾ closed Sun dinner & Mon lunch) This upscale eatery gets attention for swift service and ample options. The extensive menu includes salads, pasta, seafood and *parrilla*, as well as a full wine list.

Club Británico (☎ 427320; Av Roca 935; mains AR$30) If Chatwin couldn't resist it, how can you? There's a smoky allure to this old boy's club, ideal for an after-dinner whiskey, since the fine dining tends toward the drab side.

El Horreo (☎ 426462; Av Roca 862; mains AR$34; ⬚) Dangling vines, low lights and crisp linens add spark to this historic Sociedad Española building with a pleasant upstairs bar. It's the kind of place to see and be seen; while you're at it you can try Spanish specialties.

Shopping

Rincón Gaucho (☎ 420669; Av Roca 619) Aspiring gauchos and gauchitas can outfit themselves with the luxuriant leathers and embossed designs that are the signature of this upscale leather shop. You can also find nice gifts ranging from knives with molded handles and chaps to *mate* paraphernalia. The owner enthusiastically explains the purpose and customs of every stylish hat.

Getting There & Away
AIR
Río Gallegos' **Stand International Airport** (RGL; ☎ 442340) is 7km northwest of town. Airport tax is AR$6.

Aerolíneas Argentinas (☎ 422020/21; Av San Martín 545) flies daily to Buenos Aires (AR$675) and frequently to Ushuaia (AR$276). **LADE** (☎ 422316; Fagnano 53/57) flies several times a week to Río Grande (AR$114), El Calafate (AR$118), Comodoro Rivadavia (AR$184), Ushuaia (AR$174) and Buenos Aires (AR$318).

BUS
Río Gallegos' **bus terminal** (☎ 442159; cnr RN 3 & Av Eva Perón) is 3km southwest of the center. Companies include **El Pingüino** (☎ 442169), **Líder** (☎ 442160), **Bus Sur** (☎ 442687), **Andesmar** (☎ 442195), **Sportman** (☎ 442595) and **TAC** (☎ 442042). Companies going to Chile include

Ghisoni (☎ 442687), **Pacheco** (☎ 442765) and **Tecni-Austral** (☎ 442427). **Taqsa** (☎ 423130; www.taqsa.com .ar in Spanish; Estrada 71) beelines straight from the airport to Puerto Natales and El Calafate.

Destination	Cost (AR$)	Duration (hr)
Buenos Aires	290-348	36-40
Caleta Olivia	90	7-10
Comodoro Rivadavia	100-127	9-11
El Calafate	40	4-5
El Chaltén	60	9
Esquel	160	19
Los Antiguos	140	12
Puerto Madryn	160	15-20
Puerto Natales (Chile)	32	5-7
Punta Arenas (Chile)	35	5-6
Río Grande	85	7-8
Río Turbio	35	5
San Julián	42	4½
Trelew	155-186	14-17
Ushuaia	125	12-14

Getting Around

It's easy to share metered taxis (AR$15) between downtown, the bus terminal and the airport. From Av Roca, buses marked 'B' or 'terminal' link the center and the bus terminal (AR$1.30).

Car rental is expensive due to the poor conditions of the roads to most places of interest. Despite exchange rates, rental deals are often better in Punta Arenas, Chile – see p506. For local rentals, try **Riestra Rent A Car** (☎ 421321; Av San Martín 1504).

ESTANCIAS AROUND RÍO GALLEGOS

Visiting a working *estancia* affords an intimate glimpse into the unique Patagonian lifestyle. These are not luxury hotels, but homes that have been converted into comfortable lodgings. Meals are often shared with the owners, and token participation in the daily working life is encouraged. Booking ahead is essential, since most places are open only in summer and fill up fast. For *estancias* in Santa Cruz province, contact the provincial tourist office in Río Gallegos (p461) or see www.estanciasdesantacruz.com.

Dedicated to anglers, **Estancia Güer Aike** (☎ in Río Gallegos 02966-423895, in Buenos Aires 011-4394-3486; 4 nights & 3 days regular/angler AR$1050/2101; ⏰ Oct-Apr) has a lovely renovated lodge, Truchaike, enjoying 12km of private river frontage in a world-famous trout-fishing destination. Rates include all meals, drinks, fishing permits and

guided fishing. Day-trippers can visit the ranch for lunch or dinner (AR$63) – call in advance. It's at the junction of northbound RN 3 and westbound RP 5, 35km west of Río Gallegos.

Estancia Monte Dinero (☎ 02966-426900; www.monte dinero.com.ar in Spanish; day trip AR$180, per person with breakfast/full board AR$330/400; ⏰ Oct-Apr), named for gold once found on the coast, is a comfortable, old-world lodging with intricate hand-painted doors, billiards and well-appointed rooms. On RP 1, 120km south of Río Gallegos, it's been run by the same English-speaking family for five generations. Dudes see the typical *estancia* activities – dog demos, shearing etc – and can also take trips to **Cabo Vírgenes**, where Magellanic penguins nest September through March. A museum at the *estancia* displays an intriguing assortment of goods salvaged from the wreckage of the ship that sunk soon after the family Greenshyls sailed here from Ireland in 1886. Travel agencies in Río Gallegos offer day trips to the *estancia* starting in mid-November, usually making a quick stop at the *estancia's casco*.

INLAND PATAGONIA (ALONG RN 40)

Save for the travel hubs of El Calafate and El Chaltén, rutted RN 40 is every bit a no-man's-land. It parallels the backbone of the Andes, where ñandús doodle through sagebrush, trucks kick up whirling dust and gas stations rise on the horizon like oases. It is the ultimate road trip.

The paving of RN 40 will clearly mark the identity of a generation. At present, travel is long and hard but small hamlets along the way benefit. When the pavement settles, most motorists are likely to whiz from point A to point B, missing the quirky, unassuming settlements. For now, public transport stays limited to a few summer-only tourist shuttle services, and driving requires both preparation and patience.

RN 40 parallels the Andes from north of Bariloche to the border with Chile near Puerto Natales, then cuts east to the Atlantic Coast. Highlights include the Perito Moreno and Los Glaciares national parks, the rock art of Cueva de los Manos and remote *estancias*. This section picks up RN 40 in Esquel, from where it continues paved until south of

Gobernador Costa, where it turns to gravel. From there on down, it's gravel most of the way, with some paved sections, mainly near population centers.

ESQUEL

☎ 02945 / pop 36,000 / elev 570m

If you have tired of the gnome-in-the-chocolate-shop ambience of Bariloche and other cutesy Lakes District destinations, regular old Esquel will feel like a breath of fresh air. Set in western Chubut's dramatic, hikable foothills, Esquel mainly attracts visitors stopping over on their way to Parque Nacional Los Alerces and other Andean recreation areas. Most people zip through en route to Bariloche or Chile, but it's an easy-going and exceedingly friendly base camp for abundant adventure activities – the perfect place to chill for a few days after hard traveling on RN 40.

Founded at the turn of the 20th century, Esquel is the region's main livestock and commercial center. It's also the historic southern end of the line for La Trochita, the narrow-gauge steam train (see the boxed text, p468). The town takes its name from a term of the language of the Mapuche meaning either 'bog' or 'place of the thistles.'

Orientation

RN 259 zigzags through town to the junction with RN 40, which heads north to El Bolsón and south to Comodoro Rivadavia. South of town, RN 259 passes a junction for Parque Nacional Los Alerces en route to Trevelin.

Information

ACA (Automóvil Club Argentino; ☎ 452383; cnr 25 de Mayo & Av Ameghino) Inside YPF gas station; sells fishing licenses.

Banco de la Nación (cnr Av Alvear & General Roca) Has ATM and changes traveler's checks.

Banco del Chubut (Av Alvear 1131) Has ATM.

Biblioteca Publica (San Martín, btwn Mitre & Moreno; ☼ 8:30am-7:30pm) Free internet.

Cyber Club (Av Alvear 961; ☼ 10:30am-midnight Mon-Fri, noon-12:30am Sat, 4pm-midnight Sun) Internet access.

Hospital Zonal (☎ 451074; 25 de Mayo 150)

Laverap (Mitre 543; per load AR$12) Self- or full-service laundry.

Post office (cnr Avs Fontana & Alvear)

Tourist office (☎ 451927; www.esquel.gov.ar in Spanish; Av Alvear 1220; ☼ 7am-11pm) Well organized, helpful and multilingual.

Sights & Activities

Esquel's best attractions are of the outdoor variety, notably Parque Nacional Los Alerces and La Hoya. In town, there is **Museo de Culturas Originarias Patagónicas** (☎ 451929; Belgrano 330; admission by donation; ☼ 8:30am-1pm & 2:30-8pm Mon-Fri, 9am-noon & 5-8pm Sat, 5-8pm Sun), displaying a modest collection of Mapuche artifacts.

The Roca train station houses a free **train museum** (☎ 451403; www.latrochita.org.ar; cnr Roggero & Urquiza; ☼ 8am-2pm Mon-Sat). Even travelers arriving by bus or air should try to witness the arrival or departure of **La Trochita**, Argentina's famous narrow-gauge steam train.

Esquel's nearby lakes and rivers offer excellent **fly-fishing**, with the season running from November to April. You can purchase a license at most gas stations, including the **YPF gas station** (cnr 25 de Mayo & Av Ameghino; ☼ daylight hours) that houses the ACA.

Full-day **white-water rafting** trips go to upper and lower sections of the glacial-fed Río Corcovado for float trips (class II) and serious white-water assaults (class IV). **Mountain biking** is a good way to get out of town and explore the surrounding hills and trails. For **skiing** information, see the La Hoya section (p469).

Tours

Numerous travel agencies, including **Esquel Tours** (☎ 452832; esqueltours@ar.inter.net; Pellegrini 881), sell tickets for the Circuito Lacustre boat excursion in Parque Nacional Los Alerces (see p475); buying a ticket in Esquel assures a place on the often-crowded trip. Full-day excursions, including the lake cruise, cost AR$85 when sailing from Puerto Chucao or AR$110 from Puerto Limonao, including transfers to and from the park.

Excursions to El Bolsón/Lago Puelo and Corcovado/Carrenleufú (full day AR$85) are also offered. Half-day trips include La Hoya's winter-sports complex; the nearby Welsh settlement of Trevelin and the Futaleufú hydroelectric complex (AR$40); and the narrow-gauge railway excursion to Nahuel Pan.

For rafting and outdoor adventures, **Expediciones Patagonia Aventura** (EPA; ☎ 454366, 02945-15-684085; www.grupoepa.com in Spanish; Av Fontana 482) offers myriad options. Since the Río Corcovado is 90km away, rafting trips (class III/IV AR$145/210) spend two to four hours on the river; the harder trips are shorter, though they're usually action-packed. Half-day trips are available as well. Once you're

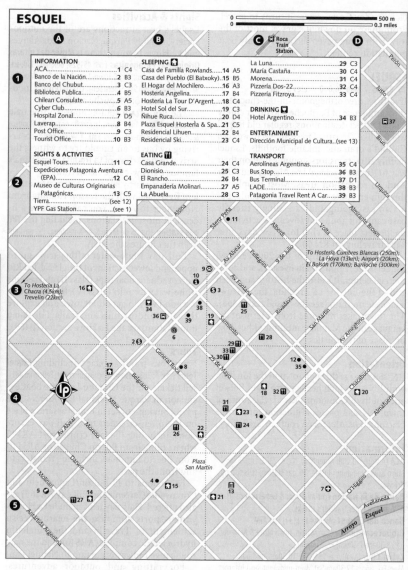

ESQUEL

INFORMATION	
ACA	1 C4
Banco de la Nación	2 B3
Banco del Chubut	3 C3
Biblioteca Publica	4 B5
Chilean Consulate	5 A5
Cyber Club	6 B3
Hospital Zonal	7 D5
Laverap	8 B4
Post Office	9 C3
Tourist Office	10 B3

SIGHTS & ACTIVITIES	
Esquel Tours	11 C2
Expediciones Patagonia Aventura (EPA)	12 C4
Museo de Culturas Originarias Patagónicas	13 C5
Tierra	(see 12)
YPF Gas Station	(see 1)

SLEEPING	
Casa de Familia Rowlands	14 A5
Casa del Pueblo (El Batxoky)	15 B5
El Hogar del Mochilero	16 A3
Hostería Angelina	17 B4
Hostería La Tour D'Argent	18 C4
Hotel Sol del Sur	19 C3
Ñihue Ruca	20 D4
Plaza Esquel Hosterla & Spa	21 C5
Residencial Lihuen	22 B4
Residencial Ski	23 C4

EATING	
Casa Grande	24 C4
Dionisio	25 C3
El Rancho	26 B4
Empanadería Molinari	27 A5
La Abuela	28 C3

La Luna	29 C3
María Castaña	30 C4
Morena	31 C4
Pizzería Dos-22	32 C4
Pizzería Fitzroya	33 C4

DRINKING	
Hotel Argentino	34 B3

ENTERTAINMENT	
Dirección Municipal de Cultura	(see 13)

TRANSPORT	
Aerolíneas Argentinas	35 C4
Bus Stop	36 B3
Bus Terminal	37 D1
LADE	38 B3
Patagonia Travel Rent A Car	39 B3

there you might want to take advantage of the peaceful surroundings: one interesting option is to stay at EPA's riverside hostel.

In summer EPA also offers canopy tours, horseback riding (full day AR$110) and trekking (full day AR$110) at its mountain center, an attractive wooden lodge (full pension AR$150) based in Parque Nacional Los Alerces. Ask about the new boat/hike combination to Río Frei.

Ski rentals are available through **Tierra** (454366; www.grupoepa.com in Spanish; Av Fontana 482) for AR$30 to AR$70 per day, with performance skis at the high end. In summer they rent bikes and can hook you up with a mountain-biking guide or trail details.

Festivals & Events

Semana de Esquel A weeklong February event that celebrates the city's 1906 founding.

Fiesta Nacional de Esquí (National Skiing Festival) Takes place in mid-September at La Hoya.

Sleeping

BUDGET

El Hogar del Mochilero (☎ 452166; www.cpatagonia .com.ar in Spanish; General Roca 1028; dm AR$15, camping per person AR$10) Follow the life-sized plaster backpacker to these cheaper-than-dirt ac-commodations. When we visited, they were undergoing renovations and adding doubles. There's an enormous group bunk room (bring a sleep sack), shady backyard camp-ing, a kitchen, free firewood and hot showers. If no one is around, check the house across the street.

our pick **Casa del Pueblo** (El Batxoky; ☎ 450581; www.grupoepa.com in Spanish; San Martín 661; dm/d/tr AR$33/80/111) Run with dedication and affec-tion, this slightly sagging hostel offers cool shared spaces but would do well to dump the ashtrays. Perks include kitchen use, a laundry room, mountain bike rentals and a grassy yard. Connected with EPA tour agency, it has handy connections for active pursuits. Breakfast is AR$3.

Casa de Familia Rowlands (☎ 452578; Rivadavia 330; r per person AR$35) This affable family home offers three basic rooms (only one with pri-vate bathroom). It's about seven blocks from the center.

MIDRANGE

Residencial Lihuen (☎ 452589; San Martín 822; s/d AR$85/95) These ample rooms tend to be dated and mismatched, but serviceable. They're well located near the leafy Plaza San Martín. Breakfast is AR$5.

Residencial Ski (☎ 451646; San Martín 961; s/d AR$70/110) Clean and friendly Ski doesn't win any style points with its faux-wood paneling, but rooms include cable TV and parking is available.

Hostería Angelina (☎ 452763; www.hosteriaangel ina.com.ar; Av Alvear 758; s/d standard AR$120/160, supe-rior AR$140/180; 🖳) Hospitable and polished, Angelina follows international standards with professional service and a good breakfast buf-fet. Superior rooms offer extra space and there is a courtyard with fountain.

Ñihue Ruca (☎ 452891; nihuerca@ciudad.com.ar; Chacabuco 1253; 2-person apt AR$140) This vaguely Swiss apartment hotel offers immaculate ac-commodations lorded over by granny style. Snug and fully equipped, apartments are sharply discounted in low season.

Hostería La Chacra (☎ 452802; rinilachacra@ciudad .com.ar; RN 259, Km 4; d/tr AR$150/180; 🖳 🐾) If you want a shot of local culture, nothing is better than this country lodging in a 1970s home with ample bright rooms, generous gringo breakfasts and thick down bedding. Owner Rini Griffiths, who sings in Esquel's Welsh chorus, is a real joy. Get here via taxi or Trevelin bus – they pass hourly.

Hostería La Tour D'Argent (☎ 454612; www.latour dargent.com.ar in Spanish; San Martín 1063; d AR$180) Some rooms are avidly depressing here, with brown terrycloth bedspreads, but others are cheery and comfy so have a look around. The restau-rant offers an extensive take-out menu and uses organic farm-fresh products.

TOP END

Hotel Sol del Sur (☎ 452189; www.hsoldelsur.com.ar in Spanish; 9 de Julio 1086; s/d with buffet breakfast AR$170/200, superior d AR$230) Geared towards groups, this hotel travels time, with leather-paneled doors, and dated wood and vinyl decor. On the upside, it is clean, with minibars and a big breakfast spread. Superior rooms are a nota-ble step up. There's a 10% cash discount.

Plaza Esquel Hostería & Spa (☎ 457002; http:// patagoniaandesgroup.com.ar; Av Ameghino 713; s/d/tr AR$181/228/310; 🖳) A new addition in front of the plaza, this attractive *hostería* offers mod-ern rooms with new fixtures, free internet access and wi-fi. Spa services include access to a Jacuzzi and sauna.

Hostería Cumbres Blancas (☎ 455100; www .cumbresblancas.com.ar in Spanish; Av Ameghino 1683; s/d AR$395/450; 🖳) Esquel's best inn is shiny and lavish, but does not surpass its packaged feel. Sportsmen and women will enjoy having their own fly-casting pond and putting green for a few days. Indoor pampering starts with the health club's sauna and steam bath. Rooms are decked out in crisp colors and fresh-feeling linens. Service is attentive and there's wi-fi throughout.

Eating

María Castaña (☎ 451752; cnr 25 de Mayo & Rivadavia; snacks AR$8) A favorite at this frilly café is waffles with *dulce de leche*; it's also good for breakfast, sandwiches and ice-cream sundaes. Grab an overstuffed chair in the back.

LA TROCHITA: THE OLD PATAGONIAN EXPRESS

Clearly an anachronism in the jet age, Ferrocarril Roca's **La Trochita** (☎ 02945-451403 in Esquel; www.latrochita.org.ar), Argentina's famous narrow-gauge steam train, averages less than 30km/h on its meandering weekly journey between Esquel and El Maitén – if it runs at speed. Despite the precarious economics of its operations, the project has survived even the most concerted efforts to shut it down. In its current incarnation, subsidized by the city of Esquel and the governments of Río Negro and Chubut, La Trochita – which Paul Theroux facetiously called *The Old Patagonian Express* – provides both a tourist attraction and a service for local citizens.

Like many other state projects, completion of the line seemed an interminable process. In 1906 the federal government authorized the southern branch of the Roca line, between Puerto San Antonio on the Atlantic coast and Lago Nahuel Huapi. In 1922 Ferrocarriles del Estado began work on the narrow-gauge section; it didn't reach the halfway point of Ñorquinco until 1939. In 1941 the line made it to the workshops at El Maitén, and in 1945 it reached the end of the line at Esquel.

Since then, the line has suffered some of the oddest mishaps in railroad history. Three times within a decade, in the late 1950s and early 1960s, the train was derailed by high winds, and ice has caused other derailments. In 1979 a collision with a cow derailed the train at Km 243 south of El Maitén; the engine driver was the appropriately named Señor Bovino.

In full operation until 1993, La Trochita's 402km route between Esquel and Ingeniero Jacobacci was probably the world's longest remaining steam-train line, with half a dozen stations and another nine *apeaderos* (whistle-stops). The Belgian Baldwin and German Henschel engines refilled their 4000L water tanks at strategically placed *parajes* (pumps) every 40km to 45km. Most of the passenger cars, heated by wood stoves, date from 1922, as do the freight cars.

During summer, the **Tren Turístico** (adult/student AR$30/24; ☺ 10am Wed & Sat) travels from Roca station in Esquel to Nahuel Pan, the first station down the line, 20km east. The trip takes 45 minutes. It's popular with groups so book ahead. For a small additional charge, you can organize with one of the Esquel travel agencies to return by minibus. La Trochita also offers infrequent passenger service between Esquel and El Maitén, a nine-hour ride. Verify the current timetable online.

Morena (☎ 02945-15-695-139; cnr San Martín & General Roca; www.morenorestobar.com.ar; mains AR$12; ☺ noon-midnight) Relaxed and warm, this brick yuppie watering hole is ideal for a glass of wine or cup of joe. Cheap victuals include decent sandwiches, pasta and pizzas.

our pick La Luna (☎ 453800; www.lalunarestobar .com.ar in Spanish; Rivadavia 1080; mains AR$15, pizzas AR$30; ☺ noon-4pm & 7pm-1am) This homey rock-n-roll restaurant-bar offers tasty spinach pizzas and heaping portions of steak and fries. The evening crowd spills out of wooden booths and brick nooks, drinking Patagonia's artisan beers.

Empanadería Molinari (☎ 454687; Molinari 633; dozen empanadas AR$15) Belcha and Jorge bake mouthwatering take-out empanadas. If you can wait for a few minutes they'll heat them up.

La Abuela (☎ 451704; Rivadavia 1109; main AR$15) Shoehorn yourself into this family nook decked out in lace tablecloths, and enjoy cheap gnocchi and home-cooked classics like *puchero* (vegetable and meat stew) with a carafe of passable house wine.

Casa Grande (☎ 452370, 02945-15-469712; General Roca 445; mains AR$22) Dig into flavorful *jabalí* (wild boar) and baked trout at this fine-dining spot, specializing in regional cuisine. The rambling house with burlwood chandeliers offers plenty of atmosphere. Portions are generous and there are some good vegetarian options on offer.

Dionisio (☎ 02945-15-507749; Av Fontana 656; mains AR$24) Enjoy the eclectic, artsy atmosphere in this yellow house, ideal for a *sobre mesa* (table talk). There are vegetarian options but crepes, both savory and sweet, are the house specialty. The restaurant re-opens after lunch at 6pm for tea.

El Rancho (☎ 451931; cnr Rivadavia & Belgrano; parilla AR$30) A satisfying corner grill offering plates of mixed meats and sausages in addition to salads and varied pastas. Follow your nose –

the smoky smells of barbecue permeate the block at lunch hour.

Worthwhile pizzerias (mains AR$15 and up) include **Pizzería Fitzroya** (☎ 450512; Rivadavia 1050) and **Pizzería Dos-22** (☎ 454995; cnr Av Ameghino & Sarmiento).

Drinking & Entertainment

Dirección Municipal de Cultura (☎ 451929; Belgrano 330) Sponsors regular music, cinema, theater and dance.

Hotel Argentino (☎ 452237; 25 de Mayo 862; ☺ 4pm-5am) This lanky and lowbrow Wild West saloon is much better suited to drinking than sleeping. By all means stop by: the owner is friendly, the 1916 construction is stuffed with relics and sculptures, and the place gets more than a little lively on weekends. Pool tables are available.

See the restaurant-bars listed under Eating for other options.

Getting There & Around

AIR

Esquel's **airport** (ESQ; ☎ 451676) is 20km east of town off RN 40. Taxis cost AR$35.

Aerolíneas Argentinas (☎ 453614; Av Fontana 406) flies to Bariloche (AR$1539) and Buenos Aires (AR$1256) several times a week.

LADE (☎ 452124; Av Alvear 1085) flies several times weekly to Bariloche (AR$103), Comodoro Rivadavia (AR$176) and Buenos Aires (AR$395), and at least once a week to Puerto Madryn (AR$181), Río Gallegos (AR$411) and El Calafate (AR$411).

BUS

Esquel's full-service **bus terminal** (☎ 451477/79; cnr Av Alvear & Brun) is an easy walk from the center.

Transportes Jacobsen (☎ 453528) goes to Futaleufú, Chile (AR$15, 1½ hours), Monday and Friday at 8am and 6pm. Buses go hourly to Trevelin (AR$3, 30 minutes), stopping near the corner of Av Alvear and 25 de Mayo on the way out of town. Buses to El Maitén (AR$16, two hours) leave at 1:30pm Tuesday, Thursday and Saturday, returning at 4pm.

In summer, **Transportes Esquel** (☎ 453529) goes through Parque Nacional Los Alerces (AR$9, 1¼ hours) to Lago Futalaufquen daily at 8am and 4pm. The first bus goes all the way to Lago Puelo (AR$23, six hours), stopping in Lago Verde (AR$13) at 10:30am and Cholila at noon. If you plan on exploring the area by

bus, purchase an open ticket (AR$30), which allows passengers to make stops along the way between Esquel and Lago Puelo or vice-versa. Service is reduced off-season.

There are daily departures to the following destinations:

Destination	Cost (AR$)	Duration (hr)
Bariloche	37	4¼
Buenos Aires	203	30
Comodoro Rivadavia	61	8-9
El Bolsón	19	2½
Neuquén	100	10
Puerto Madryn	115	7-9
Río Gallegos	160	19
Trelew	81	8-9

TRAIN

The narrow-gauge steam train La Trochita (also known by the Spanish diminutive El Trencito) departs from the diminutive **Roca train station** (☎ 451403; www.latrochita.org.ar; cnr Roggero & Urquiza; ☺ 8am-2pm Mon-Sat). There's a frequent tourist-oriented service to Nahuel Pan (see the boxed text, opposite) and infrequent passenger service to the railroad workshops at El Maitén (nine hours). For the timeless *Old Patagonian Express* feeling, it's best to catch a bus to El Maitén for the less touristy excursion to Desvío Thomae, but this service is sporadically available. Confirm schedules online or via the tourist office.

CAR

Compact rental rates start around AR$100 a day, including 100km and insurance. Try **Patagonia Travel Rent A Car** (☎ 455811, 02945-15-692174; www.patagoniatravelrentacar.com in Spanish; Av Alvear 1041), which has a good range of vehicles.

AROUND ESQUEL
La Hoya

Only 13km north of Esquel, with a base elevation of 1350m, the winter-sports area of **La Hoya** (☎ 02945-453018; www.esquelonline.com/esqui.htm; full-day lift pass AR$52) is a family-friendly favorite of Argentines and Chileans. The addition of new lifts has doubled the terrain and the powder skiing is some of Argentina's best.

The terrain consists of open bowls, with most trails above the tree line, allowing for a longer season than most ski areas. While it's cheaper and less crowded than Bariloche, experienced skiers will find it smaller and

PATAGONIA

SURVIVING RUTA NACIONAL 40

Patagonia's RN 40 is the quintessential road trip. No one gets anywhere fast here – the weather can be wily and the gravel loose. It can seem to go on forever. But it can also be magical when you've been rattling along for hours and the interminable flatline of steppe suddenly bursts open with views of glacial peaks and gem-colored lakes.

The road is half-paved, and plans to finish the job are long overdue. When it is finished, the life that slow travel brought to the small roadside towns is bound to diminish. So, if you want to drive this dirt behemoth, now is the time to giddy up.

Conditions from December to March are generally fine, but heavy precipitation can render some parts inaccessible. Most of the mythic route's unpaved stretches are wide and compacted, although some of the paved sections already show serious wear. Just be thankful you didn't set out on a bike or motorcycle.

Be Prepared

Everyone should travel with necessary repair equipment. If renting a car, carry two full-size *neumáticos* (spare tires), make sure that the headlights work and that suspension, tires and brakes are in good shape. The gravel can puncture gas tanks so be sure to have some extra fuel on hand, as well as oil and generous supplies of food and water. Gas is subsidized in Patagonia, so fill up the tank when you get the chance.

Dodging flying rocks can be difficult and many potential damages are not covered under the insurance policies offered by rental agencies. Those that aren't must be paid out of pocket. Be sure to check with the agency about coverage and deductibles.

Road Rules

The law requires that headlights are on during daylight hours. Respect speed limits: 65km/h or 80km/h is a safe maximum speed.

Sheep *always* have the right of way. While most will scurry out of the way, some are not so quick. Guanacos and ñandús are another potential hazard. Slow down, give them distance and watch out for unsigned *guardaganados* (cattle guards).

Driving Etiquette

Signal hello to oncoming drivers by flashing your headlights or raising an index finger with your hand on the steering wheel. Unwritten rule: stop to help anyone stranded on the side of the road. There's no 'roadside assistance' here and mobile phones are useless in the mountains and along most west–east stretches. Along windy roads, toot your horn before barreling through blind curves.

comparatively tame. The season lasts from June until October, with the **National Ski Festival** in the second week of September. Summer activity options include hiking, riding the chairlift and horseback riding.

Equipment can be rented on site or at sport shops in Esquel, including Tierra (p466). Minibuses can take you to La Hoya from Esquel lodgings for AR$17 per person; taxis may be a better deal for groups.

Cholila

Butch Cassidy, the Sundance Kid and Ethel Place tried settling down and making an honest living (see the boxed text, p472) near this quiet farming community outside the northeast entrance to Parque Nacional Los Alerces. Bruce Chatwin's travel classic *In Patagonia* recounts the tale. The bandits' partially restored homestead is just off RP 71 at Km 21, near the turnoff to the Casa de Piedra teahouse, 8km north of Cholila. Cholila's enthusiastic **Casa de Informes** (☎ 02945-498040/131; RP 71, at RP 15; ⏱ summer only) has a helpful regional map and will gladly point you in the right direction.

Transportes Esquel buses from Esquel to El Bolsón pass close enough for a fleeting glimpse of the cabin on the west side of the highway, but visitors with their own vehi-

When another car approaches, slow down and move to the side of the road to avoid stones flying out from under the wheels. For maximum security, consider adding a windshield screen for protection. Another recommendation is to cover headlights with transparent, industrial-strength tape to minimize the cracking should a stone hit.

Flash your headlights to signal a desire to pass. The car in front should slow down to let you by. If you're being overtaken, move over and slow down until the cloud of dust has settled. If you need to stop, don't slam on the brakes, an act that will send the car skidding along the road. Instead, slow down and use the gears to lower the speeds until you can safely park on the side of the road.

Letting Someone Else Deal with It

A group of travel agencies (www.corredorpatagonico.com in Spanish) coordinates two-day minivan transport along RN 40 from El Calafate to Bariloche, via El Chaltén, Perito Moreno and Los Antiguos. Service follows fair weather, from mid-October/November to early April, depending on demand and road conditions. Some departures may include a stop at Cueva de las Manos.

Based in Bariloche at Periko's hostel (p411), **Overland Patagonia** (www.overlandpatagonia .com) offers trips down to El Calafate: AR$950 for the four-day trip, including lodging. **Corredor Patagónico** (www.corredorpatagonico.com in Spanish) offers the same trip in two days (AR$365 to AR$405 including lodging) or four days (AR$570 to AR$590 including lodging). The company also stretches the trip to six relaxed days and charges AR$2270, including food and stays on *estancias*. Both companies offer several variations on these trips. Corredor Patagónico tailors one of its trips to seniors.

Chaltén Travel (☎ 011-4326-7282; www.chaltentravel.com; Sarmiento 559, piso 8, Buenos Aires) runs northbound two-day shuttles, leaving at 8am from El Calafate, with accommodation in Perito Moreno. Southbound three-day shuttles leave Bariloche at 6:45am on odd-numbered days, with accommodations in Perito Moreno and El Chaltén. Buses stop in Los Antiguos as well. For the whole trip, prices start at AR$970 per person (including accommodation). It's possible to hop on and off along the route, but space on the next shuttle is neither reservable nor guaranteed. Chaltén also has branches in El Calafate (☎ 02902-492212/480), El Chaltén (☎ 02962-493092) and Bariloche (☎ 02944-423809).

For a more personal approach, small, multilingual outfitters **Ruta 40** (☎ 0297-446-5337; www .ruta-40.com; Comodoro Rivadavia) and **Las Loicas** (☎ 02963-490272, 02963-15-421-3194; http://lasloicas .com; Lago Posadas) organize well-informed and personalized trips on RN 40 with opportunities to stop and explore further.

cle or time to spare can stop for a look at the overlapping log construction, typical of North America but unusual in this region. Without museum status, it remains locked, although the congenial caretaker, Daniel Sepulveda, is open to showing visitors around. Close any gates you open and ask permission from the caretaker before looking around or taking photographs.

Afterwards, you can follow the signs for 1km to the Calderón family's **Casa de Piedra** (☎ 02945-498056; RP 71, Km 20; 🕙 Dec-Mar), a beautiful stone farmhouse offering tea, sweets and preserves, as well as information. The hospitable Calderóns, of Spanish-Welsh-English-French-Basque-Mapuche descent, let double rooms for around AR$140 per person with breakfast. Call ahead to let them know you are coming.

To return to Esquel, if driving, you can follow unpaved RP 71 north for 20km to the pavement at the first crossroads, and continue 116km on paved RN 40 back to Esquel. On the way you will pass the **Museo Leleque** (☎ in Buenos Aires 011-4326-5156; www.benetton .com/patagonia; RN 40, Km 1440; 🕙 11am-5pm Thu-Tue Mar-Dec, to 7pm Jan & Feb), which has many Mapuche artifacts and narrates the history of the region from the perspective of the Benetton family.

PATAGONIA

BUTCH & SUNDANCE'S PATAGONIAN REFUGE   *Daniel Buck & Anne Meadows*

The only standing relics of Butch Cassidy and the Sundance Kid's South American adventure are the rough-hewn log ranch buildings by the Río Blanco in Chubut's Cholila Valley.

Butch and Sundance – and Sundance's chum, Ethel Place – arrived in the Cholila Valley in 1901, at a time when Argentina was attracting immigrants from all over the world and its government was eager to settle the sparsely populated southern territories. US newspapers rhapsodized about 'a land of wild apples and wild strawberries, of hill and dale, of beautiful scenery, of pastoral and mineral wealth.' Best of all, the land was free.

By all accounts, Butch and Sundance had every intention of giving up their delinquent ways and settling permanently in Cholila. They bought livestock, filed land petitions and built a ranch. In 1902 Butch wrote to a friend in Utah that 'the country is first class.' They had '300 cattle, 1500 sheep, and 28 good saddle horses,' and would soon be sending cattle over the Andes to a slaughterhouse in Chile.

Another hint of what their life was like comes from Primo Capraro, a Bariloche architect who spent a night with the trio in 1904 at their ranch. He later recalled: 'The house was simply furnished and exhibited a certain painstaking tidiness, a geometric arrangement of things, pictures with cane frames, wallpaper made of clippings from American magazines, and many beautiful weapons and lassos. The men were tall, slender, laconic, and nervous, with intense gazes. The lady, who was reading, was well-dressed.'

Their neighbors, some of whose descendants still live in the valley, were from Chile, Wales, England, Ireland, Scotland and Texas. One of the Texans had even been a sheriff back home, but among expatriate settlers, amity was the rule. When the territorial governor came through on an inspection tour, Butch and Sundance hosted a party. The governor danced with Ethel while Sundance played guitar.

Their idyll was smashed in early 1905, when they were wrongly suspected of a bank robbery in Río Gallegos and forced to flee. A few months later, as a departing thumb-in-the-eye, they held up a bank in Villa Mercedes, near Mendoza. Ethel returned to the US and vanished, while Butch and Sundance migrated to Chile and Bolivia. In November 1908, after a couple of years working in a mine camp, they robbed another mine's payroll and died in a shootout with a Bolivian military patrol.

TREVELIN

☎ 02945 / pop 6400 / elev 735m

Historic Trevelin (treh-*veh*-lehn), from the Welsh for town *(tre)* and mill *(velin)*, is the only community in interior Chubut with a notable Welsh character. Easygoing and postcard-pretty, this pastoral village makes a tranquil lodging alternative to the much busier Esquel (remember, everything is relative here), or an enjoyable day trip for tea. The surrounding countryside is ripe for exploration.

Orientation

Just 22km south of Esquel via paved RN 259, Trevelin's urban plan is unusual for an Argentine city: at the north end of town, eight streets radiate like the spokes of a wheel from Plaza Coronel Fontana. The principal thoroughfare, Av San Martín, is the southward extension of RN 259, which forks west 50km to the Chilean border and Futaleufú, 12km beyond.

Information

Banco del Chubut (cnr Av San Martín & Brown) Just south of the plaza, with an ATM.

Gales al Sur (☎ 480427; trevelin@galesalsur.com.ar; Patagonia 186) Esquel buses stop at this travel agency, which arranges tours.

Post office (Av San Martín) Just south of the plaza.

Telefónica (cnr Av San Martín & El Malacara) *Locutorio*, next to Gales al Sur. Open late, with dial-up internet.

Tourist office (☎ 480120; www.trevelin.org in Spanish; Plaza Fontana; ☺ 8am-9pm) Helpful, with a free town map, information on local hikes and English-speaking staff.

Sights & Activities

The **Museo Regional Molino Viejo** (☎ 02945-480189; cnr 25 de Mayo & Molino Viejo; admission AR$2; ☺ 11am-8:30pm Dec-Mar, to 6:30pm Apr-Nov) occupies the restored remains of a 1922 grain mill and is stuffed with interesting historic artifacts. It's a couple of blocks east of the plaza, at the end of 25 de Mayo.

Horse lovers pay their respects at **Tumba de Malacara** (☎ 480108; admission AR$10; Malacara s/n; ☽ 10am-8pm), the monument holding the remains of a brave horse whose swift retreat saved its owner's hide. As the story goes, town founder John Evans escaped with Malacara from murder-bent Araucanians, who were retaliating for an attack by the Argentine army during the Conquista del Desierto. It's two blocks northeast of Plaza Coronel Fontana. Here there's also the **Cartief Taid**, a museum replica of Evans' home.

Festivals & Events

An **artisan market** fills Plaza Coronel Fontana on Sundays in summer and on alternate Sundays the rest of the year. On March 19, the **Aniversario de Trevelin** celebrates the founding of the city. The biggest Welsh celebration of the year is the multilingual **Eisteddfod**, a festival that takes place at the end of October and sees bards competing in song and poetry. Other dates that bring out the Welsh flag include July 28, the date the first ship with 143 Welsh pilgrims docked in Patagonia in 1865. Every April 30, the community commemorates its decision to choose Argentine residency. November 25 marks the discovery of the valley with a flurry of afternoon teas and an evening concert.

Sleeping

Camping Policial (Costanera Río Percy & Holdich; campsites per person AR$6; ☽ closed winter) These fine, grassy sites offer good shade. From Av San Martín 600 block, walk two blocks west on Coronel Holdich and turn left down the gravel road. The Esquel bus goes beyond the plaza and stops at the intersection of Holdich and San Martín.

our pick **Casaverde Hostal** (☎ 480091, 02945-15-691535; www.casaverdehostel.com.ar; Los Alerces s/n; dm HI member/nonmember AR$30/35, s/d with bathroom AR$105/120, 6-person cabin AR$350; 🖳) A convivial retreat perched above town, Casaverde is homey and helpful, but the secret's out, so book ahead! Guests relax in the spacious rooms and sunny common areas, and wake up to breakfast (AR$12) with bottomless mugs of real coffee, homemade bread and jams. This is the place for bike rentals (AR$8 per hour), Spanish classes and fly-fishing lessons. It's a 10-minute walk from the plaza, off Av Fontana.

Cabañas Oregon (☎ 480408; www.oregontrevelin .com.ar in Spanish; cnr Av San Martín & JM Thomas; 4-person cabin AR$150) Scattered around an apple or-chard on the south side of town, these appealing log cabins come with kitchen, TV and private bathroom.

Hostería Casa de Piedra (☎ 480357; www.casadepiedra trevelin.com in Spanish; Brown 244; d AR$220, 5-person apt AR$320, 6-person cabin AR$320) This new stone lodge is a haven for anglers. A huge stone fireplace, tribal motifs and rustic touches create a warm ambience. Luis, the enthusiastic owner, offers fly-fishing trips and worthwhile excursions to rural home stays in Palena, Chile.

Cabañas Wilson (☎ 480803; www.wilsonpata gonia.com.ar; RP 259 at RP 71; 2-/4-/6-person cabins AR$240/260/280) Savor the serenity surrounding these newly built wood-and-brick cabins on the edge of town. Administration is friendly and the cabins include daily cleaning service, extra covers and a barbecue deck.

Eating

Just as visitors to Trelew flock to Gaiman, so visitors to Esquel head to Trevelin for Welsh tea. Tea houses are typically open from 3pm to 8pm. Often the portions are big enough to share – ask first if it's OK. In low season, confirm hours before heading out from Esquel.

Nain Maggie (☎ 480232; Perito Moreno 179; tea service AR$30; ☽ 10am-12:30pm & 3:30-8pm) Javier de la Fuente recreates granny's recipes in this, Trevelin's oldest teahouse. Though it occupies a modern building, Nain Maggie maintains high traditional standards. Along with a bottomless pot, there's outstanding cream pie, *torta negra* and scones hot from the oven.

Las Mutisias (☎ 480165; Av San Martín 170; tea service AR$24) The only other teahouse where everything is reliably homemade.

Getting There & Away

The **bus terminal** (cnr Roca & RN 40), located on a corner of the wheel, has buses to Comodoro Rivadavia (AR$53) at 11:30pm Sunday through Friday. **Gales del Sur** (☎ 480427; RN 259) has hourly buses to Esquel (AR$3, 30 minutes). Buses cross the border to Chile's Futaleufú (AR$18, one hour) on Mondays and Fridays at 8:30am and 6pm. Buses go to the village of Carrenleufú (AR$24, two hours), just before the border crossing to Palena in Chile, on Mondays, Wednesdays and Fridays at 10:30am.

PARQUE NACIONAL LOS ALERCES
☎ 02945

This collection of spry creeks, verdant mountains and mirror lakes resonates as

PATAGONIA

unadulterated Andes. The real attraction, however, is the alerce tree *(Fitzroya cupressoides)*, one of the longest-living species on the planet, with specimens that have survived up to 4000 years. Following the acclaim of well-known parks further north and south, most hikers miss this gem, which makes your visit here all the more enjoyable.

Resembling California's giant sequoia, the alerce flourishes in middle Patagonia's temperate forests, growing only about one centimeter every twenty years. Individual specimens of this beautiful tree can reach over 4m in diameter and exceed 60m in height. Like the giant sequoia, it has suffered over-exploitation because of its valuable timber. West of Esquel, this 2630-sq-km park pro-tects some of the largest alerce forests that still remain.

Environment & Climate

Hugging the eastern slopes of the Andes, the peaks of Parque Nacional Los Alerces reach up to 2300m, bearing glaciers whose retreat formed the series of nearly pristine lakes and streams below. These lakes all drain south-ward via the huge hydroelectricity reservoir of Lago Amutui Quimei into the Río Futaleufú, which flows westward into Chile. The area offers beautiful vistas and excellent fishing.

Because the Andes are relatively low here, westerly storms deposit nearly 3m of rain annually. The park's eastern sector, though, is much drier. Winter temperatures average

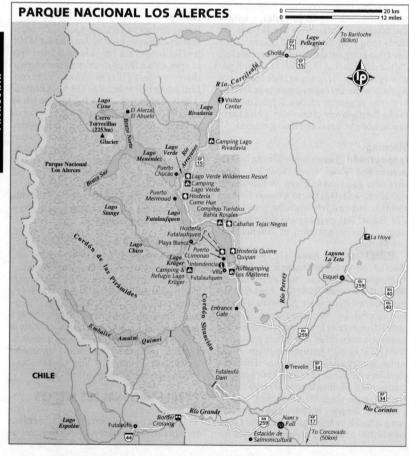

PARQUE NACIONAL LOS ALERCES

2°C, but can be much colder. The summer mean high reaches 24°C, but evenings are usually cool.

Plants & Animals

While its wild backcountry supports the seldom-seen huemul (Andean deer) and other wildlife, Los Alerces functions primarily as a trove of botanical riches. Besides the alerce, other important coniferous evergreens and deciduous broadleaf trees characterize the dense Valdivian forest, such as ñire, coihue and lenga. Most of the larger broadleaf tree species in the park belong to the genus *Nothofagus* (commonly known as southern beech), abiding only in the southern hemisphere. Hikers will find an almost impenetrable undergrowth of chusquea, a solid bamboo, coniferous cypress and the aromatic Chilean incense cedar. Another interesting species is the arrayán, whose foliage and peeling cinnamon-colored bark bear resemblance to the madrone *(Arbutus menziesii)* of the western US coastal states and British Columbia.

Information

During the high season (Christmas to Semana Santa) foreigners pay AR$12 admission. In Villa Futalaufquen you'll find the **Intendencia** (park office; ☎ 471015/20; ☼ 8am-9pm in summer, 9am-4pm rest of year), where rangers have details about hiking, camping and guided excursions. Get your fishing permits here. The headquarters also house the Museo y Centro del Interpretación, a natural-history museum. The visitor center at the northern end of the park is only open December through February.

Activities

As well as sailing and hiking, travel agencies in Esquel offer fishing, canoeing, mountain-biking, snorkeling and horseback-riding trips.

SAILING

Traditionally, **Circuito Lacustre** is Los Alerces' most popular excursion and involves sailing from Puerto Limonao up Lago Futalaufquen, then through the narrow channel of the Río Arrayanes to Lago Verde.

Low water levels now make it necessary to hike the short distance between Puerto Mermoud, at the north end of Lago Futalaufquen, and Puerto Chucao on Lago Menéndez. Launches from Puerto Chucao handle the second segment of the trip (1½ hours) to the nature trail **El Alerzal**, the most accessible stand of alerces. Another option (recommended) is to arrive to Puerto Chucao via a 1500m trail that crosses the bridge over Río Arrayanes: the scenery is well worthwhile.

The launch remains docked for over an hour at El Alerzal trailhead, sufficient for an unhurried hike around the loop trail that passes **Lago Cisne** and an attractive waterfall to end up at **El Abuelo** (Grandfather), a 57m-tall, 2600-year-old alerce.

From Puerto Limonao, the excursion costs AR$110; from Puerto Chucao it's AR$85. Departures are at 10am from Limonao and noon from Chucao, returning to Chucao at 5pm and to Limonao at 7pm. In summer, purchase tickets in Esquel to ensure a seat.

HIKING

Because of fire hazard, authorities allow camping only at authorized campsites. Even for short treks, it is compulsory to sign in at the one of the ranger stations before heading out.

Day hikes can be undertaken from several interpretive trails located near **Lago Futalaufquen**. The only trekking option is the 25km trail from **Puerto Limonao** along the south shore of Futalaufquen to **Refugio Lago Krüger** (p476), which can be done in a long day, or broken up by camping at **Playa Blanca**. Boat excursions from Puerto Limonao to Lago Krüger cost AR$70 per person.

For longer hikes, see Lonely Planet's *Trekking in the Patagonian Andes*.

Sleeping & Eating

En route to the park, watch for roadside signs advertising ideal picnic goods: homemade bread, delicious Chubut cheese, fresh fruit and Welsh sweets. In Villa Futalaufquen there are a couple of basic grocery stores and a summer-only restaurant, but it's best to bring your own provisions. The following accommodations are listed from north to south, not by price.

CAMPING

Los Alerces has several full-service, drive-in campgrounds, all of which have hot showers, grocery stores and restaurants on-site or nearby. Free (no services) and semi-organized campsites exist near most of these fee sites.

Camping Lago Rivadavia (☎ 454381; adult/child AR$14/7) Idyllic spots at Lago Rivadavia's south end, sheltered in the trees with picnic tables and a boat launch. There's an electricity hookup too. It's 42km north of the Villa.

Camping Lago Verde (☎ 471015/20, ext 23; camping per person AR$20, 6-person cabin AR$1000) With deluxe remodeled cabins and full-service camping, this campground flanks the eastern shore of its namesake lake, 35km northwest of Villa Futalaufquen. Camping with electrical hookups is extra. Besides nearby Lago Verde Wilderness Resort, it's the only option on this tranquil lake. The resort offers dining and tea service.

Complejo Turístico Bahía Rosales (☎ 471044; camping per person AR$18, 4-person refugio AR$160, 6-person cabin AR$360) This sprawling complex has flat campsites by the water, other lodging options and sporting facilities. At the north end of Lago Futalaufquen, it is 1.5km from the main road via a dirt path and 15km from the Intendencia.

Autocamping Los Maitenes (☎ 471006; per person AR$16) On a slip of grass between the main road and the lake, these spots have lovely water views. Sites include shade, electricity hookup and fire pits, 200m from the Intendencia.

Camping & Refugio Lago Krüger (☎ 471015/20, ext 23; www.krugerlodge.com.ar; camping per person AR$15, full-pension refugio per person AR$180) This relatively isolated lakefront *refugio* (rustic shelter) complex is accessible by the 25km trail that leaves from Hostería Futalaufquen (see p475), or by launch from Puerto Limonao.

CABAÑAS & HOSTERÍAS

With a group, cabins can be an affordable option.

Lago Verde Wilderness Resort (☎ in Buenos Aires 011-4312-7415; www.hosteriaselaura.com; camping per person AR$14-28, per car AR$6, 2-/3-/4-person cabins AR$942/1224/1507) Rustic yet ritzy, these raspy stone cabañas feature big cozy beds, panoramic forest views and earthy motifs. Anglers can rent motorized rafts with driver (AR$471 per day) to cast from the lake's every nook and cranny. A new gourmet restaurant and teahouse caters to travelers and guests. It's 35km north of the Villa.

Hostería Cume Hue (☎ 450503; www.cumehue.com.ar; full board per person AR$210; ⊗ year-round) Anglers fill up this family-run inn, 27km north of the Villa. Shared bathrooms and single beds lend a somewhat monastic quality to these dull lodgings with limited electricity; to boot, all guests pay full board, which makes it somewhat overpriced. Still, the family is kind and

since there is no phone on site, the park can communicate with the *hostería* via radio to help guests with last-minute reservations.

Cabañas Tejas Negras (☎ 471012, 471046; tejas negras@ciudad.com.ar; 4-/5-person cabins AR$400/500; ⊗ year-round) With a lawn like a golf course and a handful of prim A-frames, Nilda and Hector have hosted guests for 40 years. Think retreat: there are no football matches on these greens where tranquility is savored.

Hostería Quime Quipan (☎ 471021; www.cpatagonia .com/quimequipan in Spanish; d with/without view AR$300/270, 6-person cabin AR$350; ⊗ Nov-Apr) In a breathtaking setting, this old-fashioned guesthouse offers pleasant but dated rooms – splurge for those with lake views. Fishing and 4WD excursions are also offered. Nonguests can dine at the cozy, sunlit restaurant (meals AR$45), a popular après-fishing pit stop.

Hostería Futalaufquen (☎ 471008/9; www.brazo sur.com.ar/hosteria.htm in Spanish; d with half-pension low/ high season AR$587/800, 4-/5-person apt AR$1200/1600) Exclusive and elegant, this country inn is on the quieter western shore of the lake, 4.5km north of the Villa at the end of the road. It offers nine well-appointed doubles and three log cabins (without kitchens). Activities – from kayaking to rappelling – abound; collapse by the fire afterwards with a plate of dessert. The teahouse and superb dining room Lahuan are open to the public. Reservations can be made at Av Alvear 442 in Esquel.

Getting There & Away

For information on getting to/from the park, see p469.

GOBERNADOR COSTA
☎ 02945 / pop 2000

When you find a town where a child snaps the tourist's picture (and not the reverse), you've discovered something of an anomaly. This rusted little cattle town abuts the yawning stretch of RN 40 between Esquel and Río Mayo, at the intersection of RP 20 for Sarmiento and Comodoro Rivadavia. Some 20km west of town, RP 19 leads to **Lago General Vintter** and several smaller blue-ribbon lakes near the Chilean border; camping is possible along the shores.

Traveler services are few but reasonable. On the edge of fields, **Camping Municipal** (per person AR$6) has electricity and hot water. The motel-style **Mi Refugio** (☎ 491087; Av Roca s/n; s/d/tr/q AR$50/75/95/120) has dark but clean rooms with central heating and TV. The downstairs grill is friendly and its food filling. If it's booked out, check **Residencial El Jair** (☎ 02945-15-680414; cnr San Martín & Sarmiento; per person AR$30), with basic rooms and special rates for families.

The **bus terminal** (Av Roca s/n) is next to Mi Refugio. Buses go to Esquel (AR$22), continuing to Bariloche, at 3:45am every day except for Saturday. For Comodoro Rivadavia (AR$53), buses leave at 11:30pm every day except Sunday. To reach Río Mayo, most buses skip this portion of bumpy (and boring) RN 40 by taking RP 20 south, paralleling Río Senguer to the Río Mayo cutoff.

RÍO MAYO
☎ 02903 / pop 3500 humans, 800,000 sheep

The national capital of sheepshearing is a surprisingly humdrum place, save for the petroleum workers and waylaid gauchos practicing their wolf-whistles on unsuspecting female *turistas*. This barren pit stop is 200km south of Gobernador Costa, 135km north of Perito Moreno and 274km west of Comodoro Rivadavia.

The **Casa de Cultura** (☎ 420400; Ejército Argentino s/n; 🕙 9am-noon & 3-6pm) houses a tourist office, with information on local mountain biking. The town website (www.riomayo.gov.ar in Spanish) has some useful information for visitors. **Banco del Chubut** (cnr Yrigoyen & Argentina) has an ATM.

January's **Festival Nacional de la Esquila** features merino wool quality competitions and even guanaco shearing. But the main event is the long-anticipated crowning of the national sheepshearing queen.

Camping Municipal (☎ 420400; Av E Argentino s/n; per vehicle AR$15) flanks the river. Run-down but respectable, the four-room **Aurora** (☎ 420193; Fontana 750; d without bathroom AR$60) is clean and cared for by a sweet-natured matron. It's around the corner from the YPF station.

The following lodgings both offer meals, otherwise the YPF is a good bet for a quick sandwich and coffee. Funky and rambling **El Viejo Kavadonga** (☎ 420020; San Martín 573; per person with/without bathroom AR$70/50) features rooms with good down covers but varying in quality. Its coveted feature is the orange vinyl bar. **Hotel Akatá** (☎ 420054; San Martín 640; per person AR$70; 🖳) has internet but little else; its wood-panel rooms are dark and airless.

There are daily morning services from the **bus terminal** (☎ 420174; cnr Fontana & Irigoyen) to Comodoro Rivadavia (AR$24, four hours) and Sarmiento (AR$14) at 6am and 11am. Buses to Coyhaique, Chile (AR$50), go on Wednesdays and Saturdays at 12:30pm. The only regularly scheduled services on the rugged stretch of RN 40 to Perito Moreno are summer-only backpacker shuttles (see p478).

PERITO MORENO
☎ 02963 / pop 3500

Those who confuse this dull agricultural village with the jaw-dropping national park of the same name or the glacier near El Calafate might wonder why the only tourist attraction is cruising the strip on Saturday night. Perito Moreno is a brief stopover en route to the more inviting Andean oasis of Los Antiguos. It also makes a good launch pad for visiting Cueva de las Manos and Parque Nacional Perito Moreno. The main drag, San Martín, leads north to RP 43 and south to RN 40; it's 128km south to Bajo Caracoles and 135km north to Río Mayo.

The town's glory came in 1898, when explorer Perito Moreno challenged Chile's border definition of '*divortum aquarum continental*' (which claimed the headwaters of Pacific-flowing rivers as Chilean territory) by rerouting the Río Fénix, which flows through town, to Atlantic-bound Río Deseado. The river and the area remained Argentine, and the town took his name.

Information
Banco de la Nación (cnr San Martín & Perito Moreno)
Banco de Santa Cruz (cnr San Martín & Rivadavia) Has an ATM.
CTC (Perito Moreno 1032) Cheap internet access.
Hospital Distrital (☎ 432040; Colón 1237)
Post office (cnr JD Perón & Belgrano)
Telefónica (cnr San Martín & Saavedra)
Tourist office (☎ 432732; turismoperitomoreno@ yahoo.com.ar; San Martín 1766; 🕙 7am-11:30pm Mon-Fri, 8am-3pm Sat & Sun) There is also a desk at the bus terminal.
Zoien (☎ 432207; cnr San Martín & Saveedra) Travel agency with trips to Cueva de las Manos in high season.

Tours
The experienced **GuanaCondor Tours** (☎ 432117, 02963-15-452-6224, 02963-15-452-6224; jarinauta@santacruz .com.ar; Perito Moreno 1087; 🕙 10am-noon & 4-8pm Mon-Wed & Sat, 5-8pm Sun) runs tours to Cueva de las Manos (AR$120 per person), accessing the park via the former Estancia Los Toldos, with a challenging hike that adds considerably to the experience. Ask about trips to Monte Zeballos, a high mesa

PATAGONIA

with excellent views, and an overnight trip to Paso Tehuelche that's in the works.

Sleeping & Eating

Camping Municipal (Laguna de los Cisnes, off Mariano Moreno; sites AR$30, plus AR$5 per person, 4-person cabañas per person AR$100) The cheapest option for backpackers is this campground with rustic cabins on the south side of town. It's shaded by breezy poplars and has hot showers. The *cabañas*, while private, are cramped.

Hotel Americano (☎ 432074; San Martín 1327; s/d/tr AR$60/90/120) Cozy and family-run, Americano also has a decent restaurant. Rooms vary widely – some lack windows, others can be quite cozy – so ask to see a few before deciding.

Hotel Belgrano (☎ 432019; San Martín 1001; s/d/tr AR$90/140/180) This big, boxy corner hotel has spacious cement rooms with decent mattresses but not much ambience. Most folks shuffle in during the wee hours from Chaltén Travel shuttles. The downstairs restaurant serves good coffee and breakfast is AR$8.

Posada el Caminante (☎ 432204; Rivadavia 937; s/d/tr AR$100/140/180) The best bet in town, Señora Ethiel's inn fills up fast. This welcoming hostess has four spacious rooms with comfy beds, heating and private bathrooms. An abundant breakfast (AR$9 extra) is worthwhile, especially during fruit season.

There are a couple of well-stocked *panaderías* (bakeries) and grocery stores along San Martín.

Getting There & Away

LADE (☎ 432055; San Martín 1065) flies to El Calafate, Río Gallegos, Río Grande and Ushuaia.

The pristine bus terminal sits behind the YPF rotunda at the northern entrance to town. Taxis (AR$4) provide the only transport between here and the center, other than a flat 15-minute walk. Buses leave daily at 10:30am and 1:40am for Los Antiguos (AR$13, 40 minutes), and at 1:50am for Comodoro Rivadavia (AR$49, five hours) via Caleta Olivia (AR$42, four hours). Buses to El Calafate (AR$153, 19 hours) via RN 3 go at 5:05pm, stopping at Caleta Olivia.

Several shuttle services also offering excursions serve travelers on RN 40. From November to April, **Chaltén Travel** (☎ /fax in El Calafate 2902-492-212/492-480; www.chaltentravel.com) goes north to Bariloche (11 hours), departing from Hotel Belgrano in Perito Moreno at 8pm on even-

numbered days. Shuttles leave Hotel Belgrano at 8am to head south to El Chaltén (11 hours) on odd-numbered days. Year-round, **Las Loicas** (☎ 02963-490272, 0297-15-421-3194; http://lasloicas.com in Spanish) leaves Perito Moreno on Thursdays at 6pm for Bajo Caracoles (AR$40, two hours) and Lago Posadas (AR$50, four hours). **Condor Patagonico** (☎ 02944-525488) continues north to Bariloche (AR$157) in connection with shuttles coming from the south. For more information on all options, see p471.

LOS ANTIGUOS
☎ 02963 / pop 2500

Situated on the windy shores of Lago Buenos Aires, the agricultural oasis of Los Antiguos is framed with rows of Lombardy poplars sheltering *chacras* (small independent farms) of cherries, strawberries, apples, apricots and peaches. Before the arrival of Europeans, ageing Tehuelche frequented this 'banana belt' – the town's name is a near-literal translation of the Tehuelche name 'I-Keu-khon,' meaning Place of the Elders. Travelers come to cross the border into Chile, but getting here via RN 40 can be an adventure in itself.

Volcán Hudson's 1991 eruption covered the town in ash, but farms have bounced back. In summer **Lago Buenos Aires**, South America's second-biggest lake, is warm enough for a brisk swim. The stunning **Río Jeinemeni** is a favored spot for trout and salmon fishing.

Orientation

Los Antiguos occupies the delta formed by Río Los Antiguos and Río Jeinemeni, which constitutes the border with Chile. Most services are on or near east–west Av 11 de Julio, which heads west to the Chilean frontier at Chile Chico, the region's most convenient border crossing. Perito Moreno and RN 40 are 60km to the east.

Information

Banco de Santa Cruz (Av 11 de Julio 531) Has a 24-hour ATM.

Ciber Patagonia (cnr Patagonia Argentina & Fierro) Open late for internet access.

Locutorio (Alameda 436) Also has internet.

Mario Rodríguez (☎ 0229-63-491123, 02966-15-514923) Spanish-speaking local fishing guide.

Post office (Gregores 19)

Tourist information office (☎ 491261; www.losan tiguos.gov.ar in Spanish; Av 11 de Julio 446; ☒ 8am-8pm) Helpful, with a map of town and farms selling fresh produce.

Festivals & Events

The fun **Fiesta de la Cereza** (Cherry Festival), featuring rodeos and live music, celebrates its favorite crop during the second weekend of January. Artisan goods are sold and *peñas folkloricas* (Argentine folk music concerts) at private farms go on all night long – see the tourist information office for more information.

Sleeping & Eating

Camping Municipal (☎ 491265; RP 43; camping/cabins per person AR$4/40) Windbreaks help considerably at this lakeshore site 1.5km east of town. The windowless cabins have dorm-style accommodations, and hot showers are available in the evening.

Albergue Padilla (☎ 491140; San Martín 44; s/d/tr AR$30/70/90) Chaltén Travel shuttles deposit lodgers at this family-run institution after dark. Dorms share bathrooms (with plenty of hot water) and an attractive cooking area. In summer ask about cherry picking on the

family farm. They have RN 40 shuttle tickets and the latest Chilean border crossing and ferry details.

Cabañas Rincon de los Poetas (☎ 491051; Patagonia Argentina 226; d/tr/q AR$100/120/130) These snug wooden cabins equipped with kitchenettes are nothing fancy, but they prove good value for couples and families. It's located two blocks from the center.

Hotel Argentino (☎ 491132; Av 11 de Julio 850; s/d AR$85/115) Modern rooms all feature private bathroom and TV, and hearty meals satisfy a regular crowd of farmers, gauchos and businessmen.

Hostería Antigua Patagonia (☎ 491038; www.antiguapatagonia.com.ar in Spanish; RP 43 Acceso Este; s/d AR$190/230) This plush lakefront complex is decked out in rustic touches. Rooms feature four-poster beds and wooden trunks, though the snuggest spot is by the stone fireplace. Diversions include a telescope, sauna, gym, bikes and billiards. Meals feature local lamb

---

ESTANCIAS IN PATAGONIA

Most assume *estancias* are all about livestock, but these offbeat offerings prove otherwise.

A Wealth of Wildlife

- Meet the neighbors – that would be the penguins, seabirds and elephant seals – around Península Valdés' **Estancia Rincón Chico** (p442).
- Reel in the big one at the exclusive, world-renowned trout mecca **Estancia Güer Aike** (p464), near Río Gallegos.
- View the diverse fauna of Magellanic penguins, sea lions, guanacos and pumas at **Hostería Monte León** (p460).

Breathtaking Beauty

- Luxuriate among glaciers, lakes and the ragged Mt Fitz Roy in the exclusive **Hostería Estancia Helsingfors** (p497).
- Gallop the rugged splendor surrounding Parque Nacional Perito Moreno at the hospitable **Estancia Menelik** (p482).
- Hike narrow canyons and shout from the precipitous plateaus at **Estancia Telken** (p480).

Just Like Indiana Jones

- Travel back to the Pleistocene and explore 84 caves with prehistoric rock art at **Estancia La María** (p460), near Puerto San Julián.
- Trek to Unesco World Heritage site Cueva de las Manos from **Hostería Cueva de las Manos** (p480), via the serpentine red-rock canyon of Río de las Pinturas.

The Bargain Bin

- Grab your zzzs in a bunk bed and save some bucks: Estancias Menelik (p482), La María (p460) and Casa de Piedra (p481) all offer affordable *refugio* (rustic shelter) lodgings.

PATAGONIA

on a spit and fresh produce. It's 2km east of town, off the road to Perito Moreno.

Agua Grande (☎ 491165; Av 11 de Julio 871; mains AR$25) The best restaurant in town, offering a daily special and menu of pastas, meats and sandwiches.

Getting There & Away

The gradual paving of RN 40 and subsequent future services will keep transport options in flux, so get current information.

Various bus companies go to nearby Perito Moreno (AR$13, 40 minutes) at 6am, 3pm and 4pm. **Sportman** (☎ 491175; Senador Molina 690) has buses to Río Gallegos (AR$110, 16 hours) and Comodoro Rivadavia (AR$58, six hours) at 4pm daily. Ask about intermediary stops. **La Unión** (☎ 491078; cnr Av 11 de Julio & San Martín) buses head to Comodoro Rivadavia (AR$58) at 5:45am and 3pm Monday to Saturday and 4pm on Sunday.

Transportes Padilla (☎ 491140; San Martín 44) crosses the border (open 8am to 9pm or 10pm daily, often closed noon to 2pm) to Chile Chico (AR$4) several times daily.

From November to March, **Chaltén Travel** (www.chaltentravel.com) goes to El Chaltén (AR$160, 13 hours) on even-numbered days at 9am, stopping first in Perito Moreno. See p471 for northbound schedules.

Ferry **El Pilchero** (☎ in Chile 56-67-411864) crosses Lago Buenos Aires daily from Chile Chico to Puerto Ibáñez (CH$4000, vehicles CH$23,500 per meter, three to six hours), weather depending, on Monday at 8am and 4:30pm, Thursday at 3:30pm, Friday at 5:30pm and Sunday at 2:30pm. Alternatively, it's possible to continue overland around the lake's southern shore to Carretera Austral and Coyhaique.

ESTANCIA TELKEN

A highlight of traveling along this stretch, **Estancia Telken** (☎ 02963-432079; telkenpatagonia@ yahoo.com.ar; RN 40; camping per person/tent AR$15, d AR$240; ☉ Oct-Apr) offers a welcoming repose in pretty countryside. This 1915 working sheep and horse ranch, 25km south of Perito Moreno, is run by the charming Coco and Petti Nauta. Coco's family is descended from Dutch settlers, while Petti hails from a New Zealand clan and spins many a yarn about ranch life. Delicious, abundant meals are served family-style, and English and Dutch are spoken. Recently two new doubles have been added.

There are about 210 sq km of horseback riding and hiking possibilities, including a worthwhile meander along a creek bed up to the basalt plateau **Meseta de Lago Buenos Aires**. Ask Petti to take you to **Cueva de Piedra**, a small cave snuggled in a silent valley of guanacos, eagles and the occasional armadillo.

Controversial gold mining allowed by government concession has closed **Cañadon Arroyo del Feo**, a deep red-rock river canyon that narrows into steep ravines, to the public. This used to be an excellent opportunity to see well-preserved cave art that has been around for approximately 7000 years.

GuanaCondor Tours in Perito Moreno (p477) organizes trips.

CUEVA DE LAS MANOS

The incredible rock art of **Cueva de las Manos** (Cave of the Hands; admission AR$50; ☉ 9am-7pm) was proclaimed a Unesco World Heritage site in 1999. Dating from about 7370 BC, these polychrome rock paintings cover recesses in the near-vertical walls with imprints of human hands as well as drawings of guanacos and, from a later period, more-abstract designs. Of around 800 images, more than 90% are of left hands; one has six fingers.

The approach is via rough but scenic provincial roads off RN 40, abutting Río de las Pinturas. Drivers should have caution: guanacos are abundant, bounding across the steppe. There are two points of access: a more direct route via Bajo Caracoles, 46km away on the south side of the river; and another from Hostería Cueva de las Manos, on the north side, via a footbridge. Guides in Perito Moreno organize day trips, usually around AR$140 per person plus park entrance fee. Free guided walks are given every hour by knowledgeable staff. There's an information center and a basic *confitería* at the reception house near the southern entrance, but it's best to bring your own food.

On the doorstep of Argentina's best deposit of rock art, the budding **Hostería Cueva de las Manos** (☎ 02963-432730, in Buenos Aires 011-5237-4043; www.cuevadelasmanos.net; dm/d AR$35/255; ☉ Nov-Apr), formerly Estancia Los Toldos, is a short distance off RN 40, 52km south of Perito Moreno. Guests can stay in cabins, the *hostería* or a 20-person dormitory. Rooms are plain but well appointed, with hardwood details. There's restaurant service or lunchboxes for hikers. Guests and tour groups can

---

DETOUR TO LAGO POSADAS

Want to dust off Patagonia's forgotten corners? Try adventuring to turquoise Lago Posadas and the bright blue Lago Puerreydon, flanked by fossil remains, scenic trekking and steady gusts of wind. You can arrive at the hamlet of Hipolito Yrigoyen (Lago Posadas) via RP 39, 70km west from RN 40 and Bajo Caracoles. There is camping on Lago Puerreydon (called Lago Cochrane on the Chilean side). From there, locals can direct you to area walks.

Outfitter **Las Loicas** (☎ 02963-490272, 0297-15-421-3194; http://lasloicas.com; cnr Las Lengas & Condor Andino, Lago Posadas) has the scoop on hiking, climbing and horseback riding in the greater area. It can also provide transportation, with high-season departures on Thursday from Perito Moreno (AR$50) at 6pm and Bajo Caracoles (AR$20) at 8pm.

---

approach Cueva de los Manos via a scenic but challenging hiking trail (summer only) that starts from the *hostería*, descends the canyon and crosses Río de las Pinturas.

Rustic but welcoming **Estancia Casa de Piedra** (☎ 02963-432-1990; off RN 40; camping per person AR$25, dm AR$60; ❤ Dec-Mar), a basic ranch 76km south of Perito Moreno, has plain rooms and allows camping. Campers can shower; all meals cost extra. It's a good spot for trekkers to hunker down: there are nearby volcanoes and the walk to Cueva de las Manos is approximately two hours via Cañon de las Pinturas. Guides can be contracted here but the trail is clear enough to go without one.

BAJO CARACOLES

Blink and you'll miss this dusty gas stop. Little has changed since Bruce Chatwin described this hamlet as 'a crossroads of insignificant importance with roads leading all directions apparently to nowhere' in *In Patagonia* in 1975. If you're headed south, fill the tank, since it's the only reliable gas pump between Perito Moreno (128km north) and Tres Lagos (409km south). From here RP 39 heads west to Lago Posadas and the Paso Roballos to Chile.

Lodgers put on a brave face for **Hotel Bajo Caracoles** (☎ 02963-490100; d AR$140), a severely overpriced flophouse with old gas heating units that require a watchful eye. It also stocks basic provisions and has the only private telephone in town.

Heading south, RN 40 takes a turn for the worse: it's 100km to Las Horquetas, a blip on the radar screen where RN 40, RP 27 and RP 37 intersect. From here it's another 128km southeast via RP 27 to Gobernador Gregores.

PARQUE NACIONAL PERITO MORENO

Wild and windblown, Parque Nacional Perito Moreno is an adventurer's dream. Approaching from the steppe, the massive snowcapped peaks of the Sierra Colorada rise like sentinels. Guanacos graze the tufted grasses, condors circle above and wind blurs the surfaces of Technicolor aquamarine and cobalt lakes. If you come here you will be among 1200 yearly visitors – that is, mostly alone. Solitude reigns and, save for services offered by local *estancias*, you are entirely on your own.

Honoring the park system's founder, this remote but increasingly popular park encompasses 1150 sq km, 310km southwest of the town of Perito Moreno. Don't confuse this gem with Parque Nacional Los Glaciares (home to the Perito Moreno glacier) further south.

The sedimentary Sierra Colorada has a painter's palette of rusty hues. Beyond the park boundary, glacier-topped summits such as 3706m Cerro San Lorenzo (the highest peak in the area) tower over the landscape. The highest peak within the park is Cerro Mié (2254m).

Besides guanacos, the park is also home to pumas, foxes, wildcats, chinchillas and huemul (Andean deer). The abundant bird population includes condors, rheas, flamingos, black-necked swans, cauquén (upland geese) and caranchos (crested cara caras). Predecessors of the Tehuelche left evidence of their presence with rock paintings in caves at Lago Burmeister.

As precipitation increases toward the west, the Patagonian steppe grasslands along the park's eastern border become sub-Antarctic forests of southern beech, lenga and coihue. Because the base altitude exceeds 900m, weather can be severe. Summer is usually comfortable, but warm clothing and proper gear are imperative in any season. The water is pure but you must bring all food and supplies.

PATAGONIA

Information

Visitors must register at the park's information center on the eastern boundary; it's stocked with informative maps and brochures. Rangers offer a variety of guided hikes; they can also be contacted via the national parks office in Gobernador Gregores (right), where it may be possible to arrange a ride.

Sights & Activities

Behind the information center, a one-hour interpretive trail leads to **Pinturas Rupestres**, a small number of cave paintings with interpretive signs in English. Consult park rangers for backpacking options and guided walks to the pictographs at **Casa de Piedra** on Lago Burmeister, and to **Playa de los Amonites** on Lago Belgrano, where there are fossils. Lago Burmeister also has a small museum worth a peek.

From Estancia La Oriental, it's a 2½-hour hike to the summit of 1434m **Cerro León**, from where there's a dazzling panorama. Immediately east of the summit, the volcanic outcrop of **Cerro de los Cóndores** is a nesting site for the Andes' totem species. Pumas have also been spotted here and guanacos down below.

Sleeping & Eating

There are free campgrounds at the information center (barren and exposed, no fires allowed); at Lago Burmeister, 16km from the information center (more scenic, and well sheltered among dense lenga forest, fires allowed); and at El Rincón, 15km away (no fires). None have showers, but there are pit toilets.

Estancia Menelik (☎ satellite phone 011-4152-5500, in Buenos Aires 011-4836-3502; www.cielospatagonicos.com; s/d/q AR$188/251/377, refugio per person AR$63; ☼ Oct-Mar) With a panorama of Parque Nacional Perito Moreno, this 1920 working ranch is a prime destination for horseback riding; highlights include overnight trips to the high camp of Veranada de Jones. Accomodations range from rustic to comfortable and a new bunkhouse promises cozy changes. A seasoned staff provides courteous and hospitable service.

Estancia La Oriental (☎ 02962-452196, in Buenos Aires 011-4343-2366/9568; gesino@fibertel.com; AR$204/267/314/393, camping per person AR$47; ☼ Oct-Mar; ☒) At the foot of Cerro León, at the end of the road on the north shore of Lago Belgrano, La Oriental is the ideal base camp for exploring the park's varied backcountry. Excursions

to Cerro San Lorenzo (first by car, then on foot or horseback) are a highlight. Condors are easy to sight from Cerro León's 1000m cliffs. Attention is not exactly personalized: the ranch caters to group tours. The *estancia* requires a minimum two-night stay and will not sell gasoline to nonguests. Horseback riding (nonguests/guests AR$220/157, guide AR$220) is available. Meals are well praised.

Getting There & Away

Public-transport options change often; check with tourist offices in Perito Moreno, Los Antiguos and El Calafate for updates. Las Loicas (p481) can take travelers here from Perito Moreno. In summer hitchhiking is possible from the RN 40 junction, but the park is so large that getting to trailheads presents difficulties. From April to November the road becomes impassable at times. If you're driving, carry spare gas and tires.

GOBERNADOR GREGORES
☎ 02962 / pop 2521

Gobernador Gregores is a sleepy pit stop that beckons principally when your gas tank dips toward E. But as RN 40 is paved and re-routed here, its tourist services should expand. For now, the hours of siesta remain holy.

Gregores is 60km east of RN 40 on RP 25. It's the nearest town to Parque Nacional Perito Moreno, still 200km west. It is an ideal spot to get supplies and arrange transportation. There's a **tourist office** (☎ 491192; San Martín 409; ☼ 8am-2pm Mon-Fri) and **national parks administration office** (☎ 491477; San Martín 882; 9am-4pm Mon-Fri).

Seventy kilometers west of town via RP 29, the waters of **Lago Cardiel** are well loved by anglers for blue-ribbon salmon and rainbow trout fishing. From the junction to the lake it's another 116km to **Tres Lagos**, where a jovial couple run a 24-hour YPF station, then another 123km west to El Chaltén.

Summer-only **Camping Nuestra Señora del Valle** (cnr Roca & Chile; sites AR$4) has showers, hot water and stone grills. Hot meals (*plato del día* AR$25) and firm beds are found at **Cañadón León** (☎ 491082; Roca 397; s/d/tr AR$90/120/150), with 11 tidy rooms that are ample and spotless. Reserve ahead if possible. Just outside town, the pleasing **Cabañas María Abril** (☎ 491016; losluck ysma@yahoo.com.ar; Av Cañadon León 608; d without bathroom AR$80, d/tr/q AR$120/150/250) offers tranquility with a village of A-frames in the poplars.

LADE (☎ 491008; Colón 544) has popular Monday flights to Perito Moreno (AR$138), El Calafate (AR$139), Comodoro Rivadavia (AR$139) and Buenos Aires (AR$373).

Cerro San Lorenzo (cnr San Martín & Alberdi) buses leave for Puerto San Julián (AR$45, five hours) Monday to Saturday at 4pm. **El Pulgarcito** (☎ 491474; San Martín 704) goes to Río Gallegos (AR$55, six hours) daily at 7am, while **El Pegaso** (☎ 491494; Pejkovic 520) goes to Río Gallegos (AR$62) at 4am Monday to Saturday.

EL CHALTÉN & PARQUE NACIONAL LOS GLACIARES (NORTH)
☎ 02962

The Fitz Roy Range, with its rugged wilderness and shark-tooth summits, is the de-facto mountaineering mecca of Argentina. World-class climbers consider Cerro Torre and Monte Fitz Roy epic ascents, notorious for brutal weather conditions. Occupying the northern half of Parque Nacional Los Glaciares, this sector offers numerous, well-marked trails for trekking and jaw-dropping scenery – that is, when the clouds clear.

At the entrance to the northern sector, the ragtag village of **El Chaltén** (population 600) serves the thousands of visitors who make summer pilgrimages to explore the range. The packs of dogs roaming the streets are a reminder that this is a frontier town: it was slapped together in 1985 to beat Chile to the land claim. As Argentina's youngest town, it still has to sort out details like banks (there are no ATMs), roads and zoning. Hiker services continue to evolve rapidly; the recent paving of RP 23 may improve them, even as it makes way for large-scale tourism.

El Chaltén is named for Cerro Fitz Roy's Tehuelche name, meaning 'peak of fire' or 'smoking mountain,' an apt description of the cloud-enshrouded summit. Perito Moreno and Carlos Moyano later named it after the *Beagle's* Captain FitzRoy, who navigated Darwin's expedition up the Río Santa Cruz in 1834, coming within 50km of the cordillera.

Every October 12, on the wet heels of winter with the streets mired in mud, El Chaltén celebrates **Fiesta del Pueblo**, the town anniversary, with dancing in the school gym, barbecues and live music. In the last week of February the **Fiesta Nacional de Trekking** comes to town, bringing a circus of outdoor freaks for rock-climbing, bouldering and woodcutting competitions, as well as running and

mountain-bike races. **Capilla de los Escaladores**, a simple chapel of Austrian design, memorializes the many climbers who have lost their lives to the precarious peaks since 1953.

Parque Nacional Los Glaciares is divided into geographically separate northern and southern sectors. El Calafate (p490) is the gateway town for the southern sector of the park.

Information
Newspapers, cell phones and money exchange have yet to hit El Chaltén, but there's now mercurial satellite internet, a gas station, long-distance call centers – and land set aside for an ATM, bus terminal and cell-phone antennae. There's even a cemetery plotted out…but nobody's been buried there yet. Credit cards are virtually useless, but traveler's checks, euros and US dollars are widely accepted; ask around to find out who's changing money. Surf www.elchalten.com for a good overview of town.

Chaltén Travel (☎ 493005/92; Av San Martín 724) Books airline tickets and offers weather-dependent internet service for AR$12 an hour.

Municipal tourist office (☎ 493270; comfomelchalten@ yahoo.com.ar; Av MM De Güemes 21; ☷ 8am-8pm) Friendly and extremely helpful, with lodging lists and good information on town and tours. English is spoken.

Park ranger office (☎ 493004/24; admission free, donations welcome; ☷ 8am-7pm) Daytime buses all stop for a short bilingual orientation at this new visitor center, just before the bridge over the Río Fitz Roy. Park rangers distribute a map and town directory and do a good job of explaining the park's ecological issues. Climbing documentaries are shown at 3pm daily – great for rainy days. Rangers can answer questions about the area's hikes and issue climbing permits. They also post a lodging list.

Puesto Sanitario (☎ 493033; AM De Agostini, btwn McLeod & Av MM De Güemes) Provides basic health services.

Viento Oeste (☎ 493021/200; Av San Martín 898) En route to Campamento Madsen, this shop sells books, maps and souvenirs and rents a wide range of camping equipment, as do several other sundries shops around town.

Activities
HIKING
Before heading out on the trail, hikers should stop by the park ranger office for updated trail conditions. The most stable weather for hiking comes not in summer but in March and April, when there is less wind (and fewer people). During the winter months of June and July trails may be closed – check first with the park ranger office.

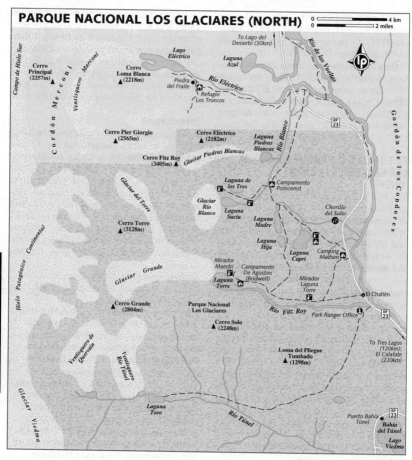

PARQUE NACIONAL LOS GLACIARES (NORTH)

Experienced backpackers can register to hike in the remote areas, which require some route-finding but reward with getting you off the central circuits and away from the crowds. A first-person ranger update is necessary for these hikes. For more information on hiking, read Lonely Planet's *Trekking in the Patagonian Andes*.

Laguna Torre

If you have good weather (ie little wind) and clear skies, make this hike (three hours one way) a priority, since the toothy Cerro Torre is the most difficult local peak to see on normal blustery days.

Hikers have the option of taking two different trails to make this trek (they later merge).

One starts at the northwestern edge of El Chaltén. From a signpost on Av San Martín, just south of Campamento Madsen, head west on Eduardo Brenner and then right to find the signposted start of the track. The Laguna Torre track winds up westwards around large boulders on slopes covered with typical Patagonian dry-land plants, then leads southwest past a *mallín* (wet meadow) to a junction with a trail coming in from the left (see the following start) after 35 to 45 minutes.

If you start from the southern end of El Chaltén, follow Lago del Desierto west past the edge of town, then drop to the riverbed and continue past a tiny hydroelectric installation. At a signpost the route climbs away from the river and leads on through scattered lenga and ñire woodland (with the odd wire fence to step over) before merging with a more prominent (signposted) path coming in from the right.

Continue up past a rounded bluff to the **Mirador Laguna Torre**, a crest giving you the first clear view up the valley to the extraordinary 3128m rock spire of Cerro Torre standing above a sprawling mass of intersecting glaciers. Look for the 'mushroom' of snow and ice that caps the peak. This precarious formation is the final obstacle for hard-core climbers, who often spend weeks waiting for decent weather.

The trail dips down gently through beautiful stands of stout ancient lengas, before cutting across open scrubby river flats and old revegetated moraines to reach a signposted junction with the Sendero Madre e Hija, a shortcut route to Campamento Poincenot, 40 to 50 minutes on. Continuing up the valley, bear left at another signposted fork and climb over a forested embankment to cross a small alluvial plain, following the fast-flowing glacial waters of the Río Fitz Roy. You'll arrive at **Campamento De Agostini** (formerly Campamento Bridwell) after a further 30 to 40 minutes. This free campground (with pit toilet) gets busy; it serves as a base camp for Cerro Torre climbers. The only other park-authorized place to camp in the vicinity is in a pleasant grove of riverside lengas below Cerro Solo.

Follow the trail along the lake's north side for about an hour to **Mirador Maestri** (no camping).

Laguna de los Tres

This hike to a high alpine tarn is a bit more strenuous (four hours one way). The trail starts from the yellow-roofed pack station at **Campamento Madsen**. After about an hour, there's a signed lateral to excellent free backcountry **campsites** at Laguna Capri. The main trail continues gently through windswept forests and past small lakes, meeting up with the trail from Lagunas Madre and Hija. Carrying on through wind-worn ñire forest (a small, deciduous southern beech species) and along boggy terrain leads to **Río Blanco** (three hours) and the woodsy, mice-plagued **Campamento Poincenot**, exclusively reserved for climbers. The trail splits before Río Blanco to head to Río Eléctrico (there is an alternative, parallel trail after Río Blanco but markings are sparse and it is not recommended). Stay left to reach

a climbers' base camp. From here the trail zigzags steeply up the tarn to the eerily still, glacial **Laguna de los Tres** and an extraordinary close view of 3405m Cerro Fitz Roy. Clouds ever huddle in the rocky crevasses, whipping up with a change in wind. Be prepared for high, potentially hazardous winds and allow time for contemplation and recovery. Scurry down 200m to the left of the lookout for an exceptional view of the emerald-green **Laguna Sucia**.

Piedra del Fraile

At Campamento Poincenot, the trail swings west to Laguna de los Tres or northeast along Río Blanco to Valle Eléctrico and Piedra del Fraile (eight hours from El Chaltén; five hours from the Río Blanco turnoff). From the turnoff, the trail leads to **Glaciar Piedras Blancas** (four hours), the last part of which is a scramble over massive granite boulders to a turquoise lake with dozens of floating icebergs and constant avalanches on the glacier's face. The trail then passes through pastures and branches left up the valley along **Río Eléctrico**, enclosed by sheer cliffs, before reaching the private **Refugio Los Troncos** (campsites AR$25, refugio beds AR$70-120). Reservations are not possible since there are no phones – simply show up. The campground has a kiosk, restaurant and excellent services, and the owners can give information on recommended nearby trails.

Rather than backtrack to Río Blanco and the Laguna de los Tres trail, it's possible to head east, hopping over streams to RP 23, the route back to El Chaltén. You'll pass waterfall **Chorillo del Salto** shortly before reaching Campamento Madsen.

Buses to Lago del Desierto (below) drop hikers at the Río Eléctrico bridge (AR$25).

Loma del Pliegue Tumbado

Heading southwest from the park ranger office, this trail (four to five hours one way) skirts the eastern face of Loma del Pliegue Tumbado going toward Río Túnel, then cuts west and heads to Laguna Toro. It offers the best views of Cerros Torres and Fitz Roy. In fact, it's the only hike that allows views of both peaks at once. The hike is rather gentle, but be prepared for strong winds and carry extra water.

Lago del Desierto & Beyond

Some 37km north of El Chaltén is Lago del Desierto, near the Chilean border, a nice day-trip option when it's raining and there's no chance of catching a glimpse of the Fitz. A 500m trail leads to an overlook that often has fine views of the lake, surrounding mountains and glaciers.

Las Lengas (☎ 493044; Antonio de Viedma 95) offers minibus service to Lago del Desierto, leaving El Chaltén at 7am daily. On the half-day trip (AR$50) the bus stops for two hours at the lake so passengers can trek to Glaciar Huemul or do the boat trip (extra). The all-day trip (AR$90) stays at the lake for six hours. A *remise* charges AR$140 roundtrip for three passengers, plus AR$10 per hour to wait. At the south end of the lake, travelers can dine at **Hostería El Pilar** (☎ 493002; www.hosteriaelpilar.com.ar) in the inviting restaurant.

Patagonia Aventura (☎ 493110; www.patagonia-aventura.com.ar in Spanish; per person AR$120) navigates Lago del Desierto. The alternative to the boat tour is a five-hour walking track between the south end and the north end of the lake.

From the lake's north end, it's increasingly popular to walk or bicycle to the Chilean border post, with hundreds of travelers now using the crossing each year. It's particularly popular with cyclists traveling on to the Chilean frontier outpost Candelaria Mansilla via cargo boat from the southernmost outpost of Villa O'Higgins, in Chile's Aisén region. In Candelaria Mansilla a family offers meals, camping and basic farmhouse accommodations; bring Chilean pesos from El Calafate, if possible. If you leave El Chaltén first thing in the morning, it's possible to cross the Chilean border and reach Candelaria Mansilla in one long day.

A Chilean **excursion boat** (www.villaohiggins.com in Spanish) goes from Candelaria Mansilla to see Glaciar O'Higgins (CH$25,000) on the Southern Ice Shelf, and continues on to Villa O'Higgins (CH$33,000) via Puerto Bahamondez. From Puerto Bahamondez, bus service to Villa O'Higgins is CH$1500. The Villa O'Higgins **municipalidad** (☎ 56-7721-1849) may be able to help with further information and sleeping options. In El Chaltén, Albergue Patagonia (p488) and the tourist office can supply current details on this ever-evolving adventure option.

ICE CLIMBING & TREKKING

Several companies offer ice-climbing courses and ice treks, some including sleds pulled by Siberian huskies. **Fitzroy Expediciones** (☎ 493017; www.fitzroyexpediciones.com.ar; Lionel Terray 145, El

Chaltén) runs glacier-trekking excursions from Campamento De Agostini (Bridwell). The trek usually begins at 9:30am, starting with a 1½-hour walk to Glaciar Grande, then three hours on the glacier, returning to the campground around 5pm. Some groups head out the same day from El Chaltén, which makes for a very arduous trip. It is advisable to make reservations in town, but head to De Agostini on your own the night prior and camp. Bring extra food and water.

Another friendly and professional outfitter, **Casa de Guias** (☎ 493118; Av San Martín s/n; www.casadeguias.com.ar) has guides who are AAGM (Argentine Association of Mountain Guides) certified and speak English. They specialize in small groups and simple camps. Offerings include mountain traverses, mountain ascents for the very fit and rock-climbing classes.

Patagonia Aventura (☎ 493110; www.patagonia-aventura.com.ar in Spanish) offers trekking (AR$230) and ice climbing ($270) on Glaciar Viedma. Trips include a six-hour hike with views of the glacier, a 2½-hour ice trek and all-day instruction in ice climbing. Ice trekkers get to trudge with their crampons through some truly awesome lunar landscapes of ice and learn the basics of safety on ice.

Multiday guided hikes over the **Hielo Patagónico Continental** (Continental Ice Field) offer a unique experience for those of us not versed in polar expeditions. Catering to serious trekkers, this route involves technical climbing, including use of crampons and some strenuous river crossings. One-week packages start at AR$3925.

Certified guide **Pablo Gallego** (payosur@yahoo.com.ar) speaks English and French and commands fun treks at reasonable prices (AR$300 per day).

HORSEBACK RIDING

Horses can be used to trot around town and to carry equipment with a guide (prices negotiable), but are not allowed unguided on national-park trails. Outfitter **El Relincho** (☎ 493007, in El Calafate 02902-491961; San Martín 505, El Chaltén) takes riders to the pretty valley of Río de las Vueltas (AR$110, three hours).

KAYAK & CANOE TRIPS

As El Chaltén grows, so will the aquatic offerings. **Fitzroy Expediciones** (☎ 493017; www.fitzroy expediciones.com.ar; Lionel Terray 145, El Chaltén) offers half-day guided kayaking trips on the Río de

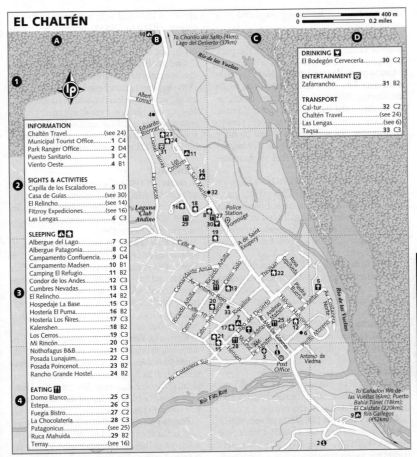

EL CHALTÉN

INFORMATION	
Chaltén Travel	(see 24)
Municipal Tourist Office	**1** C4
Park Ranger Office	**2** D4
Puesto Sanitario	**3** C4
Viento Oeste	**4** B1

SIGHTS & ACTIVITIES	
Capilla de los Escaladores	**5** D3
Casa de Guías	(see 30)
El Relincho	(see 14)
Fitzroy Expediciones	(see 16)
Las Lengas	**6** C3

SLEEPING	
Albergue del Lago	**7** C3
Albergue Patagonia	**8** C2
Campamento Confluencia	**9** D4
Campamento Madsen	**10** B1
Camping El Refugio	**11** B2
Condor de los Andes	**12** C3
Cumbres Nevadas	**13** C3
El Relincho	**14** B2
Hospedaje La Base	**15** C3
Hostería El Puma	**16** B2
Hostería Los Ñires	**17** C3
Kalenshen	**18** B2
Los Cerros	**19** C3
Mi Rincón	**20** C3
Nothofagus B&B	**21** C3
Posada Lunajuim	**22** C3
Posada Poincenot	**23** B2
Rancho Grande Hostel	**24** B2

EATING	
Domo Blanco	**25** C3
Estepa	**26** C3
Fuegia Bistro	**27** C2
La Chocolatería	**28** C3
Patagonicus	(see 25)
Ruca Mahuida	**29** B2
Terray	(see 16)

DRINKING	
El Bodegón Cervecería	**30** C2

ENTERTAINMENT	
Zafarrancho	**31** B2

TRANSPORT	
Cal-tur	**32** C2
Chaltén Travel	(see 24)
Las Lengas	(see 6)
Taqsa	**33** C3

las Vueltas and two-day trips to Río La Leona. Daily trips go to Lago del Desierto for three-hour canoe and kayak excursions.

LAKE CRUISES
Contact **Patagonia Aventura** (☎ 493110; www .patagonia-aventura.com.ar in Spanish) about tourist launches from the teahouse at Puerto Bahía Túnel on the north shore of Lago Viedma. The trip (per person AR$75, plus AR$40 transfer) takes in impressive views of the 40m Glaciar Viedma, grinding from Cerro Fitz Roy. Boat trips leave at 3:30pm and last 2½ hours.

Sleeping
Reservations should be made at least one month in advance for the January–February high season – demand here is that great. Plus it's particularly depressing to arrive in the middle of the night with the wind howling and no bed waiting. One solution is to bring a bombproof tent – there's always space in the campgrounds. Except for the backcountry campgrounds, all the following sleeping options are located in El Chaltén.

BUDGET
Camping
Free backcountry campgrounds are very basic, with one pit toilet. Bury human waste as far from water sources as possible. Some sites have dead wood with which to create windbreaks. Fires are prohibited. Water is pure as glacial melt; make sure all cleaning is done

downstream from the campground and pack out all trash.

Campamento Confluencia (sites free) A zero-amenity campground across from the park ranger office and visitor center.

Campamento Madsen (sites free) Near the start of the Fitz Roy hike, at the north end of Av San Martín, this windy and exposed campground sits on the banks of Río de las Vueltas. There are a few trees and plenty of spots to access water. Showers (AR$4) and laundry service (AR$20) are available for all campers at Rancho Grande Hostel (below) between 8am and 4pm.

Camping El Refugio (☎ 493221; Av San Martín s/n; sites per person AR$15, dm AR$35) This private campground is attached to a basic hostel – hot showers for campers are included in the fee. Sites are exposed and there is some sparse firewood (fires are OK). It's across from Rancho Grande Hostel.

Albergue del Lago (☎ 493245; Lago del Desierto 135; sites per person AR$15, dm AR$35) Partying seems to be the priority of campers outside this hostel, which offers a shared kitchen and funky showers.

El Relincho (☎ 493007; Av San Martín 505; sites per person AR$16) Another private campground, similarly wind-whipped.

Hostels

Dorm beds fill up fast in summer. Unless otherwise noted, thin walls, cramped dorms and insufficient shared facilities are the norm.

Albergue Patagonia (☎ 493019; patagoniahostel@ yahoo.com.ar; Av San Martín 493; dm AR$35, d with/without bathroom AR$180/100; ⏳ Sep-May; ✖) This welcoming wooden farmhouse has a dormitory building with spacious, modern dorms and common areas. Services are good and the atmosphere is humming. The doubles with bathroom are worth coveting. Credit cards and traveler's checks are accepted. HI members get a slightly better rate.

Rancho Grande Hostel (☎ 493092; www.hostelspata gonia.com; Av San Martín 724; dm/d/tr/q AR$35/180/195/230; ✖ 🖥) Serving as Chaltén's Grand Central Station (Chaltén Travel buses stop here), this bustling backpacker factory has a little something for everyone, from bus reservations to internet (AR$12 per hour) and café service. Clean four-bed rooms are stacked with blankets and bathrooms sport rows of shower stalls. The shared kitchen is tiny, and the common dining area bright, but both

are often crowded with nonguests. The café (meals AR$13 to AR$30), offering *milanesas*, mains and desserts, is a sure bet for grub in the off-hours. HI members get a discount.

Condor de Los Andes (☎ 493101; www.condordelosandes .com; cnr Río de las Vueltas & Halvor Halvorsen; dm/d AR$40/180; ⏳ Oct-Apr) This homey hostel has the feel of a ski lodge, with worn bunks, warm rooms and a roaring fire. Service is good, the guest kitchen is immaculate and there are comfortable lounge spaces. Extras include breakfast (AR$7), lunch boxes (AR$22) and laundry (AR$15).

MIDRANGE

Mi Rincón (☎ 493099; Cabo 1ero García 115; s/d/tr without bathroom AR$70/100/120) This adorable lodging has only a few rooms in the annex of a family home, but they are cozy and share an ample bathroom between them.

Hospedaje La Base (☎ 493031; labase@elchaltenpata gonia.com.ar; cnr Lago del Desierto & Hensen; d AR$150) These spacious, good-value rooms all face outside and have kitchen access. Large groups should book rooms 5 and 6, which share an inside kitchen with dining area. The reception area has a popular video loft with a multilingual collection.

Hostería Los Ñires (☎ 493009; www.losnireschalten.com .ar in Spanish; cnr Lago del Desierto near Hensen; d/tr AR$165/220; ⏳ mid-Oct–mid-Apr; 🖥) El Chaltén's first hotel has remodeled. Its 33 spotless rooms are ample and plain, with some showers oddly cramped. Hosts Tomas and Shirley are hospitable and can tell you about El Chaltén way back when.

Posada Poincenot (☎ 493022; www.chaltentravel .com; Av San Martín 615; s/d/tr/q AR$150/180/195/230) Adjacent to Rancho Grande Hostel, Poincenot is a small, serene inn with conscientious owners. The larger rooms are ideal for families; all have private bathrooms.

OUR PICK Nothofagus B&B (☎ 493087; www.elchalten .com/nothofagus; cnr Hensen & Riquelme; s/d/tr AR$170/180/220; ⏳ Sep-Apr; ✖) Attentive and adorable, this chalet-style inn offers a great green retreat. It is one of few Patagonian lodgings to separate organic waste and replaces towels only when asked. Wooden-beam rooms have carpet and some views, but most have bathrooms shared with one other room. Owners Eva and Gerardo, former guides, offer top service.

TOP END

Kalenshen (☎ 493108; www.kalenshen.com.ar in Spanish; Lionel Terray 50; s/d AR$270/300; 🖥) Bring your swim cap, because steep rates at Kalenshen are probably due to this average hotel boasting the town's only heated indoor swimming pool. Decent tiled rooms come with log beds and a breakfast buffet.

Cumbres Nevadas (☎ 493160; Cerro Solo 95; 4–5–person cabins AR$320) This midtown compound of yellow *cabañas* is ideal for groups: each has a kitchen, bathroom and TV. Low-season rates are AR$50 less, but cabins may be occupied by seasonal workers.

Posada Lunajuim (☎ 493047; www.elchalten.com /lunajuim; Trevisan s/n; s/d/tr AR$325/386/463) Combining modern comfort with a touch of the off-beat, this artist-owned inn gets good reviews from guests. The halls are lined with the owner's monochrome sculptures and textured paintings, and a stone fireplace and library provide a rainy-day escape. Check out the rooms in the new wing.

Hostería El Puma (☎ 493095; www.hosteriaelpuma .com.ar; Lionel Terray 212; s/d/tr AR$330/420/460) This luxury lodge with 12 comfortable rooms offers intimacy without pretension. The rock-climbing and summit photographs and maps lining the hall may inspire your next expedition, but lounging by the fireplace is the most savory way to end the day. There's attentive service, a good breakfast and the gourmet restaurant Terray (right) on site.

Los Cerros (☎ 493182; www.loscerrosdelchalten.com; Av San Martín s/n; r per person AR$550; ☯ Oct-Apr; 🖳) New and chic, this top-end *hostería* perched on a hill has sweeping views of the valley that holds El Chaltén. Think tribal-modern: the thick woven wall-hangings and natural fibers show an eye for style. The absence of TVs and phones in rooms is meant to bring you back to nature (but the gourmet meals, wine selections and wi-fi will surely zip you right back to civilization). Package rates are available.

Eating & Drinking

Groceries, especially produce, are limited and expensive. Bring what you can from El Calafate.

Domo Blanco (☎ 493036; Av MM De Güemes s/n; scoops AR$6) Homemade ice cream made with fruit harvested from a local *estancia* and calafate bushes in town.

La Chocolatería (☎ 493008; Lago del Desierto 104; snacks AR$6-15) This irresistible chocolate factory tells the story of local climbing legends on the walls. It makes for an intimate evening out, with options ranging from spirit-spiked hot cocoa to wine and fondue.

El Bodegón Cervecería (☎ 493109; Av San Martín s/n; snacks AR$12) That aprés-hike pint usually evolves into a night out in this humming pub with *simpatico* staff and a feisty female beer-master. Savor a stein of unfiltered blond pilsner or turbid bock with a bowl of popcorn. Pizza, pastas and *locro* (a spicy stew of maize, beans, beef, pork and sausage) are available.

Fuegia Bistro (☎ 493019; Av San Martín 493; mains AR$18-34; ✗) Favored for its warm ambience and savory mains, this upscale eatery boasts good veggie options and a reasonable wine list. Try the lamb in ginger sauce or trout with sage butter. It's also open for breakfast.

Patagonicus (☎ 493025; cnr Av MM De Güemes & Andreas Madsen; pizzas AR$21) The best pizza in town, with 20 kinds of pie, salads and wine served at sturdy wood tables. Cakes and coffee are also worth trying.

Estepa (☎ 493069; cnr Cerro Solo & Av Antonio Rojo; mains AR$22-35) Local favorite Estepa cooks up consistent, flavorful dishes like lamb with calafate sauce, trout ravioli or spinach crepes. Pizza is popular, and hikers can order lunch boxes.

Terray (☎ 493095; Lionel Terray 212; mains AR$28-38; ☯ 7:30-10:30pm Oct-May) Named in tribute to the Chamonix guide who first climbed Fitz Roy, this high-end kitchen at Hostería El Puma cooks up hearty and original homemade meals like lima-bean risotto, chicken and grilled-fig salad, and lamb osso buco. Reserve ahead.

Ruca Mahuida (☎ 493018; Lionel Terray 104; mains AR$36-57; ☯ 7-11pm) Some worry that this stone house with gourmet fare has lost its touch, but dishes like squash soufflé and salmon ravioli are a welcome departure from typical fare. The sheepskin benches, though, are pure Patagonia.

Entertainment

Zafarrancho, behind Rancho Grande Hostel (opposite), is a bar-café that has internet and screens movies.

Getting There & Away

El Chaltén is located 220km from El Calafate via newly paved roads.

For El Calafate (AR$60, 3½ hours), Chaltén Travel (☎ 493005/92; cnr San Martín 724) has daily departures in summer at 6:30am, 7am, 1pm and 6pm from Rancho Grande Hostel. **Cal-tur** (☎ 493079; San Martín 520) and **Taqsa** (☎ 493068; Av Antonio Rojo 88) also make the trip, but none of these companies will take advance reservations. Service is less frequent off-season.

Las Lengas (☎ 493023/227; Antonio de Viedma 95) runs minivans at 5:30am to coastal destinations on RN 3, including Piedrabuena (AR$95, six hours), from where travelers can take transportation to Parque Nacional Monte León.

Chaltén Travel heads north via RN 40 to Perito Moreno, Los Antiguos (up to 15 hours, both AR$160) and Bariloche (AR$360, two days) on even-numbered days at 8am.

EL CALAFATE
☎ 02902 / pop 15,000

Named for the berry that, once eaten, guarantees your return to Patagonia, El Calafate hooks you with another irresistible attraction: Glaciar Perito Moreno, 80km away in Parque Nacional Los Glaciares. The glacier is a magnificent must-see, but its massive popularity has encouraged tumorous growth and rapid upscaling in the once-quaint El Calafate. At the same time, it's a fun place to be with a range of traveler services. The town's strategic location between El Chaltén and Torres del Paine (Chile) makes it an inevitable stop for those in transit.

Located 320km northwest of Río Gallegos, and 32km west of RP 11's junction with northbound RN 40, El Calafate flanks the southern shore of Lago Argentino. The main strip, Av del Libertador General San Martín (typically abbreviated to Av Libertador), is dotted with cutesy knotted-pine souvenir shops, chocolate shops, restaurants and tour offices. Beyond the main street, pretensions melt away quickly: muddy roads lead to ad-hoc developments and open pastures.

January and February are the most popular (and costly) months to visit, but as shoulder-season visits grow steadily, both availability and prices stay a challenge.

Information
LAUNDRY
El Lavadero (☎ 492182; 25 de Mayo 43; per load AR$15)

MEDICAL SERVICES
Hospital Municipal Dr José Formenti (☎ 491001; Av Roca 1487)

MONEY
Withdraw your cash before the weekend rush – it isn't uncommon for ATMs to run out on Sundays.

Banco Santa Cruz (Av Libertador 1285) Changes traveler's checks and has ATM.

Thaler Cambio (9 de Julio s/n; ☯ 10am-1pm Mon-Fri, 5:30-7:30pm Sat & Sun) Usurious rates for traveler's checks, but open weekends.

POST
Post office (Av Libertador 1133)

INTERNET ACCESS
Cyberpoint (Av Libertador 1070; ☯ 24hr)

TELEPHONE
Cooperativa Telefónica (CTC; cnr Espora & Moyano) There's another branch on Av Libertador, near Perito Moreno.

TOURIST INFORMATION
ACA (Automóvil Club Argentino; ☎ 491-004; cnr 1 de Mayo & Av Roca) Argentina's auto club; good source for provincial road maps.

Municipal tourist office (☎ 491090/466; www .elcalafate.gov.ar in Spanish; ☯ 8am-10pm) At the bus terminal; has some English-speaking staff.

Parque Nacional Los Glaciares office (☎ 491005/755; Av Libertador 1302; ☯ 8am-7pm Mon-Fri, 10am-8pm Sat & Sun) Offers brochures and a decent map of Parque Nacional Los Glaciares. It's better to get info here than at the park.

TRAVEL AGENCIES
Most agents deal exclusively with nearby excursions and are unhelpful for other areas.

Tiempo Libre (☎ 491207; tiempolibre@cotecal.com.ar; 25 de Mayo 43) Books flights.

Sights & Activities
In shuffled disrepair, **Museo de El Calafate** (Av Libertador 575; admission free; ☯ 8am-7pm Mon-Fri, 10am-4pm Sat & Sun) displays arrowheads, stuffed birds and early photographs. Alongside the lakeshore, north of town, **Laguna Nimez** (admission AR$3; ☯ 9am-9pm) is prime avian habitat, but watching birds from El Calafate's shoreline on Lago Argentino can be just as good. Hiking up **Cerro Calafate** (850m) is possible, but the route behind Hostel del Glaciar Pioneros passes through marginal neighborhoods. While they are not considered dangerous, it is not exactly the ideal setting for hiking. To avoid them, ask a taxi to take you part way.

Anglers can take to the lakes with **Calafate Fishing** (☎ 493311; Av Libertador 1826; ☯ 10am-7pm Mon-Sat), offering fun fly-fishing trips to Lago Roca (full day AR$450) and Lago Strobbel, where you can test rumors that the biggest rainbow trout in the world lives here.

PATAGONIA

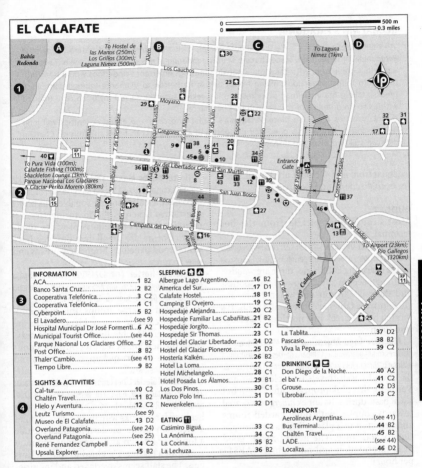

EL CALAFATE

Renting a **bike** (see Albergue Lago Argentino, p492) is an excellent way to get a feel for the area and cruise the dirt roads by the lake. Tour outfitters offer **4WD trips** to fossil beds as well as stays at regional **estancias**, where you can hike, ride horses or relax.

Tours

Some 40 travel agencies arrange excursions to the glacier and other local attractions. Tour prices for Glaciar Perito Moreno (around AR$90 per person) don't include the park entrance fee. Ask agents and other travelers about added benefits, like extra stops, boat trips, binoculars or multilingual guides. For other boat and tour operators based in El Calafate, see p495.

Cal-tur (☎ 491368; Av Libertador 1080) Specializes in El Chaltén tours and lodging packages.

Chaltén Travel (☎ 492212/480; www.chaltentravel.com; Av Libertador 1174) Recommended tours to the glacier, stopping for wildlife viewing (binoculars provided); also specializes in RN 40 trips.

Overland Patagonia (☎ 491243, 492243; www.glaciar.com) Operates out of both branches of Hostel del Glaciar Libertador (p492); organizes recommended 'alternative' and full-moon trips to the glacier, plus guided trekking, camping and ice-hiking combos in El Chaltén.

Sleeping

In spite of abundant lodgings, there are always shortages here. Book ahead, even outside of peak season. The core high season is January–February, although some places

IN CHATWIN'S PATAGONIA

'It's their Bible,' whispers a Welsh teahouse owner, spying a tourist-gripped tattered copy of *In Patagonia*. Thirty years on, Bruce Chatwin's cubist rendering of this southern extreme has become a pilgrim's guide to it. Who knew that Chatwin's musings on errant wanderings would transform them into tourist attractions: hiking from Estancia Harberton to Viamonte (guided with snack breaks); taking tea in Gaiman (hundreds do it weekly); even the sacred mylodon cave (marred with a life-sized replica of this prehistoric Chewbacca).

Not to worry. It's a big place. Patagonia's willful landscape and exiled eccentrics will long remain, and anyone with a good pair of boots and a willingness to break them in (as Chatwin did) can still find plenty to discover.

extend it from mid-October until April. Look for deep discounts in low season.

BUDGET

Most hostels offer pickup from the bus terminal.

Camping El Ovejero (☎ 493422; campinglovejero@ hotmail.com; José Pantín; sites per person AR$10-15) Hosted by the charming Humberto, these are woodsy, well-kept, secure sites. Showers are spotless and there is 24-hour hot water. Extras include private tables, electricity and grills. It's located by the creek just north of the bridge into town.

Albergue Lago Argentino (☎ 491423; www.los glaciares.com/lagoargentino; Campaña del Desierto 1050; dm/d without bathroom AR$30/80, s/d with bathroom AR$110/160; 🖳) Run by well-traveled couple Javier and Veronica, this pink property offers clean but squat basic dorms. Its annex *albergue* is geared towards couples, with quiet garden rooms and breakfast in a plant-filled nook with antique wood stove. The hosts provide good local information and bike rentals (AR$13 per hour).

Hospedaje Jorgito (☎ 491323; Moyano 943; dm/d/tr without bathroom AR$30/80/90) This mango home feels family-oriented in a way best described by the vintage Barbies, doilies and synthetic flowers providing animated decoration. Rooms vary in size but are bright and well kept. Guests can use the large kitchen.

Los Dos Pinos (☎ 491271/632; www.calafate.com /losdospinos; 9 de Julio 358; camping per person AR$12, dm/ d/tr without bathroom AR$30/80/120, d/tr with bathroom AR$150/180) With bargain doubles, this labyrinthine lodging has a supermarket selection of rooms, all adequate if not charming. Dorms lack insulation but have clean bathrooms and kitchen facilities. The full-service campground is sheltered but can get crowded.

Hostel de las Manos (☎ 492996; www.hostelde lasmanos.com.ar; Feruglio 59; dm AR$30, d with bathroom AR$150) Immaculate and personable, this hostel alternative is across the footbridge from 9 de Julio. A wall of windows provides ample light. Dorms are small but doubles have white wood paneling, bright bedspreads and new fixtures.

Calafate Hostel (☎ 492450/2; www.hostelspata gonia.com; Moyano 1226; dm AR$30-34, s/d/tr/q standard AR$100/140/160/180, superior AR$120/150/200/240; 🖳) Best suited to large groups, this mammoth log cabin ends up feeling blander than the competition. Double-bunk dorms are cozy, while the new annex features tidy brick doubles. It has airport pickup, café service and bilingual desk staff.

Hostel del Glaciar Libertador (☎ 491792; www.glaciar .com; Av Libertador 587; dm/s/d HI member AR$31/183/200, nonmember AR$37/220/241; ✗ 🖳) The best deals here are dorm bunks with thick covers. Behind a Victorian facade, modern facilities include a top-floor kitchen and a spacious common area with a plasma TV glued to sports channels. The staff seems overtaxed and inquiries take patience.

Hostel del Glaciar Pioneros (☎ 491243; www.glaciar .com; Los Pioneros 251; dm/d AR$34/193; 🖳) A 15-minute walk from town, this sociable hostel offers comfortable common areas and small dorms. In low season it closes, funneling backpackers to its sister hostel, Hostel del Glaciar Libertador.

Marco Polo Inn (☎ 493899; www.marcopoloinncala fate.com; Calle 405, No 82; dm/d/tr HI member AR$38/200/250, nonmember AR$40/220/270; 🖳) A new addition with attentive service and spacious dorms featuring quilted bedspreads and wood-finished bunks. Doubles have bathrooms and extra amenities like hair dryers and TVs. A pool table and telescope provide extra diversion.

OURPICK **America del Sur** (☎ 493525; www.america
hostel.com.ar; Puerto Deseado 151; dm/d AR$40/140; 🖳)
This backpacker favorite boasts top-tier service and a stylish lodge setting with views. One
thing you won't find here is solitude – it's
bustling at every hour. All-you-can-eat barbecues are put on nightly (AR$35), to the rave
reviews of guests. Reserve ahead.

Hospedaje Alejandra (☎ 491328; Espora 60; d/tr
without bathroom AR$50/75, 5-person cabin AR$280) A
charming family lodging smack in the center,
Alejandra offers small, dark doubles with im-
peccable housekeeping and a delightful knick-
knack collection that includes Hello Kitty and
plastic fruit.

MIDRANGE

The tourist office has a complete list of
cabañas and apartment hotels, which are the
best deals for groups and families.

Los Grillos (☎ 491160, Los Condores 1215; d with/with-
out bathroom AR$140/110, 4-person cabin AR$180) A quiet
B&B with fresh rooms, soft beds and attentive
service. Guests can serve themselves coffee,
tea and spring water in the dining nook. The
backyard cabin offers shaggy bedspreads and
all-new fixtures and appliances. A *quincho*
(thatched-roof building) under construction will give guests an ample cooking and
recreation space.

Hospedaje Sir Thomas (☎ 492220; www.cotecal
.com.ar/hospedajesirthomas in Spanish; Espora 257; d AR$135)
Quiet and central, this friendly picket-fence
B&B offers 10 tidy rooms with thin carpet,
tiled bathrooms and beds clad in plaid blankets. It lacks a common space; a cramped
breakfast area serves packaged muffins with
tea or coffee.

Hospedaje Familiar Las Cabañitas (☎ 491118;
lascabanitas@cotecal.com.ar; Valentín Feilberg 218; d/tr/q
AR$160/210/240) Run by the endearing Giordano
family, these storybook A-frames are somewhat dated but snug, with spiral staircases
leading to loft beds. Sweet touches include
English lavender and a sheltered dining patio
brimming with plants. There's hot-beverage
service, kitchen use and meals upon request.

Hotel La Loma (☎ 491016; www.lalomahotel.com;
Av Roca 849; s/d standard AR$140/170, superior AR$175/265;
🐾) Colonial furnishings and a lovely rock
garden enhance this rambling ranch-style
retreat. While its exterior is nondescript,
superior rooms are spacious and bright.
Antiques fill the creaky hallways and the re-

ception area boasts an open fire and plenty of
books. Breakfast includes homemade bread,
and guests can take dips in the only indoor
pool in town.

Newenkelen (☎ 493943; www.newenkelen.com.ar;
Puerto Deseado 223; d AR$180) Perched on a hill above
town, this intimate option features a handful of immaculate brick rooms with tasteful
bedding and mountain views. The *porteña*
owner can be convinced to give tango lessons
in low season.

TOP END

Luxury hotels are being added at a quick clip,
though not all offer the same standard.

Hotel Michelangelo (☎ 491045; www.michaelangelo
hotel.com.ar in Spanish; Moyano 1020; s/d AR$210/272; 🖳)
Tour groups favor this Swiss-chalet-style
lodging in the center of town. Dimly lit and
somewhat dated, its identical rooms have
heavy drapes, high ceilings and full amenities. The hallways smell of cigarette smoke but
there's a good restaurant, buffet breakfast and
multilingual service.

Hostería Kalkén (☎ 491073/687; www.losglaciares
.com/kalken; Valentín Feilberg 119; s/d AR$264/291; 🖳)
This hush Spanish-style hotel is understated
and elegant, with a full bar and fireplace to
greet tired travelers. Staff are well disposed
and prim doubles keep the rays out with thick
curtains. The continental breakfast is abundant and good.

Hotel Posada Los Álamos (☎ 491144; www.posada
losalamos.com; Moyano 1355; s/d/ste AR$604/658/967; 🖳)
Calafate's original resort swims in luxury:
plush rooms, overstuffed sofas, spectacular
gardens, tennis courts, putting greens and
a spa. It's enough to make you almost forget about seeing that glacier. Some find the
walls a bit thin for a four-star getaway. It features rooms accessible for disabled travelers
as well.

Eating

For a quick bite, try the ice-cream parlors and
chocolate shops along Av Libertador.

La Anónima (cnr Av Libertador & Perito Moreno) Cheap
take-out and groceries.

La Lechuza (☎ 491610; Av Libertador 1301; pizzas
AR$18) A classic selection of empanadas, sal-
ads and pizzas is served on round wooden
plates – try the sheep cheese and olive pizza.
Microbrew beers and a warm brick ambience
cement its favor with the public.

La Cocina (☎ 491758; Av Libertador 1245; mains AR$20-30) This classic pasta factory makes satisfying noodles with savory sauces and serves up a whopping *lomo a la pobre* (steak and eggs) for the carb-adverse.

Viva la Pepa (☎ 491880; Amado 833; mains AR$21-40; ☯ 10am-midnight, closed Wed) Decked out in children's drawings, this cheerful café specializes in crepes but also offers great sandwiches with homemade bread (try the chicken with apple and blue cheese), fresh juice and gourds of *mate*.

La Tablita (☎ 491065; Coronel Rosales 24; mains AR$30-50) Steak and spit-roasted lamb are the stars at this satisfying *parrilla*, popular beyond measure. For average appetites a half-steak will do, rounded out with a good malbec, fresh salad or garlic fries. Reserve ahead.

Pura Vida (☎ 493356; Av Libertador 1876; mains AR$32-49; ☯ dinner Thu-Tue) Whole grains and abundant vegetarian dishes make this ambient eatery a traveler's treat. Tables are candlelit and the kitchen serves healthy food in huge portions. Try the gnocchi with saffron, rabbit with cream or pumpkin stew served in an enormous gourd. It's a ten-minute walk west of the center.

Casimiro Biguá (☎ 492590; Av Libertador 963; mains AR$35) With warm copper accents and a hustling staff, this chic eatery and *vinoteca* (wine bar) offers an impressive list of 180 Argentine wines. The chef creates wonderful homemade pastas, risotto, lamb stew and grilled trout, but the star feature is the grill. It's no wonder the Kirchners often drop by; their weekend house is nearby.

Pascasio (☎ 492055; 25 de Mayo 52; mains AR$48) In an elegant, pared-down setting, this local star offers tasty innovations like wok seafood and ginger noodles, as well as exotic dishes like ñandú, wild boar and hare. Save room for decadent desserts, such as the serious 'study in chocolate.'

Drinking

el ba'r (9 de Julio s/n; snacks AR$8-17) This trendy patio café is the hotspot for you and your sweater-clad puppy to order espresso, *submarinos* (hot milk with melted chocolate bar), green tea or sandwiches.

Grouse (☎ 491281; Av Libertador 351; drinks AR$4-12) This Celtic pub/karaoke hub aims to appeal to all whims. Look for live acts in summer, generous mixed drinks and cans of Guinness.

Librobar (☎ 491464; Av Libertador 1015) Upstairs in the gnome village, this hip book-bar serves coffee and bottled beers alongside a stack of quality reads in English and Spanish.

Shackleton Lounge (☎ 493516; Av Libertador 3287) This laid-back lounge, 3km from the center, pleases crowds with good music and strong daiquiris.

Don Diego de la Noche (Av Libertador 1603; ☯ until 5am) This perennial favorite serves dinner and features live music like tango, guitar and *folklore* (Argentine folk music).

Getting There & Away
AIR

The modern **Aeropuerto El Calafate** (ECA; ☎ 491220/30) is 23km east of town off RP 11; the departure tax is US$18.

Aerolíneas Argentinas (☎ 492814/16; 9 de Julio 57) flies every day to Bariloche (AR$879), Ushuaia (AR$350), Trelew (AR$820) and both Aeroparque and Ezeiza in Buenos Aires (AR$380 to AR$675).

LADE (☎ 491262; at bus terminal) flies a few times a week to Río Gallegos (AR$118), Comodoro Rivadavia (AR$203), Ushuaia (AR$280), Esquel (AR$412), Puerto Madryn (AR$335), Buenos Aires (AR$336) and other smaller regional airports.

BUS

El Calafate's hilltop **bus terminal** (Av Roca s/n) is easily reached by a pedestrian staircase from the corner of Av Libertador and 9 de Julio. Book ahead in high season, as outbound seats can be in short supply.

For El Chaltén (AR$55, 3½ hours), several companies share passengers and leave daily at 7:30am, 8am and 6:30pm, stopping midway at Estancia La Leona for coffee and tasty pies.

For Puerto Natales (AR$50, five hours), **Cootra** (☎ 491444) departs daily at 8:30am, crossing the border at Cerro Castillo, where it may be possible to connect to Torres del Paine.

For Río Gallegos (AR$20 to $40, four hours), buses go daily at 3am, 4am, noon, 12:30pm and 2:30pm. **Freddy** (☎ 452671) and Interlagos offer connections to Bariloche and Ushuaia that require leaving in the middle of the night and a change of buses in Río Gallegos.

From mid-October to April, **Chaltén Travel** (☎ 492212/480; www.chaltentravel.com; Av Libertador 1174) goes to El Chaltén (AR$100 roundtrip, three hours) daily at 8am and 6:30pm. It also runs shuttles north along RN 40 to Perito Moreno and Los Antiguos (AR$215, 12 hours), departing on even-numbered days at 8am, to connect with onward service to Bariloche (AR$395, two days from El Calafate) the next morning. The same service also leaves from El Chaltén.

Getting Around

Airport shuttle **Ves Patagonia** (☎ 494355) has no office; call for door-to-door service (one way/roundtrip AR$15/25). There are several car-rental agencies at the airport. **Localiza** (☎ 491398, 02902-15-622565; www.localiza.com.ar; Av Libertador 687) offers car rentals for AR$186 daily with 200km.

AROUND EL CALAFATE

From El Calafate, paved RN 40 cuts southeast across vast steppe for 95km, then jogs south at **El Cerrito** and turns to gravel. Staying on paved RP 5 means a slow-going, five-hour, 224km bore of a trip southeast to **Río Gallegos**. Halfway along RP 5, at Km 146, is the utilitarian **Hotel La Esperanza** (☎ 02902-499200; per person AR$60; ⊙ year-round), a gas-station diner (daily special AR$25) with quick, friendly service. If you plan to stay, ask for a room in the newer cabin. From here, paved RP 7 connects back to RN 40 for the Chilean border crossing at Cerro Castillo–Cancha Carrera, Parque Nacional Torres del Paine and Puerto Natales.

PARQUE NACIONAL LOS GLACIARES (SOUTH)

Among the Earth's most dynamic and accessible ice fields, **Glaciar Perito Moreno** is the stunning centerpiece of the southern sector of **Parque Nacional Los Glaciares** (admission AR$30). Locally referred to as Glaciar Moreno, it measures 30km long, 5km wide and 60m high, but what makes it exceptional in the world of ice is its constant advance – up to 2m per day, causing building-sized icebergs to calve from its face. In some ways, watching the glacier is a very sedentary park experience, but it manages to nonetheless be thrilling.

The glacier formed as a low gap in the Andes allowed moisture-laden Pacific storms to drop their loads east of the divide, where they accumulate as snow. Over millennia, under tremendous weight, this snow has recrystallized into ice and flowed slowly eastward. The 1600-sq-km trough of **Lago Argentino**, the country's largest single body of

water, is unmistakable evidence that glaciers were once far more extensive than today.

While most of the world's glaciers are receding, Glaciar Moreno is considered 'stable.' Regardless, 17 times between 1917 and 2006, as the glacier has advanced, it has dammed the Brazo Rico (Rico Arm) of Lago Argentino, causing the water to rise. Several times, the melting ice below has been unable to support the weight of the water behind it and the dam has collapsed in an explosion of water and ice. To be present when this spectacular cataclysm occurs is unforgettable.

Visiting Glaciar Moreno is no less an auditory than a visual experience, as huge icebergs on the glacier's face calve and collapse into the **Canal de los Témpanos** (Iceberg Channel). This natural-born tourist attraction is ideally located at Península de Magallanes – close enough to guarantee great views, but far enough away to be safe. A series of recently improved catwalks and vantage points allow visitors to see, hear and photograph the glacier. Sun hits its face in the morning and the glacier's appearance changes as the day progresses and shadows shift.

A massive makeover is in the works at Glaciar Moreno. At the time of writing, a hotel was being built near the glacier lookout; look for a new *confitería* and parking as well. Since trash is difficult and costly to remove from the area, please pack yours out.

The main gateway town to the park's southern sector, El Calafate (p490), is 80km east of the glacier by road.

Activities

GLACIAR PERITO MORENO

Boat trips allow you to sense the magnitude of Glaciar Moreno, even though the boats keep a distance. **Hielo y Aventura** (☎ 02902-492094/205; www.hieloyaventura.com; Av Libertador 935, El Calafate) runs Safari Nautico (AR$35), a one-hour tour of Brazo Rico, Lago Argentino and the south side of Canal de los Témpanos. Catamarans crammed with up to 130 passengers leave hourly between 11:30am and 3:30pm from Puerto Bajo de las Sombras.

Hielo y Aventura also offers **minitrekking** (AR$275) on the glacier, a five-hour trek for groups of up to 20, involving a quick boat ride from Puerto Bajo de las Sombras, a walk through lenga forests, a quick chat on glaciology and then a 1½-hour ice walk using crampons. The more extensive **big ice**

PATAGONIA

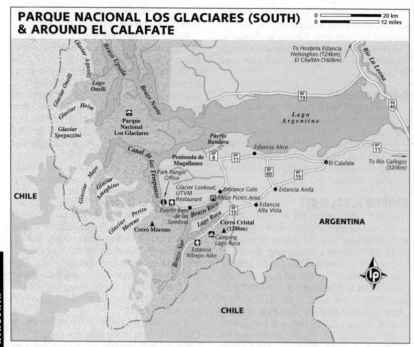

PARQUE NACIONAL LOS GLACIARES (SOUTH) & AROUND EL CALAFATE

(AR$375) offers a worthwhile four-hour ice trek. Children under eight are not allowed; reserve ahead and bring your own food.

To see the glacier's main north face, **René Fernandez Campbell** (☎ 02902-492340; www.fernandez campbell.com; Av Libertador 867, El Calafate) operates 320-passenger boats (AR$38) from below the UTVM restaurant near the main lookout, hourly between 10:30am and 2:30pm.

Beyond a short walk that parallels the shoreline at the boat dock and climbs to the lookout area, there are no trails in this sector of the park accessible without boat transportation.

GLACIAR UPSALA & LAGO ONELLI

Glaciar Upsala – 595-sq-km huge, 60km long and some 4km wide in parts – can be admired for its monumental dimensions alongside the strange and graceful forms of the nearby icebergs. The downside is that it can only be enjoyed from the crowded deck of a massive catamaran: just you and nature and 300 of your closest friends. On an extension of the Brazo Norte (North Arm) of Lago Argentino, it's accessible by launch from Puerto Bandera, 45km west of Calafate by RP 11 and RP 8.

Upsala Explorer (☎ 02902-491034; 9 de Julio 69, El Calafate) runs boat tours (AR$377) to Upsala that end with a visit to the isolated Estancia Cristina. Prices do not include transfer (AR$38) and park entry fee.

For the grand tour, **René Fernandez Campbell** (☎ 02902-492340; www.fernandezcampbell.com; Av Libertador 867, El Calafate) does an all-glacier tour (AR$240) from Punta Bandera, visiting Glaciar Upsala, Bahía Onelli and Glaciar Spegazzini. If icebergs are cooperating, boats may allow passengers to disembark at Bahía Onelli to walk 500m to iceberg-choked **Lago Onelli**, where the Onelli and Agassiz glaciers merge. Meals are expensive, but you can bring your own picnic.

LAGO ROCA

The serene south arm of Lago Argentino offers a great escape into lakeshore forests and mountains. Good hikes, pleasant camping and *estancia* accommodations occupy this most southerly section of the park, where most visitors rarely travel. No entrance fee is charged to access this section. Hikers can climb **Cerro Cristal**, a rugged but rewarding 3½-hour hike. It begins at the education camp at La Jerónima, just before the Camping Lago Roca entrance, 55km southwest of El Calafate along RP 15. On a clear day, you can see Glaciar Moreno and the Torres del Paine.

Horseback-riding trips with **Cabalgatas del Glaciar** (☎ 495447; www.cabalgatasdelglaciar.com) offer glacier panoramas; they can also be booked through **Cal-tur** (☎ 02902-491368; Av Libertador 1080, El Calafate). **Leutz Turismo** (☎ 02902-492316; leutzturismo@cotecal.com.ar; 25 de Mayo 43, El Calafate) takes visitors on day trips to Estancia Nibepo Aike (AR$155) from El Calafate. The morning or afternoon visits include tea, *mate* and fresh pastries, a sheepshearing demonstration and an hour of horseback riding.

Sleeping & Eating

Unfortunately, the campground at Bahía Escondida has been closed for recovery, since unattended campfires were threatening the area. Inquire about changes at the park.

Camping Lago Roca (☎ 02902-499500; www.losglaciares.com/campinglagoroca; per person AR$16, cabin dm for 2/4 AR$80/140) An excellent option for independent travelers, this full-service campground with restaurant-bar, located a few kilometers past the education camp, makes a good base to explore the area. The clean cement-walled dorms provide a snug alternative to camping. In summer singles pay the double rate in dorms. Hiking trails abound, and the center rents fishing equipment and bikes and coordinates horseback riding at the nearby *estancia*.

Estancia Nibepo Aike (☎ 02966-492858/9; www.nibepoaike.com.ar; RP 15, Km 60; half-pension 2 nights s/d AR$905/1187; ☒ Oct-Apr) This working sheep and cattle ranch offers the usual assortment of *estancia* highlights. In addition to horseback riding, guests have the option to explore the surroundings on two wheels from the bicycle stash. The original *casco* of this Croatian ranch offers modern comforts: elegant rooms have private bathrooms and beds draped in woven blankets. Homemade bread, scones and jam brighten the breakfast table. Nibepo Aike overlooks the southern arm of Lago Argentino, 5km past the campground on RP 15.

Hostería Estancia Helsingfors (☎ in Buenos Aires 011-4315-1222; www.helsingfors.com.ar; s/d AR$1068/1727; ☒ Oct-Apr) The simply stunning location ogling Cerro Fitz Roy from Lago Viedma makes for lots of love-at-first-sight impressions. Intimate and welcoming, this former Finnish pioneer ranch is a highly regarded luxury destination, though it cultivates a relaxed, unpretentious ambience. Guests pass the time on scenic but demanding mountain treks, rides and visits to Glaciar Viedma. Vintage wines accompany gourmet meals made with fresh garden produce. Rates represent a two-day, one-night stay, with transfers, an excursion and meals. It's on Lago Viedma's southern shore, 170km from El Chaltén and 180km from El Calafate.

UTVM Restaurant (☎ 02902-499400; snacks AR$9-16, mains AR$20; ☒ 10am-6pm) At the glacier lookout, this year-round restaurant offers sandwiches,

PATAGONIA

GLACIOLOGY 101

Ribbons of ice, stretched flat in sheets or sculpted by weather and fissured by pressure, glaciers have a raw magnificence that is boggling to behold.

As snow falls on the accumulation area, it compacts to ice. The river of ice is slugged forward by gravity, which deforms its layers as it moves. When the glacier surges downhill, melted ice mixes with rock and soil on the bottom, grinding it into a lubricant that keeps pushing the glacier along. At the same time, debris from the crushed rock is forced to the sides of the glacier, creating features called moraines. Movement also causes cracks and deformities called crevasses.

The ablation area is where the glacier melts. When accumulation outpaces melting at the ablation area, the glacier advances; when there's more melting or evaporation, the glacier recedes. Since 1980, global warming has contributed greatly to widespread glacial retreat.

Another marvel of glaciers is their hue. What makes some blue? Wavelengths and air bubbles. The more compact the ice, the longer the path that light has to travel and the bluer the ice appears. Air bubbles in uncompacted areas absorb long wavelengths of white light so we see white. Where glacier melt calves into lakes, it dumps a 'glacial flour' comprised of ground-up rock that gives the water a milky, grayish color. This same sediment remains unsettled in some lakes and diffracts the sun's light, creating a stunning palette of turquoise, pale mint and azure.

coffee and desserts, and a set lunch for which reservations are advised.

Getting There & Away

Glaciar Moreno is 80km west of El Calafate via paved RP 11, passing through the breathtaking scenery around Lago Argentino. Bus tours (AR$90 roundtrip) are frequent in summer; see p491, or simply stroll down El Calafate's Av Libertador. Buses leave El Calafate in the early morning and afternoon, returning around noon and 7pm.

CHILEAN PATAGONIA

Rugged seascapes rimmed with glacial peaks, the stunning massifs of Torres del Paine and howling steppe characterize the other side of the Andes. If you have come this far, it is well worth it to cross the border. Chilean Patagonia, a mountainous region sculpted by westerly winds, consists of the isolated Aisén and Magallanes regions, separated by the southern continental ice field. This section covers Punta Arenas, Puerto Natales and spectacular Parque Nacional Torres del Paine. For in-depth coverage of Chile, pick up Lonely Planet's *Chile & Easter Island*.

Most nationals of countries that have diplomatic relations with Chile don't need a visa to enter the country. Upon entering, customs officials will issue you a tourist card, valid for 90 days and renewable for another 90; authorities take it seriously, so guard it closely to avoid the hassle of replacing it. If arriving by air, US citizens must pay a one-time reciprocal entry fee of US$132, valid for the life of the passport; Canadians pay US$132 and Australians US$56.

Temperature-sensitive travelers will quickly notice a difference after leaving energy-rich Argentina: in public areas and budget accommodations central heating is rare; warmer clothing is the norm indoors.

Chile is slightly more expensive than Argentina, and US cash is not as widely accepted. Prices here are given in Chilean Pesos (CH$).

PUNTA ARENAS
☎ 61 / pop 130,136

Today's Punta Arenas is a confluence of the ruddy and the grand, witnessed in the elaborate wool-boom mansions, the thriving petrochemical industry and its port status. Visitors will find it the most convenient base to travel around the remote Magallanes region, with good traveler services. In truth, the city's increasing prosperity has sanded down and polished off its former roughneck reputation. Watch for more cruise-ship passengers and trekkers to replace the explorers, sealers and sailors of yesterday at the barstools – but save a spot for the old guard.

Founded in 1848 as a penal settlement and military garrison, Punta Arenas proved to be conveniently situated for ships headed to Alta California during the gold rush. The economy foundered during its early years, taking off only in the last quarter of the 19th century, after the territorial governor authorized the purchase of 300 pure-bred sheep from the Falkland Islands. This successful experiment encouraged the proliferation of sheep farming and, by the turn of the century, nearly two million animals grazed the territory.

Information

Travel agencies in the center, along Roca and Lautaro Navarro, change cash and traveler's checks. All are open weekdays and Saturday, with a few open on Sunday morning. Banks with ATMs dot the city center.

Chill-e (Av Colón 782; ☼ 9:30am-12:30am Mon-Fri, 11am-12:30am Sat, 3-11pm Sun) A comfy art deco space for internet access, with long hours and wireless connections.

Conaf (☎ 223841; José Menéndez 1147) Has details on the nearby parks.

Hospital Regional (☎ 205000; cnr Arauco & Angamos)

Information kiosk (☎ 200610; www.puntaarenas.cl in Spanish; Plaza Muñoz Gamero; ☼ 8am-7pm Mon-Sat, 9am-7pm Sun) South side of the plaza.

Lavasol (☎ 243607; O'Higgins 969) Laundry service. Hostels do laundry for a bit less.

Post office (Bories 911)

Sernatur (☎ 241330; www.sernatur.cl; Waldo Seguel 689; ☼ 8:15am-8pm Mon-Fri Dec-Feb, 8:15am-6pm Mon-Thu, 8:15am-5pm Fri rest of year) With friendly, well-informed, multilingual staff, and lists of accommodations and transportation. Also has a list of recommended doctors.

Telefónica (Nogueira 1116)

World's End (☎ 213117; Plaza Muñoz Gamero 1011) Maps, photo books, souvenirs and Lonely Planet guides in English and Spanish.

Sights & Activities
PLAZA MUÑOZ GAMERO

In the heart of Punta Arenas, this central plaza is lined with magnificent conifers and

PUNTA ARENAS

0 — 500 m
0 — 0.3 miles

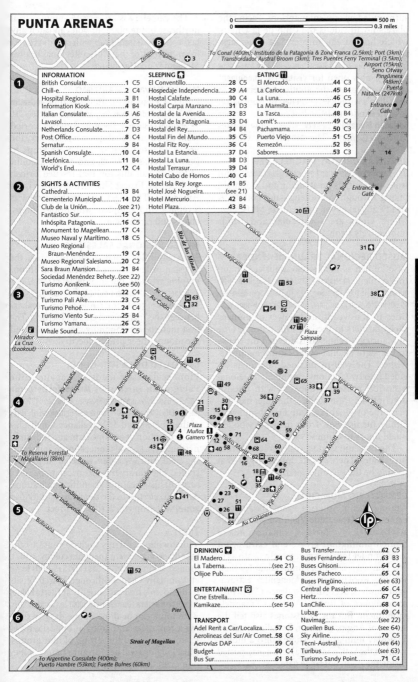

INFORMATION	
British Consulate	**1** C5
Chill-e	**2** C4
Hospital Regional	**3** B1
Information Kiosk	**4** B4
Italian Consulate	**5** A6
Lavasol	**6** C5
Netherlands Consulate	**7** D3
Post Office	**8** C4
Sernatur	**9** B4
Spanish Consulate	**10** C4
Telefónica	**11** B4
World's End	**12** C4

SIGHTS & ACTIVITIES	
Cathedral	**13** B4
Cementerio Municipal	**14** D2
Club de la Unión	(see 21)
Fantastico Sur	**15** C4
Inhóspita Patagonia	**16** C5
Monument to Magellean	**17** C4
Museo Naval y Marítimo	**18** C5
Museo Regional Braun-Menéndez	**19** C4
Museo Regional Salesiano	**20** C2
Sara Braun Mansion	**21** B4
Sociedad Menéndez Behety	(see 22)
Turismo Aonikenk	(see 50)
Turismo Comapa	**22** C4
Turismo Pali Aike	**23** C5
Turismo Pehoé	**24** C4
Turismo Viento Sur	**25** B4
Turismo Yamana	**26** C5
Whale Sound	**27** C5

SLEEPING	
El Conventillo	**28** C5
Hospedaje Independencia	**29** A4
Hostal Calafate	**30** C4
Hostal Carpa Manzano	**31** D3
Hostal de la Avenida	**32** B3
Hostal de la Patagonia	**33** D4
Hostal del Rey	**34** B4
Hostal Fin del Mundo	**35** C5
Hostal Fitz Roy	**36** C4
Hostal La Estancia	**37** D4
Hostal La Luna	**38** D3
Hostal Terrasur	**39** D4
Hotel Cabo de Hornos	**40** C4
Hotel Isla Rey Jorge	**41** B5
Hotel José Nogueira	(see 21)
Hotel Mercurio	**42** B4
Hotel Plaza	**43** B4

EATING	
El Mercado	**44** C3
La Carioca	**45** B4
La Luna	**46** C5
La Marmita	**47** C4
La Tasca	**48** B4
Lomit's	**49** C4
Pachamama	**50** C3
Puerto Viejo	**51** C5
Remezón	**52** B6
Sabores	**53** C3

DRINKING	
El Madero	**54** C3
La Taberna	(see 21)
Olijoe Pub	**55** C5

ENTERTAINMENT	
Cine Estrella	**56** C3
Kamikaze	(see 54)

TRANSPORT	
Adel Rent a Car/Localiza	**57** C5
Aerolíneas del Sur/Air Comet	**58** C4
Aerovías DAP	**59** C4
Budget	**60** C4
Bus Sur	**61** B4
Bus Transfer	**62** C5
Buses Fernández	**63** B3
Buses Ghisoni	**64** C4
Buses Pacheco	**65** C4
Buses Pingüino	(see 63)
Central de Pasajeros	**66** C4
Hertz	**67** C5
LanChile	**68** C4
Lubag	**69** C4
Navimag	(see 22)
Queilen Bus	(see 64)
Sky Airline	**70** C5
Tecni-Austral	(see 64)
Turbus	(see 63)
Turismo Sandy Point	**71** C4

To Conaf (400m); Instituto de la Patagonia & Zona Franca (2.5km); Port (3km); Transbordador Austral Broom (3km); Tres Puentes Ferry Terminal (3.5km); Airport (15km); Seno Otway Pingüinera (48km); Puerto Natales (247km)

Mirador La Cruz (Lookout)

To Reserva Forestal Magallanes (8km)

To Argentine Consulate (400m); Puerto Hambre (53km); Fuerte Bulnes (60km)

Plaza Sampaió

Plaza Muñoz Gamero

Strait of Magellan

Pier

PATAGONIA

surrounded by opulent mansions. Facing the plaza's north side is the Club de la Unión, which houses the former **Sara Braun mansion** (☎ 241489; admission CH$1000; ☉ 10:30am-1pm & 5-8:30pm Tue-Fri, 10:30am-1pm & 8-10pm Sat, 11am-2pm Sun), now open for visits. The **monument** commemorating the 400th anniversary of Magellan's voyage was donated by wool baron José Menéndez in 1920. Just east is the former **Sociedad Menéndez Behety**, which now houses Turismo Comapa. The **cathedral** sits west.

RESERVA FORESTAL MAGALLANES

This **reserve** (admission free; ☉ daylight hours), 8km from town, offers great hiking and mountain biking through dense lenga and coihue. A steady slog takes you to the top of Mt Fenton, where views are spectacular and winds impressively strong.

MUSEO REGIONAL BRAUN-MENÉNDEZ

Also known as the Palacio Mauricio Braun, this opulent **mansion** (☎ 244216; Magallanes 949; admission CH$1000, free Sun; ☉ 10:30am-5pm Mon-Sat, 10:30am-2pm Sun in summer, to 2pm daily in winter) testifies to the wealth and power of pioneer sheep farmers in the late 19th century. One of Mauricio Braun's sons donated the house to the state against other family members' wishes. The well-maintained interior is divided into two sections: one half is a regional historical museum (booklets with English descriptions are available); the other half displays the original exquisite French-nouveau family furnishings, from intricate wooden inlaid floors to Chinese vases.

The museum is most easily accessed from Magallanes. There's a café downstairs in what used to be the servants' quarters.

CEMENTERIO MUNICIPAL

Among South America's most fascinating cemeteries, **Cementerio Municipal** (main entrance at Av Bulnes 949; ☉ 7:30am-8pm) contains a mix of humble immigrant graves and extravagant tombs under topiary cypresses. In death as in life, Punta Arenas' first families flaunted their wealth – wool baron José Menéndez' extravagant tomb is, according to Bruce Chatwin, a scale replica of Rome's Vittorio Emanuele monument. But the headstones also tell the stories of Anglo, German, Scandinavian and Yugoslav immigrants. There's also a monument to the Selk'nam (Ona) and a map posted inside the main entrance gate.

The cemetery is an easy 15-minute stroll northeast of the plaza, or you can catch any taxi *colectivo* (shared cab with specific route) from in front of the Museo Regional Braun-Menéndez on Magallanes.

MUSEO NAVAL Y MARÍTIMO

Punta Arenas' naval and maritime **museum** (☎ 205479; Pedro Montt 981; adult/child CH$1500/800; ☉ 9:30am-12:30pm & 3-6pm Tue-Sat) has varied exhibits on model ships, naval history, the unprecedented visit of 27 US warships to Punta Arenas in 1908, and a fine account of the Chilean mission that rescued British explorer Sir Ernest Shackleton's crew from Antarctica. The most imaginative display is a replica ship complete with bridge, maps, charts and radio room.

MUSEO REGIONAL SALESIANO

Especially influential in settling the region, the Salesian order collected outstanding ethnographic artifacts, but their **museum** (☎ 221001; Av Bulnes 336; admission CH$1500; ☉ 10am-12:30pm & 3-6pm Tue-Sun) touts their role as peacemakers between the Yaghan and Ona and settlers. The best materials are on indigenous groups and the mountaineer priest Alberto de Agostini.

INSTITUTO DE LA PATAGONIA

Pioneer days are made real again at the Patagonian Institute's **Museo del Recuerdo** (☎ 207056; www.umag.cl in Spanish; Av Bulnes 01890; admission CH$1000; ☉ 8:30-11am & 2:30-6pm Mon-Fri), part of the Universidad de Magallanes. On display are a collection of antique farm and industrial machinery, a typical pioneer house and shearing shed, and a wooden-wheeled shepherds' trailer. The library has historical maps and a series of historical and scientific publications. Any taxi *colectivo* to the *zona franca* (duty-free zone) will drop you across the street.

Tours

Worthwhile day trips include tours to the **Seno Otway** *pingüinera* (penguin colony; p507), located 48km north. Tours (CH$15,000) leave at 4pm daily October through March. Visits to the town's first settlements at **Fuerte Bulnes & Puerto Hambre** (admission CH$1000) leave at 10am. Both tours can be done in one day; by sharing a rental car and going at opposite times visitors can avoid the strings of tour groups. Most lodgings will help arrange tours – if they don't run their own operation.

Torres del Paine tours are abundant from Punta Arenas, but the distance makes for a very long day; it's best to head to Puerto Natales and organize transport from there.

If you have the time, a more atmospheric alternative to Seno Otway is the thriving Magellanic penguin colonies of **Monumento Natural Los Pingüinos** (p507) on Isla Magdalena. Five-hour tours on the *Barcaza Melinka* (adult/child CH$15,000/7500) land for an hour at the island and depart the port on Tuesday, Thursday and Saturday, December through February. Confirm times in advance. Book tickets through **Turismo Comapa** (☎ 200200; www.comapa.com; Magallanes 990) and bring a picnic.

Recommended agencies:

Fantastico Sur (☎ 710050; www.fantasticosur.com; Magallanes 960)

Inhóspita Patagonia (☎ 224510; Lautaro Navarro 1013) Offers trekking trips to Cabo Froward, the southernmost point on mainland South America.

Turismo Aonikenk (☎ 228332; www.aonikenk.com; Magallanes 619) English-, German- and French-speaking guides.

Turismo Pali Aike (☎ 223301; www.turismopaliaike .com; Lautaro Navarro 1129)

Turismo Pehoé (☎ 244506; www.pehoe.com; José Menéndez 918)

Turismo Viento Sur (☎ 226930; www.vientosur.com; Fagnano 565)

Turismo Yamana (☎ 221130; www.yamana.cl; Errazuriz 932) Kayaking trips on Magellan Strait.

Whale Sound (☎ 221076; www.whalesound.com; Navarro 1163) Supports science with study-based sailing and kayak trips to the remote Coloane Marine Park.

Sleeping

The rates at midrange and top-end establishments include breakfast but don't reflect the additional 18% IVA charge, which foreigners in Chile aren't required to pay if paying with US cash, traveler's checks or credit card. Off-season (mid-April to mid-October) rates can drop by up to 40%.

BUDGET

Hospedaje Independencia (☎ 227572; Av Independencia 374; dm CH$4500, camping CH$1500) Shoestring travelers pack this cheaper-than-cheap lodging, run by a young couple. Rooms are good, the atmosphere is casual and guests get kitchen use and reasonable bike rentals.

Hostal La Estancia (☎ 249130; http://www.backpackers chile.com/en/hostel-estancia.php in English; O'Higgins 765; dm/d without bathroom CH$6500/20,000; 🖳) This rambling old home offers ample rooms and tidy shared bathrooms. Guests benefit from the helpful and warm nature of owners Alex and Carmen. It is nearly always booked, even in off-season. Reserve ahead.

Hostal Fitz Roy (☎ 240430; www.hostalfitzroy.com; Lautaro Navarro 850; dm/s/d/tr without bathroom CH$7000/ 12,000/20,000/25,000; 🖳) This country house in the city offers rambling, good-value rooms and an inviting, old-fashioned living room to pore over books or sea charts. Rooms have phones, TVs and wireless connections. Credit cards are accepted.

El Conventillo (☎ 242311; www.hostalelconventillo .com; Pasaje Korner 1034; dm CH$8000; 🖳) A new addition, this cool brick hostel in the reviving waterfront district has remodeled, carpeted dorms and clean row showers. Bright colors mask the fact that there is little interior light; rooms are windowless. Yogurt and cereal are part of a big breakfast. There's 24-hour reception, a laundry and a library of cool Chilean flicks.

Hostal La Luna (☎ 221764; hostalluna@hotmail.com; O'Higgins 424; s/d CH$8000/12,000; 🖳) Goose-down comforters and a scruffy tabby spell home at this friendly family lodging. Six tidy rooms have shared bathrooms and guests get kitchen and laundry privileges.

Hostal del Rey (☎ 223924; www.chileaustral .com/hdelrey; Fagnano 589; s/d/tr without bathroom CH$8000/16,000/24,000, d with bathroom CH$20,000, 2-person apt CH$24,000) Amid a haphazard decor of indigenous portraits, lace and kitsch, this cramped home features decent rooms with down-comforter beds. Apartments have full kitchens, hot water and TV.

Hostal Fin del Mundo (☎ 710185; www.alfindel mundo.cl; O'Higgins 1026; s/d/tr CH$10,000/20,000/24,000) On the 2nd and 3rd floors of a creaky downtown building, these cheerful rooms share bathrooms with hot showers and a large kitchen, but the shared space is rather dull.

MIDRANGE

Hostal Calafate (☎ 241281; www.calafate.cl in Spanish; Magallanes 922; s/d without bathroom CH$17,000/27,000, with bathroom CH$27,000/38,500; 🖳) This downtown hub bustles with traffic. Guests can choose from a selection of plain but good rooms that are not quite insulated from the street noise below. Perks include phones, TVs and central heating. A continental breakfast is included and there's a popular internet café in the lobby.

PATAGONIA

Hostal Carpa Manzano (☎ 710744; www.hotelcarpa manzano.com; Lautaro Navarro 336; s/d CH$30,000/35,000) These snappy-colored rooms feature private bathroom, carpet and cable TV. A comfortable house, it's run more like a hotel, with uniformed staff and a certain formality.

Hostal de la Patagonia (☎ 249970; www.ecotourpata gonia.com; O'Higgins 730; s/d CH$30,000/35,000) This unmistakable turquoise lodging offers a number of sunny rooms with light wood accents, and a decent buffet breakfast.

Hostal de la Avenida (☎ 710744; Av Colón 534; s/d CH$28,000/37,000) Chintzy but cozy, this mustard-yellow home has plants sprouting from a claw-foot tub and other funky installations. The staff is pleasant and there's cable TV and central heating.

Hostal Terrasur (☎ 247114; www.hostalterrasur.cl; O'Higgins 123; s/d CH$28,500/38,500; 🖳) The slightly upscale Terrasur nurtures a secret-garden atmosphere, from its rooms with flowing curtains and flower patterns to the miniature green courtyard. There's also friendly desk service.

Hotel Mercurio (☎ 242300; www.chileaustral.com/ mercurio; Fagnano 595; s/d/tr CH$45,000/53,000/62,000) A well-kept and proper corner hotel with wide staircases and slightly dated stucco rooms. The staff is bilingual and very accommodating.

Hotel Plaza (☎ 241300; www.hotelplaza.cl; Nogueira 1116; s/d CH$50,000/62,000; 🖳) This converted mansion boasts vaulted ceilings, plaza views and historical photos lining the hall. Inconsistent with such grandeur, the country decor is unfortunate. But service is genteel and the location unbeatable.

TOP END

Hotel Isla Rey Jorge (☎ 248220; www.hotelislareyjorge .com; 21 de Mayo 1243; s/d/ste CH$60,000/74,000/100,000; 🖳) Elegant and relaxed, this 1918 house exudes character; we just wonder about the cannon on the lawn. Traditional British style is flaunted, with 25 attractive rooms and a sun room for reading.

Hotel José Nogueira (☎ 248840; www.hotelnogueira .com; Bories 959; s/d CH$80,000/95,000; 🖳) This high-end hotel in the Sara Braun mansion lacks the original grandeur, but staff ghost sightings and the beautiful atrium dining room rescue some of the romance. Modern amenities combine with period furnishings in rooms, and the lobby is wired for wi-fi.

Hotel Cabo de Hornos (☎ 242134; www.hoteles-aus tralis.com/cabo_hornos/html/ingles.asp; Plaza Muñoz Gamero 1025; s/d CH$90,000/100,000; ✗ 🖳) This smart business hotel begins with a cool interior of slate and sharp angles, but rooms are more relaxed, with bright color accents and top-notch views. The well-heeled bar just beckons you to have a scotch.

Eating

The port's seasonal seafood is an exquisite treat: go for *centolla* (king crab) between July and November or *erizos* (sea urchins) between November and July. If heading to Torres del Paine, get groceries here beforehand.

La Carioca (☎ 224809; José Menéndez 600; sandwiches AR$2500) Cold lager and sandwiches are the mainstay at this downtown institution.

Lomit's (☎ 243399; José Menéndez 722; mains CH$3000; ⏲ 10am-2:30am) Chile's answer to the sidecar diner is this atmospheric café where cooks flip made-to-order burgers at a center-stage griddle. Portions are generous but the service dallies.

Sabores (☎ 227369; Mejicana 702, 2nd fl; mains CH$3500) Lacking pretension, this cozy café serves up hearty Chilean fare such as grilled fish, seafood stews and pasta to a full house.

La Marmita (☎ 222056; Plaza Sampaio 678; mains CH$5000-8000) Unbeatable for its ambience as well as its tasty fare, Marmita has fresh salads and hearty, home-cooked creations. The two small rooms are cozy and bright and the chef-owners sometimes circulate among guests. For a light main, try Pablo Neruda's *caldillo de congrio* (conger eel soup).

El Mercado (☎ 247415; Mejicana 617, 2nd fl; mains CH$6000; ⏲ 24hr) A late-night institution with heaping seafood specials, from scallops stewed in garlicky sauce to *chupe de centolla* (crab casserole). There's a full bar, English menu and cheaper sandwiches.

Puerto Viejo (☎ 225103; O'Higgins 1176; mains CH$5000-8000) With curved walls like a ship's hull and raw-wood details, this chic eatery sets sail with fresh options like hake in cider and warm abalone salad. It isn't cheap but the attention is notable.

Remezón (☎ 241029; 21 de Mayo 1469; mains CH$10,000) Take a cue from locals and start with a tart pisco sour (grape brandy with lemon). Then dive into the chef's game and seafood innovations: oysters and clams au gratin or salmon smoked with black tea, to name a couple. Service is unpretentious and welcoming.

Also recommended:

Pachamama (☎ 226171; Magallanes 619-A) Bulk trail-mix munchies and organic products.

La Luna (☎ 228555; O'Higgins 974; mains AR$4000-7000) A wide variety of fresh seafood and pastas.

La Tasca (☎ 242807; Plaza Muñoz Gamero 771; mains AR$4000-8000) In the stylish Casa España, with good views, a set lunch on weekdays and fresh seafood.

Drinking

La Taberna (☎ 241317; Sara Braun Mansion; ⏱ 7pm-2am, to 3am weekends) A magnet for travelers, this dark and elegant pub is a classic old-boys' club, with no old boys in sight. Ambience is tops, but the mixed drinks could be better.

Olijoe Pub (☎ 223728; Errázuriz 970; ⏱ 6pm-2am) Leather booths and mosaic tabletops lend pretension, but this is your usual pub with good beer and bad service. Mix it up with the house special, Glaciar – a mix of pisco, *horchata* (cinnamon rice milk), milk and curaçao.

El Madero (Bories 655) A warm-up spot for clubbers, Madero gets packed with crowds sipping stiff drinks.

Entertainment

Kamikaze (☎ 248744; Bories 655; cover CH$3000 with a free drink) Tiki torches warm up this most southerly dance club and, if you're lucky, the occasional live rock band. It's upstairs from El Madero.

Cine Estrella (Mejicana 777) Shows first-run movies.

Shopping

Zona Franca (Zofri; ⏱ closed Sun) The duty-free zone is a large, polished conglomeration of shops that is worth checking out if you're looking for electronics, outdoor gear, computer accessories or camera equipment. *Colectivos* shuttle back and forth from downtown along Av Bulnes throughout the day.

Getting There & Away

The tourist offices distribute a useful brochure which details all forms of transport available.

AIR

Punta Arenas' airport (PUQ) is 21km north of town.

LanChile (☎ 241100, 600-526-2000; www.lan.com; Lautaro Navarro 999) flies several times daily to Santiago (CH$194,000) with a stop in Puerto Montt (CH$124,000), and on Saturday to the Falkland Islands (CH$250,000 round-trip). A new service goes direct to Ushuaia (CH$107,500) three times a week. For national flights, book ahead online for the best deals.

Smaller **Aerolíneas del Sur/Air Comet** (☎ 227776; Roca 809) offers direct, nonstop flights twice daily between Santiago and Punta Arenas (CH$90,000). **Sky Airline** (☎ in Santiago 02-353-3169, 600-600-2828, in Punta Arenas 710645; Roca 935; www.skyairline.cl in Spanish) flies daily between Santiago and Punta Arenas, with a stop in either Puerto Montt or Concepción. At the time of research **Aerolíneas Argentina** (☎ 0810-222-86527; www.aerolineas.com.ar) had added an office in Punta Arenas, offering flights from various cities in Argentina.

From November to March, **Aerovías DAP** (☎ 223340, airport 213776; www.dap.cl; O'Higgins 891) flies to Porvenir (CH$19,000) Monday through Saturday, and to Puerto Williams (CH$52,000) Wednesday through Saturday and Monday. Luggage is limited to 10kg per person. DAP also offers charter flights over Cape Horn (seven-passenger plane CH$1,825,000) and to other Patagonian destinations, including Ushuaia and El Calafate. Charters to Chile's Teniente Marsh air base in Antarctica tour Base Frei (one/two days CH$1,250,000/1,750,000); weather depending, the schedule permits one night in Antarctica before returning to Punta Arenas.

BOAT

The car ferry *Melinka*, operated by **Transbordador Austral Broom** (☎ 218100; www.tabsa.cl in Spanish; Av Bulnes 05075), sails to Porvenir in Tierra del Fuego (CH$4300, 2½ to four hours) from the Tres Puentes ferry terminal north of town; catch taxi *colectivos* in front of Museo Regional Braun-Menéndez. Boats usually depart in the early morning and return in the late afternoon; schedules and travel time depend on the mercurial weather. Make reservations to ferry your vehicle (CH$28,000) by calling the office.

A faster way to get to Tierra del Fuego is the Punta Delgada–Bahía Azul ('Cruce Primera Angostura') crossing, northeast of Punta Arenas. Broom ferries (CH$1500, 20 minutes) sail every 90 minutes between 8:30am and 10pm. Call ahead for vehicle reservations (CH$12,000).

Broom is also the agent for ferries from Tres Puentes to Puerto Williams (reclining seat/bunk CH$72,500/87,500 including meals, 38 hours), on Isla Navarino. Ferries sail three or four times per month on Wednesday only, returning Saturday, both at 7pm. Trust us, the extra cost of a bunk is worthwhile.

THE FALKLAND ISLANDS/ISLAS MALVINAS
☎ 500 / pop 3200 permanent nonmilitary, 600,000 sheep

The sheep boom in Tierra del Fuego and Patagonia owes its origins to a cluster of islands 500km to the east in the South Atlantic Ocean. Known as Las Islas Malvinas to the Argentines or the Falkland Islands to the British, they had been explored, but never fully captured the interest of either country until Europe's mid-19th-century wool boom. After the Falkland Islands Company (FIC) became the islands' largest landholder, the islands' population of stranded gauchos and mariners grew rapidly with the arrival of English and Scottish immigrants. In an unusual exchange, in 1853 the South American Missionary Society began transporting Yaghan Indians from Tierra del Fuego to Keppel Island to catechize them.

Argentina has laid claim to the islands since 1833, but it wasn't until 1982 that Argentine President Leopoldo Galtieri, then drowning in economic chaos and allegations of corruption, decided that reclaiming the islands would unite his country behind him. However, British Prime Minister Margaret Thatcher (also suffering in the polls) didn't hesitate in striking back, thoroughly humiliating Argentina in what became known as the Falklands War. A severe blow to Argentina's nationalist pride, the ill-fated war succeeded in severing all diplomatic ties between the two nations.

On July 14, 1999, a joint statement issued by the British, Falkland Islands and Argentine governments promised closer cooperation on areas of economic mutual interest. In August 2001, British Prime Minister Tony Blair visited Argentina in an effort to further improve ties between the countries. Nevertheless, relations with Argentina remain cool, with most South American trade going via Chile.

Besides their status as an unusually polemical piece of property, what do the Falklands offer the intrepid traveler? Bays, inlets, estuaries and beaches create a tortuous, attractive coastline flanked by abundant wildlife. Striated and crested caracaras, cormorants, oystercatchers, snowy sheathbills and a plethora of penguins – Magellanic, rockhopper, macaroni, gentoo and king – share top billing with elephant seals, sea lions, fur seals, five dolphin species and killer whales.

Stanley (population 2000), the islands' capital on East Falkland, is an assemblage of brightly painted metal-clad houses and a good place to throw down a few pints and listen to island lore. 'Camp' – as the rest of the islands are known – hosts settlements that began as company towns (hamlets where coastal shipping could collect wool) and now provide rustic backcountry lodging and a chance to experience pristine nature and wildlife. Though there are 400km of roads, the islands have no street lights.

Planning
The best time to visit is from October to March, when migratory birds (including penguins) and marine mammals return to the beaches and headlands. The first cruise ships to South Georgia and Antarctica turn up in early November and the last ones depart around the end of March. It's worth visiting during the annual sports meetings, which feature horse racing, bull riding and sheepdog trials. The events take place in Stanley between Christmas and New Year, and on East and West Falkland at the end of the shearing season, usually in late February. Summer never gets truly hot (the maximum high is 24°C or 75°F), but high winds can bring a chill to the air. For more details, pick up Lonely Planet's *Falklands & South Georgia Island* guide.

Information
Stanley's **Jetty Visitors Centre** (☎ 27019; jettycentre@horizon.co.fk), at the public jetty on Ross Rd, distributes excellent brochures describing activities in and around Stanley. The *Visitor Accommodation Guide* lists lodgings and camping areas around the Islands. Another helpful source of information is **Falkland Islands Tourism** (☎ 22215; www.visitorfalklands.com). In the UK, contact **Falkland House** (☎ 020-7222-2542; www.falklandislands.com; 14 Broadway, Westminster, London SW1H 0BH).

Visas & Documents
Visitors from Britain and Commonwealth countries, the EU, North America, Mercosur countries and Chile don't need visas. If coming from another country, check with the British Consulate. All

nationalities must carry a valid passport, an onward ticket, and proof of sufficient funds (credit cards are fine) and pre-arranged accommodations. In practice, arrivals who don't have prebooked accommodations are held in the arrivals area while rooms are found.

Money
There's no ATM on the Falklands and only one bank in Stanley, so bring plenty of cash. Pounds sterling and US dollars in cash or traveler's checks are readily accepted, but the exchange rate for US currency is low. There's no need to change money to Falkland pounds (FK£), which are not accepted off the islands. In peak season, expect to spend US$150 to US$300 per day, not including airfare; less if camping or staying in self-catering cottages.

Getting There & Away
From South America, **LanChile** (www.lan.com) flies to Mt Pleasant International Airport (MPA; near Stanley) every Saturday from Santiago, Chile, via Puerto Montt, Punta Arenas and – one Saturday each month – Río Gallegos, Argentina. Roundtrip fares are CH$525,000 from Santiago and CH$250,000 from Punta Arenas with advance booking.

From **RAF Brize Norton** (www.raf.mod.uk/rafbrizenorton), in Oxfordshire, England, there are regular Royal Airforce flights to Mt Pleasant (18 hours, including a two-hour refueling stop on tiny Ascension Island in the South Atlantic). One-way fares are UK£949/1530/1550 for 30-day advance purchase/standard/business class. Travelers continuing on to Chile can purchase one-way tickets for half the fare. Bookings from the UK can be made through the **Falkland Islands Government Office** (☎ 020-7222-2542; fax 020-7222-2375; travel@figo.u-net.com; Falkland House, 14 Broadway, Westminster, London SW1H 0BH). Payment can be by cash or by personal or bank cheque; credit cards are not accepted. On each flight only 28 seats are reserved for nonmilitary personnel.

Getting Around
From Stanley, **Figas** (☎ 27219; figas.fig@horizon.co.fk) serves outlying destinations in eight-seater aircraft. Travel within the Falklands costs around US$2 per minute.

Several Stanley operators run day trips to East Falkland settlements, including **Discovery Tours** (☎ 21027; www.discoveryfalklands.com), **Ten Acre Tours** (☎ 21155; www.tenacrestours.horizon.co.fk) and **South Atlantic Marine Services** (☎ 21145; www.falklands-underwater.com).

Falkland Frontiers (☎ 51561; falklandfrontiers@horizon.co.fk) conducts fishing and wildlife tours. **Adventure Falklands** (☎ 21383; pwatts@horizon.co.fk) specializes in wildlife (featuring king, gentoo and Magellanic penguins) and historical tours.

Trekking and camping are feasible; however, there are no designated trails and getting lost is not unheard of. Always seek permission before entering private land.

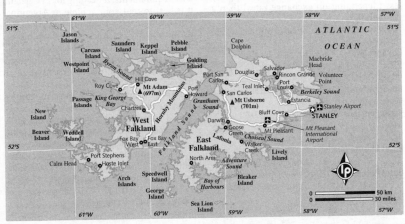

From September to May, **Cruceros Australis** (☎ in Santiago 02-442-3110; www.australis.com) runs breathtakingly scenic four- to seven-day luxury cruises aboard the 130-passenger *MV Mare Australis* and brand-new *MV Via Australis*, from Punta Arenas through the Cordillera de Darwin, Parque Nacional Alberto de Agostini, the Beagle Channel and Puerto Williams to Ushuaia (Argentina), and back. Rates for three nights start from CH$495,000 per person (double occupancy) in low season (September–October and mid-March–April) and reach CH$1,100,000 for a high-season single. Most passengers only sail one leg. Departures from Ushuaia include a possibility of disembarking at Cape Horn. Turismo Comapa (p501) handles local bookings.

Navimag (☎ 200200; www.navimag.com; Magallanes 990), which runs ferries from Puerto Natales to Puerto Montt via the spectacular Chilean fjords, is also represented by Comapa. For fares and schedules, see p511.

BUS

A central terminal is perennially promised. In the meantime, buses depart from company offices, most within a block or two of Av Colón. Buy tickets at least a couple of hours (if not a day or two during summer) in advance. The **Central de Pasajeros** (☎ 245811; cnr Magallanes & Av Colón) is the closest thing to a central booking office.

For Ushuaia, Ghisoni continues direct, but travelers report Pacheco stops too long in Río Grande. In Río Grande, minivans (Lider or Transportes Montiel) go to Ushuaia throughout the day and may cost slightly less (depending on exchange rates) than a through ticket.

Companies and daily destinations include the following:
Bus Sur (☎ 614224; www.bus-sur.cl; José Menéndez 552) El Calafate, Puerto Natales, Río Gallegos, Río Turbio, Ushuaia, Puerto Montt.
Bus Transfer (☎ 229613; Pedro Montt 966) Puerto Natales and airport transfers.
Buses Fernández/Buses Pingüino (☎ 221429/812; www.busesfernandez.com; Armando Sanhueza 745) Puerto Natales, Torres del Paine, Río Gallegos.
Buses Ghisoni/Queilen Bus (☎ 222714; Lautaro Navarro 975) Río Gallegos, Río Grande, Ushuaia, Puerto Montt.
Buses Pacheco (☎ 225527; www.busespacheco.com; Av Colón 900) Puerto Natales, Puerto Montt, Río Grande, Río Gallegos, Ushuaia.

Tecni-Austral (☎ 222078; Lautaro Navarro 975) Río Grande.
Turibus (☎ 227970; www.busescruzdelsur.cl in Spanish; Armando Sanhueza 745) Puerto Montt, Osorno, Chiloé.

Destination	Cost (CH$)	Duration (hr)
Puerto Montt	40,000	36
Puerto Natales	4000	3
Río Gallegos	7000	5-8
Río Grande	15,000	7
Ushuaia	24,000	10

Getting Around
TO/FROM THE AIRPORT
To get to Puerto Natales, there's no need to go into town since buses depart directly from the airport. **Turismo Sandy Point** (☎ 222241; Pedro Montt 840) runs door-to-door shuttle services (CH$3000) to/from town to coincide with flights. Buses Fernández does regular airport transfers (AR$2500), and Aerovías DAP also provides a shuttle service (CH$1500).

BUS & COLECTIVO
Taxi *colectivos*, with numbered routes, are only slightly more expensive than buses (about CH$450, a bit more late at night and on Sundays), far more comfortable and much quicker.

CAR
Cars are a good option for exploring Torres del Paine, but renting one in Chile to cross the border into Argentina can become prohibitively expensive due to international insurance requirements. If heading for El Calafate, it is best to rent your vehible in Argentina. Purchasing a car to explore Patagonia has its drawbacks, as Chilean Patagonia has no through roads that link northern and southern Patagonia, so it is entirely dependent on the roads of Argentina or expensive ferry travel.

Punta Arenas has Chilean Patagonia's most economical rental rates, and locally owned agencies tend to provide better service. Recommended **Adel Rent a Car/Localiza** (☎ 235471/2, 09-882-7569; www.adelrentacar.cl; Pedro Montt 962) provides attentive service, competitive rates, airport pickup and good travel tips. Other choices include **Budget** (☎ 225983; O'Higgins 964), **Hertz** (☎ 248742; O'Higgins 987) and **Lubag** (☎ 242023; Magallanes 970).

AROUND PUNTA ARENAS
Penguin Colonies

There are two substantial Magellanic penguin colonies near Punta Arenas. Easier to reach is **Seno Otway** (Otway Sound), with about 6000 breeding pairs, about an hour northwest of the city. The larger (50,000 breeding pairs) and more interesting **Monumento Natural Los Pingüinos** is accessible only by boat to Isla Magdalena in the Strait of Magellan (see above). Neither are as impressive as the larger penguin colonies in Argentina or the Falkland Islands. Tours to Seno Otway usually leave in the afternoon; however, visiting in the morning is best for photography because the birds are mostly backlit in the afternoon.

Since there is no scheduled public transport to either site, it's necessary to rent a car or join a tour. Admission to Seno Otway is CH$2000, while admission to Isla Magdalena is included in the tour price. Of the two options, the trip to Isla Magdalena is more often recommended.

Río Verde
🕾 61 / pop 300

About 50km north of Punta Arenas, a graveled lateral leads northwest toward Seno Skyring (Skyring Sound), passing this former sector of *estancias* before rejoining Ruta 9 at Villa Tehuelches at Km 100. Only visitors with a car should consider this interesting detour to one of the region's best-maintained assemblages of Magellanic architecture.

Ranch life spills from the pores of **Estancia Río Verde** (🕾 311131, 311123; www.estanciarioverde.cl; Ruta Y50, Km 97; d CH$47,500), an interesting stop on the shores of Seno Skyring. English-speaking hosts Josefina and Sergio keep a relaxed atmosphere and manage to be gracious hosts while running the ranch hands-on. A ride around the property affords a close look at operations on this sheep *estancia* that also breeds fine Chilean horses. Several times each summer there are rodeos at the *medialuna* (a traditional half-moon stadium). Sailing, fishing and sightseeing trips are also arranged. Guests stay in a beautiful restored *casco* with 14 rooms with private bathrooms. The kitchen cooks up regional delicacies, including Patagonian lamb, with fresh bread, garden vegetables and plenty of wine. Passersby can stop for lunch (CH$5000) and check out

the small museum. It's 43km north of Punta Arenas via Ruta 9; follow gravel road Y50 to Km 97.

Río Rubens

Roughly midway between Villa Tehuelches and Puerto Natales on blustery, paved Ruta 9, Río Rubens is a fine trout-fishing area and, for travelers with their own transport, an ideal spot to break the 250km journey from Punta Arenas.

Hotel Río Rubens (🕾 09-640-1583; Ruta 9, Km 183; s/d/cabins CH$10,000/15,000/40,000) is a comfy, welcoming, old country-style inn that offers good rates but can be hard to get a hold of. The restaurant serves outstanding meals, including lamb and seafood.

Parque Nacional Pali Aike

Rugged volcanic steppe pocked with craters, caves and twisted formations, Pali Aike, translated from the Tehuelche language, means 'devil's country.' This dry and desolate landscape is a 50-sq-km park along the Argentine border, west of the Monte Aymond border crossing to Río Gallegos. Lava rocks can be red, yellow or green-gray, depending on their mineral content. Fauna includes abundant guanacos, ñandús, gray foxes, armadillos and bats. In the 1930s Junius Bird's excavations at 17m-deep **Cueva Pali Aike** (Pali Aike Cave) yielded the first Paleo-Indian artifacts associated with extinct New World fauna such as the milodón and the native horse *Onohippidium*.

The **park** (admission CH$1000) has several hiking trails, including a 1.7km path through the rugged lava beds of the **Escorial del Diablo** to the impressive **Crater Morada del Diablo**; wear sturdy shoes or your feet could be shredded. There are hundreds of craters, some as high as a four-story building. There's also a 9km trail from Cueva Pali Aike to **Laguna Ana**, where there's another shorter trail to a site on the main road, 5km from the park entrance.

The **portería** (entrance gate) has a basic **refugio** (CH$6000) that holds four guests. Parque Nacional Pali Aike is 200km northeast of Punta Arenas via Ch (rural road) 9, Ch 255 and a graveled secondary road from Cooperativa Villa O'Higgins, 11km north of Estancia Kimiri Aike. There's also an access road from the Chilean border post at Monte Aymond. There is no public transport, but

Punta Arenas travel agencies offer full-day tours from CH$38,000.

PUERTO NATALES
☎ 61 / pop 15,500

On the windswept shores of Seno Última Esperanza (Last Hope Sound), this once-dreary fishing village now lives under assault by Gore-tex and Vibram soles as the well-trodden hub of the continent's number-one national park, Torres del Paine. But Natales does manage to maintain backwater charm (especially in the shoulder seasons), even while the tourist industry transforms its rusted tin storefronts one by one into gleaming facades. Nonetheless, the town sits at the edge of a magnificent frontier of wilderness whose accessibility continually increases.

The Navimag ferry through Chile's fjords ends and begins its trips here. Located 250km northwest of Punta Arenas via Ruta 9, Puerto Natales also offers frequent transport to El Calafate, Argentina.

Information
BOOKSTORES
World's End (☎ 414725; Blanco Encalada 226-A) Tip-of-the-world souvenirs, books and Torres trekking maps.

LAUNDRY
Most hostels also offer laundry service.
Servilaundry (☎ 412869; Bulnes 513) Full-service laundry.

MEDICAL SERVICES
Hospital (☎ 411533; cnr O'Higgins & Pinto)

MONEY
Most banks in town have ATMs.
Casa de Cambios (Bulnes 692; ☺ 10am-1pm & 3-7pm Mon-Fri, 10am-1pm & 3:30-7pm Sat) Best rates on cash and traveler's checks.

POST
Post office (Eberhard 429)

TELEPHONE & INTERNET ACCESS
Internet is widespread but slow throughout town.
Entel (Baquedano 270) Telephone office.

TOURIST INFORMATION
The best bilingual portal for the region is www.torresdelpaine.cl.

Conaf (☎ 411438; O'Higgins 584) National parks service administrative office.
Municipal tourist office (☎ 411263; Bulnes 285; ☺ 8:30am-12:30pm & 2:30-6pm Tue-Sun) In the Museo Histórico, with attentive staff and region-wide lodgings listings.
Sernatur (☎ 412125; infonatales@sernatur.cl; Costanera Pedro Montt 19; ☺ 9am-7pm) Not as helpful as the municipal tourist office.

TRAVEL AGENCIES
Most travel agencies ply similar services: park tours, maps and equipment rental. The following have some bilingual staff:
Antares Patagonia (☎ 414611; www.antarespatago nia.com; Barros Arana 111) Specializes in trekking in El Calafate, El Chaltén and Torres del Paine. Can facilitate climbing permits, science expeditions and made-to-order trips.
Baqueano Zamora (☎ 613531; www.baqueanozamora .com in Spanish; Baquedano 534) Runs horseback-riding trips and owns the Posada Río Serrano in Torres del Paine.
Erratic Rock (☎ 410355; Baquedano 719) Offers good park information, talks and gear rentals. Guide service specializes in treks to Cabo Froward, Isla Navarino and lesser-known destinations.
Fortaleza Expediciones (☎ 410595; www.fortale zapatagonia.cl; Arturo Prat 234) Knowledgeable; rents camping gear.
Indomita Big Foot (☎ 414525; www.indomitapata gonia.com; Bories 206) Popular kayaking, trekking and mountaineering trips, plus ice- and rock-climbing seminars.
Knudsen Tour (☎ 414747; knudsentour@yahoo. com; Blanco Encalada 284) Well regarded, with trips to El Calafate, Torres del Paine and alternative routes along Seno Último Esperanza.
Path@gone/Andescape/Onas Patagonia (☎ 413290/1; www.pathagone.com; Eberhard 595) The central point for reserving *refugios*, campsites and transport to Torres del Paine.
Turismo 21 de Mayo (☎ 411978; www.turismo 21demayo.cl in Spanish; Eberhard 560) Organizes day-trip cruises and treks to Balmaceda and Serrano glaciers.
Turismo Comapa (☎ 414300; www.comapa.com; Eberhart 555; ☺ 9am-1pm & 3-7pm Mon-Fri, 10am-2pm Sat) Navimag ferry and airline bookings.
Via Terra (☎ 410775; www.viaterra.cl; Baquedano 558) Runs tours (roundtrip CH$21,500) to Torres del Paine, departing 7:30am daily and arriving at Administración at 11:30am. It returns to Natales at 7:30pm and can do drop-offs.

Sleeping
For a small town, Puerto Natales brims with lodgings. Prices at nonbudget establishments don't reflect the additional 19% IVA, which foreigners are not required to pay if paying

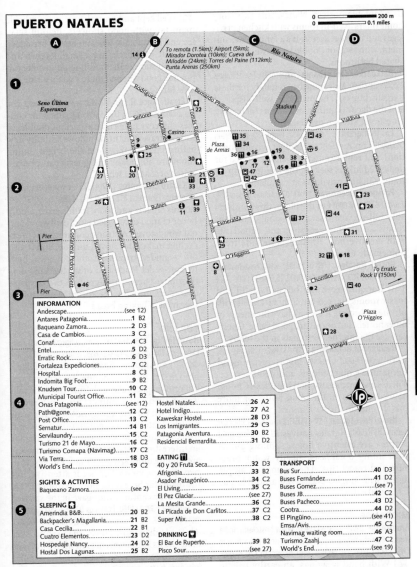

PUERTO NATALES

P A T A G O N I A

with US dollars or credit cards. In the off-season, many places drop prices by as much as 40%. Reserve ahead if you are arriving on the ferry.

BUDGET

Many budget accommodations are in quirky family homes. Hostels often rent equipment and help arrange transport. Most rates include a basic breakfast.

Kaweskar Hostel (☎ 414553; Blanco Encalada 754; dm CH$3000) A bargain hostel with bare rooms, bag storage and kitchen use. Gear rentals and bus tickets are also available.

Hospedaje Nancy (☎ 410022; www.nateslodge.cl; Ramírez 540; per person CH$5000; 💻) Oft-praised for its adoptable hostess, Nancy, this two-story home offers lived-in rooms with kitchen privileges and internet access. It's a family environment, with twin or double beds available with shared bathroom.

Backpacker's Magallania (☎ 414950; Tomás Rogers 255; dm CH$6000) A sleeping bag is handy for these bargain bunks. The owner is well disposed and the decor is quirky, but dorms fill up fast. Guests get kitchen privileges.

Los Inmigrantes (☎ 413482; Pinto 480; per person CH$7000) This *residencial* (budget accommodation) and rental center is a smart choice for dedicated hikers seeking the inside scoop on trails. Kitchen privileges are available.

Patagonia Aventura (☎ 411028; Tomás Rogers 179; dm/d CH$7500/18,000) On the plaza, this comfortable full-service hostel has small, ambient rooms, an attached gear shop and a good café with creative fare. Breakfasts include fresh homemade bread.

Hostel Natales (☎ 0410081; www.hostelnatales .cl; Ladrilleros 209; dm/d/tr CH$9000/25,000/33,000; ☐) This tranquil green inn boasts tasteful and toasty rooms, decked out in neutrals, all with private bathroom. It doesn't have the energy of other hostels, but dorms are good value. Guests can use the internet terminals in the lobby.

Residencial Bernardita (☎ 411162; O'Higgins 765; s/d CH$9000/18,000) Guests highly recommend Bernardita's quiet rooms and good service. There's also kitchen use and breakfast. Choose between rooms in the main house or more private ones in the back annex.

Hostal Dos Lagunas (☎ 415733; Barros Arana 104; r per person CH$10,000) Natales natives Alejandro and Andrea are attentive hosts, spoiling guests with filling breakfasts, steady water pressure and travel tips. The rooms are ample and warm; singles occupying a double pay CH$5000 extra.

MIDRANGE

Amerindia B&B (☎ 411945; www.hostelamerindia .com; Barros Arana 135; s/d/tr without bathroom CH$15,000/20,000/30,000; d with bathroom CH$30,000; ☐) With hand weavings, an earthy palette and retro touches, this guesthouse is a stylish retreat. Breakfast includes homemade bread and fruit. Guests can use the backyard grill, there's laundry service, and new doubles with bathrooms are on offer.

Casa Cecilia (☎ 613560; www.casaceciliahostal.com; Tomás Rogers 60; d with/without bathroom CH$30,000/20,000;

⊠) Well kept and central, Cecilia is a reliable mainstay with good showers, helpful service and homemade wheat toast for breakfast. The only drawbacks are a small kitchen and cramped rooms. Its multilingual owners can provide good tips and there's quality camping gear for hire.

Erratic Rock II (☎ 412317; www.erraticrock2.com; Benjamín Zamora 732; d CH$25,000; ☐) Ideal for couples, this cozy home offers spacious doubles in soft neutrals with throw pillows and tidy new bathrooms. Breakfasts in the bright dining room are abundant and guests can prepare coffee or tea on a whim.

Cuatro Elementos (☎ 415751; www.4elementos.cl in Spanish; Esmeralda 813; s/d/tr CH$20,000/25,000/37,000) Rooms are few and spare in this eco-friendly house crafted of recycled zinc, driftwood and old woodstoves. A strong commitment to recycling makes this hostel unique, and it also offers guided trips with an ecological bent to Torres del Paine and other trekking destinations. There's no sign: find the Japanese characters marking the entrance and follow the smell of baking bread.

TOP END

Hotel Indigo (☎ 418718; www.indigopatagonia.com; Ladrilleros 105; d/standard/ste CH$97,500/110,000/132,500; ⊠ ☐) A pampered finale to your trip. Hikers head first to Indigo's rooftop Jacuzzis and spa, but restful spaces abound, from the dark hallways dotted with hammocks to plush rooms with down duvets and candles lit for your return. Materials like eucalyptus, slate and iron overlap the modern with the natural for an interesting effect. Standard corner rooms are slightly more spacious than doubles, with two window views. Service is attentive, but the main star here is the fjord in front of you, which even captures your gaze in the shower.

remota (☎ 414040, bookings 02-387-1500; www.remota.cl; Ruta 9, Km 1.5; 3 nights s/d CH$840,000/1,160,000; ☐ ☐) Unlike most hotels, the exclusive remota draws your awareness to what's outside: silence broadcasts the gusty winds, irregular window patterns imitate old stock fences and a crooked passageway pays tribute to *estancia* sheep corridors. This vast postmodern addition to Puerto Natales offers sumptuous but spare comfort. Though rooms are cozy, you'll probably want to spend all your time at 'the beach,' a glass-walled barn room with lounge futons to gape at the wild surroundings.

Eating

La Picada de Don Carlitos (☎ 414232; Blanco Encalada 444; menú del día CH$2000) Hearty Chilean fare, like chicken stew and heaped mashed potatoes, is served at this down-home eatery bursting with locals at lunchtime.

El Living (Arturo Prat 156; mains CH$3500) Homemade soups and gourmet teas and coffee make this gringo den with comfy couches worth a leisurely stop.

Afrigonia (☎ 412232; Eberhard 343; mains CH$4200) If you're bored with local fare, try this romantic gem. Run by a Zambian/Chilean couple, its offerings include tasty mint lamb brochettes or chicken with creamy ginger sauce, spiced to your wishes.

La Mesita Grande (Arturo Prat 196; pizzas CH$5000; ☯ lunch & dinner) Happy diners share one long, worn table for outstanding thin-crust pizzas, quality pastas and organic salads. Toppings have a twist, like arugula and proscuitto or lemon-spiked salmon.

El Pez Glaciar (Ladrilleros 105; mains CH$5000) Attached to Hotel Indigo, this sleek seafood restaurant emphasizes freshness: the fish on your plate was probably hauled in with that morning's catch. Pared-down but creative preparations showcase the distinct flavor of each dish, from sesame conger eel to crisp silverside. Don't miss the spicy Peruvian seviche.

Asador Patagónico (☎ 413553; Arturo Prat 158; mains CH$8000) If trekking has left you with a mastodon appetite, splurge on flame-seared lamb, steak and salads at this upscale grill on the plaza.

Shoppers can hit **40 y 20 Fruta Seca** (☎ 210661; Baquedano 443) for dried fruits and nuts perfect for the trail. **Super Mix** (☎ 210661; Bulnes s/n) has groceries.

Drinking

El Bar de Ruperto (☎ 410863; cnr Bulnes & Magallanes; ▣) Ideal for a rainy day, this typical bar entertains you with foosball, chess and other board games. Guinness and other imports help you forget you're so far from home.

Pisco Sour (Ladrilleros 105, 2nd fl; ☯ 10am-11pm; ▣) For sunset cocktails, hit this stylish bar in the Hotel Indigo complex, with gaping views of the mountain-clad sound. Innovations on the bar's namesake drink shouldn't be missed: try the Nippon pisco sour (spiked with green tea).

Getting There & Away

AIR

Aerovías DAP (www.dap.cl) offers charter flights to El Calafate, Argentina, from the small airfield (PNT), a few kilometers north of town on the road to Torres del Paine. The closest LanChile office is in Punta Arenas (p503).

BOAT

For many travelers, a journey through Chile's spectacular fjords aboard Navimag's car and passenger ferry becomes a highlight of their trip. This four-day and three-night northbound voyage has become so popular it should be booked well in advance.

You can also try your luck. To confirm when the ferry is due, contact Turismo Comapa (p508) a couple of days before your estimated arrival date. The *Magallanes* leaves Natales early on Friday and stops in Puerto Edén (or the advancing Glaciar Pía XI on southbound sailings) en route to Puerto Montt. It usually arrives in Natales in the morning of the same day and departs either later that day or on the following day, but schedules vary according to weather conditions and tides. Disembarking passengers must stay on board while cargo is transported; those embarking have to spend the night on board.

High season is November to March, midseason is October and April, and low season is May to September. Most folks end up in dorm-style, 22-bed berths, but often wish they had sprung for a private cabin. Fares vary according to view, cabin size and private or shared bathroom, and include all meals (including veggie options if requested while booking, but bring water, snacks and drinks anyway) and interpretive talks. Per-person fares range from CH$170,000 for a bunk berth in low season to CH$975,000 for a triple-A cabin in high season; students and seniors receive a 10% to 15% discount. Check online (www.navimag.com) for current schedules and rates.

BUS

Puerto Natales has no central bus terminal, though several companies stop at the junction of Valdivia and Baquedano. In high season book at least a day ahead, especially for early-morning departures. Services are greatly reduced in the off-season.

A new road has been opened to Torres del Paine and, although gravel, it is much more direct. For now the only transportation service using it is Via Terra, but look for others to follow soon. This alternative entrance goes alongside Lago del Toro to the Administración (park headquarters).

Otherwise, for Torres del Paine, most buses leave two to three times daily at around 7am, 8am and 2:30pm. If you are headed to Mountain Lodge Paine Grande in the off-season, take the morning bus (CH$8000) to meet the catamaran (CH$11,000 one way, two hours). These schedules are in constant flux, so double-check them before heading out.

Bus Sur goes to Río Gallegos, Argentina, on Tuesday and Thursday; El Pingüino goes at 11am Wednesday and Sunday. To El Calafate, Zaahj, Cootra and Bus Sur have the most services.

Companies and destinations include the following:

Bus Sur (☎ 614221; www.bus-sur.cl in Spanish; Baquedano 658) Punta Arenas, Torres del Paine, Puerto Montt, El Calafate, Río Turbio, Ushuaia.

Buses Fernández/El Pingüino (☎ 411111; www .busesfernandez.com; cnr Esmeralda & Ramirez) Torres del Paine, Punta Arenas.

Buses Gomez (☎ 411971; www.busesgomez.com in Spanish; Arturo Prat 234) Torres del Paine.

Buses JB (☎ 412824; busesjb@hotmail.com; Arturo Prat 258) Torres del Paine.

Buses Pacheco (☎ 414513; www.busespacheco.com; Baquedano 244) Punta Arenas, Río Grande and Ushuaia.

Cootra (☎ 412785; Baquedano 456) Goes to El Calafate daily at 7:30am.

Turismo Zaahj (☎ 412260/355; www.turismozaahj .co.cl in Spanish; Arturo Prat 236/270) Torres del Paine, El Calafate.

Destination	Cost (CH$)	Duration (hr)
El Calafate	11,000	5
Punta Arenas	4000	2-3
Torres del Paine	8000	2
Ushuaia	28,000	12

Getting Around

Car rental is expensive and availability is limited; you'll get better rates in Punta Arenas or Argentina. Try **Emsa/Avis** (☎ 241182; Bulnes 632). **World's End** (☎ 414725; Blanco Encalada 226-A) rents bikes.

CUEVA DEL MILODÓN

Just 24km northwest of Puerto Natales, Hermann Eberhard discovered the remains of an enormous ground sloth in the 1890s. Nearly 4m tall, the herbivorous milodón survived on the succulent leaves of small trees and branches, but became extinct in the late Pleistocene. The 30m-high **cave** (admission CH$4000) pays homage to its former inhabitant with a life-size plastic replica of the animal. It's not exactly tasteful, but still worth a stop, whether to appreciate the grand setting and ruminate over its wild past or to take an easy walk up to a lookout point.

Camping (no fires) and picnicking are possible. Torres del Paine buses pass the entrance, which is 8km from the cave proper. There are infrequent tours from Puerto Natales; alternatively, you can hitchhike or share a taxi (CH$15,000). Outside of high season, bus services are infrequent.

PARQUE NACIONAL BERNARDO O'HIGGINS

Virtually inaccessible, O'Higgins remains the elusive and exclusive home of glaciers and waterfowl. The national park can only be entered by boat. Full-day boat excursions (CH$45,000 without lunch) to the base of Glaciar Serrano are run by **Turismo 21 de Mayo** (☎ 061-411978; www.turismo21demayo.cl in Spanish; Eberhard 560, Puerto Natales) and longer trips by **Path@gone** (☎ 061-413290/1; www.pathagone.com; Eberhard 595, Puerto Natales).

You can access Torres del Paine via boat to Glaciar Serrano. Passengers transfer to a Zodiac (a rubber boat with a motor), stop for lunch at Estancia Balmaceda (CH$12,000) and continue up Río Serrano, arriving at the southern border of the park by 5pm. The same tour can be done leaving the park, but may require camping near Río Serrano to catch the Zodiac at 9am. The trip costs CH$75,000 with Turismo 21 de Mayo or **Onas Patagonia** (☎ 061-413290/1; www.pathagone.com; Eberhard 595, Puerto Natales).

PARQUE NACIONAL TORRES DEL PAINE
☎ 61

Soaring almost vertically to nearly 3000m above the Patagonian steppe, the Torres del Paine (Towers of Paine) are spectacular granite pillars that dominate the landscape of what may be South America's finest **national park**

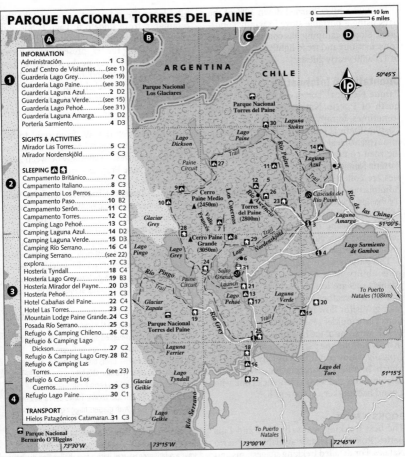

PARQUE NACIONAL TORRES DEL PAINE

0 — 10 km
0 — 6 miles

INFORMATION
Administración...........................1 C3
Conaf Centro de Visitantes......(see 1)
Guardería Lago Grey...............(see 19)
Guardería Lago Paine...............(see 30)
Guardería Laguna Azul.............2 D2
Guardería Laguna Verde...........(see 15)
Guardería Lago Pehoé............(see 31)
Guardería Laguna Amarga........3 D2
Portería Sarmiento....................4 D3

SIGHTS & ACTIVITIES
Mirador Las Torres.....................5 C2
Mirador Nordenskjöld................6 C3

SLEEPING
Campamento Británico...............7 C2
Campamento Italiano.................8 C3
Campamento Los Perros............9 B2
Campamento Paso....................10 B2
Campamento Serón...................11 C2
Campamento Torres..................12 C2
Camping Lago Pehoé.................13 C3
Camping Laguna Azul................14 D2
Camping Laguna Verde..............15 D3
Camping Río Serrano.................16 C4
Camping Serrano......................(see 22)
explora....................................17 C3
Hostería Tyndall.......................18 C4
Hostería Lago Grey...................19 B3
Hostería Mirador del Payne........20 D3
Hostería Pehoé.........................21 C3
Hotel Cabañas del Paine............22 C4
Hotel Las Torres.......................23 C2
Mountain Lodge Paine Grande....24 C3
Posada Río Serrano...................25 C3
Refugio & Camping Chileno.......26 C2
Refugio & Camping Lago
  Dickson................................27 C2
Refugio & Camping Lago Grey....28 B2
Refugio & Camping Las
  Torres..................................(see 23)
Refugio & Camping Los
  Cuernos................................29 C3
Refugio Lago Paine...................30 C1

TRANSPORT
Hielos Patagónicos Catamaran...31 C3

(www.pntp.cl in Spanish; admission high/low season in Chilean pesos only CH$15,000/5000).

Before its creation in 1959, the park was part of a large sheep *estancia*, and it's still recovering from nearly a century of over-exploitation of its pastures, forests and wildlife. Part of Unesco's Biosphere Reserve system since 1978, it shelters flocks of ostrich-like rheas (known locally as ñandús), Andean condors, flamingos and many other bird species. The park's conservation success is most evident with the guanaco (*Lama guanicoe*), which grazes the open steppe where its predator, the puma, cannot approach undetected. After over a decade of effective protection from poachers, the large and growing herds of guanacos don't even flinch when humans or vehicles approach.

For hikers and trekkers, this 1810-sq-km park is an unequaled destination. Weather can be wildly changeable. Some say you get four seasons in a day here, and sudden rainstorms and knock-down gusts are part of the hearty initiation. Bring high-quality foul-weather gear, a synthetic sleeping bag and, if you're camping, a good tent.

Guided day trips from Puerto Natales are possible, but permit only a bus-window glimpse of what the park has to offer. Instead, plan to spend anywhere from three to seven days to enjoy the hiking and other activities.

In 2005 a hiker burned down 10% of the park using a portable stove in windy conditions. Sloppy camping has consequences. Be conscientious and tread lightly – you are one of 120,000 yearly guests.

Orientation & Information

Parque Nacional Torres del Paine is 112km north of Puerto Natales via a decent but sometimes bumpy gravel road. At Cerro Castillo there is a seasonal border crossing into Argentina at Cancha Carrera. From here the road continues 40km north and west to **Portería Sarmiento**, the main entrance where fees are collected. It's another 37km to the Administración and the **Conaf Centro de Visitantes** (☻ 9am-8pm in summer), with good information on park ecology and trail status. A new road from Puerto Natales to the Administración (park headquarters) provides a shorter, more direct southern approach to the park.

The park is open year-round, subject to your ability to get there. Transportation connections are less frequent in low season and winter weather adds extra challenges to hiking. Visitor flow is edging toward regulation. The shoulder seasons of November and March are some of the best times for trekking. In both months, the park is less crowded, with typically windy conditions usually abating in March. Internet resources include www.torresdelpaine.com and www.erraticrock.com, with a good backpacker equipment list.

BOOKS & MAPS

The best trekking maps, by JLM and Luis Bertea Rojas, are widely available in Puerto Natales. For detailed trekking suggestions and maps, consult Lonely Planet's *Trekking in the Patagonian Andes*.

Activities
HIKING

Torres del Paine's 2800m granite spires inspire a mass pilgrimage of hikers from around the world. Most go for the circuit or the 'W' to soak in these classic panoramas, leaving other incredible routes deserted. Doing the circuit (the 'W' plus the backside of the peaks) requires seven to nine days, while the 'W' (named for the rough approximation to the letter that it traces out on the map) takes four to five. Add another day or two for transportation connections.

Most trekkers start either route from Laguna Amarga and head west. You can also hike from the Administración or take the catamaran from Pudeto to Lago Pehoé and start from there; hiking roughly southwest to northeast along the 'W' presents more views of black sedimentary peaks known as Los Cuernos (2200m to 2600m). Trekking alone, especially on the backside of the circuit, is inadvisable and restricted by Conaf.

The 'W'

Most people trek the 'W' from right to left (east to west), starting at Laguna Amarga, but hiking east to west – especially between Lago Pehoé and Valle Francés – provides superior views of Los Cuernos.

Refugio Las Torres to Mirador Las Torres Four hours one way. A moderate hike up Río Ascencio to a treeless tarn beneath the eastern face of the Torres del Paine proper. This is the closest view you will get of the towers. The last hour is a knee-popping scramble up boulders (covered with knee- and waist-high snow in winter). There are camping and *refugios* at Las Torres and Chileno, with basic camping at Campamento Torres. In summer stay at Campamento Torres and head up at sunrise to beat the crowds.

Refugio Las Torres to Los Cuernos Seven hours one way. Hikers should keep to the lower trail (many get lost on the upper trail, unmarked on maps). There's camping and a *refugio*. Summer winds can be fierce.

To Valle Francés Five hours one way from Los Cuernos or Lago Pehoé. In clear weather, this hike is the most beautiful stretch between 3050m Cerro Paine Grande to the west and the lower but still spectacular Torres del Paine and Los Cuernos to the east, with glaciers hugging the trail. Camp at Italiano and at Británico, right in the heart of the valley.

Mountain Lodge Paine Grande to Refugio Lago Grey Four hours one way from Lago Pehoé. This hike follows a relatively easy trail with a few challenging downhill scampers. The glacier lookout is another half-hour's hike away. There are camping and *refugios* at both ends.

Mountain Lodge Paine Grande to Administración Five hours. Up and around the side of Lago Pehoé, then through extensive grassland along Río Grey. This is not technically part of the 'W,' but after completion of the hike you can cut out to the Administración from here and avoid backtracking to Laguna Amarga. Mountain Lodge Paine Grande can radio in and make sure that you can catch a bus from the Administración back to Puerto Natales. You can also enter the 'W' this way to hike it east to west.

The Circuit

The whole loop takes in the 'W' (described above), plus the backside between Refugio Grey and Refugio Las Torres. The landscape is desolate yet beautiful. Paso John Garner (the most extreme part of the trek) sometimes offers knee-deep mud and snow. There's one basic refugio at Los Perros; the rest is rustic camping.

Refugio Lago Grey to Campamento Paso Four hours from Refugio Grey to Paso; about two hours going the opposite way. Hikers might want to go left to right (west to east), which means ascending the pass rather than slipping downhill.

Campamento Paso to Campamento Los Perros Approximately four hours. This route has plenty of mud and sometimes snow. Don't be confused by what appears to be a campsite right after crossing the pass; keep going until you see a shack.

Campamento Los Perros to Campamento Dickson Around 4½ hours. A relatively easy but windy stretch.

Campamento Lago Dickson to Campamento Serón Six hours. As the trail wraps around Lago Paine, winds can get fierce and the trails vague; stay along the trail furthest away from the lake. It's possible to break the trek at Campamento Coiron, although it is currently recovering from the 2005 fire.

Campamento Serón to Laguna Amarga Four to five hours. You can end the trek with a chill-out night and a decent meal at Refugio Las Torres.

Day Hikes
Walk from Guardería Lago Pehoé, on the main park highway, to **Salto Grande**, a powerful waterfall between Lago Nordenskjöld and Lago Pehoé. Another easy hour's walk leads to **Mirador Nordenskjöld**, an overlook with superb views of the lake and mountains. For a more challenging day hike, try the four-hour trek leading to **Lago Paine**, whose northern shore is accessible only from Laguna Azul. The route offers tranquility and gorgeous scenery.

KAYAKING
Paddle your way to pristine corners of the park on multiday trips with **Indomita Big Foot** (☎ 414525; www.indomitapatagonia.com; Bories 206, Puerto Natales). Few see the sights around Río Serrano, and these trips aren't budget travel but they can be a lot of fun. It's a great way to get up close to glaciers.

HORSEBACK RIDING
The park is certainly a beautiful place to ride. Due to property divisions within the park, horses cannot cross between the western sections (Lagos Grey and Pehoé, Río Serrano)

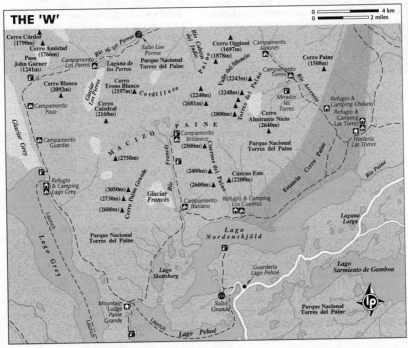

and the eastern part managed by Hostería Las Torres (Refugio Los Cuernos is the approximate cut-off). **Baqueano Zamora** (☎ 413953; www.baqueanozamora.com in Spanish; Baquedano 534, Puerto Natales) runs excursions to Lagos Pingo, Paine and Azul, and Laguna Amarga (half-day CH$27,500, lunch included).

Sleeping & Eating

Make reservations! Arriving without them, especially in high season, limits you to camping in the few free options. Travel agencies offer reservations, but it's best to deal directly with the various management companies. **Path@ gone/Andescape** (☎ 413290/1; Eberhard 595, Puerto Natales) manages Lagos Grey and Dickson. **Vertice Patagonia** (☎ 412742; www.verticepatagonia .cl) owns and runs Mountain Lodge Paine Grande. **Fantastico Sur** (☎ 710050; www.fantastico sur.com; Magallanes 960, Punta Arenas; ☒ 9am-5pm Mon-Fri, 10:30am-1:30pm & 3-5pm Sat & Sun) owns Las Torres, Chileno and Los Cuernos, and their associated campgrounds.

Some *refugios* may require photo ID (ie a passport) upon check-in. Photocopy your tourist card and passport for all lodgings in advance to expedite check-in. Staff can radio ahead to confirm your next reservation. Given the huge volume of trekkers, snags are inevitable, so practice your Zen composure.

CAMPING

Camping at the *refugios* costs CH$4000 per site. *Refugios* rent equipment – tent (CH$7000 per night), sleeping bag (CH$4500) and mat (CH$1500) – but potential shortages in high season make it prudent to pack your own gear. Small kiosks sell expensive pasta, soup packets and butane gas. Sites administered by Conaf are free and very basic. Many campers have reported wildlife (in rodent form) lurking around campsites, so don't leave food in packs or in tents – hang it from a tree instead.

REFUGIOS

Refugio rooms have four to eight bunk beds each, kitchen privileges (for lodgers and during specific hours only), hot showers and meals. A bed costs CH$12,500 to CH$17,500, sleeping-bag rental CH$4500, and meals CH$4000 to CH$7500. Should a *refugio* be overbooked, staff provide all necessary camping equipment. Most *refugios* close by the end of April. Mountain Lodge Paine Grande is the

only one that stays open year-round, but it has very limited operations.

HOTELS & HOSTERÍAS

The following have high-season prices listed.

Mountain Lodge Paine Grande (☎ 412742; www .verticepatagonia.cl; dm CH$20,600, full board CH$38,000, camping per person CH$3500; ☒) Sometimes referred to as Pehoé (its predecessor), this boxy hotel reveals a smart interior made to give sublime Los Cuernos views to all rooms. Between Lago Grey and Valle Francés, it is a perfect day hike from either. It can also be reached by boat across Lago Pehoé. The lodge is partially open year-round and is a godsend to cold, wet winter hikers. It also offers camping.

Posada Río Serrano (☎ 02-193-0338, 061-613531 in Puerto Natales; www.baqueanozamora.com in Spanish; dm CH$15,000, d with/without bathroom CH$55,000/40,000) Restored but still rustic, this rambling 19th-century ranch house has 13 rooms, a restaurant, a bar and a cozy living room focused on a fireplace. It's a popular base camp for horseback riding (arranged through the same company that owns the posada) and fishing trips to nearby lakes and rivers.

Hotel Tyndall (☎ 239401; www.hoteltyndall.com; d CH$70,000-80,000) This smart wooden lodge on the Río Serrano offers rooms or fully equipped cabins, as well as excursions for guests.

Hotel Cabañas del Paine (☎ 220174; www.cabanas delpaine.cl; d CH$75,000-100,000) On the banks of the Río Serrano, these modern wood cabins have hardwood details and offer views of the Paine massif and river. Access is via the new road into the park.

Hostería Pehoé (☎ 244506, 248888; www.pehoe .com; d CH$80,000-90,000) On the far side of Lago Pehoé, toward explora, this *hostería* is linked to the mainland by a long footbridge. It enjoys five-star panoramas of Los Cuernos and Paine Grande, but unfortunately the rooms are a bit dated. The restaurant and bar are open to the public.

Hostería Lago Grey (☎ 225986; www.lagogrey .cl; booking address Lautaro Navarro 1061, Punta Arenas; d CH$90,000-100,000) Although at the outlet of ice-berg-dotted Lago Grey, the crowded rooms at this year-round retreat are cut off from the views by thick windbreaking trees. The café (open to the public), however, overlooks the grandeur. Zodiac boat tours are available on the lake, but not to the glacier.

Hostería Mirador del Payne (☎ 226930; www.mira dordelpayne.com; booking address Fagnano 585, Punta Arenas; s/d/tr CH$80,000/97,500/108,000) On the Estancia El Lazo in the seldom-seen Laguna Verde sector, this comfortable inn is known for its serenity, proximity to spectacular viewpoints and top-rate service – but not for easy park access. Activities include bird watching, horseback riding and sport fishing. Call to arrange a ride from the road junction.

Hotel Las Torres (☎ 710050; www.lastorres.com; booking address Magallanes 960, Punta Arenas; d CH$635,000-1,463,000) A luxurious choice just 7km west of Guardería Laguna Amarga. Wings are interconnected by spacious living rooms with grand fireplaces. One end of the hotel has an interesting and educational interpretive center about the park. The restaurant (buffet CH$15,000) serves elaborate dishes of salmon, crab and steak. The spa has a sauna and Jacuzzi, and offers massages and revitalizing treatments.

explora (☎ 02-206-6060 in Santiago; www.explora.com; d per person 4 nights CH$1,195,000; 💻 📷) Strutting with style, Torres del Paine's most sophisticated (and expensive) digs sit perched above the Salto Chico waterfall at the outlet of Lago Pehoé. Rates include airport transfers, full gourmet meals and a wide variety of excursions led by young, affable, bilingual guides.

Views of the entire Paine massif pour forth from every inch of the hotel. But is it worth shelling out? Before you decide, check out the spa with heated lap pool, sauna, massage rooms and open-air Jacuzzi.

Getting There & Away

For details of transportation to the park, see p511. Going to El Calafate from the park on the same day requires joining a tour or careful advance planning, since there is no direct service. Your best bet is to return to Puerto Natales.

Getting Around

Buses drop off and pick up passengers at Laguna Amarga, at the Hielos Patagónicos catamaran launch at Pudeto, and at park headquarters.

The catamaran leaves Pudeto for Mountain Lodge Paine Grande (one way/roundtrip per person CH$11,000/17,000) at 9:30am, noon and 6pm December to mid-March, at noon and 6pm in late March and November, and at noon only in September, October and April. Another launch travels Lago Grey between Hostería Lago Grey and Refugio Lago Grey (roundtrip CH$70,000, 1½ to two hours) a couple of times daily; contact the *hostería* for the current schedule.

PATAGONIA

Tierra del Fuego

A storied past of shipwrecks, failed religious missions and indigenous extinction contributes to the powerful mystique of this end-of-the-earth location. Travelers flock here to glimpse the final reaches of the continent, and ah – what a view it is! The northern barren plains of Tierra del Fuego give way to peat bogs and moss-draped lenga forests that rise into ragged snowy mountains. At Ushuaia, the Andes meet the southern ocean in a sharp skid, making way for the city before reaching a sea of lapping currents.

While assuming a complex and sometimes conflicted identity, Tierra del Fuego still manages to remain beautiful, ancient and strange. The curved bandera tree, waving like a hankie, is a reminder that it's the toying weather that defines this place and most travelers' visits to it.

While it is isolated and hard to reach, Tierra del Fuego is by no means cut off from the mainland. Ports bustle with commerce, oil refineries chug and adventure seekers descend in droves to fly-fish, hike and start Antarctic cruises. Separated from the mainland by the Strait of Magellan, this archipelago shared with Chile is comprised of one large island, Isla Grande de Tierra del Fuego, and many smaller ones, most of them uninhabited. This chapter covers both the Argentine and Chilean sections of the territory, including Chilean Isla Navarino.

HIGHLIGHTS

- Kayak alongside sea lions in the gunmetal-gray waters of the **Beagle Channel** (p529)
- Speed through frozen valleys on a **dog-sledding tour** (p529) near Ushuaia
- Round up the sheep on a working **estancia** (p523) around Río Grande
- Relive grim times in Ushuaia's once-isolated prison turned museum, **Museo Marítimo & Museo del Presidio** (p527)
- Explore the ancient Fuegian forests in **Parque Nacional Tierra del Fuego** (p535)

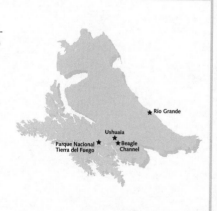

- POPULATION: 106,062 (INCL CHILE)
- AREA: 47,992 SQ KM (ISLA GRANDE)

Climate

Unrelenting winds sweep the relatively arid northern plains of Isla Grande, while high rainfall supports dense deciduous and evergreen forests in the mountainous southern half. The maritime climate is surprisingly mild, even in winter, but its unpredictability makes foul-weather gear essential year-round. The Cordillera Darwin and Sierra de Beauvoir mountains, reaching up to 2500m in the west, intercept Antarctic storms, leaving the plains around Río Grande much drier than the storm-battered bogs characteristic of the archipelago's remote southern and western zones.

National Parks

Isla Grande is home to Parque Nacional Tierra del Fuego (p535), Argentina's first shoreline national park.

Getting There & Around

The most common overland route from Patagonia is via the ferry crossing at Punta Delgada (p503). Unlike the rest of Argentina, Tierra del Fuego has no designated provincial highways, but has secondary roads known as *rutas complementarias*, modified by a lower-case letter. References to such roads in this chapter are given as 'RC-a,' for example.

If renting a car in mainland Argentina, be aware that you must cross in and out of Chile a couple of times to reach Tierra del Fuego, and that this requires special documents and additional international insurance coverage. Most rental agencies can arrange this paperwork if given advance notice.

Visitors can fly into Río Grande or Ushuaia. Buses take the ferry from Chile's Punta Delgada; all pass through Río Grande before arriving to Ushuaia.

PORVENIR (CHILE)

☎ 61 / pop 5465

'Nothing happens in Porvenir,' proclaimed one Chilean, 'but that's exactly the point!' If you want a slice of home-baked Fuegian life, this is it. Most visitors come on a quick daytrip from Punta Arenas that's often tainted by a touch of seasickness from the crossing. But spending a night in this rusted village of metal-clad Victorian houses affords you an opportunity to explore the nearby bays and countryside and absorb a little of local life.

Porvenir's heritage is rather peculiar. When gold was discovered in 1879, waves of immigrants arrived, many from Croatia, and most did not strike it rich. When sheep *estancias* began to spring up, the immigrants found more reliable work. Chilotes (from the Chilean island of Chiloé) appeared in droves for the fishing and *estancia* work, and the chance of a better life. Today's population is a unique combination of the two.

Information

Banco de Estado (cnr Philippi & Croacia) Has a 24-hour ATM.
Hospital (☎ 580034; Wood, btwn Señoret & Guerrero)
Post office (Philippi 176) Faces the verdant plaza.
Telefónica (Philippi 277) Next to the bank.
Tourist office (☎ 580094/8; Zavattaro 402; ☟ 9am-5pm Mon-Fri, 11am-5pm Sat & Sun) Information is also available at the handicrafts shop on the *costanera* (seaside road) between Philippi and Schythe.

Sights

On the plaza, the intriguing **Museo de Tierra del Fuego** (☎ 580094/8; Zavattaro 402; admission CH$500; ☟ 8am-5pm Mon-Thu, 8am-4pm Fri) has some unexpected materials, including Selk'nam skulls and mummies, musical instruments used by the mission Selk'nams on Isla Dawson and an exhibit on early Chilean cinematography.

Tours

Gold-panning, horseback-riding and 4WD tours can be arranged through the tourist office. Outfitter **Cordillera Darwin Expediciones** (☎ 580167, 09-888-6380; www.cordilleradarwin.com; Bahía Chilote s/n) organizes cool outings to view Peale's dolphins around Bahía Chilote in a traditional Chilote-style fishing boat (CH$15,000, including meals). Longer, well-recommended camping and horseback-riding trips include visits to Río Condor (three days/two nights CH$150,000), and an intense weeklong adventure that includes kayaking, *centolla-* (king crab) and fly-fishing, and riding to Glaciar Marinelli (groups of seven or more, November to May). Trips leave only with a minimum number of participants. The office is in front of the ferry landing in a restaurant; ask for the friendly Pechuga.

Sleeping & Eating

Residencial Colón (☎ 581157; Riobó 198; per person with shared bathroom CH$8000) Often filled with fisheries employees, this rickety pension offers the cheapest digs in town. Cheap meals can also be arranged.

TIERRA DEL FUEGO

TIERRA DEL FUEGO

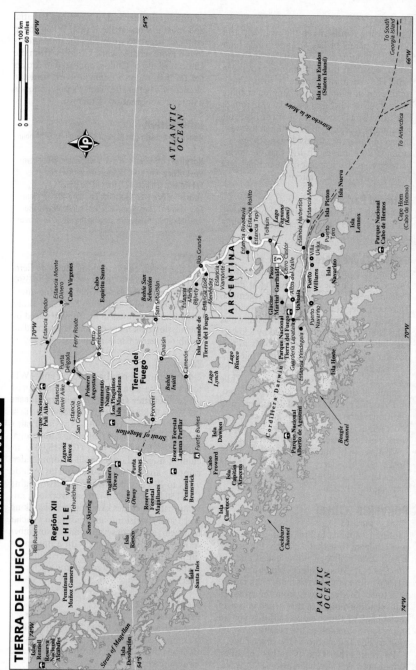

Hotel Central (☎ 580077; Philippi 298; s/d CH$12,000/20,000) Facing Hotel Rosas, this unassuming option brims with matronly charm on the inside. Snug rooms have hardwood floors and good beds. There is a comfortable sitting area as well.

Hotel Rosas (☎ 580088; hotelrosas@chile.com; Philippi 296; s/d CH$14,000/20,000) Eleven clean and pleasant rooms offer heat and cable TV. Alberto, the owner, knows heaps about the region and arranges tours to Circuito del Loro, a historical mining site. The restaurant (*plato del día* CH$3500) gets crowded for meals, serving fresh seafood and more.

Hotel España (☎ 580160; Croacia 698; s/d/tr CH$15,000/25,000/36,000) This ambling hotel has spacious, impeccably kept rooms with views of the bay. Rooms have Berber carpets, TV and central heating. There is a downstairs café and parking in the back.

La Chispa (☎ 580054; Señoret 202; plato del día CH$3000) In a century-old aquamarine firehouse, La Chispa packs with locals for salmon dinners, lamb and mashed potatoes, and other home-cooked fare. There are also several basic rooms (single/double CH$7000/12,000) upstairs, often filled with workers. It's a couple of blocks uphill from the water.

Club Croata (☎ 580053; Señoret 542; mains CH$2500-5000; ⏲ 11am-4pm & 7-10:30pm Tue-Sun) Formal to the verge of stuffy, this traditional restaurant nonetheless puts together good seafood meals at reasonable prices, in addition to Croat specialties like pork chops with *chucrut* (sauerkraut). The polished pub section stays open until 3am.

Getting There & Away
Aerovías DAP (☎ 580089; www.dap.cl; Señoret near Gamero) flies to Punta Arenas (CH$19,000, 15 minutes) Monday through Saturday from November to March, with fewer flights in the low season. For the airport, 6km north of town, DAP runs a door-to-door shuttle (CH$1500) and taxis charge CH$3000.

Transbordador Austral Broom (☎ 580089; www .tabsa.cl) operates the car/passenger ferry *Melinka* to/from Punta Arenas (CH$4300/28,000 per person/vehicle, 2½ to four hours). It usually leaves at 9am but has some afternoon departures: check the current online schedule. The bus to the ferry terminal (CH$500), 5km away, departs from the waterfront kiosk an hour before the ferry's departure.

The gravel road east, along Bahía Inútil to the Argentine border at San Sebastián, is in good shape. From San Sebastián (where there's gas and a motel), northbound motorists should avoid the heavily traveled and rutted truck route directly north and instead take the route from Onaisín to the petroleum company town of Cerro Sombrero, en route to the crossing of the Strait of Magellan at Punta Delgada–Puerto Espora.

RÍO GRANDE
☎ 02964 / pop 68,776
A monster trout sculpture at the entrance to town announces that you have come to the de facto fly-fishing capital of Tierra del Fuego, with some of the world's best blue-ribbon angling for colossal sea-run trout. Exclusive fly-in lodges on nearby *estancias* lure the likes of Hollywood heavy hitters and former US presidents with dreams of the big one. But if you didn't come with rod in hand, the longest that you will likely stay in windswept Río Grande is a few hours, before hopping on a bus to Ushuaia, 230km southwest.

Río Grande has always had a prominent role in Fuegian history. In 1886 the villainous gold seeker Julius Popper stumbled across the mouth of the Río Grande, home to Selk'nam (or Ona) people. As wool baron José Menéndez' sheep stations developed (see p523), it became a growing makeshift service town. In 1893 the Salesian order, under the guidance of Monseñor Fagnano, set up a mission in an unsuccessful attempt to shelter the Selk'nam from the growing infringement.

As a petroleum service center, Río Grande has an industrial feel: even the public art looks like giant, grim tinker toys. Duty-free status, meant to foster local development, has brought in electronics manufacturing plants and wholesale appliance stores. In the Falklands War the military played an important role here; many memorials around town pay tribute to fallen soldiers.

Information
Most visitor services are along Avs San Martín and Belgrano.

Banco de la Nación (cnr San Martín & 9 de Julio) Has an ATM; there are several others nearby.

Don Pepe (cnr 9 de Julio & Rosales; ⏲ 24hr) Supermarket with a burger grill, *locutorio* (telephone office) and internet access.

El Lavadero (Moreno 221) Laundry.

Farmacía Central (cnr San Martín & Piedrabuena; ☻ 24hr)

Instituto Fueguino de Turismo (Infuetur; ☎ 424326; www.tierradelfuego.org.ar; Espora 533; ☻ 9am-9pm) On the south side of the plaza.

Mariani Travel (☎ 426010; Rosales 281) Books flights and represents nearby *estancias*.

Municipal tourist kiosk (☎ 431324; rg-turismo@netcombbs.com.ar; ☻ 9am-8pm) Helpful kiosk on the plaza, with maps, *estancia* brochures and fishing details.

Post office (Rivadavia, btwn Moyano & Alberdi)

Thaler Cambio (☎ 421154; Rosales 259) Changes traveler's checks.

Sights

In a restored *galpón* (sheepshearing shed), the **Museo de la Ciudad** (☎ 430414; Alberdi 555; admission free; ☻ 9am-5pm Mon-Fri, 3-7pm Sat) has impressive exhibits, from logging to military displays, postal communications to cartography, indigenous artifacts to yet another milodón.

Ten kilometers north of town on RN 3, the 1893 Misión Salesiano houses the **Museo Histórico y Natural Monseñor Fagnano** (☎ 421642; adult/child AR$2/1; ☻ 9-11:30am & 3-6pm Tue-Fri, 4-6pm Sat & Sun, 3-6pm Mon), an ethnographic museum with geological and natural-history exhibits. The mission's work to protect the Selk'nam dissolved with their extinction. The mission then became an agrotechnical school, now considered the region's best. Visitors can buy fresh Salesian cheeses and produce may be purchased in the tearoom. Owing to the local soccer games on the grounds, there is usually *parrilla* (mixed grill including steak) on Sunday afternoon. Horseback rides may be available, and students (female students were not admitted until 1997) conduct informal tours of the greenhouses and dairy farms. To get here, take *colectivo* (local bus) Línea B, which runs downtown every hour from San Martín.

Sleeping

Catering to suits and anglers, lodging tends to be overpriced, not to mention sparse. There are a number of cheap but unsavory lodgings; those that are recommendable fill up fast. High-end places give discounts of 10% for cash payments.

Hostel Argentino (☎ 422546; www.interpatagonia.com; San Martín 64; dm AR$40, d with/without bathroom AR$110/80; ☐) Locals and travelers kick back in this friendly hostel hosted by the effervescent Graciela. Guests get hot showers, a shared kitchen, breakfast and luggage storage. A new wing contains small, neat doubles with twin beds and fresh paint. Long-distance cyclists even have a spot to store their bikes inside.

Hotel Isla del Mar (☎ 422883; isladelmar@arnet.com.ar; Güemes 963; s/d AR$150/170; ☐) This dilapidated flamingo-pink hotel facing the bay would do well with a makeover. The hallways smell of cigarettes and carpets are worn. Rooms are comparatively good, with the best options upstairs.

Hotel Ibarra (☎ 430071, 430883; www.federicoibarrahotel.com.ar in Spanish; Rosales 357; s/d/tr AR$163/198/230; ☐) Aimed at the business crowd, this hotel fronting the plaza has a cozy lobby with a gas-lit fireplace and carpeted, well-maintained rooms. Rooms without the plaza view are much quieter.

Hotel Villa (☎ 424998; hotelvillarg@hotmail.com, San Martín 281; d/tr AR$170/200; ☐) Opposite Casino Status, this newly refurbished place has a popular restaurant, a dozen spacious and stylish rooms outfitted with down duvets, and breakfast with *medialunas* (croissants).

Posada de los Sauces (☎ 432895; www.posadadelossauces.com.ar; Elcano 839; s/d/tr AR$195/235/290; ☐) Catering mostly to high-end anglers, this warm and professional hotel fosters a lodge atmosphere, with fresh scents and woodsy accents. Deluxe rooms have Jacuzzis. The upstairs bar-restaurant, decked out in dark wood and forest green, is just waiting for stogies and tall tales to fill the air.

Apart Hotel Keyuk'n (☎ 424435, 434073; www.keyukn.com.ar; Colón 630; d AR$200, 6-person apt AR$250) A great deal for groups, these spacious, two-floor apartments are fully equipped with kitchen, comfortable beds, living and dining room, and cable TV. Housekeeping service is included.

Eating & Drinking

Epa!!! (☎ 425334; Rosales 445; mains AR$6-21) Deep leather booths and a curved bar mark this popular café-bar that sparks up when soccer is on the tube. The set lunch is well priced and there's a laundry list of cocktails to tempt the evening crowd.

La Nueva Piamontesa (☎ 424366; Belgrano 601; mains AR$6-22; ☻ 24hr) This deli stocks home-cooked food: a selection of *parrilla*, pizza, pasta, sandwiches and dessert for take-out or in-store dining. In off-hours the food tends to wilt on the grill, so check out the cold case selection of meats and cheeses.

CONSULTING THE FUEGIAN TROUT ATLAS

You know a place takes fishing seriously when the tourism board posts a trout map online (www.tierradelfuego.org.ar/funcardio/trutamap.jpg). Hollywood stars, heads of state and former US presidents all flock to the desolate stretch of the island around Río Grande in search of the perfect day of angling. Usually they are in luck.

In 1933 pioneer John Goodall stocked the rivers around Río Grande with brown, rainbow and brook trout. Fish populated the rivers and, like the region's sheep stations, the sport-fishing industry took off. European brown trout ventured out to sea, returning to these rivers to spawn. Over the decades this back-and-forth migration has fostered one of the world's best sea-run trout-fishing areas, with some local specimens weighing in at 15kg. Rainbow trout from the western US are nearly as impressive, with individual fish reaching 9kg.

Fishing excursions are mostly organized through outside agents, many in the US. 'Public' fishing rivers, on which trips can be organized, include the Fuego, Menéndez, Candelaria, Ewan and MacLennan. Many of the more elite angling trips are lodged in *estancias*, which snatch exclusive use of some of the best rivers.

There are two types of license. License 1 is valid for fishing throughout the province, except in the national park. Contact **Asociación Caza y Pesca** (☎ 02901-423168; cazapescaush@infovia.com.ar; Maipú 822) in Ushuaia, or **Club de Pesca John Goodall** (☎ 02964-424324; Ricardo Rojas 606) in Río Grande. License 2 is valid for fishing in the national park and in Patagonia areas. Contact the **National Parks office** (☎ 02901-421315; San Martín 1395) in Ushuaia. Other useful information:

Flies Rubber legs and woolly buggers.
License fees AR$50 per day or AR$300 per season, depending on where you fish.
Limit One fish per person per day, catch and release.
Methods Spinning and fly casting; no night fishing.
Season November 1 to April 15, with catch-and-release restrictions from April 1 to April 15.

our pick La Nueva Colonial (☎ 425353; cnr Lasserre & Belgrano; mains AR$18-30) Enough reason to delay your departure, Cesar's outstanding pastas (we recommend the *sorrentinos* with pesto) are divine creations, served with fresh foccacia bread and a bottle of red. And if you don't like it, it's free (but a hard argument to make). He also does massive pepper steaks, salads and generous-sized desserts.

Ibarra Hotel (☎ 430071; Rosales 357; mains AR$25) Sunny and central, this bustling hotel *confitería* (café) is ideal for coffee or a light meal. Offerings range from rather dry sandwiches to raviolis and garlic chicken.

El Rincón de Julio (☎ 02964-15-604261; Elcano 805; all you can eat AR$35) Dive into this ambient wood shack with seven tables for the best *parrilla* in town. It's in front of the YPF service station.

Karma Café Bar (cnr Lasserre & Belgrano; drinks AR$6) Ideal for a *café con leche* (coffee with milk) or glass of wine, this elegant nook has just a few tables. It's located next to La Nueva Colonial.

Getting There & Away

The **airport** (RGA; ☎ 420699) is off RN 3, a short cab ride from town. **Aerolíneas Argentinas**

(☎ 424467; San Martín 607) flies direct daily to Buenos Aires (AR$568). **LADE** (☎ 422968; Lasserre 445) flies a couple of times weekly to Río Gallegos (AR$174), El Calafate (AR$280) and Buenos Aires.

At the time of writing there was no central bus terminal, but plans for one were in the works. **Tecni-Austral** (☎ 432885, 430610; Moyano 516) goes to Ushuaia (AR$25, four hours, daily) from 6am to 8pm, with a stop in Tolhuin (AR$20, 1½ hours); to Río Gallegos (AR$85, eight hours, daily); and to Punta Arenas (AR$85, eight hours) on Monday, Wednesday and Friday. **Buses Pacheco** (☎ 425611; 25 de Mayo 712) goes to Punta Arenas (AR$80, eight hours) several times a week.

A better option for Ushuaia (AR$40, four hours) and Tolhuin (AR$20, 1½ hours) is the door-to-door minivan service run by **Lider** (☎ 420003, 424-2000; Moreno 1056) and **Transportes Montiel** (☎ 427225; 25 de Mayo 712) several times daily. Call to reserve a seat; tickets must be paid for in person.

ESTANCIAS AROUND RÍO GRANDE

Much of Tierra del Fuego was once the sprawling backyard of wool baron José Menéndez.

TIERRA DEL FUEGO

His first *estancia* – La Primera Argentina (1897), now known as **Estancia José Menéndez**, 20km southwest of Río Grande via RN 3 and RC-b – covered 1600 sq km, with over 140,000 head of sheep. His second and most-treasured venture was La Segunda Argentina, totaling 1500 sq km. Later renamed **Estancia María Behety** (☎ 011-4331-5061 in Buenos Aires; www.maribety.com.ar in Spanish) after his wife, it's still a working ranch, 17km west of Río Grande via RC-c. Besides boasting the world's largest shearing shed, it is considered a highly exclusive (and pretentious) lodge, catering mainly to tour groups and elite anglers. Fishing lodge La Villa is a beautiful Magellanic home with lattice trim and luxuriant details. With only six bedrooms, it overlooks the Río Grande. Lodge María Behety is a newer, comfortable construction with less of the old-time allure.

Several area *estancias* have opened to small-scale tourism, offering a unique chance to learn about the area's history and enjoy its magic. Reserve as far in advance as possible.

The sons of early settler Thomas Bridges (see p537) established **Estancia Viamonte** (☎ 02964-430861, 02964-15-616813; www.estanciaviamonte .com; per person with breakfast & dinner AR$360, full board AR$750; ☷ Oct-Apr & by arrangement) in 1902 at the request of the Selk'nam, in part to protect the indigenous group. The *estancia* is alongside RN 3, 45km south of Río Grande, on the northern end of the Lucas Bridges Trail, which eventually leads to Harberton, near Ushuaia. The Goodalls, descendents of the Bridges, now run it as a working ranch, with 22,000 head of sheep on 400 sq km. The family tradition of hospitality continues with warm, unpretentious receptions and hearty meals. Guests stay in Lucas' original dwelling, the Sea View, a comfortable English-style home within earshot of the crashing waves. Guided activity possibilities include horseback riding, hiking and fly-fishing the Río Ewan. Advance reservations are greatly appreciated and highly recommended.

Croatian sheep ranch **Estancia Rivadavia** (☎ 02901-492186; www.estanciarivadavia.com; RC-h, Km 22; day tour/overnight package per person AR$330/690) has 100 sq km of valleys, lakes and mountains. Guests can participate in agrotourism as well as hikes to lakes and an adventure tour to the Río Claro. The ambience in the 1925 *casco* (ranch house) is intimate, with four well-appointed rooms and a comfortable living

area with fireplace. Notoriety found this remote stop when Paraguayan general Lino Oviedo sought political refuge in Argentina during a 1999 stay. It's 100km from Río Grande; take RN 3 to RC-h (formerly Ruta 18) until Km 22.

Founded by Tierra del Fuego's first rural doctor, the Basque-Provençal-style **Estancia Tepi** (☎ 02964-427245, 02964-15-504-2020; www.estancia tepi.com.ar in Spanish; RC-a, Km 5; day trip/B&B/full board per person AR$150/240/330; ☷ Dec-Mar) is a working, 100-sq-km ranch. Flowers surround the lodging, which is both rustic and elegant, with high-backed armchairs and sighing single beds. Horseback riding (AR$120) is offered for all levels, with traditional Patagonian mounts heaped with sheepskins. The property also boasts thermal baths, treks and tours. It's 80km from Río Grande and 150km from Ushuaia.

The rustic and charismatic **Estancia Rolito** (☎ 02901-437351, 02901-432419; www.tierradelfuego .org.ar/rolito in Spanish; RC-a, Km 14; per person with half/full board AR$188/251) is very Argentine and very inviting. Guests rave about the horseback-riding trips and hikes through ñire and lenga forest. There's a welcoming family ambience accompanied by meals of homemade bread, garden greens and heaping plates of Fuegian lamb. Day trips from Ushuaia (with Turismo de Campo) stop by for lunch or dinner and guided horseback riding. Rolito is 100km from Río Grande and 150km from Ushuaia.

TOLHUIN & LAGO FAGNANO
☎ 02901

Named for the Selk'nam word meaning 'like a heart,' Tolhuin (population 2000) is a lake town nestled in the center of Tierra del Fuego, 132km south of Río Grande and 104km northeast of Ushuaia via smooth pavement. This fast-growing frontier town of small plazas and sheltering evergreens fronts the eastern shore of Lago Fagnano, also known as Lago Kami. Most travelers tend to skip right over it, but if you are looking for a unique and tranquil spot, Tolhuin is well worth checking out.

Shared with Chile, the glacial-formed Lago Fagnano offers 117km of beach, with most of its shoreline remote and roadless. Plans to put a catamaran here are developing; look for this new cruising option, which might be combined with trekking on the far side of the lake. Otherwise, there is boating and fishing.

FUEGIAN RITES OF PASSAGE

Part of traveling to Tierra del Fuego is searching for clues to its mystical, unknowable past. Souvenir shops sell a postcard of abstract intrigue: there's a naked man painted black. Fine horizontal white stripes cross his body from chest to foot. His face remains covered, hidden. So, what's this all about?

For people who lived exposed to the elements, dependent on their wits and courage, initiation ceremonies were a big deal. Those of the seafaring Yaghan (or Yamaná) were surprisingly similar to those of the fierce northern neighbors they wanted little to do with, the nomadic hunters called Selk'nam (or Ona to the Yaghan). Both celebrated a male rite of passage that reenacted a great upheaval when the men stole the women's secrets to gain power over them. In the Kina, Yaghan men interpreted the spirits by painting their bodies with black carbon and striped or dotted patterns that used the region's white and red clays. The Selk'nam undertook their Hain ceremony similarly adorned, taking young men into huts where they were attacked by spirits. In related ceremonies men showed their strength to women by fighting the spirits in theatrical displays, each acting with the characteristics of a specific spirit. These manly displays did not always achieve their desired effect of subjugation: one account tells of spirits dispatched to menace female camps that instead evoked hilarity.

With European encroachment, these ceremonies became more abbreviated and much of their detailed significance was lost. When the last Hain was celebrated in the early 20th century in the presence of missionaries, it had already crossed the line from ritual to theatre.

Tolhuin's nascent **tourist office** (☎ 492380, 492125; www.tierradelfuego.org.ar/tolhuin; Av de los Shelknam 80), behind the gas station, has information on local tours and rentals. Those coming from Ushuaia might get more complete information from Ushuaia's tourist office (p527). **Banco Tierra del Fuego** (Calle s/n) has an ATM.

Sleeping & Eating

Camping Hain (☎ 02901-15-603606; www.campinghain .com.ar; Lago Fagnano; camping per person AR$10, 8-person refugios AR$130) Located on Lago Fagnano, this excellent campground offers grassy sites sheltered with wooden windbreaks, a huge barbecue pit and a *fogon* (sheltered firepit and kitchen area). There are bathrooms and showers with hot water. Roberto, the conscientious owner, can recommend local excursions and guides.

La Posada de los Ramirez (☎ 02901-492382/492110; Av de los Shelknam 411, Tolhuin; dm AR$45, 4-person cabin AR$150; ☐) This welcoming family lodging sits in the center of town. The family's onsite restaurant (mains AR$30) serves pasta, local trout and meat dishes.

Hostería Kaikén (☎ 492372; www.hosteriakaiken .com.ar; Lago Fagnano, Km 2942; d AR$235-290, 2-person cabin AR$175; ☐) This gorgeous lakeside inn is both refined and rustic, with beautiful colonial furniture, neutral tones and snug down bedcov-

ers. There's a stylish bar with panoramas of the lake and a dining room serving high-end cuisine. The cabins (without kitchens) are simpler but provide an extra dose of privacy.

Panadería La Unión (☎ 492202; www.panaderiala union.com.ar in Spanish; Jeujepen 450, Tolhuin; snacks AR$3; ☽ 24hr) First-rate *facturas* (pastries) and second-rate Nescafé cappuccinos keep this roadside attraction hopping. You may or may not recognize the Argentine celebrities gracing the walls (hint: the men are ageing rock stars, the women surgically enhanced). Buses break here to pick up passengers and hot water for *mate* (a tealike beverage). There are also public phones, internet access and newsstand fodder.

Within walking distance of the *panadería* are Capricho Bar and Pizza, restaurant La Amistad, and a *parrilla* (steak restaurant) firing up loads of lamb.

Getting There & Away

Throughout the day, buses and minivans passing along RN 3 (often full in high season) all stop at the *panadería* en route to Ushuaia or Río Grande (AR$20).

USHUAIA

☎ 02901 / pop 58,000

A busy port and adventure hub, Ushuaia is a sliver of steep streets and jumbled buildings set between the Beagle Channel and the snowcapped Martial Range. It's a location matched by few, and chest-beating Ushuaia takes full advantage of its end-of-the-world status as an increasing number of Antarctica-bound vessels call in to port. Its endless mercantile hustle knows no irony: the souvenir shop named for Jeremy Button (a native kidnapped for show in England), the ski center

named for a destructive invasive species... you get the idea. That said, with a pint of the world's southernmost microbrew in hand, you can happily plot the dazzling outdoor options: hiking, sailing, skiing, kayaking and even scuba diving are just minutes from town.

In 1870 the British-based South American Missionary Society set its sights on the Yaghan,

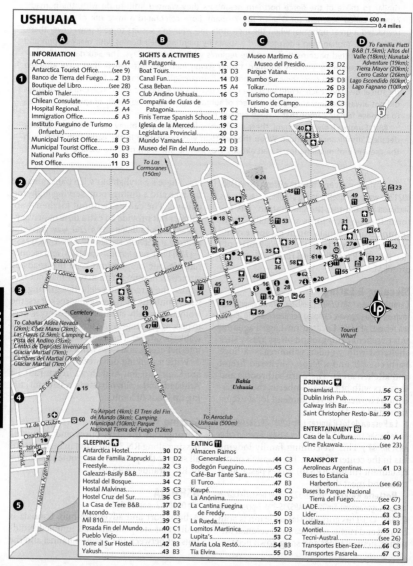

USHUAIA

0 _____ 600 m
0 _____ 0.4 miles

To Familia Piatti B&B (1.5km); Altos del Valle (18km); Nunatak Adventure (19km); Tierra Mayor (20km); Cerro Castor (26km); Lago Escondido (60km); Lago Fagnano (100km)

To Los Cormoranes (150m)

Beauvoir

Cemetery

To Cabañas Aldea Nevada (2km); Chez Manu (2km); Las Hayas (2.5km); Camping La Pista del Andino (3km); Centro de Deportes Invernales Glaciar Martial (7km); Cumbres del Martial (7km); Glaciar Martial (7km)

To Airport (4km); El Tren del Fin de Mundo (8km); Camping Municipal (10km); Parque Nacional Tierra del Fuego (12km)

To Aeroclub Ushuaia (500m)

Bahía Ushuaia

Tourist Wharf

TIERRA DEL FUEGO

a people whom Charles Darwin had deemed 'the lowest form of humanity on earth.' The mission made Ushuaia its first permanent Fuegian outpost, but the Yaghan, who had survived 6000 years without contact, were vulnerable to foreign-brought illnesses and faced increasing infringement by sealers, settlers and gold prospectors. These days, the legacy of Ushuaia's original inhabitants has been reduced to shell mounds, Thomas Bridges' famous dictionary of the Yaghan language and the Jeremy Button souvenir shop.

Between 1884 and 1947 Argentina imitated Britain's example with Australia and made the city a penal colony, incarcerating many of its most notorious criminals and political prisoners here and on remote Isla de los Estados (Staten Island). In 1906 the military prison was moved to Ushuaia, and in 1911 it was combined with the Carcel de Reincidentes, which had incarcerated civilian recidivists since 1896. Since 1950 the town has been an important naval base.

Tierra del Fuego's comparatively high wages draw Argentines from all over to resettle here, and some locals lament the loss of the small-town culture that existed until recently. Meanwhile, expansion means a jumble of housing developments advancing in the few directions the mad geography allows.

Orientation

Paralleling the Beagle Channel, Maipú becomes Malvinas Argentinas west of the cemetery, then turns into RN 3, continuing 12km to Parque Nacional Tierra del Fuego. To the east, public access ends at Yaganes, which heads north to meet RN 3 going north toward Lago Fagnano. Most visitor services are on or within a couple blocks of San Martín, a block inland from the waterfront.

Information

BOOKSTORES

Boutique del Libro (☎ 432117; 25 de Mayo 62) Comprehensive, multilingual selection of literature, guidebooks and pictorials.

IMMIGRATION

Immigration office (☎ 422334; Beauvoir 1536; ☒ 9am-noon Mon-Fri)

MEDICAL SERVICES

Hospital Regional (☎ 107, 423200; cnr Maipú & 12 de Octubre)

MONEY

Several banks on Maipú and San Martín have ATMs.

Banco de Tierra del Fuego (San Martín 396) Best rates for traveler's checks.

Cambio Thaler (San Martín 778; ☒ 10am-1pm & 5-8pm Mon-Sat, 5-8pm Sun) Convenience equals slightly poorer exchange rates.

POST

Post office (cnr San Martín & Godoy)

TELEPHONE & INTERNET ACCESS

Internet access (around AR$3 per hour) is available at call centers along San Martín.

TOURIST INFORMATION

ACA (☎ 421121; cnr Malvinas Argentinas & Onachaga) Argentina's auto club; good source for provincial road maps.

Instituto Fueguino de Turismo (Infuetur; ☎ 421423; www.tierradelfuego.org.ar; Maipú 505) On ground floor of Hotel Albatros.

Municipal tourist office (☎ 432000, at airport 423 970, outside of Tierra del Fuego 0800-333-1476; www.e -ushuaia.com in Spanish; San Martín 674) Very helpful, with English- and French-speaking staff, a message board and multilingual brochures, as well as good lodging, activities and transport info. Also at the airport and pier.

National Parks office (Administración de Parques Nacionales; ☎ 421315; San Martín 1395; ☒ 9am-4pm Mon-Fri)

Sights

MUSEO MARÍTIMO & MUSEO DEL PRESIDIO

When convicts were moved from Isla de los Estados (Staten Island) to Ushuaia in 1906, they began building the national prison, which was finished in 1920. The spokelike halls of single cells were designed to house 380, but in the prison's most active period held up to 800. It closed as a jail in 1947 and now houses the **Museo Marítimo & Museo del Presidio** (☎ 437481; www.ushuaia.org; cnr Yaganes & Gobernador Paz; adult/student AR$35/20; ☒ 9am-8pm). It's a fine port of call on a blustery day. Halls showing penal life are intriguing, but mainly because of the informative plaques, which are only in Spanish. Two of the more illustrious inmates were author Ricardo Rojasand and Russian anarchist Simón Radowitzky.

On the upper floor of one hall is a display on Antarctic exploration. Perhaps the most worthwhile part of the museum is the exhibit containing incredibly detailed scale models of famous ships, spanning 500 years and providing a unique glimpse into the region's history.

Informative pamphlets in English about this exhibit are available at reception. In the courtyard are the remains of the world's narrowest-gauge freight train, which transported prisoners between town and work stations.

MUNDO YAMANÁ

More an experience than a museum, the modest **Mundo Yamaná** (☎ 422874; Rivadavia 56; adult/child AR$8/5; ☿ 10am-8pm) explores Fuegians' attempts to bring the Yamaná (Yaghan) culture to life. Some of the expertly detailed dioramas (details in English and Spanish) are based on accessible bays and inlets of the national park; coming here before hiking in the park will give you new bearings.

MUSEO DEL FIN DEL MUNDO

Built in 1903 for the territorial governor Manuel Fernández Valdés, this building was a branch of the Banco de la Nación up until 1978, when it was transformed into the **Museo del Fin del Mundo** (☎ 421863; cnr Maipú & Rivadavia; admission AR$10; ☿ 9am-8pm). Exhibits on Fuegian natural history, stuffed birdlife, aboriginal life and the early penal colonies, and replicas of an early general store and bank, are of moderate interest.

PARQUE YATANA

Part art project, part urban refuge, **Parque Yatana** (Fundación Cultiva; ☎ 425212; cnr Magallanes & 25 de Mayo; admission free; ☿ 2:30-8pm Tue-Sat) is a city block of lenga forest preserved from the encroaching development by one determined family. After checking in, guests can walk the forest paths dotted with small benches. Signs with reflections on forests are well done.

HISTORIC BUILDINGS

The tourist office distributes a free city-tour map with information on many of the historic houses around town. The 1894 **Legislatura Provincial** (Provincial Legislature; Maipú 465) was the governor's official residence. The century-old **Iglesia de la Merced** (San Martín & Don Bosco) was built with convict labor. **Casa Beban** (cnr Maipú & Pluschow; admission free; ☿ 10am-8pm Mon-Fri, 4-8pm Sat & Sun) was built in 1911 using parts ordered from Sweden, and sometimes hosts local art exhibits.

Activities
HIKING & CANOPY TOURS

Hiking possibilities should not be limited to Parque Nacional Tierra del Fuego; the entire mountain range behind Ushuaia, with its lakes and rivers, is a hiker's high. However, many trails are poorly marked or not marked at all, and some hikers who have easily scurried uphill have gotten lost trying to find the trail back down.

Club Andino Ushuaia (☎ 422335; Juana Fadul 50; ☿ 10am-12:30pm & 2-9:30pm Mon-Fri, 10am-2pm Sat) sells a map and bilingual trekking, mountaineering and mountain-biking guidebook with rough maps and plenty of trail descriptions. The club occasionally organizes hikes and can recommend hiking guides. Unguided trekkers are strongly encouraged to register with the club or the tourist office before heading out – and check in after a safe return. In an emergency, contact the **Civil Guard** (☎ 103, 22108).

Compañía de Guías de Patagonia (☎ 437753, 02901-15-618426; www.companiadeguias.com.ar; Campos 795) organizes treks and is often recommended as a reliable information source.

Cerro Martial & Glaciar Martial

A hearty hike from downtown leads up to Glaciar Martial, with fantastic panoramas of Ushuaia and the Beagle Channel; in fact, the views are possibly more impressive than the actual glacier. Catch a taxi up the hill for under AR$20 or jump aboard a one of the minivans that leave from the corner of Maipú and Juana Fadul every half-hour from 8:30am to 6:30pm (AR$15 round-trip) to Cerro Martial. Or if you're up for an all-day hike, follow San Martín west and keep ascending as it zigzags (there are many hiker shortcuts) to the ski run 7km northwest of town. At this point either take the **aerosilla** (AR$20; ☿ 10am-4pm) chairlift or walk another two hours to make a full day of it. The cozy **Refugio de Montaña** (snacks AR$7) offers coffee, desserts and beer at the *aerosilla* base. The weather is changeable so take warm, dry clothing and sturdy footwear.

A recent addition, **canopy tours** (escuela@iterra delfuego.org.ar; Refugio de Montaña; AR$80; ☿ 10am-5:30pm Oct-Jun) run from the base of the *aerosilla* and offer an hour's worth of Tarzan time, zipping through the forest with 11 zipline cables and two hanging bridges. The highest cable is 8m.

BOATING

Navigating the Beagle Channel's gunmetal waters, with glaciers and rocky isles in the distance, offers a fresh perspective and decent wildlife watching. On the wharf a string of operators hawk similar offerings: four-hour morning or afternoon excursions (AR$95 to AR$120) that visit the sea-lion colony at Isla de los Lobos and the extensive cormorant colonies at Isla de Pájaros. An alternative tour takes hikers to the Parque Nacional Tierra del Fuego; they return via private transfer after hiking. Quality may vary: ask about the number of passengers, whether food is served and which sights are visited. A highlight is an island stop to hike and look at *conchales,* shell mounds left by the native Yaghan. The tourist wharf is on Maipú between Lasserre and Roca.

Patagonia Adventure Explorer (☎ 02901-15-465842; www.patagoniaadvent.com.ar; tourist wharf) has comfortable boats with snacks and a short hike on Isla Bridges. For extra adventure, set sail in the 18ft sailboat. Full-day sails with wine and gourmet snacks or multiday trips are also available.

Resembling a bathtub toy, the sturdy but small vessel of **Tres Marías Excursiones** (☎ 421897; www.tresmariasweb.com; tourist wharf) takes a maximum of eight passengers. It's the only outfitter with permission to land on Isla 'H' in the Isla Bridges natural reserve, which has shell mounds and a rock-cormorant colony.

Alternatively, try a more expensive catamaran trip or the historic 70-passenger **Barracuda** (☎ 437606), which chugs to the Faro Les Eclaireurs lighthouse and Isla de los Lobos and Isla de los Pájaros (AR$115, three hours).

KAYAKING

Professional guide **Daniel Urriza** (☎ 433613, 02901-15-618777; danyurriza@hotmail.com; day trip per person AR$450) has plenty of experience; rounding Cape Horn in a kayak might be the most noteworthy. Excursions can be tailor made, but expect to explore the channel and see penguins and sea lions or to head to Lago Escondido. Kayaking is also a component of many tours to Parque Nacional Tierra del Fuego; see the Nunatak Adventure and Canal Fun listings under Tours (right).

DOGSLEDDING

Wrap yourself in thermal layers and put Fido in the driver's seat. Outfitter **Nunatek Adventure** (☎ 437454; www.nunatakadventure.com; RN 3, Km 3018; guided ride AR$50) at Tierra Mayor takes dogsleds bumping across the valley floor on 2km and 6km rides. Your speed depends on the dogs (Siberian and Alaskan huskies) and conditions: heavy snow means a mild ride

while gliding over packed snow feels a little like levitation.

Ski area **Altos del Valle** (☎ 02901-15-616383; www.gatocuruchet.com.ar) teaches sledding and is the primary sponsor of popular annual dogsled races at the end of August, where kids also compete. Owner Gato Curuchet was the first South American to participate in Alaska's Iditarod race.

SKIING

With the surrounding peaks loaded with powder, winter visitors should jump at the chance to explore the local ski resorts. Accessed from RN 3, resorts offer both downhill and crosscountry options. The ski season runs from June through to September, with July (during schools' winter vacation) the busiest month. Ushuaia's biggest ski event is the annual **Marcha Blanca**, a symbolic re-creation of San Martín's historic August 17, 1817 crossing of the Andes.

The largest resort is **Cerro Castor** (☎ 02901-15-605604/6; www.cerrocastor.com in Spanish; full-day lift ticket adult/child AR$110/75), 26km from Ushuaia, with 15 runs spanning 400 hectares. Rentals are available for skis, boards, blades and crosscountry skis. There's a good restaurant at the base and a summit lodge conducive to afternoon coffee breaks.

The closest ski area to Ushuaia, **Altos del Valle** (☎ 02901-15-616383; www.gatocuruchet.com.ar) has good cross-country and snowshoeing areas, equipment rentals and full-moon trips. Extreme skiers can check out the snowcat skiing.

For a quick run near town, Club Andino Ushuaia (opposite) runs cross-country and downhill slopes only 3km and 5km away. The family-oriented **Centro de Deportes Invernales Glaciar Martial** (☎ 421423, 423340), 7km northwest of town, has downhill runs well suited for beginners; it also rents equipment.

Transportes Pasarela and Buses Alvarez run hourly shuttles (AR$25) from the corner of Juana Fadul and Maipú to the ski centers along RN 3, from 9am to 2pm daily. Each resort also provides its own transportation from downtown Ushuaia.

Tours

Many travel agencies sell tours around the region. You can go horseback riding, visit Lagos Escondido and Fagnano, stay at an *estancia,* spy on birds and beavers, and even get pulled by husky-dog sleds (winter only).

TIERRA DEL FUEGO

ANTARCTICA: THE ICE

For many travelers, a journey to Antarctica represents a once-in-a-lifetime adventure. Despite its high price tag, it is much more than just a continent to tick off your list. You will witness both land and ice shelves piled with hundreds of meters of undulating, untouched snow. Glaciers drop from mountainsides and icebergs form sculptures as tall as buildings. The wildlife is thrilling: you will see thousands of curious penguins and an extraordinary variety of flying birds, seals and whales.

Tourism to the icy land of Antarctica is red hot and growing fast. In 2007 around 33,000 tourists cruised the ice from Ushuaia – a stunning contrast to the continent's population of 5000 (summer) or 1200 (winter) scientists and staff. But travel here is not without its costs. On November 23, 2007, the MS *Explorer* was holed by ice but evacuated successfully before sinking. The circumstances were highly unusual, although the incident will likely provoke more safety measures. We can only hope that careful management will assure that this glorious continent remains intact.

So long as you've got two or three weeks to spare, hopping on board a cruise ship is not out of the question. Some voyages take in the Falkland Islands and South Georgia (human population 10 to 20, estimated penguin population two to three million!); some go just to the Antarctic Peninsula; others focus on retracing historic expeditions. A small but growing handful of visitors reach Antarctica aboard private vessels. All are sailboats (although obviously equipped with auxiliary engines).

The season runs from mid-October to mid-March, depending on ice conditions. It used to be that peak-season voyages sold out; now most trips do. When shopping around, ask how many days you will actually spend in Antarctica, as crossing the Southern Ocean takes up to two days each way. And how many landings will there be? The smaller the ship, the more landings there are per passenger (always depending on the weather, of course). Tour companies charge anywhere from US$7000 to US$70,000, although some ships allow walk-ons, which can cost as little as US$5000.

Due to Ushuaia's proximity to the Antarctic Peninsula, most cruises leave from here. Last-minute bookings can be made through **Ushuaia Turismo** (☎ 436003; ushuaiaturismo@speedy.com.ar; Gobernador Paz 865). Other travel agencies offering packages include **Rumbo Sur** (☎ 422275; www.rumbosur .com.ar; San Martín 350), **All Patagonia** (☎ 433622; www.allpatagonia.com; Juana Fadul 60) and **Canal Fun** (☎ 437395; www.canalfun.com; Rivadavia 82), though there are many more.

Check that your company is a member of **IAATO** (www.iaato.org), which mandates strict guidelines for responsible travel to Antarctica. The following are just a few companies that go to Antarctica.

Adventure Associates (www.adventureassociates.com) Australia's first tour company to Antarctica, with many ships and destinations.

Clipper Cruise Line (www.clippercruise.com) Longer voyages on a 122-passenger ship that include the Falklands and South Georgia Islands.

Heritage Expeditions (www.heritage-expeditions.com) Award-winning New Zealand company that also goes to the Ross Sea/East Antarctica regions.

Peregrine Adventures (www.peregrineadventures.com) Offers unique trips that include visiting the Antarctic Circle, with kayaking and camping options.

Quark Expeditions (www.quarkexpeditions.com) Three kinds of ships, from an icebreaker to a 48-passenger small ship for close-knit groups.

WildWings Travel (www.wildwings.co.uk) UK-based company that focuses on birding and wildlife in Antarctica.

For more information see Lonely Planet's *Antarctica* guidebook. Online, check out www.70south .com for up-to-date information and articles. In Ushuaia, consult the very helpful **Antarctica tourist office** (☎ 421423; infoantartida@tierradelfuego.org.ar) at the pier. And one last thing: bring more film and/or extra memory cards than you think you'll need. You'll thank us later.

All Patagonia (☎ 433622; www.allpatagonia.com; Juana Fadul 60) Amex rep offering more conventional and luxurious trips.

Canal Fun (☎ 437395; www.canalfun.com; Rivadavia 82) Run by hip young guys, these popular all-day outings include hiking and kayaking in Parque Nacional Tierra del Fuego (AR$220), off-roading around Lago Fagnano (AR$280), and a multisport outing around Estancia Harberton that includes kayaking and a visit to the penguin colony (AR$390).

Compañía de Guías de Patagonia (☎ 437753, 02901-15-618426; www.companiadeguias.com.ar; Campos 795) Organizes full-day treks with climbing and ice-hiking on Glaciar Vinciguerra (AR$175), and two-day high-mountain treks to Cerro Alvear with glacier camping (AR$520).

Nunatak Adventure (☎ 430329; www.nunatak adventure.com) Offers competitively priced adventure tours and has its own mountain base.

Rumbo Sur (☎ 422275; www.rumbosur.com.ar; San Martín 350) Ushuaia's longest-running agency specializes in more conventional activities.

Tolkar (☎ 431408/12; www.tolkarturismo.com.ar; Roca 157) Another helpful, popular, all-round agency, affiliated with Tecni-Austral buses.

Turismo Comapa (☎ 430727; www.comapa.com; San Martín 245) Confirm Navimag and Cruceros Australis passages here.

Turismo de Campo (☎ 437451; www.turismo decampo.com in Spanish; 25 de Mayo 64) Organizes light trekking, Beagle Channel sailing trips and visits to Estancia Rolito near Río Grande. Also sells a wide variety of nine- to 12-night Antarctica passages.

Ushuaia Turismo (☎ 436003; ushuaiaturismo@speedy .com.ar; Gobernador Paz 865) Offers last-minute Antarctica cruise bookings.

Courses

Study Spanish at **Finis Terrae Spanish School** (☎ 433871; www.spanishpatagonia.com; cnr Triunvirato & Magallanes; 1 week lodging & 20 hours of classes AR$1177). Courses last from one to six weeks and private classes are available as well. The school can also arrange homestays.

Sleeping

Lodging is scarce in the January and February high season and during early March's Fin del Mundo Marathon. During these periods, reserving ahead is essential. Most lodgings offer free transfers in; check when you reserve. In winter those places that stay open drop their rates a bit. Most hotels offer laundry service.

The municipal tourist office (p527) has lists of B&Bs and *cabañas*, and also posts a list of available lodgings outside after closing time.

BUDGET

Hostels abound, all with kitchens and most with internet access. Rates typically drop 25% in the low season (April to October).

Camping Municipal (RN 3) Ten kilometers west of town, en route to Parque Nacional Tierra del Fuego, this free campground boasts a lovely setting but minimal facilities.

Camping La Pista del Andino (☎ 435890; www .lapistadelandino.com.ar in Spanish; Alem 2873; per person AR$15; ⊙ Oct-Apr) A steep, uphill, 3km trek leads to this pleasant campground offering grassy or forested sites with views. While it's short on showers and toilets, perks include decent cooking facilities, a bar-restaurant, good common areas and bikes for rent (AR$25). It's at Club Andino Ushuaia's ski area. Call for free pickup from the airport or town center. Bus C to the center costs AR$1.25.

Torre al Sur Hostel (☎ 430745; www.torrealsur.com.ar; Gobernador Paz 1437; dm HI member/nonmember AR$27/29; ▣) Perched on a hilltop, this tower with gingerbread trim is ideal for eating in – see the large kitchen with stainless-steel countertops. Don't expect privacy: the small, mazelike dorm rooms can be noisy. Its crowning glory is the tower room with grand vistas.

Los Cormoranes (☎ 423459; www.loscormoranes.com; Kamshen 788; dm/d/tr AR$35/150/160; ▣) Mellower than the competition, this friendly HI hostel is a 10-minute (uphill) walk north of the center. Good, warm, six-bed dorms face outdoor plank hallways – making that midnight bathroom dash a bear. Modern doubles have polished cement floors and bright down duvets – the best is Room 10, with bay views. The abundant breakfast includes toast, coffee, do-it-yourself eggs and fresh-squeezed orange juice. Rates include an hour of internet, and free airport/town pickup.

Yakush (☎ 435807; www.hostelyakush.com.ar; Piedrabuena 118; dm/d AR$35/150) Exuding warmth and skillfully adorned with whimsical drawings, this colorful hostel is well kept and exceedingly friendly. It's a prime choice: dorms have fresh sheets and good beds, and social spaces include an ample upstairs lounge with futons and slanted ceilings. Breakfast includes *medialunas*, coffee and *mate*, with leftovers left out for nibbling.

Hostel Cruz del Sur (☎ 423110; www.xdelsur.com .ar; Deloquí 636; dm AR$35; ▣) Cramped but cozy, this popular hostel lines its walls with old postcards and primary hues. The four- to six-bed dorms (with heaters, thin mattresses

TIERRA DEL FUEGO

and bedding) can get loud, and when filled to capacity the bathrooms are taxed to the max. But the welcoming hosts do a fine job of rounding up groups to explore nearby areas. Kitchens are well stocked, there's a pleasant library and hot drinks are always available. Some rooms have a view.

Antarctica Hostel (☎ 435774; www.antarcticahostel .com; Antártida Argentina 270; dm/d/tr AR$40/150/180; ▢) An open floor plan and beer on tap make this trendy backpacker hub conducive to making friends. Guests play cards in the common room and cook in a cool balcony kitchen. The cement rooms are the biggest drawback; though ample in size, some smell of insecticide. Doubles share bathrooms but there are plenty of showers (check the fluctuating temperature before climbing in).

Freestyle (☎ 432874; www.ushuaiafreestyle.com; Gobernador Paz 866; dm/d/apt AR$40/180/220; ▢) This five-star hostel boasts immaculate dorms with cozy fleece blankets, a marble-countertop cooking area, and a sprawling, sunny living room with leatherette sofas and gaping panoramic views. Backpacker-owner Emilio strives to keep travelers content, and why shouldn't they be? If it's howling outside, cue up a billiards game or lounge in a comfy beanbag chair. Doubles are a bit cramped and darker.

MIDRANGE

La Casa de Tere B&B (☎ 422312, 435913; www.lacasa detere.com.ar; Rivadavia 620; d with/without bathroom AR$150/120) Tere showers her guests with attention in this beautiful modern home with great views. Its three tidy rooms fill up fast. Guests can cook, and there's cable TV and a fireplace in the living room. It's a short but steep walk uphill from the center.

Galeazzi-Basily B&B (☎ 423213; www.avesdelsur .com.ar; Valdéz 323; tw AR$120, 5-person cabin AR$180; ▢) The best feature of this elegant wooded residence is its warm and hospitable family. Rooms are small but offer a personal touch; some share a bathroom. Since beds are twin-sized, couples may prefer one of the modern cabins out back. It's a peaceful spot, and where else can you practice your English, French, Italian and Portuguese? Book ahead.

Pueblo Viejo (☎ 432098; www.puebloviejo.info; Deloquí 242; d with shared bathroom AR$150; ▢) A great value, this snug and relaxed eight-room lodging is actually two renovated houses (1920 and 1926) now joined by a passageway. Tasteful

rooms have firm mattresses and central heating. Manager Freddy gives guests the local lowdown. Cars can also be rented here; guests get discount rates.

Familia Piatti B&B (☎ 437104, 02901-15-613485; www .interpatagonia.com/familiapiatti in Spanish; Bahía Paraíso 812, Bosque del Faldeo; s/d/tr AR$155/215/275; ▢) If idling in the forest sounds good, head for this friendly B&B with warm down duvets and native lenga-wood furniture. Hiking trails nearby lead up the mountains. The friendly owners are multilingual (English, Italian and Portuguese) and can arrange transport and guided excursions. Extras include massage and babysitting service.

Hostal Malvinas (☎ 422626; www.hostalmalvinas .net; Deloquí 615; s/d/tr AR$160/190/220) A good value but nothing 'wow,' Malvinas offers standard hotel amenities at OK prices and happens to be central. The staff is hospitable and rooms are well kept – some have excellent harbor views. Clunky gas heaters, worn carpets and dated decor are the shortcomings. But you can enjoy hot drinks and pastries, available all day in the breakfast nook.

Casa de Familia Zaprucki (☎ 421316; Deloquí 271; 2-person apt AR$180; ✗) Well-crafted and tenderly cared for, these garden apartments surrounded by zinnias and rose bushes are a delightful find. Guests get a warm reception. Kitchens are well equipped and cabin apartments have nice wood details and area rugs.

TOP END

Posada Fin del Mundo (☎ 434847, 437345; www .posadafindelmundo.com.ar; cnr Rivadavia & Valdéz; d/tr AR$210/300) A welcoming and well-traveled couple welcome guests into this lovely home. The enchantment starts with a snuggly living room with expansive water views. Eight fresh, tiled rooms tend toward the small side but beds are long. A big breakfast includes eggs, oatmeal, fruit and yogurt. It's on a quiet street, a good four-block walk uphill out of town.

Cabañas Aldea Nevada (☎ 422851/68; www.aldea nevada.com.ar; Martial 1430; d AR$250, 3-night minimum; ▢) You expect the elves to arrive here any minute. This beautiful patch of lenga forest is discreetly dotted with 13 log cabins with outdoor grills and rough-hewn benches contemplatively placed by the ponds. Interiors are rustic but modern, with functional kitchens, wood stoves to fire up and hardwood details. Guests can use wi-fi in the reception area.

Macondo (☎ 437576; www.macondohouse.com; Gobernador Paz 1410; tr AR$280) This sleek red house offers up a soothing refuge with dazzling views of the bay. Paper lanterns, geometric furniture and abstract art create a minimalist feel. Rooms have vaulted ceilings, king-sized beds with down duvets and TV.

Hostal del Bosque (☎ 430777; www.hostaldel bosque.com.ar; Magallanes 709; 2-/3-person apt AR$377/471; ✗ ⌨) These tasteful, upscale apartments surrounded by pine trees have kitchenettes, tables and sofas in muted earth tones. The hillside location affords views but non-Argentines are charged steeper rates.

Mil 810 (☎ 437710; www.hotel1810.com; 25 de Mayo 245; d/tr AR$550/620; ⌨) This sleek boutique hotel plays with nature and modern style. It's not subtle: guests are first welcomed by a retention wall of river stones and a rock face trickling with water. Its 38 rooms feature brocade walls, rich tones, luxuriant textures and touches of abstract art. Rooms have flat-screen TVs and safes, and halls are monitored. If you didn't know, 1810 celebrates Argentina's independence, but in this case it seems to be also celebrating the freedom to luxuriate.

ourpick Cumbres del Martial (☎ 424779; www .cumbresdelmartial.com.ar in Spanish; Martial, Km 5; r/ste AR$550/848; ⌨) A getaway that you may never want to leave, this stylish place sits at the base of the Glaciar Martial. Standard rooms have a touch of the English cottage, while the two-story wooden cabins are simply stunners, with stone fireplaces, Jacuzzis and dazzling vaulted windows. Lush robes, optional massages (extra) and your country's newspaper delivered to your mailbox are some of the delicious details. To top it all off, the breakfast treats are homemade.

Las Hayas (☎ 430710/8; www.lashayas.com.ar; Martial 1650; d AR$863, ste AR$1105-1633; ⌨ 🐾) Serving the likes of Nelson Mandela and Mercosur presidents, Ushuaia's only five-star resort is dramatically perched 3km above town. Its elegant, traditional rooms have fine monochrome patterns, some canopy beds and great bay views. If you can swing the upgrade, suites offer Jacuzzi tubs and linen towels.

Eating

La Anónima (cnr Gobernador Paz & Rivadavia) Grocery store with cheap take-out.

Almacen Ramos Generales (☎ 427317; Maipú 749; snacks AR$7) The real draw of this rustic general store and museum is its baked goods: the

French pastry chef bakes crusty baguettes, croissants and desserts. There is also grain coffee and a wine bar.

Lomitos Martinica (San Martín 68; mains AR$9-13; ☾ 11:30am-3pm & 8:30pm-midnight) Dive dining at its best, this cheap *parrilla* with grillside seating serves enormous *milanesa* (breaded fish) sandwiches and offers an economical lunch special.

Café-Bar Tante Sara (☎ 423912; San Martín 701; mains AR$15-25) Serving up burgers and sandwiches, this popular corner bistro offers classic atmosphere.

El Turco (☎ 424711; San Martín 1040; mains AR$18; ☾ closed Sun lunch) This busy lunch spot is not very central, but popular for its cheap meats, pizza and pasta.

Lupita's (☎ 437675; 25 de Mayo 323; pizzas AR$25) This sliver-sized pizza shop delivers crisp thin-crust pizzas hot out of a brick oven. Consider it the perfect take-out.

La Cantina Fueguina de Freddy (☎ 421887; San Martín 326; mains AR$25) Say hello to your meal in the tank as you walk in. This reliably good seafood joint serves tasty king crab with herbs or parmesan, as well as pizza, pastas and stews.

Bodegón Fueguino (☎ 431972; San Martín 859; mains AR$25-40; ☾ Tue-Sun) A great gathering spot for wine and appetizers, this century-old Fuegian home is cozied up with sheep-skin-clad benches, cedar barrels and ferns. A *picada* (shared appetizer plate) for two includes eggplant, lamb brochettes, crab and bacon-wrapped plums. An early dinner crowd chows down on fresh grilled fish, salad and lots of veggie options.

ourpick María Lola Restó (☎ 421185; Deloquí 1048; mains AR$35; ☾ noon-midnight Mon-Sat) 'Satisfying' defines the experience at this creative café-style restaurant overlooking the channel. Locals pack this silver house for homemade pasta with seafood or strip steak in rich mushroom sauce. Service is good and portions tend toward humongous: desserts can easily be split.

Chez Manu (☎ 432253; Martial 2135; mains AR$35) If you are headed to Glaciar Martial, don't miss this gem on the way. Chef Emmanuel puts a French touch on fresh local ingredients like Fuegian lamb or mixed plates of cold *fruits de mer*. The three-course set lunch is the best deal. Views are a welcome bonus. It's 2km from town.

Tía Elvira (☎ 424725; Maipú 349; mains AR$35-65) This highly regarded traditional venue produces

TIERRA DEL FUEGO

seafood favorites like grilled trout or scallops in garlic sauce. Before eating, take a peek at the small museum lining the entrance hall.

La Rueda (☎ 436540; San Martín 193; buffet AR$36) This good *tenedor libre* (all-you-can-eat restaurant) offers a variety of salads alongside tasty *parrilla* grilled over coals in the window. Ordering a drink is mandatory with the buffet, which includes dessert.

Kaupé (☎ 422704; Roca 470; mains AR$40) For an out-of-body seafood experience, head to this candlelit house. Chef Ernesto Vivian employs the freshest of everything and service is nothing less than impeccable. Good options include mero (Patagonian sea bass) sashimi drizzled with soy, scallop seviche and black sea bass in blackened butter. The steaks shine too. The wine list is extensive, and the views of the bay…well, we doubt you'll bother to notice them. Reservations are advised.

Drinking

Geographically competitive drinkers should note that the southernmost bar in the world is not here but on a Ukrainian research station in Antarctica.

Dreamland (☎ 421246; www.dreamlandushuaia.com .ar; cnr 9 de Julio & Deloquí; drinks AR$9; ☻ 11am-late; ▣) The bar du jour, this ambient house mixes it up with DJs, free tango nights and happy hours. During the day it's a quiet café with lunch specials and wireless internet access.

Dublin Irish Pub (☎ 430744; cnr 9 de Julio & Deloquí) Dublin doesn't feel so far away with the lively banter and Guinness at this dimly lit foreigners' favorite. Look for occasional live music. There are a couple of other Irish bars around town, including the Galway.

Saint Christopher Resto-Bar (☎ 422423; Maipú 822) This boat-shaped restaurant, complete with nautical theme, serves food during the day but becomes more of a drinking spot at night. Note the rusty hulking shipwreck just offshore.

Galway Irish Bar (☎ 422355; Lasserre 108) This big bar affords less ambience but recovers favor with its dart board and Beagle beer (Ushuaia's own beer) on tap.

Entertainment

Cine Pakawaia (☎ 436500; cnr Yaganes & Gobernador Paz; tickets AR$6) First-run movies are shown at the Presidio's fully restored hangar-style theater.

Casa de la Cultura (☎ 422-417; Malvinas Argentinas near 12 de Octubre) Hidden behind a gym, this center hosts occasional live music shows.

Getting There & Away

AIR

Aerolíneas Argentinas (☎ 421218; Roca 116) jets several times daily to Buenos Aires (AR$703, 3½ hours), sometimes stopping in Río Gallegos (AR$266, one hour) or El Calafate (AR$506, 70 minutes). **LADE** (☎ 421123; San Martín 542) flies to Buenos Aires (AR$363), Comodoro Rivadavia (AR$280), El Calafate (AR$280) and Río Gallegos (AR$163). The airport departure tax is AR$213.

Chilean airline **Aerovías DAP** (www.dap.cl) offers charter-only flights to destinations in Patagonia, as well as overflights of Cape Horn and trips to Chile's Frei base in Antarctica.

Aeroclub Ushuaia (☎ 421717, 421892; www.aeroclub ushuaia.org.ar) offers scenic flightseeing tours (AR$150 to AR$300 per person).

BOAT

Charter boats anchored in Ushuaia's harbor may take passengers to Puerto Williams (AR$377) the next time they are heading out.

A number of private yachts charter trips to Cape Horn, Antarctica and, less often, South Georgia Island. These trips must be organized well in advance. The most popular weeklong charter, rounding Cape Horn, costs upwards of AR$5400 per person. A recommended option is **Mago del Sur** (☎ 02901-15-5148-6463, charter per person per day AR$750), captained by Alejandro Damilano, whose lifetime of sailing ensures skill and safety at the helm. Individuals can join scheduled trips (check online) to Las Islas Malvinas, Antarctica, Cape Horn, Puerto Natales and beyond.

From September through May, **Cruceros Australis** (☎ 02-442-3110 in Santiago; www.australis .com) runs luxurious four-day (starting from AR$3109/3925 per person in low/high season) and five-day sightseeing cruises to Punta Arenas and back, catering mostly to mature travelers. Saturday departures from Ushuaia include the possibility of disembarking at Cape Horn. Low season is considered to be September–October and mid-March–April. The cruise visits many otherwise inaccessible glaciers, but time alone and hiking opportunities are limited; the focus is more on nature talks and group excursions. **Turismo Comapa** (☎ 430727; www.comapa.com; San Martín 245) handles local bookings.

BUS

Ushuaia has no bus terminal. Book outgoing bus tickets with as much anticipation as possible; many readers have complained about getting stuck here in high season. Depending on your luck, long waits at border crossings can be expected.

Tecni-Austral (☎ 431408/12; Roca 157) buses for Río Grande (AR$25, four hours) leave from the travel agency Tolkar at 5:30am daily except Sunday, stopping in Tolhuin. There's an onward connecting service on Monday, Wednesday and Friday to Punta Arenas (AR$125, 11 hours), and on weekdays to Río Gallegos (AR$125, 12 hours).

Lider (☎ 436421; Gobernador Paz 921) and **Montiel** (☎ 421366; Deloquí 110) run door-to-door minivans to Tolhuin (AR$20, 2½ hours) and Río Grande (AR$40, four hours) six to eight times daily, with less frequent departures on Sunday.

Transportes Pasarela (☎ 433712; cnr Maipú & Juana Fadul) runs round-trip shuttles to Lago Esmeralda (AR$25), Lago Escondido (AR$80) and Lago Fagnano (AR$80), leaving at 10am and returning at 2pm and 6:30pm. If you're planning to stay overnight, ask to pay just one way (more likely if there are many people traveling) and arrange for pickup.

Transportes Eben-Ezer offers a similar service and leaves from nearby.

For transport to Parque Nacional Tierra del Fuego, see p537.

Getting Around

Taxis to/from the modern airport (USH), 4km southwest of downtown on the peninsula across from the waterfront, cost AR$18. Taxis can be chartered for around AR$60 per hour. There's local bus service along Maipú.

Rental rates for compact cars (including insurance) start at around AR$150; try Pueblo Viejo (p532) or **Localiza** (☎ 430739; Sarmiento 81). Some agencies may not charge for drop off in other parts of Argentine Tierra del Fuego.

PARQUE NACIONAL TIERRA DEL FUEGO

Banked against the channel, the hushed, fragrant southern forests of Tierra del Fuego are a stunning setting to explore. West of Ushuaia by 12km, **Parque Nacional Tierra del Fuego** (via RN 3; admission AR$20), Argentina's first coastal national park, extends 630 sq km from the Beagle Channel in the south to beyond Lago Fagnano in the north. However, only a couple

PARQUE NACIONAL TIERRA DEL FUEGO (LAPATAIA SECTOR)

HIKING
1 Senda Hito XXIV
2 Senda Costera
3 Senda Palestra
4 Senda Pampa Alta
5 Isla El Salmón
6 Laguna Negra

of thousand hectares along the southern edge of the park are open to the public, with a min-uscule system of short, easy trails that are designed more for day-tripping families than backpacking trekkers. The rest of the park is protected as a *reserva natural estricta* (strictly off-limits zone). Despite this, a few scenic hikes along the bays and rivers, or through dense native forests of evergreen coihue, canelo and deciduous lenga, are worthwhile. For truly spectacular color, come in the fall when hillsides of ñire burst out in red.

Birdlife is prolific, especially along the coastal zone. Keep an eye out for condors, albatross, cormorants, gulls, terns, oyster-catchers, grebes, kelp geese and the comi-cal, flightless, orange-billed steamer ducks. Common invasive species include the European rabbit and the North American beaver, both of which are wreaking ecologi-cal havoc in spite of their cuteness. Gray and red foxes, enjoying the abundance of rabbits, may also be seen.

Hiking

After running 3242km from Buenos Aires, RN 3 reaches its terminus at the shores of Bahía Lapataia. From here, trails **Mirador Lapataia** (500m), with excellent views, and **Senda Del Turbal** (400m) lead through winding lenga forest further into the bay. Other short walks include the self-guided nature trail **Senda Laguna Negra** (950m), through peat bogs, and the **Senda Castorera** (400m), showcasing mas-sive beaver dams, now abandoned, on a few small ponds.

SENDA HITO XXIV

From Camping Lago Roca, a flat 10km (four-hour) round-trip trek leads around Lago Roca's forested northeast shore to Hito XXIV – that number is *veinticuatro* in Spanish – the boundary post that marks the Argentina–Chile frontier. It is illegal to cross the frontier, which is patrolled regularly.

From the same trailhead you can reach **Cerro Guanaco** (973m) via the steep and difficult 8km trail of the same name; it's a long uphill haul but the views are excellent.

SENDA COSTERA

This 8km (four-hour) trek leads west from Bahía Ensenada along the coastline. Keep an eye out for old middens (archaeologically im-portant mounds of shells left by Yaghan inhab-itants), now covered in grass. The trail meets RN 3 a short way east of the park administra-tion *(guardería)* center at Lapataia. From here it is 1.2km further to Senda Hito XXIV.

It might be tempting to roll up the cuffs and go clamming, but be aware that occasional red tides *(marea roja)* contaminate mollusks (such as clams and mussels) along the shore of the Beagle Channel.

SENDA PALESTRA

This 4km (three-hour) round-trip trek from Bahía Ensenada follows a path eastward past an old copper mine to the popular rock-climbing wall of Palestra, near a *refugio* (rustic shelter) that is out of use.

SENDA PAMPA ALTA

The low heights of Pampa Alta (around 315m) grant long views across the Beagle Channel to Isla Navarino and Isla Hoste. RN 3 meets the trailhead 1.5km west of the Río Pipo and Bahía Ensenada road turn-offs (3km from the entrance gate). The 5km round-trip trail first climbs a hill, passing a beaver dam along the way. Enjoy the impressive views at the look-out. A quick 300m further leads to a trail par-alleling the Río Pipo and some waterfalls.

ISLA EL SALMÓN & LAGUNA NEGRA

From the road 2km southwest of Lapataia, a trail leads north along the western side of Río Lapataia to a fishing spot opposite Isla El Salmón. Laguna Negra, a lovely lake in the forest, is easily accessible via a 1km circuit loop signposted 200m past the trail to Isla El Salmón.

Sleeping & Eating

Campgrounds are the only lodging in the park. Most are free, lack services and get crowded, which means sites can get unreasonably messy. Do your part to pack out trash and follow a leave-no-trace ethic. Camping Ensenada is 16km from the park entrance and nearest the Costera trail; Camping Río Pipo is 6km from the entrance and easily accessed by either the road to Cañadon del Toro or the Pampa Alta trail. Camping Las Bandurrias, Camping Laguna Verde and Camping Los Cauquenes are on the islands in Río Lapataia.

The only fee-based campground is **Camping Lago Roca** (per person with shower AR$9), 9km from the park entrance. It's also the only one that has hot showers, a good *confitería* and a tiny (expensive) grocery store. However, there's plenty of room in the park to rough it at wild sites. Note that water at Lago Roca is not potable; boil it before using.

Getting There & Away

Buses leave from the corner of Maipú and Juana Fadul in Ushuaia several times daily from 9am to 6pm, returning approximately every hour between 8am and 8pm. Depending on your destination, a round-trip fare runs ARS$30 to AR$40, and you need not return the same day. Private tour buses cost AR$90 for a round-trip. Taxi fares shared between groups can be the same price as bus tickets.

The most touristy and, beyond jogging, the slowest way to the park, **El Tren del Fin de Mundo** (☎ 02901-431600; www.trendelfindemundo.com.ar; one way/round-trip AR$65/70, plus park entrance fee) originally carted prisoners to work camps. It departs (sans convicts) from the Estación del Fin de Mundo, 8km west of Ushuaia (taxis AR$25 one way), three or four times daily in summer and once or twice in winter. The one-hour, scenic, narrow-gauge train ride comes with historical explanations in English and Spanish. Reserve in January and February, when cruise-ship tours take over. If you are not a train fanatic, take it one way and return via minibus.

Hitchhiking to the park is feasible, but many cars will already be full.

ESTANCIA HARBERTON

Historic **Estancia Harberton** (☎ in Ushuaia 02901-422742, tours through Aves del Sur 01901-423213; tour AR$20; ☽ 10am-7pm Oct 15-Apr 15) was founded in 1886 by missionary Thomas Bridges and his family. As Tierra del Fuego's first *estancia* it contains the island's oldest house – still in use. The location earned fame from a stirring memoir written by Bridges' son Lucas, titled *Uttermost Part of the Earth* (see the boxed text, below). The *estancia* is now owned and run by the Goodalls, direct descendants of the Bridges.

Harberton is a working station, although only a handful of sheep and 1000 cattle remain on 200 sq km. The location is splendid and the history alluring. A one-hour guided tour (at 11am, 1:30pm, 3pm and 5pm) takes in the family cemetery and a garden where foliage names are given in Yaghan, Selk'nam and Spanish. There's also an abundant farmhouse tea service (AR$20), complete lunch (AR$45), optional excursions to the Reserva Yecapasela penguin colony and a replica of a Yaghan dwelling. It's also a popular destination for birders. At the time of research, there were plans for a new grill house, Acawaya Parrillada, to open in summer, though it is owned and run separately from the *estancia*.

TALES FROM THE UTTERMOST PART OF THE EARTH

Imagine a childhood where your backyard is the Beagle Channel, your playmates are unclothed Yaghans and your initiation into adulthood includes hunting wild bulls, saving shipwrecks and surviving bandit raids. Welcome to the life of E Lucas Bridges, as fraught and daring as any adventure penned by Stephenson or Krakauer.

Bridges' classic memoir, *Uttermost Part of the Earth,* starts with his British father establishing an Anglican mission in untamed Ushuaia. Little house on the prairie it wasn't. Once they moved from Ushuaia to ranch remote Harberton, the family lived in lean-tos until a house could be shipped in pieces from England (it now stands as the oldest structure in Tierra del Fuego). Bridges spent the late 1800s growing up among the now-extinct Selk'nam and Yaghan people. He learned their languages and was one of the few who, unlike Darwin, recorded indigenous customs with respect and insight.

By the time Bridges' book was published in 1947, the native population of Tierra del Fuego had nosedived to fewer than 150. *Uttermost Part of the Earth* captures the last years of Tierra del Fuego's native peoples and the island's transformation from an untouched wilderness to a frontier molded by fortune seekers, missionaries and sheep ranching. After years out of print, the book's recent re-release rescues Tierra del Fuego's powerful history and wild landscape from oblivion, reminding us of the riches that still remain.

Though he is buried in Recoleta Cemetery in Buenos Aires, traces of Lucas Bridges live on throughout the island, from his family *estancia* of Harberton to his own Estancia Viamonte (near Río Grande) and the jagged peaks backing Ushuaia that bear his name.

TIERRA DEL FUEGO

Worth the trip is the impressive **Museo Acatushún** (www.acatushun.com; admission AR$10; ⏲ hours vary, confirm with estancia), created by Natalie Prosser Goodall, a North American biologist who married into the family. Emphasizing the region's marine mammals, the museum has thousands of mammal and bird specimens inventoried; among the rarest specimens is a Hector's beaked whale. Much of this vast collection was found at Bahía San Sebastián, north of Río Grande, where a difference of up to 11km between high and low tide leaves animals stranded.

Volunteers and interns, mostly advanced university students studying tourism or biology, are taken on to work as tour guides and research assistants for the museum. Volunteers stay one month and get food, lodging and the occasional opportunity to work in the field. Competition is fierce and preference is given to Argentines.

Harberton has no phones on site so make reservations well in advance. With advance permission, free primitive camping is allowed at Río Lasifashaj, Río Varela and Río Cambaceres. Lodging is offered in the 1950 **Shepards' house** (per person AR$300) and remodeled 1901 **Cook house** (per person AR$180-240, shared bathroom); full board costs an extra AR$90.

Harberton is 85km east of Ushuaia via RN 3 and rough RC-j, a 1½- to two-hour drive one way. Shuttles leave from the base of 25 de Mayo at Av Maipú in Ushuaia at 9am, returning around 3pm (AR$100 round-trip); alternatively, take a taxi (AR$300 round-trip). Daylong catamaran tours are organized by agencies in Ushuaia.

PUERTO WILLIAMS (CHILE)

☎ 61 / pop 2500

Forget Ushuaia: the end of the world starts where colts roam Main St and yachts rounding Cape Horn take refuge. Naval settlement Puerto Williams is the only town on Isla Navarino, the official port of entry for vessels en route to Cape Horn and Antarctica, and home to the last living Yaghan speaker.

The village centers on a freshly sodded green roundabout and a concrete-slab plaza called the Centro Comercial. But just outside Puerto Williams is some of the Southern Cone's most breathtaking scenery. With over 150km of trails, Isla Navarino is a rugged backpacker's paradise, with slate-colored lakes, mossy lenga forests and the ragged

spires of the Dientes de Navarino. Trails lead past beaver dams, bunkers and army trenches as they climb steeply up into the mountains and deeper into forests. Some 40,000 beavers introduced from Canada in the 1940s now plague the island; they're even on the menu, if you can find an open restaurant.

Mid-19th-century missionaries, followed by fortune-seekers during the 1890s gold rush, established a permanent European presence here. The remaining mixed-race descendants of the Yaghan (Yamaná) people are established in a small seaside village called Villa Ukika.

Information

Near the main roundabout, the Centro Comercial contains the post office, internet access, Aerovías DAP's representative and a couple of call centers. Money exchange (US cash only, US$100 minimum) and Visa advances are possible at Banco de Chile, where there is also an ATM.

Friendly Wolf at **Turismo SIM** (☎ 621150/062; www.simltd.com; Austral 74) has details about the rampant sailing, trekking and expedition possibilities south of the 54th parallel, including Cape Horn, the Cordillera Darwin, Isla Navarino, South Georgia Island and the Antarctic Peninsula. **Fueguia** (☎ 621251; Prado 245) has recommended French-speaking guiding of the trekking circuits. The **municipalidad** (☎ 621011; www.municipalidadcabodehornos.cl in Spanish; O'Higgins 165) runs a rarely staffed **tourist info kiosk** (☎ 621012) at the roundabout.

Sights & Activities

Near the entrance to the military quarters is the original bow of the **Yelcho**, which rescued Ernest Shackleton's Antarctic expedition from Elephant Island in 1916.

The free **Museo Martín Gusinde** (☎ 621043; cnr Araguay & Gusinde; donation requested; ⏲ 9am-1pm & 2:30-7pm Mon-Fri, 2:30-6:30pm Sat & Sun), honoring the German priest and ethnographer who worked among the Yaghans from 1918 to 1923, focuses on ethnography and natural history.

A 15-minute walk east of town along the waterfront leads to the settlement of Villa Ukika. Its modest crafts shop, **Kipa-Akar** (House of Woman), sells language books, jewelry and whale-bone knives. Ask a villager for help if it's closed.

Latin America's southernmost ethnobotanical park, **Omora** (www.omora.org) has trails with plant names marked in Yaghan, Latin and

Spanish. Take the road to the right of the Virgin altar, 4km (an hour's walk) toward Puerto Navarino. Donations help advocate for the creation of a Cape Horn Biosphere Reserve.

Hiking to **Cerro Bandera** affords expansive views of the Beagle Channel. Start this four-hour round-trip at the Navarino Circuit. The trail ascends steeply through lenga to blustery stone-littered hilltops. Self-supported backpackers can continue on for the whole four- to five-day **Dientes de Navarino** circuit, enjoying impossibly raw and windswept vistas under Navarino's toothy spires. For details on trekking possibilities, refer to Lonely Planet's *Trekking in the Patagonian Andes.*

Many local lodgings can arrange tours of the island. For yacht tours to Antarctica and around the Beagle Channel, as well as trekking, climbing and riding expeditions, contact Turismo SIM.

Sleeping

Restaurant & Lodging Patagonia (☎ 621075, 621294; pedroortiz@chilesat.net; Yelcho 230; s with/without bathroom CH$9000/6500; 💻) The salty owner of the Club de Yates Micalvi bar rents out rooms and will cook up a menagerie of wild game (goose, octopus, even beaver) on request.

Hostal Lajuwa (☎ 621267; Villa Ukika; dm CH$10,000) These clean dorm-style rooms in the Yaghan community are a bit isolated but make for an interesting cultural exchange.

Residencial Pusaki (☎ 621116; Piloto Pardo 242; s/d CH$10,500/25,000) This fun family lodging is well cared for. Guests get kitchen privileges but shouldn't give up the chance to try Pati's fantastic seafood creations.

Hotel Lakutaia (☎ 621733; www.lakutaia.cl; d CH$100,000) Three kilometers east of town toward the airport, this modern full-service lodge will arrange transportation from Punta Arenas, and can organize day hikes to the Navarino Circuit and trips to Cape Horn. The library contains tons of interesting history and nature references. Its only disadvantage is its isolation; you might leave without getting much of a feel for the quirky town of Puerto Williams.

Eating

Dientes de Navarino (plaza; mains CH$3000) This hole-in-the-wall dining hall may offer few options

but they are well prepared. Seafood platters, *combinados* (pisco brandy and colas) and box wine please the hungry.

Restaurant Cabo de Hornos (☎ 621067, 621232; Maragano 146; mains CH$3000-5000) With views over the town, this is the place to try local wild game (beaver, crab, goose, guanaco and rabbit), plus organic salmon, lamb and more traditional Magellanic meats.

Of the few supermarkets, Simon & Simon is the best, with fresher vegetables, fast food and great pastries.

Drinking

Club de Yates Micalvi (beer CH$2000; 🕒 open late, Sep-May) As watering holes go, this may be like no other. A grounded German cargo boat, the *Milcalvi* was declared a regional naval museum in 1976 but found infinitely better use as a floating bar, frequented by navy men and yachties.

Getting There & Away

The only way to get to Puerto Williams is by plane or by boat. **Aerovías DAP** (☎ 621051; www.dap.cl; Plaza de Ancla s/n) flies to Punta Arenas (CH$52,000, 1¼ hours) Wednesday through Saturday and Monday from November to March, with fewer flights in winter. DAP flights to Antarctica may make a brief stopover here.

The **Transbordador Austral Broom** (www.tabsa.cl) ferry *Patagonia* sails from the Tres Puentes sector of Punta Arenas to Puerto Williams two or three times a month on Saturdays (reclining seat/bunk CH$72,500/87,500 including meals, 38 hours). Travelers rave about the trip: if the weather holds there are good views on deck and the possibility of spotting dolphins or whales. Booking a bunk is worth the extra dollars, since passenger berths are small and the reclining Pullman seats are not as comfortable as one might wish on such a long trip.

Zodiac boats head to Ushuaia daily from September to March. Book with **Akainij** (☎ 621173; www.turismoakainij.com, Centro Comercial Sur 156). The 25-minute trip (CH$60,000 one way) departs at 9am, but a transfer bus must first take passengers to Puerto Navarino. Private yachts making the trip can sometimes be found at the Club de Yates Micalvi.

TIERRA DEL FUEGO

Uruguay

Squished like a tiny grape between Brazil's gargantuan thumb and Argentina's long fore-finger, South America's smallest Spanish-speaking country is easily overlooked but well worth discovering. Ignored by the Spanish for its lack of mineral wealth, batted about like a ping-pong ball at the whim of its more powerful neighbors and bypassed by modern-day travelers preferring Argentina's mountains or Brazil's tropical allure, Uruguay has always been an underdog. Yet it remains a delightfully low-key, hospitable place where visitors can melt into the background and experience the everyday life of a different culture – whether caught in a cow-and-gaucho traffic jam on a dirt road to nowhere or strolling with *mate*-toting locals along Montevideo's beachfront.

For its diminutive size, Uruguay is surprisingly diverse. Cosmopolitan Montevideo is ex-periencing a renaissance of youthful energy while maintaining many long-standing cultural traditions. The streets erupt in a frenzy of drumming every February during Carnaval, and newly renovated Teatro Solís is among dozens of venues hosting dance, music and theater year-round at astonishingly affordable prices. Seventeenth-century Colonia seduces visitors with its cobblestoned charms, while trendy Punta del Este draws glitterati from around the globe to its sandy beaches, chichi restaurants and party-till-you-drop nightclubs.

Whatever you do, don't limit yourself to these three tourist hubs. Get out under the big sky of Uruguay's vast interior, where fields spread out like oceans dotted with little cow and eucalyptus islands. Ride horses to a river at sunset, stargaze at a 19th-century *estancia* (ranch), or watch the moonrise over the dunes at Cabo Polonio's seal colony. Out here, amid Uruguay's endless open spaces, you can still feel South America's wild grandeur.

HIGHLIGHTS

- Dance to a different drummer during Montevideo's monthlong **Carnaval** (p554)

- Admire sunset over the Atlantic from Carlos Páez Vilaró's extravagantly whimsical studio, **Casapueblo** (p588)

- Trek over sand dunes to see the lighthouse and abundant marine life at **Cabo Polonio** (p591)

- Ride a horse, roast a cow and see how the gaucho half lives at **Estancia La Sirena** (p570)

- Sunbathe on the 18th-century town wall, or dine in a vintage car on the cobblestones in picturesque **Colonia del Sacramento** (p562)

★ Estancia La Sirena

★ Colonia del Sacramento

★ Casapueblo

★ MONTEVIDEO

Cabo Polonio ★

- POPULATION: 3.5 MILLION

- AREA: 176,220 SQ KM

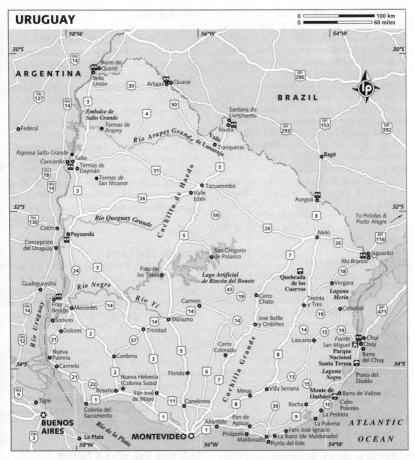

HISTORY
Early Settlement

Uruguay's aboriginal inhabitants were the Charrúa along the coast and the Guaraní north of the Río Negro. The hunting-and-gathering Charrúa discouraged European settlement for more than a century by killing Spanish explorer Juan de Solís and most of his party in 1516. In any event there was little to attract the Spanish, who valued these lowlands along the Río de la Plata only as an access route to gold and other quick riches further inland.

The first Europeans to settle on the Banda Oriental (Eastern Shore) were Jesuit missionaries near present-day Soriano, on the Río Uruguay. Next came the Portuguese, who established present-day Colonia in 1680 as a beachhead for smuggling goods into Buenos Aires. Spain responded by building its own citadel at Montevideo in 1726.

Birth of a Nation

For the next century the Portuguese, Spanish and British fought to get a foothold. This three-way rivalry eventually led to Uruguayan independence. José Gervasio Artigas, Uruguay's greatest national hero, allied with the United Provinces of the River Plate against Spain, but was unable to prevent Uruguay's takeover by Brazil. Exiled to Paraguay, Artigas inspired the famous '33 Orientales,' Uruguayan patriots under General Juan Lavalleja who, with Argentine support, crossed the Río Uruguay on April 19, 1825, and launched a campaign to liberate modern-day Uruguay from Brazilian control. In 1828, after three years' struggle, a British-mediated treaty established Uruguay as a small independent buffer between the emerging continental powers.

For most of the 19th century, Uruguay's independence was fragile. There was civil war between Uruguay's two nascent political parties, the Colorados and the Blancos (named, respectively, for the red and white bands they wore); Argentina besieged Montevideo from 1838 to 1851; and Brazil was an ever-present threat.

By the mid-19th century the economy was largely dependent on beef and wool production. The rise of the latifundios (large landholdings) and commercialization of livestock led to the gradual demise of the independent gaucho.

Rising Prosperity

In the early 20th century, visionary president José Batlle y Ordóñez introduced such innovations as pensions, farm credits, unemployment compensation and the eight-hour workday. State intervention led to the nationalization of many industries, the creation of others and a new era of general prosperity. However, Batlle's reforms were largely financed through taxing the livestock sector, and when exports faltered mid-century, the welfare state crumbled.

Economic Decline & Political Breakdown

By the 1960s economic stagnation and massive inflation were reaching crisis points, and social unrest was increasing, particularly in Montevideo, which had become accustomed to middle-class prosperity. In 1967 the country began sliding into dictatorship under President Jorge Pacheco, who outlawed leftist parties, closed newspapers and invoked state-of-siege measures in response to the 'Tupamaros' guerrilla movement – a clandestine socialist faction with roots in the urban middle class. At first the Tupamaros enjoyed public support, but this eroded quickly. After they executed suspected CIA agent Dan Mitrione and engineered a major prison escape, Pacheco put the military in charge of counterinsurgency. In 1971 Pacheco's chosen successor, Juan Bordaberry, handed control of the government over to the army.

Military Rule

The military virtually eliminated free expression. Torture became routine, and more than 60,000 citizens were arbitrarily detained. The armed forces determined eligibility for public employment, subjected political offenses to military courts, censored libraries and even required prior approval for large family gatherings.

Attempts by the military to institutionalize their political role failed. Voters rejected a military-drawn constitution in 1980, and four years later elected Colorado candidate Julio María Sanguinetti as president under the existing constitution. Sanguinetti's election implied a return to democratic traditions, although he supported a controversial amnesty for military human-rights abuses, grudgingly ratified by voters in 1989.

Into the 21st Century

In March 2000, Uruguayans elected the outspoken Colorado Jorge Batlle Ibáñez, grand-nephew of José Batlle y Ordóñez, as president. Ibañez immediately established himself as a maverick, dismissing the head of the army for suggesting that another coup might be in order, and promising to search for the remains of dissidents who disappeared under military rule. Decrying Uruguay's welfare state as cumbersome, he began implementing policies aimed at privatization and free trade. In response, the Frente Amplio (Broad Front) – a coalition of leftist parties – became a serious political contender, winning popularity for its antiprivatization, prowelfare stance.

Inflation, Recession & Bailout

In July 2002, spillover from Argentina's economic crisis triggered a run on Uruguayan banks. Uruguayans watched in horror as their economy – previously one of the strongest in South America – crumbled, and inflation (3.6% in 2001) rocketed to 40% by the end of 2002. The tourist industry (heavily reliant on prosperous Argentines) suffered. The peso plummeted in value, the economy minister resigned and the government declared a bank holiday to prevent further chaos.

What followed was a massive bailout – Ibáñez' emergency measures (cutting public spending, increasing sales tax) were rewarded with a series of loans from the US, the IMF and the World Bank totaling US$1.5 billion.

PULP FRICTION: URUGUAY'S CELLULOSE WAR WITH ARGENTINA

Who knew that a pulp mill could provoke an international crisis? At the time of writing, Uruguayan-Argentine relations had reached a 50-year low, thanks to an ongoing dispute over Finnish paper company Botnia's newly opened pulp mill on the Río Uruguay north of Fray Bentos. Ever since plans for the mill were announced in 2005, Argentine environmental groups and government officials have been protesting that it will pollute the Argentine side of the river near Gualeguaychú. Uruguay's government, intent on safeguarding this major foreign investment, has steadfastly countered that the mill, governed by strict international environmental standards, is perfectly safe.

On November 9, 2007, after multiple delays and inconclusive mediation efforts by King Juan Carlos of Spain, the pulp mill finally opened, only heightening tensions. As this book goes to press, Argentina still has a case pending against Uruguay in the International Court of Justice, and nerves are still frayed after Argentina's outgoing president accused Uruguayan President Vázquez of stabbing Argentina in the back.

Meanwhile, the bridge between Fray Bentos and Gualeguaychú remains closed by protestors for the third straight summer, and periodic blockades of the Paysandú–Colón bridge further north compound the havoc. By the time this book hits the shelves, the issue may be closer to resolution…or it may not. Regardless, the scars will probably linger for some time.

Recent Events

In March 2005 the leftist Frente Amplio swept to power under President Tabaré Vázquez, riding a wave of support from unions, youth and community groups. It was the first time in Uruguay's 175-year history that a third party had won the presidency. Things didn't start smoothly: Vázquez' early initiatives included seeking a free-trade deal with the US (surprising and alienating Uruguay's Mercosur trade partners), banning smoking in public (annoying pretty much everybody in this nicotine-crazed land) and granting leases to two foreign multinationals to build paper factories on the Río Uruguay.

Controversy over the paper mills quickly took on international implications (see the boxed text, above), and the resulting dispute with Argentina has yet to blow over. Meanwhile, on the home front, the Frente Amplio government has presided over two small social revolutions. In November 2007 abortion was legalized, and in January 2008 Uruguay became the first Latin American country to sanction civil unions between same-sex partners.

THE CULTURE
The National Psyche

The one thing that Uruguayans will tell you that they're *not* is anything like their *porteño* cousins across the water. In many ways they're right. Where Argentines can be brassy and sometimes arrogant, Uruguayans are more humble and relaxed. Where the former have always been a regional superpower, the latter have always lived in the shadow of one. Those jokes about Punta del Este being a suburb of Buenos Aires don't go down so well on this side of the border. There are plenty of similarities, though – the near-universal appreciation for the arts, the Italian influence and the gaucho heritage. Indeed, the rugged individualism and disdain that many Uruguayans hold for *el neoliberalismo* (neoliberalism) can be traced directly back to those romantic cowboy figures.

Lifestyle

Uruguayans like to take it easy and pride themselves on being the opposite of the hotheaded Latino type. They're big drinkers, but bar-room brawls are rare. Sunday's the day for family and friends, to throw half a cow on the *asado* (barbecue), sit back and sip some *mate* (a tealike beverage). The population is well educated, although public-school standards are slipping. The once-prominent middle class is disappearing as private universities become the main providers of quality education, and the country's recent economic crisis is still fresh in most Uruguayans' minds (and wallets).

Population

With 3.5 million people, Uruguay is South America's smallest Spanish-speaking country.

The population is predominately white (88%) with 8% mestizo (people with mixed Spanish and indigenous blood) and 4% black. Indigenous peoples are practically nonexistent. The average life expectancy (just over 75 years) is one of Latin America's highest. The literacy rate is also high, at 98%, while population growth is a slow 0.5%. Population density is 18.5 people per sq km.

Sports

> Sexo, droga y Peñarol
>> *Montevideo graffito*

Uruguayans, like all Latin Americans, are crazy about soccer (*fútbol*). If you suddenly notice that all the streets are empty and the bars are full, you can bet there's a game on.

Uruguay has won the World Cup twice, including the first tournament, played in Montevideo in 1930. The most notable teams are Montevideo-based Nacional and Peñarol. If you go to a match between these two, sit on the sidelines, not behind the goal, unless you're up for some serious rowdiness.

The **Asociación Uruguayo de Fútbol** (☎ 02-400-7101; Guayabo 1531) in Montevideo can provide information on matches and venues.

Religion

Sixty-six percent of Uruguayans are Roman Catholic. There's a small Jewish minority, numbering around 25,000. Evangelical Protestantism has made some inroads and Sun Myung Moon's Unification Church owns the afternoon daily, *Últimas Noticias*.

Arts

Uruguay has an impressive literary and artistic tradition, and its small population produces a surprising number of talented artists and literary figures. Uruguay's most famous philosopher and essayist is probably José Enrique Rodó, whose 1900 essay *Ariel,* contrasting North American and Latin American civilizations, is a classic of the country's literature. Major contemporary writers include Juan Carlos Onetti, and poet, essayist and novelist Mario Benedetti. Onetti's novels *No Man's Land, The Shipyard, Body Snatcher* and *A Brief Life* are available in English translations, as is *The Tree of Red Stars,* Tessa Bridal's acclaimed novel set in Montevideo during the 1970s. Most young Uruguayans have a big soft spot

for Eduardo Galeano, who has written many books and poems.

Probably the most famous Uruguay-related film is Costa-Gavras' engrossing *State of Siege* (1973), filmed in Allende's Chile, which deals with the Tupamaro guerrillas' kidnapping and execution of suspected American CIA officer Dan Mitrione. Among the best movies to come out of Uruguay recently are *Whisky* (2004), which won a couple of awards at Cannes, and *El Baño del Papa* (2007).

Theater is popular and playwrights such as Mauricio Rosencof are prominent. The most renowned painters are the late Juan Manuel Blanes and Joaquín Torres García. Sculptors include José Belloni, whose life-size bronzes can be seen in Montevideo's parks.

Tango is big in Montevideo – Uruguayans claim tango legend Carlos Gardel as a native son, and one of the best-known tangos, 'La Cumparsita,' was composed by Uruguayan Gerardo Matos Rodríguez. During Carnaval, Montevideo's streets reverberate to the energetic drumbeats of *candombe*, an African-derived rhythm brought to Uruguay by slaves from 1750 onwards. As far as contemporary music goes, ska punk is big in Uruguay, with groups like El Congo, La Vela Puerca and Once Tiros getting plenty of airplay.

Access to the arts is relatively inexpensive. Museums are mostly free, and theater and music events often cost as little as UR$80. Even the very best seats for performances at Montevideo's elegant Teatro Solís rarely exceed UR$500.

FOOD & DRINK
Uruguayan Cuisine

Breakfast to a Uruguayan generally means *café con leche* (coffee with milk) and a croissant or two, followed by serious amounts of *mate*. Any later than, say, 10am huge slabs of beef are the norm, usually cooked over hot coals on a *parrilla* (grill or barbecue). The most popular cut is the *asado de tira* (ribs) but *pulpo* (fillet steak) is also good. Seafood is excellent on the coast.

Uruguay's classic snack is a cholesterol bomb called the *chivito* (a steak sandwich with cheese, lettuce, tomato, bacon, ham, olives, pickles and more!). Vegetarians often have to content themselves with pizza and pasta, although there are a few veggie restaurants lurking about. Desserts are a dream (or nightmare, depending on your perspective) of meringue,

DAY OF THE GNOCCHI

Most Uruguayan restaurants make a big deal out of serving gnocchi on the 29th of each month. In some places this is the only day you can get them.

The tradition dates back to tough economic times when everybody was paid at the end of the month. By the time the 29th rolled around, the only thing that people could afford to cook were these delicious potato dumplings. So, in their ever-practical way, Uruguayans turned a hardship into a tradition and the 29th has been the Day of the Gnocchi ever since. Something to bear in mind next time you're paying US$25 a plate at your favorite Italian restaurant back home.

For Argentines, gnocchi have another meaning (see the boxed text, p45).

dulce de leche (milk caramel), burnt sugar and custard. The same ingredients get recombined in endless configurations, with names like *Principe Humberto* (Prince Humbert), *isla flotante* (floating island), *Massini* and *chajá*.

In major tourist destinations like Punta del Este and Colonia, restaurants charge *cubiertos* (cover charges of UR$20 or more). Theoretically these pay for the basket of bread offered before your meal – oh, by the way, that yellowish-white accompaniment is mayonnaise, not butter!

Drinks
ALCOHOLIC DRINKS

Local beers, including Pilsen, Norteño and Patricia, are decent but nothing special. The 330ml bottles are rare outside tourist areas – generally *cerveza* (beer) means a 1L bottle and some glasses, which is a great way to meet your neighbors.

Tannat, a red wine produced only in Uruguay and southwestern France, is excellent and universally available.

Clericó is a mixture of white wine and fruit juice, while *medio y medio* (half and half) is a mixture of sparkling wine and white wine. A shot of *grappa con miel* (grappa with honey) is worth a try – you might just like it.

NONALCOHOLIC DRINKS

Tap water's OK to drink in most places, but bottled water is cheap if you still have your doubts. Soft drinks are inexpensive: try the *pomelo* (grapefruit) flavor – it's very refreshing and not too sickly sweet. *Jugos* (juices) and *licuados* (juices mixed with milk or water) are available everywhere.

Coffee is generally good, coming mostly *de la máquina* (from the machine). Uruguayans consume even more *mate* than Argentines and Paraguayans. If you get the chance, try to acquire the taste – there's nothing like whiling away an afternoon passing the *mate* with a bunch of newfound friends.

ENVIRONMENT
The Land

Though one of South America's smallest countries, Uruguay is quite large by European standards. Its area of 176,220 sq km is greater than England and Wales combined, or slightly bigger than the US state of Florida.

Uruguay's two main ranges of interior hills are the Cuchilla de Haedo, west of Tacuarembó, and the Cuchilla Grande, south of Melo; neither exceeds 500m in height. West of Montevideo the terrain is more level. The Río Negro flowing through the center of the country forms a natural dividing line between north and south. The Atlantic coast has impressive beaches, dunes, headlands and lagoons. Uruguay's grasslands and forests resemble those of Argentina's pampas or southern Brazil, and patches of palm savanna persist in the east, along the Brazilian border.

Wildlife

It seems fitting that Uruguay's name can be translated as 'river of the birds'. The country is rich in birdlife, especially in the coastal lagoons of Rocha department. Most large land animals have disappeared, but the occasional ñandu (rhea) still races across northwestern Uruguay's grasslands. Whales, fur seals and sea lions are common along the coast.

CLIMATE

Since Uruguay's major attraction is its beaches, most visitors come in summer. Along the coast, daytime temperatures average 28°C in January, and nighttime temperatures average 17°C. Along the Río Uruguay, summer temperatures can be smotheringly hot, while the interior hill country is slightly cooler (January's average maximum is between 21°C and 26°C).

Annual rainfall, evenly distributed throughout the year, averages about 1m over the whole

---

CHANGING PHONE NUMBERS

Phone numbers throughout Uruguay are moving to a new 8-digit format, effective summer 2008. For details, see the boxed text in the Uruguay Directory (p599).

---

country. Between late April and November, strong winds sometimes combine with rain and cool temperatures (July's average temperature is a chilly 11°C).

Late spring and early fall are nice times to visit, as the weather is agreeable and prices (especially along the coast) tend to be lower.

NATIONAL PARKS

Uruguay's only national parks are the military-administered Parque Nacional Santa Teresa (p594) and Parque Nacional San Miguel in Rocha department. Five other natural areas are nominally protected under the Sistema Nacional de Áreas Protegidas (SNAP; National System of Protected Areas) program – see the boxed text, p577.

GETTING THERE & AWAY

There are a few direct international flights to Montevideo (p560) and Punta del Este (p587), but most airlines require a connection through Buenos Aires. Many visitors to Uruguay arrive by ferry from Buenos Aires, to either Colonia (p566) or Montevideo (p560).

MONTEVIDEO

☎ 02 / pop 1.3 million

Uruguay's capital and by far its largest city, Montevideo is a vibrant, eclectic place with a rich cultural life. Stretching nearly 20km from east to west, the city wears many faces, from its industrial port to the exclusive residential suburb of Carrasco near the airport. In the historic downtown business district, art deco and neoclassical buildings jostle for space alongside grimy, worn-out skyscrapers that appear airlifted from Havana or Ceauşescu's Romania, while across town the shopping malls and modern high-rises of beach communities like Punta Carretas and Pocitos bear more resemblance to Miami or Copacabana.

If you're coming from Colonia or Uruguay's northern beaches, Montevideo's polluted air and honking taxis may feel a bit jarring, but stick around. The capital's active and resurgent urban culture is a palpable force, and locals are justifiably proud to share it with you. In Ciudad Vieja, the heart of historic Montevideo, old buildings are being restored to make room for boldly painted cafés, hostels and galleries, while down by the port the municipal administration has spruced up the Mercado del Puerto to accommodate a new city tourist office and Carnaval museum. Montevideo serves as administrative headquarters for Mercosur, South America's leading trading bloc, and the capital's many embassies and foreign cultural centers add to the international flavor. Meanwhile, the city's music, theater, art and club scenes continue to thrive, from elegant older theaters and cozy little tango bars to modern beachfront discos.

ORIENTATION

Montevideo lies almost directly across the Río de la Plata from Buenos Aires. For many visitors, the most intriguing area is the Ciudad Vieja, the formerly walled colonial grid straddling the western tip of a peninsula between the sheltered port and the wide-open river. Just east of the old town gate Puerta de la Ciudadela, the Centro (downtown) begins at Plaza Independencia, surrounded by historic public buildings of the republican era. Av 18 de Julio, a major thoroughfare and traditionally the capital's main commercial and entertainment zone, runs east from here through Plaza del Entrevero and Plaza Cagancha before reaching the Intendencia (town hall) at the Centro's eastern edge. Street numbering is easy to follow – each city block represents a range of 50 numbers. Note that some streets change their name on either side of Av 18 de Julio.

From Plaza del Entrevero, Av Libertador General Lavalleja leads diagonally northeast to the imposing Palacio Legislativo, home of Uruguay's General Assembly. At the northeastern end of Av 18 de Julio are Montevideo's Tres Cruces bus terminal and Parque José Batlle y Ordóñez, home to the city's 75,000-seat soccer stadium. Running north–south from the bus terminal to the beach and lighthouse at Punta Carretas is Bulevar Artigas, another major artery, while the nearby Av Italia becomes the Interbalnearia, the main highway east to Punta del Este and the rest of the Uruguayan Riviera.

Many points of interest lie beyond downtown. Westward across the harbor, 132m

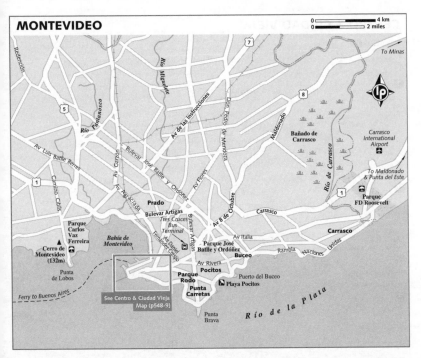

Cerro de Montevideo was a landmark for early navigators and still offers outstanding views of the city. Eastward, the Rambla, or waterfront road, leads past attractive Parque Rodó at the southern end of Bulevar Artigas, then snakes through a series of sprawling beach suburbs that are very popular with the capital's residents in summer and on weekends. These include Punta Carretas, Pocitos (sometimes likened to Rio's Copacabana), Buceo (home of the yacht club) and Carrasco, an exclusive residential district near the airport.

INFORMATION
Bookstores
Availability of non-Spanish titles is limited.

Al Faro de Lou (☎ 902-6889; cnr Zelmar Michelini & Soriano) Carries Lonely Planet titles.

Librería Linardi y Risso (☎ 915-7129; Juan Carlos Gómez 1435) Good source for history, literature, out-of-print items and photo essays on Montevideo and Uruguay.

Librería Puro Verso (☎ 901-6429; Av 18 de Julio 1199) Excellent Spanish-language bookstore with a small café downstairs.

MVD Bookstore (☎ 901-1510; Av 18 de Julio 1261) Has a small selection of novels in English, French and Italian.

Cultural Centers
Alianza Cultural Uruguay–Estados Unidos
(☎ 902-5160, theater 908-1953, library 901-7423; www.alianza.edu.uy in Spanish; Paraguay 1217) The American-Uruguayan cultural center contains a bookstore, theater and library with books and newspapers in English. The center also sponsors special programs and lectures.

Alianza Francesa (☎ 400-0505; www.alliancefrancaise .edu.uy in Spanish; Bulevar Artigas 1229)

Centro Cultural de España (☎ 915-2250; www.cce .org.uy in Spanish; Rincón 629) Spanish cultural center in the Ciudad Vieja. Hosts art exhibits and other cultural events.

Complejo Multicultural Mundo Afro (☎ 915-0247; Ciudadela 1229) Montevideo's Afro-Uruguayan community cultural center, upstairs in the Mercado Central just south of Plaza Independencia.

Instituto Cultural Anglo-Uruguayo (☎ 902-3773; www.anglo.edu.uy in Spanish; San José 1426) One of 47 branches around the country. Operates an English-language library and a theater.

Instituto de Cultura Uruguayo-Brasileño (☎ 901-1818; www.icub.edu.uy in Spanish; Av 18 de Julio 994, 6th fl) Brazilian cultural center next to the Museo del Gaucho, with an excellent library.

CENTRO & CIUDAD VIEJA

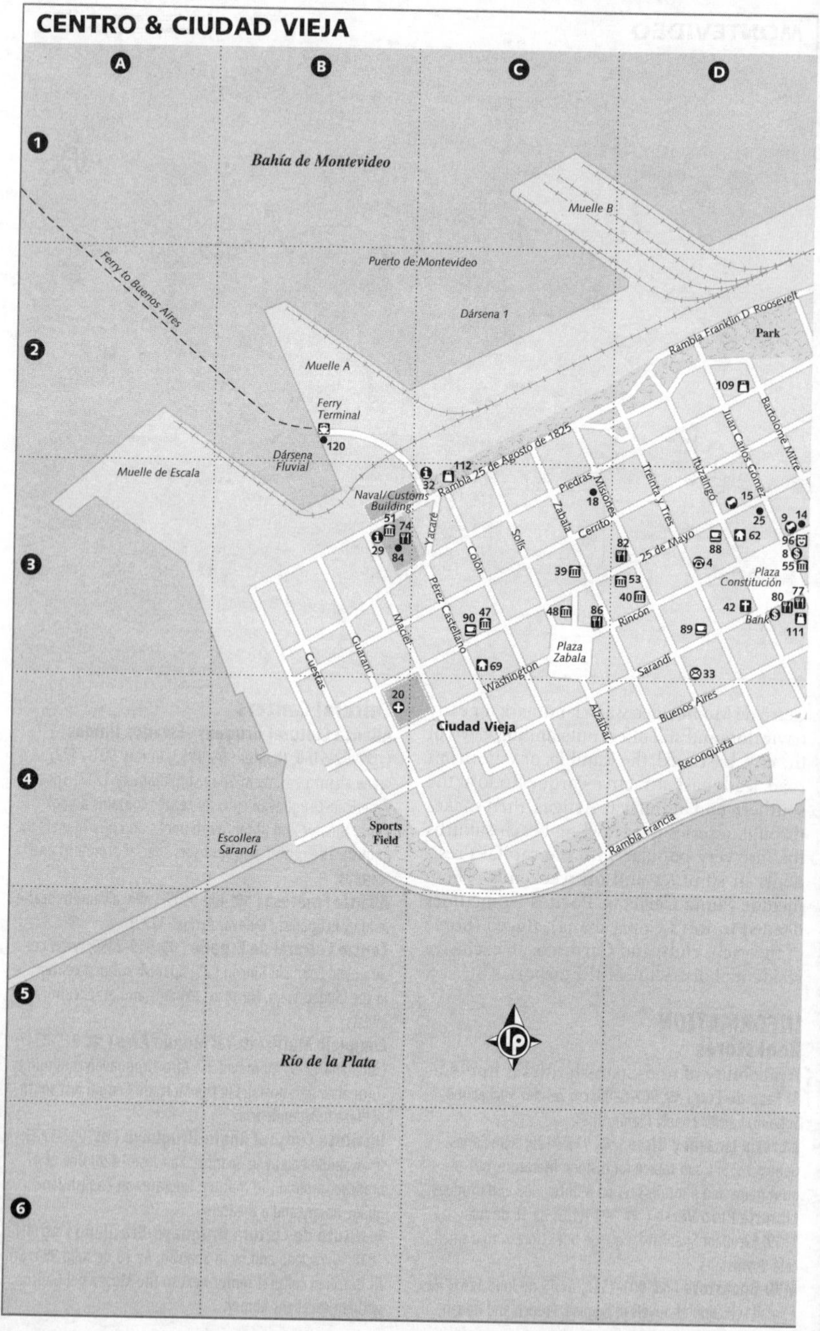

Bahía de Montevideo

Muelle B

Puerto de Montevideo

Dársena 1

Rambla Franklin D Roosevelt

Park

109

Muelle A

Ferry to Buenos Aires

Ferry
Terminal
120

*Dársena
Fluvial*

Muelle de Escala

112
32

Rambla 25 de Agosto de 1825

Piedras
18

Juan Carlos Gómez

Bartolomé Mitre

15

9 14
96
8
55

Naval/Customs
Building
51 74

29 84

Yacaré

Misiones

Zabala

Cerrito

Treinta y Tres

Ituzaingó

25 de Mayo

25
62

Colón

Solís

82
88

53
40

Plaza
Constitución
80 77

Bank
111

Perez Castellano

39

48 86
Rincón

4

42

Maciel

90 47

Plaza
Zabala

89

33

Cuareim

Washington
69

20

Ciudad Vieja

Sarandí

Buenos Aires

Alzáibar

Reconquista

*Escollera
Sarandí*

Sports
Field

Rambla Francia

Río de la Plata

URUGUAY

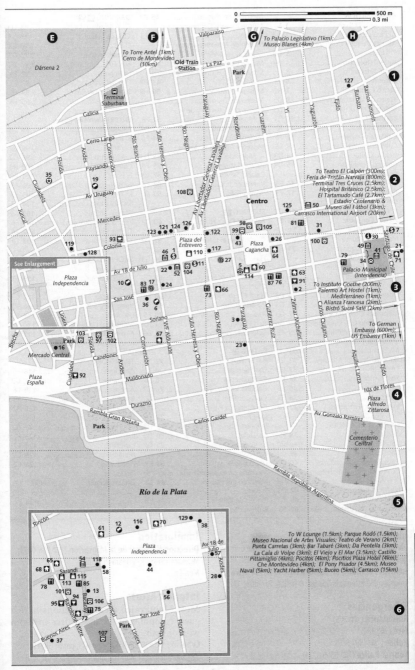

Instituto Goethe (☎ 410-5813; www.goethe
.de/ins/uy/mot/esindex.htm; Canelones 1524) The German
government's cultural center in Montevideo.
Instituto Italiano de Cultura (☎ 900-3354; www.ii
cmontevideo.esteri.it in Spanish & Italian; Paraguay 1177)

Emergencies
Ambulance (☎ 105)
Fire (☎ 104)
Police (☎ 109)
Tourist Police (☎ 0800 8226)

Immigration
Dirección Nacional de la Migración (☎ 916-0471;
Misiones 1513; ☒ 9:15am-2:30pm
Mon-Fri).

Internet Access
Most Montevideo accommodations have a
guest computer in the lobby, free in-room
wi-fi or both.
Cyberia (☎ 908-8808; San José 933; per hr UR$15;
☒ noon-midnight Mon-Fri, 6pm-midnight Sat & Sun)

URUGUAY

Provides many digital services, including computers with cameras, headphones and microphones.

Millenium Internet Café (☎ 901-4701; Av 18 de Julio 1066, Local 53; per hr UR$15; 24hr) Hidden off the street in the Galerías Delondon shopping complex, also accessible from Paraguay.

Laundry

Montevideo City Lavandería (☎ 903-0369; Andes 1333; wash & dry per load UR$85; 8am-8pm Mon-Fri, to 3pm Sat) One block east of Plaza Independencia.

Media

Montevideo dailies include the morning *El Día, La República, La Mañana* and *El País. Gaceta Comercial* is the voice of the business community. Afternoon papers are *El Diario, Mundocolor* and *Últimas Noticias.*

Medical Services

Hospital Británico (☎ 487-1020; Av Italia 2420) A highly recommended private hospital with English-speaking doctors.

Hospital Maciel (☎ 915-3000; cnr 25 de Mayo & Maciel) The public hospital, located in Ciudad Vieja.

Money

Countless exchange houses line Av 18 de Julio, with rates clearly posted. ATMs are everywhere, including the bus terminal.

ABN-AMRO Bank (Av 18 de Julio 999) Opposite Plaza del Entrevero.

Banco Comercial (cnr Av 18 de Julio & Santiago de Chile) At eastern edge of downtown.

Banco de la Nación Argentina (Juan Carlos Gómez 1378) In Ciudad Vieja, on Plaza Constitución.

Cambio Gales (Av 18 de Julio 1046) Cashes traveler's checks.

Indumex (Tres Cruces Bus Terminal)

Post

Post office Centro (cnr Ejido & San José); Ciudad Vieja (Misiones 1328)

Telephone

Antel Telecentro Centro (cnr San José & Paraguay); Ciudad Vieja (Rincón 501); Tres Cruces bus terminal (cnr Bulevar Artigas & Av Italia)

Tourist Information

Municipal tourist office Centro (☎ 1950; cnr Av 18 de Julio & Ejido; 10am-7pm Mon-Fri, 11am-6pm Sat & Sun); Ciudad Vieja (☎ 1950 ext 1830; cnr Rambla 25 de Agosto & Maciel; 10am-6pm) At the time of writing, plans were underway to close the downtown branch and move all operations to the new waterfront location next to Museo del Carnaval.

National Tourism Ministry Carrasco airport (☎ 604-0386; 8am-10pm); Ciudad Vieja (☎ 1885 ext 111; cnr Rambla 25 de Agosto & Yacaré; 9am-6pm Mon-Fri); Tres Cruces bus terminal (☎ 409-7399; cnr Bulevar Artigas & Av Italia; 8am-10pm) The national tourist office provides information about Montevideo and destinations throughout Uruguay.

Travel Agencies

Turisport Centro (☎ 902-0829; San José 930); Pocitos (☎ 712-4797; Juan B Blanco 837) The local Amex representative.

Viajeros Sin Fronteras (☎ 916-5466; www .sinfronteras.com.uy in Spanish; Buenos Aires 618, Oficina 001) Specializes in student and youth travel services.

DANGERS & ANNOYANCES

While Montevideo is pretty sedate by Latin American standards, you should exercise caution as in any large city. Wallet- and purse-snatchings are not uncommon in the Ciudad Vieja, and certain areas should be avoided at night, notably the Mercado del Puerto. You may also encounter some aggressive panhandling along the pedestrian streets Bacacay and Sarandí.

SIGHTS

All sights below are listed from west to east. Note that many Montevideo museums are known by their acronyms. Admission is free except where noted.

Ciudad Vieja
MUSEO DEL CARNAVAL

This **museum** (☎ 916-5493; Rambla 25 de Agosto 218; 11am-5pm Tue-Sun) houses a wonderful collection of costumes, drums, masks, recordings and photos documenting the 100-plus-year history of Montevideo's Carnaval. At the time of writing, all exhibits were in Spanish, with English translations planned.

MERCADO DEL PUERTO

No visitor should miss Montevideo's old port market building, at the foot of Pérez Castellano, whose impressive wrought-iron superstructure shelters a gaggle of reasonably priced *parrillas* (steak restaurants; see p556). Especially on Saturday afternoons, it's a lively, colorful place where the city's artists, craftspeople and street musicians hang out.

URUGUAY

MUSEO DE ARTE PRECOLOMBINO E INDÍGENA

This **museum** (MAPI; ☎ 916-9360; 25 de Mayo 279; ⏲ noon-6pm Tue-Sat) displays artifacts and information about Uruguay's earliest inhabitants, including the impact of Jesuit missionaries on native cultures.

MUSEO DE ARTES DECORATIVAS

The Palacio Taranco, a wealthy merchant's residence dating from 1810, is now home to the **Museo de Artes Decorativas** (☎ 915-1101; 25 de Mayo 376; ⏲ 12:30-6pm Tue-Sat, 2-6pm Sun). Free guided tours of the palatial building and its exquisite furnishings are given (in Spanish) at 4:30pm.

MUSEO HISTÓRICO NACIONAL

The National Historical Museum consists of several dispersed Ciudad Vieja houses. The centerpiece is 19th-century **Casa Rivera** (☎ 915-1051; Rincón 437; ⏲ 11am-5pm Mon-Fri, noon-5pm Sat), the former home of Uruguay's first president and founder of the Colorado Party, Fructuoso Rivera. The collection of paintings, documents, furniture and artifacts traces Uruguayan history from indigenous roots through to independence.

The 18th-century **Museo Romántico** (☎ 915-3361; 25 de Mayo 428; ⏲ 11am-5pm Mon-Fri) is filled with paintings and antique furniture. **Casa Lavalleja** (☎ 915-1028; Zabala 1469; ⏲ 11am-4pm Sat) was the home of General Lavalleja from 1830 until his death in 1853.

PLAZA CONSTITUCIÓN

Also known as Plaza Matriz, this was the heart of colonial Montevideo. On its east side stands the **Cabildo** (finished in 1812), a neoclassical stone structure that contains the **Museo y Archivo Histórico Municipal** (Municipal Archive & Historical Museum; ☎ 915-9685; Juan Carlos Gómez 1362; ⏲ noon-5:30pm Tue-Sun). Opposite the Cabildo is the **Iglesia Matriz**, Montevideo's oldest public building. It was begun in 1784 and completed in 1799.

MUSEO TORRES GARCÍA

This **museum** (☎ 916-2663; Sarandí 683; donation requested; ⏲ 9am-7pm Mon-Fri, 10am-6pm Sat & Sun) showcases the work of 20th-century Uruguayan painter Torres García and has revolving exhibitions featuring other contemporary artists.

TEATRO SOLÍS

Just off Plaza Independencia, elegant **Teatro Solís** (☎ 1950 ext 3323; www.teatrosolis.org.uy in Spanish; Buenos Aires 678) is Montevideo's premier performance space (see p559 and p559). First opened in 1856, and completely renovated during the past decade, it has superb acoustics. Regularly scheduled tours (11am, noon and 4pm Wednesday, Friday, Saturday and Sunday) are free on Wednesdays, UR$20 other days, which is the only way to see the actual performance space without attending a show.

Centro

PLAZA INDEPENDENCIA

In the middle of this downtown plaza is the **Mausoleo de Artigas**, whose aboveground portion is a 17m, 30-ton statue of the country's independence hero. Below street level an honor guard keeps 24-hour vigil over Artigas' remains.

The 18th-century **Palacio Estévez**, on the south side of the plaza, was the Government House until 1985. On the east side of the plaza, the 26-story structure with the crazy beehive hairdo is **Palacio Salvo**, the continent's tallest building when it opened in 1927. At the west end of the plaza is the **Puerta de la Ciudadela**, a stone gateway that is one of the only remnants of the colonial citadel demolished in 1833.

MUSEO DE ARTE CONTEMPORÁNEO

Across from the gaucho museum, the **Museo de Arte Contemporáneo** (MAC; ☎ 900-6662; Av 18 de Julio 965; ⏲ 2-8pm Tue-Sun, 2-6:30pm Mon), displays a small collection of modern Uruguayan painting and sculpture.

MUSEO DEL GAUCHO Y DE LA MONEDA

Housed in the ornate Palacio Heber, the **Museo del Gaucho y de la Moneda** (☎ 900-8764; Av 18 de Julio 998; ⏲ 10am-5pm Mon-Fri) eloquently conveys the deep attachments and interdependent relationships between the gauchos, their animals and the land. The excellent collection features a range of artifacts from Uruguay's gaucho history, including horse gear, silver work, and *mates* and *bombillas* in whimsical designs. Downstairs there is also a display of banknotes, coins, and exhibits about the volatile history of the Uruguayan economy.

MUSEO DEL AUTOMÓVIL
The Automóvil Club del Uruguay's **Museo del Automóvil** (☎ 902-4792; Colonia 1251, 6th fl; ☼ 5-7pm) has a superb collection of vintage cars, including a mint 1910 Hupmobile.

MUSEO DE LA HISTORIA DEL ARTE
In the basement of Montevideo's Palacio Municipial (known as Intendencia or town hall), the **Museo de la Historia del Arte** (MuHAr; ☎ 1950 ext 2191; Ejido 1326; ☼ noon-5:30pm Tue-Sun), features a wide-ranging collection of art from Egypt, Mesopotamia, Persia, Greece, Rome and numerous Native American cultures.

CENTRO MUNICIPAL DE FOTOGRAFÍA
Rotating contemporary photo exhibits can be seen at the **Centro Municipal de Fotografía** (CMDF; ☎ 1950 ext 1219; San José 1360; ☼ 10:30am-7pm Mon-Fri, 9:30am-2:30pm Sat). There are also two computers where visitors can browse the collection of 80,000 historic photos.

North of Centro
For great views out across the city, take the elevator to the top of the soaring, wedge-shaped **Torre Antel** (☎ 928-4417; Guatemala 1075; ☼ 3:30-5pm Mon, Wed & Fri, 10:30am-noon Tue & Thu), Montevideo's most dramatic modern skyscraper, northeast of the port. Free tours are available Tuesday and Thursday mornings, as well as Monday, Wednesday and Friday afternoons.

Dating from 1908, the three-story neoclassical **Palacio Legislativo** (☎ 200-1334; Av Libertador General Lavalleja) is one of Montevideo's most impressive landmarks. Guided tours take place hourly between 8:30am and 6:30pm weekdays. Citizens lobbying the legislature on various issues maintain a tent encampment across the street.

Museo Blanes (☎ 336-2248; Av Millán 4015; ☼ noon-6pm Tue-Sun), housed in an old mansion in the suburb of Prado, shows the work of Uruguay's most famous painter, Juan Manuel Blanes, including many historical scenes of the Río de la Plata region.

East of Centro
A must-see for any soccer fan, the **Museo del Fútbol** (☎ 480-1259; Estadio Centenario, Av Ricaldoni s/n, Parque José Batlle y Ordóñez; admission UR$50; ☼ 10am-6pm Wed-Fri, 9am-2pm Sat & Sun) displays memorabilia from Uruguay's 1930 and 1950 World Cup championships. The price of admission includes a stadium tour with visits to the stands, locker rooms and playing field.

Uruguay's largest collection of paintings is housed in the **Museo Nacional de Artes Visuales** (MNAV; ☎ 711-6124; www.mnav.gub.uy in Spanish; cnr Av Herrera y Reissig & T Giribaldi; ☼ 2-6:45pm Tue-Sun) in Parque Rodó. The large rooms are graced with works by Blanes, Cúneo, Figari and Torres García.

La Rambla & Eastern Beaches
La Rambla, Montevideo's multi-kilometer coastal promenade, is one of the city's defining elements, connecting downtown to the eastern beach communities of Punta Carretas, Pocitos, Buceo and Carrasco. This is Montevideo's social hub on Sunday afternoons, when the place is packed with locals cradling thermoses of *mate* and socializing with friends.

Castillo Pittamiglio (☎ 712-0284; Rambla Gandhi 633; ☼ 10:30am-7pm Mon-Fri, 9:30am-2:30pm Sat), on the Rambla between Punta Carretas and Pocitos, is the eccentric legacy of local alchemist and architect Humberto Pittamiglio. Its quirky facade alone is worth a look; tours of the interior (UR$30) are also available on Tuesday and Thursday afternoons at 4pm.

Museo Naval (☎ 622-1084; cnr Rambla Costanera & LA de Herrera; ☼ 8am-noon & 2-6pm Fri-Wed), along the eastern waterfront in Buceo, traces the role of boats and ships in Uruguayan history, from the indigenous Charrúa's canoe culture to the dramatic sinking of the German *Graf Spee* offshore of Montevideo in 1939.

The **Yacht Harbor** in Buceo, just east of Pocitos beach, is a picturesque spot for a stroll and a popular Sunday afternoon hangout.

ACTIVITIES
Get yourself a **bike** and go cruising along the walking-jogging-cycling track that follows the riverfront Rambla; bikes can be rented at both the Montevideo Hostel and the Ciudad Vieja Hostel. After about 2km you'll get to Playa Pocitos, which is best for **swimming** and where you should be able to jump in on a game of **beach volleyball**. A couple of bays further along at Puerto del Buceo you can get **windsurfing** lessons at the yacht club. If all that seems a bit too energetic, bus 64 goes from Av 18 de Julio along the coast road – just jump off when you see a beach you like.

URUGUAY

CARNAVAL IN MONTEVIDEO

If you thought Brazil was South America's only Carnaval capital, think again! Montevideanos cut loose in a big way every February, with music and dance filling the air for a solid month.

Not to be missed is the early-February **Desfile de las Llamadas**, an all-night parade of *comparsas* (neighborhood Carnaval societies) through the streets of Palermo and Barrio Sur districts just south of the Centro. *Comparsas* are made up of *negros* (persons of African descent) and *lubolos* (whites who paint their faces black for Carnaval, a long-standing Uruguayan tradition). Neighborhood rivalries play themselves out as wave after wave of dancers whirl to the electrifying rhythms of traditional Afro-Uruguay *candombe* drumming, beaten out on drums of three different pitches: the *chico* (soprano), *repique* (contralto) and *piano* (tenor). The heart of the parade route is Isla de Flores, between Salto and Gaboto. Spectators can pay for a chair on the sidewalk (UR$40) or try to snag a spot on one of the balconies overlooking the street.

Another key element of Montevideo's Carnaval is the *murgas*, organized groups of 15 to 17 gaudily dressed performers, including three percussionists, who perform original pieces of musical theater, often satirical and based on political themes. (During the dictatorship in Uruguay, *murgas* were famous for their subversive commentary.) All *murgas* use the same three instruments: the *bombo* (bass drum), *redoblante* (snare drum) and *platillos* (cymbals). *Murgas* play all over the city, and also compete throughout the month of February at the **Teatro de Verano** in Parque Rodó (admission from UR$70). The competition has three rounds, with judges determining who advances and who gets eliminated.

The fascinating history of Montevideo's Carnaval is well documented in the city's recently opened **Museo del Carnaval** (p551). This is a great place to soak up some of the Carnaval feeling if you can't attend the real thing. On display are costumes, drums and photos, along with recorded music from Carnavals past.

Another great way to experience Carnaval out of season is by attending one of the informal *candombe* practice sessions that erupt in neighborhood streets throughout the year. A good place to find these is at the corner of Isla de Flores and Gaboto in Palermo. Drummers usually gather between 7pm and 7:30pm on Sunday nights. If you show up a little late, just follow your ears.

COURSES

The following courses don't cater for the casual learner – you'd want to be staying at least a month to get your money's worth.

Berlitz (☎ 901-5535; Plaza Independencia 1380) One-on-one Spanish classes.

Joventango (☎ 901-5561; Mercado de la Abundancia, cnr San José & Aquiles Lanza) Tango classes for all levels, from beginner to expert.

Complejo Multicultural Mundo Afro (☎ 915-0247; Mercado Central, Ciudadela 1229) Classes in African drumming, capoeira and *candombe* dance.

TOURS

Most hostels and higher-end hotels can arrange city tours.

On Saturday afternoons, a photogenic (but stinky!) vintage bus makes half-hour circuits of the Ciudad Vieja (UR$20) from Plaza Constitución, with running commentary. Departures are announced by megaphone – don't worry, you'll hear it!

FESTIVALS & EVENTS

Much livelier than its Buenos Aires counterpart, Montevideo's late-summer **Carnaval** is the cultural highlight of the year – see the boxed text, above.

At Parque Prado, north of downtown, Semana Criolla festivities during **Semana Santa** (Holy Week) include displays of gaucho skills, *asados* and other such events.

In October, Joventango's **Festival Internacional Viva El Tango** is a 10-day celebration of Montevideo's tango heritage, combining free events on the streets, nightly dances at Mercado de la Abundancia and formal concerts at sit-down venues such as Teatro Solís and Sala Zitarrosa.

SLEEPING

Montevideo's burgeoning hosteling scene is a dream come true for budget travelers. Most hostels also offer city tours, plus advice on museums and nightlife.

Ciudad Vieja

BUDGET

Ciudad Vieja Hostel (☎ 915-6192; www.ciudadviejahostel .com; Ituzaingó 1436; dm HI member/nonmember UR$220/240, r UR$615/660; 🖳) This relative newcomer to Montevideo's hostel scene has friendly staff, a homey, hip atmosphere, and an appealing layout on two upper floors of an older Ciudad Vieja building. There are separate kitchens and lounging areas on each level, a DVD library, roof deck, bikes for rent, city tours and a helpful bulletin board of cultural events.

Posada al Sur (☎ 916-5287; www.posadaalsur.com.uy; Pérez Castellano 1424; dm UR$330, r with/without bathroom UR$770/660; 🖳) A few blocks above Mercado del Puerto, this lovingly restored older building has one six-bed dorm and three private rooms. Discounts are available for friends traveling together or for extended stays. Proceeds help support the owners' newly established ecotourism business.

Spléndido Hotel (☎ 916-4900; www.splendidohotel .com.uy; Bartolomé Mitre 1314; without breakfast s UR$350-500, d UR$400-800, tr UR$700; 🖳) The faded but friendly Spléndido offers excellent value for budget travelers preferring privacy over a hostel-style party vibe. There's a remarkable variety of rooms, all with wi-fi. Penny-pinchers will appreciate the ultracheap ones tucked away on claustrophobic half-floors reminiscent of *Being John Malkovich*. Pricier rooms have 15-foot ceilings and French doors opening to balconies, some overlooking Teatro Solís. Bars on the street below can get noisy on weekends, and the Montevideo Philharmonic Orchestra rehearses next door some mornings (free concert anyone?).

Hotel Palacio (☎ 916-3612; www.hotelpalacio.com.uy; Bartolomé Mitre 1364; r with/without bathroom UR$550/330) This ancient hotel has sagging brass beds, antique furniture and a vintage elevator. Try for one of the two 6th-floor rooms; the views of the Ciudad Vieja from the large balconies are superb.

TOP END

Plaza Fuerte Hotel (☎ 915-6651; www.plazafuerte .com; Bartolomé Mitre 1361; s/d standard UR$1200/1450, ste UR$1900/2100; 🗱 🖳) Housed in a stately building dating to 1913, the Plaza Fuerte has red-carpeted marble stairs, decorative tile floors and dramatic views from its 5th-floor bar and terrace. All rooms have 5m-high ceilings; the suites (some split over two levels, some with Jacuzzis) are especially elegant.

Centro

BUDGET

Montevideo Hostel (☎ 908-1324; www.montevideohostel .com.uy in Spanish; Canelones 935; per person with/without HI or ISIC card UR$200/250; 🖳) With musical instruments strewn everywhere, good internet facilities, a cellar bar, a nice fireplace and a spiral staircase connecting all three levels of the spacious central common area, this older hostel, managed by the same family for years, remains one of Montevideo's best budget options.

Che Lagarto Hostel (☎ 903-0175; www.chelagarto .com; Plaza Independencia 713; dm HI member/nonmember UR$250/275, s/tw without bathroom UR$360/625, d with bathroom UR$875; 🖳) Centrally located, in a cheerfully painted neoclassical building, Che Lagarto is part of a four-hostel South American chain. The common areas and tiny kitchen are not as welcoming as at other area hostels, but front-room balconies have great views of Plaza Independencia, and the singles are among the best deals in town.

ourpick Red Hostel (☎ 908-8514; www.redhostel .com; San José 1406; dm/s/d UR$275/550/750; 🖳) The bright orange walls, roof deck, plants and natural light pouring in through stained-glass skylights make this Montevideo's cheeriest hostel, with an energetic, friendly young staff ready to answer any questions about local goings-on. Some of the five internet computers are ready for retirement, and the TV room and kitchen could be a tad bigger, but it's highly recommended overall.

MIDRANGE

Hotel Lancaster (☎ 902-1054; www.lancasterhotel .com.uy; Plaza Cagancha 1334; s/d/tr from UR$750/900/1100; 🗱) This centrally located three-star on Plaza Cagancha is good value. Despite the unpromising exterior and bland, functional lobby decor, the rooms are clean and comfortable, many with views of the square below.

London Palace Hotel (☎ 902-0024; www.lphotel .com; Río Negro 1278; s/d UR$900/1100; 🗱 🖳) Spotless, quiet, comfortable and central, this hotel is a solid midrange option with business facilities.

TOP END

Hotel Embajador (☎ 902-0012; www.hotelembajador .com; San José 1212; s/d UR$1000/1300; ✖ 🖳 🖳) The four-star Embajador offers comfortable accommodation without a monster price tag. There's wi-fi in all rooms, a rooftop pool and sauna, and plenty of other amenities.

Balmoral Plaza Hotel (☎ 902-2393; www.balmoral .com.uy; Plaza Cagancha 1126; s/d/tr from UR$1450/1650/2100; ✖ 🖳) All rooms have minibars, safes, big TVs and double-glazed, soundproof windows, and many have bird's-eye views of leafy Plaza Cagancha. You'll also find a garage, gym, sauna and business center.

Radisson Victoria Plaza (☎ 902-0111; www .radisson.com/montevideouy; Plaza Independencia 759; s/d UR$3200/3500, ste UR$3800; ✖ 🖳 🖳) A true five-star hotel, with luxurious rooms, a semi-Olympic (25m) swimming pool, and remarkable city views from the 25th-floor restaurant. The central location on Plaza Independencia can't be beat.

East of Centro

Palermo Art Hostel (☎ 410-6519; www.palermoart hostel.com; Gaboto 1010; dm/s/d UR$275/550/700; 🖳) The newly opened Palermo compensates for its out-of-the-way location with welcoming, artsy touches like colorfully painted rooms and pretty comforters. Wi-fi is available, and there's an attractive kitchen and a downstairs pub. It's also the perfect base for experiencing Montevideo's Sunday *candombe* drum sessions (see the boxed text, p554).

La Rambla & Eastern Beaches

Pocitos Plaza Hotel (☎ 712-3939; www.pocitosplaza hotel.com.uy; Benito Blanco 640, Pocitos; s/d standard UR$1650/1750, superior UR$2000/2200; ✖ 🖳) This comfortable four-star is replete with services for the business traveler, although vacationers will also appreciate its sauna, sundeck and proximity to the beach. Superior rooms have sofas, whirlpool tubs and big closets.

Cala di Volpe (☎ 710-2000; www.hotelcaladivolpe .com.uy; cnr Rambla Gandhi & Parva Domus, Punta Carretas; r from UR$3300, ste UR$5000; ✖ 🖳 🖳) This classy newcomer across from the beach boasts one of Montevideo's most exclusive locations. Boutique features abound: comfy couches, writing desks, wi-fi, gleaming tile-and-marble bathrooms, and floor-to-ceiling picture windows with sweeping river views. There's a small rooftop pool and a nice restaurant.

EATING

Montevideo's restaurants are largely unpretentious and offer excellent value.

Ciudad Vieja

BUDGET

Mercado del Puerto (Pérez Castellano) *The* classic place to eat in Montevideo is the market on the Ciudad Vieja waterfront. The densely packed *parrillas* here cater to every budget, competing like rutting elk to show off their obscenely large racks – of roasted meat and veggies, that is! Weekends are the best time to savor the market's vibrant, crowded energy, but lunching executives and tourists keep the place buzzing on weekdays too.

Café Roldós (☎ 915-1520; Mercado del Puerto; sandwiches UR$40; ✆ 9am-7pm) This historic café is a perennial market favorite. Since 1886 they've been pouring their famous *medio y medio* (UR$25), a refreshing concoction made from half wine, half sparkling wine. Throw in a few tasty sandwiches, and you've got a meal!

Rincón de Zabala (☎ 915-1617; Rincón 387; sandwiches UR$40, lunch UR$99; ✆ 9am-5:30pm Mon-Fri) This modern corner place serves up free wi-fi along with affordable breakfasts, sandwiches and cafeteria-style daily specials.

MIDRANGE

Confitería La Pasiva (☎ 915-8261; Sarandí 600; meals from UR$110) This perfectly placed branch of Uruguay's famous chain *confitería* has outdoor seating on Ciudad Vieja's main square, with excellent, reasonably priced *minutas* (short orders) and good breakfast specials.

Las Misiones (☎ 915-4495; 25 de Mayo 449; daily specials UR$110-130; ✆ 6am-6pm Mon-Fri) Even before you walk in the door, this eye-catching corner café wins points for its lovely green-and-yellow tiled exterior dating back to 1907. *Chivitos*, salads and *sugerencias del día* (daily specials) are all good value.

Don Peperone (☎ 915-7493; Sarandí 650; meals from UR$128; ✆ 10am-2am) Another high-quality chain restaurant in Ciudad Vieja, Don Peperone serves excellent, moderately priced food late into the night, with occasional live music. Vegetarians will appreciate the unlimited salad bar for UR$179, and nicotine fiends will rejoice at the comfortable smoking section.

ourpick Café Bacacay (☎ 916-6074; Bacacay 1306; dishes UR$100-240; ✆ 9am-late Mon-Sat) This chic little café across from Teatro Solís serves a variety of mouthwatering goodies: fish of the day with wasabi or *limoncello* (lemon liqueur) sauce, build-your-own salads with tasty ingredients like grilled eggplant, spinach and smoked salmon, and a wide-ranging drinks menu. Desserts include chocolate cake, pear tart and lemon pie.

TOP END

La Corte (☎ 916-0435; Sarandí 586; dishes UR$250-325; ✆ lunch Mon-Fri, dinner Thu-Sat) OK, so maybe you'd rather not eat in a place once patronized by George W Bush, but the food is excellent at this elegant twin-level restaurant on Plaza Constitución. The lunchtime *menu ejecutivo* (business lunch) is a bargain at UR$175.

Panini's (☎ 916-8760; Bacacay 1339; dishes UR$250-400) For fine dining, Italian style, try this place in the pedestrian zone just off Plaza Independencia. Pasta lovers will appreciate the *degustación de pastas* – a veritable smorgasbord of noodley delights.

Centro
BUDGET

La Vegetariana (☎ 902-3178; Yí 1369; meals UR$70-95) Grab a plate and help yourself from the steam trays, salad bar and dessert table – it's not fine dining, but it's one of the few truly veggie options in this meat-crazed country.

Bar Hispano (☎ 908-0045; San José 1050; daily specials UR$85-100; ✆ 7am-1am) Old-school neighborhood *confiterías* (cafés offering light meals) like this are disappearing fast. The bow-tied, grouchy waiters can take pretty much any order you throw at them – a stiff drink to start the day, a full meal at 5pm or a chocolate binge in the early hours.

MIDRANGE

Club Brasilero (☎ 902-4344; Av 18 de Julio 994, 2nd fl; daily specials UR$100-120; ✆ 8:30am-10pm Mon-Fri, to 4pm Sat) Inside the Brazilian cultural center, reasonably priced meals are served in an elegant 2nd-floor salon with high ceilings and stained glass.

Cantina Vasca (☎ 902-3519; San José 1168; dishes UR$100-180, ✆ noon-4pm & 8:30pm-late) Eat among the card-players at this cozy 2nd-floor Basque social club overlooking a leafy street. Daily seafood specials, pasta and paellas are complemented by glasses of house wine (UR$15).

Ruffino Pizza y Pasta (☎ 908-3384; San José 1166; dishes UR$100-210; ✆ noon-3pm & 8pm-midnight Mon-Fri, dinner only Sat, lunch only Sun) Extremely popular for Sunday lunch, Ruffino's is a good midrange Italian option. Try the Caruso (mushroom and cream) sauce, a uniquely Uruguayan specialty created for Italian tenor Enrico Caruso during his 1915 visit to Montevideo.

The **Mercado de la Abundancia** (cnr San José & Aquiles Lanza) features four low-key eateries surrounding an open space where locals come to dance every Saturday night to tango, salsa and more. **El Rincón de los Poetas** (☎ 901-5102; dishes UR$100-170; ✆ 10am-late), with its red-and-white checked tablecloths, epitomizes the Mercado's cozy, relaxed ambience. All four restaurants feature the classic Uruguayan trinity of pasta, pizza and (of course) roast meat.

TOP END

Los Leños Uruguayos (☎ 900-2285; San José 909; dishes UR$250-340; ✆ noon-4pm & 7:30pm-12:30am Sun-Thu, to 2am Fri & Sat) This tony little restaurant is a favorite with the business set. It has a nice salad bar, and there's always a big rack of meat roasting on the fire up front. The lunchtime *menu ejecutivo* (UR$135) and *sugerencia del día* (UR$185) are both great deals, including *cubierto*, main dish, dessert and coffee.

East of Centro

Bistró Sucré Salé (☎ 402-7779; Blvd Artigas 1229, Parque Rodó; snacks & pastries from UR$65; meals UR$105-230; ✆ 8am-9pm Mon-Fri, 9am-5pm Sat) Wonderful European influences abound at this little café behind the Alianza Francesa: French music, brioches, tarts, Illy espresso, Van Gogh posters, a courtyard with fountain, iron gazebo and climbing roses. Oh, and napkins that actually work!

Mediterráneo (☎ 413-3212; Maldonado 1766, Palermo; dishes UR$115-240; ✆ noon-4pm & 8pm-midnight Mon-Fri, 8pm-midnight Sat) This trendy, dimly lit pizzeria in Palermo, with brick walls and high beamed ceilings, is on the expensive side, but the lunchtime *menu ejecutivo* (UR$140) is a great deal.

La Rambla & Eastern Beaches

El Viejo y El Mar (☎ 710-5704; Rambla Gandhi 400, Punta Carretas; dishes from UR$140; ✆ noon-1am) This waterfront eatery specializes in fish, served at thatched shelters in a grassy area outdoors.

Che Montevideo (☎ 710-6941; Rambla Gandhi 630, Pocitos; dishes from UR$150; ⏱ noon-2am Sun-Thu, to 3am Fri & Sat) The menu here features seafood with an international twist, but the big attraction is the open-air deck, with its spectacular views of the Río de la Plata and its sailboats at sunset.

Da Pentella (☎ 712-0981; cnr Luis de la Torre & Francisco Ros, Punta Carretas; dishes from UR$200; ⏱ 10am-1am) Near Punta Carretas Shopping, this is one of Montevideo's finest Italian restaurants, with over a century of history.

Bar Tabaré (☎ 712-3242; Zorrilla de San Martín 152, Punta Carretas; meals UR$300; ⏱ 8pm-late Mon-Sat) This tastefully remodeled traditional neighborhood bar, first opened in 1919, gets top marks for atmosphere and for its international array of salads, pasta, meat and fish.

DRINKING

Ciudad Vieja and Centro offer an intriguing mix of venerable old cafés and up-and-coming recent arrivals. Bars are concentrated along Bartolomé Mitre in Ciudad Vieja, and south of Plaza Independencia in the Centro.

Cafés

Oro del Rhin (☎ 902-2833; Convención 1403, Centro; ⏱ 8:30am-8:30pm Mon-Sat) With over 75 years in business, you know they're doing something right! It's worth a visit just to ogle the gorgeous collection of cakes and pastries in the window.

Café Brasilero (☎ 915-8120; Ituzaingó 1447, Ciudad Vieja; ⏱ 9am-7:30pm Mon-Fri) A delightfully old-fashioned 1877 café with little wooden tables and chairs, chandeliers, and historic photos and posters gracing the walls.

El Beso (☎ 916-6141; 25 de Mayo 263, Ciudad Vieja; ⏱ 12:30-7pm) This stylish café in Ciudad Vieja has electric-purple walls, youthful energy and the artsy Imaginario Sur boutique next door.

Café de la Pausa (☎ 915-3856; Sarandí 493, 1st fl, Ciudad Vieja; ⏱ 11am-5pm Mon-Sat) A cozy hideaway tucked upstairs just west of Plaza Constitución.

Bars

Shannon Irish Pub (☎ 916-9585; Bartolomé Mitre 1318, Ciudad Vieja; ⏱ 8pm-late Tue-Sun) A perennial favorite, the Shannon pours a good pint and features live music on weekends.

Viejo Mitre (☎ 916-8259; Bartolomé Mitre 1321, Ciudad Vieja; ⏱ 6pm-late Tue-Sun) With comfy couches on the sidewalk, this is a great place to kick back and contemplate Ciudad Vieja street life.

Fun Fun (☎ 915-8005; Ciudadela 1229, Mercado Central, Ciudad Vieja; ⏱ 7pm-late Tue-Fri, 9pm-late Sat) Since 1895, this informal venue in the Mercado Central has been serving its famous *uvita* (a sweet wine drink) while hosting tango and other live music on a tiny stage. The front deck is very pleasant.

La Ronda (☎ 902-6962; Ciudadela 1182, Centro; ⏱ noon-late Mon-Sat, 7pm-late Sun) Ultracool Ronda is always animated and jam-packed, with a turntable spinning hypnotic tunes. Patrons straddle the windowsills between the dark interior plastered with vintage album covers and the sidewalk tables cooled by breezes off the Rambla.

El Lobizón (☎ 901-1334; Zelmar Michelini 1264, Centro; ⏱ 7pm-late Sun-Thu, 8pm-late Fri & Sat) Lobizón's cellar-bar atmosphere, free-flowing pitchers of sangría and *clericó*, and tasty snacks like the famous *gramajo* (potatoes, ham and eggs) make it a very popular gathering place for young, artistic types.

ENTERTAINMENT

The useful weekly *Guía del Ocio* (UR$10, published Fridays) lists Montevideo cultural events, cinemas, theaters and restaurants. Websites with entertainment listings include the following (all are in Spanish):

■ www.pimba.com.uy
■ www.eltimon.com.uy
■ www.cartelera.com.uy
■ www.espectador.com.uy
■ www.aromperlanoche.com

Nightclubs

W Lounge (☎ 712-2671; Rambla Wilson, Parque Rodó; ⏱ 11pm-6am Fri & Sat) With two dance floors accommodating 3000 people, this nightclub in Parque Rodó is *the* place to shake your thang to rock, *cumbia* and techno beats. A taxi from the center should cost about UR$75.

AlmodóBar (☎ 916-6665; Rincón 626, Ciudad Vieja; ⏱ midnight-late) People line up around the block to dance at this trendy club.

El Pony Pisador Ciudad Vieja (☎ 916-2982; Bartolomé Mitre 1325; ⏱ 8pm-late); Pocitos (☎ 622-1885; José Iturriaga 3497; ⏱ 8pm-late) This thriving bar and disco has two locations in Montevideo and one in Punta del Este.

La Otra Ronda (☎ 902-6962; Soriano 776, Centro; ⏱ midnight-late Fri & Sat) Around the corner from La Ronda bar (above), this sister enterprise features live dance music of all kinds.

BJ Bar (☎ 908-5703; Soriano 820, Centro; ⌚ 10pm-late Wed-Sun) Features an eclectic mix of DJs, live acts and films.

La Bodeguita del Sur (☎ 901-1034; Soriano 840, Centro; ⌚ 11pm-late Fri-Sun) For live salsa, hit this place on weekend nights.

Live Music & Dance

The legendary Carlos Gardel spent time in Montevideo, where the tango is no less popular than in Buenos Aires. Music and dance venues abound downtown.

Teatro Solís (☎ 1950 ext 3323; www.teatrosolis.org.uy in Spanish; Buenos Aires 678, Ciudad Vieja; admission from UR$80) The city's top venue is home to the Montevideo Philharmonic Orchestra and hosts formal concerts of classical, jazz, tango and other music, plus music festivals, ballet and opera.

Sala Zitarrosa (☎ 901-7303; Av 18 de Julio 1008, Centro) Montevideo's best informal auditorium venue for big-name music and dance performances, including zarzuela, tango, rock, flamenco and reggae.

Cine Teatro Plaza (☎ 901-5385; Plaza Cagancha 1129, Centro) Occasionally brings in big international acts like Brazil's Milton Nascimento.

Central (☎ 908-0847; Rondeau 1383, Centro) This converted movie theater is now a multi-use space hosting live music, theater and film.

El Tartamudo Café (☎ 480-4332; 8 de Octubre 2543 & Presidente Berro, Tres Cruces; ⌚ 9pm-late Thu-Sun) Performances at this place just east of Tres Cruces bus terminal run the gamut from rock to tango to *candombe* to jazz.

Theater

Montevideo's active theater community spans many worlds: from classical to commercial to avant-garde.

Teatro Solís (☎ 1950 ext 3323; www.teatrosolis.org.uy in Spanish; Buenos Aires 678, Ciudad Vieja; admission from UR$80) Home to the Comedia Nacional, Montevideo's municipal theater company. Tours of the theater are available; see p552 for details.

Teatro Sobre Ruedas (☎ 915-8618; Bacacay 1318, Ciudad Vieja; admission UR$150) Fifteen years old and going strong, this company presents *Barro Negro*, an interactive theater piece that literally takes place on a bus whizzing through Montevideo's streets.

Teatro Circular (☎ 901-5952; Rondeau 1388, Centro; admission from UR$120) Just north of Plaza Cagancha, the venerable Circular recently celebrated its 50th anniversary.

Teatro Victoria (☎ 901-9971; Rio Negro 1479, Centro; admission from UR$150) This historic downtown theater, north of Plaza del Entrevero, sometimes mounts classics such as Lope de Vega's *Gatomaquia*.

Teatro El Galpón (☎ 408-3366; Av 18 de Julio 1618, Centro; admission from UR$120) Montevideo's most commercial theater always stages multiple shows concurrently.

Cinema

Cinemateca Uruguaya (☎ 900-9056; Av 18 de Julio 1280; membership per month UR$111) For art-house flicks, this film club charges a modest membership allowing unlimited viewing at its five cinemas. It hosts the two-week Festival Cinematográfico Internacional del Uruguay every March, and smaller film festivals throughout the year.

The rest of Montevideo's cinema scene is concentrated in the shopping malls east of downtown.

Spectator Sports

Soccer, a Uruguayan passion, inspires large and regular crowds. The main stadium, the **Estadio Centenario** (Av Ricaldoni s/n, Parque José Batlle y Ordóñez), opened in 1930 for the first World Cup, in which Uruguay defeated Argentina 4–2 in the title game.

SHOPPING

Central Montevideo's traditional downtown shopping area is Av 18 de Julio, although plenty of upmarket new stores are beginning to pop up in Ciudad Vieja. Montevideanos also flock to three major shopping malls east of downtown: Punta Carretas Shopping, Tres Cruces Shopping (above the bus terminal) and Montevideo Shopping (in the Pocitos/Buceo neighborhood).

Feria de Tristán Narvaja (Tristán Narvaja, Cordón) This colorful Sunday-morning outdoor market is a decades-long tradition begun by Italian immigrants. It sprawls from Av 18 de Julio northwards along Calle Tristán Narvaja, spilling over onto several side streets. You can find used books, music, clothing, jewelry, live animals, antiques and souvenirs in its dozens of makeshift stalls.

Saturday Flea Market (Plaza Constitución, Ciudad Vieja) Every Saturday vendors take over Ciudad Vieja's central square, selling antique door knockers, saddles, household goods and just about anything else you can imagine.

Mercado de los Artesanos (Plaza Cagancha, Centro) For attractive handicrafts at reasonable prices, this market is worth a look.

Manos del Uruguay Centro (☎ 900-4910; San José 1111); Ciudad Vieja (☎ 915-5345; Sarandí 668) This national cooperative is famous for its quality goods, especially woolens.

Imaginario Sur (☎ 916-0383; 25 de Mayo 265, Ciudad Vieja) This colorful, trendy shop features art, fashion and design work by dozens of Uruguayan artists.

Hecho Acá (☎ 915-4341; cnr Rambla 25 de Agosto & Yacaré, Ciudad Vieja) Woolen goods and other handicrafts from around the country are nicely displayed here.

Corazón al Sur (☎ 901-1714; Plaza del Entrevero, Centro) This kiosk downtown sells music CDs by a wide variety of Uruguayan artists. It sponsors live performances in the square Friday through Sunday.

El Galeón (☎ 915-6139; Juan Carlos Gómez 1327, Ciudad Vieja) With maps, engravings and rare books piled everywhere, this place is fun to explore.

Casa Mario (☎ 916-2356; Piedras 641, Ciudad Vieja) Specializing in Uruguayan leather since 1945, Casa Mario is quite touristy but has a wide selection.

Louvre (☎ 916-2686; Sarandí 652, Ciudad Vieja) Louvre has three floors packed with antiques, including gaucho paraphernalia, paintings, furniture and jewelry.

GETTING THERE & AWAY
Air

Montevideo's **Carrasco international airport** (☎ 604-0272) is served by far fewer airlines than Ezeiza in Buenos Aires.

Pluna, Sol and Aerolíneas Argentinas fly frequently between Carrasco and Buenos Aires' Aeroparque. Nonstop service from Montevideo to other international destinations is provided by Pluna (to Madrid and several South American cities), American Airlines (to Miami), Gol (to Porto Alegre, Brazil), Iberia (to Madrid), LanChile (to Santiago), TACA (to Lima) and TAM (to Rio, São Paulo and Asunción).

Several other airlines maintain offices in Montevideo but have no direct flights to/from Uruguay.

Aerolíneas Argentinas (☎ 902-3691; Plaza Independencia 749 bis, ground fl, Centro)

Air France/KLM (☎ 902-5013; Río Negro 1354, 1st fl, Centro)

American Airlines Ciudad Vieja (☎ 916-3929; Sarandí 699 bis); Pocitos (☎ 708-5205; Benito Blanco 1261)

Delta (☎ 900-7776; Colonia 981, Oficina 201, Centro)

Gol (☎ 000-405-5127; Carrasco airport)

Iberia (☎ 908-1032; Colonia 975, Centro)

LanChile (☎ 902-3881; Colonia 993, 4th fl, Centro)

Pluna (☎ 902-1414, 900-9999; Colonia 1013, Centro)

Qantas/Alitalia (☎ 903-1760; Río Negro 1354, 4th fl, Centro)

Sol (☎ 000-405-210053; Carrasco airport)

TACA (☎ 000-405-1004; Plaza Independencia 831, Oficina 807, Centro)

TAM (Transportes Aéreos de Mercosur; ☎ 901-8451; Colonia 820, Centro)

United/Lufthansa (☎ 901-3370; Plaza Independencia 831, Oficina 409, Centro)

Boat

Buquebus (☎ 130) Centro (cnr Colonia & Florida); Ciudad Vieja (Terminal Puerto); Tres Cruces bus terminal (cnr Bulevar Artigas & Av Italia) runs daily high-speed ferries direct from Montevideo to Buenos Aires (2¾ hours). Fares are UR$1560 in *turista*, UR$1860 in *primera* (UR$200 less for seniors, UR$400 less for children aged three to 10).

Tickets for less expensive bus-boat combinations to Buenos Aires via Colonia (UR$1005 adult, UR$845 child or senior, four hours) can be purchased at the **Ferryturismo office** (☎ 900-6617; Río Negro 1400) on Plaza del Entrevero.

Trans Uruguay (☎ 401-9350; www.transuruguay.com in Spanish; Tres Cruces bus terminal, Boletería 32), with its partner Cacciola, runs a twice-daily scenic bus-launch service to Buenos Aires via the riverside town of Carmelo and the Argentine Delta suburb of Tigre. The eight-hour trip costs UR$599 one way.

Bus

Montevideo's modern **Tres Cruces bus terminal** (☎ 401-8998; cnr Bulevar Artigas & Av Italia) is about 3km east of downtown. It has tourist information, decent restaurants, clean toilets, a luggage check (UR$83 per 24 hours for up to three bags), public telephones, ATMs and a shopping mall upstairs.

A taxi from the terminal to downtown costs around UR$100. A cheaper alternative is to take city bus 21, 64, 187 or 330, all of which go from the terminal to Plaza Independencia via Av 18 de Julio (UR$13.50, 15 minutes).

All destinations below are served daily (except as noted) and most several times a day.

A small *tasa de embarque* (terminal charge) is added to the ticket prices below. Travel times are approximate.

Destination	Cost (UR$)	Duration (hr)
Asunción (Par)	1832	18
Barra de Valizas	251	4½
Buenos Aires (Arg)	760	8
Carmelo	201	4
Chuy	285	6
Colonia	151	3
Córdoba (Arg)	1290	15½
Curitiba (Bra)	2591	24
Florianópolis (Bra)	2129	18
Fray Bentos	259	4½
La Paloma	201	4
Maldonado	117	2
Mendoza (Arg)	1736	21
Mercedes	234	4
Minas	100	2
Nueva Helvecia	109	2
Pan de Azúcar	84	1½
Paraná (Arg)	896	10
Paysandú	318	4½
Pelotas (Bra)	996	8
Piriápolis	84	1½
Porto Alegre (Bra)	1398	11½
Punta del Este	121	2½
Punta del Diablo	251	5
Rocha	176	3
Salto	419	6½
Santa Fe (Arg)	937	12
Santiago de Chile	2373	28
São Paulo (Bra)	2996	31
Tacuarembó	326	4½
Treinta y Tres	243	4½

Among Argentine destinations, Corrientes and Mendoza have at least two departures a week, and Paraná, Santa Fe and Rosario at least four. There are at least two weekly departures to Santiago, Chile.

Expreso Brújula (☎ 401-9350) goes to Asunción, Paraguay, on Tuesday and Friday, while **Coit** (Centro ☎ 908-6469; Río Branco 1389; Tres Cruces bus terminal ☎ 401-5628) goes on Wednesday and Saturday.

GETTING AROUND
To/From the Airport
From **Terminal Suburbana** (☎ 1975; cnr Río Branco & Galicia), five blocks north of Plaza del Entrevero, Copsa buses 700, 710 and 711 run to Carrasco airport (UR$22, 45 minutes). Coming from the airport, look for the covered Copsa bus stop on a little island in front of the arrivals hall.

A taxi to the airport from downtown Montevideo costs approximately UR$500.

Bus
Montevideo's city buses go almost everywhere for UR$13.50 per ride. The *Guía de Montevideo Eureka*, available at bookstores or kiosks, lists routes and schedules, as do the yellow pages of the Montevideo phone book. For additional information, contact **Cutcsa** (☎ 204-0000; www.cutcsa.com.uy in Spanish).

Car
Avis, Hertz, Europcar and other international companies have counters at Carrasco airport. In downtown Montevideo, the following Uruguayan companies with nationwide branches offer good deals.

Multicar (☎ 902-2555; www.redmulticar.com; Colonia 1227, Centro)

Punta Car (www.puntacar.com in Spanish) Centro (☎ 900-2772; Cerro Largo 1383); Carrasco airport (☎ 604-1111)

Taxi
Montevideo's black-and-yellow taxis are all metered, and amazingly cheap by world standards. It costs UR$20 to drop the flag and just over UR$1 per unit thereafter. All cabbies carry two official price tables, one effective on weekdays, the other (only slightly higher) used nights (between 10pm and 6am), weekends and holidays. Even for a long ride, you'll rarely pay more than UR$150, unless you're headed to Carrasco airport (about UR$500 from downtown).

WESTERN URUGUAY

From Colonia's tree-shaded cobblestone streets to the hot springs of Salto, the slow-paced river towns of western Uruguay have a universally relaxing appeal, with just enough urban attractions to keep things interesting. Here, the border with Argentina is defined by the Río de la Plata and the Río Uruguay, and the region is commonly referred to as *el litoral* (the shore).

Further inland you'll find the heart of what some consider the 'real' Uruguay – the gaucho country around Tacuarembó, with *estancias* sprinkled throughout the rural landscape and some beautiful, rarely visited nature preserves.

COLONIA DEL SACRAMENTO
☎ 052 / pop 22,000

Colonia is an irresistibly picturesque town whose colonial-era Barrio Histórico is a Unesco World Heritage site. Pretty rows of sycamores offer protection from the summer heat, and the Río de la Plata provides a venue for spectacular sunsets. Colonia's charm and its proximity to Buenos Aires draw thousands of Argentine visitors; on weekends, especially in summer, prices rise and it can be difficult to find a room.

Colonia was founded in 1680 by Manuel Lobo, the Portuguese governor of Rio de Janeiro, and occupied a strategic position almost exactly opposite Buenos Aires across the Río de la Plata. The town grew in importance as a source of smuggled trade items, undercutting Spain's jealously defended mercantile monopoly and provoking repeated sieges and battles between Spain and Portugal.

Although the two powers agreed over the cession of Colonia to Spain around 1750, it wasn't until 1777 that Spain took final control of the city. From this time, the city's commercial importance declined as foreign goods proceeded directly to Buenos Aires.

Orientation

Colonia sits on the east bank of the Río de la Plata, 180km west of Montevideo, but only 50km from Buenos Aires by ferry. Its Barrio Histórico, an irregular colonial nucleus of narrow cobbled streets, occupies a small peninsula jutting into the river. The town's commercial center, around Plaza 25 de Agosto, and the river port are a few blocks east, while the Rambla Costanera (named Rambla de las Américas at the edge of town) leads north along the river to the Real de San Carlos, another area of interest to visitors. The diagonal Av Roosevelt becomes Ruta 1, the main highway to Montevideo.

Information

Antel Telecentro Barrio Histórico (Av General Flores 172); Centro (cnr Lavalleja & Rivadavia)

Cámara Hotelera y Turística (☎ 27302; cnr Av General Flores & Rivera; ☻ 9am-7pm, to 8pm in summer) Adjacent to main municipal tourist office; helps with hotel bookings.

Cambio Dromer (cnr Av General Flores & Intendente Suárez; ☻ 9am-8pm Mon-Fri, 9am-6pm Sat, 10am-1pm Sun) Cashes traveler's checks.

Crédit Agricole (Av General Flores 299) One of several ATMs along General Flores.

Hospital Colonia (☎ 22994; 18 de Julio 462) Just west of the bus terminal.

HSBC (Portugal 183) Most convenient ATM in the historical center.

Lavandería Nueva Arco Iris (Intendente Suárez 196; per basket UR$100) Reasonably priced laundry service.

Municipal tourist office (☎ 26141; ☻ 9am-7pm, to 8pm in summer) Barrio Histórico (Manuel Lobo s/n); Centro (cnr Av General Flores & Rivera) The Barrio Histórico branch is just outside the old town gate.

National Tourism Ministry (☎ 24897) In front of the ferry terminal.

Post office (Lavalleja 226)

Sights & Activities
BARRIO HISTÓRICO

Colonia's Barrio Histórico is filled with visual delights. It's fun to just wander the streets and the waterfront. The most dramatic way to enter is via the reconstructed 1745 city gate, the **Portón de Campo** (Manuel Lobo). From here, a thick fortified wall runs south along the Paseo de San Miguel to the river, its grassy slopes popular with sunbathers. Other famous streets include the narrow, roughly cobbled **Calle de los Suspiros** (Street of Sighs), lined with tile-and-stucco colonial houses, and the riverfront **Paseo de San Gabriel**.

A single UR$25 ticket covers admission to Colonia's seven **historical museums** (☎ 25609; museoscolonia@gmail.com; ☻ 11:15am-4:45pm) All keep the same hours and are open six days a week. Closing day varies by museum as noted in parentheses below.

The **Museo Portugués** (Plaza Mayor 25 de Mayo 180; ☻ closed Wed), in a beautiful old house, holds Portuguese relics including porcelain, furniture, maps, Manuel Lobo's family tree and the old stone shield that once adorned the Portón de Campo.

The **Museo Municipal** (Plaza Mayor 25 de Mayo 77; ☻ closed Tue) houses an eclectic collection of treasures including a whale skeleton, an enormous rudder from a shipwreck, historical timelines and a scale model of Colonia c 1762.

On the northwest edge of the plaza, the **Archivo Regional** (Misiones de los Tapes 115; ☻ closed Wed) contains historical documents and a bookstore.

The **Casa Nacarello** (Plaza Mayor 25 de Mayo; ☻ closed Tue) is one of the prettiest colonial homes in town, with period furniture, thick whitewashed walls, wavy glass, original lintels (duck if you're tall!) and a nice courtyard.

COLONIA DEL SACRAMENTO

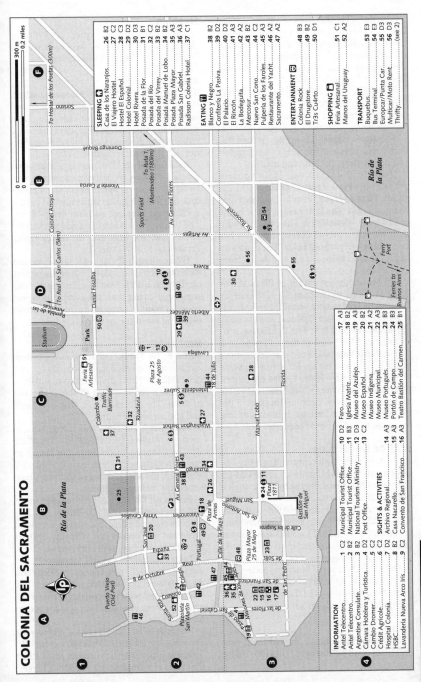

URUGUAY

The **Museo Indígena** (Comercio s/n; ♡ closed Thu) houses Roberto Banchero's personal collection of Charrúa stone tools, exhibits on indigenous history, and an amusing map upstairs showing how many European countries could fit inside Uruguay's borders (it's six!).

The dinky **Museo del Azulejo** (cnr Misiones de los Tapes & Paseo de San Gabriel; ♡ closed Wed) is a 17th-century stone house with a sampling of colonial tile work.

The **Museo Español** (San José 164; ♡ closed Thu), under renovation at the time of writing, has colonial pottery, clothing and maps.

Historic Colonia's two main squares are the vast **Plaza Mayor 25 de Mayo** and the shady **Plaza de Armas**, also known as Plaza Manuel Lobo. The latter plaza is the home of Colonia's **Iglesia Matriz**. The church, begun in 1680, is Uruguay's oldest, though it has been completely rebuilt twice. The plaza also holds the foundations of a house dating from Portuguese times.

Off the southwest corner of Plaza Mayor 25 de Mayo are the ruins of the 17th-century **Convento de San Francisco**, within which stands the 19th-century **faro** (lighthouse; admission UR$15; ♡ 10:30am–noon Sat & Sun). The lighthouse provides an excellent view of the old town.

The **Puerto Viejo** (Old Port) is now Colonia's yacht harbor and makes for a very pleasant stroll. The nearby **Teatro Bastión del Carmen** (Rivadavia s/n; admission free; ♡ 10am–11pm) is a theater and gallery complex incorporating part of the city's ancient fortifications. It hosts rotating art exhibits and periodic concerts.

REAL DE SAN CARLOS

At the turn of the 20th century, Argentine entrepreneur Nicolás Mihanovich spent US$1.5 million building an immense tourist complex 5km north of Colonia at Real de San Carlos. The attractions included a 10,000-seat bullring (made superfluous after Uruguay outlawed bullfights in 1912), a 3000-seat fronton (court) for the Basque sport of jai alai, a hotel-casino and a racecourse.

Only the racecourse functions today, but the ruins of the remaining buildings make an interesting excursion, and the adjacent beach is popular with locals on Sundays.

Tours

The tourist office outside the old town gate organizes good **walking tours** (UR$100) led by local guides.

Sleeping

Some hotels charge higher rates Friday through Sunday. Summer weekends are best avoided or booked well in advance. HI members get 10% off.

BUDGET

Hostel El Español (☎ 30759; hostelespaniol@hotmail.com; Manuel Lobo 377; dm/d without bathroom UR$150/300, with bathroom UR$180/400; ▯) Popular with young Latin Americans, this hostel's large, dark rooms are redeemed by the bright, spacious dining/internet area. HI members get 10% off.

Hotel Colonial (☎ 30347; hostelling_colonial@hotmail .com; Av General Flores 440; dm/d without bathroom HI member UR$150/360, nonmember UR$170/400; ▯) A rather drab but friendly hostel with four-bed dorms, a kitchen, a fireplace and laundry facilities. The Colonial offers free bikes and internet for guests' use, and organizes horseback-riding excursions (UR$400 per day).

El Viajero Hostel (☎ 22683; www.elviajerohostels.com; Washington Barbot 164; dm UR$240/270 HI member/nonmember; ▯) Colonia's newest hostel is brighter and somewhat cozier than the competition, but you may want to compare for yourself before plunking down the extra pesos.

MIDRANGE

Hostal de los Poetas (☎ 31643; www.guiacolonia .com.uy/hostaldelospoetas in Spanish; Mangarelli 677; s/d/tr UR$375/650/850) This simple family-run place is a bargain, if you're willing to hoof it 1km out of town. The breakfast area, fireplace room and garden are charming.

Hotel Rivera (☎ 20807; www.guiacolonia.com.uy /rivera in Spanish; Rivera 131; s/d/tr/q UR$500/750/950/1200; ▨ ▯) A stone's throw from the ferry and bus terminals, with clean rooms, cable TV and wi-fi, the Rivera is one of Colonia's least expensive midrange options.

Posada del Río (☎ 23002; hdelrio@adinet.com.uy; Washington Barbot 258; s/d/tr UR$430/790/1090; ▨) This peaceful place on a dead-end street is somewhat faded but still good value. The tiny upstairs breakfast room has partial river views.

Posada San Gabriel (☎ 23283; psangabriel@adinet .com.uy; Comercio 127; r downstairs/upstairs UR$800/1000; ▯) This sweet posada (inn) with stone walls, brass beds and wi-fi is surprisingly affordable given its prime location. Two upstairs rooms have river views.

Posada de la Flor (☎ 30794; posada_delaflor@yahoo .com.ar; Ituzaingó 268; r UR$1100; s UR$800 weekdays; ▨) Serenely situated on a sycamore-lined street that ends at a small beach, the Flor's biggest draw is its upstairs terrace with lounge chairs overlooking the river.

Casa de los Naranjos (☎ 24630; www.posadalosnaranjos .com in Spanish; 18 de Julio 219; r from UR$1100; ✿ ☺) A grassy yard with swimming pool and a 200-year-old orange tree grace this quiet colonial posada in the Barrio Histórico. The suite in a small house out back is charming.

TOP END

Posada del Virrey (☎ 22223; www.posadadelvirrey.com; España 217; s/d from UR$1050/1250, ste s/d UR$2150/2400; ✿ ☺) The marble floors, stone walls, high ceilings and spacious antique-furnished rooms at this 1850 residence make you feel like a 'modern-day king,' as their motto says. There's wi-fi throughout, plus Jacuzzis, river views and (what else?) king-size beds in the upstairs suites.

Posada Manuel de Lobo (☎ 22463; www.posada manueldelobo.com in Spanish; Ituzaingó 160; d/tr/q/ste UR$1550/1750/2000/2200; ✿ ☺) The historical charms of this 150-year-old house include heavy wooden furniture, antique tilework, beamed ceilings, brick walls, fountains and twin patios out back. All rooms have wi-fi, and suites have Jacuzzis.

Posada Plaza Mayor (☎ 23193; www.posadaplaza mayor.com; Comercio 111; r from UR$1900, ste UR$3300; ✿ ☺) Near the river in the heart of historic Colonia, the Playa Mayor comprises two colonial houses. The stone-walled, high-ceilinged 19th-century Spanish rooms surround a beautiful courtyard with a fountain; the adjoining 18th-century Portuguese structure houses several lovely common areas.

Radisson Colonia Hotel (☎ 30460; www.radisson.com /coloniauy; Washington Barbot 283; s/d from UR$2500/2750, ste s/ d UR$3750/4300; ✿ ☺ ☺) If you value chain-hotel comforts over colonial charm, the Radisson has what you're looking for. This all-in-one facility features two pools and a spacious deck overlooking the river, plus sauna, gym, solarium, children's play area and garage.

Eating

BUDGET

Mercosur (☎ 24200; Av General Flores 252; light meals UR$49-125; ✆ 10am-2am) For low-priced fast food near the historic center, try this convenient corner eatery.

El Palacio (☎ 29753; Av General Flores 466; dishes from UR$53; ✆ 10am-3am) Long hours, affordable burgers and pizza, and fixed-price daily specials (about UR$120 including wine and dessert) draw a youthful, budget-minded crowd.

Confitería La Pasiva (☎ 20331; Av General Flores 444; dishes from UR$65; ✆ 9am-2am) This bright, bustling chain *confitería* is great for breakfast, pizza or sandwiches any time of day.

Nuevo San Cono (☎ 28964; cnr Intendente Suárez & 18 de Julio; dishes UR$70-90; ✆ noon-midnight) With a well-stocked bar and a roaring fire, this traditional neighborhood *parrilla* is a cozy place to pass a chilly evening.

MIDRANGE & TOP END

La Bodeguita (☎ 25329; Comercio 167; meals UR$125-260; ✆ 8pm-late daily, plus 12:30-4pm Sat & Sun) Nab a table out back on the sunny two-level deck and soak up the sweeping river views while drinking sangría or munching on La Bodeguita's trademark pizza.

El Rincón (☎ 099-675202; Misiones de los Tapes 41; dishes UR$130-250; ✆ noon-5pm) El Rincón is best enjoyed on a sunny weekend afternoon, lounging out back under a big tree between stone and red-stucco walls, listening to Brazilian music or tango, and watching the riverfront scene as the outdoor grill exudes intoxicating smoky smells.

Pulpería de los Faroles (☎ 30271; Misiones de los Tapes 101; dishes UR$140-250; ✆ noon-midnight) Specializing in seafood and pasta, this reader-recommended eatery has a rainbow of colorful tablecloths in the artsy interior dining room, plus a sea of informal outdoor seating on Plaza Mayor 25 de Mayo.

Blanco y Negro (☎ 22236; Av General Flores 248; dishes UR$150-330; ✆ 11:30am-3:30pm & 7:30pm-1am Thu-Tue) This upmarket *parrilla* and pasta joint in a pretty stone-and-brick building has live music on weekends.

Restaurante del Yacht (☎ 31354; Santa Rita s/n; dishes UR$250-360; ✆ 11am-1am Mon-Sat, noon-5pm Sun) This somewhat snooty place serves up excellent seafood and afternoon teas, and the pierside deck affords stunning river views.

Sacramento (☎ 29245; cnr Comercio & Calle de la Playa; dishes UR$200-280; ✆ noon-4pm daily, plus 8pm-late Fri & Sat) Sacramento earns its reputation as one of Colonia's best restaurants, with tasty creations such as risotto in champagne with sesame-marinated spider crabs, or ricotta, leek, and bacon ravioli.

Entertainment

El Drugstore (☎ 25241; Portugal 174; ✆ 12:30pm-1am) This corner place on Plaza de Armas, with frequent live music, is Colonia's most enjoyable, funkiest nightspot. It has vividly colored, eclectically decorated walls, an open kitchen, fridges painted with clouds and elephants, and a vintage car on the cobblestones doubling as a romantic dining nook. Half of the 24-page menu is devoted to drinks; the other half to tapas (from UR$120) and full meals (mains UR$200 to UR$320), including a few vegetarian offerings.

Colonia Rock (☎ 28189; Misiones de los Tapes 157; ☻ 11:30am-1am) Always buzzing, this is Colonia's attempt at a Hard Rock Café. The bar/restaurant occupies a colonial building, with indoor and outdoor courtyard seating.

Tr3s Cu4rto (☎ 29664; Alberto Méndez 295) Colonia's disco for the young and restless.

Shopping

Polished agate, ornate *mate* gourds and Portuguese-style ceramics are popular items.

Feria Artesanal (cnr Intendente Suárez & Daniel Fosalba; ☻ 10am-7pm or 8pm) This handicrafts market, open daily, is on the northern waterfront.

Manos del Uruguay (☎ 21793; Av General Flores 89) Colonia's branch of the national handicrafts store is in the Barrio Histórico.

Getting There & Away

BOAT

From the port at the foot of Rivera, **Buquebus** (☎ 22975; corner of Manuel Lobo & Av FD Roosevelt) and **Ferrylíneas** (☎ 22919) run multiple daily ferries to Buenos Aires. Slow boats leave at 5:30am and 8:30pm, taking three hours, while the more frequent fast boat takes only one hour. Base fares for adults are UR$823 for the fast boat, UR$530 for the slow boat. Children and seniors get a 20% discount. The 1st-class surcharge is UR$180 for either boat.

Immigration for both countries is handled at the port before boarding.

BUS

Colonia's modern **bus terminal** (cnr Manuel Lobo & Av Roosevelt) is conveniently located near the port, within easy walking distance of the Barrio Histórico. The following destinations are served at least twice daily.

Destination	Cost (UR$)	Duration (hr)
Carmelo	67	1¼
Nueva Helvecia	59	1
Mercedes	152	3
Montevideo	151	2½-3
Paysandú	276	6
Salto	387	8

Getting Around

Walking is enjoyable in compact Colonia, but motor scooters, bicycles and gas-powered buggies are popular alternatives. Local buses go to the beaches and bullring at Real de San Carlos (UR$13) from along Av General Flores.

Colonia also makes a convenient starting point for touring western Uruguay by car – rates under UR$700 a day are available, and it's easy to get out of town. **Thrifty** (☎ 22939; Av General Flores 172; bicycle/scooter/golf cart per hr UR$35/150/250, per day UR$200/550/1050) rents everything from beater bikes to cars. Several other agencies rent cars and motorbikes near the bus and ferry terminals, including **Multicar/ Moto Rent** (☎ 24893/22266; Manuel Lobo 505), **Punta Car** (☎ 22353; Ferry Port) and **Europcar** (☎ 28454; Ferry Port).

NUEVA HELVECIA
☎ 055 / pop 10,000

Nueva Helvecia (also known as Colonia Suiza) is a quiet, pleasant destination with a demonstrably European ambience – where else in Uruguay would you find street names like Guillermo (William) Tell and Frau Vögel? Lying 120km west of Montevideo and 60km east of Colonia del Sacramento, it was settled in 1862 by Swiss immigrants attracted by the temperate climate, good land, freedom of worship and opportunity to gain Uruguayan citizenship without renouncing their own. The country's first interior agricultural colony, Nueva Helvecia provided wheat for Montevideo's mills and today produces more than half of Uruguay's cheese.

Orientation

The center of town is Plaza de los Fundadores, with a clock made of flowers and a grandiose sculpture commemorating the original Swiss pioneers. Nueva Helvecia's hotel zone is a few kilometers southeast of the plaza.

Information

Antel (cnr Artigas & Dreyer)

Banco de la República Oriental (Treinta y Tres 1210) Diagonally across from the central plaza.

Cyber Pez (☎ 47630; Treinta y Tres 1246; per hr UR$15; ☻ 9am-noon & 3-11pm Mon-Sat) Internet access, and fish too!

Hospital (☎ 44057; cnr 18 de Julio & C Cunier)

Post office (cnr F Gilomen & Treinta y Tres)

Tourist information (Plaza de los Fundadores; ☻ 3-6pm Mon-Fri, 10am-1pm & 3-6pm Sat & Sun) In the

Movimiento Nuevas Generaciones building on the main square.

Festivals & Events

The best time to visit Nueva Helvecia is during one of its festivals. On August 1 the **Fiesta Suiza** attracts visitors from around the country for Swiss dances and artisan exhibits. Every October Uruguay's bovine bounty is on full display at **Expoláctea**, an agricultural festival featuring live music, cooking demos, wine- and cheese-tasting, kids' events and a giant fondue dinner. December's **Bierfest** celebrates the town's Alpine traditions, with music and dance performances, and of course enormous steins of beer.

Sleeping & Eating

Hotels are concentrated on the southeastern outskirts of town, making access difficult for those without a vehicle. Conveniently, most have their own restaurants.

Hotel del Prado (☎ 44169; www.nuevahelvecia.com /hoteldelprado.htm in Spanish; Erwin Hodel s/n; dm/s/d/tr UR$200/400/650/850; 🏊) Dating from 1896, this 80-room hotel is a grand if declining building with balconies, a pool and some hostel rooms. Its illustrious history is chronicled in old photos lining the walls.

Granja Hotel Suizo (☎ 44002; www.hotelsuizo nuevahelvecia.com in Spanish; Av Federico Fischer s/n; s/d UR$1100/1650; 🍴 🏊) Nueva Helvecia's oldest tourist hotel has ample grounds, a pool, a sauna and a renowned restaurant. All rooms have balconies, TV and heating.

Hotel Nirvana Resort & Spa (☎ 44081, in Montevideo 02-902-4124; www.hotelnirvana.com; Av Batlle y Ordóñez s/n; r from UR$2900, half/full board extra per person UR$350/$700; 🍴 💻 🏊) Truly a world apart, ritzy Nirvana has two swimming pools, tennis courts, horseback riding and 25 hectares of beautifully landscaped grounds.

L'Arbalete (☎ 44081; Hotel Nirvana; dishes UR$97-245; ☑ 12:30-2:30pm & 9-11pm) The varied international menu features gazpacho, crepes, and Alpine specialties such as fondue and *rösti* (Swiss potato pancakes). Save room for the scrumptious desserts, including warm apple tart, pears poached in wine, and chocolate fondue.

Getting There & Away

Some bus schedules refer to the town as Colonia Suiza. COT, Turil and Colonia offer frequent bus service to Montevideo (UR$109, two hours) and Colonia del Sacramento

(UR$59, one hour). All three companies' offices are near the plaza.

CARMELO

☎ 0542 / pop 17,000

Carmelo, dating from 1816, is a laid-back town of cobblestone streets and low old houses, a center for yachting, fishing and exploring the Paraná Delta. It lies opposite the delta just below the Río Uruguay's confluence with the Río de la Plata, 75km northwest of Colonia del Sacramento and 235km from Montevideo. Launches connect Carmelo to the Buenos Aires suburb of Tigre.

Orientation

Carmelo straddles the Arroyo de las Vacas, a stream that widens into a sheltered harbor on the Río de la Plata. North of the arroyo, shady Plaza Independencia is now the commercial center. Most of the town's businesses are along 19 de Abril, which leads to the bridge over the arroyo, across which lies a large park with open space, camping, swimming and a huge casino.

Information

Antel (Barrios 329, btwn Uruguay & Zorrilla de San Martín)
Banco Comercial (Uruguay 403) On Plaza Independencia.
Hospital (☎ 2107; cnr Uruguay & Artigas)
Municipal tourist office (☎ 2001; Casa de Cultura, 19 de Abril 246; ☑ 9am-7pm) Four blocks north of the bridge over the arroyo.
New Generation Cyber Games (Uruguay 373; internet per hr UR$15; ☑ 8am-3am)
Post office (Uruguay 360)

Sights & Activities

The arroyo, with large, rusty boats moored along it, makes for a great ramble, as does strolling out to the beaches across the bridge. The **Santuario del Carmen** (Barrios, btwn Varela & del Carmen) dates from 1830. Next door, the **Archivo y Museo Parroquial** (Barrios 208; admission free; ☑ hours vary) contains documents and objects of local historical importance.

Festivals & Events

Local wines have an excellent reputation, and in early February the town hosts the **Fiesta Nacional de la Uva** (National Grape Festival).

Sleeping & Eating

Camping Náutico Carmelo (☎ 2058; Arroyo de las Vacas s/n; sites UR$100) South of Arroyo de las Vacas, this campground with hot showers caters to yachties but accepts walk-ins too.

Hotel Rambla (☎ 2390; www.ciudadcarmelo.com/ramblahotel in Spanish; Uruguay 55; s/d/tr/q from UR$490/650/950/1200) The blocky Rambla won't win any design awards, but it's conveniently close to the launch docks. The upstairs doubles with balconies facing the arroyo are much cheerier than the interior rooms.

Hotel Casino Carmelo (☎ 2314; www.hotelcasinocarmelo.com in Spanish; Av Rodó s/n; r/ste per person UR$550/750; 🏊 🐾) This hotel and casino across the arroyo is getting a bit worn around the edges, but the views toward the river are good. It has two pools, plus a small animal park with peacocks, flamingos and rheas.

Fay Fay (18 de Julio 358; dishes from UR$60; 🍴 lunch & dinner Tue-Sun) With outside tables right on the square, this local favorite has the best atmosphere in town (although the jury's still out on the Guns N' Roses soundtrack).

Piccolino (☎ 4850; cnr 19 de Abril & Roosevelt; dishes UR$60-120; 🕐 9am-midnight) This corner place has decent *chivitos* and nice views of the square.

Getting There & Away

All the bus companies are on or near Plaza Independencia. **Chadre** (☎ 2987) has the most services, with seven daily departures to Montevideo (UR$201, 3½ hours), plus two to Colonia (UR$67, one hour), Mercedes (UR$84, two hours), Fray Bentos (UR$117, 2¾ hours), Paysandú (UR$201, five hours) and Salto (UR$301, seven hours).

Cacciola (☎ 7551; www.cacciolaviajes.com; Constituyentes 263; 🕐 9am-7:30pm) runs daily launches to the Buenos Aires suburb of Tigre. The 2½-hour trip costs UR$384 one way for adults, and UR$333 for children aged three to nine.

FRAY BENTOS
☎ 056 / pop 23,000
Capital of Río Negro department, Fray Bentos is (or was!) the southernmost overland crossing over the Río Uruguay from Argentina.

This former company town, with its pretty riverfront promenade, was once dominated by an enormous English-run meat-processing plant, now preserved as a museum. The big news here in recent years has been construction of the controversial Botnia pulp mill northeast of town and the regular blockades of the bridge connecting Fray Bentos to Gualeguaychú, Argentina (see the boxed text, p543).

Information

Antel (Zorrilla 1127)
Credit Uruguay (cnr Treinta y Tres & 18 de Julio) One of several banks near central Plaza Constitución.
Hospital Salúd Pública (☎ 22742; cnr Oribe & Echeverría)
LA Cyber (18 de Julio 1106; per hour UR$20; 🕐 8am-midnight Mon-Fri, 8am-1pm & 5pm-midnight Sat-Sun) Internet access just west of Plaza Constitución.
Municipal tourist office (☎ 22233; turismo@rionegro.gub.uy; Treinta y Tres s/n, near 18 de Julio; 🕐 9am-9pm) Just north of Plaza Constitución.
Post office (Treinta y Tres 3271)

THE LITTLE BEEF CUBE THAT CIRCLED THE GLOBE

In 1865 the Liebig Extract of Meat Company located its pioneer South American plant southwest of downtown Fray Bentos. It soon became Uruguay's most important industrial complex. British-run El Anglo took over operations in the 1920s and by WWII the factory employed 4000 people, slaughtering cattle at the astronomical rate of 2000 a day.

Looking at the abandoned factory today, you'd never guess that its signature product, the Oxo beef cube, once touched millions of lives on every continent. On the factory's ground floor, the Museo de la Revolución Industrial brings this history to life with colorful displays painting a fascinating portrait of the company's scale and international influence. Oxo cubes sustained WWI soldiers in the trenches, Jules Verne sang their praises in his book *Around the Moon*, Stanley brought them on his search for Livingstone, Scott and Hillary took them to Antarctica and Everest. More than 25,000 people from over 60 countries worked here, and at its peak the factory was exporting nearly 150 different products, using every part of the cow except its moo.

Museum displays range from the humorous to the poignant: a giant cattle scale where school groups are invited to weigh themselves; or the old company office upstairs, left exactly as it was when the factory closed in 1979, with grooves rubbed into the floor by the foot of an accountant who sat at the same desk for decades.

WORKING HISTORY: AN INTERVIEW WITH RENÉ BORETTO OVALLE

René Boretto Ovalle, a journalist and native of Fray Bentos, was instrumental in converting the town's former meat-processing factory (once known as 'El Anglo') into a museum. He has been the director of the Museo de la Revolución Industrial since its founding over two decades ago.

How did you first get interested in 'El Anglo', and what aspects of its history do you find most fascinating? I became interested in 'El Anglo' because I recognized its transcendent impact. More than just feeding Europe – we were the 'world's kitchen' – we also created a society of workers, respectful and community-minded. Studying this heritage is important, to remind nations that are now industrialized and powerful that when they were suffering through wars, Uruguay's resources and the labors of its people helped them survive.

What changes have you seen in Uruguay during your lifetime? I'm 60 years old, and I lived through Uruguay's last golden age as a post-war industrialized society. I regret that radical, deep changes in the world have come about more in the realms of technology and economics than in the valuing of human beings and their work. The difficulty of accessing new technologies has caused Uruguay to lose its earlier international importance.

What are some unique elements of the Uruguayan national character? Uruguay's greatest national treasure is its people. Despite developments in the outside world, the Uruguayan national character remains fundamentally unchanged: pleasant, communicative, respectful, caring and receptive to outsiders. Ours is a rich culture, one that has adopted African and European immigrant traditions, and has become a Latin American leader in caring for the environment.

Sights & Activities

Fray Bentos' star attraction, on the waterfront 2km west of town, is the **Museo de la Revolución Industrial** (☎ 23690; Barrio Histórico del Anglo; admission UR$30; ☺ 8am-7pm Mon-Sat, 10am-5:30pm Sun) – see the boxed text, opposite, for details. Guided tours (year-round at 10am and 3pm, afternoon only on Sunday, more in summer) grant access to the intricate maze of passageways, corrals and abandoned slaughterhouses behind the museum.

The municipal **Museo Solari** (☎ 22233; Treinta y Tres s/n; admission free; ☺ 8am-2pm & 4-10pm) is on the west side of Plaza Constitución and features the satirical works of painter and engraver Luis Solari, many of which contain fanciful human figures with the heads of animals.

One block off the square, the 400-seat **Teatro Young** (cnr 25 de Mayo & Zorrilla) dates from the early 1900s and hosts cultural events throughout the year. Visits can be arranged at the theater itself or at the tourist office.

Sleeping & Eating

Club Atlético Anglo (☎ 22787; Rambla Cuervo s/n) This club maintains a campground with hot showers and beach access, picturesquely sited among shade trees on the waterfront between Plaza Constitución and the Museo de la Revolución Industrial. Under renovation at the time of writing, it expected to reopen in 2008 (prices to be announced).

Nuevo Hotel Colonial (☎ 22260; 25 de Mayo 3293; s/d/tr/q from UR$300/400/490/540, breakfast per person UR$50) Long popular with budget travelers, the Colonial is basic but well run, with wi-fi and high-ceilinged (if sometimes windowless) rooms surrounding a sunny interior patio.

La Posada del Frayle Bentos (☎ 28541; www .grupocarminatti.com in Spanish; 25 de Mayo 3434; s/d/tr/ q UR$750/1200/1650/2100; ☒ ▢ ▢ ▢) This lovely posada occupies a restored colonial building with patios, fountain, pool and bouganvilleas. Rooms are filled with modern amenities.

Pizzería 33 (☎ 28617; Treinta y Tres 3188; dishes UR$50-115; ☺ 11:30am-2:30pm & 7:30pm-midnight) This popular place just off the main square has a bilingual menu and specializes in pizza, pasta and sandwiches.

La Estancia (☎ 22078; Rincón 1359; dishes UR$50-155; ☺ noon-2:30pm & 8pm-midnight Wed-Mon) A simple *chivitería* on weekdays, and a fully fledged *parrilla* nights and weekends, this cozy local hangout serves good food at affordable prices. Don't miss the *torta estanciera* (UR$30), a tall three-layer cake loaded with strawberries and cream.

URUGUAY

Entertainment

Tango Feroz (Treinta y Tres 3270; ☽ 11pm-late Fri & Sat) Just north of the main square, this disco draws a lively weekend crowd.

Teatro Municipal de Verano (Parque Roosevelt, 18 de Julio) On the banks of the river, this open-air venue seats 4000 and has excellent acoustics. It hosts a diverse range of musical concerts.

Getting There & Around

Buses depart from the **bus terminal** (18 de Julio, btwn Varela & Blanes), 10 blocks east of central Plaza Constitución. When the bridge to Argentina is open, ETA goes to Gualeguaychú (UR$71, 1¼ hours). It also has a midnight departure Monday, Wednesday and Friday for Tacuarembó (UR$360, six hours).

Several buses a day go to Mercedes (UR$25, 45 minutes) and Montevideo (UR$259, 4½ hours). Buses Chadre has two *línea litoral* (river route) buses daily in each direction: northbound, destinations include Salto (UR$184, four hours) and Paysandú (UR$84, two hours); southbound, they stop in Mercedes, Carmelo (UR$117, three hours) and Colonia (UR$184, four hours).

MERCEDES

☎ 053 / pop 42,000

Only 30km east of Fray Bentos, Mercedes is a livestock center and capital of the department of Soriano. There are cobblestoned streets and a small pedestrian zone around central Plaza Independencia, but the town's most appealing feature is its leafy waterfront along the south bank of the Río Negro.

Information

Antel (Roosevelt 681)

Banco Comercial (Giménez 719) ATM on central Plaza Independencia.

Cyber Area 51 (cnr Giménez & Artigas; internet per hr UR$10; ☽ 9:30am-11pm Mon-Sat)

Hospital Mercedes (☎ 22177; cnr Sánchez & Rincón)

Municipal tourist office (☎ 22733; Detomasi 415; ☽ 8am-6:30pm Mon-Fri) In a crumbling white building near the bridge to the campground.

Post office (cnr Rodó & 18 de Julio)

Sights & Activities

The waterfront area is Mercedes' biggest attraction. Principal activities are boating, fishing and swimming along the sandy beaches, or simply strolling along the Rambla (especially popular on Sunday afternoons).

On Plaza Independencia, the imposing **Catedral de Nuestra Señora de las Mercedes** dates from 1788. The nearby **Biblioteca Museo Eusebio Giménez** (Giménez 560, at Sarandí) displays paintings by the local artist.

About 6km west of town is the **Museo Paleontológico Alejandro Berro** (Zona Mauá; admission free; ☽ 11am-5pm), displaying a substantial fossil collection in an old, white, castlelike building.

Sleeping

Camping del Hum (☎ 22733; Isla del Puerto; camping per adult/child UR$9/6, plus UR$11 per tent; ☽ Dec-Mar) Mercedes' spacious campground, one of the region's best, occupies half the Isla del Puerto in the Río Negro. Connected to the mainland by a bridge, it offers excellent swimming, fishing and sanitary facilities.

Hotel Marín (☎ 22115; Roosevelt 627; s/d/tr/q UR$350/600/750/850; ☒) The older front part of this hotel has high ceilings, French doors and a nice breakfast room with fireplace. Upstairs rooms without heat or air-con cost UR$100 less.

Estancia La Sirena (☎ 099-102130, in Montevideo 02-606-2924; www.lasirena.com.uy in Spanish; Ruta 14, Km 4.5; r with breakfast UR$1550; s/d with full board UR$1750/3500) Surrounded by rolling open country 15km upriver from Mercedes, this *estancia* is one of Uruguay's oldest and most beautiful. The spacious 1830 ranch house, with its cozy parlor and fireplaces, makes a perfect base for relaxation and excursions to the nearby river on foot or horseback. The isolated setting is perfect for stargazing, and the homemade food, often cooked on a giant outdoor grill, is delicious. Hosts Rodney and Lucía Bruce speak English, French and Spanish.

Eating

Club Remeros Mercedes (☎ 22534; de la Ribera 949; breakfast UR$35, meals UR$65-160; ☽ 7am-1am) The restaurant at this sports club near the river (also offering hostel accommodation) is open morning, noon and night, serving a varied menu.

La Churrasquera (☎ 24036; Careaga 792; dishes UR$70-220; ☽ noon-3pm & 8:30pm-midnight) You can't miss this place – the *parrilla* and its firewood are proudly displayed in the front window. Large portions are served, and the atmosphere is delightfully old-timey.

Parador Rambla (☎ 20877; Rambla Costanera s/n; dishes UR$95-195; ☽ noon-3pm & 8:30pm-1:30am) This riverfront restaurant at the foot of Colón serves delicious Spanish specialties like garlic prawns, *patatas bravas* (fried potatoes with a spicy sauce) and paella. The fabulous European-influenced desserts include profiteroles, chocolate crepes, tiramisu and orange flan.

Getting There & Away

Mercedes' modern **bus terminal** (Don Bosco) is about 10 blocks from Plaza Independencia. It has a shopping center, a supermarket, an ATM, luggage storage and even an emergency medical clinic. No local buses serve the terminal; getting downtown involves walking or taking a cab.

All destinations below are served at least once daily, and most several times a day.

Destination	Cost (UR$)	Duration (hr)
Buenos Aires (Arg)	561	7
Carmelo	84	2
Colonia	155	3
Fray Bentos	25	¾
Gualeguaychú *	154	1¾
Montevideo	234	3½–4½
Paysandú	100	2
Salto	226	4
Tacuarembó	351	6½

* when bridge reopens

PAYSANDÚ

☎ 072 / pop 73,000

For most travelers, Uruguay's third-largest city is just a stopover en route to or from Argentina. Founded as a mid-18th-century outpost of cattle herders from the Jesuit mission at Yapeyú (in present-day Argentina), Paysandú gradually rose to prominence as a meat-processing center. Repeated sieges of the city during the turbulent 1800s (the last in 1864–65) earned it the local nickname 'the American Troy.'

Despite its turbulent history and its ongoing status as a major industrial center, modern-day Paysandú is easy-going and surprisingly sedate. To see the city's wilder side, visit during Carnaval or the annual weeklong beer festival (held during Semana Santa).

Orientation

On the east bank of the Río Uruguay, Paysandú is 370km from Montevideo via Ruta 3 and 110km north of Fray Bentos via Ruta 24. The Puente Internacional General Artigas, 15km north of town, connects it with Colón in Argentina.

The center of activity is Plaza Constitución, six blocks north of the bus terminal. From

---

ESTANCIA TOURISM IN URUGUAY

Estancias, the giant farms of Uruguay's interior, are a national cultural icon and now a big contender for the tourist dollar. In recent years, dozens of *estancias turísticas* have opened their doors, from traditional working farms to opportunistic wannabes. Typically, *estancias* organize daily activities with a heavy emphasis on horseback riding; many provide overnight accommodations as well. Most are difficult to reach without a vehicle, although they'll often pick guests up with advance notice. The Uruguayan Ministry of Tourism has designated 'Estancia Turística' as a distinct lodging category and posts a full list on its website (www.turismo.gub.uy in Spanish – under 'Operadores' choose 'Estancias Turísticas').

The granddaddy of Uruguayan tourist *estancias* is **San Pedro de Timote** (☎ 0310-8086; www .sanpedrodetimote.com.uy in Spanish; r per adult/child UR$2400/1200; ☒). Its remarkable setting, 14km up a dirt road amid endless rolling cattle country, is greatly enhanced by the complex of historic structures, some dating back to the mid-1800s: a gracious white chapel, a courtyard with soaring palm trees, a library with gorgeous tilework, and a circular stone corral. Common areas feature parquet wood floors, big fireplaces and comfy leather armchairs. Two pools and a sauna add to the luxurious feel. Accommodation prices include three meals, afternoon tea and two daily horseback-riding excursions (plus night rides on the full moon). With 253 hectares of grounds, the possibilities are virtually limitless. Non-overnight guests can pay UR$1100 for lunch, afternoon tea and a horseback ride. The nearest town is Cerro Colorado, 160km northeast of Montevideo on Ruta 7.

Other tourist *estancias* covered in this book are listed under the city or town closest to them – the highly recommended La Sirena (opposite), La Paz (p573), San Nicanor (p575) and Fortín de San Miguel (p595).

In Montevideo, **Lares** (☎ 02-901-9120; www.lares.com.uy; WF Aldunate 1320, Local 15) and **Cecilia Regules Viajes** (☎ 02-916-3011; www.ceciliaregulesviajes.com; Bacacay 1334, Local C) are travel agencies specializing in *estancia* tourism.

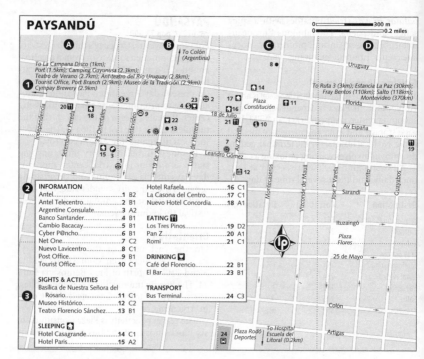

PAYSANDÚ

INFORMATION	
Antel	1 B2
Antel Telecentro	2 B1
Argentine Consulate	3 A2
Banco Santander	4 B1
Cambio Bacacay	5 B1
Cyber P@ncho	6 B1
Net One	7 C2
Nuevo Lavicentro	8 C1
Post Office	9 B1
Tourist Office	10 C1

SIGHTS & ACTIVITIES	
Basílica de Nuestra Señora del Rosario	11 C1
Museo Histórico	12 C2
Teatro Florencio Sánchez	13 B1

SLEEPING	
Hotel Casagrande	14 C1
Hotel París	15 A2

Hotel Rafaela	16 C1
La Casona del Centro	17 C1
Nuevo Hotel Concordia	18 A1

EATING	
Los Tres Pinos	19 D2
Pan Z	20 A1
Romi	21 C1

DRINKING	
Café del Florencio	22 B1
El Bar	23 B1

TRANSPORT	
Bus Terminal	24 C3

here, 18 de Julio, the main commercial street, runs west to the port. Except for a small developed area, directly west of downtown, the entire riverfront remains open parkland due to regular flooding.

Information

Antel Main office (Montevideo 875); Telecentro (Luis A de Herrera 964)

Banco Santander (18 de Julio 1137) One of several ATMs along Paysandú's main street.

Cambio Bacacay (18 de Julio 1039) Changes traveler's checks.

Cyber P@ncho (19 de Abril s/n; internet per hr UR$10; 🕑 10am-10pm daily)

Hospital Escuela del Litoral (☎ 24836; Montecaseros 520)

Net One (Leandro Gómez 1193; internet per hr UR$10; 🕑 24hr) Noisy with adolescent gamers, but open all night.

Nuevo Lavicentro (☎ 22826; Montecaseros 1043; per kilo UR$45; 🕑 8am-noon & 3-7pm Mon-Fri, 8am-1pm Sat) Same-day laundry service.

Post office (cnr 18 de Julio & Montevideo)

Tourist office Centro (☎ 26220, ext 184; turismo@ paysandu.gub.uy; 18 de Julio 1226; 🕑 8am-7pm Mon-Fri, 8am-6pm Sat & Sun); Port (☎ 29235; plandelacosta@

paysandu.gub.uy; Av de Los Iracundos; 🕑 11am-7pm Mon-Fri, 1-6pm Sat & Sun) First office is on Plaza Constitución; latter is next to the Museo de la Tradición.

Sights & Activities

Dating from 1860, chunky **Basílica de Nuestra Señora del Rosario** (Plaza Constitución) has one of the more ornately decorated interiors in Uruguay.

The 1876 **Teatro Florencio Sánchez** (☎ 26220, ext 170; 19 de Abril 926), Uruguay's oldest theater outside of Montevideo, has many original features (including the curtain) and hosts occasional music and dance events.

The **Museo Histórico** (☎ 26221, ext 247; Av Zorrilla 874; admission free; 🕑 8am-5pm Mon-Fri, 9am-2pm Sat) displays evocative images from the multiple 19th-century sieges of Paysandú: women exiled to an island offshore watching the city's bombardment, the bullet-riddled shell of the cathedral and more.

In parkland near the riverfront, the **Museo de la Tradición** (☎ 23125; Av de Los Iracundos 5; admission free; 🕑 9am-5:45pm) features a small but well-displayed selection of anthropological artifacts and gaucho gear.

Sleeping

Camping Guyunusa (Av de Los Iracundos s/n) Camping is free in the municipal park near the river's edge, just south of the Museo de la Tradición. Get a permit from the tourist office before pitching your tent. The bare-bones amenities include cold showers, toilets, picnic tables and grills.

Nuevo Hotel Concordia (☎ 22417; 18 de Julio 984; r per person with/without bathroom UR$240/180) The sweeping marble staircase, plant-filled patio and wooden floorboards make up for obvious signs of wear in this central hotel.

Hotel Paris (☎ 23774; Leandro Gómez 1008; s/d UR$250/390) You gotta love the facade on this place – dating from 1870, it still retains some character despite its run-down condition.

La Casona del Centro (☎ 22998; Av Zorrilla 975; dm/s/d UR$250/350/500) Right on Plaza Constitución, La Casona offers clean, safe, hostel-style accommodation with a family vibe – most beds are two-tier bunks newly installed in the grown kids' former bedrooms.

Hotel Rafaela (☎ 24216; 18 de Julio 1181; s/d/tr/q UR$450/620/750/880) The Rafaela is decent value close to the main square; its rooms are dark but large, and some have their own small patios.

Hotel Casagrande (☎ 24994; www.paysandu .com/hotelcasagrande in Spanish; Florida 1221; s/tw/d UR$990/1380/1585; ⚡ 🖥) The extremely homey and conveniently located Casagrande is Paysandú's nicest downtown hotel. Comfy armchairs, marble tabletops and big brass beds are among the boutique hotel amenities justifying the higher price tag.

Estancia La Paz (☎ 02272; www.estancialapaz .uy; Ruta 24, Km 86.5; s/d with full board UR$1950/3900; ⚡ 🖥 ⚛) The tennis courts, swimming pool and muzak-filled common areas feel incongruous among the historic buildings and pristine natural setting at this tourist *estancia* 30km south of Paysandú. Serious equestrians will appreciate the horseback-riding excursions, lasting from one day to two weeks. Access is via a long dirt road: turn off at Km 86.5 on Ruta 24 or Km 336 on Ruta 3.

Eating & Drinking

Pan Z (☎ 29551; cnr 18 de Julio & Setembrino Pereda; dishes UR$70-260; ⏱ noon-3pm & 8pm-1am) Popular 'Panceta' serves pizza, *chivitos* stacked high with every ingredient imaginable, and tasty Italian desserts like *torta di ricota* and tiramisu.

Romi (☎ 42244; cnr 18 de Julio & Av Zorrilla; dishes UR$80-225; ⏱ 10am-4pm & 8pm-2am) This lively pizzeria-*parrilla* seamlessly blends modern and old-fashioned touches of class, with bow-tied, black-and-white-clad waiters moving through a landscape of plum-colored brick walls and checkerboard tile floors.

Los Tres Pinos (☎ 41211; Av España 1474; dishes UR$85-180; ⏱ 11:30am-3pm & 8:30pm-12:30am Mon-Sat, lunch only Sun) The *parrilla* here is excellent; carnivores will appreciate specialties like *pollo supremo Andrés* (chicken stuffed with green apples, ham and cheese) and *lechón a las brazas* (roast suckling pig).

El Bar (☎ 37809; Herrera 955; dishes UR$75-175; ⏱ 6:30am-late) This atmospheric corner place has a wide-ranging drinks menu and brings in live music on weekends.

Café del Florencio (☎ 28512; 19 de Abril 930) This historic café has seen better days, but the faded elegance of its 1870s décor makes it an appealing choice for beer or coffee.

Entertainment

La Campana Disco (cnr Brasil & Manuel Ledesma; ⏱ midnight-7am Fri & Sat) Pumping out live music every weekend, this is the newest and largest of several late-night venues down by the port.

Further north along the waterfront, Paysandú's intimate, tree-encircled Teatro de Verano is just across the street from the larger Anfiteatro del Río Uruguay, which seats up to 20,000 people and hosts major concerts during Paysandú's annual beer festival. Check with the tourist office for details of upcoming events.

Getting There & Away

Paysandú's **bus terminal** (☎ 23325; cnr Artigas & Av Zorrilla) is directly south of Plaza Constitución. Uruguayan destinations in the following table are served at least once daily. International departures are less frequent, as detailed below.

Destination	Cost (UR$)	Duration (hr)
Asunción (Par)	1832	15
Carmelo	201	5
Colón (Arg)	55	¾
Colonia	276	6
Concepción del Uruguay (Arg)	75	1½
Córdoba (Arg)	1097	10
Fray Bentos	84	2
Mercedes	100	2
Montevideo	318	4½
Paraná (Arg)	579	4½
Salto	100	2
Santa Fe (Arg)	610	5½
Tacuarembó	201	3½

URUGUAY

Flecha Bus goes to Paraná, Santa Fe and Córdoba every Wednesday and Saturday evening. EGA serves the same three Argentine cities on Fridays, and also travels to Asunción, Paraguay, on Wednesday and Saturday nights. Empresa Paccot serves Colón and Concepción del Uruguay. At the time of writing, buses to Rosario, Argentina (UR$648, six hours), were also passing through Paysandú due to the bridge closing at Fray Bentos.

Getting Around

Bus 104, marked 'Zona Industrial,' runs every half-hour between downtown and the waterfront, serving the campground, museum and brewery.

SALTO

☎ 073 / pop 101,000

Built near the falls where the Río Uruguay makes its 'big jump' (Salto Grande), Salto is Uruguay's second-largest city and the most northerly crossing point to Argentina. It's a relaxed place, surrounded by citrus orchards, with some 19th-century architecture and a pretty riverfront. People come here for the nearby hot springs, and the recreation area above the enormous Salto Grande hydroelectric dam.

Information

Antel (Artigas 895) Across from the post office.

Banco Comercial (cnr Uruguay & Lavalleja) One of several banks at this intersection.

Cyberm@ni@ (Uruguay 1082; per hour UR$15; ☻ 9am-midnight Mon-Sat) Air-conditioned internet access.

Hospital Regional Salto (☎ 32155; cnr 18 de Julio & Varela)

Lavadero Magnolias (Agraciada 786; per load UR$75) Same-day laundry service.

Post office (cnr Artigas & Treinta y Tres)

Tourist office (turismo@salto.gub.uy) bus terminal (☎ 40843; ☻ 6am-midnight); Centro (☎ 34096; Uruguay 1052; ☻ 7:30am-8:30pm Mon-Sat)

Sights & Activities

Admission to Salto's museums is free.

The **Museo de Bellas Artes y Artes Decorativas** (☎ 29898; Uruguay 1057; ☻ 3-8pm Tue-Sat, 5-8pm Sun) displays a nice collection of Uruguayan painting and sculpture in a historic two-story mansion with grand staircase, stained glass and back garden.

The **Museo del Hombre y la Tecnología** (☎ 29898; cnr Av Brasil & Zorrilla; ☻ 2-7pm), housed in a historic market building, features excellent displays on local cultural development and history upstairs, and a small archaeological section downstairs.

The **Teatro Larrañaga** (☎ 29898; Joaquín Suárez 39; ☻ 2-8pm Mon-Sat), a red velvet- and chandelier-bedecked theater dating to 1882, is open for visits daily except Sunday and hosts occasional dance and theater performances (UR$45 to UR$60).

Sleeping

Salto's downtown accommodation options are generally a bit faded; spiffier alternatives include the many nearby hot springs and the five-star lakeside Hotel Horacio Quiroga.

Hostal del Jardín (☎ 32325; hostaldeljardin@hotmail .com; Colón 47; s/d/tr without breakfast UR$300/500/700) Convenient to the port, this place has simple, clean rooms lined up motel-style along a small, grassy side yard.

Gran Hotel Concordia (☎ 32735; www.granhotel concordia.com.uy in Spanish; Uruguay 749; r per person UR$300) This 1860s relic is a national historical monument and indisputably Salto's most atmospheric downtown hotel. A life-size wooden cutout of Carlos Gardel, who once stayed in room 32, greets you at the end of a marble corridor opening into a leafy courtyard filled with murals, sculptures and cats. Front rooms with tall French-shuttered windows overlook the courtyard. Back rooms flank a wrought-iron terrace shaded by climbing vines.

Hotel Los Cedros (☎ 33984; www.hotelloscedros .com in Spanish; Uruguay 657; s/d with fan UR$380/660, with air-con from UR$530/870; ☒) The padded vinyl elevator door hints at the bad taste awaiting upstairs, where dark rooms suffocate under dull brown and mustard decor. The pluses? It's centrally located and comfortable enough, with wireless internet throughout and good city views from the 4th-floor breakfast area.

Hotel Horacio Quiroga (☎ 34411; www.hotel horacioquiroga.com; Parque del Lago, Salto Grande; s/d/tr/q from UR$1900/2300/3000/3500, full board from UR$2600/3600/5000/6200; ☒ ☐ ☒) On the lake above the dam, the luxurious Quiroga has its own thermal baths and spa facilities. Lakeview rooms are especially nice, with balconies overlooking the swimming pools and flowery grounds planted with trees from around the world. Van transfers from town can be provided, with advance notice.

Eating

Azabache (☎ 32337; Uruguay 702; mains UR$52-108, set meals UR$128-164; ☺ 9am-midnight) The ample outdoor seating and privileged corner location make Azabache a popular choice for morning coffee, evening drinks and good-value fixed-price meals.

La Caldera (☎ 24648; Uruguay 221; dishes UR$70-155; ☺ noon-3pm & 9pm-midnight) With fresh breezes blowing in off the river and sunny outdoor seating on funky stools, this *parrilla* makes a great lunch stop.

Casa de Lamas (☎ 29376; Chiazzaro 20; dishes UR$85-240; ☺ noon-3pm & 9pm-midnight Thu-Mon, dinner only Wed) Also near the waterfront, this swank eatery is housed in a 19th-century building painted an eye-catching shade of purple, with pretty vaulted brickwork in the dining room. It has several vegetarian offerings, and a *menú de la casa* (set menu) for UR$195.

Getting There & Away

BOAT

Transporte Fluvial San Cristóbal (☎ 32461; cnr Av Brasil & Costanera Norte) runs launches across the river to Concordia (UR$55, 15 minutes) four times a day in winter, five in summer, between 8:45am and 6:30pm Monday to Saturday (no service on Sunday).

BUS

From the **bus terminal** (☎ 32909; Salto Shopping Center, cnr Ruta 3 & Av Batlle) east of downtown, two daily buses go to Concordia (UR$69, one hour), with connections to many other Argentine destinations. Chadre, Núñez and El Norteño offer frequent services to Montevideo (UR$419, 6½ hours) and Paysandú (UR$100, two hours). Chadre also has twice-daily services to Colonia (UR$387, eight hours). On Mondays and Fridays direct buses run to Tacuarembó (UR$253, four hours).

AROUND SALTO

Represa Salto Grande

This massive **hydroelectric project** (☎ 26131; ☺ 8am-5pm Mon-Sat) at Salto Grande, 14km north of town, provides 65% of Uruguay's electricity and is a symbol of national pride. Free hour-long guided tours of the dam visit both the Uruguayan and Argentine sides (no minimum group size, maximum wait 20 minutes). There's no public transport; a taxi from Salto costs about UR$500 roundtrip. En route,

check out the stands selling fresh-squeezed local orange juice for UR$12 a liter!

Termas de Daymán

☎ 073

Eight kilometers south of Salto, Termas de Daymán is a Disneyland of thermal baths, the most developed of several such complexes in northwestern Uruguay. Surrounded by motels and restaurants, it's popular with Uruguayan and Argentine tourists, who roam the town's block-long main street in bathrobes.

The **Complejo Médico Hidrotermal Daymán** (☎ 69090; admission UR$150; ☺ 10am-8pm) provides body wraps, facials, massages, mud treatments and physical therapy. A full package including 40-minute massage costs UR$570. At the end of the hotel row are the **municipal baths** (☎ 69711; admission UR$50; ☺ 7am-11pm), a vast complex of pools interspersed with grassy picnic areas. **Acuamanía** (☎ 69222; www.acuamania .com in Spanish; admission UR$120; ☺ 10:30am-6:30pm) is a water park with gargantuan slides.

The former monastery **La Posta del Daymán** (☎ 69801; www.lapostadeldayman.com in Spanish; campsite per person UR$65, dm/r per person with breakfast UR$440/660, half board UR$600/800, full board UR$700/900; ☒) has everything – a campground, hostel, spacious hotel rooms, Jacuzzi, sauna, thermal swimming pool and good-value attached restaurant. Out of season prices drop dramatically.

Hostal Canela (☎ 69121; hcanela@internet.com.uy; Los Sauces s/n; dm UR$270; ☒) is a family-run HI hostel with swimming pool on a quiet residential street 1km north of the springs.

Between 6:30am and 10:30pm COSA operates hourly buses (UR$13.50) from Salto's port to the baths, returning hourly from 7am to 11pm. Stops in Salto are along Av Brasil outbound and Av 19 de Abril inbound.

Estancia San Nicanor

Surrounded by a landscape of cows, fields and water reminiscent of a Flemish painting, **Estancia San Nicanor** (☎ 0730-2209; Ruta 3, Km 475; www.sannicanor.com.uy in Spanish; campsite per person UR$250, dm/r/tr/q UR$440/1300/1750/2200; ☒) offers more tranquility than neighboring Daymán. Prized by New Agers, it has a gigantic outdoor thermal pool, plus camping (tents available onsite), hostel and cabin accommodation, and a recently converted *estancia* house with gorgeous high-ceilinged rooms, outlandishly large fireplaces and peacocks strolling the grounds. The 14km unpaved access road is just south of Termas del Daymán. They'll pick you up if you call ahead.

Termas de Arapey

In the middle of nowhere, 90km northeast of Salto, Termas de Arapey is another popular hot springs resort. Its multiple pools are surrounded by gardens, fountains and paths leading down to the Río Arapey Grande. Despite the electric lighting and dizzying profusion of lodging options, the natural setting remains supremely serene.

Rooms at **Hotel Municipal** (☎ 073-34096; instur@ adinet.com.uy; s/d/tr UR$800/1100/1300, with half board UR$1050/1600/1980; ❄) have phone, satellite TV, and hot and cold thermal water. There are also cheaper motel and bungalow accommodations, plus campsites ($120 for up to two people, UR$60 each additional person).

Two morning buses serve Arapey daily from Salto (UR$95, 1½ hours).

TACUAREMBÓ

☎ 063 / pop 51,000

This is gaucho country. Not your 'we pose for pesos' types, but your real-deal 'we tuck our baggy pants into our boots and slap on a beret just to go to the local store' crew. It's also the alleged birthplace of tango legend Carlos Gardel. Capital of its department, Tacuarembó has sycamore-lined streets and attractive plazas that make it one of Uruguay's most agreeable interior towns.

Orientation

In the rolling hill country along the Cuchilla de Haedo, Tacuarembó is 230km east of Paysandú and 390km north of Montevideo. The town center is Plaza 19 de Abril, but the streets 25 de Mayo and 18 de Julio both lead south past the almost equally important Plazas Colón and Rivera.

Information

Antel (Sarandí 242)

Banco Santander (18 de Julio 258) One of several banks with ATMs near the northeast corner of central Plaza Colón.

Departmental tourist office (☎ 27144; ❄ 7:30am-7pm Mon-Fri, 10:30am-3:30pm Sat & Sun) Just outside the bus terminal.

Hospital Regional (☎ 22955; cnr Treinta y Tres & Catalogne)

Post office (Ituzaingó 262)

Sights & Activities

Tacuarembó's **Museo del Indio y del Gaucho Washington Escobar** (cnr Flores & Artigas; admission free; ❄ 12:30-6:30pm Tue, Wed & Fri, 8am-6:30pm Thu, 2-6pm Sat & Sun) pays romantic tribute to Uruguay's gauchos and indigenous peoples. The collection includes stools made from leather and cow bones, elegantly worked silver spurs and other accessories of early rural life.

Festivals & Events

In the first week of March, the colorful five-day **Fiesta de la Patria Gaucha** attracts visitors from around the country to exhibitions of traditional gaucho skills, music and other activities. It takes place in Parque 25 de Agosto, north of town.

Sleeping & Eating

Hotel Plaza (☎ 27988; 25 de Agosto 247; s/d/tr/q UR$375/600/890/1075; ❄ ▯) Painted a bright and cheery yellow, with fish on the shower curtains and wireless internet in the rooms, the centrally located Plaza is the most welcoming place in town.

Hotel Central (☎ 22341; fax 22841; Flores 300; s/d/tr/q UR$410/580/1020/1360; ❄ ▯) Bland but comfortable, the Central's large, clean rooms have cable TV.

La Sombrilla (☎ 23432; cnr 25 de Mayo & Suárez; snacks from UR$16) This reasonably priced confitería is good for breakfast and late-night snacking.

La Rueda (☎ 22453; W Beltrán 251; dishes UR$70-140; ❄ 11am-3pm & 7pm-1am Mon-Sat, lunch only Sun) With its thatched roof and walls covered with gaucho paraphernalia (and ewww…animal skins), La Rueda is a friendly neighborhood parrilla.

Getting There & Around

The **bus terminal** (cnr Ruta 5 & Av Victorino Pereira) is 2km northeast of the center. A taxi into town costs about UR$40. Turil, Chadre and Nuñez offer direct service to Montevideo (UR$326, 4½ hours). Chadre and Toriani have direct but infrequent service to Salto (UR$253, four hours); an alternative is to take one of the daily buses to Paysandú (UR$201, 3½ hours) and change for Salto there.

VALLE EDÉN

☎ 063

Valle Edén, a lush valley 24km southwest of Tacuarembó, is home to the **Museo Carlos Gardel** (☎ 22898; admission UR$15; ❄ 9:30am-6:30pm).

URUGUAY'S OFF-THE-BEATEN-TRACK NATURE PRESERVES

Uruguay's interior, with its vast open spaces, is a naturalist's dream. The Uruguayan government has designated five locations around the country as especially worthy of protection under its Sistema Nacional de Áreas Protegidas (SNAP) program. Alas, funding to actually preserve these areas is still sadly lacking, and tourist infrastructure remains rudimentary, but intrepid travelers will be richly rewarded for seeking out these little-visited spots. Here are some details on the two preserves that best capture the spirit of Uruguay's wild gaucho country.

Valle del Lunarejo

This gorgeous valley, 95km north of Tacuarembó, is a place of marvelous peace and isolation, with birds and rushing water providing the only soundtrack.

Enchanting **Posada Lunarejo** (☎ 099-826348; www.posadalunarejo.com in Spanish; Ruta 30, Km 238; r with breakfast per person UR$540, other meals UR$200 each) occupies a lovingly restored 1880 building 2km off the main road, 3km from the river and a few steps from a garza (crane) colony. Further up the road, local guide Mario Padern's company **Balcones de Lunarejo** (☎ 0650-6353, 099-450653; Ruta 30, Km 230; tour with lunch UR$350 walking, UR$520 horseback) leads hiking and horseback-riding tours from the canyon's edge down to a series of natural pools near the river's headwaters.

Valle del Lunarejo is served by Turil's twice-daily Montevideo–Tacuarembó–Artigas bus (from Montevideo UR$419, six hours; from Tacuarembó UR$92, 1½ hours). Ask to get off at the relevant kilometer marker (see above). Posada Lunarejo can meet your bus if you call ahead.

Quebrada de los Cuervos

This hidden little canyon cuts through the rolling hill country 40km northwest of Treinta y Tres (325km northeast of Montevideo), providing an unexpectedly moist and cool habitat for a variety of plants and birds. There's a nature trail looping through the park (two hours roundtrip), plus a shady hilltop campground (UR$100 per person) at park headquarters.

A perfect base for exploring this region is **Cañada del Brujo** (☎ 099-297448; cdelbrujo@latinmail .com; dm UR$170, meals UR$115 each), an ultrarustic hostel in an old schoolhouse 12km from the park. Hostel owner Pablo Rado can take you hiking to nearby waterfalls and introduce you to the simple joys of gaucho life: living by candlelight, drinking *mate,* sleeping under a wool poncho, eating simple meals cooked on the wood stove and watching spectacular sunsets under the big sky. With advance notice, he'll meet you in Treinta y Tres and drive you to the hostel in his old VW bug.

For bus travel to Treinta y Tres, see Getting There & Away under Montevideo (p560), Chuy (p595), Minas (p580) and Maldonado (p582).

Reached via a drive-through creek spanned by a wooden suspension footbridge, and housed in a former *pulpería* (the general store/bar that used to operate on many *estancias*), the museum documents Tacuarembó's claim as birthplace of the revered tango singer – a claim vigorously contested by Argentina and France!

Accommodation in Valle Edén is available at **Camping El Mago** (☎ 27144; campsite per person UR$10) and at the lovely historic mud-and-stone **Posada Valle Edén** (☎ 099-810567; www.posada valleeden.com.uy in Spanish; r per person UR$380-780).

Empresa Calibus runs infrequent buses from Tacuarembó to Valle Edén (UR$25, 20 minutes).

EASTERN URUGUAY

The gorgeous 340km sweep of beaches, dunes, forests and lagoons stretching northeast from Montevideo to the Brazilian border is one of Uruguay's national treasures. Still largely unknown except to Uruguayans and their immediate neighbors, this part of Uruguay lies nearly dormant for 10 months out of the year, then explodes with summer activity from Christmas to Carnaval, when it seems like every bus out of Montevideo is headed somewhere up the coast. For sheer fun-in-the-sun energy, there's nothing like the peak season, but if you can make it here slightly off-season, you'll experience all the same beauty for literally half the price.

Near the Brazilian border, amid the wide-open landscapes and untrammeled beaches of Rocha department, abandoned hilltop fortresses and shipwrecks offer mute testimony to the time when Spain and Portugal struggled for control of the new continent. Where lookouts once scanned the wide horizon for invading forces, a new wave of invaders has taken hold, from binocular-wielding whale-watchers in Cabo Polonio to camera-toting celebrity-watchers in Punta del Este. This part of Uruguay has something for everyone: surfers flock to Punta del Diablo and La Paloma, ornithologists go cuckoo over the endless string of coastal lagoons, families with kids frolic in the waves at La Pedrera or Piriápolis, and party animals find their nirvana in the all-night club scene at Punta del Este.

PIRIÁPOLIS

☎ 043 / pop 7500

With its elegant old hotel and beachfront promenade backed by small mountains, Piriápolis is vaguely reminiscent of a Mediterranean beach town and is arguably Uruguay's most picturesque coastal resort. Less pretentious and more affordable than Punta del Este, it was developed for tourism in the 1930s by Argentine entrepreneur Francisco Piria, who built the imposing landmark Argentino Hotel and an eccentric hillside residence known as Castillo de Piria (Piria's Castle; opposite).

The surrounding countryside holds many interesting features, including two of Uruguay's highest summits.

Orientation

Piriápolis is very compact. Almost all the action happens near the beachfront, in the 10-block stretch between Av Artigas (the access road from Ruta 9) and Av Piria, where the coastline makes a broad curve southwards. Streets back from the beach quickly become residential. The Argentino Hotel is the town's most prominent landmark.

Information

Antel (cnr Tucumán & Buenos Aires; internet per hr UR$19; ☉ 8am-11pm)

Asociación de Fomento y Turismo (☎ 22560; info@ turismopiriapolis.com; Rambla de los Argentinos s/n; ☉ 9am-9pm Jan & Feb, 10am-8pm Mar-Dec) Off the street, in the Paseo de la Pasiva building.

Banco de la República (Rambla de los Argentinos, btwn Sierra & Sanabria) Convenient ATM.

Centro de Hoteles y Restaurantes de Piriápolis (☎ 22218; chryp@adinet.com.uy; Rambla de los Argentinos; ☉ 9am-11pm) Adjacent to tourist office; provides local hotel info and booking assistance.

Lavadero Familiar (cnr Piria & Reconquista; wash & dry per load UR$65; ☉ 9am-9pm)

Post office (Av Piria) Just south of Tucumán.

Sights & Activities

Swimming and **sunbathing** are the most popular activities, and there's good **fishing** off the rocks at the west end of the beach, where Rambla de los Argentinos becomes Rambla de los Ingleses.

For a great view of Piriápolis, take the **chairlift** (adult/child UR$60/40; ☉ 9am-8pm) to the summit of **Cerro San Antonio** at the east end of town.

Sleeping

Camping Piriápolis FC (☎ 23275; cnr Misiones & Niza; camping per person UR$85; ☉ Dec-Apr) Opposite the bus terminal, this seasonal campground has sports facilities, a restaurant, electricity and hot showers.

Albergue Antón Grassi (☎ 20394; piriapolis@hostel uruguay.org; Simón del Pino 1106-36; dm/s/d HI member UR$180/290/390, nonmember surcharge per person UR$100) This 270-bed hostel, South America's second-largest, has dozens of dorms and a few doubles. It's desolate as an airplane hangar when empty, but full of life (and often booked solid) in January and February.

Bungalows Margariteñas (☎ 22245; www.marga ritenias.com in Spanish; cnr Zufriategui & Piedras; d/tr/q from UR$836/910/1070) Near the bus terminal, this place has beautifully equipped, individually decorated bungalows that sleep two to four. The owners speak English.

Hotel Rex (☎ 22543; Manuel Freire 968; www.hotel rex.com.uy; s/d/tr/q UR$900/1350/2000/2500; ✕ ▣) The Rex, with its colorful decor, immaculate housekeeping and location half a block from the beach, makes for a very comfortable stay.

Hotel Colón (☎ 22508; www.hotelcolonpiriapolis.com in Spanish; Rambla 950; r/tr/q from UR$1550/2300/2750; ▣) Built in 1910 by Francisco Piria, this faux-Tudor mansion by the waterfront boasts fine views, gorgeous art nouveau details and an old-fashioned sitting room with fireplace.

Argentino Hotel (☎ 22791; www.argentinohotel.com in Spanish; Rambla de los Argentinos s/n; s/d with breakfast from UR$1500/2100, half board UR$1750/2600, full board UR$2000/3100; ✕ ▣ ▣) Even if you don't stay here, you should visit this elegant 350-room European-style spa with two heated river-water pools, a casino, ice-skating rink and other luxuries.

Eating

Most restaurants are within a block of the Rambla.

Sal y Pimienta (☎ 22244; cnr Tucumán & Sierra; set meals UR$99-119) This corner eatery one block back from the beach offers affordable set menus with an emphasis on pasta and seafood.

Restaurante Yoyo (☎ 22948; cnr Sanabria & Tucumán; dishes UR$99-235; ☉ 9:30am-4:30pm & 7:30pm-late) Yoyo specializes in pizza and seafood, brews its own beer and has live music in summer.

Terra Nova (☎ 27879; cnr Rambla de los Argentinos & Sanabria; dishes UR$115-350; ☉ 9am-midnight, to 3am in summer) Smack in the center of the waterfront promenade, this trendy *parrilla* with turquoise brick walls framing a blazing fire buzzes with activity year-round.

Getting There & Away

The **bus terminal** (cnr Misiones & Niza) is a few blocks back from the beach. COT and COPSA run frequent buses to Montevideo (UR$84, 1½ hours), Maldonado (UR$42, 40 minutes) and Punta del Este (UR$50, 50 minutes). COOM runs multiple buses daily to Minas (UR$59, 1¼ hours) and Pan de Azúcar, where there are connections to Rocha and other points northeast.

AROUND PIRIÁPOLIS
Castillo de Piria & Pan de Azúcar

North of town, visitors can tour **Castillo de Piria** (☎ 043-23268; Ruta 37, Km 4; admission free; ☉ 10am-5pm Tue-Sun), Francisco Piria's outlandishly opulent residence. One kilometer further up Ruta 37, the **Reserva de Fauna Autóctona** (Ruta 37, Km 5; admission free; ☉ sunrise-sunset) showcases native species such as the capybara, gray fox and ñandú. From here, hikers can climb Uruguay's fourth-highest 'peak,' **Cerro Pan de Azúcar** (389m). The trail (three hours roundtrip) starts as a gradual dirt road, then narrows to a steep path marked with red arrows. Ask for directions at Parador Drago, in the reserve's parking lot.

Sierra de las Animas

Increasingly popular with Uruguayan hikers, the privately operated nature preserve **Sierra de las Ánimas** (☎ 094-419891; www.sierradelasanimas.com in

Spanish; Ruta 9, Km 86) is just off the Interbalnearia, 25km towards Montevideo from Piriápolis. Activities include climbing to the 501m summit (Uruguay's second-highest), swimming in the **Espejo del Guardián** (a natural pool below a waterfall), mountain biking and camping. Coming from Montevideo by bus, get off at Parador Los Cardos restaurant and cross the highway.

SOS Rescate de Fauna Marina

Ten kilometers south of Piriápolis is Uruguay's premier marine-animal rescue and rehabilitation center, **SOS Rescate de Fauna Marina** (☎ 094-330795; sos-faunamarina@adinet.com.uy; admission UR$50; ☉ by appointment). Run entirely by volunteers, its emphasis is on educating schoolchildren, who can assist with daily feedings and observe penguins, sea lions, turtles and other rescued wildlife. Visitors willing to support the center's mission with the requested UR$50 donation (or more) are welcome with advance notice.

MINAS
☎ 044 / pop 38,000

If Uruguay has been making you feel starved for hills, Minas will come as a welcome surprise. Surrounded by the lovely undulating landscape of the Cuchilla Grande in Lavalleja department, 120km northeast of Montevideo and 60km north of Piriápolis, Minas is named for nearby granite quarries.

Information

Antel (Treinta y Tres 765; ☉ 7am-11pm) Across from the bus terminal.

Cyber Arroba (☎ 32122; Treinta y Tres 591; internet per hr UR$15; ☉ 9am-midnight Mon-Sat, 2:30pm-midnight Sun) Just off of Plaza Libertad.

Municipal tourist office (☎ 29796; www.lavalleja .gub.uy in Spanish; Treinta y Tres s/n; ☉ 8am-8pm)

Post office (W Beltrán 612) At corner with 25 de Mayo.

Sights & Activities

Among the eucalyptus groves 10km west of town, **Parque Salus** (☎ 31652; Ruta 8, Km 109; admission free; ☉ 10.15am-4pm Oct-Feb & 9am-6pm Mar-Sep) is the source of Uruguay's best-known mineral water and site of the Patricia brewery. Buses for the complex (which includes an upmarket hotel, reasonable restaurant and small botanical garden) leave regularly from Minas' bus terminal.

Gruta Arequita (☎ 0440-2731; info@complejoarequita .com; tours UR$50; ☉ tours 11am & 4pm Mon-Fri, 11am,

2pm, 4pm & 6pm Sat, Sun & holidays, or by arrangement) is a privately operated cave 10km north of town in beautiful Parque Arequita. Public buses (UR$25, 30 minutes) run to/from Minas at least once daily (more in summer).

Turismo Aventura (☎ 27686) organizes hikes into the surrounding hills and rappelling trips down abandoned mineshafts.

Festivals & Events

Every April 19, up to 70,000 pilgrims visit the **Cerro y Virgen del Verdún**, 6km west of town. The festival, dating back to the early 20th century, draws in pilgrims from all over Uruguay, who pack the mountains above Minas for a series of masses and other religious rituals.

Sleeping & Eating

Parque Arequita (☎ 02503; camping per person UR$29-43, 2-/3-/4-/6-bed cabañas without bathroom UR$192/265/338/386; 🏊) This municipal-run park 11km north of town has grassy campsites and cabins set amid trees, hills and rocky outcroppings. Llamas and ñandus roam about, there's a cold-water swimming pool, and you can rent horses (UR$1 per minute) or hike to nearby Gruta Arequita.

Posada Verdún (☎ 24563; posadaverdun@hotmail .com; W Beltrán 715; s/d/tr/q UR$320/560/830/1100, breakfast per person UR$60) Convenient for the bus terminal, this welcoming family-run posada has been in business over 25 years. Simple, clean rooms come with cable TV, and there's a flowery patio.

Casa Rica (☎ 31492; cnr Ituzaingó & Roosevelt; snacks from UR$15) This corner place on Plaza Rivera makes delicious empanadas, cakes and light meals.

Confitería Irisarri (☎ 22639; Treinta y Tres 618; sandwiches UR$45-73; 🕘 9am-10pm) Family-run since 1898, this café on Plaza Libertad is famous for its *alfajores* (cookie sandwiches) and *serranitos* (sweets made from vanilla-flavored caramel, fruit pulp, chocolate and peanuts).

Kijoia (☎ 25884; Domingo Pérez 483; meals UR$90-280; 🕚 11:30am-midnight) All you need is a whiff of the delightful smoky smell coming from this *parrilla* on Plaza Libertad to understand why it's so popular.

Getting There & Away

The **bus terminal** (Treinta y Tres s/n) is between Sarandí and Williman. CUT and Minuano provide frequent services to Montevideo (UR$100, two hours). Minuano also runs

twice daily to Treinta y Tres (UR$151, 2½ hours). COOM has several daily departures to Piriápolis (UR$59, 1¼ hours). Emtur goes to Maldonado (UR$67, 1½ hours) and Punta del Este (UR$75, 1¾ hours). Nuñez runs once daily to Chuy (UR$184, four hours).

VILLA SERRANA
☎ 044

Those seeking an off-the-beaten-track retreat will love the serenity of this little village nestled in hills above a small lake, 25km northeast of Minas. Nearby attractions include **Salto del Penitente**, a 60m waterfall.

The simple **Albergue Villa Serrana** (☎ 099-085677, in Montevideo 02-9013587; vserrana@hostel uruguay.org; Camino Molles s/n; dm HI member/nonmember UR$150/200) hostel has an intimate fairy-tale quality, with a thatched roof, fireplace and ladders climbing to sleeping decks under the eaves. There's a tiny guest kitchen (bring food). Advance notice is essential – in summer it's often fully booked; in the off-season you may be the only visitor and will need to fetch the key down the street.

Picturesquely perched above the valley, **La Calaguala** (☎ 02347, 099-387519; www.paysandu.com /lacalaguala in Spanish; Ruta 8, Km 145; campsite UR$150, r per person with breakfast/half board/full board UR$400/580/800) is a friendly family-run posada with attached restaurant, which also arranges horseback-riding and hiking excursions (from UR$80 per person). The slightly more expensive room with whirlpool tub and fireplace is extremely cozy on chilly nights.

Direct buses to Villa Serrana (UR$25, 30 minutes) leave Minas Tuesdays and Thursdays at 9am and 5:30pm, returning at 9:45am and 6:15pm. On other days, any northbound bus from Minas along Ruta 8 can drop you at Km 140 or Km 145, from where it's a stiff 4km uphill walk into town. Area accommodations can meet you at the highway with advance notice.

MALDONADO
☎ 042 / pop 55,000

Capital of its namesake department, Maldonado nowadays feels like Punta del Este's poor cousin. Dating from 1755, it has retained a few shreds of colonial atmosphere, but it's unlikely to keep you engaged for more than an afternoon. Once considered an economical alternative to Punta, its prices are no longer so attractive. Perhaps the most

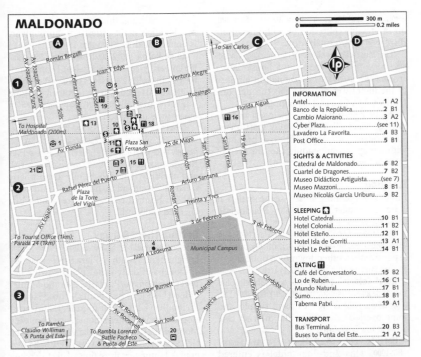

MALDONADO

INFORMATION
Antel...............................1 A2
Banco de la República...............2 B1
Cambio Maiorano...................3 A2
Cyber Plaza......................(see 11)
Lavadero La Favorita...............4 B3
Post Office.........................5 B1

SIGHTS & ACTIVITIES
Catedral de Maldonado..............6 B2
Cuartel de Dragones...............7 B1
Museo Didáctico Artiguista........(see 7)
Museo Mazzoni.....................8 B1
Museo Nicolás García Uriburu......9 B2

SLEEPING
Hotel Catedral....................10 B1
Hotel Colonial....................11 B1
Hotel Esteño......................12 B1
Hotel Isla de Gorriti.............13 A1
Hotel Le Petit....................14 B1

EATING
Café del Conversatorio............15 B2
Lo de Ruben.......................16 C1
Mundo Natural.....................17 B1
Sumo..............................18 B1
Taberna Patxi.....................19 A1

TRANSPORT
Bus Terminal......................20 B3
Buses to Punta del Este...........21 A2

---

compelling reason to visit is to eat at one of its two superb restaurants, Lo de Ruben and Taberna Patxi.

Orientation

Maldonado is 130km east of Montevideo and only 30km from Piriápolis. Other than the beaches south of the center, most points of interest are within a few blocks of its central Plaza San Fernando. Rambla Claudio Williman and Rambla Lorenzo Batlle Pacheco are coastal thoroughfares that converge from northwest and northeast, respectively. Locations along the Ramblas are usually identified by numbered *paradas* (bus stops).

Information

Antel (cnr Av Joaquín de Viana & Av Florida; 8am-11pm)

Banco de la República (Av Florida 774) ATM on the main square.

Cambio Maiorano (Av Florida 860; 9am-7:30pm Mon-Sat) One of many exchange houses along Av Florida.

Cyber Plaza (223346; 18 de Julio 841; per hr UR$20; 8am-2am) Internet café serving drinks, run by Hotel Colonial.

Hospital Maldonado (225889; Ventura Alegre) About eight blocks west of Plaza San Fernando.

Lavadero La Favorita (223763; Juan A Ledesma s/n) Laundry service just west of Sarandí.

Post office (18 de Julio 965) Just north of Ventura Alegre.

Tourist office (230050; www.maldonado.gub.uy in Spanish; Parada 24; 8am-7pm) Maldonado has closed its downtown tourist office and moved operations to beachside Rambla Claudio Williman.

Sights & Activities

The **Catedral de Maldonado** (Plaza San Fernando) was completed in 1895 after nearly a century of construction. On Rafael Pérez del Puerto, the **Plaza de la Torre del Vigía** features a colonial watchtower built with peepholes for viewing the approach of hostile forces.

Another colonial relic, the **Cuartel de Dragones** is a block of military fortifications with stone walls and iron gates, built between 1771 and 1797. Inside, the **Museo Didáctico Artiguista** (225378; admission free; 10am-6pm) displays colorful maps tracing the peripatetic military campaigns of Uruguay's independence hero. Next door is the fine-arts **Museo Nicolás García Uriburu** (225378; 25 de Mayo s/n;

URUGUAY

admission free; 10:15am-5:45pm Tue-Sat, 2-6pm Sun), an impressive collection of sculpture nicely displayed in two small wings.

The **Museo Mazzoni** (221107; Ituzaingó 789; admission free; 1-6pm Tue-Sun), in a house dating from 1782, provides a fascinating glimpse of the life of wealthy colonials through one family's furniture and belongings.

Popular pastimes along the coast include **surfing**, **windsurfing**, **diving** and **sportfishing**. The tourist office publishes a brochure with a map recommending sites for each of these activities.

Sleeping

Punta's burgeoning hostel scene makes it a better budget choice than Maldonado these days.

Hotel Isla de Gorriti (245218; cnr Zelmar Michelini & Ituzaingó; d/q UR$790/1100;) A bit musty but less expensive than other downtown options. All rooms surround a little courtyard.

Hotel Colonial (223346; www.elhotelcolonial.com; 18 de Julio 841; s/d/tr/q UR$550/900/1100/1300) The Colonial's rooms are clean and simple, and some overlook the plaza. The internet café downstairs is a bonus.

Hotel Le Petit (223044; cnr Av Florida & Sarandí; r UR$1000) This 2nd-floor hotel is entered through a little shopping mall on the plaza. It gets some street noise, but has well-kept rooms with cable TV.

Hotel Esteño (225222; Sarandí 881; s/d UR$750/1100) The Esteño's rooms, with aging carpeting and very small bathrooms, don't live up to the promise of its entryway.

Hotel Catedral (242513; hotelcatedral@adinet.com.uy; Av Florida 830; s/d/tr/q UR$1300/1650/2000/2500) Downtown Maldonado's classiest hotel has Japanese-pattern bedspreads, ultraclean bathrooms and art posters in the hallways. Front rooms overlook the cathedral.

Eating

Mundo Natural (Román Guerra 918; items from UR$20) This cheerful hole-in-the-wall has been serving vegetarian treats since 1992.

Café del Conversatorio (220478; Sarandí s/n; snacks UR$20-90; 8am-10pm Mon-Thu, to 1am Fri-Sun) This spirited little café adjoining a music conservatory has a nice garden patio with tiled fountain. It features live music on weekend nights.

Sumo (223959; cnr Sarandí & Av Florida; dishes UR$60-230; 8am-1am) Perfectly situated for people-watching, this corner restaurant on Maldonado's main pedestrian thoroughfare is popular with local youth.

Lo de Ruben (223059; Santa Teresa 846; dishes UR$105-320; noon-4pm & 8pm-late) From humble origins selling sausages off a cart with his father twenty-odd years ago, Ruben has built one of the area's most wildly popular *parrillas*, a true local institution.

Taberna Patxi (238393; José Dodera 944; dishes UR$195-330; noon-3pm & 8pm-midnight Thu-Sat, dinner only Wed, lunch only Sun) Taberna Patxi serves fine Basque food with an emphasis on fish and shellfish. The delightfully atmospheric cellar environment features stone-and-brick walls, a beamed ceiling, and red-and-white checked tablecloths.

Getting There & Away

The **bus terminal** (250490; cnr Av Roosevelt & Sarandí) is eight blocks south of Plaza San Fernando.

Dozens of daily buses ply the route between Maldonado/Punta del Este and Montevideo (UR$121, two hours); some stop in Piriápolis (UR$42, 40 minutes), and most stop at Carrasco International Airport outside Montevideo. COT has two daily buses to Rocha (UR$75, 1½ hours) and Chuy (UR$184, 3½ hours). Emtur goes three times daily to Treinta y Tres (UR$184, 3½ hours) and twice daily to Minas (UR$67, 1½ hours). COOM sells tickets to Buenos Aires (UR$770, 11 hours) and other international destinations.

Getting Around

Local buses (blue Codesa, yellow Olivera and green Maldonado Turismo) run between Maldonado and Punta del Este (UR$13.50, 15 to 30 minutes) via various routes. In summer they run around the clock, as often as every 15 minutes. Olivera's westbound Línea 8 connects Maldonado with Punta Ballena, Portezuelo and the airport, while eastbound Línea 14 hits the bus terminals in both Maldonado and Punta del Este, the eastern beaches, La Barra and José Ignacio.

PUNTA DEL ESTE
042 / pop 7500

OK, here's the plan: tan it, wax it, buff it at the gym, then plonk it on the beach at 'Punta.' Once you're done there, go out and shake it at one of the town's famous clubs.

Punta del Este – with its many beaches, elegant seaside homes, yacht harbor, high-rise apartment buildings, pricey hotels and glitzy restaurants – is one of South America's most glamorous resorts and easily the most expensive place in Uruguay. Extremely popular with Argentines and Brazilians, Punta suffered a period of decline during the Uruguayan and Argentine recessions, but has come back with a vengeance.

Celebrity-watchers have a full-time job here. Punta is teeming with big names. Early sightings in 2008, as this book went to press, included Ralph Lauren, soccer star Zinedine Zidane and Metallica's lead singer James Hetfield. And then of course there's the ongoing speculation about when exactly Shakira will marry at her nearby *estancia*…

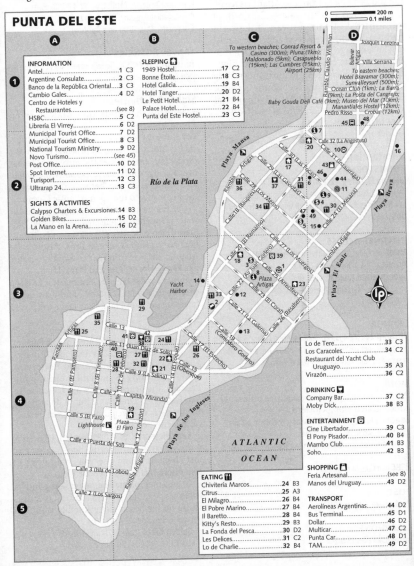

PUNTA DEL ESTE

INFORMATION

Antel	1 C3
Argentine Consulate	2 C3
Banco de la República Oriental	3 C3
Cambio Gales	4 D2
Centro de Hoteles y Restaurantes	(see 8)
HSBC	5 C2
Librería El Virrey	6 D2
Municipal Tourist Office	7 D2
Municipal Tourist Office	8 C3
National Tourism Ministry	9 D2
Novo Turismo	(see 45)
Post Office	10 D2
Spot Internet	11 D2
Turisport	12 C3
Ultrarap 24	13 C3

SIGHTS & ACTIVITIES

Calypso Charters & Excursions	14 B3
Golden Bikes	15 D2
La Mano en la Arena	16 D2

SLEEPING

1949 Hostel	17 C2
Bonne Étoile	18 C3
Hotel Galicia	19 B4
Hotel Tanger	20 D2
Le Petit Hotel	21 B4
Palace Hotel	22 B4
Punta del Este Hostel	23 C3

EATING

Chivitería Marcos	24 B3
Citrus	25 A3
El Milagro	26 B4
El Pobre Marino	27 B4
Il Baretto	28 B4
Kitty's Resto	29 B3
La Fonda del Pesca	30 D2
Les Delices	31 C2
Lo de Charlie	32 B4
Lo de Tere	33 C3
Los Caracoles	34 C2
Restaurant del Yacht Club Uruguayo	35 A3
Virazón	36 C2

DRINKING

Company Bar	37 C2
Moby Dick	38 B3

ENTERTAINMENT

Cine Libertador	39 C3
El Pony Pisador	40 B4
Mambo Club	41 B3
Soho	42 B3

SHOPPING

Feria Artesanal	(see 8)
Manos del Uruguay	43 D2

TRANSPORT

Aerolíneas Argentinas	44 D2
Bus Terminal	45 D1
Dollar	46 D2
Multicar	47 C2
Punta Car	48 D1
TAM	49 D2

URUGUAY

Surrounding towns caught up in the whole Punta mystique include the famed club zone of La Barra to the east and Punta Ballena to the west.

Orientation

Punta itself is relatively small, confined to a narrow peninsula that officially divides the Río de la Plata from the Atlantic Ocean. The town has two separate grids: north of a constricted isthmus just east of the yacht harbor is the high-rise hotel zone; the southern area is largely residential. Street signs in Punta del Este bear both names and numbers, though locals refer to most streets only by their number. An exception is Av Juan Gorlero (Calle 22), the main commercial street, universally referred to as just 'Gorlero' (not to be confused with Calle 19, *Comodoro Gorlero*).

Information

BOOKSTORES

Librería El Virrey (Calle 30, btwn Gorlero & Calle 20; ☉ 9am-2:30am daily Dec-Mar, 10am-9pm Thu-Tue Apr-Nov) Friendly staff and a small selection of English-language bestsellers.

INTERNET ACCESS

Antel (cnr Calles 25 & 24) The most dependable spot for internet access in low season.

Spot Internet (Calle 30, btwn Gorlero & Calle 24; ☉ 24hr Dec-Mar) One of several seasonally operating internet places.

LAUNDRY

Ultrarap 24 (☎ 445595; Calle 24, btwn Calles 19 & 21; wash & dry per basket UR$150; ☉ 8:30am-midnight daily in summer, 9am-7pm Mon-Sat rest of year)

MONEY

Punta's many banks and exchange offices are concentrated along Gorlero.

Banco de la República Oriental (cnr Gorlero & Calle 25) One of two ATMs on this corner.

Cambio Gales (cnr Gorlero & Calle 29) Changes traveler's checks.

HSBC (cnr Gorlero & Calle 28)

POST

Post office (Gorlero 1035)

TELEPHONE

Antel (cnr Calles 25 & 24)

TOURIST INFORMATION

Centro de Hoteles y Restaurantes (☎ 440512; www .puntadelestehoteles.com; Plaza Artigas; ☉ 8am-midnight Dec-Mar, 10am-6pm Apr-Nov) Helps with hotel bookings.

Municipal tourist office (☎ 446510; www.maldo nado.gub.uy in Spanish; cnr Calle 31 & the Rambla; ☉ 8am-midnight Dec 15-Mar 1, 10am-4pm rest of year) Maintains a second branch on Plaza Artigas.

National Tourism Ministry (☎ 441218; punta deleste@mintur.gub.uy; Gorlero 942; ☉ 9am-2pm & 5-10pm Dec-Mar, 10am-6pm Apr-Nov)

TRAVEL AGENCIES

Turisport (☎ 445500; Gorlero, btwn Calles 21 & 23) The local Amex representative.

Sights & Activities

Beaches are the big daytime draw in sunny Punta, and there are plenty to choose from. On the west side of town, Rambla Artigas snakes along the calm **Playa Mansa** on the Río de la Plata, then passes the busy **yacht harbor**, overflowing with boats, restaurants, nightclubs and beautiful people, before circling around the peninsula to the open Atlantic Ocean.

On the eastern side of the peninsula the water is rougher, as reflected in the name **Playa Brava** (Fierce Beach); the waves and currents here have claimed several lives. Also on the Atlantic side, you'll find surfer-friendly beaches like **Playa de los Ingleses** and **Playa El Emir**.

Punta's most famous landmark is **La Mano en la Arena**, a giant sculpted hand protruding from the sand on Playa Brava (see the boxed text, opposite).

From Playa Mansa, west along Rambla Williman, the main beach areas are La Pastora, Marconi, Cantegril, Las Delicias, Pinares, La Gruta at Punta Ballena, and Portezuelo. Eastward, along Rambla Lorenzo Batlle Pacheco, the prime beaches are La Chiverta, San Rafael, La Draga and Punta de la Barra. In summer, all have *paradores* (small restaurants) with beach service.

Sunvalleysurf (☎ 481388; Parada 3, Playa Brava) rents wetsuits, surfboards, bodyboards and just about anything else you could want. It also offers surf and bodyboard lessons.

In summer, **parasailing**, **water skiing** and **jet skiing** are possible on Playa Mansa. Operators set up on the beach along Rambla Williman between Paradas 2 and 20.

Golden Bikes (Calle 24, btwn Calles 28 & 29) rents bikes for UR$40/150 per hour/day.

THE HAND IN THE SAND

Punta del Este's most famous landmark is the monster-sized hand emerging from the sands of Playa Brava. La Mano en la Arena (Hand in the Sand), sculpted in iron and cement by Chilean artist Mario Irarrazabal in 1982, won first prize in a monumental art contest that year and has been a Punta fixture ever since. The hand exerts a magnetic attraction over visitors to Punta, who climb and jump off its digits and pose for thousands of photos with it every year.

Up close, the hand is starting to show its age. There's graffiti scrawled all over it, and its ungraceful cement base often gets exposed by shifting sands. But watch out – the hand's still likely to reach out and grab you!

Tours

Calypso Charters & Excursiones (☎ 446152; www .calypso.com.uy in Spanish; cnr Rambla Artigas & Calle 21; tours adult/child UR$1300/650) One of several companies offering two-hour tours to Isla de Lobos.

Novo Turismo (☎ 493154; www.novoturismo.com in Spanish; bus terminal) Runs city tours of Punta del Este and arranges excursions to surrounding attractions such as Casapueblo, Faro José Ignacio and Cabo Polonio.

Sleeping

In summer Punta is jammed with people, and prices are astronomical. In winter it's a ghost town, and places that stay open lower their prices considerably. Prices listed below are for high season. Because Punta is so much more expensive than other Uruguayan summer resorts, you'll find that hotels marked midrange actually charge top-end rates in summer. Off-season visitors will find prices more in keeping with the midrange and top-end ranges defined on p596.

BUDGET

Punta del Este Hostel (☎ 441632; www.puntadeleste hostel.com; Calle 25 544; dm from UR$350; 🖳) This centrally located hostel is about the cheapest lodging in Punta. It makes a good first impression, with a bright facade and a homey front sitting room (converted to a dorm in summer). Then there's the dark side: the minuscule kitchen, the often sullen staff, and the claustrophobic 11-bed dorm downstairs, with a scary-looking triple-decker bunk!

1949 Hostel (☎ 440719; www.1949hostel.com; cnr Calles 30 & 18; dm/d UR$350/900; 🖳) Punta's best value, this ultracool hostel is a magnet for international youth, with hammocks out front, river views, surfboard rentals, breakfast till noon and a corner bar. Light sleepers who don't plan to party till dawn, beware: it can get pretty rowdy here – witness the duct-taped guitar dangling from the wall!

Manantiales Hostel (☎ 774427; www.manantiales hostel.com; Ruta 10, Km 164; dm/d per person UR$350/450; 🖳 🏊) At the time of writing this hostel looked like a construction site, with a pool and additional dorms going in, and a surf camp in the works. Only 600m from surfer-recommended Bikini Beach, it's frustratingly far from everything else – a 400m walk to the main road, plus five minutes by bus to La Barra, or 20 to Punta.

MIDRANGE

Hotel Galicia (☎ 440547; www.hotelgalicia.com.uy; Plaza El Faro; s/d/tr UR$1200/1600/2300) This small two-star sits in a quiet residential district south of the port. Three of the cheerfully painted rooms face the plaza and have fine views of Punta's lighthouse.

Le Petit Hotel (☎ 441412; www.petithotel -puntadeleste.com in Spanish; Calle 9 717; d/tr/q from UR$1650/2200/3000; 🖳 🏊) This two-star in one of Punta's oldest buildings has recently been remodeled, adding a pool, wi-fi and other upgrades. The newer rooms out back surround a grassy courtyard.

Hotel Bravamar (☎ 480559; www.hotelespunta deleste.com in Spanish; Parada 2, Playa Brava; s/d/tr UR$1300/1750/2300; 🖳) One of the best deals on Playa Brava, the Bravamar has two rooms overlooking the beach…sort of. Unfortunately, the little red Astroturf terraces and intervening highway don't do much to enhance the view!

Bonne Étoile (☎ 440301; www.hotelbonneetoile .com in Spanish; Calle 20, btwn Calles 23 & 25; s/d/tr UR$1750/2000/2300; 🖳) In a 1940s beach house adjoining a more modern six-story tower, Bonne Étoile has clean, spacious rooms, some with river views. The location between Gorlero and the port is hard to beat.

Palace Hotel (☎ 441919; jdlpunta@hotmail.com; cnr Gorlero & Calle 11; s/d/tr/q UR$2000/2100/2400/3300; 🖳 🏊) Just one block up from the yacht harbor, the Palace has a palm-shaded central courtyard and a pretty shared veranda overlooking Calle 11. Rooms are a bit dowdy, but it's hard to argue with the location.

Hotel Tanger (☎ 441333; www.hoteltanger .com in Spanish; Calle 31, btwn Calles 18 & 20; d/tr/q UR$2200/3600/4000; ✄ ▯ ▣) This recommended family-run hotel has ample, comfortable rooms with minibars, safes and wi-fi. The rooftop sundeck and swimming pool have good beach views.

TOP END

La Posta del Cangrejo (☎ 770021; www.lapostadel cangrejo.com; La Barra; s/d from UR$3300/4400, ste UR$10,500; ✄ ▯ ▣) This beachside hotel in the heart of La Barra has whitewashed adobe walls, an award-winning French restaurant and a poolside terrace within earshot of the ocean. The upstairs suites are especially alluring, with fireplaces, Jacuzzis, 29in TVs and nice sound systems.

Casapueblo (☎ 578611; www.clubhotel.com.ar /cas-eng; Punta Ballena; d/q apt UR$3800/7600, d hotel room UR$5400, d/q ste UR$8000/16,000; ✄ ▯ ▣) Artist Carlos Páez Vilaró's whimsical, splurge-worthy architectural masterpiece is like a Mediterranean fantasyland. Rooms cascade down nine levels – numbered zero to negative nine – to a brilliant turquoise, mosaic-floored pool surrounded by a vast sun terrace. Package deals including ferry from Argentina are available online.

our pick **Las Cumbres** (☎ 578689; www.cumbres.com .uy; Ruta 12, Km 3.9, Laguna del Sauce; r UR$3200-4700, ste UR$6700-10,900; ✄ ▯ ▣) Near Punta Ballena, this understatedly luxurious hilltop paradise is eclectically decorated with treasures from the owners' world travels. Rooms abound with special features like writing desks, fireplaces and outdoor whirlpool tubs. Three-hour spa treatments cost UR$1800, and the tearoom terrace (open to the public) has magnificent sunset views.

Conrad Resort & Casino (☎ 491111; www.conrad hotels.com; Parada 4, Playa Mansa; d from UR$7400; ✄ ▯ ▣) If you're looking for five-star amenities in downtown Punta, the high-rise, ultramodern Conrad is the obvious choice. Better rooms have terraces with sea views, the pool and spa complex is fabulous, and the casino offers entertainment extravaganzas.

Eating

BUDGET & MIDRANGE

El Milagro (☎ 443866; Calle 17, btwn Gorlero & Calle 24; dishes UR$60-110; ◷ 11am-midnight) This humble chivitería and pizzeria is about as affordable as things get in Punta. There's a *menu del día* (daily specials menu) for UR$60 and (gasp!) no cover charge.

La Fonda del Pesca (☎ 449165; Calle 29, btwn Gorlero & Calle 24; dishes UR$65-180; ◷ noon-11pm) A vividly painted hole-in-the-wall specializing in fish, La Fonda also serves up plenty of local color. Owner-chef Pesca makes personal appearances at diners' tables to make sure they're enjoying themselves.

El Pobre Marino (☎ 443306; cnr Calles 11 & 12; dishes from UR$95; ◷ lunch & dinner) Decked out with nets and glass floats, this is one of the few affordable sit-down places near the port – where else are you going to find *rabas* (calamari) for UR$95?

Chivitería Marcos (☎ 449932; Rambla Artigas, btwn Calles 12 & 14; made-to-order chivitos UR$120; ◷ 11am-4am Dec-Mar, 11am-4pm & 8pm-late Apr-Nov) Montevideo-based Marcos earned its fame building mega-sandwiches to order. Just tell the *chivito*-sculptor behind the counter which of the 12 toppings and nine sauces you want, then try to balance the thing back to your table.

Les Delices (☎ 443640; cnr Calles 20 & 29; cakes from UR$130; ◷ 8am-10pm, closed May) Great juices, pastries, cakes and salads explain the success of this corner *confitería*, which recently received the Geneva-based International Quality Star award.

Baby Gouda Deli Café (☎ 771874; Ruta 10, Km 161, La Barra; dishes from UR$150; ◷ 11am-7:30pm Mon-Thu, to 1am Fri-Sun) An ultracool deli with an inviting outdoor deck, on the main drag in La Barra, a couple of blocks up from the beach.

TOP END

Kitty's Resto (☎ 446197; Marina 3-4; dishes UR$250-350; ◷ 9am-6pm year-round, plus dinner Dec-Mar) So close to the water, you might as well be dining on a yacht. Seafood is the specialty, but homesick travelers may also appreciate the full American breakfasts for UR$180.

Los Caracoles (☎ 440912; cnr Calles 20 & 28; dishes UR$250-400; ◷ lunch & dinner) Waiters in white jackets and bow ties set the classy tone at this popular corner *parrilla*.

Restaurant del Yacht Club Uruguayo (☎ 447181; cnr Rambla Artigas & Calle 8; dishes UR$250-495; ◷ noon-4pm & 8pm-midnight) This popular traditional fish restaurant is across from the port.

Virazón (☎ 443924; cnr Rambla Artigas & Calle 28; dishes UR$275-565; ◷ 9am-late) Virazón serves great seafood. Grab a spot on the beachside deck, and have fun watching the waiters try to look dignified as they cross the street with loaded trays.

our pick **Lo de Charlie** (☎ 444183; Calle 12, No 819; dishes UR$275-550; ⏱ 11am-4pm & 8pm-1am Thu-Sun) Owned by a fishing buddy of local artist Carlos Páez Vilaró and decorated with some of his work, this is one of Punta's premier restaurants. The endless culinary delights include gazpacho, risotto, homemade pasta, fish and shellfish.

Il Baretto (☎ 447243; cnr Calles 9 & 10; dishes UR$280-570; ⏱ noon-4pm & 8pm-late Thu-Sun) Il Baretto's supercolorful menu features some of the best pasta in Punta and desserts to die for. The lunchtime special (two dishes for UR$355, including cover charge) counts as a good deal by Punta's extravagant standards.

Lo de Tere (☎ 440492; Rambla Artigas, btwn Calles 19 & 21; dishes UR$340-785; ⏱ noon-4pm & 7:30pm-midnight) Even with early-bird discounts of 20% to 40%, Tere's can put a hurtin' on your wallet (at the time of writing they had a bottle of Spanish wine on the menu for US$776!), but the food is truly world-class.

Citrus (☎ 447006; cnr Rambla Artigas & Calle 11; meals UR$375-750; ⏱ 11:30am-5am) Studiedly stylish Citrus bases its appeal on big comfy armchairs, an incomparable 2nd-floor view, and an intriguing fusion of Asian, French, Italian and Mexican flavors.

Drinking & Entertainment

Bear in mind that it's social suicide to turn up at a nightclub before 2am here. A good place to meet up with other travelers beforehand is the bar of the 1949 Hostel (p585). In general, Punta's bars stay open as long as there's a crowd and sometimes have live music on weekends.

The most fashionable clubs are clustered in Punta's port area and along the beach road to La Barra. Ironically, considering Punta's reputation for nightlife, many clubs only stay open for the mid-summer superpeak period. Also, clubs commonly change names or disappear altogether from year to year.

Moby Dick (☎ 441240; Calle 13, btwn Calles 10 & 12) A local fixture, this classic bar near the yacht harbor is where Punta's dynamic social scene kicks off every evening.

Soho (Calle 13, btwn Calles 10 & 12) Next door to Moby Dick, Soho is a dependable year-round dance spot pumping out techno beats (weekends only in low season).

Mambo Club (☎ 448956; cnr Calle 13 & Calle 10) Yet another nightspot down by the port. As the sign says, there's a party every summer night at the Mambo!

El Pony Pisador (☎ 447889; Calle 10, btwn Calles 9 & 11) Around the corner from the other portside venues, this is a branch of Montevideo's famous bar and disco.

Company Bar (☎ 440130; Calle 29, btwn Calles 18 & 20) In downtown Punta, this place is open all year for drinks and live music (weekends only in low season).

Ocean Club (☎ 484869; Parada 12, Playa Brava) On the beach between Punta and La Barra, this club is always hopping, although the name tends to change from year to year.

Crobar (Camino Urquiza, La Barra) A dance place mixing DJs and live music, inland from La Barra on the road to San Carlos.

Medio y Medio (☎ 578791; Camino Lussich s/n, Punta Ballena) This jazz club and restaurant near the beach in Punta Ballena brings in performers from Uruguay, Argentina and Brazil.

Cine Libertador (Gorlero 796) Open year-round with movies on two screens.

Shopping

Manos del Uruguay (☎ 441953; Gorlero, btwn Calles 30 & 31) This is the local branch of Uruguay's national cooperative, selling fine woolens.

Feria Artesanal (Plaza Artigas) This artisan's fair, moved temporarily to the corner of Calles 9 and 14 due to construction in Plaza Artigas, should be back on the main square by the time you read this.

Getting There & Away

AIR

Aeropuerto Internacional de Punta del Este (☎ 559777) is at Laguna del Sauce 25km west of Punta del Este.

Pluna (☎ 492050, 490101; cnr Av Roosevelt & Parada 9; ⏱ 9am-6pm Mon-Sat) offers the most frequent flights between Punta and Buenos Aires' Aeroparque. In summer it also flies to Brazil and Chile, with plans for new services to Córdoba, Argentina, and Asunción, Paraguay.

Aerolíneas Argentinas (☎ 444343; Edificio Santos Dumont, Gorlero, btwn Calles 30 & 31; ⏱ 9am-11pm daily Dec-Mar, 10am-12:30pm & 2:30-6pm Mon-Fri Apr-Nov) flies to Aeroparque several times daily in season, and once a day on Friday and Sunday off-season.

TAM (☎ 442920; Calle 29, btwn Gorlero & Calle 24; ⏱ Dec-Mar) operates a limited number of flights to/from São Paulo in summer.

BUS

Most services to Punta's **bus terminal** (☎ 489467; cnr Calle 32 & Bulevar Artigas) are an extension of those to Maldonado; see p582.

Getting Around

TO/FROM THE AIRPORT

COT runs direct minivans to the airport (UR$90, 30 minutes), leaving 1½ hours before each flight. Alternatively, any Piriápolis-bound bus will drop you at the airport entrance on the main highway (UR$25, 30 minutes), a ten-minute walk from the terminal.

BUS

See p582 for details of the frequent transport between Maldonado and Punta. *Micros* (minibuses) leave every 15 minutes in summer from Bay 1 at Punta's bus terminal and serve the eastern beaches and nightspots on Rambla Batlle Pacheco on their way to La Barra (UR$25, 20 minutes); others run to points west, including Punta Ballena and Piriápolis.

CAR

Car rental outlets are ubiquitous near the bus terminal and along Gorlero. Some of the better deals include **Punta Car** (☎ 482112; cnr Bulevar Artigas & Pedro Risso), **Multicar** (☎ 443143; Gorlero 860) and **Dollar** (☎ 443644; Gorlero 961).

AROUND PUNTA DEL ESTE
Isla Gorriti

Boats leave every half-hour or so (daily in season, weekends in off-season) from Punta del Este's yacht harbor for the 15-minute trip to this island, which has excellent sandy beaches, a couple of restaurants and the ruins of the **Baterías de Santa Ana**, an 18th-century fortification.

Isla de Lobos

About 10km offshore, Isla de Lobos is home to the world's second-largest southern sea-lion colony (200,000 at last count), as well as South America's tallest lighthouse. The island is protected and can only be visited on an organized tour (see p585).

Museo del Mar

This **museum** (☎ 042-771817; Calle de los Corsarios, La Barra; admission UR$50; 🕙 10am-8:30pm Dec-Mar, 11am-6pm Apr-Nov) is 1km inland from the ocean at La Barra. Its diverse collection includes seashells, whale skeletons, kooky-looking fish, a pirate room

for kids, and quotes about the sea from famous personages like Da Vinci and Beaudelaire.

Casapueblo

At Punta Ballena, a jutting headland 15km west of Punta del Este, Uruguayan artist Carlos Páez Vilaró built this exuberantly whimsical **villa and art gallery** (☎ 042-578041; admission UR$100; 🕙 10am-sunset). Gleaming white in the sun and cascading nine stories down a cliffside, it's one of Uruguay's most unique attractions. Visitors can tour five rooms, view a film on the artist's life and travels, and eat up the spectacular views at the upstairs bar-cafeteria. There's a hotel (p586) and restaurant too. It's a 2km walk from the junction where Olivera's Línea 8 bus drops you.

Faro José Ignacio

The rich and famous flock to this increasingly fashionable little beachside town with a pretty lighthouse 30km east of Punta. There's limited tourist infrastructure, but if your goal is to luxuriate by the sea, it's hard to find a nicer place than **La Posada del Faro** (☎ 0486-2110; www.posadadelfaro.com; cnr de la Bahía & Timonel; r UR$4600-9900; 🕙 🔲 🖳). The pricier rooms have fireplaces and private ocean-view terraces. For fine beachside dining, **Parador La Huella** (☎ 0486-2279; Playa Brava; 🕙 lunch & dinner Dec-Apr, lunch Fri-Sun & dinner Fri & Sat May-Nov) specializes in sushi, grilled fish and clay-oven-fired pizza. Two buses daily make the 45-minute trip from Punta (UR$47), stopping in the main square near the **tourist office** (☎ 0486-2409; ligafaro@dedicado.net.uy; 🕙 7am-2:30pm).

ROCHA
☎ 047 / pop 25,000

Rocha is capital of its namesake department and a transport hub for visitors to nearby La Paloma.

There's a helpful departmental **tourist office** (☎ 29728) on Ruta 9, 2km from the center. All other services are concentrated near central Plaza Independencia, including **Antel** (cnr General Artigas & Rodó), the **post office** (18 de Julio 131) and **Banco Comercial** (cnr General Artigas & 25 de Mayo).

Rocha's hotels can be handy if things get booked up in La Paloma. **Hotel Trocadero** (☎ 22267; 25 de Agosto 114; s/d/tr UR$630/1170/1510; 🕙 🔲) has spacious rooms with parquet floors, cable TV, writing desks and 1950s-vintage bathrooms.

For a bite between buses, there are some decent restaurants on the main square. Friendly local eatery **City Café** (☎ 24974; JP Ramírez 112; meals UR$60-120; ☯ 8am-2am) has daily lunchtime specials for UR$85, with a pleasant upstairs balcony overlooking the plaza.

All buses stop on Plaza Independencia. **Cynsa** (cnr Ramírez & 25 de Mayo) has frequent services to La Paloma (UR$29, 30 minutes). **Rutas del Sol** and **COT** (cnr Ramírez & 25 de Agosto) each run several buses daily to Montevideo (UR$176, three hours) and Chuy (UR$117, two hours). Rutas del Sol also serves Punta del Diablo (UR$84, 1½ hours); COT has three daily buses to Maldonado (UR$75, 1¼ hours) and Punta del Este (UR$84, 1½ hours), and also goes to Barra de Valizas (UR$75, 1½ hours), stopping en route at La Paloma, La Pedrera (UR$39, 45 minutes) and the Cabo Polonio turnoff (UR$75, 1¼ hours).

LA PALOMA
☎ 0479 / pop 5000

Placid La Paloma, 28km south of Rocha and 250km from Montevideo, is less developed, less expensive and much less crowded than Punta del Este. It has attractive sandy beaches, great surfing and almost every important amenity except for Punta's hyperactive nightlife. On summer weekends the town often hosts free concerts down on the beach, making accommodation bookings essential.

Orientation

La Paloma occupies a small peninsula at the south end of Ruta 15. Its center, flanking Av Nicolás Solari, is small and compact. Streets radiating diagonally off Av Nicolás Solari

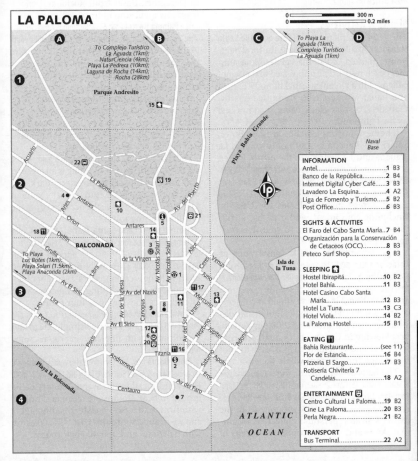

LA PALOMA

0 — 300 m
0 — 0.2 miles

To Complejo Turístico
La Aguada (1km);
Naturn. encia (4km);
Playa La Pedrera (10km);
Laguna de Rocha (14km);
Rocha (28km)

To Playa La
Aguada (1km);
Complejo Turístico
La Aguada (1km)

Parque Andresito

Naval
Base

Playa Bahía Grande

Isla de
la Tuna

To Playa
Los Botes (1km);
Playa Solari (1.5km);
Playa Anaconda (2km)

Playa la Balconada

ATLANTIC
OCEAN

INFORMATION
Antel...**1** B3
Banco de la República...............**2** B4
Internet Digital Cyber Café.......**3** B3
Lavadero La Esquina..................**4** A2
Liga de Fomento y Turismo.......**5** B2
Post Office.................................**6** B3

SIGHTS & ACTIVITIES
El Faro del Cabo Santa María....**7** B4
Organización para la Conservación
   de Cetaceos (OCC)................**8** B3
Peteco Surf Shop.......................**9** B3

SLEEPING
Hostel Ibirapitá........................**10** B2
Hotel Bahía..............................**11** B3
Hotel Casino Cabo Santa
   María....................................**12** B3
Hotel La Tuna...........................**13** C3
Hotel Viola...............................**14** B2
La Paloma Hostel......................**15** B1

EATING
Bahía Restaurante...............(see **11**)
Flor de Estancia........................**16** B4
Pizzeria El Sargo.......................**17** B3
Rotisería Chivitería 7
   Candelas...............................**18** A2

ENTERTAINMENT
Centro Cultural La Paloma.......**19** B2
Cine La Paloma.........................**20** B3
Perla Negra..............................**21** B2

TRANSPORT
Bus Terminal............................**22** A2

URUGUAY

are named after classical deities, making for funny-sounding intersections like Eros and Adonis.

Information

Antel (Av Nicolás Solari)

Banco de la República (cnr Av Nicolás Solari & Titania) Has an ATM.

Internet Digital Cyber Café (cnr Av Nicolás Solari & de la Virgen; internet per hr UR$10; ☼ 11am-10pm) Upstairs off the main street.

Lavadero La Esquina (☎ 8176; cnr Antares & Aries; wash & dry per basket UR$80; ☼ 10am-8pm Mon-Sat)

Liga de Fomento y Turismo (☎ 6088; www.ligalapal oma.com in Spanish; Av Nicolás Solari; ☼ 9am-11pm daily Dec-Easter, 10am-3pm Mon-Sat rest of year) On the traffic circle at the north end of Av Nicolás Solari.

Post office (Av Nicolás Solari)

Sights & Activities

The 1874 completion of **El Faro del Cabo Santa María** (admission UR$15; ☼ 8am-8pm), the local lighthouse, marked La Paloma's genesis as a summer beach resort. The unfinished first attempt collapsed in a violent storm, killing 17 French and Italian workers who are buried nearby. Outside is a solar clock using shadows cast by the lighthouse.

The best surfing beaches are Los Botes, Solari and Anaconda south of town, and La Aguada and La Pedrera to the north. Ruben at the very friendly **Peteco Surf Shop** (☎ 099-626726; petecosurf@adinet.com.uy; Av Nicolás Solari, btwn Av El Sirio & Av del Navío) rents boards for UR$250 a day, offers surfing classes for UR$500 (including equipment) and even has a couple of beachfront houses to rent. His staff speaks English.

The **Organización para la Conservación de Cetáceos** (OCC; ☎ 8318; www.occ.org.uy in Spanish; Av Nicolás Solari; ☼ 7pm-1am Tue-Sun Dec-Mar, 9am-noon & 2-5pm Wed-Sun Apr-Nov) sponsors scientific research and educational initiatives aimed at conserving the southern right whale. It offers all-day whalewatching tours (UR$1500 per person, best viewing in October). Its small museum in La Paloma's median strip is easy to spot – just look for the giant whale skeleton.

The **NaturCiencia** (☎ 9065; www.naturciencia.com in Spanish; Ruta 15, Km 7.2; adult/child UR$50/30; ☼ 11am-8pm daily Dec-Apr, 11am-6pm Sat & Sun May-Nov) science museum north of town grew from the owner's sizable personal collection of animal skulls and now incorporates dozens of brainteasing hands-on exhibits inspired by San Francisco's Exploratorium.

Laguna de Rocha, an ecological reserve protected under Uruguay's SNAP program (see the boxed text, p577), is a vast wetland 10km west of La Paloma with populations of black-necked swans, storks, spoonbills and other waterfowl. Local guide **Cecilia Olivet** (☎ 099-269775; colivet9@adinet.com.uy) offers tours in Spanish.

Sleeping

Complejo Turístico La Aguada (☎ 6239; www.complejo laaguada.com in Spanish; Ruta 15, Km 2.5; camping per 2 people UR$240, 2-/4-/6-/8-bed cabañas UR$600/1080/1680/2150) This complex of campsites and cabins just outside town offers excellent access to Playa La Aguada and hosts its own reggae festival in December. Buses from Rocha and *micros* from town will stop in front.

La Paloma Hostel (☎ 6396; lapaloma@hosteluruguay .org; Parada 7, Parque Andresito; dm adult/child/youth UR$260/130/240; ☼ Dec-Apr) Just north of town, this thatch-roofed hostel in shady Parque Andresito has large dorms, plus a small common room and kitchen.

Hostel Ibirapitá (☎ 9303; www.hostelibirapita.com in Spanish; La Paloma s/n; dm/d per person UR$250/350; ☐) A bit cramped, but closer to town than other area hostels, Ibirapitá has dorms and doubles, and rents bikes and surfboards.

Hotel La Tuna (☎ 6083; cnr Neptuno & Juno; s/d/tr/q UR$500/990/1200/1540) The building is an eyesore, and some rooms are oppressively dark, but you can't get much closer to the water without a boat. Four rooms face the ocean, as does the 3rd-floor dining room.

Hotel Casino Cabo Santa María (☎ 6004; cabo santamaria@redfacil.com.uy; Av Nicolás Solari; s/d/tr/q in hotel UR$1100/1300/1650/1900, d/tr/q in bungalow UR$1500/1800/2000) This rambling hotel attached to La Paloma's casino offers a variety of accommodations, including bungalows with kitchenettes housing up to four people.

Hotel Viola (☎ 6020; hviola@adinet.com.uy; Av Nicolás Solari; r UR$1250) The Viola is a simple, clean and friendly place with ample, breezy rooms, some with balconies.

Hotel Bahía (☎ 6029; www.elbahia.com.uy in Spanish; cnr Av del Navío & Av del Sol; s/d/tr from UR$1300/1400/1600) For central location and overall comfort, Bahía is hard to beat. Rooms are clean and bright, with firm mattresses, bedside reading lights and wi-fi. Superior rooms cost UR$200 extra, with balconies and updated bathrooms.

Eating

The places below are open year-round. Many additional eateries open in summer.

Rotisería Chivitería 7 Candelas (☎ 8253; Av Delfín s/n; dishes from UR$70; ⏰ 10am-4pm & 7pm-late) This unpretentious local hangout serves *chivitos*, chicken and *milanesas* (breaded fish). Eat in the cheerfully decorated interior room or on the tree-shaded front patio.

Flor de Estancia (☎ 9812; cnr Av Nicolás Solari & Titania; dishes UR$75-180; ⏰ 11am-3:30pm Mon-Thu, 11am-late Fri-Sun) Close to the lighthouse, this *parrilla* and seafood place has pleasant outdoor seating on a covered patio and in a grassy side yard.

Pizzería El Sargo (☎ 7922; cnr Mercurio & Ceres; dishes UR$95-190; ⏰ noon-3pm & 7:30pm-late) The menu is wide-ranging at this corner place, but pizza is the specialty.

Bahía Restaurante (☎ 6029; cnr Av del Navío & Av del Sol; dishes UR$150-270; ⏰ noon-4pm & 7pm-late) Repeatedly recommended by locals as La Paloma's best restaurant, the Bahía specializes in seafood.

Entertainment

Perla Negra (Av del Puerto) A leading nightspot with live music year-round.

Cine La Paloma (Av Nicolás Solari) Has twin screens showing movies throughout the summer.

Centro Cultural La Paloma (Parque Andresito) Shows movies every Friday at 7pm in off-season and hosts other cultural events.

Getting There & Around

All buses use the new bus terminal near Aries and La Paloma. At least seven daily buses serve Montevideo (UR$201, four hours). Other destinations include La Pedrera (UR$25, 15 minutes), Cabo Polonio (UR$50, 45 minutes), Barra de Valizas (UR$50, one hour), Punta del Diablo (UR$100, two hours) and Chuy (UR$134, three hours). The most frequently served destination is Rocha (UR$29, 30 minutes), from where better connections are available.

LA PEDRERA

☎ 0479 / pop 1000

Beautifully sited La Pedrera is popular with artists, surfers and families. The main street entering from Ruta 10 dead-ends atop a bluff with magnificent long views north toward Cabo Polonio and south toward La Paloma. Tourist services are limited.

Sleeping & Eating

Rates drop dramatically in the off-season.

La Pedrera Hostel (☎ 099-057560; www.lapedrerahostel.com; Ruta 10, Km 230; dm/d UR$330/1300; 🖳) This hostel north of La Pedrera is tricky to find – ask the driver on any Cabo Polonio–bound bus to drop you at Km 230, then walk toward the coast. There's a guest laundry and a comfy common area with internet, DVD player and fireplace, plus three upstairs doubles with distant ocean views. Bikes and surfing classes are available.

Posada del Barco (☎ 2028; posadadelbarco@adinet.com.uy; Playa del Barco; s/d/tr/q UR$1500/1900/2400/3200; 🖳) Classy, comfortable Posada del Barco has sweeping views of La Pedrera's southern beach. Its annual Easter Week jazz festival has attracted performers from Argentina, Brazil and Cuba.

El Club (☎ 099-806444; Calle Principal; meals UR$95-150; ⏰ 11am-late) Open year-round, this restaurant-café exudes vibrant, youthful energy, with trendy music and decor, an outdoor deck and a working antique foosball table. El Club doubles as La Pedrera's cultural and social center, hosting live music, art exhibitions, yoga and dance classes, children's events and an annual short-film festival in January.

Costa Brava (☎ 2051; meals UR$150-350; ⏰ lunch & dinner daily in summer, Fri dinner through Sun lunch rest of year) Perched atop the bluffs overlooking the Atlantic, Costa Brava is all about seafood accompanied by an unbeatable view.

Getting There & Away

Regular buses to La Pedrera leave from Rocha and La Paloma. Some stop only at the town entrance on Ruta 10, from where it's a 15-minute walk. Others continue down La Pedrera's main street to the beachfront.

CABO POLONIO

☎ 0470 / pop 500

Northeast of La Paloma at Km 264.5 on Ruta 10 lies the turnoff to Cabo Polonio, one of Uruguay's wildest areas and home to its second-biggest sea-lion colony, near a tiny fishing village nestled in sand dunes.

Sights & Activities

Cabo Polonio's striking lighthouse, **Faro Cabo Polonio** (admission UR$15; ⏰ 8:30am-sunset), provides a fabulous perspective on the point itself, the sea-lion colony, and the surrounding dunes and islands.

URUGUAY

Wildlife viewing is excellent year-round. Below the lighthouse, southern sea lions *(Otaria flavescens)* and South American fur seals *(Arctocephalus australis)* frolic on the rocks every month except February. You can also spot southern right whales just offshore in October and November, penguins on the beach in July, and the occasional southern elephant seal *(Mirounga leonina)* between January and March on nearby Isla de la Raza.

Surfing classes (UR$350 per hour) are available in high season. Inquire at the surf shop, in the square where trucks from Ruta 10 drop you off.

Local hotels can arrange **horseback rides** along the beach and into the surrounding dunes.

Sleeping & Eating

Hotels listed here are open year-round and serve food in their attached restaurants. In summertime, locals rent houses as well (from about UR$800). The hardest time to find accommodation is during the first two weeks of January. Off-season, prices drop as much as 80%.

Posada Mariemar (☎ 5164, 099-875260; mariemar@cabopolonio.com; r downstairs/upstairs UR$1600/1800) In business for nearly half a century, Posada Mariemar is right on the beach, and all rooms have ocean views. The restaurant serves tasty fish and homemade *buñuelos de algas* (seaweed fritters). It's a few hundred meters north of the lighthouse; just look for the beautiful angel mural out front.

La Perla del Cabo (☎ 5125, 099-921037; rosariocalimares1313@hotmail.com; r UR$2000) Next to Mariemar, this place has also been around for decades and is a bit more upscale. Even if you don't stay here, it's fun to eat on the beachside deck.

Getting There & Away

Buses between La Paloma and Barra de Valizas stop at the access road to Cabo Polonio, where waiting 4WD trucks offer rides across the dunes into town (UR$60, 30 minutes). Alternatively, you can walk from the bus stop to Cabo Polonio, a strenuous 7km hike taking about two hours (bring water). Other ways to reach Cabo Polonio include the pretty 12km beach walk from Barra de Valizas (see the boxed text, opposite) or organized tours originating in neighboring towns.

MONTE DE OMBÚES

North of Cabo Polonio, at Km 267 on Ruta 10, is Uruguay's largest concentration of ombúes, graceful treelike plants whose anarchic growth pattern results in some rather fantastic shapes. In other parts of Uruguay the ombú is a solitary plant, but specimens here – some of them centuries old – grow in clusters, insulated by the Laguna de Castillos from the bovine trampling that has spelled their doom elsewhere. Brothers Marcos and Juan Carlos Oliveros, whose family received this land from the Portuguese crown in 1793, lead 2½- to three-hour excursions (UR$1300 for up to six people, UR$300 each additional person). Tours begin with a 20-minute boat ride through a wetland teeming with cormorants, ibis, cranes and black swans, followed by a hike through the ombú forest. Departures are frequent in summer (anytime six people show up); other times of year, advance notice is required by phoning **Monte Grande/Monte de Ombúes** (☎ 099-295177).

BARRA DE VALIZAS

This tiny beach town 4km off Ruta 10 has largely escaped the development creeping eastward from Punta del Este. Slow-paced Valizas has friendly dogs and inquisitive horses wandering the streets, and dunes stretching toward Cabo Polonio.

The Valizas-Polonio area is rich in history. This notoriously treacherous stretch of coastline caused numerous shipwrecks over the centuries. South toward Cabo Polonio, the tallest point on the horizon is 58m-high **Cerro Buena Vista**, a rocky outcropping draped in sand that once formed the border between Spanish and Portuguese America, as agreed in the Madrid Treaty of 1750. The base of the stone that marked the border is still embedded here; the carved part bearing the names of Spain and Portugal is displayed at Fortaleza de Santa Teresa (p594), 35km north.

Businesses listed below are on Valiza's main dirt street, which runs perpendicular to the waterfront. The town's bus stop is on a parallel street one block south.

The very basic **Valizas Hostel** (☎ 099-610267; www.valizashostel.com; dm HI member/nonmember UR$195/220; ☼ Nov-Mar) has multibed dorms, kitchen facilities and hot showers. Raúl, the friendly manager, knows the local area well.

Nearby are Supermercado El Puente (a year-round grocery store) and Restaurante Ipocampo, open daily in summer and cooking meals upon request in the off-season – just knock!

MAKING TRACKS ON URUGUAY'S NORTHERN BEACHES

With so many kilometers of uninterrupted white sand, Uruguay's northern department of Rocha is a great place for beach walks.

Barra de Valizas to Cabo Polonio

This adventurous approach to Cabo Polonio allows you to fully appreciate the town's isolation and the dramatic visual impact of its lighthouse. From Barra de Valizas, follow the beach south to the river (about 20 minutes). Locals will ferry you across for about UR$50 – knock on doors if necessary. From here it's a stunningly wild and beautiful 12km walk along the ocean. The beach is more or less flat, but sand dunes rise steeply just inland. Depending on the season you may see sea lions or whales offshore, or cows grazing on the dune grasses. Near the halfway mark, you'll round a point and get your first view of Cabo Polonio's lighthouse, at the far end of a seemingly endless beach. Follow the light on into town.

Punta del Diablo to Parque Nacional Santa Teresa

From the Punta del Diablo bus stop, stroll down to the waterfront and turn north. Within half an hour you'll cross over a point and descend to Playa Grande, a long sandy beach at the southernmost edge of Parque Nacional Santa Teresa. Just beyond a wooden observation platform on the left, look for a campground and a road coming down to meet the beach. You can continue exploring north along the beach (the park goes on for several kilometers), or follow the road 45 minutes inland through a hilly eucalyptus forest to the Capatacía (park headquarters), where any Rutas del Sol or Cynsa bus will whisk you back to Punta del Diablo (UR$25, 15 minutes).

Rutas del Sol operates at least three buses daily to/from Montevideo (UR$251, 4½ hours).

PUNTA DEL DIABLO

☎ 0477 / pop 1000

In recent years, Punta del Diablo has morphed from a sleepy fishing village into one of Uruguay's prime coastal getaways. The beautiful shoreline remains intact, and the influx of outsiders has added an infectious dose of youthful energy, but inland the place is beginning to feel choked by endless waves of seemingly uncontrolled development. It's still a very pleasant spot to spend a few days; just don't come expecting to escape the crowds.

Sights & Activities

A big part of Punta del Diablo's appeal is simply taking life as it comes. During the day you can rent surfboards or horses along the town's main beach, or take the hour-long trek north to Parque Nacional Santa Teresa (see the boxed text, above). In the evening there are sunsets to watch, spontaneous bonfires and drum sessions to drop in on…you get the idea.

On the shores of Laguna Negra, 10km northwest of town, the **Estación Biológica**

Potrerillo de Santa Teresa harbors a rich variety of bird and plant life and several 3000-year-old indigenous burial mounds. Three-hour tours can be arranged by calling ☎ 0470-6028.

Sleeping

Cabañas are the accommodation of choice in Punta del Diablo. Note that this term applies to just about anything: from rustic-to-a-fault shacks to custom-built designer condos with all modern conveniences. Most *cabañas* have kitchens and require you to bring your own bedding. A couple of nice ones are listed below, but available offerings literally change month to month. Between Christmas and Carnaval, prices start around UR$1100; off-season rates are much cheaper. If you need help finding something, ask at the bus stop for El Vasco, a local guru of the *cabaña* realty market, or check online at www.portaldeldiablo.com.uy.

Albergue El Nagual (☎ 2009, 099-824164; Parada 2, Bulevar Santa Teresa; dm UR$250) Well inland from the beach, this hostel has affordable rates, laundry facilities, bicycles and other nice amenities. Arriving by bus, get off at Parada 2, 1km before town.

El Diablo Tranquilo (☎ 2647; www.eldiablotranquilo .com; dm/d per person UR$350/500) This welcoming hostel near the beach north of the bus stop is run by an expatriate American and has an attached bar.

El Barco (☎ 096-705042; cabañas for up to 4 UR$1100-1300; ✹ Sep-Apr) These brightly hued *cabañas* are easy to spot – entering town by bus, look for the boat-shaped deck and fake masts on the right side at the last big curve.

Del Norte Vengo y En El Sur Me Quedo (☎ 099-878357; www.portaldeldiablo.com.uy; cabañas for up to 4 UR$1300) Two blocks north of the bus stop, these colorful two-level *cabañas* have upstairs decks, ocean views, and satiny curtains and bedspreads. The young owners have lived in the US and speak good English.

La Posada (☎ 2041; www.portaldeldiablo.com.uy; r with/without ocean views UR$2000/1200) The front rooms have awesome sea views in this quaint little hotel perched on top of the bluff.

Eating

El Tiburón (Calle Principal; meals from UR$120; ✹ closed in winter) Just across from the beach, this place is a local favorite.

Al Pairo (Playa de los Pescadores; meals from UR$150; ✹ closed in winter) Also right on the waterfront, Al Pairo serves delicious seafood with a fabulous view.

El Viejo y El Mar (Playa de la Viuda; fish & wine UR$200; ✹ lunch & dinner) This ramshackle restaurant is suffused with a carefully calculated rustic-hip atmosphere – its candlelit walls are adorned with fishing nets, wine bottles, lanterns and guitars, and a friendly dog roams from room to room. You're offered whatever they're serving that night, with fish and wine sure to feature prominently.

Getting There & Away

Buses stop in a small square a few hundred meters inland from the ocean, from where small dirt roads fan out in all directions. Rutas del Sol and Cynsa each run at least two daily buses to Montevideo (UR$251, 4½ hours), Rocha (UR$84, 1½ hours) and Chuy (UR$42, one hour). For Parque Nacional Santa Teresa (UR$25, 15 minutes), take any Chuy-bound bus, and get off at either the Capatacía (park headquarters) or Fortaleza de Santa Teresa, near the park's northwestern corner.

PARQUE NACIONAL SANTA TERESA

This **national park** (☎ 0477-2101; www.turismo.gub .uy/santateresa/index.htm), 35km south of Chuy, is administered by the army and attracts many Uruguayan and Brazilian visitors to its relatively uncrowded beaches. It offers 1200 dispersed campsites in eucalyptus and pine groves, a very small zoo and a plant conservatory. Camping costs UR$150/50 per site in summer/winter, for up to six people. There are also various grades of *cabañas* for rent from UR$450 to UR$1200.

Many buses between Chuy and Rocha stop at the Capatacía (park headquarters), where there's a phone, post office, market, bakery and **restaurant** (meals UR$60-250; ✹ 9am-10pm).

The park's star attraction, 4km further north on Ruta 9, is the impressive hilltop **Fortaleza de Santa Teresa** (admission UR$10; ✹ 10am-7pm daily Dec-Mar, 10am-5pm Fri-Sun Apr-Nov), begun by the Portuguese in 1762 and finished by the Spaniards after its capture in 1793. At the park's northeastern corner is **Cerro Verde**, a coastal bluff protected under Uruguay's SNAP program (see the boxed text, p577).

BARRA DEL CHUY

☎ 0474 / pop 500

The beach stretches as far as the eye can see at this town near the mouth of Arroyo San Miguel, 20km from Chuy and a stone's throw south of the Brazilian border.

In a pine grove 1km back from the beach, deluxe **Complejo Turístico Chuy** (☎ 8113, in Montevideo 02-900-6122; www.complejoturisticochuy.com in Spanish; campsite for 2/3/4 people UR$250/360/440, A-frame q UR$850, bungalow d/tr/q UR$1350/1500/1850, hotel d/tr/q from UR$1250/1650/1900; 🏊) offers a dizzying array of accommodations. There's a pool and spa, and guests get 50% off the UR$160 entry fee at the adjacent water park.

Some buses traveling between Montevideo and Chuy service Barra. Local buses from Chuy (UR$25, 30 minutes) also come here several times daily.

CHUY

☎ 0474 / pop 11,000

Warning: if you're not on your way to or from Brazil, you're seriously lost, buddy. Turn around and go back. But while you're here you may as well check out the pirated CDs, contraband cigarettes and duty-free shops lining both sides of Chuy's main street.

Orientation

Av Artigas is the main drag into town from Ruta 9. Crossing north into Brazil, it becomes Av Argentina (for a full list of name changes, see the maps posted throughout town). Chuy's main square is one block south of the border. Running east–west along the border itself is the town's four-lane commercial thoroughfare, called Av Brasil on the Uruguayan side, Av Uruguaí on the Brazilian side.

Information

If proceeding beyond Chuy into Brazil, complete Uruguayan emigration formalities at the **customs post** (Ruta 9), 1km south of town, where you'll also find the **National Tourism Ministry** (☎ 4599).

Uruguayan currency is worthless any distance into Brazil. There are several exchange houses along the border and on Av Artigas. **Banco de la República Oriental** (cnr Av Artigas & Ventura) has an ATM just across from the main square. The **post office** (Av Artigas 322) is a few blocks further south.

Sleeping & Eating

If you've got a long layover between buses, Chuy has several affordable hotels and eateries, plus a fancy tourist *estancia* west of town.

Hotel Vitoria (☎ 2280; Numancia 143; r per person UR$250) Simple, clean, and family-run, it's far enough east of the hubbub to offer a decent night's sleep.

Fortín de San Miguel (☎ 6607; www.elfortin.com in Spanish; Ruta 19, Km 8; r UR$1300; ⊠) You'll think you've died and gone to – well, someplace much nicer than Chuy – when you see the palatial rooms and pool at this colonial-style *estancia* in verdant countryside across from Fuerte San Miguel. The attached restaurant is reasonably priced.

Panaderia Giannini (cnr Av Artigas & Guaiba; snacks from UR$15; ⊠ 7am-9pm) Just follow your nose to this aromatic bakery, which also sells sandwiches, yogurt and juice.

Miravos (☎ 4180; Av Brasil 507; dishes UR$65-250) Miravos serves a varied menu, with comfortable indoor booths and sunny sidewalk seating.

Getting There & Away

Bus companies **Cotec/Rutas del Sol** (Olivera 121) and **Cynsa/Núñez** (Olivera 125) operate out of adjoining offices half a block south of the border. Several daily buses go to Montevideo (UR$285, six hours), stopping at intermediate points along the coast. Tureste (tickets sold by Cotec) serves Treinta y Tres (UR$134, three hours) twice daily.

The Brazilian *rodoviária* (bus terminal) is at the corner of Venezuela and Chile, two blocks north of the border. Destinations include Rio Grande (R$31, four hours), Pelotas (R$28.50, four hours), Porto Alegre (R$62 regular, R$72.45 semidirect, seven hours) and São Paulo (R$197, 32 hours).

FUERTE SAN MIGUEL

This pink-granite **fortress** (Ruta 19, Km 9; admission UR$10; ⊠ 9am-5pm), 9km west of Chuy, was built in 1734 during hostilities between Spain and Portugal. Today it forms the centerpiece of Parque Nacional San Miguel. Its entrance, guarded by a moat, overlooks the border from a high, isolated point. When it's closed you can still glimpse the interior and visit the nearby Museo Criollo/Museo Indígena, with indoor and outdoor displays relating to gaucho, indigenous and pioneer life, and an impressive array of carts and machinery. Cotec runs a few daily buses from Chuy to the fortress (UR$25, 10 minutes), or you can pay UR$80 for a taxi.

URUGUAY DIRECTORY

ACCOMMODATIONS

Uruguay has an excellent network of hostels and campgrounds, especially along the coast. Some offer discounts to ISIC or HI cardholders. General hostel information is available in Montevideo from **HI Uruguay** (☎ 02-900-5749; www.hosteluruguay.org; Paraguay 1212). Other low-end options include *hospedajes* (family homes) and *residenciales* (budget hotels).

Posadas (inns) are available in all price ranges and tend to be homier than hotels. Hotels are ranked from one to five stars, according to amenities.

In the countryside, *estancias turísticas* (marked with blue National Tourism Ministry signs) provide lodging on farms (see the boxed text, p571).

ACTIVITIES

Uruguay's Atlantic coast is a paradise for surfers and wildlife watchers. Punta del Diablo, La Paloma and Punta del Este all get excellent waves, while Cabo Polonio and the coastal lagoons of Rocha department are great for whale- and bird-watching, respectively.

Punta del Este is the place to head for the upmarket beach scene, bars and snazzier beach activities, like parasailing, windsurfing and jet skiing.

Horseback riding is very popular in the interior and can be arranged on most tourist *estancias* (see the boxed text, p571). Natural areas like Quebrada de los Cuervos and Valle del Lunarejo (see the boxed text, p577) are prime hiking and bird-watching destinations.

BOOKS

Compared with neighboring countries, surprisingly little material is available on Uruguay in English. William Henry Hudson's novel *The Purple Land* (1916) is a classic portrait of 19th-century Uruguayan life. A good starting point for looking at the politics of modern Uruguay is Martin Weinstein's *Uruguay, Democracy at the Crossroads*. For an account of Uruguay's Dirty War, see Lawrence Weschler's *A Miracle, A Universe: Settling Accounts with Torturers*. For a sympathetic explanation of the rise of the 1960s guerrilla movements, see María Esther Gilio's *The Tupamaro Guerrillas*.

For Uruguayan literature, see p544.

BUSINESS HOURS

Most shops open weekdays and Saturday from 8:30am to 1pm, then close until mid-afternoon and reopen until 7pm or 8pm. Banks are generally open weekday afternoons only.

If serving breakfast, restaurants open around 8am. Lunch is generally between noon and 3pm, and dinner is generally not eaten until after 9pm or even as late as midnight in urban areas. Bars may open as early as 6pm, but often remain empty until at least 1am, when everybody finally gets around to going out.

COSTS

Throughout this chapter, accommodations are generally categorized by price: budget (up to UR$500 per double), midrange (UR$500 to UR$1200 per double), and top end (over UR$1200 per double). Unless otherwise mentioned, prices include tax and are high-season rates. Please note that summertime prices in glitzy Punta del Este will often be at least double what you'd pay elsewhere in Uruguay.

For eating reviews, listings are categorized by the average price of a main course: budget (up to UR$100), midrange (UR$100 to UR$250), and top end (over UR$250).

Travelers' costs are generally lower than in Argentina. The inflation rate in 2006 was 6.4%, compared to Argentina's 10.9%.

COURSES

Cafés in tourist areas often have notice boards advertising private Spanish lessons. Formal language classes are also available in Montevideo (see p554).

DANGERS & ANNOYANCES

Uruguay is still one of the safest countries in South America, but petty street crime in Montevideo has risen in recent years. Visitors to the capital should take precautions as in any large city.

ELECTRICITY

Uruguay runs on 220V, 50Hz. The most common plug uses two round pins with no earthing/grounding pin.

EMBASSIES & CONSULATES

Unless otherwise specified, the following addresses and telephone numbers are in Montevideo (area code ☎ 02); many are east and south of downtown.

Argentina Montevideo (Map pp548-9; ☎ 902-8623; WF Aldunate 1281); Colonia (Map p563; ☎ 052-22093; Av General Flores 209); Fray Bentos (☎ 056-23225; Treinta y Tres 3237); Paysandú (Map p572; ☎ 072-22253; Leandro Gómez 1034); Punta del Este (Map p583; ☎ 042-440789; cnr Gorlero & Calle 19); Salto (☎ 073-32931; Artigas 1162)

Belgium (Map pp548-9; ☎ 916-2719; Rincón 625, 5th fl)

Bolivia (☎ 708-3573; Prudencio de Pena 2469)

Brazil Montevideo (Map pp548-9; ☎ 901-2024; Convención 1343, 6th fl); Chuy (☎ 0474-2049; Fernández 147)

Canada (Map pp548-9; ☎ 902-2030; Plaza Independencia 749, Oficina 102)

Chile (Map pp548-9; ☎ 916-2346; 25 de Mayo 575)

France (Map pp548-9; ☎ 902-0077; Av Uruguay 853)

Germany (☎ 902-5222; La Cumparsita 1435)

Israel (☎ 400-4164; Bulevar Artigas 1585)

Italy (☎ 480-7080; Jorge Canning 2535)

Japan (☎ 418-7645; Bulevar Artigas 953)

Netherlands (☎ 711-2956; Leyenda Patria 2880, 2nd fl)

Paraguay (☎ 707-2138; Bulevar Artigas 1525)

Peru (☎ 707-1420; Obligado 1384)

Spain (☎ 708-0048; Libertad 2738)

Sweden (☎ 917-0289; Rambla 25 de Agosto 508, 5th fl)

Switzerland (☎ 711-5545; Federico Abadie 2936, 11th fl)

UK (☎ 622-3630; Marco Bruto 1073)

USA (☎ 419-7854; Lauro Muller 1776)

FESTIVALS & EVENTS

Uruguay's Carnaval lasts for over a month and is livelier than Argentina's (see p554). Semana

Santa (Holy Week) has become known as Semana Turismo – many Uruguayans travel out of town, and accommodation is tricky during this time. Other noteworthy events include Paysandú's beer festival (p571), Tacuarembó's Fiesta de la Patria Gaucha (p576) and Montevideo's Semana Criolla (p554).

GAY & LESBIAN TRAVELERS

Uruguay has gotten more GLBT-friendly in recent years. In January 2008 it became the first Latin American country to recognize same-sex civil unions.

An excellent English-language web resource is **Out in Uruguay** (www.outinuruguay.com).

HOLIDAYS

Año Nuevo (New Year's Day) January 1
Epifanía (Epiphany) January 6
Viernes Santo/Pascua (Good Friday/Easter) March/April (dates vary)
Desembarco de los 33 (Return of the 33 Exiles) April 19; honors the exiles who returned to Uruguay in 1825 to liberate the country from Brazil with Argentine support
Día del Trabajador (Labor Day) May 1
Batalla de Las Piedras (Battle of Las Piedras) May 18; commemorates a major battle of the fight for independence
Natalicio de Artigas (Artigas' Birthday) June 19
Jura de la Constitución (Constitution Day) July 18
Día de la Independencia (Independence Day) August 25
Día de la Raza (Columbus Day) October 12
Día de los Muertos (All Souls' Day) November 2
Navidad (Christmas Day) December 25

INTERNET ACCESS

Internet cafés are commonplace in cities and larger towns; access costs UR$10 to UR$15 an hour. Many Antel (state telephone company) offices also provide internet for UR$19 an hour.

INTERNET RESOURCES

Mercopress News Agency (www.mercopress.com) Montevideo-based internet news agency.
National Tourism Ministry (www.turismo.gub.uy in Spanish) Government tourist information.
Olas y Vientos (www.olasyvientos.com.uy in Spanish) Everything you need to know about Uruguay's surf scene.
Red Uruguaya (www.reduruguaya.com in Spanish) A guide to Uruguayan internet resources.
Uruguayan Embassy in Washington, DC (www.uruwashi.org) Historical, cultural and economic information on Uruguay.

LANGUAGE

Spanish is the official language and is universally understood. Uruguayans fluctuate between use of the *voseo* and *tuteo* in everyday speech (see the boxed text 'El Voseo' in the Language chapter, p638), and both are readily understood. Along the Brazilian border, many people are Spanish-Portuguese bilingual or speak *portuñol*, an unusual hybrid of the two. One common influence from Brazilian Portuguese is the Uruguayan usage of 'ta,' short for 'está bien' ('OK'), often in question form. See the Language chapter (p637) for more on Latin American Spanish.

LEGAL MATTERS

Drugs are freely available in Uruguay, but getting caught with them is about as much fun as anywhere else in the world, and Uruguayan police and officials are not as bribe-hungry as many of their South American counterparts.

MAPS

ITMB (http://shop.itmb.ca) publishes a useful map depicting Montevideo on one side and Uruguay on the other (also available from online retailers like Amazon). In Uruguay, Ancap service stations sell good road maps. Two other good sources in Montevideo are the **Automóvil Club del Uruguay** (☎ 02-1707; Av Libertador 1532) and **Instituto Geográfico Militar** (☎ 02-481-6868; cnr 8 de Octubre & Abreu).

MONEY

The unit of currency is the *peso uruguayo* (UR$). Banknote values are five, 10, 20, 50, 100, 200, 500 and 1000. There are coins of 50 centavos, and one, two, five and 10 pesos.

US dollars are commonly accepted in major tourist hubs, where top-end hotels and even some budget accommodations quote US$ prices. However, beware of bad exchange rates at hotel desks. In many cases, you'll still come out ahead paying in pesos. Away from the touristed areas, dollars are of limited use.

ATMs

In all but the smallest interior towns, getting cash with your ATM card is easy. Machines marked with the green Banred or blue Redbrou logo serve all major international banking networks, including Cirrus, Visa, MasterCard and Maestro.

ATMs dispense bills in multiples of 100 pesos. It's advisable to request smaller bills whenever possible (ie take out UR$900 rather than UR$1000, UR$1900 rather than UR$2000 etc) to avoid getting stuck with large bills. The UR$1000 notes, in particular, can be difficult to change even in big cities.

Many ATMs also dispense US dollars, designated as U$S, not to be confused with Uruguayan pesos, which are designated with a stand-alone $ symbol.

Credit Cards

Most better hotels, restaurants and shops accept credit cards.

Exchange Rates

Exchange rates at press time included the following:

Country	Unit	UR$
Argentina	AR$1	6.99
Australia	A$1	19.30
Brazil	R$1	12.53
Canada	C$1	22.15
Euro zone	€1	32.37
Japan	¥100	20.13
New Zealand	NZ$1	16.93
UK	UK£1	43.34
US	US$1	21.95

Exchanging Money

There are *casas de cambio* in Montevideo, Colonia, the Atlantic beach resorts and border towns like Chuy. They keep longer hours than banks but often offer lower rates.

Traveler's Checks

Traveler's checks can still be cashed at some banks and *casas de cambio*, but you'll get better rates and avoid commissions by simply withdrawing cash on your ATM card.

POST

Postal rates are reasonable, though service can be slow. If something is truly important, send it by registered mail or private courier.

The main post office in Montevideo will hold poste restante for up to a month, or two months with authorization.

SHOPPING

Bargains include leather clothing and accessories, woolen clothing and fabrics, agates and gems, ceramics, woodcrafts and decorated *mate* gourds.

Bargaining isn't part of Uruguayan culture, and serious red-in-the-face, veins-out-on-forehead haggling is completely out of phase with the whole Uruguayan psyche. Chances are you're paying exactly what the locals are.

TELEPHONE

Uruguay's country code is ☎ 598. Antel is the state telephone company, with offices in every town. There are also private *locutorios* (telephone offices) everywhere.

Most public phones require prepaid cards, sold in values of 25, 50, 100 and 200 pesos, available at Antel offices or newspaper kiosks. Montevideo still has a few coin-operated phones as well.

Many internet cafés have headphones and microphones, allowing you to make very inexpensive international calls using programs like Skype.

All Uruguayan phone numbers are scheduled to change to eight digits in July 2008 (see the boxed text, opposite).

TOILETS

Toilets in Uruguay are generally clean and of a similar design to what you're probably used to. If there's a wastepaper basket next to the toilet, put used toilet paper in there to avoid clogging the system.

TOURIST INFORMATION

The **National Tourism Ministry** (www.turismo.gub.uy in Spanish) operates 13 offices around the country. They distribute excellent free maps for each of Uruguay's 19 departments, along with specialized brochures on *estancia* tourism, Carnaval and other subjects of interest to travelers. Most towns also have a municipal tourist office on the plaza or at the bus terminal. Materials are generally in Spanish only.

TOURS

Montevideo-based **Lares** (Map pp548-9; ☎ 02-901-9120; www.lares.com.uy; WF Aldunate 1320, Local 15) offers *estancia*-based tours with an emphasis on horseback riding, birding and other outdoor activities. For travelers 55 and older, **Elderhostel** (www.elderhostel.org) operates several educational tours.

TRAVELERS WITH DISABILITIES

A modern country in many other ways, Uruguay hasn't kept up with developments for travelers with special needs. Sidewalks are level(ish), but ramps and easy-access buses are nonexistent. Many budget hotels have at

---

URUGUAY'S NEW EIGHT-DIGIT PHONE NUMBERS

Uruguayan phone numbers are in the midst of a major makeover. As this book goes to press, plans are underway to convert landlines nationwide to an eight-digit format. The goal is to standardize phone numbers so they can be dialed identically from any point within Uruguay, and so that they all begin with either 2 (for Montevideo) or 4 (for elsewhere in Uruguay).

It's anybody's guess whether the conversion will actually take place by the projected July 2008 effective date. Uruguay's national regulatory agency URSEC, which hatched the plan, is more enthusiastic about the switchover than national telephone company Antel, which has responsibility for implementing it and is showing signs of serious foot-dragging.

Given all the uncertainty, phone numbers in this book have been left in the old format. However, by the time you read this, the change may very well have taken place. Converting to the eight-digit format is easy. Here's how it works:

- **Seven-digit Montevideo numbers** Simply add a 2 at the beginning (the old city code 02, with the zero dropped). So the old (02) 123-4567 becomes 2-1234567.
- **Six-digit Maldonado and Punta del Este numbers** Add 42 at the beginning (again the city code with the zero dropped). So (042) 123456 becomes 42-123456.
- **Four- and five-digit numbers elsewhere in the country** Add a 4 at the beginning, plus the old city code with zero dropped, plus the number. So in Colonia (052) 12345 becomes 4-52-12345, and in Punta del Diablo (0477) 1234 becomes 4-477-1234.
- **Cell phones** These will continue to use their traditional nine-digit format (for example 099-123456).

Got it?

---

least one set of stairs and no elevator. On the bright side, taxis are cheap and locals are glad to help however they can.

VISAS

Nationals of Western Europe, Australia, the USA, Canada and New Zealand automatically receive a 90-day tourist card, renewable for another 90 days. Other nationals may require visas. For extensions, visit the **Dirección Nacional de la Migración** (Map pp548-9; ☎ 02-916-0471; Misiones 1513; ☷ 9:15am-2:30pm Mon-Fri) in Montevideo or local offices in border towns.

VOLUNTEERING

All Uruguayan organizations accepting volunteers require a minimum commitment of one month, and many require at least basic Spanish proficiency. Following are some Montevideo-based NGOs:

Comisión de la Juventud (☎ 1950, ext 2046; cnr Santiago de Chile & Soriano) Social workers concentrating on youth issues.

Cruz Roja (Red Cross; ☎ 02-480-0714; 8 de Octubre 2990) The Red Cross helps people avoid, prepare for and cope with emergencies.

Liga Uruguaya de Voluntarios (☎ 02-481-3763; Joanicó 3216) Cancer prevention and education.

UNICEF (☎ 02-707-4972; España 2565) The local branch of the UN children's fund.

WOMEN TRAVELERS

Uruguayans are no slouches when it comes to *machismo*, but women are generally treated with respect, and traveling alone is safer here than in many other countries.

TRANSPORTATION IN URUGUAY

GETTING THERE & AWAY
Entering the Country

Uruguay requires passports of all foreigners, except those from neighboring countries (who need only national identification cards).

Passports are necessary for many everyday transactions, such as checking into hotels and cashing traveler's checks.

Air

International passengers leaving from Montevideo's Carrasco airport pay a departure tax of US$29. For addresses and telephone numbers of airline offices, see p560.

URUGUAY

CONTINENTAL EUROPE

Both Iberia and the Uruguayan carrier Pluna have direct flights between Montevideo and Madrid. Air France, KLM and Lufthansa connect to other European destinations via Buenos Aires or São Paulo.

SOUTH AMERICA

There are frequent flights between Carrasco and Buenos Aires' Aeroparque, as well as between Aeroparque and Punta del Este. Pluna and Aerolíneas Argentinas offer the most flights.

Other South American countries served by direct flights from Montevideo include Brazil, Chile, Paraguay and Peru. See p560 for more details.

USA

American Airlines has direct flights between Montevideo and Miami. LanChile has flights from Los Angeles, Miami and New York with a change of planes in Santiago. Other airlines connect through Buenos Aires' Ezeiza airport or São Paulo, Brazil.

Land

Uruguay shares borders with the Argentine province of Entre Ríos and the southern Brazilian state of Rio Grande do Sul. Major highways and bus services are generally good.

ARGENTINA

Three bridges cross the Río Uruguay between Uruguay and Argentina: from Fray Bentos to Gualeguaychú (closed indefinitely at time of writing); from Paysandú to Colón; and from Salto to Concordia. Direct buses from Montevideo to Buenos Aires (traveling via Paysandú–Colón until the Fray Bentos–Gualeguaychú bridge reopens) are slower and less convenient than the land/river combinations across the Río de la Plata.

BRAZIL

There are five land crossings between Uruguay and Brazil. The most popular one connects Chuy, Uruguay, to Chuí, Brazil (described on p595). The remaining crossings, from east to west, are: Río Branco to Jaguarão; Aceguá to Bagé, Rivera to Santana do Livramento; Artigas to Quaraí; and Bella Unión to Barra do Quaraí. It's possible to use the latter cross-

ing as a route to Iguazú Falls, but the trip through Brazil is slow and difficult.

Sea

ARGENTINA

The most common way of traveling between Uruguay and Argentina is by launch or ferry (the latter sometimes involving bus connections through Colonia). The three routes are: Montevideo to Buenos Aires (p560); Colonia to Buenos Aires (p566); and Carmelo to Tigre (p568).

GETTING AROUND
Bus

Buses are comfortable, fares are reasonable and distances are short. Most companies distribute free timetables. In the few cities that lack terminals, all companies are within easy walking distance of each other, usually around the main plaza.

Buses leave frequently for destinations all around the country, so reservations are unnecessary except during holiday periods. Be aware that on peak travel dates a single company may run multiple departures at the same hour, in which case they'll mark a bus number on your ticket; check with the driver to make sure you're boarding the right bus, or you may find yourself in the 'right' seat on the wrong bus!

Most towns with central bus terminals have a fee-based left-luggage facility. Where there's no terminal you can usually leave your bags with the company you're ticketed to leave with later in the day.

Car & Motorcycle

Uruguayan drivers are extremely considerate. The only exception is Montevideo, where many drivers are eager to get ahead, and the lines dividing lanes serve as mere decoration. Even so, it's quite sedate compared with Buenos Aires.

AUTOMOBILE ASSOCIATIONS

The **Automóvil Club del Uruguay** (☎ 02-902-4792; Av Libertador General Lavalleja 1532, Montevideo) has good maps and information.

DRIVER'S LICENSE

Visitors to Uruguay who are staying less than 90 days need only bring a valid driver's license from their home country.

FUEL

Uruguay imports all its oil. Unleaded premium gasoline costs UR$30.40 a liter at the time of research, making driving more expensive than in Argentina.

HIRE

Economy cars rent for as little as UR$900 a day in the low season, with tax and insurance included. If you shop around, multiweek rentals can work out even less (as low as UR$700 per day), sometimes with discounts for cash payment.

Annoyingly, some agencies will rent you a car with an empty tank, asking you to return it the same way. Also, beware: many rental-car radios will run down the battery if not removed overnight, and it can be quite difficult to get a jump start!

ROAD HAZARDS

Outside the capital and coastal tourist areas, traffic is minimal and poses few problems. Roads are generally in good shape, but some interior roads can be rough. Keep an eye out for livestock and wildlife. Even in Montevideo's busy downtown, horse-drawn carts still operate, hauling trash or freight.

ROAD RULES

Drivers are expected to use headlights in daytime on all highways. People will flash their lights to remind you. In most towns, alternating one-way streets are the rule, with an arrow marking the allowed direction of travel. Outside of Montevideo, most intersections have neither a stop sign nor a traffic light; right of way is determined by who reaches the corner first. This can be nerve-wracking for the uninitiated! Arbitrary police stops and searches are rare.

Hitchhiking

It's common to see locals hitchhiking in rural areas, as gas is expensive and relatively few people own cars. Safety is not as serious a concern as in most other countries, although foreigners looking to hitch a ride may encounter some raised eyebrows.

Local Transportation

Taxis, *remises* (radio-dispatched taxis) and local buses are similar to those in Argentina. Taxis are metered, and drivers calculate fares using meter readings and a photocopied chart. Between 10pm and 6am, and on weekends and holidays, fares are 20% higher. There's a small additional charge for luggage, and passengers generally tip the driver by rounding fares up to the next multiple of five or ten pesos. City bus service is excellent in Montevideo and urban hubs such as Maldonado–Punta del Este, while *micros* (minibuses) form the backbone of the local transit network in smaller coastal towns like La Paloma.

Directory

CONTENTS

ACCOMMODATIONS

Accommodations in Argentina range from campgrounds to five-star luxury hotels, with excellent options in all categories. At the more tourist-oriented hotels, the staff usually speaks a smattering of English, though at more provincial accommodations you'll need to learn the Spanish basics.

All but the cheapest hotels have private bathrooms, and most hotels include breakfast – usually *medialunas* (croissants) and weak coffee or tea – in the price. Generally, assume both are included as you flip through listings

in this book. Many hotels provide temporary luggage storage for travelers with late afternoon or evening flights or bus trips.

Some hotels, particularly pricier hotels in tourist hotspots such as Patagonia, operate on a two-tier price system (see the boxed text, below), charging foreigners more than nationals.

For long-term rentals in the capital, see p114. For information on relocating to Argentina, see p613. Also note that many hotels offer discounted rates for extended stays, usually a week or more. Make sure to negotiate this *before* you begin your stay.

Prices

Throughout this book, accommodations are generally categorized by price: budget (up to AR$60 per double), midrange (up to AR$180 per double), and top end (over AR$180 per double). Prices in Argentina have increased steadily over the last several years (many places charge twice what they did in 2003), and they may continue to do so. To avoid getting sticker shock, it's helpful to supplement your book research with a good dose of internet research. For information on the rising cost of travel in Argentina, see p19. That said, in Buenos Aires you can land excellent accommodations for under AR$200, and throughout the country, AR$130 will buy you a comfort-

---

TWO-TIER PRICING

With the devaluation of the peso in 2002, Argentina became a highly affordable destination practically overnight. With the subsequent upswing in tourism, however, the good ol' annoying two-tier pricing system emerged: businesses in certain areas (mostly in Buenos Aires, but also in Patagonia and parts of the Lake District) charge Argentines one price, and foreigners a higher price, regardless of whether they're banking euros, pounds or dollars. While you won't find this everywhere, you will encounter it at museums in Buenos Aires, *estancias*, national parks, the national airline (Aerolíneas Argentinas) and upscale hotels throughout the country.

PRACTICALITIES

▪ Argentina uses the metric system for weights and measures.

▪ Electrical current is 220 volts, 50 cycles, and there are two types of electric plugs: either with two rounded prongs or with three angled flat prongs. Adapters from one to the other are available.

▪ Buenos Aires' two leading daily newspapers, available throughout Argentina, are *Clarín* and *La Nación*. The English-language daily *Buenos Aires Herald* covers Argentina and the world from an international perspective and is available in most large cities. Also see p94.

▪ In Buenos Aires, tune into FM 92.7 for 24-hour tango or FM 92.3 for Argentine *folklore* (folk music).

▪ In Argentine addresses, the word *local* refers to a suite or office. If an address has 's/n,' short for *sin numero* (without number), the address has no street number.

---

able double room. Hostels in Buenos Aires charge AR$25 to AR$30 per bed and around AR$90 for a private double. Rates are lower outside the capital: figure on about AR$22 for a dorm bed and AR$60 for private double.

Accommodations prices in this book, to the best of our knowledge, all include tax and are high-season rates. Budget and midrange hotels almost always include taxes when quoting their prices. If you're inquiring on your own into a top-end hotel, however, be sure to ask; pricier hotels often quote fares before tax – a whopping 21%! High season is generally July and August (except in Patagonia), Semana Santa (Easter week) and January and February (when Argentines take their summer breaks). Outside these times, prices can drop anywhere from 20% to 40% from the rates quoted in this book.

Camping & Refugios

Camping can be one of the most splendid ways to experience Argentina, particularly the Lake District and Patagonia, where there are countless outstanding campgrounds. Nearly every Argentine city or town has fairly centralized municipal campgrounds, where you can pitch a tent for under AR$10 per night and sometimes for free; these are hit-and-miss, sometimes delightfully woodsy, sometimes crowded and ugly. Free campgrounds are often excellent, especially in the Lake District, though they lack facilities.

Private campgrounds usually have good facilities: hot showers, toilets, laundry, a barbecue for grilling, a restaurant or *confitería* (café), a grocery store, and sometimes even a swimming pool. Personal possessions are generally secure, since attendants keep a watchful eye on the grounds, but don't leave anything lying around unnecessarily.

For comfort, invest in a good tent before coming to South America, where camping equipment is costlier and often inferior, even in Argentina. A three-season sleeping bag should be adequate for almost any weather. A good petrol- or kerosene-burning stove is also a good idea, since white gas (called *bencina* in Spanish) is expensive and available only at chemical-supply shops, hardware stores and some camping stores in larger cities. Bring mosquito repellent, since many campgrounds are near rivers or lakes; the stuff is essential if you're camping in hotter places in north-central and northeast Argentina.

Backpacking and backcountry camping opportunities abound in and around the national parks, especially from the Lake District and south. Some parks have *refugios* (basic shelters for hikers in the high country), which have some sort of cooking facilities and are filled with saggy but welcome bunks. Most *refugios* are free, but some charge. Some fill up fast in high season, so do your local research and arrive early to score a bed if necessary.

Estancias

Few experiences feel more typically Argentine than staying at an *estancia* (a traditional ranch, often called *fincas* in the northwest). *Estancias* are a wonderful way to spend time in remote areas of the country – and wine, horses and *asados* (traditional barbecues) are almost always involved. *Estancias* are especially common in the area around Buenos Aires; near Esteros del Iberá; and throughout the Lake District and Patagonia. In the latter, they're often geared toward

anglers. Costs rarely dip below AR$250 per
day, but the rates generally include room,
board and some activities. To easily locate
many of the *estancias* covered in this book,
see the boxed texts on p150, p316 and p479.
Estancias are also listed in Sleeping sections.
If you're investigating *estancias* from within
Argentina, the provincial tourist offices (p616)
in Buenos Aires are an excellent resource.
Helpful websites listing *estancias* around
Argentina include www.estanciastravel.com
and www.estanciasargentinas.com.

Those lacking the time, money or inclina-
tion to spend the night on an estancia can still
experience one by partaking in a *día de campo*
(day in the country). Offered by many of the
estancias that offer accommodations, the *día
de campo* usually consists of a giant *asado*,
horseback riding and other traditional activities associated with *estancias*. Also see p150.

Hospedajes, Pensiones & Residenciales

Aside from hostels, these are Argentina's
cheapest accommodations, and the differences among them are sometimes ambiguous,
to the point that they're often simply called
hotels. However, if you're flipping through a
tourist office's list of accommodations, they
won't fall into the Hotel category.

A *hospedaje* is usually a large family home
with a few extra bedrooms (and, generally, a
shared bathroom). Similarly, a *pensión* offers
short-term accommodations in a family home
but may also have permanent lodgers. Meals
may be available. *Residenciales* figure more
commonly in tourist-office lists. In general,
they occupy buildings designed for short-stay
accommodations, although some (known euphemistically as *albergues transitorios*) cater
to clientele who intend only *very* short stays
– of two hours maximum. Prostitutes occasionally use them, but they're mostly used
by young Argentine couples with no other

indoor alternative or by someone who cannot,
for whatever reason, get busy at home.

Rooms and furnishings at these accommodations are modest, often basic and usually clean, and rooms with shared bathrooms
are the cheapest. *Hospedajes* and *residenciales* are usually as good as or better than
one-star hotels.

Hostels

Hostels have sprouted up throughout Argentina
like grass in the pampas, and nearly every town
with tourist appeal has at least one. Most are
excellent places to stay, where you can meet and
hang out with fellow travelers, get travel advice
and enjoy one of the fun *asados* that are practically de rigueur. Like hostels throughout much
of the world, those in Argentina usually have
common kitchens and living spaces, shared
bathrooms, and, more often than not, at least
one private double. What's more, most hostels
are run by an enthusiastic, conscientious staff
with its finger on the pulse of Argentine travel,
meaning few establishments in all of Argentina
are as helpful in finding out the best places to
visit. But remember that Argentines are night
owls and hostellers tend to follow suit, so ear-
plugs can be handy indeed.

Many hostels offer private doubles that,
were it not for their predominantly dorm-
room style accommodations, would fall into
our midrange sections. Those who crave the
camaraderie of a hostel but actually wish to
sleep (and have their own bathroom) should
consider these options. They can offer the best
of both worlds: the community of a hostel and
the privacy of a hotel.

Card-carrying Hostelling International
(HI) members will save a nominal AR$1 to
AR$3 on a bed at HI facilities. Most hostels,
however, are private, and few travelers carry
HI cards.

There are some excellent online resources,
including **Argentina Hostelling International** (www
.hostels.org.ar), **Hostel World** (www.hostelworld.com)
and **Argentina Top Hostels** (www.hostelsar.com.ar).
All three allow you to book online.

Hotels

Argentine hotels vary from depressing, utilitarian one-star accommodations to luxurious
five-star hotels. Oddly enough, many one- and
two-star hotels can prove better value than
three- and four-star lodgings. In general, ho-

tels provide a room with private bathroom, often a telephone, and usually a TV. Normally they have a *confitería* or restaurant and almost always include breakfast in the price. In the top categories you will have room and laundry service, a swimming pool, a bar, shopping galleries and perhaps a gym (which, in the three- to four-star range, amounts to little more than a pile of dumbbells and a squeaky exercise bike).

Rentals & Homestays

House and apartment rentals can save you money if you're staying in one place for an extended period. In resort locations, such as towns along the Atlantic coast (Mar del Plata, Pinamar etc) or Bariloche, you can lodge several people for the price of one by seeking an apartment and cooking your own meals. Tourist offices and newspapers are good sources for listings. For rental resources in Buenos Aires, see p114.

During the tourist season, mostly in the interior, families rent rooms to visitors. Often these are excellent bargains, permitting access to cooking and laundry facilities and hot showers, as well as encouraging contact with Argentines. Generally, we do not cover homestays in this book, since they change regularly. Tourist offices in most smaller towns, but even in cities as large as Salta and Mendoza, maintain lists of such accommodations.

ACTIVITIES

Argentina has a cornucopia of outdoor activities, offering everything from trekking in the Lake District and Patagonia, mountaineering in Mendoza and San Juan, to snow sports, cycling and fishing. For more information, see p70.

BUSINESS HOURS

Traditionally, business hours in Argentina commence by 8am and break at midday *siesta* (rest) for three or even four hours, during which people return home for lunch and a brief nap. After siesta, shops reopen until 8pm or 9pm. This schedule is still common in the provinces, but government offices and many businesses in Buenos Aires have adopted a more conventional 8am to 5pm schedule in the interests of 'greater efficiency.'

Throughout this book, we list opening hours for businesses only when they deviate from the standard business hours listed inside the front cover.

CHILDREN

Argentina is extremely child-friendly in terms of travel safety (except when it comes to car safety seats), health, people's attitudes and family-oriented activities. This is also a country where people frequently touch each other, so don't be surprised when your child is patted on the head or caressed on the cheek.

When it comes to public transport, Argentines are usually very helpful. It's common for someone sitting to give up a seat for a parent and child, and occasionally an older person may offer to put the child on his or her lap.

Most nonflashy restaurants provide a wide selection of food suitable for children (vegetables, pasta, meat, chicken, fish, French fries etc), but adult portions are normally so large that small children rarely need a separate order. Waiters are accustomed to providing extra plates and cutlery for children, though some places may add a small additional charge. Whatever you do, don't forget to take the kids out for ice cream – it's a real Argentine treat!

FUN FOR THE KIDS

Art museums? Boring. Churches (yawn). Bus rides – ouch. But worry not. There are plenty of ways to keep your kiddos' spirits high in Argentina. The following make great bargaining chips to keep the kids in check.

- Dinosaur exhibits – including multi-story-tall skeletons and massive footprints – in Neuquén (p386).

- Shopping for zany, unique and affordable kids clothes in Palermo Viejo, Buenos Aires (p130).

- Horseback rides during a stay on an *estancia* (p603).

- Glaciar Perito Moreno and icebergs in Parque Nacional Los Glaciares (p495).

- Tandem paragliding flight in La Cumbre, Córdoba (p329).

- Two words: ice cream. It's outstanding in Argentina.

Breast-feeding in public is not uncommon, though most women are discreet and cover themselves. Poorly maintained public bathrooms may be a concern for some parents. Always carry toilet paper and baby wipes. While a woman may take a young boy into the ladies' room, it would be socially unacceptable for a man to take a girl of any age into the men's room.

On buses, small children can share a seat with their parents to save money; on sleeper buses (see p625), this rarely proves uncomfortable.

CLIMATE CHARTS

From the scorching subtropical summers of Chaco and Formosa provinces, to the freezing, gale-force winter winds of Tierra del Fuego, Argentina has wildly varied climates. For information on the best time to visit the country, see p18.

COURSES

Most opportunities for Spanish-language instruction are based in Buenos Aires (see p106), though larger cities such as Mendoza (p351) and Córdoba (p320) are also excellent places to kick-start or hone your Spanish. Córdoba is a city of students, meaning you will feel right at home going to school, and you will also find plenty of opportunities to set up learning exchanges with local students.

Small-group instruction or individual tutoring offer the best opportunities for improving language skills, and are affordable options. Rates average around AR$40 per hour (one-on-one) or AR$300 to AR$400 per week.

Tango classes are hugely popular in Buenos Aires, where group lessons cost around AR$20. For more information see the boxed text, p123.

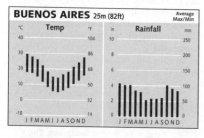

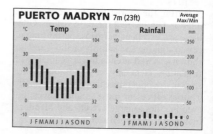

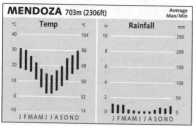

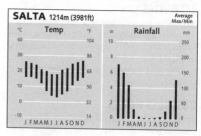

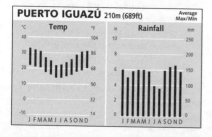

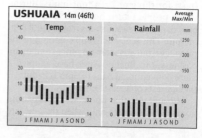

CUSTOMS

Argentine officials are generally courteous and reasonable toward tourists. Electronic items, including laptops, cameras and cell phones, can be brought into the country duty free, provided they are not intended for resale. You may also bring in, duty free, up to 2L of alcohol, 400 cigarettes and 50 cigars. If you're entering with expensive computer, photographic and/or other electronic equipment, you should play it safe and declare it. Folks rarely have problems entering with the usual electronic items.

If you're entering Argentina from a neighboring country, officials focus on different things. Travelers southbound from the central Andean countries may be searched for drugs, while those from bordering countries will have fruits and vegetables confiscated. Carrying drugs will pretty much get you into trouble no matter which country you're coming from.

DANGERS & ANNOYANCES

For tourists, Argentina is probably the safest country in Latin America. This isn't to say you should skip down the street drunk with your money belt strapped to your head, but, with a little common sense, you can visit Argentina's big cities as safely as you could London, Paris or New York. That said, crime has been on the rise.

Petty Crime

The economic crisis of 1999–2001 plunged a lot of people into poverty, and street crime (pickpocketing, bag-snatching and armed robbery) has subsequently risen, especially in Buenos Aires (see p95) and, more recently, Mendoza (see p347). Still, most people feel perfectly safe in Buenos Aires. In the small towns of the provinces you'd have to *search* for a crook to rob you.

Bus terminals are the most common places tourists become separated from their possessions. For the most part, bus terminals are safe, as they're usually full of families traveling and saying goodbyes, but they're also prime grounds for bag-snatchers. Always keep an eagle eye on your goods. This is especially true in Buenos Aires' Retiro station.

Pickets & Protests

Street protests have become part of daily life in Argentina, especially in Buenos Aires, so it's wise to be aware of current political events.

Generally these have little effect on tourists other than blocking traffic or making it impossible to see Buenos Aires' Plaza de Mayo and the Casa Rosada (where protests occur almost weekly). The country has many *gremios* or *sindicatos* (trade unions), and it seems like one of them is always on strike. Transportation unions sometimes go on strike, which can effect travelers directly by delaying domestic flights and bus services. It's always a good idea to keep your eye on the news before traveling.

Drivers

Being a pedestrian in Argentina is perhaps one of the country's more difficult ventures. Many Argentine drivers jump the gun when the traffic signal is about to change to green, drive extremely fast and change lanes unpredictably. Even though pedestrians at corners and crosswalks have legal right-of-way (ha!), very few drivers respect this and will hardly slow down when you are crossing. Be especially careful of buses, which can be reckless and, because of their large size, particularly painful.

Police & Military

The police and military have a reputation for being corrupt or irresponsible, but, while a foreign visitor may experience petty harassment (usually to procure payment of a bribe), both are generally helpful and courteous to tourists. If you feel you're being patted down for a bribe, you can respond by tactfully paying up (see p610), or asking the officer to accompany you to the police station to take care of it. The latter may lead the officer to drop it, or lead you in to the labyrinthine bureaucracy of the Argentine police system.

Smoking

Many Argentines are heavy smokers, and you can't help but be exposed to it on the street. The good news for nonsmokers is that Argentina passed a smoking ban for restaurants, cafés, internet cafés, bars and other public places in 2006. Regulations and enforcement differ throughout the country. Smoking is prohibited on buses and all domestic flights.

Kidnapping

Kidnappings in Buenos Aires received a lot of press a few years back, but the crimes were *rarely* aimed at foreigners. Your odds of being kidnapped are extremely low.

DISCOUNT CARDS

The International Student Identity Card (ISIC), available for US$11.05 (or about AR$35) through the student and discount travel agency **Asatej** (Map pp84-5; ☎ 011-4114-7500; www.asatej.net; Florida 835, Room 320, 3rd fl, Buenos Aires), can help travelers obtain discounts on public transportation and admissions to museums. Often any official-looking university identification may be an acceptable substitute. An HI card, available for US$14 (about AR$44) at the **HI office** (Map pp84-5; ☎ 011-4511-8723; www .hostels.org.ar; Florida 835, Room 319, 3rd fl, Buenos Aires), will get you small discounts on your stay at any HI facility (see p604).

Travelers over the age of 60 can sometimes obtain senior-citizen discounts on museum admissions and the like. Usually a passport with date of birth is sufficient evidence of age.

EMBASSIES & CONSULATES
Argentine Embassies & Consulates

Argentina has diplomatic representation throughout the world. A quick internet search will turn up the *embajada Argentina* (Argentine embassy) in your home country with nearest consulates to you.

Embassies & Consulates in Argentina

Following is a list of embassies and consulates in Buenos Aires. Some countries have both an embassy and a consulate here, but only the most central location is listed. Diplomatic offices in other Argentine cities are listed after their respective name.

Australia Buenos Aires (Map pp88-9; ☎ 011-4779-3500; Villanueva 1400, Palermo)

Bolivia Buenos Aires (Map pp84-5; ☎ 011-4381-0539; Adolfo Alsina 1886, Balvanera); Jujuy (Map p248; ☎ 0388-424-0501; Independencia 1098; ⊗ 9am-1pm Mon-Fri); La Quiaca (☎ 0388-422 283; cnr Árabe Siria & 9 de Julio; ⊗ 7am-4pm Mon-Fri); Salta (Map p262; ☎ 0387-421-1040; Mariano Boedo 34, Salta; ⊗ 9am-2pm Mon-Fri); Tucumán (off Map p287; ☎ 0381-425-2224; Av Aconquija 1117)

Brazil Buenos Aires (Map pp84-5; ☎ 011-4515-6500, 011-4394-5264; Carlos Pellegrini 1363, 5th fl, Retiro); Paso de los Libres (☎ 03772-425444; vclibres@arnet.com.ar; Calle Bartolomé Mitre 894 at Sarmiento); Puerto Iguazú (Map p226; ☎ 03757-421348; conbrasil@iguazunet .com; Córdoba 264)

Canada Buenos Aires (Map pp88-9; ☎ 011-4808-1000; Tagle 2828, Recoleta)

Chile Buenos Aires (Map pp84-5; ☎ 011-4394-6582;

San Martín 439, 9th fl, San Nicolás); Bariloche (Map p407; ☎ 02944-423050; Av Juan Manuel de Rosas 180); Esquel (Map p466; ☎ 02945-451189; Molinari 754); Jujuy (Map p248; ☎ 0388-426-1985; Pacará 50, Los Perales; ⊗ call for appointment); Mendoza (off Map pp348-9; ☎ 0261-425-4844; Paso de los Andes 1147); Neuquén (Map p383; ☎ 0299-442-2727; La Rioja 241); Río Gallegos (Map p461; ☎ 02966-422364; Mariano Moreno 148); Salta (Map p262; ☎ 0387-431-1857; www.cgchilesalta.com .ar; Santiago del Estero 965; ⊗ 9am-1:15pm Mon-Fri); Ushuaia (Map p526; ☎ 02901-430909; Jainén 50) The Ushuaia branch is southwest of town.

France Buenos Aires (Map pp84-5; ☎ 011-4312-2409; Santa Fe 846, 4th fl, Retiro); Mendoza (off Map pp348-9; ☎ 0261-423-1542; Av Houssay 790); Salta (Map p262; ☎ 0387-423-5797; Santa Fe 38; 5-7pm Tue & Thu); Tucumán (Map p287; ☎ 0381-421-8202; Crisóstomo Álvarez 471; ⊗ 6:30pm Mon & Fri only, appointment necessary)

Germany Buenos Aires (Map pp88-9; ☎ 011-4778-2500; Villanueva 1055, Belgrano); Mendoza (Map pp348-9; ☎ 0261-429-6539; Montevideo 127, 1st fl, No 6); Posadas (Map p215; ☎ 03752-435508; Junín 1811, 1st fl; ⊗ 8am-noon Mon-Fri); Salta (Map p262; ☎ 0387-422-9088; consusal@arnet.com.ar; Las Heras 03; ⊗ 9-11am Mon, Wed & Fri); Tucumán (off Map p287; ☎ 0381-421-9102; 9 de Julio 1015; ⊗ 4-8pm Mon & Wed)

Israel Buenos Aires (Map pp84-5; ☎ 011-4338-2500; Av de Mayo 701, 10th fl, Montserrat); Mendoza (off Map pp348-9; ☎ 0261-428-2140; Lamadrid 738)

Italy Buenos Aires (Map pp88-9; ☎ 011-4114-4800; Calle Billinghurst 2577, No 1425); Mendoza (Map pp348-9; ☎ 0261-423-1640; Necochea 712); Salta (Map p262; ☎ 0387-432-1532; Santiago del Estero 497; ⊗ 4-7pm Mon & Wed-Fri, 9am-2pm Tue); Tucumán (Map p287; ☎ 0381-422-3830; fax 0381-431-0423; San Martín 623, 5th fl; ⊗ 9:30am-5pm Tue)

Japan Buenos Aires (Map pp84-5; ☎ 011-4318-8200; Bouchard 547, 17th fl, Microcentro)

Netherlands Buenos Aires (☎ 011-4338-0050; Olga Cossenttini 831, 3rd fl, Edificio Porteño II, Puerto Madero)

Paraguay Buenos Aires (Map pp84-5; ☎ 011-4814-4803; Viamonte 1851, Balvanera); Corrientes (☎ 03783-426576; Córdoba 969); Posadas (Map p215; ☎ 03752-423858; San Lorenzo 179) Puerto Iguazú (Map p226; ☎ 03757-424230; Córdoba 370)

Peru Buenos Aires (Map pp84-5; ☎ 011-4334-0970; Florida 165, Galería Güemes, 2nd fl) Enter from Bartolome Mitre.

Spain Buenos Aires (Map pp84-5; ☎ 011-4814-9100; Guido 1760, Recoleta); Mendoza (off Map pp348-9; ☎ 0261-420-2252; Agustín Alvarez 455); Río Gallegos (Casa España; Map p461; ☎ 02966-422131; Av Roca 866); Tucumán (off Map p287; ☎ 0381-435-3042; Mate de Luna 4107; ⊗ 9am-noon Mon, Tue, Thu & Fri)

UK Buenos Aires (Map pp84-5; ☎ 011-4808-2200; Dr Luis Agote 2412, Recoleta)

Uruguay Buenos Aires (Map pp84-5; ☎ 011-4807-3040;
Av Las Heras 1915, Recoleta); Colón (☎ 03447-421999; San
Martín 417; ☒ 8am-2pm Mon-Fri) Concordia (Map p211;
☎ 0345-421-0380; Pellegrini 709); Gualeguaychú (Map p205;
☎ 03446-422466; Rivadavia 510; ☒ 8am-2pm Mon-Fri)
USA Buenos Aires (Map pp88-9; ☎ 011-5777-4533;
Colombia 4300, Palermo)

FOOD

For a mouthwatering idea of all the food you
can eat while traveling in Argentina, see p53.
Compared to Europe and North America,
restaurant prices in much of Argentina are
quite affordable. However, in places such as
Buenos Aires and especially Patagonia, good-
value meals are harder to come by.

Eating sections throughout this book are
arranged by budget, with the most economical
options listed first. Restaurants that charge up
to AR$15 for a main course (what we abbrevi-
ate as 'mains' in listings) fall into the budget
category. Budget restaurants are usually modest, often family oriented and, more often
than not, serve Argentine standbys like pastas, *milanesas* (breaded fried veal or chicken)
and sandwiches. Ordering house wine by the
glass or *jarra* (carafe) keeps the price down. If
you're pinching pesos, you can almost always
find budget restaurants and keep your eating costs low. (Remember, there are a lot of
Argentines trying to do the same.)

Our midrange category includes restaurants that charge AR$16 to AR$30 for main
courses. You can eat very well at midrange
eateries and usually get out the door having
spent under AR$45 for a complete meal, often
including dessert and wine. Top-end restaurants charge over AR$30 for a main course.
These are plentiful in Buenos Aires (thanks to
all the money in the city and the higher cost
of living) and in Patagonia (thanks to tourism
and the region's isolation).

For the standard opening hours of restaurants, see the inside front cover.

GAY & LESBIAN TRAVELERS

Since the end of military rule, and with the
declining influence of the Catholic church,
Argentina has become increasingly gay-
friendly. Buenos Aires is one of the world's
top gay destinations – with gay hotels and
B&Bs, gay bars and nightclubs, gay restaurants and even gay cruises calling at the port.
The capital is home to South America's largest
annual gay pride parade and has numerous
gay and lesbian organizations and clubs. In
2003 Buenos Aires became the first city in
Latin America to legalize civil unions between
same-sex couples, granting civil-union rights
nearly equal to those held by heterosexual
couples. In 2007 legislation was introduced
to the senate which, if passed, will legalize
same-sex marriage nationwide.

Although Buenos Aires (and, to a lesser
extent, Argentina's other large cities) is becoming increasingly tolerant, most of the rest
of Argentina still feels uncomfortable with
homosexuality. Homophobia rarely takes the
form of physical violence, however; instead
it manifests through inappropriate jokes and
chatty disapproval any time the subject comes
up. That said, gay people regularly travel
throughout the country to return home with
nothing but praise.

When it comes to public affection, Argentine men are more physically demonstrative
than their North American and European
counterparts. Behaviors such as kissing on the
cheek in greeting or a vigorous embrace are
innocuous even to those who express unease
with homosexuality. Lesbians walking hand
in hand should attract little attention, since
heterosexual Argentine women frequently
do so, but this would be very conspicuous
behavior for men. When in doubt, it's best
to be discreet.

For gay-oriented activities in Buenos Aires,
check out the **Gay Guide** (www.thegayguide.com.ar).
Pride Travel (Map pp84-5; ☎ 011-5218-6556; www.pride
-travel.com; Paraguay 523, Room 2E) is a gay-oriented
travel agency in the capital that specializes in
travel throughout Argentina and to Uruguay,
Brazil and Chile. It also offers short tours in
and around the capital and helps arrange
short- or long-term stays in Buenos Aires. For
much more on what's gay in Buenos Aires, see
the boxed text on p126.

Also check out the following websites:
Gayscape (www.gayscape.com) Handful of useful links on
the Argentina page.
Global Gayz.com (www.globalgayz.com) Has a South
America section full of news, tips and links about gay travel
in the region, with a small section on Argentina.
International Lesbian and Gay Association (ILGA;
www.ilga.org) Click 'Countries' and find the Argentina
page for excellent news and information. Also links to
international lesbian, gay and transgender organizations.
Mundo Gay (www.mundogay.com in Spanish) Noteworthy online publication out of Buenos Aires; club listings,
chat, blog and more. Mostly for men.

HOLIDAYS

Government offices and businesses are closed on Argentina's numerous public holidays. If the holiday falls on a midweek day or weekend day, it's often bumped to the nearest Monday. Public transport options are also more limited and fill up fast. The following list does not include provincial holidays, which may vary considerably. For Argentina's best festivals and events, see p22.

New Year's Day January 1.

Semana Santa (Easter week) March/April, dates vary; most businesses close on Good Friday; major travel week.

Día de las Malvinas April 2; commemorates the day in 1829 that Argentina claimed military rule over the Islas Malvinas (Falkland Islands).

Labor Day May 1.

Revolución de Mayo May 25; commemorates the 1810 revolution against Spain.

Día de la Bandera (Flag Day) June 20.

Independence Day July 9.

Día de San Martín August 17; marks the anniversary of José de San Martín's death (1778–1850).

Día de la Raza (Columbus Day) October 12.

Día de la Concepción Inmaculada December 8; religious holiday that celebrates the immaculate conception of the Virgin Mary.

Christmas Day December 25.

INSURANCE

In addition to health insurance (p630) and car insurance (p627), it's wise to purchase travel insurance that protects baggage, valuables and cancelled flights. Keep in mind that some insurance policies do not cover certain 'high risk' activities, usually of the extreme sport type, which can be anything from rock climbing to paragliding. Be sure to read the fine print and choose a policy that best suits your needs.

Keep your insurance records separate from other possessions in case you have to make a claim (a good trick is to email them to yourself and keep them accessible in your Inbox). Worldwide travel insurance is available at www.lonelyplanet.com/travel_services. You can buy, extend and claim online anytime – even if you're already on the road.

INTERNET ACCESS

For Sleeping listings throughout this book, we've included a 🖳 symbol for those accommodations that provide internet access for their guests. If a hotel offers wireless service but no guest computers (meaning you need your own computer to get online), we still include the icon, but describe the situation in the review. For a list of recommended internet resources, see p21.

Rarely is an Argentine town – no matter how small it is – without an internet café. In cities, internet cafés seem to occupy every other building, with even the smallest *locutorios* (telephone centers) having a few computers. Internet cafés charge about AR$2 per hour in most cities, while in smaller towns where competition is slimmer, prices can top AR$5 per hour.

Some Spanish keyboards can be a little tricky, especially when trying to find the '@' symbol (called *arroba* in Spanish). First try substituting the Alt-Gr key for Shift (that is: Alt-Gr + @). If that doesn't work, try holding down the Alt key and typing 64 on the number pad (with Number Lock on). If all else fails, ask the attendant '¿Cómo se hace la arroba?' ('How do you make the @ sign?'). Gr is a function key on most Spanish keyboards.

Open, free wireless networks (such as wi-fi) have become commonplace at cafés and hotels (usually midrange and up) throughout Argentina, even in small towns. Traveling with a laptop can be convenient, but unless you know what you're doing, it's fraught with potential problems. Remember, the power supply in Argentina (220 volts) may differ from that at home, so if your laptop doesn't have an internal voltage converter (many do), you'll have to purchase one. If you do buy a converter, be sure you buy one that's rated for the electronic devices you're using – the standard power converters sold at most luggage and travel stores are meant only for hairdryers, battery chargers and the like.

Argentina uses US-type RJ-11 telephone wall jacks. If you hope to access the internet at a hotel via a hard line connection, be sure you're plugging in with an RJ-11 socket or that you have an RJ-11 adaptor. For more information on traveling with laptops and other electronics check out Steve Kropla's excellent website at www.kropla.com.

LEGAL MATTERS

Argentina presently enjoys civilian government, but the police and military both have a reputation for corruption and abuse of power. However, as a tourist it is very unlikely you will ever experience this if you obey the law. Police, however, can demand identification at any moment and for whatever reason. Always carry your documents and always be courteous and cooperative.

The legal drinking age is 18. Though it's not uncommon to see folks drinking beer on the street or in plazas, it's technically illegal to do so. Marijuana is illegal in Argentina and can land you in jail. Cocaine and other substances that are illegal in the US and most European countries are also illegal here. Though constitutionally a person is innocent until proven guilty, people are regularly held for years without a trial. If arrested, you have the constitutional right to a lawyer, a telephone call and to remain silent.

No Argentine in their right mind would offer a *coima* (bribe) to a police officer. The police do not accept them. However, things are often taken care of on the spot by asking '*¿Con cuanto podemos arreglar este malentendido?*' ('How much to fix up this misunderstanding?') or '*¿Como podemos arreglar esto mas rápido?*' ('What can we do to expedite this situation?').

MAPS

Tourist offices throughout the country provide free city maps that are good enough for tooling around town. **International Travel Maps** (www.itmb.com) publishes fairly useful Buenos Aires and Argentina maps.

With offices in nearly every Argentine city, the Automóvil Club Argentino (ACA; p626) publishes excellent, regularly updated maps of provinces and cities that are particularly good for driving and trip planning. The provincial maps cost about AR$19 (AR$14 for card-carrying members of foreign automobile clubs). Not as good, but still handy are the red *Argenguide* maps, which are sold for AR$15 to AR$20 at most YPF (gas or petrol) stations.

Geography nerds will adore the topographic maps available from the **Instituto Geográfico Militar** (☎ 4576-5576; www.igm.gov.ar; Cabildo 381, Palermo, Buenos Aires; ☼ 8am-1pm Mon-Fri). To get there, take the Subte to the Ministro Carranza stop, or take bus 152. These maps are difficult to obtain outside the capital.

MONEY

The Argentine unit of currency is the peso (AR$). Prices in this book are quoted in Argentine pesos unless otherwise noted. See the inside front cover for exchange rates. Also see p18 for information on costs.

Since 2002, when the Argentine government devalued the peso amid an economic crisis that rocked the nation, the peso has been hovering steadily at about three to the US dollar, though visitors should keep an eye on current economic events.

Carrying cash and an ATM card is the way to go in Argentina.

ATMs

Cajeros automáticos (ATMs) are found in nearly every city and town in Argentina and can also be used for cash advances on major credit cards. They're the best way to get money, and nearly all have instructions in English. Almost all ATMs use Cirrus, Plus or Link systems. The downside to ATMs is that most machines only allow a maximum withdrawal of AR$300 per transaction. You can withdraw AR$300 several times from the same machine (simply make another transaction), but most home banks charge a withdrawal fee of AR$15 or equivalent – *per transaction*. Some people have reported that cards using the Cirrus/MasterCard aren't subject to fees. Others avoid withdrawal fees by taking cash advances on their credit cards (though interest rates on cash are high). Whatever system you use, be sure to check with your bank about fees to avoid surprises later on.

Cash

Paper money comes in denominations of two, five, 10, 20, 50 and 100 pesos. One peso equals 100 *centavos;* coins come in denominations of one (rare), five, 10, 25 and 50 *centavos,* and one peso. At present, US dollars are accepted by many tourist-oriented businesses, but you should always carry some pesos.

Counterfeiting, of both local and US bills, has become a problem in recent years, and merchants are very careful when accepting large denominations. You should be too; look for a clear watermark or running thread on the largest bills.

Changing large denomination bills is a huge problem throughout the country (and a major gripe for Argentines and tourists alike). Whenever you can, change your AR$100 and AR$50 bills at the bank to avoid problems. Taxi drivers, kiosks and small stores rarely change them, and you could easily find yourself without a means of paying.

Credit Cards

The most widely accepted credit cards are Visa and MasterCard, though American Express and a few others are also valid in many establishments. Before you leave home, warn your credit-card company that you'll be using it abroad or it may put a hold on the card thinking it was lost.

Some businesses add a *recargo* (surcharge) of 5% to 10% toward credit-card purchases. Also, the actual amount you'll eventually pay depends upon the exchange rate not at the time of sale, but when the purchase is posted to an overseas account, sometimes weeks later.

If you use a credit card to pay for restaurant bills, be aware that tips can't usually be added to the bill. Some lower-end hotels and private tour companies will not accept credit cards. Holders of MasterCard and Visa can get cash advances at Argentine banks and most ATMs.

Exchanging Money

US dollars are by far the preferred foreign currency, although Chilean and Uruguayan pesos can be readily exchanged at the borders. Cash dollars and euros can be changed at *cambios* (exchange houses) in most larger cities, but other currencies can be difficult to change outside Buenos Aires.

Taxes & Refunds

Under limited circumstances, foreign visitors may obtain refunds of the *impuesto al valor agregado* (IVA; value-added tax) on purchases of Argentine products upon their departure from the country. A 'Tax Free' (in English) window decal identifies merchants participating in this program. Hang on to your invoice and you can obtain refunds in Buenos Aires at Ezeiza, Aeroparque Jorge Newbery and the Buquebus terminal at Darsena Norte.

Tipping & Bargaining

In restaurants it's customary to tip about 10% of the bill, but in times of economic distress (ie, these days), many Argentines overlook the custom. In general, waiters are poorly paid, so if you can afford to eat out, you can probably afford to tip. Even a small *propina* (tip) will be appreciated, but note that restaurant tips can't be added to a credit card bill. Taxi drivers don't expect tips, but it's customary to round up to the nearest peso. Unlike many other South American countries, bargaining is generally not the norm in Argentina.

Traveler's Checks

Very high commissions are levied on traveler's checks, which are difficult to cash anywhere

and specifically *not* recommended for travel in Argentina. Stores will *not* accept traveler's checks, and outside Buenos Aires it's even harder to change them.

PHOTOGRAPHY

For tips on how to photograph people, cities, landscapes and more, pick up a copy of Lonely Planet's easy-to-carry *Travel Photography* book by Richard I'Anson. Avoid taking photos of military or police, as you may have your camera confiscated.

Digital

If you're shooting digital and plan to be taking a lot of photos, invest in a portable hard drive. It's the best way to back up your files. If you don't plan to travel with a portable hard drive, you can easily back up your photos to CD, DVD or flash drive at an internet café (see p610). Nearly all internet cafés have at least one machine with usable USB ports and a CD burner.

Film

Film in Argentina is comparable to that in North America and Europe, both in quality and price. But it's generally cheaper to develop film here than it is in Europe or the US. Developing quality is generally high, so do it before you leave for home and save yourself a bundle. Developing 36 midsize color prints costs AR$30 to AR$40. Print developing is widely available in Argentina. For slide developing, you'll have fewer choices except in Buenos Aires.

POST

Correo Argentino, the privatized postal service, has become more reliable over the years but mail still regularly gets waylaid and occasionally gets lost. International letters and postcards under 20g cost AR$4; a letter over 20g costs AR$12.60. Certified letters to the US cost AR$13.50 for up to 100g, and AR$14.25 to the rest of the world. For essential overseas mail, send it *certificado* (certified) or use one of the local courier services.

Domestic couriers, such as **Andreani** (www .andreani.com.ar) and **OCA** (www.oca.com.ar), and international couriers, like DHL and FedEx, are far more dependable than the post office. But they're also far more expensive. The last two have offices only in the largest cities, while the former two usually serve as their connections to the interior of the country.

You can receive mail via *poste restante* or *lista de correos*, both equivalent to general delivery, at any Argentine post office. Instruct your correspondents to address letters clearly (capitalizing your last name) and to indicate a date until which the post office should hold them; otherwise, the mail will be returned or destroyed. Charges are AR$4 per letter. To receive mail in Buenos Aires have your letter sent like this:

Sarah SMITH (last name in capitals)
Lista de Correos
Correo Central
Sarmiento 189
(1003) Capital Federal
Argentina

If a package is being sent to you, expect to wait a long time for it to turn up within the system (or to receive notice of its arrival). All parcels sent to Buenos Aires go to the international Retiro office, near the Buquebus terminal. To collect the package you'll have to wait (sometimes hours) first to get it and then to have it checked by customs. There's also an AR$4 processing fee.

RELOCATING TO ARGENTINA

After the devaluation of the peso in 2002, foreigners began moving to Argentina – where the cost of living for those earning dollars, euros or pounds was extremely low – in huge numbers. Although prices for just about everything (including food, apartments and transportation) have been on the rise, Argentina is still an extremely popular destination for expats on the make. Levels of relocation vary: countless folks simply rent an apartment in Buenos Aires for a year or two and leave the country every three months to renew their visa. Others go the full route, purchasing property and jumping through the hoops of legal residency. Whatever you decide to do, don't expect to find work in Argentina, unless you'll be employed by a foreign company (for more on work, see p618).

Opening a bank account in Argentina is a bit of a hassle. You can't just walk in with AR$1000 and open one. Requirements vary by bank, but generally you need the minimum equivalent of US$500, plus a picture ID, plus – and here's the kicker – a CDI (a national ID card number) or CUIT/CUIL (employment and tax ID numbers). Obtaining these requires proof of residency and/or legal employment

and are available through the **Administración Federal de Ingresos Públicos** (AFIP; www.afip.gov.ar) in Buenos Aires. Basically, if you just want to open an account to avoid withdrawal fees from your home-country bank, it may not be worth the trouble.

For those considering the long-term relocation, including buying property, there are some excellent resources out there. They include the following:

BANewcomers (http://groups.yahoo.com/group/BANewcomers/) Yahoo newsgroup; good place to throw out questions to expats in Argentina.

BABlackJumpers (http://groups.yahoo.com/group/BABlackJumpers/) Sometimes zany newsgroup for expats in Argentina.

Escape Artist (www.escapeartist.com) General info site for folks moving abroad with helpful Argentina links.

Expat Argentina (www.expat-argentina.blogspot.com) Excellent, thoroughly researched blog written by several expats in Argentina.

Moving and living in ... Argentina (http://movingtoargentina.typepad.com) Although primarily an outlet for her e-book about moving to Argentina, expat Laura Zurro's blog is still full of useful links.

Transitions Abroad (www.transitionsabroad.com) Excellent, longtime resource for folks living, working and studying abroad.

Yes BA (www.yesba.org) Excellent mailing list with job info, apartment listings, entertainment and more.

For a list of apartment rental services in Buenos Aires, see p114. For internet resources specific to Buenos Aires, see p93.

SHOPPING

Argentina is a great place to shop, especially for anyone traveling on strong foreign currencies. When it comes to fashion, Buenos Aires is one of the world's best cities to shop, with everything from boutique and independent designers who sell their wares at street fares, to big-name brands in BA's slickest shopping centers. The city's Palermo Viejo neighborhood is arguably the city's best area to shop.

Argentina is also famous for its leather, and downtown Buenos Aires is home to countless leather shops (p131) that cater to the tourist trade, selling leather jackets, handbags and shoes. Quality and prices can vary greatly, so shop around before buying.

Found everywhere, *mate* paraphernalia makes great souvenirs. Gourds and *bombillas* (metal straws with filters for drinking *mate*) range from inexpensive aluminum to elaborate and expensive gold and silver. Another great buy of the traditional sort is the gaucho (or criollo) knife. These usually have intricately woven leather or bone handles, and the blades vary widely. They're sold throughout the country, but the pampas town of Tandil (p148) is particularly famous for its cutlery.

In artisans *ferias* (fairs), found throughout Argentina, the variety of handicrafts is extensive and interesting. The best *ferias* are likely those in Córdoba (p324) and El Bolsón (p419). The Lake District town of Bariloche (p406) is well known for its woolen goods, but the local chocolate is what will really rock your world. In the province of Salta, the distinctive *ponchos de Güemes* make for memorable purchases.

Argentines are well read and interested in both national and world literature, and Buenos Aires has a good selection of general- and special-interest bookstores. Since the end of the military dictatorship, the capital has re-established itself as a publishing center; April's Feria del Libro (book fair; p108) is South America's largest, with over 600 exhibitors drawing over a million visitors.

Foreign-language books tend to be very expensive, but there's a good selection (including this and other Lonely Planet guides) at Buenos Aires' better bookstores and, occasionally, those in the interior.

Wine, of course, is another fabulous buy, but bringing it home is no longer as easy as it once was, primarily because most international airlines now prohibit passengers from carrying bottles aboard. You can pack a few bottles into your checked luggage, but you'd better be sure they're well padded. Most upscale wine stores in Buenos Aires and Mendoza will package bottles in bubble wrap and cardboard, free of charge. Finer wines are available in wooden boxes.

Many places add a surcharge to credit-card purchases; ask before you pay.

SOLO TRAVELERS

Traveling alone can be one of the most rewarding experiences in life. You're far more likely to meet locals and fellow travelers – which is really what travel's all about – without the shell of companionship. Mind you, it can get lonely at times, and it's certainly nice to have a mate to watch your bags for you (or your back when you're snapping photos) but these benefits are often outweighed by the joy of meeting locals. Argentines are quick to invite solo travelers to an *asado* or elsewhere, and even quicker to strike up conversation. What's more, with Argentina's abundance of new hostels, you can easily hook up with other travelers when you're feeling lonely.

Traveling alone as a woman, unfortunately, inherently entails more risk than traveling as a man. But countless women travel alone safely in Argentina every day; it's one of the safest countries in South America to do so. For more information for women travelers, see p617.

TELEPHONE & FAX

Two companies, Telecom and Telefónica, split the country's telephone services. For emergencies dial ☎ 107, police ☎ 101, fire ☎ 100. Directory Assistance is ☎ 110.

The easiest way to make a local phone call is to find a *locutorio,* which has private cabins where you make your calls, and then pay all at once at the register. *Locutorios* can be found on practically every other block. They cost about the same as street phones, are much quieter and you won't run out of coins. Most *locutorios* are supplied with phone books.

To use street phones, you'll pay with regular coins or *tarjetas telefónicas* (magnetic phone cards available at many kiosks). You'll only be able to speak for a limited time before you get cut off, so carry enough credit.

International collect calls or calls by credit card are not necessarily cheaper than calling from long-distance telephone offices. Long-distance offices are usually busy during evenings and weekends, when overseas calls are cheaper. Prices for Europe and Australia can be as high as AR$1.35 per minute; calling the USA costs approximately AR$0.90. Your best option is to use a phone card (see opposite).

Faxes are widely used in Argentina and available at most *locutorios* and internet cafés. Costs are the price of the call plus about AR$1.50 per page.

MOBILE PHONES

Argentina operates on the GSM 1900 standard, so, if you have a tri-band GSM cell phone (sometimes called a 'world phone' in the USA), you should be able to use it in Argentina. There are various ways to do this. If you plan to use your own provider, you probably have to contact the company to have your phone unlocked for international use. Unless you have a plan tailored specifically toward international use, your rates on calls made and accepted in Argentina will likely be high.

Another option for folks with tri-band GSM phones is to purchase a prepaid SIM card in Argentina (from a company such as CTI Móvil) and insert it into your phone. Prepaid SIM cards cost anywhere from AR$10 to AR$100 and charge you from AR$0.35 to AR$0.65 (the more minutes you buy, the cheaper they cost).

Another option is purchasing a new cell phone in Argentina. You can pick one up for as little as AR$99, usually with the equivalent in minutes already on the phone. Most companies require you to pay up to three months in advance, but it can still work out to be economically feasible. Cell-phone rentals are also available in Buenos Aires for around AR$45 per week, including a chunk of free minutes.

Finally, you can purchase an international phone or a prepaid international SIM card from one of numerous companies that likely operate in your home country. These can easily be found by doing an internet search for 'international cell phone.'

Other cellular systems in use in Argentina are CDMA and TDMA.

This is a fast-changing field so check the current situation before you travel; take a look at www.kropla.com or do an internet search on GSM cell phones for the myriad of products on the market.

It is generally impossible to call an Argentine cell phone from outside South America.

PHONE CODES

When dialing abroad from Argentina, you must first dial '00,' followed by the country code. The *característica* (area code) for Buenos Aires is ☎ 011, and all telephone numbers in the Greater Buenos Aires area have eight

---

digits. Area codes vary wildly throughout the provinces; those of larger cities have four digits (always beginning with a zero), followed by a seven-digit telephone number. Smaller towns have six-digit telephone numbers and five-digit area codes (again, always beginning with a zero). Basically, when calling from outside an area code, you're always going to dial 11 numbers.

Cellular phone numbers in Argentina are always preceded by '15'. After that simple fact, it gets confusing. Usually you just dial the regional code corresponding to the person's location, regardless of where the phone was purchased. Other times, the regional code you must dial depends on where the person bought the cellular phone. So you may have to try more than once to get through. Your best bet is starting with the regional code where the person is located, followed by '15', then the number. If you're calling a cell phone from within the same regional code, you don't have to dial the regional code. We've listed regional codes with cell numbers throughout this book, so always try that option first when calling from another region. When calling a cellular phone from abroad, first you dial Argentina's country code (54), then '9' (instead of '15'), then the regional code, followed by the telephone number itself.

Toll-free numbers begin with ☎ 0800 or ☎ 0810.

PHONECARDS

Telephone calling cards (such as Asimon, Hablé Mas, Llamada Directa and Momentos de Telecom) are sold at nearly all kiosks and make domestic and international calls far cheaper (for AR$10 you can talk to the US for over an hour). However, they must be used from a fixed line such as a home or hotel telephone (provided you can dial outside the hotel). They cannot be used at most pay phones. Some *locutorios* allow you to use them, and although they levy a surcharge, the call is still far cheaper than dialing direct. When purchasing one, tell the clerk the country you will call so they give you the right card.

TIME

Argentina is three hours behind GMT and does not observe daylight saving time. When it's noon in Argentina, it's 10am in New York, 7am in San Francisco, 3pm in London and 1pm the next day in Sydney (add one

---

COUNTRY CODES

To call a number in Argentina from another country, dial your international access code, then the country code for Argentina (☎ 54), then the area code (without the zero) and number.

To call a telephone number in Chile from another country, the country code is ☎ 56. The country code for Uruguay is ☎ 598; for Brazil the code is ☎ 55 and for Bolivia ☎ 591.

hour to these times during daylight saving). Argentina tells time by the 24-hour clock. See also p674.

TOILETS

Public toilets in Argentina are better than in most of South America, but there are certainly exceptions. For the truly squeamish, the better restaurants and cafés are good alternatives. Large shopping malls often have public bathrooms as do international fast-food chains. Always carry your own toilet paper, since it often runs out in public restrooms, and don't expect luxuries like soap, hot water and paper towels either.

TOURIST INFORMATION

Argentina's national tourist board is the **Secretaría Nacional de Turismo** (www.turismo.gov.ar). Almost every city or town has a tourist office, usually on or near the main plaza or at the bus terminal. Each Argentine province also has its own representation in Buenos Aires; most, though not all, of these are well organized, often offering a computerized database of tourist information, and are well worth a visit before heading for the provinces.

Another excellent source of information and generally indispensable resource is **South American Explorers** (www.saexplorers.org), which maintains a clubhouse in Buenos Aires (p95).

The offices listed here are all provincial tourist offices located in Buenos Aires (area code ☎ 011).

Buenos Aires (Map pp84-5; ☎ 4373-2508; Av Callao 235)
Catamarca (Map pp84-5; ☎ 4374-6891; Córdoba 2080)
Chaco (Map pp84-5; ☎ 4372-5209; Av Callao 328)
Chubut (Map pp84-5; ☎ 200-666-2904, 4382-2009; Sarmiento 1172)
Córdoba (Map pp84-5; ☎ 4371-1688, 4373-4277; Av Callao 332)
Corrientes (Map pp84-5; ☎ 4394-7418; San Martín 333, 4th fl)
Entre Ríos (Map pp84-5; ☎ 4328-2284; Suipacha 844)
Formosa (Map pp84-5; ☎ 4381-7048; Hipólito Yrigoyen 1429)
Jujuy (Map pp84-5; ☎ 4393-6096; Av Santa Fe 967)
La Pampa (Map pp84-5; ☎ 4326-0511; Suipacha 346)
La Rioja (Map pp84-5; ☎ 4815-1929; Av Callao 745)
Mendoza (Map pp84-5; ☎ 4371-7301, 4371-0835; Av Callao 445)
Misiones (Map pp84-5; ☎ 4322-0686; Av Santa Fe 989)
Neuquén (Map pp84-5; ☎ 4343-2324/95, ext 1004/5; Maipú 48)

Río Negro (Map pp84-5; ☎ 4371-5599, 4371-7273; Tucumán 1916)
Salta (Map pp84-5; ☎ 4326-1314; Diagonal Norte/ Roque Sáenz Peña 933)
San Juan (Map pp84-5; ☎ 4382-9241; Sarmiento 1251)
San Luis (Map pp84-5; ☎ 5778-1621; Azcuénaga 1087)
Santa Cruz (Map pp84-5; ☎ 4325-3098; Suipacha 1120)
Santa Fe (Map pp84-5; ☎ 4342-0408; 25 de Mayo 168)
Santiago del Estero (Map pp84-5; ☎ 4326-3733; Florida 274)
Tierra del Fuego (Map pp84-5; ☎ 4328-7040; Esmeralda 783)
Tucumán (Map pp84-5; ☎ 4322-0010, ext 124; Suipacha 140)

With offices throughout the country, the Automóvil Club Argentino (ACA) is a useful source of good, up-to-date maps of provinces and cities that are useful for driving and trip planning. For more information, see p626.

TRAVELERS WITH DISABILITIES

Travelers with disabilities will find things somewhat difficult in Argentina. Those in wheelchairs in particular will quickly realize that many cities' narrow, busy and uneven sidewalks are difficult to negotiate. Crossing streets is also a problem, since not every corner has ramps and Argentine drivers don't have much patience for slower pedestrians, disabled or not. Nevertheless, Argentines with disabilities do get around, and in Buenos Aires there exists a few buses described as *piso bajo*, which lower to provide wheelchair lifts. Wheelchair curb ramps exist at many corners in Buenos Aires, but they're often broken beyond use.

Except at four- and five-star properties, hotels usually do not have wheelchair-accessible rooms (at least as they're known in other parts of the world), meaning doors are narrow and there is little space to move around inside the room. Bathrooms at midrange and budget hotels are notoriously small, making it difficult for anyone (disabled or not) to get around in. For truly accessible rooms, you'll have better luck in pricier hotels. Call ahead and ask specific questions – even if a hotel defines a room as wheelchair accessible, it may not be up to standards to which you're accustomed.

Other than the use of brail on ATMs little effort has been dedicated to bettering accessibility for the blind. Stoplights are rarely equipped with sound alerts. The **Biblioteca Argentina Para Ciegos** (BAC; Argentine Library for the

Blind; ☎ 4981-0137; www.bac.org.ar in Spanish; Lezica 3909, Buenos Aires) maintains a brail collection of over 3000 books, as well as other resources.

In Buenos Aires, **Movidisc** (☎ 011-4328-6921; www .movidisc-web.com.ar in Spanish; Av Roque Sáenz Peña 868, 3rd fl) offers private transport and day tours in vans fully equipped for wheelchair users. If you're taking a tour with another agency, Movidisc can provide transport alone, provided you ask your tour company to arrange it with Movidisc.

Also check out the following organizations online, all of which offer countless links to other resources.

accesible.com (www.accesible.com)
Access-able Travel Source (www.access-able.com)
Mobility International (www.miusa.org)
National Information Communication Awareness Network (www.nican.com.au)

VISAS

Nationals of the USA, Canada, most Western European countries, Australia and New Zealand do not need visas to visit Argentina. In theory, upon arrival all non-visa visitors must obtain a free tourist card, good for 90 days and renewable for 90 more. In practice, immigration officials issue these only at major border crossings, such as airports and on the ferries and hydrofoils between Buenos Aires and Uruguay. Although you should not toss your card away, losing it is no major catastrophe; at most exit points, immigration officials will provide immediate replacement for free.

Dependent children traveling without *both* parents theoretically need a notarized document certifying that both parents agree to the child's travel. Parents may also wish to bring a copy of the custody form; however, there's a good chance they won't be asked for either document.

Very short visits to neighboring countries usually do not require visas. Despite what a travel agency might say, you probably don't need a Brazilian visa to cross from the Argentine town of Puerto Iguazú to Foz do Iguaçu and/or Ciudad del Este, Paraguay, if you return the same day, although you should bring your passport. The same is true at the Bolivian border town of Villazón, near La Quiaca. Officials at the Paraguayan crossing at Encarnación, near Posadas (p214), have been known to extract cash 'fees' from crossers who don't have a Paraguayan visa (British, Australian, Canadian and US nationals need

them), assuming you stop or get stopped at the border.

Visa Extensions

For a 90-day extension on your tourist visa, visit the **Dirección Nacional de Migraciones** (Map pp84-5; immigration office; ☎ 011-4317-0200; Antártida Argentina 1355; ◷ 7:30am-1:30pm Mon-Fri) in Buenos Aires. You must do so during the week that your tourist visa is scheduled to expire. The fee is AR$100.

Another option if you're staying more than three months is to cross into Colonia or Montevideo (both in Uruguay) or into Chile for a day or two before your visa expires, then return with a new 90-day visa. However, this only works if you don't need a visa to enter the other country (Australians need visas for Uruguay).

VOLUNTEERING

Argentina isn't a hotbed for volunteerism, but there are some opportunities. Most Argentine NGOs provide volunteer opportunities for travelers, sometimes in the form of internships that can go towards tertiary degree credits. You can contact NGOs directly, or use the referral service provided by organizations such as the South American Explorers (see p95), which maintains a clubhouse in Buenos Aires, has excellent resources and catalogs volunteer ops throughout the country. Also check out **Help Argentina** (www.help argentina.org), which places volunteers in positions throughout the country. Although it charges a hefty placement fee, it also assists with language courses and housing. It waives the fee for people with special skills.

The **Foundation for Sustainable Development** (www.fsdinternational.org) also links volunteers up with local NGOs, while those interested in sustainable and organic farming can flex their muscles (and enjoy some free digs) with **Organic Volunteers** (www.organicvolunteers.org).

WOMEN TRAVELERS

Being a woman in Argentina is a challenge, especially if you are young, traveling alone and/or maintaining an inflexibly liberal attitude. In some ways Argentina is a safer place for a woman than Europe, the USA and most other Latin American countries, but dealing with this machismo culture can be a real pain in the ass.

Some males brimming with testosterone feel the need to comment on a woman's attractiveness. This often happens when the woman is alone and walking by on the street; it occasionally happens to two or more women walking together, but never to a heterosexual couple. Verbal comments include crude language, hisses, whistles and *piropos* (flirtatious comments), which many Argentine males consider an art of complimenting a woman. *Piropos* are often vulgar, although some can be creative and even eloquent. Much as you may want to kick them where it counts, the best thing to do is completely ignore the comments. After all, many *porteñas* (women from Buenos Aires) do enjoy getting these 'compliments,' and most men don't necessarily mean to be insulting; they're just doing what males in their culture are taught to do.

Another issue foreign women may find themselves struggling to come to terms with is the endless barrage – in advertising, news stands and signs – of select areas of the female anatomy. For many women, it gets old quick. Those who make a conscious effort to not let it bother them are least affected.

On the plus side of machismo, expect men to hold a door open for you and always let you enter first, including getting on buses; this gives you a better chance at grabbing an empty seat, so get in there quick.

WORK

Argentina is *very* short on jobs – many locals are unemployed or underemployed – and foreign travelers shouldn't expect to find any work other than teaching English. Working out of an institute, native English speakers (certified or not) can earn about AR$10 to AR$20 per hour, hardly a livable wage and definitely one that won't reap you any savings. When planning, you should take into account slow periods like January and February, when many locals leave town on vacation. Most teachers work 'illegally,' heading over to Uruguay every three months for a new visa.

Transportation

CONTENTS

Getting There & Away	**619**
Entering the Country	619
Air	619
Land	621
River	622
Sea	622
Getting Around	**623**
Air	623
Bicycle	623
Boat	625
Bus	625
Car & Motorcycle	626
Hitchhiking	628
Local Transportation	628
Train	629

GETTING THERE & AWAY

ENTERING THE COUNTRY

Entering Argentina is straightforward; immigration officials at airports are generally quick to the point and waste few words, while those at border crossings may take a little more time scrutinizing your passport before stamping it. Anyone entering the country is required to have a valid passport. Once you're in the country, police can still demand identification at any moment. It's a good idea to carry at least a photocopy of your passport around town at all times. For information on visa requirements, see p617.

When entering by air, you officially must have a return ticket, though this is rarely asked for once you're in Argentina. However, it is commonly asked for by the airline in the country of origin. Most airlines prohibit from boarding any passengers without proof of onward travel, regardless of whether the person was sold a one-way ticket or not. They do this because the airline would be responsible for flying you back home should you be denied entrance (which is highly unlikely) once you're in Argentina. For those planning to travel indefinitely, the only way out of this predicament is to buy a cheap, *fully refundable* onward flight (say, Mendoza to Santiago,

Chile) and either use it or get the refund once you're in Argentina. The refund, however, can take months to process.

AIR

Argentina has direct flights between countries including North America, the UK, Europe, Australia, New Zealand, Japan, Italy, Spain and South Africa, and from all South American countries except the Guianas. Alternatively, you can fly to a neighboring country, such as Chile or Brazil, and continue overland to Argentina.

Airports & Airlines

Aerolíneas Argentinas, the national carrier, enjoys a good reputation for its international flights (although it's national flights are notoriously prone to delay; see p623). Except for flights from Santiago, Chile to Mendoza or Córdoba nearly all international flights arrive at Buenos Aires' **Aeropuerto Internacional Ministro Pistarini** (Ezeiza; ☎ 011-5480-6111, tourist information 011-4480-0224), which is about a 40-minute bus or cab ride out of town. Airports in several provincial capitals and tourist destinations are earmarked as 'international': this usually means they receive flights from neighboring countries. Basic information on most Argentine airports can be found online at **Aeropuertos Argentina 2000** (www.aa2000.com.ar in Spanish). Airports include the following:

Bariloche (code BRC; ☎ 02944-422767)
Córdoba (code COR; ☎ 0351-475-0392)
El Calafate (code ECA; ☎ 02902-491-220/30)
Jujuy (code JUJ; ☎ 0388-491-1102)

THINGS CHANGE...

The information in this chapter is particularly vulnerable to change. Check directly with the airline or a travel agent to make sure you understand how a fare (and ticket you may buy) works and be aware of the security requirements for international travel. Shop carefully. The details given in this chapter should be regarded as pointers and are not a substitute for your own careful, up-to-date research.

Mendoza (code MDZ; ☎ 0261-448-2603)
Puerto Iguazú (code IGR; ☎ 03757-420595)
Río Gallegos (code RGL; ☎ 02966-442340/4)
Rosario (code ROS; ☎ 0341-451-2997)
Salta (code SLA; ☎ 0387-424-2904)
San Juan (code UAQ; ☎ 0264-425-4133)
Tucumán (code TUC; ☎ 0381-426-4906)
Ushuaia (code USH; ☎ 0291-424422)

AIRLINES FLYING TO & FROM ARGENTINA

The following airlines fly to and from Argentina and are listed here with their telephone numbers in Argentina; all numbers that aren't toll-free are Buenos Aires numbers.

Aerolíneas Argentinas (code ARG; ☎ 0810-222-86527; www.aerolineas.com)

AeroSur (code ASU; ☎ 011-4516-0999; www.aerosur.com)

Air Canada (code ACA; ☎ 011- 4327-3640/44; www.aircanada.ca)

Air France (code AFR; ☎ 011-4317-4700/11/22; www.airfrance.com)

Alitalia (code AZA; ☎ 0810-777-2548, 011-4310-9970; www.alitalia.com)

American Airlines (code AAL; ☎ 011-4318-1111; www.aa.com)

Avianca (code AVA; ☎ 011-4322-2731; www.avianca.com)

British Airways (code BA; ☎ 0800-666-1459; www.britishairways.com)

Continental (code COA; ☎ 0800-333-0425; www.continental.com)

Copa (code CMP; ☎ 0810-222-2672; www.copaair.com)

Delta (code DAL; ☎ 0800-666-0133; www.delta.com)

Gol (code GLO; ☎ 0810-266-3232; www.voegol.com.br)

KLM (code KLM; ☎ 0800-222-2600, 011-4326-8422; www.klm.com)

LAN Airlines (code LAN; ☎ 011-4378-2222; www.lan.com)

Líneas Aéreas del Estado (LADE) (code LDE; ☎ 0810-810-5233, 011-5129-9000; www.lade.com.ar)

Lloyd Aéreo Boliviano (code LAB; ☎ 011-4323-1900/05; www.labairlines.com)

Lufthansa (code DLH; ☎ 011-4319-0600; www.lufthansa.com)

Pluna (code PUA; ☎ 011-4120-0530; www.pluna.com.uy)

Qantas Airways (code QFA; ☎ 011-4144-5800; www.qantas.com)

TACA (code TAI; ☎ 0810-333-8222; www.taca.com)

Transportes Aéreos de Mercosur (code TAM; ☎ 0810-333-3333; www.tam.com.py)

United Airlines (code UAL; ☎ 0810-777-8648; www.united.com.ar)

Varig (code VRG; ☎ 0810-266-6874; www.varig.com.br)

Tickets

From almost everywhere, South America is a relatively costly destination, but discount fares can reduce the bite considerably. Contacting a travel agency that specializes in Latin American destinations often turns up the cheapest fares.

INTERCONTINENTAL (RTW) TICKETS

Some of the best deals for travelers visiting many countries on different continents are Round-the-World (RTW) tickets. Itineraries from the USA, Europe or Australia usually include five or six stopovers (including Buenos Aires). Similar 'Circle Pacific' fares allow excursions between Australasia and South America. These types of tickets are certain to have restrictions, so check the fine print carefully. For an idea of the varying fares and itinerary policies for both types of tickets, check out the following sites.

Airtreks (www.airtreks.com) US based.
Air Brokers International (www.airbrokers.com) US based.
Bridge the World (www.bridgetheworld.com) UK based.
One World (www.oneworld.com) US based.
Round the World Flights (www.roundtheworldflights.com) UK based.

Australia & New Zealand

Qantas flies direct to Santiago, Chile, making the connection to Buenos Aires in conjunction with Aerolíneas Argentinas or LanChile. Aerolíneas Argentinas flies direct to Buenos Aires from Sydney and Auckland. Yet another way to get to Buenos Aires is to travel via the USA (Los Angeles, Dallas or Miami) with either American Airlines or United Airlines, but it's a much longer flight.

Canada

Air Canada operates the only nonstop flight from Canada to Buenos Aires, which leaves from Toronto. Booking flights with connec-

---

DEPARTURE TAX

Departure taxes on international flights out of Argentina are generally *not* included in the price of your ticket. Make sure you ask. If the departure tax is not included, you must pay it in Argentine pesos ($54) or US dollars (US$18) after check-in and have the tax sticker placed on your ticket.

CLIMATE CHANGE & TRAVEL

Climate change is a serious threat to the ecosystems that humans rely upon, and air travel is the fastest-growing contributor to the problem. Lonely Planet regards travel, overall, as a global benefit, but believes we all have a responsibility to limit our personal impact on global warming.

Flying & Climate Change

Pretty much every form of motorized travel generates CO_2 (the main cause of human-induced climate change) but planes are far and away the worst offenders, not just because of the sheer distances they allow us to travel, but because they release greenhouse gases high into the atmosphere. The statistics are frightening: two people taking a return flight between Europe and the US will contribute as much to climate change as an average household's gas and electricity consumption over a whole year.

Carbon Offset Schemes

Climatecare.org and other websites use 'carbon calculators' that allow travelers to offset the level of greenhouse gases they are responsible for with financial contributions to sustainable travel schemes that reduce global warming – including projects in India, Honduras, Kazakhstan and Uganda.

Lonely Planet, together with Rough Guides and other concerned partners in the travel industry, support the carbon offset scheme run by climatecare.org. Lonely Planet offsets all of its staff and author travel.

For more information check out our website: www.lonelyplanet.com.

---

tions through a US carrier (such as American Airlines and Continental via New York, Miami or Los Angeles) may offer more flexibility.

Continental Europe

To Buenos Aires, there are direct flights from Paris (with Air France or Aerolíneas Argentinas), Madrid (with Aerolíneas Argentinas) and Frankfurt (with Lufthansa). Flights from other European countries are usually to Sao Paolo, Brazil or Santiago, Chile. You may be able to purchase a connection through to Buenos Aires if the airline works in conjunction with a South American airline that flies to the Argentine capital.

South America

Buenos Aires is well connected to most other capital cities in Latin America. Prices range from a US$120 one-way hop to/from Montevideo, Uruguay, to a US$450 flight to/from La Paz, Bolivia or Quito, Ecuador. The Bolivian airline, AeroSur, flies between Santa Cruz, Bolivia, and the northwest Argentine cities of Tucumán, Salta and Jujuy.

UK & Ireland

Direct services to Buenos Aires are available with Aerolíneas Argentinas and many other airlines. Varig has connections via Rio de Janeiro and São Paulo. **Journey Latin America** (☎ in UK 020-8747 3108, in Ireland 1800 818 126; www .journeylatinamerica.co.uk) specializes in travel to Latin America and is a good place to start your inquiries.

USA

The principal gateways are Miami, Dallas, New York, Los Angeles and, since 2007, Chicago. Aerolíneas Argentinas, Delta, American Airlines and United fly to Buenos Aires. Latin American travel specialist **eXito Travel** (☎ in US 800-655-4053; www.exitotravel.com) offers some of the cheapest fares around as well as personal service (such as flight changes from abroad, travel recommendations and more) from an impressively well-informed staff.

LAND
Border Crossings

There are numerous border crossings from neighboring Chile, Bolivia, Paraguay, Brazil and Uruguay; the following lists are only the principal crossings. Generally, border formalities are straightforward as long as all your documents are in order. For info on necessary visas and documents, see p617.

Current weather conditions, hours of service and other useful information for Argentina's border crossings are provided online by the **Gendarmería Nacional de Argentina** (www.gendarmeria.gov. ar/pasos/pasos1.htm).

BOLIVIA
La Quiaca to Villazón Many buses go from Jujuy and Salta to La Quiaca, where you must walk or take a taxi across the Bolivian border.
Aguas Blancas to Bermejo From Orán, reached by bus from Salta or Jujuy, take a bus to Aguas Blancas and then Bermejo, where you can catch a bus to Tarija.
Pocitos to Yacuiba Buses from Jujuy or Salta go to Tartagal and then on to the Bolivian border at Pocitos/Yacuiba, where there are buses to Santa Cruz.

BRAZIL
The most common crossing is from Puerto Iguazú (p225) to Foz do Iguaçu (p229). Check both cities for more information on the peculiarities of this border crossing, especially if you're crossing the border into Brazil only to see the other side of Iguazú Falls. For specifics, see the boxed text on p226. There are also border crossings from Paso de los Libres (Argentina; p212) to Uruguaiana (Brazil) to São Borja (Brazil).

CHILE
There are numerous crossings between Argentina and Chile. Except in far southern Patagonia, every land crossing involves crossing the Andes. Due to weather, some high-altitude passes close in winter; even the busy Mendoza–Santiago route over RN 7 can close for several days (sometimes longer) during a severe storm. Always check road conditions, especially if you have a flight scheduled on the other side of the mountains. The following are the most commonly used crossings.
Salta to San Pedro de Atacama (via Purmamarca) Twelve-hour bus ride through the altiplano with stunningly beautiful scenery.
Mendoza to Santiago The most popular crossing between the two countries, passing 6962m Aconcagua en route.
Bariloche to Puerto Montt The famous, scenic 12-hour bus-boat combination runs over the Andes to Chile. Takes two days in winter. See p414.
Los Antiguos to Chile Chico Those entering from Chile can access the rugged RN 40 from here and head down to El Chaltén and El Calafate. Best in summer, when there's actually public transport available.
El Calafate to Puerto Natales & Parque Nacional Torres del Paine Probably the most beaten route down here, heading from the Glaciar Perito Moreno (near El Calafate) to Parque Nacional Torres del Paine (near Puerto

Natales). Several buses per day in summer; one to two daily in the off-season.
Ushuaia to Punta Arenas Daily buses in summer, fewer in winter, on this 12- to 18-hour trip (depending on weather conditions), which includes a ferry crossing at either Porvenir or Punta Delgada/Primera Angostura.

URUGUAY & PARAGUAY
There are two direct border crossings between Argentina and Paraguay: Clorinda (p241) to Asunción, and Posadas (p214) to Encarnación. From Puerto Iguazú, Argentina, you can also cross through Brazil into Ciudad del Este, Paraguay.

Border crossings from Argentine cities to Uruguayan cities include Gualeguaychú (p204) to Fray Bentos; Colón (p208) to Paysandú; and Concordia (p210) to Salto. All involve crossing bridges. Buses from Buenos Aires to Montevideo and other waterfront cities, however, are slower and less convenient than the ferries (or ferry–bus combinations) across the Río de la Plata (see below). The crossings at Gualeguaychú and Paysandú may be closed due to conflict surrounding the construction of a pulp mill on the Uruguayan side of the river. For more information, see the boxed text, p543.

Bus
Travelers can bus to Argentina from most bordering countries. Buses are usually comfortable, modern and fairly clean. Crossing over does not involve too many hassles; just make sure that you have any proper visas (p617) beforehand.

RIVER
There are several river crossings between Uruguay and Buenos Aires that involve ferry or hydrofoil, and often require combinations with buses.
Buenos Aires to Montevideo High-speed ferries carry passengers from downtown Buenos Aires to the Uruguayan capital in only 2¾ hours. See p560.
Buenos Aires to Colonia Daily ferries (50 minutes to three hours) head to Colonia, with bus connections to Montevideo (additional three hours). See p566.
Tigre to Carmelo Regular passenger launches speed from the Buenos Aires suburb of Tigre to Carmelo (services also go to Montevideo from Tigre). See p568.

SEA
Arriving in Argentina by sea is uncommon indeed, although Chilean company **Navimag**

(www.navimag.com) operates the famous ferry from Puerto Montt, Chile (near Bariloche), down the length of Chilean Patagonia to Puerto Natales, Chile, near Parque Nacional Torres del Paine (due west of Río Gallegos).

GETTING AROUND

AIR

Airlines in Argentina

The national carrier, **Aerolíneas Argentinas/ Austral** (☎ 0810-222-86527; www.aerolineas.com), offers the most domestic flights, but it's not necessarily better than its competitors. In fact, the airline's reputation for delays has gotten so bad that you should never rely on an Aerolíneas Argentinas flight to make a connection. Aerolíneas also maintains a two-tier pricing system: only residents qualify for the cheapest tickets. Other airlines with domestic flights are **LanChile** (LAN; ☎ 011-4378-2222; www.lan.com) and **Líneas Aéreas del Estado** (LADE; ☎ 011-5129-9001; www.lade.com.ar), the air force's passenger service. The latter has some of the least expensive air tickets (probably because its offices still have the same decor they did in 1974) and specializes in Patagonia.

One way to avoid the higher fee Aerolíneas Argentinas charges foreigners is by taking advantage of the discounted airfares the airline offers to those who fly to Argentina with Aerolíneas. However, you must purchase these tickets from outside Argentina, usually at the time of purchasing your international flight. The promotion is most convenient for travelers who can set their schedule prior to visiting the country.

A new airline, **AirPampas**, was set to begin service on the eve of this book's publication. There was no website at the time, but it's worth checking into for competitive rates. Other domestic airlines open and close with surprising frequency (Southern Winds and American Falcon are both gone), so always do a little research.

Nearly all domestic flights (except for LADE's hops around Patagonia) have connections only through **Aeroparque Jorge Newbery** (☎ 011-5480-6111; www.aa2000.com.ar), a short distance from downtown Buenos Aires. Flying with certain airlines on certain flights can be financially comparable or even cheaper than covering the same distance by bus, but demand is heavy and flights, especially to Patagonian destinations in summer, are often booked well in advance.

BICYCLE

If you dig cycling your way around a country, Argentina has some good potential. It will also save you some money: partnered with camping, cycling can cut the costs of your trip significantly. And of course you'll see the landscape in greater detail, you'll have far greater freedom than you would if beholden to public transportation, and you'll likely meet more locals.

Road bikes are suitable for many paved roads, but these byways are often narrow, and surfaces can be rough. A *todo terreno* (mountain bike) is often safer and more convenient, allowing you to use the unpaved shoulder and the very extensive network of graveled roads throughout the country. Argentine bicycles are improving in quality but are still far from equal to their counterparts in Europe or the USA.

There are two major drawbacks to long-distance bicycling in Argentina. One is the wind, which in Patagonia can slow your progress to a crawl. The other is Argentine motorists: on many of the country's straight, narrow, two-lane highways, they can be a serious hazard to cyclists. Make yourself as visible as possible, and wear a helmet.

Bring an adequate repair kit and extra parts (and the know-how to use them), and stock up on good maps (see p611), which is usually easier to do once you're in Argentina (there are plenty of places to get good maps in Buenos Aires). Even if you have 10 maps for a region, always confirm directions and inquire about conditions locally; maps can be unreliable, and conditions change regularly. In Patagonia, a windbreaker and warm clothing are essential. Don't expect much traffic on some back roads.

For ideas on where you might want to ride, see p74.

Purchase

Many towns have bike shops, but high-quality bikes are expensive, and repair parts can be hard to come by. If you do decide to buy while you're here, you're best off doing so in Buenos Aires. Selection in other major cities – even Córdoba and Mendoza – is pretty slim, and prices for an imported bike (which you'll want if you're doing serious cycling) are much

DOMESTIC AIR ROUTES

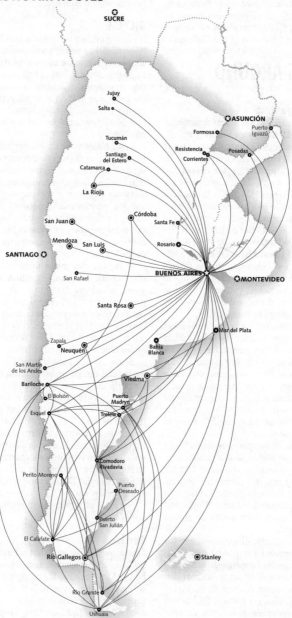

higher than in their country of origin. If you're staying for a while and you just need a bike for tooling around the city, you'll find Argentine bikes are great value. You can pick up a beach cruiser for under AR$300, and a multi-speed townie won't cost much more.

Rental

Reasonable bicycle rentals (mostly mountain bikes) are available in many popular tourist destinations, such as Mendoza, Bariloche and other towns throughout the Lake District and Córdoba's Central Sierras. Prices are affordable, setting renters back no more than AR$10 per hour.

BOAT

Opportunities for boat or river travel in and around Argentina are limited, though there are regular international services to/from Uruguay (see p600) and to/from Chile via the Lake District (see p413). The classic sea route south along the Patagonian Andes is the Navimag boat trip (see p622); although the journey is in Chile, many people combine the trip with a visit to Argentina. Further south, from Ushuaia, operators offer sailing trips on the Beagle Channel in Tierra del Fuego; see p528.

Otherwise, if you must be on the water, head to the Buenos Aires suburb of Tigre (p136), where there are numerous boat excursions around the delta of the Río de la Plata.

BUS

If you're doing any serious traveling around Argentina, you'll become very familiar with the country's excellent bus network, which reaches almost everywhere. Buses are fast, surprisingly comfortable and can be a rather luxurious experience. It's the way most Argentines get around. Larger luggage is stowed in the hold below, security is generally good (especially on the first-class buses) and attendants always tag your bags (and should be tipped). If you have a long way to go – say Buenos Aires to Mendoza – overnight buses are the way to go, saving you a night's accommodations and the daylight hours for fun.

Hundreds of bus companies serve different regions but a few bigger lines (listed here) really dominate the long-haul business.

Andesmar (☎ 0261-412-2710, 011-6385-3031; www .andesmar.com in Spanish) Serves the entire country.

Chevallier (☎ 011-4016-7000; www.nuevachevallier .com in Spanish) Serves the entire country.

El Rápido International (☎ 011-4313-3757, 011-4315-0804; www.elrapidoint.com.ar in Spanish) Buenos Aires, Mendoza, Córdoba, Rosario. International service to Santiago and Viña del Mar, Chile, and Lima, Peru.

Via Bariloche (☎ 0800-333-7575; www.viabariloche .com.ar) Serves most destinations in La Pampa province, the Lake District and Patagonia.

Most cities and towns have a central bus terminal where each company has its own ticket window. Some companies post fares and schedules prominently, and the ticket price and departure time is always on the ticket you buy. Expect (Argentine) fast-food stalls, kiosks and newspaper vendors inside or near almost every terminal. There are generally few hotel touts or other traveler-hassling types at terminals.

Classes

This is where it gets fun. Better bus lines such as Chevallier and Andesmar (not to mention dozens of others) have modern Mercedes or Volvo coaches with spacious, cushy leather seats, large windows, air-conditioning, toilets, TVs and sometimes an attendant serving coffee and snacks. Spend a little money and you'll be playing bingo for wine as you roll across the pampas (no kidding!).

On overnight trips it's well worth the extra AR$20 to AR$50 to go *coche cama* (sleeper class), though the cheaper *coche semi-cama* (semisleeper) is definitely manageable. In *coche cama,* seats are wider, recline almost flat and are far more comfortable. If you want to lay totally flat, you can go *ejecutivo* (executive) or *coche super cama* (supersleeper), which is available on a few popular runs such as Buenos Aires–Córdoba or Buenos Aires–Rosario. If pinching pesos, *común* (common) is the cheapest class. For trips under about five hours, there's usually no choice and buses are *común* or beat-up *semi-cama,* which are both usually just fine.

Costs

Bus fares vary widely depending on season, class and company, and can cost anywhere from about AR$6 to AR$8 per hour on *común* or *semi-cama,* to AR$9 to AR$11 for *coche cama*. Prices given in the Getting There & Away sections throughout this book are approximate and are mid- to high-season fares, generally in *semi-cama*. Patagonia runs tend to be the most expensive. Many

TRANSPORTATION

TRANSPORTATION

companies accept credit cards. Following are sample fares from Buenos Aires.

Destination	Cost (AR$)
Bariloche	180
Comodoro Rivadavia	189
Córdoba	75-100
Mar del Plata	65
Mendoza	100-140
Puerto Iguazú	110-175
Puerto Madryn	180-210
Rosario	35-40

Reservations

Often you don't need to buy bus tickets ahead of time unless you're traveling on a Friday between major cities, when overnight *coche cama* services sell out fast. During holiday stretches such as late December, January, July and August, tickets sell quickly, so you're best off buying yours ahead of time. As soon as you arrive somewhere, especially if it's a town with limited services, find out which companies go to your next destination and when, and plan your trip out around that.

Seasonal Services

In the Lake District and northern Patagonia, bus services are outstanding during summer (November through March), when there are many microbus routes to campgrounds, along lake circuits, to trail heads and to other destinations popular with tourists. Outside summer, however, these services stop, and getting around becomes much more difficult.

In Patagonia the famed stretch of RN 40, or *Ruta Cuarenta* (Route Forty), south of Gobernador Costa, is infrequently traveled, rough and blessed with zero public transport – well, almost. Recently, several businesses have sprung up offering seasonal service (really they're just microbus tours) along the route. For more information, see p470.

CAR & MOTORCYCLE

Because Argentina is so large, many parts are accessible only by private vehicle, despite the country's extensive public transport system. This is especially true in Patagonia, where distances are great and buses can be infrequent. Besides, with your own wheels, you can stop for photo ops or bathroom breaks at the side of the road whenever you want.

Although motorbikes have become fashionable among some Argentines, they are very expensive, and there appears to be no motorcycle-rental agencies in Argentina.

Automobile Associations

Whenever driving in Argentina, it's worth being a member – in fact, you may *already* be a member – of the **Automóvil Club Argentino** (ACA; Map pp88-9; ☎ 011-4802-6061; www.aca.org.ar in Spanish; Av del Libertador 1850, Palermo, Buenos Aires), which has offices, service stations and garages throughout the country, offering free **road service** (☎ 0800-888-84253) and towing in and around major destinations. ACA recognizes members of most overseas auto clubs and grants them privileges, including road service and discounts on maps and accommodations. Bring your card. Otherwise ACA membership costs AR$55 per month.

Bring Your Own Vehicle

Chile is probably the best country on the continent for shipping a vehicle from overseas, though Argentina is feasible. Getting the vehicle out of customs typically involves routine but time consuming paperwork.

Driver's License & Documents

Technically you're supposed to have an international driving permit to supplement your national or state driver's license. If you are stopped, police will inspect your automobile registration and insurance and tax documents, all of which must be up to date. Except in Buenos Aires, security problems are few.

Drivers of Argentine vehicles must carry their title document (*tarjeta verde* or 'green card'); if it's a rental, make sure it's in the glove box. For foreign vehicles, customs permission is the acceptable substitute. Liability insurance is obligatory, and police often ask to see proof of insurance at checkpoints.

Fuel & Spare Parts

Nafta (gas) costs roughly AR$1.90 to AR$2.50 per liter depending on the grade you choose. *Normal* or *común* (regular) is about 86 octane, while super is 96 octane, and *premium* (often called Fangio) runs about 97.5 octane. In Patagonia (where much of Argentina's oil fields are) gas prices are nearly half what they are elsewhere. *Estaciones de servicio* (gas stations) are fairly common (especially YPFs), but outside the cities keep an eye on your gas gauge. In Patagonia it's a good idea to carry extra fuel. Tolls on privatized highways cost on average AR$2 per 100km.

Insurance

Liability insurance is obligatory in Argentina, and police ask to see proof of insurance at checkpoints. Fortunately, coverage is reasonably priced. Insuring a US$20,000 car with basic liability insurance costs about AR$250 per month. The cost is lower, of course, if you have an older vehicle. If you plan on taking the car to neighboring countries, make sure it will remain covered (you'll have to pay extra). Among reputable insurers in Argentina are **Mapfre** (☎ 0800-999-7424; www.mapfre.com.ar in Spanish) and the **ACA** (☎ 011-4802-6061; www.aca.org.ar in Spanish).

Purchase

If you are spending several months in Argentina, purchasing a car is an alternative worth exploring. If you resell the car at the end of your stay, it may turn out even more economical. On the other hand, any used car can be a risk, especially on Patagonia's rugged back roads, and the process of purchasing a car can be a real headache.

If you buy a car, you must deal with the exasperating Argentine bureaucracy. You must have the title *(tarjeta verde),* and license tax payments must be up to date. As a foreigner, you may find it useful to carry a notarized document authorizing your use of the car, since the bureaucracy moves too slowly to change the title easily. Argentines themselves rarely change the title over because of the expense involved.

As a foreigner you may own a vehicle in Argentina but, in theory at least, you may not take it out of the country (even to Chile) without a notarized authorization, which can be nearly impossible to obtain. Dependable used cars rarely cost under AR$10,000.

Rental

Renting a car in Argentina, if you can cough up the cash, is well worth it because it allows you the freedom to go and stop wherever you please and to visit those backcountry places that buses don't. The best deals are almost always with the locally owned agencies (when you can find them) rather than the ever-present international ones. To rent a car, you must be at least 21 years of age and have a valid driver's license and a credit card. To

ROAD DISTANCES (KM)

	Buenos Aires	Córdoba	Corrientes	Formosa	Jujuy	La Rioja	Mendoza	Neuquén	Resistencia	Río Gallegos	Salta	San Juan	San Luis	Tucumán
Córdoba	715													
Corrientes	1025	900												
Formosa	1190	1045	190											
Jujuy	1545	930	885	960										
La Rioja	1150	435	995	1135	770									
Mendoza	1050	670	1565	1656	1345	615								
Neuquén	1158	1137	2046	2060	2200	1470	855							
Resistencia	1023	875	23	170	860	970	1587	2012						
Río Gallegos	2635	3635	3365	3550	3565	3070	2800	1930	3390					
Salta	1510	897	805	948	340	695	1227	2082	780	3530				
San Juan	1110	500	1395	1545	1220	450	165	1020	1420	2860	1145			
San Luis	850	455	1320	1465	1320	550	260	885	1295	2540	1245	320		
Tucumán	1205	590	790	936	340	388	1005	1860	765	3225	307	840	505	
Ushuaia	3171	3228	3960	4150	4155	3665	3393	2353	3983	595	4125	3455	3135	3820

drive you must have an international driving permit, but renters rarely ask for this.

The cheapest and smallest vehicles cost anywhere from AR$150 to AR$170 per day with 150km to 200km included. Although unlimited-kilometer deals do exist, they are much more expensive. A 4WD vehicle is significantly more expensive. One of the cheapest places to rent a car is Bariloche; if you're heading down to Patagonia or plan to drive for a while, this is a good place to rent. Reserving a car with one of the major international agencies in your home country sometimes gets you lower rates.

Road Rules & Hazards

Anyone considering driving in Argentina should know that Argentine drivers are aggressive and commonly ignore speed limits, road signs and even traffic signals. That said, once you're out of the city, driving is a joy.

Though most Argentine highways have a speed limit of 80km/h, and some have been raised to 100km/h or more, hardly anybody pays attention to these – or any other regulations. During the pampas harvest season, pay particular attention to slow-moving farm machinery, which, though not a hazard in its own right, brings out the worst in impatient Argentine motorists. Night driving is not recommended; in many regions animals hang out on the road for warmth, and plowing into an Argentine cow is not fun.

Have on hand some emergency reflectors *(balizas)*, and a 1kg fire extinguisher. Headrests are required for the driver and passengers, and seatbelts are now obligatory (though few people wear them). Motorcycle helmets are also obligatory, although this law is rarely enforced.

You won't often see police patrolling the highways, but you will meet them at major intersections and roadside checkpoints where they conduct meticulous document and equipment checks. Equipment violations can carry heavy fines, but such checks are more commonly pretexts for graft. For instance, if the police ask to check your turn signals (which almost no Argentine bothers to use), brake lights or hand brake, it may well be a warning of corruption in progress. The police may claim that you must pay the fine at a local bank, which may not be open until the following day, or if it's on a weekend, until Monday. If you are uncertain about your rights, state in a very matter-of-fact manner your intention to contact your embassy or consulate, or feign such complete ignorance of Spanish that you're more trouble than the police think it's worth. It may be possible to pay the fine on the spot (wink, wink). Ask, *'¿Puedo pagar la multa ahora?'* ('Can I pay the fine right now?').

HITCHHIKING

Hitchhiking is never entirely safe in any country in the world. Travelers who decide to hitch should understand that they are taking a small but potentially serious risk. People who do choose to hitch will be safer if they travel in pairs and let someone know where they are planning to go.

Along with Chile, Argentina is probably the best country for hitching in all of South America. The major drawback is that Argentine vehicles are often stuffed full with families and children, but truckers will frequently pick up backpackers. At the *estaciones de servicio* (gas stations) at the outskirts of large Argentine cities, where truckers gas up their vehicles, it's often easy to solicit a ride.

Women can and do hitchhike alone, but should exercise caution and especially avoid getting into a car with more than one man. In Patagonia, where distances are great and vehicles few, hitchers should expect long waits and carry warm, windproof clothing.

There are a few routes along which hitching is undesirable. RN 40, from El Calafate to Perito Moreno and Río Mayo, is one. Up north, the scenic route from Tucumán to Cafayate is difficult past Tafí del Valle. Throughout the Lake District, hitching is common, especially out in the country where locals regularly get around by thumbing it.

LOCAL TRANSPORTATION
Bus

Local Argentine buses, called *colectivos*, are notorious for charging down the street, gobbling up coins and spewing clouds of black smoke while traveling at breakneck speeds. Riding on one is a good way to see the cities and get around, providing you can sort out the often complex bus systems. Buses are clearly numbered and usually carry a placard indicating their final destination. Since many identically numbered buses serve slightly different routes (especially in bigger cities), pay attention to these placards. To ask 'Does this bus go (to the town center)?' say *'¿Va este colectivo (al centro)?'*

Most city buses operate on coins; you pay as you board. In some cities, such as Mendoza, you must buy prepaid bus cards or – in the case of Córdoba – *cospeles* (tokens). In both cases, they can be bought at any kiosk.

Subway

Buenos Aires is the only Argentine city with a subway system (known as the Subte), and it's the quickest way of getting around the city center. For details, see p134.

Taxi & Remise

The people of Buenos Aires make frequent use of taxis, which are digitally metered and, compared to the US and Europe, cheap. Outside Buenos Aires, meters are common but not universal, and it may be necessary to agree upon a fare in advance. Drivers are generally polite and honest, but there are exceptions; be sure the meter is set at zero, and be sure it's on. Also be sure to read it closely: tagging an extra zero on to the end is not unheard of. It is customary to round up the fare as a tip.

Where public transportation can be scarce, it's possible to hire a cab with a driver for the day to visit places off the beaten track. If you bargain, this can actually be cheaper than a rental car, but negotiate the fee in advance.

Remises are radio taxis without meters that generally offer fixed fares within a given zone. They are usually cheaper than taxis. They don't cruise the city in search of fares, as taxis do, but hotels and restaurants will phone them for you if you ask.

TRAIN

Despite major reductions in long-distance train service, rail lines continue to serve most of the Buenos Aires suburbs and some surrounding provinces. There are longer rail services between Buenos Aires and the towns of Posadas and Córdoba. During the holiday periods like Christmas or national holidays, buy tickets in advance. Train fares tend to be lower than comparable bus fares, but trains are slower and there are fewer departure times and destinations.

Train buffs will want to take the narrow-gauge La Trochita (see the boxed text, p468), which runs from Esquel to El Maitén. Another legendary ride is Salta's spectacular Tren a las Nubes (Train to the Clouds; p269), but service is extremely sporadic. A scenic stretch of track (and luxurious service aboard the Tren Patagónico) also connects the Lake District hub of Bariloche (p414) to Viedma (p430), on the Atlantic coast of Patagonia.

Health Dr David Goldberg

CONTENTS

Medically speaking, there are two South Americas: tropical South America, which includes most of the continent except for the southernmost portion, and temperate South America, which includes Chile, Uruguay, southern Argentina and the Falkland Islands. The diseases found in tropical South America are comparable to those found in tropical areas in Africa and Asia. Particularly important are mosquito-borne infections, including malaria, yellow fever and dengue fever, which are not a significant concern in temperate regions.

Prevention is the key to staying healthy in Argentina. Travelers who receive the recommended vaccines and follow common-sense precautions usually come away with nothing more than a little diarrhea.

BEFORE YOU GO

Bring medication in its original, clearly labeled container. A signed, dated letter from your physician describing your medical conditions and medications, including generic names, is also a good idea. If carrying syringes or needles, be sure to have a physician's letter documenting their medical necessity.

INSURANCE

If your health insurance doesn't cover you for medical expenses abroad, consider getting extra insurance. Find out in advance if your insurance plan will make payments directly to providers or reimburse you later for overseas health expenditures. (In many countries doctors expect payment in cash.)

MEDICAL CHECKLIST

- acetaminophen (Tylenol) or aspirin
- adhesive or paper tape
- antibacterial ointment (eg Bactroban; for cuts and abrasions)
- antibiotics
- antidiarrheal drugs (eg loperamide)
- antihistamines (for hay fever and allergic reactions)
- anti-inflammatory drugs (eg ibuprofen)
- bandages, gauze, gauze rolls
- DEET-containing insect repellent for the skin
- iodine tablets (for water purification)
- oral rehydration salts
- permethrin-containing insect spray for clothing, tents and bed nets
- pocket knife
- scissors, safety pins, tweezers
- steroid cream or cortisone (for poison ivy and other allergic rashes)
- sunblock
- syringes and sterile needles
- thermometer

INTERNET RESOURCES

There is a wealth of travel health advice on the Internet. For further info, the **Lonely Planet website** (www.lonelyplanet.com) is a good place to start. The **World Health Organization** (www.who.int/ith) publishes a superb book called *International Travel and Health*, which is revised annually and is available online at no cost. Another website of general interest is **MD Travel Health** (www.mdtravelhealth.com), which provides complete travel-health recommendations for every country and is updated daily.

It's usually a good idea to consult your government's travel health website before departure, if one is available:

Australia www.smartraveller.gov.au
Canada www.hc-sc.gc.ca/english/index.html
UK www.doh.gov.uk/traveladvice
US www.cdc.gov/travel

RECOMMENDED VACCINATIONS

Since most vaccines don't produce immunity until at least two weeks after they're given, visit a physician four to eight weeks before departure. No vaccines are required for Argentina, but a number are recommended.

Vaccine	Recommended For	Dosage	Side Effects
chickenpox	travelers who've never had chickenpox	2 doses 1 month apart	fever; mild case of chickenpox
hepatitis A	all travelers	1 dose before trip; booster 6-12 months later	soreness at injection site; headaches; body aches
hepatitis B	long-term travelers in close contact with the local population	3 doses over 6-month period	soreness at injection site; low-grade fever
measles	travelers who have never had measles or completed a vaccination course	1 dose	fever; rash; joint pains; allergic reactions
rabies	travelers who may have contact with animals and may not have access to medical care	3 doses over 3-4 week period	soreness at injection site; headaches; body aches
tetanus	all travelers who haven't had booster within 10 years	1 dose lasts 10 years diphtheria	soreness at injection site
typhoid	all travelers	4 capsules by mouth, 1 taken every other day	abdominal pain; nausea; rash
yellow fever	travelers to the northeastern forest areas	1 dose lasts 10 years	headaches; body aches; severe reactions are rare

FURTHER READING

For further information, see Lonely Planet's *Healthy Travel Central & South America*. If you're traveling with children, Lonely Planet's *Travel with Children* may be useful. The *ABC of Healthy Travel*, by E Walker et al, is another valuable resource.

IN TRANSIT

DEEP VEIN THROMBOSIS (DVT)

Blood clots may form in the legs (deep vein thrombosis or DVT) during plane flights, chiefly because of prolonged immobility. The longer the flight, the greater the risk. Though most blood clots are reabsorbed uneventfully, some may break off and travel through the blood vessels to the lungs, where they could cause life-threatening complications.

The chief symptom of DVT is swelling or pain of the foot, ankle or calf, usually – but not always – on just one side. When a blood clot travels to the lungs, it may cause chest pain and difficulty breathing. Travelers with any of these symptoms should immediately seek medical attention.

To prevent the development of DVT on long flights, you should walk about the cabin, perform isometric contractions of the leg muscles (ie flex the leg muscles while sitting), drink plenty of fluids and avoid alcohol and tobacco.

JET LAG & MOTION SICKNESS

Jet lag is common when crossing more than five time zones, resulting in insomnia, fatigue, malaise or nausea. To avoid jet lag try drinking plenty of (nonalcoholic) fluids and eating light meals. Upon arrival, get exposure to natural sunlight and readjust your schedule (for meals, sleep etc) as soon as possible.

Antihistamines such as dimenhydrinate (Dramamine) and meclizine (Antivert, Bonine) are usually the first choice for treating motion sickness. Their main side effect is drowsiness. An herbal alternative is ginger, which works like a charm for some people.

IN ARGENTINA

AVAILABILITY & COST OF HEALTH CARE

Good medical care is available in Buenos Aires but may be variable elsewhere, especially in rural areas. Most doctors and hospitals expect payment in cash, regardless of whether you have travel health insurance.

HEALTH

The US Embassy website at http://usem bassy.state.gov/posts/ar1/wwwhdoctors.html has an extensive list of physicians, dentists, hospitals and emergency services. If you're pregnant, be sure to check this site before departure to find the name of one or two obstetricians in the area you'll be visiting.

If you develop a life-threatening medical problem, you'll probably want to be evacuated to a country with state-of-the-art medical care. (For an ambulance, call ☎ 107.) Since this may cost thousands of dollars, be sure you have insurance to cover this before you depart. You can find a list of medical evacuation and travel-insurance companies on the US State Department website at www.travel.state.gov/medical.html.

Most pharmacies in Argentina are well supplied. Many medications that require a prescription in the USA and Canada are available over the counter, though they may be relatively expensive. If you're taking any medication on a regular basis, be sure you know its generic (scientific) name, since many pharmaceuticals go under different names in Argentina.

INFECTIOUS DISEASES
Dengue Fever
Dengue fever is a viral infection found throughout South America. In Argentina, dengue occurs in Salta province in the northwestern part of the country. Dengue is transmitted by Aedes mosquitoes, which prefer to bite during the daytime and are usually found close to human habitations, often indoors. They breed primarily in artificial water containers, such as jars, barrels, cans, cisterns, metal drums, plastic containers and discarded tires. As a result, dengue is especially common in densely populated, urban environments.

Dengue usually causes flu-like symptoms, including fever, muscle aches, joint pains, headaches, nausea and vomiting, often followed by a rash. The body aches may be quite uncomfortable, but most cases resolve uneventfully in a few days. Severe cases usually occur in children under the age of 15 who are experiencing their second dengue infection.

There is no treatment for dengue fever except to take analgesics such as acetaminophen/paracetamol (Tylenol) and drink plenty of fluids. Severe cases may require hospitalization for intravenous fluids and supportive care. There

is no vaccine. The cornerstone of prevention is insect protection measures (see p635).

Hepatitis A
Hepatitis A is the second most common travel-related infection (after traveler's diarrhea). It's a viral infection of the liver that is usually acquired by ingestion of contaminated water, food or ice, though it may also be acquired by direct contact with infected persons. The illness occurs throughout the world, but the incidence is higher in developing nations. Symptoms may include fever, malaise, jaundice, nausea, vomiting and abdominal pain. Most cases resolve without complications, though hepatitis A occasionally causes severe liver damage. There is no treatment.

The vaccine for hepatitis A is extremely safe and highly effective. If you get a booster six to 12 months later, it lasts for at least 10 years. You really should get it before you go to Argentina. The safety of the hepatitis A vaccine has not been established for pregnant women or children under two years; instead, they should be given a gammaglobulin injection.

Hepatitis B
Like hepatitis A, hepatitis B is a liver infection that occurs worldwide but is more common in developing nations. Unlike hepatitis A, the disease is usually acquired by sexual contact or by exposure to infected blood, generally through blood transfusions or contaminated needles. The vaccine is recommended only for long-term travelers (on the road more than six months) who expect to live in rural areas or have close physical contact with the local population. Additionally, the vaccine is recommended for anyone who anticipates sexual contact with the local inhabitants or a possible need for medical, dental or other treatments while abroad, especially if a need for transfusions or injections is expected.

The hepatitis B vaccine is safe and highly effective. However, a total of three injections are necessary to establish full immunity. Several countries added the hepatitis B vaccine to the list of routine childhood immunizations in the 1980s, so many young adults are already protected.

Malaria
Malaria occurs in every South American country except Chile, Uruguay and the Falkland

Islands. It's transmitted by mosquito bites, usually between dusk and dawn. The main symptom is high spiking fevers, which may be accompanied by chills, sweats, headache, body aches, weakness, vomiting or diarrhea. Severe cases may involve the central nervous system and lead to seizures, confusion, coma and death.

For Argentina, taking malaria pills is strongly recommended for travel to rural areas along the borders with Bolivia (lowlands of Salta and Jujuy provinces) and Paraguay (lowlands of Misiones and Corrientes provinces). There is a choice of three malaria pills, all of which work about equally well. Mefloquine (Lariam) is taken once weekly in a dosage of 250mg, starting one to two weeks before arrival and continuing through the trip and for four weeks after return. The problem is that a certain percentage of people (the number is controversial) develop neuropsychiatric side effects, which may range from mild to severe. Atovaquone/proguanil (Malarone) is a newly approved combination pill taken once daily with food starting two days before arrival and continuing through the trip and for seven days after departure. Side effects are typically mild. Doxycycline is a third alternative, but may cause an exaggerated sunburn reaction.

In general, Malarone seems to cause fewer side effects than mefloquine and is becoming more popular. The chief disadvantage is that it has to be taken daily. For longer trips, it's probably worth trying mefloquine; for shorter trips, Malarone will be the drug of choice for most people.

Protecting yourself against mosquito bites is just as important as taking malaria pills (for recommendations see p635), since none of the pills are 100% effective.

If you do not have access to medical care while traveling, you should bring along additional pills for emergency self-treatment, which you should take if you can't reach a doctor and you develop symptoms that suggest malaria, such as high spiking fevers. One option is to take four tablets of Malarone once daily for three days. However, Malarone should not be used for treatment if you're already taking it for prevention. An alternative is to take 650mg quinine three times daily and 100mg doxycycline twice daily for one week. If you start self-medication, see a doctor at the earliest possible opportunity.

If you develop a fever after returning home, see a physician, as malaria symptoms may not occur for months.

Rabies

Rabies is a viral infection of the brain and spinal cord that is almost always fatal. The rabies virus is carried in the saliva of infected animals and is typically transmitted through an animal bite, though contamination of any break in the skin with infected saliva may result in rabies. Rabies occurs in all South American countries.

The rabies vaccine is safe, but a full series requires three injections and is quite expensive. Those at high risk for rabies, such as animal handlers and spelunkers (cave explorers), should certainly get the vaccine. In addition, those at lower risk for animal bites should consider asking for the vaccine if they might be traveling to remote areas and might not have access to appropriate medical care if needed. The treatment for a possibly rabid bite consists of the rabies vaccine with rabies immune globulin. It's effective, but must be given promptly. Most travelers don't need rabies vaccine.

All animal bites and scratches must be promptly and thoroughly cleansed with large amounts of soap and water and local health authorities contacted to determine whether or not further treatment is necessary. Also see p635.

Typhoid Fever

Typhoid fever is caused by ingestion of food or water contaminated by a species of salmonella known as *Salmonella typhi*. Fever occurs in virtually all cases. Other symptoms may include headache, malaise, muscle aches, dizziness, loss of appetite, nausea and abdominal pain. Either diarrhea or constipation may occur. Possible complications include intestinal perforation, intestinal bleeding, confusion, delirium or (rarely) coma.

Unless you expect to take all your meals in major hotels and restaurants, a typhoid vaccine is a good idea. It's usually given orally, but is also available as an injection. Neither vaccine is approved for use in children under two years.

The drug of choice for typhoid fever is usually a quinolone antibiotic such as ciprofloxacin (Cipro) or levofloxacin (Levaquin), which many travelers carry for treatment of traveler's diarrhea. However, if you self-treat for typhoid fever, you may also need to self-treat for malaria, since the symptoms of the two diseases may be indistinguishable.

Yellow Fever

Yellow fever is a life-threatening viral infection transmitted by mosquitoes in forested areas. The illness begins with flu-like symptoms, which may include fever, chills, headache, muscle aches, backache, loss of appetite, nausea and vomiting. These symptoms usually subside in a few days, but one person in six enters a second, toxic phase characterized by recurrent fever, vomiting, listlessness, jaundice, kidney failure and hemorrhage, leading to death in up to half of the cases. There is no treatment except for supportive care.

The yellow fever vaccine is strongly recommended for all travelers greater than nine months of age who visit the northeastern forest areas near the border with Brazil and Paraguay. For an up-to-date map showing the distribution of yellow fever in Argentina, go to the Center for Disease Control (CDC) website at www.cdc.gov/travel/diseases/maps /yellowfever_map2.htm.

The yellow fever vaccine is given only in approved yellow fever vaccination centers, which provide validated International Certificates of Vaccination (yellow booklets). The vaccine should be given at least 10 days before any potential exposure to yellow fever and remains effective for approximately 10 years. Reactions to the vaccine are generally mild and may include headaches, muscle aches, low-grade fevers, or discomfort at the injection site. Severe, life-threatening reactions have been described but are extremely rare. In general, the risk of becoming ill from the vaccine is far less than the risk of becoming ill from yellow fever, and you're strongly encouraged to get the vaccine.

Taking measures to protect yourself from mosquito bites (p635) is an essential part of preventing yellow fever.

Other Infections

Argentine hemorrhagic fever occurs in the pampas, chiefly from March through October. The disease is acquired by inhalation of dust contaminated with rodent excreta or by direct rodent contact.

Brucellosis is an infection of domestic and wild animals that may be transmitted to humans through direct animal contact or by consumption of unpasteurized dairy products from infected animals. Symptoms may include fever, malaise, depression, loss of appetite, headache, muscle aches and back pain. Complications may include arthritis, hepatitis, meningitis and endocarditis (heart-valve infection).

Chagas' disease is a parasitic infection that is transmitted by triatomine insects (reduviid bugs, which look like long-legged beetles), which inhabit crevices in the walls and roofs of substandard housing in South and Central America. In Argentina, Chagas' disease occurs north of latitude 44° 45'. Transmission is greatest during late spring (November and December). The triatomine insect lays its feces on human skin as it bites, usually at night. A person becomes infected when he or she unknowingly rubs the feces into the bite wound or any other open sore. Chagas' disease is extremely rare in travelers. However, if you sleep in a poorly constructed house, especially one made of mud, adobe or thatch, you should be sure to protect yourself with a bed net and a good insecticide.

Cholera is extremely rare in Argentina. A cholera vaccine is not recommended.

Hantavirus pulmonary syndrome is a rapidly progressive, life-threatening infection acquired through exposure to the excretions of wild rodents. Most cases occur in those who live in rodent-infested dwellings in rural areas. In Argentina, hantavirus infections are reported from the north-central and southwestern parts of the country.

HIV/AIDS has been reported from all South American countries. Be sure to use condoms for all sexual encounters.

Leishmaniasis occurs in the mountains and jungles of all South American countries except for Chile, Uruguay and the Falkland Islands. The infection is transmitted by sandflies, which are about one-third the size of mosquitoes. In Argentina, most cases occur in the northeastern part of the country and are limited to the skin, causing slowly growing ulcers over exposed parts of the body. A more severe type of Leishmaniasis disseminates to the bone marrow, liver and spleen. The disease may be particularly severe in those with HIV. There is no vaccine. To protect yourself from sandflies, follow the same precautions as for mosquitoes (see right), except that netting must be finer mesh (at least 18 holes per 2.54cm or to the linear inch).

Louse-borne typhus occurs in mountain areas, and **murine typhus**, which is transmitted by rat fleas, occurs in warmer rural and jungle areas in the north.

Tick-borne relapsing fever, which may be transmitted by either ticks or lice, is caused by bacteria that are closely related to those which cause Lyme disease and syphilis. In Argentina, tick-borne relapsing fever occurs in the northern part of the country. The illness is characterized by periods of fever, chills, headaches, body aches, muscle aches and cough, alternating with periods when the fever subsides and the person feels relatively well. To minimize the risk of relapsing fever, follow tick precautions (see p636) and practice good personal hygiene at all times.

TRAVELER'S DIARRHEA

To prevent diarrhea, avoid tap water unless it has been boiled, filtered or chemically disinfected (with iodine); only eat fresh fruits or vegetables if cooked or peeled; be wary of dairy products that might contain unpasteurized milk; and be highly selective when eating food from street vendors.

If you develop diarrhea, be sure to drink plenty of fluids, preferably an oral rehydration solution containing lots of salt and sugar. A few loose stools don't require treatment but if you start having more than four or five stools a day, you should start taking an antibiotic (usually a quinolone drug) and an antidiarrheal agent (such as loperamide). If diarrhea is bloody, persists for more than 72 hours or is accompanied by fever, shaking chills or severe abdominal pain you should seek medical attention.

ENVIRONMENTAL HAZARDS
Animal Bites

Do not attempt to pet, handle or feed any animal, with the exception of domestic animals known to be free of any infectious disease. Most animal injuries are directly related to a person's attempt to touch or feed the animal.

Any bite or scratch by a mammal, including bats, should be promptly and thoroughly cleansed with large amounts of soap and water, followed by application of an antiseptic such as iodine or alcohol. The local health authorities should be contacted immediately for possible post-exposure rabies treatment, whether or not you've been immunized against rabies. It may also be advisable to start an antibiotic, since wounds caused by animal bites and scratches frequently become infected. One of the newer quinolones, such as levofloxacin (Levaquin), which many travelers carry in case of diarrhea, would be an appropriate choice.

Snakes and leeches are a hazard in some areas of South America. In the event of a bite from a venomous snake, place the victim at rest, keep the bitten area immobilized, and move the victim immediately to the nearest medical facility. Avoid tourniquets, which are no longer recommended.

Mosquito Bites

To prevent mosquito bites, wear long sleeves, long pants, hats and shoes (rather than sandals). Bring along a good insect repellent, preferably one containing DEET, which should be applied to exposed skin and clothing, but not to eyes, mouth, cuts, wounds or irritated skin. Products containing lower concentrations of DEET are as effective, but for shorter periods of time. In general, adults and children over 12 years should use preparations containing 25% to 35% DEET, which usually lasts about six hours. Children between two and 12 years of age should use preparations containing no more than 10% DEET, applied sparingly, which will usually last about three hours. Neurologic toxicity has been reported from DEET, especially in children, but appears to be extremely uncommon and generally related to overuse. DEET-containing compounds should not be used on children under the age of two.

Insect repellents containing certain botanical products, including oil of eucalyptus and soybean oil, are effective but last only 1½ to two hours. DEET-containing repellents are preferable for areas where there is a high risk of malaria or yellow fever. Products based on citronella are not effective.

For additional protection, you can apply permethrin to clothing, shoes, tents and bed nets. Permethrin treatments are safe and remain effective for at least two weeks, even when items are laundered. Permethrin should not be applied directly to skin.

HEALTH

TRADITIONAL MEDICINE

Some common traditional remedies:

problem	treatment
altitude sickness	gingko
jet lag	melatonin
mosquito-bite prevention	eucalyptus oil; soybean oil
motion sickness	ginger

Don't sleep with the window open unless there is a screen. If sleeping outdoors or in accommodations that allows entry of mosquitoes, use a bed net, preferably treated with permethrin, with edges tucked in under the mattress. The mesh size should be less than 1.5mm. If the sleeping area is not otherwise protected, use a mosquito coil, which will fill the room with insecticide through the night. Repellent-impregnated wristbands are not effective.

Tick Bites

To protect yourself from tick bites, follow the same precautions as for mosquitoes, except that boots are preferable to shoes, with pants tucked in. Be sure to perform a thorough tick check at the end of each day. You'll generally need the assistance of a friend or mirror for a full examination. Ticks should be removed with tweezers, grasping them firmly by the head. Insect repellents based on botanical products, described above, have not been adequately studied for insects other than mosquitoes and cannot be recommended to prevent tick bites.

Water

Tap water is generally not safe to drink. Vigorous boiling for one minute is the most effective means of water purification. At altitudes greater than 2000m, boil for three minutes.

Another option is to disinfect water with iodine. You can add 2% tincture of iodine to 1L of water (five drops to clear water, 10 drops to cloudy water) and let stand for 30 minutes. If the water is cold, longer times may be required. Or you can buy iodine pills such as Globaline, Potable-Aqua and Coghlan's, available at most pharmacies. Instructions are enclosed and should be carefully followed. The taste of iodinated water may be improved by adding vitamin C (ascorbic acid). Iodinated water should not be consumed for more than a few weeks. Pregnant women, those with a history of thyroid disease, and those allergic to iodine should not drink iodinated water.

A number of water filters are on the market. Those with smaller pores (reverse osmosis filters) provide the broadest protection, but they are relatively large and are readily plugged by debris. Those with somewhat larger pores (microstrainer filters) are ineffective against viruses, although they remove other organisms. Manufacturers' instructions must be carefully followed.

TRAVELING WITH CHILDREN

When traveling with young children, be particularly careful about what you allow them to eat and drink, because diarrhea can be especially dangerous in this age group and because the vaccines for hepatitis A and typhoid fever are not approved for use in children under two years.

In general, children under nine months should not be brought to northeastern forest areas near the border with Brazil and Paraguay, where yellow fever occurs, since the vaccine is not safe in this age group.

Chloroquine, which is the main drug used to prevent malaria, may be given to children, but insect repellents must be applied in lower concentrations.

WOMEN'S HEALTH

You can find an English-speaking obstetrician in Argentina by going to the US Embassy website at http://usembassy.state.gov/posts/ar1/wwwhdoctors.html. However, medical facilities will probably not be comparable to those in your home country. In general, it's safer to avoid travel to Argentina late in pregnancy.

Language

Spanish (known as *castellano* in Argentina and the rest of South America) is the official language and it is spoken throughout the country.

A number of immigrant communities have retained their languages as a badge of identity. In central Patagonia, for instance, there are pockets of Welsh speakers, but despite having undergone a bit of a revival in Argentina, the language is in danger of disappearing. Welsh cultural traditions remain strong in these regions, however, even reaching into the tourist industry.

English is studied, spoken and understood by many Argentines (especially in the capital). Italian is the language of the largest immigrant group and also understood by some, as is French. German speakers are numerous enough to support a weekly *porteño* newspaper, *Argentinisches Tageblatt*.

Argentina has over a dozen indigenous tongues, though some are spoken by very few individuals. In the Andean northwest, Quechua speakers are numerous, and most of these are also Spanish speakers. In the southern Andes, there are at least 40,000 Mapuche speakers. In northeastern Argentina, there are about 15,000 speakers of both Guaraní and Toba.

ARGENTINE SPANISH

In addition to their flamboyance, an Argentine's Italian-accented Spanish pronunciation and other language quirks readily identify them throughout Latin America and abroad. The most prominent peculiarities are the usage of the pronoun *vos* in place of *tú* for 'you,' (see El Voseo on p638) and the trait of pronouncing the letters **ll** and **y** as 'zh' (as in 'azure') rather than 'y' (as in 'you') as in the rest of the Americas. Note that in American Spanish, the plural of the familiar *tú* or *vos* is *ustedes,* not *vosotros,* as in Spain.

There are many vocabulary differences between European and American Spanish, and among Spanish-speaking countries in the Americas. The speech of Buenos Aires, in particular, abounds with words and phrases from the colorful slang known as *lunfardo*. Although you shouldn't use *lunfardo* words unless you are supremely confident that you know their every implication (especially in formal situations), you should be aware of some of the more common everyday usages (see Lunfardo on p642). Argentines normally refer to the Spanish.

Every visitor should make an effort to speak Spanish; the basic elements are easily acquired. If possible, take a brief night course at your local university or community college before departure. Even if you can't speak very well, Argentines are gracious folk and will encourage your use of Spanish, so there is no need to feel self-conscious about vocabulary or pronunciation. There are many common cognates, so if you're stuck, try Hispanicizing an English word – it's unlikely you'll make a truly embarrassing error. Do not, however, admit to being *embarazada* unless you are in fact pregnant. (See Cognates & Condoms on p640 for other usages to avoid.)

PHRASEBOOKS & DICTIONARIES

Lonely Planet's *Latin American Spanish Phrasebook* is not only amusing but can also get you by in many adventurous situations. Another very useful language resource is the University of Chicago *Spanish-English,*

EL VOSEO

Spanish in the Río de la Plata region differs from that of Spain and the rest of the Americas, most notably in the informal of the word 'you.' Instead of *tuteo* (the use of *tú*), Argentines commonly speak with *voseo* (the use of *vos*), a relic from 16th-century Spanish requiring slightly different grammar. All verbs change in spelling, stress and pronunciation. Examples of *-ar*, *-er* and *-ir* verbs are given below – the pronoun *tú* is included for contrast. Imperative forms (commands) also differ, but negative imperatives are identical in both *tuteo* and *voseo*.

The Spanish phrases included in this book use the *vos* form. An Argentine inviting a foreigner to address him or her informally will say *Me podés tutear* (literally, 'You can call me *tú*') even though they'll use the *vos* forms in subsequent conversation.

Verb	Tuteo	Voseo
hablar (to speak): **You speak/Speak!**	*Tú hablas/¡Habla!*	*Vos hablás/¡Hablá!*
soñar (to dream): **You dream/Dream!**	*Tú sueñas/¡Sueña!*	*Vos soñás/¡Soñá!*
comer (to eat): **You eat/Eat!**	*Tú comes/¡Come!*	*Vos comés/¡Comé!*
poner (to put): **You put/Put!**	*Tú pones/¡Pon!*	*Vos ponés/¡Poné!*
admitir (to admit): **You admit/Admit!**	*Tú admites/¡Admite!*	*Vos admitís/¡Admití!*
venir (to come): **You come/Come!**	*Tú vienes/¡Ven!*	*Vos venís/¡Vení!*

English-Spanish Dictionary. Its small size, light weight and thorough entries make it perfect for travel.

PRONUNCIATION

Pronunciation of Spanish is not difficult. Many Spanish sounds are similar to their English counterparts, and the relationship between pronunciation and spelling is clear and consistent. Unless otherwise indicated, the English examples used below take standard American pronunciation.

Vowels & Diphthongs

a	as in 'father'
e	as in 'met'
i	as the 'i' in 'police'
o	as in British English 'hot'
u	as the 'u' in 'rude'
ai	as the 'ai' in 'aisle'
au	as the 'ow' in 'how'
ei	as the 'ei' in 'vein'
ia	as the 'ya' in 'yard'
ie	as the 'ye' in 'yes'
oi	as the 'oi' in 'coin'
ua	as the 'wa' in 'wash'
ue	as the 'we' in 'well'

Consonants

Spanish consonants are generally as they are in English, with the exceptions listed on this page. The consonants **ch**, **ll** and **ñ** are generally considered distinct letters, but in dictionaries **ch** and **ll** are now often listed alphabetically under **c** and **l** respectively. The letter **ñ** still has a separate entry after **n** in alphabetical listings.

b	similar to English 'b,' but softer; referred to as *b larga*
c	as in 'celery' before **e** and **i**; elsewhere as the 'k' in 'king'
ch	as in 'choose' before **a**, **o** and **u**; elsewhere as the 'k' in 'king'
d	as in 'dog'; between vowels and after **l** or **n**, it's closer to the 'th' in 'this'
g	as the 'ch' in the Scottish *loch* before **e** and **i** (*kh* in our pronunciation guides); elsewhere, as in 'go'
h	invariably silent
j	as the 'ch' in the Scottish *loch* (*kh* in our pronunciation guides)
ll	as the 'y' in 'yellow'
ñ	as the 'ni' in 'onion'
r	as in 'run,' but strongly rolled
rr	very strongly rolled
v	similar to English 'b,' but softer; referred to as *b corta*
x	usually pronounced as **j** above; as in 'taxi' in other instances
y	as the 'sh' in ship when used as a consonant
z	as the 's' in 'sun'

Word Stress

In general, words ending in vowels or the letters **n** or **s** are stressed on the second-last syllable, while those with other endings have stress on the last syllable. Thus *vaca* (cow) and *caballos* (horses) are both stressed on the next-to-last syllable, while *ciudad* (city) and *infeliz* (unhappy) are stressed on the last syllable.

Written accents generally indicate words that don't follow the rules above, eg *sótano* (basement), *América* and *porción* (portion).

GENDER & PLURALS

In Spanish, nouns are either masculine or feminine, and there are rules to help determine gender (there are of course some exceptions). Feminine nouns generally end with -**a** or with the groups -**ción**, -**sión** or -**dad**. Other endings typically signify a masculine noun. Endings for adjectives also change to agree with the gender of the noun they modify (masculine/feminine -**o**/-**a**). Where both masculine and feminine forms are included in this language guide, they are separated by a slash, with the masculine form first, eg *perdido/a* (lost).

If a noun or adjective ends in a vowel, the plural is formed by adding **s** to the end. If it ends in a consonant, the plural is formed by adding **es** to the end.

ACCOMMODATIONS

I'm looking for ...
Estoy buscando ...   e·*stoy* boos·*kan*·do ...

Where is ...?
¿Dónde hay ...?   don·de ai ...
  a hotel
  un hotel   oon o·*tel*
  a boarding house
  una residencial   oo·na re·si·den·si·*al*
  a youth hostel
  un albergue de juventud   oon al·*ber*·ge de khoo·ven·*tood*

Are there any rooms available?
¿Tienen habitaciones libres?
tye·nen a·bee·ta·*syon*·es lee·bres

I'd like a ...	*Quisiera una*	kee·*sye*·ra oo·na
room.	*habitación ...*	a·bee·ta·*syon* ...
double	*doble*	do·ble
single	*individual*	een·dee·vee·*dwal*
twin	*con dos camas*	kon dos *ka*·mas

How much is it	*¿Cuánto cuesta*	kwan·to kwes·ta
per ...?	*por ...?*	por ...
night	*noche*	no·che
person	*persona*	per·so·na
week	*semana*	se·ma·na

MAKING A RESERVATION
(for phone or written requests)

To ...	*A ...*
From ...	*De ...*
Date	*Fecha*
I'd like to book ...	*Quisiera reservar ...* (see the list under 'Accommodations' for bed and room options)
in the name of ...	*en nombre de ...*
for the nights of ...	*para las noches del ...*
credit card ...	*... tarjeta de crédito*
number	*número de*
expiry date	*fecha de vencimiento de*
Please confirm ...	*Puede confirmar ...*
availability	*la disponibilidad*
price	*el precio*

private/shared bathroom	*baño privado/ compartido*	ba·nyo pree·va·do/ kom·par·tee·do
full board	*pensión completa*	pen·syon kom·ple·ta
too expensive	*demasiado caro*	de·ma·sya·do ka·ro
cheaper	*más económico*	mas e·ko·no·mee·ko
discount	*descuento*	des·kwen·to

Does it include breakfast?
¿Incluye el desayuno?   een·*kloo*·she el de·sa·*shoo*·no

May I see the room?
¿Puedo ver la habitación?   pwe·do ver la a·bee·ta·*syon*

I don't like it.
No me gusta.   no me *goos*·ta

It's fine. I'll take it.
Está bien. La alquilo.   es·*ta* byen la al·*kee*·lo

I'm leaving now.
Me voy ahora.   me *voy* a·o·ra

CONVERSATION & ESSENTIALS

Hello.	*Hola.*	o·la
Good morning.	*Buenos días.*	bwe·nos dee·as
Good afternoon.	*Buenas tardes.*	bwe·nas tar·des
Good evening/ night.	*Buenas noches.*	bwe·nas no·ches
Bye.	*Chau.*	chow
See you soon.	*Hasta luego.*	as·ta lwe·go
Yes.	*Sí.*	see
No.	*No.*	no
Please.	*Por favor.*	por fa·vor
Thank you.	*Gracias.*	gra·syas
Many thanks.	*Muchas gracias.*	moo·chas gra·syas
You're welcome.	*De nada.*	de na·da

LANGUAGE

COGNATES & CONDOMS

False cognates are words that appear to be very similar but have different meanings in different languages. In some instances, these differences can lead to serious misunderstandings. The following is a list of some of these words in English with their Spanish cousins and their meaning in Spanish. Note that this list deals primarily with the Río de la Plata region, and usages may differ elsewhere in South America. Also, be careful with some words from Spain, like *coger*, which in Mexico and South America doesn't mean 'to get or catch' but 'to fuck.' It will take only one instance of being laughed at for claiming you need to fuck the bus before you quickly learn what to really say.

English Spanish	Meaning in Spanish
actual	
actual	current (at present)
carpet	
carpeta	looseleaf notebook
embarrassed	
embarazada	pregnant
fabric	
fábrica	factory
to introduce	
introducir	to introduce (eg an innovation)
notorious	
notorio	well known, evident
to present	
presentar	to introduce (a person)
precise	
preciso	necessary
preservative	
preservativo	condom
sensible	
sensible	sensitive
violation	
violación	rape

Pardon me.	*Perdón.*	per·*don*
Excuse me.	*Permiso.*	per·*mee*·so

(used when asking permission, eg to get by someone)

Forgive me.	*Disculpe.*	dees·*kool*·pe

(used when apologizing)

How are you?

¿Cómo está? (pol)	co·mo es·*ta*
¿Cómo estás? (inf)	co·mo es·*tas*

What's your name?

¿Cómo se llama? (pol)	ko·mo se *sha*·ma
¿Cómo te llamás? (inf)	ko·mo te sha·*mas*

My name is ...

Me llamo ...	me *sha*·mo ...

It's a pleasure to meet you.

Mucho gusto.	moo·cho *goos*·to

The pleasure is mine.

El gusto es mío.	el *goos*·to es *mee*·o

Where are you from?

¿De dónde es? (pol)	de *don*·de es
¿De dónde sos? (inf)	de *don*·de sos

I'm from ...

Soy de ...	soy de ...

Where are you staying?

¿Dónde estás alojado/a?	*don*·de es·*tas* a·lo·*kha*·do/a

May I take a photo?

¿Puedo tomar una foto?	*pwe*·do to·*mar* oo·na *fo*·to

DIRECTIONS

How do I get to ...?

¿Cómo puedo llegar a ...? ko·mo *pwe*·do she·*gar* a ...

Is it far?

¿Está lejos?	es·*ta le*·khos

Go straight ahead.

Siga derecho.	*see*·ga de·*re*·cho

Turn left.

Voltée a la izquierda.	vol·*te*·e a la ees·*kyer*·da

Turn right.

Voltée a la derecha.	vol·*te*·e a la de·*re*·cha

Can you show me (on the map)?

¿Me lo podría indicar (en el mapa)?	me lo po·*dree*·a een·dee·*kar* (en el *ma*·pa)

north	*norte*	*nor*·te
south	*sur*	soor
east	*este*	*s*·te
west	*oeste*	o·*es*·te
here	*aquí*	a·*kee*
there	*allí*	a·*shee*
avenue	*avenida*	a·ve·*nee*·da
block	*cuadra*	*kwa*·dra
street	*calle*	*ka*·she

SIGNS

Entrada	Entrance
Salida	Exit
Información	Information
Abierto	Open
Cerrado	Closed
Prohibido	Prohibited
Comisaria	Police Station
Baños	Toilets
Hombres/Caballeros	Men/Gentlemen
Mujeres/Damas	Women/Ladies

EMERGENCIES

Help!
  ¡Ayuda!   a·*shoo*·da
Go away!
  ¡Déjeme!   de·khe·me
Get lost!
  ¡Váyase!   va·sha·se
It's an emergency.
  Es una emergencia.   es oo·na e·mer·*khen*·sya
Could you help me, please?
  ¿Me puede ayudar,   me pwe·de a·yoo·*dar*
  por favor?   por fa·*vor*
I'm lost.
  Estoy perdido/a. (m/f)   es·toy per·*dee*·do/a
Where are the toilets?
  ¿Dónde están los baños?   don·de es·*tan* los
                                 ba·nyos

Call ...!
  ¡Llame a ...!   sha·me a
    an ambulance
    una ambulancia   oo·na am·boo·*lan*·sya
    a doctor
    un médico   oon me·dee·ko
    the police
    la policía   la po·lee·*see*·a

HEALTH

I'm sick.
  Estoy enfermo/a.   es·toy en·*fer*·mo/a
I need a doctor.
  Necesito un médico.   ne·se·*see*·to oon me·dee·ko
Where's the hospital?
  ¿Dónde está el hospital?   don·de es·*ta* el os·pee·*tal*
I'm pregnant.
  Estoy embarazada.   es·toy em·ba·ra·*sa*·da
I've been vaccinated.
  Estoy vacunado/a.   es·toy va·koo·*na*·do/a

I'm allergic to ...	*Soy alérgico/a a ...*	soy a·*ler*·khee·ko/a a ...
antibiotics	*los antibióticos*	los an·tee·*byo*·tee·kos
nuts	*las frutas secas*	las *froo*·tas se·kas
peanuts	*los maníes*	los ma·*nee*·es·
penicillin	*la penicilina*	la pe·ni·see·*lee*·na

I'm ...	*Soy ...*	soy ...
asthmatic	*asmático/a*	as·*ma*·tee·ko/a
diabetic	*diabético/a*	dya·*be*·tee·ko/a
epileptic	*epiléptico/a*	e·pee·*lep*·tee·ko/a

I have ...	*Tengo ...*	*ten*·go ...
a cough	*tos*	tos
diarrhea	*diarrea*	dya·*re*·a
a headache	*un dolor de cabeza*	oon do·*lor* de ka·*be*·sa
nausea	*náusea*	*now*·se·a

LANGUAGE DIFFICULTIES

Do you speak (English)?
  ¿Habla/Hablás (inglés)?   a·bla/a·*blas* (een·*gles*) (pol/inf)
Does anyone here speak English?
  ¿Hay alguien que hable   ai al·*gyen* ke a·ble
  inglés?   een·*gles*
I (don't) understand.
  (No) Entiendo.   (no) en·*tyen*·do
How do you say ...?
  ¿Cómo se dice ...?   ko·mo se *dee*·se ...
What does ... mean?
  ¿Qué quiere decir ...?   ke *kye*·re de·*seer* ...

Could you please ...?	*¿Puede ..., por favor?*	pwe·de ... por fa·vor
repeat that	*repetirlo*	re·pe·*teer*·lo
speak more slowly	*hablar más despacio*	a·*blar* mas des·*pa*·syo
write it down	*escribirlo*	es·kree·*beer*·lo

NUMBERS

0	*cero*	ce·ro
1	*uno/a*	oo·no/a
2	*dos*	dos
3	*tres*	tres
4	*cuatro*	kwa·tro
5	*cinco*	seen·ko
6	*seis*	seys
7	*siete*	sye·te
8	*ocho*	o·cho
9	*nueve*	nwe·ve
10	*diez*	dyes
11	*once*	on·se
12	*doce*	do·se
13	*trece*	tre·se
14	*catorce*	ka·tor·se
15	*quince*	keen·se
16	*dieciséis*	dye·see·seys
17	*diecisiete*	dye·see·sye·te
18	*dieciocho*	dye·see·o·cho
19	*diecinueve*	dye·see·nwe·ve
20	*veinte*	vayn·te
21	*veintiuno*	vayn·tee·oo·no
30	*treinta*	trayn·ta
31	*treinta y uno*	trayn·tai oo·no
40	*cuarenta*	kwa·ren·ta
50	*cincuenta*	seen·kwen·ta

LANGUAGE

60	*sesenta*	se·*sen*·ta
70	*setenta*	se·*ten*·ta
80	*ochenta*	o·*chen*·ta
90	*noventa*	no·*ven*·ta
100	*cien*	syen
101	*ciento uno*	syen·to oo·no
200	*doscientos*	do·syen·tos
1000	*mil*	meel

SHOPPING & SERVICES

I'd like to buy ...
Quisiera comprar ... kee·*sye*·ra kom·*prar* ...
I'm just looking.
Sólo estoy mirando. so·lo es·*toy* mee·*ran*·do
May I look at it?
¿Puedo mirarlo? pwe·do mee·*rar*·lo
How much is it?
¿Cuánto cuesta? kwan·to kwes·ta
That's too expensive for me.
Es demasiado caro es de·ma·*sya*·do ka·ro
para mí. pa·ra mee
Could you lower the price?
¿Podría bajar un poco po·*dree*·a ba·khar oon po·ko
el precio? el pre·syo
I don't like it.
No me gusta. no me goos·ta
I'll take it.
Lo llevo. lo ye·vo

Do you *¿Aceptan ...?* a·sep·tan ...
accept ...?
  credit cards *tarjetas de* tar·*khe*·tas de
    crédito kre·dee·to
  traveler's *cheques de* che·kes de
    checks *viajero* vya·khe·ro

less *menos* me·nos
more *más* mas
large *grande* gran·de
small *pequeño* pe·ke·nyo

I'm looking *Estoy buscando ...* es·toy boos·kan·do
for (the) ...
  ATM *el cajero* el ka·khe·ro
    automático ow·to·ma·tee·ko
  bank *el banco* el ban·ko
  bookstore *la librería* la lee·bre·ree·a
  embassy *la embajada* la em·ba·kha·da
  exchange office *la casa de* la ka·sa de
    cambio kam·byo
  general store *la tienda* la tyen·da
  laundry *la lavandería* la la·van·de·ree·a
  market *el mercado* el mer·ka·do
  pharmacy *la farmacia* la far·ma·sya
  post office *los correos* los ko·re·os

LUNFARDO

Below are are some of the spicier *lunfardo* (slang) terms that you may hear on your travels in Argentina.

boliche – disco or nightclub
boludo – jerk, asshole, idiot; often used in a friendly fashion, but a deep insult to a stranger
bondi – bus
buena onda – good vibes
carajo – asshole, prick, bloody hell
chabón/chabona – kid, guy/girl (term of endearment)
che – hey
fiaca – laziness
guita – money
macanudo – great, fabulous
mango – one peso
masa – a great, cool thing
mina – woman
morfar – eat
pendejo – idiot
piba/pibe – cool young guy/girl
piola – cool, clever
pucho – cigarette
re – very, as in *re interesante* (very interesting)

Some Lunfardo Phrases

¡Ponete las pilas! – Get on with it! (literally 'Put in the batteries!')
Diez puntos – OK, cool, fine (literally 'Ten points')
Me mataste – I don't know; I have no idea (literally 'You've killed me')
Le faltan un par de jugadores – He's not playing with a full deck (literally 'He's a couple of players short (of a team)')
Che boludo – the most *porteño* phrase on earth. Ask a friendly local youth to explain.

---

supermarket *el supermercado* el soo·per·mer·ka·do
tourist office *la oficina de* la o·fee·see·na de
  turismo too·rees·mo

What time does it open/close?
¿A qué hora abre/cierra?
a ke o·ra a·bre/sye·ra
I want to change some money/traveler's checks.
Quiero cambiar dinero/cheques de viajero.
kye·ro kam·byar dee·ne·ro/che·kes de vya·khe·ro
What's the exchange rate?
¿Cuál es el tipo de cambio?
kwal es el tee·po de kam·byo

I want to call ...
  Quiero llamar a ...
  kye·ro ya·mar a ...
Where's the local internet cafe?
  ¿Dónde hay un cibercafé por acá?
  don·de ai oon sy·ber·ka·fay por a·ka
I'd like to get internet access.
  Quisiera usar internet.
  kee·sye·ra oo·sar in·tair·net

airmail	*correo aéreo*	ko·re·o a·e·re·o
letter	*carta*	kar·ta
registered mail	*certificado*	ser·tee·fee·ka·do
stamps	*estampillas*	es·tam·pee·shas

TIME & DATES

What time is it?	*¿Qué hora es?*	ke o·ra es
It's (one) o'clock.	*Es la (una).*	es la (oo·na)
It's (six) o'clock.	*Son las (seis).*	son las (seys)
midnight	*medianoche*	me·dya·no·che
noon	*mediodía*	me·dyo·dee·a
half past two	*dos y media*	dos ee me·dya
now	*ahora*	a·o·ra
today	*hoy*	oy
tonight	*esta noche*	es·ta no·che
tomorrow	*mañana*	ma·nya·na
Monday	*lunes*	loo·nes
Tuesday	*martes*	mar·tes
Wednesday	*miércoles*	myer·ko·les
Thursday	*jueves*	khwe·ves
Friday	*viernes*	vyer·nes
Saturday	*sábado*	sa·ba·do
Sunday	*domingo*	do·meen·go
January	*enero*	e·ne·ro
February	*febrero*	fe·bre·ro
March	*marzo*	mar·so
April	*abril*	a·breel
May	*mayo*	ma·sho
June	*junio*	khoo·nyo
July	*julio*	khoo·lyo
August	*agosto*	a·gos·to
September	*septiembre*	sep·tyem·bre
October	*octubre*	ok·too·bre
November	*noviembre*	no·vyem·bre
December	*diciembre*	dee·syem·bre

TRANSPORT
Public Transport

What time does	*¿A qué hora ...*	a ke o·ra ...
... leave/arrive?	*sale/llega?*	sa·le/she·ga
the bus	*el autobús*	el ow·to·boos
the plane	*el avión*	el a·vyon
the ship	*el barco*	el bar·ko

airport	*el aeropuerto*	el a·e·ro·pwer·to
bus station	*la estación de autobuses*	la es·ta·syon de ow·to·boo·ses
bus stop	*la parada de autobuses*	la pa·ra·da de ow·to·boo·ses
luggage check room	*la guardería de equipaje*	la gwar·de·ree·a de e·kee·pa·khe
ticket office	*la boletería*	la bo·le·te·ree·a

I'd like a ticket to ...
  Quiero un boleto a ...   kye·ro oon bo·le·to a ...
What's the fare to ...?
  ¿Cuánto cuesta hasta ...? kwan·to kwes·ta a·sta ...

student's (fare)	*de estudiante*	de es·too·dyan·te
1st class	*primera clase*	pree·me·ra kla·se
2nd class	*segunda clase*	se·goon·da kla·se
one-way	*ida*	ee·da
return	*ida y vuelta*	ee·da ee vwel·ta
taxi	*taxi*	tak·see

Private Transport

pickup (truck)	*camioneta*	ka·myo·ne·ta
truck	*camión*	ka·myon
hitchhike	*hacer dedo*	a·ser de·do
I'd like to hire a/an ...	*Quisiera alquilar ...*	kee·sye·ra al·kee·lar ...
bicycle	*una bicicleta*	oo·na bee·see·kle·ta
car	*un auto*	oon ow·to
4WD	*un todo terreno*	oon to·do te·re·no
motorbike	*una moto*	oo·na mo·to

Is this the road to ...?
  ¿Se va a ... por esta carretera?   se va a ... por es·ta ka·re·te·ra
Where's a petrol station?
  ¿Dónde hay una gasolinera?   don·de ai oo·na ga·so·lee·ne·ra
Please fill it up.
  Lleno, por favor.   she·no por fa·vor
I'd like (20) liters.
  Quiero (veinte) litros.   kye·ro (vayn·te) lee·tros

diesel	*diesel*	dee·sel
gas/petrol	*gasolina*	ga·so·lee·na

(How long) Can I park here?
  ¿(Por cuánto tiempo)   (por kwan·to tyem·po)
  Puedo estacionar aquí?   pwe·do e·psta·syon·ar a·kee
Where do I pay?
  ¿Dónde se paga?   don·de se pa·ga
I need a mechanic.
  Necesito un mecánico.   ne·se·see·to oon me·ka·nee·ko

ROAD SIGNS

Acceso	Entrance
Estacionamiento	Parking
Ceda el Paso	Give Way
Despacio	Slow
Dirección Única	One-Way
Mantenga Su Derecha	Keep to the Right
No Adelantar	No Passing
Peaje	Toll
Peligro	Danger
Prohibido Estacionar	No Parking
Prohibido el Paso	No Entry
Stop	Stop
Salida de Autopista	Exit Freeway

The car has broken down (in ...).
El auto se ha averiado   el *ow*·to se a a·ve·*rya*·do
(en ...).   (en ...)

The motorbike won't start.
No arranca la moto.   no a·*ran*·ka la *mo*·to

I have a flat tyre.
Tengo un pinchazo.   *ten*·go oon peen·*cha*·so

I've run out of petrol.
Me quedé sin gasolina.   me ke·*de* seen ga·so·*lee*·na

I've had an accident.
Tuve un accidente.   *too*·ve oon ak·see·*den*·te

TRAVEL WITH CHILDREN

I need ...
Necesito ...   ne·se·*see*·to ...

Do you have ...?
¿Hay ...?   ai ...

a car baby seat
un asiento de seguridad para bebés
oon a·*syen*·to de se·goo·ree·*dad* pa·ra be·*bes*

a child-minding service
un servicio de cuidado de niños
oon ser·*vee*·syo de kwee·*da*·do de *nee*·nyos

a creche
una guardería
oo·na gwar·de·*ree*·a

(disposable) diapers/nappies
pañales (de usar y tirar)
pa·*nya*·les (de oo·*sar* ee tee·*rar*)

an (English-speaking) babysitter
una niñera (de habla inglesa)
oo·na nee·*nye*·ra (de a·bla een·*gle*·sa)

formula (infant milk powder)
leche en polvo
le·che en *pol*·vo

a highchair
una trona
oo·na *tro*·na

a potty
una pelela
oo·na pe·*le*·la

a stroller
un cochecito
oon ko·che·*see*·to

Do you mind if I breast-feed here?
¿Le molesta que dé de pecho aquí?
le mo·*les*·ta ke de de *pe*·cho a·*kee*

Are children allowed?
¿Se admiten niños?
se ad·*mee*·ten *nee*·nyos

Also available from Lonely Planet:
Latin American Spanish Phrasebook

Glossary

For an explanation of food-related terms, see p53, for accommodation terms, p602, and for language in general, p637.

abuelos – grandparents
ACA – Automóvil Club Argentino, which provides maps, road service, insurance and other services, and operates hotels and campgrounds throughout the country
acequia – irrigation canal
aerosilla – chairlift
alcalde – mayor
alerce – large coniferous tree, resembling a California redwood, from which Argentina's Parque Nacional Los Alerces takes its name
apeadero – whistle-stop
arrayán – tree of the myrtle family, from which Argentina's Parque Nacional Los Arrayanes takes its name
arroyo – creek, stream
arte rupestre – cave paintings
asado – the famous Argentine barbecue
autopista – freeway or motorway

baliza – emergency reflector
balneario – any swimming or bathing area, including beach resorts, river beaches and swimming holes
balsa – ferry
bandoneón – an accordion-like instrument used in tango music
barra brava – fervent soccer fan; the Argentine equivalent of Britain's 'football hooligan'
bencina – white gas, used for camp stoves; also known as *nafta blanca*
bicho – any small creature, from insect to mammal; also used to refer to an ugly person
boleadoras – weighted, leather-covered balls attached to a length of thin rope, historically used as a hunting weapon by gauchos and some of Argentina's indigenous peoples; thrown at a guanaco or rhea's legs, they entangle the animal and bring it down
boliche – nightclub or disco
bombachas – a gaucho's baggy pants; can also mean women's underwear
bombilla – metal straw with filter for drinking *mate*
buena onda – good vibes

cabildo – colonial town council; also, the building that housed the council
cacerolazo – a form of street protest; it first occurred in December 2001 where people took to their balconies in Buenos Aires banging pots and pans *(cacerolas)* to show

their discontent; the banging moved to the streets, then to cities throughout Argentina, and culminated in the resignation of President de la Rua
cajero automático – ATM
caldén – a tree characteristic of the dry pampas
camarote – 1st-class sleeper
cambio – money-exchange office; also *casa de cambio*
campo – the countryside; alternately, a field or paddock
característica – telephone area code
carnavalito – traditional folk dance
carpincho – capybara, a large (but cute) aquatic rodent that inhabits the Paraná and other subtropical rivers
carrovelismo – land sailing
cartelera – an office selling discount tickets
casa de cambio – money-exchange office, often shortened to *cambio*
casa de familia – family accommodations
casa de gobierno – literally 'government house,' a building now often converted to a museum, offices etc
castellano – the term used in much of South America for the Spanish language spoken throughout Latin America; literally refers to Castilian Spanish
catarata – waterfall
caudillo – in 19th-century Argentine politics, a provincial strongman whose power rested more on personal loyalty than political ideals or party affiliation
centro cívico – civic center
cerro – hill, mountain
certificado – certified mail
chacarera – traditional folk dance
chacra – small, independent farm
chamamé – folk music of Corrientes
chusquea – solid bamboo of the Valdivian rainforest in Patagonia
coche cama – sleeper class
coima – a bribe; one who solicits a bribe is a *coimero*
colectivo – local bus
combi – long-distance bus
comedor – basic cafeteria
común – common class
Conaf – Corporación Nacional Forestal, Chilean state agency in charge of forestry and conservation, including management of national parks like Torres del Paine
confitería – café serving light meals
conjunto – a musical band
Conquista del Desierto – Conquest of the Desert, a euphemism for General Julio Argentino Roca's late-19th-century war of extermination against the Mapuche of northern Patagonia
contrabajo – double bass

correo – post office

corriente – current

cospel – token used in public telephones

costanera – seaside, riverside or lakeside road or walkway

criollo – in colonial period, an American-born Spaniard, but now used for any Latin American of European descent; the term also describes the feral cattle and horses of the pampas

cruce – crossroads

cuatrerismo – cattle rustling

día de campo – 'day in the country', spent at an *estancia;* typically includes an *asado,* horseback riding and use of the property's facilities

desaparecidos (los) – the disappeared; the victims (estimated at up to 30,000) of Argentina's *Guerra Sucia* who were never found

dique – a dam; the resultant reservoir is often used for recreational purposes; can also refer to a drydock

Dirty War – see *Guerra Sucia*

dorado – large river fish in the Paraná drainage, known among fishing enthusiasts as the 'Tiger of the Paraná' for its fighting spirit

duende – gnome

edificio – a building

ejecutivo – executive class

encomienda – colonial labor system, under which Indian communities were required to provide laborers for Spaniards *(encomenderos),* and the Spaniards were to provide religious and language instruction; in practice, the system benefited Spaniards far more than native peoples

epa – an exclamation meaning 'Hey! Wow! Look out!'

ERP – Ejército Revolucionario del Pueblo, a revolutionary leftist group in the sugar-growing areas of Tucumán province in 1970s that modeled itself after the Cuban revolution; it was wiped out by the Argentine army during the *Guerra Sucia*

esquina – street corner

estación de servicio – gas station

estancia – extensive ranch for cattle or sheep, with an owner or manager *(estanciero)* and dependent resident labor force; many are now open to tourists for recreational activities such as riding, tennis and swimming, either for weekend escapes or extended stays

este – east

facón – a knife used by gauchos that is traditionally worn in the small of the back behind the belt

folklore – Argentine folk music; also known as folklórico

fútbol – soccer

gasolero – motor vehicle that uses diesel fuel, which is much cheaper than ordinary gasoline in Argentina

guardaganado – cattle guard (on a road or highway)

guardia – watchman

Guerra Sucia – the Dirty War of the 1970s, of the Argentine military against left-wing revolutionaries and anyone suspected of sympathizing with them; also referred to as the 'military period'

guitarrón – an oversized guitar used for playing bass lines

horario – schedule

ichu – bunch grass of the Andean altiplano

ida – one-way

ida y vuelta – roundtrip

iglesia – church

interno – internal bus-route number; also a telephone extension number

IVA – *impuesto al valor agregado;* value-added tax, often added to restaurant or hotel bills in Argentina

jejenes – annoying biting insects

jineteada – rodeo

libro de reclamos – complaint book

locutorio – private long-distance telephone office; usually offers fax and internet services as well

lunfardo – street slang

manta – a shawl or bedspread

manzana – literally, 'apple'; also used to define one square block of a city

Maragatos – inhabitants of Carmen de Patagons

mate – tea made from *yerba mate* leaves; Argentina is the world's largest producer and consumer of *mate* and preparing and drinking the beverage is an important social ritual; the word also refers to the *mate* gourd the tea is prepared in

mazorca – political police of 19th-century Argentine dictator Juan Manuel de Rosas

mercado artesanal – handicraft market

meseta – interior steppe of eastern Patagonia

mestizo – a person of mixed Indian and Spanish descent

milonga – in tango, refers to a song, a dance or the dance salon itself

minutas – snacks or short orders

mirador – scenic viewpoint, usually on a hill but often in a building

monte – scrub forest; the term is often applied to any densely vegetated area

Montoneros – left-wing faction of the Peronist party that became an underground urban guerrilla movement in 1970s

municipalidad – city hall

nafta – gasoline or petrol

neumático – spare tire

norte – north

oeste – west

Ovnis – UFOs

parada – a bus stop

paraje – pump

parrilla – mixed grill; also *parrillada*

paseo – an outing, such as a walk in the park or downtown

pato – duck; also a gaucho sport where players on horseback wrestle for a ball encased in a leather harness with handles

peatonal – pedestrian mall, usually in the downtown area of major Argentine cities

pehuén – araucaria, or 'monkey puzzle' tree of southern Patagonia

peña – club that hosts informal folk-music gatherings

percha – perch, also means coathanger

picada – in rural areas, a trail, especially through dense woods or mountains; in the context of food, hors d'oeuvres or snacks

pingüinera – penguin colony

piqueteros – picketers

piropo – a flirtatious remark

piso – floor

porteño/a – inhabitant of Buenos Aires, a 'resident of the port'

precios patagónicos – Patagonian prices

precordillera – foothills of the Andes

primera – 1st class on a train

Proceso – short for El Proceso de Reorganización Nacional, a military euphemism for its brutal attempt to remake Argentina's political and economic culture between 1976 and 1983

propina – a tip, for example, in a restaurant or cinema

pucará – in the Andean northwest, a pre-Columbian fortification, generally on high ground commanding an unobstructed view in several directions

pulpería – a country store or tavern

puna – Andean highlands, usually above 3000m

puntano – a native or resident of Argentina's San Luis province

quebracho – literally, 'ax-breaker'; tree common to the Chaco that's a natural source of tannin for the leather industry

quebrada – a canyon

quincho – thatch-roof hut, now often used to refer to a building at the back of a house used for parties

rambla – boardwalk

rancho – a rural house, generally of adobe, with a thatched roof

recargo – additional charge, usually 10%, that many Argentine businesses add to credit-card transactions

reducción – an Indian settlement created by Spanish missionaries during the colonial period; the most famous are the Jesuit missions in the triple-border area of Argentina, Paraguay and Brazil

refugio – a usually rustic shelter in a national park or remote area

remise – radio taxi without a meter that generally offer fixed fares within a given zone; also *remís*

riacho – stream

ripio – gravel

rotisería – take-out shop

rotonda – traffic circle, roundabout

RN – Ruta Nacional; a national highway

RP – Ruta Provincial; a provincial highway

ruta – highway

s/n *-sin número,* indicating a street address without a number

sábalo – popular river fish in the Paraná drainage

salar – salt lake or salt pan, usually in the high Andes or Argentine Patagonia

samba – traditional folk dance

semi-cama – semisleeper class

sendero – a trail in the woods

servicentro – gas station

siesta – lengthy afternoon break for lunch and, sometimes, a nap

Subte – the Buenos Aires subway system

sur – south

surubí – popular river fish frequently served in restaurants

tahona – flour mill

tapir – large hoofed mammal of subtropical forests in northern Argentina and Paraguay; a distant relative of the horse

tarjeta magnética – magnetic bus card

tarjeta telefónica – telephone card

tarjeta verde – 'green card'; title document for Argentine vehicles that drivers must carry

teleférico – gondola cable-car

telera – textile workshop

tenedor libre – all you can eat

todo terreno – mountain bike

tola – high-altitude shrubs in the altiplano of northwestern Argentina

torrontés – dry white wine from Cafayate

trapiche – sugar mill

turista – 2nd class on a train, usually not very comfortable

vicuña – wild relative of domestic llama and alpaca, found in Argentina's Andean northwest only at high altitudes

vinoteca – wine bar

vino tinto – red wine

yacaré – South American alligator, found in humid, subtropical areas

YPF – Yacimientos Fiscales Petrolíferos, Argentina's former national oil company

yungas – in northwestern Argentina, transitional subtropical lowland forest

zapateo – folkloric tap dance

zona franca – duty-free zone

zonda – a hot, dry wind descending from the Andes

The Authors

DANNY PALMERLEE
Coordinating Author

Danny is a freelance writer and photographer based in Portland, Oregon. He lived in Buenos Aires for a year and, since his first visit to Argentina in 1999, has traveled extensively throughout the country. From his most recent trip – this time into the Impenetrable region – he brought home a body full of ticks. Danny's travel writing has appeared in the *Los Angeles Times, Miami Herald, San Francisco Chronicle* and the *Dallas Morning News*, as well as other publications throughout the US and the world. He is the main author of numerous Lonely Planet books, including *South America on a Shoestring, Best of Buenos Aires, Ecuador & the Galápagos Islands* and *Baja California & Los Cabos*. Danny wrote the front- and back-matter chapters for this edition.

SANDRA BAO

Sandra's mom escaped China's communist regime after WWII, then hopped on a freighter to Argentina. After months at sea she arrived in Buenos Aires – two days after Evita's death (1952). Mourning workers meant luggage wasn't processed for a week. Sandra's dad had a better welcome in 1955. Sandra's parents met, got married and had two kids (Sandra was one of them). In 1974 Argentina was in turmoil, so once again the family emigrated to greener pastures – this time the USA. Sandra remains proud to be a *porteña* and has often returned to her homeland. She's the author of Lonely Planet's *Buenos Aires* guidebook, and has contributed to *Argentina* and *South America on a Shoestring*. Sandra wrote the Buenos Aires chapter.

GREGOR CLARK

Gregor's magnetic attraction to South America dates back to adolescence, when a high-school Spanish teacher filled him with starry-eyed notions of hiking the Inca Trail. A veteran of nine Latin American trips, he's traveled the continent from tip to tail and developed a special fondness for Brazil and Argentina, but somehow Uruguay kept eluding him...till now. Favorite memories from this trip are getting caught in a cow-and-gaucho traffic jam, wandering Rocha's northern beaches and taste-testing *chivitos*. He recently co-authored Lonely Planet's *Brazil 7* and wrote about Machu Picchu and Easter Island for Lonely Planet's *Middle of Nowhere*. Already scheming his next trip back, he lives in Vermont with his family. Gregor wrote the Uruguay chapter.

LONELY PLANET AUTHORS

Why is our travel information the best in the world? It's simple: our authors are independent, dedicated travelers. They don't research using just the internet or phone, and they don't take freebies, so you can rely on their advice being well researched and impartial. They travel widely, to all the popular spots and off the beaten track. They personally visit thousands of hotels, restaurants, cafés, bars, galleries, palaces, museums and more – and they take pride in getting all the details right, and telling it how it is. Think you can do it? Find out how at lonelyplanet.com.

SARAH GILBERT

Sarah fell in love at first sight twice in Argentina – once with a *porteño*, and once with Buenos Aires, where she now lives and works as a journalist and travel writer. Originally from Sydney, Australia, Sarah earned her masters in journalism at New York's Columbia University and cut her teeth on the Big Apple's tabloids. This was Sarah's first Lonely Planet assignment, and she wrote the Pampas & Atlantic Coast chapter. When she's not writing, she teaches her Argentine to throw seafood on the *asado* and he teaches her to ride a horse. They are living happily ever after.

CAROLYN MCCARTHY

Author and journalist Carolyn McCarthy got her start to travel writing while searching for the Yanomami in Venezuela. Since then she has spent the last nine years cruising around the Americas but makes her home in malaria-free southern Chile, where she enjoys hiking and the long rainy season. Her work has appeared in *National Geographic*, the *Boston Globe*, *Salt Lake Tribune*, Lonely Planet online and other publications. For Lonely Planet, she has co-authored *Chile*, *Costa Rica*, *Ecuador*, *El Salvador* and *Yellowstone & Grand Teton National Parks*. You can visit her blog at www.carolynswildblueyonder .blogspot.com. Carolyn wrote the Tierra del Fuego and Patagonia chapters.

ANDY SYMINGTON

Andy's relationship with Argentina is a story of four generations: his grand-mother lived there in the '20s, and her father had a *mate* plantation in Misiones. Andy first visited the country with his own father, the start of a long love affair with South America that has involved many trips all around the continent, a spell living and working in Buenos Aires, a deep-rooted respect for provincial Argentina that he renewed on this research trip, and a debatable addiction to barbecued intestines. Andy hails from Australia, lives in northern Spain, and has contributed to many Lonely Planet guidebooks. Andy wrote the Northeast Argentina and Andean Northwest chapters.

LUCAS VIDGEN

Lucas has been working, traveling and living in Latin America for more than a decade. He first fell in love with Argentina's wide open spaces and cosmopolitan cities back in 2001 and now jumps at any excuse to go back. Among other Lonely Planet titles, he has contributed to *South America on a Shoestring*, *Guatemala* and *Central America on a Shoestring*. Lucas currently lives in Quetzaltenango, Guatemala. His Spanish is OK, but he misses his potato cakes and his mum. Lucas wrote the Córdoba & the Central Sierras, Mendoza & the Central Andes and Lake District chapters.

Behind the Scenes

THIS BOOK

The 6th edition of *Argentina* was researched and written by Danny Palmerlee (coordinating author), Sandra Bao, Gregor Clark, Sarah Gilbert, Carolyn McCarthy, Andy Symington and Lucas Vidgen. Danny, Sandra and Lucas also wrote the previous edition, along with Andrew Dean Nystrom and contributing Food & Drink author Dereck Foster. Also contributing to this edition were David Labi (Going to a Fútbol Game boxed text in the Buenos Aires chapter), Daniel Buck and Anne Meadows (Butch & Sundance's Patagonian Refuge boxed text in the Patagonia chapter) and Dr David Goldberg (Health). This guidebook was commissioned in Lonely Planet's Oakland office, and produced by the following:

Commissioning Editors Jay Cooke, Jennye Garibaldi, Kathleen Munnelly
Coordinating Editor Rosie Nicholson
Coordinating Cartographers Owen Eszeki, Valentina Kremenchutskaya
Coordinating Layout Designer Carol Jackson
Managing Editor Bruce Evans
Managing Cartographer Alison Lyall

Managing Layout Designer Celia Wood
Assisting Editors Sasha Baskett, Kate Evans, Penelope Goodes, Paul Harding, Stephanie Pearson, Martine Power, Sarah Stewart
Assisting Cartographers Alissa Baker, Karen Grant, Sam Sayer, Lyndell Stringer
Assisting Layout Designers Yvonne Bischofberger, Wibowo Rusli
Cover Designer Karina Dea
Project Manager Rachel Imeson
Language Content Coordinator Quentin Frayne

Thanks to Melanie Dankel, Heather Dickson, Ryan Evans, Mark Germanchis, Mark Griffiths, Jim Hsu, Lisa Knights, Adam McCrow, Naomi Parker, Adam Stanford, Gerard Walker

THANKS
DANNY PALMERLEE

First, a huge, huge thanks to my wife Aimee for goin' it alone with our five-month-old daughter while I ran off to Argentina again. In Buenos Aires, thanks heaps to Yanina Ronconi for putting me up (and putting up with me), and to Agustin for his

---

THE LONELY PLANET STORY

Fresh from an epic journey across Europe, Asia and Australia in 1972, Tony and Maureen Wheeler sat at their kitchen table stapling together notes. The first Lonely Planet guidebook, *Across Asia on the Cheap*, was born.

Travelers snapped up the guides. Inspired by their success, the Wheelers began publishing books to Southeast Asia, India and beyond. Demand was prodigious, and the Wheelers expanded the business rapidly to keep up. Over the years, Lonely Planet extended its coverage to every country and into the virtual world via lonelyplanet.com and the Thorn Tree message board.

As Lonely Planet became a globally loved brand, Tony and Maureen received several offers for the company. But it wasn't until 2007 that they found a partner whom they trusted to remain true to the company's principles of traveling widely, treading lightly and giving sustainably. In October of that year, BBC Worldwide acquired a 75% share in the company, pledging to uphold Lonely Planet's commitment to independent travel, trustworthy advice and editorial independence.

Today, Lonely Planet has offices in Melbourne, London and Oakland, with over 500 staff members and 300 authors. Tony and Maureen are still actively involved with Lonely Planet. They're travelling more often than ever, and they're devoting their spare time to charitable projects. And the company is still driven by the philosophy of *Across Asia on the Cheap*: 'All you've got to do is decide to go and the hardest part is over. So go!'

time and the delicious *asado*. Thanks and a heart-felt *abrazo* to German and Carina, from Córdoba, for accompanying me on an epic journey through the Impenetrable. To my editor, Kathleen Munnelly, a giant thanks for sending me off to beautiful Argentina once again. And to my co-authors, a round of Quilmes and a big ¡Salud! Thanks for everything!

SANDRA BAO

Muchas gracias to my *porteño* family, Elsa, Jorge and Christina, for hospitality and wonderful meals. Thanks to Mindy for fun times, and Nicole for that fabulous Thanksgiving! And Lucas – what an amazing *asado*! Bob and Flor, great seeing you always. Graciela, you're a hoot (and so is your sister) – thanks for showing me a bit of my past. Talya Frost, you certainly know your way around the nightclubs. Thanks also to David Labi, Sylvia Zapiola and all my co-authors. Finally, David, Fung and Daniel – you're always in my thoughts, as is my dear monkey husband, Ben Greensfelder.

GREGOR CLARK

Thanks to the dozens of warm-hearted Uruguayans who shared their country's beauty with me, especially Enrique Frade, Pablo Rado and Marujita, Mario Padern, Lucia and Rodney Bruce, René Boretto, Cecilia Olivet, Sergio Dessa, Dahianna and José Assanelli, Ibero Laventure, Eric at the 1949 Hostel and the guardian angels at Palermo and Cyberia. Thanks to my predecessor Lucas Vidgen, whose humorous prose frequently made me burst out laughing, to my wonderful editor Kathleen Munnelly and coordinating author Danny Palmerlee. Finally, big hugs to Gaen, Meigan and Chloe, whose love and companionship always make coming home the best part of the trip.

SARAH GILBERT

Thanks to my BA amigos – Lou and Cam for the welcome, Will and Tiff for the car, Viv for egging me on, Prue for saving my sanity, Mercedes *por mi español*, Annie and Ed for showing up and Paula for her dance moves. Thanks to my Lonely Planet colleagues for helping me through my first guide. I'll always be grateful to my loving and beloved parents, Danny and Kathleen, and my brother and sister James and Mary. *Mil gracias a mi familia Argentina por todo su cariño*. Thanks most particularly to my dearest Nico, my reason for being in Argentina and for loving it as my own.

CAROLYN MCCARTHY

Unforseen events always make your experience on the road and this was the longest road trip ever. Profuse appreciation goes out to the new friends who made my job much easier. The biggest thank you goes to Joe Ray, who did a good share of driving and proved an indispensable comrade in adventure. Huge appreciation goes to Don Manuel Pardo for *mate* and stories in a snowstorm and to Agustin Smart for logistical support. Ditto to the anonymous fellow who loaned his tire jack and even invited us home for mussels (we couldn't find the house!). Gus Wagemeister, Salvo Tavella and Graciela and Silvia Guzman offered valuable support in Buenos Aires. On the home front, my appreciation goes to Kathleen Munnelly, my editor, Danny Palmerlee, my music consultant, and the rest of the Argentina book team.

ANDY SYMINGTON

I would like to thank the many warm-hearted people that made this trip such a pleasurable one, in particular those who went beyond the call of duty to provide information, advice, and help. These include: Gilda Hernández and Eze Bariffo, Virginia Getino and Graciela Chávez, Adriana Luraschi and Oscar Rodríguez, Luis Lovrincevich, Ramón Mercado, Jorge Guasp and the APN in Salta, Juan Carlos Delgado, Silvia Tocco, Osvaldo Leveratto, Lucas, Paula, and Matias from El Escaño in León, Héctor 'Guiso' Morales, Andrea and Marcos in Resistencia, and Mariano Juanche, as well as the tourist offices in Rosario, Paraná riverside, Concepción, Resistencia, Foz do Iguaçu, Tucumán, Santa María, Salta, and Jujuy. Profuse thanks also to my family for their support, to readers and fellow travelers who offer advice and corrections, to Kathleen Munnelly and the Lonely Planet team, to Danny and all my fellow authors – particularly Sarah Gilbert for taking notes while on holiday – and to all those friends whom I never thank but who keep in regular and much-appreciated touch when I'm on the road.

LUCAS VIDGEN

Special thanks to Melina Cardenas, Ignacio Mitre and Paula Piatti, all the travelers who wrote in or that I met along the way with snippets of info, and fellow authors Danny, Sandra, Carolyn, Gregor, Andy and Sarah. To Emma Vidgen for her ace photography and navigation skills (the other left...), Chris Perras and Ana Marie Madison for keeping the home fires burning and América Hernández

BEHIND THE SCENES

BEHIND THE SCENES

and Sofia Vidgen for being there and, more importantly, being here when I returned.

Also, my undying gratitude to the extra sweater I packed for Patagonia. Thanks, ol' bluey – I think you saved my life.

OUR READERS

Many thanks to the travelers who used the last edition and wrote to us with helpful hints, useful advice and interesting anecdotes:

A Kate Adlam, Christina (Tina) Alefounder, John Alexander, Joe Allanmeyer, Andrea Alonso, Sogol Aminan, Debbie Amos, Steve Anderson, Amma Aning, Wally Apostolakis, Patrik Aqvist, Pirmin Aregger, Kathleen Armstrong, Rebecca Arthur, Daniel Aruca, Nadav Atik, Ariona Aubrey **B** Carl Ba, Graham Balch, Justin Bannister, Barbara Bansemer, Richard Barclay, Geoffrey Bard, Arlen L Barn, Philipp Baumann, Tobias Baumgartner, Reni Beishuizen, John Bell, Udy Bell, Nancy Benjamin, Matthew David Bennett, Tim & Trish Bermon, Alaya Binder, Monique Birenbaum, Caroline Blackmon, Michele Bocacci, Giorgio Boccia, Sanne Bogers, Inge Boland, Andrea Bonanomi, Carlos Borgialli, Andy Bornmann, Maree Bourke, Jaap Bouwer, Jenny Boyd, Meike Ter Braak, Andrew Bresler, Jan Willem Ten Brinke, Russ Brompton, Jeff Browitt, Richard Bru, James Bryant, Simon Burges, Soeren Buschmann, Sibylle Von Busekist, Sandra & Diego Bustillo, Frank Böhm **C** Matteo Candaten, Mell Carey, Douglass M Carver, Raphael Cecchi, Fernando Cendron, Ken & Barbara Cerotsky, Cy Chadley, Geoff Chadwick, Anthony Chant, Graham Chapman, Dave Chappell, Rodrigo Chia, Dino Chivilo, Adriana Cipolletti, Bjørn Clasen, Ian Clegg, Andrew Cohan, Simon Collard-Wexler, Claudio Conca, Carlos Connolly, Patricia Cook, Charles Cosgrave, Hannah Della Costa, Zach Cowan, Simone Crok, Kori Crow, Pam Crowest, Clare Cuthbertson **D** Luciano D`Angelo, Shari Das, Annemarie Dautzenberg, Joana David, Annalisa Deeney, Josan Derix, Karin Dielemans, Sarah Dixon, Alexis Dodin, Darragh Dolan, Cynthia Mac Donald, Niels Donker, Chris Donovan, Sander Doolaard, Lasse Doring, Christoph Dorn, Niels Doun, Simon Drath, Gil Dryden, Andrew Duncan, Elizabeth Dunningham, Nicolas Dupont, Han Pieter Duyverman **E** Roger Paul Edmonds, Tineke Eikelenboom, John Elliott, Christa Ellis, Stephen Ellis, Paula Ely, Roger Emanuels, Barbara Exley **F** Jan Faassen, Lucas Farnbach, Lizzy Fawns, María Aparecida Da Costa Felipe, Marcelo Figueredo, Joseph Filicetti, Paul Fish, Ruth Fisher, Adrian Flash, Jennifer Flood, Mike Flory, Mary Flynn, Elisabeth Folkunger, Adriana Fontan, Susannah Ford, Maria Fortiz-Morse, Claire Francis, Robert La Franco, Catherine Franks, Roger Franquesa, Jay Freistadt, Petra Frodyma, Leandro Funes, Glòria Furdada **G** Chen G, Paulo Gaeta, Matthew Galbraith, Patrick Garvey, John Gaukroger, Julia Gaylard, Olivier Geffroy, Marc Gerard, Griet Gillard, Ann Givens, Cecile Golden, Ana Cristina Cavalcante Goncalves, Eltonio Aralijo Goncalves, Laura Gottlieb, Benoit Gouzi, Patrick Graham, Narelle & Gez Green, Loredana Grindlay, Adriana Guevara, Andree Guilhen, Paul Gurn, Pierre Guyot, Pamela Gómez **H** Christa Haelterman, Dr Bashar Hamarneh, Rainer Hamet, Arjan Hanekamp, Tessa Hanevelt, Paola Hanna, Chris Hanour, Peter Hansen, Michael Harrington, Rachael Harris, Pragyana Hartig, Philipp Haselbach,

Natasha Haverty, Simon Hawliczek, Andrew Hazlett, Nick Healing, Laura Heckman, Christine Hendrix, Sian Herbert, Mike Herren, Agnes Hevesi, Peter Hills, Theresa Hilpert, Jodie Hine, Steven Hines, Teja Hlacer, Laure Hofmann, Nadine Holinski, John Horton, Steve Horton, Clarissa Horwood, Melanie Howlett, Ian Humphreys, Elizabeth Hunt, Cecilia Hvarfner, Susanne Höllwarth **I** Blanche Iberg, Cleide Pires Inácio, Vera Isachsen, Debbie Isbell, Can Isik, Maciek Izbicki **J** Alexander Jarrett, Maria De La Paz Jaureguizar, Joyce Jeffery, Peter Jensen, Sanne Jespersen, Rolf Johansson, Peter Johnson, Luke Jones, Wade Jones, Irene Jordet, Simidjiyski Julian, Nicole Jurmo **K** Einat Kadoury, Nico Kamm, David Kaplan, Mary Kelly, Paul Kennedy, Nicola Kettelz, Mark Kimerer, Kattie Kingsley, Florian Kirchhoff, Sven Kistner, Lucas Klamert, Marcy Klapper, Robert Jam Klop, Lisa Knappich, Konstanee Kogler, Marika Konings, Jacqueline Kostick, Harald Kraschina **L** Edith Lackner, Donna Lancaster, Fritz Lanz, Amber Larkin, Helma Larkin, Ian Lavoie, Alan Law, Mark Lawrence, Angela Lawson, Ron Leach, Graeme Lee, Joann Lee, Stephen Lee, Ronen Leibovich, Nick Leitch, Kate Lena, Hugh Leschot, Markus Leuchs, Yossi Lev, Jonathan Levin, Emma Lewis, Yen Lien, Uri Lifshitz, Jerry Livson, Gregor Loesbrock, Frederic Lopez, Martin L Lorenzo, Peter Luescher **M** Cyntia Machado, Danilo Machado, Bev Mackenzie, Sebastian Madina, Rene Mantel, Antonio Maria, Martinez Marina, Lynn Marino, Richard Mark, Ana Marquis, Valentina Martinez, Manuela Maschke, Adam Masojada, Tünde Mathe, Ashley Mawhonney, Pamela Mazza, Margaret Mcaspurn, Rick Mccharles, Fred Mcgary, Susie Mckee, Pablo Meglioli, Shirit Menashe, Ivenise Aparecida Mendes, David Merriman, James Mill, James Millership, David Mills, Anna Mitchell, Lara Mockewitz, Michael Modlock, Truus Moelker, Ruth Molloy, Andrew Moody, Braulio Moreira, Philip Morris, Gail Morrison, Jennifer Murby, Maria Paz Muriel, Riccardo Musella **N** Edith & Doug Naegele, Brian Nancarrow, Philip Nash, Suzanne Natelson, William Nelson, Hilda Neutel, K Nielsen, Anne-Pascale Niez, Tanja Nijhoff, Caroline Ninnes, Valentina Nobili, Jaymie Noble, Rickard Nordin, Sue Norman, Mia Nyamundanda **O** Giorgio Olivo, Malene Lykke Olsen, Pilar Ortega, Alejandro Ostera **P** Zsolt Palotas, Rocio Panelo, Carla Paoloni, Cecilia Pardo, Alice Parham, Martin Parkes, Rodrigo Pastor, Albergue Patagonia, Edward Perkin, Bill Phelan, Fernanda Pirani, Will Pizzolato, Bastian Platt, Will Price, Marc Pruijn, Lindsay Purifoy **R** Maggie Racklyeft, Julia Rahman, Nyoka Rajah, Alejandro Rascovan, Raphael Rashid, Sheikh Rasul, Mark Raymond, Tom Reed, Christian Reh, Stefan Reichenberger, Wolfgang Reiter, Anna Reschreiter, M Husam Rezek, Fernando Rezende, Roberto Ricca, Dean Richardson, Philip Riches, Anna Rinoldi, Markus Riutta, Catherine Robinson, Yosef Robinson, Seamus Roche, Martin Rodriguez, Joachim Rose, Stephan Roy, Fritz Rudolph, Dagmar Ruehl, Steph Russell, Gabriel Rusu, Matthias Ryser **S** Joan Safford, Janet L Sanfilippo, Evelyn Santoro, Cristiane Rodrigues Santos, Chris Sasha, Corinne & Cedric Saugy, Fred Schaebsdau, Beate Schmahl, Niek Schmitz, Katharina Schneider, Markus Schober, Brian Schreiber, Ann Schumacher, Meike Seele, Christine Seichter, Joel Selwood, Kurt Shearer, Brian Sheehy, Max Shue, Anni Siesing, Stuart Sill, Maxine Simmons, Adam Smith, Brian Smith, Kaiyote Snow, Candid Soldevila, Pablo Soledad, Elizabeth Sommers, Nicholas Southey, Murray Sparks,

SEND US YOUR FEEDBACK

We love to hear from travelers – your comments keep us on our toes and help make our books better. Our well-travelled team reads every word on what you loved or loathed about this book. Although we cannot reply individually to postal submissions, we always guarantee that your feedback goes straight to the appropriate authors, in time for the next edition. Each person who sends us information is thanked in the next edition – and the most useful submissions are rewarded with a free book.

To send us your updates – and find out about Lonely Planet events, newsletters and travel news – visit our award-winning website: **www.lonelyplanet.com/contact**.

Note: we may edit, reproduce and incorporate your comments in Lonely Planet products such as guidebooks, websites and digital products, so let us know if you don't want your comments reproduced or your name acknowledged. For a copy of our privacy policy visit www.lonelyplanet.com/privacy.

BEHIND THE SCENES

Carsten Steger, Claudia Stocker-Waldhuber, Fiédéric Stoven, Will Stroll, Ricardo Daniel Svitek **T** Brian Taaffe, Karina Tahiliani, Suzanne Tallon, Nana Taylor, Penny Taylor, Marjorie Tenchavez, Emily Tew, Anjali Thakariya, Gord Thompson, Ryan Thompson, Bruce Thomson, Linda Thomson, Martin Thygesen, Luca Toscani, Gerald Tsui, Chris Tuck, John Tuckwell, Nathalie Tzaud **V** Jérémie Vachon, Ana Teresa Vale, Emmanuelle Valmy, Patricio Valsecchi, Koenraad van Brabant, Carola van Lamoen, Dave De van Lindeloof, Thomas van Luijtelaar, Daphne van Meningen, Jan van Ravens, Hester van Santen, Carien van den Berg, Marieke van den Oever, Dave Vassar, Janaína Vergara, Jasper Verschuure, Thomas Vogt, Jens Vrang **W** Jan Waclawek, Anna Walkington, Mike Wallace, Sonja Walper, Jillian Warburton, Michal Warcholik, Carla Ward, Garth Ward, Tony Watton, Mareen Weber, Frank Weidenmueller, Alexander Weissmann, Amanda Wells, Matthias Wenger, Rico Werner, Stephen G Wesley, Paul White, Lisa Whitworth, David Wickham, Henrietta Wilkins, Tim Wilson, Simon Winterburn, Elias Wolfberg, Sandra Wolff, Jennifer Worsham, Katie Worters, Gabriella Wortmann, Miriam Wunderwald **Y** Ariel Yablon, Maite Yael, Wendy & Colin Young **Z** Laura Zamboni, Lut Zhasmann, Tania Zulkoskey

ACKNOWLEDGMENTS
Many thanks to the following for the use of their content:

Globe on title page ©Mountain High Maps 1993 Digital Wisdom, Inc.

Internal photographs p6 (#1 bottom), p12 (#1), p284 Danny Palmerlee; p7 (#7) © Chad Ehlers /Alamy; p9 (#3), p282, Andy Symington; p278, Carolyn McCarthy; p280 Sandra Bao; p281, Lucas Vidgen. All other photographs by Lonely Planet Images, and by Michael Taylor, p5, p9 (#2) ; Andrew Peacock p7 (#3); Michael Coyne p6 (#1 top), p10 (#1), p277; Olivier Cirendini p8 (#1); Terry Carter p11 (#2); Grant Dixon p11 (#3).

Index

INDEX

INDEX

GreenDex